# THE LAW OF TRUSTS AND EQUITABLE OBLIGATIONS

This book is dedicated to the memory of our fathers

Walter Charles Pearce
8 March 1922 – 22 April 1993

Alan Hugh Stevens
3 March 1938 – 13 August 1993

# THE LAW OF TRUSTS AND EQUITABLE OBLIGATIONS

*Fourth Edition*

**PROFESSOR ROBERT PEARCE, BCL, MA**

*Vice Chancellor, University of Wales, Lampeter*

**JOHN STEVENS, BCL, MA**

*Senior Lecturer in Law, University of Birmingham*

OXFORD

UNIVERSITY PRESS

## OXFORD
### UNIVERSITY PRESS

Great Clarendon Street, Oxford OX2 6DP

Oxford University Press is a department of the University of Oxford.
It furthers the University's objective of excellence in research, scholarship,
and education by publishing worldwide in

Oxford New York

Auckland Cape Town Dar es Salaam Hong Kong Karachi
Kuala Lumpur Madrid Melbourne Mexico City Nairobi
New Delhi Shanghai Taipei Toronto

With offices in

Argentina Austria Brazil Chile Czech Republic France Greece
Guatemala Hungary Italy Japan Poland Portugal Singapore
South Korea Switzerland Thailand Turkey Ukraine Vietnam

Oxford is a registered trade mark of Oxford University Press
in the UK and in certain other countries

Published in the United States
by Oxford University Press Inc., New York

© Robert Pearce and John Stevens 2006

British Library Cataloguing in Publication Data
Data available

Library of Congress Cataloging in Publication Data
Data available

Typeset by RefineCatch Limited, Bungay, Suffolk
Printed in Great Britain
on acid-free paper by
Ashford Colour Press Ltd, Gosport, Hampshire

ISBN 978–0–19–928535–8

3 5 7 9 10 8 6 4

# Preface to the fourth edition

The law of trusts and equitable obligations is frequently seen by students as alien and intimidating because of its abstract concepts and unfamiliar terminology. It is, however, a subject which is at the heart of the common law of property, and underpins a wide variety of personal and commercial arrangements. It is a living and dynamic area of the law, and this is reflected in the substantial rewriting which has been necessitated by legislative and judicial developments since the last edition four years ago.

Our approach has remained the same as in previous editions. We have sought to bring the subject alive to students by placing the law in context. We have sought to produce a book which is clear and comprehensible and thus accessible to students. The arrangement of the book therefore adopts an analytical structure which recognises the important distinction between the distributive and asset management function of trusts and which deals separately with the creation of equitable obligations and the checks and controls used to enforce them. In our style we have endeavoured to use accessible language, to explain core concepts before building upon them, and to provide examples and diagrams by way of illustration. At the same time we have sought not to sacrifice academic depth for the sake of simplicity. We have drawn attention to all significant areas of academic controversy, and have sought to add our own scholarly contribution to these debates, and made suggestions for reform where we consider this is needed. We have continued to draw upon case law in other jurisdictions to demonstrate the differing solutions which are possible to common problems.

We have sought to take account of all major developments in the law up until 1st February 2006, although in some places it has been possible to include even more recent changes. The most significant legislative changes have been the updating of the system of land registration by the Land Registration Act 2002, the introduction of civil partnerships by the Civil Partnerships Act 2004, the reform of pension trusts by the Pensions Act 2004, and the proposed reforms of the law of charity by the Charity Bill 2006, which is anticipated to become law in the near future. The most important developments through case law are in the field of constructive trusts, where the decision of the Court of Appeal in *Oxley v Hiscock* [2004] 3 All ER 703 has radically changed the way in which the quantum of an interest arising by way of a constrictive trust is assessed. There have been significant developments in regard to the accountability of trustees and the right of access of beneficiaries to trust documents, and in the application of the defences of limitation and laches to liability for breach of trust and an account of profits obtained in breach of fiduciary duty. The meaning of 'dishonesty' for the purposes of liability for dishonest receipt has also been reconsidered by the Privy Council in *Barlow Clowes v Eurotrust* [2006] 1 All ER 333, which addresses the confusions introduced by the House of Lords in *Twinsectra v Yardley* [2002] 2 All ER 377, which were identified in the previous edition. The Law Commission has been particularly active in the last four years, and has published a number of reports or consultation papers within the subject area of this book, including Home Sharing (*Sharing Homes*, Law Com. No. 278 (2002)), Trustee Exemption Clauses (*Trustee Exemption Clauses*, Law Commission Consultation

Paper No. 171 (2003)), Forfeiture (*The Forfeiture Rule and the Law of Succession*, Law Com. No. 295 (2005)), and the rule in *Howe v Dartmouth* (*Capital and Income in Trusts: Classification and Apportionment*, Law Com. CP No. 175 (2004)). These are considered and evaluated. One of the interesting features of the past four years is the absence of any seminal authorities examining the relationship between restitution and property, especially in regard to knowing receipt and tracing. Note has been taken of the many minor decisions in these areas, but the uncertainties identified in the last edition remain.

It is now 11 years since the first edition of this book was published, and 13 since we were short listed for the Butterworths Prize and commissioned to write it. We are extremely grateful for the support and assistance we have received from Butterworths over the years, and for their production and marketing of the text. Together with the rest of Butterworths textbook catalogue, the baton has now been passed to OUP. We are very grateful to then for their enthusiastic support for this new edition, and the high quality of the production procedures they have applied to it. They have been able to turn around the manuscript in very short order. We are especially grateful to Sophie Baird, our editor, for her patience and efficiency.

We are, as always, very grateful to our families for their support, and for putting up with the distractions that producing a new edition inevitably involves. We are also grateful for the support of our colleagues, institutions and the students who have encouraged us in the production of this new edition. We are also very grateful to our fellow Trusts teachers, who have recommended and adopted this book for their courses over the years. We hope they will long continue to do so!

Robert Pearce
University of Wales, Lampeter

John Stevens
University of Birmingham

May 2006

# Contents

## PART III   ALLOCATION OF BENEFIT

# Table of statutes

Page references in **bold** indicate where a statute has been set out in part or in full

# Table of cases

# PART I

# INTRODUCTORY

# 1
# Historical introduction

## 1 What is equity?

### (1) A layman's understanding

To the layman the term 'equity' connotes justice and fairness, so that to act 'equitably' is synonymous with acting 'fairly.' For example, Psalm 96 speaks of God's justice in such terms:

> 'The LORD reigns.
> The world is firmly established, it
> cannot be moved;
> he will judge the peoples with equity.'[1]

The idea of 'equity' has always been particularly associated with judicial decisions, and emphasises that cases should be decided in a way which is fair and right, so that justice is achieved between the parties. However, although the branch of English law known as 'Equity' may have its origins in such concepts of fairness and justice, it carries specific and technical meaning.

### (2) A legal definition

Rather than referring to an abstract concept of justice or fairness, in English law the term 'Equity' describes a particular body of law, consisting of rights and remedies, which evolved historically through the Courts of Chancery. Until the late nineteenth century there were two parallel systems of law operating in England, each recognising, upholding and applying its own distinct rights and remedies. The Common Law Courts applied the common law and the Courts of Chancery applied equity. Although this division between courts was removed by the Judicature Acts of 1873 and 1875,[2] those rights and remedies which are today described as 'equitable' were either originally developed by and enforced through the Chancery courts, or have evolved by extension from such rights and remedies.

---

[1] Psalm 96 v 10: New International Version.    [2] See below, p 9.

## 2  The historical development of equity[3]

### (1)  The common law

#### (a)  History and emergence

Prior to the Norman Conquest of 1066 there was no developed legislature or judicature operating throughout England. Instead a system of 'custom' was applied by a variety of decision making bodies, ranging from the King's Council to village meetings. Custom inevitably varied with geographical location. However, the notion had already begun to evolve that justice was the prerogative of the Crown. This laid the jurisprudential foundation for the emergence of the common law in the twelfth century. The focus of the common law was the *Curia Regis*, the King's Court. During the 1180s Sir Ranulf de Glanvill wrote a treatise on 'the laws and customs of England' based on the workings of the King's Court, and produced 'a coherent system of English law deriving ultimate authority from the king'.[4] By 1234 the two common law courts, the Court of Common Pleas and the King's Bench, had developed.

#### (b)  Writs, actions and remedies

A plaintiff who wished to start an action in the Court of Common Pleas or the King's Bench needed to obtain a royal writ authorising the commencement of proceedings. These writs were purchased from the King's Chancery. As plaintiffs sought redress for novel legal problems new writs were developed to meet their needs until the Provisions of Oxford in 1258 prevented the issue of new writs without the permission of the King's Council. This closed the categories of writ which were available, confining plaintiffs to bringing cases within the terms of the recognised writs thus severely limiting the ability of the common law to develop effective redress for new types of case. The common law therefore became stultified and inflexible. Furthermore, the common law also offered only a limited range of remedies, predominantly monetary damages, to redress the wrong suffered by a successful plaintiff. This straight-jacketing of the common law was the predominant motive for the emergence of 'equity' as administered by the Courts of Chancery.

### (2)  The Courts of Chancery

#### (a)  The Chancery and the Chancellor

The Chancery was essentially a department of State. The Chancellor was the Keeper of the Great Seal, a Minister of the Crown who sometimes acted in a Prime Ministerial capacity to the King.

---

[3] See Holdsworth, *A History of English Law* (7th edn, 1956), Vol 1, Ch V; Baker, *An Introduction to English Legal History* (2nd edn, 1979), Ch 6.
[4] Baker, *An Introduction to English Legal History* (2nd edn, 1979), p 12.

### (b) Emergence of the judicial role of the Chancellor

Despite the development of the Common Law, justice remained a royal prerogative, and therefore the King retained a residuum of justice which enabled aggrieved parties to appeal directly to him for redress. These appeals were initially heard by the King in Council, but by the fourteenth century they were delegated to the Chancellor, who acted on behalf of the King. By 1473 the Chancellor had begun to issue decrees by his own authority in his own name.

### (c) Motivation for the emergence of the Courts of Chancery

The Chancery courts and their equity jurisdiction emerged because of the defects and rigidity of the common law, typified by the limited range of writs and the tendency to apply the strict rules of the common law even when this caused hardship, or seemed to do injustice, on the particular facts. For example, a debtor who had paid his debt but who had not ensured that his sealed bond was cancelled could be compelled by the common law to pay his creditor a second time because the bond was incontrovertible evidence of the debt. Again, the common law courts would not enforce an oral contract where the law required formalities such as proof in writing or a deed. Baker concludes that:

'It was not that the common law held that a debt was due twice, or that a promise of trust could be broken; such propositions would have been as absurd then as now. It was a matter of observing strict rules of evidence, rules which might exclude the merits of the case from consideration but which could not be relaxed without destroying certainty and condoning carelessness.'[5]

In contrast, the Court of Chancery developed as a court of 'conscience' to remedy these defects of the common law system. In the *Earl of Oxford's Case*,[6] heard in 1615, Lord Ellesmere explained why there was a Chancery:

'. . . [M]en's actions are so diverse and infinite that it is impossible to make any general law which may aptly meet with every particular and not fail in some circumstances. The office of the Chancellor is to correct men's consciences for frauds, breaches of trust, wrongs and oppression of what nature so ever they be, and to soften and mollify the extremity of the law.'

This corresponds with the conception of equity in classical writings where Aristotle had defined 'equity' as 'a correction of law where it is defective owing to its universality'.

### (d) Commencing an action in the Chancery Court

Unlike the Common Law Courts, where an action could only be commenced by means of a writ, actions in the Chancery Court were commenced by an informal bill of complaint, and process was begun by means of a *subpoena*. Proceedings were characterised by informality, and the court could sit outside of the legal terms which determined when the Common Law Courts sat. It could sit anywhere, including the Chancellor's house.

---

[5] Baker, *An Introduction to English Legal History* (2nd edn, 1979), p 88.    [6] (1615) 1 Rep Ch 1 at 6.

## (3) Character of the equity jurisdiction

### (a) A court of conscience

The Chancery Courts initially functioned as courts of conscience. In 1452 Fortescue CJ responded to a legal argument presented in the Court of Chancery: 'We are to argue conscience here, not the law.'[7] The Chancellor decided cases on the basis of his own sense of justice. Inevitably, different Chancellors had different conceptions of justice so that, in Selden's well-known phrase, equity varied with the length of the Chancellor's foot.[8] In the sixteenth century Cardinal Wolsey, who was Chancellor between 1515 and 1529 despite his lack of academic training, was the cause of particular complaint because of the arbitrary nature of the justice he dispensed. Blackstone summarised the condition of the equitable jurisdiction of the Court of Chancery at the end of the fifteenth century:

'No regular judicial system at that time prevailed in the court; but the suitor when he thought himself aggrieved found a desultory and uncertain remedy, according to the private opinion of the Chancellor.'[9]

### (b) Court of Equity

By the seventeenth century the Chancellor[10] tended to be a lawyer rather than a churchman. Decisions were reported, leading to a system of precedent and the development of a settled body of law, with distinct rights and remedies, that was almost as rigid as the common law. The Court of Chancery was no longer a simple court of conscience, but a court of 'equity' in the technical sense. For example, in *Honywood v Bennett*[11] in 1675 it was said that a contract without consideration was binding in conscience but not in equity. At the beginning of the nineteenth century the process was complete. Lord Eldon, Chancellor between 1801–06 and 1807–27, reflected in *Gee v Pritchard*[12] that:

'The doctrines of [the Court of Chancery] ought to be well settled, and made as uniform, almost, as those of the common law, laying down fixed principles, but taking care that they are to be applied according to the circumstances of each case. I cannot agree that the doctrines of this court are to be changed by every succeeding judge. Nothing would inflict on me greater pain in quitting this place than the recollection that I had done anything to justify the reproach that the equity of this court varies like the Chancellor's foot.'

In 1878 Jessel MR stated in *Re National Funds Assurance Co*[13] that the Chancery Division of the High Court 'is not, as I have often said, a Court of Conscience, but a Court of Law'. The process of an evolutionary development of settled principle was more recently recognised by the House of Lords in *Co-operative Insurance Society Ltd v*

---

7   Mich 31 Hen VI, Fitz Abr Subpoena, pl 23.
8   *Table talk of John Selden* (F Pollock edn, 1927), p 43.       9   *Comm* iii 53.
10   The last non-legal chancellor was Lord Shaftesbury (1673–82).
11   (1675) Nottingham Rep (73 ss) 214.       12   (1818) 2 Swan 402 at 414.
13   (1878) 10 Ch D 118; see also *Re Telescriptor Syndicate Ltd* [1903] 2 Ch 174 at 196, per Buckley J.

*Argyll Stores (Holdings) Ltd*,[14] which concerned the availability of the equitable remedy of specific performance. Lord Hoffmann stated:

'Of course the grant or refusal of specific performance remains a matter for the judge's discretion. There are no binding rules, but this does not mean that there cannot be settled principles, founded on practical considerations . . . which do not have to be re-examined in every case, but which the courts will apply in all but exceptional circumstances.'[15]

## (4) The relationship between equity and the common law

### (a) Equity not in conflict with the law

Initially equity avoided conflict with the common law and the common law courts. One fundamental maxim of equity is that it acts in personam,[16] so that it does not overturn the common law. For example, if the common law regards a defendant as the owner of land, whereas equity would find the plaintiff owner, equity does not say that the common law is wrong. Rather it orders the defendant, as legal owner, to deal with the land in a way which recognises that the plaintiff is the true owner. If the defendant fails to obey such an order he will be in contempt of court and subject to the appropriate penalties, including imprisonment.

### (b) The common injunctions

With two parallel systems of law administered by separate courts it was inevitable that there would be conflict as each struggled for dominance over the other. This struggle came to a head in the early seventeenth century during the reign of James I, when the primacy of equity was finally established. It had become frequent practice for the Court of Chancery to issue so called 'common injunctions', either ordering a party to a dispute to restrain his action at common law, or, if judgment had already been given in his favour by the common law court, to prevent him enforcing it. Refusal to obey these injunctions would be a contempt of court, deterred by the threat of imprisonment. These 'common injunctions' were a direct threat to the jurisdiction of the common law courts and their supremacy was at stake. Sir Edward Coke, the Chief Justice of the King's Bench, held that imprisonment for disobedience of the Chancery injunctions was unlawful, and ordered the release of those affected under the writ of *Habeas Corpus*.[17] The Chancery Court argued that the injunctions did not interfere with the common law, as any judgment still stood, but rather concerned only the conduct of the parties. This jurisdictional civil war was finally ended in 1616, when James I issued an order in favour of the Chancery Court and the common injunctions. Despite some subsequent attempts to reverse this resolution,[18] the primacy of the Chancery Courts was well established by the end of the century. The primacy of equity has been

---

[14] [1997] 3 All ER 297.    [15] [1997] 3 All ER 297 at 305.    [16] See below, p 23.
[17] See *Heath v Rydley* (1614) Cro Jac 335.
[18] Eg in 1690 a Bill was introduced in the House of Lords enacting that no Court of Equity should entertain any suit for which the proper remedy was at common law. However, the Bill was dropped when it was shown that it would make equity unworkable, which would lead to injustice.

preserved and was reaffirmed by statute in s 25 of The Supreme Court of Judicature Act 1873.[19]

## (5) Equity in the eighteenth and nineteenth centuries

### (a) Defects

Although the supremacy of equity was firmly established by the end of the seventeenth century, its administration was affected by severe procedural defects causing extreme delay. The Chancellor was the sole judge and the court officers abused their positions. The Chancery offices, in particular that of the Master, were lucrative for the holders. The offices were sold and the purchasers appointed by the Chancellor.[20] A fee system operated for tasks performed by the officers, leading to inefficiency. For example, clerks paid by the page to produce copies of documents required by litigants developed large handwriting and made use of wide margins to maximise their income. The Masters' reports were lengthened by reciting the whole of previous proceedings verbatim. In 1824 these difficulties led to the establishment of a Commission headed by Lord Eldon, who was himself notorious for delay. At that time some £39 million derived from cases awaiting decision was held by the court.

### (b) Reforms

In order to improve the administration of the equity jurisdiction a number of reforms were introduced.

*(i) Reform of the personnel of the Chancery Courts.* The number of persons competent to exercise the equity jurisdiction was increased. In 1813 a Vice Chancellor was appointed to assist the Chancellor, followed by a further two in 1843. In 1833 the Master of the Rolls was granted jurisdiction to sit concurrently with the Chancellor. In 1851 a Court of Appeals in Chancery was created. The other court offices were also reformed. In 1833 the office of Master became a Crown appointment with a fixed salary. In 1842 the six Clerks were abolished as were the Masters in 1852.

*(ii) Limited reform of the jurisdiction of the Chancery Courts.* The Common Law Procedure Act 1854 introduced changes marking a step towards the fusion of the common law and equity jurisdictions. The effect of this Act was summarised in the report of the Judicature Commission:

'The Court of Chancery is now not only empowered, but bound to decide for itself all questions of common law without having recourse as formerly to the aid of a Common Law Court . . . The Court is further empowered to take evidence orally in open court, and in certain cases to award damages for breaches of contract, or wrongs, as at common law; and trial by jury, the great distinguishing feature of the common law, has recently been introduced into the Court of Chancery. On the other hand, the Courts of Common Law are now authorised to compel discovery in all cases in which a court of Equity would have enforced it in a suit instituted for that purpose. A limited power has been conferred on Courts of

---

[19] See below, p 10.    [20] For up to £5,000.

Common Law to grant injunctions, and to allow equitable defences to be pleaded, and in certain cases to grant relief from forfeitures.'

However, the progress towards fusion was slight as the Act only applied where a court of equity would have granted an absolute and perpetual injunction. True fusion was only effected by the dramatic reform of the English legal system by the Judicature Acts of 1873 and 1875.

# 3 The Judicature Acts 1873 and 1875

## (1) Restructuring the system of courts

The Judicature Acts effected a radical restructuring of the English court system. The Courts of Chancery, King's Bench, Common Pleas, Exchequer, Admiralty, Probate and the London Court of Bankruptcy were consolidated and merged to form a single Supreme Court, divided into the High Court and the Court of Appeal. As a matter of convenience, rather than of jurisdiction, the High Court was organised into divisions, comprising the Chancery Division; King's Bench Division; Common Pleas Division; Exchequer Division; and the Probate, Divorce and Admiralty Division.

## (2) Uniform jurisdiction given to judges of the Supreme Court

Although the High Court divisions reflected the former distinction between the common law and Chancery courts, the central feature of the reform was that all the judges of the Supreme Court, irrespective of the division in which they sat, were to have both common law and equitable jurisdiction. This was achieved by s 24 of the 1873 Act, which provided that all judges were to give effect to such equitable estates, rights, relief, defences, duties and liabilities as would have been given effect by the Court of Chancery, and also to recognise and give effect to all estates, titles, rights, duties, obligations and liabilities existing by the common law.[21] This combined jurisdiction was more recently re-enacted in s 49(1) of the Supreme Court Act 1981, which provides:

'. . . every court exercising jurisdiction in England and Wales in any civil cause or matter shall continue to administer law and equity . . .'

## (3) Procedural implications of the reforms

The concurrent common law and equity jurisdiction conferred on the Supreme Court by the Judicature Acts revolutionised the process of litigation. It was no longer necessary to commence a separate action in the Chancery Court to gain recognition of an equitable right or to obtain an equitable remedy.

---

[21] Judicature Act 1925, ss 36–44; Supreme Court Act 1981, s 49.

## (4) Supremacy of equity enshrined

### (a) Supreme Court of Judicature Act 1873, s 25

It has been seen that historically the supremacy of equity was maintained by the power of the Chancery Court to grant common injunctions. These were abolished by the Supreme Court of Judicature Act 1873, s 24(5), since the concurrent jurisdiction granted to judges under s 24 rendered them unnecessary. The supremacy of equity was itself placed on a statutory footing by s 25, which provided that in a number of specific instances[22] the existing equitable rule was to supersede the common law rule. Section 25(11) provided somewhat more generally that:

'. . . in all matters not herein-before particularly mentioned, in which there is any conflict, or variance, between the Rules of Equity and the Rules of the Common Law with reference to the same matter, the Rules of Equity will apply.[23]

### (b) Operation of s 25(11)

Section 25(11) only operates if there is a genuine conflict between the rules of equity and the rules of common law. It was applied in the leading case *Walsh v Lonsdale*,[24] where the defendant had agreed to grant the plaintiff a lease of a weaving mill. The rent[25] was payable yearly in advance. No legal lease was ever executed[26] but the plaintiff was allowed into possession of the mill and paid rent quarterly in arrears to the defendant. Under the common law the plaintiff had thereby become a periodic tenant of the mill. Under the terms of this periodic tenancy the rent was payable in arrears. In equity, however, the contract between the defendant and plaintiff gave rise to an equitable lease,[27] under the terms of which the rent was payable in advance as agreed in the contract. The defendant demanded payment of rent in advance and exercised the remedy of distress to secure payment.[28] The plaintiff claimed that this distress was improper. Whether the defendant's exercise of distress was lawful or improper depended on whether the parties' relationship as landlord and tenant was governed by the legal or equitable rule. If there was a legal periodic tenancy the distress was improper as the rent was not due, whereas under an equitable lease the rent was in arrears and the defendant was entitled to exercise his right to recover it. The Court of Appeal held that as there was a conflict between the respective legal and equitable rules, s 25(11) of the Judicature Act applied and the equitable rule prevailed. The defendant's exercise of distress was therefore proper.

---

[22]  S 25(1)–(10).

[23]  This provision is retained by Supreme Court Act 1981, s 49(1), which provides that: 'wherever there is any conflict or variance between the rule of equity and the rules of the common law with reference to the same matter, the rules of equity shall prevail.'

[24]  (1882) 21 Ch D 9; see also *Job v Job* (1877) 6 Ch D 562; *Lowe & Sons v Dixon & Sons* (1885–86) 16 QBD 455.

[25]  Of 30 shillings per loom per annum, with the plaintiffs agreeing to run not less than 540 looms.

[26]  A legal lease would only have been created if the defendant had executed a deed.

[27]  This is because the defendant's contract to grant the lease was specifically performable. The equitable lease arises as a consequence of the maxim that 'equity treats as done that which ought to be done'. See below, p 22.

[28]  Distress is a common law remedy which entitles the landlord to seize goods on the rented land and sell them to recoup any arrears of rent owed by the tenant.

A further situation in which the equitable rule has been held to prevail over the legal equivalent is in the context of contractual terms as to the time when performance is expected. Whereas at common law requirements as to time were regarded as of the essence of the contract, in equity they were not, so that a party in breach of a requirement of time was not entitled to repudiate the contract for breach. Outside of commercial contracts, where stipulations as to time are regarded as crucial, the equitable rule has been held to prevail over the common law rule where there is no express agreement that time is to be of the essence.[29]

# 4 The fusion of law and equity

## (1) The effect of the Judicature Acts

One question arising from the reforms instituted by the Judicature Acts is whether there has been a 'fusion' of law and equity. Jurisprudential debate has questioned whether there is now one single body of 'English law', which has its heritage in the rules, rights and remedies of the previously distinct bodies of 'common law' and 'equity', or whether there has been a mere fusion of the administration of these two distinct bodies of law so that 'common law' and 'equity' are now administered by a single court replacing the pre-existing duality of courts. The traditional view is that the Judicature Acts effected only a fusion of administration, though more recent judicial sentiments seem to favour the view that there has been a substantive fusion in some sense. As this issue is examined it will become apparent that the central differences of opinion revolve around the meaning attributed to the concept of 'fusion'.

## (2) Fusion of administration[30]

Traditionalists hold that the Judicature Acts merely fused the administration of equity and the common law. In the famous words of Ashburner the result is that:

'. . . the two streams of jurisprudence, though they run in the same channel, run side by side, and do not mingle their waters.'[31]

This view enjoys the support of judicial dicta contemporaneous with the passing of the Acts. For example, in *Salt v Cooper* Jessel MR commented:

'. . . the main object of the Act was to assimilate the transaction of Equity business and Common Law business by different Courts of Judicature. It has been sometimes inaccurately called "the fusion of Law and Equity"; but it was not any fusion, or anything of the kind; it was the vesting in one tribunal of the administration of Law and Equity in every cause, action or dispute which should come before that tribunal.'[32]

---

[29] *United Scientific Holdings Ltd v Burnley Borough Council* [1978] AC 904.

[30] See (1954) 70 LQR 326 (Lord Evershed); (1961) 24 MLR 116 (V T H Delaney); (1977) 93 LQR 529 (P V Baker); (1977) 6 AALR 119 (T G Watkin); (1994) 14 LS 313 (David Capper), pp 315–317.

[31] Snell, *Principles of Equity* (2nd edn), p 18.      [32] (1880–81) 16 Ch D 544 at 549.

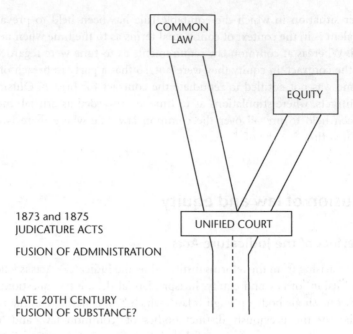

1873 and 1875
JUDICATURE ACTS

FUSION OF ADMINISTRATION

LATE 20TH CENTURY
FUSION OF SUBSTANCE?

The Attorney General at the time that the Acts were passed disavowed the object of fusion when explaining their effect to the House of Commons during the second reading of the Judicature Bill:

'Law and Equity therefore, would remain if the Bill passed, but they would be administered concurrently, and no one would be sent to get in one court the relief which another court had refused to give . . .'[33] More recent statutory language also implies that law and equity remain distinct bodies of law. Section 49(1) of the Supreme Court Act 1981, which re-enacts many of the central provisions of the Judicature Acts regarding the place of equity and the common law, speaks of the 'rules of equity and the rules of the common law'.

## (3) Fusion in substance

Although contemporaneous opinion may have favoured the view that the Judicature Acts had not led to the fusion of law and equity more recent dicta have expressed the view that there has been a substantive fusion of equity and the common law, producing a single body of legal rules, not a mere fusion of their administration. This has been particularly clearly accepted in Commonwealth jurisdictions.

### (a) Early dicta

Even some early dicta suggested that something beyond a simple fusion of the administration of law and equity had taken place. For example, in *Walsh v Lonsdale*,[34] which was considered above, Jessel MR stated:

[33]  Hansard 3rd Series, Vol 216, pp 644–645.    [34]  (1882) 21 Ch D 9.

'There are not two estates as there were formerly, one estate at common law by reason of the payment of the rent from year to year, and an estate in equity under the agreement. There is only one Court and the equity rule prevails in it.'

## (b) More recent cases

As time passed and the separate administration of law and equity became little more than a distant memory, an increasing number of judges advocated practical realism and declared that law and equity had been fused. In the middle years of the twentieth century Lord Denning regarded law and equity as unified, and manipulated this as a justification for law reform. In *Errington v Errington and Woods*[35] he stated that 'law and equity have been fused for nearly eighty years'. In *Boyer v Warbey*[36] he argued that such fusion demanded that the common law principle of privity of estate, which allows leasehold covenants to be enforced between successors in title to an original landlord and tenant despite the fact that they are not privy to the contractual terms of the lease, should be extended so as to apply to equitable leases:[37] 'I know that before the Judicature Act 1873 it was said that the doctrine of covenants running with the land only applied to covenants under seal[38] and not to agreements under hand[39] . . . But since the fusion of law and equity the position is different. The distinction between agreements under hand and covenants under seal has largely been obliterated.'[40]

Some 20 years later, members of the House of Lords expressed similar sentiments in *United Scientific Holdings Ltd v Burnley Borough Council.*[41] Lord Diplock specifically commented on Ashburner's metaphor:

'. . . by 1977 this metaphor has in my view become both mischievous and deceptive. The innate conservatism of English lawyers made them slow to recognise that by the Supreme Court of Judicature Act 1873 the two systems of substantive and adjectival law formerly administered by the Courts of Law and Courts of Chancery . . . were fused. As at the confluence of the Rhone and Saone, it may be possible for a short distance to discern the source from which each part of the combined stream came, but there comes a point at which this ceases to be possible. If Professor Ashburner's fluvial metaphor is to be retained at all, the waters of the confluent streams of law and equity have surely mingled now.'

Lord Simon also held that the Judicature Acts had 'truly . . . brought about a fusion of common law and equity'[42] but considered that there were institutional reasons why English lawyers had been slow to accept this conclusion. First, there had been some dovetailing of the systems before the Acts themselves.[43] Secondly, the High Court had continued to sit in administrative divisions. Thirdly, the conservatism of lawyers and their training tended to minimise the change that had been made.

---

[35] [1952] 1 KB 290 at 298.     [36] [1953] 1 QB 234.     [37] [1953] 1 QB 234 at 245–246.

[38] In other words, to covenants made by deed, and therefore enforceable at common law. A seal was one of the formal requirements for a deed before the Law of Property (Miscellaneous Provisions) Act 1989.

[39] In other words, a covenant enforceable only in equity on the basis of a written agreement not made by deed.

[40] See also [1978] CLJ 98 (Smith).     [41] [1978] AC 904.     [42] [1978] AC 904 at 944.

[43] See above.

## (c) Commonwealth approaches

The courts in some Commonwealth jurisdictions have been far more strident in declaring the practical fusion of equity and the common law. For example, in *Aquaculture Corpn v New Zealand Green Mussel Co Ltd*,[44] the New Zealand Court of Appeal addressed the question whether damages, historically a common law remedy, should be available as a remedy for breach of an equitable duty of confidence. Cooke P stated:

'For all purposes now material, equity and common law are mingled or merged. The practicality of the matter is that in the circumstances of the dealings between the parties the law imposes a duty of confidence. For its breach a full range of remedies should be available as appropriate, no matter whether they originated in common law, equity or statute.'[45]

The New Zealand courts have similarly held that breach of an equitable duty can lead to exemplary damages or damages for mental distress,[46] which were historically only available at common law, and that an award of equitable compensation may be subject to reduction by application of the common law principles of contributory negligence.[47] This contrasts with the more conservative approach taken in England, where the award of damages for breach of an equitable duty of confidence has been justified under the Chancery Amendment Act 1858 in lieu of an injunction,[48] without the need to find an autonomous right to equitable compensation paralleling the common law right to compensatory damages for breach of duty or obligation.

The approach advocated by Lord Diplock in *United Scientific Holdings Ltd v Burnley Borough Council*[49] was also adopted by the Canadian courts in *Le Mesurier v Andrus*[50] and *Canson Enterprises Ltd v Broughton & Co*,[51] where the common law principle of remoteness of damage was held applicable to an equitable claim for damages for breach of fiduciary duty.[52] La Forest J, however, recognised that in some circumstances it is still necessary to differentiate between equitable rights and remedies and those which historically originated at common law:

'There might be room for concern if one were indiscriminately attempting to meld the whole of the two systems. Equitable concepts like trusts, equitable estates and consequent equitable remedies must continue to exist apart, if not in isolation, from common law rules.'[53]

## (4) A single coherent body of law[54]

Whilst the debate has not been settled clearly in favour of either view, it seems that the central problem is often the meaning invested in the term 'fusion'. If 'fusion' means that

---

[44] [1990] 3 NZLR 299.

[45] [1990] 3 NZLR 299 at 301. See also *Catt v Marac Australia Ltd* (1986) 9 NSWLR 639 (NSW); *LAC Minerals v International Corona Resources Ltd* (1989) 61 DLR (4th) 14 (Canada). See: (1994) 14 LS 313 (David Capper).

[46] *Mouat v Clark Boyce* [1992] 2 NZLR 559.      [47] *Mouat v Clark Boyce* [1992] 2 NZLR 559.

[48] *Saltman Engineering Co Ltd v Campbell Engineering Co Ltd* (1948) 65 RPC 203; *Seager v Copydex Ltd* [1967] 2 All ER 415; *A-G v Observer Ltd* [1990] AC 109.

[49] [1978] AC 904.      [50] (1986) 54 OR (2d) 1.      [51] (1991) 85 DLR (4th) 129.

[52] See also *Bristol and West Building Society v Mothew* [1996] 4 All ER 698 at 711.

[53] (1991) 85 DLR (4th) 129 at 152.      [54] See also (1997) 113 LQR 601 (Duggan).

any distinction between equity and common law, and especially between equitable and legal rights and remedies, has been completely removed so that adjectivally the term 'equitable' has no continuing relevance, then it has not occurred. The law still distinguishes between legal and equitable ownership, the foundation of the trust concept which is the main subject of this book.[55] However, it is also clear that English law no longer preserves the strict distinction between equitable and legal rules that was maintained before the Judicature Acts. The law has developed as a whole, so that there has been some synthesis of legal and equitable rights and remedies and cross-fertilisation between them, and some of the old distinctions between rights and remedies historically equitable in origin and those historically of common law origin have ceased to be significant. The adjectives 'equitable' and 'common law' are useful to distinguish the different rights and remedies that make up English law but it is submitted that Lord Diplock was correct to observe in *United Scientific Holdings Ltd v Burnley Borough Council* that:

'. . . if, by "rules of equity" is meant that body of substantive and adjectival law that prior to 1875, was administered by the Court of Chancery but not by courts of common law, to speak of the rules of equity as being part of the law of England in 1977 is about as meaningful as to speak similarly of the Statute of Uses or of Quia Emptores. Historically, all three have in their time played an important part in the development of the corpus juris into what it is today; but to perpetuate a dichotomy between rules of equity and rules of common law which it was a major purpose of the Supreme Court of Judicature Act 1873 to do away with, is, in my view, conducive to erroneous conclusions as to the ways in which the law of England has developed in the last hundred years.'[56]

The approach which best represents the prevailing judicial attitude is that the long fusion of the administration of law and equity has produced a single, coherent, body of rules which operate harmoniously together, even though some historically have their origin in equity and others in the common law. Those historical roots can often still be discerned, and in some cases may still remain significant. In other cases it may indeed be accurate to describe the rules as having merged or melded. This middle approach was articulated by the House of Lords in *Tinsley v Milligan*,[57] which concerned the question whether a plaintiff could assert a claim to an equitable interest in land by way of a resulting trust where she had acted illegally.[58] It was argued that the traditional equitable maxim that a person seeking to assert an equitable entitlement must come with 'clean hands' prevented the plaintiff asserting her right. In contrast, the common law had concluded that a person whose acquisition of property was tainted by illegal conduct was entitled to assert his common law right to ownership provided that he did not need to rely on his illegal conduct to establish his title.[59] Lord Browne-Wilkinson[60] considered that such a distinction was inappropriate in the modern law:

'. . . to draw such distinctions between property rights enforceable at law and those which

---

[55] See Chapter 3 for a discussion of the nature of a trust.    [56] [1978] AC 904 at 924.
[57] [1993] 3 All ER 65.    [58] The facts are set out below at p 19.
[59] *Bowmakers Ltd v Barnet Instruments Ltd* [1945] KB 65.
[60] With whom Lord Jauncey and Lord Lowry concurred.

require the intervention of equity would be surprising. More than 100 years has elapsed since the fusion of the administration of law and equity. The reality of the matter is that, in 1993, English law has one single law of property made up of legal and equitable interests. Although for historical reasons legal estates and equitable estates have differing incidents, the person owning either type of estate has a right of property, a right in rem not merely a right in personam. If the law is that a party is entitled to enforce a proprietary right acquired under an illegal transaction, in my judgement the same rule ought to apply to any property right so acquired, whether such right is legal or equitable.'[61]

Although he referred to the 'fusion of the administration of law and equity', which could be taken as supporting the orthodox position, his analysis that English law has 'one single law of property made up of legal and equitable interests' is of greater significance. This presupposes that there has been a degree of fusion in substance, but not so as to completely eradicate all distinctions. There are different types of ownership, different rights and remedies in English law which by historical origin are equitable and legal, and although they form one coherent body of law they must still be distinguished or identified as such because of the different 'incidents' that accompany them. A similar approach was also taken by the House of Lords in *Lord Napier and Ettrick v Hunter*,[62] where Lord Goff considered the relationship between equitable proprietary rights and personal rights and obligations deriving from a contract of insurance:

'No doubt our task nowadays is to see the two strands of authority, at law and in equity, moulded into a coherent whole; but for my part I cannot see why this amalgamation should lead to the rejection of the equitable proprietary right . . .'

Examples of situations where there is a need to draw a distinction between legal and equitable rights and remedies are abundant in English law. In relation to land, the entire scheme of the Law of Property Act 1925 is predicated upon the distinction between legal and equitable estates and interests in land,[63] and the character of an interest determines its ability to endure through transfers of the legal title. Specific perform-ance, an equitable remedy, is only available where a contract has been entered in return for valuable consideration and not of a promise made by deed, which would be enforced by the common law. A promise to create a trust will not therefore be enforced by equity in favour of a volunteer,[64] although such a promise contained in a deed, to which the intended beneficiary was a party, will entitle the beneficiary to an award of common law damages if the covenantor fails to create the promised trust.[65] The rules governing the passing of the benefit and burden of a covenant affecting freehold land are different in law and in equity, so that at law the burden of a covenant is incapable of passing to a successor in title to the original covenantor, whereas in equity the burden of a restrictive covenant is capable of passing with the land.[66] It is impossible to combine the legal and equitable rules governing the passing of the benefit and burden of such

---

[61]  [1993] 3 All ER 65 at 86.        [62]  [1993] 1 All ER 385 at 401.

[63]  Law of Property Act 1925 s 1.

[64]  *Donaldson v Donaldson* (1854) Kay 711; *Re Plumptre's Marriage Settlement* [1901] 1 Ch 609; *Re Cooks' Settlement* [1965] Ch 902.

[65]  *Cannon v Hartley* [1949] Ch 213.        [66]  See Stevens and Pearce, *Land Law* (3rd edn, 2005) Ch 16.

covenants, so that a covenant will not be enforceable between successors in title to the land of the original covenantor and covenantee if the benefit of the covenant has passed at law but not in equity, and the burden has passed in equity but not at law. The rules which enable a person to trace property which has been misappropriated from them are also different at law and in equity. Whereas at common law it is impossible to trace money once it has become mixed with other money,[67] equity allows tracing through a mixed fund provided that a sufficient fiduciary relationship to justify the intervention of equity can be shown.[68] In the very significant case *Westdeutsche Landesbank Girozentrale v Islington London Borough Council*[69] the majority of the House of Lords held that whereas equity enjoys a limited jurisdiction to award compound interest when a remedy is granted,[70] the common law has no such jurisdiction and is only capable of awarding simple interest.[71] Therefore, a plaintiff seeking restitution was held not to be entitled to compound interest because his cause of action in unjust enrichment arose at common law and not in equity. This reinforces the view that it is not irrelevant where a cause of action originates. As has already been noted above, the trust emerged because, through the parallel systems of law and equity, English law developed the abstract concept of the double-ownership of property. Thus, legal and equitable title can exist simultaneously in the same item of property, enjoyed by different persons as owners.

# 5  The maxims of equity[72]

The maxims of equity are an attempt to formulate in short pithy phrases the key principles which underlie the exercise of the equitable jurisdiction. They are not binding rules, nor do they provide guidance for every situation in which equity operates. Nevertheless, they provide useful illustrations of some of the principal recurrent themes which can be identified within the corpus of the rules of equity.

## (1)  Equity will not suffer a wrong to be without a remedy

This maxim provides the philosophical foundation of equity, namely that wrongs should be redressed by the courts if possible. Equity developed as a response to defects of the common law to provide relief where none was available. For example,

---

[67] *Taylor v Plumer* (1815) 3 M & S 562; *Agip (Africa) Ltd v Jackson* [1990] Ch 265; *Bank Tejarat v Hong Kong and Shanghai Banking Corpn (CI) Ltd* [1995] 1 Lloyd's Rep 239.

[68] *Re Diplock* [1948] Ch 465.

[69] [1996] 2 All ER 961. See also [1996] RLR 3 (Birks); [1996] LMCLQ 441 (Stevens)

[70] *President of India v La Pintada Compania Navegacion SA (La Pintada)* [1985] AC 104.

[71] The Law Reform (Miscellaneous Provisions) Act 1934, s 3(1) and Supreme Court Act 1981, s 35A expressly enable the award of simple interest on claims at common law, where historically the common law had no general power to award interest at all: *London, Chatham and Dover Rly Co v South Eastern Rly Co* [1893] AC 429.

[72] See Snell's *Principles of Equity* (30th edn, 2000), pp 27–44.

equity intervened to allow a person to escape from a contract which they had entered having been misled by a mistake of fact, even though the contract was enforceable at common law.[73] Similarly, through a trust[74] equity enabled a beneficiary to enforce an obligation to use property in a particular way where there was no remedy at common law.

## (2) Equity follows the law[75]

The Court of Chancery did not override the Courts of Common Law except to remedy an injustice, and could not depart from statute. Equity does not unnecessarily depart from legal principles.[76] The fact that equity follows the law is well illustrated in the context of land[77] by the fact that the equitable estates and interests largely correspond to those at law.[78]

## (3) Where the equities are equal the law prevails

This maxim means that where there are two persons with competing rights to the same item of property, one with a legal right and the other an equitable right, the legal right will take priority over the equitable right even if the equitable right had pre-existed it. In *Wortley v Birkhead*[79] Lord Hardwicke LC explained that that this was 'by reason of that force [the Court of Chancery] necessarily and rightly gives to the legal title'.[80] In the context of land, issues of priority between competing rights, whether legal or equitable, are governed by statutory rules which have displaced the operation of this maxim and the next.[81]

## (4) Where the equities are equal the first in time prevails

This maxim means that if two parties have competing equitable rights in the same item of property, and neither has the legal estate, the right which was created first enjoys priority.[82] This maxim mirrors the common law rule as to priority between competing legal rights.

---

[73]  See eg *Cooper v Joel* (1859) 1 De G F & J 240; *Torrance v Bolton* (1872) 8 Ch App 118.

[74]  See Chapter 3 for a consideration of trusts.

[75]  See [1995] CLJ 60 (Gardner).

[76]  *Burgess v Wheate* (1759) 1 Eden 177 at 195, per Clarke MR; *Sinclair v Brougham* [1914] AC 398 at 414–415, per Lord Haldane LC.

[77]  See Stevens and Pearce, *Land Law* (3rd edn, 2005) p33.

[78]  See Chapter 3. However, equity recognised a range of future interests in land not recognised at law: see Megarry and Wade, *The Law of Real Property* (6th edn, 2000), pp 104–107.

[79]  (1754) 2 Ves Sen 571 at 574.

[80]  Compare also *Marsh v Lee* (1670) 2 Vent 337; *E Pfeiffer Weinkellerei-Weineinkauf GmbH & Co v Arbothnot Factors Ltd* [1988] 1 WLR 150.

[81]  See Chapter 3.

[82]  *Willoughby v Willoughby* (1756) 1 Term Rep 763; *Brace v Duchess of Marlborough* (1728) 2 P Wms 491; *Rice v Rice* (1854) 2 Drew 73; *Phillips v Phillips* (1861) 4 De GF & J 208.

## (5) He who seeks equity must do equity

This maxim looks to a plaintiff's future conduct. If a plaintiff seeks equitable relief he must be prepared to act fairly toward the person against whom it is sought.[83] For example, if a purchase is set aside in equity the purchase money must be repaid with interest.[84]

## (6) He who comes to equity must come with clean hands

In contrast, this maxim looks to the past conduct of the plaintiff. If the plaintiff's conduct is tainted by illegal or inequitable conduct he may be denied the relief to which he would otherwise be entitled. For example, a tenant will not be granted specific performance of an agreement for a lease if he is in breach of the covenants it contains.[85] The maxim does not apply to conduct in general, but only that which has 'an immediate and necessary relation to the equity sued for'.[86] Therefore in *Argyll (Duchess) v Argyll (Duke)*[87] the plaintiff's adultery, which caused a divorce, was no bar to her claim for an injunction to restrain the defendant from publishing confidential material. The rationale for this maxim, as for the parallel common law rule against illegality, is to deter persons from entering transactions which involve a dimension of illegality. However, since these rules may in practice allow one person who was party to an illegal purpose to arbitrarily retain the entire benefit of property transferred to him, because another equally guilty party is prevented from asserting any entitlement to it, the courts have systematically ameliorated their strictness through exceptions.

The operation of the equitable maxim was considered by the House of Lords in *Tinsley v Milligan*,[88] where a house was purchased jointly by a lesbian couple. Only one of them was registered as the legal proprietor to enable the other to dishonestly claim social security benefits by appearing to be a mere lodger. After the breakdown of the relationship, the partner who did not enjoy a share of the legal title claimed that she was entitled to a half-share of the house in equity arising by way of a resulting trust implied from her contribution to the purchase price.[89] The registered proprietor argued that she was prevented from asserting her equitable right because she was tainted by their illegal purpose, so that she did not come to equity with 'clean hands'. The House of Lords held by a bare majority that she was entitled to succeed in her claim. The essential disagreement between the majority and minority was not as to the existence of the maxim 'he who comes to equity must come with clean hands', but how it should be applied in circumstances where a plaintiff's claim is not itself founded on the alleged illegality. Lord Goff, who dissented,[90] took the view that the maxim should apply in its full force, since it was well established by authority and there was no justification

---

[83] See eg *Lodge v National Union Investment Co Ltd* [1907] 1 Ch 300; *Solle v Butcher* [1950] 1 KB 671; *Chappell v Times Newspapers Ltd* [1975] 1 WLR 482.

[84] *Peacock v Evans* (1809–10) 16 Ves 512.    [85] *Coatsworth v Johnson* (1886) 54 LT 520.

[86] *Dering v Earl of Winchelsea* (1787) 2 White & Tud LC 488 at 489.    [87] [1967] Ch 302.

[88] [1994] 1 AC 340.    [89] See Chapter 8.    [90] With whom Lord Keith concurred.

for introducing a change,[91] even though it produced an admittedly harsh result for the plaintiff.[92] Lord Browne-Wilkinson, with whom Lord Jauncey and Lord Lowry concurred, held that the maxim should prevent a plaintiff asserting equitable title to property only if he had to rely on his illegal conduct to establish the entitlement, thus ensuring uniformity with the common law rule against illegality as interpreted in *Bowmakers Ltd v Barnet Instruments Ltd.*[93] He concluded that:

'. . . although there is no case for overruling the wide principle . . . as the law has developed the equitable principle has become elided into the common law rule. In my judgement the time has come to decide clearly that the rule is the same whether a plaintiff founds himself on a legal or equitable title: he is entitled to recover if he is not forced to plead or rely on the illegality, even if it emerges that the title on which he relied was acquired in the course of carrying through an illegal transaction.'[94]

With the operation of the maxim circumscribed in this way, the plaintiff was held entitled to succeed, since she could establish her entitlement to an equitable interest by way of a resulting trust merely by showing that she had contributed to the purchase price of the property. She did not need to rely on her illegal conduct because the underlying purpose of the purchase was irrelevant to her claim against the registered proprietor. Despite the differing approaches adopted the House of Lords rejected any wholesale change to a general 'public conscience' test as had been proposed by the Court of Appeal,[95] as this would have required the court to weigh the adverse consequences of granting relief against those of refusing relief.

The application of the maxim was further weakened in *Tribe v Tribe,*[96] where the Court of Appeal held a father entitled to assert an equitable entitlement to shares, the legal title to which he had transferred to his son as part of a scheme to defraud his creditors. Because the shares had been transferred by a father to his son there was a presumption that the father had intended to make a gift,[97] thereby disposing of his entire interest in them. He could only demonstrate that he had retained the equitable ownership of the shares through a resulting trust if this presumption of gift was rebutted. The underlying purpose of the transaction was clearly sufficient to rebut the presumption because there was no intention that the son should own the shares for himself, but to so rebut it would require the father to rely on the illegal purpose behind the transfer. The equitable maxim would therefore apply, preventing him from claiming any equitable entitlement. In the event, however, the feared creditors never materialised to be defrauded and the father demanded the re-transfer of the shares. The Court of Appeal surprisingly held that the father was not prevented from asserting a resulting trust of the shares, on the ground that the illegal purpose had not been carried out. This was a somewhat generous finding, since as Nourse LJ stated, this exception to the full rigour of the maxim only applies if 'the illegal purpose has not been carried into effect

[91] *Curtis v Perry* (1802) 6 Ves 739; *Groves v Groves* (1828) 3 Y & J 163; *Childers v Childers* (1857) 3 K & J 310; *Tinker v Tinker* [1970] P 136; *Cantor v Cox* (1976) 239 Estates Gazette 121.

[92] Which Lord Goff recognised: [1993] 3 All ER 65 at 80.        [93] [1945] KB 65.

[94] [1945] KB 65 at 91.        [95] [1992] 2 All ER 391.

[96] [1996] Ch 107, [1995] 4 All ER 236.

[97] Technically, their relationship gave rise to a presumption of advancement.

in any way', and the central act required to defraud the creditors, namely transferring the legal title of the shares to the son, had undeniably occurred. The conclusion that the illegal purpose had not been carried into effect was therefore artificial. It was merely fortuitous for the father that the perceived threat against which he had taken pre-emptive action was illusory.

## (7) Delay defeats equity

Equity will not assist a plaintiff who has failed to assert his rights within a reasonable time. As Lord Camden LC said in *Smith v Clay*:

'. . . [equity] has always refused its aid to stale demands, where a party has slept upon his right and acquiesced for a great length of time. Nothing can call forth this court into activity, but conscience, good faith, and reasonable diligence; where these are wanting, the Court is passive and does nothing.'[98] This is the foundation of the equitable defence of laches, which was recently applied in *Nelson v Rye*,[99] where it was held that a musician could not claim an account of earnings wrongfully retained by his manager in breach of fiduciary duty because he had waited for more than six years before commencing an action. The operation of this defence must today be considered in conjunction with the statutory rules concerning limitation of actions under the Limitation Act 1980.[100]

## (8) Equality is equity

Where persons enjoy concurrent entitlement to identical interests in property, and there is no express provision, agreement or other basis as to how it should be divided amongst them, equity prescribes that equal division should occur, so that each receives an equal share in the property.[101] This maxim is reflected in the preference of equity for a tenancy in common, which will sometimes be implied in equity even where the common law holds that there is a joint tenancy,[102] namely[103] where joint purchasers contribute to the purchase in equal shares and there is no express allocation of the equitable interest; where persons have jointly lent money on mortgage;[104] and where property is acquired as part of a joint business venture.[105]

## (9) Equity looks to the intent rather than the form

The principle behind this maxim was well stated by Romilly MR in *Parkin v Thorold*:

---

[98] (1767) 3 Bro CC 639n at 640.    [99] [1996] 2 All ER 186; [1997] Conv 225 (J Stevens).

[100] See Chapter 22.

[101] *Petit v Smith* (1695) 1 P Wms 7; *Re Dickens* [1935] Ch 267; *Re Bradberry* [1943] Ch 35; *Hampton & Sons v Garrard Smith (Estate Agents) Ltd* [1985] 1 EGLR 23; see also *McPhail v Doulton* [1971] AC 424, discussed in Chapter 16.

[102] See Stevens and Pearce, *Land Law* (3rd edn 2005), p 319.

[103] See *Malayan Credit Ltd v Jack Chia-MPH Ltd* [1986] AC 549.

[104] *Morley v Bird* (1798) 3 Ves 628. This applies only to where there are joint lenders, not to the more common situation of joint borrowers.

[105] *Lake v Craddock* (1732) 2 White & Tud LC 876.

'Courts of equity make a distinction between that which is matter of substance and that which is matter of form; and if it finds that by insisting on the form, the substance will be defeated, it holds it to be inequitable to allow a person to insist on such form, and thereby defeat the substance.'[106]

More recently, in *Foskett v McKeown* Sir Richard Scott V-C stated that:

'The availability of equitable remedies ought . . . to depend upon the substance of the transaction in question.'[107]

Therefore, equity categorises a covenant affecting freehold land as 'restrictive', even though worded in a positive way, if in substance it is negative.[108] Similarly, equity will not grant an injunction to enforce a negative covenant entered by an employee agreeing not to work for others if in substance this would amount to an order of specific performance of their contract of employment,[109] since equity will not enforce contracts of personal service.[110] It is not necessary to use the precise word 'trust' to create a trust, provided that in substance the settlor intended to subject the legal owner of the property to a mandatory obligation regarding its use.[111] Similarly, equity will look to the substance, and not the wording used, to determine if a clause in a contract providing for the payment of a specific sum in the event of breach is a penalty or a genuine pre-estimate of damages.[112]

## (10) Equity regards as done that which ought to be done[113]

Where a contract is specifically enforceable,[114] equity regards the promisor as having already done what he has promised to do, because he can be compelled to do it. Therefore, as was seen in *Walsh v Lonsdale*,[115] a contract to grant a lease is treated as creating an equitable lease on the same terms. Similarly, because of the availability of specific performance, a contract for the purchase of land,[116] or of unique personal property,[117] will give rise to an immediate constructive trust vesting the equitable ownership in the purchaser by way of a constructive trust at the very moment that the contract is entered. The maxim also underlies the general doctrine of conversion, and the rule in *Howe v Earl Dartmouth*,[118] which requires that a trustee convert unauthorised investments into authorised investments.[119] In *A-G for Hong Kong v Reid*[120] the maxim has been held to have the implication that a fiduciary who receives

---

[106] (1852) 16 Beav 59 at 66.      [107] [1997] 3 All ER 392 at 399.

[108] *Tulk v Moxhay* (1848) 18 LJ Ch 83; *Rhone v Stephens* [1994] 2 AC 310.

[109] *Page One Records Ltd v Britton* [1967] 3 All ER 822.

[110] *Lumley v Wagner* (1852) 1 De GM & G 604.

[111] *Re Kayford Ltd* [1975] 1 WLR 279; see Chapter 11.

[112] *Kembel v Farren* (1829) 6 Bing 141; *Pye v British Automobile Commercial Syndicate* [1906] 1 KB 425; *Diestal v Stevenson* [1906] 2 KB 345; *Cellulose Acetate Silk Co Ltd v Widnes Foundry (1925) Ltd* [1933] AC 20; *Robert Stewart & Sons Ltd v Carapanayoti & Co Ltd* [1962] 1 WLR 34.

[113] See [1995] CLJ 60 (Gardner).      [114] See pp 32–44.

[115] (1882) 21 Ch D 9. See above, p 10.      [116] *Lloyds Bank plc v Carrick* [1996] 4 All ER 630.

[117] Eg in *Oughtred v IRC* [1960] AC 206, where there was a contract for the purchase of a beneficiary's equitable interest in shares in a private company.

[118] (1802) 7 Ves 137.      [119] See Chapter 12.      [120] [1994] 1 AC 324.

an unauthorised profit in breach of his duty of loyalty will hold the profit on constructive trust for his principal because he is subject to an equitable duty to account for the profit he received.

## (11) Equity imputes an intention to fulfill an obligation

Equity places the most favourable construction on a man's acts, so that if he does something which could be construed as fulfilling an obligation he owes, equity will regard it as having this effect. For example, if a debtor leaves a legacy to his creditor, this is presumed to be a repayment of the debt.[121] The doctrines of performance and satisfaction are founded on this maxim.

## (12) Equity acts in personam

This maxim refers to the fact that, as has been noted above, equity enforces its decisions by means of a personal order against the defendant, for example by an order to perform a contract, observe a trust or refrain from some behaviour by means of an injunction. If the defendant breaches the order he will be in contempt of court.[122] The court may exercise jurisdiction over any person within the power of the court,[123] even though the order may relate to property which is situated abroad.[124] The potential extra-territoriality of the equity jurisdiction has been recognised by the Court of Justice of the European Community. In *Webb v Webb*[125] a father bought a flat in Antibes in his son's name, intending to retain the ownership. The European Court held that even though the usual rule was that matters of title to immovable property, such as buildings, had to be settled in accordance with the law of the country in which it was situated, the father was entitled to pursue his claim to a share in the property under a resulting trust[126] through the English courts because it was a personal claim. It therefore upheld the decision, on the merits, of the English High Court[127] that the son held the flat on a resulting trust for his father. In *Re Hayward*[128] it was said that it was significant that the plaintiff in *Webb v Webb* was not making any claim based on legal ownership of the property concerned. In *Re Hayward* a trustee in bankruptcy claimed to be entitled to a half share in a villa in Spain which had belonged to the bankrupt and his wife in indivisible halves[129] but which had subsequently been transferred to the defendant by the bankrupt's widow, who claimed to be entitled to do so in her own right and as intestate successor to her husband's share. The property had then been registered in the name of the defendant in the property register in Minorca. The basis of the trustee in bankruptcy's claim was that the bankrupt's rights had vested in him so that there was

---

121  *Thynne v Glengall* (1848) 2 HL Cas 131; *Chichester v Coventry* (1867) LR 2 HL 71; *Re Horlock* [1895] 1 Ch 516.

122  See *Co-operative Insurance v Argyll Stores* [1997] 3 All ER 297 at 302–303.

123  Ie someone who is within the jurisdiction or on whom the court order can be served outside of it.

124  *Penn v Lord Baltimore* (1750) 1 Ves Sen 444; *Ewing v Orr Ewing* (1883–84) 9 App Cas 34, HL; *Richard West & Partners (Inverness) Ltd v Dick* [1969] 1 All ER 289; affd [1969] 2 Ch 424, CA.

125  [1994] QB 696.   126  See Chapter 28.   127  [1992] 1 All ER 17.

128  [1997] 1 All ER 32.   129  The Spanish equivalent of a legal tenancy in common.

nothing which should have passed to the bankrupt's wife and thence to the defendant. The trustee in bankruptcy was therefore seeking to have the Minorcan property register rectified to show him as half owner. Rattee J held that, under Article 16 of the 1968 Convention on Jurisdiction and the Enforcement of Judgments in Civil and Commercial Matters (adopted as law by the Civil Jurisdiction and Judgments Act 1982), the Spanish courts had exclusive jurisdiction over the matter since the proceedings had as their object 'rights in rem in immovable property'. Rattee J rejected the argument that a claim for an order to reverse the registration could be treated as a claim in personam. In his view, although English law did not recognise as sharply as some other jurisdictions the distinction between rights in rem and rights in personam, 'it is difficult to contemplate any right more clearly a right in rem than a right to legal ownership such as is claimed by the trustee [in bankruptcy] in the present case'.[130] The relationship of this case with *Webb v Webb* raises interesting questions. Since one of the rights of the beneficiaries under a trust is a right to call for a vesting in them of the legal estate, it is difficult to see why the claim of a beneficiary under a resulting or constructive trust (as in *Webb v Webb*) should not be seen as a right in rem, just like the claim in *Re Hayward*. On the other hand, the two cases differed in the way in which they were pleaded, and it may be that this is a sufficient (although unsatisfactory) distinction between them.

# 6  The creativity of equity

## (1)  Equity and the creation of rights and remedies

From a historical perspective one of the outstanding characteristics of equity has been its capacity to develop new rights and remedies for the benefit of plaintiffs. The need for such creativity within English law was the very reason for equity's genesis, and it led in particular to the evolution of the trust. The following chapters will examine the contribution of equity to modern English law through the remedies and rights to which it gave birth. Today, despite its undisputed and revered pedigree, the question has arisen whether equity retains such dynamic creative capacity. The need for ongoing creativity by equity was recognised by Jessel MR in *Re Hallet's Estate*:

'It must not be forgotten that the rules of equity are not, like the rules of the common law, supposed to have been established from time immemorial. It is perfectly well known that they have been established from time to time—altered, improved, and refined from time to time. In many cases we know the name of the Chancellor who invented them . . . Take such things as these: the separate use of a married woman, the restraint on alienation, the modern rule against perpetuities, and the rules of equitable waste. We can name the Chancellors who first invented them, and state the date when they were first introduced into equity jurisprudence; and therefore, in cases of this kind, the older precedents in equity are of very little

---

[130]  [1997] 1 All ER 32 at 43.

value. The doctrines are progressive, refined and improved; and if we want to know what the rules of equity are, we must look, of course, rather to the more modern than the more ancient cases.'[131]

However, these remarks are more than a hundred years old and reflect the immediate aftermath of the Judicature Acts, and in more recent times it has been questioned whether equity retains the capacity to 'invent' new rights and remedies which seem appropriate to meet the justice of a plaintiff's case. To borrow a favourite metaphor of Lord Denning, is equity 'past the age of childbearing'?

## (2) 'Equity is not past the age of childbearing'

Through the third quarter of the twentieth century Lord Denning was the strongest judicial exponent of the creativity of equity and he utilised this capacity to justify new rights and remedies to meet social needs and perceived injustices. In the context of matrimonial property he attempted to introduce a 'deserted wife's equity' entitling a woman deserted by her husband to remain in occupation of their matrimonial home, a right which would be enforceable against strangers who acquired the property, or a mortgage over it, from the husband. This equitable right was emphatically rejected by the House of Lords, which held that the right of a wife to be provided with accommodation by her husband lacked the characteristics of identifiability, stability and permanence which would enable it to be enforced against third parties.[132] However, in a matter of years they had taken note of the need for a means by which women and cohabitees could gain proprietary entitlements to property shared with their spouses or partners by a widening of the doctrines of resulting and constructive trusts, and Parliament enacted a statutory right entitling spouses to occupy their matrimonial home. With the introduction of a wider jurisdiction to establish resulting and constructive trusts, Lord Denning went a step further and sought to establish a whole new type of constructive trust, which he described as the 'New Model Constructive Trust', based on American restitutionary principles. The essence of this 'new model' constructive trust was that equity could impose a trust 'whenever justice and good conscience' demanded it.[133] The proposed operation of this trust is considered later in this book, but it is already noticeable that Lord Denning felt it proper for judges to create such new rights where required to meet the needs of justice. In *Eves v Eves*, which concerned a woman cohabiting with her partner, he summarised how he considered equity had been responsive to the needs of practical justice:

'. . . a few years ago even equity would not have helped her. But things have altered now. Equity is not past the age of child bearing. One of her latest progeny is a constructive trust of a new model. Lord Diplock brought it into the world[134] and we have nourished it . . .'[135]

---

[131] (1880) 13 Ch D 696 at 710.     [132] *National Provincial Bank v Ainsworth* [1965] AC 1175.
[133] *Hussey v Palmer* [1972] 1 WLR 1286.     [134] [1975] 1 WLR 1338.
[135] In *Gissing v Gissing* [1971] AC 886.

### (3) The creativity of equity circumscribed

Although Lord Denning championed the creativity of equity by developing the 'new model constructive trust', other judges expressed a more cautious and restrictive approach. Some judges have stated extra-judicially their feeling that equity has lost its creative power altogether. For example, in 1953 Lord Evershed expressed his opinion that:

'. . . the passing of the Judicature Act, and section 25(11) in particular, put a stop to, or at least a very severe limitation on, the inventive faculties of future Chancery judges.'[136]

In 1952 Lord Denning himself expressed his concern, which he later strove to overcome, that:

> 'The Courts of Chancery are no longer courts of equity . . . They are as fixed and immutable as the courts of law ever were.'[137]

Two main fears seem to have influenced the courts against a creative role for equity.

### (a) Reluctance to countenance judicial law-making

First, some judges fear that a willingness to create new equitable rights and remedies threatens the delicate constitutional balance between the legislative and judicial arms of government because it usurps the proper function of Parliament. This fear is not unique to equity, but affects English law as a whole. This fear was expressed by Megaw LJ in *Western Fish Products v Penwith District Council*:

'. . . As Harman LJ pointed out in *Campbell Discount Co Ltd v Bridge*[138] the system of equity has become a very precise one. The creation of new rights and remedies is a matter for Parliament, not the judges.'[139]

This reluctance to undermine Parliament was evident in *Westdeutsche Landesbank Girozentrale v Islington London Borough Council*.[140] The unwillingness of the majority to extend the jurisdiction of equity to award compound damages was grounded in the concern that such an extension would be an unjustifiable usurpation of the functions properly belonging to Parliament, because Parliament had twice legislated to grant the common law the power to award simple interest but had not felt it necessary to go further. As Lord Lloyd explained:

'To extend the equitable jurisdiction for the first time to cover a residual injustice at common law, which Parliament chose not to remedy, would, I think, be as great a usurpation of the role of the legislature, and as clear an example of judicial lawmaking as it would have been in *President of India*.[141] If it is thought desirable that the courts should have a power to award compound interest in common law claims for actions for money had and received, then such a result can now only be brought about by Parliament.'[142]

In the more recent case of *Great Peace Shipping Ltd v Tsavliris Salvage (International) Ltd*[143] the Court of Appeal similarly stated that the introduction of a wider jurisdiction

---

[136] (1953) 6 CLP 1 at 12.     [137] (1952) 5 CLP 8.     [138] [1961] 1 QB 445 at 459.
[139] [1981] 2 All ER 204.
[140] [1996] 2 All ER 961. See also [1996] RLR 3 (Birks); [1996] LMCLQ 441 (Stevens).
[141] *President of India v La Pintada Cia Navigacion SA* [1985] AC 104.
[142] [1996] 2 All ER 961 at 1021.     [143] [2004] 4 All ER 689.

to set contracts aside on the grounds of common mistake than that available at common law[144] would require legislation, and could not be achieved through the development of an equitable jurisdiction.

## (b) Danger of uncertainty

Some judges have equally expressed their concern that radical creativity by equity, generating new rights and remedies to do justice in individual cases, would result in uncertainty. The courts are reluctant to allow the situation to develop where equity could again appear subjective and attract the criticism of varying with the length of the Chancellor's foot. This concern to avoid uncertainty was particularly apposite in the context of the new model constructive trust, as the concept of a powerful proprietary remedy to be awarded on the basis of what the judge felt was 'just', without reference to clear guiding principles, was inherently uncertain. As Bagnall J stated in *Cowcher v Cowcher*:

'I am convinced that in determining rights, particularly property rights, the only justice that can be attained by mortals, who are fallible and are not omniscient, is justice according to law; the justice that flows from the application of sure and settled principles to proved or admitted facts. So in the field of equity the length of the Chancellor's foot has been measured or is capable of measurement . . .'[145]

He observed that the practical difficulty of allowing equity do justice on a case by case basis was that in the realm of property 'no lawyer could safely advise on his client's title'. More recently, in *Westdeutsche v Islington London Borough Council* Lord Browne-Wilkinson refused to countenance the extension of equitable resulting trust principles to provide proprietary restitution where a payment had been made under a contract which was ultra vires and void because of the dangers of uncertainty:

'I do not think it right to make an unprincipled alteration to the law of property (ie the law of trusts) so as to produce in the law of unjust enrichment the injustices to third parties . . . and the consequential commercial uncertainty which any extension of proprietary interests in personal property is bound to produce.'[146]

In *Taylor v Dickens* Judge Weeks QC somewhat intemperately vented his fear of uncertainty when he suggested that the evolution of a broad doctrine of proprietary estoppel founded on the notion of 'unconscionability' would have the effect that:

'. . . one might as well forget the law of contract and issue every judge with a portable palm tree. The days of justice varying with the size of the Chancellor's foot would have returned.'[147]

## (4) Evolution of new rights and remedies from existing principles

Despite the reluctance of the court to 'invent' new rights and remedies this does not mean that equity is stagnant and incapable of flexible development to meet new

---

[144] *Bell v Lever Bros Ltd* [1932] AC 161.     [145] [1972] 1 WLR 425 at 430.
[146] [1996] 2 All ER 961 at 992.     [147] [1998] 1 FLR 806, [1998] Conv 210 (Thompson).

circumstances. The inevitability of the development of existing law was recognised by Glass JA in the Australian case *Allen v Snyder*, together with the necessary limitations on such development:

'It is inevitable that judge made law will alter to meet the changing conditions of society. That is the way it has always evolved. But it is essential that new rules should be related to fundamental doctrine. If the foundations of accepted doctrine be submerged under new principles, without regard to the interaction between the two, there will be high uncertainty as to the state of the law, both old and new.'[148]

The law is a coherent and dynamic whole, subject to constant re-evaluation and adjustment, sometimes culminating in the birth of new principles and doctrines. Equity has made a tremendous contribution to this whole and the continuous process of remoulding equitable rights and remedies should be seen as an essential part of this overall process of legal development. Rights and remedies which are in practice 'new' can be developed from existing principles and precedents. In *Re Diplock* the Court of Appeal said that an equitable claim:

'. . . must be shown to have an ancestry founded in the practice and precedents of the courts administering equity jurisdiction. It is not sufficient that because we think that the justice of the present case requires it, we should invent such a jurisdiction for the first time.'[149]

In *Cowcher v Cowcher*[150] Bagnall J affirmed that equity was not past the age of childbearing, remaining fertile and capable of developing new rights and remedies. However, he considered that its reproductive capacity should be circumscribed so that 'its progeny must be legitimate—by precedent out of principle'. Ultimately, the 'new model' constructive trust in its broadest form was rejected by the Court of Appeal on the grounds that it did not have sufficient ancestry in the principles and precedents of equity, and was 'at variance with the principles stated in *Gissing v Gissing*'.[151]

The emergence of new rights and remedies labelled 'equitable' must be viewed within the framework of judicial development of the law as a whole. Equity does not enjoy any special ability to be more creative than other branches of law, and in recent years one of the most radical developments has occurred within what was historically the province of the common law through the recognition by the House of Lords of the right to restitution founded upon an autonomous cause of action in unjust enrichment.[152] This development parallels past common law achievements such as the acceptance of a general law of negligence in *Donoghue v Stevenson*.[153]

The fears which have been expressed in relation to the ability of equity to create new rights and remedies have also curtailed the willingness of the court to introduce changes to traditional common law doctrines. For example, in *Prudential Assurance Co Ltd v London Residuary Body*[154] the House of Lords refused to overrule the ancient common law rule that a lease is void if it is not created with an ascertainable maximum

---

148  [1977] 2 NSWLR 685 at 689.        149  [1948] Ch 465.        150  [1972] 1 WLR 425 at 430.
151  *Grant v Edwards* [1986] Ch 638, per Nourse LJ.
152  *Lipkin Gorman v Karpnale Ltd* [1991] 2 AC 548; *Woolwich Equitable Building Society v IRC* [1993] AC 70; *Westdeutsche Bank v Islington London Borough Council* [1996] AC 669.
153  [1932] AC 562.        154  [1992] 3 All ER 504.

duration, despite the fact that it served no useful purpose and they could find no satisfactory rationale for its existence, because of fear that so doing might 'upset long-established titles'.

## (5) Examples of the creativity of equity

Despite the caution that has often been expressed about the development of new law, there have been a number of significant developments in the past half-century where judges have created new 'equitable' rights or remedies, or expanded existing principles to such a degree that a virtually new right has emerged. The majority of new developments have occurred incrementally, by progressive evolution from existing doctrines and principles. This has sometimes happened to enable old principles to apply to modern situations. For instance, the principles of resulting and constructive trusts have been reworked, so that they are unrecognisable from the concepts known by those names at the time of the Judicature Acts or the Law of Property Act 1925, to determine property rights between unmarried cohabiting partners who have acquired a home by their joint effort, without any formal legal agreement as to how the ownership should be shared. In some cases, notably in relation to Mareva and Anton Piller orders considered below, the development has been much more rapid in response to an urgent and important problem. Even in these cases, however, the courts have sought to proceed cautiously and carefully on the basis of clear criteria, to minimise the risk of uncertainty.

### (a) Creation of new rights and remedies

Two examples of remedies which have been developed by equity in the past twenty-five years are the Mareva injunction (Freezing Order) and the Anton Piller order (Search Order).[155] These are specialised injunctions which respectively prevent a defendant from disposing of his assets to avoid meeting a possible judgment against him, or destroying material evidence. Although unknown prior to their creation in two Court of Appeal decisions, they have come to be essential elements of civil procedure and litigation, and have been described by Donaldson LJ as the 'law's two "nuclear" weapons'.[156] Lord Denning MR was instrumental in the creation of both, and he has subsequently described them as 'the greatest piece of judicial law reform in my time'.[157] They are considered in detail in the following chapter.

### (b) Extension and development of existing principles

Outside of the general flexibility of the trust to meet changing family, financial and commercial circumstances, existing principles of equity have been extended and developed to meet modern social needs in a number of specific areas.

*(i) Resulting and constructive trusts.* As has been noted, the traditional concepts of resulting and constructive trusts have been developed and extended to form the

---

[155] See Chapter 2. See also J Stevens 'Equity's Manhattan Project' [1999] Denning LJ 25.
[156] *Bank Mellat v Nikpour* [1985] FSR 87 at 91–92, CA.
[157] *The Due Process of Law* (1980), p 134; *The Closing Chapter* (1983), p 225.

foundations for dealings with the shared acquisition of residential property by married and cohabiting couples. These developments reflected the changing needs of society as social mores shifted from the paradigm family unit of husband and wife, where the husband alone owned the matrimonial home, to modern partnerships. The fundamental principles were set down by the House of Lords in two 1970s cases, *Pettitt v Pettitt*[158] and *Gissing v Gissing*.[159] These principles and their implications are examined in detail in Chapters 8 and 9.

*(ii) Proprietary estoppel.* Also operating in the context of rights and interests in land, the doctrine of proprietary estoppel has been developed from nineteenth-century principles,[160] to create proprietary interests in circumstances which do not otherwise meet the criteria for establishing a resulting or constructive trust. Proprietary estoppel is considered in Chapter 10.

## (c) Rejected new rights and remedies

Some proposed new rights and remedies have been aborted by the higher courts after a brief tentative life. It has already been noted how the House of Lords rejected Lord Denning's notion of the existence of a deserted wife's right to occupy her matrimonial home. Similarly, the Court of Appeal has regarded the 'new model' constructive trust as inconsistent with orthodox principles because of its inherent uncertainty, and in *Ashburn Anstalt v Arnold*[161] rejected Lord Denning's concerted judicial effort to confer the status of equitable proprietary interests on contractual licences.[162] In *Great Peace Shipping Ltd v Tsavliris Salvage (International) Ltd*[163] the House of Lords more recently rejected a supposed equitable jurisdiction to grant rescission of a contract on the grounds of mistake wider than that available at common law,[164] which Lord Denning had propounded in the case of *Solle v Butcher*.[165]

## (d) Potential for future development

It is perhaps somewhat ironic that where the proposed 'new model' constructive trust led to rigorous doubt as to the creative ability of equity, the House of Lords more recently indicated the possible future adoption into English law of the 'remedial constructive trust', which, as a trust imposed on property by the court as a remedial response to effect restitution, shares some characteristics of the 'new model' constructive trust. In *Westdeutsche Landesbank Girozentrale v Islington London Borough Council* Lord Browne-Wilkinson remarked:

'Although the resulting trust is an unsuitable basis for developing proprietary restitutionary remedies, the remedial constructive trust, if introduced into English law, may provide a more satisfactory road forward . . . However, whether English law should follow the United States and Canada by adopting the remedial constructive trust will have to be decided in some future case when the point is directly in issue.'[166]

---

[158] [1970] AC 777.    [159] [1971] AC 886.
[160] *Dillwyn v Llewelyn* (1862) 4 De G F & J 517; *Willmott v Barber* (1880) 15 Ch D 96.
[161] [1989] Ch 1.    [162] *Binions v Evans* [1972] Ch 359.    [163] [2002] 4 All ER 689.
[164] *Bell v Lever Brothers Ltd* [1932] AC 161.    [165] [1950] 1 KB 671.
[166] [1996] 2 All ER 961 at 999.

Although subsequent cases have chosen not to take this step,[167] the willingness of Lord Browne-Wilkinson to anticipate the ability of equity to incorporate such a remedy into English law is a strong reminder that equity's potential for childbearing has not yet passed.

[167]  *Re Polly Peck International (No 5)* [1998] 3 All ER 812.

# 2

# Equitable remedies in modern English law

## 1 Introduction to equitable remedies

The previous chapter has charted the historical development of equity and the Court of Chancery. Although this is important, the prime concern of this book is with the present contribution that equity makes to English law. This chapter will examine the most significant remedies developed by equity and Chapter 3 will then consider the role that equity plays in the law of property through its creation of equitable rights. This will culminate in a consideration of the trust, which is the principal concern of the remainder of the book.

## 2 Specific performance[1]

At common law the only remedy for breach of contract was damages. A defendant who had breached his contract would not be compelled to perform, but was liable to compensate the plaintiff for any loss he suffered as a consequence of the breach.[2] This might be his 'expectation loss' or 'reliance loss'. The plaintiff was expected, at common law, to use his compensation to purchase alternative performance, for instance by buying replacement goods on the open market, or by finding an alternative supplier of services. As Lord Diplock observed in *Photo Production Ltd v Securicor Transport Ltd*, this means the defendant has the option of either performing the contract or breaching the contract and paying damages:

'Every failure to perform a primary obligation is a breach of contract. The secondary obligation on the part of the contract-breaker to which it gives rise by implication of the common law is to pay monetary compensation to the other party for the loss sustained by him in consequence of the breach . . .'[3]

In effect, therefore, the defendant can buy his way out of performance of the contract.

---

[1] See *Snell's Principles of Equity* (31st edn, 2005), pp 345–379; Treitel, *The Law of Contract* (11th edn, 2004), pp 1019–1049; Hanbury and Martin, *Modern Equity* (17th edn, 2005), pp 732–763; Pettitt, *Equity and the Law of Trusts* (9th edn, 2001), pp 628–655.

[2] *Tai Hing Cotton Mills Ltd v Kanmsing Knitting Factory* [1979] AC 91.      [3] [1980] 1 All ER 556.

However, equity intervened where the common law remedy was inadequate,[4] because it would have been unjust to allow the defendant to avoid performance and merely pay damages. By means of an order of specific performance the court can compel the defendant to perform his contractual obligations. The court is also willing to order specific performance of a contract to confer benefits on third parties.[5] Specific performance is an order made personally against the defendant, and illustrates how equity acts in personam.[6] If the defendant fails to comply, he will be in contempt of court and faces the possibility of imprisonment.

As specific performance is an equitable remedy it may only be obtained by a person who has provided valuable consideration and is not therefore a volunteer. Thus specific performance may not be obtained by a volunteer who is a party to a covenant, even though a promise made by deed is enforceable at common law.[7] Although the Contracts (Rights of Third Parties Act) 1999 provides that a third party who is entitled to enforce a contract may obtain any remedy 'that would have been available to him in an action for breach of contract if he had been a party to the contract', it seems that a volunteer third party will still be unable to obtain specific performance. Section 1(5) provides that the 'rules relating to . . . specific performance . . . shall apply accordingly', thereby incorporating the long established rule that a volunteer may not obtain specific performance.[8]

## (1) When is specific performance available?

Specific performance is not generally available as a remedy for breach of contract. As Lord Selbourne LC said in *Wilson v Northampton and Banbury Junction Rly Co*:

'The court gives specific performance instead of damages, only when it can by that means do more and complete justice.'[9]

In *Co-operative Insurance v Argyll Stores*[10] this perspective was reiterated by the House of Lords. Lord Hoffmann stated:

'Specific performance is traditionally regarded in English law as an exceptional remedy, as opposed to the common law damages to which a successful plaintiff is entitled as of right . . . by the nineteenth century it was orthodox doctrine that the power to decree specific performance was part of the discretionary jurisdiction of the Court of Chancery to do justice in cases in which the remedies available at common law were inadequate.'[11]

There are a number of well recognised circumstances in which it is recognised that damages would not provide an adequate remedy so that specific performance is ordinarily available.

---

[4] *Hutton v Watling* [1948] Ch 26; affd [1948] Ch 398.

[5] *Beswick v Beswick* [1968] AC 58; *Gurtner v Circuit* [1968] 2 QB 587.

[6] See *Penn v Lord Baltimore* (1750) 1 Ves Sen 444; *Richard West & Partners (Inverness) Ltd v Dick* [1969] 1 All ER 289.

[7] See, for example, *Cannon v Hartley* [1949] Ch 213.

[8] See, Hanbury & Martin, *Modern Equity* (17th edn), at p 734.

[9] (1874) 9 Ch App 279 at 284.　　　[10] [1997] 3 All ER 297.　　　[11] [1997] 3 All ER 297 at 301.

## (a) Contracts concerning land

Land is always deemed to be unique as it is assumed that there is no identical market alternative.[12] Therefore, as Lord Diplock observed in *Sudbrook Trading Estate Ltd v Eggleton*, damages would:

'. . . constitute a wholly inadequate and unjust remedy for the breach. That is why the normal remedy is by a decree of specific performance . . .'[13]

Specific performance is therefore available in respect of a contract for the sale of land, for the grant of an interest in land or even for the grant of a licence to occupy land.[14] A contract for the sale of land, or the disposition of an interest in land, must be made in writing in accordance with the provisions of s 2 of the Law of Property (Miscelaneous Provisions) Act 1989. Specific performance will not therefore be avaialble of an oral contract in respect of an interest in land, although such and agreement might give rise to a remedy by way of proprietary estoppel.[15]

## (b) Contracts for the sale of unique personal property

Specific performance will not normally be granted to enforce a contract for the sale of personal property because a market substitute can readily be obtained. However, if the item is unique and there is no available alternative the court may grant a decree of specific performance. For example, in *Falcke v Gray*[16] Kindersley V-C would have granted specific performance of a contract for the sale of two oriental jars which were of 'unusual beauty, rarity and distinction' if he had not found that the consideration was inadequate.[17] A contract to sell shares may also be specifically enforceable if they are not available in the general market.[18]

## (c) Practical unavailability of market substitutes

Specific performance has also been granted of contracts for the sale of goods which are not unique and are normally readily available in the market where special circumstances have meant that substitutes are in fact unobtainable. In *Sky Petroleum Ltd v VIP Petroleum Ltd*[19] the plaintiff sought an injunction to prevent the defendants from breaching their contract as the exclusive supplier of petrol and diesel for the plaintiff's garages. Goulding J granted the injunction, which amounted to specific performance of the contract, because the market in petroleum had changed considerably since the contract had been entered and the plaintiff had no market alternative:

---

[12] Equity treated land as unique before the practice developed in Georgian and later periods of building large estates of houses of identical or near-identical design.

[13] [1983] 1 AC 444 at 478.

[14] *Verrall v Great Yarmouth Borough Council* [1981] QB 202. This is so even though a contractual licence does not create an interest in the land capable of binding successors in title of the licensor: *Ashburn Anstalt v Arnold* [1989] Ch 1.

[15] *Yaxley v Gotts* [2000] Ch 162. See Chapter 10.     [16] (1859) 4 Drew 651.

[17] See also *Pearne v Lisle* (1749) Amb 75; *Thorn v Public Works* (1863) 32 Beav 490; *Behnke v Bede Shipping Co Ltd* [1927] 1 KB 649; *Phillips v Lamdin* [1949] 2 KB 33. Contrast *Cohen v Roche* [1927] 1 KB 169.

[18] *Duncuft v Albrecht* (1841) 12 Sim 189; *Oughtred v IRC* [1960] AC 206; *Neville v Wilson* [1997] Ch 144.

[19] [1974] 1 All ER 954. Compare also *Howard E Perry & Co Ltd v British Railways Board* [1980] 1 WLR 1375.

'. . . the petroleum market is in an unusual state in which a would-be buyer cannot go out into the market and contract with another seller, possibly at some sacrifice as to price. Here, the defendant company appears for practical purposes to be the plaintiff company's sole means of keeping its business going . . .'[20]

## (d) Contracts where the quantification of damages would be difficult[21]

Specific performance has been ordered of contracts to sell or pay annuities because the value of the rights is uncertain,[22] and of contracts to execute a mortgage for money already lent because the value of having security for the loan cannot be quantified.[23] Specific performance has also been awarded where the loss is difficult to prove,[24] or where the defendant is unlikely to be able to pay damages.[25]

## (e) Plaintiff entitled only to nominal damages

Specific performance has been ordered where the plaintiff would only be entitled to recover nominal damages for his loss. In *Beswick v Beswick*[26] Mr Beswick had made a contract with his nephew to pay a pension to his wife. On his death the nephew refused to pay. Although Mrs Beswick could not sue in her own right because she was not privy to the contract, she was entitled to sue in her capacity as Mr Beswick's personal representative. The court ordered the nephew to perform the contract because damages would be an inadequate remedy. Mr Beswick had not personally suffered any loss and would therefore have been entitled only to nominal damages. That would not have compensated his widow, who had suffered a substantial loss.

## (2) Contracts where specific performance is not available

In some well recognised situations it is clear that the court will not enforce a contract by means of a decree of specific performance.

## (a) Contracts of personal service

Equity will not specifically enforce a contract of personal service requiring the defendant to work for the plaintiff because this would infringe his liberty.[27] As Fry LJ observed in *De Francesco v Barnum*:

'The courts are bound to be jealous, lest they should turn contracts of service into contracts of slavery.'[28]

---

[20] [1974] 1 All ER 954 at 956.

[21] *Société des Industries Metallurgiques SA v Bronx Engineering Co Ltd* [1975] 1 Lloyd's Rep 465, CA.

[22] *Ball v Coggs* (1710) 1 Bro Parl Cas 140, HL; *Kenney v Wexham* (1822) 6 Madd 355; *Adderly v Dixon* (1824) 1 Sim & St 607; *Clifford v Turrell* (1841) 1 Y & C Ch Cas 138; *Beswick v Beswick* [1968] AC 58.

[23] *Ashton v Corrigan* (1871) LR 13 Eq 76; *Swiss Bank Corpn v Lloyds Bank Ltd* [1982] AC 584.h

[24] *Decro-Wall International SA v Practitioners in Marketing Ltd* [1971] 1 WLR 361.

[25] *Evans Marshall & Co v Bertola SA* [1973] 1 All ER 992.      [26] [1968] AC 58.

[27] *Lumley v Wagner* (1852) 1 De GM & G 604; *Johnson v Shrewsbury and Birmingham Rly* (1853) 3 De GM & G 914; *Brett v East India and London Shipping Co Ltd* (1864) 2 Hem & M 404; *Britain v Rossiter* (1879) 11 QBD 123; *Rigby v Connol* (1880) 14 Ch D 482; *De Francesco v Barnum* (1890) 45 Ch D 430. See also Trade Union and Labour Relations Act 1974, s 16.

[28] (1890) 45 Ch D 430.

The court will also refuse to grant an injunction[29] to give effect to a contractual provision that the defendant is not to work for anyone else, as this would indirectly amount to specific performance of the contract.[30] Therefore, in *Page One Records Ltd v Britton*[31] Stamp J refused to grant an injunction to indirectly enforce a contractual term in an exclusive management agreement by which a pop group agreed not to work for any other manager.

In some cases it has been questioned whether equity will always decline to order specific performance of contracts for personal services, particularly given the radical change in the nature of employment over the century and a half since the rule was adopted. In *CH Giles & Co Ltd v Morris* Megarry J was at pains to emphasis that there was no absolute 'rule' that there could never be specific performance of a contract for personal services. He reconsidered the basis upon which it has been justified:

'Such a rule is plainly not absolute and without exception . . . The reasons why the court is reluctant to decree specific performance of a contract for personal services (and I would regard it as a strong reluctance rather than a rule) are, I think, more complex and more firmly bottomed in human nature. If a singer contracts to sing, there could no doubt be proceedings for committal if, ordered to sing, the singer remained obstinately dumb. But if instead the singer sang flat, or sharp, or too fast, or too slowly, or too loudly, or too quietly . . . the threat of committal would reveal itself as a most unsatisfactory weapon: for who could say whether such imperfections of performance were natural or self-induced.'[32]

He considered that 'not all contracts of personal service . . . are as dependant as this on matters of opinion and judgment, nor do all such contracts involve the same degree of the daily impact of person upon person', and that therefore in some circumstances specific performance might be available because 'the matter is one of the balance of advantage and disadvantage in relation to the particular obligations in question'.[33]

In *Hill v C A Parsons & Co Ltd*[34] the court prevented an employer from dismissing an employee shortly before the date at which he was due to retire since this would have serious implications for his entitlement to a pension which could not adequately be compensated in damages. However, in *Scandinavian Trading Tanker Co AB v Flota Petrolera Ecuatoriana, The Scaptrade*[35] the House of Lords, in the context of a shipping time charter, reaffirmed the equitable principle that a contract for services will not be specifically enforced.[36] It is noteworthy that, under employment legislation, an employee may be entitled to reinstatement. This may give cause to believe that in future the courts will be less reluctant to order specific performance of contracts of employment.

---

[29] An injunction is an order of the court prohibiting the person enjoined from a particular course of conduct. It is considered more fully below: see p 44.

[30] *Warner Bros Picture Inc v Nelson* [1937] 1 KB 209.        [31] [1967] 3 All ER 822

[32] [1972] 1 WLR 307 at 318.

[33] See also *Hill v CA Parsons & Co Ltd* [1972] Ch 305; *Powell v London Borough of Brent* [1987] IRLR 446; *Hughes v London Borough of Southwark* [1988] IRLR 55.

[34] [1972] Ch 305.        [35] [1983] 2 AC 694.

[36] [1983] 2 AC 694 at 700–701, per Lord Diplock.

## (b) Contracts requiring constant supervision

In *Ryan v Mutual Tontine Westminster Chambers Association*[37] it was held that the court will not grant specific performance of a contract that will require its constant supervision. The defendants, who were the lessors of a block of residential flats, covenanted to provide a resident porter who would be in constant attendance. The Court of Appeal held that this covenant could not be specifically enforced because 'the execution of it would require constant superintendence by the Court, which the Court in such cases has always declined to give'.[38] The rationale for the refusal of specific performance in such circumstances was recently examined by the House of Lords in *Co-operative Insurance v Argyll Stores (Holdings) Ltd.*[39] Lord Hoffmann held such refusal was not because the court would have to literally supervise the execution of the order, but because the court might have to give an 'indefinite series of rulings' whether the order had been kept or broken.[40] He emphasised that the only means by which the court could enforce the order was through the 'quasi-criminal procedure of punishment for contempt', and that given the seriousness of a finding of contempt litigation would be likely to be 'heavy and expensive'. Thus, he held that:

'The possibility of repeated applications over a period of time means that, in comparison with a once and for all inquiry as to damages, the enforcement of the remedy is likely to be expensive in terms of costs to the parties and the resources of the judicial system.'[41]

The refusal to grant specific performance where constant supervision was required had been followed in many cases.[42] However, in *Tito v Waddell (No 2)*[43] Megarry V-C considered that the prohibition was not absolute. He suggested that the real issue 'is whether there is a sufficient definition of what has to be done in order to comply with the order of the court'.[44] In *Posner v Scott-Lewis*[45] Mervyn Davies J was therefore prepared to grant an order for specific performance where the defendant landlords had covenanted to employ a resident porter solely for the purposes of keeping the common parts clean, looking after the central heating and carrying rubbish to the dustbins. He held that the key questions determining whether an order should be granted were:

'(a) is there a sufficient definition of what has to be done in order to comply with the order of the court? (b) Will enforcing compliance involve superintendence by the court to an unacceptable degree? (c) What are the respective prejudices or hardships that will be suffered by the parties if the order is made or not made?'[46]

However, in *Co-operative Insurance v Argyll Stores (Holdings) Ltd*[47] the House of Lords held that Megarry V-C had wrongly rejected the difficulty of supervision as an

---

[37] [1893] 1 Ch 116.    [38] [1893] 1 Ch 116 at 123, per Lord Esher MR.
[39] [1997] 3 All ER 297; (1998) 61 MLR 421 (Phang); [1997] CLJ 488 (Jones).
[40] [1997] 3 All ER 297 at 302.    [41] [1997] 3 All ER 297 at 303.
[42] *Rayner v Stone* (1762) 2 Eden 128; *Blackett v Bates* (1865) 1 Ch App 117; *Powell Duffryn Steam Coal Co v Taff Vale Rly Co* (1874) 9 Ch App 331; *Phipps v Jackson* (1887) 56 LJ Ch 550; *Dominion Coal Co v Dominion Iron & Steel Co Ltd and National Trust Co Ltd* [1909] AC 293; *Dowty Boulton Paul Ltd v Wolverhampton Corpn* [1971] 1 WLR 204; *Braddon Towers Ltd v International Stores Ltd* [1987] 1 EGLR 209.
[43] [1977] Ch 106.    [44] See also *Wolverhampton Corpn v Emmons* [1901] 1 KB 515.
[45] [1987] Ch 25.    [46] Ibid at 36.    [47] [1997] 3 All ER 297.

objection to specific performance which would require the defendant to carry on an activity. It held that in such cases specific performance should be refused. Lord Hoffmann explained:

'This is a convenient point at which to distinguish between orders which require a defendant to carry on an activity, such as running a business over a more or less extended period of time, and orders which require him to achieve a result. The possibility of repeated applications for rulings on compliance with the order which arises in the former case does not exist to anything like the same extent in the latter. Even if the achievement of the result is a complicated matter which will take some time, the court, if called upon to rule, only has to examine the finished work and say whether it complies with the order.'[48]

This distinction explains why the courts have decreed specific performance of building contracts[49] and repairing covenants,[50] since the performance of such obligations requires a result to be achieved. However, Lord Hoffmann held that even a contract requiring mutual supervision may be enforced by way of specific performance if a defendant had committed a gross breach of personal faith in breaching his obligation.[51]

### (c) Contracts to carry on a business

In *Co-operative Insurance v Argyll Stores (Holdings) Ltd*[52] the House of Lords held that specific performance should not be granted of a contract to carry on a business. The defendants were a company which lease a shop unit in a Sheffield shopping centre where they operated a Safeway supermarket. In their lease they had covenanted to keep the premises open for 'retail trade'. Following a review of their national operations the defendants decided to close the store along with other loss-making supermarkets. The plaintiff landlords sought specific performance of the contract. The first instance judge refused to order specific performance on the grounds that the authorities revealed a 'settled practice' that orders would not be made requiring a defendant to run a business. The majority of the Court of Appeal held that specific performance should be decreed, arguing that any objection on the grounds that such an order would require constant supervision was outmoded.[53] The House of Lords granted the defendant's appeal and held that specific performance should not be ordered, reiterating that there was a 'settled practice'[54] to this effect and that such an order requiring the defendant to conduct an activity would require constant supervision by the court. Lord Hoffmann also considered that the grant of an order might 'cause injustice by allowing the plaintiff to enrich himself at the defendant's expense' by requiring the defendant to run a business at a loss far greater than the plaintiff would suffer by reason of the breach of contract,[55] and that from the wider perspective of public policy it was not in the public

---

48   Ibid at 303.         49   *Wolverhampton Corp v Emmons* [1901] 1 KB 515.

50   *Jeune v Queens Cross Properties Ltd* [1974] Ch 97.

51   [1997] 3 All ER 297 at 307–308. He held that the defendant had not in fact acted in such a way. See also *Greene v West Cheshire Rly Co* (1871) LR 13 Eq 44.

52   [1997] 3 All ER 297.         53   [1996] Ch 286.

54   [1997] 3 All ER 297 at 301, citing *Braddon Towers Ltd v International Stores Ltd* [1987] 1 EGLR 209.

55   [1997] 3 All ER 297 at 304, approving the comments of Millet LJ who dissented in the Court of Appeal [1996] Ch 286 at 303–305.

interest 'to require someone to carry on business at a loss if there is any plausible alternative by which the other party can be given compensation'.[56]

## (d) Agreements made without consideration

Since 'equity will not assist a volunteer',[57] the court will not grant specific performance in favour of a person who has not provided consideration, even though the agreement may be binding and enforceable at law because it has been made by deed.[58]

## (e) Contractual terms are insufficiently precise

A contractual obligation will not be enforced by way of specific performance if its terms are insufficiently precise to enable an order to be drawn which will clearly define what the defendant must do to comply therewith.[59] The scope of this limitation was examined by Lord Hoffmann in *Co-operative Insurance v Argyll Stores (Holdings) Ltd*:

'If the terms of the court's order, reflecting the terms of the obligation, cannot be precisely drawn, the possibility of wasteful litigation over compliance is increased. So is the oppression caused by the defendant having to do things under threat of proceedings for contempt. The less precise the order, the fewer the signposts to the forensic minefield which he has to traverse. The fact that the terms of a contractual obligation are sufficiently definite to escape being void for uncertainty, or to found a claim for damages, or to permit compliance to be made a condition of relief against forfeiture, does not necessarily mean that they will be sufficiently precise to be capable of being specifically performed.'[60]

The degree of certainty of the obligation in question is, however, only a factor to be taken into account by the court in relation to the exercise of its discretion, and where the plaintiff's merits are strong the courts have 'shown themselves willing to cope with a certain degree of imprecision in cases of orders requiring a result'.[61]

## (f) Contracts for transient interests

Traditionally, equity would not specifically enforce agreements for transient interests, such as tenancies at will or short tenancies.[62] In *Lavery v Pursell*[63] the court would not grant specific performance of an agreement for a tenancy for one year because it was normally impossible to get the action heard within that period.[64] However, in the modern case of *Verrall v Great Yarmouth Borough Council*[65] the Court of Appeal upheld an order for the specific performance of a contract to grant a licence for two days. Roskill LJ stated that, in his judgment:

---

[56] [1997] 3 All ER 297 at 305.      [57] See Chapter 6.

[58] *Jefferys v Jefferys* (1841) Cr & Ph 138; *Cannon v Hartley* [1949] Ch 213.

[59] *Wolverhampton Corpn v Emmons* [1901] 1 KB 515 at 525, per Romer LJ; *Redland Bricks Ltd v Morris* [1970] AC 652 at 666, per Lord Upjohn.

[60] [1997] 3 All ER 297 at 303.      [61] [1997] 3 All ER 297 at 304.

[62] *Glasse v Woolgar and Roberts (No 2)* (1897) 41 Sol Jo 573: tenancy for a day.

[63] (1888) 39 Ch D 508.

[64] See *Lever v Koffler* [1901] 1 Ch 543; *Manchester Brewery Co v Coombs* [1901] 2 Ch 608 (agreement for a tenancy from year to year is specifically enforceable).

[65] [1981] QB 202.

'. . . the old view . . . that courts of equity would not protect a so-called transient interest can no longer be supported, at any rate to its full extent.'[66]

### (g) Contracts for partnership

Such contracts will not be specifically enforced unless the partners have begun to act upon their agreement.[67]

### (h) Contracts to transfer goodwill

The court will not specifically enforce a contract to transfer merely the goodwill of a business,[68] unless annexed to an agreement to sell the premises or other asset of the business.

### (i) Contracts to exercise a testamentary power of appointment[69]

The court will not grant specific performance of a contract to exercise a testamentary power in favour of a specific person because this would undermine the intention of the person who had granted the power (the donor) that the donee should be able to exercise it until his death.[70]

### (j) Indivisible contracts

The court will not specifically enforce part of a contract if it is not possible to specific-ally enforce another part which cannot be separated. In *Ogden v Fossick*[71] there was an agreement to grant the plaintiffs a lease of a wharf and to appoint the defendant as manager. The court would not specifically enforce the contract for the lease because it could not be separated from the agreement to appoint the defendant manager. The management agreement could not be specifically enforced because this was a contract for personal services. If the parts of a contract can be separated the court may enforce one part but not the other.[72]

### (k) Contracts referring to arbitration

The court will not specifically enforce a contract to refer a matter to arbitration,[73] but it may stay proceedings under s 9 of the Arbitration Act 1996. This will indirectly enforce the agreement because the plaintiff will have no option other than to seek arbitration if he wishes to obtain a remedy. A decision made by an arbitrator can be enforced by means of specific performance.

---

[66] [1981] QB 202 at 220.

[67] *England v Curling* (1844) 8 Beav 129; *Sichel v Mosenthal* (1862) 30 Beav 371; *Scott v Rayment* (1868) LR 7 Eq 112.

[68] *Baxter v Conolly* (1820) 1 Jac & W 576; *Darbey v Whitaker* (1857) 4 Drew 134: the reason is because of the uncertainty of the subject matter.

[69] See Chapter 15.        [70] *Re Parkin* [1892] 3 Ch 510; *Re Coake* [1922] 1 Ch 292.

[71] (1862) 4 De GF & J 426.

[72] See *Lewin v Guest* (1826) 1 Russ 325; *Wilkinson v Clements* (1872) LR 8 Ch App 96; *Odessa Tramways Co v Mendel* (1878) 8 Ch D 235.

[73] *Re Smith and Service and Nelson & Sons* (1890) 25 QBD 545; *Doleman & Sons v Ossett Corpn* [1912] 3 KB 257.

## (l) Illegal or immoral contracts

The court will not grant specific performance if the contract is illegal or contrary to public policy.[74]

## (3) Mutuality

Historically, it was thought that the court could not grant specific performance in favour of a plaintiff unless it could also have granted specific performance in favour of the defendant. For example, the court would not grant specific performance in favour of a minor, because it would not have specifically enforced the contract against him.[75] The relevant date was thought to be the date that the contract was made.[76] However, in more recent cases it has been held that lack of mutuality is not an absolute bar to specific performance. In *Price v Strange*[77] Goff LJ stated the 'true principle':

'. . . one judges the defence of want of mutuality on the facts and circumstances as they exist at the hearing, albeit in the light of the whole conduct of the parties in relation to the subject matter, and in the absence of any other disqualifying circumstances the court will grant specific performance if it can be done without injustice or unfairness to the defendant.'[78]

The defendant had agreed to grant the plaintiff a new lease of premises he occupied if he carried out some internal and external repairs. At the time of trial the plaintiff had completed the internal repairs and had only been prevented from completing the external repairs by the defendant, who had done them herself. In these circumstances the Court of Appeal ordered specific performance, even though at the date of the agreement the defendant could not have compelled the plaintiff to carry out his promises to repair. There was no risk of hardship to the defendant in granting specific performance because the plaintiff's contractual undertakings had been performed.

## (4) Defences to specific performance

Even though the contract may be one where specific performance would be available, there are a number of defences available to a defendant.

## (a) Absence of necessary formalities

Specific performance will not be available to a plaintiff where a contract was entered without the necessary formalities. Section 40 of the Law of Property Act 1925 required a contract for the sale or disposition of land or an interest in land to be in writing, or for there to be a memorandum or note of the agreement. The absence of such writing would be a defence to an action for specific performance, unless the defendant were

---

[74] *Ewing v Osbaldiston* (1837) 2 My & Cr 53; *Sutton v Sutton* [1984] Ch 184.

[75] *Flight v Bolland* (1828) 4 Russ 298; *Lumley v Ravenscroft* [1895] 1 QB 683.

[76] Fry, *Specific Performance* (6th edn, 1921), p 219. See also *Clayton v Ashdown* (1714) 2 Eq Cas Abr 516; *Hoggart v Scott* (1830) 1 Russ & M 293; *Wilkinson v Clements* (1872) 8 Ch App 96.

[77] [1978] Ch 337; (1978) 128 NLJ 569 (Glover). See also *Sutton v Sutton* [1984] Ch 184.

[78] [1978] Ch 337 at 357.

guilty of fraud[79] or the plaintiff had partly performed the contract.[80] However, for contracts made after 26 September 1989, the Law of Property Act 1925, s 40 has been abolished and replaced by the Law of Property (Miscellaneous Provisions) Act 1989, s 2, which requires that the contract must be made in writing. There is no longer any place for the doctrine of part performance.

### (b) Misrepresentation by the plaintiff

Any misrepresentation by the plaintiff to the defendant, whether innocent or fraudulent, which would entitle the defendant to rescind the contract, will be a defence to an action seeking specific performance.[81]

### (c) Mistake

Where the defendant has made a mistake, which does not prevent the formation of a contract, this will generally be no defence to specific performance. However, the court may refuse the order if it would cause the defendant 'a hardship amounting to injustice'.[82]

### (d) Hardship

Specific performance is a discretionary remedy,[83] and the courts may refuse to grant it if it would cause great hardship to the defendant[84] or a third party.[85] In *Patel v Ali*[86] Mr and Mrs Ali had entered into a contract to sell their house to Mr and Mrs Patel. Mr Ali was then adjudicated bankrupt and spent a year in prison. Mrs Ali was diagnosed as having bone cancer, had a leg amputated just before the birth of her second child, and then subsequently had a third child. In these circumstances Goulding J refused an order for specific performance on the grounds of the hardship to the plaintiffs. He stressed that:

'The important and true principle . . . is that only in extraordinary and persuasive circumstances can hardship supply an excuse for resisting performance of a contract for the sale of immoveable property . . .'[87]

### (e) Misdescription of the property

If the property has been misdescribed in a contract for sale, the defendant will be entitled to rescind the contract[88] and resist a claim for specific performance if the

---

79  *Maxwell v Lady Mountacute* (1719) Prec Ch 526; *Wakeham v Mackenzie* [1968] 1 WLR 1175.

80  Law of Property Act 1925, s 40(2); *Lester v Foxcroft* (1701) Colles 108, HL; *Steadman v Steadman* [1976] AC 536.

81  *Walker v Boyle* [1982] 1 WLR 495.

82  *Tamplin v James* (1880) LR 15 Ch D 215 at 221, per James LJ. Compare *Malins v Freeman* (1836) 2 Keen 25; *Webster v Cecil* (1861) 30 Beav 62.

83  *Co-operative Insurance v Argyll Stores* [1997] 3 All ER 297 at 299.

84  *Denne v Light* (1857) 8 De GM & G 774; *Pegler v White* (1864) 33 Beav 403; *Tamplin v James* (1880) 15 Ch D 215; *Warmington v Miller* [1973] QB 877; *Mountford v Scott* [1975] Ch 258; *Francis v Cowcliff Ltd* (1977) 33 P & CR 368; *Shell UK Ltd v Lostock Garage Ltd* [1977] 1 All ER 481; *Cross v Cross* (1983) 12 Fam Law 182.

85  *Earl of Sefton v Tophams Ltd* [1965] Ch 1140; *Sullivan v Henderson* [1973] 1 WLR 333; *Watts v Spence* [1976] Ch 165; *Cedar Holdings Ltd v Green* [1981] Ch 129.

86  [1984] Ch 283.        87  [1984] Ch 283 at 288.

88  *Flight v Booth* (1834) 1 Bing NC 370; *Charles Hunt Ltd v Palmer* [1931] 2 Ch 287. See below, p 71.

property he would be forced to buy was different in substance. For example, if the contract was for the grant of a lease, the purchaser would not be compelled to take an underlease.[89] Similarly, if the contract was for the sale of 'registered freehold property', the purchaser would not be compelled to take a merely possessory title.[90] The purchaser may, however, choose to take the interest under the contract subject to an abatement of the purchase price in compensation.[91] If the misdescription is slight, so that the purchaser receives substantially what he is entitled to under the contract, the court will order specific performance, subject to the vendor compensating the purchaser, as for example in *Scott v Hanson*,[92] where there was a contract for the sale of fourteen acres of watermeadow, but only twelve could be so described.[93]

### (f) Delay

Equity does not regard time as of the essence of a contract[94] and therefore specific performance may be granted after the due date for performance. Although there is no statutory time limit to a claim for specific performance, the plaintiff must not delay unduly. Thus, in *Huxham v Llewellyn*[95] a delay of five months prevented specific performance.[96] However, in *Lazard Bros & Co Ltd v Fairfield Properties Co (Mayfair) Ltd*[97] Megarry V-C rejected a strict approach and held that if it was just that between the plaintiff and the defendant, the plaintiff should obtain the remedy, the court ought not to withhold it merely because the plaintiff had been guilty of delay. Delay will be no defence where the plaintiff has entered into possession of the property and is simply seeking a transfer of the legal title.[98] For example, in *Williams v Greatrex*[99] specific performance was granted where there had been a delay of ten years. A failure to perform a contract by its due date is a breach for which common law damages may be payable whether or not specific performance is available.[100]

## (5) Damages in lieu of specific performance

### (a) Jurisdiction to award damages

The Court of Chancery was given the power to award damages in lieu of specific performance by s 2 of the Chancery Amendment Act 1858.[101] This had the procedural

---

[89] *Madeley v Booth* (1848) 2 De G & Sm 718; *Re Russ and Brown's Contract* [1934] Ch 34.

[90] *Re Brine and Davies' Contract* [1935] Ch 388.

[91] *Mortlock v Buller* (1804) 10 Ves 292 at 315–316, per Lord Eldon LC; *Hill v Buckley* (1811) 17 Ves 394; *Barnes v Wood* (1869) LR 8 Eq 424; *Horrocks v Rigby* (1878) 9 Ch D 180; *Basma v Weekes* [1950] AC 441.

[92] (1829) 1 Russ & M 128.

[93] See also *M'Queen v Farquhar* (1805) 11 Ves 467; *Re Fawcett and Holmes Contract* (1889) 42 Ch D 150.

[94] *United Scientific Holdings Ltd v Burnley Borough Council* [1978] AC 904.

[95] (1873) 21 WR 570.

[96] See also *Milward v Earl of Thanet* (1801) 5 Ves 720n; *Walker v Jeffreys* (1842) 1 Hare 341; *Mills v Haywood* (1877) 6 Ch D 196; *Cornwall v Henson* [1900] 2 Ch 298.

[97] (1977) 121 Sol Jo 793; [1978] Conv 184.

[98] *Crofton v Ormsby* (1806) 2 Sch & Lef 583; *Shepheard v Walker* (1875) LR 20 Eq 659.

[99] [1957] 1 WLR 31.

[100] *United Scientific Holdings Ltd v Burnley Borough Council* [1978] AC 904.

[101] Lord Cairns' Act.

advantage that if a plaintiff was not awarded specific performance he would not have to start a separate action for damages in the common law courts. After the Judicature Acts of 1873 and 1875 there was no need to rely on the earlier provision, except where damages would not have been available at common law. The Chancery Amendment Act 1858 has been repealed, but its provisions are preserved in the Supreme Court Act 1981, s 50.

## (b) Assessment of damages

In *Wroth v Tyler*[102] Megarry J held that the measure of damages awarded in lieu of specific performance need not be the same as that at common law. He refused an order for specific performance of a contract for the sale of a bungalow, and calculated damages as the difference between the contract price and the value at the date of the judgment, which was £5,500. This was more than the common law measure, which would be the difference between the contract price and the value at the date of the breach, which would have been £1,500. This approach was doubted by the House of Lords in *Johnson v Agnew*,[103] where Lord Wilberforce held that the award of damages under the Chancery Amendment Act was not to be calculated on a different basis than common law damages. However, the result in *Wroth v Tyler*[104] is supportable on the basis that it is not a fixed rule that common law damages must be assessed as at the date of breach.[105] This approach has been recently approved by the House of Lords in *AG v Blake*[106] where Lord Nicholls explained that the jurisdiction under Lord Cairn's Act enables a court to assess damages to include losses likely to follow from the anticipated future continuance of the wrong as well as losses already suffered.

## 3 Injunctions[107]

By means of an order of specific performance the court may compel a person to perform his contractual obligations. In contrast, by means of an injunction the court may order a person[108] to refrain from a particular activity or conduct. For example, in the *Taittinger SA v Allbev Ltd*[109] the Court of Appeal granted an injunction preventing the defendants from selling their non-alcoholic drink under the name 'Elderflower Champagne' because this would amount to passing-off their product as genuine 'champagne'. Failure to comply with an injunction will constitute a contempt of court,

---

[102] [1974] Ch 30.      [103] [1980] AC 367.      [104] [1974] Ch 30.

[105] *Horsler v Zorro* [1975] Ch 302; *Radford v de Froberville* [1978]1 All ER 33; *Malhotra v Choudhury* [1980] Ch 52; *Johnson v Agnew* [1980] AC 367; *Suleman v Shahsavari* [1989] 2 All ER 460.

[106] [2001] 1 AC 268.

[107] See *Snell's Principles of Equity* (31st edn, 2005), pp 379–427; Hanbury and Martin, *Modern Equity* (17th edn, 2005), pp 765–849; Pettit, *Equity and the Law of Trusts* (9th edn, 2001), pp 588–627.

[108] An injunction may also be granted against an unnamed person (*Bloomsbury Publishing Group plc v News Group Newspapers* [2003] 1 WLR 1633) or against the members of a class or organisation (*M Michaels (Furriers) Ltd v Askew* (1983) Times, 25 June)

[109] [1994] 4 All ER 75.

which may lead to sanctions including imprisonment, sequestration of property, or a fine. A third party who aids and abets a breach of an injunction will also be guilty of contempt,[110] and third parties who nullify the effect of a injunction, for example by publishing information which others have been ordered not to publish, will be in contempt of court by virtue of their knowing interference with the administration of justice.[111]

## (1) Types of injunction

### (a) Prohibitory and mandatory

A prohibitory injunction orders a person to refrain from, or to discontinue, a wrongful act. A mandatory injunction requires a person to perform some act, and is often given after the wrong has been done and orders its reversal. For example, if a defendant is about to build in circumstances which would be wrongful, a prohibitory injunction would order him not to build. However, if he had already built, a mandatory injunction would order the building to be pulled down. Historically all injunctions had to be given in a prohibitory form, but since *Jackson v Normanby Brick Co*[112] an injunction which is mandatory in substance will be given in a mandatory form.

### (b) Perpetual and interlocutory

A perpetual injunction is granted to defend a plaintiff's rights after a full hearing. It is a final remedy, even if it does not last for ever as its name might suggest. An interlocutory injunction is granted in order to preserve the status quo pending a full trial and before the parties' rights have finally been established.

### (c) Injunctions without notice

In urgent cases a defenedant will be able to apply for an injunction without giving notice to the defendant (formerly called an ex parte injuction).[113] Where such an injunction is granted, the defendant will subsequently have chance to have the order set aside or varied.[114]

### (d) Quia timet[115] injunctions

This is an injunction to prevent a threatened infringement of the plaintiff's rights which has not yet taken place.[116]

---

[110] *Acro (Automation) Ltd v Rex Chainbelt Inc* [1971] 1 WLR 1676.
[111] *AG v Times Newspapers Ltd* [1992] 1 AC 191; *AG v Punch* [2003] 1 AC 1046.
[112] [1899] 1 Ch 438
[113] The change was introduced by the Civil Procedure Rules 1998.     [114] CPR 23.9, 23.10, 25.3
[115] The name comes from the Latin and means 'he who fears'.
[116] See *Redland Bricks Ltd v Morris* [1970] AC 652.

## (2) General principles governing the grant of a perpetual injunction

### (a) Damages would be an inadequate remedy

An injunction will only be awarded if damages would prove an inadequate remedy.[117] They are generally available as a response to continuing infringements of the plaintiff's rights, for example nuisance or trespass. An injunction is not available for a past infringement which will not be repeated. Damages may be inadequate merely because the defendant is a pauper.[118]

### (b) An infringement of the plaintiff's rights

In *Paton v British Pregnancy Advisory Service Trustees* Sir George Baker P stated:

'. . . the first and basic principle is that there must be a legal right enforceable in law or in equity before the applicant can obtain an injunction from the court to restrain an infringement of that right.'[119]

It is therefore necessary that the plaintiff demonstrate that he is entitled to a legal or equitable right which the courts can protect by means of an injunction.[120] In *Day v Brownrigg*[121] the Court of Appeal refused to grant an injunction restraining the defendant from giving his house the same name as the plaintiff, his next door neighbour, had given to his, because there was no infringement of any legal or equitable right of the plaintiff. In *Paton v British Pregnancy Advisory Service Trustees*[122] the court refused to grant a husband an injunction to prevent his pregnant wife having a lawful abortion because he had no right that was thereby infringed.[123]

### (c) Grant of an injunction is discretionary

As an equitable remedy the award of an injunction is at the court's discretion, although as a general rule a party who establishes the infringement of his right will be entitled to an injunction.[124] However, some prohibitory injunctions are in practice available almost as of right. For example, with reference to an injunction to restrain a breach of a negative contract, Lord Cairns LC said in *Doherty v Allman*:

'. . . it is not a question of the balance of convenience or inconvenience, or of the amount of damage or injury—it is the specific performance, by the Court, of that negative bargain which the parties have made, with their eyes open, between themselves.'[125]

The fact that a plaintiff has only suffered nominal or very small damage from the infringement of his right does not prevent the court awarding an injunction,[126]

---

117 *London and Blackwall Rly Co v Cross* (1886) 31 Ch D 354.
118 *Hodgson v Duce* (1856) 28 LTos 155.    119 [1979] QB 76.
120 *North London Rly Co v Great Northern Rly Co* (1883) 11 QBD 30, CA; *Re C* [1991] 2 FLR 168.
121 (1878) 10 Ch D 294.    122 [1979] QB 276.    123 See also *C v S* [1988] QB 135.
124 *Imperial Gas Light and Coke Co v Broadbent* (1859) 7 HL Cas 600; *Fullwood v Fullwood* (1878) LR 9 Ch D 176; *Pride of Derby and Derbyshire Angling Association Ltd v British Celanese Ltd* [1953] Ch 149 at 181, per Evershed MR; *Harrow London Borough Council v Donohue* [1995] 1 EGLR 257.
125 (1878) 3 App Cas 709 at 720.
126 *Rochdale Canal Co v King* (1851) 2 Sim NS 78; *Wood v Sutcliffe* (1851) 2 Sim NS 163; *Marriott v East Grinstead Gas and Water Co* [1909] 1 Ch 70; *Woollerton & Wilson Ltd v Richard Costain Ltd* [1970] 1 WLR 411.

although it is a factor to be taken into account. In *Society of Architects v Kendrick*[127] the members of the Society placed the letters MSA after their name. Joyce J refused to grant them an injunction against the defendant, who placed the letters after his name even though he was not a member of the society, because he considered the matter 'too trivial for the granting of an injunction'. In *Behrens v Richards*[128] Buckley J refused an injunction against the defendants who were trespassing on the plaintiff's land because their use of a path caused no damage. However, a more strict approach to trespass seems to have been taken in *Patel v WH Smith (Eziot) Ltd*,[129] where the Court of Appeal held that only in very rare cases would an injunction be refused to restrain a continuing trespass. With regard to mandatory injunctions, Lord Upjohn stated the principle in *Redland Bricks Ltd v Morris*:

'. . . the grant of a mandatory injunction is . . . entirely discretionary and unlike a negative injunction can never be "as of course". Every case must depend essentially upon its own particular circumstances.'[130]

He held that the question of the cost to the defendant to do the works necessary was an element to be taken into account in determining whether an injunction should be granted. For this reason the House of Lords refused to grant a mandatory injunction requiring the defendants to perform remedial work costing some £35,000 to their land, to provide support for the plaintiff's land which was only worth £1,500. In *Wrotham Park Estate Co Ltd v Parkside Homes Ltd*[131] Brightman J refused to grant a mandatory injunction requiring the demolition of houses which had been built in contravention of a restrictive covenant because he felt that it would be 'an unpardonable waste of much needed houses'.[132] Obviously, the defendant's conduct is a major factor that will be taken into consideration in determining whether a mandatory injunction should be awarded. As Lord Upjohn said in *Redland Bricks Ltd v Morris*:

'. . . where the defendant has acted without regard to his neighbour's rights and has tried to steal a march on him or has tried to evade the jurisdiction of the court or . . . has acted wantonly and quite unreasonably in relation to his neighbour he may be ordered to repair his wanton and unreasonable acts by doing positive work to restore the status quo even if the expense to him is out of all proportion to the advantage thereby accruing to the plaintiff.'[133]

The courts are reluctant to grant mandatory injunctions in the context of industrial disputes, as Geoffrey Lane J said in *Harold Stephen & Co Ltd v Post Office*:

'It can only be in very rare circumstances and in the most extreme circumstances that this court should interfere by way of mandatory injunction in the delicate mechanism of industrial disputes and industrial negotiations.'[134]

---

[127] (1910) 26 TLR 433. See also *Society of Accountants and Auditors v Goodway* [1907] 1 Ch 489.

[128] [1905] 2 Ch 614.

[129] [1987] 2 All ER 569. See also *Trenberth (John) Ltd v National Westminster Bank Ltd* (1980) 39 P & CR 104.

[130] [1970] AC 652 at 665.     [131] [1974] 1 WLR 798.     [132] [1974] 1 WLR 798 at 811.

[133] [1970] AC 652 at 666. See *Woodhouse v Newry Navigation Co* [1898] 1 IR 161, CA.

[134] [1977] 1 WLR 1172 at 1180. See *Parker v Camden London Borough Council* [1986] Ch 162, CA, where the court was willing to grant a mandatory injunction for the defendants to turn on boilers where tenants had no heat or hot water, because of a boilermen's strike.

## (d) Delay and acquiesence

The court may refuse an injunction if the plaintiff has delayed for an inordinate time,[135] although where an injunction is refused for reasons of delay, a plaintiff may be entitled to damages in lieu.[136] His failure to seek interlocutory relief may also be relevant to a refusal to grant an injunction.[137] Equally, there will be no injunction if the plaintiff has acquiesced and waived his rights.[138] In *Shaw v Applegate*[139] Goff LJ expressed the opinion that it was easier to establish acquiescence in the case of an equitable rather than a legal right.

## (e) Plaintiff must come with 'clean hands'

A plaintiff will only be granted an injunction if he himself comes seeking the aid of equity with 'clean hands'. Breach of his own obligations or unfair conduct[140] will disentitle him to relief, as will his own refusal to carry out his future obligations.[141]

## (f) Damages in lieu of an injunction

Under the Chancery Amendment Act 1858 the court has jurisdiction to award damages in substitution for the award of an injunction. Although the Act itself has been repealed, the jurisdiction remains.[142] In general, the courts will only award damages in substitution in exceptional circumstances.[143] A 'good working rule' as to when damages should be awarded in substitution was set out by AL Smith LJ in *Shelfer v City of London Electric Lighting Co (No 1)*:

'(1) If the injury to the plaintiff's legal rights is small;
(2) and is one which is capable of being estimated in money;
(3) and is one which can be adequately compensated by a small money payment;
(4) and the case is one in which it would be oppressive to the defendant to grant an injunction.'[144]

It must be stressed that these guidelines were given in the context of the understanding that where the plaintiff's legal right has been invaded he is prima facie entitled to an injunction.[145] Although the rule has at times been severely criticised, it has been applied

---

135  *H P Bulmer Ltd and Showerings Ltd v J Bollinger SA* [1977] 2 CMLR 625, CA. *Cf Newport Association Football Club Ltd v Football Association of Wales Ltd* [1995] 2 All ER 87.

136  *Shelfer v City of London Electric Lighting Co (No 1)* [1895] 1 Ch 287; *Bracewell v Appleby* [1975] Ch 408; *Gooden v Ketley* [1996] EGCS 47.

137  See *Shaw v Applegate* [1977] 1 WLR 970, CA.

138  *Parrott v Palmer* (1834) 3 My & K 632; *Johnson v Wyatt* (1863) 2 De G J & Sm 18; *Blue Town Investments Ltd v Higgs and Hill plc* [1990] 1 WLR 696.

139  [1977] 1 WLR 970 at 979.

140  *Shell UK Ltd v Lostock Garage Bros Ltd* [1977] 1 All ER 481. The conduct must concern the subject matter of the dispute in relation to which the injunction is sought: *Argyll v Argyll* [1967] Ch 302.

141  *Measures v Measures* [1910] 2 Ch 248; *Chappell v Times Newspapers Ltd* [1975] 1 WLR 482.

142  Supreme Court Act 1981, s 50; *Leeds Industrial Co-operative Society Ltd v Slack* [1924] AC 851, HL.

143  *Imperial Gas Light and Coke Co v Broadbent* (1859) 7 HL Cas 600; *Shelfer v City of London Electric Lighting Co (No 1)* [1895] 1 Ch 287, CA; *Leeds Industrial Co-operative Society v Slack* [1924] AC 851, HL; *Achilli v Tovell* [1927] 2 Ch 243; *Sefton v Tophams Ltd* [1965] Ch 1140.

144  [1895] 1 Ch 287.

145  See *Slack v Leeds Industrial Co-operative Society Ltd* [1924] 2 Ch 475, CA.

in many cases and was accepted by the Court of Appeal in *Kennaway v Thompson*,[146] where the court reversed the decision of the judge at first instance to award damages in substitution because the first three criteria of the rule had not been met. Similarly, it was applied by the Court of Appeal in *Jaggard v Sawyer*,[147] although Millett LJ emphasised that it provided 'only a working rule and does not purport to be an exhaustive statement of the circumstances in which damages may be awarded instead of an injunction'.[148] In *Woollerton & Wilson Ltd v Richard Costain Ltd*[149] Stamp J doubted that the criteria would be satisfied where there was a trespass which founded a claim to nominal damages only as the payment of damages in lieu of an injunction would amount to the award of a licence to continue trespassing. However, this approach was rejected by the Court of Appeal in *Jaggard v Sawyer*,[150] which held that the principles identified in *Shelfer v City of London Electric Lighting Co*[151] are applicable to cases of trespass.

The measure of damages which may be awarded in lieu of an injunction has been a matter of some controversy. In *Johnson v Agnew*[152] the House of Lords held that where damages would have been available at common law the court only possessed the jurisdiction to award damages on the same compensatory basis. However in some cases the courts awarded damages in lieu of an injunction or specific performance even where there had been no loss. For example, in *Wrotham Park Estate Co Ltd v Parkside Homes Ltd*[153] Brightman J refused an injunction to demolish houses built in breach of covenant but granted the plaintiff damages in substitution. Although at common law damages would have been purely nominal because the plaintiff had suffered no loss in terms of a reduction in the value of his land, substantial damages were awarded, equivalent to the sum of money which might reasonably have been demanded by the plaintiffs for relaxing the restrictive covenant. In *Surrey County Council v Bredero Homes Ltd*[154] Dillon LJ questioned whether this measure of compensation was consistent with *Johnson v Agnew*, but in *Jaggard v Sawyer*[155] the Court of Appeal held that the assessment of damages in *Wrotham Park Estate Co Ltd v Parkside Homes Ltd*[156] had been conducted on a compensatory basis and that it represented an appropriate means by which a judge could assess damages where he declined to prevent the commission of a future wrong by the award of an injunction.[157] The issue was recently re-examined by the House of Lords in *A-G v Blake*.[158] Lord Nicholls explained that although Lord Cairns Act did not alter the measure to be employed in assessing damages, it did enable the court to award damages in respect of the future as well as the past, so that the damages awarded in lieu of an injunction could include losses likely to follow from the anticipated future continuance of the wrong as well as losses already suffered. He summarised as follows:

'The measure of damages awarded in this type of case is often analysed as damages for loss of a bargaining opportunity or, which comes to the same, the price payable for the

---

[146] [1981] QB 88. See also *Wakeham v Wood* (1982) 43 P & CR 40, CA.
[147] [1995] 2 All ER 189.     [148] [1995] 2 All ER 189 at 208.     [149] [1970] 1 WLR 411.
[150] [1995] 2 All ER 189.     [151] [1895] 1 Ch 287.     [152] [1980] AC 367.
[153] [1974] 1 WLR 798     [154] [1993] 3 All ER 705.     [155] [1995] 2 All ER 189.
[156] [1974] 1 WLR 798.
[157] [1995] 2 All ER 189 at 201–202, per Sir Thomas Bingham MR.
[158] [2000] 4 All ER 385.

compulsory acquisition of a right. This analysis is correct. The Court's refusal to grant an injunction means that in practice the defendant is thereby permitted to perpetuate the wrongful state of affairs he has brought about.'[159]

The House of Lords has therefore approved Wrotham Park Estates and doubted *Surrey County Council v Breredo Homes.*

## (g)  Suspension of injunctions

In some circumstances the court will suspend an injunction so that it does not have immediate effect.[160] This may be because it would be impossible immediately to cease the infringement that called for the grant of an injunction. For example, in *Pride of Derby and Derbyshire Angling Association Ltd v British Celanese Ltd*,[161] the Court of Appeal suspended an injunction made against the defendants who polluted a river with sewerage, giving them time to remedy the nuisance they were causing. In *Waverley Borough Council v Hilden*[162] Scott J suspended an injunction requiring gypsies to remove their caravans from an unauthorised site for three months to give them 'a reasonable time to comply with the order'. However, the courts have disapproved of the suspension granted in *Woollerton and Wilson Ltd v Richard Costain Ltd*,[163] which amounted to a licence for the defendants to continue trespassing in the plaintiff's airspace.[164]

## (h)  Declarations

In *Greenwich Healthcare National Health Service Trust v London and Quadrant*[165] Lightman J held that the court has power to grant a declaration that a defendant will not be entitled to an injunction if the plaintiff engages in a particular course of conduct. The plaintiffs wanted to redevelop their hospital, but this would involve a realignment of a private right of way. The dominant owners entitled to the easement had been informed of the proposals and had raised no objection; but neither had they given any positive consent. The plaintiffs were afraid that an injunction might be sought in the future. Lightman J was prepared to make the declaration that no future injunction would be granted, and that the defendants would in the future be limited to redress by means of damages. This was because the realignment was no less commodious than the original route (indeed, it constituted an improvement); the potential dominant owners had been informed and had raised no objection; and the realignment was necessary to achieve an object of substantial public and local importance and value. Lightman J observed:

---

[159]  [2000] 4 All ER 385 at 394.

[160]  *A-G v Birmingham Borough Council* (1858) 4 K & J 528; *A-G v Colney Hatch Lunatic Asylum* (1868) 4 Ch App 146; *Jones v Llanrwst UDC* [1911] 1 Ch 393; *Stollmeyer v Petroleum Development Co Ltd* [1918] AC 498n, PC; *Pride of Derby and Derbyshire Angling Association Ltd v British Celanese Ltd* [1953] Ch 149, CA; *Halsey v Esso Petroleum Co Ltd* [1961] 1 WLR 683; *Miller v Jackson* [1977] QB 966, CA; *Waverley Borough Council v Hilden* [1988] 1 WLR 246.

[161]  [1953] Ch 149.        [162]  [1988] 1 WLR 246.        [163]  [1970] 1 WLR 411.

[164]  Disapproved in *Charrington v Simons & Co Ltd* [1971] 1 WLR 598, CA; *Trenberth (John) Ltd v National Westminster Bank Ltd* (1980) 39 P & CR 104; *Jaggard v Sawyer* [1995] 2 All ER 189 at 199. Contrast *Kelsen v Imperial Tobacco Co of Great Britain and Ireland Ltd* [1957] 2 QB 334.

[165]  [1998] 3 All ER 437.

'The jurisdiction of the court to grant declarations must extend to entitlement both to proprietary rights and to particular remedies. Circumstances may exist when a declaration, eg that a defendant is not entitled to specific performance, rectification or an injunction, is necessary if a period of damaging (or indeed paralysing) uncertainty is to be voided, and indeed the occasion for an unwarrented ransom demand is to be removed. The law is sufficiently adaptable to grant declarations which are necessary to dispel uncertainties and remove obstacles to progress and legitimate activities.'[166]

## (3) General principles governing the grant of an interlocutory injunction

Unlike permanent injunctions, which are granted to protect a plaintiff's established rights, an interlocutory injunction is granted to preserve the status quo between the plaintiff and the defendant before their respective rights can be determined at trial. As Lord Wilberforce said in *Hoffmann-La Roche (F) & Co AG v Secretary of State for Trade and Industry*:

'The object is to prevent a litigant, who must necessarily suffer the law's delay, from losing by that delay the fruit of his litigation.'[167]

### (a) When should an interlocutory injunction be granted?

The principles by which the court should determine whether to grant an interlocutory injunction were outlined by Lord Diplock in the leading case *American Cyanamid Co v Ethicon Ltd*.[168] Subsequent cases have held that the principles are not 'rules,' but rather guidelines with room for flexibility.[169] Until recently, the orthodox interpretation was that in *American Cyanamid* the House of Lords had rejected earlier authorities holding that a plaintiff was required to demonstrate a prima facie case before an interlocutory injunction could be granted[170] in favour of a lower threshold which required the plaintiff to merely demonstrate that there was a 'serious question to be tried'. However, in *Series 5 Software Ltd v Clarke*[171] Laddie J questioned this orthodoxy and provided a reinterpretation of *American Cyanamid* requiring the court to take into account the strength of the parties' respective cases on the evidence. He especially pointed to the decision of the House of Lords in *Hoffmann-La Roche (F) & Co AG v Secretary of State for Trade and Industry*,[172] which had been decided a few months before *American Cyanamid* but was not cited in the subsequent case, where Lord Diplock had suggested that the award of an interlocutory injunction was conditional upon the plaintiff demonstrating a 'strong prima facie case that he will be entitled to a final order'.[173]

---

[166] [1998] 3 All ER 437 at 444.     [167] [1975] AC 295 at 355.

[168] [1975] AC 396, HL; (1975) 91 LQR 168 (Prescott); (1975) 38 MLR 672 (Gore); (1976) 35 CLJ 82 (Wallington); (1981) 40 CLJ 307 (Gray).

[169] See *Fellowes & Son v Fisher* [1976] QB 122, CA; *Cayne v Global Natural Resources plc* [1984] 1 All ER 225, CA; *Cambridge Nutrition Ltd v BBC* [1990] 3 All ER 523, CA; *Factortame Ltd v Secretary of State for Transport (No 2)* [1991] 1 All ER 70; *Kirklees MBC v Wickes Building Supplies Ltd* [1993] AC 227.

[170] *Preston v Luck* (1884) 27 Ch D 497; *Smith v Grigg Ltd* [1924] 1 KB 655, CA; *JT Stratford & Son Ltd v Lindley* [1965] AC 269. Compare also *Fellowes & Son v Fisher* [1976] QB 122; *Hubbard v Pitt* [1976] QB 142.

[171] [1996] 1 All ER 853.     [172] [1975] AC 295.     [173] [1975] AC 295 at 360–361.

Having concluded that the prospects of success at trial were relevant, Laddie J indicated the matters which he thought the court should take into account in deciding whether to grant an injunction:

'(1) The grant of an interlocutory injunction is a matter of discretion and depends on all the facts of the case. (2) There are no fixed rules as to when an injunction should or should not be granted. The relief must be kept flexible. (3) Because of the practice adopted on the hearing of applications for interlocutory relief, the court should rarely attempt to resolve complex issues of disputed fact or law. (4) Major factors the court can bear in mind are (a) the extent to which damages are likely to be an adequate remedy for each party and the ability of the other party to pay, (b) the balance of convenience, (c) the maintenance of the status quo, and (d) any clear view the court may reach as to the relative strengths of the parties' cases.'[174]

He refused to award an interlocutory injunction despite the fact that the plaintiff's case was 'arguable in the sense that it is possible that the facts at the trial may support the allegation it makes' because he was 'not impressed with its strength'.[175] It is unclear whether this re-interpretation will be adopted. However, as will be seen, there are a number of special cases where there is a long-standing practice of considering the strength of the plaintiff's case. In addition, Laddie J's view has been praised as restoring judicial discretion to an area that was in danger of becoming 'so encrusted with expectations as to how that discretion should be exercised that it too had established a tyranny'.[176]

### (b) The orthodox interpretation of American Cyanamid

Under the orthodox interpretation of *American Cyanamid* the following factors must be taken into account by the court to determine whether an interlocutory injunction should be granted.

*(i) 'A serious question to be tried'*. Although the plaintiff does not need to establish a prima facie case, Lord Diplock held that 'the court . . . must be satisfied that the claim is not frivolous or vexatious; in other words that there is a serious question to be tried'. Only if the plaintiff fails to show any real prospect of succeeding in his claim at trial should the court refuse the injunction without going on to consider the balance of convenience.

*(ii) The 'balance of convenience'*. Once the plaintiff has shown that there is a serious issue, the court must weigh the balance of convenience between granting and refusing an injunction, and the effect that this would have on the respective parties if the issue was determined in favour of that party at trial. The court must assess the adequacy of damages as a remedy for any loss they may suffer in consequence of the grant or refusal of an injunction. Lord Diplock explained the issues to be considered:

'. . . the court should first consider whether, if the plaintiff were to succeed at the trial in establishing his right to a permanent injunction, he would be adequately compensated by an

---

174 [1996] 1 All ER 853 at 865.      175 [1996] 1 All ER 853 at 867.
176 Phillips [1997] JBL 486 at 487, reviewing the cases decided since *Series 5 Software*.

award of damages for the loss he would have sustained as a result of the defendant's continuing to do what was sought to be enjoined between the time of the application and the time of the trial. If damages in the measure recoverable at common law would be adequate remedy and the defendant would be in a financial position to pay them, no interlocutory injunction should normally be granted, however strong the plaintiff's claim appeared to be at that stage. If, on the other hand, damages would not provide an adequate remedy for the plaintiff in the event of his succeeding at the trial, the court should then consider whether, on the contrary hypothesis that the defendant were to succeed at the trial in establishing his right to do that which was sought to be enjoined, he would be adequately compensated under the plaintiff's undertaking as to damages for the loss he would have sustained by being prevented from doing so between the time of the application and the time of the trial. If damages in the measure recoverable under such an undertaking would be an adequate remedy and the plaintiff would be in a financial position to pay them, there would be no reason upon this ground to refuse an interlocutory injunction.'[177]

He concluded that where the factors appear to be evenly balanced 'it is a counsel of prudence to take such measures as preserve the status quo'. This exercise of weighing the 'balance of convenience' has also been described as the 'balance of the risk of doing an injustice'.[178]

*(iii) 'Other special factors to be taken into consideration'.* Lord Diplock also recognised that there 'may be many other special factors to be taken into consideration in the particular circumstances of individual cases'.[179] For example, in *American Cyanamid*[180] itself, which concerned an interlocutory injunction to prevent the defendants launching a surgical product claimed to be in breach of the plaintiffs' patent, a number of additional factors were taken into account, including the fact that the defendants as yet had no business which would be brought to a stop by the injunction; that the launch of the defendants' product would prevent the plaintiffs' patented product becoming established in the market; and that if the defendants' product was allowed on the market before trial and patients and doctors became used to it, it might be impracticable for the plaintiffs to insist on a permanent injunction at trial. For these reasons the House of Lords held that an interlocutory injunction should be granted. The public interest, and the interests of the public in general may also be factors to be taken into account in determining whether an interlocutory injunction should be granted.[181] In *Themehelp Ltd v West*[182] the Court of Appeal was asked to grant an interlocutory injunction preventing the enforcement of a performance bond pending a fraud trial. The court was prepared to grant the order, but recognised that the situations in which such orders should be granted had to be considered with care lest they

---

[177] [1975] AC 396 at 408.

[178] *Cayne v Global Natural Resources plc* [1984] 1 All ER 225 at 237, per May LJ.

[179] *Bryanston Finance Ltd v de Vries (No 2)* [1976] Ch 63; *Dunford and Elliot Ltd v Johnson and Firth Brown Ltd* [1977] 1 Lloyd's Rep 505, CA; *Roussel-Uclaf v G D Searle & Co Ltd* [1977] FSR 125; *A-G v Guardian Newspapers Ltd* [1987] 1 WLR 1248.

[180] [1975] AC 396.

[181] See *Smith v Inner London Education Authority* [1978] 1 All ER 411, CA; *Factortame Ltd v Secretary of State for Transport (No 2)* [1991] 1 All ER 70 at 118–119, per Lord Goff.

[182] [1995] 4 All ER 215.

disturb the mercantile practice that performance bonds should normally be treated as autonomous guarantees which could be enforced regardless of any problems extraneous to the guarantee itself.

*(iv) 'Real prospect of trial'.* Although an interlocutory injunction is intended to preserve the status quo before the final determination of the issue at trial, it is inevitable that in many cases the matter will go no further and the parties will settle on the basis of the injunction granted.[183] With the rejection of the requirement that the plaintiff must establish a prima facie case there is now no need for the court to inquire too deeply into the merits of the plaintiffs' claim, and the consequence is that the plaintiff may force the defendant to settle without ever having to prove his case. To address this problem the Court of Appeal held in *Cayne v Global Natural Resources plc*[184] that a future trial must be likely to take place. Kerr LJ stated the limitation:

'The second pre-requisite . . . is that a trial is in fact likely to take place, in the sense that the plaintiff's case shows that they are genuinely concerned to pursue their claim to trial, and that they are seeking the injunction as a means of a holding operation pending the trial.'[185]

*(v) Freedom of expression.* The principles by which it is determined whether an interlocutory injunction should be granted are different in cases involving a breach of confidence, privacy or libel because of the effect of the Human Rights Act 1998, which incorporates into English Law art 10 of the European Convention on Human Rights protecting freedom of expression. Section 12(3) of the Human Rights Act provides that the court should not grant relief unless the court 'is satisfied that the applicant is likely to reestablish that the publication should not be allowed'. It follows that in such cases the courts must look at the strength of the claimant's case before granting an interlocutory injunction, and not simply apply the usual 'balance of convenience' test. An interlocutory injunction will therefore only be granted if the claimant can show that he would probably succeed at trail, unless the consequences of publication would be especially serious.[186] Even where the claimant can demonstrate the likelihood of success, the court may refuse an injunction and leave the claimant to a remedy in damages if the 'balance of convenience' favours refusing the award of an injunction.[187]

## (c) Undertaking in damages

On the grant of an interlocutory injunction the plaintiff is generally required to give an undertaking in damages to the defendant. By this undertaking, made to the court,[188] the plaintiff is liable to pay the defendant damages for any loss he has suffered as a result of the grant of the interlocutory injunction prior to the full hearing if at the subsequent

---

[183] See *Fellowes & Son v Fisher* [1976] QB 122 at 133, per Lord Denning MR, who suggested that 99 cases out of 100 go no further than the grant of an interlocutory injunction.

[184] [1984] 1 All ER 225.      [185] [1984] 1 All ER 225 at 234.

[186] *Cream Holdings Ltd v Banerjee* [2004] 3 WLR 918

[187] *Douglas v Hello! Ltd* [2001] QB 967.See Morgan, 'Confidence and Horizontal Effect; "Hello" Trouble' [2003] 62 CLJ 444

[188] Therefore, any breach is a contempt and not merely a breach of contract: *Hussain v Hussain* [1986] Fam 134, CA. Compare *Balkanbank v Taher* [1994] 4 All ER 239.

trial it appears that the injunction should not have been granted.[189] There is no need for an undertaking in damages in matrimonial proceedings,[190] or where the crown seeks an injunction to enforce the general law[191] rather than its own proprietary right.[192]

### (d) Mandatory interlocutory injunctions

The courts are more reluctant to award mandatory interlocutory injunctions, and it seems that a higher test may have to be satisfied than that set out in *American Cyanamid*,[193] which involved a prohibitory injunction. In *De Falco v Crawley Borough Council*[194] Lord Denning MR held that a mandatory interlocutory injunction should not be granted unless the plaintiffs made out a 'strong prima facie case',[195] and in *Shepherd Homes Ltd v Sandham*[196] Megarry J held that 'the case has to be unusually strong and clear before a mandatory injunction will be granted'. His suggestion that 'the court must ... feel a high degree of assurance that at the trial it will appear that the injunction was rightly granted'[197] was approved and applied by the Court of Appeal in *Locabail International Finance Ltd v Agroexport & Atlanta (UK) Ltd*,[198] which felt that the statements of principle relating to mandatory interlocutory injunctions were not affected by *American Cyanamid*.[199] Where the requirements are met the court will grant such an injunction.[200]

### (e) Interlocutory injunctions in the context of trade disputes

By s 221(2) of the Trade Union and Labour Relations Act 1992, in determining whether to grant an interlocutory injunction the court must have regard to the likelihood of the defendant establishing at trial that the action was in contemplation of a trade dispute and therefore entitled to statutory immunity. The defendant must be able to show a high degree of probability that the statutory defence will succeed if the consequences of refusing the injunction will be severe damage to the plaintiff.[201]

### (f) Interlocutory injunctions in the context of libel

The courts will generally refuse to award an interlocutory injunction in cases of alleged libel if the defendant intends to justify (ie to prove the truth of the defamatory statement).[202] This has not been altered by *American Cyanamid*.[203]

---

[189] See *Chappell v Davidson* (1856) 8 De G M & G 1; *Smith v Day* (1882) 21 Ch D 421; *Digital Equipment Corpn v Darkcrest* [1984] Ch 512.

[190] *Practice Direction (Injunction: Undertaking as to Damages)* [1974] 1 WLR 576.

[191] *Hoffman La Roche (F) & Co AG v Secretary of State for Trade and Industry* [1975] AC 295.

[192] See *A-G v Wright* [1988] 1 WLR 164.

[193] [1975] AC 396, HL.    [194] [1980] QB 460, CA.    [195] [1980] QB 460 at 478.

[196] [1971] Ch 340 at 349.    [197] [1971] Ch 340 at 351.    [198] [1986] 1 WLR 657.

[199] See also *Films Rover International Ltd v Cannon Film Sales Ltd* [1987] 1 WLR 670, where Hoffmann J held that a mandatory interlocutory injunction could be granted where refusal carried a greater risk of injustice than granting it, even though the 'high degree of assurance' test was not met.

[200] *NWL Ltd v Woods* [1979] 1 WLR 1294, HL.

[201] See *Smith v Peters* (1875) LR 20 Eq 511; *Esso Petroleum Co Ltd v Kingswood Motors (Addlestone) Ltd* [1974] QB 142; *Sky Petroleum v VIP Petroleum Ltd* [1974] 1 WLR 576; *Astro Exito Navegacion SA v Southland Enterprise Co Ltd (No 2)* [1982] QB 1248; *Parker v Camden London Borough Council* [1986] Ch 162; *Hemingway Securities Ltd v Dunraven Ltd* [1995] 1 EGLR 61.

[202] *Bonnard v Perryman* [1891] 2 Ch 269, CA.

[203] *Bestobell Paints Ltd v Bigg* (1975) 119 Sol Jo 678; *J Trevor & Sons v P R Solomon* [1978] 2 EGLR 120; *A-G v BBC* [1981] AC 303; *Gulf Oil (GB) Ltd v Page* [1987] Ch 327.

## (4) General principles governing the grant of a quia timet injunction

Quia timet injunctions are available where, although there has as yet been no infringement of the plaintiff's rights, such an infringement has been threatened or is apprehended. In *Redland Bricks Ltd v Morris* Lord Upjohn distinguished two circumstances in which a quia timet injunction would be appropriate:

'. . . first, where the defendant has as yet done no hurt to the plaintiff but is threatening and intending (so the plaintiff alleges) to do works which will render irreparable harm to him or his property if carried to completion . . . Secondly, the type of case where the plaintiff has been fully compensated both at law and in equity for the damage he has suffered but where he alleges that the earlier actions of the defendant may lead to further causes of action.'[204]

In order for the court to grant a quia timet injunction the plaintiff must satisfy a relatively high burden of proof that the threatened or apprehended infringement will occur. As Lord Dunedin said in *A-G for the Dominion of Canada v Ritchie Contracting and Supply Co Ltd*[205] 'no one can obtain a quia timet order by merely saying "Timeo" '.[206] In *A-G v Manchester Corpn* Chitty J stated:

'The principle which I think may be properly and safely extracted from the quia timet authorities is, that the plaintiff must show a strong case of probability that the apprehended mischief will, in fact, arise.'[207]

In *Redland Bricks Ltd v Morris*[208] Lord Upjohn said that 'a mandatory injunction can only be granted where the plaintiff shows a very strong probability upon the facts that grave damage will accrue to him in the future'.[209] However, in *Hooper v Rogers* Russell LJ suggested a different formulation:

'In different cases differing phrases have been used in describing circumstances in which . . . quia timet injunctions will be granted. In truth it seems to me that the degree of probability of future injury is not an absolute standard: what is to be aimed at is justice between the parties having regard to all the relevant circumstances.'[210]

Where the defendant cannot demonstrate a strong probability of the threatened or apprehended infringement the court will refuse to grant an injunction. For example, in *A-G v Nottingham Corpn*[211] an application for a quia timet injunction to prevent the defendant using a building as a smallpox hospital on the grounds that it would constitute a public and private nuisance was refused because the plaintiff had failed to show 'a strong probability almost amounting to moral certainty' that there would be an actionable nuisance.[212] In contrast in *Goodhart v Hyett*[213] the plaintiff owned, by virtue of an

---

[204] [1970] AC 652 at 665.     [205] [1919] AC 999 at 1005.

[206] 'Timeo' means 'I am afraid' and comes from the same Latin verb as quia timet.

[207] [1893] 2 Ch 87 at 92.     [208] [1970] AC 652.

[209] See also *A-G v Manchester Corpn* [1893] 2 Ch 87; *A-G v Rathmines and Pembroke Joint Hospital Board* [1904] 1 IR 161.

[210] [1974] 3 WLR 329 at 334.

[211] [1904] 1 Ch 673. See also *Worsley v Swann* (1882) 51 LJ Ch 576; *Fletcher v Bealey* (1885) 28 Ch D 688; *A-G v Manchester Corpn* [1893] 2 Ch 87; *Draper v British Optical Association* [1938] 1 All ER 115.

[212] See also *A-G v Rathmines and Pembroke Joint Hospital Board* [1904] 1 IR 161.

[213] (1883) 25 Ch D 182.

easement, a pipe running across the defendant's land. North J granted a quia timet injunction to prevent the defendant building a house above the pipe, because the plaintiff had shown that this would prevent him repairing the pipe.[214]

## (5) Rights which will be protected by the grant of an injunction

Having examined the general requirements governing the grant of perpetual, interlocutory and quia timet injunctions, it is appropriate to consider the most important practical circumstances in which they are available as a remedy.

### (a) Trespass

A landowner will normally[215] be entitled to a prohibitory injunction to prevent trespassers entering his land, and a mandatory injunction ordering trespassers to be removed. These remedies are available even though he has suffered no damage from the trespass.[216]

### (b) Nuisance

An injunction is an important remedy available to the occupier of land where the defendant is causing a private nuisance, or to a private individual who suffers particular damage from a public nuisance.[217]

### (c) Waste

Waste is a tort committed when by any action, or inaction, a tenant for years or tenant for life of land permanently alters the physical character of land in his possession.[218] An injunction will be granted to restrain voluntary[219] and equitable waste,[220] but not ameliorative[221] or permissive waste.[222]

### (d) Libel

The court possesses the jurisdiction to award an injunction to prevent the publication of defamatory material.[223] However, such an injunction will only be granted if it is clear

---

[214] See also *Emperor of Austria v Day* (1861) 3 De G F & J 217; *Dicker v Popham, Radford & Co* (1890) 63 LT 379; *Torquay Hotel Co Ltd v Cousins* [1969] 2 Ch 106.

[215] *Jaggard v Sawyer* [1995] 2 All ER 189 is an example of an exception.

[216] See *Kelsen v Imperial Tobacco* [1957] 2 QB 334; *Patel v WH Smith (Eziot) Ltd* [1987] 1 WLR 853, CA; *Trenberth (John) Ltd v National Westminster Bank Ltd* (1980) 39 P & CR 104; *Harrow London Borough Council v Donohue* [1995] 1 EGLR 257.

[217] *Lyon v Fishmongers' Co* (1875–76) 1 App Cas 662, HL; *Vanderpant v Mayfair Hotel Co Ltd* [1930] 1 Ch 138.

[218] See Gray & Gray, *Elements of Land Law* (3rd edn, 2001), pp 69–70.

[219] Any acts which positively diminish the value of the land, for example quarrying or cutting timber.

[220] Equitable waste is malicious or wanton destruction of the land or buildings exceeding the licence conferred by a clause exempting the tenant from liability for voluntary waste: *Vane v Lord Barnard* (1716) 2 Vern 738; *Weld-Blundell v Wolseley* [1903] 2 Ch 664.

[221] Where the land is improved: *Doherty v Allman* (1878) 3 App Cas 709.

[222] Defaults of maintenance and repair: *Powys v Blagrave* (1854) 4 De GM & G 448; *Re Cartwright* (1889) 41 Ch D 532.

[223] *Quartz Hill Consolidated Gold Mining Co v Beall* (1881–82) LR 20 Ch D 501; *Bonnard v Perryman* [1891] 2 Ch 269; *Hubbard v Pitt* [1976] QB 142; *Gulf Oil (Great Britain) Ltd v Page* [1987] Ch 327; *Femis-Bank (Anguilla) Ltd v Lazer* [1991] Ch 391.

that the material to be published is false, since the court is concerned to protect the public interest in knowing the truth.[224] As was noted above,[225] since the award of an injunction to prevent a libel may affect the right to freedom of expression, where an interlocutory injunction is sought the principles identified in *American Cyanamid* are inapplicable.[226] An injunction will rarely be granted if the defendant intends to justify statements published.[227] In *Greene v Associated Newspapers*[228] the Court of Appeal held that the Human Rights Act 1998 had not changed the rule in *Bonnard v Perryman*[229] that a court would not impose a prior restraint on publication unless it was clear that no defence would succeed at trial. A quia timet injunction may be granted to prevent a threatened libel, but in *British Data Management plc v Boxer Commercial Removals plc*[230] the Court of Appeal held that such an injunction should only be granted if the plaintiff could demonstrate with 'reasonable certainty' the threatened words which are allegedly defamatory.[231] In the case of *Holley v Smyth*[232] the Court of Appeal held that an interlocutory injunction should not be granted to restrain the threatened publication of an allegedly libellous allegation that the plaintiff had caused a loss of £200,000 from a trust through a fraudulent misrepresentation, unless it could be shown that the allegation was 'plainly untrue' at the interlocutory stage. Where the untruthfulness of the statement could not be so proved the law would allow publication. If it was subsequently proved that the allegation was libellous, then the plaintiff would be entitled to receive compensation, which might include an award of aggravated damages,[233] if warranted, to punish his motives for publication.[234]

### (e) Breach of contract

An injunction is an appropriate remedy against a party who is in breach of a negative contractual term.[235] For example, in *Nordenfelt v Maxim Nordenfelt Guns and Ammunition Co Ltd*[236] the House of Lords granted an injunction to enforce a contractual stipulation that the defendant would not engage in the business of manufacturing guns or ammunition for 25 years after he had sold his patents and business to the plaintiffs.[237] The court will also grant injunctions to enforce the terms of partnership

---

[224]   *Fraser v Evans* [1969] 1 QB 349; *Woodward v Hutchins* [1977] 1 WLR 760; *A-G v BBC* [1981] AC 303.
[225]   See p 54.
[226]   *Herbage v Pressdram Ltd* [1984] 1 WLR 1160; *Kaye v Robertson* [1991] FSR 62.
[227]   *Bonnard v Perryman* [1891] 2 Ch 269.        [228]   [2005] 1 All ER 30.
[229]   [1891] 2 Ch 269.        [230]   [1996] 3 All ER 707.
[231]   [1996] 3 All ER 707 at 717, per Hirst LJ. The plaintiff does not therefore need to be able to plead the actual words that the defendant has threatened to use.
[232]   [1998] 2 WLR 742.        [233]   *Rookes v Barnard* [1964] AC 1129.
[234]   [1998] 2 WLR 742 at 758–759, per Auld LJ.
[235]   The term need not be expressed in a negative way as the court will look to the substance and not the form: *Wolverhampton and Walsall Rly Co Ltd v London and North Western Rly Ltd* (1873) LR 16 Eq 433. In exceptional circumstances breach of a negative term of a contract may give rise to the restitutionary remedy of an account of profits: *A-G v Blake* [2001] 1 AC 268; *Experience Hendrix LLC v PPX Enterprises Inc* [2003] 1 All ER (Comm) 830.
[236]   [1894] AC 535.
[237]   A world-wide prohibition would normally be invalid as being in restraint of trade, but it was upheld in this case because of the international scale and nature of the businesses concerned.

agreements.[238] The court will not grant an injunction to enforce a contractual term in a contract for personal services which would indirectly amount to specific performance of the contract because the employee will have no option but to perform the contract or remain idle.[239]

## (f) Restrictive covenants

The court may grant an injunction to enforce a restrictive covenant[240] over land. For example, in *Wakeham v Wood*[241] a mandatory injunction was granted requiring the defendant to demolish a building which obstructed the view of the sea from the plaintiff's house contrary to a restrictive covenant.

## (g) Breach of trust

The court will grant an injunction to restrain trustees from committing a breach of trust.[242]

## (h) Breach of confidence[243]

In *Campbell v MGN Ltd* the House of Lords held that a duty of confidence arisies 'whenever a person receives information he knows or ought to know is fairly and reasonably to be regarded as confidential.'[244] The court may grant an injunction to prevent a breach of confidence by restraining the publication of confidential information.[245] For example, in *Prince Albert v Strange*[246] the Prince obtained an injunction to prevent the publication of etchings which had been obtained in breach of confidence. In *Duchess of Argyll v Duke of Argyll*[247] an injunction was granted to prevent the plaintiff publishing details of her marriage to the defendant. In the *Spycatcher* case an interlocutory injunction was granted to prevent the publication of a book on the basis of the public interest of maintaining confidentiality.[248] An injunction may also be available in a commercial context where a company has received confidential information. For example, in *Peter Pan Manufacturing Corpn v Corsets Silhouette Ltd*[249] the plaintiffs were granted an injunction to prevent the defendants manufacturing a brassiere to a design which they had been shown in confidence. The right to confidence can extend to

---

[238] *Hall v Hall* (1850) 12 Beav 414.

[239] See *Lumley v Wagner* (1852) 1 De GM & G 604; *Rely-a-Bell Burglar and Fire Alarm Co v Eisler* [1926] Ch 609; *Warner Bros Pictures Inc v Nelson* [1937] 1 KB 209; *Page One Records Ltd v Britton* [1967] 3 All ER 822; *Evening Standard Co Ltd v Henderson* [1987] IRLR 64.

[240] See Gray & Gray, *Elements of Land Law* (3rd edn, 2001), pp 1181–1184.

[241] (1982) 43 P & CR 40, CA.

[242] *Fox v Fox* (1870) LR 11 Eq 142; *Dance v Goldingham* (1872–73) 8 Ch App 902; *Waller v Waller* [1967] 1 All ER 305.

[243] See Chapter 29.      [244] [2004] 2 All ER 995, at [14], per Lord Nicholls.

[245] See *Lord Ashburton v Pape* [1913] 2 Ch 469, CA; *Foster v Mountford* [1978] FSR 582; *Woodward v Hutchins* [1977] 1 WLR 760, CA; *Lion Laboratories v Evans* [1985] QB 526, CA; *X (HA) v Y* [1988] 2 All ER 648; *W v Egdell* [1990] Ch 359.

[246] (1849) 1 Mac & G 25.      [247] [1967] Ch 302.

[248] *A-G v Guardian Newspapers Ltd* [1987] 1 WLR 1248; *A-G v Guardian Newspapers Ltd (No 2)* [1990] 1 AC 109.

[249] [1964] 1 WLR 96.

preventing the publication of photographs[250] or of tape recordings of private conversations.[251] Protection of confidential information is now seen as part of a rapidly developing law of privacy,[252] and the protection of such information involves consideration of the relationship between the right to privacy and the right to freedom of expression under arts 8 and 10 of the European Convention on Human Rights, incorporated into English Law by the Human Rights Act 1998. In *Campbell v MGN Ltd*[253] the House of Lords held that neither art 8 nor art 10 were to be given pre-eminence, so that the right of the media to provide information to the public had to be balanced against the respect to be given to private life. The difficulty of determining where the balance between these competing rights should lie is well illustrated by the fact that the Law Lords were split 3–2 as to whether publication of photographs of Naomi Campbell attending Narcotic's Anonymous meetings infringed her right to privacy. The majority[254] held that details of her treatment should be protected, since they considered that the assurance of privacy was essential to the effectiveness of the therapy being received. However the minority[255] held that the disclosure of the nature of the treatment she was receiving was unremarkable, and followed consequentially from the fact that it was in the public interest to disclose the fact that she was receiving treatment for drug addiction because she had previously denied using drugs. As was noted above, as a result of the Human Rights Act 1998 the award of an interlocutory injunction to restrain publication of information on the grounds of breach of confidence will not be determined by the application of the usual *American Cyanamid* principles, so that an injunction will only be granted if the claimant can demonstrate a likelihood of success at trial.[256]

## (i) Intellectual property rights

An injunction will be granted to prevent a defendant passing-off a product so that it appears to be the plaintiff's,[257] using his trade mark or infringement of his patent, registered design or copyright.[258]

## (j) Expulsion from clubs and societies

The court will grant an injunction to restrain the wrongful expulsion of a member from a club, for example where the rules of natural justice have been breached.[259] The court will clearly act if the member has a proprietary interest in the club,[260] but even where

---

[250]  *Douglas v Hello* [2003] 3 All ER 996; *D v L* [2003] EWCA Civ 1169.

[251]  *D v L* [2003] EWCA Civ 1169.

[252]  See Phillipson, 'Transforming Breach of Confidence? Towards a Common Law Right of Privacy Under the Human Rights Act' (2003) 66 MLR 726.

[253]  [2004] 2 All ER 995. See also *Douglas v Hello! Ltd* [2003] 3 All ER 996 and [2005] EWCA Civ 595.

[254]  Lord Hope, Baronness Hale, Lord Carson.        [255]  Lord Nicholls, Lord Hoffman.

[256]  See above p 54.

[257]  *GG Spalding & Bros v AW Gamage Ltd* (1915) 32 RPC 273, HL; *Erven Warnick BV v J Townend & Sons (Hull) Ltd* [1979] AC 731; *Taittinger SA v Allbev Ltd* [1994] 4 All ER 75, CA.

[258]  See Trade Marks Act 1938; Patents Act 1949; Registered Designs Act 1949; Patents Act 1977; Copyright, Design and Patents Act 1988.

[259]  *Labouchere v Earl of Wharncliffe* (1879–80) 13 Ch D 346.

[260]  *Rigby v Connol* (1880) 14 Ch D 482.

there is no proprietary interest[261] an injunction is available to protect his right to work[262] or if a matter of public importance is involved.[263] One particular area where injunctions have been granted is to prevent wrongful expulsion from trade unions.[264]

### (k) Judicial review

An injunction is one remedy[265] available where the decision of a public body is subject to 'judicial review', for instance because it has acted outside the scope of its powers. The House of Lords held in *O'Reilly v Mackman*[266] that an application for judicial review claiming a public body has infringed public rights must be brought under RSC Ord 53. However, where a private law right is infringed an injunction may be sought in the ordinary way.[267]

### (l) Family matters

The court has statutory jurisdiction under the Family Law Act 1996[268] to grant injunctions excluding a spouse or partner from the matrimonial home, and to restrain one spouse molesting the other. Injunctions may also be used to protect minors. An injunction cannot, however, be obtained by a husband or partner to prevent a woman having an abortion.[269] A detailed consideration of these issues is outside the scope of this text.

# 4 Freezing injunctions[270]

## (1) Definition

### (a) Nature of the Freezing Injunction

Although basically an injunction similar to those considered in the preceding section, the freezing injunction is sufficiently important to merit a consideration of its own. If granted, it prevents a defendant (or a third party holding a defendant's assets[271]) from dissipating or removing his assets from the jurisdiction so that there will be nothing

---

[261] See *Baird v Wells* (1890) 44 Ch D 661, CA; *Rowe v Hewitt* (1906) 12 OLR 13; *Lee v Showmen's Guild of Great Britain* [1952] 2 QB 329; *Gaiman v National Association for Mental Health* [1971] Ch 317.

[262] *Edwards v Society of Graphical and Allied Trades* [1971] Ch 354.

[263] *Woodford v Smith* [1970] 1 WLR 806.

[264] *Osborne v Amalgamated Society of Railway Servants* [1911] 1 Ch 540; *Edwards v Society of Graphical and Allied Trades* [1971] Ch 354; *Breen v Amalgamated Engineering Union* [1971] 2 QB 175; *Shotton v Hammond* (1976) 120 Sol Jo 780.

[265] Others are a declaration or prerogative order.      [266] [1983] 2 AC 237.

[267] *R v BBC, ex p Lavelle* [1983] 1 WLR 23; *Law v National Greyhound Racing Club Ltd* [1983] 1 WLR 1302; *R v East Berkshire Health Authority, ex p Walsh* [1985] QB 152; *R v Derbyshire County Council, ex p Noble* [1990] ICR 808.

[268] Extending and replacing earlier legislation including the Matrimonial Causes Act 1973 and Matrimonial and Family Proceedings Act 1984.

[269] *Paton v Trustees of British Pregnancy Advisory Service* [1979] QB 76; *C v S* [1988] QB 135.

[270] See *Snell's Principles of Equity* (31st edn, 2005), pp 415–420; Hanbury and Martin, *Modern Equity* (17th edn, 2005), pp 842–849; Pettit, *Equity and the Law of Trusts* (9th edn, 2001), pp 608–618.

[271] See [1996] LMCLQ 268 (Devonshire).

remaining to satisfy a judgment which might be obtained against him at trial.[272] Until recently freezing injunctions were known as 'Mareva' Injunctions, taking their name from the case in which they were first exercised, *Mareva Compania Naviera SA v International Bulk Carriers SA*.[273] The new nomenclature was introduced in the Civil Procedure Rules.[274] The injunction is granted in an interlocutory form and is usually obtained ex parte. As Kerr LJ stated in *Z Ltd v A-Z*:

'Mareva injunctions should be granted … when it appears to the court that there is a combination of two circumstances. First, when it appears likely that the plaintiff will recover judgment against the defendant for a certain or approximate sum. Secondly, when there are also reasons to believe that the defendant has assets within the jurisdiction to meet the judgment, in whole or in part, but may well take steps designed to ensure that these are no longer available or traceable when judgment is given against him.'[275]

As Lord Donaldson MR said in *Derby & Co v Weldon (Nos 3 & 4)*[276] the fundamental principle underlying the jurisdiction to grant a freezing injunction is that 'no court should permit a defendant to take action designed to ensure that subsequent orders of the court are rendered less effective than would otherwise be the case'.[277] Where a freezing injunction is granted the defendant is entitled to draw upon his assets to fund his legitimate expenses,[278] including his reasonable legal expenses in defending the subsequent action. Where the plaintiff seeks to assert a proprietary claim to property in the defendant's hands, for example asserting that he was a constructive trustee, and a freezing injunction has been granted, the mere fact that the defendant will not act in breach of the injunction by applying the property towards his expenses will not prevent him being held liable for breach of trust if the proprietary claim is upheld and the property has been wholly or partial dissipated.[279] Similarly, the recipients of such property, for example solicitors whose legal fees are paid from it, will not be protected from possible future claims on the grounds that they had knowingly received trust property.[280]

## (b) History

The freezing injunction is a relatively recent creation of equity.[281] It was traditionally thought that *Lister & Co v Stubbs*[282] prevented the court from granting the plaintiff such

---

[272] It has recently been suggested that the jurisdiction extends to future assets of a defendant as well as those in existence at the date that the injunction is granted: *Sonico SACI v Novokuznetsk Aluminium Plant* [1998] QB 406, per Coleman J.

[273] [1975] 2 Lloyd's Rep 509.     [274] CPR 25.1(1)(f).     [275] [1982] QB 558 at 585.

[276] [1990] Ch 65 at 76.

[277] See also *Camdex International Ltd v Bank of Zambia (No 2)* [1997] 1 All ER 728 at 733, per Sir Thomas Bingham MR.

[278] Cf *Fitzgerald v Williams* [1996] 2 All ER 171, where the Court of Appeal held that a defendant was not permitted to draw on frozen funds to which the plaintiff asserted a proprietary claim unless he had no other funds on which he could draw.

[279] *United Mizrahi Bank Ltd v Doherty* [1998] 2 All ER 230.

[280] *United Mizrahi Bank Ltd v Doherty* [1998] 2 All ER 230.

[281] However, in *The Siskina* [1979] AC 210 Lord Denning MR suggested that the Mareva injunction was a 'rediscovery' of the earlier procedure of 'foreign attachment'.

[282] (1890) LR 45 Ch D 1.

an injunction, but in *Nippon Yusen Kaisha v Kaageorgis* and *Mareva Compania Naviera SA v International Bulkcarriers SA*[283] the Court of Appeal held that the court enjoyed the jurisdiction to grant such an order under the predecessor to s 37(1) of the Supreme Court Act 1981.[284] Lord Denning MR described the development of the order as 'the greatest piece of judicial law reform in my time'.[285] A freezing injunction may be granted in aid of proceedings within the jurisdiction or of proceedings in a foreign jurisdiction.[286]

### (c) Practical illustrations

Two cases illustrate the practical application of the freezing injunction. *Re BCCI SA (No 9)*[287] concerned the collapse of the BCCI banking group as the consequence of a massive fraud. A world-wide Mareva injunction was granted against 'Mahfouz', a director of BCCI and 'Kahlon', an employee, whom the liquidators sought to make personally liable for the debts of BCCI on the basis of their allegedly fraudulent management. In *Balkanbank v Taher*[288] a bank was granted a world-wide Mareva injunction against the defendants, who were alleged to have acted fraudulently in respect of a joint venture, an allegation which later failed in the Irish courts.

## (2) Guidelines for the grant of a freezing injunction

In *Re BCCI SA (No 9)*,[289] following the judgment of Parker LJ in the Court of Appeal in *Derby & Co Ltd v Weldon*,[290] Rattee J stated that there were 'three issues on which the court has to be satisfied before granting a Mareva injunction'.

### (a) 'Has the applicant a good arguable case?'

Although the freezing injunction is generally interlocutory, a stricter standard is applied concerning the strength of the plaintiff's claim. Under the test set down in *American Cyanamid Co v Ethicon Ltd*,[291] a plaintiff merely has to demonstrate that there is a serious question to be tried. Before a freezing injunction will be granted, he must demonstrate that he has a 'good arguable case'.[292] In *Third Chandris Shipping Corpn v Unimarine SA*[293] Lord Denning MR said that a plaintiff seeking a Mareva injunction 'should make full and frank disclosure of all matters in his knowledge which are material for the judge to know',[294] and 'give particulars of his claim against the defendant, stating the grounds of his claim and the amount thereof, and fairly stating the

---

[283] [1980] 1 All ER 213, [1975] 2 Lloyd's Rep 509. A 'Mareva' injunction was first granted in the earlier case of *Nippon Yusen Kaisha v Karageorgis* [1975] 1 WLR 1093.

[284] Supreme Court of Judicature (Consolidation) Act 1925, s 45(1).

[285] *The Due Process of Law* (1980), p 134

[286] Civil Jurisdiction and Judgments Act 1982, s 25. See *The Siskina* [1979] AC 210; *Rosseel NV v Oriental Commercial and Shipping (UK) Ltd* [1990] 3 All ER 545; *Mercedes-Benz AG v Leiduck* [1996] AC 284.

[287] [1994] 3 All ER 764.      [288] [1994] 4 All ER 239; on appeal [1995] 2 All ER 904, CA.

[289] [1994] 3 All ER 764 at 785.      [290] [1990] Ch 48 at 57.      [291] [1975] AC 396, HL.

[292] A distinction which Parker LJ said was 'incapable of definition'.

[293] [1979] QB 645

[294] See *Negocios Del Mar SA v Doric Shipping Corpn SA, The Assios* [1979] 1 Lloyd's Rep 331; *Brinks-MAT Ltd v Elcombe* [1988] 3 All ER 188; *Tate Access Floors Inc v Boswell* [1990] 3 All ER 303.

points made against it by the defendant'. If subsequently it appears that he had not made full disclosure, the injunction will normally be discharged.[295]

## (b) 'Has the applicant satisfied the court that there are assets within and, where an extra-territorial order is sought, without the jurisdiction'

A freezing injunction is available against both movable[296] or immovable property.[297] Originally, it was only available against assets within the jurisdiction, but today an order may be made with world-wide effect.[298]

## (c) 'Is there a real risk of dissipation or secretion of assets so as to render any judgment which the applicant may obtain nugatory'

The plaintiff should give some grounds for believing that there is a real risk that the assets of the defendant will be removed or dissipated before the judgment or award is satisfied.[299] In *Camdex International Ltd v Bank of Zambia (No 2)*[300] the Court of Appeal held that it was inappropriate to grant a Mareva injunction against the Zambian government freezing a large quantity of new banknotes which had been printed for Zambia in England because the notes were of no value to the plaintiff (or other creditors of the defendant) on the open market. Thus, they were not an asset which might be dissipated so as to avoid satisfaction of a judgment debt. It was inappropriate to use a Mareva injunction merely to hold a defendant to ransom in the hope that he would be compelled to satisfy the judgment debt.

## (3) Undertakings in damages

When a freezing injunction is granted the plaintiff must also give an undertaking in damages. As Lord Denning MR explained in *Third Chandris Shipping Corpn v Unimarine SA*:

'The plaintiff must, of course, give an undertaking in damages—in case he fails in his claim or the injunction turns out to be unjustified. In a suitable case this should be supported by a bond or security.'[301]

The undertaking in damages follows from the fact that the freezing injunction is an interlocutory injunction.[302] If the plaintiff fails to establish his case at trial the defend-

---

[295] *Ali & Fahd Shobokshi Group Ltd v Moneim* [1989] 2 All ER 404; *Dubai Bank Ltd v Galadari* [1990] 1 Lloyd's Rep 120, CA.

[296] 'Assets' includes a wide range of chattels. See *Allen v Jambo Holdings Ltd* [1980] 1 WLR 1252 (aeroplanes); *The Rena K* [1979] QB 377 (ships); *Rasu Maritima SA v Persuahaan Pertambangan Minyak Dan Gas Bumi Negara* [1978] QB 644 (machinery); *CBS United Kingdom Ltd v Lambert* [1983] Ch 37 (jewellery, objects d'art, other valuables and choses in action); *Darashah v UFAC (UK) Ltd* (1982) Times, 30 March, CA (goodwill of a business).

[297] *Derby & Co Ltd v Weldon (Nos 3 and 4)* [1990] Ch 65 (disposition of a freehold interest in a house).

[298] See below, p 65.

[299] In *Ketchum International Plc v Group Public Relations Holdings Ltd* [1996] 4 All ER 374 at 383 the Court of Appeal, per Stuart-Smith LJ, held that there was no need to demonstrate the a defendant intends to deal with his assets so as to ensure that a judgment remains unsatisfied.

[300] [1997] 1 All ER 728.    [301] [1979] QB 645.    [302] See above, p 61.

ant may then be entitled to damages. However, as was made clear in *Balkanbank v Taher*,[303] the undertaking is made to the court and not the defendant and the 'court has a discretion whether to order the plaintiff to pay damages where the defendants have sustained loss caused by the injunction'.[304] The court is not bound to order damages, and whether it does will depend on the circumstances of the case.

## (4) Disclosure of assets

In *Derby & Co Ltd v Weldon*[305] the Court of Appeal made clear that the court has jurisdiction to grant a 'disclosure' order against the defendant in respect of assets both within and without the jurisdiction, as ancillary to a Mareva injunction. This 'disclosure' order may be made both before[306] and after[307] judgment. However, the court will protect the position of the defendant by requiring the plaintiff to grant an undertaking that he will not use information so obtained to start civil or criminal proceedings in other jurisdictions.[308] In *Den Norske Bank ASA v Antonatos*[309] the Court of Appeal held that a defendant would be entitled to refuse to provide information on the grounds that such disclosure would infringe his privilege against self-incrimination.[310] This privilege is available in respect of any piece of information or evidence on which the prosecution might wish to rely in establishing guilt or in making their decision whether to prosecute or not.

## (5) The 'world-wide' freezing injunction

### (a) Development of the jurisdiction

Initially, the Mareva injunction was only granted to prevent the defendant from removing assets that were within the jurisdiction of the court.[311] However, in a number of cases the court has held that it possesses the jurisdiction to grant a Mareva injunction with world-wide effect.[312] In *Derby & Co Ltd v Weldon (Nos 3 and 4)* Neill LJ concluded:

'. . . the time has come to state unequivocally that in an appropriate case the court has power to grant an interlocutory injunction even on a world-wide basis against any person who is properly before the court, so as to prevent that person by the transfer of his property frustrating a future judgment of the court. The jurisdiction to grant such injunctions is one which the court requires and it seems to me that it is consistent with the wide words of Supreme Court Act 1981, s 37(1).'[313]

---

[303] [1994] 4 All ER 239.    [304] Per Clarke J.    [305] [1990] Ch 48.
[306] *Republic of Haiti v Duvalier* [1990] 1 QB 202.
[307] *Interpool Ltd v Galani* [1988] QB 738; *Maclaine Watson & Co Ltd v International Tin Council (No 2)* [1989] Ch 286, CA.
[308] See *Practice Direction* [1994] 4 All ER 52.    [309] [1998] 3 All ER 74.
[310] See also below, p 71, where the availability of the privilege against self-incrimination in the context of Anton Pillar orders is discussed.
[311] See *Ashtiani v Kashi* [1987] QB 888; *South Carolina Insurance Co v Assurantie Maatschappij De Zeven Provincien NV* [1987] AC 24.
[312] *Babanaft International Co SA v Bassatne* [1990] Ch 13; *Republic of Haiti v Duvalier* [1990] 1 QB 202, CA; *Derby & Co Ltd v Weldon* [1990] Ch 48; *Derby & Co v Weldon (Nos 3 and 4)* [1990] Ch 65.
[313] [1990] Ch 65 at 93.

## (b) Circumstances where the jurisdiction will be exercised

Although the court recognised the jurisdiction to grant world-wide freezing injunctions in *Derby & Co Ltd v Weldon*,[314] May LJ emphasised that 'it will only be in an exceptional case that the court will make such an order'. On the facts, which involved claims that the defendants, who were directors of the plaintiff company, had dealt in commodities on their own behalf causing the company huge trading losses,[315] the Court of Appeal held that a world-wide injunction was justified. As Parker LJ summarised:

'The defendants are clearly sophisticated operators who have amply demonstrated their ability to render assets untraceable and a determination not to reveal them. In those circumstances it appears to me that there is every justification for a world-wide Mareva . . .'[316]

Similarly, in *Re BCCI SA (No 9)*[317] Rattee J, granting a world-wide injunction, held that the case was 'exceptional . . . having regard, in particular, to the complex international nature of the financial dealings in the past to both respondents and that both claim not to be resident in this country'. Where a freezing injunction is sought in aid of proceedings in a foreign jurisdiction, the Court of Appeal has also held that the order should not be world-wide except in 'very exceptional circumstances'.[318] However, in the more recent case of *Crédit Suisse Fides Trust v Cuoghi*[319] the Court of Appeal questioned whether it was necessary to demonstrate such exceptional circumstances, and suggested that the sole question was whether 'it would be inexpedient to make the order'.[320]

## (c) Safeguards for the defendant when a world-wide injunction is granted

Although the court may grant a world-wide order in exceptional circumstances, such an order is of so devastating an effect that it insists that certain safeguards are built into the order in the form of undertakings by the plaintiff. In *Derby & Co Ltd v Weldon* Parker LJ stated that the order should contain the following protection:

'(a) oppression of the defendants by way of exposure to multiplicity of proceedings is avoided, (b) the defendants are protected against the misuse of information gained from the ordinary order for disclosure in aid of the Mareva, and (c) the position of third parties is protected.'[321]

These limitations were approved by the Court of Appeal in *Re BCCI SA (No 9)*,[322] where the key issue was whether the form of the order granted by Rattee J contained sufficient protection against the multiplicity of proceedings in foreign jurisdictions. The usual

---

314  [1990] Ch 48 at 55, CA.
315  The grounds of the plaintiff's claim included: breach of contract, negligence, breach of fiduciary duty, deceit and conspiracy to defraud.
316  [1990] Ch 48 at 57.        317  [1994] 3 All ER 764 at 787.
318  *Rosseel NV v Oriental Commercial and Shipping (UK) Ltd* [1990] 3 All ER 545 at 546, per Lord Donaldson MR. See *S & T Bautrading v Nordling* [1997] 3 All ER 718, where the Court of Appeal held that the circumstances were not sufficiently exceptional to justify the grant of a worldwide Mareva order.
319  [1997] 3 All ER 724.
320  [1997] 3 All ER 724 at 732, per Millett LJ, citing s 25(2) of the Civil Jurisdiction and Judgments Act 1982.
321  [1990] Ch 48.        322  [1994] 3 All ER 764.

protection is an undertaking by the plaintiff not to seek to enforce the freezing injunction in any country other than England and Wales without the leave of the court. The defendants argued that this was insufficient and that the plaintiff should also undertake not to start any fresh proceedings in foreign courts arising out of the same subject matter. Dillon LJ stated the principle:

'It does not automatically follow, as a matter of logic, that if a person obtains a worldwide Mareva injunction and to prevent oppression in the enforcement of the injunction he is required to give an undertaking not to make any application to a foreign court to enforce the injunction without first obtaining the leave of the English court, he must also be required to give a further undertaking as a safeguard against a somewhat different form of possible oppression, not to issue any fresh proceedings in a foreign court arising out of the same subject matter without first obtaining the leave of the English court. But it may none the less be reasonable that he should be required to give such an undertaking if it seems prima facie oppressive that he should be free to start further proceedings in other jurisdictions founded on the same facts as are the basis of the English proceedings.'

In the circumstances the court felt that it was reasonable that the plaintiff give an undertaking not to start fresh civil proceedings in foreign courts.[323]

The standard form for the world-wide freezing injunction contains undertakings that the plaintiff 'will not without the leave of the court begin proceedings against the defendant in any other jurisdiction or use information obtained as a result of an order of the court in this jurisdiction for the purpose of civil or criminal proceedings in any other jurisdiction' and 'will not, without the leave of the court, seek to enforce this order in any country outside England and Wales'.[324]

## (6) Uniformity of orders

In *Re BCCI SA (No 9)*[325] Dillon LJ expressed the view that it was desirable that 'the practice in these matters should develop uniformly' and suggested that there was no good reason why the form of the order granted in *Derby & Co Ltd v Weldon*[326] should not be followed. On 28 July 1994 the Lord Chief Justice issued a *Practice Direction*[327] including standard forms for world-wide Mareva injunctions and those limited to assets within the jurisdiction: 'These forms of order should be used save to the extent that the judge hearing a particular application considers there is a good reason for adopting a different form.' A revised form of order was introduced on 28 October 1996.[328]

## (7) Limits to the grant of freezing orders

Freezing injunctions can be granted in support of prospective proceedings in the superior courts, but as the jurisdictional limits of the inferior courts are increased, it

---

[323] With the exception of Luxembourg, where BCCI was being liquidated.
[324] *Practice Direction* [1994] 4 All ER 52.   [325] [1994] 3 All ER 764.
[326] [1990] Ch 48.   [327] [1990] Ch 48.   [328] [1994] 4 All ER 52.

becomes important to know how far they can be used in support of cases brought in other courts. An order can almost certainly be made in support of proceedings in a magistrates' court,[329] but no order will be issued in aid of a comprehensive statutory scheme such as that set out in the Child Support Act 1991 and which implicitly excludes other enforcement mechanisms.[330]

# 5 Search orders[331]

## (1) Definition

Whereas a freezing injunction restrains a defendant from dissipating his assets, a search order prevents a defendant from destroying vital evidence before an issue comes to trial by requiring him to allow the plaintiff to enter his premises and search for, examine, remove or copy articles specified in the order. Until recently such injunctions were known as Anton Piller orders, and the new nomenclature was introduced by the Civil Procedure Rules. The rationale for the order was explained by Lord Denning MR in *Anton Piller KG v Manufacturing Processes Ltd*:

'. . . such an order can be made by a judge ex parte, but it should only be made where it is essential that the plaintiff should have inspection so that justice can be done between the parties: and when, if the defendant were forewarned, there is a grave danger that vital evidence will be destroyed, that papers will be burnt or lost or hidden.'[332]

The first such order was granted in *EMI Ltd v Kishorilal Pandit*,[333] and the first by the Court of Appeal in *Anton Piller KG v Manufacturing Processes Ltd*.[334] They were approved by the House of Lords in *Rank Film Distributors Ltd v Video Information Centre*.[335] Search orders have been particularly appropriate in cases where it is suspected that 'pirating' of music or films has taken place.[336]

## (2) Pre-conditions to the grant of a search order

Search orders are granted ex parte, as the element of surprise is essential to prevent defendants destroying or hiding the evidence. As was said in *Rank Film Distributors Ltd v Video Information Centre*:[337]

---

[329] [1997] 1 All ER 288, [1996] 1 WLR 1552.

[330] *Department of Social Security v Butler* [1995] 4 All ER 193 at 204–205.

[331] See *Snell's Principles of Equity* (31st edn, 2005), pp 420–421; Hanbury and Martin, *Modern Equity* (17th edn, 2005), pp 839–841; Pettit, *Equity and the Law of Trusts* (9th edn, 2001), pp 618–624.

[332] [1976] Ch 55 at 61.        [333] [1975] 1 All ER 418.        [334] [1976] Ch 55.

[335] [1982] AC 380.

[336] Eg *Ex p Island Records Ltd* [1978] Ch 122, CA; *Rank Film Distributors Ltd v Video Information Centre* [1982] AC 380; *Columbia Picture Industries Ltd v Robinson* [1986] 3 All ER 338.

[337] [1982] AC 380.

'If the stable door cannot be bolted, the horse must be secured . . . If the horse is liable to be spirited away, notice of an intention to secure the horse will defeat the intention.'[338]

Given the powerful effect of the order, as well as the fact that it will be granted without hearing the defendant, the court has laid down relatively strict criteria that the plaintiff must satisfy. In *Anton Piller KG v Manufacturing Processes Ltd*[339] Ormrod LJ said that there are 'three essential pre-conditions' for the granting of an order. To these a fourth requirement suggested by Lord Denning MR can be added.

### (a) Strong prima facie case

There must be 'an *extremely* strong prima facie case'. This represents a much higher standard than that required for interlocutory injunctions in *American Cyanamid*.

### (b) Serious potential damage

The damage, potential or actual, must be very serious for the applicant.

### (c) Real possibility evidence will be destroyed

There must be clear evidence that the defendants have in their possession incriminating documents or things, and that there is a real possibility that they may destroy such material before any application inter partes can be made.'

### (d) No real harm to the defendant

Lord Denning held that an order should only be granted when it 'would do no real harm to the defendant or his case'. In *Coca-Cola v Gilbey*[340] Lightman J held that the risk of violence against a defendant if forced to disclose information will not generally justify the refusal to award an Anton Piller order. An order had been granted against the defendant, who had been involved in an operation to counterfeit Coca-Cola products, but he refused to disclose information concerning the operation because such disclosure would jeopardise his safety and that of his family. Lightman J held that such threats were 'a factor' to be considered when deciding whether to grant an order, but that in most cases it would be outweighed by the interests of justice:

'I cannot think that in any ordinary case where the plaintiff has a pressing need for the information in question, the existence of the risk of violence against the potential informant should outweigh the interest of the plaintiff in obtaining the information. In case of any unlawful threat or action directed at a party, a witness or their families, the rule of law requires that the law should in no wise be deflected from following its ordinary course and the court should proceed undeterred. Police protection is the appropriate remedy . . .'[341]

---

[338] [1982] AC 380 at 418 per Templeman LJ.     [339] [1976] Ch 55 at 62.
[340] [1995] 4 All ER 711.     [341] [1995] 4 All ER 711 at 716.

### (3) Protection for the defendant

Because of the 'draconian and essentially unfair nature of search orders from the point of view of the defendant'[342] there are a number of limitations and restrictions as to its execution intended to protect the defendant. Many of these were stated by Dillon LJ in *Booker McConnell plc v Plascow*[343] and Scott J in *Columbia Picture Industries v Robinson,* who recognised that:

'. . . a decision whether or not an Anton Piller order should be granted requires a balance to be struck between the plaintiff's need that the remedies allowed by the civil law for the breach of his rights should be attainable and the requirement of justice that a defendant should not be deprived of his property without being heard.'[344]

Many of these limitations are incorporated in the standard form order issued under a *Practice Direction* of the Lord Chief Justice.[345]

#### (a) Service and explanation by a solicitor

The order must be served by an independent supervising solicitor accompanying the plaintiff,[346] who must also explain what it means to the defendant in everyday language.[347] If the premises are likely to be occupied by an unaccompanied woman and the supervising solicitor is a man, one of the persons accompanying him must be a woman.

#### (b) Times of service

The order may only be served between 9.30 am and 5.30 pm on a weekday.

#### (c) Application to vary or discharge

The defendant may apply to the court at short notice for variation or discharge of the order, provided that the plaintiff and his solicitor, and the supervising solicitor have been allowed to enter the premises, although not commenced the search.

#### (d) Items to be removed

No item may be removed from the premises until a list of the items to be removed has been prepared, and a copy of the list has been supplied to the person served with the order, and he has been given a reasonable opportunity to check the list.

#### (e) Search in the presence of the defendant

The premises must not be searched, and items must not be removed from them, except in the presence of the defendant or a person appearing to be a responsible employee of the defendant.

---

[342]   *Columbia Picture Industries Ltd v Robinson* [1986] 3 All ER 338 at 371. See also *Lock International plc v Beswick* [1989] 1 WLR 1268; *Bhimji v Chatwani* [1991] 1 WLR 989.

[343]   [1985] RPC 425, CA.        [344]   [1986] 3 All ER 338

[345]   [1994] 4 All ER 52; [1997] 1 All ER 288, [1996] 1 WLR 1552.

[346]   *ITC Film Distributors Ltd v Video Exchange Ltd* [1982] Ch 431.

[347]   *Bhimji v Chatwani* [1991] 1 WLR 989.

## (f) Undertaking in damages

The plaintiff must make an undertaking in damages to compensate the plaintiff for any loss he suffers as a result of the carrying out of the order if the court decides that he should be compensated.

## (4) The privilege against self-incrimination

In *Rank Film Distributors Ltd v Video Information Centre*[348] the House of Lords held that a plaintiff would not be granted an Anton Piller order requiring the defendants to answer questions or disclose documents which would have the effect of incriminating him, as he is entitled to the privilege against self-incrimination.[349] In *IBM United Kingdom Ltd v Prima Data International Ltd*[350] Sir Mervyn Davies QC refused to set aside sections of an Anton Piller order made against a company director from whom IBM sought damages for conspiracy to extract goods without payment because the solicitor serving the order had adequately explained his right to claim privilege against self-incrimination. However, this privilege was removed as regards proceedings for the infringement of intellectual property rights and passing off by s 72 of the Supreme Court Act 1981.[351] In *Cobra Golf Ltd v Rata*[352] Rimer J therefore held that a defendant had no right to assert an entitlement to the privilege against self-incrimination where proceedings for civil contempt had been commenced by a manufacture of golf equipment alleging that he had infringed their trade marks.

# 6 Rescission[353]

Rescission is the right of a party to a contract[354] to have the contract set aside and to be restored to his former position, which is known as *restitutio in integrum*. The House of Lords held in *Johnson v Agnew*[355] that this is to be distinguished from the situation also described as 'rescission' where a contract is treated as never having come into existence in law, for example because of mistake, fraud or lack of consent, where there is rescission ab initio. The right of a party to rescind a contract may be wider in equity than at common law. By defining the circumstances in which a contract may be rescinded, equity serves the very important function of setting the standards of acceptable

---

[348] [1982] AC 380.

[349] See also *Tate Access Floors Inc v Boswell* [1991] Ch 512; *IBM United Kingdom Ltd v Prima Data International Ltd* [1994] 4 All ER 748; *Cobra Golf Ltd v Rata* [1997] 2 All ER 150; *Den Norske Bank ASA v Antonatos* [1999] QB 271.

[350] [1994] 4 All ER 748.    [351] See *Istel (AT & T) Ltd v Tully* [1993] AC 45, HL.

[352] [1998] Ch 109.

[353] See *Snell's Principles of Equity* (31st edn, 2005), pp 317–331.

[354] Or a voluntary deed: *Gibbon v Mitchell* [1990] 1 WLR 1304; *Dent v Dent* [1996] 1 WLR 683; *Wolff v Wolff* [2004] STC 1633.

[355] [1980] AC 367 at 392–392.

behaviour in commercial transactions, thus protecting the vulnerable from exploitation at the hands of those who are more capable but lack scruples.[356]

## (1)  Rescission of contracts entered under mistake[357]

### (a)  Mistake at common law

The position at common law was stated in *Bell v Lever Bros Ltd*,[358] where the House of Lords held that only a very narrow range of mistakes shared between the parties to a contract would render it void ab initio. In essence, only those mistakes which would make the performance of the contract as agreed impossible render the contract void. This was well summarised by Denning LJ in *Solle v Butcher*:

'The correct interpretation of that case . . . is that, once a contract has been made, that is to say, once the parties, whatever their inmost state of mind, have to all outward appearances agreed with sufficient certainty in the same terms on the same subject matter, then the contract is good unless and until it is set aside for failure of some condition on which the existence of the contract depends, or for fraud or on some equitable ground.'[359]

Therefore, a contract will be void at common law if the subject matter of the contract no longer existed at the time of contracting,[360] if the purchaser is in fact already the owner of the property to be transferred under the contract[361] or where the mistake is such that one party would be unable to perform so as to amount to a total failure of consideration. However, shared mistakes as to the mere quality of the subject matter of the contract would not render it void. Thus, in *Leaf v International Galleries*[362] a contract for the sale of a painting believed to be a Constable was not void for mistake.[363]

### (b)  Mistake in equity

In *Solle v Butcher*[364] Denning LJ suggested the existence of a wider jurisdiction in equity, supplemental to the narrow common law jurisdiction of *Bell v Lever Bros Ltd*, which would allow a party to rescind a contract which was entered under a shared fundamental mistake. He stated the basis of this jurisdiction as follows:

'A contract is also liable in equity to be set aside if the parties were under a common misapprehension either as to facts or as to their relative and respective rights, provided that the misapprehension was fundamental and that the party seeking to set it aside was not himself at fault.'[365]

---

356  For a consideration of the proprietary consequences of rescission see *Worthington* [2002] RLR 28.

357  See Treitel, *The Law of Contract* (11th edn, 2003), pp 286–329; Goff and Jones, *The Law of Restitution* (6th edn, 2002), pp 247–287.

358  [1932] AC 161.        359  [1950] 1 KB 671 at 691.

360  *Couturier v Hastie* (1856) 5 HL Cas 673; *Strickland v Turner* (1852) 7 Exch 208; *Galloway v Galloway* (1914) 30 TLR 531; *Associated Japanese Bank (International) Ltd v Crédit du Nord SA* [1988] 3 All ER 902.

361  *Cooper v Phibbs* (1867) LR 2 HL 149.

362  [1950] 2 KB 86, CA.

363  See also *Frederick E Rose (London) Ltd v William H Pim Jnr & Co Ltd* [1953] 2 QB 450.

364  [1950] 1 KB 671, CA. Denning LJ relied on *Cooper v Phibbs* (1867) LR 2 HL 149 and *Huddersfield Banking Co Ltd v Henry Lister & Sons Ltd* [1895] 2 Ch 273, CA.

365  [1950] 1 KB 671.

It is to be noted that the two main requirements of this supposed equitable jurisdiction are that the mistake must be 'mutual', in the sense that it is shared by both parties, and that it must be 'fundamental'. Unlike mistake at common law, which renders the contract void ab initio, the right to rescind in equity would only render the contract voidable. A number of subsequent cases accepted the existence of this more generous equitable jurisdiction.[366] However in the recent case *Great Peace Shipping v Tsavliris Salvage (International) Ltd*[367] the Court of Appeal disapproved of the decision in *Solle v Butcher*, and doubted the existence of any equitable jurisdiction to rescind a contract wider than that granted at common law in *Bell v Lever Brothers Ltd*. The Court of Appeal did not find it conceivable that the House of Lords had overlooked an equitable right to rescind the agreement in *Bell v Lever Bros*, notwithstanding that the agreement was not void for mistake at common law,[368] and concluded that there was no authority for the proposition that there are two categories of mistake, one that renders a contract void at law and one that renders it voidable in equity.[369] The Court of Appeal further found that it was impossible to distinguish between the requirement of a 'fundamental' mistake, as stated to be the basis of the equitable jurisdiction in *Solle v Butcher*, and a mistake as to quality which 'makes the thing contracted for essentially different from the thing that it was believed to be,' which is the basis of the common law right in *Bell v Lever Bros Ltd*.[370] The Court of Appeal held that the decision in *Solle v Butcher* had been an unwarranted intrusion of equity where the common law had clearly drawn the line as to when relief might be given for common mistake, such that the effect was not to supplement or mitigate the common law, but to say that *Bell v Lever Bros Ltd* was wrongly decided. Lord Phillips MR therefore summarised:

'Our conclusion is that it is impossible to reconcile *Solle v Butcher* with *Bell v Lever Bros Ltd*. The jurisdiction asserted in the former case has not developed. It has been a fertile source of academic debate. But in practice it has given rise to a handful of cases that have merely emphasised the confusion in this area of our jurisprudence . . . If coherence is to be restored to this area of our law, it can only be by declaring that there is no jurisdiction to grant rescission of a contract on the ground of common mistake where that contract is valid and enforceable on ordinary principles of contract law.'[371]

Having rejected the existence of the equitable jurisdiction, the Court of Appeal did express sympathy for the desire for the greater flexibility that it would give to grant rescission on terms where a common fundamental mistake has induced a contract, in contrast to the common law doctrine which holds the contract void in such circumstances. However the introduction of such a jurisdiction would require legislation.[372]

---

[366] *Grist v Bailey* [1967] Ch 532; *Magee v Pennine Insurance Co Ltd* [1969] 2 QB 507; *Associated Japanese Bank (International) Ltd v Credit du Nord SA* [1988] 3 All ER 902; *West Sussex Properties Ltd v Chichester District Council* [2000] NPC 74.

[367] [2003] QB 679; [2002] 4 All ER 690; [2002] LMCLQ (McMeel); (2003) 119 LQR 177 (Reynolds); (2003) 62 CLJ 29 (Hare); [2003] Conv 247 (Phang); [2003] 1 RLR 93 (Cartwright).

[368] Ibid at [118].      [369] Ibid at [153].      [370] [1932] AC 161 at 218, per Lord Atkin.

[371] [2002] 4 All ER 689 at [157].      [372] Ibid at [161].

## (2) Rescission of contracts induced by misrepresentation[373]

### (a) Meaning of misrepresentation

In *Behn v Burness*[374] Williams J defined a representation as 'a statement or assertion, made by one party to the other before or at the time of the contract, of some matter or circumstance relating to it'. A misrepresentation does not render a contract void, but the other contracting party may be entitled to rescind it. The representation must be of fact,[375] and not simply an expression of intention[376] or opinion.[377] Although there is no general duty on a contracting party to reveal all known relevant facts, in the case of some contracts, known as contracts *uberrimae fidei*, there is such a duty. These include contracts for insurance[378] and family settlements.[379]

### (b) Fraudulent misrepresentation

A party is entitled to rescind a contract he entered on the basis of a fraudulent misrepresentation by the other, which means a false statement made knowingly, or without belief in its truth, or reckless whether it is true or not.[380]

### (c) Innocent misrepresentation

Innocent misrepresentation occurs where the party making the misrepresentation honestly believes it to be true. The other party has the right to rescind the contract,[381] although by s 2(2) of the Misrepresentation Act 1967 the court has the discretion to award damages in lieu of rescission and declare the contract subsisting.

## (3) Rescission of contracts entered under undue influence[382]

### (a) Meaning of undue influence

Rescission in equity is available whenever a contract has been entered by one party acting under the undue influence of the other. The essence of undue influence is that the party making the contract was dominated by the other so that he was not acting of his own free choice.

---

[373] See Treitel, *The Law of Contract* (11th edn, 2003), pp 364–385; Goff and Jones, *The Law of Restitution* (6th edn, 2002), pp 247–277.

[374] (1863) 3 B & S 751.      [375] *Ship v Crosskill* (1870) LR 10 Eq 73.

[376] *Edgington v Fitzmaurice* (1885) 29 Ch D 459, CA.      [377] *Bisset v Wilkinson* [1927] AC 177, PC.

[378] See *Lambert v Co-operative Insurance Society* [1975] 2 Lloyd's Rep 485, CA.

[379] *Gordon v Gordon* (1816) 3 Swan 400.      [380] *Derry v Peek* (1889) 14 App Cas 337.

[381] *Reese River Silver Mining Co v Smith* (1869) LR 4 HL 64; *Torrance v Bolton* (1872) 8 Ch App 118; *Redgrave v Hurd* (1881) 20 Ch D 1, CA; *Walker v Boyle* [1982] 1 All ER 634. By s 2(1) of the Misrepresentation Act 1967 he is also entitled to recover damages unless the defendant had reasonable grounds to believe that his statement was true: *Esso Petroleum v Mardon* [1976] QB 801; *Royscot Trust Ltd v Rogerson* [1991] 2 QB 297; *Smith New Court Securities Ltd v Scrimgeour Vickers (Asset Management) Ltd* [1997] AC 254.

[382] See Treitel, *The Law of Contract* (11th edn, 2003), pp 405–428; Goff and Jones, *The Law of Restitution* (6th edn, 2002), pp 347–360.

## (b) Actual undue influence

Actual undue influence arises where one party has in fact applied improper pressure to the other, which falls short of that necessary to constitute duress.[383] In *Bank of Credit and Commerce International SA v Aboody*[384] the court held that it was also necessary for the party alleging actual undue influence to demonstrate that they had suffered a 'manifest disadvantage' from the transaction, but this requirement was rejected by the House of Lords in *CIBC Mortgages plc v Pitt.*[385]

## (c) Presumed undue influence

In some circumstances, the nature of the relationship between the parties itself gives rise to the presumption of undue influence, and the burden falls on the defendant to demonstrate that no such influence was exercised.[386] Examples of relationships where influence will be presumed include parent and child,[387] spiritual adviser and disciple,[388] doctor and patient,[389] married and cohabiting couples[390] or couples in a close, stable, sexual and emotional relationship[391] or between solicitor and client.[392] In the case of other relationships, for example bank and customer[393] and pop artist and manager,[394] it may be possible to show that there was in fact a relationship of influence. Undue influence has increasingly been presumed where a relationship of confidence has been shown to have existed between family members or relations.[395] Similarly, the fact that a person agrees to act as surety of the debts of another will give rise to a presumption of a relationship of confidence if the surety gained no personal advantage from so acting.[396] In *Crédit Lyonnais Bank Nederland NV v Burch*[397] the Court of Appeal held that an abuse of a relationship of confidence was presumed from the mere fact that a junior employee had executed an 'extravagantly improvident' unlimited guarantee of all her employer's debts, and that there was no need to show any sexual or emotional tie. In *National Westminster Bank Plc v Morgan*[398] the House of Lords held that a party relying on presumed undue influence must also demonstrate that he had suffered a manifest disadvantage from the transaction. However in the more recent case of *Royal Bank of*

---

[383]  See eg *Re Craig* [1971] Ch 95; *Cheese v Thomas* [1994] 1 All ER 35.

[384]  [1990] 1 QB 923, CA.

[385]  [1994] 1 AC 200. See also *Barclays Bank v O'Brien* [1994] 1 AC 180.

[386]  See *Allcard v Skinner* (1887) 36 Ch D 145. See also *Hammond v Osborn* [2002] WTLR 1125; [2003] LMCLQ 145 (Scott); (2003) 119 LQR 34 (Birks).

[387]  [1934] 1 KB 380, CA.

[388]  *Allcard v Skinner* (1887) 36 Ch D 145; *Tufton v Sperni* [1952] 2 TLR 516, CA; *Roche v Sherrington* [1982] 1 WLR 599.

[389]  *Dent v Bennett* (1839) 4 My & Cr 269.         [390]  *Barclays Bank v O'Brien* [1994] 1 AC 180.

[391]  *Massey v Midland Bank plc* [1995] 1 All ER 929.

[392]  *Wright v Carter* [1903] 1 Ch 27, CA.         [393]  *Lloyds Bank v Bundy* [1975] QB 326, CA.

[394]  *O'Sullivan v Management Agency and Music Ltd* [1985] QB 428.

[395]  *Simpson v Simpson* [1992] 1 FLR 601; *Cheese v Thomas* [1994] 1 WLR 129; *Langton v Langton* [1995] 2 FLR 890; *Mahoney v Purnell* [1996] 3 All ER 61.

[396]  *Barclays Bank v O'Brien* [1994] 1 AC 180; *CIBC v Pitt* [1994] 1 AC 200; *Massey v Midland Bank plc* [1995] 1 All ER 929; *Allied Irish Bank plc v Byrne* [1995] 2 FLR 325; *Banco Exterior Internacional SA v Thomas* [1997] 1 All ER 46; *Dunbar Bank plc v Nadeem* [1998] 3 All ER 876. But cf. *Mumford v Bank of Scotland* 1996 SLT 392.

[397]  [1997] 1 All ER 144; [1997] LMCLQ 17 (Hooley and O'Sullivan).         [398]  [1985] AC 686.

*Scotland v Etridge (No 2)*[399] the House of Lords held that the requirement of 'manifest disadvantage' was ambiguous and should be discarded.

### (d) Influence exercised by third parties[400]

In an ever expanding number of recent cases it has been held that a transaction can be set aside where the circumstances are such that the person benefiting from the transaction was aware of circumstances in which the other party may have been acting under the undue influence of a third party. Most typically this has occurred where a wife has executed some kind of financial guarantee of her husband's debts in favour of a bank. For example, in *Barclays Bank v O'Brien*[401] a husband whose business was in difficulties executed a second mortgage over the family home he jointly owned with his wife to provide additional security for the company's debts. The House of Lords held that the wife had signed the mortgage documents acting under the undue influence of her husband. Since the bank had failed to take reasonable steps to satisfy itself that she had entered the transaction freely, they had constructive notice of the undue influence and she was therefore able to set the transaction aside.[402] A person will not be affixed with constructive notice of such undue influence if they ensure that the party they contract with received independent advice as to the effect of the transaction.[403] A creditor may also be put on notice where the undue influence has been exercsied by a co-surety of the mortgagor rather than the debtor.[404]

Following an explosion of litigation, the House of Lords clarified the circumstances in which such surety transactions may be set aside on the grounds of undue influence in *Royal Bank of Scotland v Etridge (No 2)*.[405] It was held that a bank would be put on inquiry whenever a wife offers to stand surety for her husband's debts. To avoid the transaction being impugned on the grounds of undue influence the bank must merely take reasonable steps to satisfy itself that the practical implications of the proposed transaction have been brought home to the wife, especially the risks involved, so that she is able to enter the transaction with her eyes open as to its basic elements. This does not require a meeting between the bank and the wife. The bank is entitled to rely upon confirmation from a solicitor acting for the wife that he has advised her appropriately.

If a mortgage is executed to replace an earlier mortgage which could be set aside because the mortgagee had constructive notice that it was effected by undue influence,

---

[399] [2001] 4 All ER 449.    [400] See Stevens and Pearce, *Land Law* (3rd edn, 2005), pp 506–519.

[401] [1994] 1 AC 180.

[402] See also *Massey v Midland Bank plc* [1995] 1 All ER 929; *Banco Exterior Internacional SA v Mann* [1995] 1 All ER 936; *TSB Bank plc v Camfield* [1995] 1 All ER 951. In Scotland constructive notice is insufficient and the transaction will only be set aside if the contracting party had actual notice of the undue influence: *Mumford v Bank of Scotland* 1996 SLT 392.

[403] *Barclays Bank plc v O'Brien* [1994] 1 AC 180; *Midland Bank plc v Kidwai* [1995] NPC 81; *Banco Exterior Internacional v Mann* [1995] 1 All ER 936; *Massey v Midland Bank plc* [1995] 1 All ER 929; *Bank of Baroda v Rayarel* [1995] 2 FLR 376; *Hemsley v Brown (No 2)* [1996] 2 FCR 107; *Banco Exterior Internacional SA v Thomas* [1997] 1 All ER 46; *Crédit Lyonnais Bank Nederland NV v Burch* [1997] 1 All ER 144.

[404] *First National Bank v Achampong* [2003] EWCA Civ 487; [2003] LMCLQ 307 (Enonchong).

[405] [2001] 4 All ER 449. See Capper, 'Banks, Borrowers, Sureties and Undue Influence—a Half-Baked Solution to a Thoroughly Cooked Problem' [2002] RLR 100; (2002) 65 MLR 435 (Bigwood); Phang and Tijo, 'The uncertain boundaries of undue influence' [2002] LMCLQ 231.

the subsequent mortgage could also be set aside, even if relates to another property. The two mortgages are inseparable, and the principle that a contract of insurance can be set aside for misrepresentation if it has been renewed, even though each renewal constitutes a fresh contract, can be applied by analogy.[406]

## (4) Setting aside unconscionable bargains[407]

### (a) A bargain is not unconscionable merely because its terms are unfair

Equity will set aside bargains[408] which have been entered in circumstances that can be regarded as 'unconscionable'. The scope of the doctrine is relatively narrow, and in *National Westminster Bank plc v Morgan*[409] the House of Lords rejected the comprehensive principle of 'inequality of bargaining power' advocated by Lord Denning MR in *Lloyds Bank Ltd v Bundy*.[410] In *Boustany v Piggott*[411] the Privy Council stated that a bargain will not be held to be unconscionable merely because it was 'hard, unreasonable or foolish', and Lord Templeman adopted a number of propositions outlining the circumstances in which relief would be available:[412]

'(1) It is not sufficient to attract the jurisdiction of equity to prove that a bargain is hard, unreasonable or foolish; it must be proved to be unconscionable, in the sense that "one of the parties to it has imposed the objectionable terms in a morally reprehensible manner, that is to say, in a way which affects his conscience".[413]

(2) "Unconscionable" relates not merely to the terms of the bargain but to the behaviour of the stronger party, which must be characterised by some moral culpability or impropriety.[414]

(3) Unequal bargaining power or objectively unreasonable terms provide no basis for equitable interference in the absence of unconscientious or extortionate abuse of power where exceptionally, and as a matter of common fairness, "it was not right that the strong should be allowed to push the weak to the wall".[415]

(4) A contract cannot be set aside in equity as "an unconscionable bargain" against a party innocent of actual or constructive fraud. Even if the terms of the contract are "unfair" in the sense that they are more favourable to one party than the other ("contractual imbalance"), equity will not provide relief unless the beneficiary is guilty of unconscionable conduct.[416]

(5) In situations of this kind it is necessary for the plaintiff who seeks relief to establish unconscionable conduct, namely that unconscientious advantage has been taken of his disabling condition or circumstances.'[417]

---

[406] *Yorkshire Bank plc v Tinsley* [2004] 3 All ER 463; [2005] 64 CLJ 42 (Gravells).

[407] Burrows, *The Law of Restitution* (2nd edn 2002), pp 260–272; Goff and Jones, *The Law of Restitution* (6th edn, 2002), pp 361–373.

[408] The jurisdiction does not extend to gifts: *Langton v Langton* [1995] 2 FLR 890.

[409] [1985] AC 686.     [410] [1975] QB 326, CA.

[411] (1993) 69 P & CR 288. See [1995] LMCLQ 538 (Bamforth).

[412] (1995) 69 P & CR 288 at 303.     [413] *Multiservice Bookbinding Ltd v Marden* [1979] Ch 84.

[414] *Alec Lobb (Garages) Ltd v Total Oil (Great Britain) Ltd* [1983] 1 WLR 87 at 94.

[415] *Alec Lobb (Garages) Ltd v Total Oil (Great Britain) Ltd* [1985] 1 WLR 173 at 183.

[416] *Hart v O'Connor* [1985] AC 1000; *Nichols v Jessup* [1986] 1 NZLR 226.

[417] *Commercial Bank of Australia Ltd v Amadio* (1983) 46 ALR 402 at 413, per Mason J.

## (b) Factors which render a bargain unconscionable

*(i)  A personal disadvantage.* A bargain will only be set aside if the party contracting was subject to some personal disadvantage which rendered him substantially less capable than ordinary members of society. This may include a mental incapacity such as senile dementia,[418] illiteracy or unfamiliarity with a language or culture,[419] age,[420] or youth and inexperience. Equity has also long recognised that a transaction may be set aside if it was entered by a person who was 'poor and ignorant'. This principle was stated by Kay J in *Fry v Lane*, where the court set aside a sale of a reversionary interest of land at an undervalue:

'. . . where a purchase is made from a poor and ignorant man at a considerable undervalue, the vendor having no independent advice, a court of equity will set aside the transaction.'[421]

This principle was translated into a modern context in *Cresswell v Potter*,[422] where a wife, who was a telephonist, released her interest in the matrimonial home for inadequate consideration on divorce. Megarry J stated:

'Eighty years ago, when *Fry v Lane* was decided, social conditions were very different from those which exist today. I do not, however, think that the principle has changed, even though the euphemisms of the 20th century may require the word "poor" to be replaced by "a member of the lower income group" or the like, and the word "ignorant" by "less highly educated" . . .'[423]

In the more recent case of *Crédit Lyonnais Bank Nederland NV v Burch*,[424] Millett LJ speculated that the principle could have operated in favour of a junior employee who had entered a contract to act as unlimited surety of her employer's debts.

*(ii)  Conscious exploitation of vulnerability.* A transaction will only be regarded as unconscionable if the one contracting party was aware of the personal disadvantage of the other, so that his conscience was affected by actual or constructive notice thereof.[425] Such exploitation will not be demonstrated if the contracting party received independent legal advice before entering the bargain.[426]

*(iii)  Objective unfairness of the bargain.* A bargain will only be set aside if it was actually unfair. This will most easily be demonstrated if the contracting party has received no personal advantage from a transaction,[427] or if his property has been purchased at a substantially lower price than might reasonable have been expected in the market place.[428]

---

[418]  *Archer v Cutler* [1980] 1 NZLR 386; *Hart v O'Connor* [1985] AC 1000.
[419]  *Commercial Bank of Australia Ltd v Amadio* (1983) 46 ALR 402.
[420]  *Watkin v Watson-Smith* (1986) Times, 3 July.       [421]  (1888) 40 Ch D 312 at 322.
[422]  [1978] 1 WLR 255n.
[423]  [1978] 1 WLR 255n at 257. See also *Boustany v Pigott* (1993) 69 P & CR 288 where the Privy Council held that a contract would be set aside as unconscionable if the party was 'poor or ignorant'.
[424]  [1997] 1 All ER 144.       [425]  *Hart v O'Connor* [1985] AC 1000.
[426]  *Fry v Lane* (1888) 40 Ch D 312; *Butlin-Sanders v Butlin* [1985] Fam Law 126.
[427]  *Crédit Lyonnais Bank Nederland v Burch* [1997] 1 All ER 144.
[428]  *Fry v Lane* (1888) 40 Ch D 312.

## (5) Limitations on the availability of rescission

There are a number of circumstances where it will not be possible for a plaintiff to rescind a contract.

### (a) Restitutio in integrum is impossible

When a contract is rescinded the parties must be returned to their former positions as far as is practically possible.[429] As Lord Blackburn said in *Erlanger v New Sombrero Phosphate Co*:

'It is . . . clear on principles of general justice, that as a condition to a rescission there must be *restitutio in integrum*. The parties must be put in *status quo* . . .'[430]

For example, in *Clarke v Dickson*[431] the court held that a party could not rescind a contract to purchase shares in a partnership which had been converted into a limited liability company.[432] Equity approaches the question flexibly, and is particularly ready to grant rescission where there was fraud.[433] In granting rescission the court may impose terms,[434] for example to account for profits or allow for deterioration.[435] The overall objective is for the courts to do 'what is practically just'.[436] Thus, in *O'Sullivan v Management Agency and Music Ltd*[437] a contract for the management of a pop singer was rescinded on the grounds of undue influence. The managers were allowed to retain a reasonable remuneration for the work they had done which had contributed to his success. In *Cheese v Thomas*[438] an uncle and his great-nephew had purchased a house for £83,000. The uncle had contributed £43,000 and the remainder had been borrowed by the nephew by way of a mortgage. The uncle was held entitled to set the transaction aside on the grounds of undue influence exercised by the nephew. However, when the house was sold its value had fallen considerably and only £55,000 was received. This was sufficient to discharge the mortgage but even if the balance was paid to the uncle he would remain £25,000 out of pocket. The Court of Appeal rejected the uncle's submission that his nephew should repay him the entire £43,000 he had contributed to the property. Nicholls V-C explained that, although the transaction was to be reversed on the grounds of undue influence, it was impossible to restore the parties to the precise position they were in before the contract had been entered. The court would thus 'do what is practically just' by restoring the uncle 'as near to his original position as is now possible'. It was thus held that the uncle was entitled to receive a share of the net proceeds of sale received from the property proportionate to his original contribution,

---

[429] *Spence v Crawford* [1939] 3 All ER 271, HL; *Cheese v Thomas* [1994] 1 All ER 35 at 412, per Nicholls V-C. See also *Maguire v Makaronis* (1997) 71 ALJR 781; (1997) 114 LQR 9 (Moriarty).

[430] (1878) 3 App Cas 1218 at 1278. See [1997] RLR 89 (Halson).

[431] (1858) EB & E 148.

[432] See also *Thorpe v Fasey* [1949] Ch 649; *Butler v Croft* (1973) 27 P & CR 1.

[433] *Spence v Crawford* [1939] 3 All ER 271, HL.      [434] See [1996] RLR 71 (Proksch).

[435] *Lagunas Nitrate Co v Lagunas Syndicate* [1899] 2 Ch 392; *Armstrong v Jackson* [1917] 2 KB 822; *Wiebe v Butchart's Motors Ltd* [1949] 4 DLR 838. See *TSB Bank plc v Camfield* [1995] 1 All ER 951.

[436] *Spence v Crawford* [1939] 3 All ER 271 at 288, per Lord Wright; *Cheese v Thomas* [1994] 1 All ER 35 at 412, per Nicholls V-C; *Vadasz v Pioneer Concrete* (SA) Pty Ltd (1995) 130 ALR 570.

[437] [1985] QB 428.      [438] [1994] 1 All ER 35.

ie 43:40. As such, he would bear a proportionate share of the loss caused by the fall in value thereof.

## (b) Affirmation

A party cannot rescind a contract which he has subsequently affirmed. In *Long v Lloyd*[439] a purchaser was taken to have affirmed a contract for the sale of a lorry when he used it a second time having discovered there were faults. He could not rescind on the grounds of the seller's misrepresentation. Similarly, a person cannot rescind a contract entered under undue influence if he affirms it after the influence has stopped.[440]

## (c) Third party rights

The right to rescind is lost once third parties have acquired rights in the property in good faith for value.[441]

## (d) Delay

In *Allcard v Skinner*[442] the plaintiff was held not to be entitled to rescind gifts of stock to a religious order five years after she left because of her delay. Lindley LJ stated that the victim must 'seek relief within a reasonable time after the removal of the influence'.[443] Similarly, in *Leaf v International Galleries*[444] a plaintiff was not entitled to rescind a contract for innocent misrepresentation after a delay of five years.

# 7 Rectification[445]

Rectification is a discretionary[446] equitable remedy which allows for the correction of a document so that it reflects the real intention of the parties. It is an exception to the 'parol evidence rule' so that oral evidence may be admitted to demonstrate that a written instrument is incorrect. For example, in *Joscelyne v Nissen*[447] the Court of Appeal ordered the rectification of an agreement between a daughter and her father which they intended should include a provision that she was to pay the household expenses, which she had refused to pay claiming that she was not required to do so on a true construction of the written agreement they had entered. A wide range of documents have been rectified, including a conveyance,[448] a bill of exchange,[449] a marriage settlement,[450] a transfer of shares[451] and, by statute, wills.[452]

---

[439] [1958] 2 All ER 402, CA.    [440] *Mitchell v Homfray* (1881) 8 QBD 587.

[441] See *Oakes v Turquand* (1867) LR 2 HL 325; *Bainbrigge v Browne* (1881) 18 Ch D 188; *Re Scottish Petroleum Co (No 2)* (1883) 23 Ch D 413; *Coldunell Ltd v Gallon* [1986] 1 All ER 429.

[442] (1887) 36 Ch D 145.    [443] (1887) 36 Ch D 145 at 187.    [444] [1950] 2 KB 86.

[445] See *Snell's Principles of Equity* (31st edn, 2005), pp 331–345; Hanbury and Martin, *Modern Equity* (17th edn, 2005) 870–877; Goff and Jones, *The Law of Restitution* (6th edn, 2002) 288–294.

[446] *Re Butlin's Will Trusts* [1976] Ch 251.    [447] [1970] 2 QB 86.

[448] *Beale v Kyte* [1907] 1 Ch 564.    [449] *Druiff v Lord Parker* (1867–68) LR 5 Eq 131.

[450] *Bold v Hutchinson* (1855) 5 De GM & G 558.

[451] *Re International Contract Co* (1872) 7 Ch App 485.

[452] Administration of Justice Act 1982, s 20(1). See *Wordingham v Royal Exchange Trust Co* [1992] Ch 412; *Re Segelman* [1996] Ch 171, [1995] 3 All ER 676.

## (1) Requirements for rectification

### (a) Mistake in written document

Rectification is only possible where a written document mistakenly fails to state what the parties had intended to agree. It is not necessary that the parties had actually entered a contract orally prior to the incorrect instrument. In *Joscelyne v Nissen*[453] the Court of Appeal held that all that is necessary is a prior common intention as to what the written agreement was to be.[454] There are grounds for rectification if that common intention does not appear in the written document.[455] Rectification is only available for a mistake of the actual terms of the parties' agreement. Thus, in *Frederick E Rose (London) Ltd v William Pim Jnr & Co Ltd*[456] rectification was not possible where the parties had entered a written contract for the sale of 'horsebeans', which they had mistakenly believed were the same as 'feveroles'. The contract was a correct record of their agreement.

### (b) Common mistake

Generally, an instrument will only be rectified if it records the agreement contrary to the intentions of both parties.[457]

### (c) Unilateral mistake

Rectification is not normally available where a mistake is unilateral.[458] However, rectification will be available if the party who was not mistaken had acted fraudulently[459] or is estopped from resisting rectification. In *Thomas Bates & Son Ltd v Wyndham's (Lingerie) Ltd*[460] Buckley LJ set out the circumstances in which a person will be estopped from resisting rectification:

'. . . it must be shown: first, that one party, A, erroneously believed that the document sought to be rectified contained a particular term or provision which, mistakenly, it did contain; second, that the other party, B, was aware of the omission or the inclusion and that it was due to a mistake on the part of A; third, that B has omitted to draw the mistake to the notice of A. And I think there must be a fourth element involved, namely, that the mistake must be one calculated to benefit B. If these requirements are satisfied, the court may regard it as inequitable to allow B to resist rectification to give effect to A's intention on the ground that the mistake was not . . . a common mistake.'[461]

A line of authorities which suggested that the party who was not mistaken has the option of accepting rectification or rescission of the contract has been disapproved by the Court of Appeal in *Riverlate Properties Ltd v Paul*.[462]

---

[453] [1970] 2 QB 86.     [454] *Crane v Hegeman-Harris Co Inc* [1939] 1 All ER 662.
[455] *Earl v Hector Whaling Ltd* [1961] 1 Lloyd's Rep 459.     [456] [1953] 2 QB 450.
[457] *Murray v Parker* (1854) 19 Beav 305; *Fowler v Fowler* (1859) 4 De G & J 250.
[458] *Sells v Sells* (1860) 1 Drew & Sm 42.
[459] *Ball v Storie* (1823) 1 Sim & St 210; *Lovesy v Smith* (1880) LR 15 Ch D 655.
[460] [1981] 1 All ER 1077, CA.     [461] [1981] 1 All ER 1077 at 1086.     [462] [1975] Ch 133.

### (d)  Burden of proof

For rectification the mistake must be established with 'a high degree of conviction'.[463] In *Joscelyne v Nissen*[464] Russel LJ said that there must be 'convincing proof' of the mistake. Thus, in *Re Segelman*[465] Chadwick J held that a testator's will should be rectified where extrinsic evidence of the his intentions demonstrated convincingly that it had failed to carry out his intentions.

## (2)  Defences to rectification

Rectification will not be granted where it would affect the position of third parties who have acquired rights bona fides for value.[466] Delay may also bar a claim.[467]

# 8  Account

Where someone has obtained a benefit to which they are not entitled, or has incurred an expense which should be payable by another, an account in equity may be ordered, either on its own, or as an adjunct to another substantive remedy. An account may be ordered, for instance, where equitable co-owners are entitled to share the occupation of residential property, but only one of them has been paying the bills,[468] or where land held by co-owners has been let or exploited for profit.[469] Similarly, a fiduciary who has made improper use of information acquired as adviser to a trust may be obliged by means of an account to give up to the beneficiaries any profits which he has made.[470]

## (1)  Ancillary orders in support of legal rights

In some instances, the order for account will not be sought in its own right, but in order to make effective some other remedy of the plaintiff. The plaintiff owed a debt might seek an account, for instance, to verify the amount owing. There were some instances where an account of this kind could be ordered at common law, but the superior procedures of equity[471] meant that the equitable order largely displaced the common

---

[463]  *Crane v Hegeman-Harris Co Inc* [1939] 4 All ER 68, CA. See also *Countess of Shelburne v Earl of Inchiquin* (1784) 1 Bro CC 338; *Fowler v Fowler* (1859) 4 De G & J 250.

[464]  [1970] 2 QB 86, CA. See *Brimican Investments Ltd v Blue Circle Heating Ltd* [1995] EGCS 18; *Racal Group Services Ltd v Ashmore* [1995] STC 1151; *Re Segelman* [1995] 3 All ER 676.

[465]  *Re Segelman* [1995] 3 All ER 676 at 684.

[466]  *Garrard v Frankel* (1862) 30 Beav 445; *Smith v Jones* [1954] 1 WLR 1089; *Thames Guaranty Ltd v Campbell* [1985] QB 210.

[467]  *Beale v Kyte* [1907] 1 Ch 564.

[468]  *Leake v Bruzzi* [1974] 1 WLR 1528; *Leigh v Dickeson* (1884) 15 QBD 60. See also *Henderson v Eason* (1851) 17 QB 701 at 721, per Parke B.

[469]  *Henderson v Eason* (1851) 17 QB 701; *Job v Potton* (1875) LR 20 Eq 84; *Jacobs v Seward* (1872) LR 5 HL 464.

[470]  *Boardman v Phipps* [1967] 2 AC 46, HL. See Chapter 29.

[471]  See *A-G v Dublin Corpn* (1827) 1 Bli NS 312 at 337; *Beaumont v Boultbee* (1802) 7 Ves 599.

law jurisdiction.[472] Following the amalgamation of the courts of law and the courts of equity, and the prevailing judicial view about the effect of that fusion,[473] there is now probably no reason to distinguish between the legal and equitable jurisdictions.[474]

An order for account may be used as an adjunct to the obligation of an agent to answer to his principal under a contract of agency. The principal could, by means of account, obtain disclosure of any sums owing to him by his agent.[475] Equity was prepared to intervene because a principal places confidence in his agent, and without disclosure by the agent may have no means of knowing what is owing.[476] For similar reasons, an inventor seeking by injunction to prevent the infringement of a patent[477] may use an account in order to discover what profits have been made from the unauthorised exploitation of the invention. Equity also offered aid through an action in account where the affairs of the parties were especially complicated[478] or where mutual accounts were involved.[479]

## (2) Ancillary orders in support of equitable rights

Equity would, of course, order an account where this was necessary to support a purely equitable right, such as the right of a beneficiary against a trustee in respect of trust property, the right of a landlord against a tenant for equitable waste,[480] or the right of a mortgagor to obtain the best return reasonably possible from property of which the mortgagee has taken possession. In this last instance, the mortgagee is held accountable not only for what has in fact been received, but also for the sums which he ought to have received if he had fulfilled his duty. The mortgagee would thus be accountable for rents which could have been obtained if the property had been let as it ought[481] and for the full market rent which could have been obtained if the property had not been let subject to a disparaging condition.[482]

Where a trustee's inaction amounts to a breach of duty[483] (for instance, where a trustee has taken inadequate steps to recover sums owing to the trust fund[484]), the

---

[472]  *Sturton v Richardson* (1844) 13 M & W 17; *Shepard v Brown* (1862) 4 Giff 203.

[473]  See above, pp 12–17.

[474]  The distinction could, before the fusion of the courts of law and of equity, be of significance. For instance, equity would not order an account in favour of a customer against his banker, since the relationship between them was in the nature of a simple contract without any fiduciary character: *Foley v Hill* (1848) 2 HL Cas 28.

[475]  *Beaumont v Boultbee* (1802) 7 Ves 599; *Mackenzie v Johnston* (1819) 4 Madd 373.

[476]  That would not generally be the case where the agent brings an action against the principal: *Padwick v Stanley* (1852) 9 Hare 627.

[477]  *Price's Patent Candle Co v Bauwen's Patent Candle Co Ltd* (1858) 4 K & J 727; *De Vitre v Betts* (1873) LR 6 HL 319. See Patents Act 1977, s 61.

[478]  *O'Connor v Spaight* (1804) 1 Sch & Lef 305; *Taff Vale Rly Co v Nixon* (1847) 1 HL Cas 111; *North-Eastern Rly Co v Martin* (1848) 2 Ph 758.

[479]  *Phillips v Phillips* (1852) 9 Hare 471.

[480]  *Duke of Leeds v Earl of Amherst* (1846) 2 Ph 117. Equitable waste is deliberate and malicious injury to land or buildings affecting its permanent value. See above, p 57.

[481]  *Noyes v Pollock* (1886) 32 Ch D 53 at 61

[482]  *White v City of London Brewery Co* (1889) 42 Ch D 237.

[483]  *Re Stevens, Cooke v Stevens* [1898] 1 Ch 162, CA. See Chapter 28.

[484]  See *Re Vickery* [1931] 1 Ch 572.

trustee can be held liable, by means of account, for the losses which have arisen through this failure to act, or 'wilful default' as it is described.[485] As with any action for breach of trust, at least one breach must be proved or admitted,[486] but if there is reason to believe that there may have been other instances of default, the court may order a general account rather than limiting it to the particular instance proved.[487]

## (3) Substantive orders to account

There are some instances in which the order to account appears to be used as a substantive remedy: that is, it is ordered even though there is no separate remedy such as damages in respect of which the order is sought.[488] The order of account therefore both quantifies the measure of profit or loss, and also imposes a liability to pay it.[489] The absence of any separate remedy may reflect the absence of an antecedent and independent cause of action apart from the taking of an account. Whether the payment of the sum owing should be described as 'damages' or 'compensation' or 'restitution' is a matter of debate, and for most purposes the description of the obligation is a matter of no significance. What is significant is that the order for account is being used in some situations as a remedy in its own right. It has long been a feature of English law that the availability of a remedy has been a key feature in the development of new rights. As account is used in novel situations, we are therefore observing the development of new rights, some of which in due course will be absorbed either into existing classifications of rights and obligations, or into the developing autonomous doctrine of restitution based on unjust enrichment.

Three principal examples can be given of the use of account in a substantive way. First, an obligation to account will be imposed on a fiduciary who has made a profit from a breach of confidence. Secondly, a formally appointed or constructive trustee will be obliged to account for any personal advantage gained through a position of trust. Finally, an agent will be obliged to account for an illicit bribe. These cases can all be subsumed under the general rubric of unauthorised profits made by a fiduciary, although it is not clear how far the existence of a fiduciary relationship is an essential requirement.

### (a) Accounting for profits from breach of confidence

We have already observed that equity was prepared to lend support, by means of taking an account, to an action for infringement of a patent. Similarly, where the originator of an idea or invention has disclosed it in confidence to a manufacturer who has exploited it without permission, the courts have been prepared to intervene by means of an

---

[485]  See Stannard [1979] Conv 345.

[486]  *Sleight v Lawson* (1857) 3 K & J 292; *Re Youngs* (1885) 30 Ch D 421.

[487]  *Re Tebbs* [1976] 2 All ER 858.

[488]  Eg in *Mouat v Clark Boyce* [1992] 2 NZLR 559 at 566 Sir Robin Cooke included an account of profits in a list of remedies available to the court alongside other remedies such as damages.

[489]  For a recent discussion of the extent to which equity is able to award damages or compensation for the breach of purely equitable rights see (1994) 14 LS 313–334 (Capper), esp at pp 313–328.

injunction or an account of profits.[490] The same remedies have been given to actresses whose idea for a television series was used without their consent.[491] The remedies are available independently of any contract or other substantive basis for a remedy. In *Coco v AN Clark (Engineers) Ltd*[492] it was said that three requirements had to be met: (i) that the information imparted was of a confidential nature; (ii) that it was communicated in circumstances importing an obligation of confidence; and (iii) that there had been an unauthorised use of the information. In the *Spycatcher* case[493] the House of Lords agreed that the obligation to account could be extended to a newspaper which had published extracts from a book written by a former member of the British secret service. There was no doubt that Peter Wright, the member of MI5 concerned, had acted in breach of confidence. It appears to have been considered by the Lords that it was enough that the newspaper was aware of this to impose on it an obligation to account for any profits made from its publication. Lord Goff would have gone further and imposed a duty to keep confidence independently of the circumstances in which the information was acquired. He was prepared to contemplate applying an obligation to keep confidence in certain situations 'beloved of law teachers, where an obviously confidential document is wafted by an electric fan out of a window into a crowded street, or when an obviously confidential document, such as a private diary, is dropped in a public place, and is then picked up by a passer-by'.[494] The opinions come close to according the status of property to confidential information.

## (b) Accounting for personal advantage from breach of trust

The second situation in which the order of account appears to be used as a substantive remedy, namely in cases of personal advantage gained through a position of trust, is discussed more fully in Chapter 29. A person who is appointed director of a company through the use of a shareholding of which he is trustee may be obliged to account to the trustees for any fees which he receives in that capacity,[495] unless the trust instrument authorises the trustee to retain it.[496] This liability arises in order to prevent any potential conflict between the self-interest of a trustee and the proper administration of the trust. It is not clear from the cases whether the obligation is personal, or whether proprietary. The mere fact that the obligation is phrased in the language of account does not mean that any fees received by the trustee-director are trust property and are recoverable by the beneficiaries for that reason. It is equally possible that equity uses the mechanism of account as a means of imposing a personal obligation on the trustee to pay to the beneficiaries either the sum which he has received in fees or a sum of equal value. The remedy of account is therefore being used as a means of enforcing a money payment.[497]

---

[490] *Coco v A N Clark (Engineers) Ltd* [1969] RPC 41; *Seager v Copydex Ltd (No 1)* [1967] 1 WLR 923; (No 2) [1969] 1 WLR 809.

[491] *Fraser v Thames Television Ltd* [1984] QB 44. [492] [1969] RPC 41.

[493] *A-G v Guardian Newspapers Ltd (No 2)* [1988] 3 All ER 545.

[494] [1988] 3 All ER 545 at 658–659. [495] *Re Gee* [1948] Ch 284.

[496] *Re Llewellin's Will Trusts* [1949] Ch 225.

[497] In other words, the equitable remedy of account is being used as equity's equivalent of the common law action for debt.

## (c) Accounting for bribes or secret profits

A long line of authority holds that where an agent[498] or other person in a fiduciary position, such as a company director[499] or trustee,[500] receives a bribe or makes some other secret profit, he must account for the sum received to his principal. In the case of the accountability of agents for bribes or secret profits which they have received, it used to be thought, on the authority of *Lister & Co v Stubbs*,[501] that the obligation of the agent was personal only. The court held that an employee of a company who had received bribes for favouring a third party in negotiating contracts on behalf of his employer was liable to account to his employers for the sums he had received, but only as a debtor to them, not as a trustee. Similarly, in *A-G's Reference (No 1 of 1985)*,[502] the Court of Appeal held that the manager of a public house who was permitted to sell only beverages supplied by his employers was under an obligation to account for profits which he made by selling drinks obtained from other sources, but that he was not a trustee of the sums which he received. The Court of Appeal held that the employer has no proprietary interest in the illicit profits which the manager makes.[503] In the words of Lord Lane CJ, delivering the opinion of the court:

'The fact that A may have to account to B for money he has received from X does not mean necessarily that he received the money on account of B.'

However, in *A-G for Hong Kong v Reid*[504] the Privy Council considered that the decision in *Lister & Co v Stubbs* was wrong in principle in holding that a bribe received by an agent did not belong to his principal. Charles Reid, a New Zealander working in the government legal service in Hong Kong, supplemented his income by taking illicit payments in return for obstructing the prosecution of certain criminals. The Attorney General for Hong Kong, acting on behalf of the Crown, sought to assert a right to three freehold properties in New Zealand which it was alleged had been acquired with the bribes. The Privy Council held that the Crown was entitled, not merely to an account from Charles Reid, but that, provided that the assets derived from the bribes were separately identifiable, the Crown could claim proprietary rights over them.

Two reasons were given. First, if the fiduciary is not to benefit from his wrong, he must be accountable not only for the value of any property received by way of bribe, but also for any profits made through its retention in kind if it appreciates in value, or for any profits made through its advantageous reinvestment. Secondly, the maxim 'equity considers as done that which ought to have been done' applied. As soon as the bribe was received by the bribee, it should have been paid over to the person injured. The false fiduciary was therefore a constructive trustee of it. It was no objection that by giving the Crown employer a proprietary right to the bribe, it would not be available to any of Charles Reid's creditors. The bribe was money which he should never have received.

---

[498]  *Lister & Co v Stubbs* (1890) LR 45 Ch D 1, CA.

[499]  *Regal (Hastings) Ltd v Gulliver* [1942] 1 All ER 378, HL; *Industrial Development Consultants Ltd v Cooley* [1972] 2 All ER 162.

[500]  See Chapter 26.     [501]  (1890) LR 45 Ch D 1.     [502]  [1986] 2 All ER 219.

[503]  Unless, perhaps, the profit can be identified as a separate piece of property rather than as part of a mixed fund: [1986] 2 All ER 219 at 225.

[504]  [1994] 1 All ER 1. See also Chapter 29.

There is a sharp division of opinion as to whether the conclusion reached by the Privy Council in Reid is correct, but there is some support in *A-G v Guardian Newspapers (No 2)*[505] (the *Spycatcher* case) for conferring proprietary rights on plaintiffs entitled to seek an account from a wrongdoer. There are indications in the House of Lords opinions that they would have been prepared to give the Crown proprietary rights in order to deprive Peter Wright of the benefits he received by publishing confidential information acquired during his employment in the security service.[506] Similarly, the House of Lords held in *Lord Napier and Ettrick v Hunter*[507] that a stop-loss insurer of a Lloyd's underwriter had an equitable lien over money recovered by the underwriter[508] to the extent that they represented sums paid by the insurer under the stop-loss insurance.

A problem which remains to be resolved is when a wrongdoer who receives an illicit benefit will be held personally liable only, and when the courts will consider that the injured party has proprietary rights to the sums received by the wrongdoer. No clear guidance on this matter is to be found in any of the recent decisions.

## (4) Settled accounts

Since the essence of all the cases in which an account is sought is that the defendant owes a sum of money to the plaintiff, and the purpose of the taking of an account is to ascertain that sum, it will be a defence to the request for an account either that nothing is due, or that the sum due has already been agreed between the parties. The agreement as to the sum owing does not need to be in any particular form,[509] but if the nature of the settlement of account involves the making of concessions, it will not be binding unless it has effect as a contract supported by consideration. That will usually be the case where there are mutual dealings. In the words of Romer J in *Anglo-American Asphalt Co v Crowley Russell & Co*:[510]

'Where A owes, or may owe, B money, and B owes, or may owe, A money, and in their accounts they strike a balance and agree that balance, that truly represents the financial result of their transactions. There is mutuality in it, and . . . they expressly or by implication agree to a conventional position which is established by striking a balance, and that results in what is called a settled account. But that has no application . . . where the whole accounting is to be rendered by one party to another.'

---

[505]  [1988] 3 All ER 545.

[506]  See Lord Keith at 645, Lord Griffiths at 654 and Lord Goff at 664. See also Scott J at first instance at 567 and Dillon LJ in the Court of Appeal at 621, explaining more fully the reasons for imposing a constructive trust. These remarks are directed at the question of whether the Crown has an equitable copyright in a book written in breach of confidence by a crown servant, but Scott J also says at 584 that the profit made through the use of confidential information 'in equity, belongs to the owner of the information'.

[507]  [1993] 1 All ER 385 at 402.

[508]  That is, a first right to payment from those funds. An equitable lien of this kind is a proprietary right falling short of full ownership. Liens are discussed in the context of the right to trace in Chapter 25.

[509]  *Yourell v Hibernian Bank* [1918] AC 372, HL; *Phillips-Higgins v Harper* [1954] 1 All ER 116; affd [1954] 2 All ER 51n, CA.

[510]  [1945] 2 All ER 324 at 331.

Where the agreement on a settled account has been reached as a result of fraud, then the agreement may be set aside and the accounts reviewed.[511] Similarly, the accounts may be reviewed where there has been a mistake or oversight.[512] In the case of fraud or serious error, the court will normally reopen the account and order that it be taken anew. Where the error or mistake is less substantial, the court may direct that the account stands, subject to 'surcharge and falsification',[513] that is, subject to the addition (surcharge) of items wrongly omitted and to the deletion (falsification) of items wrongly included. A settled account will not exclude the statutory jurisdiction to reopen extortionate credit bargains.[514]

## (5) Delay

The right to an account lapses after the expiration of the statutory time limit applicable to the cause of action which it supports.[515] In other cases, no express limitation period applies, although it might be expected that the general six-year limitation period would apply by analogy with other claims, subject to the ordinary general exceptions.

---

[511] *Vernon v Vawdrey* (1740) 2 Atk 119; *Oldaker v Lavender* (1833) 6 Sim 239; *Millar v Craig* (1843) 6 Beav 433; *Gething v Keighley* (1878) 9 Ch D 547; *Allfrey v Allfrey* (1849) 1 Mac & G 87.

[512] *Pritt v Clay* (1843) 6 Beav 503; *Williamson v Barbour* (1877) 9 Ch D 529.

[513] *Pit v Cholmondeley* (1754) 2 Ves Sen 565.

[514] Consumer Credit Act 1974, ss 137–140.

[515] Limitation Act 1980, s 23.

# 3

# Equity and the law of property

## 1 Introduction

In the previous chapter the remedial contribution of equity to English law has been examined. The remainder of this book will largely be concerned with the contribution equity has made to the law of property, in particular through the trust. The English law of property law comprises a synthesis of legal and equitable rights and interests, reflecting its historical genesis in the bifurcated legal system described in Chapter 1. Whereas the common law developed and applied it own rules regulating the ownership of things, the Chancery courts developed and enforced a parallel regime of equitable rights. As Lord Browne-Wilkinson has observed:

'In 1993, English law has one single law of property made up of legal and equitable interests.'[1]

## 2 What is property?[2]

### (1) The basic concept

At its most basic, the term property is simply a more technical expression describing 'things'. Things can readily be distinguished from 'persons'. Persons are either individual human beings or abstract entitles, such as companies or corporations, which are treated as enjoying independent legal personhood. In general, persons are capable of owning things, whereas things have no capacity to own other things. Since the abolition of slavery, human persons are incapable of being owned as such. Body parts are also incapable of ownership.[3] Companies are owned by their shareholders, but the separate identity of the company is maintained so that it is not treated as synonymous with its shareholders. Animals are regarded as things and are capable of being owned, whereas they are not capable of owning.

---

[1] *Tinsley v Milligan* [1993] 3 All ER 65 at 86. See above, p 15.

[2] See Lawson and Rudden, *The Law of Property* (1982), pp 1–38; Penner, *The Idea of Property in Law* (1997); (1998) 18 LS 41 (Rotherham).

[3] See Skene, 'Proprietary rights in human bodies, body parts and tissue: regulatory contexts and proposals for new laws' (2002) 22 LS 102.

Lawson and Rudden have commented that 'the law of property deals with the legal relations between people with regard to things'.[4] It addresses such questions as the following: Who owns the thing? What is the owner entitled to do with the thing he owns? How can the owner of the thing transfer it to someone else so that they become the owner in his place? Can the owner continue to assert his ownership of the thing even when a third person has taken it from him without permission, or against a person who has acquired the thing from such a third person?

For example, imagine that Kevin is the owner of a car. He purchased the car from the manufacturers and is therefore the owner of the car. If he lends the car to his friend Leon, for the weekend does Leon become the owner of the car? If Leon gives the car to Michael while he is borrowing it does Michael become the owner of the car thus depriving Kevin of his ownership? Does it make any difference if Leon sells the car to Michael, who believed that it belonged to him? The answers to these issues are determined by the law of property.

## (2) Classification of types of property

Although property comprises 'things', the law differentiates between different types, or categories, of thing. The law applicable to a particular item of property will be dependent upon its nature.

### (a) Real and personal property

English law distinguishes between what are termed 'real' and 'personal' property. Real property comprises land and interests in land, whereas personal property comprises everything which is not land. Items of tangible personal property, for example cars or furniture, are termed chattels. If chattels are attached to land so as to become part of the land, they lose their identity as personal property and become 'fixtures'.[5] Historically, the distinction between real and personal property was extremely significant, as the rules of succession, which determine what happens to property on the death of its owner, were different.

### (b) Movable and immovable property

Many continental legal systems, based on Roman law, distinguish not between real and personal property but between 'movable' and 'immovable' property—terms which speak for themselves. Although similar to the English distinction between real and personal property, this classification is not synonymous with it, as some interests that English law would regard as personal would be characterised as immovable.[6] For the purposes of private international law English law abandons its domestic classification and distinguishes between movable and immovable property.[7]

---

[4]  *The Law of Property* (1982), p 1.

[5]  See Gray & Gray, *Elements of Land Law* (3rd edn, 2001), pp 44–55.

[6]  Eg the interest of a leaseholder is regarded as personal rather than real, whereas it is immovable rather than movable: *Freke v Lord Carbery* (1873) LR 16 Eq 461; *Duncan v Lawson* (1889) 41 Ch D 394.

[7]  *Re Hoyles* [1911] 1 Ch 179, CA. See Cheshire and North, *Private International Law* (12th edn, 1992); pp 779–783.

## (c) Tangible and intangible property

A further distinction is drawn between things which are tangible and those which are not. A thing which is tangible is physical in nature, whereas intangible property only exists in abstract, comprising a bundle of rights and entitlements. Intellectual property rights, such as copyrights, patents and trademarks, are good examples of intangible property. Others include negotiable instruments,[8] debts, and shares. These types of property are also described as choses in action.

# 3 Proprietary rights[9]

Proprietary rights are those rights and entitlements which exist in reference to things. The most important and absolute right is that of ownership, but there are many lesser interests that may be enjoyed in respect of an item of property.

## (1) Ownership

A person who owns a thing in which nobody else has any interests is the absolute owner thereof. Such ownership is the 'greatest possible interest in a thing which a mature system of law recognises'.[10] The rights of an owner are best understood in terms of the legal powers which are conferred in relation to the thing. Lawson and Rudden identify three main elements of ownership:

'(a) the right to make physical use of a thing; (b) the right to the income from it, in money, in kind, or in services; and (c) the power of management, including that of alienation.'[11]

By virtue of ownership a person is entitled to do as he wishes with his property. He can possess, use, enjoy and exploit it as he pleases. He is even free to destroy it. He can give it away, or sell it to a third person. The person who owns property is said to have 'title' to it, a term derived from the fact that he is 'entitled' to it. In many cases the ownership of property will be more complex. For example, there may be multiple owners of the thing, termed co-owners, who enjoy concurrent ownership.

## (2) Other rights in property

Although the most important right in property is ownership, there are a large range of other proprietary rights that a person may enjoy over a thing. The complexity of property law follows from the fact that, often, a number of persons may have different, sometimes competing, rights in the same thing. Such subsidiary rights may qualify or limit the absolute entitlement of the owner to do as he chooses with the thing. This

---

[8] Bills of exchange, promissory notes and cheques.
[9] See (1996) 16 OJLS 31 (Eleftheriadis); (1998) 18 OJLS 361 (Chambers).
[10] Honore, 'Ownership', in Guest (ed), *Oxford Essays in Jurisprudence* (1961).
[11] Lawson and Rudden, *The Law of Property* (1982), p 8.

multiplicity of proprietary rights in the same thing is most clearly illustrated in the context of land. Assume that Norman is the owner of a piece of land, Blackacre, which he purchased with the help of a Building Society loan secured by a mortgage. He has leased the land to Owen for twenty-five years. He has granted his next-door neighbour, Penelope, the right to walk to her garage across his back garden, and reached an agreement with his other next-door neighbour, Quentin, that he will not use the land for business purposes. In this simple scenario Norman, Owen, Penelope, Quentin and the Building Society all have different proprietary interests in the same land.

## (3) Proprietary and personal rights

### (a) The need to distinguish proprietary and personal rights

Whilst noting that there are a wide range of rights that might be enjoyed in relation to an item of property, it is important to draw a more fundamental distinction between those rights and interests recognised and enforced by the law which are proprietary in nature and those which are personal. The essence of a proprietary interest is that it is a right subsisting in relation to a thing, and not as against a particular individual. For example, if Kevin owns a car, his ownership is a right which subsists in relation to the car itself. In the event that his car is stolen, and sold by the thief to Michael, his entitlement to the car persists. He can demand that it be returned to him. It has remained his throughout, irrespective of the fact that his possession was interrupted.

In contrast, a personal right is a right which is only enforceable against a specific individual. For example, a contract creates a purely personal right enforceable only against the person who made the relevant promise. If Kevin contracted to buy a specific car from a garage, and the garage subsequently sold the car to Michael, Kevin would have no rights in that car itself[12] which he could enforce against Michael. The car would not be his but Michael's and his only right would lie against the garage for breach of contract. Proprietary rights are described as rights in rem,[13] whereas personal rights are rights in personam.

### (b) The defining characteristic of proprietary rights

Whilst it is possible to point to the differing characteristics which attach to a right, depending upon whether it is personal or proprietary, it is much more difficult to identify any conceptual principle which operates to determine whether particular rights or entitlements enjoy proprietary status. To some extent, the characterisation of rights as either proprietary or personal has been a process of historical accident. For example, leases, which are in many respects merely contracts by which an owner of land agrees to allow a tenant to occupy and use it, have long been regarded as conferring a proprietary

---

[12] Unless the contract was specifically enforceable, in which case he would acquire an interest in the property by way of a constructive trust: see Chapter 9. There would be no such constructive trust in the case of a contract to purchase a readily available model of car where there would be alternatives available in the market place.

[13] Meaning 'in the thing', from the Latin word 'res', meaning 'thing'.

right in the land on the tenant. Similarly, a covenant entered into by the owner of land with a neighbouring land-owner whereby he promises to restrict the potential use to which he may put his land is regarded as a species of proprietary right known as a restrictive covenant. Because such covenants enjoy proprietary status, they are capable of binding a successor in title to the original covenantor, thus circumventing the doctrine of privity of contract which prevents the enforcement of personal contractual obligations against anyone but the original promisor. These rights have both made the transition from mere contract into property, but other contractual obligations concerning things have not made this transition. For instance, a person leasing a car or a computer must rely on contract and has no proprietary interest in the car or computer which he is renting.

In this century, the courts have shown a marked reluctance to accord proprietary status to rights traditionally characterised as personal. In *National Provincial Bank Ltd v Ainsworth*[14] a husband had deserted his wife, leaving her living in their erstwhile matrimonial home, which he owned. He subsequently mortgaged the house to a bank, realising its value for himself. The House of Lords held that although the deserted wife enjoyed a right to occupy her husband's house, known as the 'deserted wife's equity', this right was purely personal and not proprietary. Thus, it did not subsist in the house itself but only as against her husband. It was therefore incapable of detracting from the rights of the bank which had taken a mortgage.[15] In the course of his judgment Lord Wilberforce identified the essential characteristics of a property right:

'Before a right or an interest can be admitted into the category of property, or of a right affecting property, it must be definable, identifiable by third parties, capable in its nature of assumption by third parties, and have some degree of permanence or stability.'[16]

The central characteristic of a proprietary right is therefore that it is *capable* of enduring though changes in the ownership of the property to which it relates.

## (c) Examples contrasting personal and proprietary rights

*(i) Leases and licences.*[17] Although leases and licences are functionally similar, in that they both confer a right to occupy land owned by another, leases are proprietary interests whereas licences are purely personal.[18] For example, if David owns a house, grants Edward a lease and subsequently sells the house to Fiona, Edward's lease will be capable of enduring through the change of ownership so that it will detract from Fiona's ownership. She will not be entitled to evict David and he will still be able to enjoy his rights as tenant of the land.[19] His right is as effective against the land in her

---

[14] [1965] AC 1175.

[15] As an overriding interest under the Land Registration Act 1925, s 70(1)(g). See now Land Registration Act 2002, s 29.

[16] [1965] AC 1175 at 1248.

[17] See Stevens & Pearce, *Land Law* (3rd edn, 2005) Ch 9; *Street v Mountford* [1985] AC 809; *Bruton London & Quadrant Housing Trust* [2001] 1 AC 406.

[18] See *Ashburn Anstalt v W. J. Arnold & Co* [1989] Ch 1.

[19] In some instances the lease will not be binding owing to special registration roles of land law, which are beyond the scope of this book.

hands as it was when David was the owner. However, if instead David had granted Edward a mere licence to occupy the house, he would have had no proprietary interest in the land but a personal right to occupy enforceable only against David. Such a right could not detract from Fiona's ownership rightfully acquired from David. Vis-à-vis Fiona, Edward would be a trespasser, and his only remedy would be an action for damages for breach of contract against David.[20] As has already been noted, the courts have rejected the suggestion that contractual licences should be elevated to the status of proprietary rights.[21]

*(ii) Retention of title clauses.*[22] When one party enters into a contract for the supply of goods to another, an important question is the time at which the title to the goods passes from the buyer to the seller. Once the title to the goods has passed the seller retains no entitlement to the goods themselves, but has only a personal contractual claim against the buyer for the payment of the price. However, if the contract contains a 'retention of title clause' the seller will retain a proprietary interest in the goods supplied even after they have been delivered, until the price has been paid. Such entitlement will be of particular importance if the buyer becomes insolvent after delivery but before payment. If the property in the goods has passed he will rank only as one of the buyer's creditors, and is likely to receive only a small percentage of the amount owed. However, if he has retained his proprietary interest in the goods he will be able to claim them as his own, and they will not form part of the buyer's assets available for distribution amongst his general creditors. For example, in *Aluminium Industrie Vaassen BV v Romalpa Aluminium Ltd*[23] the plaintiffs supplied the defendants with aluminium foil, of which the defendants had stock worth £50,000. Under the terms of the contract, title was not to pass to the defendants until they had paid all that was owing to the plaintiffs, and they were required to store the foil in such a way that it could be identified as the plaintiffs' property. It was held that the plaintiffs were entitled to the foil in the defendants' hands. This has been followed in subsequent cases, for example *Hendy Lennox (Industrial Engines) Ltd v Grahame Puttick Ltd.*[24] Here, the plaintiffs sold engines to the defendants with the contract containing a retention of title clause until the full purchase price had been paid. The defendants became insolvent, and owed the plaintiffs some £46,000. They were unlikely to recover anything in an insolvency, as the defendants owed the debenture holders some £700,000. However, they were held entitled to claim one engine remaining on the defendants' premises which had not been appropriated to any contract of sub-sale. This proprietary right stands in contrast to the purely personal right to the repayment of the money owed.[25]

---

[20] Unless Fiona was bound by a constructive trust: see Chapter 9 and *Ashburn Anstalt v Arnold* [1989] Ch 1. See also *Strand Securities v Caswell* [1965] Ch 958, CA.

[21] *Ashburn Anstalt v Arnold* [1989] Ch 1

[22] See Worthington, *Proprietary Interests in Commercial Transactions* (1996,) pp 7–42.

[23] [1976] 1 WLR 676.      [24] [1984] 1 WLR 485.

[25] See also *Borden (UK) Ltd v Scottish Timber Products Ltd* [1981] Ch 25; *Re Peachdart Ltd* [1984] Ch 131; *Re Andrabell Ltd* [1984] 3 All ER 407; *Clough Mill Ltd v Martin* [1985] 1 WLR 111; *Armour v Thyssen Edelstahlwerke AG* [1991] 2 AC 339, HL; *Re Weddell New Zealand Ltd* (1995) 5 NZBLC 104.555; *Chaigley Farms Ltd v Crawford, Kaye & Grayshire Ltd* [1996] BCC 957; [1997] CLJ 28 (Sealey).

*(iii) Loans and trusts.* Retention of title clauses apply to the delivery of physical goods. Similar principles have also been developed where a loan of money was made. If one person loans money to another, their relationship as creditor and debtor respectively is one of contract only. For example, if a bank lends £10,000 to a company, and the company uses the money to buy a car for its managing director, the bank can have no claim to the car. Instead, it enjoys a purely personal right to repayment of the debt by the company. However, in some circumstances where a loan has been made, it has been held that the lender retains a proprietary interest in the money lent. This is particularly important if the creditor subsequently becomes insolvent. For example, if a bank makes a loan to a company for a specific purpose, such as for the payment of a dividend declared on its shares[26] or the purchase of new machinery,[27] with a stipulation that the money is only to be used for that purpose, the bank retains a proprietary interest in the money lent by way of a resulting trust.[28] If the purpose fails and the company goes into liquidation, the bank will be able to claim the return of the specific money lent. In the absence of such a proprietary right, the money would form part of the general assets of the company to be distributed on insolvency, and the bank would be limited to a personal claim for repayment, ranking as one of the company's general creditors.

## (d) Proprietary and personal rights in the context of insolvency[29]

As has been evident in the last two examples, the significance of the distinction between personal and proprietary rights is especially important where the person against whom a right is claimed is insolvent. If it can be shown that the claimant enjoys a proprietary right to some specific asset in the bankrupt's possession, it will not form part of the bankrupt's general assets for distribution amongst his creditors. As such he will gain priority over all the other creditors, and avoid the basic principle that all unsecured creditors should share their losses pari passu (ie equally). The practical importance of proprietary claims in such cases is well illustrated by the facts of *Chase Manhattan Bank NA v Israel-British Bank (London) Ltd.*[30] Chase Manhattan owed the defendants $1m, which they paid. Unfortunately, due to a clerical error, they paid the same amount again a day later. The Israeli-British Bank subsequently became insolvent and Chase Manhattan sought to recover the $1m that had been overpaid. There was no doubt that Chase Manhattan were entitled to return of the money paid by mistake by way of a claim to restitution. Such a restitutionary claim was personal in nature, imposing an obligation on the payee to return the mistaken payment to the payor. A personal claim would not enable Chase Manhattan to recover the whole of the money paid because Chase Manhattan would have to share any assets with the other creditors in the insolvency. The court held that Chase Manhattan were entitled to assert a proprietary claim to the overpaid $1m which was still held by the insolvent bank by way of a constructive trust, and were thus entitled to the return of the sum mistakenly paid in full. As the $1m did not form part of the bankrupt's assets, it was not to be divided amongst their

---

[26] *Barclays Bank plc v Quistclose Investments Ltd* [1970] AC 567, HL.
[27] *Re EVTR Ltd* [1987] BCLC 646.     [28] See Chapter 8.     [29] See [1995] CLJ 377 (Oakley).
[30] [1981] Ch 105.

creditors. In this way Chase Manhattan were able to gain priority over the rights of the other creditors of the Israeli-British Bank.

It is by no means clear the court was right to find that Chase Manhattan enjoyed a proprietary right by way of a trust in the money mistakenly paid, but this is an issue that will be examined in the context of the creation of trust interests. For the moment it is sufficient to illustrate the importance of establishing a proprietary right where a person against whom a claim is maintained is insolvent. The automatic priority gained over general creditors where a proprietary right can be asserted has been a major factor motivating plaintiffs to assert, and the courts to recognise, equitable interests in commercial contexts where previously it might have been thought that no such rights existed.

## 4  Equitable proprietary rights[31]

Proprietary rights described as 'equitable' are those which were historically recognised and enforced by the Courts of Chancery,[32] or have been developed by process of extension from such rights. In contrast, legal proprietary rights are those which were historically recognised and enforced by the common law courts. As has been seen, following the Judicature Acts[33] the courts are required to give effect to both legal and equitable proprietary rights, and legal and equitable rights together form a coherent law of property. By far the most important of the proprietary rights developed by equity is the trust.

### (1)  Equitable proprietary rights corresponding to legal rights

The common law only recognised the creation of proprietary rights if appropriate formalities were satisfied. This generally required the grant of the right using the special formality of a deed.[34] For example, under the Real Property Act 1845, a legal lease would not be created unless made by deed.[35] Today, a legal mortgage must be created by means of a charge by deed.[36] Similarly, a legal easement will only be created by an express or implied grant by deed.[37] However, equity, which looks to the substance rather than the form of transactions, was prepared to recognise and enforce proprietary interests even if the requisite formalities for creation at law had not been observed. It has already been seen that equity regards a mere contract for a lease as creating an equitable

---

[31] See (1955) 19 Conv 343 (Crane), cited by Lord Upjohn in *National Provincial Bank Ltd v Ainsworth* [1965] AC 1175 at 1238.

[32] See Chapter 1.      [33] See above, p 9.

[34] This originally required the document to be 'signed, sealed and delivered'. Because of this, the grant was sometimes said to be made 'under seal'. See now Law of Property (Miscellaneous Provisions) Act 1989, s 1.

[35] See now Law of Property Act 1925, s 2(1). By s 52(2)(d) and s 54(2) there is no need for a deed for the creation of a legal lease for less than three years at the best rent which can reasonably be obtained.

[36] Law of Property Act 1925, s 85(1).

[37] A legal easement may also be acquired by statute or prescription.

lease despite the absence of a deed.[38] Similarly, a contract to create an easement will give rise to an equitable easement[39] and a contract to create a legal mortgage will generate an equitable mortgage if the money advanced is paid to the mortgagor.[40]

## (2) Equitable proprietary rights without a legal equivalent

The creativity of equity also allowed it to develop proprietary interests which were not parasitic equivalents of correspondent common law rights. For example, in law the burden of a covenant affecting the use of freehold land is enforceable only against the original covenantor because of the doctrine of privity of contract.[41] However, following *Tulk v Moxhay*,[42] equity elevated freehold covenants restrictive of the owner's use of his land to the status of proprietary interests, with the consequence that they are capable of passing with the title of the land so as to bind subsequent purchasers.[43] Other contracts concerning rights over land have also been given the status of proprietary interests rather than merely personal rights. An equitable mortgage could be created by the simple deposit of the title deeds to the property with the mortgagee.[44] Similarly, a contract to purchase an interest in land is an equitable proprietary interest known as an 'estate contract', which will be binding against subsequent purchasers of the land, subject to any legislative requirements of registration.[45]

## (3) Equitable ownership

Alongside equitable proprietary interests such as leases, mortgages and restrictive covenants, equity spawned a general right of ownership of property through the development of the trust. Where property is subject to a trust, equity treats the persons for whose benefit the trust exists as the owners of the property, even though they are not the owners of it at law. Where property is subject to a trust, there is a duality of ownership, or 'double dominium', and a distinction must be drawn between the legal ownership and the equitable ownership. This capacity for dual ownership at law and in equity is the most distinctive feature of English property law. It emerged as a product of the historical divide between equity and the common law. Duality of ownership of property is the essential characteristic of a trust. A person enjoying the legal ownership of the trust property is referred to as a 'trustee', and a person enjoying the equitable ownership is a 'beneficiary'. The majority of this book will be devoted to an examination of the modern trust, and in particular to the means by which such a relationship

---

[38] *Parker v Taswell* (1858) 2 De G & J 559; *Walsh v Lonsdale* (1882) 21 LR Ch D 9.

[39] *McManus v Cooke* (1887) 35 Ch D 681; *May v Belleville* [1905] 2 Ch 605.

[40] *Tebb v Hodge* (1869) LR 5 CP 73.

[41] *Austerberry v Oldham Corpn* (1885) 29 Ch D 750, CA; *Rhone v Stephens* [1994] 2 AC 310.

[42] (1848) 2 Ph 774.

[43] For some reason, English law has failed to recognise restrictions on the use of land as capable of existing as easements, the nearest equivalent right recognised by the common law.

[44] *Russel v Russel* (1783) 1 Bro CC 269. Following the Law of Property (Miscellaneous Provisions) Act 1989, the contract supporting this equitable mortgage must be made in writing.

[45] See *Midland Bank Trust Co Ltd (No 1) v Green* [1981] AC 513, HL.

can be brought into existence and the nature of the rights and duties of trustees and beneficiaries. The remainder of this sub-section will consider the genesis of the trust in the Chancery courts.

## (a) History of the trust[46]

*(i) The feudal system of land holding.*[47] An understanding of the origins of the trust requires an elementary grasp of the feudal system of landowning operative during the medieval period. All land was technically owned by the King, whilst others enjoyed the right to use it as tenants. Individuals were granted 'tenure' of land by their 'over-lord', who would himself enjoy tenure from his 'over-lord'. These levels of tenure formed a feudal pyramid of landholdings stretching from the King, who was at its pinnacle because he had no 'over-lord', downwards. The terms of 'tenure' defined the conditions under which the tenant was entitled to enjoy the land, generally requiring the performance of services on behalf of his lord. These might include the provision of military forces,[48] religious functions[49] or agricultural services.[50] On the death of a tenant, the person who succeeded to his tenure and thereby inherited his position on the feudal ladder was required to make a payment to his over-lord. These medieval inheritance taxes, termed 'feudal incidents', provided the Crown with a significant source of revenue. Whilst the doctrine of tenure defined the terms under which land was held, the parallel doctrine of 'estates' determined the duration for which a grant of tenure was to last.[51] An estate in fee simple[52] was a grant of tenure for ever, and within the feudal structure the right to tenure of land in fee simple was tantamount to absolute ownership.

*(ii) Development of the 'use'.* In the context of this feudal structure, the ancestor of the modern trust, the 'use', was developed by the Chancery courts. If land was conveyed to X 'to the use of Y' this had the effect that, whilst X became the owner of the land, X was obliged to apply it for the benefit of Y and was prevented from treating it as his own. X was termed the 'feoffee' and Y the 'cestui que use'. The common law did not recognise, and would not enforce, a 'use' of land, but rather regarded the feoffee, in whom the legal estate was vested, as the absolute owner. From the perspective of equity, however, the feoffee was bound in conscience to apply the property for the benefit of the cestui que use, because of the undertaking he had given. The Court of Chancery was

---

[46] See Holdsworth, *History of English Law* (7th edn, 1956), pp 407–480; Baker, *Introduction to English Legal History* (2nd edn, 1979), pp 210–219 and 242–244. See also (1998) 61 MLR 162 (Pottage).

[47] See Gray & Gray, *Elements of Land Law* (3rd edn, 2001), pp 72–77; Cheshire and Burn, *Modern Law of Real Property* (16th edn, 2000), pp 9–38.

[48] Eg the tenure of 'Knight's service' which required the provision of armed horsemen for battle.

[49] 'Spiritual tenure'.

[50] Tenures in socage.

[51] See *Walsingham's Case* (1579) 2 Plowd 547 at 555: 'the land itself is one thing, and an estate in the land is another thing, for an estate in the land is a time in the land, or land for a time, and there are diversities of estates, which are no more than diversities of time . . .'

[52] To be distinguished from a 'fee tail' (or 'entailed interest'), which was only to last for so long as the grantee had lineal descendants, and the life interest, which was only to last for the length of the grantee's life.

therefore prepared to enforce the use in personam, requiring the feoffee to apply the property vested in him to the benefit of the cestui que use. Equity did not deny the reality of the ownership of the feoffee at common law, but instead prevented him from exercising the entitlements concomitant with his legal ownership in a manner inconsistent with the interests of the cestui que use. Thus, the use shared a central characteristic of the modern trust, namely that the formal ownership of the property subject to it was separated from the right to enjoy the benefit derived from such ownership. The use evolved as a popular mechanism for landholding because of the positive advantages it offered. It provided a means of making gifts to charities that were technically unable to own property. For example, the monastic order of St Francis was forbidden to own property by its rule, but land could be given to feoffees for its use. Though technically it would not 'own' the property, it would be entitled to derive the benefits flowing from such ownership. A landowner could avoid the strict legal rules of inheritance by directing feoffees in his will to hold the land as he wished. The use also offered a mechanism for primitive tax-planning through the avoidance of feudal dues. If land was vested in a group of feoffees, who would never die as a group because each individual feoffee would be replaced on death, the legal title would never have to be pass by way of succession. The feudal incidents payable on inheritance would thus be avoided altogether.

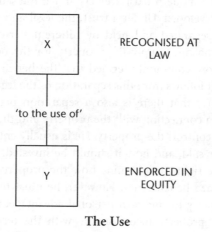

The Use

*(iii) The development of the trust.* The financial advantages attendant upon a use were so attractive to landowners that by 1500 the majority of land in England was held in use.[53] This inevitably led to a serious diminution in the King's feudal revenue. In order to close this tax-avoidance loophole, legislation (the Statute of Uses 1535) was introduced to abolish uses by 'executing' them, ie vesting the legal estate in the cestui que use. However, it did not take the ingenuity of lawyers long to find ways around the Statute of Uses and, indeed, to turn it to their advantage. The statute did not apply to uses where the feoffee had active duties to perform, for example the collection and distribution of profits and the management of an estate.[54] A further means to avoiding

[53] YB Mich 15 Hen VII, 13, p 1, per Frowyk Sjt.
[54] A use of leasehold land, a term of years, was also not executed.

'execution' of a use under the statute was to create a double use, termed a 'use upon a use', whereby the legal estate in land would be conveyed 'to X, to the use of Y, to the use of Z'. Although the first use would be executed by the Statute of Uses, so that Y would be treated as the legal owner, the second use remained unexecuted. The Court of Chancery would then enforce the second use, requiring Y to hold the land for the benefit of Z. This second use was termed a 'trust', providing the modern terminology.[55] The 'use upon a use' was accepted as valid by the latter part of the sixteenth century,[56] by which time it had come to serve different social functions than the mere avoidance of feudal dues. Common objectives were to protect estates from spendthrift sons, and to enable married women to enjoy property independently of their husbands. The effect of the trust to avoid the execution of uses was so successful that in 1739 Lord Hardwicke was able to observe that the Statute of Uses 'has had no other effect than to add at most, three words to a conveyance'.[57] Although the trust had emerged as a recognised legal instrument by the end of the sixteenth century, it flourished in the nineteenth century, when it served as the foundation for property holding by families and as a device to preserve family estates.

## (b) The modern trust

The cardinal features of a modern trust are very much the same as those of the early use from which it has developed. Under a trust, the legal and equitable ownership of the trust property are separated and held by different persons.[58] The legal title is vested in the trustee, who must apply the property for the benefit of someone else, the cestui que trust, more commonly termed the 'the beneficiary', who is regarded as the equitable owner. It follows from this separation of the legal and equitable owner-ship of the trust property that there is also a separation between the management responsibilities arising in connection with the property and the enjoyment thereof. As legal owner, the trustee controls the property. He is usually entitled to decide whether it should be retained or sold, and how it should be invested. In some types of trust the trustee even has the right to determine how the property should be distributed amongst a class of defined beneficiaries. However, he must not exercise his rights to deal with the trust property for his own personal advantage, and equity will prevent him applying the trust property inconsistently with the terms of the trust, which define the entitlement of the beneficiary or beneficiaries. This capacity of the trust to separate the management of property from its enjoyment, while preserving the own-ership of both the trustee and beneficiary, renders it a perfect vehicle to facilitate complex arrangements involving property, as will be seen in the following chapters. Its tremendous flexibility has enabled it to adapt through the centuries and into new social and commercial contexts. Maitland was of the opinion that the trust was 'the greatest and most distinctive achievement performed by Englishmen in the field of jurisprudence'.

---

[55]  In fact, the term was also used for a single 'use' prior to the development of the 'use upon a use'.
[56]  See (1966) 82 LQR 215 (Barton); (1977) 93 LQR 33 (Baker).
[57]  *Hopkins v Hopkins* (1739) 1 Atk 581.      [58]  *Selby v Alston* (1797) 3 Ves 339.

## (4) Mere equities

Equity further recognises a category of entitlements described as 'equities' or 'mere equities'. This terminology is intended to distinguish them from fullblown equitable proprietary interests. They have been held to include the right to have a transaction set aside for fraud[59] or undue influence,[60] the right to have a document rectified[61] and the deserted wife's right to occupy the matrimonial home.[62] When mere equities relate to property, they have a limited capacity to affect third parties who acquire ownership of it, but they are not true interests in the property itself.

# 5  The durability of proprietary rights[63]

As has been noted above, one of the defining characteristics of a proprietary right is that it is capable of enduring through changes in the ownership the thing to which it relates. However, the durability of a specific proprietary right will depend upon its character. Different rules developed in equity and the common law to govern the durability of their respective proprietary rights. In general, legal rights are more durable than their equitable equivalents. A statutory scheme has been introduced which determines issues of priority between legal and equitable rights and interests in land, the details of which are beyond the scope of this text, but the traditional rules developed by equity and the common law remain operative in relation to personal property.

## (1) Legal ownership

Of all types of ownership, legal ownership is the most durable, subject to a few exceptions at common law and to rather more which have been introduced by statute. The basic rule is that the ownership or rights of a legal owner will continue indefinitely until the owner has transferred them to someone else. Where two people claim legal rights to the same thing, the better rights are those of the person with the earlier claim. So, for instance, if Alf steals a car belonging to Mary and sells it to Peter, neither Alf nor Peter become the owner of the car. It continues to belong to Mary. If Peter still has the car in his hands, Mary can demand that it be returned to her, vindicating her continuing legal ownership. Only if the car is destroyed will Mary's legal ownership be terminated, as there will no longer be any subject matter in which the right can continue to subsist.

There are some other situations in which a legal owner can lose legal ownership against his will. For instance, a special rule which applies to currency (coins of the realm and banknotes) is that even a thief can pass ownership in them to someone who takes

---

[59]  *Ernest v Vivian* (1863) 33 LJ Ch 513.
[60]  *Bainbrigge v Browne* (1881) 18 Ch D 188; *Barclays Bank v O'Brien* [1994] 1 AC 180.
[61]  *Shiloh Spinners Ltd v Harding (No 1)* [1973] AC 691 at 721, per Lord Wilberforce.
[62]  *National Provincial Bank Ltd v Ainsworth* [1965] AC 1175.
[63]  See Worthington, *Personal Property Law* (2000), pp 457–473.

them in good faith and for value. Another special rule which applies to land is that a legal owner's right can be defeated by a person who takes physical possession without permission for a sufficient period of time. After twelve years of such 'adverse possession' the owner's rights are extinguished by s 15 of the Limitation Act 1980, which provides that he may no longer bring an action to vindicate his rights. In effect, this allows a squatter to steal land from an owner who has failed to take steps to protect his rights. This is a special rule which applies only to land. In relation to a chattel, legal ownership will only be displaced by a third party taking possession if the owner had previously abandoned it.[64] When a chattel has been lost, a finder will not acquire a right to it superior to that of the legal owner.[65]

In relation to some forms of property, such as land or shares, legal ownership is determined by means of a register. In such cases the statutory rule is that the person registered is the owner, even where that registration has wrongly been obtained. For instance, if a thief forges a transfer of land into his own name, and has himself registered, then he becomes the owner, even though the person he has swindled has the right to have the error in the register rectified. Until that rectification, by virtue of the statutory rule, the person registered is deemed to be the legal owner.

Apart from those situations where a special rule applies, the rule relating to legal ownership is therefore that 'legal rights bind the world'. In consequence, where two people can assert a claim with a lawful origin, 'the first in time prevails'.

## (2) Subsidiary legal proprietary rights

Although ownership is the most significant legal proprietary interest, it has been seen that other subsidiary proprietary interests can exist with legal status. For example, if Trevor, the legal owner of land, grants Ursula a legal lease, her lease will obviously bind Trevor and detract from his right to enjoy the immediate possession and enjoyment of his land. If Trevor sells the land to Victor, so that Victor becomes the legal owner, the principle that 'legal rights bind the world' ensures that her lease will equally bind Victor. The mere fact that he acquired legal title to the land from Trevor is incapable of defeating it. Trevor's rights are the first in time, but he has transferred them in part to Ursula. The sale to Victor is subject to Ursula's rights because her rights were created before he acquired his. As between Ursula and Victor, Ursula's rights are the first in time, and therefore prevail over Victor's.

This simple rule that legal rights bind the world was abandoned in the context of rights and interests in land when a system of registration was introduced in 1925. In many cases, the system of registration has the effect that subsidiary proprietary rights, such as long leases and mortgages, can only be validly created with legal status if they are entered on the register of title of the land they affect. If not so registered they take effect in equity only. Those rights which can be created at law without the need for registration, for example leases for a period of less than twenty-one years and easements, tend to be binding on any subsequent transferee of the land because they are accorded the status of overriding interests under s 70(1) of the Land Registration Act

---

[64] *The Crystal* [1894] AC 508.    [65] *Parker v British Airways Board* [1982] QB 1004.

1925. As such, their durability is statutory rather in consequence of their intrinsic legal character.

## (3) Equitable proprietary rights[66]

### (a) Priority between equitable interests

Equity followed the law when it was dealing with the relative status of claims based in equity. It therefore accepted the principle that competing claims should be judged on the footing that where they all had a lawful origin 'the first in time prevails'. For instance, suppose that before the rules were changed by the introduction of registration systems, Oliver, the owner of a freehold cottage, had contracted to sell it both to Peter and to Paul, and they each sought an order for specific performance. The court would have granted the decree in favour of the first of them to have signed a binding contract with Oliver. The other would have to make do with a remedy in damages against Oliver.

### (b) The doctrine of notice

When it came to dealing with the relative status of rights, some of which were legal and some equitable, equity again adopted the root philosophy that they should be judged in accordance with the time order of their creation. However, this philosophy is applied with one very important qualification. A pre-existing equitable interest will not subsist in property which is acquired by a bona fide purchaser of a legal interest who was not aware at the time of its acquisition of the earlier equitable interest. This principle is known as the 'doctrine of notice'. To pursue the example used above, if Trevor had granted Ursula an equitable rather than a legal lease, and subsequently sold the legal title of his land to Victor, Ursula's equitable lease would not have been binding against the land in Victor's hands if he had not known of its existence when he purchased the legal title. An equitable interest which is so defeated by the operation of the doctrine of notice is extinguished and no longer exists.

The operation of the doctrine of notice to destroy equitable proprietary interests is rooted in concepts of good conscience. In the view of equity, a person who was aware of a pre-existing interest subsisting in property cannot acquire it free from such interest. He has no grounds for complaint when equity requires him to continue to give effect to it because he knew what he was getting. Only if he purchased the property without knowing of its existence is his conscience unaffected so as to justify the conclusion that he should not be bound by it. As Lord Browne-Wilkinson explained in *Barclays Bank plc v O'Brien*:[67]

'The doctrine of notice lies at the heart of equity. Given that there are two innocent parties, each enjoying rights, the earlier right prevails against the later right if the enquirer of the later right knows of the earlier right (actual notice) or would have discovered it had he taken

---

[66] *London and South Western Rly Co v Gomm* (1882) 20 Ch D 562; *Re Nisbet and Potts' Contract* [1906] 1 Ch 386.
[67] [1994] 1 AC 180.

proper steps (constructive notice). In particular, if the party asserting that he takes free of the earlier rights of another knows of certain facts which put him on enquiry as to the possible existence of the rights of that other and he fails to make such enquiry or take such other steps as are reasonable to verify whether such earlier right does or does not exist, he will have constructive notice of the earlier right and take subject to it.'

### (c) Requirements of the equitable doctrine of notice

The equitable doctrine of notice only operates in favour of a person who can demonstrate that he was the bona fide purchaser of the legal ownership of the property for value without notice. Each component element of this formula must be satisfied.

*(i) Bona fides.* The doctrine of notice only operates in favour of a person who acted in good faith. However this requirement adds little to the element that he must not have notice of the equitable interests in the property.

*(ii) Purchase for value.* The doctrine of notice will only operate in favour of a person who purchased the property in which there was a pre-existing equitable interest for valuable consideration. The concept of consideration in equity is different to that at common law. In equity, nominal consideration, which would be sufficient to establish an enforceable contractual obligation at common law,[68] is insufficient. It follows from this requirement of valuable consideration that the doctrine of notice will never operate in favour of a volunteer. Thus, a person who receives property by way of gift or succession will always acquire the legal ownership subject to any pre-existing equitable interests.

*(iii) Of the legal title.* The doctrine of notice only protects a purchaser of the legal title to the property. In the case of land, the purchase must be of a legal estate or interest.[69] A person who purchases an equitable interest in property will therefore take subject to all other pre-existing equitable interests, since between competing equitable entitlements 'the first in time prevails'.

*(iv) Without notice.*[70] This is the most important of the requirements. It concerns the extent to which the purchaser was aware or ignorant of the existence of any pre-existing equitable interests subsisting in the property acquired. Clearly, he will have 'notice' of such interests if he consciously knew of their existence, for example if the seller had informed him. Such awareness is termed 'actual notice'. However, the concept of notice has been given a wider ambit in equity, so that a person is treated as if he was actually aware of all pre-existing equitable interests that he would have discovered if he had taken all reasonable steps to investigate the property concerned by making 'such inquiries and inspections . . . as ought reasonably to have been made'.[71] This prevents

---

[68] Eg a peppercorn. However, there is no need for the consideration to be 'adequate' as equity only insists that the consideration be valuable. Marriage consideration is also regarded as valuable consideration in equity.
[69] Under the Law of Property Act 1925 s 1 this means a fee simple absolute in possession (freehold) or a terms of years absolute (leasehold) or one of the subsidiary legal interests listed in the section.
[70] See Law of Property Act 1925, s 199.
[71] Law of Property Act 1925, s 199(1)(ii)(*a*). See *Jones v Smith* (1841) 1 Hare 43; *Northern Bank Ltd v Henry* [1981] IR 1.

a person claiming the benefit of the doctrine of notice simply by seeking to avoid receiving actual notice of such rights. Such deemed notice is termed 'constructive notice'. A person will also be treated as having notice if the purchase was conducted by an agent acting on his behalf if the agent had actual or constructive notice of the existence of the equitable interest. Such notice is termed 'imputed notice'.

### (d) Destruction of equitable proprietary interests by the doctrine of notice

Where all the requisite elements of the doctrine of notice are satisfied, it operates so as to completely destroy any subsisting equitable interests in the property concerned. Even if the property is subsequently transferred to a person with notice of the relevant interest, it will not revive. This can be seen from the facts of *Wilkes v Spooner*.[72] Spooner was the tenant of a pork butcher's shop. Wilkes was the beneficiary of an equitable restrictive covenant, affecting the shop, preventing its use as a general butcher's. Spooner surrendered his lease of the shop to the landlord.[73] As the landlord was unaware of the restrictive covenant he was protected by the doctrine of notice, with the consequence that his legal ownership was not encumbered by it. Subsequently, the landlord granted a new lease of the shop to Spooner's son, who had actual notice of the restriction. Since the doctrine of notice had operated so as to destroy the right altogether, he too acquired the shop free from the restriction.

## (4)  Trusts and the doctrine of notice

It has been noted above that when property is subject to a trust the beneficiaries enjoy the equitable ownership thereof. As proprietary rights with equitable character, such beneficial interests arising under a trust are equally subject to the operation of the doctrine of notice. If the trustee transfers the trust property to a bona fide purchaser who was unaware that it was subject to a trust, that person will acquire his legal title free from the entitlements of the beneficiaries. He will be the absolute and unencumbered legal owner of the property. The beneficiaries will be entitled to a person remedy for breach of trust against the trustee if the trust property was wrongfully transferred, but they will have no continuing proprietary entitlements in the erstwhile trust property.

### (a)  Trusts of personal property

Where personal property is subject to a trust, the doctrine of notice operates, so that a bona fide purchase of the trust property will entirely destroy the proprietary interest of the beneficiaries. For example, if Robert holds shares on trust and sells and transfers them to Kevin, the equitable entitlement of the beneficiaries will be destroyed if Kevin had no knowledge, actual or constructive, that Robert was holding the shares as a trustee. The extension of the principles of constructive notice to commercial

---

[72] [1911] 2 KB 473.

[73] The surrender of the lease satisfied the requirement that the landlord be a purchaser of a legal estate for value.

transactions involving personal property rather than land has sometimes been questioned. In *Manchester Trust v Furness* Lindley LJ stated:

'The equitable doctrines of constructive notice are common enough in dealing with land and estates with which the Court is familiar; but there has always been repeated protest against the introduction into commercial transactions of anything like an extension of those doctrines and the protest is founded on perfect good sense. In dealing with estates in land title is everything and it can be leisurely investigated; in commercial transactions possession is everything and there is no time to investigate title; and if we were to extend the doctrine of constructive notice to commercial transactions we should be doing infinite mischief and paralysing the trade of the country.'[74]

However, the better view seems to be that the principle of constructive notice operates even where a commercial purchaser acquired legal title to personal property. In *Macmillan Inc v Bishopsgate Investment Trust Plc*[75] shares were held on trust for Macmillan by Bishopsgate Investment Trust (BIT), an investment trust controlled by Robert Maxwell. In breach of trust, and without the consent or knowledge of Macmillan, BIT transferred legal title to the trust shares to various banks and financial institutions as security for the debts of other Maxwell companies. Millet J held that, if English law applied,[76] the transferees of these shares would only have acquired them free from the equitable interests of Macmillan if they had no constructive notice that they were trust shares:

'It is true that many distinguished judges in the past have warned against the extension of the equitable doctrine of constructive notice to commercial transactions . . . but they were obviously referring to the doctrine in its strict conveyancing sense with its many refinements and its insistence on a proper investigation of title in every case. The relevance of constructive notice in its wider meaning cannot depend on whether the transaction is "commercial": the provision of secured overdraft facilities to a corporate managing director is equally "commercial" whether the security consists of the managing director's house or his private investments. The difference is that in one case there is, and in the other there is not, a recognised procedure for investigating the mortgagor's title which the creditor ignores at his peril.'[77]

Whilst this affirms the relevance of constructive notice to transactions involving personal property, it makes clear that the level of inquiry and investigation reasonably to be expected from a purchaser varies in relation to the nature and context of the transaction in issue. Where there is no recognised procedure for investigation into the title of the type of property offered for sale, a bona fide purchaser will satisfy the requirements of the doctrine of notice unless he had actual knowledge of the existence of the trust, was suspicious that the seller did not have the right to transfer, or had reason to know or be suspicious. If there is a recognised procedure the purchaser will not be protected by the doctrine of notice if he has failed to follow it.

---

[74] [1895] 2 QB 539 at 545.    [75] [1995] 3 All ER 747.

[76] In the event, he concluded that the priority of proprietary rights to the shares was to be determined by the law of New York. See: (1996) 59 MLR 741 (Stevens).

[77] (1996) 59 MLR 741 at 769.

## (b) Trusts of land

*(i) Priority determined by the doctrine of notice.* Historically, issues of priority between competing interests in land were also governed by application of the twin principle that the first in time prevailed, subject to the equitable doctrine of notice. A bona fide purchaser for value without notice of a legal estate in land would take free from any pre-existing equitable interests. For example, in *Pilcher v Rawlins*[78] trustees held £8,373 on trust for Jeremiah Pilcher which they lent to Rawlins by way of a mortgage. The mortgage was secured by the transfer of the legal title to the mortgaged land to the trustees. The trustees subsequently re-conveyed the legal title to Rawlins to enable him to fraudulently borrow a further £10,000 by granting a mortgage to Stockwell and Lambe. Jeremiah Pilcher, as beneficiary of the trust, claimed that Stockwell and Lambe were bound to observe the trust. However, the Court of Appeal held that they were bona fide purchasers without notice of the existence of the trust. They had therefore acquired their legal mortgage free from his equitable interest. James LJ explained:

'I propose simply to apply myself to the case of a purchaser for valuable consideration, without notice, obtaining, upon the occasion of his purchase, and by means of his purchase deed, some legal estate, some legal right, some legal advantage; and according to my view of the established law of this court, such a purchaser's plea of a purchase for valuable consideration without notice is an absolute, unqualified, unanswerable defence, and an unanswerable plea to the jurisdiction of this court.'

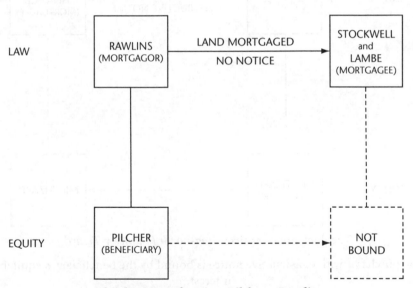

The doctrine of notice: *Pilcher v Rawlins*

**The bona fide purchaser without notice is not bound by the beneficiary's equitable interest.**

---

[78] (1871–72) LR 7 Ch App 259.

In contrast, a purchaser with notice, whether actual or constructive, will be required to yield priority to a beneficiary of a pre-existing trust. In *Kingsnorth Finance Co Ltd v Tizard*[79] a husband held the legal title to his matrimonial home on trust for himself and his wife. After they separated she no longer lived at the house, although she visited for part of each day. He mortgaged the house and absconded with the money raised. Prior to accepting a mortgage, the mortgage company had sent a surveyor to inspect the house. He visited on a Sunday afternoon, a time arranged by the husband when he knew that his wife would not be present. He told the surveyor that he and his wife had separated many months before and that she had no interest in the property. The court held that in these circumstances the mortgage company was bound by the wife's equitable interest under the trust. It had not made all the inquiries that were reasonably required from a potential mortgagee, and it was therefore affixed with constructive notice. Judge John Finlay QC concluded that the inspection had been inadequate:

'What is such an inspection "as ought reasonably to be made" must, I think, depend on all the circumstances. In the circumstances of the present case I am not satisfied that the pre-arranged inspection on a Sunday afternoon fell within the category of "such inspections which ought reasonably to have been made", the words in s 199 of the Law of Property Act 1925 . . .'[80]

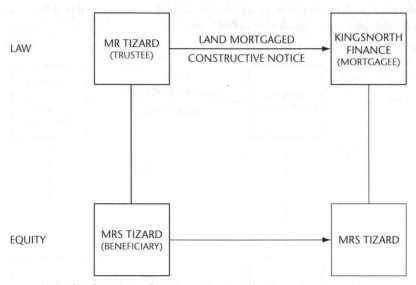

The doctrine of notice: *Kingsnorth Finance v Tizard*

**The purchaser with constructive notice is bound by the beneficiary's equitable interest.**

*(ii) Priority determined by statute.* Statutory reform, starting in 1925 and culminating in the Land Registration Act 2002, has largely displaced the doctrine of notice as a means of determining whether a purchaser of land acquires his legal title free from

---

[79] [1986] 1 WLR 783; [1986] Conv 283 (Thompson).    [80] [1986] 1 WLR 783 at 795.

pre-existing equitable trust interests. The Law of Property Act 1925 provides that where land is held on trust the interests of the beneficiaries are automatically eliminated if it is transferred to a purchaser who pays any purchase moneys arising to two or more trustees holding the legal title. This process is called 'overreaching', and it operates irrespective of whether the purchaser had knowledge, actual or constructive, of the existence of the trust. When overreaching occurs the beneficiaries' equitable interests are not eliminated altogether, but they are displaced from the land and continue to subsist as rights in rem only in the purchase moneys paid to the trustees. Where overreaching occurs, a purchaser of land need not be concerned by the possible existence of any trusts affecting the land he acquires. He can be sure that, provided any purchase money arising from the transaction is paid to two trustees, no pre-existing trust interests will endure in the land to affect his legal ownership. The operation and effect of overreaching were considered in *City of London Building Society v Flegg*.[81] A house had been purchased in the name of Mr and Mrs Maxwell-Brown with the financial help of Mrs Maxwell-Brown's parents, Mr and Mrs Flegg. Mr and Mrs Maxwell-Brown therefore held the house on trust for themselves and Mr and Mrs Flegg. The Maxwell-Browns subsequently mortgaged the house to the Building Society without the Fleggs' consent or knowledge. The House of Lords held that since Mr and Mrs Maxwell-Brown were trustees for sale, and since the mortgage company had advanced the money borrowed to them, the Fleggs' equitable interest had been overreached.

Where trust interests in land are not overreached by a transfer of the legal title, for example if the land was owned by a sole trustee so that the qualifying condition of payment to two or more trustees was not satisfied,[82] the question whether the trust

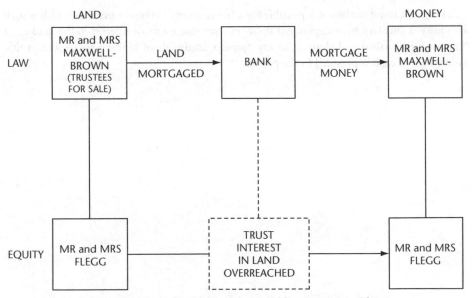

Overreaching: *City of London Building Society v Flegg*

[81] [1988] AC 54.

[82] See *Williams & Glyn's Bank Ltd v Boland* [1981] AC 487, HL; *Kingsnorth Finance Co v Tizard* [1986] 1 WLR 783.

subsists in the land in the hands of the transferee is determined by the relevant rules under the provisions of the Land Registration Act 2002.[83] If title to the land is already registered, and a registered disposition takes place, for example where the land is sold, a lease for more than seven years is granted, or the land is mortgaged, the beneficial interest will enjoy priority if it is an overriding interest.[84] The trust interest will only be overriding if the beneficiary was in actual occupation of the land at the date of the disposition, and either the occupation would have been obvious from a reasonably careful inspection of the land or the person to whom the disposition was made had actual notice of it.[85] The interest will cease to be overriding if the disponee had made enquiry of the beneficiary before the disposition took place, and the beneficiary had failed to disclose his beneficial interest when he could reasonably have been expected to do so. If the land is unregistered at the time of a disposition, and has to be registered for the first time, other special rules are applicable.[86] In this increasingly less common situation a trust interest affecting the land will bind the first registered proprietor as an overriding interest if the beneficiary was in actual occupation of the land.[87]

## (5) Mere equities

Whereas it has been seen that equitable interests are only destroyed if the legal title to the property in which they subsist is acquired by a bona fide purchaser for value without notice, mere equities relating to property are incapable of binding a person who purchases an interest in it, whether legal or equitable, irrespective of whether they have notice. As Lord Upjohn stated in *National Provincial Bank Ltd v Ainsworth.*

'. . . I myself cannot see how it is possible for a "mere equity" to bind a purchaser unless such an equity is ancillary to or dependent upon an equitable estate or interest in the land . . . a "mere equity" naked and alone is, in my opinion, incapable of binding successors in title even with notice; it is personal to the parties.'[88]

---

[83] See Stevens & Pearce, *Land Law* (3rd ed 2005), Ch 7.
[84] Land Registration Act 2002, s 29(2)(a)(ii).    [85] Land Registration Act 2002, Sch 3, para 2.
[86] Land Registration Act 2002, s 11(4)(b) and s 12(4)(c).
[87] Land Registration Act 2002, Sch 1, para 2.    [88] [1965] AC 1175 at 1238.

# 4

# Equitable obligations: trusts and powers

## 1 Introduction

The previous chapters have charted the historical importance of equity, and its contribution to the range of remedies available in English law and the law of property. In particular, the preceding chapter noted that the most significant contribution of equity to English property law has been the trust, and detailed its evolution from a medieval progenitor, the use. This chapter will examine the fundamental characteristics of the modern trust, and draw comparisons between it and other equitable obligations relating to property.

## 2 Fundamental characteristics of trusts[1]

### (1) The hybrid nature of trusts

It is difficult to categorise the essential nature of a trust. As a legal concept a trust does not fit neatly into either the category of 'obligations' or of 'proprietary rights'. Rather, the trust shares some characteristics of obligations and some characteristics of proprietary rights. In this sense it is a hybrid, and can best be regarded as a sui generis 'proprietary obligation'. Despite difficulties of classification, three essential characteristic of trusts can be identified. First, a trust can only exist in relation to specific property. Secondly, this property must be held by trustees subject to mandatory obligations governing how it should be used and applied. Third the trustees must owe these mandatory obligations to legal persons who are entitled to enforce them. These persons are termed the beneficiaries of the trust, and they are entitled to the trust property in equity. These three elements all appear in the definition of a 'trust' in art 2 of the Hague Convention on the Law Applicable to Trusts and on their Recognition, incorporated into English law by the Recognition of Trusts Act 1987:

'For the purposes of this Convention, the term "trust" refers to the legal relationship created—inter vivos or on death—by a person, the settlor, when assets have been placed under the control of a trustee for the benefit of a beneficiary or for a specified purpose.

---

[1] See [1996] Conv 186 (Bartlett); Hayton, 'Developing the Obligation Characteristics of the Trust' (2001) 117 LQR 96; Parkinson, 'Reconceptualising the Express Trust' [2002] 61 CLJ 657.

A trust has the following characteristics—

(a) the assets constitute a separate fund and are not part of the trustee's own estate;

(b) title to the trust assets stands in the name of the trustee or in the name of another person on behalf of the trustee;

(c) the trustee has the power and the duty, in respect of which he is accountable, to manage, employ or dispose of the assets in accordance with the terms of the trust and the special duties imposed upon him by law.

The reservation by the settlor of certain rights and powers, and the fact that the trustee may himself have rights as a beneficiary, are not necessarily inconsistent with the existence of a trust.'

## (2) Property subject to the trust

### (a) A trust can only exist in relation to specific property

A trust can only exist in relation to specific property, whether land or personal property. As Lord Browne-Wilkinson stated in *Westdeutsche Landesbank Girozentrale v Islington London Borough Council*:[2] 'In order to establish a trust there must be identifiable trust property.' This requirement is reflected in a number of principles limiting the circumstances in which there will be a valid trust will. A trust cannot be effectively created over 'future property', which is property not yet in existence but merely expected as a possibility in the future. For example, a trust cannot be created over property that a person expects to receive under the will of a relative who has not yet died,[3] or over money that a person might win from the national lottery. In both cases it is uncertain whether the alleged property will ever materialise. It is possible to promise to create a trust of such future property in the event that it materialises, which may create a contractual obligation so to do, but this is essentially different from the creation of an immediate trust. Similarly, a trust cannot be created over unascertained property. For example, in *Re Goldcorp Exchange Ltd (In Receivership)*[4] a company received money from customers which it invested in the purchase of gold and other precious metals. The Privy Council held that customers could not establish that the company was holding the metal on trust for them because it was impossible to identify the specific metal derived from each customer's individual investment. The customers unable to establish a trust were therefore limited to a contractual claim against the company for the return of their investment. A trust will also cease to exist if all the property subject to it is destroyed or dissipated.[5]

### (b) The concept of a 'trust fund'[6]

Although a trust may exist in relation to a single specific asset, for example a sum of money, a piece of land or shares in a company, often the property to which the trust relates will comprise a wide range of different assets. In both cases, the trustees may be

---

[2] [1996] 2 All ER 961 at 988.    [3] See *Re Ellenborough* [1903] 1 Ch 697.
[4] [1994] 2 All ER 806.
[5] See *Re Diplock* [1948] Ch 465; *Bishopsgate Investment Management v Homan* [1995] 1 All ER 347.
[6] See Nolan, 'Property in a Fund' (2004) 120 LQR 108.

permitted to sell the assets and exchange them for new ones. For this reason the property subject to the trust is generically identified as the trust 'fund'. Often the precise content of the fund will be fluid, because the individual assets comprising the fund are frequently being substituted by means of sale and reinvestment. For example, if trustees hold capital under a trust requiring them to invest it and pay any income to the beneficiaries, the capital need not necessarily remain in the same investments throughout the life of the trust. Indeed, there will be some instances, such as with unit trusts and pension schemes, where the benefits of collective investment would largely be lost without a regular review of the investment portfolio. The trustees therefore have powers of disposition over the investments held and they will move or change those investments from time to time. Provided that the proceeds from the realisation of any investment are immediately reinvested, the value of the investment portfolio will remain unchanged, apart from any gains or losses which have been made on individual investments within the portfolio. This fluidity of the trust assets was recognised in *Re Earl of Strafford (Deceased)*, where the discussion concerned a disputed claim which formed part of the trust assets. Buckley LJ said that:

'The trustees may enforce the claim, sell it, compromise it or compound it, or (if it be worthless) abandon it. In any case but the last, the fruit of enforcing, selling or compromising the claim will replace the claim as an asset of the trust. None of these transactions involves any variation of the trusts or of the beneficial interests under them; there is merely a change in the composition of the trust fund. If the trustees compromise the claim at an unduly low level, they may be liable for breach of trust, but no variation of the trusts is involved. The trust fund will thenceforth comprise, in addition to other assets, the fruit of the compromise plus a claim against the culpable trustees.'[7]

This concept of trust assets forming a collective investment fund is a core principle in equity. It lies at the root of unit trusts and pension funds. In more domestic contexts it provides a means by which parents with sufficient money to invest can make provision for their children, preserving wealth within the family, but giving flexibility to the trustees as to how it will be managed and invested. The fund concept has also been employed in a corporate context, where equity has recognised that it is possible to create a floating charge over the assets of a company.[8] This operates to use the assets of the company as security for an obligation, in a similar way to in that in which a house can be mortgaged to secure the repayment of a loan. Instead of freezing any particular asset, however, a floating charge treats all the assets of the company as a fund, and applies to the fund as a whole. So long as it continues to trade in the ordinary course of business, so that assets disposed of are balanced by assets acquired, the company retains freedom of disposition over individual assets. Should the company cease to trade in the ordinary way, or if some other specified event occurs, then the charge settles and crystallises by attaching to the specific assets then forming part of the fund.[9]

---

[7] [1980] Ch 28, CA.

[8] In principle, it should also be possible for an individual to create a floating charge. See also the possibility of creating a floating trust in cases of mutual wills discussed in Chapter 11.

[9] *Governments Stock and Other Securities Co v Manila Railway Co* [1897] AC 81 at 86, per Lord MacNaghten; *George Barker (Transport) Ltd v Eynon* [1974] 1 All ER 900 at 905, per Edmund Davies LJ.

## (c) Property which is the product of trust property will also be trust property

A feature of a fund is that it includes accretions as well as substitutions. Property produced by trust property itself becomes subject to the trust. For example, if the trust property includes shares in a company any dividends paid on such shares will also comprise trust property. It has already been noted that property acquired by the sale and reinvestment of trust property will belong to the trust fund.[10] As an extension of this principle, any unauthorised profits earned by the exploitation of opportunities arising from the trust property will also be trust property. For example, where the trust property comprises shares in a company, those shares inevitably carry voting rights in the company general meeting which are controlled by the trustees in virtue of their legal title to the shares. If a trustee is then appointed director through the use of those voting rights any personal remuneration he receives in that capacity will prima facie constitute trust property.

## (3) Trustees subject to the obligations of the trust

### (a) The trust as a species of obligation

The essence of a trust is that the owner of specific property is subject to mandatory personal obligations governing how it should be used and applied. A trustee is therefore someone who owns property subject to personal obligations to manage and apply it in accordance with the terms of the trust to the advantage of the beneficiaries thereof. As such, he does not enjoy the right to treat the property as if it were his own. The precise nature of the trustee's obligations and duties in relation to the trust property are dependent upon the terms of the particular trust. His rights and duties may be both positive and negative. In other words, there may be some things that a trustee should do in relation to the trust property, and others that he should not. The obligations imposed by a trust are not such as to limit the capacity of the trustee to deal with the property. His unencumbered capacity to deal with the trust property derives simply from the fact that he owns it. The trust obligations merely dictate what he should or should not do, and dealings with the trust property in contravention of these obligations are not ultra vires and void. A trustee who deals with the trust property inconsistently with the terms of the trust will instead become personally liable to the beneficiaries for 'breach of trust' and, in the absence of any defences, will be required to compensate them for any loss they suffer in consequence. The relationship between the capacity of the trustee to deal with the trust property and the trust obligations was summarised by Lord Browne-Wilkinson in *Hammersmith and Fulham London Borough Council v Monk*.

'The fact that a trustee acts in breach of trust does not mean that he has no capacity to do the act he wrongly did.'[11]

### (b) The source of the trust obligations

A trust arises when property is held by trustees subject to obligations owed in favour of beneficiaries. Such obligations will arise either where the owner of property deliberately

---

[10] See Chapter 22.    [11] [1992] 1 AC 478 at 493.

subjects it to a trust, is presumed to have subjected it to a trust, or if a trust is imposed by law.

*(i) Express intention to impose trust obligations.* Property may be subjected to a trust obligation by the deliberate act of its owner. An absolute owner of property may create a trust either by subjecting himself to trust obligations, by declaring that he holds it for specified beneficiaries, or by transferring the ownership to someone else, specifying that they are intended to hold it on trust. For example, if Mike owns shares in a company and wishes to create a trust of them in favour of Norma, he can either declare himself a trustee of the shares or transfer them to Owen, directing him to hold them on trust for her. In either case the trust is said to be express, as it was created by the deliberate intention of the owner. The person creating an express trust is described as the 'settlor', as he is said to 'settle' the property on trust for the benefit of the beneficiaries.

*(ii) Implied intention to impose trust obligations.* Whilst the paradigm source of trust obligations is the express intention of the settlor, there are some circumstances in which equity presumes that a person intended to subject property to a trust, even though in fact no such intention was expressed. If a presumption of a trust arises, and it is not rebutted by counter-evidence that no trust was intended, the property will be subject to a resulting trust. Resulting trusts arise in two main circumstances, which were identified by Lord Browne-Wilkinson in *Westdeutsche Landesbank Girozentrale v Islington London Borough Council*:

'Under existing law a resulting trust arises in two sets of circumstances:

(a) where A makes a voluntary payment to B or pays (wholly or partly) for the purchase of property which is vested either in B alone or in the joint names of A and B, there is a presumption that A did not intend to make a gift to B; the money or property is held on trust for A (if he is the sole provider of the money) or in the case of a joint purchase by A and B in shares proportionate to their contributions . . .

(b) where A transfers property to B on express trusts, but the trusts declared do not exhaust the whole beneficial interest.'[12]

*(iii) Imposed trust obligations.* In some cases property will be regarded as subject to trust obligations despite the lack of either express or presumed intention on the part of the owner because his unconscionable conduct demands that he be required to hold the property for the benefit of others. In such circumstances the law imposes a constructive trust.

## (c) The content of the trustees' obligations under the trust

The precise obligations imposed on any particular trustee will vary with the terms of the trust. In many cases the obligations of the trustees will be specified by the settlor creating the trust. However, in the absence of express exclusion some powers and duties are granted and imposed by statute. Two main categories of obligation can be identified.

---

[12] [1996] 2 All ER 961 at 990.

*(i) The obligation to allocate the trust property.* The most important obligation imposed by a trust is the obligation of the trustees to apply the trust property for the benefit of the beneficiaries in accordance with the terms of the trust. Under some trusts the trustees have no part to play in deciding how the trust property should be allocated amongst the beneficiaries because the terms of the trust themselves stipulate how the beneficial interest is to be shared. Such a trust is described as a 'fixed trust' because the settlor who created it has specified the respective entitlements of the beneficiaries in the terms of the trust, and the trustees' duty is merely to carry out his instructions. In other cases, the trustees have a role to play in determining how the beneficial interest is to be allocated. Rather than fixing the specific entitlements of the beneficiaries, the settlor may confer on the trustees the right to decide how the trust property should be allocated amongst a class of beneficiaries. Such a trust is called a 'discretionary trust' because the entitlement of any individual beneficiary to share in the trust fund is at the discretion of the trustees. Where the terms of a discretionary trust require the trustees to distribute the whole of the trust property amongst the beneficiaries the trust is said to be 'exhaustive', whereas if the trustees have the power to decide not to distribute the whole of the trust property, but rather to retain and invest it, the trust is said to be 'non-exhaustive'. Where property is held on trust for children who have not yet reached the age of majority, so that they do not enjoy vested interests in the trust property or the income generated from it, the trustees may enjoy the power to apply such income to their benefit, or even to allow them to receive part of the trust property itself ahead of time. These powers are respectively termed the power of 'maintenance' and the power of 'advancement'. These powers may be granted expressly to the trustees by the settlor creating the trust, but in the absence of an express grant they are conferred by statute under the Trustee Act 1925, ss 31 and 32.

*(ii) The obligation to manage the trust property.* The second category of trustees' obligations concerns their duties to manage the trust property and to maintain the integrity of the fund. The trustees enjoy complete control of the trust property by virtue of their legal ownership of the assets which comprise the fund. Management functions include decisions on how the trust fund should be invested, and on whether assets held should be realised and the proceeds of sale reinvested. The precise scope of the trustees' management powers are determined by the terms of the particular trust. For example, the terms of the trust may expressly specify the investment powers that the trustees are to enjoy in relation to the trust property, perhaps limiting the type of investments that the trustees are entitled to pursue. In the absence of such express powers of investment, statute intervenes to grant the trustees standard investment powers.[13] The trust may also specify the means by which new or replacement trustees can be appointed, and statute empowers the trustees to delegate some of their functions to an agent acting on their behalf.

### (d) The mandatory character of the trustees' obligations under the trust

The obligations of a trustee are mandatory in nature. This means that trustees are required to carry the terms of the trust into effect. In the event that they fail to carry out

---

[13] Trustee Act 2000. See Chapter 22 below.

their obligations, especially the obligation to allocate the trust fund amongst the beneficiaries, the court will intervene to ensure that the trust is carried out, either by ordering them to act as required by the terms of the trust, or, if necessary, by finding an alternative means of enforcing the trust, for example by appointing new trustees. In this sense trust obligations can be distinguished from powers of appointment, which are discretionary rather than mandatory in character. The mandatory character of the trust obligations is also seen in the operation of the maxim that 'equity will not allow a trust to fail for want of a trustee'. If a settlor transfers property to a person who refuses to accept the office of trustee, or if he leaves property by will to a trustee who predeceases him, equity will not allow the trust to fail but will instead find an alternative person to act as trustee.

### (e) The trustees' liability for breach of trust

As has been noted above, trustees do not lack capacity to deal with the trust property in a manner inconsistent with the terms of the trust. However, if they do act inconsistently with the terms of the trust, their breach of obligation will render them personally liable to compensate the beneficiaries for any loss caused by the breach.[14] The trustees may commit a breach of trust in three circumstances. First, they commit a breach of trust if they act in a manner inconsistent with the terms of the trust by doing something they were not authorised to do. Secondly, they commit a breach of trust by omission if they fail to do what the terms of the trust require them to do. Thirdly, they commit a breach of trust if they fail to act with the requisite objective standard of care expected of them, namely that of 'the ordinary prudent man of business'.

### (f) The ability of the beneficiaries to override the terms of the trust

Although trustees are placed under personal obligations as to how the trust property should be allocated and managed, the terms of the trust stipulated by the settlor are not sacrosanct, and can be overridden by the wishes of the beneficiaries. If the trustees act in breach of trust with the authorisation of the beneficiaries, they will not be liable to them for any losses that ensue from the breach. The trustees will only enjoy complete immunity from liability if all the beneficiaries authorise the breach, and they remain liable to any beneficiaries who do not give valid authorisation. Valid authorisation can only be given by beneficiaries who are of age and legally competent. The power of the beneficiaries to override the terms of the trust is most vividly illustrated by the operation of the rule in *Sanders v Vautier*,[15] by which the beneficiaries are entitled to insist that the trust is brought to an end by requiring the trustees to transfer the legal title to the trust property to them. They will thus become the absolute owners of the trust property and it will be free from the control of the trustees. In *Sanders v Vautier* property was held on trust for a beneficiary who was aged 21. The terms of the trust required the trustees to accumulate the income generated by the trust fund for the

---

[14] The beneficiaries may also have a claim against someone who receives the trust property knowing of the breach, or dishonestly assists in the breach.
[15] (1841) 4 Beav 115.

beneficiary, who was only to be entitled to receive it on reaching the age of 25.[16] It was held that, as the beneficiary had attained the age of majority, he was entitled to demand that the trustees transfer the trust property to him, thus negating the age restriction imposed by the settlor. Similarly, the beneficiaries of a trust can countenance variations in its terms, again potentially undermining the wishes of the settlor embodied therein. The Variation of Trusts Act 1958 even permits the court to grant approval to variations on behalf of beneficiaries who are incapable of consenting for themselves, either because they lack the capacity to consent, are not yet in existence or cannot be ascertained, provided that the proposed variations are for their 'benefit'.

### (g) The fiduciary obligations of trustees

Whilst the trustees are subject to the specific obligations imposed by the terms of the trust, they are also subject to a general fiduciary duty imposed by equity. Equity recognises that trustees may be tempted to take advantage of their position as the legal owners of the trust property and utilise it to their own advantage rather than in the interests of their beneficiaries. It therefore imposes a strict duty of exclusive loyalty on trustees, obliging them to act solely in the interests of their beneficiaries, and assumes that any personal profit derived from their position as trustee was only obtained by allowing their own interests to prevail over those of their beneficiaries. Trustees are therefore obliged to make restitution to the beneficiaries of any unauthorised profits that they received in virtue of their position, or in circumstances where there was a mere possibility of a conflict of interest between their duty and their personal interests. Trustees will be entitled to retain such profits received in breach of their fiduciary duty if they acted with the informed consent or authorisation of the beneficiaries.

## (4) Beneficiaries entitled to the benefit of the trust

The third essential characteristic of a trust is that there must be objects for whose benefit the property is held, and to whom the obligations of the trustees are owed. With the exception of trusts for charitable purposes, and a very small number of other anomalous trusts for purposes, trusts must exist for the benefit of persons rather than purposes. The reason for this limitation is that only legal persons, whether human individuals, companies or corporations, possess the necessary capacity to enjoy and enforce the obligation of the trustees. Therefore, a trust cannot be validly created for the abstract purpose of 'promoting good journalism' because there is no person to whom the obligation is owed, and no one who possesses sufficient locus standi to complain to the court if the trustees fail to apply the trust property to the specified purpose. In the case of charitable trusts, the trustees' obligations are supervised on behalf of the Crown by the Attorney General and the Charity Commissioners.

---

[16] The beneficiary had a vested right to the fund. In other words, there was only a direction to postpone payment. The beneficiary's entitlement was not conditional on reaching the age specified.

## (a) The beneficiaries have the right to enforce the trust obligations

The prime entitlement of the beneficiaries of a trust is that the trustees carry out the terms of the trust. They are entitled to enforce the trust, either by preventing the trustees acting in breach or by requiring them to perform their obligations if they are refusing to do so. In effect, they are entitled to require specific performance of the trust in their favour. Once property has been validly subjected to a trust in their favour, the beneficiaries are entitled to enforce it irrespective of whether they provided consideration or not in return for the creation of the trust.

## (b) The beneficiaries have the right to override the terms of the trust

As has already been noted, the beneficiaries enjoy the right to override the terms of the trust as stipulated by the settlor. They can authorise and require the trustees to act in a way which would otherwise be a breach of trust, or a breach of their fiduciary duty, and if they are all of age and legally competent they can demand that the trust be brought to an end in accordance with the rule in *Saunders v Vautier*.[17]

## (c) The beneficiaries enjoy a proprietary entitlement to the trust fund

The beneficiaries of a trust enjoy more than merely personal rights to have the trust obligations carried out in their favour by the trustees. Despite some historical debate, the better view is that beneficiaries are also entitled to proprietary rights in the trust property.

*(i) The beneficial interest as a mere interest in personam.* Some have argued that the fact that the beneficial interest behind a trust is destroyed by the bona fide purchase of the trust property proves that it is a mere interest in personam. Maitland stated that equity had never regarded the beneficiary as 'owner' of the trust property, but only as entitled to enforce the personal obligation of the trustee to carry out the terms of the trust:

'. . . [the trustee] is the owner, the full owner, of the thing, while the cestui que trust has no rights in the thing . . .'[18]

More recent support for the view that beneficial interests behind a trust are mere rights in personam can be derived from the decision in *Webb v Webb*,[19] where the central issue was whether a father's assertion, that his son held a holiday home in France on resulting trust for him, was a claim founded on a right in rem for the purposes of art 16(1) of the Convention on Jurisdiction and the Enforcement of Judgments in Civil and Commercial Matters 1968. Following the advice of Advocate General Damon, the Court of Appeal held that the father's claim was not founded on a right in rem but merely on the existence of a personal fiduciary relationship. However, little weight should be placed upon this decision, as the classification of the nature of claims for the purposes of settling whether the English courts have jurisdiction when the property in dispute is situated abroad should not be determinative of the jurisprudential character of beneficial interests for domestic purposes.

---

[17] (1841) 4 Beav 115.      [18] Maitland, *Equity*, (1936), p 17.
[19] [1994] QB 696; [1995] Conv 125 (MacMillan). See pp 23–24 above.

*(ii)  The beneficial interest as a proprietary interest in rem.* In reality, it seems that the beneficial interest behind a trust is more than a mere personal interest enforceable against the trustee. A beneficiary's interest is enforceable against anyone acquiring the trust property except a bona fide purchaser, who is protected by the doctrine of notice. In this sense the beneficial interest shares the essential characteristic of proprietary rights identified by Lord Wilberfoce in *National Provincial Bank Ltd v Ainsworth*,[20] namely that they are capable of enduring through changes in ownership. Beneficial interests are certainly not as durable as legal ownership, but the mere fact that in some circumstances they are defeated by superior rights should not prevent the recognition that they are essentially proprietary in nature. Even Maitland later acknowledged that a beneficiary was entitled to more than a merely personal obligation:

'. . . I believe that for the ordinary thought of Englishmen "equitable ownership" is just ownership pure and simple, though it is subject to a peculiar, technical and not very intelligible rule in favour of bona fide purchasers . . . so many people are bound to respect these rights that practically they are almost as valuable as if they were *dominium*.'[21]

The essentially proprietary nature of the beneficial interest under a trust is also supported by the fact that the beneficiary is entitled to deal with it in ways characteristic of property owners. He can transfer his equitable interest by assignment, either by way of sale or as a gift. He can dispose of it by will, or in the event of his dying intestate it will pass to his heirs under the rules governing intestate succession. It can be used to provide security for a loan. He may be required to pay tax on its value. The proprietary character of the beneficial interest under a trust was clearly stated in *Westdeutsche Landesbank Girozentrale v Islington London Borough Council*,[22] where Lord Browne-Wilkinson said:

'Once a trust is established, as from the date of its establishment the beneficiary has, in equity, a proprietary interest in the trust property, which proprietary interest will be enforceable in equity against any subsequent holder of the property (whether the original property or substituted property into which it can be traced) other than a purchaser for value of the legal interest without notice'.[23]

# 3  Powers of appointment

The trust is not the only mechanism which has been developed by equity to facilitate the management and allocation of property. A person may be granted a power of appointment in respect of specific property or a fund of property. This enables him to decide who should receive the property. The holder of the power (the donee) is able to allocate the property by exercising his power and making appointments thereof to the objects of the power. Unlike a trust, the donee of a power of appointment is under no obligation to exercise the power conferred upon him. It is discretionary rather than mandatory in character. A power of appointment may form part of a will, in which case

[20]  [1965] AC 1175.     [21]  Collected papers, Vol III, p 349.     [22]  [1996] AC 669.
[23]  [1996] AC 669 at 705.

it allows the donee to nominate beneficiaries to whom the personal representatives must give the property concerned. Alternatively, the power may be used to give similar instructions to trustees holding property on trust to give effect to the directions of the donee. Finally, a power may be given to the trustees themselves.

## (1) Classification of powers by reference to the donee's duties

Where a power is not held by the donee in a fiduciary capacity it is termed a 'bare' or 'mere' power. The donee of such a mere power enjoys an absolute discretion whether or not to allocate the fund, or part of the fund, to the objects of the power by making appointments. He is under no enforceable duty to do so, and the courts will only intervene if he makes a wrongful allocation. The objects cannot complain to the court if the donee fails to make any allocations, and the court will not compel him to do so. The donee is not even under a duty to consider whether allocations should be made. Where the donee holds the power in a fiduciary capacity, often because he is a trustee of the property to which it relates, the power is termed a 'fiduciary power'. Whilst such a power remains substantively discretionary in character the donee is subject to a duty to consider from time to time whether he should exercise it in favour of the objects and to make appointments in their favour.

## (2) Classification of powers by reference to the range of objects

A power of appointment is described as a 'general power' if the donee is entitled to appoint the relevant property to anyone in the world, including himself. There is no specified restricted class of objects. If a power is general in nature, the donee cannot make an appointment to someone who is outside of the scope of the power, since by definition there is none in such a position. In contrast, a 'special power' can only be exercised in favour of an identified class of persons. The donee can only make valid appointments to persons who fall within that class. A 'hybrid power' arises where a donee is authorised to make appointments to anyone except the members of a specified class. Unlike the beneficiaries of a trust, the objects of a power enjoy no proprietary entitlement to the property over which the power is enjoyed by the donee. The rule in *Saunders v Vautier*[24] has no application in the context of powers so that the objects cannot demand that the property be transferred to them. No object is entitled to any interests in the fund unless and until the donee exercises the power and makes an appointment in his favour.

## 4 Classification of equitable obligations

In the trust and the power, equity has developed two mechanisms which facilitate a separation between the functions of the management and allocation of property and

---

[24] (1841) 4 Beav 115.

the right to the enjoyment of property. In the absence of either a trust or a power, these entitlements are enjoyed in a unitary manner by the owner of the property. However, despite a degree of functional similarly between trusts and powers, it was historically important to draw a sharp distinction between them. Conceptually, a power is purely discretionary, imposing no obligations upon the donee and conferring no proprietary rights upon the objects. In contrast, a trust is mandatory in character, imposing an obligation to act upon the trustees and conferring a proprietary entitlement to the trust fund upon the beneficiaries. Equity has tended to differentiate between trusts and powers by examining any given situation and characterising the mechanism created as either a trust or a power. The rights and duties of the parties are thus determined by that characterisation. Traditionally, the two mechanisms were clearly distinguishable from each other. However, over time such a simple bifurcation has proved insufficiently flexible, and equity has extended the boundaries of existing obligations and developed new obligations. As a result, the distinction between different categories of equitable mechanism may be extremely fine. In the light of these developments, although convenient from the point of view of analysis, it is questionable whether it is still valid to regard the law as comprising a fixed group of categories of obligation into which each fact situation must be fitted, with the inevitable result that the categorisation will determine the rights and duties. Instead, a 'scale' of equitable obligations seems to be emerging, and the courts will be willing to construe any particular fact situation as falling somewhere along the scale, not necessarily within a fixed traditional category, and then finding the appropriate rights and duties.

## (1) A traditional categorisation

### (a) Trust or power

As has been described, the two main classes of obligation traditionally recognised in equity were the trust and the power. They were seen as being conceptually distinct with only a limited scope for overlap. In construing a document, it was therefore simply a question of determining whether an obligation fell within the category of a trust or power. This would be determined by a consideration of the language used in the instrument creating it. In some circumstances the characterisation of an arrangement as a trust or a power would determine whether the arrangement was valid or invalid.

For both trusts and powers it is necessary for the court to supervise the arrangement by ensuring that the fund is allocated only to those who fall within the terms of the original disposition. This requires that the beneficiaries of the trust, or the objects of the power, be defined with sufficient clarity and certainty. If this certainty of objects is lacking, then the whole arrangement will be void. Until the decision of the House of Lords in *McPhail v Doulton*,[25] the test of certainty of objects for powers was more generous than the test of certainty for trusts. Thus, it was often the case

---

[25]  [1971] AC 424.

that an arrangement would be valid if characterised as a power but invalid if it was a trust.

## (b) Limitations of a traditional categorisation

One major limitation of the traditional categorisation was the difficulty of determining whether a particular obligation was to be classed as a trust or a power, which could have such significant consequences for all the parties involved. The mere use of the words 'trust' or 'power' would not necessarily be conclusive, since what was important was the intention of the property owner creating the arrangement. If he intended to impose mandatory obligations, a trust would be created, but if he intended to give discretion, then a power would be conferred. The difficulty lay in the fine distinction between these two alternatives. As Lord Wilberforce acknowledged in *McPhail v Doulton*, this is an area of 'delicate shading'.[26] No particular words were (or are) needed to create a trust or a power. There is therefore no easy way of telling whether a particular disposition (even if professionally drafted) creates a trust or a power, and the law reports are full of cases where even the courts have found it difficult to decide which is created in a given case. In *McPhail v Doulton* itself, the judge at first instance and the Court of Appeal found that the settlor had intended to create a power. These conclusions were influenced by the fact that the arrangement would be valid if characterised as a power, but void for want of certainty if it was a trust. The House of Lords ultimately held that the mandatory character of the language used indicated an intention to create a trust, but proceeded to revise the test of certainty applicable to trusts to ensure that it was not invalidated.

## (c) Trusts combined with powers

The difficulty of making a distinction between trusts and powers is compounded by the fact that a power will always be associated with a trust. This is because a power of appointment is essentially the right to give directions to trustees as to how or for whom they are to hold trust property. This can happen in one of several ways. First, trustees could be directed to hold property for whoever the donee of the power selects. In the absence of the power being exercised, there may be a defined trust in default of appointment. Secondly, there might be a fixed trust, subject to the donee of a power being able to divest the beneficiaries of their interests by exercising the power. Finally, there might be an obligation to make a selection, so that the 'power' is really itself a trust. In each case, the power of selection could either be held by the trustees of the trust fund themselves, or by a separate donee.

## (2) The evolution of intermediate obligations

The development of trusts and powers by equity was driven by the desire to enable property owners to deal with their property as they wish. The power enabled a property owner to delegate to another the control over the distribution of his property, within

---

[26] [1970] 2 All ER 228 at 240. See also Sir Richard Arden MR in *Brown v Higgs* (1800) 5 Ves 495 at 505 citing *Duke of Marlborough v Lord Godolphin* (1750) 2 Ves Sen 61.

the limits he had specified. The trust enabled the owner of property to distribute his property to pre-determined individuals by giving the legal title to a trustee and specifying the beneficial interests. However, as owners' intentions changed with time and they sought to distribute their property in more complex ways, a simple analysis of equitable obligations proved inadequate. Equity was able to develop new obligations which combined aspects of both the power and the trust. The prime example is the emergence of the discretionary trust. Despite its lengthy heritage the effect of the development was not fully felt until the decision of the House of Lords in *McPhail v Doulton*.[27]

## (a)  Early developments akin to discretionary trusts

The existence of hybrid obligations was recognised by Lord Eldon LC in the leading case of *Brown v Higgs*:[28]

'There are not only a mere trust and a mere power, but there is also known to the court a power which the party to whom it is given is intrusted and required to execute; and with regard to that species of power, the court considers it as partaking so much of the nature and qualities of a trust, that if the person who has that duty imposed on him does not discharge it, the court will to a certain extent discharge the duty in his room and place.'

A relatively early example of such an arrangement is *Crockett v Crockett*.[29] A testator had left his entire estate to 'be at the disposal of his most true and lawful wife, Caroline Crockett, for herself and children'. Sir James Wigram V-C held this to confer equal shares on Caroline and the children, so that when the eldest child came of age he could call for his share.[30] Lord Cottenham LC, on appeal, disagreed. He did not need to categorise the arrangement exactly, but in his view one possible interpretation of the will was that Caroline was 'a trustee, with a large discretion as to the application of the fund'.[31] Sir John Romilly, who had been counsel in *Crockett v Crockett*, followed the case in *Hart v Tribe*,[32] after his appointment as Master of the Rolls. He gave a similar interpretation to a gift by will to the testator's wife Maria 'to be used for her own and the children's benefit, as she shall in her judgment and conscience think fit'. Within just a few years the concept was sufficiently clearly established for Thomas Smith MR, in the Irish Court of Chancery, to describe it as a discretionary trust.[33]

However, as might be expected, the early development was uncertain. This is evident in the decision in *Burrough v Philcox*.[34] John Walton left property to his two children for life and granted them a power to dispose of it by will in favour of his nephews and nieces. His two children died without making any appointment and the question arose whether the nephews and nieces could claim the property or whether it would pass to the residuary legatees of John Walton's will. The arrangement was clearly a power, but the court found that there was a general intention in favour of the class by John Walton

---

27  [1971] AC 424.      28  (1799) 4 Ves 708; re-heard (1800) 5 Ves 495; affd (1803) 8 Ves 561.
29  (1848) 2 Ph 553.      30  (1842) 1 Hare 451; (1847) 5 Hare 326.      31  (1848) 2 Ph 553 at 561.
32  (1854) 18 Beav 215.      33  *Gray v Gray* (1862) 13 I Ch R 404.      34  (1840) 5 My & Cr 72.

and since that intention had failed because a selection had not been made by his children, the court would carry into effect the general intention and divide the property equally between the nephews and nieces. The court chose to analyse this disposition as a power with a trust in favour of the class should the power fail to be exercised. It could equally well have been treated as a discretionary trust.

## (b) The enforcement of hybrid obligations

Whilst equity seemed willing to contemplate the emergence of mechanisms which were hybrid in nature, in that they were not exclusively mandatory or exclusively discretionary, there was uncertainty as to how the court could intervene if a trustee failed to exercise his discretion under a discretionary trust. In *Hart v Tribe* Sir John Romilly, had said:[35]

'There is no question but that this court will sometimes execute a trust, where a fund is originally given to a trustee to be disposed of in favour of certain objects, according to his judgment and discretion . . . I am of opinion that the court will not control this discretion, when it sees that it is *bona fide* exercised. I am far from saying, that this court would not compel the wife duly to perform the condition on which the gift was made to her, if it found that one child was really left destitute and in want, nothing being applied for its benefit—that the objects contemplated by the testator were disregarded, and the benefits which he intended the children to receive, were, in point of fact, withheld.'

Were any such neglect to occur, Romilly MR said that an application could be made to the court 'and I shall know how to deal with it'. An application was subsequently made on behalf of one of the children for whom Maria had made no provision.[36] Sir John Romilly ordered Maria to make an annual payment from the income of the fund to meet the majority of the boy's school fees.[37] There are other cases in which the court compelled a trustee under a discretionary trust to act,[38] or substituted its own judgment for that of a discretionary trustee who had failed to act.[39]

In other cases, though, the court disclaimed the ability to substitute its own opinion for that of the trustee. An example is *Gray v Gray*,[40] where Thomas Smith MR, ironically following a dictum of Romilly MR in *Hart v Tribe*, held that the only means by which the court could execute a discretionary trust where the trustee had failed to do so was by ordering equal division between all the objects. A similar view was taken by Sir Richard Arden MR in *Kemp v Kemp*.[41] The cases adopting a more flexible approach were condemned as anomalous by the Court of Appeal in 1954 in *IRC v Broadway Cottages Trust*.[42] The orthodox view adopted in that case was that the court had no right to substitute its discretion for that of the designated trustees should they fail or refuse to

---

[35] (1854) 18 Beav 215 at 217–218.

[36] The child, Frederick, had been informally adopted by the testator. Maria had hoped that he would remain with her, but he was taken away by his blood relatives.

[37] (1854) 19 Beav 149.

[38] See *Gisborne v Gisborne* (1877) 2 App Cas 300, HL; *Tempest v Lord Camoys* (1882) 21 Ch D 571.

[39] *Mosely v Mosely* (1673) Cas temp Finch 53; *Clarke v Turner* (1694) Freem Ch 198; *Warburton v Warburton* (1702) 4 Bro Parl Cas 1; *Richardson v Chapman* (1760) 7 Bro Parl Cas 318.

[40] (1862) 13 I Ch R 404.      [41] (1795) 5 Ves Jr 849.      [42] [1955] Ch 20, [1954] 3 All ER 120.

act. The discretion being conferred on and exercisable by the trustees alone, the court could not do other than authorise a distribution in equal shares. To this there might have been a limited exception that where the testator or settlor had laid down pointers or guides to the exercise of the discretion, this could form a basis for the exercise of a more flexible order by the court.[43]

### (3) *McPhail v Doulton*: a modern watershed

Despite the early developments outlined above, the decision in the House of Lords in *McPhail v Doulton* marks the major break from the traditional dichotomy between trust and powers. Mr Bertram Baden settled property on trust to enable the trustees to make grants in favour of the staff of Matthew Hall and Co Ltd and their relatives and dependants. It was obvious that Mr Baden did not intend each and every member of staff and their dependants and relatives to have a share in the property left on trust, as there would simply not be enough for them each to receive any meaningful sum. The trustees were to have discretion which of the members of staff and their relatives and dependants were to benefit. The House of Lords held by a majority that this was a trust and not a power. Most significantly, it held that if the trustees failed to exercise their discretion, the court could intervene to compel them, or to ensure by some other means that the trust was carried out. Lord Wilberforce stated that:

'The court, if called upon to execute the trust power, will do so in the manner best calculated to give effect to the settlor's or testator's intentions. It may do so by appointing new trustees, or by authorising or directing representative persons of the classes of beneficiaries to prepare a scheme of distribution, or even, should the proper basis for distribution appear by itself directing the trustees so to distribute.'

### (4) The contemporary classification of equitable obligations

*McPhail v Doulton*[44] overturned the orthodox view that there were a limited number of categories of equitable obligation and that regard would be had to the wishes of the settlor by allocating the arrangement which he had created into the most appropriate box or category. Some of the categories recognised before *McPhail v Doulton* did, of course, contain the potential for fine-tuning. The settlor could specify what discretions he was conferring upon his trustees, but the lack of anything but the crudest form of enforcement through equal division in the case of a failure by his trustees to exercise a discretion meant that the settlor's freedom of invention was comparatively limited. *McPhail v Doulton*[45] marked a watershed not merely because it changed the certainty requirement for discretionary trusts, but also because it altered the basis on which the courts would enforce fiduciary obligations. By recognising that equal division was not the only remedy available where a trustee failed to act, the House of Lords opened the

---

[43] See the dissenting judgment of Lord Hodson in *McPhail v Doulton* [1970] 2 All ER 228 at 234.
[44] [1971] AC 424.    [45] [1971] AC 424.

possibility of more varied and sophisticated obligations in equity. The possibilities opened up by the case have been confirmed and exploited since.

## (a) Blurring distinctions

The historic categories of the mandatory fixed trust, discretionary trust and mere power provided the beginnings of a broader scale of obligations. *McPhail v Doulton* has led to the exploitation of the grey areas existing between them. This has happened both by the evolution of new mechanisms filling the gaps between the old constructs, and also by expansion within the categories themselves. For example, within the category of discretionary trust, it is possible to distinguish between those under which the trustees are obliged to distribute the assets of the trust, and those where there is no such obligation. Since *McPhail v Doulton* the difference matters. The way in which the court is likely to intervene may differ markedly according to whether the trustees' obligation does or does not require the exhaustion of the trust fund. The availability of a sophisticated response to a failure by trustees to fulfill their obligation makes the difference in the nature of that obligation significant. In a similar vein, it has long been recognised that some powers are fiduciary, in the sense that the donee is unable to agree voluntarily or by contract not to exercise the power. It is said, to use the technical term, that the power cannot be released. That was as far as the court was willing to intervene when the traditional dichotomy between mandatory trusts and permissive powers held sway. However, in *Mettoy Pension Trustees Ltd v Evans*[46] Warner J held that in some circumstances the courts might be willing to compel the donee of a fiduciary power to exercise it using the same methods of enforcement that were suggested by Lord Wilberforce as applicable to discretionary trusts in *McPhail v Doulton*.[47] The case is fully discussed in a later chapter[48] but at this stage it is sufficient to recognise that this runs against the tenor of previous cases which have maintained the orthodox position that the exercise of fiduciary powers[49] cannot be enforced by the courts.[50] There has also been a blurring between the traditional categories. Discretionary trusts themselves represent a blurring between the poles of the trust and power. The House of Lords in *McPhail v Doulton* described the arrangement which Bertram Baden had set up as a 'trust power'. That phrase encapsulates the hybrid nature of the discretionary trust, which draws in elements both of trusts, in the obligation which is placed upon the trustees, and of power, in relation to the discretions which are conferred upon the trustees and the lack of defined rights, even in default, upon the part of the beneficiaries. The decision in the *Mettoy Pension* case suggests a further blurring. Rather than there being a sharp conceptual distinction between discretionary trusts and fiduciary powers, there appears to be a 'grey area' where obligations are neither distinctly one nor the other, but where they enjoy characteristics of both. The distinctions are particularly indistinct between the fiduciary power, where following *Mettoy*[51] the donee has a discretion whether or not

---

[46] [1991] 2 All ER 513.    [47] [1971] AC 424.    [48] See Chapter 15.
[49] As opposed to the consideration of the exercise of the power.
[50] *Re Gulbenkian's Settlement Trusts (No 1)* [1968] Ch 126; *McPhail v Doulton* [1971] AC 424; *Re Hay's Settlement Trusts* [1981] 3 All ER 786.
[51] [1991] 2 All ER 513.

to exercise the power but an obligation to consider whether to do so which may be enforced by the court, and a non-exhaustive discretionary trust, where the trustee has a mandatory duty to distribute the fund subject to a power to accumulate the income. It is almost impossible to discern a clear conceptual distinction between these different obligations. The more recent decision of the Privy Council in *Schmidt v Rosewood Trust Ltd*[52] further confirms the blurring of the traditional distinction between trusts and powers. In this case it was held that no distinction should be drawn between the rights of the object of a discretionary trust or of a fiduciary power in regard to the entitlement to the disclosure of trust documents. Thus a right which was formerly predicated upon the proprietary right of the beneficiary to the trust property was extended to the objects of a power of appointment who have no proprietary interest. In reaching this conclusion Lord Walker referred to the way in which Lord Wilberforce had demonstrated in *McPhail v Doulton* that the differences between trusts and powers were 'a good deal less significant than the similarities.'[53]

The increasingly sophisticated use of trusts and powers further suggests the inevitability of a blending and melding between some of the old categories. Take, for instance, the pension scheme. The trustees of a pension fund will generally be under a binding obligation to pay pension benefits to the widow or dependant children of a contributing member if he dies in service, that is, while still in employment. A capital sum will usually also be available. With most pension schemes, the trustees hold any capital sum upon discretionary trusts to distribute it amongst a class of beneficiaries including the member's near family, any dependants and any person the member may have nominated. The trustees may also have powers to establish trusts containing discretions and powers where they are applying a lump sum on death in service. In considering what to do, the trustees may have received directions from the member. In one typical scheme, it is stated: 'In the exercise of their discretionary powers the Trustees may have regard to but shall not be bound by any wishes notified to them by the member.' In a single arrangement, therefore, one can find fixed trusts, discretionary trusts, powers and directions with no express binding force alongside each other.

## (b) Determining rights and duties

Given the blurring of the distinctions between the recognised equitable mechanisms and the difficulty of drawing conceptual distinctions between them, the traditional approach of categorising obligations into a small number of well-defined categories seems inappropriate. In the past there was a temptation to allow the classification of an arrangement to dictate the parties' rights and duties. However, this is a circular activity and the fallacy of it is evident by examining an illustration. In *Re Gestetner Settlement*[54] Harman J indicated that in addition to a discretionary trust where the trustees were under an obligation to distribute, there could also be a situation where trustees were simply under an obligation to consider whether a power to distribute should be exercised, without being obliged to part with any income or capital. This is sometimes described as a non-exhaustive discretionary trust, to distinguish it from

---

[52] [2003] 3 All ER 76.    [53] Ibid at [66].    [54] [1953] Ch 672, [1953] 1 All ER 1150.

the case where the trustees are under a duty to distribute and exhaust the fund (an exhaustive discretionary trust). In *McPhail v Doulton* Lord Wilberforce drew a distinction between a discretionary trust (which he described as a trust power) and a mere power which was conferred on trustees. In the latter case he stated that 'although the trustees may, and normally will, be under a fiduciary duty to consider whether or in what way they should exercise their power, the court will not normally compel its exercise'. Lord Wilberforce did not consider this to be a discretionary trust (or a trust power, in the terminology which he used in the case), but it is difficult to see how it differs in any real respect from a non-exhaustive discretionary trust.[55]

The extent of the obligation to review the range of objects can also vary. Again, in *McPhail v Doulton* Lord Wilberforce said that:

'. . . as to the trustees' duty of enquiry or ascertainment, in each case the trustees ought to make such a survey of the range of objects or possible beneficiaries as will enable them to carry out their fiduciary duty. A wider and more comprehensive range of enquiry is called for in the case of trust powers than in the case of powers.'

Earlier in his opinion, he had indicated that the distinction was a functional one:

'Such distinction as there is would seem to lie in the extent of the survey which the trustee is required to carry out; if he has to distribute the whole of a fund's income, he must necessarily make a wider and more systematic survey than if his duty is expressed in terms of a power to make grants . . . The difference may be one of degree rather than of principle; in the well-known words of Sir George Farwell,[56] trusts and powers are often blended, and the mixture may vary in its ingredients.'

*(i) A traditional categorisation*

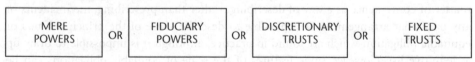

*(ii) A scale of obligations*

THE DISCRETIONARY EXTREME

THE MANDATORY EXTREME

**The emergence of a scale of equitable obligations**

---

[55] See, however, Hayton's definition of a non-exhaustive discretionary trust as one in which 'the trustees must distribute the income amongst class 'A' only if they fail to exercise a power to withhold the income for some purpose such as accumulating it or using it for class 'B': Hayton and Marshall, *Cases and Commentary on the Law of Trusts* (11th edn, 2001), p 152, n 90.

[56] *Farwell on Powers* (3rd edn, 1916), p 10.

## (c) A scale of equitable obligations?

The mix of trusts and powers, and the nature of the obligations which can be imposed on the donee of a fiduciary power, makes it undesirable to insist upon a rigid classification. There are, moreover, difficulties in locating some arrangements clearly under one category or another. As the litigation in *McPhail v Doulton* indicates, what one person sees as a trust in favour of a class with a power to accumulate may by another be seen as a trust to accumulate with a power to make grants in favour of a class. The House of Lords recognised that not only are the distinctions fine, but also that they are not determinative of the obligations of the donee or trustee. In the words of Lord Wilberforce:

'It is striking how narrow and in a sense artificial is the distinction . . . between trusts . . . and powers . . . And if one considers how in practice reasonable and competent trustees would act, and ought to act, in the two cases, surely a matter very relevant to the question of validity, the distinction appears even less significant. To say that there is no obligation to exercise a mere power and that no court will intervene to compel it, whereas a trust is mandatory and its execution may be compelled, may be legally correct enough, but the proposition does not contain an exhaustive comparison of the duties of persons who are trustees in the two cases.'[57]

This marks a fundamental shift from a simple conceptual framework of equitable obligations, where characterisation as either a trust or a power determines the rights and duties of the parties, to a functional analysis where the courts will construe an arrangement in the way best capable of fulfilling the intention of the owner of the property. The absence of a rigid hierarchy of equitable obligations means that there is instead a wide spectrum of arrangements, the characteristics of which depend upon the terms and circumstances of their creation. Any classification can be adopted only as a matter of convenience as a way of describing, rather than prescribing, the incidents of any particular arrangement. It is possible to describe some of the principal kinds of equitable obligation which are found in practice, although it is impossible to draw up a definitive list. However, some features of the scale of equitable obligations can be identified.

*(i) The mandatory extreme.* At one end of the spectrum of equitable mechanisms for property management and holding is the bare trust. The trustee may well have no independent powers of management or investment, and the shares in which the property is to be enjoyed are predetermined. The freedom of the trustee is constrained, and control is at its highest. But even here the position may be qualified. For instance, it is not unusual for a trust providing for fixed successive interests to contain a power enabling the trustee to draw down some of the capital and to pay it by way of an advancement to a beneficiary who has only a presumptive interest in the fund. There may also be a power to make applications of income (and sometimes capital) for the education and maintenance of an infant beneficiary who would otherwise have only a deferred right to those funds.

---

[57] [1970] 2 All ER 228 at 240.

*(ii) The discretionary extreme.* At the other end of the spectrum is a mere power, the donee of which enjoys an unfettered discretion whether to exercise it and, if it is exercised, how to exercise it. Even here, however, the donee does not have complete freedom, for the court will ensure that the power is exercised only within its terms.

*(iii) Intermediate points on the scale.* Between the bare fixed trust and the mere power there lies an almost infinite variety of intermediate arrangements. These include: trusts in favour of a fixed class, but with a power to make a selection between them in unequal shares;[58] a discretionary trust where the trustee is under an obligation to make a selection and which will be exercised by some means by the court if the trustee fails to exercise it;[59] a fiduciary power where the donee need not make a distribution but must at least consider periodically whether it should be exercised;[60] and a power or discretionary trust in favour of a class with a power to extend that class by appointing new members of the class.[61] Most of these possibilities can be combined in one form or another.

---

[58] *Wilson v Duguid* (1883) 24 Ch D 244 (where the gift to the class in equal shares was implied); *Burroughs v Philcox* (1840) 5 My & Cr 72; *Re Llewellyn's Settlement* [1921] 2 Ch 281; *Re Arnold* [1947] Ch 131.

[59] *Brown v Higgs* (1803) 8 Ves 561; *McPhail v Doulton* [1971] AC 424.

[60] *Re Manisty's Settlement Trusts* [1974] Ch 17; *Re Hay's Settlement Trusts* [1982] 1 WLR 202.

[61] *Re Hay's Settlement Trusts* [1982] 1 WLR 202

# 5

# Equity and the management of property

## 1 The modern significance of trusts

In the previous chapter the key characteristics of trusts and powers have been examined. However, at this stage the reader may no doubt be wondering why they have come into existence, and why they are relevant to the modern law. Trusts, and to a lesser extent powers, have evolved to enable property owners to accomplish objectives that they wish to achieve in respect of their property. Whilst they first emerged in an entirely different social environment, where their primary use was as a means of ensuring that property remained within a family, they have proved extremely adaptable to modern family and commercial contexts. The majority of people enjoy some interaction with trusts, even though they may not be aware of it. Every person who is a co-owner of land is a beneficiary under a trust. Every person who has a pension fund, or who has investments in a unit trust or an ISA will find that the underlying assets behind their investment are held under a trust. Persons with considerable wealth may utilise trusts as a means of efficient tax planning. Every person who makes a donation to a charitable organisation will in many cases unknowingly interact with the law of trusts. Most of these objectives are possible because trusts facilitate a separation between the management and enjoyment of property. It is the purpose of this chapter to sketch some of the more important practical usages of trusts.

## 2 Hiding the identity of the true owner of property

The fact that a trust enables the separation of the legal and beneficial ownership of property means that it can be used as an effective mechanism for hiding the identity of the true owner of property. If property is held on trust it may appear to all the world that the trustee is in fact the absolute legal owner, and others will have no knowledge of the existence of a trust. There is no obligation to publicly disclose the existence of a trust and therefore this mechanism will be particularly important where the legal ownership is made public, for example in the case of land where ownership is constituted by registration on a public register. For example, if a famous pop star wishes to purchase a cottage in a village without attracting attention, he may arrange for the house to be purchased on his behalf by a trustee, which would create what is known as a 'bare trust'.[1] Similarly, if a man wishes to make provision for his mistress on his death without members of his family discovering that she exists, he can leave the property he intends to give her in his will to a trusted friend who will take it as trustee on behalf of the mistress. There is no need for the identity of the mistress to appear in the will, which would become a public document as a consequence of the probate procedure, and nor is there any need for the will to make mention of the trust. Such trusts are known as secret trusts and are discussed fully in Chapter 7.

## 3 Transferring the ownership of property

One of the simplest dealings with property is an outright transfer of ownership, whether by gift or sale. The requirements for effective transfer of ownership vary with the type of property involved. Some forms of property, including banknotes and ordinary goods like books and furniture, can be transferred by the simple handing over of possession with the intention of transferring ownership. Other forms of property require more. The transfer of land, for instance, requires the transfer to be made in a prescribed form, and in most cases the transferee must then be registered as the new owner by the Land Registry.[2]

Equity normally has no role to play in outright transfers, except where the form of property concerned is recognised only in equity, for example a transfer of a share in a trust fund. In some cases equity will treat an attempted transfer as effective, even though some of the special formal requirements for the transfer of that form of property have not been used. Equity will, for instance, treat a transfer of land as being effective for some purposes after all the necessary documents have been completed and signed, even though the statutory rules require the transfer to be registered.[3] Conversely, in some special cases the principles of equity may become involved to deprive an apparent transfer of its full effect by imposing a resulting or constructive trust so that the original owner retains the equitable interest in the property transferred. For example, in *Bannister v Bannister*[4] Mrs Bannister sold two cottages to her brother-in-law for a third less than their full market value. He promised orally to let Mrs Bannister stay on in one of the cottages rent-free for the rest of her life, but four years later he sought to evict her. The oral promise could not be enforced as a contract since it was not in writing, or proved in writing, as the statutory rules required.[5] The Court of Appeal held, however, that in view of the promise which the brother-in-law had made, he acquired the cottage as trustee during the life of Mrs Bannister. He could not evict her so long as she desired to occupy the cottage. Similarly, in *Hodgson v Marks*,[6] Mrs Hodgson, an 83-year-old widow, had been persuaded by her lodger, Mr Evans, to transfer her house to him to prevent him from being evicted by her nephew. The transfer was not intended to be a gift, but to leave Mrs Hodgson as the effective owner.

---

[1] See Chapters 6 and 14.     [2] See p 102.
[3] *Mascall v Mascall* (1985) 50 P & CR 119 and see Chapter 26.     [4] [1948] 2 All ER 133.
[5] Law of Property Act 1925, s 40.     [6] [1971] Ch 892.

Although on the surface it appeared that Mr Evans was the owner because his name had been entered as proprietor in the register kept by the Land Registry, equity imposed a trust on him to give effect to the intention that Mrs Hodgson was to remain entitled to the full benefit of the property. Mrs Hodgson's interest was protected against a purchaser to whom Mr Evans fraudulently sold the house.

# 4　Sharing ownership of property

## (1)　Concurrent ownership of property

Trusts also provide a mechanism by which the ownership of property can be shared between a number of persons. Their interests are said to be concurrent because they are enjoyed at the same time. Co-ownership can be effected by means of either a joint tenancy or a tenancy-in-common.

### (a)　Joint tenancy[7]

Where the ownership of property is shared by means of a joint tenancy, all of the co-owners are jointly entitled to the whole of the co-owned property, so that they do not have specific shares in it. In the event of the death of one joint tenant, his interest passes automatically to the other remaining joint tenants under the principle of survivorship. A joint tenancy can be converted into a tenancy-in-common in equity by means of severance,[8] where the joint tenant severs his 'share', and the rules of survivorship no longer apply.

### (b)　Tenancy-in-common[9]

Where the ownership of property is shared by means of a tenancy-in-common the co-owners enjoy 'undivided shares' in the co-owned property. This means that they have specific notional shares in the property, which may be equal or unequal, and survivorship has no application. However, all the co-owners enjoy the right to use and enjoy the property, and no co-owner can regard part of it as representing his 'share' alone.

### (c)　Trusts and co-ownership

In relation to some property, the ownership can be shared concurrently by means of a joint-tenancy or a tenancy-in-common without the need for a trust. For example, two students who purchase a car together may become the joint owners thereof and no trust

---

[7] See Stevens and Pearce, *Land Law* (3rd edn, 2005) pp 311–313, Gray & Gray, *Elements of Land Law* (3rd edn, 2001), pp 822–833.

[8] See Stevens and Pearce, *Land Law* (3rd edn, 2005) pp 321–341; Gray & Gray, *Elements of Land Law* (3rd edn, 2001), pp 851–877.

[9] See Stevens and Pearce, *Land Law* (3rd edn, 2005), p 314; Gray & Gray, *Elements of Land Law* (3rd edn, 2001), pp 833–851.

is involved. In the case of personal property, the legal title may be held by co-owners either as joint tenants or tenants-in-common. Therefore, where the chattels of two owners are commingled to form an indistinguishable whole, they share the whole as tenants-in-common in proportion to their contributions.[10] However, in general the common law preferred the mechanism of a joint tenancy, and thus a tenancy-in-common is relatively rare without a trust. Where the property concerned is land any form of co-ownership will inevitably give rise to a trust of land. By statute only the legal title to land can be held by joint-tenants,[11] and therefore a tenancy in common can only exist in equity. The only situation in which land will not be held on trust is where there is a single absolute owner. This means that the trust is the foundation of most land holding under English law.

## (2) Successive ownership of property

It has been seen how the trust can provide a mechanism to facilitate the shared con-current ownership of property. An owner of property may wish to divide the ownership of property so that it is enjoyed successively rather than concurrently. For example, imagine that Alice, an elderly lady with a significant shareholding, has one daughter, Claire, and three grandchildren. On her death she wants Claire to enjoy the benefit of the shares, but ultimately she wants to ensure that they pass to her grandchildren. Alice can grant Claire a life-interest in the shares which will entitle her to receive the income they produce for the duration of her life, but without any right to their capital value. On her death the shares will become the property of the grandchildren. Such an arrangement, sharing the enjoyment of the property successively, can only be achieved by means of a trust, irrespective of whether the property concerned is land or personal property.[12]

# 5 Delegating management functions

Many of the most significant uses of trusts arise because they enable an owner to delegate some of the management responsibilities attendant upon the ownership of property to a third person who will become the trustee. In some cases such delegation will be chosen for reasons of convenience, whilst in others it may be a matter of necessity because the owner of property is incapable of managing it for himself.

---

[10] See *Spence v Union Marine Insurance Co* (1868) LR 3 CP 427; *Indian Oil Corpn Ltd v Greenstone Shipping SA* [1987] 3 All ER 893; cf *F S Sandeman & Sons v Tyzack and Branfoot Shipping Co* [1913] AC 680, HL.

[11] Law of Property Act 1925, ss 1(6), 36(2).

[12] It was once possible to create limited interests in land without using a trust, but since the Law of Property Act 1925, a trust is now required whenever limited interests in land are created. It has always been the case that limited interests in property other than land can only be created by means of a trust. See Stevens and Pearce, *Land Law* (2nd edn, 2005) pp 371–396.

## (1) Delegation for reasons of convenience

The owner of property may choose to create a trust of his property for reasons of convenience. Thus, a person owning a substantial share portfolio may transfer his shares to his stock-broker or a professional trustee to facilitate dealing transactions. In the case of such a bare trust, the trustee may not enjoy any active powers of management over the trust property but will act on the instructions of the beneficiary.

## (2) Delegation of allocation

An owner may know that he wants to transfer the ownership of his property but not yet know who he wants to transfer it to. By means of a trust, combined with a power of appointment, the owner can effectively delegate the responsibility for choosing who should receive the ultimate benefit of his property to someone else, the donee of the power. Often, the donee of the power or the trustee of the discretionary trust will be in a better position than the original owner to determine how it should be distributed, either by reason of the time at which they can make the decision, or because of their superior knowledge. For example, imagine that Henry has no children of his own but has a large number of nieces and nephews. He only has a small estate and he wants to ensure that his property goes to those who really need it. In his will he can leave his property to his sister Frances for life, giving her a power of appointment to choose which of his nephews and nieces are to receive the property on her death. By this means Henry is able to delegate the task of selecting who is to benefit, whilst at the same time stipulating the class of persons amongst whom allocations can be made. Alternatively, Henry could leave his estate to Frances on trust for such of his nephews and nieces in such shares as she determines. By means of this discretionary trust Henry has imposed a mandatory obligation on Frances to allocate the property amongst the class of his nephews and nieces, but has left her the decision as to which specific members of that class should benefit and to what extent.

Again, a discretionary trust or a power of appointment can be used on a larger scale. For instance, William is the owner of a large business with some 10,000 employees. He wishes to establish a fund to provide for the education of the children of his employees. Obviously, he cannot provide for them all, so he is able to create a trust in which the fund is transferred to trustees who have the discretion to select which of his employees' children should receive this benefit. The result is that only some of the 10,000 will benefit, but William has delegated to others the task of deciding which.[13]

*McPhail v Doulton* provides an example of such delegated allocation.[14] Bertram Baden wanted to give property for the benefit of the employees and ex-employees, and their relatives and dependants, of a company he owned. Rather than determining how the property should be allocated, he left the property to trustees, giving them the discretion as to which of the potential beneficiaries should actually receive a share of the property. In this way he delegated to them the task of allocating the property. Similarly,

---

[13]  Eg *Oppenheim v Tobacco Securities Trust Co Ltd* [1951] AC 297.    [14]  [1971] AC 424.

in *Re Diplock*[15] Caleb Diplock left his residuary estate to his executors to be applied to 'such ... charitable or benevolent objects' as they shall 'in their absolute discretion select'. Again, this was an attempt to delegate the decision as to how the property should actually be allocated to others, namely the executors.[16]

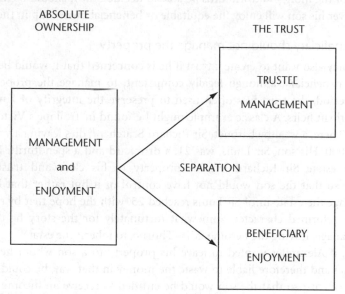

Trusts: facilitating the separation of the management and enjoyment of property

## (3) Providing for vulnerable individuals

An owner may want to take deliberate advantage of the possibility of separating the legal and equitable ownership of property through a trust to gain the advantage of ensuring that the beneficial owner does not have control of the management of the property. There are a number of reasons why this may be the case.

### (a) The beneficiary cannot manage the property

An owner may wish someone to enjoy the benefit of property who is not capable of managing it adequately for himself. The device of the trust enables the owner to transfer the legal title, and therefore the management responsibility, to someone who is capable of looking after the interests of the beneficiary.

*(i) Infancy.* An owner may want to create a trust because the intended beneficiary is an infant, and is therefore incapable of managing the property for himself. This would be the case, for example, if parents die leaving their property to infant children. The trustee will have the control of the property which will be invested and managed for their benefit until they reach the age of majority.

*(ii) Incapacity.* A trust may also be employed where the intended beneficiary lacks the

---

[15] [1948] Ch 465.

[16] In fact the gift failed because it was not exclusively charitable: see Chapter 19.

capacity to conduct his own affairs for reasons other than infancy. Suppose that John has a handicapped adult son for whom he wishes to make provision in his will. John knows that his son is unable to make decisions for himself. By means of a trust John can nominate a trustee to hold the property for his son. The trustee will have the legal ownership of the money and will thus be able to decide how it should be invested and used. However his son will enjoy the equitable or beneficial ownership in the money.

### (b) The beneficiary should not manage the property

An owner may also want to create a trust if he is concerned that it would be unwise to permit the beneficiary, although legally competent, to manage the property. In the Victorian period, the trust was often used to preserve the integrity of family estates from spendthrift heirs. A classic example might be found in Trollope's Victorian novel *Dr Thorne*. There, a wealthy baronet, Sir Richard Scatcherd, dies leaving a vast estate of some £300,000. His son, Sir Louis, was 21, a drunkard and a spendthrift. In order to protect the estate Sir Richard left his property to his close and trusted friend, Dr Thorne, so that the son would not have control of it but rather that Dr Thorne would manage the estate until Sir Louis reached 25, with the hope that by such age he would be a reformed character. Somewhat fortunately for the story he died before reaching that age, leaving the heroine, Miss Thorne, to inherit the estate!

Similarly, if Alexander wanted to leave his property to a son whom he knew was a drug addict and therefore liable to waste the money in that way, he could leave it on some form of trust so that the son would be entitled to receive an income but not to rapidly dissipate the property.

### (c) Protective trusts

A spendthrift may also be protected from the dangers of his own bankruptcy by a special type of trust, the protective trust. Under such a trust property is held by the trustees with a direction that the beneficiary is to receive the income from the trust. In the case of a conventional trust, if the beneficiary became insolvent his trustee in bankruptcy will be entitled to receive the income from the trust. However, the terms of a protective trust provide that in the event of insolvency the beneficiary's entitlement to the income automatically fails or determines, so that he is no longer entitled to it as of right. Instead, the income is to be held by the trustees under a discretionary trust to be used for the support of a range of persons, including the original beneficiary. This means that the trustee in bankruptcy will only receive the income if the trustees of the settled fund make an appointment to the bankrupt beneficiary. By means of this device the trust property and income are protected from the consequences of the beneficiary's bankruptcy.

It has been held that a settlor cannot create a trust to protect himself from his own bankruptcy.[17] However, a trust created by a third party which will protect the beneficiary from the consequences of his bankruptcy has been held to be valid.[18] Although a

---

[17] *Re Burroughs-Fowler* [1916] 2 Ch 251.
[18] *Billson v Crofts* (1873) LR 15 Eq 314; *Re Aylwin's Trusts* (1873) LR 16 Eq 585; *Re Ashby*, ex p Wreford [1892] 1 QB 872 QBD.

protective trust may be created expressly, a statutory form has been introduced. Section 33(1) of the Trustee Act 1925 provides that where any income is directed to be held on 'protective trusts' for the benefit of any person, then the property is to be held upon the terms set out in the section. These provide for a primary trust, and then a secondary trust which will only come into being if the primary trust fails.

*(i) The terms of the primary trust.* Section 33(1)(i) provides that the income will be held:

'Upon trust for the principal beneficiary during the trust period or until he ... does or attempts to do anything, or until any event happens ... whereby, if the said income were payable during the trust period to the principal beneficiary absolutely during that period, he would be deprived of the right to receive the same or any part thereof, in any of which cases ... this trust of the said income shall fail or determine.'

This primary trust entitles the principal beneficiary to receive the income from the trust, which entitlement determines automatically if he for any reason loses the right to retain it, for example if he becomes bankrupt, in which case his trustee in bankruptcy would be entitled to the income from the trust.[19] Other events have included the sequestration of the income[20] and the trustees impounding the income to repay capital wrongly advanced to the beneficiary.[21] In contrast, the fact that a beneficiary was resident in enemy occupied territory, with the consequence that income could not be paid to her, was held not to be sufficient to determine the trust.[22]

*(ii) The terms of the secondary trust.* If the primary trust is determined, then the income is to be held on the terms of a secondary trust set out in s 33(1)(ii):

'If the trust aforesaid fails or determines during the subsistence of the trust period, then, during the residue of that period, the said income shall be held upon trust for the application thereof for the maintenance or support, or otherwise for the benefit, of all or any one or more exclusively of the other or others of the following persons—

(a) the principal beneficiary and his or her wife or husband, if any, and his or her children or more remote issue, if any; or

(b) if there is no wife or husband or issue of the principal beneficiary in existence, the principal beneficiary and the persons who would, if he were actually dead, be entitled to the trust property or the income thereof or to the annuity fund, if any, or arrears of the annuity, as the case may be;

as the trustees in their absolute discretion, without being liable to account for the exercise of such discretion, think fit.'

This secondary trust takes the form of a discretionary trust, so that the principal beneficiary no longer has the right to the income of the trust, but the trustees may at their discretion give him some or even all of that income, or otherwise use it for the

---

[19] *Trappes v Meredith* (1871) 7 Ch App 248; *Re Evans* [1920] 2 Ch 304; *Re Walker* [1939] Ch 974; *Re Forder* [1927] 2 Ch 291.

[20] *Re Baring's Settlement Trusts* [1940] Ch 737.     [21] *Re Balfour's Settlement* [1938] Ch 928.

[22] *Re Hall* [1944] Ch 46.

support of his family. At any event, it will be possible to ensure his family's support without the income being seized by his trustee in bankruptcy.[23]

# 6 Gifts to be applied for purposes

It is a general principle of property that only a person[24] may be an owner. The owner of property might, however, wish to transfer it not to specified individuals, but for the carrying out of a specified purpose. Clearly, an owner can apply his own property in the furtherance of whatever purpose he chooses, but the problem arises when he wishes to oblige a transferee of the property to so apply it. Whilst it might be thought that a trustee could be obliged to use trust property in furtherance of a specified purpose, equity has adopted the general rule that, subject to limited exceptions, a trust can only be validly created in favour of persons rather than purposes.[25] A trust for the benefit of a pure purpose will be void. For example, in *Re Astor's Settlement Trusts*[26] a trust was established for the purpose of the 'maintenance of . . . good understanding sympathy and co-operation between nations' and 'the preservation of the independence and integrity of newspapers'. This was held to be invalid, as it was a gift for a purpose and not persons.

The most important exception to this principle is that property can be transferred on trust for purposes which are regarded as charitable in law, and the facilitation of charitable giving is one of the most important functions of the trust today. For example, in *Re Delius*[27] the widow of the composer Frederick Delius left her residuary estate[28] to trustees to promote the musical works of her late husband. This was upheld as a charitable gift, even though there was no person who would directly benefit from this gift. Where the trust is charitable in status, it attracts certain privileges. Charitable trusts are examined in detail in Chapter 18.

# 7 Collective investment

As has been seen, because the trust enables the responsibilities for the management of property to be severed from its ownership and enjoyment, and because they enable the ownership of property to be shared concurrently, trusts are an effective vehicle by which individuals can pool their resources for collective investment. One example of how

---

[23] In some circumstance the trustee in bankruptcy will be entitled to income that is received by the bankrupt principal beneficiary as the assignee of his interests under the discretionary trust. See *Re Coleman* (1888) LR 39 Ch D 443; *Re Neil* (1890) 62 LT 649; *Re Ashby*, ex p Wreford [1892] 1 QB 872.

[24] This includes a company which is treated as having legal personality and therefore the capacity to hold property.

[25] See Chapter 12.       [26] [1952] Ch 534.       [27] [1957] Ch 299.

[28] The residuary estate is the balance of a deceased person's assets after their debts have been paid and all specific gifts by will have been made.

trusts may be used in this way is the formation of a syndicate to enter the national lottery. Rather than entering as single individuals, a number of persons may come together to pool their resources and increase their chances of winning by financing the purchase of multiple combinations of numbers which they could not afford individually. Fundamental to the operation of such a syndicate would be the collection of the 'stakes' from the members, the purchase of the tickets and the distribution of any winnings. Since the ticket will be purchased in the name of only one member, that member will hold any winnings on trust for the members of the syndicate who have contributed, in proportion to the size of their stake.[29] More significantly, the ability of equity to facilitate collective investment lies at the heart of two important institutions, the unit trust and some pension schemes.

## (1) Unit trusts

Unit trusts have grown in significance since the middle of this century as a means of making modest investments on the stock exchange or in other securities. Suppose that Adrian has £1,000 to invest. He wishes to invest in stocks and shares, rather than to deposit his money with a bank or building society, because he believes that he will be better protected against the ravages of inflation. He knows the dangers of dealing on the stock market and wants to be able to spread the risk of his investment over a variety of securities, but his investment is too small to enable that. By buying units in a unit trust, Adrian is able to join together with other investors so that collectively they can spread their investments across the market. A management company, acting as a trustee, takes subscriptions from Adrian and other individual investors. They are allocated units in the trust assets in proportion to the sums which they have contributed. The subscriptions are pooled and used to purchase shares or to make other investments. In this way the investors are able to share in a far wider portfolio than if they were to invest alone. Although the management company is responsible for making investment decisions, it is the investors collectively who have beneficial entitlement. Sophisticated provisions enable Adrian or the other investors to withdraw from the trust by being paid back a sum which represents the proceeds of their initial investment. New investors may buy into the trust at a price which reflects the current value of units.

## (2) Pension schemes

Pension schemes can work in a very similar way, enabling members of the scheme to pool their contributions for the purpose of making investments which will later pay the pensions. Individuals pay into a collective investment fund, managed by trustees, knowing that they will receive better returns than if they each attempted to invest individually. It is the separation of ownership from the management of property that makes this possible.

---

[29] See (1995) NLJ 217 (Wilkinson).

### (3) The interface with contract

Although unit trusts and pension schemes are able to operate through mechanisms developed by the law of equity, the rights of individual investors and contributors may be dependent on the law of contract, not equity. For example, when a contributor to a pension scheme retires, he may have a contractual entitlement to receive a pension throughout his retirement based upon his final salary, rather than receiving back that proportion of the investments which represents his contributions. If he dies soon after retirement, he may draw less in pension than he has contributed. If he lives to a ripe old age, he may draw significantly more by way of pension than he has contributed. The contractual aspect of the arrangement is just as important as the trust or property aspects. Chapter 23 analyses the interrelationship between equity and contract in this area.

## 8 Property holding by clubs and societies

Clubs and societies which are not incorporated as companies are not capable of owning property in their own right since they lack the necessary legal personality. This raises the question as to how the funds of the society are to be held. In most cases they can be treated as belonging to the whole membership of the club, subject to the rules of the club.[30] Where the assets are vested in the members of the committee or some other group of individuals on behalf of the members of the club, those holding the club assets will be trustees for the members.

## 9 Trusts arising to protect legitimate expectations

Most of the situations examined concern the deliberate choice of a trust or power by an owner to achieve his objective. However, not every trust arises as a result of the owner's overt intention. For example, trusts commonly arise informally where a couple pool their resources in order to buy a home together, but the legal ownership of the home is put in the name of one of them alone. Often the couple will have given no thought as to how their arrangement would be characterised by the law. Provided that there is some common understanding that both of the couple were intended to have a share in the ownership of the property, the court will impose a trust to give effect to this intention.[31] Even in cases where there is no clear agreement, a trust will be imposed if the contributions made by each of the couple are such that the only reasonable inference is that, if asked, the couple would have said they intended to be joint owners.[32] *Grant v Edwards*[33] is a clear example. Mrs Linda Grant left her husband and moved in

---

[30]  *Re Recher's Will Trusts* [1972] Ch 526.      [31]  See Chapter 29.
[32]  *Lloyds Bank plc v Rosset* [1991] 1 AC 107.      [33]  [1986] Ch 638.

with Mr George Edwards. A modest house was purchased with the aid of a mortgage to provide a home for the couple. The purchase was made in the name of George Edwards and his brother Arthur. Mrs Grant's name was not included in the purchase, since Mr Edwards suggested that it might complicate her divorce proceedings. Mrs Grant helped with the purchase by contributing to the repayment of the mortgage and in other ways. The court imposed a trust on George and Arthur to give effect to the understanding that Mrs Grant would be entitled to a half share in the net value of the house.

# 10 Trusts which are remedial in effect

The examples above illustrate how equity enables a property owner to achieve more complicated objectives than making a simple outright transfer. Those dealing with informal situations also show how equity sometimes acts to protect legitimate expectations. But equity also serves a powerful remedial function by protecting the rights which it creates. In some situations equity protects an existing proprietary right, whereas in others it generates a new proprietary right. Although not universally accepted, some writers would characterise these proprietary rights as remedial or restitutionary trusts.[34] The use of remedial trusts has proved especially significant in the context of commercial transactions.

## (1) Misappropriated property

Where property is subject to a trust, the proprietary rights of the beneficiaries to the trust property will not be defeated unless the property is acquired by a bona fide purchaser for value. The trust property can be traced through mixtures and substitutions. However, where property is not subject to an express trust, the rights of the owner have traditionally been governed by the common law. These rights have proved less than adequate because the common law has not developed a sophisticated means of identifying the proceeds and substitute-products thereof. Thus, where property has been misappropriated, owners may seek relief in equity by the demonstration that a constructive trust relationship has come into being. Where, for example, money has been misappropriated from a company by one of its senior employees, the fiduciary relationship between the company and the employee fastens a constructive trust on the stolen funds in favour of the company, and thus the company can seek remedies in equity against the recipients of the money even though it has passed through a mixed bank account.[35] In *Westdeutsche Landesbank Girozentrale v Islington London Borough Council*[36] Lord Browne-Wilkinson suggested that a constructive trust would arise whenever money was stolen, irrespective of whether there was a fiduciary relationship or not.

---

[34] See Oakley, *Constructive Trusts (3rd edn, 1996); Birks, An Introduction to the Law of Restitution* (1985).
[35] *Agip (Africa) Ltd v Jackson* [1992] 4 All ER 451.      [36] [1996] AC 669.

## (2) Avoiding the effects of insolvency

Creditors have also sought to use trusts as a means of avoiding the consequences of the insolvency of their debtors. If a creditor can demonstrate that he enjoys an equitable proprietary interest in some property in the bankrupt's hands, in other words that the bankrupt debtor was holding it on trust for him, then, as has been seen, it will not form part of the bankrupt's assets to be distributed amongst his general creditors and the beneficiary will gain priority in the insolvency as if he were a protected creditor. Thus, where one bank made a mistaken payment to another bank which became insolvent, it was held that the payee bank held the payment on trust for the payor.[37] Similarly, where a loan is made for a specific purpose the money advanced will be held on trust for the creditor if the purpose has failed.[38] Where a customer has ordered goods from a supplier they may be held on trust for him if they have been separated from the bulk so as to be identifiable as his property.[39] Where a fiduciary has earned an illegitimate profit at the expense of his principal, his duty to account for the profit received will give rise to a constructive trust in favour of the principal, thus ensuring that the principal would obtain priority over the fiduciary's other creditors in the event of his insolvency.[40]

# 11 Trusts and tax avoidance

As already discussed, trusts have evolved to enable owners to deal with their property flexibly. However, one of the major motivations for the use of trusts is that they can be used effectively and creatively to reduce taxation. They are an essential aspect of tax planning which aims to achieve legitimate tax avoidance.[41] As Lord Tomlin said in *IRC v Duke of Westminster*:

'Every man is entitled if he can to order his affairs so that the tax attaching under the appropriate Act is less than it otherwise would be. If he succeeds in ordering them so as to secure that result, then, however unappreciative the Commissioners of Inland Revenue or his fellow taxpayers may be of his ingenuity, he cannot be compelled to pay an increased tax.'[42]

This general principle has been qualified by more recent House of Lords' decisions which have held that where steps are inserted into a pre-ordained series of transactions which have no commercial or business purpose but are inserted solely to avoid tax, the transaction will be treated as a single whole and taxed as such.[43] This limitation applies to trusts.[44]

---

37  *Chase Manhattan Bank NA v Israel-British Bank (London) Ltd* [1981] Ch 105.
38  *Barclays Bank Ltd v Quistclose Investments Ltd* [1970] AC 567.
39  *Re Goldcorp Exchange* [1995] 1 AC 74.      40  *A-G of Hong Kong v Reid* [1994] 1 AC 324.
41  Which is to be distinguished from illegitimate tax evasion.
42  [1936] AC 1. See also *IRC v Willoughby* [1997] 1 WLR 1071.
43  *W T Ramsay Ltd v IRC* [1982] AC 300; *Furness v Dawson* [1984] AC 474; *Craven (Inspector of Taxes) v White (Stephen)* [1989] AC 398; *Ensign Tankers (Leasing) Ltd v Stokes (Inspector of Taxes)* [1992] 1 AC 655; *IRC v McGuckian* [1997] STC 908; *MacNiven (HM Inspector of Taxes) v Westmoreland Investments Ltd* [2003] 1 AC 311. See Lord Walker, 'Ramsay 25 Years On: Some Reflections on Tax Avoidance' (2004) 120 LQR 412.
44  *Countess Fitzwilliam v IRC* [1992] STC 185.

A detailed consideration of taxation is outside the scope of this book,[45] but it is essential to have an elementary grasp of the tax structure and an appreciation of how trusts have historically been used to minimise liability to taxation. There has been an ongoing 'battle' between the government seeking to raise revenue, and those attempting to use the trust to avoid paying tax, and new statutory provisions tighten the tax regime to bring what were tax efficient trusts into tax liability.

There are three main types of taxation which will affect a trust: income tax, capital gains tax and inheritance tax. Each will be briefly examined and their applicability to trusts considered.

## (1) Income tax

### (a) Definition of income tax

Income tax, as Lord Macnaghten somewhat unnecessarily pointed out,[46] 'is a tax on income'. However, income tax is not payable on a person's whole income, but only his 'taxable income'. For example, a single person presently enjoys a tax-free allowance of £5,035 and is only taxable on his income above that figure. The rates of income tax on taxable income in the tax year 2005–2006 were:

| Taxable Income | Rate |
| --- | --- |
| £0–2,090 | 10% |
| £2,091–32,400 | 22% |
| £32,401 and above | 40% |

Income from savings, excluding share dividends, is taxed at 20%.

### (b) Income tax and trusts

For the purposes of income tax the trustees are liable to pay income tax at the basic rate (22%) on the income of the trust except where the income is savings income excluding dividends, for example bank interest, when a 20% rate applies. Dividend income is taxed at 10%. There is no personal allowance, and no lower band. Equally, the basic rate applies even if the trust income far exceeds the limit for the basic rate of taxation of personal income. One exception is that a special rate, known as the rate applicable to trusts, is chargeable against discretionary trusts and those where the income is accumulated. Where the rate applicable to trusts applies, the first £500 of the trust income is chargeable at the basic rate of 22% and the remainder at 40%.[47] Dividend income received by such trusts is taxed at 32.5%. This reduces the attractiveness and efficiency of discretionary trusts as means of avoiding income tax.

---

[45] For further reading see: Whitehouse, *Revenue Law—Principles and Practice* (19th edn, 2001); Moffat, *Trusts Law: Text and Materials* (3rd edn, 1999), Chs 3 and 8; Maudsley and Burn, *Trusts and Trustees: Cases and Materials* (6th edn, 2002), Part 3; Shipwright and Keeling, *Textbook on Revenue Law* (2nd edn, 1998).

[46] *LCC v A-G* [1901] AC 26 at 35.

[47] Income and Corporation Taxes Act 1988, s 686, added by Finance Act 1993.

### (c)  The receipt of trust income by trust beneficiaries

When trust income is paid out to trust beneficiaries they are not liable to pay further tax, provided that the trust income does not take their total taxable income outside of the basic rate. However, if they are liable to pay income tax at the higher rate, they are liable to make up the difference between the tax which was paid by the trustees (either 22% or 40%) and the higher rate of income tax (40%). A beneficiary who pays tax at a lower rate than that already paid by the trust will conversely be able to claim a refund of the difference.

### (d)  Trusts as a means of avoiding income tax

Trusts have proved a particularly popular and effective means of avoiding income tax. This is particularly the case with discretionary trusts, which can be used to distribute the income to those who have a low rate of personal taxation, for example the settlor's spouse or children, and avoid the higher rates that he himself would have to pay on that income. It has already been seen how the revenue authorities have responded by the imposition of a higher rate of taxation on the income of discretionary trusts and those where it is accumulated. To further limit tax avoidance, the Income and Corporation Taxes Act 1988, Pt XV provides that income under a trust is treated as the income of the settlor unless the income arises from property in which the settlor has no interest. A settlor is treated as having an interest in property if that property or any property derived from it can or might be payable to or for the benefit of the settlor or the settlor's spouse in any circumstances whatsoever. Property or derived property might be payable to the settlor where there is a power to revoke the settlement, or where a reversionary interest (whether vested or contingent) is conferred on the settlor. The settlor is also chargeable to tax on any income payable under the settlement to his unmarried minor children. There is no restriction on trusts of income for the benefit of adult children, and married minor children and grandchildren, and income tax may therefore be avoided by settlements in their favour.

## (2)  Capital gains tax

### (a)  Definition of capital gains tax

Capital gains tax is payable on the increase in value of 'chargeable assets' when they are realised. What is taxable is the difference in value of the asset between the date of acquisition and of disposal.[48] The tax is governed by the Taxation of Chargeable Gains Act 1992, and is levied at the rate of the disposer's income tax, subject to an annual exemption which is currently £7,500 per year for individuals.

---

[48] In the past inflation was taken into account in calculating the gain. Under the Finance Act 1998, ss 121–122, this was replaced with taper relief under which the proportion of gains subject to tax will be reduced year by year over a ten year period.

## (b) Capital gains tax and trusts

A settlor will be liable to pay capital gains tax personally when he settles property on trust, as this is considered a disposal.[49] Trustees pay capital gains tax on disposals by the trust at the rate applicable to trusts, namely 40% in the tax year 2005–2006. The trust enjoys an exemption equivalent to half of the personal exemption, ie £4,250. The trustees will be liable when they dispose of assets as part of the administration of the trust, and where the beneficiary becomes absolutely entitled to the property held on trust, other than by the death of the life tenant, which is a 'deemed disposal'.[50] This deemed disposal means that capital gains tax is payable whenever a settlement is brought to an end and the property resettled, which increases the costs of terminating or resettling property.[51]

## (3) Inheritance tax

### (a) Definition and history of inheritance tax

Inheritance tax is, in essence, a tax payable on capital which passes on death, but it also applies to inter vivos gifts that were made less than seven years before the death occurred. It is something of a combination of two earlier taxes: estate duty and capital transfer tax. Prior to 1974 there was just one tax, estate duty, which was payable on death.[52] Transfers inter vivos would be liable to estate duty if made seven years before the death.[53] Estate duty was payable on the whole trust fund on the death of a life tenant, but was easily avoided by the creation of a discretionary trust where the beneficiaries had no interest in the fund itself.[54] In 1974 estate duty was replaced by capital transfer tax, which was to be payable on any transfer of capital either inter vivos or on death, although higher rates applied to transfers on death. In 1986 capital transfer tax was replaced by inheritance tax.

### (b) The operation of inheritance tax

Section 1 of the Inheritance Tax Act 1984 provides:

'Inheritance Tax shall be charged on the value transferred by a chargeable transfer.'

A number of key features of the inheritance tax system must be considered in order to understand how it applies.

*(i) 'Transfers of value'.* Inheritance tax is only payable where there has been a 'transfer of value' which is defined in s 3(1) of the Inheritance Tax Act as 'a disposition made by a person as a result of which the value of his estate immediately after the disposition is less than it would be but for the disposition'.

*(ii) 'Value transferred'.* Tax is only payable on the 'value transferred', which is also defined in s 3(1) as the amount by which the transferor's estate is reduced by the transfer of value to the transferee.

---

[49] Taxation of Chargeable Gains Act 1992, s 53.    [50] Ss 54(1), 71.    [51] See Chapter 18.
[52] Finance Act 1894, ss 1, 2.    [53] Finance Act 1968, s 35.
[54] *Gartside v IRC* [1968] AC 553; see Chapter 17.

*(iii) 'Chargeable transfers'*. Not every transfer of value will attract inheritance tax. Only a 'chargeable transfer', which is defined in s 2(1) as 'a transfer of value which is made by an individual but is not an exempt transfer', is liable. Exempt transfers include gifts of up to £3,000 per annum and gifts between spouses.

*(iv) 'Potentially exempt transfers'*. Some transfers do not attract immediate inheritance tax, for example some inter vivos gifts will not incur tax if they are made seven years before the death of the transferor. However, before the seven-year period has elapsed, such gifts are described as 'potentially exempt transfers', since it is not yet clear whether they will in fact attract liability to tax.

*(v) Cumulation*. Tax is payable on the cumulative total of chargeable transfers made by the transferor, so that the gross value of all transfers of value over the relevant period are added together. Only those transfers made in the previous seven years will be cumulated in this way to determine the amount liable to taxation.

*(vi) The rate of inheritance tax*. In the case of transfers of value on death, the present rate of tax is 40% on cumulative transfers of value greater than the £275,000 (nil-rate band). This 40% rate also applies to gifts made inter vivos within three years prior to death, and for those made between seven and three years prior to the death there is a sliding scale of tax payable. Where an inter vivos transfer is initially chargeable, the rate is 20%.

*(vii) 'Interests in possession'*.[55] When the inheritance tax regime is applied to trusts there is a crucial distinction drawn between trusts in favour of beneficiaries who have an 'interest in possession' and those where the beneficiaries do not. Simply, the 'interest in possession' means that the beneficiary is immediately entitled to an interest in the trust fund or the income from it. This will therefore include successive interests where there is a life tenant who is entitled to the income from the capital of the trust. Broadly, this distinguishes fixed trusts from discretionary trusts where the beneficiaries have no immediate entitlement to any of the trust fund unless the trustees have decided to exercise their discretion and allocate shares of the trust fund to them. By means of this distinction different tax consequences apply to fixed and discretionary trusts.

## (c) Inheritance tax and fixed trusts[56]

*(i) Chargeable transfers*. Where the beneficiaries have 'interests in possession' and that interest comes to an end, this is treated as a transfer of value. This will include the death of the life tenant or disposal or assignment of the beneficiary's interest. Inheritance tax is then payable on the relevant proportion of the trust capital to which the beneficiary's interest relates. For this purpose, the life tenant is treated as entitled to the share of the trust capital from which his income derives, and inheritance tax will be payable on the death of the life tenant.

*(ii) Potentially exempt transfers*. In some cases the transfer will not attract immediate

---

[55]  *See Pearson v IRC* [1981] AC 753.     [56]  Inheritance Tax Act 1984, ss 49–57.

taxation but will be a 'potentially exempt transfer' and no tax will be payable if the transfer took place seven years or more before death. These include the inter vivos creation of a trust with an interest in possession by the settlor, and where an interest is terminated by the beneficiary with the consequence that another individual becomes entitled to the property.[57]

## (d) Inheritance tax and discretionary trusts[58]

The inheritance tax regime, and its predecessor capital transfer tax, has had a major impact on the effectiveness of discretionary trusts to avoid liability to taxation. Many of the provisions are intended to bring discretionary trusts within the scope of the tax. The legislation does not actually use the term 'discretionary trust' but speaks of 'relevant property' which is defined in s 58(1) as 'settled property in which no qualifying interest in possession exists'. This will largely cover discretionary trusts because the beneficiaries of a discretionary trust have no rights to the property held on trust until the trustee decides to make an allocation in their favour.[59]

*(i) Inter vivos transfers on discretionary trusts.* Where a gift is made inter vivos subject to a discretionary trust the transfer of value is immediately chargeable at the rate of 20%. This is because the transfer does not qualify as a potentially exempt transfer as described above.

*(ii) A periodic charge.* The property held on discretionary trust is subject to a periodic charge of up to a maximum of 6% of the value of the 'relevant property' to be levied on each tenth anniversary of the commencement of the settlement.[60]

*(iii) Exit charge.* Inheritance tax is also payable whenever the property ceases to be 'relevant property' within the meaning of the Act, which includes the termination of the discretionary trust or the allocation and distribution of property to beneficiaries.

*(iv) Exempted discretionary trusts.* Some discretionary trusts are exempt from this regime and enjoy a favoured status. Most important are accumulation and maintenance trusts, which are defined in s 71 as 'those trusts for the benefit of persons who have no interest in possession in the property but who will become entitled to either the property or an interest in possession before the age of 25, and that the income of the trust is in the meantime to be accumulated rather than distributed to them'.[61] All the potential beneficiaries of the trust must also share a common grandparent,[62] confining the exception to family trusts. Unlike other discretionary trusts, the inter vivos transfer of property to an accumulation and maintenance trust is not immediately chargeable, but a potentially exempt transfer. Similarly, there is no periodic charge and there is no exit charge when a beneficiary becomes entitled to the property or an interest in possession.

---

[57] Either absolutely, entitled to an interest in possession or held on accumulation and maintenance trusts: Finance (No 2) Act 1987, s 96.

[58] Inheritance Tax Act 1984, ss 58–85.    [59] See Chapter 17.    [60] Inheritance Tax Act 1984, s 64.

[61] Except the income that may be used for their maintenance, education or benefit; see Chapter 16.

[62] Or their widows, widowers or children if they have died.

### (e) Tax planning and discretionary trusts

Despite the narrowing of the opportunities of tax avoidance through discretionary trusts, they still offer the opportunity to minimise liability to inheritance tax. For example, a settlor can establish a discretionary trust of £275,000 or less without incurring any inheritance tax because they are within the 'nil band rate'. This will be particularly effective if the assets of the trust are expected to increase rapidly in value, for example shares or insurance policies, because the value of the assets is pegged at the date the settlement was created for the purpose of calculating any exit charge within the first ten years. Similarly, advantage can be taken of the favourable position of accumulation and maintenance trusts for the benefit of members of the family.

## 12 Distinguishing other mechanisms which facilitate a separation between the management and ownership of property

It has been seen that the practical usage of trusts largely derives from their ability to separate the management responsibilities from the ownership of property. However, this ability is not unique to trusts. This section will provide a brief examination of some situations where such a separation may be facilitated by other means.

### (1) Companies

One means by which such a such a separation can be made in practice is through public companies.[63] The capital for establishing a public company is provided by the shareholders who originally subscribed to the shares. They own the company. If it is wound up, any surplus funds remaining after the payment of the company's creditors will be distributed amongst them. Any profits which the company makes which are not capitalised by being retained to develop the business will also be distributed by way of a dividend to the shareholders. In a very real sense, therefore, the company belongs to the shareholders. It is they who benefit from its capital value and from the income which it produces. Yet the shareholders of a public company will very rarely be involved in its day-to-day management. Instead, they will appoint directors at a general meeting to whom they delegate the everyday management of the enterprise. The directors (unless they are also shareholders) will not themselves have a stake in the assets of the company, although within the limits of the authority given to them they will be able to decide how the assets of the company should be used. The directors will, of course, be under an obligation to exercise their powers of management honestly and properly. This is a duty which they owe, through the company, to the shareholders.

---

[63] The analysis given here applies equally to private companies, although it is more likely with private companies that the same individuals will be both shareholders and directors.

## (2) Agency

### (a) The agency relationship

The relationship of agency is the major means by which the common law enables the management and enjoyment of property to be separated. For example, Jake is the owner of a car he wishes to sell. Rather than arranging a contract of sale himself, he can delegate the task to another. He could authorise a garage to display the car on their forecourt and to sell the car to any purchaser prepared to pay more than a price arranged in advance. Here, Jake would be the principal and the garage would be acting as his agent. The relationship between the principal and the agent is contractual, and under this contract ownership in the car never passes to the agent. The agent is empowered to enter a contract with the purchaser on the principal's behalf, and property in the car will pass directly from the principal to the purchaser under that contract. Although he was not a party to the contract, the essence of agency is that it brings about a contract which is binding on the principal. For example, if the garage agreed to sell the car to Keith, this would bring about a contract with Jake, and if he refused to deliver the car for personal reasons, Keith would be entitled to maintain an action against him for breach of contract. Again, subject to any special arrangement between them, the agent owes a duty to his principal to act honestly and properly. An agent will be liable to his principal under the tort of negligence even where the agent is acting gratuitously.[64]

Agency is most commonly found in commercial situations. All company directors are treated as agents of the company, authorised to make decisions and to enter into engagements on behalf of the company. The manager of a shop, and the sales staff in the shop, will be agents of the proprietor, whether that proprietor is an individual or a company. Agency is less commonly found in non-commercial contexts,[65] and where it is, it is most likely to be used to support a single transaction.

### (b) Automatic termination of agency

In an agency relationship the agent represents his principal for the limited purposes for which the principal has granted him authority. However, the agent cannot enjoy a greater authority than the principal has given him, or than the principal himself enjoys. For this reason, if the principal loses his contractual capacity the agent automatically loses his authority to enter into contracts with third parties that are binding on the principal. He cannot enjoy the capacity to enter into contracts that the principal could not have entered himself. Thus, if the principal dies, or loses mental capacity, the authority of the agent is automatically terminated, whether or not the agent is aware of the principal's situation.[66]

### (c) Powers of attorney

Where a principal wishes an agent to be empowered to enter into a transaction requiring a deed, the authority must itself be conferred by way of deed termed a power of

---

[64] *Chaudhry v Prabhakar* [1988] 3 All ER 718, CA.

[65] Although see *Conservative & Unionist Central Office v Burrell* [1982] 1 WLR 522, discussed below, Chapter 11.

[66] See *Drew v Nunn* (1879) 4 QBD 661; *Yonge v Toynbee* [1910] 1 KB 215.

attorney. An agent so appointed is described as an attorney. The phrase 'power of attorney', as well as describing the deed and arrangement under which an agent is permitted to execute a deed on the principal's behalf, is also used to describe a general authority given by a principal permitting an agent to undertake any business concerning property on behalf of the principal. Such an authority could be given by a principal who was expecting to spend some time abroad during which it would be impracticable for him to manage his own affairs.

## (d) Enduring powers of attorney

*(i) The need for enduring powers of attorney.* Since a power of attorney is a form of agency, it will also terminate automatically if the principal loses his capacity. This poses particular difficulties for a society with an increasingly large elderly population, many of whom may go on to develop senile dementia, or other types of mental incapacity. An older person may wish to grant someone she trusts, perhaps a child or other relative, a comprehensive power of attorney over her affairs because she may feel that she is no longer able to cope. However, although the power of attorney will be effective as long as she retains capacity, if she becomes mentally incapable the authority will automatically terminate and the attorney will no longer be able to deal with her property. For this reason, the enduring power of attorney has been introduced by statute. The chief characteristic of the enduring power is set out in s 1(1)(a) of the Enduring Powers of Attorney Act 1985, namely that:

'. . . the power shall not be revoked by any subsequent mental incapacity [of the individual creating the power].'

*(ii) Creation of enduring powers of attorney.* An enduring power can only be created in accordance with the prescribed form set out in regulations made by the Lord Chancellor.[67] These include the requirement that the document creating the power contains explanatory information of the general effect of the power, to make clear the effect to both the principal and to the attorney.[68] The form must be signed by both principal and attorney in the presence of a witness.

*(iii) Supervision by the court.* Clearly, the enduring power of attorney gives the attorney tremendous power over the affairs of the person who created it, and there is a real danger of abuse, particularly after the creator has become incapable and is not able to supervise the exercise of the power. For this reason, the Court of Protection[69] exercises a supervisory function. By s 4 the attorney is under a duty to apply to the court for the registration of the instrument creating the power if he 'has reason to believe that the donor is or is becoming mentally incapable'.[70] Once the power has been registered it cannot be revoked by the donor[71] unless he clearly revokes the power 'and was mentally capable . . . when he did so'.[72]

---

[67] S 2(2).      [68] S 2(2)(*a*).

[69] The Court of Protection is an office of the Supreme Court responsible for administering the affairs of those who are incapable of doing so for themselves by virtue of mental incapacity.

[70] S 4(1).      [71] S 7(1).      [72] S 8(3).

*(iv) Notice to relatives.* When the attorney applies to the court for the power to be registered, he is under a duty to give notice to the donor's relatives in accordance with Sch 1 to the Act.[73] This enables the relatives, who are those most likely to be affected by the way that the attorney deals with the donor's property, the opportunity to object to the registration.

### (e) Agency and equity

Agency and powers of attorney are common law concepts, but both are supported by equity. The common law remedies for a failure by an agent or attorney to act in accordance with the terms of the authority conferred, or to break the duty of loyalty and care owed to the principal, are to deprive a purported but improper transaction of effect[74] and to impose on the agent or attorney an obligation to compensate the principal in damages for any loss. In some cases a third party suffering loss will have a right of redress against the agent by way of damages for breach of warranty of authority. Equity recognises agency by treating agents or attorneys, and company directors, as fiduciaries,[75] standing in such a position of trust with regard to their principal that they can be held liable to account for any abuse of their position. Thus, if they make an unauthorised profit, they can be obliged to hand the benefit over to their principal. In this respect, there is a clear analogy between the position of an agent and the position of a trustee.

### (f) Agency and ownership

Although agency provides a means by which powers of management can be divorced from the rights of enjoyment of property, it is generally considered to leave ownership in the principal unless the agent exercises his authority to pass ownership to himself or a third party. Even though the principal has conferred rights of disposal on the agent, this does not normally deprive him of his own rights of management and disposal. The agency is simply an authority which the principal gives to someone else to do some of those things which he can do himself. Moreover, apart from some limited exceptions, the principal retains the right to give instructions to the agent and to terminate the agency. The divorce between management and enjoyment is accordingly neither complete nor permanent.

### (g) Mandate

Agency is normally used to permit someone entrusted by the principal to enter into contracts on behalf of the principal. The common law recognises, however, a form of agency in which an agent is permitted to dispose of property belonging to the principal. This form of agency is known as mandate. For instance, Howard might authorise his wife, Winnie, to sign cheques payable from his own bank account. Similarly, Elizabeth,

---

[73] S 4(3).

[74] This will be the case both where the transaction lies outside the limits of the agent's authority and where there has been some procedural impropriety.

[75] See Chapter 23.

wishing to distribute a sum of money to the poor, might give a sum in cash to Philip, authorising him to choose the recipients. In each case, the agent may not be entering into contracts with third parties but is given authority to transfer title in the principal's property to a third party. Unless and until this authority is exercised, the title in the property remains with the principal.

# PART II

# CREATING THE RELATIONSHIP

# 6

# Substantive and formal requirements for the creation of express trusts

## 1 Introduction

The preceding section has examined the history of equity, its contribution to English law and in particular outlined the nature of the trust relationship. This section will consider how the trust relationship is created. This chapter will consider the creation of express trusts: ie trusts which are brought into existence by the deliberate act of the owner of property. Resulting and constructive trusts, which arise other than by the deliberate act of the owner, will be considered in Chapters 8 and 9.

## 2 Creating a valid trust

A trust only arises where there is a separation of the legal and beneficial ownership of property, in other words where a trustee holds property on trust for beneficiaries or recognised purposes. This trust relationship can be brought about in two ways, which were identified by the Court of Appeal in *Milroy v Lord*.[1]

*(i) Declaration of self as trustee*. A trust will be created if the person who holds the legal title to property effectively declares himself trustee of it in favour of specified beneficiaries. From the moment of the declaration he will hold the property on trust, and, although he retains the legal title, the beneficiaries will enjoy the equitable interest in the property. If a trust is created by such a declaration there is no need for any transfer of the property. Instead, the owner has simply changed his status vis-à-vis the property from that of absolute legal owner to that of trustee.

*(ii) Transfer of the property on trust to trustees*. If the legal owner of property wishes to subject it to a trust in favour of beneficiaries, but does not wish to serve as trustee himself, he can create a trust by transferring it to someone else, requiring them to hold it as trustee for the intended beneficiaries. In such circumstances the original owner ceases to have any interest in the property and the transferee of the property receives it

---

[1] (1862) 4 De GF & J 264.

(i)  The absolute owner declares himself trustee

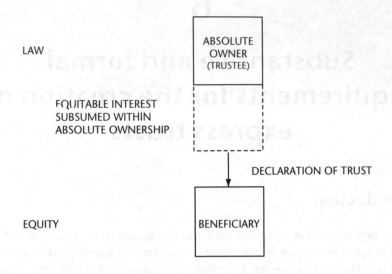

(ii)  The absolute owner transfers the property to a trustee on trust

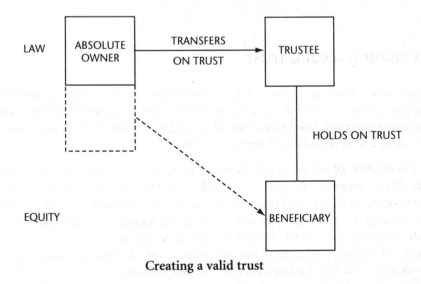

**Creating a valid trust**

as trustee subject to the trust obligations. After the transfer has occurred, the beneficiaries enjoy the equitable interest in the property.

Whichever method is used to create the trust, a number of requirements must be satisfied.

## (a)  Intention

An express trust will only be created if the owner of property wishes it to be subjected to a trust obligation. Therefore, he must clearly intend to create the trust, whether by declaration or by transfer.

## (b) Trust property

A trust obligation can only subsist in relation to specific property which is to be subject to the trust. Mere intention to create a trust will be of no effect if it is not also clearly indicated which property is intended to comprise the trust property.

## (c) Beneficiaries

As a consequence of the beneficiary principle, a trust can only exist in favour of individuals or legal persons. With some exceptions, the most notable of which is a trust for a charitable purpose, it is not possible to create a trust for abstract purposes with no ascertainable human beneficiaries.[2] Where the owner of property has indicated an intention to create a trust but has not specified who the beneficiaries are to be, no trust will come into existence and, if the property has been transferred to a third party as trustee, the equitable interest will revert back to him by means of a resulting trust.[3] The 'beneficiary principle' is examined in detail in Chapter 12.

## (d) Constitution[4]

A trust will only come into existence if the intended separation between the legal and equitable title has in fact occurred. In the case of an express trust created by the owner of the property declaring himself to be a trustee, this will only be so if the declaration was effective. Alternatively, if the trust was intended to be created by transferring the property to the trustee, then the trust will only come into existence if the property was effectually transferred and the intention to impose a trust communicated. Provided that such a declaration and transfer is effective, the trust relationship comes into being and the trust is described as completely constituted. If there was no effective declaration or transfer, the trust relationship will not have come into being, and the trust is described as incompletely constituted.

## (e) Formalities

Where the owner of property intends to create a trust of it during his lifetime, it may be necessary for him to comply with statutory provisions requiring the declaration to be made or evidenced by certain formalities. This is especially so if the intended trust property is land.[5] If these formalities are not followed, then the inter-vivos declaration of trust may be void or unenforceable and the trust will not come into existence. Where the owner intends to make a trust of property on his death, he must comply with the statutory formalities required for a valid will.

---

[2]  See below, p 378.    [3]  See Chapter 8.    [4]  See below, p 168.
[5]  Law of Property Act 1925, s 53.

## 3 The requirement of certainty

### (1) The three certainties

An express trust will not be validly created unless the 'three certainties'[6] are present. These classic requirements for a valid trust were identified by Lord Langdale MR in *Knight v Knight*,[7] where he said that a trust would only come into existence if there was certainty of words, certainty of subject matter and certainty of objects.[8] If a trust is uncertain in any of these respects it will be invalid. In the case of a purported declaration of trust the owner of the intended trust property will remain the absolute owner thereof. If the property was transferred to a trustee the equitable ownership will revert to the original owner by means of an automatic resulting trust.[9]

### (2) Certainty of intention

#### (a) Meaning of the requirement

Although the term 'certainty of words' was used by Lord Langdale MR in *Knight v Knight*[10] the modern meaning is probably better captured by the term 'certainty of intention'. The essence of the requirement is that an express trust will only arise if the owner of the property can be shown to have intended to subject it to a trust obligation. As Megarry J said in *Re Kayford Ltd (In Liquidation)*:

'. . . the question is whether in substance a sufficient intention to create a trust has been manifested.'[11]

There is thus no need for the word 'trust' to be used to create a trust. In *Re Kayford Ltd (In Liquidation)* a mail-order company was in financial difficulties and used a separate bank account to deposit money received from customers whose goods had not yet been delivered. When the company became insolvent the question arose whether the money in that account was held on trust for the customers, in which case it would not form part of the general assets of the company. Megarry J held that a trust had been created, stating:

'As for the requisite certainty of words, it is well settled that a trust can be created without using the words "trust" or confidence or the like . . .'[12]

An intention to create a trust can be deduced from the use of language which makes it clear that the recipient cannot hold property for his own benefit, but holds it for the benefit of others. It must demonstrate an intention to impose a mandatory obligation

---

6 See *Re Kayford Ltd (In Liquidation)* [1975] 1 All ER 604 at 607; *Hunter v Moss* [1994] 3 All ER 215 at 219.
7 (1840) 3 Beav 148 at 173.
8 See *Wright v Atkyns* (1823) Turn & R 143 at 157, per Lord Eldon.
9 See Chapter 19. A failure to communicate any trust on a transfer will give the transferee title free from the trust.
10 (1840) 3 Beav 148.    11 [1975] 1 WLR 279 at 282.    12 [1975] 1 All ER 604 at 607.

on the recipient of property as opposed to a purely moral obligation. In *Re Snowden (Deceased)*[13] an elderly lady who could not decide how to leave her property among her nephews and nieces left it all to her brother, Bert, telling him that he would 'know what to do.' It was held that she had not intended to impose a mandatory obligation on him to hold the property on secret trust for her nephews and nieces, but merely expressed a moral obligation to distribute the property among her family. In contrast in *Gold v Hill*[14] it was held that man who orally directed the beneficiary of his life insurance policy to 'look after Carol [his former wife] and the kids' had intended to impose a mandatory obligation and created a trust. In *McPhail v Doulton*[15] the House of Lords held that the mandatory character of the language used in a deed establishing a fund to provide for the benefit of the employees and ex-employees of a company, and their relatives and dependents, meant that the deed created a trust and not a mere power. The deed stated that the 'trustees shall apply the net income of the fund in making at their absolute discretion grants' to the specified class. The presence of the word 'shall' demonstrated that the recipients were under a mandatory duty to make grants, although they had a discretion as to who they were to be made to. In *R v Clowes*[16] it was held that a trust had arisen where an investment company had declared in its brochure that all monies received from clients would be held in a designated client account and only used to purchase specified government stock. In contrast in *Duggan v Governor of Full Sutton Prison*[17] no trust was found to have been created where a prison governor held money in an account for a life prisoner in accordance with r 43(3) of the Prison Rules 1999, which provides that any cash which a prisoner had at a prison should be paid into an account under the control of the governor and the prisoner should be credited with the amount in the books of the prison. Hart J concluded that the language of the rules did not disclose an intention to create a trust, with a concomitant duty to 'invest' the money, but only to create the relationship of debtor and creditor.

Even if the language used in an agreement is inadequate to create a trust, a trust may be held to have been created if this would fulfill the settlor's overriding intention. In *Don King Productions Inc v Warren (No 1)*[18] Lightman J held that such an intention could be deduced as a 'matter of business common sense' from the commercial background and the commercial purpose of agreements for the assignment of promotion and management of a number of boxers.[19]

## (b) Precatory words

Although there is no need for the settlor to use the technical term 'trust' to create a valid trust, in earlier cases the question arose whether the use of certain words would automatically give rise to a trust. In older authorities it was held that if a settlor or testator used certain key words or phrases, called 'precatory words', this would create a trust.[20] For example, if a testator had expressed his 'confidence', 'desire', 'wish', or 'hope' that a

---

[13] [1979] 2 All ER 172.   [14] [1999] 1 FLR 54.   [15] [1971] AC 424.
[16] [1994] 2 All ER 316.   [17] [2003] 2 All ER 678.
[18] [1998] 2 All ER 608; affd [2000] Ch 291, CA.   [19] [1998] 2 All ER 608 at 625.
[20] Even if the terms of the gift seemed to be absolute: *Malim v Keighley* (1795) 2 Ves 529; *Gully v Cregore* (1857) 24 Beav 185; *Curnick v Tucker* (1874) LR 17 Eq 320.

gift in his will be used in a particular way this would be held to impose a trust on the recipient of the gift. The difficulty with this approach is that such words do not seem to impose any obligation on the recipient of the property, but merely express the wish of the transferor or testator as to how he would like to see the property used. They imply a purely moral obligation[21] and not the legally enforceable mandatory obligation which is the essential characteristic of a trust.

However, in a number of late nineteenth-century authorities this approach was rejected and it was held that a trust would not be created merely by the use of such 'precatory words'.[22] In *Re Adams and Kensington Vestry*[23] a testator left all his property to his wife 'in full confidence that she would do what was right as to the disposal thereof between his children'. The issue was whether this language was effective to create a trust in favour of the children, or whether the wife took the property absolutely. The Court of Appeal held that the precatory words alone were insufficient to give rise to a trust. The position was summarised by Cotton LJ:

'... I think that some of the older authorities went a deal too far in holding that some particular words appearing in a will were sufficient to create a trust. Undoubtedly confidence, if the rest of the context shows that a trust is intended, may make a trust, but what we have to look at is the whole of the will which we have to construe, and if the confidence is that she will do what is right as regards the disposal of the property, I cannot say that that is, on the true construction of the will, a trust imposed upon her.'[24]

The consequence of these decisions is not that precatory words can never create a trust, but that they do not automatically create a trust. Instead, the whole context of the instrument alleged to give rise to a trust must be examined to determine whether there was an intention to subject the property to mandatory obligations.[25]

In the rather unusual case of *Re Steele's Will Trusts*[26] it was held that precatory words were sufficient to create a trust. A testatrix left a diamond necklace to her son by will. Her will contained a clause intended to make the necklace a family heirloom which ended with the expression 'I request my said son to do all in his power by his will or otherwise to give effect to this my wish'. This form of words had been copied exactly from the will at issue in the earlier case of *Shelley v Shelley*,[27] where they had been held effective to create a trust. Wynn-Parry J concluded that although subsequent cases had held that mere precatory words were not sufficient to create a trust, in the circumstances a trust had been created. The very fact that the precedent of *Shelley v Shelley* had been followed verbatim afforded the strongest indication that the testatrix had intended to create a trust. Thus, the rationale for this decision was not the use of the precatory

---

[21] In *Mussoorie Bank Ltd v Raynor* (1882) 7 App Cas 321 at 331 the use of precatory words such as 'confidence' was described simply as an 'appeal to the conscience of the taker'. See also *Re Snowden (Deceased)* [1979] Ch 528.

[22] See *Lambe v Eames* (1871) 6 Ch App 597; *Re Hutchinson and Tenant* (1878) 8 Ch D 540; *Mussoorie Bank Ltd v Raynor* (1882) 7 App Cas 321; *Re Diggles* (1888) LR 39 Ch D 253; *Re Hamilton* [1895] 2 Ch 370; *Re Johnson* [1939] 2 All ER 458.

[23] LR (1884) 27 Ch D 394.        [24] LR (1884) 27 Ch D 394 at 410.

[25] *Comiskey v Bowring-Hanbury* [1905] AC 84, HL.        [26] [1948] Ch 603.

[27] (1868) LR 6 Eq 540.

words per se, but the intention evidenced by following an established precedent for the creation of a trust of a family heirloom. It is unlikely that anyone would now be sufficiently foolish to attempt to create a trust in the same way.

## (c) 'Sham' intention

Although an express intention will usually be effective to create a trust, provided that the appropriate formalities have been observed, the court may refuse to find that a trust was validly created if such an intention was a 'sham' and that at the time it was made the owner had no real intention to subject his property to a trust. In *Midland Bank plc v Wyatt*[28] Mr and Mrs Wyatt were the joint legal owners of their matrimonial home. In 1987 they executed a formally valid declaration of trust of the house in favour of Mrs Wyatt and their daughters. The trust deed was dated 17 June 1987 and signed by both husband and wife, although Mrs Wyatt had not been aware of its effect. The declaration of trust was not acted upon in any way but was placed in a safe. Subsequently, Mr Wyatt obtained loans to finance his business, secured by his interest in the house. The banks were unaware of the existence of the declaration. The declaration was only produced after the business had gone into receivership and the secured creditors sought a charging order against the house. D E M Young QC held that in these circumstances the purported declaration of trust in favour of the wife and children was a sham and had therefore been ineffective to divest him of the entire beneficial interest in the house:

'I do not believe that Mr Wyatt had any intention when he executed the trust deed of endowing his children with his interest in Honer House, which at the time was his only real asset. I consider the trust deed was executed by him, not to be acted upon but to be put in the safe for a rainy day ... As such I consider the declaration of trust was not what it purported to be but a pretence or, as it is sometimes referred to, a "sham" ... Accordingly, I find that the declaration of trust sought to be relied upon by Mr Wyatt is void and unenforceable.'[29]

*Midland Bank plc v Wyatt* concerned a situation where a settlor purported to declare himself a trustee. Where the settlor and the trustee are distinct, the trust will only be invalidated on the basis of a sham intention if the trustee shared the intention of the settlor.[30]

## (3) Certainty of subject matter

A trust only exists if a separation of the legal and equitable ownership of property was brought about. Specific property must therefore be identified which is intended to be subject to the trust obligation. An imprecise definition of the intended trust property will render the trust invalid for uncertainty of subject matter.

## (a) No specific property has been indicated

Since a trust cannot exist in abstract, but only in relation to specific assets, the failure to identify any specific property as the trust property will prevent the creation of a valid

---

[28] [1995] 1 FLR 697.    [29] [1995] 1 FLR 697 at 707.

[30] *Shalson v Russo (Tracing Claims)* [2003] WTLR 1165; *Re Esteem Settlement* [2004] WTLR 1.

trust. In *Hemmens v Wilson Browne (a firm)*,[31] which primarily concerned the duty of care owed by a solicitor, it was held that an agreement allowing a person to call for a payment of £110,000 at any time could not create a trust of such a sum arising over their general assets because no specific property had been identified as the subject matter of the obligation. As Judge Moseley QC observed: 'there was no identifiable fund to which any trust could attach'.[32]

### (b)  The trust property has not been clearly defined

A trust will fail for uncertainty if it is impossible to ascertain the property intended to be subject to it from the definition given. In essence, there must be no 'conceptual uncertainty' as to the subject matter of the trust. For example, in *Palmer v Simmonds*[33] a testatrix attempted to create a trust of 'the bulk of my said residuary estate'. Kindersley V-C held that this did not create a trust because the term 'bulk' did not identify a definite, clear and certain part of her estate. Similarly, in *Re Jones*[34] it was held that a gift by a testator of the parts of his residuary estate which were not spent or disposed of by his wife did not create a trust.[35] In the more recent case of *Anthony v Donges*[36] a husband made a gift to his wife by will of 'such minimal part of my estate of whatsoever kind and wheresoever situate save as aforesaid she may be entitled to under English law for maintenance purposes'. Lloyd J held that this provision was void for uncertainty on the grounds that it was impossible to determine what she was entitled to under English law for maintenance purposes.

In contrast, if the property is capable of being ascertained from the definition used a valid trust will be created. For example, in *Re Golay's Will Trusts*[37] a testator provided in his will that a legatee was to receive a 'reasonable income' from his properties. Ungoed-Thomas J held that this was not uncertain because the term 'reasonable income' was sufficiently objective to be capable of quantification, noting that the court is regularly required to make objective assessments of what is reasonable.[38] In *T Choithram International SA v Pagarani*[39] the Privy Council expressed no view as to whether a settlor's gift of 'all my wealth' was void for uncertainty, as the particular assets at issue in the case had been clearly identified by the settlor as being included in the gift, and they were therefore held on trust.

### (c)  It is impossible to identify the trust property

A trust will fail for uncertainty if it is impossible to identify the property subject to the trust. In *Boyce v Boyce*[40] a testator bequeathed his two houses to trustees, one to be held on trust for each of his two daughters. The terms of the trust required the trustees to convey to Maria whichever house she chose and then to convey the other to Charlotte.

---

[31]  [1995] Ch 223.        [32]  [1995] Ch 223 at 232.        [33]  (1854) 2 Drew 221.
[34]  [1898] 1 Ch 438.
[35]  See also *Sprange v Barnard* (1789) 2 Bro CC 585; *In the Estate of Last* [1958] P 137. The authorities on mutual wills are developing in a way which suggests that (at least in some cases) a valid trust can exist where a beneficiary has a limited entitlement to draw down capital. See Chapter 11.
[36]  [1998] 2 FLR 775.        [37]  [1965] 2 All ER 660.
[38]  See *Jackson v Hamilton* (1846) 3 Jo & Lat 702.
[39]  [2001] 2 All ER 492, [2001] 1 WLR 1.        [40]  (1849) 16 Sim 476.

However, as Maria had died during his lifetime the court held that no valid trust of either house was created in favour of Charlotte because it was impossible to ascertain which should comprise the trust property. Where there is a discretionary trust, and the trustees have the discretion to determine the extent of the beneficiaries' entitlement to the trust property, no such uncertainty will occur.[41]

A comparable problem arose in *MacJordan Construction Ltd v Brookmount Erostin Ltd*,[42] where a builder's employer was entitled by contract to retain 3% of the contract price as trustee for a builder, to ensure that the work done was satisfactory, but had failed to establish any retention fund of specific money due under the contract. When the employer subsequently became insolvent it was impossible to identify any specific money as subject to the trust obligation, and therefore the builder was not entitled to priority.

### (d) The trust property is unascertained property[43]

Where the property intended to be subject to the trust is of an unascertained nature, it will not be subjected to a trust. In *Re London Wine Co (Shippers) Ltd*[44] a wine merchant held large stocks of wine in various warehouses. When a customer ordered a consignment, it was intended that the bottles ordered should become the property of the customer and that from that moment they would be held on trust for him by the company. However, there was no segregation of the bottles ordered from the general stocks until actual delivery to the customer. No beneficiary was able to identify which of the bottles were his or hers. In these circumstances, Oliver J held that the intended express trust of wine in favour of customers whose orders had not yet been delivered failed for lack of certainty of subject matter because the wine had not been appropriated from the general stock.[45] More recently, this requirement was affirmed and applied by the Privy Council in *Re Goldcorp Exchange Ltd (In Receiveship)*,[46] where a company dealing in gold and other precious metals had used investors' money to acquire bullion. As the company had not appropriated or segregated any specific parcels of bullion to the individual purchasers, but rather held it in bulk, the Privy Council held that it was not held on trust for the investors, so that when the company became insolvent they ranked merely as general unsecured creditors.

A rather different view was taken in *Hunter v Moss*.[47] The Court of Appeal held that an oral declaration of trust by Mr Moss, who owned 950 shares in a private company, of 5% of the issued share capital in favour of Mr Hunter, was not void for want of certainty of subject matter because the shares had not been segregated or appropriated. As the issued share capital was 1,000 shares, Moss held 50 of his shares on trust for Hunter. Since the shares had been sold he was accountable for an equivalent percentage

---

[41] See Chapter 16.      [42] [1992] BCLC 350

[43] See Parkinson, 'Reconceptualising the Express Trust' [2002] 61 CLJ 657, at 667–676.

[44] (1975) 126 NLJ 977.

[45] Compare *Re Stapylton Fletcher Ltd (In Administration Receivership)* [1995] 1 All ER 192, where a legal tenancy in common was found because bottles of wine for a group of customers had been segregated from the bulk.

[46] [1995] 1 AC 74. See [1995] RLR 83 (Birks).

[47] *Hunter v Moss* [1994] 1 WLR 452; [1994] 3 All ER 215, CA, (1994) 110 LQR 335 (Hayton); [1996] Conv 223 (Martin).

of the consideration received. The reason for this decision is not entirely clear. One interpretation is that the declaration of trust was to be treated as of a fractional share of Mr Moss's holding, like a tenancy in common. Another is that the requirement of the appropriation of the trust property from a common stock only applies in the case of tangible property but has no application to intangible property, provided that there is an identifiable bulk from which the property allegedly subject to the trust can be drawn. *Hunter v Moss* had been argued and decided before the decision had been given in *Re Goldcorp Exchange Ltd*. It has therefore been subjected to criticism[48] on the grounds that it is inconsistent with the ringing endorsement by the Privy Council of *Re London Wine Co (Shippers) Ltd*. However in *Re Harvard Securities Ltd (In Liquidation)* Neuberger J held that he was required to follow the decision in Hunter, and that it could be distinguished from the earlier cases on the grounds that it concerned shares and not chattels.[49]

It should be noted that as a consequence of the Sale of Goods (Amendment) Act 1995 purchasers of unascertained goods held in bulk become tenants in common of the legal title if the good are interchangeable. Although this does not generate a trust, it ensures that the purchaser enjoys a proprietary interest in the goods purchased, with the consequence that they will enjoy priority over other general creditors if the seller subsequently becomes insolvent before the goods are segregated from the bulk.

## (e) Future property

It is impossible for a settlor to create a presently existing trust of future property. 'Future property' means property which a person does not presently own, but which he hopes or expects will come into his ownership sometime in the future. Examples of future property include: the interest a person hopes to receive under the will or on the intestacy of a living person;[50] property a person may receive under the exercise of a special power of appointment;[51] future royalties;[52] a part, rather than a share, of future income;[53] and damages expected to be recovered in future litigation.[54] Future property should be distinguished from a residuary interest where a property right has already been conferred subject to the expiry of some prior right. A person with a vested or contingent right to property at some future date has an immediate proprietary interest in the property. Since it is not 'future property' he may subject it to an immediate trust.[55] For example, the person entitled to the remainder interest of property subject to a life interest may create a trust of his remainder interest.

In *Re Ellenborough*[56] Miss Emily Towry Law, who was the sister of Lord Ellenborough,

---

[48]  See, for example, Underhill & Hayton, *Law Relating to Trusts and Trustees* (16th edn, 2003) at p 79. See also [2003] LMCLQ 379 (Goode).

[49]  [1997] 2 BCLC 369, 381–384.

[50]  *Re Ellenborough* [1903] 1 Ch 697; *Re Lind* [1915] 2 Ch 345.

[51]  *Re Brooks' Settlement Trusts* [1939] Ch 993. See Chapter 15.        [52]  *Re Trytel* [1952] 2 TLR 32.

[53]  *Williams v CIR* [1965] NZLR 395: The settlor assigned the first £500 of his income to a charitable purpose. The New Zealand Court of Appeal held that this was future property, because it was not certain there would be such income. If he assigned a proportion of his annual income this would have been valid.

[54]  *Glegg v Bromley* [1912] 3 KB 474.

[55]  *Re Midleton's Will Trusts* [1969] 1 Ch 600; *Re Ralli's Will Trusts* [1964] Ch 288.

[56]  [1903] 1 Ch 697.

had executed a settlement in 1893 granting trustees any property she might become entitled to on the deaths of her brother and sister. When her brother died in 1902 she decided not to transfer the property to the trustees. Buckley J held that no trust had been created by the execution of the settlement. It amounted rather to a mere promise to create a trust. The trustees could not compel her to transfer the property to the trustees because no consideration had been given for the promise and 'equity will not assist a volunteer'.[57] Similarly, in *Re Brooks' Settlement Trusts*[58] a son assigned all the property which he might receive under the exercise of a power of appointment by his mother over property held on her marriage settlement to trustees in 1929. An appointment of £3,517 was made in his favour in 1939. Farwell J held that no trust had been created in 1929 because the property was a 'mere expectancy' and that since the settlement had been voluntary it could not be enforced.[59]

### (f) The inter-relationship between certainty of intention and of subject matter

Although the certainties of 'intention' and 'subject matter' refer to different aspects of the trust relationship, they are not to be considered independently of each other. Doubt over the certainty of the subject matter of a trust will exacerbate any doubt over the certainty of intention. This was recognised by the Privy Council in *Mussoorie Bank Ltd v Raynor*,[60] where the question at issue was whether the use of precatory words had been effective to create a trust:

'Now these rules are clear with respect to the doctrine of precatory trusts, that the words of gift used by the testator must be such that the court finds them to be imperative . . . If there is uncertainty as to the amount or nature of the property that is given over, two difficulties at once arise . . . the uncertainty in the subject of the gift has a reflex action upon the previous words and throws doubt upon the intention of the testator, and seems to show that he could not possibly have intended his words of confidence, hope, or whatever they may be . . . to be imperative words.'[61]

## (4) Certainty of objects

### (a) General

With the exception of charitable trusts and the small number of anomalous unenforceable trusts which are valid as exceptions to the beneficiary principle, a trust will only be valid if it exists for the benefit of identified legal persons who possess the locus standi to enforce the trust obligations, and for whom the property is held. If an owner of property attempts to declare himself trustee without specifying any valid beneficiaries, he will retain the absolute ownership of his property, whereas if he attempts to create a trust by transferring the property to a trustee without specifying any valid beneficiaries, the equitable interest in the property transferred will revert back to him by means of a resulting trust.[62] The beneficiaries must be defined in such a way that it is possible for the trustees, or in the event of their default the court, to know who they are. The trustee

---

[57] See pp 182–184 below      [58] [1939] Ch 993.
[59] See also *Norman v Federal Comr of Taxation* [1964] ALR 131; *Williams v CIR* [1965] NZLR 395.
[60] (1882) 7 App Cas 321.      [61] (1882) 7 App Cas 321 at 331.      [62] See Chapter 8.

will only be capable performing his functions, by allocating and transferring the trust property to them, if they are capable of certain identification. Problems of uncertainty generally arise where the beneficiaries are defined by means of a 'class definition'. Such a definition must be sufficiently certain, and the criterion used to identify the class sufficiently objective, to enable determination who is within, and who is outside, the class, thus ensuring that allocations of trust property are only made to genuine beneficiaries. The requirement of certainty of objects will be fully considered in Part III, with reference to the different types of equitable obligation. This section will only briefly review the relevant tests of certainty applying to trusts.

### (b) Fixed trusts[63]

In the case of a fixed trust, where the beneficial interests of each beneficiary have been predetermined by the settlor, it must be possible to draw up a 'complete list' of all the beneficiaries.[64] This means that the definition of the beneficiaries must be 'conceptually certain', and that there must also be 'evidential certainty' of who is within the class.

### (c) Discretionary trusts[65]

In the case of discretionary trusts, the trustees enjoy the discretion to determine how the trust property should be allocated amongst the class of potential beneficiaries. In *McPhail v Doulton*[66] the House of Lords held that the test for certainty of beneficiaries in discretionary trusts should be 'similar' to that used for the certainty of objects of powers,[67] namely that it must be possible to say of any given individual that he is, or is not, within the class. The Court of Appeal subsequently held in *Re Baden's Deed Trusts (No 2)*[68] that when this test is applied, a discretionary trust will be valid provided that the beneficiaries are defined with 'conceptual certainty', and that it is not invalidated by the absence of 'evidential certainty'. A discretionary trust will also be invalid if it is administratively unworkable because of the sheer size of the class of potential beneficiaries.[69]

## 4 Constitution of trusts

### (1) The meaning of constitution

#### (a) Fully constituted trusts

As was mentioned above, there are two methods by which the owner of property, termed the settlor, can create a trust over it. He may either declare himself to be the trustee of the property, or alternatively transfer it to a third party who is intended to

---

[63] See Chapter 13.    [64] *IRC v Broadway Cottages Trust* [1955] Ch 20, CA.
[65] See Chapter 16.    [66] [1971] AC 424.
[67] *Re Gulbenkian's Settlement Trusts (No 1)* [1968] Ch 126. See Chapter 15.    [68] [1972] Ch 607.
[69] *McPhail v Doulton* [1971] AC 424; *R v District Auditor, ex p West Yorkshire Metropolitan County Council* [1986] RVR 24.

hold it on trust for the specified beneficiaries and not to receive it for himself. If such a declaration is made, or transfer occurs, the trust is brought into existence, and from that moment the trustee holds the legal title to the property subject to the trust obligations, and the beneficiaries enjoy the equitable ownership of the trust property. Such a trust is described as 'fully-constituted,' meaning simply that the trust has in fact come into existence.

## (b) Incompletely constituted trusts

In contrast, if for any reason the settlor fails effectively to declare himself trustee of the intended trust property, or if the property is never transferred by the settlor to the intended trustee, the trust does not come into being. The settlor remains the absolute owner of the property and it is not held by him subject to the trust obligations. In consequence, the beneficiaries have no subsisting proprietary entitlement to the intended trust property. No effective separation of the legal title and equitable ownership has occurred. In such circumstances the trust is described as 'incompletely constituted'. This terminology may be confusing, as in fact no trust exists. The Privy Council has recently indicated that equity should not 'strive officiously to defeat a gift' so as to render a trust unconstituted.[70]

## (c) Beneficiaries' remedies

Where a trust remains incompletely constituted, the reality is often that a settlor has previously promised that he will create a trust in favour of the beneficiaries but he has not fulfilled his promise by failing to make an effective declaration or transfer. In such circumstances the main concern of the beneficiaries will be whether they have any means of requiring the settlor to constitute the trust in their favour. The basic position is that the beneficiaries cannot force the settlor to constitute the trust if they are volunteers who have not provided valuable consideration in return for his promise to settle the property on trust for them. This follows from the rule that 'equity will not assist a volunteer'. However, it will be seen that this general restriction is subject to a number of limited exceptions. Alternatively, even if the beneficiaries are volunteers and not entitled to any equitable remedies, they may be able to seek common law remedies to compensate them for the loss they have suffered because the trust has not been constituted.

## (2) Constituting the trust by declaration

### (a) Requirements of effective declaration

In *Re Cozens*, Neville J indicated what would be required by the court to establish that a settlor had declared himself trustee of his property:

'. . . in each case where a declaration of trust is relied on the Court must be satisfied that a present irrevocable declaration of trust has been made.'[71]

---

[70] *Choithram (T) International SA v Pagarani* [2001] 2 All ER 492, 501 per Lord Browne-Wilkinson.
[71] [1913] 2 Ch 478 at 486.

This emphasises that an expression of intent to create a trust in the future does not create an immediate fully constituted trust. In *Richards v Delbridge* Jessel MR made clear that the settlor does not need to use particular words or technical expressions to create a trust by declaration:

'. . . he need not use the words "I declare myself a trustee", but he must do something which is equivalent to it, and use expressions which have that meaning.'[72]

In *Paul v Constance* Scarman LJ accepted as a statement of principle that 'there must be clear evidence from what is said or done of an intention to create a trust'.[73]

### (b) Formalities[74]

In general, an inter vivos declaration of trust will be valid and effective to create a fully constituted trust, even though it is made orally and without consideration.[75] However, in the case of land s 53(1)(*b*) of the Law of Property Act 1925 provides:

'. . . a declaration of trust respecting any land or any interest therein must be manifested and proved by some writing signed by some person who is able to declare such trust or by his will.'

A purported declaration of a trust of land which is not evidenced in writing will generally be ineffective, although this general rule is subject to exceptions, which are discussed below in the context of the formalities required for the creation of express trusts.[76]

### (c) Cases illustrating effective declaration

It is ultimately a question of fact whether in any particular case an effective declaration of trust has occurred. A number of general indications can be drawn from the authorities:

*(i) Loose conversation. Jones v Lock*[77] suggests that words spoken in what was merely 'loose conversation' will not amount to an effective declaration of trust because the necessary intention to create a trust is lacking. Jones was an ironmonger who had returned from a business trip to Birmingham. The nurse of his infant son complained that he had not brought anything back as a present for the baby. Jones then produced a cheque for £900, payable to himself, which was the result of his business negotiations and handed it to the baby saying: 'Look you here, I give this to baby; it is for himself, and I am going to put it away for him, and will give him a great deal more along with it.' A few days later he died. The question was whether in the circumstances the father had created a trust of the money represented by the cheque for the son. The cheque had not been effectively transferred to the son, as this would have required the father's endorsement. Lord Cranworth LC held that there was equally no effective declaration of trust:

---

[72] (1874) LR 18 Eq 11 at 14.     [73] [1977] 1 WLR 527, CA.     [74] See below, p 195.
[75] See *Jones v Lock* (1865) LR 1 Ch App 25 at 28, per Lord Cranworth LC: 'a parol declaration of trust of personality may be perfectly valid even when voluntary'.
[76] See below, p 196.     [77] (1865) LR 1 Ch App 25.

'. . . the case turns on the very short question whether Jones intended to make a declaration that he held the property in trust for the child; and I cannot come to any other conclusion than that he did not. I think it would be of very dangerous example if loose conversation of this sort, in important transactions of this kind, should have the effect of declarations of trust.'

*(ii) Words repeated over a period of time.* Although isolated 'loose conversation' will not alone effect a valid declaration of trust, *Paul v Constance*[78] suggests that the repetition of such words in conversation over a period of time may be sufficient to create a trust. Dennis Constance was separated from his wife and living with Doreen Paul. In 1974 he received £950 damages as compensation for a an injury he had sustained at work. He deposited the money in a bank account and on a number of occasions told Paul that the money was 'as much yours as mine'. Constance died without leaving a will and his wife, from whom he had not been divorced, claimed that she was entitled to the money in the account on the grounds that it formed part of his estate, to which she was entitled by the rules of intestate succession. The Court of Appeal held that she was not entitled to the money because it was held upon a validly declared express trust in favour of Paul. Scarman LJ said that although 'it is not easy to pin-point a specific moment of declaration' the 'use of those words on numerous occasions' between Constance and Paul was sufficient to constitute an express declaration of trust.

*Paul v Constance* was followed in the more recent case of *Rowe v Prance*.[79] Mr Prance and Mrs Rowe had conducted a relationship over many years. Although Prance had promised to divorce his wife to live with Mrs Rowe, he had remained married. He purchased a yacht where he said he would live with Mrs Rowe, and in which they could sail the world. The yacht was registered in his sole name, allegedly because Mrs Rowe did not have an Ocean Master's certificate. Over a period of time Mr Prance regularly used the word 'our' in relation to the yacht. Nicholas Warren QC held that in these circumstances the yacht was held on trust by Mr Prance for himself and Mrs Rowe in equal shares.

*(iii) Words of gift by the settlor to himself.* In the recent case of *Choithram (T) International SA v Pagarani*[80] the Privy Council was forced to consider a novel situation which did not fall squarely within either of the methods of constitution identified in *Milroy v Lord.* The case concerned a wealthy philanthropist ('TCP') who wished to set up a charitable foundation to receive much of his wealth, consisting of company shares and deposit balances, when he died. In February 1992, knowing that he was dying, he signed a trust deed establishing the foundation. The deed stated that he was the settlor, and appointed seven trustees, of which he was one. After signing the deed he orally stated that he was giving all his wealth to the foundation. He died a month later, but had not executed any share transfers to the foundation, nor had he executed a formal declaration of trust. The judge at first instance, and the Court of Appeal of the British Virgin Islands, held that no trust had been created because of the absence of either an effective declaration or an effective transfer. The Privy Council allowed an appeal, advising that the settlor had constituted the trust. Lord Browne-Wilkinson explained

---

[78] [1977] 1 WLR 527.    [79] [1999] 2 FLR 787.    [80] [2001] 2 All ER 492, [2001] 1 WLR 1.

that his words of gift to the foundation could only have been intended to establish a trust:

'Although the words used by TCP are normally appropriate to an outright gift—"I give to X"—in the present context there is no breach of the principle in *Milroy v Lord* if the words of TCP's gift (ie to the foundation) are given their only possible meaning in this context. The foundation has no legal existence apart from the trust declared by the foundation trust deed. Therefore the words "I give to the foundation" can only mean "I give to the trustees of the foundation trust deed to be held by them on the trusts of the foundation trust deed." Although the words are apparently words of outright gift they are essentially words of gift on trust.'[81]

In effect the settlor made a gift of the intended trust property to himself in his capacity as trustee, which had the effect of constituting the trust. The trust was enforceable even though the trust property had only been vested in one of the trustees. Since it is somewhat artificial to regard the settlor as having made a gift to himself, as there was no need for any transfer of the assets concerned, it might be better to treat the settlor as having declared himself a trustee of the assets which were already his. Thus words of gift by the settlor to himself on trust should be regarded in substance as a declaration of self as trustee

*(iv) Declaration by conduct.* An effective declaration of trust may also be inferred from conduct, even though no words approximating to such a declaration are used. In *Re Vandervell's Trust (No 2)*[82] the Vandervell Trust Company held a share option on trust for Mr Vandervell. The option was exercised using £5,000 that the trust company held on separate trusts for Vandervell's children. Thereafter, the trustees wrote to the Inland Revenue saying that the shares would be held on trust for the children's settlement, and dividends arising from the shares were henceforth paid into the children's settlement. Given that this was all done with the full assent of Mr Vandervell, the Court of Appeal held that the evidence of the intention to declare a trust was clear and manifest and that the trustee company held the shares on trust for the children.

*(v) Overarching intention to create a trust.* In *Don King Productions Inc v Warren (No 1)*[83] Lightman J was faced with the task of interpreting two multi-million pound contracts between the leading boxing promoters in the UK and the USA. The judge remarked that 'the drafting of the first agreement is somewhat primitive for a transaction of this size and importance for the parties'.[84] By the agreements, Frank Warren, the UK boxing promoter, purported to assign his promotion, management and associated contracts ('PMA contracts') to a partnership with Don King, the 'larger than life' American promoter. Because the contracts related to personal services, no assignment could take place. However, Lightman J held that the benefit of the PMA contracts had been subjected to a trust in favour of the partnership since this had been the overriding intention of the parties:

---

[81] [2001] 2 All ER 492 at 501.    [82] [1974] Ch 269.    [83] [1998] 2 All ER 608.
[84] [1998] 2 All ER 608 at 615.

'. . . the clear intent of the parties manifested in the first and second agreements was that the promotion management and associated agreements should be held by the partnership or by the partners for the benefit of the partnership absolutely, and that this intent should be given the fullest possible effect. The agreements have accordingly at all times been held by the partners as trustees for the partnership.'[85]

## (3) Constituting the trust by transfer

### (a) Requirements for effective transfer

Where a settlor wishes to create a trust of which a third party is the trustee, the trust will only be constituted if the trust property is vested in the trustee by means of an effective transfer of his legal or beneficial title. In *Choithram (T) International SA v Pagarani* the Privy Council recently held that where the settlor intends to establish a trust with a body of trustees it will be sufficient to constitute the trust if the property is transferred to at least one of the intended trustees, since that recipient will be bound by the trust and must give effect to it by transferring the trust property into the name of all the trustees.[86] The requirements for an effective transfer of the settlor's title vary, depending on the type of property involved.

*(i) Land.* By s 52 of the Law of Property Act 1925 all conveyances of land, or of interests in land, are void unless made by deed. Therefore an attempted oral transfer of land, a transfer by mere writing, or even granting the trustees physical possession of the land will be insufficient to create a constituted trust. In *Richards v Delbridge*[87] a grandfather attempted to create a trust of a leasehold interest for his grandson by assigning the lease to the boy's mother. Although the assignment was in writing, it was not made by deed. There was therefore no effective transfer of the lease and the trust remained incompletely constituted. Where land is registered, the transfer of the legal title must be perfected by the registration of the transferee as the 'registered proprietor'.[88]

*(ii) Shares.* As in the case of registered land, shares are owned at law by the person who is registered as the owner thereof on the 'share register' of the company to which they relate. The legal ownership of shares can only be transferred by means of the registration of the transferee on the share register of the company issuing them. The possession of share certificates is merely evidence of the ownership of the shares but does not itself constitute ownership. Registration of a transferee as legal owner of the shares may occur either following the completion of an appropriate share transfer form,[89] or by means of an appropriate instruction if the shares are held electronically in the CREST system.[90] In either case, mere delivery of the share certificates by the settlor to an intended trustee will not create a completely constituted trust. This was established in the leading case,

---

85   [1998] 2 All ER 608 at 635.
86   [2001] 2 All ER 492 at 502. See also *Re Ralli's Will Trust* [1964] Ch 288, considered below.
87   (1874) LR 18 Eq 11.
88   See Land Registration Act 2002; *Mascall v Mascall* (1984) 50 P & CR 119, CA.
89   Companies Act 1985, ss 182, 183; Stock Transfer Act 1963, s 1.
90   (1996) 146 NLJ 964 (Pinner).

*Milroy v Lord*.[91] Thomas Medley attempted to create a trust of 50 shares in the Bank of Louisiana in favour of the plaintiffs by transferring them on trust to Samuel Lord. By the constitution of the bank the shares were only transferable in the books of the company. Although Medley had executed a deed of assignment and delivered the share certificates to Lord, the view of the court was that title had not been effectively transferred and the trust remained incompletely constituted.

*(iii) Copyrights*. By s 1 of the Copyright, Designs and Patents Act 1988, a copyright must be transferred in writing.

*(iv) Chattels*. Title to chattels, ie tangible personal property, may be effectively transferred by means either of a deed or gift, or delivery of possession of the chattel to the intended transferee.

*(v) Bills of exchange*. A bill of exchange may only be transferred by endorsement. Mere physical delivery to the intended trustee will not constitute the trust. This was evident in *Jones v Lock*,[92] where the mere fact that the father had handed his cheque to his infant son was insufficient to transfer title to him.

*(vi) Equitable interests*. If the intended trust property is an equitable interest enjoyed in property by the settlor, it can only be transferred to the trustee by writing, as required by s 53(1)(c) of the Law of Property Act 1925, which provides:

'. . . a disposition of an equitable interest or trust subsisting at the time of the disposition, must be in writing signed by the person disposing of the same, or by his agent thereunto lawfully authorised in writing or by will.'[93]

## (b) Transfers where registration by a third party is required

As has been seen above, the legal title to some forms of property such as shares or land can only be transferred by registration of the transferee as the new legal owner. Prior to the very recent decision of the Court of Appeal in *Pennington v Waine*[94] it was thought that the mere completion of the relevant transfer documents by the transferor would be ineffective to transfer any interest to a volunteer transferee, since equity would not act to perfect an imperfect gift. The only exception, known as the rule in *Re Rose*, was that equity would treat a transfer as complete if the transferor had done everything in his power to transfer the property to the transferee. However in *Pennington v Waine* the Court of Appeal held that mere completion of the relevant transfer documents may be capable of giving rise to an equitable assignment of the property concerned even where the transferor has not strictly done everything in his power to transfer the property.

*(i) Transfer complete in equity when the transferor has done everything in his power to transfer the legal title to the transferee*.[95] It is well established that where the legal title to property can only be effectively transferred by registration of the transferee

---

[91]  (1862) 4 De GF & J 264.      [92]  (1865) LR 1 Ch App 25.      [93]  See below, p 199.

[94]  [2002] 1 WLR 2075; [2002] LMCLQ 296 (Tijo & Yeo); (2003) 17 TLI 35 (Ladds); (2003) 62 CLJ 263 (Doggett); [2003] Conv 364 (Garton); [2003] Con 192 (Halliwell).

[95]  See [1998] CLJ 46 (Lowrie and Todd). See also *Hunter v Moss* [1994] 3 All ER 215, 220; *Re Harvard Securities Ltd (In Liquidation)* [1997] 2 BCLC 369, 375.

as the substitute owner on a register maintained by a third party equity will treat the transfer as complete from the moment that the transferor has done 'everything within his power' to facilitate the transfer of the property. This principle emerged in *Re Rose (Deceased)*,[96] where Eric Rose had transferred 10,000 shares to his wife. The share transfer form was completed on 30 March 1943 and forwarded to the company. The transfer was registered in the books of the company on 30 June. To avoid estate duty the transfer would have had to have been completed prior to 10 April. The Court of Appeal held that the transfer had in fact been completed on 30 March, since at that time the transferor had done everything within his power to divest himself of his interest in the shares. Estate duty was not therefore payable.

The concept of the transferor having done 'everything within his power' to transfer legal title to his property does not merely mean that he had done all that he was practically able to do, or had been capable of doing, in the circumstances he faced. The rule in *Re Rose* operates where the only acts which remain to achieve the transfer of the legal title to the transferee are those of third parties. The transferor must have gone beyond the point of no return so that he is no longer able to prevent the transfer being completed. The principle was explained by Jenkins LJ:

'[Rose] had done all in his power to divest himself of and to transfer to the transferees the whole of his right, title and interest, legal and equitable, in the shares in question. He had, moreover, complied strictly with the procedure prescribed by the company's articles. Nevertheless, he had not transferred the full legal title, nor could he do so by the unaided operation of any instructions of his . . . [He] had thus done all he could, in appropriate form, to transfer the whole of his interest, but so far as the legal title was concerned, it was not in his power himself to effect the actual transfer of that, inasmuch as it could only be conferred on the transferees in its perfect form by registration of the transfers.'[97]

The rule was not therefore held to operate in *Re Fry*[98] because the transferor had failed to do everything which was necessary to transfer title. The owner of shares in an English company, who was domiciled in America, had executed a share transfer form and sent it to England to be registered. Under legislation in force the company was prohibited from registering the transfer without the consent of the Treasury. Although the transferee had obtained, completed and returned the appropriate forms seeking such consent, he had died before it was given. In these circumstances Romer J held that he had not done everything within his power to transfer title to the shares, and that they therefore remained his at the date of his death:

'Now I should have thought it was difficult to say that the testator had done everything that was required to be done by him at the time of his death, for it was necessary for him to obtain permission from the Treasury for the assignment and he had not obtained it. Moreover the Treasury might in any case have required further information of the kind referred to in the questionnaire which was submitted to him, or answers supplemental to those which he had given in reply to it.'[99]

---

[96] [1952] Ch 499.     [97] [1952] Ch 499 at 515.     [98] [1946] Ch 312.
[99] [1946] Ch 312 at 317–318

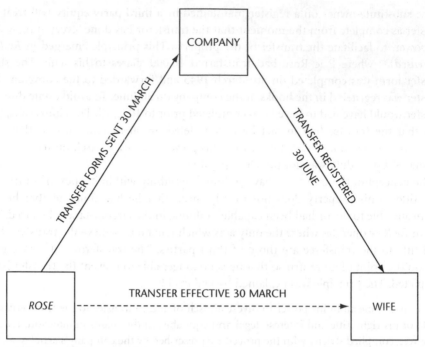

The settlor has done everything within his power to transfer the property: *Re Rose*

The rule in *Re Rose* was applied to a transfer of registered land in *Mascall v Mascall*.[100] William Mascall wanted to transfer his house to his son. He filled in all the relevant parts of a form of transfer supplied by the Land Registry to effect a transfer of the land and handed it to his son. The son completed those parts that the intended transferee was required to complete and sent the form to the Stamp Office. He then had a row with his father, who sought a declaration that the transfer was void. The transfer form had not yet been sent to the Land Registry. The Court of Appeal held that the father had done everything in his power to transfer the title to his son, and that the transfer was therefore completed when he handed the transfer form to him, having completed all the parts that were required of the transferor. Although it had not yet been sent to the Land Registry, this was the responsibility of his son as transferee, and therefore he had done everything within his power, or more precisely everything that was necessary by him, to transfer the title. All that remained were the acts of third parties, the son sending the form to the Land Registry and their registering him as the proprietor, which were out of his control. The principle was stated by Browne-Wilkinson LJ:

'A gift is complete as soon as the settlor or donor has done everything that the donor has to do, that is to say, as soon as the donee has within his control all those things necessary to enable him, the donee, to complete his title.'[101]

The rule has also been held to apply to an assignment of a lease which must be completed by registration.[102]

---

[100] (1984) 50 P & CR 119.    [101] (1984) 50 P & CR 119 at 126.
[102] *Brown & Root Technology Ltd v Sun Alliance and London Assurance Co Ltd* [1996] Ch 51.

Although *Re Rose*[103] and *Mascall v Mascall*[104] concerned absolute transfers of property which was not intended to become subject to a trust, the rule would equally operate in favour of a transferee who was intended to acquire then legal title as a trustee. In such a case the trust would be completely constituted from the very moment that the settlor had done everything within his power to transfer title. Although this is not an exception to the rule that 'equity will not assist a volunteer', because there is no need for the court to intervene and order the trust to be constituted on behalf of the beneficiaries, the rule in *Re Rose*[105] does indirectly operate to assist volunteers by widening the circumstances in which equity will regard a trust as having come into existence.

*(ii) Transfer complete in equity when it would be unconscionable for the transferor to recall the gift to the transferee.* Until recently it was thought that an attempted transfer of shares would only be regarded as complete if the strict requirements of the rule in *Re Rose* were satisfied. However in *Pennington v Waine*[106] the Court of Appeal held that, in appropriate circumstances the execution of a share transfer form might be sufficient to give rise to an equitable assignment of the beneficial interest in the shares, so that the transferor henceforth holds the shares on trust for the transferee, even though the completed form has not been delivered to the transferee or the third part registrar. In September 1998 Ada Crampton executed a share transfer form in favour of her nephew, Harold Crampton, in respect of 400 shares in a family company. The share transfer form had been drawn up for her by a partner in the Company's auditors. She returned the form to him and it was placed on the company's file. Ada also wanted Harold to become a director of the company, and the auditor wrote to him enclosing instructions to complete form 288A (a prescribed form of consent to act as a director), and also stating that Ada had instructed him to arrange the transfer to him of 400 shares in the company, adding that this did not require any action on his part. The auditor took no further action to transfer the shares prior to Ada's death in November 1998. The Court of Appeal held that, despite the fact that Ada had not done everything in her power to transfer the shares to Harold because the transfer form had not been sent to the company for registration, the gift was effective in equity. Arden LJ, with whom Schiemann LJ agreed, held that it was not necessary for Ada to have delivered the share transfer form either to Harold or the company. The gift was complete because Ada had intended to make an immediate gift and it would have been unconscionable for her to recall the gift.[107] Clarke LJ held that the execution of the share transfer form could be taken as a complete assignment of her equitable interest in the shares, thus generating a trust under which she could have been compelled to procure the registration of the shares in Harold's name.[108]

In the view of the majority the crucial element which renders a transfer complete in equity is that it would be unconscionable for the transferor to recall the gift. Arden LJ identified the circumstances which she considered had made it unconscionable for Ada to recall the gift:

---

[103] [1952] Ch 499.    [104] (1984) 50 P & CR 119.    [105] [1952] Ch 499.
[106] [2002] 1 WLR 2075.    [107] Ibid at [66].    [108] Ibid at [110].

'There can be no comprehensive list of factors which makes it unconscionable for the donor to change his or her mind: it must depend on the court's evaluation of all the relevant considerations. What then are the relevant facts here? Ada made the gift of her own free will: there is no finding that she was not competent to do this. She not only told Harold about the gift and signed a form of transfer which she delivered to Mr Pennington for him to secure registration; her agent also told Harold that he need take no action. In addition Harold agreed to become a director of the Company without limit of time, which he could not do without shares being transferred to him. If Ada had changed her mind on (say) 10 November 1998, in my judgement the court could properly have concluded that it was too late for her to do this as by that date Harold signed the form 288A.'[109]

However it is submitted that this case dangerously undermines the well established principle that equity will not act to perfect an imperfect gift nor assist a volunteer. The mere fact that a donor intended to make a immediate gift does not mean that an immediate gift was made. The rules enable a transferor to change his or her mind whether to make a gift even after they have completed many of the steps necessary to effect a transfer. Whilst it might have been clear that Ada had not changed her mind about the intended transfer, in other cases the evidence will be more equivocal. The effectiveness of alleged transfers of property should not be determined by the vagaries of whether the court considers that it would be 'unconscionable' for the transferee to change his or her mind. Arden LJ held that if she had been wrong to hold that the delivery of the share transfers to the company or donee was not required, then the case could have been decided that same way by finding that Ada and the Company auditor had become agents for Harold for the purpose of submitting the share transfer to the company.[110] It is submitted that this analysis would have been preferable to the amelioration of the well established strict requirements of the rule in *Re Rose*. Alternatively it might have been argued that Harold had provided valuable consideration by agreeing to become a director of the company without limit of time in return for the gift of shares, thus entitling equity to act on his behalf. It remains to be seen whether the new approach founded on unconscionability finds favour with higher courts.

## (4) Constitution of a trust through co-incidental receipt of the trust property by the trustee

In most cases, a trust will only be fully constituted if the trust property is transferred to the trustee by the deliberate act of the settlor. However, in some very rare cases it seems that a trust will be fully constituted if the trustee received the legal title to the trust property as a matter of coincidence. In *Re Ralli's Will Trusts*[111] a number of trusts were created by the members of a family. The patriarch, Ambrose Ralli, died in 1899. Under his will his wife was to enjoy a life interest of his residuary estate which was to be held on trust, and on her death it would pass to his daughters, Helen and Irene, in equal shares. In 1924 Helen executed a marriage settlement, under which she promised to settle any after-acquired property for the benefit of the beneficiaries of the settlement. This would include the remainder interest in her father's estate to which she would

---

[109]  Ibid at [64].        [110]  2002 WL 45513 at [67].        [111]  [1964] Ch 288.

become entitled on the death of her mother. The beneficiaries under the marriage settlement were her sister Irene's children. Helen died in 1956 and the testator's widow in 1961. The plaintiff, who had been appointed a trustee of Ambrose Ralli's will in 1946, was at that date the sole surviving trustee of the trusts established under the will. He was, coincidentally, also the sole surviving trustee of Helen's marriage settlement. On Ambrose's widow's death the remainder interest in his residuary estate was vested in him as trustee under the will. The central question was whether he held Helen's half share as part of Helen's estate, in which case it would pass under her will, or whether he held it under the terms of her marriage settlement, in which case it would pass to Irene's children. Although there had been no intentional transfer of the property to the plaintiff in his capacity as trustee of the marriage settlement, Buckley J held that the fact that he had received it in his capacity as the trustee of the will was sufficient to constitute the trust, and the property was therefore held on the terms of the marriage settlement. He concluded that it did not matter how the trustee had come to receive the legal title to the trust property:

'In my judgment the circumstance that the plaintiff holds the fund because he was appointed a trustee of the will is irrelevant. He is at law the owner of the fund, and the

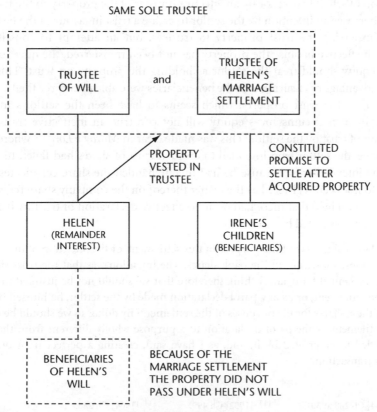

SAME SOLE TRUSTEE

TRUSTEE OF WILL and TRUSTEE OF HELEN'S MARRIAGE SETTLEMENT

PROPERTY VESTED IN TRUSTEE

CONSTITUTED PROMISE TO SETTLE AFTER ACQUIRED PROPERTY

HELEN (REMAINDER INTEREST)

IRENE'S CHILDREN (BENEFICIARIES)

BENEFICIARIES OF HELEN'S WILL

BECAUSE OF THE MARRIAGE SETTLEMENT THE PROPERTY DID NOT PASS UNDER HELEN'S WILL

**Re Ralli's Will Trusts**

means by which he became so have no effect on the quality of his legal ownership. The question is: For whom, if anyone, does he hold the fund in equity?'[112]

In the circumstances that transpired, it was a fortuitous coincidence that the plaintiff had enjoyed a double capacity as trustee of both the will and of the marriage settlement. It meant that Helen could not claim the property from him without breaking her promise to give it to him on trust. On a narrow reading of the case this was an essential part of the decision. On a wider reading, the case supports the view that it is not essential for a trustee to obtain the legal title to the trust property by way of a deliberate transfer from the settlor.

As with the principle in *Re Rose*[113] examined above, *Re Ralli's Will Trusts*[114] does not provide an example of equity assisting a volunteer. The trust is completely constituted, so there is no need for equity to assist the beneficiaries. However, the effect of the principle is to broaden the circumstances in which equity will regard a trust as having been constituted which indirectly assists the position of volunteers.

## (5) Relationship between constitution by transfer and constitution by declaration

It has been seen that a fully constituted trust may be created either by an effective declaration of self as trustee, or by an effective transfer of the property to the trustee on trust. If there was an intention by the settlor to create a trust in favour of the beneficiaries by transferring the trust property to trustees, but an attempt to constitute the trust was ineffective because the property has not been transferred, the question arises whether equity should treat the settlor as holding the property on trust. This would have the advantage of ensuring that the beneficiaries were able to enforce their equitable entitlement to the trust property, which seems to have been the settlor's intention. However, in such circumstances equity will not construe an ineffective transfer as a declaration of trust by the settlor. This was made clear in *Milroy v Lord*[115] where, as was noted above, the settlor who intended to create a trust of shares had failed to transfer title to the intended trust because he had merely handed the share certificates to him and he had not been registered as the owner thereof on the company share register. The Court of Appeal held that there had been no effective declaration of trust by the settlor. The principle was stated by Turner LJ:

'. . . it is plain that it was not the purpose of this settlement, or the intention of the settlor, to constitute himself a trustee of the bank shares. The intention was that the trust should be vested in . . . Samuel Lord, and I think therefore that we should not be justified in holding that by the settlement, or by any parol declaration made by the settlor, he himself became a trustee of these shares for the purposes of the settlement. By doing so we should be converting the settlement or the parol declaration to a purpose wholly different from that which was intended to be created by it, and, as I have said, creating a perfect trust out of the imperfect transaction.'[116]

---

[112] [1964] Ch 288 at 301.    [113] [1952] Ch 499.    [114] [1964] Ch 288.
[115] (1862) 4 De GF & J 264.    [116] (1862) 4 De GF & J 264 at 275.

In *Choithram (T) International SA v Pagarani*,[117] which was discussed above, the Privy Council dealt with a situation which did not easily fit into the two categories identified in *Milroy v Lord*. The decision does not, however, undermine the traditional principle that a failed transfer will not be construed as a declaration of trust. Instead it is submitted that the highly unusual situation of a settlor's words of gift to himself should be construed in substance as a declaration of trust.

## (6) Enforcing a trust

### (a) Enforcing fully constituted trusts

Where a trust has been fully constituted, whether in consequence of a settlor's declaration or through an effective transfer of the intended trust property to trustees, the beneficiaries are immediately entitled to the equitable interest in the property held on trust for them. They can seek the aid of equity to compel the trustees to perform the trust obligations by virtue of their interest as beneficiaries, irrespective of whether they were volunteers or whether they had provided consideration to the settlor in return for the creation of the trust. Once the trust has been created the settlor cannot change his mind.[118]

This can be seen from the following two cases. *Paul v Paul*[119] concerned a marriage settlement executed by parties who had since separated. Under the terms of the settlement as husband and wife they were entitled to enjoy the income derived from the trust property for life, with the remainder interest passing on their deaths to the children of the marriage. If there were no children and the wife predeceased her husband she enjoyed a general power to appoint over the trust property by will, subject to an express provision in default of appointment in favour of her next of kin. As there were no children, the husband and wife applied to have the capital of the trust paid over to themselves, arguing that the only other persons with any interest in it were the next of kin, who were volunteers. The Court of Appeal held that although the next of kin were volunteers, they enjoyed an immediate equitable interest in the capital because the trust was fully constituted and they were beneficiaries under it. As such, the trust could not be brought to an end without their consent. In *Re Bowden*[120] Catherine Bowden agreed to settle any property to which she might become entitled under her father's will on trust. Her father died in 1869, and between 1871 and 1874 the property to which she was entitled under his will was transferred to the trustees. In 1935 she requested that the trustees transfer the trust funds to her absolutely. Bennett J held that she was not entitled to the transfer because the property had become impressed with the trust the moment that it had been received by them.

---

[117] [2001] 2 All ER 492, [2001] 1 WLR 1.

[118] See *Jefferys v Jefferys* (1841) Cr & Ph 138; *Bentley v Mackay* (1851) 15 Beav 12; *Kekewich v Manning* (1851) 1 De GM & G 176; *Milroy v Lord* (1862) 4 De GF & J 264; *Richardson v Richardson* (1867) LR 3 Eq 686; *Henry v Armstrong* (1881) 18 Ch D 668.

[119] (1882) 20 Ch D 742, CA.      [120] [1936] Ch 71.

## (b) Enforcing incompletely constituted trusts

As mentioned above, where a settlor has neither declared himself trustee of the trust property nor transferred it to trustees, the trust is said to be incompletely constituted. In reality no trust exists. The trust property is not subject to any obligations, and the legal and equitable ownership are not separated. The settlor remains the absolute owner. The beneficiaries therefore enjoy no entitlement to the putative trust property, nor can they enforce the trust obligations against the intended trustees. In substance, the beneficiaries are merely the victims of the settlor's unfulfilled promise to create a trust in their favour. In such circumstances the question arises as to whether there are any means by which the beneficiaries can compel the settlor to carry out his promise to subject the property to a trust in their favour, by in effect requiring specific performance thereof. The basic principle is that if the intended beneficiaries have provided valuable consideration in return for the settlor's promise to create a trust in their favour, then equity will compel the settlor to constitute the trust. However, if they are volunteers the rule that 'equity will not assist a volunteer' operates to prevent them compelling the settlor to constitute the trust.

*(i) Beneficiaries of an incompletely-constituted trust who have given valuable consideration.* Where the beneficiaries have given valuable consideration equity will come to their assistance and compel the settlor to constitute the trust.[121] Equity does not take the same view of consideration as the common law and will not enforce a promise made in return for merely nominal consideration. Instead, equity requires 'valuable consideration'. 'Valuable consideration' is a technical term requiring either 'money or money's worth'[122] or marriage consideration.[123] As well as excluding nominal consideration, it also excludes a deed (a covenant) which is enforceable at common law by the covenantee even where no consideration at all has been provided. The ability of equity to compel the creation of trusts which are not completely constituted on behalf of those who have provided valuable consideration can be illustrated from the context of marriage settlements. In *Pullan v Koe*[124] a wife covenanted to settle after-acquired property of a value greater than £100 on the trusts established under her marriage settlement. She subsequently received a gift of £285 from her mother, which she failed to transfer to the trustees and which was instead invested in bonds. On the death of her husband, the bonds were in the possession of his executors. Swinfen Eady J held that the trustees were entitled to enforce the trust on behalf of her children because they were within the scope of the marriage consideration and not mere volunteers. The bonds were therefore held on the terms of the marriage settlement even though they had not been transferred to the trustees.

---

[121] See *Donaldson v Donaldson* (1854) Kay 711; *Lee v Lee* (1876) 4 Ch D 175.

[122] If value was given it is irrelevant whether the consideration was adequate: *Bassett v Nosworthy* (1673) Cas temp Finch 102.

[123] Only the husband, wife and issue of the marriage are within the marriage consideration: *De Mestre v West* [1891] AC 264; *A-G v Jacobs-Smith* [1895] 2 QB 341, CA; *Rennell v IRC* [1962] Ch 329; *Re Cook's Settlement's Trusts* [1965] Ch 902.

[124] [1913] 1 Ch 9.

*(ii) Volunteer beneficiaries of an incompletely-constituted trust.* In contrast, where the beneficiaries of an incompletely constituted trust are volunteers who have provided no valuable consideration in return for the settlor's promise to create a trust, equity will not compel the constitution of the trust.[125] This is an application of a more general principle that equity will not act to complete an imperfect gift, which was explained by Page-Wood V-C in *Donaldson v Donaldson*:

'[Where there is an imperfect gift] which requires some other act to complete it on the part of the assignor or donor, the court will not interfere to require anything else to be done by him.'[126]

This limitation prevented the enforcement of a trust in *Re Plumptre's Marriage Settlement*,[127] which, like *Pullan v Koe* above, also concerned a wife's covenant in her marriage settlement to transfer any after-acquired property to the trustees. She was subsequently given certain stocks by her husband, but they were never transferred to the trustees of the marriage settlement. On her death her next of kin sought to enforce the trust. It was held that they were unable to do so because they were outside of the scope of the marriage consideration and therefore volunteers in equity. The stocks therefore remained free of the marriage settlement trusts and formed part of her estate. Similarly, in *Re Cooks' Settlement Trusts*[128] it was held that volunteer beneficiaries were not entitled to enforce a settlor's promise to create a trust, even though other beneficiaries had given consideration. Sir Francis Cook executed a covenant that he would settle the proceeds of sale of any picture he had received from his father, and which he sold in his lifetime, on trust for members of his family. The beneficiaries provided no consideration for this covenant. During his lifetime he gave Rembrandt's 'Titus' to his wife, which she wished to sell. The trustees sought the opinion of the court as to the steps they should take if the picture was sold and the proceeds were not paid over to them. Buckley J held that since the beneficiaries were volunteers, equity would not enforce the trust if it was not completely constituted by the promised transfer of the proceeds of sale.[129]

*(iii) Volunteer beneficiaries of an incompletely-constituted trust who are able to obtain specific performance of a contract to create a trust.* Where a settlor has entered a contract with a third party promising to settle specified property on trust for beneficiaries, the beneficiaries will generally be unable to obtain specific performance because they are volunteers. However, in exceptional circumstances the beneficiaries might be able to stand in the position of the third party to whom the contractual promise was made and thus obtain specific performance and enforce the trust. In *Beswick v Beswick*[130] Peter Beswick contracted to transfer his business to his nephew, John, in return for his promise to pay an annuity of £5 per week to his wife. The

---

[125] See *Jefferys v Jefferys* (1841) Cr & Ph 138; *Dening v Ware* (1856) 22 Beav 184; *Re D'Angibau* (1880) LR 15 Ch D 228; *Harding v Harding* (1886) 17 QBD 442; *Re Earl of Lucan* (1890) 45 Ch D 470.

[126] (1854) Kay 711 at 718.      [127] [1910] 1 Ch 609.      [128] [1965] Ch 902.

[129] The abrogation of the doctrine of privity of contract by the Contracts (Rights of Third Parties) Act 1999 would enable the beneficiaries to obtain common law damages for breach of contract in such a situation, but does not enable them to obtain specific performance. This is discussed more fully below.

[130] [1968] AC 58.

business was transferred, but after Peter died John refused to pay the annuity. The House of Lords held that Mrs Beswick, although a volunteer who was not privy to the contract, was entitled to an order of specific performance to compel the nephew to pay the annuity. She was not, however, entitled to this remedy in her own right, but rather because she stood in the shoes of her husband as she was the administrator of his estate. It was therefore as if Peter Beswick himself were seeking the remedy. Although *Beswick v Beswick* did not in fact involve a trust, if the nephew had agreed to settle property on Mrs Beswick, as administratrix she would have been similarly able to obtain an order of specific performance, thus enforcing the trust. Merely because she was administratrix she was able to obtain indirectly what she was not entitled to obtain directly.

## (7) Exceptions to the rule that 'equity will not assist a volunteer'

### (a) Importance of the exceptions

Although the rule that 'equity will not assist a volunteer' in general prevents the enforcement of incompletely-constituted trusts on behalf of beneficiaries who have not provided valuable consideration, in limited circumstances equity is prepared to assist a volunteer transferee of property if a transferor has failed effectively to transfer the legal title to him. The exceptions operate whether the ineffective transfer was intended as an absolute gift or whether the property was intended to be held by the transferee on trust for third party beneficiaries. If the transferee was intended to hold the property as trustee, the effect of equity compelling the perfection of the imperfect transfer is to constitute the trust.

### (b) The rule in *Strong v Bird* [131]

If a donor makes an imperfect gift during his lifetime, so that the donee does not receive the legal title to the property, the rule in *Strong v Bird* operates to perfect the gift if the donee is appointed the donor's executor, or becomes his administrator on intestacy. The gift is perfected because the donee receives legal title to all the donor's property in his capacity as executor or administrator, including the property which was the intended subject matter of the gift. This has the effect of completing the imperfect transfer.[132] *Strong v Bird*[133] concerned an incomplete release of a debt. Strong had borrowed £1,100 from his step-mother, who lived in his house and paid board to him. It was initially agreed that he would repay the sum to her by means of a deduction of £100 from the board she paid quarterly. After two quarters where the deduction was made, she told him that she did not want the money returned and reverted to paying full board. This was not effective as a release of the debt at common law, which required a deed, and Strong had not provided any consideration. Four years later she died. Strong was appointed sole executor in her will. The court held that his appointment operated to perfect the imperfect release of the debt, so that Strong was not liable to repay the loan to the estate. The principle was stated by Jessel MR:

---

[131] (1874) LR 18 Eq 315; [1982] Conv 14 (Kodilinye).
[132] See *Re Ralli's Will Trusts* [1964] Ch 288.       [133] (1874) LR 18 Eq 315.

'. . . it appears to me that there being a continuing intention to give, and there being a legal act which transferred the ownership or released the obligation—for it is the same thing— the transaction is perfected, and he does not want the aid of a court of equity to carry it out, or to make it complete, because it is complete already, and there is no equity against him to take the property away from him.'[134]

This principle was subsequently applied in *Re James*.[135] Sarah James had been the housekeeper of James for some nineteen years. Although she received no payment, he told her that his house and furniture were to be hers on his death. When he died his son John inherited the property and gave Sarah the title deeds of the house, where she continued to live with her husband. John later died intestate and Sarah was granted letters of administration. Farwell J held that this had the effect of perfecting the gift of the house, which was imperfect because there had been no conveyance to her. He held that:

'. . . by her appointment as one of the administratrices she got the legal estate vested in her . . . she needs no assistance from equity to complete her title.'[136]

A number of conditions must be satisfied before the rule in *Strong v Bird* will operate to perfect an imperfect gift:

*(i) The donor must have intended to make an inter vivos gift.* The rule will only apply if an immediate inter vivos gift of the property had been intended by the donor, which failed because the transfer was ineffective given the nature of the property. The rule has no application where the donor intended to make a gift which would only take effect on his death.

*(ii) The donor's intention to make the gift must have continued until his death.* The rule will only operate if the donor who had failed to make an effective gift of the property had a 'continuing intention' to make the gift at the time of his death. This was emphasised in *Strong v Bird*[137] and also in *Re James,*[138] where Farwell J concluded that he was 'completely satisfied that there was a continuing intention in the donor up to the time of his death to give the property to the defendant'.[139] In contrast in *Re Gonin*[140] it was held that the donor had no such continuing intention, and therefore the rule could not operate. The plaintiff, Lucy Gonin, had returned home in 1944 to look after her parents. They promised that in return she should have their house when they died. Because Lucy had been born illegitimate her mother mistakenly believed that she could not leave the property to her by will. In 1962 she therefore drew a cheque for £33,000 in Lucy's favour, which she left in an envelope which was discovered after her death. Lucy claimed that in these circumstances the imperfect gift of the house was perfected when she was granted letters of administration over her mother's estate. Walton J held that the rule in *Strong v Bird* could not apply because her mother had not had a continuing intention to make a gift of the house at the time of her death:

---

[134] (1874) LR 18 Eq 315 at 319.    [135] [1935] Ch 449.    [136] [1935] Ch 449 at 451.

[137] (1874) Lr 18 Eq 315.    [138] [1935] Ch 449.

[139] See also *Re Freeland* [1952] Ch 110; *Re Wale* [1956] 1 WLR 1346; *Choithram (T) International SA v Pagarani* [2001] 2 All ER 492.

[140] [1979] Ch 16; (1977) 93 LQR 488.

'. . . so far as the land is concerned no such continuing intention can be found . . . I think that the intention changed by the latest in 1962 when the deceased drew her cheque in favour of her daughter. I find it impossible to think that from then on what she really had in mind was anything other than that the plaintiff would inherit the cheque on the deceased's death—no immediate gift, and no gift of land.'[141]

*(iii) The donee must have been appointed an executor or granted letters of administration.* The perfection of an imperfect gift by the rule in *Strong v Bird* is only effected by the vesting of the legal title to the intended subject matter in the donee in his capacity as the executor or administrator of the donor. It is irrelevant whether the donee is a sole executor, or one of several joint executors.[142] Some doubts were expressed in *Re Gonin*[143] as to whether the rule should apply to administrators, because 'it is often a matter of pure chance which of many persons equally entitled to a grant of letters of administration finally takes them out'.[144] However, Walton J was unwilling to determine the issue and noted that the rule was applied to an administrator in *Re James*,[145] which had been cited without dissent by Buckley J in *Re Ralli's Will Trusts*.[146]

*(iv) The intended subject matter of the gift must have been capable of enduring the death of the donor.* Most property, whether tangible or intangible, is capable of enduring the death of its owner. However, a cheque which has not been endorsed by the payee constitutes nothing more than a revocable mandate of the customer on whose account it was drawn, to his bank, requesting them as his agents to make payment to the payee. On the death of the customer, this mandate is automatically terminated. Therefore a cheque which remains uncashed at the date of death of the drawer will be incapable of passing title to the money instructed to be transferred, even if the payee is appointed the executor or administrator of the estate. Thus, in *Re Gonin*[147] the daughter had no entitlement to the £33,000 cheque her mother had left for her. In contrast, if a cheque is endorsed by its payee, it becomes a negotiable instrument and is a species of property capable of enduring despite the death of the drawer.

Although the rule in *Strong v Bird*[148] is commonly cited as an example of an exception to the rule that equity will not assist a volunteer, it is questionable whether this is genuinely the case. As with the principles identified in *Re Rose*[149] and *Re Ralli's Will Trusts*,[150] it is rather an example of widened circumstances in which equity is willing to find that a transfer has in fact been completed.

## (c) Donatio mortis causa (gift on account of death)

Unlike the rule in *Strong v Bird*,[151] the donatio mortis causa provides a genuine exception to the principle that equity will not assist a volunteer. It operates where an owner wants to make a gift of property to the donee which is only intended to take effect if he dies. If, in such circumstances, the donor failed to make an effective transfer of the property to the donee during his lifetime, equity will act to compel his executors, or administrators, to perfect the donee's imperfect title, even though he is a mere

---

[141] [1979] Ch 16 at 35.     [142] *Re Stewart* [1908] 2 Ch 251.     [143] [1979] Ch 16.
[144] [1979] Ch 16 at 35.     [145] [1935] Ch 449.     [146] [1964] Ch 288 at 301.
[147] [1979] Ch 16.     [148] (1874) LR 18 Eq 315.     [149] [1952] Ch 499.
[150] [1964] Ch 288.     [151] (1874) LR 18 Eq 315.

volunteer. If the donee was intended to receive the property as a trustee, the operation of the donatio mortis causa will have the effect of constituting the trust.

In its simplest form, a donatio mortis causa is merely a gift which is conditional upon death. Where the intended subject matter of a gift is personal property, a straightforward gift (such as a birthday present) is normally made by handing the property to the recipient with the intention to make a gift. The intention will normally be unconditional. However, it is possible for the intention to be subject to some condition being satisfied. For instance, a doting father might lend a car to his daughter, telling the daughter that she can keep it if she passes her examinations. If the daughter does pass, then the gift is completed. Where the condition which has to be satisfied is the death of the donor, the gift could be described as a donatio mortis causa. In extended forms of the donatio mortis causa the gift may go beyond the simple characteristics of such a conditional gift, as will be seen from the cases described below.

The essential conditions of a valid donatio mortis causa were stated by Lord Russell CJ in *Cain v Moon*:[152]

*(i) 'The gift or donation must have been made in contemplation, though not necessarily in expectation of death'*. The special treatment granted to the donee of a donatio mortis causa is only warranted because of the unique circumstances in which the gift was made. Only if the donee made the gift in contemplation of death can a valid donatio occur. This requires something more specific than a realisation of the general truth that we are all going to die eventually. As Hale J said in the Australian case *Smallacombe v Elder's Trustee & Executor Co Ltd*:

'. . . the donor must have been contemplating a comparatively early death from some cause or other, whether it be an existing illness, a dangerous journey[153] or even extreme old age. While an immediate expectation of immediate death is not required, nevertheless something more is required than a mere recognition of the inevitability of death itself.'[154]

Where a gift is made by a donor in contemplation of death from a specific cause, it is irrelevant if he in fact dies from different causes, and this does not prevent the validity of the donatio. In *Wilkes v Allington*[155] the donor was diagnosed as suffering from cancer in 1922. Although he continued to farm, he considered himself under a sentence of death. He therefore made several incomplete gifts to his nieces. In January 1928, after coming home in a bus from Worcester market, he caught a chill and died of pneumonia. Lord Tomlin held that there was a valid donatio even though the precise cause of death was different to the contemplated cause.

It seems that a gift made in contemplation of suicide will not operate as a valid donatio mortis causa.[156] However, the Irish case *Mills v Shields*[157] held that a gift in

---

[152] [1896] 2 QB 283. See also *Re Johnson* (1905) 92 LT 357, per Farwell J; *Re Craven's Estate (No 1)* [1937] Ch 423, per Farwell J; *Delgoffe v Fader* [1939] Ch 922, per Luxmore LJ; *Birch v Treasury Solicitor* [1951] Ch 298.

[153] See *Thompson v Mechan* [1958] OR 357: the ordinary risks of air travel are not sufficient for a valid donatio.

[154] [1963] WAR 3 at 4–5.      [155] [1931] 2 Ch 104.

[156] *Agnew v Belfast Banking Co* [1896] 2 IR 204, CA; *Re Dudman* [1925] Ch 553.

[157] [1948] IR 367.

contemplation of death by natural causes was a valid donatio even if the donor sub-sequently committed suicide.

*(ii) 'There must have been delivery to the donee of the subject matter of the gift'.*
An imperfect inter vivos gift will only be perfected as a donatio mortis causa if the donor had delivered the property intended to be the subject matter of the gift to the donee before his death.[158] In the case of chattels, such delivery can usually be achieved by handing physical possession of the property to the donee.[159] However, by way of one extension of the simple concept of a conditional gift, it will also be sufficient if the donor hands the donee 'dominion' over the property by granting him the means to control it. Such dominion would have been given, for example, if the property had been kept in a locked box and the donor had handed the key to the donee.[160] In *Re Lilling-ston*[161] the donor gave the donee the key to a trunk, which contained the key to a safe deposit at Harrods, which in turn contained the key to a safe deposit at the National Safe Deposit and Trustee Co. It was held that there was a valid donatio mortis causa of jewellery in the trunk and the contents of the two safe deposit boxes. In *Woodard v Woodard*[162] the Court of Appeal held that there was a valid donatio of a car where the donor had given the donee a set of keys since these constituted sufficient dominion.

When the intended subject matter of the gift is land or intangible property it is impossible for the donor to physically deliver it to the donee, or grant him dominion over it. In such cases the prerequisite of a valid donatio is that the donor delivered the 'essential indicia or evidence of title'[163] to the donee, or gave him dominion over such indicia. For money held in a bank deposit account,[164] post office saving account[165] or national saving certificates,[166] the relevant pass book or certificates are the necessary indicia. In *Sen v Headley*[167] the Court of Appeal held that in the case of unregistered land the deeds were the essential indicia of title, and that therefore the passing of dominion over the deeds effected a valid donatio mortis causa of the land. Presumably, the 'land certificate' would be sufficient indicia of title of registered land. In respect of shares in a public company, *Staniland v Willott*[168] suggests that handing the donee an executed share transfer form is sufficient for a valid donatio of the shares, even though the formal transfer of such rights requires the appropriate form of assignment. However, it is unclear whether mere delivery of a share certificate will suffice, although Australian authority suggests that it will,[169] as does reasoning by analogy from *Sen v Healey*.

A second extension to the concept of the simple conditional gift is that where there is a valid donatio mortis causa of property such as land, or money in a deposit account,

---

[158] *Ward v Turner* (1752) 2 Ves Sen 431.       [159] *Miller v Miller* (1735) 3 P Wms 356.

[160] See *Re Wasserberg* [1915] 1 Ch 195; *Re Cole (A Bankrupt)* [1964] Ch 175; *Sen v Headley* [1991] Ch 425, CA.

[161] [1952] 2 All ER 184.       [162] [1991] Fam Law 470.

[163] *Birch v Treasury Solicitor* [1951] Ch 298, CA.

[164] *Re Dillon* (1890) 44 Ch D 76; *Birch v Treasury Solicitor* [1951] Ch 298.

[165] *Re Thompson's Estate* [1928] IR 606; *Re Weston* [1902] 1 Ch 680.

[166] *Darlow v Sparks* [1938] 2 All ER 235.       [167] [1991] Ch 425.       [168] (1852) 3 Mac & G 664.

[169] *Duffucy v Mollica* [1968] 3 NSWR 751. Compare the Irish case of *Mills v Shields (No 2)* [1950] IR 21, where Gavan Duffy P held that delivery of share certificates was not sufficient to constitute a valid donatio of the shares.

where the transfer of dominion is purely symbolic, equity will intervene to compel the personal representatives of the deceased's estate to do whatever is necessary to complete the formal transfer of the property.

*(iii) 'The gift must be made under such circumstances as show that the thing is to revert to the donor in case he should recover'*. There will be no valid donatio unless the donor only intended the gift to take effect in the event of his death. Otherwise, the gift is simply an ineffective inter vivos transfer. Thus there will be no effective donatio mortis causa if the donor intended the donee to have the property at all events. As Wynn-Parry J said in *Re Lillingston*:

'The gift should be conditional, ie, on the terms that, if the donor should not die, he should be entitled to resume complete dominion of the property the subject matter of the gift.'[170]

A donatio will not be invalid merely because the donor knows that he will not recover, and in such cases the intention to make a revocable gift is implied.[171] Where the donatio has been made in contemplation of death from an illness, the gift is automatically revoked by the donor's recovery.[172] The donor may also revoke the gift at any time during his lifetime, for example by retaking dominion over the property,[173] or giving the donee notice of revocation.[174] However, he may not revoke the gift by will.[175]

A fourth requirement may be added to the three set out by Lord Russell:[176]

*(iv) The property must be capable of forming the subject matter of a donatio mortis causa*. Even if the preceding three conditions are satisfied, it has been held that some types of property are not capable of forming the subject matter of a valid donatio mortis causa. A cheque payable to the donor is capable of forming the subject matter of a donatio,[177] but a cheque written by the donor cannot,[178] because it is merely a revocable mandate to his bank which automatically terminates on death. Similarly, the donor's promissory note is incapable of forming the subject matter of a donatio.[179] A conflict of authorities renders it unclear whether shares are capable of forming the subject matter of a donatio. Some cases adopt the view that shares cannot be the subject of a valid donatio,[180] but in *Staniland v Willott*[181] it was held that there could be a valid donatio of shares in a public company. There seems to be no reason in logic or principle why shares should not be able to form the subject matter of a donatio mortis causa.[182]

---

[170] [1952] 2 All ER 184 at 187.

[171] *Wilkes v Allington* [1931] 2 Ch 104; See also *Sen v Headley* [1991] Ch 425 where the gift was made by the donor two days after he had been readmitted to hospital, when he knew he did not have long to live and when there could have been no practical possibility of his ever returning home.

[172] *Gardner v Parker* (1818) 3 Madd 184; *Staniland v Willott* (1852) 3 Mac & G 664; *Keys v Hore* (1879) 13 ILT 58.

[173] *Bunn v Markham* (1816) 7 Taunt 224; *Staniland v Willott* (1852) 3 Mac & G 664.

[174] *Bunn v Markham* (1816) 7 Taunt 224.

[175] *Jones v Selby* (1710) Prec Ch 300; White and Tudor, *Leading Cases in Equity* (7th edn, 1897) Vol 1, p 403.

[176] *Cain v Moon* [1896] 2 QB 283.     [177] *Re Mead* (1880) LR 15 Ch D 651; *Re Mulroy* [1924] 1 IR 98.

[178] *Re Beaumont* [1902] 1 Ch 886.

[179] *Re Leaper* [1916] 1 Ch 579.

[180] *Ward v Turner* (1752) 2 Ves Sen 431 (South Sea annuities); *Moore v Moore* (1874) LR 18 Eq 474 (railway stock); *Re Weston* [1902] 1 Ch 680 (building society shares).

[181] (1852) 3 Mac & G 664.     [182] See (1966) 30 Conv 189 (Samuels).

Following dicta of Lord Eldon in *Duffield v Elwes*,[183] land was traditionally regarded as incapable of forming the subject matter of a valid donatio mortis causa because it was not thought possible to grant dominion to the donee. In *Sen v Headley*[184] the Court of Appeal held that it was possible to part with dominion over the essential indicia of title of unregistered land, namely the title deeds, and that therefore to refuse to permit a valid donatio of land would create an anomalous exception.[185] Mrs Sen had lived with Mr Hewitt for ten years and had remained very close to him after this. When he was dying he told her that his house, title to which was unregistered, was hers, and he gave her the keys to a steel box which contained the deeds. It was held that in these circumstances a valid donatio had been made in her favour, and she was therefore entitled to compel the administrator of his estate to transfer the legal title of the house into her name. Although the case concerned unregistered land, where title is constituted by the title deeds, there seems no reason why the same principle should not apply to registered land, particularly as the object of the court was to avoid anomalous exceptions. Although the land certificate to registered land is only evidence of title,[186] it is sometimes treated as the equivalent of the title deeds to unregistered land.[187]

## (8) Common law remedies which may be available to the beneficiary of an incompletely-constituted trust

### (a) Significance of common law remedies

Where a settlor has promised to create a trust which remains incompletely constituted, it has been seen that volunteer beneficiaries cannot require the constitution of the trust in equity. However, although they are unable to gain any redress in equity, such volunteer beneficiaries may be entitled to sue the settlor at common law and recover compensatory damages for his failure to constitute the trust. Where damages at common law are available, the measure recoverable will be the quantum of loss suffered in consequence of the settlor's failure to constitute the trust, which will generally be the value of the promised trust property. Historically the possibility of obtaining common law damages arose because equity and the common law treated the concept of consideration differently. Thus a promise to create a trust would be enforceable at common law if it was contained in a covenant (ie a deed)[188] or was accompanied by even nominal consideration. Such a contract or covenant might have been entered between the settlor and the intended beneficiaries, or between the settlor and the intended trustees. The ability of volunteer beneficiaries to obtain a remedy at common law has recently been significantly widened by the Contracts (Rights of Third Parties) Act 1999, which has had the effect of abrogating the doctrine of privity of contract. This will prove especially

---

[183] (1823) 1 Sim & St 239. See also *Wilkes v Allington* [1931] 2 Ch 104.

[184] [1991] Ch 425; [1991] Conv 307 (Halliwell); (1991) 50 CLJ 404 (Thornely); All ER Rev 1991, p 207 (Clarke); (1991) 1 Carib LR 100 (Kodilinye); (1993) 109 LQR 19 (Baker).

[185] [1991] Ch 425 at 440, per Nourse LJ.    [186] Land Registration Act 2002, Sch 10, para 4.

[187] See eg Land Registration Act 1925, s 66; *Thames Guaranty Ltd v Campbell* [1985] QB 210 at 233. Stevens & Pearce, *Land Law* (3rd edn, 2005) p 79.

[188] See Law of Property (Miscellaneous Provisions) Act 1989, s 1.

significant where a settlor has covenanted or contracted to create a trust with the intended trustees but not the beneficiaries. The new regime applies to contracts entered into on or after 11 May 2000.[189]

It is important to realise that the beneficiaries' entitlement to claim damages at common law is not a means by which they can constitute the trust, thus circumventing the rule that equity will not assist a volunteer. Any damages recovered are merely compensation for the fact that no trust was ever created in their favour, and they will receive such damages absolutely and free from any trust. By contrast, where a beneficiary who has given consideration recognised by equity brings a suit, the remedy will normally be to compel the constitution of the trust which will, of course, also work to the advantage of the beneficiaries who have provided no consideration. Whether beneficiaries are in fact able to recover damages for the settlor's breach of covenant will depend on the circumstances of the case.

### (b) Common law compensation where the settlor contracted or covenanted to create a trust on or after 11 May 2000

*(i) Settlor covenanted or contracted with the beneficiary to create a trust.* Where a settlor has entered into a covenant to create a trust with the intended beneficiary, or has entered into a contract with the beneficiary for nominal consideration, the beneficiary will be entitled to sue to recover damages at common law if he fails to fulfill his promise to constitute the trust. As the beneficiary is a party to the covenant or contract there is no difficulty of privity.

*(ii) Settlor covenanted or contracted with the trustee to create a trust.* The Contracts (Rights of Third Parties) Act 1999, s 1(1) provides that a third party is entitled to enforce a term of a contract if it expressly provides that he may, or if it purports to confer a benefit on him Where a settlor enters into a covenant[190] or contract to create a trust with the intended trustee the beneficiary will therefore be entitled to sue to recover damages at common law if he fails to fulfill his promise, unless the contract made clear that it was not intended to be enforceable by him.[191] Although s 1(5) provides that a third party is entitled to obtain any remedy that would have been available to him in an action for breach of contract if he had been a party to the contract, the better view appears to be that this does not mean that the beneficiary can obtain specific performance as the rule that equity will not assist a volunteer has not been abrogated.[192]

### (c) Common law compensation where the settlor covenanted to create a trust before 11 May 2000

The Contracts (Rights of Third Parties) Act 1999 does not apply to covenants granted prior to 11 May 2000. The rights of the beneficiaries to enforce such a covenant will continue to be determined by the traditional rules:

*(i) Beneficiary was a party to the settlor's covenant to create a trust.* If a beneficiary is a party to a settlor's covenant to create a trust in his favour, it is clear from *Cannon v*

---

[189] Contracts (Rights of Third Parties Act) 1999, s 10(2).    [190] S 7(3).    [191] S 1(2).
[192] Hanbury & Martin, *Modern Equity* (17th edn, 2005), p 131. See also (2001) 60 CLJ 353 (Andrews).

*Hartley* [193] that he can recover damages for breach of covenant against the settlor if the latter subsequently fails to constitute the trust. Bernard Hartley executed a covenant on his separation from his wife, to which his wife and daughter were parties. He agreed that he would settle any money or property worth more than £1,000 which he subsequently received on the death of his parents on trust for his daughter. When his parents died he received a substantial amount of money but refused to transfer it to trustees. Romer J held although the daughter was a volunteer, and therefore unable to enforce the incompletely-constituted trust in equity, she was entitled to receive damages for breach of covenant:

'The plaintiff, although a volunteer, is not only a party to the deed of separation but is also a direct convenantee under the very covenant upon which she is suing. She does not require the assistance of the court to enforce the covenant for she has a legal right herself to enforce it. She is not asking for equitable relief but for damages at common law for breach of covenant.' [194]

*(ii) Common law compensation where the trustee was party to the settlor's covenant to create a trust.* The beneficiary's position in much less certain if the intended trustee of the settlement was a party to the settlor's covenant to create a trust but he himself was not. As the beneficiary was not a party to the covenant, he cannot sue the settlor for breach in his own right. Unless the trustees hold the benefit of the covenant on trust for him [195] he similarly cannot compel them to bring an action for breach against the settlor. The central question in such a case is whether the trustee is able to sue the settlor if he so wishes and, if so, as to the quantum damages recoverable.

It is well established that where a trustee who is party to the settlor's covenant seeks the court's direction whether he should sue, he will be directed not to take proceedings to enforce the covenant. In *Re Pryce* [196] Eve J directed the trustees of a marriage settlement to take no proceedings to enforce a covenant to settle after-acquired property. In *Re Kay's Settlement Trusts* [197] Simonds J followed the decision in *Re Pryce* and held that where a spinster had failed to perform her voluntary covenant to settle after-acquired property the trustees should be directed not to take any proceedings to enforce the covenant by an action for damages for breach. These authorities were further approved in *Re Cook's Settlement Trusts*, [198] where Buckley J held that volunteer beneficiaries could not compel the trustees to sue on the settlor's covenant to settle the proceeds of sale of certain paintings, even though other beneficiaries had given consideration. The rationale underlying these decisions is that to allow trustees to recover under the settlor's deed at common law would indirectly assist volunteers who are not entitled to the direct assistance of the court in equity. [199]

Although if asked the court will direct trustees not to take proceedings against a settlor for breach of covenant, they remain free to take action on their own initiative. However, if they do decide to sue it is debatable whether they will be entitled to recover substantial damages. It has been argued that a trustee suing for breach of the settlor's

---

[193] [1949] Ch 213.    [194] [1949] Ch 213 at 223.    [195] See below, p 193.
[196] [1917] 1 Ch 234.    [197] [1939] Ch 329.    [198] [1965] Ch 902.
[199] See *Re Pryce* [1917] 1 Ch 234 at 241, per Eve J.

covenant should be entitled to recover substantial damages equivalent to the value of the property which was promised as the subject matter of the trust, and that he will hold those damages on trust for the beneficiaries.[200] This view is supported by *Re Cavendish Browne's Settlement Trusts*,[201] where a settlor had covenanted with the trustees to settle land in Canada on trust for beneficiaries who were volunteers. The trustees were held entitled to recover damages from the settlor representing the value of the land which should have been transferred to them, which were to be held on trust for the beneficiaries.[202] However, it has also been argued that, as a matter of principle, a covenantee is only entitled to recover damages as compensation for his own personal loss[203] resulting from breach of the covenant to which he was a party. A trustee who is a party to a settlor's covenant was never entitled to receive the intended trust property for his own benefit and therefore he was never going to enjoy any personal gain from the trust. As such he cannot be said to have suffered any personal loss from the breach, and therefore he should only be entitled to recover nominal damages from the settlor. Furthermore, even if such a trustee were held entitled to recover substantial damages, it has been argued that he should hold them on a resulting trust for the settlor rather than for the volunteer beneficiaries.[204] If this is not the case, the perverse result is produced that the beneficiaries will do better where trustees sue on their own initiative than where they seek directions from the court.

*(iii) Common law compensation where the trustees hold the benefit of the settlor's covenant on trust for the beneficiary.* As has been seen, beneficiaries who are not party to the settlor's covenant to settle cannot compel trustees who are parties to take proceedings. However, if the trustees can be shown to hold the 'benefit of the covenant' on trust for the beneficiaries, they can sue in their own right as the beneficiaries of a completely-constituted trust of the covenant, and the trustees can either join their action as co-plaintiffs or be joined as co-defendants. Such a trust of the benefit of the covenant is possible because a covenant is a 'chose in action', and thus a form of intangible property capable of forming the subject matter of a trust. The possibility of a trust of the benefit of a covenant therefore provides a means of avoiding the restrictive implications of the privity doctrine, which prevent a beneficiary suing in his own right.

The concept of a 'trust of the benefit of a covenant', which enables a beneficiary to enforce a settlor's covenant with the trustees, was accepted by Wigram V-C in the mid-nineteenth-century case, *Fletcher v Fletcher*:

'One question made in argument has been whether there can be a trust of a covenant the benefit of which shall belong to a third party; but I cannot think there is any difficulty in that . . . The proposition, therefore, that in no case can there be a trust of a covenant is clearly too

---

[200] See (1960) 76 LQR 100 (Elliott); (1975) 91 LQR 236 (Barton); [1982] Conv 280 (Friend); [1988] Conv 18 (Goddard).

[201] [1916] WN 341; (1979) 32 CLP 1 (Rickett).

[202] However, *Re Cavendish Browne's Settlement Trusts* is distinguishable from *Re Pryce, Re Kay* and *Re Cook* as it involved a covenant to settle identified specific property rather than after-acquired property.

[203] *Woodar Investment Developments Ltd v Wimpey Construction UK Ltd* [1980] 1 WLR 277; *Panatown Ltd v Alfred McAlpine Construction Ltd* [2000] 4 All ER 97.

[204] (1969) 85 LQR 213 (Lee).

large, and the real question is whether the relation of trustee and [beneficiary] is established in the present case.'[205]

Ellis Fletcher had executed a voluntary covenant to settle £60,000 on trust for his illegitimate sons, John and Jacob, if they survived him. He retained the deed and did not make known its existence either to the trustees with whom it was made or to his sons. After his death it was found amongst his papers. Jacob, who had survived his father and attained the age of 21, sued the executors of his father's estate for £60,000. Wigram V-C held that although Jacob was not a party to the deed himself he was entitled to recover the £60,000 from the executors because the trustees held the benefit of the covenant on trust for him. The legitimacy of the concept of a trust of a promise has been confirmed by the courts in a large number of cases;[206] most recently in *Don King Productions v Warren*,[207] where Lightman J cited the dicta of Lord Shaw in *Lord Strathcona Steamship Co Ltd v Dominion Coal Co Ltd*:

'The scope of the trusts recognized in equity is unlimited. There can be a trust of a chattel, or of a right or obligation under an ordinary legal contract, just as much as a trust of land.'[208]

However, whilst *Fletcher v Fletcher*[209] clearly establishes that the benefit of a covenant may form the subject matter of a trust, such trusts have not been found to be common-place. There is great difficulty is establishing that such a trust has in fact come into existence. There is a marked reluctance to find that such trusts have been created because they are capable of undermining the doctrine of privity of contract. *Fletcher v Fletcher* is open to criticism in that there was no evidence on the facts of an intention to create a trust of the benefit of the covenant. There was no evidence that Fletcher intended to create such a trust, and the trustees and beneficiaries were unaware of the existence of the covenant. How could the trustees be said to be holding the benefit of a covenant, the existence of which they were unaware of, on trust for beneficiaries for whom they did not know they were trustees? In more recent cases the courts have held that a trust of a covenant will only be created by clear express intention. In *Vandepitte v Preferred Accident Insurance Corpn of New York*[210] the Privy Council held that to establish a trust of the benefit of an insurance contract 'the intention to constitute the trust must be affirmatively proved', and that such an intention could not necessarily be inferred from the words of the policy. There was therefore no intention that the policy holder had any intention to create a trust in favour of the plaintiff. Similarly, in *Re Schebsman*[211] Lord Greene MR held that it was 'not legitimate to import into the contract the idea of a trust when the parties have given no indication that such was their intention'.[212] These cases suggest that a trust of the benefit of a promise will not be implied merely from the fact that a promise has been made between two parties for the benefit of a third. Such a trust will only arise if there is clear evidence of an intention on

---

[205] (1844) 4 Hare 67.
[206] See *Lloyd's v Harper* (1880) 16 Ch D 290, CA; *Vandepitte v Preferred Accident Assurance Corpn of New York* [1933] AC 70, PC; *Re Schebsman (Decd)* [1944] Ch 83, CA; *Re Cook's Settlement Trusts* [1965] Ch 902; *Swain v Law Society* [1983] 1 AC 598, HL.
[207] [1998] 2 All ER 608.     [208] [1926] AC 108 at 124.     [209] (1844) 4 Hare 67.
[210] [1933] AC 70.     [211] [1944] Ch 83.     [212] [1944] Ch 83 at 89.

the part of the parties to the promise to create such a trust.[213] Such a trust clearly cannot arise if the contract contains a term prohibiting such a declaration.[214]

One further anomalous restriction on the scope of the concept of a trust of the benefit of a covenant is that it has been held that a covenant to settle future property is incapable of forming the subject matter of a trust. In *Re Cook's Settlement Trusts*[215] Sir Francis Cook covenanted to settle the proceeds of sale of certain pictures sold during his lifetime. Because this covenant did not create a property right that would have been capable of being the subject matter of an immediate trust, Buckley J held that no trust of the covenant could have been created:

'. . . this covenant upon its true construction is . . . an executory contract to settle a particular fund or particular funds of money which at the date of the covenant did not exist and which might never come into existence. It is analogous to a covenant to settle an expectation or to settle after-acquired property. The case, in my judgment, involves the law of contract, not the law of trusts.'[216]

This limitation has been severely criticised,[217] since although the covenant concerns future property, which could not itself form the subject matter of a trust,[218] it is no less a valid chose in action than a covenant to settle existing property. The promise itself is the subject matter of a trust of the benefit of a covenant, not the property to which the promise relates.

# 5 Formalities required for the creation of trusts

As has been seen above, a valid trust may be created either by the self-declaration of the legal owner, or by the transfer of the legal title to trustees upon trust. The trust may be created either inter vivos or by will. In some circumstances legislation requires the observance of specified formalities to create a valid or enforceable trust.

## (1) Inter vivos declarations of trust

### (a) Trusts of land[219]

*(i) Formalities required.* Section 53(1)(b) of the Law of Property Act 1925[220] provides:

'. . . a declaration of a trust respecting any land or any interest therein must be manifested and proved by some writing signed by some person who is able to declare such a trust or by his will.'

---

[213] *Swain v Law Society* [1983] 1 AC 598.
[214] *Don King Productions v Warren* [1998] 2 All ER 608 at 632–633.
[215] [1965] Ch 902.        [216] [1965] Ch 902 at 914.
[217] (1965) 24 CLJ 46 (Jones); (1969) 85 LQR 213 (Lee); (1979) 32 CLP 1 and (1981) 34 CLP 189 (Rickett); (1982) 98 LQR 17 (Feltham); [1982] Conv 280 (Friend); [1982] Conv 352 (Smith).
[218] See above, pp 166–167.        [219] [1984] CLJ 306 (Youdan).
[220] Re-enacting the Statute of Frauds 1677, s 7.

Formalities are required for declarations of trusts of land to prevent the disputes and inconvenience which would result if purely oral declarations were allowed. In essence s 53(1)(b) imposes an evidential safeguard. It is important to note that a purported oral declaration of a trust of land is not void, but only unenforceable.[221] The requirement of writing applies whether the trust is created by the land owner declaring himself trustee or transferring the land to trustees. It is not necessary that the actual declaration of the trust be made in writing, nor need the writing which evidences the declaration be contemporaneous with the declaration of the trust.[222] However, the written evidence must contain all the material terms of the trust, namely the beneficiaries, the trust property and the nature of the trust.[223] Unlike the parallel provision s 53(1)(c), s 53(1)(b) will not be satisfied if the writing was signed by an agent. However, if the land is transferred subject to a trust the transferee of the land may sign the written evidence of the declaration.[224]

*(ii) The rule in Rochefoucauld v Boustead.*[225] Although s 53(1)(b) renders an orally declared trust of land unenforceable in the absence of substantiating writing, this requirement is not always strictly enforced. The courts have held that where insistence upon writing would allow the statute to be used as 'an instrument of fraud' the trust will be enforced, irrespective of the lack of writing. Such fraud arises if a person to whom land was conveyed, subject to an oral understanding that it was to be held on trust, seeks to deny the trust, and claims to be absolutely entitled to the land because the requisite formalities re lacking. In *Rochefoucauld v Boustead*[226] the Comtesse de la Rochefoucauld owned the Delmar Estates in Ceylon, subject to a mortgage of £25,000. The land was sold by the mortgagee to the defendant, who was intended to take as trustee for the Comtesse. He subsequently mortgaged the land for a further £70,000 without her consent. The Comtesse sought a declaration that the defendant had acquired the land subject to a trust in her favour. The defendant claimed that the alleged trust had not been proved by any writing signed by him, as required by the Statute of Frauds, s 7.[227] The Court of Appeal held that despite the lack of formalities compliant with the statutory provision evidence other than writing signed by the defendant would be admitted to prove the trust, since otherwise the defendant would be committing a fraud against the Comtesse. The principle was stated by Lindley LJ:

'. . . the Statute of Frauds does not prevent the proof of a fraud; and it is a fraud on the part of a person to whom land is conveyed as a trustee, and who knows it was so conveyed, to deny the trust and claim the land himself. Consequently, notwithstanding the statute, it is competent for a person claiming land conveyed to another to prove by parol evidence that it

---

[221]  *Gardner v Rowe* (1828) 5 Russ 258; *Gissing v Gissing* [1969] 2 Ch 85 at 99; *Cowcher v Cowcher* [1972] 1 WLR 425 at 430–431; *Midland Bank plc v Dobson* [1986] 1 FLR 171 at 175.

[222]  *Forster v Hale* (1798) 3 Ves 696; *Rochefoucauld v Boustead* [1897] 1 Ch 196.

[223]  *Smith v Matthews* (1861) 3 De GF & J 139; *Rochefoucauld v Boustead* [1897] 1 Ch 196.

[224]  *Gardner v Rowe* (1828) 5 Russ 258; *Smith v Matthews* (1861) 3 De GF & J 139.

[225]  See [1984] CLJ 306 (Youdan); McFarlane, 'Constructive Trusts Arising on a Receipt of Property *Sub Conditione*' (2004) 120 LQR 667.

[226]  [1897] 1 Ch 196.

[227]  Predecessor of s 53(1)(b) of the Law of Property Act 1925.

was so conveyed upon trust for the claimant, and that the grantee, knowing the facts, is denying the trust and relying upon the form and conveyance and the statute, in order to keep the land himself.'[228]

Although the principle applies where a third party seeks to deny that he received the legal title to land as a trustee, it is less likely that a fraud will be committed if the owner of land orally declares himself a trustee in favour of a volunteer beneficiary. In such a case there is no justification for finding that a fraud had been perpetrated against the purported beneficiary.

The principle adopted in *Rochefoucauld v Boustead* has the merit of justice, but clearly runs contrary to the wording of the statute. More recent cases have tended to treat the principle as an example of a situation where a constructive trust is imposed, so that the intended trustee cannot rely on the absence of writing to deny the trust because he is already a constructive trustee of the land for the intended beneficiary.[229] For example, in *Bannister v Bannister* Scott LJ described the principle as:

'. . . the equitable principle on which a constructive trust is raised against a person who insists on the absolute character of a conveyance to himself for the purpose of defeating a beneficial interest.'[230]

This analysis of the rule in *Rochefoucauld v Boustead*[231] has the attraction of not seeming to contradict the wording of s 53(1)(b) of the Law of Property Act 1925, as s 53(2) provides that formalities are not required for the creation of 'resulting, implied or constructive trusts'. Therefore, if a constructive trust of the land can be found, the court will not be seen to be enforcing a trust that the clear words of s 53(1)(b) render unenforceable. However, in *Rochefoucauld v Boustead*[232] itself, the Court of Appeal was clearly of the view that an express trust was being enforced, despite the lack of statutory formalities. Lindley LJ stated that 'the trust which the plaintiff has established is clearly an express trust'. It seems more satisfactory to regard *Rochefoucauld v Boustead*[233] as authority for the proposition that the court will enforce an express trust of land, despite an absence of writing, where to do otherwise would be to allow the statute to facilitate a fraud.

## (b) Trusts of personal property

Section 53(1)(b) has no application to declarations of trusts of personal property. An absolute owner may orally declare himself the trustee of such property without the need for any further formalities.[234]

## (c) Declaration of a sub-trust

Where property is already held on trust, the beneficiary enjoys an immediate proprietary interest in the trust property. Since equitable proprietary interests are themselves

---

[228] [1897] 1 Ch 196 at 206.

[229] *Bannister v Bannister* [1948] 2 All ER 133; *Neale v Willis* (1968) 19 P & CR 836; *Re Densham (A Bankrupt)* [1975] 1 WLR 1519.

[230] [1948] 2 All ER 133.    [231] [1897] 1 Ch 196.    [232] [1897] 1 Ch 196.

[233] [1897] 1 Ch 196.

[234] See eg *Re Kayford Ltd* [1975] 1 WLR 279; *Paul v Constance* [1977] 1 WLR 527, CA.

capable of forming the subject matter of a trust, the beneficiary is entitled to declare himself a trustee of his interest under the trust, thus creating a sub-trust. If the property held under the head trust is land, any declaration of a sub-trust will only be enforceable by the sub-beneficiary if it is evidenced in writing in compliance with s 53(1)(b), since the trust property consists of an 'interest in land'. If the property held under the head trust is personalty, formalities will only be required to create the sub-trust if s 53(1)(c) applies.[235] This section stipulates that dispositions of subsisting equitable interests can only be made in writing. The central question is therefore whether a declaration of a sub-trust is to be characterised as effecting a 'disposition' of the original beneficiary's equitable interest under the head trust. If so, any purported declaration which is not effected in writing will be void and of no effect. In addressing this question it seems that the courts have drawn a distinction between genuine declarations of a sub-trust, and transactions which, though in the form of a declaration of sub-trust, are in substance a disposition of the beneficiary's equitable interest. If the sub-trust declared is a bare trust,[236] so that the sub-trustee has no active duties to perform because the sub-beneficiary's entitlement to the trust property is identical to his own, he will be regarded as having effected a disposition of his interest. Since the sub-trust would merely amount to a duplication of the head-trustee's duties, the sub-trustee is said to drop out of the picture and the head trustee holds the property on trust for the newly declared beneficiary. This principle was recognised in *Grainge v Wilberforce*.[237] More significantly it was accepted in *Grey v IRC*,[238] where Upjohn J used the language of a sub-trustee 'disappearing from the picture'[239] when a sub-trust is declared. Where a beneficiary who declares a sub-trust 'drops out of the picture' in this manner, the reality of the transaction is that he has effected a disposition of his equitable interest under the trust to the intended sub-beneficiary, and therefore the transaction will be ineffective unless the declaration is effected in writing.

In contrast, if an intended sub-trustee has active duties to perform under the sub-trust, he does not drop out of the picture and there is no disposition. Instead, a genuine sub-trust arises. This would be the case, for example, if a beneficiary created a life-interest of his interest under the trust in favour of a sub-beneficiary. Provided that the trust property is not land, in such circumstances there is no need for the declaration to be made in writing under s 53(1)(c). A purely oral declaration of the sub-trust will be sufficient.[240]

## (2) Declarations of trusts by will

A valid trust may be declared of any property, whether land or personalty, by will.[241] The requirements of a valid will are set out in s 9 of the Wills Act 1837. A will is only valid if it is made in writing,[242] which is signed by the testator (or by some other person

---

235  See below, p 199.    236  See Chapters 4 and 5.

237  (1889) 5 TLR 436. See also: *Re Lashmar* [1891] 1 Ch 258, CA; Law Com No 260, *Trustees' Powers and Duties* (1999), para 5.4, fn 3.

238  [1958] Ch 375.    239  [1958] Ch 375 at 382, per Upjohn J.

240  (1984) 47 MLR 385 (Green).    241  S 53(1)(b) and (c).    242  S 9(a).

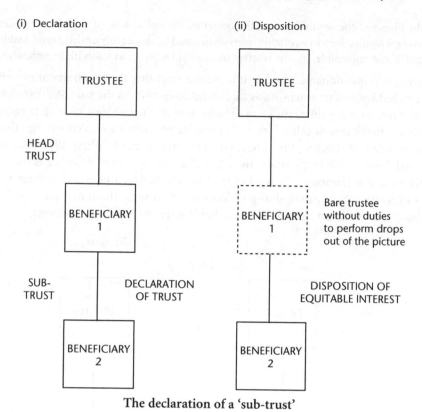

The declaration of a 'sub-trust'

acting at his direction in his presence)[243] in the presence of two witnesses, who them-selves attest and sign the will (or acknowledge their signature) in the presence of the testator.[244]

## (3) Dispositions of subsisting equitable interests

### (a) The requirement of writing

It has already been noted in the context of the difficulties associated with the declaration of sub-trusts above that a different formality requirement applies to dispositions of existing equitable interests. Section 53(1)(c) of the Law of Property Act 1925 provides that:

'. . . a disposition of an equitable interest or trust subsisting at the time of the disposition, must be in writing signed by the person disposing of the same, or by his agent thereunto lawfully authorised in writing or by will.'

This section applies whenever the beneficiary of a trust attempts to transfer his equitable interest in the trust property to someone else. In *Vandervell v IRC* Lord Upjohn provided an explanation of why formalities are required to effect such dispositions of a beneficiary's interest under a trust:

---

[243] S 9(a).     [244] S 9(c) and (d).

'. . . the object of the section, as was the object of the old Statute of Frauds, is to prevent hidden oral transactions in equitable interests in fraud of those truly entitled, and making it difficult, if not impossible, for the trustees to ascertain who are in truth his beneficiaries.'[245]

However, it is questionable whether it is truly correct that the requirement of writing prevents hidden oral transactions, as there is no obligation on the part of the transferor or transferee to bring the transfer to the attention of the trustees. Writing is required because, as in the case of other forms of intangible property such as copyrights, there is no other means of effecting a transfer, as the property cannot be physically possessed or delivered. Unlike s 53(1)(b), where the effect of a lack of written evidence is merely to render an oral declaration of a trust of land unenforceable, a failure to comply with s 53(1)(c) renders the purported disposition void.[246] As such, the transferee-beneficiary will have failed to divest himself of his equitable interest in the trust property.

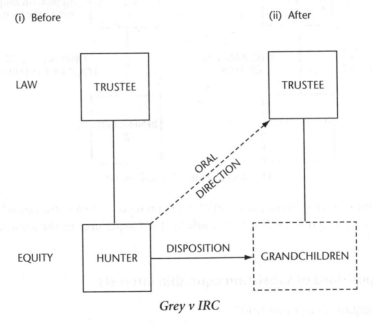

*Grey v IRC*

The following aspects of the requirement deserve attention:

*(i) 'Disposition'.* Section 53(1)(c) only encompasses dispositions of subsisting equitable interests. It therefore has no application to declarations of trust, otherwise s 53(1)(b) would be redundant in requiring a declaration of trust of land to be evidenced in writing. It is clear that an assignment of a subsisting equitable interest must be made in writing, as was held in *Re Danish Bacon Co Ltd Staff Pension Fund Trusts.*[247] However, the meaning of the term 'disposition' has been the subject of much debate, as beneficiaries have sought to avoid compliance with the requirement of writing for tax reasons. Its scope was considered by the House of Lords in *Grey v IRC,*[248] where it was

---

[245] [1967] 2 AC 291 at 311.    [246] See *Grey v IRC* [1960] AC 1; *Oughtred v IRC* [1960] AC 206.
[247] [1971] 1 WLR 248.
[248] [1960] AC 1; (1960) CLJ 31 (Thornely); See also *Re Danish Bacon Co Ltd Staff Pension Fund Trusts* [1971] 1 WLR 248 at 254, per Megarry J; *Halley v The Law Society* [2003] WTLR 845.

held that it should be given its 'natural meaning'.[249] The appellants held 18,000 shares on a bare trust as nominees for Mr Hunter. On 18 February 1955 Hunter orally directed them to henceforth hold the shares under six trusts, of 3,000 shares each, in favour of his grandchildren. On 25 March the trustees executed a declaration of trust to that effect. The central question was whether the oral direction of 18 February was effective to transfer the equitable interest in the shares to the grandchildren. The revenue argued that without writing the oral direction was void and ineffective to transfer the equitable interest in the shares. The trustees responded that the transaction did not require a written instrument because there had been no 'disposition' within the meaning of s 53(1)(c). They alleged that the Law of Property Act 1925 was merely a consolidating act, and that the word 'disposition' should be given no wider meaning than that accorded to the words 'grants and assignments' in the Statute of Frauds.[250] The House of Lords rejected this argument and held that the word 'disposition' should be given its natural meaning, in which case the oral direction to the trustees had been a disposition and was void and ineffective to transfer the equitable interest in the shares to the children. Lord Radcliffe stated:

'. . . if there is nothing more in this appeal than the short question whether the oral direction that Mr Hunter gave to his trustees on February 18th 1955 amounted in any ordinary sense to a "disposition of an equitable interest or trust subsisting at the time of the disposition", I do not feel any doubt as to my answer. I think that it did. Whether we describe what happened in technical or in more general terms the full equitable interest in the 18,000 shares concerned, which at that time was his, was . . . diverted by his direction from his ownership into the beneficial ownership of [his grandchildren] . . .'[251]

As the oral directions of 18 February were ineffective because of the absence of writing, the transfer of the equitable interest in the shares had only been effected by the deed executed on 25 March. This written declaration was therefore liable to ad valorem stamp duty.[252] A disclaimer of an equitable interest will not be regarded as a 'disposition' requiring writing,[253] whereas a surrender of an equitable interest is a disposition and will fall within the ambit of s53(1)(c).[254]

*(ii) Of an equitable interest or trust subsisting at the time of the disposition.* Section 53(1)(c) only applies to beneficial interests which actually exist at the date of the disposition. In *Re Danish Bacon Co Ltd* an employee had nominated someone to receive pension benefits if he died in pensionable service. Megarry J suggested that in these circumstances s 53(1)(c) did not apply because the employee had been dealing with something that could never be his. He had no subsisting equitable interest in the benefits he was allocating.

*(iii) In writing.* Unlike s 53(1)(b), which only requires that a declaration of trust be

---

[249] [1960] AC 1 at 13, 15, per Lord Simmonds.     [250] Statute of Frauds 1677, s 9.

[251] [1960] AC 1 at 15.

[252] By s 74 of the Finance Act 1910. Note that stamp duty was abolished by the Finance Act 2003 in respect of shares, though stamp duty land tax was introduced in respect of land.

[253] *Re Paradise Motor Co Ltd* [1968] 1 WLR 1125.

[254] See *Newlon Housing Trust v Al-Sulaimen* [1999] 1 AC 313 in the context of Matrimonial Causes Act 1973, s 37.

evidenced in writing, s 53(1)(c) requires that a disposition actually be made in writing. Such writing must obviously be contemporaneous with the intended disposition, although the disposition may be found in two or more separate documents, provided they are sufficiently connected.[255] It seems that the requirements of writing and signing may be satisfied by an electronic document.[256] This will be important where, for example, shares are held in trust and are traded electronically.

*(iv) Signed by the person disposing of the same or his agent.* Again in contrast to s 53(1)(b), the written instrument effecting a disposition need not be personally signed by the beneficiary or other person disposing of the equitable interest. It will be effective if signed by his lawfully authorised agent.

*(v) By will.* A disposition of a subsisting equitable interest may be effected by will. The requirements of a valid will were considered above.

### (b) Exceptions to s 53(1)(c)

Although the requirement of writing under s 53(1)(c) appears comprehensive, in a number of situations the courts have concluded that writing was not required to effect a transaction which was in substance a disposition of an equitable interest. These cases have largely arisen in the context of taxation, where transferees have sought to avoid stamp duty by effecting transfers of their equitable interest without using a written instrument that will attract duty. In some cases the courts have held that writing was not necessary to effect the transfer, but generally they have also found that tax remained payable.

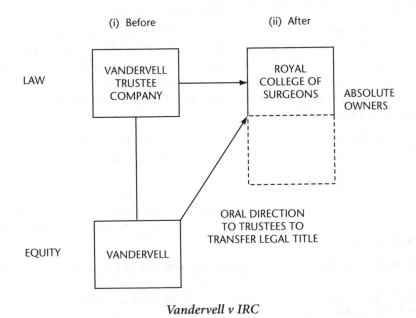

*Vandervell v IRC*

---

255  *Re Danish Bacon Co Ltd Staff Pension Fund Trusts* [1971] 1 WLR 248 at 254–255.

256  See Electronic Communications Act 2000, s 8; Pt 3 of the Advice from the Law Commission, *Electronic Commerce: Formal Requirements in Commercial Transactions* (2001).

The cases suggest that writing will not be required to effect a transfer of a subsisting beneficial interest in the following circumstances:

*(i) The beneficiary of a bare trust directs the trustees to transfer the legal title.* In *Vandervell v IRC*[257] the House of Lords held that s 53(1)(c) did not have to be satisfied where a beneficiary with a subsisting equitable interest under a bare trust directed the trustees to transfer the legal title to a third party and the transaction was completed. Mr Vandervell was the sole beneficiary of a bare trust of shares in his company, Vandervell Products Ltd, of which Vandervell Trustees Ltd were trustee. He decided to endow a chair of pharmacology at the Royal College of Surgeons and wished to do so in a tax efficient manner by transferring shares in his company to them and then declaring a special dividend on them. He therefore directed the trustee company to execute a share transfer form for the shares and to pass it to him, leaving the name of the transferee blank. The trustees duly completed the transfer form and handed it to Mr Vandervell, who entered the name of the Royal College of Surgeons as transferee. The college was then registered as the owner of the shares on he company share register. In return for the transfer of the shares, the college granted the trustees an option to repurchase the shares for £5,000. Dividends of some £250,000 were subsequently declared on the shares to provide the endowment of the chair. The Revenue claimed that Vandervell was liable to pay surtax on these dividends, arguing that the transaction amounted to a settlement of property where the settlor had not absolutely divested himself of his interest in the property.[258] One ground of the Revenue's case was that Vandervell had failed to divest himself of his equitable interest in the shares because the disposition had not been effected in writing. Addressing this argument, the House of Lords held that, in the circumstances, writing had not been necessary to effect a transfer of Vandervell's equitable interest in the shares to the college. As the beneficiary of a bare trust he was entitled to direct the trustee to transfer the legal title to the trust property, and there was no need for a separate disposition to transfer the equitable title. As Lord Wilberforce said: 'No separate transfer . . . of the equitable interest ever came to or needed to be made and there is no room for the operation of the subsection.'[259] The rationale was more fully explained by Lord Upjohn:

'I cannot agree . . . that prima facie a transfer of the legal estate carries with it the absolute beneficial interest in the property transferred; this plainly is not so, e.g., the transfer may be on a change of trustee; it is a matter of intention in each case. But if the intention of the beneficial owner in directing the trustee to transfer the legal estate to X is that X should be the beneficial owner I can see no reason for any further document or further words in the document assigning the legal estate also expressly transferring the beneficial interest; the greater includes the less. X may be wise to secure some evidence that the beneficial owner intended him to take the beneficial interest in case his beneficial title is challenged at a later date but it certainly cannot, in my opinion, be a statutory requirement that to effect its passing there must be some writing under section 53(1)(c).'[260]

---

[257] [1967] 2 AC 291; (1966) 24 CLJ 19 (Jones); (1967) 31 Conv(NS) 175 (Spencer); (1967) 30 MLR 461 (Strauss); (1975) 38 MLR 557 (Harris). More recently Nolan has argued that the decision can be explained on the basis of overreaching: '*Vandervell v IRC*; A Case of Overreaching' [2002] 61 CLJ 169.

[258] Income Tax Act 1952, Pt XVIII.       [259] [1967] 2 AC 291 at 330.       [260] [1967] 2 AC 291 at 311.

He also held that a transfer without writing in such circumstances would not offend against the policy underlying the formality requirement noted above, namely to prevent hidden oral transactions in equitable interests in fraud of those truly entitled and which might make it difficult or impossible for the trustees to ascertain their beneficiaries:

'. . . when the beneficial owner owns the whole beneficial estate and is in a position to give directions to his bare trustee with regard to the legal as well as the equitable estate there can be no possible ground for invoking the section where the beneficial owner wants to deal with the legal estate as well as the equitable estate.'[261]

Although the House of Lords held that the transfer of the equitable interest in the shares had taken place without the need for writing separate from the transfer of the legal interest, the majority went on to find Vandervell liable to surtax on the dividends declared. They held that the option to repurchase the shares granted by the College to the trustee company was, in the absence of an express declaration of trust, held on an automatic resulting trust for Vandervell himself.[262] Since he was the beneficiary of the option (as opposed to the shares themselves), he had failed to fully divest himself of all interest in the shares, thus attracting liability to surtax.

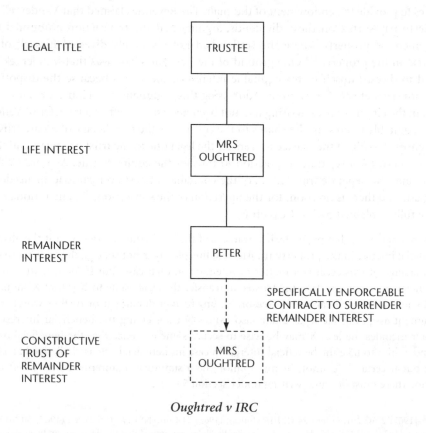

*Oughtred v IRC*

---

[261] [1967] 2 AC 291 at 311.     [262] See Chapter 8.

*(ii) A specifically enforceable contract for the transfer of the subsisting equitable interest.* Where a beneficiary enters a specifically enforceable contract to transfer a subsisting equitable interest under a trust, that interest passes to the intended transferee immediately on the making of the contract by means of a constructive trust. Since the transferee obtains the equitable interest by means of the constructive trust arising from the contract, there is no need for further writing under s 53(1)(c). In *Oughtred v IRC*[263] shares in a private company were held on trust for Mrs Oughtred for life with remainder to her son, Peter. On 18 June they entered an oral contract in which Peter agreed to release his interest in the shares subject to the settlement, so that his mother would be absolutely entitled to them, in return for which she would transfer 72,700 shares, of which she was already the absolute owner, to nominees for him. A deed of release was executed on 26 June. The central question before the House of Lords was whether ad valorem stamp duty was payable on this deed, which depended on whether the deed was a 'transfer on sale' within the provisions of the Stamp Act 1891.[264] The Oughtreds argued that the deed was not a 'transfer on sale' because the equitable remainder interest in the shares had passed to Mrs Oughtred by virtue of the contract to transfer, since, from the moment of the agreement, Peter held his interest on constructive trust. The majority of the House of Lords[265] held that irrespective of any constructive trust the deed of 26 June was a 'transfer on sale' for the purposes of the Stamp Act, and that stamp duty was therefore payable.[266] However, Upjohn J at first instance, and Lord Radcliffe in the House of Lords, took the view that the oral contract had given rise to a constructive trust which effected a transfer of the remainder interest in the shares to Mrs Oughtred without the need for further writing. Lord Radcliffe explained:

'The reasoning of the whole matter, as I see it, is as follows: On June 18 1956 the son owned an equitable reversionary interest in the settled shares: by his oral agreement of that date he created in his mother an equitable interest in his reversion, since the subject-matter of the agreement was property of which specific performance would normally be decreed by the court. He thus became a trustee for her of that interest sub modo: having regard to subsection (2) of section 53 Law of Property Act 1925, subsection (1) of that section did not operate to prevent that trusteeship arising by operation of law . . .'[267]

There has been some question whether Lord Radcliffe's comments establish that a specifically enforceable contract to transfer a subsisting equitable interest passes the interest by way of a constructive trust without the need for further writing, because the other members of the House of Lords did not express an opinion. However his approach seems to have been adopted as correct in subsequent cases. It was accepted by Megarry J in *Re Holt's Settlement*[268] and more recently by the Court of Appeal in *Neville*

[263] [1960] AC 206.
[264] Stamp Act 1891, s 54, Sch 1. Note that stamp duty was abolished by the Finance Act 2003.
[265] With the exception of Lord Denning.
[266] Per Lords Keith, Denning and Jenkins, Lords Radcliffe and Cohen dissenting.
[267] [1960] AC 206 at 227
[268] [1969] 1 Ch 100. See *DHN Food Distributors Ltd v London Borough of Tower Hamlets* [1976] 3 All ER 462, (1977) 93 LQR 170 (Sugarman and Webb); *Chinn v Collins (Inspector of Taxes)* [1981] 1 All ER 189, HL.

*v Wilson.*[269] This case concerned a trust of 120 shares in a company (U Ltd), which were held by the directors of the company as nominees for a separate family company (J Ltd). In 1969 J Ltd had been struck of the register because it had become defunct. It was claimed that in 1969 an oral agreement had been reached between the shareholders of J Ltd that the assets of the company should be divided amongst the shareholders rateably. The central question was whether this oral agreement gave rise to a constructive trust of the 120 shares in favour of the shareholders of J Ltd or whether it was void for failure to comply with the requirements of s 53(1)(c). If no such constructive trust had arisen, the shares would pass to the Crown as bona vacantia. The Court of Appeal held that the oral agreement of the shareholders had produced a constructive trust of the shares, so that they were held by the directors of U Ltd on behalf of the shareholders of J Ltd. Nourse LJ explained:

'The simple view of the present case is that the effect of each individual agreement was to constitute the shareholder an implied or constructive trustee for the other shareholders, so that the requirement for writing contained in sub-s (1)(c) of s 53 was dispensed with by sub-s (2). That was the view taken by Upjohn J at first instance and by Lord Radcliffe in the House of Lords in *Oughtred v IRC* . . . So far as it is material to the present case, what sub-s (2) says is that subs-s (1)(c) does not affect the creation or operation of implied or constructive trusts. Just as in *Oughtred v IRC* the son's oral agreement created a constructive trust in favour of the mother, so here each shareholder's oral or implied agreement created an implied or constructive trust in favour of the other shareholders. Why then should sub-s (2) not apply? No convincing reason was suggested in argument and none has occurred to us since. Moreover, to deny its application in this case would be to restrict the effect of the general words when no restriction is called for, and to lay the ground for fine distinctions in the future. With all the respect which is due to those who have thought to the contrary, we hold that sub-s (2) applies to an agreement such as we have in this case.'

Following *Neville v Wilson* it seems clear that there is a general principle that where a subsisting equitable interest is the subject of an oral contract to transfer which gives rise to a constructive trust, there is no need for further writing in satisfaction of s 53(1)(c) because the constructive trust itself effects the disposition of the subsisting equitable interest to the transferee. However, in practice this possibility will be of relatively limited scope. It will only apply to oral contracts which are specifically enforceable. Whilst contracts to transfer interests in land are specifically enforceable, giving rise to a constructive trust, there is no possibility of an oral contract to transfer a subsisting equitable interest under a trust of land avoiding formality provisions altogether, because the contract itself must be in writing.[270] In the case of personal property, contracts are not specifically enforceable unless the subject matter of the contract is unique because no market substitute is available. For example, a contract to transfer

---

[269] [1997] Ch 144; (1996) 55 CLJ 436 (Nolan); [1996] Conv 368 (Thompson); (1997) 113 LQR 213 (Milne). See also *Bishop Square Ltd v IRC* (1999) 78 P & CR 169, where the Court of Appeal applied *Oughtred v IRC* to a very similar fact situation.

[270] Law of Property (Miscellaneous Provisions) Act 1989, s 2.

shares in a public company is not usually thought to give rise to a constructive trust.[271] In *Oughtred v IRC*[272] the contract was specifically enforceable only because the shares were in a private company and were not freely available in the market.

*(iii) Extinction of a subsisting equitable interest under a resulting trust.* It further seems that there is no need for writing in satisfaction of s 53(1)(c) if the act of a third party has the effect of extinguishing a subsisting equitable interest which has arisen under an automatic resulting trust.[273] It has already been seen how, in *Vandervell v IRC*,[274] Mr Vandervell failed to divest himself absolutely of his interest in shares transferred to the Royal College of Surgeons because the option to repurchase was held on resulting trust for him by the Vandervell Trustee Company. The trustee company subsequently exercised this option using money they held on other trusts for Vandervell's children. They then informed the Revenue that they held the re-acquired shares on trust for the children, and all dividends deriving from those shares were paid to the children's settlement. In *Re Vandervell's Trusts (No 2)*[275] the Revenue claimed that Vandervell was liable to pay surtax on these dividends as well, on the grounds that he had still not divested himself absolutely of his interest in the shares. Their argument that there had been no effective declaration of trust in favour of the children was accepted by Megarry J, at first instance, but rejected by the Court of Appeal, which held that the conduct of the trustees was sufficient to amount to a declaration of trust in favour of the children. The Revenue further argued that Vandervell had never effectually disposed of his equitable interest under the resulting trust of the option, because he had never done so in writing as required by s 53(1)(c). The Court of Appeal also rejected this argument, holding that there had been no need of a written instrument to extinguish Vandervell's resulting trust interest. Lord Denning MR based his conclusion on the nature and function of the resulting trust:

'... A resulting trust for the settlor is born and dies without any writing at all. It comes into existence whenever there is a gap in the beneficial ownership. It ceases to exist whenever that gap is filled by someone becoming beneficially entitled. As soon as the gap is filled by the creation or declaration of a valid trust, the resulting trust comes to an end. In this case, before the option was exercised, there was a gap in the beneficial ownership. So there was a resulting trust for Mr Vandervell. But as soon as the option was exercised and the shares registered in the trustee's name, there was created a valid trust of the shares in favour of the children's settlement . . .'[276]

Lawton LJ took the view that the declaration of the trust of the shares in favour of the children's settlement had the effect of extinguishing Vandervell's interest under the

---

[271] See, however, *Chinn v Collins (Inspector of Taxes)* [1981] AC 533, which provides some authority that even in the case of shares in a public company a constructive trust will arise. Lord Wilberforce considered the effect of a contract to transfer the equitable interest in shares in a public company quoted on the London Stock Exchange which were held on trust by a nominee. He regarded the agreement as giving rise to a constructive trust so that dealings with the equitable interest did not require formalities. He seemed to regard it as irrelevant whether the contract would have been specifically enforceable. However, *Oughtred v IRC* was not cited.

[272] [1960] AC 206.     [273] See Chapter 8.     [274] [1967] 2 AC 291.
[275] [1974] Ch 269; (1975) 38 MLR 557 (Harris).     [276] [1974] Ch 269 at 320.

resulting trust of the option. Such an extinction was not a 'disposition' and therefore writing was not required:

'The exercise of the option and the transfer of the shares to the trustee company necessarily put an end to the resulting trust of the option. There could not be a resulting trust of a chose in action which was no more. The only reason why there ever had been a resulting trust of the option was the rule that the beneficial interest in property must be held for some one if the legal owner is not entitled to it. The legal but not the beneficial interest in the option had vested in the trustee company. The beneficial interest had to be held for some one and as the trustee company had declared no trusts of the option, the only possible beneficiary was Mr Vandervell. Once the trustee company took a transfer of the shares the position was very different. The legal title to them was vested in the trustee company and by reason of the facts and circumstances to which I have already referred it held the beneficial interest for the trusts of the children's settlement. There was no gap between the legal and beneficial interests and in consequence no need for a resulting trust in favour of Mr Vandervell to fill it. Neither the extinction of the resulting trust of the option resulting from its exercise nor the creation of a beneficial interest in the shares by the declaration of trust amounted to a disposition of an equitable interest or trust within the meaning of sections 53(1)(c) and 205(1)(ii) of the Law of Property Act 1925.'[277]

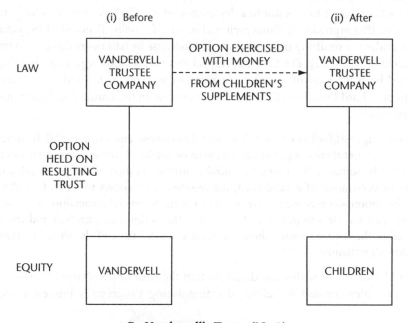

*Re Vandervell's Trusts (No 2)*

The precise impact of the decision in *Re Vandervell's Trusts (No 2)*[278] is open to question. It is doubtful whether, in reality, the acts of the trustee company were of themselves sufficient to divest Vandervell of his resulting trust of the option. As Megarry J had commented at first instance:

---

[277] [1974] Ch 269 at 326.     [278] [1974] Ch 269.

'That issue is, in essence, whether trustees who hold an option on trust for X will hold the shares obtained by exercising that option on trust for Y merely because they used Y's money in exercising the option. Authority apart, my answer would be an unhesitating no. The option belongs to X beneficially, and the money merely exercises rights which belongs to X. Let the shares be worth £50,000 so than an option to purchase those shares for £5,000 is worth £45,000, and it will be at once seen what a monstrous result would be produced by allowing trustees to divert from their beneficiary X the benefits of what they hold for him merely because they used Y's money instead of X's.'

More significantly, it is questionable whether the mere fact that the beneficial interest in the option arose under a resulting trust should provide a justification for the inapplicability of s 53(1)(c). There is no conceptual imperative for treating a disposition of a subsisting equitable interest which has arisen by way of a resulting trust any differently from a disposition of an interest arising under an express trust. The court's reasoning that the resulting trust is somehow eliminated by the act of the trustee identifying new beneficiaries is spurious. Whilst it is true that the original resulting trust arose because Vandervell had failed to specify who was to be the beneficial owner of the option, the trust is only a 'resulting trust' to the extent that it was not expressly created, and this characterisation should not colour its nature for the whole of its existence. The prime duty of a trustee, whether of a bare or active trust, is to preserve the trust fund for the beneficiary, and the beneficiary's interest cannot be transferred to different beneficiaries by the mere act of the trustees without assignment by the beneficiary, otherwise the trustee would have the effective right to dispose of the beneficial interests behind the trust without reference to the beneficiary. For example, if two friends (X and Y) contributed equally to the purchase of shares valued at £100,000 in the name of X alone, surely X should not be able to eliminate Y's beneficial half-interest under a resulting trust merely by declaring that henceforward he regards himself as holding the shares on trust for Z. To conclude that interests subsisting behind resulting trusts can be disposed of without writing would also provide an easy means of evasion of the ruling in *Grey v IRC*, which concerned an equitable interest subsisting under an express bare trust. If a settlor were to transfer property to a nominee, without specifying a beneficiary and thus giving rise to a resulting trust in his favour, he could then transfer the equitable interest to new beneficiaries by merely orally directing the trustees to declare new trusts.

If any general principle can be construed from *Re Vandervell's Trusts (No 2)* it would therefore seem that it should be limited to a case where the extinction of the equitable interest arising under a resulting trust is the act of a third party, and not of the person who enjoys the interest. It was only because the declaration of trust was made by the trustees that there was no need for writing. If Vandervell himself had sought to transfer his equitable interest under the resulting trust writing would surely have been required in satisfaction of s 53(1)(c).

## (4) Resulting and constructive trusts

The formality requirements of s 53(1) only apply in respect of declarations of express trusts and dispositions of existing equitable interests. As will be evident in the following chapters, they have no application to resulting[279] or constructive trusts.[280] This is the effect of s 53(2), which provides:

'This section does not affect the creation or operation of resulting, implied or constructive trusts.'

[279] See Chapter 8.    [280] See Chapter 9.

# 7

# Secret trusts

## 1 Distributing property on death

### (1) The function of secret trusts

It is a simple truth that a man cannot take his property with him when he dies. He may, however, wish to decide to whom it should pass when he no longer has any need of it. Secret trusts provide a mechanism by which an owner can direct how his property should be distributed on death. Whilst English law provides a number of other means by which an owner can determine the destiny of his worldly goods on his demise they generally involve some element of public scrutiny to prevent fraud or abuse, with the inevitable consequence that the identity of the ultimate recipient of the property becomes public knowledge. The cardinal feature of secret trusts is that the ultimate recipient of the property may be kept entirely secret by not being disclosed in the will. Secret trusts are probably most often used today to provide for a beneficiary who has been forgotten, and in some cases because the testator was unsure as to who should be the ultimate beneficiary when he made his will. They have historically been used by owners wishing to leave property to persons whose existence they would prefer to conceal, for example mistresses or illegitimate children.[1] Rather than leaving property directly to such a person by will, the testator chooses to leaves it to a trusted friend who has agreed in advance to pass it on to the secret beneficiary. If such an arrangement is established, the face of the will simply suggests that a bequest is made to the friend, whereas the reality behind the scenes is that provision is made secretly for the unrevealed beneficiary.

### (2) Mechanisms for distributing property on death

#### (a) General

Since 'we brought nothing into the world, and we can take nothing out of it',[2] the question arises as to what should happen to a man's property on death. As has been noted, the law provides a number of mechanisms that enable the owner of property to determine who should receive his property after death.

---

[1] Eg *Re Boyes* (1884) LR 26 Ch D 531; *Blackwell v Blackwell* [1929] AC 318.
[2] St Paul, First Letter to Timothy, Ch 6, v 7.

It is necessary to examine these mechanisms and their operation to gain a full appreciation of the advantages offered by secret trusts and the policy motivations which led to their acceptance and enforceability.

## (b) Testamentary dispositions

*(i) Formalities required.* The most important mechanism by which an owner can stipulate how his property should be distributed on his death is through a valid will. A document is only a valid will if it complies with the provisions of the Wills Act 1837. The formalities[3] there prescribed are intended to prevent fraud and to ensure that the genuine intentions of the owner are carried out. Section 9 provides that a will is only valid if it is in writing and properly attested and witnessed:

'No will shall be valid unless—

(a) it is in writing, and signed by the testator, or by some other person in his presence and by his direction; and

(b) it appears that the testator intended his signature to give effect to the will; and

(c) the signature is made or acknowledged by the testator in the presence of two or more witnesses present at the same time; and

(d) each witness either—

(i) attests and signs the will; or

(ii) acknowledges his signature, in the presence of the testator (but not necessarily in the presence of any other witnesses).'

Although it is obviously necessary to have a general requirement that wills must be executed in a specified form, the law recognises that in some circumstances it is unfair or impracticable to expect a testator to comply with such requirements. In limited cases a testator is therefore entitled to make a privileged will[4] without the need to comply with the formality provisions of s 9. Section 11 provides that 'any soldier[5] being in actual military service'[6] or 'any mariner or seaman[7] being at sea'[8] can make a valid will without any formalities.

*(ii) The process of probate.*[9] Where a person has died leaving a valid will, this does not automatically effect a distribution of his property to the named beneficiaries, nor can the beneficiaries simply seize the property left to them. Instead, on death the totality of the testator's assets pass to his executors. The executors are not entitled to distribute the

---

[3] See Mellows, *The Law of Succession* (5th edn, 1993), Ch 6; Parry and Clark, *The Law of Succession*, (10th edn, 1996), Ch 4.

[4] See Mellows, *The Law of Succession* (5th edn, 1993), Ch 7; Parry and Clark, *The Law of Succession*, (10th edn, 1996), pp 87–91.

[5] *Re Donaldson's Goods* (1840) 2 Curt 386; *Re White's Application* [1975] 2 NSWLR 125. See also Wills (Soldiers and Sailors) Act 1918, s 5 (2) (members of the RAF to be treated as soldiers).

[6] *White v Repton* (1844) 3 Curt 818; *Re Spark's Estate* [1941] P 115; *Re Gibson's Estate* [1941] P 118n; *Re Rowson's Estate* [1944] 2 All ER 36; *Re Wingham* [1949] P 187; *Re Jones* [1981] 1 All ER 1.

[7] See *Re Yate's Estate* [1919] P 93; *Re Knibb's Estate* [1962] 2 All ER 829; *Re Hale's Goods* [1915] 2 IR 362.

[8] *Re Barnes' Goods* (1926) 96 LJP 26; *Re Rapley's Estate* [1983] 1 WLR 1069.

[9] See Mellows, *The Law of Succession* (5th edn, 1993), Pt V; Parry and Clark, *The Law of Succession*, (10th edn, 1996), Ch 14.

property comprising the estate until they have been granted probate by the court. Probate will only be granted once the executor has 'proved' the will, demonstrating that it was the last effective will of the deceased. During the process of obtaining probate the will becomes a public document and is open to public scrutiny. This means that details of the value of the testator's estate, and the identity of those to whom it was left, enter the public sphere. For this reason it was possible for reporters to discover the exact details of the will of Diana, Princess of Wales. This publicity is an essential part of the probate process as it ensures effective scrutiny of the will. Interested parties can examine the will and then challenge its authenticity if the terms suggest that it is not genuine. It is the public nature of this probate process which prevents a testator making secret bequests of his property by will. The very people he would most wish to keep from discovering that he had made provision for a mistress or illegitimate child, namely his family, would be those most likely to examine the will.

## (c) Incorporation by reference[10]

Whilst a valid testamentary disposition must comply with the appropriate formalities identified above, there is in fact no need for a will to contain all the terms specifying how the deceased's property should be distributed on death. Under the doctrine of 'incorporation by reference' documents which are not themselves signed, attested and witnessed may be incorporated into a will. Where a document is effectively incorporated into the will, it 'becomes part of the will'.[11] As such, the incorporated document must also be admitted to probate, and thereby becomes a public document in the same way as the will itself. The doctrine of incorporation by reference does not, therefore, enable a testator to make secret dispositions of his property on death.

A document will only be incorporated by reference into a will if the conditions stated by Gorell-Barnes P in *Re Smart's Goods*[12] are met.

*(i) Incorporated document was in existence at the date of the will.* Only a document which was in existence at the date the will was executed can be incorporated by reference, thus becoming part of the will.[13] A document may be incorporated if it was written after the will was executed provided that a subsequent codicil is added confirming that it is to be incorporated.

*(ii) Incorporated document is referred to in the will.* To be incorporated into a will a document must not only exist at the date of the will, but it must also be referred to in the will as existing at that date. In *Re Smart's Goods*[14] the testatrix, Caroline Smart, executed a will in 1895 leaving her property to the friends she might designate in a book or memorandum. At the time that the will was executed no such book or memorandum existed. A book was written between 1898 and 1899, and in 1900 a codicil was added to the will. However, although this book was in existence at the date of the execution of the codicil it was held that it was not incorporated into the will because the codicil made no

---

[10] See Mellows, *The Law of Succession* (5th edn, 1993), pp 77–80; Parry and Clark, *The Law of Succession*, (10th edn, 1996), pp 91–93.
[11] *Re Smart's Goods* [1902] P 238 at 240.    [12] [1902] P 238.
[13] *Singleton v Tomlinson* (1878) 3 App Cas 404, HL.    [14] [1902] P 238.

reference to it as existing at the date that it was executed. The will continued to refer to the book as a future document.[15]

*(iii) Incorporated document must be clearly identified in the will.* A document will only be incorporated by reference if it is clearly identified in the will.[16]

## (d) Non-testamentary mechanisms

*(i) Intestacy.*[17] If the owner of property dies without leaving a valid will he is said to die 'intestate'. Since he has not left a valid will indicating how his property should be allocated after his death, it will be distributed on the basis of the rules of intestacy. For those dying after 31 May 1987 the rules of intestacy are found in the Administration of Estates Act 1925 and the Family Provision (Intestate Succession) Order 1987.

*(ii) Donatio mortis causa.* The principle of donatio mortis causa, which was examined in detail in the previous chapter,[18] provides a means by which an owner can allocate property on his death. He can make an inter vivos conditional gift which is only intended to become an absolute gift in the event of his death. A donatio will only occur if the donor transferred dominion of the property to the donee in contemplation of death. Provided the requirements are met, the donor's executors or administrators will be obliged to make good any defects in the donee's title.

*(iii) Secret trusts.* As has been noted, secret trusts provide a further means by which an owner can determine who is to benefit from his property after his death outside of the terms of his will.

*(iv) Inter vivos settlements.* The owner of property can settle it during his lifetime by creating a trust under which he retains only a life estate, the remainder passing to the person he desires to benefit on his death. Such a settlement confers an immediate proprietary interest on the beneficiaries which can be varied only in accordance with the terms of the trust or with the consent of all the beneficiaries.

# 2  Introduction to secret trusts

## (1) Types of secret trust

English law recognises two categories of secret trust, namely 'fully secret trusts' and 'half-secret trusts'. The central difference between these categories is the extent to which

---

[15]   See also *University College of North Wales v Taylor* [1908] P 140; *Re Bateman's Will Trusts* [1970] 3 All ER 817.

[16]   See *Croker v Marquis of Hertford* (1844) 8 Jur 863; *Re Balmes' Goods* [1897] P 261; *Re Saxton's Estate* [1939] 2 All ER 418; *Re Mardon's Estate* [1944] P 109.

[17]   See Mellows, *Law of Succession* (5th edn, 1993), Ch 12; Parry and Clark, *The Law of Succession* (10th edn, 1996), Ch 2.

[18]   See above, p 186.

the testator's will discloses that the person named as the recipient of a bequest is intended to take the property as a trustee rather than for himself. Whilst the difference might appear slight, for a long period of time it was held that only fully secret trusts should be recognised as valid, and even though half-secret trusts are now accepted, the rules governing their creation are somewhat more restrictive.

## (a) Fully-secret trusts

A fully-secret trust is created when a testator bequeaths property to a specified person in his will who has agreed that he will hold the property left to him on trust for a third party. In a fully-secret trust neither the fact of the trust nor the identity of the beneficiary are revealed in the will. For example, imagine that George has a mistress, Henrietta, for whom he wishes to make provision on his death without his wife discovering her existence. He therefore leaves £50,000 in his will to his close friend, Ian, having told him of his intention, and Ian having agreed that he will ensure that Henrietta receives the money. On the face of George's will it will appears that Ian is the absolute beneficiary of the bequest, whereas in fact, behind the scenes, Henrietta is intended to benefit. This arrangement would give rise to a fully-secret trust. On the death of George, Ian will receive the money under the terms of the will, but he will not be entitled to retain it for himself. Instead, he will be required to hold it as trustee for Henrietta. Ian is therefore the trustee of the secret trust, and Henrietta the beneficiary.

## (b) Half-secret trusts

The performance of a fully secret trust is to some extent dependent on the integrity of the beneficiary who has agreed to act as the secret trustee. There is always a danger that the secret trustee will ignore the trust and take the property left to him by will for his own benefit and refuse to apply it to the intended secret beneficiary. This danger will be avoided if the testator indicates in his will that the recipient of the bequest is not intended to take the property absolutely, but as a trustee. By this means the identity of the ultimate beneficiary remains concealed, but the beneficiary named in the will is clearly seen to be a secret trustee. Amending the example used above, if George were to leave £50,000 to Ian in his will 'on trust', without disclosing that Henrietta was the ultimate beneficiary, a half-secret trust would have been created. The trust is described as 'half-secret' because the fact that the property is subject to a trust obligation appears on the face of the will, although its terms, and especially the identity of the intended beneficiary, remain secret. In the case of a half-secret trust the secret trustee cannot ignore the trust and take the property absolutely for himself because the fact of the trust appears on the face of the will and it is clear to the court that he is not intended to take the property absolutely.

## (c) Secret trusts arising on intestacy

Although secret trusts generally arise in the context of a testamentary disposition, a secret trust may arise in a case of intestacy,[19] provided that the person entitled

---

[19]  *Stickland v Aldridge* (1804) 9 Ves 516.

to the deceased's estate on his intestacy had agreed that he would receive the speci-fied property as a trustee and not for himself absolutely. As Romer J stated in *Re Gardner (No 2)*:[20]

'. . . The principle has been applied . . . where the owner of property refrains from making a will and so allows the property to pass to the donee as on an intestacy.'

Therefore, if, under the rules of intestacy, Ian was entitled to receive a share of George's estate, George could ask him to hold that share for the benefit of Henrietta. Provided that Ian agreed, and George died without making a will, Ian would hold whatever he received from the administration of George's estate on trust for Henrietta.

### (2) Why does equity enforce secret trusts?

The enforcement of secret trusts seems at odds with the policy of public regulation and scrutiny of testamentary dispositions embodied in the Wills Act and probate process. Superficially, the enforcement of a secret trust even seems to be inconsistent with the terms of s 9, since such enforcement appears to permit a testamentary dis-position without satisfaction of the requisite formalities. Historically, equity justified the enforcement of secret trusts on the ground that to refuse to uphold them because of a lack of formality would be to allow the Wills Act to be used as an instrument of fraud. This historic explanation has been eclipsed by a more fashionable alternative, which is that a secret trust is an inter vivos trust, declared by the testator and the secret trustee, which remains incompletely constituted until the death of the testator, at which time it is constituted through the operation of the will passing title to the trust property to the secret trustee. The explanation has the advantage that it does not presuppose a conflict between the enforcement of the secret trusts and the require-ments of s 9 of the Wills Act. The secret trusts arises altogether outside of the will, which simply operates according to its terms. These rival explanations will be examined in detail below.

## 3 Requirements for the creation of secret trusts

The essential requirements of 'intention, communication and acceptance' must be satisfied to create a valid fully-secret, or half-secret, trust. It has recently been ques-tioned whether the creation of a secret trust requires a contract between the testator and the intended trustee, whereby the trustee agrees to hold the property bequeathed to him on trust for the indicated beneficiary. In *Re Goodchild (Decd)*[21] Morritt LJ suggested that the 'principles applicable to cases of a fully secret trust do, in substance, require the proof of a contract', although he accepted that they do not 'require exactly the same degree of agreement as does a contract at law'.[22] Whilst many of the authorities elucidating the meaning of these requirements are applicable to both

---

[20]  [1923] 2 Ch 230.      [21]  [1997] 3 All ER 63.      [22]  [1997] 3 All ER 63 at 75.

categories of secret trust, it should be noted in advance that there are significant differences regarding the application of the requirement of communication to half-secret trusts.

## (1) Fully-secret trusts

The leading authority stating the requirements of a fully-secret trust is *Ottaway v Norman*.[23] Harry Ottaway cohabited with Miss Hodges in his house, 'Ashcroft'. On his death, 'Ashcroft' was left to Miss Hodges in his will, and she left it in her will to Mr and Mrs Norman. Harry's son, William, claimed that the house had been left to Miss Hodges on the understanding that she would leave it to him on her death. He claimed that a secret trust had been created in his favour, so that Miss Hodges held the house on trust for him and that it had not therefore formed part of her estate. Although the case is open to criticism on the grounds that it did not really involve a secret trust, as Miss Hodges was not subjected to an immediate obligation to hold the house on trust for William on the death of Harry, it was argued and decided on the basis that the existence of a secret trust was at issue. Having examined the facts, Brightman J concluded that a fully-secret trust had been created. In the course of his judgment he used somewhat confusing terminology, referring to the secret trustee as the 'primary donee' (who would take the property under the will) and the secret beneficiary as the 'secondary donee'.[24] He held that subjection of property to a fully-secret trust required the three elements of intention, communication and acceptance.

### (a) Intention

Brightman J stated that a secret trust would not be created unless it was 'the intention of the testator to subject the primary donee to an obligation in favour of the secondary donee'.[25] This requirement is no different from the requirement that conventional express trusts must demonstrate sufficient 'certainty of intention' to create a trust.[26] It must be shown that the testator intended to subject the secret trustee to a mandatory obligation to hold the property for the benefit of the secret beneficiary. An intention to impose a purely moral obligation is insufficient, as can be seen in *Re Snowden (Decd)*,[27] where an elderly testatrix left her entire residuary estate to her older brother because she was uncertain as to how she should leave her property amongst her relatives, and she said that her brother would 'know what to do'. She died without changing her will, and six days later her brother also died, leaving all his property to his only son. The question was whether the brother had taken Mrs Snowden's residuary estate on secret trust for her nephews and nieces equally. Megarry V-C concluded that she had not possessed the necessary intention to impose a trust on her brother in favour of the nephews and nieces, but that she had merely intended to impose on him a 'moral obligation' to do what he thought best. As a result no secret trust was established, and the brother's son was entitled to the entire residue absolutely.

---

[23] [1972] Ch 698; (1972) 36 Conv 129.      [24] [1972] Ch 698 at 711.      [25] [1972] Ch 698 at 711.
[26] See above, p 216.      [27] [1979] 2 All ER 172.

## (b) Communication

The mere fact that a testator intends to create a secret trust is alone insufficient to subject the recipient of the trust property under his will to an enforceable secret trust. As Brightman J stated in *Ottaway v Norman*, creation of a valid secret trust requires 'communication of that intention to the primary donee'.[28] The conscience of a beneficiary under the will is only affected, so as to justify the imposition of a trust, if the testator made him aware that he was to receive the property bequeathed as a trustee.

Communication will only be effective to create a fully-secret trust if it satisfies the following criteria.

*(i) Communication of both the fact of the trust and the terms of the trust.* A fully-secret trust will only arise if the testator makes the intended trustee aware of both the fact that he is to hold the property bequeathed to him on trust, and the identity (or the means of discovering the identity) of the intended beneficiary thereof. Where either of these elements is missing, the property will not be held on trust. For example, in *Re Boyes*[29] George Boyes left his entire estate by will to his solicitor, Frederick Carritt. Prior to his death Boyes had informed Carritt that he was to hold the property on trust, the terms of which he said he would communicate to him by letter. No communication of the terms of the trust was made during the testator's lifetime, but after his death papers were discovered directing Carritt to hold the property for his mistress and illegitimate child. Kay J held that in these circumstances a secret trust had not been established in favour of the mistress and child. However, as the solicitor had admitted that he had agreed to receive the property left to him as a trustee, he was not entitled to take it absolutely for himself, and therefore he held it on a resulting trust for Boyes' next of kin. Whilst a complete failure to communicate the terms of the trust before the testator's death prevents the creation of a valid secret trust, it seems that communication of the terms of the trust by means of a sealed envelope, given to the trustee during the testator's lifetime with the stipulation that it was not to be opened until after his death, will be sufficient to create a secret trust. This was accepted by the Court of Appeal in *Re Keen*,[30] where Lord Wright MR considered such communication analogous with that of a ship sailing under sealed orders, which he considered is 'sailing under orders though the exact terms are not ascertained by the captain till later'. He held that a sealed envelope containing the terms of the trust which had been given to the trustee could constitute sufficient communication to create a secret trust.

*(ii) Communication of the extent of the trust.* A secret trust will only affect property bequeathed to the intended trustees to the extent that effective communication had been made. In *Re Cooper*[31] a testator left £5,000 by will to two trustees. He had previously communicated the terms of the trust to them both. He subsequently added a codicil to his will, increasing the amount of the gift to £10,000, but without communicating

---

[28] *Ottaway v Norman* [1972] Ch 698 at 711.    [29] (1884) LR 26 Ch D 531.
[30] [1937] Ch 236. See also *Re Boyes* (1884) LR 26 Ch D 531 at 536; *Re Bateman's Will Trusts* [1970] 1 WLR 1463.
[31] [1939] Ch 811.

this alteration to the trustees. The Court of Appeal held that only £5,000 of the money bequeathed to the trustees was subject to the secret trust.[32]

*(iii) Communication must be made before the death of the testator.* A valid fully-secret trust will be created provided that effective communication was made to the trustee at any time prior to the death of the testator. It has already been seen how failure to communicate the terms of the intended trust before the testator's death prevented the finding of a secret trust in *Re Boyes*.[33] In *Wallgrave v Tebbs*[34] William Coles left property by will to the defendants. From a letter he had written it appeared that he had intended that it should be applied by them for the charitable purpose of endowing a church. However, as this intention had not been communicated to them during his lifetime, Page-Wood V-C held that no trust had been created, and that the defendants were entitled to take the property bequeathed to them absolutely.

*(iv) Communication to joint trustees.* Particular difficulties of communication emerge if a testator intends to subject property to a secret trust bequeathed to two or more persons jointly in his will. The question arises whether the joint beneficiaries under the will are bound by the secret trust if communication had only been made to some of them. In answering this dilemma the law distinguishes between bequests made to the intended trustees as joint tenants, and bequests made to them as tenants-in-common. The principles were stated by Farwell J in *Re Stead*.[35] Where the intended trust property is bequeathed to two or more persons as tenants-in-common, a secret trust will only bind the respective shares of those tenants-in-common to whom the testator had communicated the terms of the trust. Those to whom the trust had not been communicated are entitled to receive their respective shares of the bequeathed property absolutely.[36] In *Re Stead* Mrs Stead had left property to Mrs Witham and Mrs Andrews as tenants-in-common. She informed Mrs Witham that £2,000 was to be held on trust for John Collett, but made no communication to Mrs Andrews. It was held that Mrs Andrews took her share of the property free from any trust. Where the intended trust property is bequeathed to joint tenants, a further distinction is made on the grounds of the timing of any communication of the trust. Farwell J held that if a testator made effective communication to any one of the joint tenants before executing the will, they would all be bound by the secret trust.[37] However, he held that where communication occurred after the will had been executed, only those to whom communication had been made would be bound by the trust, and that therefore those tenants-in-common to whom no communication had been made would be entitled to take their respective shares of the bequeathed property absolutely.[38] Although clearly representing the present law it has been persuasively argued that the rules expounded in *Re Stead*[39] are incorrect because

---

[32] As it was a half-secret trust the remaining £5,000 was held on resulting trust for the testator's residuary legatees. If it had been a fully secret trust they would have been entitled to the remaining £5,000 absolutely.

[33] (1884) LR 26 Ch D 531.     [34] (1855) 2 K & J 313.     [35] [1900] 1 Ch 237.

[36] See *Tee v Ferri* (1856) 2 K & J 357; *Rowbotham v Dunnett* (1878) LR 8 Ch D 430; *Re Young (Deceased)* [1951] Ch 344. Compare also *Geddis v Semple* [1903] 1 IR 73.

[37] *Russell v Jackson* (1852) 10 Hare 204; *Jones v Badley* (1868) 3 Ch App 362.

[38] *Burney v Macdonald* (1845) 15 Sim 6; *Moss v Cooper* (1861) 1 John & H 352.

[39] [1900] 1 Ch 237.

Farwell J developed his reasoning from a misunderstanding of earlier cases cited as authority.[40] It is suggested that, rather than distinguishing between joint tenants and tenants in common (and in the latter case also between communication before and after the execution of the will), the question in each case should be whether the testator was induced to make the joint bequest only because of the promise of some of those entitled that the property would be held on trust.[41] Clearly, it will be more difficult to show that the gift was so induced if it was made to tenants-in-common, or if the promise was only made after the will had been executed.

### (c) Acceptance

A secret trust is not imposed on property bequeathed to an intended secret trustee merely because the testator effectively communicated his intention that it should be held on trust. The property will only be subject to a secret trust if the intended trustee accepted that he would hold it on trust. As Brightman J said in *Ottaway v Norman*,[42] the third essential element for the creation of a fully-secret trust is 'the acceptance of that obligation by the primary donee either expressly or by acquiescence'. Such acceptance does not need to be active. It seems that if the terms of the trust have been communicated to the intended trustee his silence will be taken to be an acceptance of the trust. In *Moss v Cooper*[43] John Hill left property in his will to James Gawthorn, William Sedman and James Owen. He communicated his intention to all three that the property should be used for the benefit of certain charities. The trust was accepted by Gawthron and Sedman. However, Owen remained silent. Page-Wood V-C held that, having learned of the testator's intention, such silence amounted to an acceptance of the trust. He justified this conclusion the grounds that 'the legatees, as soon as they learned the intention of the testator, would be bound to elect whether they would undertake the trust or not'.

## (2) Half-secret trusts

The creation of a valid half-secret trust is dependent upon satisfaction of the same three elements of intention, communication and acceptance. However, there are significant differences concerning the application of the requirement of communication. The leading case stipulating the requirements for half-secret trusts is *Blackwell v Blackwell*,[44] where Lord Sumner stated that the essential criteria were 'intention, communication and acquiescence'.[45] As the criteria of intention and acceptance are identical to those required for a valid fully-secret trust, which have been discussed above, only the element of communication will be examined.

### (a) Communication must be made before the execution of the will

It has already been seen that property bequeathed to an intended trustee will be subject to a fully secret trust if the testator made effective communication of the trust at any

---

[40] (1972) 88 LQR 225 (Perrins).
[41] Applying the principle of *Huguenin v Baseley* (1807) 14 Ves 273 that 'No man may profit by the fraud of another.'
[42] [1972] Ch 698 at 711.    [43] (1861) 1 John & H 352.    [44] [1929] AC 318, HL.
[45] [1929] AC 318 at 334.

time before his death. In contrast, in the case of half-secret trusts it has been held that the testator must make communication to the intended trustee before his will is executed. Communication subsequent to the execution of the will, even though prior to the testator's death, will not subject the bequeathed property to an enforceable half-secret trust. This follows from the judgment of Lord Sumner in *Blackwell v Blackwell,*[46] who stated:

'... A testator cannot reserve to himself a power of making future unwitnessed dispositions by merely naming a trustee and leaving the purposes of the trust to be supplied afterwards ...'

His comments in this respect were strictly obiter, because the trust in question had been communicated to the intended trustee before the testator's will was executed. However, the limitation was accepted by the Court of Appeal in *Re Keen,*[47] followed in *Re Bateman's Will Trusts.*[48] It is hard to see the logic for this differentiation between fully- and half-secret trusts.[49] The justification provided for this insistence on communication before the execution of the will appears to arise by analogy between the doctrine of half-secret trusts and the principle of incorporation by reference. As was explained above, a document will can only be incorporated into a will if it was in existence when the will was executed. It is submitted that this analogy is false, and that there is no reason for maintaining a distinction between the rules of communication applicable to fully- and half-secret trusts. A document incorporated by reference becomes part of the will itself, whereas according to the prevailing theory a secret trust, whether fully- or half-secret, arises wholly outside of the terms of the will.[50] It may yet be open to the House of Lords to find that a half-secret trust can be validly created by communication at any time before the death of the testator, and other jurisdictions have rejected the distinction and held that the same rule applies to both fully and half-secret trusts.[51] In the Irish case *Riordan v Banon,*[52] Chatterton V-C seems to have suggested that a valid half-secret trust can be created by communication before the testator's death, and this has been supported by later cases.[53]

### (b)  Evidence will not be admissible of communication inconsistent with the face of the will

Even if a testator communicates the trust to the intended trustee of a half-secret trust before executing his will, evidence of such communication will not be admitted to

---

[46] [1929] AC 318 at 339.        [47] [1937] Ch 236.        [48] [1970] 1 WLR 1463.

[49] (1937) 53 LQR 501 (Holdsworth). In recent case of *Gold v Hill* [1999] 1 FLR 54 a man who had separated from his wife nominated a solicitor as the beneficiary of a life insurance policy, having communicated to him that the proceeds were to be held on trust for his partner and her children. This nomination and communication had taken place after the execution of his will, which had left his estate to his wife. Carnwath J held that the situation was analogous to that of a half-secret trust, but held that any doubts as to the effectiveness of communication after the execution of a will were derived from the particular rules applying to wills and should not create difficulties for nominations.

[50] See below, p 228.        [51] See Scott, *Law of Trusts* (4th edn, 1988), para 55.8.

[52] (1876) 10 IrR Eq 469.

[53] See *Re King's Estate* (1888) 21 LR Ir 273; *Re Browne* [1944] IrR 90. *Re Prendeville* (5 December 1990, unreported) (Irish High Court). See [1992] Conv 202 (Mee).

establish the trust if it is inconsistent with the face of the will. Therefore, evidence of a communication inconsistent with the manner in which the will stated that communication would be made will not be admissible to prove the existence of a half-secret trust. The application of this rule had the effect of preventing the creation of a half-secret trust in *Re Keen*.[54] Whilst the terms of the trust had in fact been communicated to the trustee before the execution of the will, by means of a sealed envelope, the Court of Appeal held that evidence of the communication was inadmissible because clause 56 of the will anticipated that communication would only be made after the will had been executed. Therefore, evidence of the prior communication was inconsistent with the face of the will. In *Re Spence*[55] a testator had communicated the trust to some of the four trustees to whom he had jointly bequeathed the intended property. Whilst such communication would have been sufficient to establish a fully-secret trust, it was held that evidence of the communication was inadmissible to establish a half-secret trust. It was inconsistent with the terms of the will, which stated that communication had been made to them all.

The validity of this restriction should also be questioned. It is inconsistent with the approach applied to fully-secret trusts, where parol evidence of communication is admissible to prove the secret trust despite the fact that it is always inconsistent with the face of the will, which suggests that an absolute gift has been made. The inconsistency should only be material where it casts significant doubt upon whether the testator had intended the communication to be an effective expression of his wishes.

## (3) The burden of proof required to establish a secret trust

Whilst it is possible to identify the requirements necessary for the creation of a valid secret trust in the abstract, in reality a secret trust will only be established if the evidence in a particular case proves that they were satisfied. The level of proof necessary to establish a secret trust has been a matter of some debate. Traditionally, secret trusts were thought to be imposed by the court to prevent the secret trustee committing a fraud by denying the existence of the trust. In *McCormick v Grogan*[56] Lord Westbury therefore held that an extremely high burden of proof must be discharged before the court would impose a secret trust:

'Now, being a jurisdiction founded on personal fraud, it is incumbent on the court to see that a fraud, a malus animus, is proved by the clearest and most indisputable evidence . . . You are obliged, therefore, to show most clearly and distinctly that the person you wish to convert into a trustee acted mala animo. You must show distinctly that the testator or the intestate was beguiled and deceived by his conduct . . .'

As will be seen below, this view of secret trusts imposed to prevent personal fraud has been rejected by more modern cases in favour of the theory that they are inter vivos trusts arising wholly outside of the testator's will.[57] It is therefore illogical that a special

[54] [1937] Ch 236.     [55] [1949] WN 237.     [56] (1869) LR 4 HL 82.
[57] See below, p 228.

standard of proof appropriate to an allegation of fraud should be required before the court will enforce a secret trust. In *Ottaway v Norman*[58] Brightman J suggested that what was required was a standard of proof 'analogous to that required before the court would rectify a written instrument'. However, in *Re Snowden*[59] Megarry V-C considered that even this was inappropriate, since it demanded a higher threshold than the ordinary civil standard of proof, and it was founded upon a false analogy between rectification of documents and the operation of secret trusts. He concluded that the standard of proof required to establish a secret trust was simply the 'ordinary standard of evidence required to establish a trust'.[60] The higher standard appropriate for fraud would only need to be satisfied in circumstances where the secret trust could only be established by holding the legatee guilty of fraud.

# 4 Failure of secret trusts

Where a testator has bequeathed property in his will intending that it should be subject to a secret trust, but having failed to satisfy the requisite criteria, the ultimate location of the ownership of the intended trust property will depend upon whether the trust was fully- or half-secret.

## (1) Failure of a fully-secret trust

If a testator fails to establish a valid fully-secret trust, the intended secret trustee will be entitled to take the property for himself absolutely. This is nothing other than his entitlement under the will because the fact of the trust does not appear from the face of the will.[61] The intended trustee will only be required to hold the property on resulting trust for the testator's residuary legatees or next of kin[62] if he admits that he was intended to receive the property as a trustee.

## (2) Failure of a half-secret trust

Unlike a fully-secret trust, a half-secret trust is evident from the face of the will. If the trust fails for any reason the trustee will therefore be prevented from retaining the property bequeathed to him by the will. Instead, he will hold it on resulting trust, either for the residuary legatees under the will or, if the bequest is of the residuary estate, for the testator's next of kin.[63]

---

[58] [1972] Ch 698 at 699.    [59] [1979] 2 All ER 172.    [60] [1979] 2 All ER 172 at 178.
[61] Eg *Wallgrave v Tebbs* (1855) 2 K & J 313; *Jones v Badley* (1868) 3 Ch App 362; *McCormick v Grogan* (1869) LR 4 HL 82; *Re Pitt Rivers* [1902] 1 Ch 403.
[62] *Re Boyes* (1884) LR 26 Ch D 531.    [63] See *Re Cooper* [1939] Ch 811, CA.

# 5  Death or disclaimer of the secret trustee

A secret trust does not come into existence until the death of the testator who has bequeathed the trust property in his will to the intended secret trustee. Inevitably there is therefore a period of time, which in some cases may be substantial, between the communication and acceptance of the trust and the death of the testator. This time interval will give rise practical difficulties if the intended secret trustee predeceases the testator, or disclaims the trust on the death of the testator. In either event, the question will arise whether the intended trust property is subjected to a valid trust on the death of the testator. The answer will be determined primarily by the nature of the secret trust concerned.

## (1)  Death of the secret trustee

### (a)  Secret trustee predeceases the testator

*(i) Fully-secret trust.* Under the law of succession, a bequest lapses and fails if the beneficiary predeceases the testator.[64] At a matter of logic, the predecease of a trustee of a fully-secret trust should therefore cause the trust to fail. This was accepted in *Re Maddock*,[65] where Cozens-Hardy LJ stated that a fully-secret trust will fail if the trustee dies during the lifetime of the testator. This is consistent with the modern explanation of the operation of secret trusts discussed below, namely that a secret trust is an expressly declared inter vivos trust which remains unconstituted until the testator's will operates to transfer the legal title to the trust property to the trustee. Since the predecease of the trustee causes the gift to lapse, the testator's will fails to effect a constitution of the trust.

*(ii) Half-secret trusts.* In the case of a fully-secret trust, the existence of the intention to subject the property bequeathed to a trust is entirely absent from the face of the will. In contrast, where the trust is half-secret the fact that the property bequeathed was intended to be subject to a trust is apparent from the will itself. It is therefore clear that the legatee was never intended to enjoy the property left to him absolutely. If the intended trustee of a half-secret trust predeceases the testator, equity will not allow the trust to fail for want of a trustee. The testator's personal representative will act as trustee in his place.[66] Provided that it is still possible to identify the terms thereof, the half-secret trust will not fail.

### (b)  Death of the secret trustee subsequent to the death of the testator

If the trustee of a secret trust, whether half- or fully-secret, dies after the testator, the trust will not fail. In both cases the testator's will operates according to its terms to transfer the legal title of the property bequeathed to the secret trustee at the moment of

---

[64] *Elliott v Davenport* (1705) 1 P Wms 83; *Mabank v Brooks* (1780) 1 Bro CC 84. See Parry and Clark, *The Law of Succession* (10th edn, 1996), Ch 11.
[65] [1902] 2 Ch 220 at 231.    [66] See *Mallott v Wilson* [1903] 2 Ch 494.

the testator's death, thus constituting the trust. As the trust is fully constituted from the death of the testator, it will not fail for want of a trustee. However, if the death of the secret trustee renders it impossible to identify the beneficiary of the trust, the property will pass by resulting trust to the testator's residuary legatees or next of kin.

## (2) Secret trustee disclaims the trust

### (a) Revocation of acceptance before the death of the testator

It has been seen that a secret trust will only be established if the intended trustee accepts that he will hold the property bequeathed to him on trust. His acceptance, however, is not irrevocable. A secret trustee is entitled to revoke a previous acceptance of the trust at any time before the death of the testator. If the trust was fully-secret, a trustee who has revoked the trust will be entitled to take the property bequeathed to him in the will absolutely for his own benefit. In contrast, if the trust was half-secret, the intended trust property will be held on resulting trust for the testator's residuary legatees or next of kin. To be effective, the trustee must communicate his change of mind to the testator. He will otherwise be estopped from asserting his revocation of the agreement to hold upon trust.

### (b) Disclaimer after the death of the testator

Whilst a secret trustee may revoke his acceptance of the secret trust at any time before the death of the testator, in principle disclaimer after the will has taken effect should not invalidate the trust. Despite dicta to the contrary by Cozens-Hardy LJ in *Re Maddock*,[67] dicta of Lord Buckmaster and Lord Warrington in *Blackwell v Blackwell*[68] suggest that a secret trust will not fail if the trustee disclaims the trust subsequent to the testator's death. This is logical because the trust is constituted by the operation of will on the death of the testator, thus crystallising the secret beneficiary's equitable entitlement to the trust property. Since the trust has come into existence, it should not be allowed to fail for want of a trustee.

## 6 Can a secret trustee benefit from a secret trust?

In some cases, the trustee of a secret trust will enjoy no personal entitlement to the trust property and will hold it entirely for others. However in others the testator may also wish to grant the trustee some entitlement to the trust property, either as a joint beneficiary of the secret trust, or by way of a right to retain any surplus funds remaining after the beneficiaries have been allocated their interests. In *Irvine v Sullivan*[69] it was held that the trustee of a fully-secret trust was entitled to retain the surplus of the trust property remaining after the trusts had been carried out. In contrast, in *Re Rees' Will Trusts*[70] the

---

[67] [1902] 2 Ch 220.     [68] [1929] AC 318 at 328, 341.     [69] (1869) LR 8 Eq 673.
[70] [1950] Ch 204.

Court of Appeal held that the trustee of a half-secret trust was not entitled to assert any entitlement to such a surplus because this would be inconsistent with the terms of the will, which suggested that all the property bequeathed to him was subject to the trust. This decision was doubted by Pennycuick J in *Re Tyler's Fund Trusts*[71] and there is no logical justification for maintaining this differentiation between fully-secret and half-secret trusts.[72] It may be significant that in *Re Rees' Will Trusts* the trustee was the testator's solicitor and a beneficial gift was therefore inherently less likely.[73]

# 7 Justifying the enforcement of secret trusts

Whilst it is easy to appreciate the practical advantages which have contributed to the evolution of secret trusts as mechanisms for allocating property on death, it is less easy to provide an adequate explanation of the legal principles justifying their enforcement. They appear to operate in contradiction of the clear policy of the Wills Act requiring testamentary dispositions to be executed in the specified form. Equity's effort to provide an adequate explanation for the enforcement of secret trusts is an ex post facto rational-isation of a mechanism which had already been allowed to emerge. Historically, equity enforced secret trusts on the grounds that to fail to do so would allow the Wills Act to be used as an instrument of fraud. However, cases subsequent to the decision of the House of Lords in *Blackwell v Blackwell*[74] have held that they are enforced as valid inter vivos trusts arising outside (dehors) the will. The advantage of this explanation is that it does not predicate a conflict between the enforcement of secret trusts and the provisions of the Wills Act. However, even this theory is not wholly satisfactory.

## (1) Secret trusts enforced to prevent fraud

In the nineteenth century equity accepted that secret trusts were enforced in order to prevent fraud. The secret trustee had induced the testator to leave property to him on the understanding that he would apply it for the benefit of the secret beneficiary. If the secret trustee were permitted to deny the trust, because of a lack of testamentary formalities, and to assert a personal entitlement to the property bequeathed to him in the testator's will, he would be using the Wills Act as an instrument of fraud. To prevent such a fraud, equity would allow the admission of parol evidence on behalf of the beneficiary to prove that the bequest had been subject to a trust. This rationale was accepted by the House of Lords in *McCormick v Grogan*,[75] where Lord Hatherley LC described the enforcement of secret trusts as:

'. . . a doctrine which involves a wide departure from the policy of . . . the [Wills Act] and it is only in clear cases of fraud that this doctrine has been applied—cases in which the court

---

[71] [1967] 1 WLR 1269.    [72] See Oakley, *Constructive Trusts* (3rd edn, 1997), p 259.
[73] See [1950] Ch 204 at 211, per Lord Evershed MR.    [74] [1929] AC 318.
[75] (1869) LR 4 HL 82.

has been persuaded that there has been a fraudulent inducement held out on the part of the apparent beneficiary in order to lead the testator to confide to him the duty which he so understood to perform.'[76]

Lord Westbury also emphasised that the enforcement of secret trusts was 'founded altogether on personal fraud'.[77]

However, despite the early acceptance of the fraud explanation by the House of Lords, it came to be thought that the fraud theory was inadequate as a justification for the enforcement of secret trusts.[78] A number of defects were identified. First, the fraud theory accepts that the enforcement of secret trusts is in direct conflict with the provisions and policy of the Wills Act. Although such conflict has been tolerated in other areas, for example where the principle of *Rochefoucauld v Boustead*[79] operates to enforce an oral declaration of a trust of land despite the lack of writing, the courts today are reluctant to adopt an analysis so directly opposed to the terms of legislation. Second, a major defect of the fraud theory was that it did not provide an adequate justification for the enforcement of half-secret trusts. In the case of a half-secret trust, the fact of the trust is evident from the face of the will, so that there is no possibility of fraud. The secret trustee cannot take the property absolutely for himself. Fraud would easily be avoided by the secret trustee holding any property received under the will on resulting trust for the residuary legatees or the testator's next of kin. Third, it is questionable whether the fraud theory is also capable of explaining why a fully-secret trust should be enforced in favour of the secret beneficiary. Whilst it might justify the refusal to allow the secret trustee to take the property bequeathed to him by the testator absolutely, it is less easy to see why the possibility of fraud justifies enforcement of the trust in favour of the secret beneficiary. Any fraud could equally be prevented if the trustee was required to hold the property on resulting trust for the residuary legatees under the will or the testator's next of kin. This would prevent the trustee benefiting by his fraud, but would not contradict the provisions of the Wills Act. Fourth, as has been noted above, adoption of the fraud theory had the effect that an unduly high burden of proof needed to be discharged if a beneficiary was to establish that property was held on secret trust. In consequence of these inadequacies, the fraud analysis has been rejected in more modern cases in favour of a theory that secret trusts arise entirely outside of the operation of the testator's will by express inter vivos declaration.

However the fraud theory continues to enjoy the support of some academics. Critchley has recently argued that the modern theory that secret trusts arise outside of the will is implausible, and argues that secret trusts are upheld to prevent fraud where this is demanded by legal policy.[80] Such enforcement will only be justified where there is a combination of personal wrongdoing on the part of the trustee, and harm would be caused to beneficiary and/or testator if the trust were not enforced. The requisite element of personal wrongdoing would only be satisfied if 'the trustee was fully aware that the property was only to be transferred to him on trust, but that he took no steps to

---

[76] (1869) LR 4 HL 82 at 89.  　　[77] (1869) LR 4 HL 82 at 99.  　　[78] See [1980] Conv 341 (Hodge).
[79] [1897] 1 Ch 196, CA. See above p 196.
[80] 'Instruments of Fraud, Testamentary Dispositions, and the Doctrine of Secret Trusts' (1999) 115 LQR 631.

deny this understanding until the transfer was completed beyond the recall of the testator'.[81] However this argument does not address all of the problems identified above. Critchley concludes that whilst the fraud maxim might justify the enforcement of a fully secret trustee where the trustee actively seeks to deny the trust, it is 'less overwhelmingly supportive' of justifying the enforcement of other fully- and half-secret trusts. She therefore suggests that these other secret trusts must be allowed to tag along in the wake of those which can be justified on the basis of fraud, since otherwise further problems, such as the increase of opportunities for fraud, or of litigation over the construction of the will, seem likely, if not bound, to emerge.[82] It is submitted that this concedes that the fraud theory, even articulated in a more sophisticated form, is incapable of adequately justifying the enforcement of secret trusts.

## (2) Secret trusts arise outside of the testator's will

The modern justification of the enforcement of secret trusts was neatly summarised by Megarry V-C in *Re Snowden*:[83]

'... the whole basis of secret trusts, as I understand it, is that they operate outside the will, changing nothing that is written in it, and allowing it to operate according to its tenor, but then fastening a trust on to the property in the hands of the recipient.'

This explanation evolved from the decision of the House of Lords in *Cullen v A-G for Ireland* where Lord Westbury said:

'... I think it very material to point out that where there is a secret trust, ... the title of the party claiming under the secret trust ... is a title dehors the will, and which cannot be correctly termed testamentary.'[84]

It was utilised and developed by the House of Lords in *Blackwell v Blackwell*[85] to justify the enforceability of half-secret trusts. Its overwhelming advantage is that it does not presuppose a contradiction between the enforcement of secret trusts and the Wills Act.[86]

The essence of this modern justification for the enforcement of secret trusts is that they come into existence entirely outside of the operation of the will to which they relate, so that the equitable interest enjoyed by the secret beneficiary is not a species of testamentary disposition. The modern theory postulates two distinguishable stages in the creation of a valid secret trust. First, the testator communicates to the secret trustee his intention to subject the property bequeathed to a trust, at which point the secret trustee accepts the trust obligation. However, at this point the secret trust has not yet come into existence. The intended subject matter of the trust remains the absolute property of the testator, and the legal title to it has not been transferred to the trustee. In effect the testator and trustee have agreed that the property will be subject to a trust when it comes into the hands of the trustee but at present the trust remains

---

[81] (1999) 115 LQR 631 at 647.   [82] (1999) 115 LQR 631 at 653.
[83] [1979] 2 All ER 172 at 177.   [84] [1866] LR 1 HL 190 at 196.   [85] [1929] AC 318.
[86] [1929] AC 318 at 340.

(i)  The trust is declared inter vivos but remains unconstituted

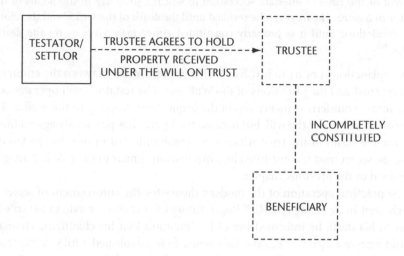

(ii)  The trust is constituted by the operation of the settlor's will

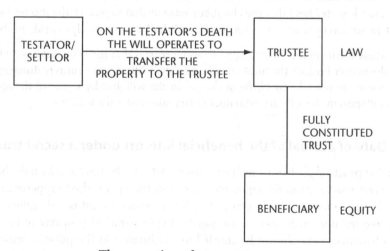

### The operation of secret trusts

incompletely constituted. Secondly, when the testator dies his will operates according to its terms to transfer the legal title to the property bequeathed to the secret trustee. His receipt of the property in this way has the effect of constituting the incompletely-constituted trust.[87] He henceforth holds the property on trust for the secret beneficiary. The secret trust does not therefore arise completely independently of the testator's will. As Kincaid has recently commented:

---

[87]  Critchley, however, argues that this analysis is 'implausible': (1999) 115 LQR 631 at 634.

'A secret trust relies on the death of the settlor to constitute the trust and the terms of the will or the rules of intestate succession to vest the property in the hands of the secret trustee or legatee. The trust can be revoked until the death of the settlor and therefore it does not stand alone until it is properly constituted either *inter vivos* or on the death of the settlor.'[88]

This explanation appears to involve no element of conflict between the enforcement of a secret trust and the provisions of the Wills Act. The testator's will operates according to its terms, transferring ownership of the bequeathed property to the legatee. The trust is enforced not under the will, but because the legatee has previously agreed that he will observe the terms of the trust which were communicated to him by the testator. In a sense the secret trust is constituted by a mechanism similar to the rule in *Strong v Bird* [89] examined in the previous chapter.

The practical operation of the modern theory for the enforcement of secret trusts is clearly seen in *Re Young (Decd)*.[90] Roger Young left his entire estate to his wife Eveleen. Prior to his death he informed her of his intention that his chauffeur, Thomas Cobb, should receive a legacy of £2,000. This prima facie established a fully-secret trust in his favour. However the chauffeur was coincidentally one of the witnesses to Roger's will. By s 15 of the Wills Act 1837 a legacy to a person attesting a will is forfeit. The central question was, therefore, whether the chauffeur's entitlement to the £2,000 subject to the secret trust should be characterised as a legacy under the will, in which case it would be void. Danckwerts J held that the chauffeur was entitled to receive the money because his entitlement was by way of a secret trust which had arisen wholly outside of the will:

'The whole theory of the formulation of a secret trust is that the Wills Act has nothing to do with the matter because the forms required by the Wills Act are entirely disregarded, since the persons do not take by virtue of the gift in the will, but by virtue of the secret trusts imposed upon the beneficiary, who does in fact take under the will.'[91]

## (3) Date of accrual of the beneficial interest under a secret trust

A further practical problem which has arisen relates to the time at which the beneficiary of a secret trust accrues the equitable interest in the bequeathed property intended as the subject matter thereof. In principle, because a secret trust is only fully constituted when the testator's will operates to transfer the bequeathed property to the trustee, a secret beneficiary should not be entitled to any interest in the putative trust property until the death of the testator. Prior to his death, the testator retains the right to change his will, enabling him to subvert the trust by bequeathing the property to someone other than the secret trustee, thus ensuring that the trust is never constituted.[92] The logic of this argument was not, however, followed in *Re Gardner (No 2)*.[93] A testatrix

---

[88] 'The tangled web: the relationship between a secret trust and the will' [2000] Conv 420 at 442.

[89] (1874) LR 18 Eq 315         [90] [1951] Ch 344.         [91] [1951] Ch 344 at 350.

[92] Pawlowski and Brown argue, however, that an estoppel equity may arise from the moment that the testator departs from his promise to benefit the secret beneficiary and changes his will: 'Constituting a Secret Trust by Estoppel' [2004] Conv 388.

[93] [1923] 2 Ch 230.

made a will leaving all her property to her husband for life, with the remainder subject to a secret trust in favour of her two nieces and nephew. At the date of the testatrix's death she had been predeceased by one of her nieces. The court was required to decide whether the personal representative of the niece was entitled to a third share of the remainder interest by way of the secret trust. Romer J held that, as a secret beneficiary, the niece had been entitled to her share of the trust property from the moment that the husband had accepted the terms of the trust. Her third share was therefore held on trust for her personal representative, notwithstanding that she had predeceased the testator. This case is open to the criticism that the niece cannot have gained an interest in the testatrix's estate until her death, since a secret trust remains unconstituted until the will operates to transfer the trust property to the trustee. Prior to the testator's death the trust does not exist. It is therefore submitted that the decision in *Re Gardner (No 2)* is incorrect and that a secret beneficiary enjoys no entitlement to the putative trust property until the trust is fully constituted through the operation of the testator's will.

## (4) Problems associated with the modern theory

The currently fashionable theory for explaining secret trusts is less elegant than it may seem and has attracted academic criticism. There appears to be no reason why the testator should not change his mind about the creation of the trust prior to his death, either by informing the trustee that he no longer wishes to create a trust, or by an amendment to his will. The secret trust therefore shares one of the characteristics of a testamentary gift, namely that it is revocable at any time prior to the testator's death. Furthermore, secret trusts are clearly intended to become operative only on the testator's death, so that they do not in any way inhibit the testator's power to deal as he wishes with his property during his lifetime. This is also a characteristic of a testamentary gift. Finally, in *Re Maddock*[94] a gift by way of a secret trust was treated as if it had been made by will in a case where the estate was insufficient to meet all the specific gifts made by the testator. The case for treating gifts under a half-secret trust in this way would be even stronger.

Critchley has therefore argued that the *dehors* the will theory cannot justify the enforcement of secret trusts.[95] She submits that secret trusts are testamentary dispositions because they possess the characteristics of ambulatoriness and revocability, in that they do not take effect until the death of the testator, and the testator can change his mind:

'. . . the *dehors* theory seems to be fatally flawed. In essence the mistake is to confuse "outside the will" with "outside the *Wills Act*". The *dehors* theory needs—and fails—to demonstrate the trust of the latter and too often ends up resting merely upon the former, which is wholly inadequate as a justificatory argument.'[96]

---

[94] [1902] 2 Ch 220.

[95] 'Instruments of Fraud, Testamentary Dispositions, and the Doctrine of Secret Trusts' (1999) 115 LQR 631.

[96] (1999) 115 LQR 631 at 641.

However, in the light of the admitted inability of the rival fraud theory to justify the enforcement of all the well established categories of secret trusts, it is submitted that the modern theory that secret trusts arise outside of the will remains the most convincing justification.[97] It is certainly the explanation which commands the support of the authorities. Whilst the fashionable modern theory explaining their operation is imperfect, it has the merit of pragmatism.

## (5) The juridical nature of secret trusts

The accepted modern justification for enforcement of secret trusts is that they arise inter vivos outside of the will. However, the acceptance of this theory does not of itself answer the question whether secret trusts should be characterised as express or constructive trusts. This is not an entirely esoteric academic question. If secret trusts are characterised as express in nature, practical difficulties arise where the intended trust property is land or an interest in land, as s 53(1)(b) of the Law of Property Act 1925 renders an oral declaration of a trust of land unenforceable without substantiating evidence in writing. In contrast, if they are characterised as constructive in nature, a secret trust of land will be enforceable without the need for further formalities as s 53(2) exempts all constructive trusts from the need of writing.

### (a) Secret trusts characterised as express trusts

The modern theory that secret trusts arise inter vivos outside of the testator's will would logically suggests that they are express in nature. The acceptance of the trust by the secret trustee amounts to an express inter vivos declaration of trust. This view has been favoured in the past by most academic writers.[98] However, such a characterisation could produce the unsatisfactory implication of rendering an oral agreement to hold land subject to a secret trust unenforceable through the absence of writing, as required by s 53(1)(b) of the Law of Property Act 1925.[99] Thus, in *Re Baillie*[100] North J held a secret trust of land unenforceable because the Statute of Frauds applied and the trust had not been indicated in writing. In other cases, for example *Ottaway v Norman*,[101] orally declared secret trusts of land have been enforced without question. Of itself the enforcement of the trusts in such cases fails to prove the point, since a trust will not fail for lack of formalities unless the absence of writing is specifically pleaded as a ground of

[97] Emma Challinor has recently argued that no logical rationale for the enforcement of secret trusts may be discerned, and that they are covert devices by which the courts avoid the statutory formalities of the Wills Act 1837, thus subverting the policy of the Wills Act: [2005] Con 493. She therefore proposes abolition or fundamental revision of the law relating to secret trusts,

[98] See Snell, *Principles of Equity* (30th edn, 2000), p 132–136; Underhill and Hayton, *Law of Trusts and Trustees* (15th edn, 1998), pp 227–237; Hayton and Marshal, *Cases and Commentary on the Law of Trusts* (11th edn, 2001), p 103–121; Pettit, *Equity and the Law of Trusts* (9th edn, 2001), p 125; Oakley, *Constructive Trusts* (3rd edn, 1997), p 263; (1991) 5 Tru LI 69 (Coughlon). See also (1951) 67 LQR 314 (Sheridan)—where half-secret trusts are held to be express, but fully-secret trusts to be constructive. Hanbury and Martin, *Modern Equity* (17th edn, 2005), pp 168–169 concludes that secret trusts can be enforced as either express trusts or constructive trusts.

[99] See Chapter 25.        [100] (1886) 2 TLR 660.        [101] [1972] Ch 698.

invalidity.[102] However, even if secret trusts are characterised as express trusts, it is submitted that an orally declared secret trust of land should not fail merely because of the lack of writing. The court should invoke the well established doctrine of *Roche-foucauld v Boustead*,[103] namely that equity will not allow the statute requiring trusts of land to be evidenced in writing to be used as an instrument of fraud, to prevent the secret trustee denying the trust because of the absence of writing. This would not mark a reversion to the fraud explanation of the enforcement of secret trusts in conflict with the terms of the Wills Act, as the rule in *Rochefoucauld v Boustead* would only be employed to prevent the use of s 53(1)(b) of the Law of Property Act as an instrument of fraud.

## (b) Secret trusts characterised as constructive trusts

Despite traditional academic consensus that secret trusts are express in nature, in *Re Cleaver*[104] Nourse J characterised them as constructive trusts. As the case concerned the doctrine of mutual wills, his expression of opinion is strictly obiter. A number of recent commentators have adopted the view that secret trusts are gratuitous promises enforced on the grounds of fraud or unconsionability.[105]

---

[102] *North v Loomes* [1919] 1 Ch 378.     [103] [1897] 1 Ch 196, CA.     [104] [1981] 1 WLR 939.

[105] Underhill and Hayton, *Law of Trusts and Trustees* (16th edn, 2003), pp 257; McFarlane, 'Constructive Trusts Arising on a Receipt of Property *Sub Conditione*' (2004) 120 LQR 667. See also Hanbury and Martin, *Modern Equity* (17th edn, 2005), pp 168–169, which concludes that secret trusts can be enforced as either express trusts or constructive trusts.

# 8

# Resulting trusts

## 1 Introduction to resulting trusts

### (1) What are resulting trusts?[1]

The previous two chapters have examined the circumstances in which a trust relationship may be created by the deliberate intention and act of the settlor. Such trusts are known as 'express trusts'. However, in some situations property will be regarded as subject to a trust despite the absence of any express intention on the part of the settlor. In English law 'resulting trusts' are one of the two main categories of such informal trusts, the other being that of 'constructive trusts'. The circumstances in which property will become subject to a resulting trust were recently examined by the House of Lords in *Westdeutsche Landesbank Girozentrale v Islington London Borough Council*.[2] Lord Browne-Wilkinson identified two circumstances in which a resulting trust would arise:

'Under existing law a resulting trust arises in two sets of circumstances: (A) where A makes a voluntary payment to B or pays (wholly or in part) for the purchase of property which is vested either in B alone or in the joint names of A and B, there is a presumption that A did not intend to make a gift to B; the money or property is held on trust for A (if he is the sole provider of the money) or in the case of a joint purchaser by A and B in shares proportionate to their contributions. It is important to stress that this is only a *presumption*, which presumption is easily rebutted either by the counter presumption of advancement or by direct evidence of A's intention to make an outright transfer . . . (B) Where A transfers property to B *on express trusts*, but the trusts declared do not exhaust the whole beneficial interest.'[3]

Resulting trusts of the second type will be examined in Chapter 19, where it will be seen that they operate to 'fill the gap' in the beneficial ownership of property where an express trust fails. This chapter will be concerned largely with resulting trusts of the first type, commonly termed 'presumed resulting trusts'.

---

[1] See Chambers, *Resulting Trusts* (1997).     [2] [1996] AC 669. See [1996] RLR 3 (Birks).
[3] [1996] AC 669 at 708.

## (2) Distinguishing resulting and constructive trusts

In some cases, the House of Lords seem to have used 'resulting' and 'constructive' trusts as interchangeable terms,[4] suggesting that it is not necessary to distinguish between them. However it is submitted that they are fundamentally different, operating on different principles, and that they need to be strictly differentiated.

Constructive trusts[5] are imposed by the court as a consequence of the conduct of the party who becomes a trustee. Resulting trusts are not imposed as a response to the conduct of the trustee, but to give effect to the implied intentions of the owner. Where a transfer of property has occurred and the legal title has been transferred, but the transferor has failed to show an intention to divest himself fully of all his interest in that property, the transferee will not be permitted to receive the property absolutely for his own benefit. Instead, he will hold it on trust for the transferor. The equitable interests is said to 'result back' to the transferor, thus ensuring that he retains his interest in the property. Practical imperatives may also demand that a distinction be drawn between beneficial entitlements taking effect under resulting and constructive trusts. *Re Densham (A Bankrupt)*[6] concerned a dispute as to the ownership of a matrimonial home. Whilst the husband was the sole legal owner of the house, his wife had contributed towards the purchase price and they had also agreed that the ownership should be jointly shared. Goff J held that, in consequence of the agreement, the wife was prima facie entitled to a beneficial half share in the ownership of the house by way of a constructive trust, and that through her direct financial contribution to the purchase price she was also entitled to a ninth share of the beneficial ownership by way of a resulting trust. However, because the husband was bankrupt, she was held unable to assert any entitlement by way of the constructive trust, because it was not a settlement made for 'valuable consideration' and therefore void against his trustee in bankruptcy.[7] Nevertheless, she was able to assert her entitlement by way of the resulting trust.

*Re Densham* therefore illustrates the need to distinguish between the operation of resulting and constructive trusts. This need was reiterated by the Court of Appeal in *Drake v Whipp*,[8] where the central issue was as to the proportion of the equitable interest that the plaintiff enjoyed in a barn owned by her erstwhile partner by virtue of her contributions to the purchase price and work done, where there was also a common intention that she was to enjoy a share of the ownership. Peter Gibson LJ remarked:

'A potent source of confusion, to my mind, has been suggestions that it matters not whether the terminology used is that of the constructive trust, to which the intention, actual or imputed, of the parties is crucial, or that of the resulting trust which operates as a presumed intention of the contributing party in the absence of rebutting evidence of actual intention.'[9]

---

[4] Eg *Gissing v Gissing* [1971] AC 886 at 905, per Lord Diplock; *Tinsley v Milligan* [1993] 3 All ER 65 at 86–87, per Lord Browne-Wilkinson.

[5] See Chapter 9.      [6] [1975] 1 WLR 1519.      [7] Bankruptcy Act 1914, s 42.

[8] [1996] 1 FLR 826.       [9] [1996] 1 FLR 826 at 827.

Thus, whilst by means of a resulting trust the plaintiff would only be entitled to a share of the beneficial interest directly equivalent to the proportion of her contribution to the purchase price of the barn (which was 19.4%), by way of a constructive trust she was entitled to a third interest.[10]

## (3) Rationale of resulting trusts

In *Westdeutsche Landesbank Girozentrale v Islington London Borough Council*[11] Lord Browne-Wilkinson stated that resulting trusts arise to fulfill the implied intentions of the parties:

'Both types of resulting trust are traditionally regarded as examples of trusts giving effect to the common intentions of the parties. A resulting trust is not imposed by law against the intentions of the trustee (as is a constructive trust) but gives effect to his presumed intention.'[12]

However, this formulation should be subject to question. Whilst it is certainly the case that a presumed resulting trust arises in consequence of the presumed intention of the transferor of the trust property (or contributor to its purchase as the case may be) it is not necessarily the case that the trustee who received the legal title intended the property to be held on trust. In many cases, a resulting trust has been found in circumstances where the transferee of the legal title anticipated that a gift had been made divesting the transferor of his entire interest in the property. This can be seen from the fact that many cases involve a dispute as to whether a presumption of resulting trust has been rebutted. As Lord Browne-Wilkinson himself observed, a resulting trust of the first type arises because 'there is a presumption that A did not intend to make a gift to B'.[13] A resulting trust will arise in favour of A in such circumstances even though B anticipated that he was the beneficiary of an absolute gift, and in this sense B will be required to hold the property on resulting trust against his intentions. More significantly, a resulting trust may even arise where the transferee of property was unaware that the transfer had occurred.[14] Therefore, it should not be thought that a resulting trust will only arise on the basis of the mutual intention of the parties. Instead, a resulting trust should arise whenever a transferee (or contributor) cannot be shown to have possessed the intention to make a gift. As Lord Goff stated, a presumed resulting trust arises when there are:

'. . . voluntary payments by A to B, or for the purchase of property in the name of B or in his and A's joint names, where there is no presumption of advancement or evidence of intention to make an out-and-out gift.'[15]

A number of earlier cases provide a less confusing analysis of the rationale for the creation of resulting trusts. In *Re Sick and Funeral Society of St John's Sunday School, Golcar*[16] Megarry V-C stated that:

---

[10] See also *Midland Bank Plc v Cooke* [1995] 4 All ER 562.   [11] [1996] AC 669.
[12] [1996] AC 669 at 708.   [13] [1996] AC 669 at 708.
[14] As, for example, in *Re Vinogradoff* [1935] WN 68. See Chambers, *Resulting Trusts* (1997), p 37.
[15] [1996] AC 669 at 689.   [16] [1973] Ch 51.

'A resulting trust is essentially a property concept: any property that a man does not effectually dispose of remains his own.'

This clearly recognises that a resulting trust arises because of the failure of the transferor to make an absolute gift of his property. As Lord Reid observed in *Vandervell v IRC*:

'... where it appears to have been the intention of the donor that the donee should not take beneficially, there will be a resulting trust in favour of the donor.'[17]

A more nuanced understanding of the operation of resulting trusts was provided by the Privy Council in *Air Jamaica Ltd v Charlton*, where Lord Millet stated:

'Like a constructive trust, a resulting trust arises by operation of law, although unlike a constructive trust it gives effect to intention. But it arises whether or not the transferor intended to retain a beneficial interest—he almost always does not—since it responds to the absence of any intention on his part to pass a beneficial interest to the recipient.'[18]

# 2 Presumed resulting trusts[19]

Presumed resulting trusts arise where it is presumed that the transferor of property did not intend to dispose of his entire ownership interest in the property transferred. Under English law there is a rebuttable presumption that a transferor of property does not intend to make a gift of it, and unless this presumption is rebutted the transferee will hold it on resulting trust for the donor. However, in some circumstances the nature of the relationship between the transferor and the transferee gives rise to an opposite presumption, namely that the transferor did intend to benefit the transferee, in which case unless the presumption of a gift is rebutted there will be no resulting trust. This counter-presumption is known as the 'presumption of advancement'.

## (1) The basic presumption of resulting trust

English law adopts two basic presumptions about the intentions of property owners, both of which are rebuttable by evidence of a contrary intention.

### (a) A presumption against gifts

First, it is presumed that, outside of certain relationships, an owner of property never intends to make a gift. If an owner voluntarily transfers the legal title of his property to a third party without receiving any consideration in return, he is presumed to have intended to retain the equitable interest for himself. The transferee will therefore hold the property on resulting trust for him. This presumption was invented by equity to

---

[17] [1967] 2 AC 291, HL.  [18] [1999] 1 WLR 1399 at 1412.
[19] See Chambers, *Resulting Trusts* (1997), pp 11–39.

defeat the misappropriation of property as a consequence of potentially fraudulent or improvident transactions.[20]

### (b) A presumption in favour of the provider of purchase money

By extension of this first presumption, it is also presumed that a person who provides the money required to purchase property intends to obtain the equitable interest in the property acquired. Therefore, when the property is purchased in the name of someone who did not provide the purchase money, he will be presumed to hold the legal title on trust for the provider thereof. This presumption is long established and was recognised in *Dyer v Dyer*, where Eyre CB stated:

'... the trust of a legal estate ... whether taken in the names of the purchasers and others jointly, or in the names of others without that of the purchaser; whether in one name of several; whether jointly or successive, results to the man who advances the purchase-money.'[21]

Where a person has only contributed a part of the purchase price of property a resulting trust will be presumed in his favour of an equivalent proportion of the equitable interest.[22]

### (2) Voluntary transfers of property

Where an owner makes a voluntary transfer of property, either into the sole name of the transferee or into the joint names of himself and the transferee, without receiving any consideration in return, a resulting trust will be presumed in his favour unless rebutted by evidence that he intended to make a gift. The presumption of a resulting trust clearly operates in the context of voluntary transfers of personal property, but it is less certain whether it operates in respect to voluntary transfers of land.

### (a) Operation of the presumption of resulting trust in the context of personal property

The operation of the presumption of a resulting trust is well illustrated by *Re Vinogradoff*.[23] Mrs Vindogradoff transferred a £800 War Loan into the joint names of herself and her infant granddaughter. Farwell J held that the stock was held on resulting trust for her,[24] and that therefore on her death it belonged in equity to her estate. In *Thavorn v Bank of Credit and Commerce International SA*[25] a resulting trust was found to exist where a woman opened a bank account in favour of her infant nephew. In 1981 Mrs Thavorn opened an account with some £20,000 in her nephew's name. She had directed the bank that she alone was to operate the account. Lloyd J held that in these circumstances there was no evidence to rebut the presumption of a resulting trust:

---

[20] *Lynch v Burke* [1995] 2 IR 159, per O'Flaherty J.     [21] (1788) 2 Cox Eq Cas 92 at 93.

[22] *Midland Bank plc v Cooke* [1995] 4 All ER 562; *Drake v Whipp* [1996] 1 FLR 826.

[23] [1935] WN 68. See also *Re Muller* [1953] NZLR 879.

[24] The granddaughter was held to be a trustee of the resulting trust despite her minority. See Law of Property Act 1925, s 20.

[25] [1985] 1 Lloyd's Rep 259. Compare also *Re Howes* (1905) 21 TLR 501.

'There was not the slightest evidence on which I could hold that, by opening the account in his name, she intended to transfer any beneficial interest to him during her lifetime.'

The bank was therefore liable to pay damages when they paid the money into his current account. A presumption of resulting trust will also arise where a person transfers money into a bank account in joint names. In the recent case of *Aroso v*

(i)  Voluntary transfer: *Re Vindogradoff*

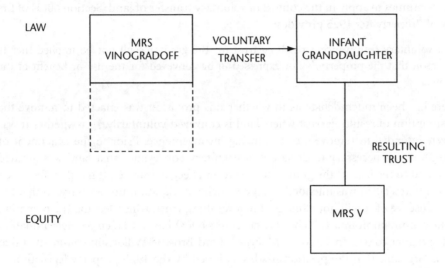

(il)  Contribution to purchase price: *Tinsley v Milligan*

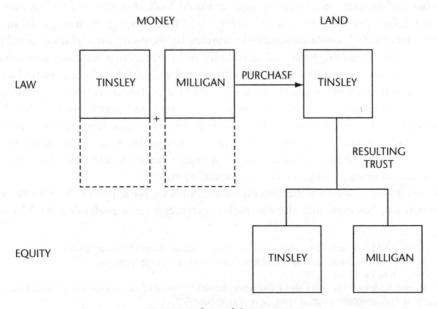

**Presumed resulting trusts**

*Coutts*[26] it was held that the presumption of resulting trusts operated when Sr Aroso transferred money into a joint account opened in the names of himself and his nephew, although the presumption was held to have been rebutted by evidence that a gift had been intended.

## (b) Operation of the presumption of resulting trust in the context of land

Whilst the presumption of resulting trust clearly operates in respect of voluntary transfers of personal property, a more difficult question is whether the presumption against gifts continues to apply in the context of voluntary transfer of land. Section 60(3) of the Law of Property Act 1925 provides:

'In a voluntary conveyance a resulting trust for the grantor shall not be implied merely by reason that the property is not expressed to be conveyed for the use or benefit of the grantee.'

There has been much debate as to whether this provision was enacted to remove the presumption of resulting trust where land is conveyed voluntarily,[27] or whether it was merely intended to remove a conveyancing inconvenience. Prior to the enactment of s 60(3), it was necessary to declare in a voluntary conveyance that land was granted 'unto and to the use of' the grantee to ensure an effective transfer. It has therefore been argued that s 60(3) was intended to render such a declaration unnecessary, so that the mere absence of it will not alone lead to a resulting trust, whilst leaving the operation of the presumption intact.[28] The true effect of s 60(3) has not fallen for determination by the higher courts. In *Tinsley v Milligan*[29] Lord Browne-Wilkinson commented that it was 'arguable that the position has been altered by the 1925 property legislation',[30] and in *Hodgson v Marks*[31] the Court of Appeal held that a resulting trust arose in favour of an elderly lady who had transferred the legal title to her house to her lodger on the basis of an oral understanding that he would look after her affairs. However in *Lohia v Lohia*[32] Nicholas Strauss QC recently held that although both proposed interpretations of s 60(3) could reasonably be adopted by the court, on a 'plain reading' the presumption of resulting trust had been abolished in respect of a voluntary conveyance of land. Thus a presumption of resulting trust will only arise if there is some fact in addition to the lack of consideration, such as that the parties are strangers. In the light of this interpretation, he held that no resulting trust had arisen where a son had conveyed his share in the family home to his father. The mere fact that there was no evidence of any sensible reason why he had so conveyed his share in the house to his father, and that he had continued to share mortgage payments and rental income, was not sufficient to lead to the inference of a resulting trust.

It remains to be seen whether this interpretation is supported by the higher courts. It is submitted, however, that the alternative interpretation is preferable. As Nicholas

---

[26] [2002] 1 All ER (Comm) 241.    [27] Chambers, *Resulting Trusts* (1997), pp 18–19.

[28] See Cheshire and Burn, *Modern Law of Real Property* (15th edn, 1994), p 161.

[29] [1993] 3 All ER 65, HL.

[30] See also *Hodgson v Marks* [1971] Ch 892, where Russell LJ described the proposition that s 60(3) has put an end to the presumption resulting trusts of land as 'debatable'.

[31] [1971] Ch 892.    [32] [2001] WTLR 101.

Strauss QC himself indicated, it is doubtful whether the differences between land and personalty, and between methods of making apparent gifts, provide meaningful bases for distinction. The presumptions of resulting trust and advancement operate in practice primarily to allocate the burden of proof where property has been transferred and there is a dispute as to the effect of the transfer. To eliminate the presumption of resulting trust in relation to land is, in effect, to introduce something akin to the presumption of advancement where land has been voluntarily conveyed. The transferor will therefore have to bring forward evidence to show that the beneficial interest was not intended to be transferred. The facts of *Lohia v Lohia* demonstrate that it may prove difficult to discharge such a burden.

## (3) Purchase money resulting trusts

The presumption of a resulting trust in favour of a contributor to the purchase price of property applies to both personal property and land.

### (a) Operation of the presumption of resulting trust in the context of personal property

The presumption of a resulting trust of personal property was raised in *Fowkes v Pascoe*.[33] John Pascoe was the son of Elizabeth Anne Pascoe, the widow of the only son of Sarah Baker. Over a period of some five years, Sarah Baker purchased annuities totalling £7,000 in the joint names of herself and John Pascoe. The Court of Appeal accepted that there was thus a presumption of a resulting trust in favour of Sarah Baker, but held the evidence rebutted this presumption and demonstrated that a gift had been intended. In *The Venture*[34] a resulting trust was held to have arisen in favour of a contributor to the purchase price of a yacht. In *Abrahams v Trustee in Bankruptcy of Abrahams*[35] it was held that a presumption of resulting trust operated where a wife, who was separated from her husband, contributed to a syndicate purchasing National Lottery tickets in the names of her husband. Since the presumption was not rebutted the husband held his share of the winnings, some £242,000, on resulting trust for his wife.

The recent case of *Foskett v McKeown*[36] concerned the question whether a contributor to the premiums of a life insurance policy thereby gained a proportionate share of the proceeds of the policy. A Mr Murphy had taken out a life insurance policy in 1986 which would provide a death benefit of £1 million. He paid the annual premiums for the first two years using his own money, but paid subsequent premiums using misappropriated trust money. He committed suicide in 1991, at which point at least 40% of the premiums had been paid using trust money. The question was whether the beneficiaries were entitled to a proportionate share of the proceeds of the policy. Whilst there was no doubt that the trust money had been used to pay premiums, under the terms of the policy the death benefit would still have been payable even if they had not been made, due to the payment of the earlier premiums. In *Re Policy No 6402 of the*

---

[33]  (1875) 10 Ch App 343.      [34]  [1908] P 218.      [35]  [1999] BPIR 637.
[36]  [2000] 3 All ER 97.

*Scottish Equitable Life Assurance Society*[37] Joyce J had held that resulting trust principles were applicable to a life policy. In the Court of Appeal[38] Scott V-C held that this case was distinguishable because the contributions giving rise to the resulting trust had been made from the outset of the policy, so that it did not apply in favour of contributors of latter premiums which would have the effect of divesting those already entitled to the proceeds of the policy.[39] Morritt LJ dissented and, whilst he was unwilling to decide whether a resulting trust could arise from the payment of some premiums due on an insurance policy taken out in the name of another,[40] he held that contributions to the purchase of property by installments could give rise to a resulting trust:

'. . . in principle if property is acquired by a series of payments a resulting trust in respect of the due proportion may arise from the payment of one or more in the series; hire purchase or installment payment transactions would be examples'.[41]

The majority of the House of Lords approved the dissenting judgment of Morritt LJ, and held that the beneficiaries were entitled to a proportionate share of the proceeds of the policy. Lord Millett explained:

'It is true that the last two premiums were not needed to provide the death benefit in the sense that in the events which had happened the same amount would have been payable even if those premiums had not been paid . . . But the fact is that Mr Murphy, who could not forsee the future, did choose to pay the last two premiums, and to pay them with the purchaser's money; and they were applied by the insurer towards the payment of the internal premiums needed to fund the death benefit. It should not avail his donees that he need not have paid the premiums, and that if he had not then (in the events which happened) the insurers would have provided the same death benefit and funded it differently.'[42]

Contribution to the premiums required under an insurance policy will therefore entitle the contributor to a proportionate share of the proceeds.

However *Foskett v Mckeown* also illustrates the potential problems of determining the exact extent of an interest acquired by resulting trust where contributions have been made to a purchase by installments. Lords Hoffman and Browne-Wilkinson held that the extent of the interest in the proceeds of the policy should be proportionate to the contributions the parties had made to the premiums. Lord Millett considered that, since the policy was unitlinked in nature, the appropriate division was in proportion to the number of units which were acquired by the respective premiums.

### (b) Operation of the presumption of resulting trust in relation to land[43]

In the context of the acquisition of land it is clear that a presumed resulting trust will arise in favour of a contributor to the purchase price. The general principle was stated by Lord Reid in *Pettitt v Pettitt*:

---

[37] [1902] 1 Ch 282.    [38] [1997] 3 All ER 392.    [39] [1997] 3 All ER 392 at 406.
[40] [1997] 3 All ER 392 at 424–425.    [41] [1997] 3 All ER 392 at 423.
[42] [2000] 3 All ER 97 at 130.
[43] See Gray & Gray, *Elements of Land Law* (3rd edn, 2001), pp 670–700. Stevens and Pearce, *Land Law* (2nd edn, 2000), pp 163–182.

'. . . in the absence of evidence to the contrary effect, a contributor to the purchase-price will acquire a beneficial interest in the property.'[44]

This was reiterated by Lord Pearson in *Gissing v Gissing*, where the issue was whether a wife was entitled to a share of the ownership of her matrimonial home, which had been purchased in the sole name of her husband:

'If [the wife] did make contribution of a substantial amount towards the purchase of the house, there would be a resulting trust in her favour. That would be the presumption as to the intention of the parties at the time or times when she made and he accepted the contributions. The presumption is a rebuttable presumption: it can be rebutted by evidence showing some other intention . . .'[45]

These cases clearly show that a contribution to the purchase price of land will give rise to a presumption of a resulting trust. The major area of controversy has concerned the nature of 'contributions' sufficient to give rise to the presumption. Whilst 'indirect' contributions may constitute sufficient detriment to call for the imposition of a con-structive trust if there was an express common intention to share the ownership of the land,[46] only 'direct' contributions to the purchase price will give rise to a presumption of resulting trust in favour of the contributor. In *Ivin v Blake* [47] the Court of Appeal therefore held that a daughter who had helped her mother to run a pub, drawing only weekly pocket money from the business, had not acquired any interest in a house purchased by her mother by way of a resulting trust because she had not made a direct contribution to the purchase price.

*(i) Contribution to the purchase price.* A direct contribution to the purchase price of the land will give rise to a presumed resulting trust, normally in proportion to the amount of the contribution. In *Tinsley v Milligan*[48] a lesbian couple purchased a house in the sole name of Tinsley. The purchase price of £29,000 was raised by way of a mortgage of £24,000, with the remainder derived from the sale of a car that they owned jointly. The House of Lords held that this direct contribution gave rise to a presumption of a resulting trust in favour of Milligan of a half share in the house.[49] In *Midland Bank plc v Cooke*[50] a house was purchased in the sole name of a husband for £8,500. Whilst the majority of the purchase price was raised by way of a mortgage, the deposit was provided largely by a wedding gift of £1,100 from the husband's parents. As this gift had been made to the husband and wife jointly, it was held that she had contributed £550 to the purchase price, and that this gave rise to a presumption of a resulting trust in her favour. Where such a direct contribution has been made to the purchaser price, the contributor will be entitled to a proportionate share of the beneficial interest mathematically equivalent to the proportion of her contribution. In *Midland Bank plc v Cooke* it was held that Mrs Cooke's contribution of £550 to the purchase price entitled her to a 6.74% share of the beneficial interest of the house by way of a presumed

---

[44] [1970] AC 777 at 794.  [45] [1971] AC 886.  [46] See Chapter 29.

[47] (1994) 67 P & CR 263.  [48] [1994] 1 AC 340.

[49] The mortgage was repaid from the proceeds of their joint business.

[50] [1995] 4 All ER 562; (1997) 60 MLR 420 (O'Hagan); [1997] Conv 66 (Dixon). See also *McHardy and Sons (A firm) v Warren* [1994] 2 FLR 338.

resulting trust. A contributor will only be able to demonstrate an entitlement to a share of the beneficial interest greater than the exact mathematical equivalent of her contribution if she can demonstrate that the land was held on constructive trust.[51] The Court of Appeal subsequently held that there was sufficient evidence to conclude that Mrs Cooke was entitled to a 50% share of the property by way of a constructive trust. This aspect of the case is discussed in the following chapter.

*(ii) Contribution to mortgage repayments.* In the majority of cases land is not purchased outright but with the help of a mortgage. In such circumstances it might be thought that a person who contributes to the mortgage repayments should be treated as having contributed to the purchase price, thus raising a presumption of resulting trust in his or her favour in proportion to his contributions. However a distinction must be drawn between contributions made to the repayment of a mortgage on the basis of an agreement made when the mortgage is taken out, and subsequent payments of mortgage installments. In the former case the payment of mortgage installments will be taken to give rise to a resulting trust. This was explained in *Cowcher v Cowcher* where Bagnall J considered the consequences of a conveyance of a house to A for £24,000, where A had provided £8,000 of his own money and the remainder was provided by a mortgage taken out in the name of B:

'. . . suppose that at the time A says that as between himself and B he, A, will be responsible for half the mortgage repayments . . . Though as between A and B and the vendor A has provided £8,000 and B £16,000, as between A and B themselves A had provided £8,000 and made himself liable for the repayment of half the £16,000 mortgage namely a further £8,000, a total of £16,000; the resulting trust will therefore be as to two-thirds for A and one-third for B.'[52]

Applying this principle, Bagnall J held that a resulting trust was presumed in favour of a wife who had made some of the repayments on a mortgage taken out by her husband.[53] Similarly in *Tinsley v Milligan*[54] the House of Lords held that there was a resulting trust where the parties had agreed that the mortgage repayments would be made form an account containing the proceeds of their joint business operation, even though this was in the sole name of Tinsley.

However, in the absence of any such prior agreement, the payment of mortgage instalments subsequent to the initial acquisition of the property will not give rise to any interest by way of a resulting trust, since they are not regarded as being contributions to the purchase price of the property. This was so held by the Court of Appeal in *Curley v Parkes.*[55] In this case Mr Curley and Miss Parkes were living together. A house was purchased in 2001 in the sole name of Parkes. The purchase was funded exclusively by the proceeds of sale of her previous solely-owned house, cash she provided and a

---

[51] See *Drake v Whipp* [1996] 1 FLR 826.    [52] [1972] 1 WLR 425.

[53] In *McQuillan v Maguire* [1996] 1 ILRM 394 a wife was held entitled to a 50% share of a matrimonial home purchased in the name of her husband because she had contributed indirectly towards the discharge of the mortgage. In *Cowcher v Cowcher* Bagnall J's analysis was based upon the intention of the parties at the date of purchase. Where there is no clear intention at that date, and a share of the ownership arises from contributions to repaying a mortgage, backward tracing appears to be operating: see Chapter 31, pp 771–772.

[54] [1994] 1 AC 340.    [55] [2004] EWCA Civ 1515.

mortgage of £138,000 which was taken out in her sole name. Curley subsequently paid some £9,000 into Park's bank account, from which the mortgage instalments were paid, as a way of assisting her with the huge commitments she was taking on. Curley claimed that these payments entitled him to an 8.5% share of the equitable ownership of the house by way of a resulting trust. The Court of Appeal rejected his claim to an interest on this basis, holding that the payments could not be regarded as a contribution to the purchase price. Peter Gibson LJ explained the relevant principles:

'The relevant principle is that the resulting trust of a property purchased in the name of another, in the absence of contrary intention, arises once and for all at the date on which the property is acquired. Because of the liability assumed by the mortgagor in a case where monies are borrowed by the mortgagor to be used on the purchase, the mortgagor is treated as having provided the proportion of the purchase price attributable to the monies so borrowed. Subsequent payment of the mortgage instalments are not part of the purchase price already paid to the vendor, but are sums paid for discharging the mortgagor's obligations under the mortgage.'[56]

This decision to exclude subsequent payments of mortgage instalments, or of capital repayments which similarly discharge the obligations of the mortgagor under the mortgage, will thus further reduce the importance of resulting trusts in determining the ownership of co-habited land. It will prevent the need for difficult calculations to determine the proportion of the ownership of property acquired by way of subsequent contributions to mortgage payments, a difficulty which was acknowledged by the House of Lords in *Gissing v Gissing*, and for which no easy solution had been found.[57]

However even though such contributions may be insufficient to gain an interest by way of a resulting trust they may be relevant for the purposes of a constructive trust, whether by way of establishing an implied common intention to share the ownership of the property, or as a 'detriment' on the part of the contributor where there was there was an express common intention between the parties to share the ownership of the land.[58] If such a constructive trust can be established, the contributor may be entitled to a share of the beneficial ownership of the land far in excess of the exact mathematical equivalent of their contributions.

*(iii) Contribution by qualification for a discount in the purchase price.* If a house is purchased at a discounted price, the amount of the discount is regarded as a contribution to the purchase price. Therefore, the person who qualified for the discount will be presumed to be the beneficiary of a resulting trust to that extent in the property. In *Marsh v Von Sternberg*[59] Bush J held that a discount gained on the market value of a long lease because one of the parties was a sitting tenant was to be treated as a

---

[56] Ibid at [14].

[57] [1971] AC 886 at 987, per Lord Reid: '. . . where [the contributor] does not make direct payments towards the purchase it is less easy to evaluate her share. If her payments are direct she gets a share proportionate to what she has paid. Otherwise there must be a more rough and ready evaluation. I agree that this does not mean that she would as a rule get a half-share . . . There will of course be cases where a half-share is a reasonable estimation, but there will be many others where a fair estimate might be a tenth or a quarter or something even more than a half.'

[58] See Chapter 10.     [59] [1986] 1 FLR 526.

contribution to the purchase price in assessing their respective interests under a resulting trust. In *Springette v Defoe*[60] a discount of 41% of the market value of a council flat obtained because the plaintiff had been a tenant for more than eleven years was counted as a contribution to the purchase price by the Court of Appeal.

*(iv) Contributions to the cost of repairs or renovation.* Where the property is repaired or renovated, and its value is thereby increased, a person who contributes towards the cost of such repairs or renovations will be entitled to an interest in the land by way of a resulting trust proportionate to the extent to which the increase was attributable to their contribution.[61] Improvements made much later than the date of purchase may give rise to a constructive trust.

*(v) Contributions to general household expenses.* In contrast to indirect contributions to the purchase price of land, it seems that contributions made to general household expenses will not give rise to a presumption of resulting trust in favour of the contributor because they are not sufficiently referable to the purchase price. In *Burns v Burns*[62] Mr and Mrs Burns began living together as man and wife in 1961. In 1963 a house was purchased in the sole name of Mr Burns, who financed the purchase by way of a mortgage. Mrs Burns began to work in 1975. She used part of her earnings to pay the rates and telephone bills and to buy various domestic chattels for the house. When they split up in 1980, she claimed to be entitled to an equitable interest in the house by reason of her contributions. The Court of Appeal held that she was not entitled to an interest by way of resulting trust because she had 'made no direct contribution to the purchase price'.[63] It should be noted that although such contributions to family expenses will not give rise to a presumption of resulting trust, they may, if substantial, constitute sufficient detriment to lead to the imposition of a constructive trust.[64]

*(vi) Contributions to removal expenses.* In *Curley v Parkes*[65] the Court of Appeal held that neither the payment of solicitor's fees and expenses, nor the payment of removal costs, were capable of giving rise to a resulting trust. Although such costs might be substantial they do not form any part of the purchase price of the property itself, and hence do not give rise to a presumption of resulting trust. They may, however, be relevant for the purposes of a constructive trust.[66]

## (4) Rebutting the presumption of resulting trust

In *Pettitt v Pettitt* Lord Diplock observed that the presumptions of resulting trust and advancement are:

'. . . no more than a consensus of judicial opinion disclosed by reported cases as to the most likely inference of fact to be drawn in the absence of any evidence to the contrary.'[67]

It therefore follows that they can be rebutted by evidence that in a specific situation the 'most likely inference' was not, in fact, intended. The presumption of a resulting trust,

---

[60] [1992] 2 FLR 388.    [61] *Drake v Whipp* [1996] 1 FLR 826.    [62] [1984] Ch 317.
[63] [1984] Ch 317 at 326, per Fox LJ.    [64] See Chapter 10.    [65] [2004] EWCA Civ 1515.
[66] See Chapter 10.    [67] [1970] AC 777 at 823.

whether arising from a voluntary transfer or a contribution to the purchase price of property, will be rebutted by evidence that the transferor or contributor had no intention to retain any beneficial interest in the property. The strength of the evidence required to rebut the presumption of a resulting trust will depend upon the strength of the presumption, which will in turn depend upon the facts and circumstances which gave rise to it.[68]

## (a) Circumstances rebutting the presumption of resulting trust

*(i) Evidence a gift was intended.*[69] It was noted above that in *Fowkes v Pascoe*[70] a presumption of a resulting trust was raised when Sarah Baker purchased annuities in the joint names of herself and John Pascoe. However, this presumption was rebutted by evidence indicating that a gift had been intended. Two initial purchases of stock were made by Sarah, one of £250 in the joint names of herself and John Pascoe, and another of £250 in the joint names of herself and her companion. She also held large quantities of the same stock in her own name, besides other property. The court considered this 'absolutely conclusive' that a gift was intended. As James LJ said:

'Is it possible to reconcile with mental sanity the theory that she put £250 into the names of herself and her companion, and £250 into the names of herself and [John Pascoe], as trustees upon trust for herself? What. . . . . object is there conceivable in doing this?'[71]

In *Re Young*[72] it was similarly held that the presumption of a resulting trust had been rebutted. Colonel and Mrs Young had a joint bank account, which contained money derived from Mrs Young's separate income. The account was used to pay for household expenses, and Colonel Young, with his wife's consent, withdrew money to purchase investments in his own name. Pearson J held that the evidence showed that the money in the account was intended to be joint, and that the investments purchased in his own name were his own property, and were not held on resulting trust for his wife.

In the recent case of *Arosos v Coutt's & Co*[73] Collins J held that the presumption of resulting trust was rebutted where a wealthy Portuguese gentleman had transferred money into a joint account in the names of himself and his nephew. The evidence, primarily the mandate establishing the account which clearly stated that the beneficial interest was to be held jointly and the evidence of the bank client relationship officer who had explained the effect of the account, established that he had intended the nephew to take the property beneficially.

It appears that a presumption of resulting trust may be rebutted even where money has been paid into a joint bank account with the intention that the transferee is not allowed to draw on the account until the death of the transferor. This approach was adopted in *Russell v Scott*,[74] where an aunt had opened a joint account in the names of herself and her nephew, but did not intend her nephew to benefit during her lifetime.

---

[68] *Vajpeyi v Yijsaf* [2003] EWHC 2339, per Peter Prescott QC at [71].

[69] See *Sekhon v Alissa* [1989] 2 FLR 94, where there was insufficient evidence of a gift to rebut the presumption of a resulting trust.

[70] (1875) LR 10 Ch App 343.      [71] (1875) LR 10 Ch App 343 at 349.      [72] (1885) 28 Ch D 705.

[73] [2002] 1 All ER (Comm) 241.      [74] (1936) 55 CLR 440.

The Australian High Court held that she had nevertheless conferred an immediate beneficial interest on him which would only fall into possession on her death through the operation of the right of survivorship. Because of her control over the account, the interest that she conferred on him remained revocable by her during her lifetime. This decision was followed in England in *Young v Sealey*.[75] In contrast in Ireland it was held in *Owens v Greene*[76] that the presumption of resulting trust could not be rebutted in such cases because the transferor's intention amounted to an intention to make a testamentary gift, and that evidence of this intention was not admissible, since otherwise the requirements for making a will would be avoided. However as many commentators have observed,[77] rebutting the presumption of resulting trust in such circumstances is no more offensive to the policy of the Wills Act than the recognition of secret trusts. *Owens v Greene* has since been overruled by the Irish Supreme Court in *Lynch v Burke*.[78] In *Arosos v Coutt's & Co*[79] Collins J indicated that he would have followed *Russell v Scott* and *Young v Sealey,* but the point did not arise for decision.

*(ii) Evidence a loan was intended.* The presumption of a resulting trust will also be rebutted where evidence shows that money was advanced by way of a loan. In *Re Sharpe (a bankrupt)*[80] Mr and Mrs Sharpe lived in a maisonette with their 82-year-old aunt, Mrs Johnson. The property had been purchased in the name of Mr Sharpe for £17,000. Mrs Johnson had contributed £12,000 towards the purchase price, whilst the remainder was raised by way of a mortgage. Mr and Mrs Sharpe were subsequently declared bankrupt and Mrs Johnson claimed to be entitled to a proprietary interest in the maisonette by means of a resulting trust presumed from her contribution to the purchase price. Browne-Wilkinson J held that the money had in fact been advanced by way of a loan, with the intention that it would be repaid. She was not therefore entitled to any share of the equitable interest of the property. A presumption of a resulting trust was also rebutted by evidence that a loan was intended in the more recent case of *Vajpeyi v Yijaf.*[81] In this case the claimant provided the defendant, who was her lover, with £10,000 to enable him to purchase a house in his sole name. At the time of the purchase in 1980 the defendant was a young man of limited means. The claimant alleged that by virtue of this payment she was entitled to a 33.89% share of the equitable ownership of the property on the basis of a presumed resulting trust, whereas the defendant claimed that the money had been advanced by way of a loan, which he had repaid. Peter Prescott QC held that the following factors had rebutted the presumption of a resulting trust in favour of a loan: the fact that the defendant had been a young man of limited means who was anxious to get on the property ladder whereas the claimant was a lady who was already on the property ladder when the money was advanced; the fact that the claimant had tolerated the defendant collecting rents from the property and keeping them for himself for some 21 years; the fact that the claimant had failed to propound her claim to an interest for 21 years and the fact that she had never said

[75] [1949] Ch 278.      [76] [1932] IR 225.

[77] For a recent example see Delaney, *Equity and Trusts in the Republic of Ireland* (1995), p 133.

[78] [1995] 2 IR 159. See (1996) ILSI Gazette March, p 70 (Mee).      [79] [2002] 1 All ER (Comm) 241.

[80] [1980] 1 WLR 219.      [81] [2003] EWHC 2339.

anything about her alleged interest in the house when it was mortgaged by the defendant to enable him to purchase her matrimonial home some years previously.

### (b) Evidence required to rebut the presumption of resulting trust

*Fowkes v Pascoe*[82] makes clear that the quality of evidence required to rebut a presumption of a resulting trust will vary depending on the circumstances in question, because the presumption of resulting trust will be given varying weight depending upon the context. As Mellish LJ stated:

'. . . the presumption must . . . be of very different weight in different cases. In some cases it would be very strong indeed. If, for instance, a man invested a sum of stock in the name of himself and his solicitor, the inference would be very strong indeed that it was intended solely for the purpose of a trust, and the court would require very strong evidence on the part of the solicitor to prove that it was intended as a gift; and certainly his own evidence would not be sufficient. On the other hand, a man may make an investment of stock in the name of himself and some person, although not a child or wife,[83] yet in such a position to him as to make it extremely probable that the investment was intended as a gift. In such a case, although the rule of law, if there was no evidence at all, would compel the Court to say that the presumption of trust must prevail, even if the court might not believe that the fact was in accordance with the presumption, yet, if there is evidence to rebut the presumption, then, in my opinion, the court must go into the actual facts.'[84]

One situation where the presumption of resulting trust is weak and easily rebutted is where a wife conveys property into the name of her husband, or when property is purchased in the name of the husband with money provided by the wife. As no presumption of advancement arises between a wife and a husband, there will be a prima facie presumption of resulting trust. However, this will be rebutted by the slightest evidence that a gift was intended. As Lord Upjohn observed in *Pettitt v Pettitt*:

'If a wife puts property into her husband's name it may be that in the absence of all other evidence he is a trustee for her, but in practice there will in almost every case be some explanation (however slight) of this (today) rather unusual course. If a wife puts property into their joint names I would myself think that a joint tenancy was intended, for I can see no other reason for it.'[85]

In *Knightly v Knightly*[86] the Court of Appeal went so far as to say there is no room for the presumption of a resulting trust in favour of a wife unless 'a wife advances money to her husband for the purchase of either realty or personality and there is no evidence of any agreement or understanding between them as to who is to own the property and no evidence from conduct and circumstances going to show what their intentions as to rights and interests were'.[87]

---

[82] (1875) LR 10 Ch App 343.
[83] Where the presumption of advancement would apply. See below, p 253.
[84] (1875) LR 10 Ch App 343 at 352–353.     [85] [1970] AC 777 at 815.     [86] (1981) 11 Fam Law 122.
[87] (1981) 11 Fam Law 122 at 123, per Lawton LJ.

### (c) Admissibility of evidence to rebut a presumption of resulting trust

Any acts or declarations by the parties forming part of the transaction to which the presumption of a resulting trust relates will be admissible in favour of, or against, the parties performing them. However, in *Shephard v Cartwright*[88] the House of Lords held, in the context of the rebuttal of a presumption of advancement, that subsequent acts and declarations are admissible only as evidence against the party who made them, and not in his favour.

## (5) Presumed resulting trust arising in the context of an illegal purpose[89]

In *Tinsley v Milligan*[90] the House of Lords was faced with the question whether a plaintiff was entitled to rely on a presumption of resulting trust arising in the context of a transaction entered to facilitate an illegal purpose. As was mentioned above, a house had been purchased in the sole name of Tinsley, using the joint money of Tinsley and Milligan. The reason for this was to enable Milligan to appear to be a mere lodger in the property, rather than a co-owner, so that she could make false claims for various state social welfare benefits. After the breakdown of their relationship, Milligan claimed that Tinsley held the house on trust for them in equal shares. Tinsley claimed that the court should not enforce Milligan's claim because of the illegal purpose for which the transaction had taken place, demanding a strict application of the maxim that 'he who comes to equity must come with clean hands'. This would obviously have the consequence that Tinsley was solely entitled to the house, despite the fact that she had been as much party to the illegality as Milligan. Whilst this might have seemed a harsh result between the specific parties, especially given that the falsely claimed social security money had been repaid, the strict rule was intended to operate as a deterrent to those who might be tempted to involve themselves in illegal transactions.

The majority of the Court of Appeal rejected the application of such a strict principle in favour of the adoption of a 'public conscience test', which would vest the court with a discretion to balance the consequences of either granting or refusing relief to the person seeking to claim an interest.[91] The House of Lords in turn rejected this discretionary approach, favouring the application of a strict rule to determine when a plaintiff could assert an interest. However it was divided as to the appropriate rule. Lord Goff and Lord Keith held that the equitable maxim requiring clean hands should be strictly applied. Lord Goff explained how this would operate:

'. . . once it comes to the attention of a court of equity that the claimant has not come to the court with clean hands, the court will refuse to assist the claimant, even though the claimant can prima facie establish his claim without recourse to underlying fraudulent or illegal purpose.'[92]

---

[88] [1955] AC 431.

[89] See J D Davies, 'Presumptions and Illegality' in Oakley, *Trends in Contemporary Trust Law* (1996); Halliwell, 'Equitable Property Rights, Discretionary Remedies and Unclean Hands', [2004] Conv 439

[90] [1994] 1 AC 340.      [91] [1992] 2 All ER 391.      [92] [1993] 3 All ER 65 at 75.

In contrast the majority adopted an evidential approach, whereby a claimant is entitled to enforce an equitable interest provided that he or she did not have to rely on the fact of the illegal purpose in order to establish that interest. Lord Browne-Wilkinson stated the principle:

'In my judgement the time has come to decide clearly that the rule is the same whether a plaintiff founds himself on a legal or equitable title: he is entitled to recover if he is not forced to plead or rely on the illegality, even if it emerges that the title on which he relied was acquired in the course of carrying through an illegal transaction.'[93]

He explained how this principle applied where the alleged equitable interest had arisen through the operation of a presumption of a resulting trust:

'The presumption of resulting trust is . . . crucial in considering the authorities. On that presumption . . . hinges the answer to the crucial question: does a plaintiff claiming under a resulting trust have to rely on the underlying illegality? Where the presumption of resulting trust applies, the plaintiff does not have to rely on the illegality. If he proves that the property is vested in the defendant alone but that the plaintiff provided part of the purchase money, or voluntarily transferred the property to the defendant, the plaintiff establishes his claim under a resulting trust unless either the contrary presumption of advancement displaces the presumption of resulting trust or the defendant leads evidence to rebut the presumption of resulting trust. Therefore, in cases where the presumption of advancement does not apply, a plaintiff can establish his equitable interest in the property without relying in any way on the underlying illegal transaction.'[94]

Applying this principle it was therefore held that Milligan was entitled to assert her entitlement to a half-share of the equitable ownership of the house, since all she needed to do to establish her interest was to prove that she had contributed to the purchase prices. This would give rise to a presumption of resulting trust in her favour, and she did not need to rely on the illegal purpose underlying the transaction.

The evidential approach adopted in *Tinsley v Milligan* has been applied in subsequent cases. In *Silverwood v Silverwood*[95] an elderly lady had transferred money to her grandchildren to enable her to claim income support to contribute towards the costs of her residential care. The Court of Appeal held that the plaintiff, who was a beneficiary under her will, was entitled to maintain that the money was held on resulting trust by the recipients, as he did not need to rely on the illegality to establish the resulting trust. Peter Gibson LJ also stated that it would be absurd and unjust if he could not lead evidence of fraud in order to disprove a spurious defence by the recipients. In *Lowson v Coombes*[96] a man had purchased a flat together with his mistress, but it was conveyed into her sole name so that his wife would not be able to maintain any claim to it. The Court of Appeal held that he was entitled to assert a half-interest by way of a resulting trust, despite the illegal purpose of frustrating any potential claim under Matrimonial Causes Act 1973, because he did not need to rely on the illegal purpose to establish his entitlement.

---

[93] [1993] 3 All ER 65 at 91.     [94] [1993] 3 All ER 65 at 87.     [95] (1997) 74 P & CR 453.
[96] [1999] Ch 373.

However it has also been subjected to criticism. In *Silverwood v Silverwood*[97] Nouse LJ described the principle adopted in *Tinsley v Milligan* as a 'straightjacket' and indicated that he would have preferred a more flexible approach. In particular the approach adopted by the House of Lords arbitrarily differentiates between situations where a presumption of resulting trust and a presumption of advancement are operative. Whilst Milligan was held able to assert her interest by way of a presumed resulting trust without the need to rely on the fact of her illegal conduct, a more difficult problem would have arisen if the countervailing presumption of advancement had applied between Tinsley and herself. In such circumstances she would only have been entitled to assert her interest if she could rebut the presumption, which would require evidence of the illegal purpose of the transaction. The Court of Appeal was forced to grapple with such a difficulty in *Tribe v Tribe*,[98] where a presumption of advancement did arise between the parties. As Nourse LJ observed in *Silverwood v Silverwood*:

'It is not at all easy to understand or to see any public or other policy or advantage behind a rule which regulates the claimant's right of recovery solely according to whether the other party to the transaction is his wife, child or fiancée on the one hand or his brother, grandchild or anyone else on the other.'[99]

Lord Goff, in his dissenting judgment, also pointed to the arbitrary consequences which might follow from the application of the principle adopted by the majority in *Tinsley v Milligan*:

'But it is not to be forgotten that other cases in this category will not evoke the same sympathy on the part of the court. There may be cases in which the fraud is far more serious than that in the present case, and is uncovered not as a result of a confession but only after a length police investigation and a prolonged criminal trial. Again there may be cases in which a group of terrorists, or armed robbers, secure a base for their criminal activities by buying a house in the name of a third party not directly implicated in those activities. In cases such as these there will almost certainly be no presumption of advancement. Is it really to be said that criminals such as these, or their personal representatives, are entitled to invoke the assistance of a court of equity in order to establish an equitable interest in property?'[100]

In the light of such criticisms the law regarding illegality has recently been reviewed by the Law Commission, which has recommended the abandonment of the 'reliance principle' adopted in *Tinsley v Milligan* in favour of granting the court a discretion to declare a trust illegal or invalid.[101] The operation of this proposed discretion is discussed in more detail below in the context of the operation of the presumption of advancement, since this has provided the context for the more serious difficulties.

---

[97] (1997) 74 P & CR 453.    [98] [1996] Ch 107.    [99] (1997) 74 P & CR 453 at 458.
[100] [1993] 3 All ER 65 at 79.
[101] 'Illegal Transactions: The Effect of Illegality on Contracts and Trusts' (1999), Law Comm CP No 154.

# 3 The presumption of advancement

## (1) Nature of the presumption

In some circumstances where a person voluntarily transfers property into the name of another, or contributes to its purchase, the law presumes that a gift was intended and that the transferor/contributor did not intend to retain any interest in the property concerned. This presumption, known as the 'presumption of advancement', displaces the presumption of resulting trust. The presumption of advancement arises as a consequence of a pre-existing relationship between the parties to the transfer or acquisition, where the transferor/contributor is regarded as morally obliged to provide for the person benefiting. As Lord Eldon stated in *Murless v Franklin*:

'The general rule that on a purchase by one man in the name of another, the nominee is a trustee for the purchaser, is subject to exception where the purchaser is under a species of natural obligation to provide for the nominee.'[102]

The range of relationships where equity recognises a presumption of advancement reflects a nineteenth-century understanding of family responsibility, and it is clear that, today, the strengths of the presumptions vary to reflect differing social circumstances. However, the state of the law in this area remains far from satisfactory.

## (2) Relationships giving rise to a presumption of advancement

### (a) Father and child

Traditionally, there was a strong presumption of advancement between a father and his child.[103] In *Re Roberts (Decd)*[104] Evershed J held that the presumption of advancement applied where a father had made payments on a policy of assurance taken out on his son's life. He said that:

'. . . It is well established that a father making payments on behalf of his son prima facie, and in the absence of contrary evidence, is to be taken to be making and intending an advance in favour of the son and for his benefit.'[105]

In *B v B*[106] a Canadian court held that the presumption of advancement applied where a father had purchased a winning lottery ticket in the name of his 12-year-old daughter. She was therefore entitled to the winnings absolutely. The rationale for the presumption of advancement between father and child is that a father, by the very nature of his position, is under a duty to provide for his child.[107] This may include the child's mother

---

[102] (1818) 1 Swan 13 at 17.
[103] See *Shephard v Cartwright* [1955] AC 431. In *Oliveri v Oliveri* (1995) 38 NSWLR 665 Powell J suggested that a presumption of advancement could operate between a step-father and step-child.
[104] [1946] Ch 1.      [105] [1946] Ch 1 at 5.      [106] (1976) 65 DLR (3d) 460.
[107] *Bennet v Bennet* (1879) LR 10 Ch D 474 at 476, per Jessel MR.

if she stands in loco parentis. There is no presumption of advancement in the case of other family relationships.[108]

The strength of this presumption of advancement between a father and child was questioned by the Court of Appeal in *McGrath v Wallis*,[109] where Nourse LJ stated:

'Ever since the decision in *Pettitt v Pettitt* it has been my understanding that, in its application to houses acquired for joint occupation, the equitable presumption of advancement has been reclassified as a judicial instrument of last resort, its subordinate status comparable to that of the contra proferentem rule in the construction of deeds and contracts ... For myself, I have been unable to recollect any subsequent case of this kind in which the presumption has proved decisive ...'[110]

### (b) Persons standing in loco parentis

A presumption of advancement also arises between a child and a person standing in loco parentis.[111] The rationale for this extension of the presumption was stated by Jessel MR in *Bennet v Bennet*:

'... as regards a child, a person not the father of the child may put himself in the position of loco parentis to the child, and so incur the obligation to make provision for the child ...'[112]

### (c) Husband and wife

The presumption of advancement also arises between a husband and his wife. The principle was stated in *Re Eykyn's Trusts*, by Malins V-C:

'The law of this court is perfectly settled that when a husband transfers money or other property into the name of his wife only, then the presumption is, that it is intended as a gift or advancement to the wife absolutely at once, subject to such marital control as he may exercise. And if a husband invests in money, stocks, or otherwise, in the names of himself and his wife, then also it is an advancement for the benefit of the wife absolutely if she survives her husband ...'[113]

The operation of the presumption in this context reflects a nineteenth-century social understanding of a husband's obligation to provide for his wife.

Although these comments were cited in *Pettitt v Pettitt*,[114] the House of Lords acknowledged that the presumption between husband and wife had reduced in significance.[115] Lord Reid suggested that the only reasonable basis for the presumption had been the economic dependence of wives on their husbands, and that given the

---

[108] Eg sister (*Noack v Noack* [1959] VR 137; *Gorog v Kiss* (1977) 78 DLR (3d) 690); son-in-law (*Knight v Biss* [1954] NZLR 55); and nephew (*Dury v Dury* (1675) 75 SS 205; *Russell v Scott* (1936) 55 CLR 440).

[109] [1995] 2 FLR 114.      [110] [1995] 2 FLR 114 at 115.

[111] *Hepworth v Hepworth* (1870) LR 11 Eq 10; *Re Orme* (1883) 50 LT 51; *Shephard v Cartwright* [1955] AC 431; *Re Paradise Motor Co Ltd* [1968] 1 WLR 1125, CA.

[112] (1878–79) LR 10 Ch D 474.      [113] (1877) 6 Ch D 115 at 118.

[114] [1970] AC 777 at 815, per Lord Upjohn.

[115] See *Silver v Silver* [1958] 1 All ER 523 at 525, per Evershed MR. The presumption of advancement between husband and wife also applies in Ireland and Australia: *Heavey v Heavey* [1971] 111 ILTR 1; *M v M* [1980] 114 ILTR 46; *Doohan v Nelson* [1973] 2 NSWLR 320; *Napier v Public Trustee (Western Australia)* (1980) 32 ALR 153.

changes in social circumstances 'the strength of the presumption must have much diminished'.[116]

Lord Diplock considered that it was not appropriate that transactions between married couples should be governed by presumptions 'based upon inferences of fact which an earlier generation of judges drew as to the most likely intentions of earlier generations of spouses belonging to the propertied classes of a different social era'.[117] The presumption of advancement also applies between a man and his fiancee.[118]

## (3) Relationships where no presumption of advancement arises

### (a) Mother and child[119]

No presumption of advancement arises between a mother and her child, and therefore if a mother transfers property voluntarily to her child the counter presumption of resulting trust will apply.[120] In *Bennet v Bennet*[121] Jessel MR explained the absence of the presumption on the basis that 'there is no moral legal obligation . . . no obligation according to the rules of equity—on a mother to provide for her child'.[122] Again, such reasoning reflects nineteenth-century concepts of the family, and in modern social conditions mothers almost invariably share the responsibility to provide for their children.[123] Despite the socially archaic rationale, more modern cases have confirmed that there continues to be no presumption of advancement between a mother and child. The presumption of resulting trust was applied by the Court of Appeal in *Gross v French*,[124] and by Hoffmann J in *Sekhon v Alissa*.[125] In the latter case, a mother had provided £22,500 to help her daughter purchase a house. In the absence of sufficient evidence to rebut the presumption of a resulting trust, the mother was held entitled to an interest in the property.

Despite the absence of a presumption of advancement between mother and child the presumption of resulting trust arising in default is relatively weak and easily rebutted. As Jessel MR said in *Bennet v Bennet*:

'We arrive then at this conclusion, that in the case of a mother . . . it is easier to prove a gift than in the case of a stranger: in the case of a mother very little evidence beyond the relationship is wanted, there being very little additional motive required to induce a mother to make a gift to her child.'[126]

---

[116] [1970] AC 777 at 792.      [117] [1970] AC 777 at 792.

[118] *Moate v Moate* [1948] 2 All ER 486; *Silver v Silver* [1958] 1 WLR 259; *Tinker v Tinker (No 1)* [1970] P 136; *Mossop v Mossop* [1989] Fam 77.

[119] See [1996] Conv 274 (Dowling).

[120] *Re De Visme* (1863) 2 De GJ & Sm 17; *Bennet v Bennet* (1878–79) LR 10 Ch D 474. See also: *Sayre v Hughes* (1867–68) LR 5 Eq 376; *Gore-Grimes v Grimes* [1937] IR 470.

[121] (1878–79) LR 10 Ch D 474.      [122] ibid at 478.

[123] Compare *Dullow v Dullow* [1985] 3 NSWLR 531.

[124] (1975) 238 Estates Gazette 39.      [125] [1989] 2 FLR 94.

[126] (1879) 10 Ch D 474 at 480. See, however, *Sekhon v Alissa* [1989] 2 FLR 94, where Hoffmann J held that the evidence was inconsistent with there being a gift.

In *Nelson v Nelson*[127] the Australian High Court has held that a presumption of advancement should operate between a mother and child.[128] In England the recent decision in *Re Cameron (Decd)*[129] suggests a possible avenue by which it might be found that the presumption should operate between a mother and child. Lindsay J held that, in the light of the difference between Victorian and modern attitudes to the owner-ship and ability to dispose of property, it would be appropriate nowadays to take both parents to be in loco parentis unless the contrary is proved for the purposes of the succession rule against double portions.[130]

## (b) Wife and husband

Similarly, no presumption of advancement operates between a wife and her husband, so that if a wife voluntarily transfers property into the name of her husband, or con-tributes to the purchase of property in his name, a presumption of resulting trust arises. Thus, in *Re Curtis*,[131] in the absence of evidence that a gift was intended, a wife was presumed to enjoy the equitable interest in shares, which she had voluntarily transferred into the name of her husband, by way of a resulting trust.[132] The absence of the presumption seems to have been accepted in the more recent case of *Mossop v Mossop*,[133] and led to the presumption of a resulting trust in *Abrahams v Trustee in Bankruptcy of Abrahams*,[134] where a wife contributed to a syndicate purchasing National Lottery tickets in the name of her husband.

The absence of the presumption of advancement between a wife and her husband reflects nineteenth-century social circumstances. As was noted above,[135] in *Pettitt v Pettitt*[136] the House of Lords held that the presumption of resulting trust between a wife and her husband was of much diminished strength and would be rebutted by very slight evidence that a gift was intended.

## (c) Co-habiting couples/mistresses

There is no presumption of advancement between cohabiting couples (whether hetero-sexual or homosexual),[137] nor between a man and his mistress.[138] The presumption of resulting trust will therefore apply if property is voluntarily transferred in such cases.

---

[127] (1995) 132 ALR 133.

[128] In *Re Dreger Estate* (1994) 97 Man R (2d) 39 it was held that in modern conditions the presumption of advancement ought to be applicable between mother and child.

[129] [1999] 2 All ER 924.    [130] [1999] 2 All ER 924 at 939.    [131] (1885) 52 LT 244.

[132] See also *Mercier v Mercier* [1903] 2 Ch 98; *Pearson v Pearson* (1965) Times, 30 November; *Pettitt v Pettitt* [1970] AC 777; *Heseltine v Heseltine* [1971] 1 WLR 342; *Northern Bank Ltd v Henry* [1981] IR 1; *Allied Irish Banks Ltd v McWilliams* [1982] NI 156.

[133] [1988] 2 All ER 202 at 206, where Lawton LJ cited the relevant principles from Snell, *Principles of Equity* (28th edn, 1982), p 183.

[134] [1999] BPIR 637.    [135] See above, p 249.    [136] [1970] AC 777.

[137] *Rider v Kidder* (1805) 10 Ves 360; *Soar v Foster* (1858) 4 K & J 152; *Allen v Snyder* [1977] 2 NSWLR 685; *Calverly v Green* (1984) 56 ALR 483.

[138] *Diwell v Farnes* [1959] 1 WLR 624.

## (4) Rebutting a presumption of advancement

### (a) Evidence required to rebut a presumption of advancement

A presumption of advancement will be rebutted by evidence that the transferor (or contributor) did not intend to make a gift but wished to retain an interest in the property transferred or acquired. In *Re Gooch*[139] Sir Daniel Gooch transferred shares into the name of his eldest son. The son paid the dividends from the shares to his father, who also retained the share certificates. Kay J held that the presumption of advancement was rebutted by evidence that the shares had been transferred to qualify the son to become a director of the company, and that no gift had been intended. In *Warren v Gurney*[140] a father purchased a house in the name of his daughter prior to her wedding. He retained the title deeds until his death. The Court of Appeal held that the presumption of advancement was rebutted by evidence that at the time of the transaction the father had intended her husband to repay the money. The retention of the title deeds was considered a very significant fact, as 'one would have expected the father to have handed them over either to [his daughter] or her husband, if he had intended the gift'.[141] In *McGrath v Wallis*[142] a house was acquired for joint occupancy by a father and son in the sole name of the son. The purchase price was provided partly by the proceeds of sale of the father's previous house and partly by means of a mortgage. The Court of Appeal held that the presumption of advancement was rebutted by evidence that the father had intended to retain an interest in the ownership of the house, including an unsigned declaration of trust which would have shared the beneficial ownership in the proportions represented by the deposit and mortgage respectively.

The mere fact that any rents and profits generated from the property concerned are returned to the purchaser or transferor will not conclusively rebut a presumption of advancement. In *Stamp Duties Comrs v Byrnes*[143] a father had purchased property in Australia in the name of his sons. They paid over to him the rents received from the properties, and he paid for rates and repairs. The Privy Council held that as it was not unusual for a father to transfer property to a son whilst continuing to receive any rents and profits during his lifetime, the presumption of advancement had not been rebutted:

'Having regard to the state of the family and the relations subsisting between Mr Byrnes and his two sons who were living at home, it seems very natural that the sons receiving advances should yet feel a delicacy in taking the fruits during their father's lifetime. They had all they wanted as things were, and if they were unduly favoured it might possibly have created some feeling of jealousy among the rest.'[144]

Although the opening of a bank account by a husband in the joint names of himself and his wife will lead to the presumption of a joint tenancy of the money therein,[145] the

---

[139] (1890) 62 LT 384.
[140] [1944] 2 All ER 472. See also *Webb v Webb* [1992] 1 All ER 17; refd [1994] 3 All ER 911.
[141] [1944] 2 All ER 472 at 473, per Morton LJ.     [142] [1995] 2 FLR 114.     [143] [1911] AC 386.
[144] [1911] AC 386 at 392.     [145] See *Re Bishop* [1965] Ch 450; *Re Figgis* [1969] 1 Ch 123.

presumption of advancement operating between them may be rebutted. In *Marshal v Crutwell*[146] it was held that the presumption of advancement was rebutted where a husband had transferred his bank account into the joint names of himself and his wife. The court held that the transfer was merely for convenience, since the husband was in ill health and could not draw cheques himself. His wife was not therefore entitled to the balance in the account on his death. In *Anson v Anson*[147] the presumption of advancement was rebutted where a husband had entered a guarantee of an overdraft on a bank account in his wife's name. After their divorce he was called to pay £500 to the bank under the guarantee, and demanded repayment from the wife. Pearson J held that the intention was that the debt would remain her debt, and the guarantee to the bank was not intended to relieve her of her obligation but merely to solve her immediate banking emergency.

## (b) Rebuttal of a presumption of advancement by evidence of an illegal purpose[148]

It has been seen above that, as a general rule, a plaintiff will not be permitted to rely on evidence of his own illegal conduct to rebut a presumption of resulting trust.[149] He will similarly be prevented from relying on evidence of an illegal purpose to rebut a presumption of advancement. In *Gascoigne v Gascoigne*[150] a husband took a lease of land in his wife's name. The judge at first instance held that the presumption of advancement was rebutted by evidence that he had not intended to make a gift of the lease to his wife because it had been taken in her name only to defeat the claims of his creditors. However, the Court of Appeal held that he was not entitled to rebut the presumption by raising evidence of the illegal purpose underlying the transaction:

'. . . what the learned judge has done is this: He has permitted the plaintiff to rebut the presumption which the law raises by setting up his own illegality and fraud, and to obtain relief in equity because he has succeeded in proving it. The plaintiff cannot do this . . .'[151]

This restriction was followed by the Court of Appeal in *Tinker v Tinker (No 1)*,[152] where a husband had purchased a house in the name of his wife, on the advice of his solicitor, again with the intention of preventing the house being seized by creditors if his business failed. On the breakdown of the marriage it was held that he could not rebut the presumption of advancement. Lord Denning MR stated:

'. . . he cannot say that the house is his own and, at one and the same time, say that it is his wife's. As against his wife, he wants to say that it belongs to him. As against his creditors, that it belongs to her. That simply will not do. Either it was conveyed to her for her own use absolutely; or it was conveyed to her as trustee for her husband. It must be one or the other. The presumption is that it was conveyed to her for her own use: and he does not rebut that presumption by saying that he only did it to defeat his creditors . . .'[153]

---

[146] (1875) LR 20 Eq 328.    [147] [1953] 1 QB 636.
[148] See J D Davies, 'Presumptions and Illegality' in Oakley, *Trends in Contemporary Trust Law* (1996).
[149] See *Tinsley v Milligan* [1993] 3 All ER 65 at 90.    [150] [1918] 1 KB 223.
[151] [1918] 1 KB 223 at 226.    [152] [1970] P 136.    [153] [1970] P 136 at 141.

In *Re Emery's Investments Trusts*[154] a husband was held unable to rebut a presumption of advancement when he had purchased American stock in the name of his American wife to avoid taxation under American Federal law, and in *Chettiar v Chettiar*[155] a father could not rebut a presumption of resulting trust where he had purchased a rubber estate in the name of his son to avoid a provision restricting the maximum area of rubber land that an individual could own.

Whilst the policy objective of this strict approach is to discourage persons from entering illegal transactions, in the more recent case of *Tribe v Tribe*[156] the Court of Appeal demonstrated a marked reluctance to disallow a father from rebutting the presumption of advancement arising when he had transferred property voluntarily to his son to achieve an illegal purpose. The father was the owner of a majority shareholding in a family company and the tenant of two properties occupied by the company as licensee. The landlord of these premises served notice of various alleged dilapidations on the father, requiring him to carry out substantial repairs. The father was advised by his solicitor that, if the claims were valid, he might be forced to sell the company shares to pay for the repairs. He therefore transferred them to his son as a means of safeguarding his assets. The transfer was stated to be made for a consideration of £78,030, but no money was ever paid. In the event, the father was never required to carry out the repairs and he sought to recover the shares from his son. The son refused to re-transfer them to him, and the father alleged that he held them on bare trust for him. The son argued that the presumption of advancement applied in his favour and that the father could not rebut it by evidence of the illegal attempt to evade his creditors. Whilst accepting that the decision of the House of Lords in *Tinsley v Milligan*[157] had the general effect that a presumption of advancement cannot be rebutted by evidence of an underlying illegal purpose, the Court of Appeal held that this general rule was subject to an exception if the 'illegal purpose has not been carried into effect'. As Nourse LJ explained:

'The judge found that the illegal purpose was to deceive the plaintiff's creditors by creating an appearance that he no longer owned any shares in the company. He also found that it was not carried into effect in any way. [Counsel for the defendant] attacked the latter finding on grounds which appeared to me to confuse the purpose with the transaction. Certainly the transaction was carried into effect by the execution and registration of the transfer. But *Wright's*[158] case shows that that is immaterial. It is the purpose which has to be carried into effect and that would only have happened if and when a creditor of the plaintiff had been deceived by the transaction. The judge said there was no evidence of that and clearly he did not think it appropriate to infer it. Nor is it any objection to the plaintiff's right to recover the shares that he did not demand their return until after the danger had passed and it was no longer necessary to conceal the transfer from his creditors. All that matters is that no deception was practised on them. For these reasons the judge was right to hold that the exception applied.'[159]

[154] [1959] Ch 410.       [155] [1962] 1 All ER 494.
[156] [1995] 4 All ER 236; (1996) 112 LQR 386 (Rose); [1996] CLJ 23 (Virgo); (1997) 60 MLR 102 (Creighton). See also (1995) 111 LQR 135 (Enonchong); [1996] RLR 78 (Enonchong).
[157] [1993] 3 All ER 65.
[158] *Perpetual Executors and Trustees Association of Australia Ltd v Wright* (1917) 23 CLR 185.
[159] [1995] 4 All ER 236 at 248.

Millet LJ reached the same conclusion but stated the principle more broadly, holding that a person is entitled to recover property transferred for an illegal purpose if he withdrew from the transaction before it was carried out. He attempted to formulate a single unitary principle derived from the equitable doctrines regarding the rebuttal of presumptions of resulting trust and advancement and common law cases where it had been held that a party was entitled to withdraw from an illegal contract. Whilst he made clear that effectual withdrawal from a transaction did not require 'genuine repentance' on the part of the wrongdoer, he held that he must have withdrawn voluntarily. There would therefore be no effective withdrawal if 'he is forced to [withdraw] because his plan has been discovered'.[160]

Despite the superficial attraction of simplicity, this proposed general approach is inadequate because it is unclear when a transaction has been carried into effect so as to prevent withdrawal. As Millet LJ noted, early common law cases indicated that a party to an illegal contract could withdraw only so long as it has not been completely performed, whereas later decisions held that any recovery under the contract was barred once partial performance had occurred.[161] He formulated his general proposition in the following terms:

'The transferor can lead evidence of the illegal purpose whenever it is necessary for him to do so provided that he has withdrawn from the transaction before the illegal purpose has been *wholly or partly* carried into effect.'[162]

It is submitted that this is extremely confusing, as it fails to indicate whether withdrawal is possible in cases where the transaction was partially carried into effect.

*Tribe v Tribe* is therefore only good authority to the extent that it decides that evidence of an illegal purpose may be admitted to rebut a presumption of advancement if the illegal purpose has not been carried into effect at all. However, even when assessed in the light of this limited proposition, the decision remains unsatisfactory. The conclusion that the illegal purpose had not been carried into effect was artificial, as in reality the act which was intended to achieve the illegal purpose was the transfer of the legal title of the shares to the son, thus on the face of it divesting the father of any interest. It is surely arguable that the illegal object was carried into effect at the very moment that the legal title was effectually transferred to the son. Far from rebutting the presumption of advancement, the very act of transferring the shares to the son with the illegal aim of defeating the creditors reinforces the presumption of a gift to the son. As Millet LJ stated:

'The only way in which a man can protect his property from his creditors is by divesting himself of all beneficial interest in it. Evidence that he transferred the property in order to protect it from his creditors, therefore, does nothing by itself to rebut the presumption of advancement; it reinforces it. To rebut the presumption it is necessary to show that he intended to retain a beneficial interest and conceal it from his creditors.'[163]

The reality is that in both *Tribe v Tribe* and *Tinsley v Milligan*[164] the respective courts

---

160 [1995] 4 All ER 236 at 259.       161 *Kearley v Thomson* (1890) 24 QBD 742.
162 [1995] 4 All ER 236 at 259.       163 [1995] 4 All ER 236 at 259.       164 [1994] 1 AC 340.

were attempting to avoid the perceived unfairness that would result from the application of a strict rule against illegality intended to serve a general public policy of deterring wrongdoers. It would seem unfair if Milligan were to be prevented from asserting any entitlement to an equitable share of the house owned at law by Tinsley when they were both parties to the illegal purpose, and the consequence would be that Tinsley received a large windfall gain at Milligan's expense. The majority of the House of Lords were conveniently able to avoid such a result by exploiting the logic that Milligan merely needed to prove that she had contributed to the purchase price of the house to raise a unrebuttable presumption of resulting trust in her favour. Whilst achieving justice between the parties, the decision represented a move away from the traditional position that a transferor could not recover property transferred in pursuit of an illegal purpose irrespective of whether the presumption of advancement or the presumption of result-ing trust applied. *Tinsley v Milligan* therefore introduced an arbitrary distinction, whereby the general rule would apply where there was a presumption of advancement between the parties, but not where there was a presumption of resulting trust. As has been noted above, the circumstances in which a presumption of advancement arises are largely derived from out-dated conceptions of family responsibility. They are riddled with inconsistency, to such an extent that the courts have tended to treat them as of relatively little weight and easily rebutted. Given the inadequacy of the law determining the circumstances in which a presumption of advancement arises, any differentiation between the effects of illegality on such grounds is highly unsatisfactory. As Judge Weekes stated at first instance in *Tribe v Tribe*:

'Finally, it is not for me to criticise their Lordship's reasoning, but with the greatest respect I find it difficult to see why the outcome in cases such as the present one should depend to such a large extent on arbitrary factors, such as whether the claim is brought by a father against a son, or a mother against a son, or a grandfather against a grandson.'[165]

What is needed is an approach which operates consistently, irrespective of the nature of the presumption applicable. Such consistency could have been obtained by retention of the traditional rule that an equitable interest cannot be asserted by a transferor of property if the purpose of the transfer was to give effect to an illegal purpose, irrespect-ive of whether there was a presumption of advancement or resulting trust. Instead, the estate would 'lie where it falls'. However, this approach was rejected by the majority in *Tinsley v Milligan* precisely because it would lead to unfairness in individual cases. It was also rejected by the High Court of Australia in *Nelson v Nelson*,[166] where Deane and Gummow JJ described it as a 'harsh and indiscriminate principle'. In that case the approach of the House of Lords in *Tinsley v Milligan* was also rejected on the grounds that it generated different results which were 'entirely fortuitous being dependent upon the relationship between the parties', and therefore 'wholly unjustifiable on any policy ground'.[167] The High Court held that a person should only be prevented from asserting an equitable right if to allow him to do so would be inconsistent with the public policy

---

[165] Quote by Nourse LJ [1995] 4 All ER 236 at 244. See also *Collier v Collier* [2003] WTLR 617 at 654–655, per Mance LJ.

[166] (1995) 132 ALR 133.        [167] (1995) 132 ALR 133 at 166, per Dawson J.

applicable to the specific right claimed. Applying this test, the High Court held that public policy did not prevent a mother asserting an equitable interest in property she had transferred to her children. Mrs Nelson had provided the purchase money for a house which was transferred into the names of her two children to enable her to obtain a subsidised advance towards the purchase of another house under the Australian housing legislation. To obtain such an advance she had to declare that she did not own, or have an interest, in any other house. After she had received the advance the first house was sold, and one of the children claimed that he was entitled to half the proceeds of sale. It was held that Mrs Nelson could rebut the presumption of advancement operating in favour of the children because the policy of the particular legislation concerned would 'not be defeated if the court enforces her equitable right'. Thus, the court was willing to allow Mrs Nelson to assert her equitable entitlement even though the illegal purpose had been carried into effect, a result which would not have been possible through an application of the principles adopted in *Tribe v Tribe*. However, the majority further held that her right to assert her equitable interest should be conditional on repayment of her unlawful benefit to the state.

As was noted above the current law regarding illegality has recently been reviewed by the Law Commission.[168] Given its unsatisfactory nature the Law Commission has recommended the abandonment of the 'reliance principle' adopted in *Tinsley v Milligan* in favour of a granting the court a discretion to declare a trust illegal or invalid. This discretion would be structured so that a court would have to take into account a number of specified factors in reaching its decisions:

'. . . those factors should be: (a) the seriousness of the illegality; (b) the knowledge and intention of the illegal trust beneficiary; (c) whether invalidity would tend to deter the illegality; (d) whether invalidity would further the purpose of the rule which renders the trust "illegal"; and (e) whether invalidity would be a proportionate response to the claimant's participation in the illegality.'[169]

It remains to be seen whether this proposal is implemented. Whilst there are undoubtedly problems with the current law, especially the arbitrary distinction between situations where the presumption of resulting trusts and the presumption of advancement apply, it should be noted that all members of the House of Lords in *Tinsley v Milligan* rejected a discretionary approach to the effect of illegality on equitable property rights, preferring strict rules which would determine whether a right could be asserted. In many ways the only logical and consistent approach was that advocated by the dissenting minority, namely that those who seek to assert equitable interests must come to the courts with clean hands.

## (c) Admissibility of evidence to rebut a presumption of advancement

As in the case of the rebuttal of presumptions of a resulting trust,[170] only evidence of the plaintiff's acts and declarations contemporaneous with the transaction are

---

[168] *'Illegal Transactions: The Effect of Illegality on Contracts and Trusts'* (1999), Law Comm CP No 154. See Enonchong, 'Illegal Transactions: The Future?' [2000] RLR 82.

[169] [2000] RLR 82 at para 8.63.    [170] See above, p 250.

admissible in his favour to rebut the presumption of advancement. Evidence of subsequent acts and declarations are only admissible as evidence against him. This principle was stated and applied by the House of Lords in *Shephard v Cartwright*,[171] where Lord Simmonds approved a summary of the law in Snell's *Equity*:

'The acts and declarations of the parties before or at the time of the purchase, or so immediately after it as to constitute a part of the transaction, are admissible in evidence either for or against the party who did the acts or made the declaration . . . But subsequent declarations are admissible as evidence only against the party who made them, and not in his favour.'[172]

In 1929 Philip Shephard subscribed for shares in the name of his children. In 1934 the shares were sold to a company promoted by him, and the children signed the requisite documents at his request without knowing what they were doing. The proceeds of sale were paid into separate deposit accounts in the children's names. They later signed documents, unaware of their contents, authorising him to withdraw money from the accounts, whereupon he withdrew money from them without their knowledge. In an action by the children against his executors the central issue was whether the presumption of advancement had been rebutted. The House of Lords held that evidence of the father's acts after the transaction of 1929 were not admissible to prove the rebuttal of the presumption of advancement as they did not form part of the original transaction.[173]

# 4 Reform of presumed resulting trusts

The presumptions of resulting trusts largely operate as a mechanism for allocating the burden of proof when there is a dispute as to intended effect of a transaction on the beneficial ownership of property. As the Australian High Court stated in *Russell v Scott*:

'The presumption of resulting trusts does no more than call for proof of an intention to confer beneficial ownership.'[174]

Thus where the presumption of resulting trust applies a transferee will have to discharge the burden of proof by demonstrating that a gift was intended, whereas if the presumption of advancement applies the transferor will bear the burden of proving that no gift was intended. The presumptions may serve the purpose of protecting vulnerable individuals where property has been transferred, or contributions made, in circumstances where there was very little evidence as to the intended nature of the transaction.

However the operation of the presumptions can be criticised on the grounds that they are archaic and anachronistic. The presumptions themselves are based on

---

[171] [1955] AC 431.

[172] [1955] AC 431 at 445; Snell, *Principles of Equity* (24th edn, 1990), p 153.

[173] Similarly, evidence of the children's acts in signing the documents at their father's request were not admissible against them, because they had been unaware of the contents.

[174] (1936) 55 CLR 440, per Dixon and Evatt JJ.

nineteenth-century concepts of the family. Despite judicial comments that they are often inappropriate to modern situations, that they have lost much of their force, or are easily rebutted, they continue to enshrine outdated paternalistic and chauvinistic values. In the area of matrimonial property the inconsistencies are glaring, for example the presumption of advancement is applied between a husband and wife, but the presumption of resulting trust between a wife and a husband. These difficulties were recognised by the Law Commission in their Report, *Family Law: Matrimonial Property*.[175] It concluded that the present law was unsatisfactory because:

'. . . its application may not result in co-ownership of property even when a married couple desire this. Actual ownership may be held to depend on factors which neither party considered significant at the time of acquisition. In its treatment of money allowances and gifts of property the law discriminates between husband and wife.'[176]

In the light of this inadequacy, the Law Commission considered a number of alternatives for reform. They rejected the wholesale introduction of community of property during marriage, whereby some or all of the property of a married couple would be automatically co-owned during the marriage, as unacceptable because it does not permit independent management during the marriage.[177] Instead, they proposed a rewriting of the presumptions between a married couple in a manner which accords more closely to their likely intentions:

'(i)  Where money is spent to buy property, or property or money is transferred by one spouse to the other, for their joint use or benefit the property acquired or money transferred should be jointly owned.

(ii)  Where money or property is transferred by one spouse to the other for any other purpose, it should be owned by that other.

In both cases, the general rule should give way to a contrary intention on the part of the paying or transferring spouse, provided that the contrary intention is known to that other spouse.'[178]

Under these revised presumptions, a presumption of advancement would apply to both husbands and wives.[179] The proposal would apply to married or engaged couples. In any event the gender bias of the presumptions may also contravene the European Convention on Human Rights.[180]

# 5 Resulting trusts operating to reverse unjust enrichment?

At the beginning of this chapter it was noted that there are two categories of resulting trusts recognised in English law, historically differentiated as 'presumed' and 'automatic' resulting trusts. However, a great deal of recent debate has been addressed to the

---

[175]  Law Com No 175 (1988).    [176]  Para 2.8.    [177]  Paras 3.3–3.6.    [178]  Para 4.1.
[179]  Para 4.19.    [180]  Law Commission Discussion Paper, *Sharing Homes* (2002), para 2.60.

question whether a third type should be recognised, namely a restitutionary resulting trust which arises for the purpose of reversing unjust enrichment. Although English law did not historically recognise a right to restitution founded on a general principle against unjust enrichment, in *Likpin Gorman v Karpnale Ltd*[181] the House of Lords held that 'unjust enrichment' should be recognised as a valid autonomous cause of action. This recognition has been reiterated in many subsequent decisions[182] and is now beyond doubt. A plaintiff will be entitled to restitution whenever he can demonstrate that the defendant was unjustly enriched at his expense. Where a plaintiff can demonstrate an entitlement to receive restitution from the defendant, the question arises as to the nature of the remedy available to him to effect such restitution. The plaintiff will generally be entitled to a personal remedy, requiring the defendant to pay over to him an amount equivalent to the enrichment that had been received, but this remedy will be of little use if the defendant is insolvent. If, however, it can be shown that property constituting the enrichment received by the defendant was subjected to a trust, the plaintiff will be able to assert a proprietary claim to any assets remaining in the defendant's hands which are the traceable proceeds of the enrichment received. Such a trust will not arise expressly and there would be no grounds for finding a presumed resulting trust.

However, in a significant article, Professor Birks argued that a resulting trust should arise whenever a defendant receives an unjust enrichment conferred by mistake or under a contract the consideration for which wholly fails.[183] If such a resulting trust were to arise from the mere fact of enrichment in such cases the plaintiff would be entitled to a proprietary remedy. This thesis was considered in *Westdeutsche Landesbank Girozentrale v Islington London Borough Council*,[184] where it was comprehensively rejected by the House of Lords, which preferred the critical approach of William Swadling.[185] The case involved an interest rate swap agreement entered between the plaintiff bank and the defendant local authority. Under the agreement the bank made a payment of £2.5m to the authority. However, as a consequence of the decision of the House of Lords in *Hazell v Hammersmith and Fulham London Borough Council*,[186] the contract between the parties was ultra vires the local authority and therefore void. The bank sought restitution of the balance of the payment it had made, less the repayments the authority had already made, together with interest. In the House of Lords the sole remaining question was as to the nature of the interest payable on the award of restitution. If the bank was only entitled to restitution at common law then the court had no jurisdiction to award compound interest. However, the bank alleged that the payment had been received subject to a resulting trust, because the contract under which it was made was void, thus rooting their claim in equity and entitling the

---

[181] [1991] 2 AC 548. See [1991] LMCLQ 473 (Birks).

[182] See *Woolwich Equitable Building Society v IRC* [1993] AC 70; *Westdeutsche Landesbank Girozentrale v Islington London Borough Council* [1996] AC 669; *Kleinwort Benson Ltd v Glasgow City Council* [1999] 1 AC 153, HL.

[183] Birks, 'Restitution and Resulting Trusts', in Goldstein (ed), *Equity: Contemporary Legal Development* (1992). See also Chambers, *Resulting Trusts* (1997), pp 93–219.

[184] [1996] AC 669; (1996) 112 LQR 521 (Cape); [1996] CLJ 432 (Jones); [1997] LMCLQ 441 (Stevens).

[185] (1996) 16 LS 133.      [186] [1992] 2 AC 1.

court to award compound interest. However, Lord Browne-Wilkinson explained that the circumstances of the payment could not have given rise to a resulting trust:

'Applying these conventional principles of resulting trust to the present case, the bank's claim must fail. There was no transfer of money to the local authority on express trusts: therefore a resulting trust of type (B) above could not arise. As to type (A) above, any presumption of resulting trust is rebutted, since it is demonstrated that the bank paid, and the local authority received, the upfront payment with the intention that the moneys so paid should become the absolute property of the local authority. It is true that the parties were under a misapprehension that the payment was made in pursuance of a valid contract. But that does not alter the actual intentions of the parties at the date the payment was made . . .'[187]

He further elucidated three reasons for rejecting Professor Birks' thesis that the concept of the resulting trust should be extended to provide a plaintiff with a proprietary remedy whenever he had transferred value to a defendant under a mistake or subject to a condition which is not subsequently satisfied. First, he held that trust interests could not arise in relation to the restitutionary concept of 'value transferred' but only in relation to defined property. Secondly, he considered that a trust would only arise at the moment that a defendant received a payment if he was aware of the circumstances alleged to give rise to the trust. Since a recipient of a payment subsequently found void for mistake or failure of consideration will not have been aware of the circumstances rendering it void at the date of receipt his conscience cannot have been effected so as to generate a trust. Thirdly, he noted that the thesis was flawed by the need to artificially exclude cases of partial failure to perform a contract, despite the fact that the wider concept logically led to a resulting trust in such cases.

Alongside these conceptual objections to the recognition of restitutionary resulting trusts, the House of Lords considered that the consequential expansion in proprietary entitlements would have unacceptable practical consequences for third parties.[188] For example, if money paid under a void contract was subject to a resulting trust, third parties who entered into transactions with the recipient of the payment might be affected by the trust interest of the payor, even though no one knew that the contract was void, so that they could not have been aware of the supposed trust. In the light of these considerations Lord Browne-Wilkinson concluded:

'If adopted, Professor Birks' wider concepts would give rise to all the practical consequences and injustice to which I have referred. I do not think it right to make an unprincipled alteration to the law of property (ie the law of trusts) so as to produce in the law of unjust enrichment the injustices to third parties . . . and the consequential commercial uncertainty which any extension of proprietary interests in personal property is bound to produce.'[189]

Although the House of Lords has rejected the adoption of a wider restitutionary

---

[187] [1996] AC 669 at 708.
[188] See [1995] RLR 15 (Burrows) for a fuller consideration of the practical implications of the adoption of restitutionary resulting trusts.
[189] [1996] AC 669 at 709.

resulting trust, this does not mean that a trust interest will never be raised for the purpose of reversing an unjust enrichment. Lord Browne-Wilkinson stated:

'Although the resulting trust is an unsuitable basis for developing proprietary restitutionary remedies, the remedial constructive trust, if introduced into English law, may provide a more satisfactory road forward.'[190]

The nature of the remedial constructive trust is examined in the following chapter.

[190]  [1996] AC 669 at 709, 716.

# 9

# Constructive trusts

## 1 Introduction to constructive trusts

### (1) Terminology

The major obstacle to any analysis of the English doctrine of constructive trusts is the wide number of circumstances that the term 'constructive trust' has been used to describe. This has led Sir Peter Millet to comment that 'the use of the language of constructive trust has become such a fertile source of confusion that it would be better if it were abandoned'.[1] It has been used to describe a range of situations as diverse as the remedy available against a fiduciary who has made an unauthorised profit in breach of his duty, to the creation of a trust where parties make mutual wills. At its simplest, the term 'constructive trust' describes the circumstances in which property is subjected to a trust by operation of law. Unlike an expressly declared trust, a constructive trust does not come into being solely in consequence of the express intention of a settlor. Unlike a resulting trust, it is not the product of an implied intention.[2] In *Westdeutsche Landesbank Girozentrale v Islington London Borough Council*[3] Lord Browne-Wilkinson identified a constructive trust as a trust 'which the law imposed on [the trustee] by reason of his unconscionable conduct'.[4]

### (2) The English concept of the 'constructive trust'

Although the terminology of 'constructive trusts' is used throughout common law jurisdictions, it does not describe identical concepts. Different jurisdictions have developed widely differing views as to the nature of constructive trusts and the circumstances in which they come into existence. One of the most significant conceptual distinctions is between what are described as 'institutional' and 'remedial' constructive trusts.

---

[1] McKendrick, *Commercial Aspects of Trusts and Fiduciary Obligations* (1992), p 3.

[2] But see, however, *Midland Bank plc v Cooke* [1995] 4 All ER 562 where the Court of Appeal failed to maintain a strict distinction between resulting and constructive trusts.

[3] [1996] AC 669; (1996) 112 LQR 521 (Cape); [1996] CLJ 432 (Jones); [1997] LMCLQ 441 (Stevens)

[4] [1996] AC 669 at 705. See also *Paragon Finance plc v D B Thakerar & Co* [1999] 1 All ER 400, 409 where Millett LJ stated that a 'constructive trust arises by operation of law whenever the circumstances are such that it would be unconscionable for the owner of property (usually but not necessarily the legal estate) to assert his beneficial interest in the property'.

## (a) The 'institutional' constructive trust

An institutional constructive trust is a trust which is brought into being on the occurrence of specified events, without the need for the intervention of the court. The trust comes into being if the facts which are necessary to give rise to it are proved to have occurred. It exists from the time that the relevant events occurred.[5] The court does not impose the trust but rather recognises that the beneficiary enjoys a pre-existing proprietary interest in the trust property. The court has no discretion to decide whether or not the property should be subject to a trust. Since an institutional constructive trust does not arise from the judgment of the court, it is capable of gaining priority over any interests acquired by third parties in the trust property during the period between the creation of the trust and its recognition by the court.

## (b) The 'remedial' constructive trust

In contrast to the 'institutional' constructive trust, other jurisdictions have come to regard constructive trusts as one of a range of remedies which may effect restitution where a defendant has been unjustly enriched at the expense of a plaintiff. Having found that there has been an unjust enrichment, the court can, in its discretion, impose a constructive trust over assets representing any remaining enrichment in the hands of the defendant if appropriate, or alternatively award a monetary remedy. A remedial constructive trust is imposed by the court, which does not merely recognise a pre-existing proprietary right. The trust arises from the date of the court's judgment and it will not therefore gain automatic priority over the rights of third parties. These characteristics of a 'remedial' constructive trust were recognised in *Metall and Rohstoff AG v Donaldson Lufkin & Jenerette Inc*,[6] where Slade LJ stated:

'. . . the court imposes a constructive trust de novo on assets which are not subject to any pre-existing trust as a means of granting equitable relief in a case where it considers it just that restitution should be made.'[7]

At present English law only recognises the 'institutional' constructive trust and has not been willing to adopt the remedial constructive trust.[8] Other jurisdictions, in particular Canada, have adopted an unjust enrichment analysis to explain the availability of constructive trusts, and the operation of the remedial constructive trust will be examined in detail at the end of this chapter.[9]

## (3) The search for a coherent theory

As the terminology of constructive trusts is utilised in so many different contexts, it is difficult to provide any coherent unifying theory that will adequately explain their

---

[5] *Re Sharpe* [1980] 1 All ER 198 at 203, per Browne-Wilkinson J.     [6] [1990] 1 QB 391.

[7] [1990] 1 QB 391 at 478. See also *Re Polly Peck (No 2)* [1998] 3 All ER 812 at 831, where Nourse LJ defined a remedial constructive trust as 'an order of the court granting, by way of remedy, a proprietary right to someone who, beforehand, had no proprietary right'.

[8] See: *Metall und Rohstoff AG v Donaldson Lufkin & Jenrette Inc* [1990] 1 QB 391; *Westdeutsche Landesbank Girozentrale v Islington London Borough Council* [1996] AC 669; *Re Polly Peck (No 2)* [1998] 3 All ER 812.

[9] See below, p 318.

incidence. English law has tended to take the view that constructive trusts arise in a range of relatively well circumscribed conditions in which the trustee's conduct is considered unconscionable. A previous edition of Snell's *Equity* concluded:

'For the present . . . constructive trusts fall for the most part in well-established categories, and it is only occasionally and in unusual circumstances that it would be necessary to take refuge in such a broad and fundamental principle [ie of unconscionability].'[10]

In the case of the remedial constructive trust, the unifying fundamental principle is that of the reversal of unjust enrichment. Although superficially attractive as a touchstone, this merely shifts the goal posts, since it becomes necessary to define when an enrichment is 'unjust'. This will require the identification of common fact situations where enrichment is regarded as 'unjust', which may of themselves have no greater coherency than those regarded as giving rise to constructive trusts in English law. In this sense the restitutionary approach may simply re-invent the wheel under a different name.

Despite the difficulty of providing any single coherent theory for the enforcement of constructive trusts, the factor which appears to connect the circumstances in which the court will find that a constructive trust has arisen is an emphasis on the conduct of the party who is required to hold property subject to the constructive trust. Constructive trusts are imposed by equity in order to satisfy the demands of justice and good conscience,[11] and where it would be unjust to allow the trustee to assert an absolute entitlement to property. As Lord Denning MR observed in *Binions v Evans*,[12] quoting the words of an American judge:

'A constructive trust is the formula through which the conscience of equity finds expression. When property has been acquired in such circumstances that the holder of the legal title may not in good conscience retain the beneficial interest, equity converts him into a trustee.'[13]

The concept of 'justice and good conscience' is too broad to be of direct practical value.[14] Analysis of the precise conduct justifying the imposition of a constructive trust can only realistically be attempted in the context of the common circumstances where constructive trusts have been found to arise. This chapter will therefore follow the common approach of identifying and describing the circumstances in which English law will find that a constructive trust has been created.

## (4) The significance of constructive trusts

### (a) Creation of proprietary interests

As a species of trust, constructive trusts inherently create equitable proprietary interests in favour of identifiable beneficiaries. A trust cannot arise in abstract, but only in

---

[10] Snell, *Principles of Equity* (29th edn, 1990), p 197.
[11] *Carl-Zeiss-Stiftung v Herbert Smith & Co (No 2)* [1969] 2 Ch 276 at 301, per Edmund Davies LJ.
[12] [1972] Ch 359 at 386.
[13] *Beatty v Guggenheim Exploration Co* 225 NY 380 (1919) at 386 per Cardozo J.
[14] See: *Snell's Equity* (13th edn, 2000), p 221.

respect of defined property.[15] Constructive trusts therefore provide a means by which a legal owner will be required to hold property on trust for beneficiaries, despite the lack of any express or implied intention that he should do so, or where an intention to create a trust is ineffective because it is not expressed in compliance with the appropriate statutory formalities.[16] This ability of constructive trusts to generate proprietary interests has been especially significant in the context of the ownership of land. Alongside resulting trusts, constructive trusts provide a means by which a person can obtain a share of the beneficial ownership where no formal declaration of trust has been made in their favour.[17] Where constructive trusts do give rise to proprietary interests, they may have far reaching effects, especially by detracting from the interests that third parties may have acquired after the trust had arisen, for example if land subject to a constructive trust has been mortgaged, and by gaining automatic priority over the rights of other creditors if the trustee is insolvent. The institutional nature of the constructive trust gives the court no flexibility to consider the potential effects of the constructive trust on such third parties or creditors.

### (b) Preservation of pre-existing equitable interests

Constructive trusts also operate to preserve the interest of the beneficiaries of an existing trust, however created, if the legal title to the trust property is wrongly transferred by the trustee. A third party who purchases the legal title to the trust property from a trustee will take free from the pre-existing trust interests of the beneficiaries if he was a bona fide purchaser for value without notice. However, if the requirements of the doctrine of notice are not fulfilled, either because the transferee of the legal title was a volunteer who had not provided consideration, or because he had notice (whether actual or constructive) of the existence of the trust, the transferee will hold the property as constructive trustee for the beneficiaries. By this means their pre-existing entitlements are preserved and the recipient will not be entitled to treat the property as if he were the absolute owner.

### (c) Misappropriated property

Constructive trusts have increasingly come to prominence in commercial contexts where property has been misappropriated from its true owner. If the misappropriated property was not previously subject to a trust, it may be rendered subject to a constructive trust in the hands of the recipient if it was misappropriated by a person standing in a fiduciary relationship to the owner,[18] or if it was received in circumstances generating a fiduciary relationship between the recipient and the owner.[19] By means of such a constructive trust, the entitlement of the true owner is preserved in equity. In *Westdeutsche Landesbank Girozentrale v Islington London Borough Council*[20] Lord Browne-Wilkinson

---

[15] *Westdeutsche Landesbank Girozentrale v Islington London Borough Council* [1996] AC 669 at 709, per Lord Browne-Wilkinson.

[16] *Rochefoucauld v Boustead* [1897] 1 Ch 196.     [17] See (1995) 15 LS 356 (Howard and Hill).

[18] As eg in *Agip (Africa) v Jackson* [1991] Ch 547.

[19] *Chase Manhattan Bank NA v Israel-British Bank* (London) Ltd [1981] Ch 105.

[20] [1996] AC 669.

held that a thief would hold the money he had stolen on constructive trust for the victim.[21]

### (d) Receipt of an unauthorised profit by a fiduciary

A constructive trust will also arise whenever a fiduciary receives an unauthorised profit in breach of the duty of loyalty that is owed to his principal.[22] A person who holds such a fiduciary position is under a duty not to abuse his position by receiving any unauthorised remuneration, or to profit by allowing his duty and his interest to conflict. Equity will compel a fiduciary to hold any unauthorised profits he receives on trust for his principal, who will be entitled to claim an equitable proprietary interest in them or their traceable proceeds. The remedies available against a fiduciary will be fully considered in Chapter 29.

### (e) Personal liability to account as a constructive trustee

Historically English law also utilised the concept of the constructive trust to impose a personal liability to account upon a fiduciary who had received an unauthorised profit, a stranger to a trust who had knowingly received and dissipated trust property, and a stranger who had knowingly assisted in the commission of a breach of trust. However in *Paragon Finance plc v D B Thakerar & Co*[23] Millett LJ considered that the terminology of constructive trusts was inappropriate to describe such liability. He distinguished between two categories of constructive trusts. The first category were those situations in which a person had assumed the duties of a trustee even thought he had not been expressly appointed as such. The second were circumstances in which the defendant was implicated in a fraud. In respect to this second category of cases he considered that the language of constructive trusts was inappropriate:

'The second class of case is different. It arises when the defendant is implicated in a fraud. Equity has always given relief against fraud by making any person sufficiently implicated in the fraud accountable in equity. In such a case he is traditionally though I think unfortunately described as a constructive trustee and said to be "liable to account as a constructive trustee". Such a person is not in fact a trustee at all, even though he may be liable to account as if he were. He never assumes the position of a trustee, and if he receives the trust property at all it is adversely to the plaintiff by an unlawful transaction which is impugned by the plaintiff. In such a case the expressions "constructive trust" and "constructive trustee" are misleading, for there is no trust and usually no possibility of a proprietary remedy; they are "nothing more than a formula for equitable relief": *Selangor United Rubber Estates Ltd v Craddock (No 3)*'.[24]

Whilst it is certainly correct that the personal liability of a person who has assisted in the commission of a breach of trust should not be characterised as the liability of a constructive trustee, as the assistor will usually never have held the trust property, it is less obvious that the terminology is inappropriate to describe the personal liability of a fiduciary who has received an unauthorised profit, or a stranger who has received and

---

[21] [1996] AC 669 at 716.    [22] *A-G for Hong Kong v Reid* [1994] 1 All ER 1, PC.
[23] [1999] 1 All ER 400.    [24] [1999] 1 All ER 400 at 409.

dissipated trust property. In both situations the liability arises because the fiduciary or stranger has failed to preserve the property which he held on trust. However, given the confusion of terminology, the personal liability of a fiduciary to account for unauthorised profits, or of a stranger to account for the value of trust property he has received, are better analysed as examples of claims to restitution in equity.[25] The personal remedies available against a fiduciary are considered in Chapter 29, and those against a stranger who has received trust property in Chapter 30.

# 2 Constructive trusts imposed to prevent a criminal benefiting from his crime[26]

## (1) The principle that no criminal may benefit from his crime

It is a basic principle of English Law that no criminal should be entitled to retain a material benefit derived from his crime. As Fry LJ said in *Cleaver v Mutual Reserve Fund Life Association*:

'. . . no system of jurisprudence can with reason include among the rights which it enforces rights directly resulting to the person asserting them from the crime of that person . . . This principle of public policy, like all such principles, must be applied to all cases to which it can be applied without reference to the particular character of the right asserted or the form of its assertion.'[27]

The principle operates to prevent property coming into the hands of a criminal as a result of his crime, and instead deflects it to others who would be entitled in his place by forfeiting his entitlement. The harsh operation of the rule was recently illustrated in *Re D W S (decd)*.[28] In this case a son had murdered his parents, who had died intestate. Clearly the son was disqualified from inheriting their estates. The Court of Appeal held that his illegitimate son was also unable to inherit his grandparent's estate because the rules of intestacy state that 'no issue shall take whose parent is living at the date of the intestate.'[29] Their estates therefore passed to more distant relatives.

Where, however, a criminal has already received property into his hands in consequence of his crime, it will be subjected to a constructive trust in favour of those who would have been entitled to it in his place. Suppose, for example, a man kills his wife and subsequently inherits property that she bequeathed to him in her will. If it is later discovered that she was murdered, he will hold what remains of the property, or its traceable proceeds, on constructive trust. The imposition of this constructive trust has

---

[25] As eg in *Re Montagu's Settlement Trusts* [1987] Ch 264.
[26] See Oakley, *Constructive Trusts* (3rd edn, 1996), pp 46–53; Goff and Jones, *The Law of Restitution* (5th edn, 1998), pp 802–814; (1973) 89 LQR 235 (Youdan); (1974) 37 MLR 481 (Earnshaw and Pace).
[27] [1892] 1 QB 147 at 156.     [28] [2001] Ch 568.
[29] Administration of Estates Act 1925, s 47 (1) (i).

the effect of depriving him of the beneficial interest in the property, although he will continue to hold the legal title as trustee.

The principle that a criminal cannot benefit from his crime could have application in two main circumstances. First, where a person receives property by theft, and secondly where he acquires property (whether by succession or survivorship) from someone who has died in consequence of a crime he committed.

## (2) Property obtained by theft

The principle has little practical application to the area of theft because a thief does not acquire legal title to the property that he steals.[30] Under s 28 of the Theft Act 1968 the court has power to order a person convicted of theft to return the property to its owner.

## (3) Property acquired by a crime causing death

A person who unlawfully kills another will not be entitled to retain property received as a result of his victim's death, whether under the victim's will, on intestacy, or through the operation of survivorship in the context of jointly owned property. Similarly, an unlawful killer will not be able to recover under an insurance policy covering the consequences of the death of the unlawfully killed person. In each of these cases the courts intervene to prevent the criminal obtaining a benefit.

### (a) Must the criminal have used or threatened violence?

The principle of forfeiture by imposition of a constructive trust will clearly apply where a person has received property from a victim he has unlawfully killed. Unlawful killing clearly includes murder, but forfeiture will not operate against a killer found innocent on the grounds of insanity because such a verdict constitutes an acquittal.[31] It has been less clear whether forfeiture applies where a killer has committed manslaughter. As Salmon LJ observed in *Gray v Barr*:

'Manslaughter is a crime which varies infinitely in its seriousness. It may come very near to murder or amount to little more than inadvertence, although in the latter class of case the jury only rarely convicts.'[32]

It remains unclear whether forfeiture operates in cases of 'involuntary manslaughter', for example where death was caused by reckless driving. The courts have shown reluctance to draw a distinction between voluntary and involuntary manslaughter.[33] For example in *Re Giles*, where a wife had been found guilty of the manslaughter of her husband on the ground of diminished responsibility, Pennycuick V-C held:

---

[30] A purchaser from a thief will only obtain good title in a few cases. See Bradgate, *Commercial Law* (3rd edn, 2000).

[31] Criminal Procedure (Insanity) Act 1964, s 1.        [32] [1971] 2 QB 554 at 581.

[33] Voluntary manslaughter is where what would otherwise be murder is reduced to manslaughter by provocation or diminished responsibility, or because the death occurred in pursuance of a suicide pact. Involuntary manslaughter is where an unlawful killing is reduced to manslaughter because there was no intent to kill or to do grievous bodily harm: see *Re K* [1985] Ch 85 at 98.

'It is sufficient to state that the rule has been established and that the deserving of punishment and moral culpability are not necessary ingredients of the type of crime to which this rule applies, that is, culpable homicide, murder or manslaughter.'[34]

Some evidence for the inapplicability of the forfeiture rule to cases of involuntary manslaughter can be derived from insurance cases where a driver had committed 'motor manslaughter' and killed through his reckless driving. In such cases the courts have held that an insured driver was not prevented from recovering under his insurance policy,[35] unless his conduct was wilful and culpable.[36]

However, in cases not involving motor manslaughter, the courts have historically held that forfeiture operates only if the killer used violence, or threats of violence, against his victim, even if the death was accidental. In *Gray v Barr*[37] Mr Barr confronted Mr Gray believing that his wife, with whom Mr Gray had been having an affair, was present. He involuntarily shot Mr Gray after falling backwards while threatening him with a loaded shotgun. The Court of Appeal held that in these circumstances the principle of forfeiture should apply. Salmon LJ stated:

'Although public policy is rightly regarded as an unruly steed which should be cautiously ridden, I am confident that public policy undoubtedly requires that no one who threatens unlawful violence with a loaded gun should be allowed to enforce a claim for indemnity against any liability he may incur as a result of having so acted.'[38]

At first instance, Geoffrey Lane J had held that the forfeiture rule should apply if a person was 'guilty of deliberate, intentional and unlawful violence or threats of violence'. This test was cited with approval by Vinelott J in *Re K*,[39] where a wife had shot and killed her husband following domestic violence. She had intended to frighten him with a loaded shotgun that was kept in their kitchen, but it had gone off when she removed the safety catch. At trial she was acquitted of murder but found guilty of manslaughter on the grounds of diminished responsibility. Vinelott J held that the forfeiture rule applied because she had threatened violence deliberately in order to frighten and deter her husband, even though his death had been wholly unintended. In *Re H*[40] Peter Gibson J held that the forfeiture rule did not apply where a offender convicted of manslaughter on grounds of diminished responsibility had not been responsible for his actions which were therefore neither deliberate nor intentional.

However, in *Dunbar v Plant*[41] the Court of Appeal rejected the view that forfeiture only operates where deliberate violence, or threats of violence, have been used and concluded that it applied where a woman had aided and abetted the suicide of her fiancé. The facts of the case were tragic. Miss Plant, who was facing a trial for theft from her employers, decided to commit suicide rather than face the prospect of jail. Mr Dunbar, her fiancé, said that he could not contemplate life without her, so they

---

[34] [1972] Ch 544 at 552. See also *R v Chief National Insurance Comr, ex p Connor* [1981] QB 758; *Re Royse* [1985] Ch 22.

[35] See *Tinline v White Cross Insurance Association Ltd* [1921] 3 KB 327; *James v British General Insurance Co Ltd* [1927] 2 KB 311.

[36] *Hardy v Motor Insurers' Bureau* [1964] 2 QB 745.    [37] [1971] 2 QB 554.

[38] [1971] 2 QB 554 at 581.    [39] [1985] 2 WLR 262 at 276.

[40] [1990] 1 FLR 441.    [41] [1998] Ch 412.

agreed that they would commit suicide together. An initial attempt to gas themselves in a car failed, as did a attempt to hang themselves with cable. On a further attempt to hang themselves with sheets, Dunbar was successful but Plant survived. Further suicide attempts, including cutting her throat and jumping out of a window, were also unsuccessful. The case concerned the question whether forfeiture should operate to prevent her obtaining the benefit of Dunbar's life insurance policy, of which she was the beneficiary. Counsel for Plant argued that the forfeiture rule should not apply at all because she had not used or threatened violence against Dunbar. This was rejected unanimously by the Court of Appeal, which held that the forfeiture rule prima facie applied. Mummery LJ explained:

'In my judgment . . . the presence of acts or threats of violence is not necessary for the application of the forfeiture rule. It is sufficient that a serious crime has been committed deliberately and intentionally. The references to acts or threats of violence in the cases are explicable by the facts of those cases. But in none of those cases were the courts legislating a principle couched in specific statutory language. The essence of the principle of public policy is that (a) no person shall take a benefit resulting from a crime committed by him or her resulting in the death of the victim and (b) the nature of the crime determines the application of the principle. On that view, the important point is that the crime that had fatal consequences was committed with a guilty mind (deliberately and intentionally). The particular means used to commit the crime (whether violent or non-violent) are not a necessary ingredient of the rule.'[42]

Given that violence was not required, it was held that the forfeiture rule operated where the offence of aiding and abetting suicide contrary to s 2(1) of the Suicide Act 1961 had been committed in the context of a suicide pact. Miss Plant had encouraged Dunbar to commit suicide, thus committing the offence and attracting the operation of the forfeiture rule.

As is evident from *Dunbar v Plant*, where Miss Plant had not been convicted of the offence of aiding and abetting, the forfeiture rule will apply even though the person causing death has not been convicted of a criminal offence. This may be because it has not been possible to bring him to trial, for example because of his own suicide.[43] In *Gray v Barr*[44] the Court of Appeal held that the forfeiture rule should apply even though Mr Barr had been acquitted at trial of both murder and manslaughter. In the civil trial the lower evidential standard of the 'balance of probabilities' applied. For this reason, Lord Denning MR was able to conclude: 'there is no doubt, to my mind, that Mr Barr was guilty of manslaughter'.[45]

## (b) Forfeiture of entitlement under the victim's will

Where the forfeiture rule operates, a criminal will not be permitted to derive any benefit under the will of his victim. In *Re Sigsworth*[46] a coroner's inquest found that Mary

---

[42] [1997] 4 All ER 289 at 300. Mummery LJ cited the Canadian case *Whitelaw v Wilson* [1934] OR 415, where it had been held that the forfeiture rule applied to the survivor of a suicide pact in which a husband and wife both drank poison.

[43] See *Re Sigsworth* [1935] Ch 89.     [44] [1971] 2 QB 554.     [45] [1971] 2 QB 554 at 568.

[46] [1935] Ch 89. See also *Re Callaway* [1956] Ch 559; *Re Peacock* [1957] Ch 310.

Sigsworth had died as a result of a fractured spine caused by her son, Thomas. He subsequently committed suicide before he could be brought to trial. She had left the whole of her property to him. On the assumption that he had murdered his mother,[47] Clauson J held that Thomas was not entitled to take any interest under the will. He stated the principle:

'. . . the claim of the [son], to the estate of the mother under her will is bound to fail by reason of the well-settled principle that public policy precludes a sane murderer from taking a benefit under his victim's will.'[48]

### (c) Forfeiture of entitlement arising on the victim's intestacy

Similarly, the forfeiture rule operates to preclude the criminal receiving any property to which he would ordinarily have been entitled on the intestacy of the deceased. In *Re Crippen*[49] Harvey Crippen was executed following his conviction for the murder of his wife, Cora. She had left no will. Before his execution he made a will leaving all his property to his mistress, Ethel Le Neve. The court held that Le Neve was not entitled to receive the property to which Crippen would have been entitled from his wife's estate under the rules of intestacy. The principle was again stated by Clauson J in *Re Sigsworth*:

'. . . the principle of public policy which precludes a murderer from claiming a benefit conferred on him by his victims will preclude him from claiming a benefit conferred on him, in case of his victim's intestacy, by statute.'[50]

### (d) Forfeiture of entitlement by survivorship

Where property is held by co-owners as joint tenants, the principle of survivorship (the *ius accrescendi*) operates, so that the property vests automatically in the surviving joint tenant or tenants. This will apply whether the joint tenancy is of the legal or the equitable title to property. Therefore, if Harry and Joan are the joint tenants of a house in law and in equity, and Harry dies, the title will vest automatically in Joan. It will make no difference if he had left all his property by will to charity, as the operation of survivorship takes precedence over the disposition by will. However, if Joan unlawfully killed Harry and survivorship were allowed to operate irrespective, she would benefit from her crime. Therefore, the forfeiture rule is applied and the principle of survivorship will not operate between the joint tenants.[51] In *Re K*[52] Vinelott J held that the principle of forfeiture applied so that a wife who was guilty of the manslaughter of her husband was not entitled to their jointly-owned matrimonial home by the operation of survivorship between them. Instead, she held the house on trust for herself and her

---

[47] The verdict of the coroner's jury was not conclusive, and the judge stressed that if the administrator of the estate acted upon his judgment he would have to take the risk that the assumption of fact may conceivably turn out to be erroneous.

[48] [1935] Ch 89 at 92.      [49] [1911] P 108.      [50] [1935] Ch 89 at 92.

[51] It should be noted that the rule does not deprive the killer of his or her own presumptive share under the joint tenancy.

[52] [1985] Ch 85.

husband's next of kin in equal shares as tenants-in-common.[53] Similarly, in *Dunbar v Plant*[54] the forfeiture rule prima facie excluded the operation of survivorship in respect of a jointly-owned house.

## (4) The court's jurisdiction to grant relief from forfeiture

Although the forfeiture rule prima facie applies where a person has died in consequence of a crime, under the Forfeiture Act 1982 the court has the discretion to grant relief from the effects of the rule. Section 2(1) provides that where the forfeiture rule has precluded a person who has unlawfully killed another from acquiring any interest in property: 'the court may make an order . . . modifying the effect of that rule'. This jurisdiction applies to property in the form of beneficial interests under the deceased's will, intestacy, a donatio morits causa or under a trust. The section has no application to persons convicted of murder.[55] Under s 2(2) the court may only exercise its jurisdiction to grant relief if satisfied that:

'. . . having regard to the conduct of the offender and of the deceased and to such other circumstances as appear to the court to be material, the justice of the case requires the effect of the rule to be modified in that case.'

The jurisdiction was exercised in *Re K*.[56] Vinelott J held that the discretion conferred by the Act requires the court to investigate the moral culpability of the killing, and he concluded that, because of the tragic circumstances of the case, and the fact that a loyal wife had suffered grave violence at the hands of her husband, it was appropriate for the court to grant relief so that she would not be deprived of the provision which her husband had made for her under his will or of the matrimonial home under the operation of survivorship. He also considered that it was relevant to take into account the relative financial position of persons claiming relief under the Act and those who would be entitled if the forfeiture rule was applied.

In *Dunbar v Plant*[57] the Court of Appeal also held that Miss Plant should be granted relief against forfeiture of the proceeds of Dunbar's life insurance policy, even though this was contested by his father. It was unanimously held that the approach of the first instance judge, who had sought to 'do justice between the parties', was an inappropriate approach to the exercise of the jurisdiction. The majority went on to conclude that, in the case of suicide pacts which were the result of irrational depression or desperation, total relief from forfeiture would be appropriate. Phillips LJ, with whom Hirst LJ agreed, concluded that there was nothing in the circumstances to require a different approach:

'The desperation that led Miss Plant to decide to kill herself, and which led to the suicide pact, was an irrational and tragic reaction to her predicament. I do not consider that the

---

[53]  See also *Schobelt v Barber* (1966) 60 DLR (2d) 519; *Re Pechar* [1969] NZLR 574. Although the forfeiture rule operates simply where there are only two joint tenants, it is much more complicated where there are three or more and one joint tenant kills another. For an analysis of this problem see: Gray &Gray, *Elements of Land Law* (3rd edn, 2001), p 876; *Rasmanis v Jurewitsch* [1970] 70 SRNSW 407.

[54]  [1997] 4 All ER 289.      [55]  S 5.      [56]  [1985] Ch 85, Vinelott J; affd [1986] Ch 180, CA.

[57]  [1997] 4 All ER 289.

nature of Miss Plant's conduct alters what I have indicated should be the normal approach when dealing with a suicide pact—that there should be full relief against forfeiture. The assets with which this case is concerned were in no way derived from Mr Dunbar's family. They are the fruits of insurance taken out by Mr Dunbar for the benefit of Miss Plant.'[58]

## (5) Reform of the forfeiture rule

The harsh consequences of the operation of forfeiture rule in *Re DWS (Decd)*[59] have led the Law Commission to recommend that the rule be reformed. Under the current law if a child kills an intestate parent, and is thereby disqualified from inheriting, the killer's children will also not be disinherited. The Law Commission has therefore proposed that the forfeiture rule should be replaced by a 'deemed predecease' rule, so that the property of the intestate would be distributed as if the child had died immediately before the intestate.[60] This rule would also extend to situations where the deceased had made a will and the potential heir is excluded because he or she has killed the deceased.[61] The proposals would not, however, have any application to the operation of the survivorship rule in joint tenancies since the deemed predecease rule would be confined to the construction of the intestacy legislation and of wills.[62]

# 3 Constructive trust arising from a specifically enforceable contract to sell property

From the very moment that a vendor enters a specifically enforceable contract to sell property, he holds it on constructive trust for the purchaser. The reason for the imposition of the trust in these circumstances is that the contract of sale renders the vendor subject to an obligation to transfer the property to the purchaser which will be enforced in equity by means of the remedy of specific performance. By applying the maxim that 'equity treats as done that which ought to be done', the constructive trust ensures that the purchaser is entitled to the equitable interest immediately, even though he will not become the full absolute owner until the vendor transfers the legal title in fulfillment of the contract. The operation of such constructive trusts was explained in *Lysaght v Edwards*[63] by Jessel MR:

'. . . the moment you have a valid contract for sale the vendor becomes in equity a trustee for the purchaser of the estate sold, and the beneficial ownership passes to the purchaser . . .'[64] Such constructive trusts will most commonly arise in the context of contracts for the

---

[58] [1997] 4 All ER 289 at 313.     [59] [2001] Ch 568.

[60] *The Forfeiture Rule and the Law of Succession*, Law Comm No 295 (2005), para 1.14–1.15.

[61] Ibid, para 1.16.     [62] Ibid, para 2.29.

[63] (1876) 2 Ch D 499; see also *Haywood v Cope* (1858) 25 Beav 140.

[64] Compare *Rayner v Preston* (1880–81) LR 18 Ch D 1, CA, where Brett LJ held that a trust did not arise; *KLDE Pty Ltd v Stamp Duties Comr (Queensland)* (1984) 155 CLR 288.

purchase of land.[65] The majority of contracts for the purchase of personal property are not specifically enforceable because the subject matter is not unique. However, if specific performance would be available, a constructive trust will arise. Such a constructive trust was found to have arisen in *Oughtred v IRC*,[66] which involved a contract for the sale of shares in a private company. This decision was reaffirmed by the Court of Appeal in *Neville v Wilson*.[67]

From the moment of contract, a genuine trust relationship is created, so that the vendor holds the title of the property on trust for the purchaser. His duties are not the same as those of an ordinary trustee,[68] for example he is entitled to retain profits arising from the property before completion of the contract.[69] However, he is under a duty to 'use reasonable care to preserve the property in a reasonable state of preservation'.[70]

## 4 Constructive trust arising from mutual wills

It is a fundamental principle that a man is entitled to make a will leaving his property to whomsoever he chooses. Any will he makes remains revocable until his death. However, if two persons enter into a contract to execute wills in a common form, and the survivor subsequently changes his will, the court will impose a constructive trust on the property in the hands of the executors of the survivor in favour of the beneficiaries of the mutual wills. The doctrine of mutual wills is fully considered in Chapter 11.

## 5 Constructive trust arising because a purchaser of land has expressly agreed to take subject to the interests of a third party

One of the central objectives of land law is to determine whether a transferee of land is bound by third party interests in the land which were valid against the transferor. Where title to the land is registered, the equitable doctrine of notice has been replaced by a scheme of registration.[71] Lesser interests must be protected by means of an entry

---

[65] Eg *Green v Smith* (1738) 1 Atk 572; *Rose v Watson* (1864) 10 HL Cas 672; *Appleton v Aspin* [1988] 1 WLR 410, CA.

[66] [1960] AC 206. See also *Re Holt's Settlement* [1969] 1 Ch 100.

[67] [1996] 3 All ER 171; (1996) 55 CLJ 436 (Nolan); [1996] Conv 368 (Thompson).

[68] *Shaw v Foster* (1872) LR 5 HL 321; *Earl of Egmont v Smith* (1877) 6 Ch D 469; *Royal Bristol Permanent Building Society v Bomash* (1887) LR 35 Ch D 390; *Cumberland Consolidated Holdings Ltd v Ireland* [1946] KB 264; *Engelwood Properties v Patel* [2005] 3 All ER 307.

[69] *Cuddon v Tite* (1858) 1 Giff 395.

[70] *Clarke v Ramuz* [1891] 2 QB 456 at 459–460, per Lord Coleridge CJ. See also *Royal Bristol Permanent Building Society v Bomash* (1887) LR 35 Ch D 390; *Phillips v Lamdin* [1949] 2 KB 33; *Lucie-Smith v Gorman* [1981] CLY 2866.

[71] Stevens and Pearce, *Land Law* (3rd edn, 2005), pp 63–84.

on the register of the title to which they relate. If an interest is unprotected, a transferee for valuable consideration of the legal title will acquire the land free from it,[72] unless it is an 'overriding interest'[73] in which case it will bind the transferee irrespective.

However, it has been held that if a transferee of the land expressly agrees that he will honour the rights of a third party, he will be bound by those rights under a constructive trust even though it had not been properly protected on the register. This constructive trust prevents the purchaser taking advantage of his strict rights under the statute. Such a constructive trust was held to have arisen in *Lyus v Prowsa Developments.*[74] Mr and Mrs Lyus entered a contract to purchase a house which was to be built on a new estate. The developers subsequently went into liquidation and the bank which held a mortgage of the land sold it to another developer. This second developer agreed in the contract to take the land 'subject to, but with the benefit of the contract made with Mr and Mrs Lyus'. This developer subsequently sold the land to a third, who agreed to the same terms. The contract entered between the first developer and Mr and Mrs Lyus was an interest in land which should have been protected on the register as a minor interest. Even though it had not been protected appropriately, Dillon J held that the developers who had purchased the land were bound by it. They had expressly agreed to take subject to the interest and therefore a constructive trust was raised to 'counter unconscionable conduct or fraud'.[75] Dillon J stressed that the agreement was not a general agreement to take the land subject to possible encumbrances but a positive stipulation in favour of a particular identified interest. A similar position was adopted by the Australian High Court in *Bahr v Nicolay (No 2).*[76]

The operation of such constructive trust was further considered in *Ashburn Anstalt v Arnold.*[77] The Court of Appeal addressed, obiter, the question whether a purchaser could be bound by a constructive trust when he had expressly agreed to acquire land subject to a third party's contractual licence. Citing *Lyus v Prowsa Developments,*[78] the court accepted that a constructive trust could arise in such circumstances, but stated that 'the court will not impose a constructive trust unless it is satisfied that the conscience of the estate owner is affected'.[79] The mere fact that land was expressly said to be conveyed 'subject to' a contractual right would not suffice alone:

'We do not think it is desirable that constructive trusts of land should be imposed in reliance on inference from slender materials.'[80]

It was suggested that other factors would be necessary to justify the imposition of a constructive trust, for example evidence that the purchaser paid a lower price for the land as a consequence of the express agreement to take subject to the interest. The

---

[72] Land Registration Act 2002, s 29.   [73] Land Registration Act 2002, Sch.3.
[74] [1982] 1 WLR 1044.   [75] [1982] 1 WLR 1044 at 1052.
[76] (1988) 78 ALR 1. Compare, however, *Hollington Bros v Rhodes* [1951] 2 All ER 578n, where a different conclusion was reached concerning an unregistered charge under the Land Charges Act 1925. See now the Land Charges Act 1972.
[77] [1989] Ch 1; [1988] Cov 201 (Thompson); (1988) 51 MLR 226 (Hill); (1988) 104 LQR 175 (Sparkes).
[78] [1982] 1 WLR 1044.   [79] [1989] Ch 1 at 25.   [80] [1989] Ch 1 at 26.

essence of the constructive trust is the purchaser's voluntary acceptance of obligations in favour of the third party.[81]

# 6  Constructive trusts arising through a common intention to share the ownership of land[82]

One of the most significant areas of operation of the doctrine of constructive trusts in the post-war period has been in the context of land ownership. Constructive trusts provide a means by which a person may obtain a share of the ownership of land despite the lack of any express declaration of trust in his favour, or where he has failed to make a substantial contribution to the purchase price this giving rise to a presumed resulting trust. The circumstances in which land will be subject to a constructive trust were identified by the House of Lords in *Gissing v Gissing*,[83] where Lord Diplock stated:

'A . . . constructive trust . . . is created by a transaction between the trustee and the [beneficiary] in connection with the acquisition by the trustee of a legal estate in land, whenever the trustee has so conducted himself that it would be inequitable to allow him to deny to the [beneficiary] a beneficial interest in the land acquired.'

Many of the reported cases concerning such constructive trusts have sought to define the precise circumstances in which it should be regarded as 'inequitable' not to impose a trust on the legal owner of land.

## (1)  The social context of constructive trusts of land[84]

The development of the principles by which a constructive trust will be imposed on the legal owner of land requires an understanding of the social circumstances in which they emerged. They evolved primarily to take account of post-war changes in society, including the massive increase in owner-occupation, and especially to challenge traditional attitudes towards women and their ownership of property. During the first half of the century the majority of matrimonial homes were purchased in the sole name of the husband, who generally worked to provide the family income while the wife brought up their children and took care of the domestic needs of the family. Divorce was less common and it was often unnecessary to determine whether the wife had any independent interest in the property. However, the increasing recognition of the equal

---

[81] There is a clear analogy with cases such as *Bannister v Bannister* [1948] 2 All ER 133 and *Binions v Evans* [1972] Ch 359. See also McFarlane, 'Constructive Trusts Arising on a Receipt of Property *Sub Conditione*' (2004) 120 LQR 667.

[82] See: Mee, *The Property Rights of Cohabitees* (1999); Hopkins, *The Informal Acquisition of Rights in Land* (2000); Megarry & Wade, *The Law of Real Property* (6th edn, 2001) pp 544–558; Gray & Gray, *Elements of Land Law* (3rd edn, 2001) pp 725–760; Stevens and Pearce, *Land Law* (2nd edn, 2000), pp 182–204.

[83] [1971] AC 886 at 905.

[84] See A J H Morris QC, 'Equity's Reaction to Modern Domestic Relationships' in Oakley, *Trends in Contemporary Trust Law* (1996).

place of women, their growing economic contribution to marriage through their participation in the labour market, and especially the growth in divorce, made it essential to determine when a wife enjoyed a share of the ownership of her matrimonial home. This was particularly important in the context of divorce, since under the regime in place at that time the court possessed no jurisdiction to divide the matrimonial property between the parties. If the husband was the sole owner of the matrimonial home, it would remain his on divorce.

In these circumstances it was often difficult for a wife to establish any entitlement to a share of the ownership of the matrimonial home. There was unlikely to be any expressly declared trust in her favour. She may have been entitled to some interest by way of a resulting trust if she had made a financial contribution to the purchase price of the house, where the share of the ownership gained would be proportional to the contribution made.[85] Since in most cases a house could only be purchased by means of a mortgage, the majority of the purchase price would have been provided from the husband's income. Against this background, it came to be seen that the reality of most marriages was one of co-operation as an economic unit. The division of labour between domestic responsibility and work should not automatically deprive a wife of a share of the ownership of her matrimonial home. Despite the conveyance of the house into the husband's name alone, there was an element of expectation that the property would be shared. The courts developed the doctrine of the constructive trust to give effect to a wife's interest in such circumstances. The possibility of a constructive trust was recognised by the House of Lords in two leading authorities in the early 1970s, *Pettitt v Pettitt*[86] and *Gissing v Gissing*.[87] Subsequent legislative reforms in the family law context have rendered the constructive trust a less significant mechanism for ensuring that a wife is entitled to a share of the ownership of her matrimonial home. The court was given jurisdiction to make orders adjusting the property rights of couples on divorce under the Matrimonial Causes Act 1973. The Civil Partnerships Act 2004 has now extended a similar jurisdiction to same-sex couples who have registered as civil parents. However, the courts have no such power where heterosexual couples are cohabiting but are not married, or where homosexual couples are cohabiting but have not registered their relationship as a civil partnership. With increasing numbers of couples choosing to live together rather than marry it seems inevitable that the property rights of many cohabitees will fall to be determined by the principles of resulting and constructive trusts.[88] Difficulties are most likely to emerge at the end of a relationship where a couple have failed to take legal steps to clarify how their shared home is to be owned. Recent evidence suggests that most cohabiting couples do not appreciate the need to take steps to clarify the ownership of their shared home because they mistakenly believe the 'common law marriage myth', that they have the same rights as married couples,[89]

Even where parties are married, resulting and constructive trusts will be significant if a spouse is claiming an equitable interest enjoying priority over the subsequently

---

[85] See Chapter 8.  [86] [1970] AC 777.  [87] [1971] AC 886.

[88] The same will obviously be the case where the parties are a homosexual couple: See eg the Australian case *W v G* (1996) 20 Fam LR 49 (NSW Supreme Court); (1997) 113 LQR 227 (Bailey-Harris).

[89] Barlow, Duncan, James, Park, *Cohabitation, Marriage and the Law* (2005);. See also [2005] Conv 555 (Cooke).

acquired interests of a third party, often a mortgagee of the land.[90] The courts have tended to restrict the circumstances in which a constructive trust can arise, and also the rules by which such an interest can gain priority, in order to prevent severe adverse consequences for banks and other mortgage lenders.[91]

The complexity of home ownership and occupation in modern British society was recognised by the Law Commission in its recent discussion paper 'Sharing Homes'.[92] The Commission summarised as follows:

'By the year 2000 seven out of ten homes in England were owned by one or more of their occupiers. Over the last quarter of a century, living arrangements within those homes have become increasingly diverse, and greater numbers of people are now living together in circumstances which are characterized by informality. While marriage remains popular, cohabitation outside of marriage continues to grow, and, as has been observed, statistics based solely on the marital status of the parties give "an increasingly incomplete picture of relationships and family circumstances" Moreover, the notion of the "traditional" family, based on one or two parents and their children living together in one unit, does not make allowance for multi-generational living arrangements within a family, where a home which may be legally owned by the head of the family is occupied by siblings, children, grand-children, and possibly even great grand-children, many of whom may be adults. As the population ages, there are many elderly siblings or friends who live together for comfort and companionship, and adult children who move in with their elderly parents to provide day-to-day care and support.'[93]

The sheer range of the circumstances in which home-sharing may occur led the Law Commission to conclude that it would be impossible to devise a statutory scheme for the determination of interests in the shared home which would operate fairly and evenly across all the diverse circumstances which are now to be encountered.[94]

Whilst many of the cases in which constructive trust principles have been developed have concerned the ownership of residential property, they are equally applicable in respect of commercial property. Thus in *Banner Homes v Luff Developments Ltd*[95] the Court of Appeal held that a constructive trust arose where two development companies had an understanding that they would form a joint venture to acquire a site and one of them subsequently acquired the site alone, because the other company had acted to its detriment by agreeing to stay out of the market for the site.

## (2) Identifying inequitable conduct

### (a) Competing objectives of justice and certainty

As has been noted, it has proved difficult to provide a workable definition of the conduct which will justify the subjection of land to a constructive trust. Central to this

---

[90] *Williams & Glyn's Bank Ltd v Boland* [1981] AC 487; *Kingsnorth Finance v Tizard* [1986] 1 WLR 783.

[91] See *City of London Building Society v Flegg* [1988] AC 54; *Abbey National Building Society v Cann* [1991] 1 AC 56

[92] See Mee, 'Property rights and personal relationships: reflections on reform' (2004) 24 LS 414.

[93] Law. Com No 278 (2002), para 1.7.

[94] See also the analysis of the concept of the 'family home' in Fox, 'Creditors and the concept of "family home": a functional analysis' (2005) 25 LS 201.

[95] [2000] 2 All ER 117.

difficulty is the inherent tension between the competing legal objectives of achieving justice between the parties and providing sufficient certainty to enable the conduct of commercial transactions. If justice between the parties were paramount, the courts should perhaps impose a constructive trust whenever this seems equitable, or fair. However, land is also an important marketable commodity and purchasers and mortgagees must be able to be protected from the danger of an undetectable and unexpected constructive trust gaining priority over their interests.

## (b) The 'new model' constructive trust

During the 1970s Lord Denning MR advocated a novel approach whereby a constructive trust should be imposed simply to achieve perceived justice between the parties. He described this principle as a 'New Model' constructive trust.[96] In *Hussey v Palmer* he expounded the nature and operation of such a trust:

'. . . it is a trust imposed by law whenever justice and good conscience require it. It is a liberal process, founded on large principles of equity, to be applied in cases where the defendant cannot conscientiously keep the property for himself alone, but ought to allow another to have the property or a share in it. The trust may arise at the outset when the property is acquired, or later on, as the circumstances may require. It is an equitable remedy by which the court can enable an aggrieved party to obtain restitution.'[97]

In essence, the 'new model' constructive trust was a trust imposed to achieve restitution, in other words to prevent the legal owner of land being unjustly enriched by refusing to acknowledge that the beneficiary was entitled to an interest. The 'new model' constructive trust was derived from the American model of constructive trusts, as stated in the Restatement of Restitution:

'Where a person holding title to property is subject to an equitable duty to convey it to another on the ground that he would be unjustly enriched if he were permitted to retain it, a constructive trust arises.'[98]

Lord Denning even claimed that in advocating the 'new model' constructive trust he was merely extending the concept that had been approved by the House of Lords in *Gissing v Gissing*. In *Eves v Eves*[99] he stated:

'Equity is not past the age of child bearing. One of her latest progeny is a constructive trust of a new model. Lord Diplock brought it into the world[100] and we have nourished it . . .'

However, on careful reading, his citation of Lord Diplock's comments was extremely selective and, as will be seen below, the House of Lords did not suggest anything approximating to the 'new model' constructive trust.

---

[96] *Eves v Eves* [1975] 1 WLR 1338 at 1341. See also *Binions v Evans* [1972] Ch 359; *Cooke v Head (No 1)* [1972] 1 WLR 518; *Hussey v Palmer* [1972] 1 WLR 1286.

[97] *Hussey v Palmer* [1972] 3 All ER 744 at 747; (1973) 37 Conv (Hayton); (1973) 89 LQR 2; (1973) 32 CLJ 41 (Fairest); (1973) 36 MLR 426 (Ridley); (1973) 26 CLP 17 (Oakley); (1978) 8 Sydney LR 578 (Davies).

[98] Para 16.    [99] [1975] 1 WLR 1338.    [100] In *Gissing v Gissing* [1971] AC 886.

## (c) Judicial rejection of the new model constructive trust

Despite Lord Denning's attempt to mould the constructive trust into a wide remedy available to do justice and prevent unjust enrichment, the 'new model' constructive trust has been comprehensively rejected by the English courts. The main objection has been the absence of a coherent principle by which it can be decided whether the imposition of a constructive trust is warranted in any particular situation, which would lead to uncertainty and unpredictability in proprietary rights. After Lord Denning had retired, the Court of Appeal held in a number of cases that, whilst the actual decisions where he had advocated the 'new model' constructive trust could be justified on other grounds, it was inconsistent with earlier authorities. For example, in *Grant v Edwards* [101] Nourse LJ suggested that Lord Denning's decision in *Eves v Eves* [102] had been 'at variance with the principles stated in *Gissing v Gissing*'. [103]

The main objection raised against the new model constructive trust was the fear that such an approach to proprietary entitlements would create uncertainty, and that decisions would depend on the personal moral feelings of the individual judge. This danger was clearly expressed by Bagnall J in *Cowcher v Cowcher*, [104] where he considered the argument that injustice could result from the narrow criteria required for a constructive trust by the House of Lords in *Pettitt v Pettitt* [105] and *Gissing v Gissing*: [106]

'In any individual case the application of these propositions may produce a result which appears unfair. So be it; in my view, that is not an injustice. I am convinced that in determining rights, particularly property rights, the only justice that can be attained by mortals, who are fallible and are not omniscient, is justice according to law; the justice which flows from the application of sure and settled principles to proved or admitted facts. So in the field of equity the length of the Chancellor's foot has been measured or is capable of measurement. This does not mean that equity is past the age of child bearing: simply that its progeny must be legitimate—by precedent out of principle. It is well that this should be so; otherwise no lawyer could safely advise on his client's title and every quarrel would lead to a law suit.'

This attitude was echoed in *Springette v Defoe*, [107] where Dillon LJ proclaimed:

'The court does not as yet sit, as under a palm tree, to exercise a general discretion to do what the man in the street, on a general overview of the case, might regard as fair.'

The new model constructive trust was also initially rejected by some Commonwealth jurisdictions on similar grounds of uncertainty and lack of principle. In Australia, *Allen v Snyder* [108] doubted whether the new model constructive trust could be supported from *Gissing v Gissing*, [109] and the High Court rejected it in *Muschinski v Dodds*. [110] In New Zealand the 'new model' constructive trust was described in *Carly v Farrelly* [111] by Mahon J:

'... a supposed rule of equity which is not only vague in its outline but which must

---

[101] [1986] Ch 638 at 647.    [102] [1975] 1 WLR 1338.    [103] [1971] AC 886.
[104] [1972] 1 WLR 425 at 430.    [105] [1970] AC 777.    [106] [1971] AC 886.
[107] [1992] 2 FLR 388 at 393.    [108] [1977] 2 NSWLR 685.    [109] [1971] AC 886.
[110] (1985) 160 CLR 583, 62 ALR 429 at 452.
[111] [1975] 1 NZLR 356; (1978) 94 LQR 347 (Samuels). See also *Avondale Printers & Stationers Ltd v Haggie* [1979] 2 NZLR 124.

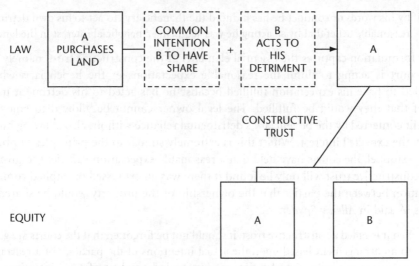

The 'common intention' constructive trust

disqualify itself from acceptance as a valid principle of jurisprudence by its total uncertainty of application and result.'

It is somewhat ironic that these jurisdictions have subsequently adopted forms of constructive trust which are imposed as remedies to prevent 'unjust enrichment' similar to the new model constructive trust as Lord Denning described it.[112]

Despite the seemingly universal rejection of the 'new model' constructive trust, in the recent case of *Oxley v Hiscock*[113] the Court of Appeal held that where the parties had a common intention to share the ownership of a property, but had not reached a common intention as to the proportions in which they should share the beneficial ownership, the court should award them such shares as it 'considers to be fair having regard to the whole course of dealings between them in relation to the property.'[114] However whilst this language seems similar to that of the 'new model' constructive trust, the element of discretion applies only to the determination of the extent of the beneficial interests of the parties, and not to the question whether there should be a constructive trust at all. A constructive trust will not be imposed by the court simply because it believes that it would be just and fair to do so. A constructive trust will only arise if certain criteria are satisfied.

## (d) Criteria prerequisite to the establishment of a constructive trust

Although the House of Lords held in *Gissing v Gissing*[115] that a constructive trust should be imposed whenever it is 'inequitable' for a legal owner to deny the beneficiary an equitable interest in land, it was further stated that such inequitability would only occur in closely-defined circumstances. Lord Diplock emphasised that a legal owner would only have acted so as to justify the imposition of a constructive trust:

---

[112] See below, p 318.   [113] [2004] 3 All ER 703.   [114] Ibid at [69].   [115] [1971] AC 886.

'. . . if by his words or conduct he has induced the [beneficiary] to act to his own detriment in the reasonable belief that by so acting he was acquiring a beneficial interest in the land.'[116]

This formulation captures the essential elements of the constructive trust, namely that the court is acting to fulfill the reasonable expectations of the beneficiary, who is entitled to have his expectation fulfilled because he has acted to his detriment in the belief that they would be fulfilled. The legal owner cannot be allowed to enjoy the benefit conferred by the beneficiary's detrimental reliance without also allowing him to enjoy the expected interest. Whilst this is extremely similar to the principles of proprietary estoppel, the courts have held that a reasonable expectation sufficient to give rise to a constructive trust will only be found if there was an expressed or implied common intention between the parties that the ownership of the property would be shared. As Glass JA said in *Allen v Snyder*:

'. . . when it is called a constructive trust, it should not be forgotten that the courts are giving effect to an arrangement based upon the actual intentions of the parties, not a rearrangement in accordance with considerations of justice, independent of their intentions and founded upon their respective behaviour in relation to the matrimonial home.'[117]

In English law two essential criteria are prerequisites of the establishment of a constructive trust. These criteria were re-affirmed in *Lloyds Bank plc v Rosset*,[118] the most recent decision of the House of Lords.

*(i) Common intention.* A constructive trust will only be established where the parties shared a common intention to share the ownership of the land concerned. This intention may either have been expressed, or the court may find that such an intention can be implied from their conduct.

*(ii) Detrimental reliance.* The mere fact of a common intention does not alone establish a constructive trust. The party claiming a beneficial interest by way of a constructive trust must demonstrate that he significantly altered his position or acted to his detriment on the basis of the common intention.

## (3) Establishing a 'common intention' constructive trust

### (a) *Lloyds Bank plc v Rosset*[119]

The most significant recent decision concerning the operation of constructive trusts of land is *Lloyds Bank plc v Rosset*, in which the House of Lords provided a framework for determining when such trusts will arise. The case concerned a married couple, and the central issue was whether the wife had acquired an interest in her matrimonial home by way of a constructive trust which was capable of gaining priority over a legal mortgage of the house which the husband had granted to a bank.

Mr and Mrs Rosset were married in 1972. In 1982 Mr Rosset became entitled to a substantial sum of money under a trust fund established by his grandmother in

---

[116] [1971] AC 886 at 905.   [117] [1977] 2 NSWLR 685 at 693.   [118] [1991] 1 AC 107.
[119] [1991] 1 AC 107.

Switzerland. They found a house which required complete renovation. It was purchased for £57,500 in the sole name of Mr Rosset because the Swiss trustee had refused to advance the money for a purchase in joint names. The cost of the renovation work was also provided by Mr Rosset alone, so that his wife made no direct financial contribution to the purchase. Mrs Rosset had, however, helped with the renovation work. She had decorated some bedrooms and prepared others for decoration. She had also supervised the work of builders who were carrying out the renovation work. In the light of this she claimed to be entitled to a share of the ownership by way of a constructive trust.[120] The judge at first instance held that, although there was no express agreement that Mrs Rosset was intended to enjoy a share of the beneficial ownership, he could infer a common intention to share from the fact that she had assisted with the renovations, as this had been work 'upon which she could not reasonably have been expected to embark unless she was to have an interest in the house'. However, the House of Lords held that no such intention could be inferred from the work she had done, and that, in the absence of an express common intention, no constructive trust had arisen in her favour and Mr Rosset remained the absolute owner of the house. In consequence, Mrs Rosset had no proprietary interest which could take priority over the rights of the mortgagee bank.

The significance of the decision lies beyond the mere conclusion that Mrs Rosset did not enjoy any interest by way of a constructive trust. Lord Bridge, with whom the other members of the House of Lords agreed, expounded the meaning and practical requirements of the concepts of 'common intention' and 'detriment', thus delimiting the scope of the constructive trust.

## (b) Common intention

A constructive trust will only be established if it can be demonstrated that there was a common intention between the parties that the ownership of the land was to be shared. Where such a common intention was present, the constructive trust arises to ensure that it is carried into effect in equity, even though legal title to the land was vested in only one of the parties.

Establishing the presence of a common intention is often the greatest hurdle to establishing a constructive trust. In *Grant v Edwards*[121] Nourse LJ observed that in most cases 'the fundamental, and invariably the most difficult, question to decide is whether there was the necessary common intention'.[122] In *Lloyds Bank plc v Rosset*[123] Lord Bridge recognised that one barrier to the establishment of a common intention is that 'spouses living in amity will not normally think it necessary to formulate or define their respective interests in the property in any precise way'. Although the expectation of the parties to a happy marriage is generally that they will share the practical benefits of occupying

---

[120]  The issue did not arise on a divorce of the parties, where it would have been open to the court to adjust their interests in the property. Instead, Mr Rosset had mortgaged the property without his wife's consent, and she was seeking to establish an overriding interest under s 70(1)(g) which would bind the bank and therefore prevent them from enforcing the sale of the house. To establish the overriding interest, Mrs Rosset would have to show that she had an interest in the property, which she claimed to have by way of a constructive trust. See Stevens and Pearce *Land Law* (2nd edn, 2001), pp 182–201.

[121]  [1986] Ch 638.    [122]  [1986] Ch 638 at 647.    [123]  [1991] 1 AC 107.

the matrimonial home, whoever owns it, he maintained that this is not identical to a common intention to sharing the ownership of the property. A true common intention to share ownership sufficient to found a constructive trust may be established either from the expressed sentiments of the parties or by inference from their conduct.

*(i) Express common intention.* Lord Bridge stated that a constructive trust can be established where the parties expressly agreed that the ownership of he land was to be shared:

'The first and fundamental question which must always be resolved is whether independently of any inference to be drawn from the conduct of the parties in the course of sharing the house as their home and managing their joint affairs, there has at any time prior to acquisition, or exceptionally at some later date, been any agreement, arrangement or understanding reached between them that the property is to be shared beneficially.'[124]

It will be a question of fact in each case whether the parties had reached such an express common intention. In *Stack v Dowden*,[125] for example, a couple purchased a property in their joint names and included in the transfer a declaration that 'the survivor of them is entitled to give a valid receipt for capital money arising from a disposition of all or part of the property.' The Court of Appeal held that this declaration did not disclose an express common intention, because other authorities have held that such a declaration cannot be regarded as a declaration of trust of the property.[126] Whilst it is binding upon the parties as against a purchaser of the land, it does not determine the beneficial interest between them.[127]

It will be harder to establish such an intention if the circumstances prima facie render it less likely that such an agreement had been reached. For example, Mrs Rosset claimed that in conversations with her husband it had been expressly agreed that the house was to be jointly owned. Lord Bridge considered that, given that Mr Rosset had provided the whole purchase price and the cost of renovation, a high standard of evidence would have been required to establish this claim:

'Mrs Rosset would . . . have encountered formidable difficulty in establishing her claim to joint beneficial ownership . . . In these circumstances, it would have required very cogent evidence to establish that it was the Rossets' common intention to defeat the evident purpose of the Swiss trustee's restriction by acquiring the property in Mr Rosset's name alone but to treat it nevertheless as beneficially owned jointly by both spouses.'[128]

In the event, the judge at first instance had held that there was no express agreement and the House of Lords merely confirmed this.

Where a genuine express agreement to share the ownership of land is found, in substance the legal owner has expressly declared, or agreed to declare, a trust in favour of the claimant. However such a declaration would be merely oral and therefore

---

[124] [1991] 1 AC 107 at 132.      [125] [2005] EWCA Civ 857; [2005] Conv 555 (Cooke).

[126] On the authority of *Huntingford v Hobbs* [1993] 1 FLR 736 and *Harwood v Harwood* [1991] 2 FLR 274.

[127] Although there was no express common intention, a constructive trust could be found because the parties had contributed to the purchase price of the property, and therefore a common intention could be inferred.

[128] [1991] 1 AC 107 at 128.

ineffective to create an enforceable trust due to the absence of compliance with the formality requirements of s 53(1)(b) of the Law of Property Act 1925.[129] Although there is no enforceable express declaration of trust, a constructive trust will be imposed if the claimant acted to her detriment on the basis of the express agreement, as it would be inequitable to allow the legal owner to deny a trust which would give effect to his intentions.

Lord Bridge considered that the earlier cases of *Eves v Eves*[130] and *Grant v Edwards*[131] were 'outstanding examples'[132] of constructive trusts created through an express common intention. In *Eves v Eves*[133] an unmarried couple, Janet and Stuart Eves,[134] moved to a new house. It was purchased solely in the name of Stuart, who told Janet that it was to be their house, and a home for themselves and their children. He also told her that the purchase could not be completed in their joint names because she was under 21, but that if she had been of age it would have been purchased in their joint names. In *Grant v Edwards*[135] a man purchased a house in his name alone to provide a home for himself and his lover. He told her that he had not purchased it in their joint names because that would prejudice her divorce proceedings.

However in both of these cases the supposed 'common intention' was in reality merely an appearance of common intention. Neither of the male parties genuinely wished their partners to enjoy a share of the ownership of their respective houses. Better examples of a true common intention can be found in the more recent cases of *Yaxley v Gotts* and *Banner Homes plc v Luff Developments Ltd*. In *Yaxley v Gotts*,[136] a case which was in fact decided on the grounds of proprietary estoppel, the Court of Appeal held that a constructive trust could have been established where a builder had carried out work to convert and refurbish a house into flats on the basis of an oral understanding that he would acquire the ground floor flat. In *Banner Homes plc v Luff Developments Ltd*[137] the Court of Appeal held that a constructive trust arose where two development companies reached an understanding that they would acquire a site as a joint venture, but one went ahead and developed the site alone.

In *Drake v Whipp*,[138] the Court of Appeal stressed that the principles identified in *Lloyds Bank plc v Rosset* did not require the parties to have reached a common intention 'as to the respective shares to be taken by the beneficial owners',[139] as this was impossible in the light of *Gissing v Gissing*.[140] Peter Gibson LJ stated:

'All that is required for the creation of a constructive trust is that there should be a common intention that the party who is not the legal owner should have a beneficial interest and that that party should act to his or her detriment in reliance thereon.'[141]

*(ii) Inferred common intention.* The absence of an express common intention is not necessarily fatal to the establishment of a constructive trust. In fact, in *Midland Bank*

---

[129] Law of Property Act 1925.   [130] [1975] 1 WLR 1338.   [131] [1986] Ch 638.

[132] [1991] 1 AC 107 at 133. See also *Hammond v Mitchell* [1992] 2 All ER 109.

[133] [1975] 1 WLR 1338.

[134] Although they shared the same name, they were unmarried. She had changed her name to his by deed poll.

[135] [1986] Ch 638.   [136] [2000] Ch 162.   [137] [2000] 2 All ER 117.

[138] [1996] 1 FLR 826.   [139] [1996] 1 FLR 826 at 830, per Peter Gibson LJ.   [140] [1971] AC 886.

[141] [1996] 1 FLR 826 at 830.

*plc v Cooke*[142] the Court of Appeal held that it was possible to infer a common intention even where the evidence proved that the parties had made no express agreement concerning the ownership property. Waite LJ explained that a wife was able to establish an interest in her matrimonial home by way of a constructive trust even though there had been no discussions between herself and her husband as to how the property should be owned when it was purchased in his name alone:

'It would be anomalous . . . to create a range of home-buyers who were beyond the pale of equity's assistance in formulating a fair presumed basis for sharing of beneficial title, simply because they had been honest enough to admit that they never gave ownership a thought or reached any agreement about it.'[143]

In *Lloyds Bank plc v Rosset* Lord Bridge made clear that in some circumstances the parties' conduct will alone entitle the court to infer that they held a common intention to share the ownership of property:

'. . . where there is no evidence to support a finding of an agreement or arrangement to share . . . the court must rely entirely on the conduct of the parties both as the basis from which to infer a common intention to share the property beneficially and as the conduct relied on to give rise to a constructive trust.'[144]

The claimant's conduct may thus be relevant in two distinct senses. First, it may constitute the evidence from which it can be inferred that there was a common intention to share the beneficial ownership. Secondly, it will also constitute the detrimental reliance which requires that intention to be carried into effect by the court recognising that the land is subject to a constructive trust.

Since the conduct of the parties may alone lead to the establishment of a constructive trust, it is vitally important to determine the type of conduct which the court will consider sufficient to give rise to the inference of a common intention. In *Lloyds Bank plc v Rosset* the House of Lords significantly concluded that a common intention should only be inferred where a claimant had made direct contributions to the purchase price of the property concerned. Lord Bridge stated that in circumstances where a common intent would have to be inferred:

'. . . direct contributions to the purchase price by the partner who is not the legal owner, whether initially or by payment of mortgage installments, will readily justify the inference necessary to the creation of a constructive trust. But, as I read the authorities, it is at least extremely doubtful whether anything less will do.'[145]

A common intention can be inferred from such a direct contribution to the purchase price because it is assumed that the contributor would not have made a contribution unless he was expecting to gain a share of the ownership of the property. This requirement of a direct financial contribution has not been altered by the more recent decision of the Court of Appeal in *Oxley v Hiscock*,[146] as this decision relates only to the quantifi-

---

[142] [1995] 4 All ER 562.     [143] [1995] 4 All ER 562 at 575.
[144] [1991] 1 AC 107 at 132–133.     [145] [1991] 1 AC 107 at 133. See *Burns v Burns* [1984] Ch 317.
[146] [2004] 3 All ER 703.

cation of the beneficial interest where a common intention has been established, and not to the issue of whether a common intention may be inferred in the first place.[147]

It is therefore clear that a common intention will be inferred in circumstances where a presumption of resulting trust might have arisen. Thus a common intention will be inferred where a person has made a financial contribution to the purchase of the property, has enabled the property to be purchased at a discounted price,[148] or had increased the value of the property by undertaking or contributing to the cost of significant improvements.[149] However relatively insignificant improvements will not be sufficient to give rise to an inference of a common intention. In *Lloyds Bank plc v Rosset* itself, the House of Lords held that Mrs Rosset's assistance with the decoration of the house 'could not possibly justify' the inference of a common intention that she was to gain a share of the ownership thereof:

'. . . Mrs Rosset was extremely anxious that the new matrimonial home should be ready for occupation before Christmas if possible. In these circumstances it would seem the most natural thing in the world for any wife, in the absence of her husband abroad, to spend all the time she could spare and to employ any skills she might have, such as the ability to decorate a room, in doing all she could to accelerate progress of the work quite irrespective of any expectation she might have of enjoying a beneficial interest in the property.'[150]

The monetary value of her work, in the light of a total purchase price exceeding £70,000, was also said to have been 'so trifling as to be almost de minimis'.[151] Cases subsequent to *Lloyds Bank plc v Rosset* have also held that the words of Lord Bridge requiring a 'direct financial contribution to the purchase price' should not be interpreted so strictly as to exclude the possibility of an inference of a common intention where a person has contributed to the payment of household expenses and this has enabled the legal owner to pay the mortgage. In *Le Foe v Le Foe*[152] Nicholas Mostyn QC held that the financial contributions of a couple to the acquisition of their home should be viewed as a whole, so that a wife's contributions towards the household expenses could be regarded as an indirect contribution to the purchase price of the property:

'Although I am sure that H earned more than W . . . I have no doubt that the family economy depended for its function on W's earnings. It was an arbitrary allocation of responsibility that he paid the mortgage, service charge and outgoings, whereas W paid for

---

[147] *Lightfoot v Lightfoot-Browne* [2005] EWCA Civ 201.

[148] As was the case in *Oxley v Hiscock* [2004] 3 All ER 703.

[149] Note that s 65 of the Civil Partnerships Act 2004 expressly provides that a civil partner who contributes in money or money's worth to the improvement of property will be entitled to a share, or an increased share, of the beneficial ownership of the property, either on the basis of what may have been agreed between the parties, or in default of such agreement on the basis of what may seem just to the court in all the circumstances.

[150] [1991] 1 AC 107 at 131.

[151] See also *W v G* (1996) 20 Fam LR 49; (1997) 113 LQR 227 (Bailey-Harris)—where the NSW Supreme Court held that a contribution of $500 towards the deposit of a house was de minimis and therefore incapable of establishing an interest by way of a constructive trust. Contrast, however, *Midland Bank plc v Cooke* [1995] 4 All ER 562, where a small contribution to the purchase price of property derived from a joint gift was sufficient to establish a common intention.

[152] [2001] 2 FLR 970.

day-to-day domestic expenditure. I have clearly concluded that W contributed indirectly to the mortgage repayments, the principal of which furnished part of the consideration of the initial purchased price.'[153]

Thus contributions to the purchase price which are, strictly speaking, indirect may still be capable of leading to the inference of a common intention if they enabled the other party to make a direct contribution.

The recent decision of the Court of Appeal in *Curley v Parkes*[154] has, however, called into question whether contributions to the payment of a mortgage, whether direct or indirect, made subsequent to the acquisition of the property can be regarded as a contribution to the purchase price at all. The case itself concerned a claim to an interest by way of a resulting trust. The Court of Appeal held that contributions made toward the payment of mortgage instalments subsequent to the acquisition of a property are simply sums paid to discharging the mortgagor's obligations under the mortgage, and as such are not a contribution to the purchase price.[155] It is unclear whether the same principle will apply in the context of constructive trusts, and in some subsequent decisions the possibility of a common intention being inferred from contributions to mortgage payments has been entertained without question.[156] In *Driver v Yorke*[157] it was held that occasional contributions to the mortgage instalments made by the two sons of the purchaser of a flat would not give rise to an inference of a common intention because the payments did not have sufficient connection with the purchase to be treated as a contribution to the purchase price. If the dicta in *Curley v Parkes* are strictly applied a claimant who moved in with an owner of a mortgaged property and then contributed to the mortgage instalments would not be able to establish an inferred common intention to share the ownership from the payments alone, and so would only be able to maintain a constructive trust if the payments were made on the basis of an express common intention to share the ownership. Since this is one of the commonest scenarios in which cohabitation may occur without the parties giving any express consideration to their respective property rights, such an application would severely reduce the ability of home sharers to establish an interest by way of a constructive trust.

The mere fact that a financial contribution has been made towards the purchase price of property does not in itself guarantee that a common intention will be inferred. No constructive trust will arise if the contribution is made in circumstances which demonstrate that there was no intention on the part of the contributor to obtain an interest in the property. A common intention will not therefore be inferred if the parties have merely done what spouses or partners would ordinarily do. As Lord Diplock observed in *Pettitt v Pettitt*:[158]

'It is common enough nowadays for husbands and wives to decorate and to make improvements in the family home themselves, with no other intention than to indulge in what is now a popular hobby, and to make the home pleasanter for their common use and enjoyment. If the husband likes to occupy his leisure by laying a new lawn in the garden or

---

[153] Ibid at 973.      [154] [2004] EWCA Civ 1515.      [155] See above p 244.
[156] *Lightfoot v Lightfoot-Browne* [2005] EWCA Civ 201.      [157] [2003] 2 P & CR 210.
[158] [1970] AC 777 at 826.

building a fitted wardrobe in the bedroom while the wife does the shopping, cooks the family dinner or bathes the children, I, for my part, find it quite impossible to impute to them as reasonable husband and wife any common intention that these domestic activities or any of them are to have any effect upon existing proprietary rights in the family home on which they are undertaken.'[159]

In *Lloyds Bank plc v Rosset*[160] the decisions of the Court of Appeal in *Eves v Eves* and *Grant v Edwards* were reviewed. In *Eves v Eves*[161] Lord Denning had considered that Janet had done 'a great deal of work to the house and garden . . . much more than many wives would do',[162] including stripping the hall of wallpaper, painting the woodwork in the lounge and kitchen, painting the kitchen cabinets, painting the brickwork, breaking up concrete in the front garden and demolishing a shed. In *Grant v Edwards*[163] Linda Grant had made a substantial contribution to housekeeping expenses. However, Lord Bridge concluded that the conduct of neither of the respective claimants had been sufficient to infer a common intention. The constructive trusts in each case were only justifiable on the basis of an express common intention. In *Driver v Yorke*[164] it was held that a person who had acted as a guarantor of the mortgage on behalf of the purchaser of a flat had not made any contribution to the purchase price because he had not shown any intention of being liable for the mortgage installments. Similarly a contribution to the purchase of property by way of a loan or a gift cannot give rise to an inference of a constructive trust.[165] Nor will a common intention be inferred where a person has made a contribution to the purchase price without the knowledge of the legal owner. In *Lightfoot v Lightfoot-Browne* a claimant who had made a payment of £41,000 towards the mortgage of a property without knowledge of the sole legal owner was therefore held unable to establish a common intention by inference from the payment.[166]

Payments which do not contribute to the purchase price of property, for example the payment of removal costs or solicitors fees,[167] will clearly be insufficient to generate an inferred common intention as they are not regarded as a contribution to the purchase price. Nor will a constructive trust be able to be inferred from conduct which, though costly in time and effort, does not contribute financially at all. Thus a constructive trust will not be inferred in favour of a person who undertakes domestic responsibilities, bears children, provides child care or looks after sick or elderly relatives. However such non-financial contributions are not entirely irrelevant, as they can be taken into account in determining the extent of the beneficial interest which will arise under a constructive trust established on the basis of a common intention inferred from a direct

---

[159] See also *Burns v Burns* [1984] Ch 317 at 344, where May LJ said: 'The court is only entitled to look at the financial contributions or their real and substantial equivalent to the acquisition of the house; that the husband may spend this weekends redecorating or laying a patio is neither here nor there, nor is the fact that the woman has spent so much of her time looking after the house, doing the cooking and bringing up the family.'

[160] [1991] 1 AC 107.      [161] [1975] 1 WLR 1338.      [162] [1975] 1 WLR 1338 at 1340.

[163] [1986] Ch 638.      [164] [2003] 2 P & CR 210.

[165] See *Re Sharpe (A Bankrupt)* [1980] 1 WLR 219.

[166] [2005] EWCA Civ 201. Note that in the light of *Curley v Parkes* [2004] EWCA Civ 1515 such a contribution to the discharge of the mortgage might not have been considered a contribution to the purchase price in any event.

[167] *Curley v Parkes* [2004] EWCA Civ 515.

financial contribution. Thus such non-financial conduct will only be irrelevant in a case where a person has acted in the absence of an express common intention and they have not made any financial contribution of any kind, no matter how small, to the purchase price of the property.

## (c) Detriment

The mere fact of a 'common intention' will not alone give rise to a constructive trust. A constructive trust will only arise in favour of a person who acted to his detriment, or substantially changed his position in reliance on the common intention. The constructive trust arises because it would be inequitable to allow the legal owner to refuse to give effect to the intention when the claimant has acted in a personally detrimental manner. It is absolutely essential to grasp that the standard of conduct sufficient to establish detrimental reliance is different from the standard of conduct required to justify an inference of a common intention. Whilst only a direct contribution to the purchase price will justify the inference of a common intention, a much wider range of conduct will constitute sufficient detriment to lead to the imposition of a constructive trust if there was an express common intention.

*(i) Detriment where there was an express common intention to share the ownership of the land.* In *Lloyds Bank plc v Rosset*[168] Lord Bridge summarised what was required in the way of detriment to establish a constructive trust founded upon an express common intention:

'. . . it will only be necessary for the partner asserting a claim to a beneficial interest against the partner entitled to the legal estate to show that he or she has acted to his or her detriment or significantly altered his or her position in reliance on the agreement in order to give rise to a trust . . .'[169]

This clearly adopts a much lower standard than the restrictive threshold of conduct from which it is possible to infer a common intention. The cases clearly support the proposition that conduct other than a direct contribution to the purchase price of the property will suffice to establish a constructive trust if there was an express common intention that the ownership of the land be shared. In *Lloyds Bank plc v Rosset*[170] itself the House of Lords held that there was no express common intention between the husband and wife as to the ownership of the house and therefore the question whether Mrs Rosset's activities would have been sufficient to establish such a trust was not addressed. The leading authority therefore remains *Grant v Edwards*,[171] where it was held that there was an express common intention that Linda Grant was to enjoy a share of the ownership of the house she cohabited with George Edwards. Whilst Edwards paid the mortgage installments, Grant made a substantial contribution from her own wages to the housekeeping and bringing up the children. The Court of Appeal held that her conduct amounted to sufficient detriment to justify a constructive trust. However, a difference of opinion appears in the judgments. Nourse LJ addressed the question as to the nature of conduct required and concluded:

---

[168] [1991] 1 AC 107.    [169] [1991] 1 AC 107 at 132.    [170] [1991] 1 AC 107.
[171] [1986] Ch 638.

'In my judgment it must be conduct on which the woman could not reasonably have been expected to embark unless she was to have an interest in the house.'[172]

He held that Grant's contribution to the housekeeping amounted to an indirect contribution to the mortgage installments, as it enabled Edwards to pay them from his own wages. This was conduct that could not have been reasonably expected unless she was to have an interest in the house. Sir Nicholas Browne-Wilkinson V-C took a more liberal view:

'Once it has been shown that there was a common intention that the claimant should have an interest in the house, any act done by her to her detriment relating to the joint lives of the parties is, in my judgment, sufficient detriment to qualify. The acts do not have to be referable to the house.'[173]

He emphasised the practical difficulties attendant on a test which required the court to find that the claimant's conduct could only be explained on the basis that a beneficial interest in the property would be thereby acquired:

'In many cases of the present sort, it is impossible to say whether or not the claimant would have done the acts relied on as a detriment even if she thought she had no interest in the house. Setting up house together, having a baby, making payments to general housekeeping expenses (not strictly necessary to enable the mortgage to be paid) may all be referable to the mutual love and affection of the parties and not specifically referable to the claimant's belief that she has an interest in the house.'

Given that Lord Bridge indicated in *Lloyds Bank plc v Rosset*[174] that 'a significant change of position by the claimant' was sufficient detriment to establish a constructive trust in fulfillment of an express common intention, it seems that the more liberal approach of Browne-Wilkinson V-C is to be preferred. This also follows from the growing recognition that the detriment required in the case of a constructive trust based on an express common intention is analogous to that required to sustain a claim to a remedy under the principles of proprietary estoppel considered in Chapter 10.[175]

In *Banner Homes Group plc v Luff Developments Ltd*[176] the Court of Appeal suggested that a constructive trust might be established even where the claimant had suffered no detriment through his reliance on a common intention or agreement, if the defendant had obtained an advantage. The case concerned an understanding between two developers that they would form a joint venture to acquire a development site. The site was to be acquired by a company owned by Luff Developments. In the event Luff acquired the site, and then informed Banner Homes that it was withdrawing from the joint

---

172 [1986] Ch 638 at 648.

173 [1986] Ch 638 at 657. Compare the similar debate on part performance in *Steadman v Steadman* [1976] AC 536.

174 [1991] 1 AC 107.

175 *Lloyd's Bank plc v Rosset* [1991] 1 AC 107 at 132. See also *Grant v Edwards* [1986] Ch 638 at 656, where Browne-Wilkinson V-C thought that 'useful guidance may in future be obtained from the principles underlying the law of proprietary estoppel which in my judgment are closely akin to those laid down in *Gissing v Gissing*'.

176 [2000] 2 All ER 117.

venture. The Court of Appeal held that Banner Homes was entitled to a constructive trust over half the shares in the company which had purchased the land. Chadwick LJ held that Banner Homes had suffered a detriment because, on the basis of the understanding with Luff Developments, it had stayed out of the market for the site. However he also opined that the trust would have arisen even if it could not have been held that Banner Homes had suffered detriment:

'It may be just as inequitable to allow the defendant to treat the property as his own when it had been acquired by the use of some advantage which he has obtained under the agreement or understanding as it is to allow him to treat the property as his own when the plaintiff has suffered some detriment under the arrangement or understanding.'[177]

*(ii) Detriment where there was an inference of a common intention to share the ownership of the land.* Where there was no express common intention but the criteria are satisfied to entitle the court to infer a common intention, the element of detriment presents much less difficulty. Given that the court can only infer a common intention from conduct constituting a direct contribution to the purchase price of the property,[178] the contributor will clearly have acted to his detriment sufficiently to justify a constructive trust. The nature of the detriment will, however, be crucial to the determination of the extent of the beneficial interest thereby acquired.

## (4)  Quantifying the beneficial interest under a common intention constructive trust

### (a)  When is it necessary for the court to quantify the beneficial interests arising by way of a constructive trust?

Where the evidence establishes that the parties had reached an express agreement as to the ownership of the property, the constructive trust will operate to fulfill that agreement. In most cases the parties will have expressly agreed to share the property equally, and the claimant will be entitled to a half-share of the equitable interest. However where there is no express common intention as to the respective shares of the parties in the property, either because they had an express common intention to share the ownership of the property but had not discussed the specific proportions in which the ownership was to be shared,[179] or because the common intention to share has had to be inferred from a contribution to the purchase price, the extent of the equitable interest arising under the constructive trust will have to be determined by the court. In *Stack v Dowden*[180] for example, it was held that the parties had not reached an express intention as to the quantum of their respective shares of the beneficial ownership of the property because they had not understood the meaning of a declaration in the transfer stating that the survivor of them 'is entitled to give a valid receipt for capital money arising from a disposition of all or part of the property.' The decision of the House of Lords in *Lloyds Bank plc v Rosset*[181] failed to address conclusively the way in which the respective

---

177  [2000] 2 All ER 117 at 141.      178  *Lloyds Bank plc v Rosset* [1991] 1 AC 107 at 133.
179  As in *Cox v Jones* [2004] EWHC 1486 and *Pinfield v Eagles* [2005] EWHC 477.
180  [2005] EWCA Civ 857.      181  [1991] 1 AC 107.

shares of the parties in the beneficial interest should be determined in such cases, and the relevant principles have had to be spelled out in subsequent cases.

### (b) How should the court quantify the beneficial interests *arising under a constructive trust?*

The starting point for analysis is the basic principle that constructive trusts arise to fulfill the intentions of the parties, so as Browne-Wilkinson V-C stated in *Grant v Edwards*[182] 'prima facie the interest of the claimant will be that which the parties intended'. This fundamental link between the intention of the parties and the quantum of the interest arising was identified by Lord Diplock in *Gissing v Gissing*.[183]

'. . . the court must first do its best to discover from the conduct of the spouses whether any inference can reasonably be drawn as to the probable common understanding about the amount of the share of the contributing spouse upon which each must have acted in doing what each did even though that understanding was never expressly stated by one spouse to the other or even consciously formulated in words by either of them independently. It is only if no such inference can be drawn that the court is driven to apply as a rule of law, and not as an inference of fact, the maxim "equality is equity", and to hold that the beneficial interest belongs to the spouses in equal shares.'

The constructive trust can thus be distinguished from the resulting trust. In the case of a presumed resulting trust, the extent of the claimant's beneficial entitlement will be determined solely by the amount of contribution made to the purchase price of the property, whereas in the case of a constructive trust the claimant may gain a share of the equitable interest far in excess of the proportion they have contributed to the purchaser price, or of the value of their action which constitutes the necessary detriment. This difference is neatly illustrated by *Midland Bank plc v Cooke*[184] where a wife who had contributed 6.74% of the purchase price of a property was held to be entitled to a half-share by way of a constructive trusts arising on the basis of a common intention to share inferred from her contribution.

Two alternative approaches have been adopted to this problem of the quantification of the beneficial interests, both of which enable the court to take into account all the aspects of the parties relationship. In *Midland Bank plc v Cooke*[185] the Court of Appeal held that the court should determine the respective interests of the parties by identifying their assumed intentions from all of the available evidence, and then implementing those intentions by way of a constructive trust. As was noted above, Mrs Cooke had contributed 6.74% of the purchase price of her matrimonial home, which had been acquired in the sole name of her husband, through her share of a joint wedding gift which they had received.[186] In the absence of an express common intention this financial contribution was sufficient to give rise to the inference of a common intention. The key question was as to the extent of her beneficial interest. The Court of Appeal held that it should consider the whole course of dealing between the parties so as to be able

---

[182] [1986] Ch 638 at 657.     [183] [1971] AC 886 at 908.     [184] [1995] 4 All ER 562.
[185] [1995] 4 All ER 562; (1997) 60 MLR 420 (O'Hagan).
[186] See also *McHardy and Sons v Warren* [1994] 2 FLR 338.

to identify their assumed intentions as to the sharing of the ownership. Waite LJ explained that the court was entitled to take account of all the circumstances of the parties' relationship:

'The general principle to be derived from *Gissing v Gissing* and *Grant v Edwards* can in my judgement be summarised in this way. When the court is proceeding, in cases like the present where the partner without legal title has successfully asserted an equitable interest through direct contribution, to determine (in the absence of express evidence of intention) what proportions the parties must be assumed to have intended for their beneficial owner- ship, the duty of the judge is to undertake a survey of the whole course of dealing between the parties relevant to their ownership and occupation of the property and their sharing its burdens and advantages. That scrutiny will not confine itself to a limited range of acts of direct contribution of the sort that are needed to found a beneficial interest in the first place. It will take into consideration all conduct which throws light on the question what shares were intended. Only if that search proves inconclusive does the court fall back on the maxim that "equality is equity".'

In the light of all the evidence, he held that they should be presumed to have intended to share the property equally. Waite LJ considered as particularly relevant the fact that she had looked after their children and maintained the property; contributed to house- hold bills from her own salary; and consented to a second mortgage of the house to guarantee her husband's business debts. He concluded:

'One could hardly have a clearer example of a couple who had agreed to share everything equally: the profits of his business while it prospered, and the risks of indebtedness suffered through its failure; the upbringing of their children; the rewards of her own career as a teacher; and most relevantly, a home into which he put his savings and to which she was to give over the years the benefit of the maintenance and improvement contribution. When to all this there is added the fact (still an important one) that this was a couple who had chosen to introduce into their relationship the additional commitments which marriage involves, the conclusion becomes inescapable that their presumed intention was to share the beneficial interest in the property in equal shares.'

Although criticised by some commentators, this more holistic approach certainly had the benefit of enabling the court to take into account non-financial conduct in deter- mining the extent of the beneficial interests of a claimant arising by way of a construct- ive trust, and was followed in subsequent cases.[187] However most recent cases have abandoned the pretence that they are seeking to establish and fulfill the assumed inten- tions of the parties in favour of the adoption of a discretion on the part of the court to decided what share of the equitable ownership would be 'fair' to award the claimant in the light of all the circumstances.

The leading authority is now *Oxley v Hiscock*,[188] in which the Court of Appeal conducted an extensive review of all the possible approaches to the quantification of the beneficial interest arising under a constructive trust. The case concerned a house pur- chased in 1991 to provide a home for Mr Hiscock and Mrs Oxley. The purchase was made in the sole name of Mr Hiscock, and was funded partly by the proceeds of sale of

---

[187]  See, for example, *Le Foe v Le Foe* [2001] 2 FLR 970.     [188]  [2004] 3 All ER 703.

a previous property owned by Mrs Oxley, partly by a direct financial contribution from Mr Hiscock's savings, and partly by way of a mortgage. The ownership of the property came to be disputed when the parties' relationship broke down and the property was sold. There was no doubt that Mrs Oxley had made a direct contribution to the purchase price which was sufficient to give rise to the inference of a common intention, and at first instance it was held that she should be entitled to a half-share of the beneficial ownership by way of a constructive trust. Mr Hiscock appealed, arguing that because the parties had not discussed the extent of their respective beneficial interests at the time of the purchase they should receive a share proportionate to their financial contributions. On this basis Mrs Oxley would have been entitled to a 22% share of the property. The Court of Appeal rejected this argument and was forced to consider how the extent of a beneficial interest arising under a constructive trust should be determined where there was no evidence as to the parties actual intentions. The Court of Appeal considered a number of possible approaches to this problem, including the assumed intentions approach of *Midland Bank plc v Cooke*[189] and found them to be wanting. Chadwick LJ adopted a new broad principle that the beneficial interests of the parties should be determined by the court on the basis of what seemed 'fair' in the light of all the circumstances:

'It must now be accepted (at least in this Court and below) the answer is that each is entitled to that share which the court considered fair having regard to the whole course of dealing between them in relation to the property. And, in that context, the "whole course of dealing between them in relation to the property" includes the arrangements which they make from time to time in order to meet the outgoings (for example, mortgage contributions, council tax and utilities, repairs, insurance and housekeeping) which have to be met if they are to live in the property as their home.'[190]

Applying this principle, the Court of Appeal concluded that Mrs Oxley should be entitled to a 40% share of the beneficial interest of the house. Chadwick LJ explained that this decision had been reached because the award of an equal share to Mrs Oxley would have been unfair to Mr Hiscock in the light of his greater direct contribution to the purchase price:

'In my view to declare that the parties were entitled in equal shares would be unfair to Mr Hiscock. It would give insufficient weight to the fact that his direct contribution to the purchase price (£60,700) was substantially greater than that of Mrs Oxley (£36,300). On the basis of the judge's findings that there was in this case "a classic pooling of resources" and conduct consistent with an intention to share the burden of the property (by which she must, I think, have meant the outgoings referable to ownership and cohabitation), it would be fair to treat them as having made approximately equal contributions to the balance of the purchase price (£30,000). Taking that into account with their direct contributions at the time of the purchase, I would hold that a fair division of the proceeds of sale of the property would be 60% to Mr Hiscock and 40% to Mrs Oxley.'[191]

The discretionary approach adopted in *Oxley v Hiscock* achieves the same objective as

---

[189] [1995] 2 FLR 915.    [190] [2004] 3 All ER 703, at [69].    [191] Ibid, at [74].

that assumed intentions approach in *Midland Bank plc v Cooke* of allowing the court
to take into account a wider range of circumstances than merely the direct financial
contributions of the parties to the property. However it owes more to the principles of
proprietary estoppel than to the traditional principles of constructive trusts.[192] Indeed
in *Pinfield v Eagles* Hart J considered the exercise of the discretion to determine a fair
share of the beneficial interest under a constructive trust to be identical to the exercise
of discretion to satisfy an equity arising by way of proprietary estoppel.[193] As will be
seen in the next chapter, proprietary estoppel has not previously been used as a means
of generating beneficial interests in land. However these recent decisions almost have
the effect of treating a financial contribution to the purchase price of property as if it
were a form of passive assurance of an interest in land, which the court can then satisfy
by the award of an appropriate share of the beneficial interest. As was noted above the
approach seems similar to that of the 'new model' constructive trust which Lord
Denning sought to introduce in the 1970s. A close comparison might be drawn with
*Eves v Eves*,[194] for example, where he held that a claimant should be entitled to a quar-
ter-share of the equitable interest by way of a constructive trust, on the grounds that
this would be just and reasonable. However a crucial difference is that the element of
discretion only emerges under the principles adopted in *Oxley v Hiscock* in relation to
the quantification of the beneficial interest, and not as to whether a constrictive trust
should arise in the first place. The principles adopted by the House of Lords in *Lloyds
Bank plc v Rosset* will continue to determine when a constructive trust may be found,
so that the pre-requisite of an express or inferred common intention remains. Whilst
the discretionary approach adopted in *Oxley v Hiscock* may seem less artificial than the
assumed intentions approach of *Midland Bank plc v Cooke*, it is arguable that it is less
liberal and generous in practice, and gives insufficient weight to the nature of the
parties' relationship and overemphasises their direct financial contributions to the
purchase of the property. As has been seen in *Midlands Bank plc v Cooke* the fact that
the parties had married and shared their lives was given great weight, and led the court
to assume that they had intended to share the property equally. Less weight seems to
have been attached in *Oxley v Hiscock* to the fact that the parties had lived together in
the property as their home for nearly 10 years. Whilst the judge at first instance held
that their relationship had been a classic case of the 'pooling of resources' the Court of
Appeal seemed to give greater importance to the fact that Mr Hiscock had provided
slightly more of the initial capital for the acquisition of the property. This difference of
perspective demonstrates that the determination of the beneficial interest arising under
a constructive trusts will ultimately turn on subjective value judgments rather than legal
principles. It should be noted that the principle adopted in *Oxley v Hiscock* is applicable
not only to the quantification of the beneficial interests arising under a constructive
trust of residential property, but also in commercial situations.[195]

---

[192] In fact the Court of Appeal relied heavily upon the judgement in *Yaxley v Gotts* [2000] Ch 162. See
Nield, 'Constructive trusts and estoppel' (2003) 23 LS 311 for an analysis of the relationship between the
common intention constructive trust and proprietary estoppel.
[193] [2005] EWHC 477 at [38]–[39].          [194] [1975] 1 WLR 1338.
[195] *Pinfield v Eagles* [2005] EWHC 477.

## (c) How has the court exercised its discretion to quantify the beneficial interests arising under a constructive trust?

The principles adopted in *Oxley v Hiscock* have been applied in a number of subsequent cases[196] which illustrate how the discretion will be exercised in practice. In *Cox v Jones*[197] two barristers in a relationship purchased a mill in Essex, which they intended to renovate as a home, in the sole name of Mr Jones. The initial purchase price was raised by way of a small financial contribution from both parties and a mortgage of £450,000. The mortgage was paid exclusively by Mr Jones, who also paid virtually all of the costs of the renovation, which were some £163,000. Miss Cox spent £1,000 on the renovations, £4,000 on services an insurance and £6,800 on furniture. She also performed a large planning, management and co-ordination role in the renovation, did a small amount of physical work, and lived at the mill for the period of the works which caused her work and earnings to decline. Mann J held that the parties had had an express common intention to share the property, but that there was no express agreement as to the share that Miss Cox would be entitled to. He therefore applied *Oxley v Hiscock* and concluded that it would be fair in all the circumstances for Miss Cox to receive a 25% share of the beneficial ownership. He reasoned as follows:

'I do not consider that a 50% share for Miss Cox would be fair in these circumstances. Mr Jones funded the entirety of the purchase and the works, and the mortgage payments (though those have fallen into arrears). Miss Cox paid virtually nothing. She did, of course, forego the income from her practice, and contributed very materially to the project, but I do not think that that entitles her to as much as 50% of the equity in the property. Scientific analysis is impossible in these cases; what the court has to do is to form an overall assessment. I think that 25% is a proper figure for her share, reflecting everything she has put in but giving due weight to Mr Jones's own considerable contributions.'[198]

In *Pinfield v Eagles*[199] Mr Eagles and Mrs Pinfield, who were living together, formed a company and went into business purchasing and managing care homes. The majority of the finance for the purchase of the care homes was raised by a commercial loan, with Mr Eagle providing the remainder. Mrs Pinfield did not contribute directly to the purchase price, but was appointed a director of the company, gave up a flower-arranging business which paid her a modest income, and ran the homes. For six months she drew no salary, but enjoyed the benefit of a company car and expenses. Thereafter she drew a salary of £20,000. Hart J held that although there was an express agreement that she was to have an interest in the business, there was no express agreement that she was to have a half-share. He therefore applied *Oxley v Hiscock* and held that she should be entitled to a 39% share, on the basis that this represented the financial contribution she had made to the initial purchase:

' "What would be a fair share for each party having regard to the whole course of dealings between them in relation to the [companies]?" My answer to that question is arrived at by

---

[196] For example *Lightfoot v Lightfoot-Browne* [2005] EWCA Civ 201, although in this case it was held that a common intention could not be inferred.
[197] [2004] EWHC 1486; [2005] Conv 168 (Probert)     [198] Ibid at [80]–[81].
[199] [2005] EWHC 447

looking at the contributions made by each of them to the initial financing. I think they should be treated as having contributed equally to the procurement of the commercial finance (£1,436,000). The balance of approximately £415,000 was procured by the efforts of Mr Eagles alone. On that basis Mr Eagles can be treated as having contributed 61% and Mrs Pinfield 39%. Those are the proportions in which I would declare the parties are respectively entitled to share in the net equity of the companies.'[200]

In *Stack v Dowden*[201] a couple purchased a house in 1993 for £190,000, £125,000 having been provided by Miss Dowden and the remainder raised by way of a mortgage. The couple lived in the property for 10 years and had four children, during which time Mr Stack paid off £27,000 of the mortgage loan. When the couple split up Mr Stack claimed that they were tenants in common of the property in equal shares. As was been noted above, the Court of Appeal held that a common intention could be inferred so as to generate a constructive trust, but the parties had not expressed any intention about the quantum of their interests. The Court of Appeal therefore applied *Oxley v Hiscock* to determine the parties' shares in the light of the 'whole course of dealings' between them. However, in exercising its discretion to determine a fair share of the beneficial ownership for Mr Stack exclusive attention was given to the financial contributions of the parties. Since Mr Stack had only contributed £27,000 of the purchase price it was held that it would not be fair for him to enjoy a half share. As Miss Dowden was only claiming a 65% share of the property there was no need to decide whether she might have been entitled to an even greater share.

## (5) Criticism of the 'common intention' constructive trust[202]

Although the common intention approach to constructive trusts was firmly entrenched by *Lloyds Bank plc v Rosset*,[203] building on the foundation laid in *Gising v Gissing*, it has been subjected to extensive criticism.[204] The major objection is that the whole process of finding, and then enforcing, the 'common intention' of the parties is highly artificial, and that despite their protestations to the contrary, the courts are effectively 'inventing' or 'discovering' an intention where they feel that a trust should arise. As Tipping J said in *Lankow v Rose* in the New Zealand Court of Appeal:

'English jurisprudence appears still to be concerned with notions of express or imputed intention or understanding. That approach, essentially contractual or quasi-contractual, is in my view unnecessarily artificial. It is better to acknowledge openly that a constructive trust is being imposed in equity without the consent, express, implied or imputed, of the constructive trustee. The trust is imposed because equity will not allow the legal owner to deny the claimant a beneficial interest.'[205]

---

[200] Ibid at [38]–[39].      [201] [2005] EWCA Civ 857.
[202] (1993) 109 LQR 263 (Gardener); [1998] Conv 202 (Riniker).      [203] [1991] 1 AC 107.
[204] Gardner, 'Rethinking Family Property' (1993) 109 LQR 263; Glover & Todd, 'The myth of common intention' (1996) 16 LS 325; Riniker, 'The Fiction of Common Intention and Detriment' [1998] Conv 202; Mee, *The Property Rights of Cohabitees* (1999) pp 117–173; Rotherham, 'The Property Rights of Unmarried Cohabitees: The Case for Reform' [2004] Conv 268,
[205] [1995] 1 NZLR 277, 293.

Thus whereas Lord Bridge described *Eves v Eves*[206] and *Grant v Edwards*[207] as 'outstanding' examples of express common intention, the facts would suggest that there was no real agreement between the parties to share the ownership of the property concerned. In both cases the men concerned had no real intention that their partners should enjoy an interest in the property. Stuart Eves refused to put Janet on the title of the house using the excuse that she was under 21. Grant would not put Edwards on the title because he said that it would prejudice her forthcoming matrimonial proceedings. Both of these excuses covered the real intention of the men that their partners were not to receive any proprietary interest in the house. They were to remain the owners and to enjoy the power and control that are necessarily commensurate with such ownership. If the relationship broke down, they wanted to be able to remove their erstwhile partner and not to be encumbered by their presence in the house. To describe the parties in these cases as enjoying a 'common intention' to share the ownership is nothing short of a fiction. The inference of common intention is similarly fraught with the danger that the court is merely inventing a justification for imposing a constructive trust. In *Westdeutsche Landesbank Girozentrale v Islington London Borough Council*[208] Lord Browne-Wilkinson suggested that, unlike a resulting trust, a constructive trust is imposed on a trustee by law against his intentions.[209] The inevitable implication of this greater realism is that the language of 'common intention' is inappropriate as a description of the true rationale for establishing a constructive trust of cohabited land.

As Gardner[210] points out, the central difficulty is that the common intention analysis focuses on the parties' own thinking as the basis for the imposition of a constructive trust, when in fact they will often have given little or no thought to the question of ownership, as was evident in *Midland Bank plc v Cooke*.[211] If the principle of a common intention was applied literally, constructive trusts would arise in virtually no domestic circumstances. It fails to take account of the nature of the relationship between the parties, which should be the main factor in determining the location of the ownership of the property held by the partners. Mee goes so far as to conclude that the English 'common intention constructive trust' is theoretically indefensible:

'The English courts have thrown into the pot three distinct doctrines (resulting trusts, estoppel and the principle in *Rochefoucauld v Boustead*) and have sealed over this unpalatable mixture with a thick crust of confusion, in the form of the misleading phrase "common intention" (with its implications of bargains and subjective consensus). Not surprisingly, even after twenty-five years in the oven, the "common intention" analysis remains stubbornly half-baked . . . Furthermore, there is the great irony that, despite the liberties it takes with legal principle, the common intention trust analysis can boast very few advantages at a practical level: it is difficult and expensive to apply and provides a remedy for claimants in only a narrow range of cases. Clearly, this ill conceived doctrine should find no place in the law of England.'[212]

The decision of the Court of Appeal in *Oxley v Hiscock*[213] in relation to the quantification of the beneficial interest arising under a constructive trust at least has the merit of

---

[206] [1975] 1 WLR 1338.     [207] [1986] Ch 638.     [208] [1996] AC 669.     [209] Ibid at 708.
[210] (1993) 109 LQR 263 at 282.     [211] [1995] 4 All ER 562.
[212] The Property Rights of Cohabitees, (1999) pp. 173–174.     [213] [2004] 3 All ER 703.

eliminating the need for the court to identify an artificial assumed intention where there was no express intention between the parties as to the sharing of the property, but the reintroduction of a broad discretion for the court to decided what share would be 'fair' in all the circumstances opens the door to the equally dangerous problems of legal uncertainty and inconsistency.

However despite the acknowledged deficiencies of the 'common intention' constructive trust, it has proved difficult to identify an alternative which is not equally problematic. In 2002 the Law Commission published a long-awaited discussion paper entitled *Sharing Homes*[214] As was noted above, the Law Commission concluded that it was impossible to devise a statutory scheme for the ascertainment and quantification of beneficial interests in shared home which would operate fairly and evenly across the diversity of domestic circumstances which are now encountered.[215] It therefore confined itself to making recommendations for the modification of the 'common intention' constructive trust.[216] It concluded that, whatever the problems of artificiality, the concept of 'common intention' should not be replaced as the basic criteria for the establishment of a constructive trust:

'While we realize that the application of "common intention" causes real difficulties to the courts and that it can lead to a highly artificial exercise, it is difficult to present a convincing case for any more effective criteria on which an assessment of beneficial interest could be based. Intention is clearly important, as it would be wholly unsatisfactory if a person were to obtain a beneficial interest where it was made extremely clear that a particular contribution, by financial or other contribution, would not be met this way.'[217]

Instead it advocated a widening of the circumstances in which a common intention would be inferred to include indirect financial contributions to the acquisition of the property:

'In many cases, a couple will not engage in discussion, but agree to an ordering of the household finances such that one pays off the mortgage while the other pays the household bills. In those circumstances, where the payment of those bills has enabled the other party to pay the mortgage installments, we believe that the payer of the bills should be given due credit. In our view, an indirect contribution to the mortgage of this kind should be sufficient to enable the courts to infer that the parties had a common intention that the beneficial entitlement to the home be shared.'[218]

On the issue of quantification the Law Commission advocated adopting a broad approach that would take account the whole course of dealing between the parties:

'We consider that there is a strong case for the courts to adopt a broad approach here as well. If the question really is one of the parties' "common intention", we believe that there is much to be said for adopting what has been called a "holistic approach" to quantification, undertaking a survey of the whole course of dealing between the parties and taking account of all conduct which throws light on the question what shares were intended.'[219]

---

[214] Law Com No 278 (2002).     [215] Ibid para 1.31(1).

[216] Craig Rotherham argues the need for reform, 'The Property Rights of Unmarried Cohabitees: The Case for Reform' [2004] Conv 268.

[217] Ibid para 4.24.     [218] Ibid para 4.26.     [219] Ibid para. 4.27.

However these recommendations have already arguably been achieved by subsequent development of the criteria set down by the by the House of Lords in *Lloyds Bank plc v Rosset*. As was noted above, the possibility that a common intention might be inferred from indirect contributions to the purchase price was adopted in *Le Foe v Le Foe*[220] and the 'holistic approach' to quantification in *Midland Bank plc v Cooke*.[221] The recent decision in *Oxley v Hiscock* has gone much further than the recommendations in abandoning the idea of common intention in relation to the quantification of the beneficial interest in favour of a broad judicial discretion to do what seems 'fair' in all the circumstances. The Law Commission's recommendations would thus have little to add to the current law.

Intellectual integrity would perhaps be better served by the rejection of 'common intention' as the touchstone for constructive trusts and replacement with some other principle, such as the fulfillment of the claimant's 'reasonable or legitimate expectation' arising in the light of the parties' relationship and conduct. A number of Commonwealth jurisdictions have rejected the 'common intention' analysis in favour of such alternative explanations for the imposition of constructive trusts these are briefly examined and evaluated below.

## (6) Commonwealth approaches

### (a) Canada[222]

The Canadian courts have moved furthest from the 'common intention' constructive trust and have introduced the concept of a remedial constructive trust to effect restitution through the reversal of unjust enrichment. The principles were stated in *Pettkus v Becker*,[223] where the Supreme Court held that a woman who had lived with a man for 14 years and worked with him on his honey farm was entitled to a half-share by way of a constructive trust. The court outlined the three elements which must be satisfied to justify the imposition of a constructive trust:

'. . . an enrichment, a corresponding deprivation and absence of any juristic reason for the enrichment.'[224]

This rationale has been accepted and followed by subsequent cases.[225]

*(i) An enrichment.* This element is satisfied when the legal owner of the land has been benefited (enriched) by the actions of the claimant of a constructive trust. In *Sorochan v Sorochan*[226] Mary and Alex Sorochan lived together as man and wife for 42 years, jointly working a farm. The Supreme Court held that Alex had been enriched because he had derived a benefit from the appellant's many years of labour in the home and on the farm. This enrichment included the valuable savings he had made as a result of having

---

[220] [2001] 2 FLR 970.     [221] [1995] 4 All ER 562.
[222] [1987] Denning LJ 151 (Welstead).     [223] (1980) 117 DLR (3d) 257.
[224] (1980) 117 DLR (3d) 257 at 274.
[225] See *Sorochan v Sorochan* (1986) 29 DLR (4th) 1; *Rawluk v Rawluk* (1990) 65 DLR (4th) 161; *Peter v Beblow* (1993) 101 DLR (4th) 621.
[226] (1986) 29 DLR (4th) 1.

essential farm services and domestic work performed without remuneration. Similarly, in *Peter v Beblow*[227] the Supreme Court held that the man had been enriched by the claimant, with whom he had lived for twelve years, acting as housekeeper, homemaker and step-mother without compensation.

*(ii) A corresponding deprivation.* This element is often simply the inverse of the requirement of enrichment. One party has been enriched and as a result the other has been deprived. As Cory J said in *Peter v Beblow*,[228] 'as a general rule, if it is found that the defendant has been enriched by the efforts of the plaintiff there will, almost as a matter of course, be deprivation suffered by the plaintiff'. In that case a woman was held to have been deprived of any compensation for her labour when she had devoted the majority of her time and energy, and some money she earned, towards the benefit of her partner, his children and his property.

*(iii) The absence of any juristic reason for the enrichment.* This final element means that the claimant must not have been obliged to provide the services or other activity which constituted an enrichment. This element is closely connected to the concept of 'reasonable expectation'. In *Pettkus v Becker*[229] Dixon J stated:

'. . . I hold that where one person in a relationship tantamount to spousal prejudices herself in the reasonable expectation of receiving an interest in property and the other person in the relationship freely accepts benefits conferred by the first person in circumstances where he knows or ought to have known of that reasonable expectation, it would be unjust to allow the recipient of the benefit to retain it.'

This Canadian approach may be contrasted with the English position adopted in *Lloyds Bank plc v Rosset*.[230] One favourable feature is the willingness of the Canadian courts to emphasise the significance of a female partner's contribution to the family, in terms of housekeeping and child-rearing, whereas these are the very things that the House of Lords held would be insufficient to lead to the inference of a common intention. In *Peter v Beblow*[231] McLachlin J considered that the argument that non-financial contributions cannot give rise to equitable claims:

'. . . is no longer tenable in Canada, either from the point of view of logic or authority. From the point of view of logic, I share the view of Professors Hovius and Youdan in *The Law of Family Property* (Toronto: Casewell, 1991), that "there is no logical reason to distinguish domestic services from other contributions". The notion that household and child care services are not worthy of recognition by the court fails to recognise the fact that these services are of great value, not only to the family, but to the other spouse.'

The Canadian approach is more willing to look to the reality of the relationship between the parties, and to assess their consequent expectations. As Cory J observed in *Peter v Beblow*:[232]

---

[227] (1993) 101 DLR (4th) 621.    [228] (1993) 101 DLR (4th) 621 at 632.
[229] (1980) 117 DLR (3d) 257 at 274.    [230] [1991] 1 AC 107.
[231] (1993) 101 DLR (4th) 621.
[232] (1993) 101 DLR (4th) 621 at 633–634. See also *Single v Macharski Estate* (1996) 107 Man R (2d) 291.

'. . . in today's society it is unreasonable to assume that the presence of love automatically implies a gift of one party's services to another. Nor is it unreasonable for the party providing the domestic labour required to create a home to expect a share in the property of the parties when the relationship is terminated. Women no longer are expected to work exclusively in the home. It must be recognised that when they do so, women forgo outside employment to provide domestic services and child care. The granting of relief in the form of a personal judgment or a property interest to the provider of domestic services should adequately reflect the fact that the income earning capacity and the ability to acquire assets by one party has been enhanced by the unpaid domestic services of the other.'

A further aspect of the Canadian approach is that if the three elements are satisfied, thus establishing an unjust enrichment, it is not inevitable that a constructive trust will arise. The court enjoys discretion to decide whether a constructive trust should be imposed, or whether some alternative remedy, for example a monetary entitlement, would be more appropriate. In *Sorochan v Sorochan*[233] the court held that a constructive trust of a third share of the farm was an appropriate remedy to reverse the unjust enrichment, and that it was not necessary to demonstrate a connection between the deprivation of the claimant and the acquisition of the land. In *Peter v Beblow*[234] a constructive trust was held to be the appropriate remedy where the legal owner was living on a war veteran's allowance, and monetary compensation would be impracticable, unrealistic and unreasonable.

Although the Canadian approach is commendable for its more enlightened approach to the reality of relationships, it is still open to criticism.[235] Wong suggests that the focus on relationships which are 'tantamount to spousal' will leave the court susceptible to value judgments, with the consequence that the common intention approach may be more flexible, as it is able to include a wider range of relationships.[236] Mee argues that the language of restitution has been misappropriated by the courts to justify a discretion to adjust the property rights of cohabitees. In his view the Canadian courts have violated restitutionary theory in three ways: by failing to adequately justify why restitution should be available in such cases; by taking into account detriments incurred by a claimant which do not enrich the land owner; and by awarding remedies which have no reference to the enrichment conferred:

'One is left to conclude that the Canadian courts have effectively arrogated to themselves a statutory-style discretion providing for the adjustment of the property rights of cohabitees upon the ending of their relationship. Whether the rule they have chosen reflects the social conditions and expectations of the people of Canada is a matter for speculation. The important point appears to be that the discretion the Canadian courts have created for themselves does extreme violence to the law of restitution. Yet, if a court had the stomach for such violence, similar results could be achieved with almost equal ease by taking the hatchet to a more familiar area of the law such as contract or trusts. Thus, one's conclusion must be

---

[233] (1986) 29 DLR (4th) 1.    [234] (1993) 101 DLR (4th) 621.

[235] See (1993) 109 LQR 263 (Gardner), pp 269–275.

[236] 'Constructive trusts over the family home: lessons to be learned from other commonwealth jurisdictions' [1998] 18 LS 369, 386.

that the appeal to the principles of unjust enrichment provides no easy answer to the problem of property disputes between unmarried couples.'[237]

In conclusion, it is unfair to compare the Canadian approach with merely the common intention constructive trust, since the Canadian restitutionary approach covers much the same ground as the combined English doctrines of the common intention constructive trust and proprietary estoppel.[238] When these two doctrines are considered together, there may be very little practical difference between the two jurisdictions. For example, in *Re Polly Peck (No 2)* Nourse LJ considered that many of the leading Canadian cases could have been decided similarly on the principles of *Gissing v Gissing*, and that English law had enabled further development through the principles of proprietary estoppel.[239]

## (b) Australia[240]

The Australian courts initially adopted the common intention approach to constructive trusts, requiring the court to find an actual or subjective common intention of the parties regarding the ownership of the property.[241] However, more recently they have favoured the imposition of constructive trusts on the grounds of 'unconscionability'. This approach to the constructive trust was explained by Deane J in *Muschinski v Dodds*:

'Viewed in its modern context, the constructive trust can properly be described as a remedial institution which equity imposes regardless of actual or presumed intention . . . to preclude the retention or assertion of beneficial ownership of property to the extent that such retention or assertion would be contrary to equitable principle.'[242]

He went on to say that the content of the principle was that where there was a joint endeavour and joint contributions to the purchase of property, 'equity will not permit [a party] . . . to assert or retain the benefit of the relevant property to the extent that it would be unconscionable for him to do so'.[243]

The principle of 'unconscionability' was applied in *Baumgartner v Baumgartner*.[244] Leo and Frances Baumgartner, who were unmarried, began to cohabit in 1978 in Leo's home. In 1979 he bought a house in his own name with a mortgage. While they lived together, Frances gave her pay packet to Leo, who paid all the expenses associated with their accommodation and household. The court found that Frances contributed 45% and Leo 55% of their common pool of earnings. When their relationship broke down in 1982, Frances left with their child and claimed that she was entitled to an interest in the property. The first instance judge held that she was not entitled to any interest. The Court of Appeal of New South Wales held that the parties had held a subjective common intention that she was to receive an interest in the property. The High Court held

---

[237] *The Property Rights of Cohabitees* (1999) p 226.    [238] Chapter 10.

[239] [1998] 3 All ER 812, 831–832.

[240] See [1990] Conv 370 (Hayton); (1997) 113 LQR 227 (Bailey-Harris).

[241] See *Allen v Snyder* [1977] 2 NSWLR 685; *Baumgartner v Baumgartner* (1988) 164 CLR 137.

[242] (1985) 160 CLR 583 at 614, 62 ALR 429 at 451.

[243] (1985) 160 CLR 583 at 614, 62 ALR 429 at 455.    [244] (1988) 164 CLR 137, 76 ALR 75.

that conflicts of evidence prevented the establishment of a common intention but nevertheless imposed a constructive trust. Given the pooled nature of the parties' resources, and that it was unrealistic to say that Frances had intended to make a gift of her earnings to Leo, the majority of the High Court concluded that:

'[Leo's] assertion, after the relationship had failed, that the [property], which was financed in part through the pooled funds, is his sole property, is his property to the exclusion of any interest at all on the part of [Frances], amounts to unconscionable conduct which attracts the intervention of equity and the imposition of a constructive trust . . .'[245]

Having decided that a constructive trust should be imposed, the court determined its terms, and concluded that the property should be held in the same shares to which they contributed their income to the common pool: ie 45% and 55%.

In Australia, 'unconscionability' has been recognised as the explanation not merely of constructive trusts, but also of the doctrine of proprietary estoppel. These doctrines, which are treated as distinct in English law, operate as aspects of one common principle.[246]

The approach of 'unconscionability' has the merit of doing away with the highly artificial concept of 'common intention'. However, in reality, the court is still required to decide whether the parties' conduct was 'unconscionable', so as to justify the imposition of a constructive trust. This involves an assessment of what the parties would have intended given the nature of the relationship. In *Baumgartner v Baumgartner* the pooling of resources and absence of any intention by Frances to make a gift of her wages were considered crucial to establishing that Leo's claim to sole legal ownership was unconscionable. *Baumgartner* concerned a situation where a partner provided direct financial contributions to the purchase of the property, and it did not answer the question whether the performance of household services or child-rearing would be sufficient by a partner to render the denial of an equitable interest unconscionable.[247] Subsequent cases have adopted a narrow view and have held a constructive trust will not be raised other than by contributions which are directly related to the acquisition of property.[248] Thus, in *W v G*[249] the plaintiff was held not to be entitled to any interest in the property of her lesbian lover by way of a constructive trust, despite the fact that she had contributed to their joint living expenses, contributed financially and physically to the improvement of the property, and looked after their children. In reality, the doctrine of 'unconscionability' may have become just as narrow in scope as the English 'common intention' constructive trust[250] and fails to provide adequate recognition of domestic contributions to family life.[251]

Whilst in many cases the same result would have been reached by the application of

---

[245] (1987) 76 ALR 75 at 85, per Mason CJ, Wilson and Deane JJ.

[246] See *Waltons Stores (Interstate) Ltd v Maher* (1988) 62 ALJR 110 (Aust HC).

[247] Later cases seem to apply the principle only to financial contributions. See *Hibberson v George* (1989) 12 Fam LR 735; *Arthur v Public Trustee* (1988) 90 FLR 203.

[248] *Bryson v Bryant* (1992) 29 NSWLR 188; *Stowe and Deveraux Holdings Pty Ltd v Stowe* (1995) 19 Fam LR 409 (Supreme Court of Western Australia).

[249] (1996) 20 Fam LR 49; (1997) 113 LQR 227 (Bailey-Harris).

[250] See (1990) 106 LQR 25 (Bryan).

[251] See *Booth v Beresford* (1993) 16 SASR 475; *Harmer v Pearson* (1993) 16 Fam LR 596.

English principles, a major difference between the English and Australian approaches concerns the effect of the award of a constructive trust on the rights of third parties. Under the common intention type of constructive trust, the court retrospectively recognises a pre-existing equitable interest in the property,[252] arising from the very moment that the claimant acted to her detriment on the basis of a common intention. As such, it can gain priority over the interests of general creditors of the legal owner, or over subsequent transferees of the legal title, including mortgagees. Where a constructive trust is imposed on the grounds of 'unconscionability' it need not have such retrospective effect. The court enjoys the discretion to determine whether the trust should have retrospective effect. As Deane J said in *Muschinski v Dodds*:

'Where competing common law or equitable claims are or may be involved, a declaration of constructive trust by way of remedy can properly be so framed that the consequences of its imposition are operative only from the date of judgement or formal court order or from some other specified date.'[253]

The Australian approach has also attracted academic criticism. Wong argues that it is only marginally more flexible than the English common intention constructive trust, and that there are remnants of gender bias in that, by requiring some evidence of commercialism in the relationship, it ignores the impact of sexual division of labour on women's employment and earning patterns.[254] Mee commends the fact that the unconscionability doctrine does not require the court to make improbable inferences concerning the intention of the claimant by focusing on the fact that one party neglected to consider her separate property rights because she put her faith in her relationship with the owner. However, he argues that the courts have distorted the joint-venture analogy so as to justify the redistribution of property rights:

'It cannot be sufficient simply for the courts to observe that an intimate cohabitation has some of the features of a joint venture and to move directly from that generalized observation to a statutory-style regime of redistribution of property upon the termination of such a cohabitation.'[255]

## (c) New Zealand

The New Zealand courts also initially adopted the 'common intention' analysis.[256] However, in *Gillies v Keogh*[257] Cooke P rejected the 'common intention' analysis because the common intentions discovered were fictitious rather than real. Instead, he stated the principle that the constructive trust is imposed to fulfill the 'reasonable expectations'[258] of the parties:

---

[252] See *Midland Bank plc v Dobson* [1986] 1 FLR 171; *Lloyds Bank plc v Rosset* [1989] Ch 350, CA; revsd [1991] 1 AC 107, HL.

[253] (1985) 160 CLR 583 at 615.

[254] 'Constructive trusts over the family home: lessons to be learned from other commonwealth jurisdictions' [1998] 18 LS 369, 382.

[255] *The Property Rights of Cohabitees* (1999) p 266.    [256] *Hayward v Giordani* [1983] NZLR 140.

[257] [1989] 2 NZLR 327.

[258] *Pasi v Kamana* [1986] 1 NZLR 603; *Oliver v Bradley* [1987] 1 NZLR 586; *Gillies v Keogh* [1989] 2 NZLR 327.

'Whatever legal label or rubric cases in this field are placed under, reasonable expectations in the light of the conduct of the parties are at the heart of the matter. It can be said that a party is unjustly enriched if he or she retains the entire fruits of contributions made by the other, notwithstanding that the other has suffered detriment or made a sacrifice and has reasonably expected from the conduct of the first party and all the circumstances that the contributions will carry rights. Similarly, to retain the sole benefit can be labelled unconscionable or contrary to equity or manifestly unjust.'

He considered that a number of factors would be relevant in determining whether a reasonable expectation had been created, including the length of the relationship and the value of contributions made by the claimant, whether in the form of money or services.[259] However, where an owner made clear that only the use of property was to be shared, but not the ownership, 'a reasonable person in the claimant's position would not expect a benefit',[260] and therefore his claim to a constructive trust would fail. Cooke P also held that the court should enjoy flexibility as to the nature of the remedy to be awarded, so that the New Zealand courts could adopt the Canadian approach of awarding monetary compensation in suitable cases.

In *Gillies v Keogh* a man moved in with a woman. A house was purchased in her sole name, using funds from her previous matrimonial property and various loans from family and friends. They both worked and their earnings were paid into a joint account which was used to pay household expenses and outgoings associated with the house, which was also extended and improved. Throughout the relationship she indicated to him that she regarded the house as hers. The Court of Appeal held that in these circumstances he had no 'reasonable expectation' of obtaining an interest in the house and he was not therefore entitled to a constructive trust.

The principles were further considered by the Court of Appeal in *Lankow v Rose*.[261] This case concerned a claimant who had been involved in a relationship for ten years. During that time she had done the housework, contributed her earnings to the household, and undertaken many thousands of dollars of unpaid work on behalf of her partner's business. On the basis of these compelling facts, it was held that she was entitled to a half interest in their family home. Tipping J indicated that four requirements must be satisfied before a constructive trust would be imposed:

'In order to be awarded a beneficial interest in property owned in law by the defendant, the claimant must first show some contribution, direct or indirect, to the property at issue. A contribution to the relationship will not qualify unless it is also, as will often be the case, a contribution to that property . . . The second thing the claimant must establish is that she expected an interest in the property. If, for any reason, she had no expectation, a constructive trust cannot be imposed in her favour. Thirdly the claimant must show that her expectation of an interest was reasonable in the circumstances. The fourth step is for the claimant to show that the defendant should reasonably expect to yield her an interest. The fact that the defendant is not willing to yield an interest or did not expect to have to do so is no bar to her claim if he should reasonably expect to do so. In that respect the Court stands as his conscience.'[262]

---

[259] [1989] 2 NZLR 327 at 334.     [260] [1989] 2 NZLR 327 at 334.     [261] [1995] 1 NZLR 277.
[262] [1995] 1 NZLR 277 at 294.

Hardie Boys J stated that a claimant would only be able to be entitled to an interest if his or her contributions manifestly exceeded any benefits derived from the relationship:

'In the first place, by contribution to assets one is not referring to those contributions to a common household that are adequately compensated by the benefits the relationship itself confers. The contributions must manifestly exceed the benefit. Putting it in conventional estoppel terms, the plaintiff's contributions must have been to his or her detriment; or in Canadian terms they must have resulted by the end of the relationship in the enrichment of one to the juristically unjustified deprivation of the other. Further, the contributions need not be in money; they may be in services or in any other respect. But there must be a causal relationship between the contributions and the acquisition, preservation or enhancement of the defendant's assets, for, as a claim to a constructive trust is a proprietary claim, a claim to an interest in property, the contributions must have been made to assets; not necessarily to particular assets, but certainly to the defendant's assets in general.'[263]

The 'reasonable expectation' approach again has the merit of avoiding any fiction of a real common intention on the part of the parties, requiring subjective inquiry into their motivations, in favour of an objective assessment of what a reasonable person would have expected in their position. However it has also been subject to criticism on both practical and theoretical grounds. Wong has commented that, whilst domestic contributions may qualify as contributions towards the acquisition of a house, the requirement that contributions must manifestly exceed benefits received will lead to gender bias, since women are generally in a weaker economic position.[264] Mee criticises the New Zealand judges for borrowing from all the other Commonwealth approaches without recognising their doctrinal flaws.[265] He argues that the refusal to choose between them has led to uncertainty as to the scope of the reasonable expectations principle, and the absurdity of one judge's suggestion that a claimant could make a claim to an interest in the family home on any of eight separate bases, namely contract; express; implied or resulting trusts; common intention; unconscionability; estoppel; and unjust enrichment.[266]

## (d) Conclusion

The fact that four Commonwealth jurisdictions have reached such different justifications for the imposition of constructive trusts demonstrates the difficulty of what Casey J described as 'the search for a credible basis on which to found a constructive trust'.[267] Although the approach taken in each jurisdiction differs, it is questionable whether in practice the outcomes of particular cases would be very different. As Cooke P said in *Gillies v Keogh*:

'Normally it makes no practical difference in the result whether one talks of constructive trust, unjust enrichment, imputed common intention or estoppel. In deciding whether any of these are established it is necessary to take into account the same factors.'[268]

---

[263] [1995] 1 NZLR 277 at 282.
[264] 'Constructive trusts over the family home: lessons to be learned from other commonwealth jurisdictions' [1998] 18 LS 369, 388.
[265] *The Property Rights of Cohabitees* (1999) p 292.
[266] *Lankow v Rose* [1995] 1 NZLR 277, 289, per Gault J.
[267] *Gillies v Keogh* [1989] 2 NZLR 327 at 348.    [268] [1989] 2 NZLR 327 at 330.

Each jurisdiction is grappling with the same issue, namely the problem of the ownership of property by partners, married or cohabiting, who have not specified how the property is to be held, and may have entirely opposite understandings. Four issues seem to be crucial in analysing the different approaches:

*(i) The extent to which the parties' thinking is relevant.* All four approaches place some degree of importance on the perceived intentions of the parties. In English law the element of intention is formalised so that it is necessary to demonstrate that the parties intended, either expressly or by necessary implication from conduct, to share the beneficial ownership of the property. 'Reasonable expectation', although concentrating on what a reasonable person would have expected to receive, also takes account of actual intention where a party has made it clear that no interest is to be gained through the contributions. In the Australian doctrine of 'unconscionability' it is necessary to consider what the parties intended, and even under the Canadian 'unjust enrichment' analysis the courts take account of the parties' reasonable expectations in determining whether there is a juristic reason for the enrichment. Therefore, however the criteria are described, it is impossible to escape the relevance of the parties' intentions altogether. Commonwealth jurisdictions may not have escaped the 'common intention' constructive trust as much as their language may suggest.

*(ii) The relevance of non-financial contributions to the relationship.* The 'common intention' constructive trust seems to adopt a very restrictive stance in respect of the relevance of non-financial contributions. Whilst non-financial conduct may constitute sufficient detriment to give rise to a constructive trust in the context of an express common intention, and may be taken into account in quantifying the extent of the beneficial interest arising under a constructive trust,[269] it will not alone entitle the court to infer a common intention. However it is noteworthy that some of the recent English cases applying the broad discretionary approach to the quantification of beneficial interests arising under a constructive trust have focused almost exclusively upon the financial contributions of the parties to the property, rather than the relationship of the parties, thus tending to marginalise the importance of non-financial contributions.[270] Only the Canadian courts seem to have clearly accepted the importance of non-financial contributions such as housekeeping and child-rearing to relationships, so that they may be sufficient to justify the imposition of a constructive trust.

*(iii) Flexibility of remedies.* The English 'common intention' constructive trust is institutional in nature so that a trust arises automatically, conferring a retrospective beneficial interest in the property. The other jurisdictions have accepted that a wider range of remedial responses are available when it is shown that a constructive trust should be imposed, so that a share of the equitable interest is not inevitable. Where appropriate, a monetary payment is an alternative remedy. Even if an equitable proprietary interest is imposed it is not retrospective in its operation.

---

[269] *Oxley v Hiscock* [2004] 3 All ER 703.

[270] *Pinfield v Eagles* [2005] EWCA 447; *Stack v Dowden* [2005] EWCA Civ 857. See [2005] Conv 555 (Cooke).

*(iv) Relationship of the constructive trust to proprietary estoppel.* Despite some judicial comments in England equating constructive trusts with proprietary estoppel, the other Commonwealth jurisdictions have more readily accepted that these two doctrines are sufficiently similar to comprise a unitary principle. However, in England they have been kept distinct. For this reason the use of the term 'constructive trust' may not be synonymous with its use in other jurisdictions, where it can describe a general remedy giving the court flexibility of remedial response. This function is achieved under English law through the doctrine of proprietary estoppel.

In conclusion, the House of Lords has confirmed[271] that English law has a very narrow concept of the constructive trust, based on the finding of a common intention between the legal owner and the person claiming an interest in the property. However, this is balanced by the much wider doctrine of proprietary estoppel, and taken together these doctrines provide English law with as wide and flexible a range of remedies as any of the other jurisdictions considered.

## (7) Legislative solutions to the problem of cohabitee's property rights

The tortured search for a satisfactory mechanism by which cohabitees can obtain an interest in land highlights the difficulty of utilising strict property concepts to solve what is essentially a social problem. Some jurisdictions have therefore adopted a legislative solution, granting the courts a discretion to adjust the property rights of cohabitees, in much the same way as the courts in England have been granted the right to adjust the property rights of married couples on divorce. For example, the New South Wales Property (Relationships) Act 1984 grants the court the discretion to adjust the property rights of those who are party to a domestic relationship.[272] Section 20 provides:

(1) On an application by a party to a domestic relationship for an order under this Part to adjust interests with respect to the property of the parties to the relationship or either of them, a court may make such order adjusting the interests of the parties in the property as to it seems just and equitable having regard to:

   (a) the financial and non-financial contributions made directly or indirectly by or on behalf of the parties to the relationship to the acquisition, conservation or improvement of any of the property of the parties or either of them or to the financial resources of the parties or either of them, and

   (b) the contributions, including any contributions made in the capacity of homemaker or parent, made by either of the parties to the relationship to the welfare of the other party to the relationship or to the welfare of the family constituted by the parties and one or more of the following, namely:

      (i)   a child of the parties,

      (ii)  a child accepted by the parties or either of them into the household of the parties, whether or not the child is a child of either of the parties.

---

[271]  *Lloyds Bank plc v Rosset* [1991] 1 AC 107.

[272]  Other examples include: Victoria Property Law (Amendment Act) 1987; Northern Territory De Facto Relationships Act 1991; ACT Domestic Relationships Act 1994.

One problem with such legislative solutions is the difficulty of formulating an adequate definition of a 'domestic' or 'de facto' relationship. Thus in New South Wales a 'de facto relationship' is defined as a relationship between two adult persons, who live together as a couple, and who are not married to one another or related by family. To determine whether two persons are in a de facto relationship all the circumstances of the relationship are to be taken into account, including: the duration of the relationship; the nature and extent of common residence; whether or not a sexual relationship exists; the degree of financial dependence or interdependence; any arrangements for financial support between the parties; the ownership, use and acquisition of property; the degree of mutual commitment to a shared life; the care and support of children; the performance of household duties; and the reputation and public aspects of the relationship.[273]

No equivalent legislation extending to all co-habitation relationships has been introduced in English law, although various proposals for such a reform have been made. Barlow and Lind, for example, have advocated the adoption of a legislative presumption of sharing where a family home is owned by one of a married couple, or by an unmarried cohabitant who, with her partner has a child, or by an unmarried cohabitant without children but who has been living with her partner for a specified period.[274] The presumptions would operate on a sliding scale, whereby the proportion of the presumed interest would be determined by the length of the relationship. Cohabitees who acted as the primary carer for minor children would receive an enhanced share, to recognise the value of their domestic work, which also reduces their earning capacity. The court would also retain a residual discretion to reallocate beneficial ownership when the presumptions would lead to 'manifest injustice'.[275] However, as was noted above, the Law Commission recently concluded that it would be impossible to devise a statutory scheme for the determination of shares in the shared home which could operate fairly and evenly across all the diverse circumstances which are now to be encountered.[276] It did recommend that further consideration be given to the adoption of a broader-based approach than marriage to personal relationships, such as the registration of certain civil partnerships and/or the imposition of legal rights and obligations on individuals who are involved in a relationship outside of marriage, but felt that it would be inappropriate for it to define a status which would lead to the vesting of rights and obligations.[277] Subsequent to this Law Commission discussion paper, the Civil Partnerships Act 2004 has accorded many of the rights of married couples to same-sex couples who register as civil partners.[278] In particular the court may adjust the property rights of the partners on the dissolution of the civil partnership in the same way that they can adjust the property rights of married couples on divorce.[279] The

---

[273] S 4. See also s 5 where a 'domestic relationship' is defined as a a de facto relationship, or a close personal relationship (other than a marriage or a de facto relationship) between two adult persons, whether or not related by family, who are living together, one or each of whom provides the other with domestic support and personal care.

[274] 'A matter of trust: the allocation of rights in the family home' (1999) 19 LS 468.

[275] See also Niles, 'Property Law v Family Law: resolving the problems of family property' (2003) 23 LS 624, where the Barlow and Lind scheme is considered.

[276] *Sharing Homes A Discussion Paper*, Law Comm No 278 (2002), para 3.100.

[277] Ibid para 5.35–5.45.     [278] Civil Partnership Acts 2004, s 1.

[279] Civil Partnership Acts 2004, s 72 and Sch 5, para 1.

legislation does not extent to heterosexual cohabiting couples, or to homosexual couples who choose to keep their relationship informal rather than registering it as a civil partnership. Since couples who choose to enter a formal civil partnership are those most likely to have given express consideration to their respective property rights in their shared home, the legislation will make little practical difference to the scope of application of constructive trusts in determining the beneficial ownership of shared homes. The principles of resulting and constructive trusts, together with the parallel doctrine of proprietary estoppel, are thus not rendered irrelevant, although the intro-duction of civil partnerships and the publicity they have attracted might help eradicate the popular notion of 'common law marriage', which may lead many vulnerable cohab-ittees to assume that they are entitled to an interest in property merely by virtue of their relationship. The Law Commission is currently examining cohabitation and this may lead to the introduction of more wide ranging reform.[280]

## (8) Conclusion

Although constructive trusts have been evolved so as to enable cohabittees to gain a beneficial interest of the home they share, the courts have stressed the need for parties embarking upon cohabitation to think carefully about the proprietary implications, and to execute an express declaration of trust so as to avoid having to rely on the vagaries of the principles of resulting and constructive trusts or proprietary estoppel. Practitioners who are involved in home purchases also bear a responsibility to try to ensure that the parties clarify their intentions with respect to the ownership. As Ward LJ stated in *Carlton v Goodman*:

'I ask in despair how often this court has to remind conveyancers that they would save the clients a great deal of later difficulty if only they would sit the purchasers down, explain the difference between a joint tenancy and a tenancy in common, ascertain what they want and then expressly declare in the conveyance of transfer how the beneficial interest is to be held because that will be conclusive and save all argument. When are conveyancers going to do this as a matter of invariable standard practice? This court has urged that time after time. Perhaps conveyancers do not always read the law reports. I will try one more time: *always try to agree on and then record how the beneficial interest is to be held.* It is not very difficult to do.'[281]

# 7 The 'remedial constructive trust'[282]

## (1) Defining the 'remedial constructive trust'

The English doctrine of constructive trusts has been subjected to much criticism. As has been seen in the context of trusts of co-owned land, English law adopts an

---

[280] See [2005] Conv 555 (Cooke) at 563–565.    [281] [2002] EWCA Civ 545 AT [44].

[282] See Birks (ed), *The Frontiers of Liability* (1994) Vol 2, pp 163–223; (1998) 114 LQR 399 (Sir Peter Millett).

'institutional' form of constructive trust, whereby the court merely recognises a pre-existing equitable interest. There is little scope for flexibility, other than by manipulation of the criteria which must be satisfied for the creation of a constructive trust, and the nature of the claim pre-determines the remedial outcome.

In other jurisdictions, an entirely different approach towards constructive trusts has emerged. An equitable proprietary right is regarded as one possible remedial response to effect restitution where a defendant has been unjustly enriched. Restitution may be effected either by a personal remedy requiring the enriched defendant to pay a monetary sum equivalent to the value of the enrichment he received to the plaintiff, or by the award of a proprietary remedy over any assets representing the enrichment which remain in the defendant's hands. The essence of the 'remedial' constructive trust is that the court enjoys the discretion to determine whether or not a proprietary remedy should be awarded. If the court exercises its discretion to award a constructive trust the resulting beneficial entitlement can be said to have been 'imposed' by the court, which does not merely recognise a pre-existing proprietary interest. The plaintiff's equitable proprietary interest does not therefore arise from the facts per se, which establish a cause of action in unjust enrichment, but from the exercise of its discretion to award such a remedy.

## (2) Development of the remedial constructive trust

The Commonwealth authorities examined above in the context of the co-ownership of land suggest a movement away from the institutional approach to constructive trusts, towards a more remedial understanding. However, the courts of Canada seem to have taken the greatest steps towards the recognition and acceptance of a general remedial constructive trust, not merely within the context of familial or quasi-familial property, but also in commercial situations. The best description of how the remedial nature of the constructive trust came to be recognised in Canada is found in the judgment of Dickson CJC in *Hunter Engineering Co Inc v Syncrude Canada Ltd*:

'The constructive trust has existed for over two hundred years as an equitable remedy for certain forms of unjust enrichment. In its earliest form, the constructive trust was used to provide a remedy to claimants alleging that others had made profits at their expense. Where the claimant could show the existence of a fiduciary relationship between the claimant and the person taking advantage of the claimant, the courts were receptive . . . Equity would not countenance the abuse of the trust and confidence inherent in a fiduciary relationship and imposed trust obligations on those who profited from abusing their position of loyalty. The doctrine was gradually extended to apply to situations where other persons who were not in a fiduciary relationship with the claimant acted in concert with the fiduciary or knew of the fiduciary obligations. Until the decision of this court in *Pettkus v Becker*, the constructive trust was viewed largely in terms of the law of trusts, hence the need for the existence of a fiduciary relationship. In *Pettkus v Becker* the court moved to an approach more in line with restitutionary principles by explicitly recognising a constructive trust as one of the remedies for unjust enrichment. In finding unjust enrichment the court . . . invoked three criteria: namely (1) an enrichment, (2) a corresponding deprivation, and (3) absence of any juristic reason for the enrichment. The court then found that in the circumstances of the case a constructive trust was the appropriate remedy to redress the unjust enrichment.'[283]

Several key points of this restatement of principle require examination.

### (a)  A restitutionary cause of action

A remedial constructive trust can only be imposed against a person who has been unjustly enriched. 'Unjust enrichment' is therefore the cause of action for which the constructive trust is available as a remedy. In the absence of an unjust enrichment, a constructive trust will not be imposed. For this reason a constructive trust was not imposed in *Hunter Engineering Co v Syncrude Canada Ltd*.[284] Syncrude ordered some specialist gearboxes from Hunter Canada Ltd, a company which fraudulently mis-represented that it acted on behalf of an American company, Hunter US. Hunter Canada placed a contract for the gearboxes with a subcontractor, Alco Sales and Engin-eering. When Hunter US discovered the circumstances they immediately alerted Syncrude and began an action against Hunter Canada for 'passing off'. Fearing a delay in the production of the gearboxes, Syncrude set up a trust fund into which they paid all the moneys which would have been payable to Hunter Canada, and agreed to pay Alco the contract price of the subcontract from this fund. The balance, representing the profit which Hunter Canada would have made, was to be distributed according to the outcome of the litigation between Hunter Canada and Hunter US. In these circum-stances, Hunter US claimed that the balance of the fund was held on constructive trust for them, because it represented the profit that Hunter Canada would have made through passing themselves off as their authorised representatives. The majority of the Supreme Court allowed an appeal against the judgment of the Court of Appeal which had imposed a constructive trust under the principle of *Pettkus v Becker*.[285] They held that there had been no enrichment of Hunter US that would call for restitution, and therefore that a constructive trust could not be justified. Any claim of Hunter US could only arise as a result of Hunter Canada's actions, and Hunter Canada would only be entitled to the surplus in the trust fund on the basis of their contract with Syncrude. Since that contract had been terminated because of the fraudulent misrepresentation, Hunter Canada were no longer entitled to any payment under the contract, and Hunter US could not be in a better position vis-à-vis Syncrude than Hunter Canada. In conclusion, rather than reversing an enrichment received by Syncrude, Dickson CJC considered that:

'. . . if Hunter US's claim prevailed, (i) Hunter US would be enriched, (ii) with a correspond-ing deprivation of Syncrude, (iii) and for no juristic reason that I am able to detect.'[286]

### (b)  A range of remedial responses

Once liability has been established by demonstrating an unjust enrichment which calls for restitution, the court is entitled to select the appropriate remedy to effect restitution. It may conclude that a proprietary remedy is appropriate. Alternatively, a purely personal

---

283  (1989) 57 DLR (4th) 321 at 348.        284  (1989) 57 DLR (4th) 321.
285  (1980) 117 DLR (3d) 257.        286  (1989) 57 DLR (4th) 321 at 353.

monetary award may be made. This flexibility was recognised by the Supreme Court in *Sorochan v Sorochan*, where Dickson CJC stated:

'The constructive trust constitutes one important judicial means of remedying unjust enrichment. Other remedies, such as monetary damages, may also be available to rectify situations of unjust enrichment. We must, therefore, ask when and under what circumstances it is appropriate for a court to impose a constructive trust . . .'[287]

This remedial flexibility was similarly adopted in *Rawluk v Rawluk*.[288] McLachlin J explained:

'The significance of the remedial nature of the constructive trust is not that it cannot confer a property interest, but that the conferring of such an interest is discretionary and dependant on the inadequacy of other remedies for the unjust enrichment in question. The doctrine of constructive trust may be used to confer a proprietary remedy, but that does not automatically presuppose a possessory property right. Thus, even where the tests for constructive trust are met—unjust enrichment, corresponding deprivation, and no juridical justification for the enrichment—the property interest does not automatically arise. Rather, the court must consider whether other remedies to remedy the injustice exist which make the declaration of a constructive trust inappropriate.'[289]

The most important decision concerning the nature and function of remedial constructive trusts is that of the Supreme Court in *LAC Minerals Ltd v International Corona Resources Ltd*.[290] This case concerned the application of the remedial constructive trust to a commercial situation rather than to the specialised circumstances of the co-ownership of familial or quasi-familial land. Corona owned the mining rights over land, and approached LAC with a view to negotiating a joint venture to exploit mineral deposits. In the course of these negotiations Corona revealed results from their exploratory drilling, from which it was clear that adjacent land was also likely to contain mineral deposits. Corona sought to purchase the neighbouring land but were defeated by a competing bid by LAC, which proceeded to exploit the deposits alone. The court held that in these circumstances LAC had been unjustly enriched by misuse of the confidential information they had received from Corona. The central question was as to the nature of the remedy that should be awarded to effect restitution and reverse their unjust enrichment. To give some idea of the size of the claims involved, the trial judge had valued the land at $700m. The Supreme Court emphasised that as the plaintiff's right to restitution had been established it possessed a remedial discretion:

'The court can award either a proprietary remedy, namely that LAC hand over the [land], or award a personal remedy, namely a monetary award. The constructive trust does not lie at the heart of the law of restitution. It is but one remedy, and will only be imposed in appropriate circumstances.'[291]

The majority of the court held that in the circumstances a constructive trust was appropriate, and that LAC should hold the land on trust for Corona.

---

[287] (1986) 29 DLR (4th) 1.     [288] (1990) 65 DLR (4th) 161.
[289] (1990) 65 DLR (4th) 161 at 185–186.     [290] (1989) 61 DLR (4th) 14.
[291] (1989) 61 DLR (4th) 14 at 48, per La Forest J.

## (3) Difficulties associated with the remedial constructive trust

Although superficially attractive, in that it seems to provide a single coherent theory to explain the imposition of constructive trusts, as well as providing flexibility of remedies, the remedial constructive trust poses difficulties which cannot be ignored. The essential problem is one of uncertainty, which arises both at the level of the cause of action and at the level of the court's remedial discretion. For these reasons, the English courts have not yet followed the Canadian lead and adopted the 'remedial constructive trust'. As has been seen, in *Lloyds Bank plc v Rosset*[292] the House of Lords reasserted a very traditional understanding of constructive trusts. Whilst some English judges have suggested that the remedial constructive trust might be introduced in the future, the most recent cases have refused to countenance its adoption.

### (a) Uncertainty as to the cause of action

The remedial constructive trust is seen as one means by which restitution may be effected. The cause of action which gives rise to it is not therefore breach of fiduciary duty or inequitable conduct, which are the triggers for a constructive trust in English law, but unjust enrichment. The Canadian courts have been quick to develop and recognise a general principle of unjust enrichment, whereas in England there has been a historic reluctance to adopt what has been seen as vague and amorphous concept. In *LAC Minerals Ltd v International Corona Resources Ltd*[293] the Supreme Court stressed that unjust enrichment was not simply a vague concept of fairness. La Forest J was keen to point out that:

'The determination that the enrichment is "unjust" does not refer to abstract notions of morality and justice, but flows directly from the finding that there was a breach of a legally recognised duty for which the courts will grant relief. Restitution is a distinct body of law governed by its own developing system of rules.'[294]

The remedial constructive trust is therefore dependent upon a highly developed and well-defined concept of unjust enrichment. Otherwise, it would evolve into the 'palm tree justice' that the courts have been so keen to avoid, and which was the prime reason for the rejection of Lord Denning's new model constructive trust. In *Korkontzilas v Soulos*[295] the majority of the Supreme Court of Canada held that a remedial constructive trust was available even where there had been no unjust enrichment, and that it could be imposed where good conscience requires. If uncertainty is to be avoided, the view of the dissenting minority that a constructive trust may only be imposed where there has been an unjust enrichment should be preferred.

### (b) Uncertainty as to the remedy

Once unjust enrichment has been established, it is for the court to determine the appropriate remedy. It is therefore impossible for the parties to determine whether a constructive trust will be imposed from the fact than an unjust enrichment had been received, although precedents might provide some guidance as to the likely remedy. In

---

[292] [1991] 1 AC 107.    [293] (1989) 61 DLR (4th) 14.    [294] (1989) 61 DLR (4th) 14 at 45.
[295] (1997) 146 DLR (4th) 214

*LAC Minerals v International Corona Resources Ltd* the court was aware of the problems of uncertainty attendant on the remedial constructive trust. La Forest J observed that:

'There is no unanimous agreement on the circumstances in which a constructive trust will be imposed.'[296]

The approach advocated by Goff and Jones, who had argued that a restitutionary proprietary remedy should be awarded when it is 'just, in the particular circumstances of the case, to impose a constructive trust',[297] was rejected unless further guidance could be given as to what those circumstances might be.[298] However, some guidelines were suggested, and it was held that there was no need to demonstrate a special relationship between the parties as a prerequisite of a constructive trust, nor that there must have been a pre-existing property right. La Forest J suggested that 'a constructive trust should only be awarded if there is reason to grant the plaintiff the additional rights that flow from the recognition of a right of property'.[299] A number of factors were identified which may be relevant in determining whether to award a proprietary remedy:

'Amongst the most important of these will be that it is appropriate that the plaintiff receive the priority accorded to the holder of a right of property in a bankruptcy. More important in this case is the right of a property owner to have changes in value accrue to his account rather than to the account of the wrongdoer . . . The moral quality of the defendant's acts may also be another consideration in determining whether a proprietary remedy is appropriate. Allowing the defendant to retain a specific asset when it was obtained through conscious wrongdoing may so offend a court that it would deny to the defendant the right to retain the property.'

Having considered these factors, La Forest J, with whom the majority concurred, concluded that a constructive trust should be imposed:

'. . . [the constructive trust] is but one remedy, and will only be imposed in appropriate circumstances. Where it could be more appropriate than in the present case, however, it is difficult to see.'[300]

However, the absolute certainty of the rightness of a proprietary remedy in this statement only serves to emphasise the difficulty of uncertainty, for whilst La Forest J and the majority considered that the facts provided the clearest possible case for a proprietary remedy, Sopinka J and McIntyre J dissented and held that a personal monetary award of restitution was sufficient to reverse the unjust enrichment.[301] This uncertainty about the correct remedy was also evident in the more recent case *Korkontzilas v Soulos*,[302] where the Supreme Court considered whether a constructive trust should be awarded against a gratuitous agent who had acted in breach of his fiduciary obligations.

---

[296] (1989) 61 DLR (4th) 14 at 49.
[297] Goff and Jones, *The Law of Restitution* (3rd edn, 1986), p 78.
[298] (1989) 61 DLR (4th) 14 at 51.     [299] (1989) 61 DLR (4th) 14.
[300] (1989) 61 DLR (4th) 14 at 48.
[301] See also Tang, 'Confidence and the constructive trust' (2003) 23 LS 135, who argues that a constructive trust should not have been imposed.
[302] (1997) 146 DLR (4th) 214.

The majority held that a constructive trust should be awarded whereas the dissenting minority held that it should not.

## (4) Prospects for the remedial constructive trust in England

Whilst the remedial constructive trust developed in Canada has to some degree been adopted in other commonwealth jurisdictions, it has yet to find a place in English law.[303] As has been evident throughout this chapter, English law seems to have been particularly sensitive to the difficulties of uncertainty, especially in the field of proprietary rights. The ability of a legal system to incorporate a concept such as the remedial constructive trust may largely be determined by the prevailing legal culture and its ability to accept a degree of remedial discretion in the interests of individual justice at the expense of absolute certainty. However, the emergence of a coherent doctrine of unjust enrichment in England has opened the door to the possible acceptance of a remedial style of constructive trust in the future. In *Lipkin Gorman v Karpnale Ltd*[304] the House of Lords took the momentous step of acknowledging the existence of an autonomous cause of action in unjust enrichment, which has been consistently affirmed in subsequent decisions.[305] The precise scope of the principle against unjust enrichment has been the subject of intense academic scrutiny, and as restitutionary claims are more frequently considered judicially it is inevitable that it will attain greater clarity. Whilst some areas remain vague, for example the practical scope of the restitutionary defence of change of position, it seems clear that English law has developed an independent law of restitution, founded on the principle against unjust enrichment, which is the necessary prerequisite of the adoption of the remedial constructive trust. The adoption of a cause of action in unjust enrichment inevitably raises the question as to the nature of the remedies available to effect restitution. Whilst personal restitutionary remedies are available, it is less clear when restitution may be effected by the award of a proprietary remedy. Traditionally, such proprietary remedies have only been available where an enrichment has been received in breach of fiduciary duty, or if the defendant enjoyed a pre-existing proprietary right, or 'proprietary base'[306] in the property from which the enrichment was derived. It was noted in the preceding chapter how Professor Birks proposed an extension of the concept of the resulting trust as a vehicle to effect restitution, which would have led to a significant expansion in the circumstances in which a proprietary remedy was available against an enriched defendant. Although this thesis was rejected by the House of Lords in *Westdeutsche Landesbank Girozentrale v Islington London Borough Council*,[307] Lord Browne-Wilkinson took the

---

[303] The possible existence of the remedial constructive trust was left open by the Privy Council in *Re Goldcorp Exchange Ltd (in receivership)* [1995] 1 AC 74.

[304] [1991] 2 AC 548.

[305] See *Woolwich Equitable Building Society v IRC* [1992] 3 All ER 737; *Westdeutsche Landesbank Girozentrale v Islington London Borough Council* [1996] AC 669; *Kleinwort Benson Ltd v Glasgow City Council* [1999] 1 AC 153.

[306] *Lonhro plc v Al-Fayed (No 2)* [1992] 1 WLR 1.

[307] [1996] AC 669; (1996) 112 LQR 521 (Cape); [1996] CLJ 432 (Jones); [1996] LMCLQ 441 (Stevens). See [1996] RLR 3 (Birks).

opportunity to suggest that English law may yet decide to adopt the remedial constructive trust:

'Although the resulting trust is an unsuitable basis for developing proprietary restitutionary
remedies, the remedial constructive trust, if introduced into English law, may provide a
more satisfactory road forward. The court by way of remedy might impose a constructive
trust on a defendant who knowingly retains property of which the plaintiff has been
unjustly deprived. Since the remedy can be tailored to the circumstances of the particular
case, innocent third parties would not be prejudiced and restitutionary defences, such as
change of position, are capable of being given effect. However, whether English law should
follow the United States and Canada by adopting the remedial constructive trust will have to
be decided in some future case when the point is directly in issue.'[308]

However in subsequent cases the Court of Appeal has rejected any suggestion that
English law should introduce the remedial constructive trust. In *Halifax Building
Society v Thomas*[309] Peter Gibson LJ refused to impose a constructive trust where a
defendant had obtained a profit by purchasing a house, which had subsequently risen in
value, using a fraudulently obtained mortgage. He stated that English Law had not
followed other jurisdictions where the constructive trust has become a remedy for
unjust enrichment, and indicated that, in the light of Parliamentary action which
presupposed that a criminal might keep the benefit of his crime without statutory
intervention, the courts should not indulge in such judicial creativity.[310]

Such objections were stated even more strongly in *Re Polly Peck (No 2)*,[311] which is
the only English case where the issue of the existence of the remedial constructive trust
has arisen for decision. The applicants, who were the owners of land in Cyprus, applied
for leave, pursuant to s 11(3)(d) of the Insolvency Act 1986, to commence proceedings
by writ against the administrators of Polly Peck International. They claimed that they
were entitled to a remedial constructive trust of the profits which Polly Peck had
obtained by wrongful exploitation of their land after it had been misappropriated by
the Turkish Republic of Northern Cyprus. As Polly Peck was in administration the grant
of a such proprietary remedy would enable them to gain priority over other creditors.
The Court of Appeal held that there was no prospect that the court would grant the
order requested. It would impose a retrospective proprietary interest on the assets of
the insolvent company, excluding those assets from pari passu distribution amongst the
general creditors, thereby modifying the statutory scheme for the distribution of the
company's assets under the Insolvency Act. Nourse LJ held that the remedial constructive trust could only be introduced into English law by an Act of Parliament. Having
noted that Lord Browne-Wilkinson had accepted the possibility that the remedial constructive trust may become part of English Law in *Westdeutsche Landesbank Girozentrale
v Islington London Borough Council* he continued:

'. . . such observations, being both obiter and tentative, can only be of limited assistance
when the question has to be decided, as it does here. There being no earlier decision, we
must turn to principle. In doing so, we must recognise that the remedial constructive trust

---

[308] [1996] AC 669 at 716.    [309] [1996] Ch 217.    [310] [1995] 4 All ER 673 at 682.
[311] [1998] 3 All ER 812.

gives the court a discretion to vary proprietary rights. You cannot grant a proprietary right to A, who has not had one beforehand, without taking some proprietary right away from B. No English court has ever had the power to do that, except with the authority of Parliament . . . It is not that you need an Act of Parliament to prohibit a variation of proprietary rights. You need one to permit it: see the Variation of Trusts Act 1958 and the Matrimonial Causes Act 1973.'[312]

He further indicated that, in his opinion, the possibility of a remedial constructive trust would not have been seriously arguable even if Polly Peck had been solvent and there was no direct conflict with the provisions of the Insolvency Act.

In the light of these recent cases, commentators have suggested that there is no prospect that the remedial constructive trust will be introduced in England.[313] Whilst in practice such an innovation is highly unlikely, it is less certain that the House of Lords lacks the jurisdiction necessary to introduce such a remedy if it so wishes.

---

[312] [1998] 3 All ER 812 at 831. Nourse LJ placed particular reliance on the judgment of Lord Simmond LC in *Chapman v Chapman* [1954] AC 429.

[313] (1998) 12 Trusts Law International 202 (Birks); All ER Rev 1998, 415; [1999] RLR 128 (Wright).

# 10

# Proprietary estoppel[1]

## 1 Introduction to proprietary estoppel[2]

### (1) A means of creating proprietary interests

In the previous chapters it has been seen how an equitable proprietary interest can be created informally by means of a resulting or constructive trust. Such trusts have proved particularly significant in the context of cohabitation. The doctrine of 'proprietary estoppel' provides another means by which a person may become entitled to a proprietary right despite the absence of express intention and appropriate formalities. As Stephen Moriarty has observed:

'The role of proprietary estoppel seems self-evident: it provides for the informal creation of interests in land whenever a person has acted detrimentally in reliance upon an oral assurance that he has such an interest. Oral grants of interests by themselves, therefore, are insufficient; but act in reliance upon some such assurance, and proprietary estoppel will validate what the Law of Property Act says has no effect.'[3]

### (2) Establishing a claim by way of proprietary estoppel

A claim by way of proprietary estoppel is not in itself a remedy. However, where a claimant can demonstrate an entitlement by way of estoppel, an appropriate remedy will be awarded. The estoppel is therefore best seen as a species of cause of action which demands an appropriate remedial response. Whilst the general doctrine of estoppel is only capable of acting as a shield to protect against a person asserting his rights, proprietary estoppel 'may be relied on as a sword, not merely as a shield'.[4]

There are therefore two essential stages to the process of claiming a remedy by way of proprietary estoppel, namely establishing an estoppel 'equity' and satisfying that equity through an appropriate remedy.

---

[1] See Hopkins, *The Informal Acquisition of Rights in Land* (2000); Finn, *Equitable Estoppel*, in Finn (ed), *Essays in Equity* (1985); Welstead, *Proprietary Estoppel and the Family Home* (Unpublished Phd Thesis), Cambridge University Library; Denning Law Library, University of Buckingham; (1997) 17 LS 258 (Cooke).

[2] Gray, *Elements of Land Law* (3rd edn, 2000), pp 753–817; Stevens and Pearce, *Land Law* (2005), pp 555–582.

[3] (1984) 100 LQR 376 at 381.    [4] *Pascoe v Turner* [1979] 1 WLR 431 at 436, per Cumming-Bruce LJ.

## (a) Establishing an 'equity'

A claimant must first demonstrate circumstances which entitle him to demand a remedy. In other words, a claimant must show that the cause of action, namely a proprietary estoppel, has been raised. Modern cases have stated that three factors are required to establish a proprietary estoppel: (1) an assurance; (2) a reliance; and (3) change of position or detriment.[5] An estoppel 'equity' will only arise if these three elements are proved. They will be discussed in detail below.

## (b) Satisfying the 'equity'

Once an estoppel 'equity' has been established, the claimant is prima facie entitled to remedial relief. However, the mere existence of an 'equity' does not predetermine the appropriate remedial response. Rather, the court must decide what specific remedy would be appropriate in the circumstances to 'satisfy' the equity raised by the estoppel.[6] The court enjoys the discretion to select from a range of possible remedies.

## (3) Scope of proprietary estoppel

The principles of proprietary estoppel have been held to operate so as to create rights and interests in land, and possibly other types of property. However, it has been suggested that they do not apply in the context of public law matters, such as the grant of planning permission. In *Western Fish Products Ltd v Penwith District Council*, Megaw LJ said:

'We know of no case, and none has been cited to us, in which the principle set out in *Ramsden v Dyson* and *Crabb v Arun District Council* has been applied otherwise than to rights and interests created in or over land. It may extend to other forms of property: see per Lord Denning MR in *Moorgate Mercantile Co Ltd v Twitchings*.[7] In our judgment there is no good reason for extending the principle further. As Harman LJ pointed out in *Campbell Discount Co Ltd v Bridge*,[8] the system of equity has become a very precise one. The creation of new rights and remedies is a matter for Parliament, not the judges.'[9]

Although Megaw LJ considered that the doctrine of proprietary estoppel had no application in a public law context, the developing doctrine of legitimate expectation in public law does, however, provide a close analogy with proprietary estoppel.

## (4) Relationship between proprietary estoppel and constructive trusts[10]

As was seen in Chapter 9, English law adopts a predominantly 'institutional' or 'substantive' approach towards constructive trusts. If the requirements for a constructive trust are demonstrated, the legal owner will be treated as having held the property

---

5  See *A-G of Hong Kong v Humphreys' Estate (Queen's Gardens) Ltd* [1987] AC 114, PC.
6  *Plimmer v City of Wellington Corpn* (1883–84) LR 9 App Cas 699.        7  [1981] 2 All ER 204 at 218.
8  [1976] QB 225 at 242.        9  [1961] 1 QB 445 at 459.
10  See Nield, 'Constructive trusts and estoppel' (2003) 23 LS 311.

subject to a trust from the time that the requirements were met. As has been seen, English law has not yet adopted the 'remedial constructive trust', which would allow the court the discretion to decide whether a trust should arise, and if so whether it should gain priority over other third party interests subsisting in the property affected. However, where a proprietary estoppel can be established, the court possesses a much wider discretion as to the range of remedies that it may award. It is arguable that one means by which the court can satisfy the equity is the imposition of a trust.[11]

Some have argued that any distinction between constructive trusts and proprietary estoppel is purely illusory, and that they should therefore be regarded as rooted in a common principle, for example the discretionary prevention of unconscionability.[12] However, even though there has been some blurring of the concepts of proprietary estoppel and constructive trusts in judicial statements, it is submitted that it remains important to maintain a distinction[13] between them. The criteria applied by the courts in relation to each concept are clearly different. To establish a constructive trust it is essential to demonstrate that the parties shared a 'common intention' as to the ownership of the property in question, whereas in the case of proprietary estoppel a mere 'assurance' is required, which is a somewhat less definite requirement. In the case of a constructive trust, only a limited range of activities will be considered sufficient to constitute detriment, whereas there is a much greater willingness to regard non-financial detriment as sufficient to establish an estoppel equity. Lastly, in the case of constructive trusts, the court possesses no remedial flexibility and cannot take account of the effect that the recognition of an equitable interest in the property will have on third parties, whereas under proprietary estoppel the court claims a discretion to determine how the equity should be satisfied, and any remedy only takes effect from the date that the court awards it in satisfaction of the equity.

In reality there is a substantial overlap between constructive trusts and proprietary estoppel. This means that the same facts might give rise either to the recognition of a constructive trust, or to the award of an estoppel remedy. This was evident in the case of *Yaxley v Gotts*[14] where a builder had refurbished and converted a house into flats on the basis of an oral agreement with the owner that he would acquire the ground floor flats for himself. The Court of Appeal upheld that decision of the first instance judge that the builder was entitled to an interest by way of proprietary estoppel, but also held that the facts entitled him to an interest under a constructive trust in accordance with the principles of *Lloyds Bank plc v Rossett*.[15]

## (5) Issues of priority relating to proprietary estoppel

The doctrine of proprietary estoppel provides a means by which proprietary rights may be created. Until recently it was unclear whether an estoppel 'equity' was an interest in land capable of binding a third party who acquired a subsequent interest in it.[16]

---

[11] See below, p 346.   [12] [1990] Conv 370 (Hayton).   [13] [1993] 109 LQR 114 (Ferguson).
[14] [2000] 1 All ER 711.   [15] [1991] 1 AC 107.
[16] See Gray & Gray, *Land Law* (3rd edn, 2001) pp 1020–1024; Stevens and Pearce, *Land Law* (3rd edn, 2005), pp 579–582; *Sledmore v Dalby* (1996) 72 P & CR 196; (1997) LQR 232 (Pawlowski).

However s 116 of the Land Registration Act 2002 now provides that 'for the avoidance of doubt' an equity by estoppel is 'an interest capable of binding successors in title'. Although there is little authority, it has recently been argued that proprietary estoppel might give rise to a continuing personal liability even after the land or property to which it relates has been sold.[17]

# 2 Establishing the equity

## (1) The essence of proprietary estoppel

The essence of proprietary estoppel is that if the legal owner of property (almost invariably land) has so conducted himself (whether by encouragement or representations) that the claimant believes that he has, or will obtain, some rights in respect of the land, and he has acted to his detriment on the basis of his induced belief, it would be unconscionable for the legal owner to assert his strict legal entitlement to the property.[18] The remedy granted in satisfaction of the estoppel equity is therefore awarded because the claimant has experienced 'frustrated expectation'.[19] The nature of the claim was summarised by Scott J in *Layton v Martin*:

'The proprietary estoppel line of cases are concerned with the question whether an owner of property can, by insisting on his strict legal rights therein, defeat an expectation of an interest in that property, it being an expectation which he has raised by his conduct and which has been relied on by the claimant.'[20]

## (2) Identifying 'unconscionability'

Although the principle of proprietary estoppel has a long historical pedigree, dating from before the nineteenth century,[21] it is only in more recent years that the courts have formulated the key requirements in a general way. The most important question is to identify the circumstances in which a legal owner's conduct can be regarded as 'unconscionable', thus calling for the court to provide the claimant with a remedy and preventing him from asserting his legal rights. The courts have recognised that at the moment the circumstances in which the equity will be established are 'ill defined'.[22]

### (a) Strict criteria

In the late nineteenth century, the courts held that there were strict and rigid criteria which must be met before an estoppel equity was raised. Despite earlier and broader

---

17 [2005] Conv 14 (Bright and McFarlane)
18 See Snell, *Principles of Equity* (29th edn, 1990), pp 573–574.
19 Gray, *Elements of Land Law* (2nd edn, 1993), p 356.     20 [1986] 2 FLR 227 at 238.
21 See *Bridges v Kilburne* (1792) (referred to in *Jackson v Cator* (1800) 5 Ves 688); *Dillwyn v Llewelyn* (1862) 4 De G F & J 517; *Ramsden v Dyson* (1866) LR 1 HL 129.
22 *Walker v Walker* (12 April 1984, unreported), per Browne-Wilkinson LJ.

statements of principle in *Ramsden v Dyson*,[23] in *Willmott v Barber*[24] Fry J stipulated five essential elements which had to be established before the court would restrain a defendant from asserting his legal rights over property:

'A man is not to be deprived of his legal rights unless he has acted in such a way as would make it fraudulent for him to set up those rights. What, then are the elements or requisites necessary to constitute fraud of that description? In the first place the plaintiff must have made some mistake as to his legal rights. Secondly, the plaintiff must have expended some money or must have done some act (not necessarily upon the defendant's land) on the faith of his mistaken belief. Thirdly, the defendant, the possessor of the legal right, must know of the existence of his own right which is inconsistent with the right claimed by the plaintiff. If he does not know of it he is in the same position as the plaintiff, and the doctrine of acquiescence is founded upon conduct with a knowledge of your legal rights. Fourthly, the defendant, the possessor of the legal right, must know of the plaintiff's mistaken belief of his rights. If he does not, there is nothing which calls upon him to assert his own rights. Lastly, the defendant, the possessor of the legal right, must have encouraged the plaintiff in his expenditure of money or in the other acts which he has done, either directly or by abstaining from asserting his legal right. Where all these elements exist, there is fraud of such a nature as will entitle the court to restrain the possessor of the legal title from exercising it, but, in my judgment, nothing short of this will do.'

These five 'probanda' came to be regarded as essential requirements of estoppel, and claims failed where it was not possible to establish all five.[25] In *Crabb v Arun District Council*[26] Scarman LJ considered that the five requirements were 'a valuable guide as to the matters of fact which have to be established in order that a plaintiff may establish this particular equity', and in *Coombes v Smith*[27] Jonathan Parker QC, sitting as a deputy High Court judge, addressed the question of whether an equity had been established by considering whether each of the five requirements were met on the facts.

Despite such judicial approval, the requirements in *Willmott v Barber*[28] should not be regarded as a comprehensive statement of the essentials of an estoppel claim. They were stipulated in the context of a situation where the claimant had acted under a mistake as to his existing rights. This should be distinguished from cases where the claimant founded his claim upon an 'expectation' created or encouraged by the legal owner. This concept of estoppel by encouragement had found expression in the judgment of Lord Kingsdown in *Ramsden v Dyson*, where he had suggested a less restrictive approach:

'If a man, under a verbal agreement with a landlord for a certain interest in land, or what amounts to the same thing, under an expectation, created or encouraged by the landlord, that he shall have a certain interest, takes possession of such land, with the consent of the landlord, and upon the faith of such promise or expectation, with the knowledge of the

---

[23] (1866) LR 1 HL 129 at 152 (Lord Cranworth LC) and at 170 (Lord Kingsdown).

[24] (1880) 15 Ch D 96 at 105–106.

[25] See *Kammins Ballroom Co Ltd v Zenith Instruments (Torquay) Ltd* [1971] AC 850 at 884; *E and L Berg Homes Ltd v Grey* (1979) 253 Estates Gazette 473.

[26] [1976] Ch 179.    [27] [1986] 1 WLR 808.    [28] (1880) 15 Ch D 96.

landlord, and without objection by him, lays out money upon the land, a Court of equity will compel the landlord to give effect to such promise or expectation.'[29]

## (b) General 'unconscionability'

The restrictive approach of *Willmott v Barber*[30] has largely given way to a much broader understanding of proprietary estoppel.[31] In *Taylor Fashions Ltd v Liverpool Victoria Trustees Co Ltd*[32] Oliver J restated the requirements of proprietary estoppel in a manner which means that not all the 'probanda' of *Willmott v Barber*[33] are necessarily applicable to every case of proprietary estoppel:

'. . . the recent cases indicate,[34] in my judgment, that the application of the *Ramsden v Dyson* principle—whether you call it proprietary estoppel, estoppel by acquiescence or estoppel by encouragement is really immaterial—requires a very much broader approach which is directed rather at ascertaining whether, in particular individual circumstances, it would be unconscionable for a party to be permitted to deny that which, knowingly or unknowingly, he has allowed or encouraged another to assume to his detriment than to inquiring whether the circumstances can be fitted within the confines of some preconceived formula serving as a universal yardstick for every form of unconscionable behaviour.'[35]

Therefore, rather than determining whether an equity had been established by application of a rigid list of requirements which must be satisfied, he held that the appropriate inquiry was simply whether the defendant's conduct had been, in all the circumstances of the case, 'unconscionable'.[36] This was also emphasised by Megarry V-C in *Appleby v Cowley*:

'. . . As the law has developed, it may be that in cases in which a claim based on proprietary estoppel is made, the real question comes down simply to whether or not the assertion of strict legal rights would be unconscionable, without any detailed conditions or criteria being specified.'[37]

This modern approach was also adopted by the Court of Appeal in *Habib Bank Ltd v Habib Bank AG*[38] and by the Privy Council in *Lim Teng Huan v Ang Swee Chuan*,[39] where Lord Browne-Wilkinson stated:

'The decision in *Taylor Fashions Ltd v Liverpool Victoria Trustees Co Ltd* showed that, in order

---

[29] (1866) LR 1 HL 129 at 170.    [30] (1880) 15 Ch D 96.

[31] However, in the recent case of *Taylor v Dickens* [1998] 1 FLR 806, Judge Weeks QC rejected the notion of a broad doctrine of estoppel founded on the principle of 'unconscionability' and that the existence of such a doctrine would mean that 'you might as well forget the law of contract and issue every judge with a portable palm tree'. His comments appear to be inconsistent with the majority of modern cases and have been severely criticised: [1998] Conv 213 (Thompson).

[32] [1982] QB 133n; *McMahon v Kerry County Council* (1981) ILRM 419; (1985) 79 ILSI Gaz 179 (Pearce).

[33] (1880) 15 Ch D 96.

[34] See *Inwards v Baker* [1965] 2 QB 29; *ER Ives Investment Ltd v High* [1967] 2 QB 379; *Crabb v Arun District Council* [1976] Ch 179; *Moorgate Mercantile Credit Co Ltd v Twitchings* [1976] QB 225, CA; *Shaw v Applegate* [1977] 1 WLR 970, CA.

[35] See also *Amalgamated Investment and Property Co Ltd (in liquidation) v Texas Commerce International Bank Ltd* [1982] QB 84.

[36] [1982] QB 84 at 155.    [37] (1982) Times, 14 April.    [38] [1981] 1 WLR 1265.

[39] [1992] 1 WLR 113.

to found a proprietary estoppel, it is not essential that the representor should have been guilty of unconscionable conduct in permitting the representee to assume that he could act as he did: it is enough if, in all the circumstances, it is unconscionable for the representor to go back on the assumption which he permitted the representee to make.'[40]

Most recently in *Gillett v Holt* Robert Walker LJ emphasised that the prevention of 'unconscionability' is the essence of proprietary estoppel:

'Moreover, the fundamental principle that equity is concerned to prevent unconscionable conduct permeates all the elements of the doctrine. In the end the court must look at the matter in the round.'[41]

### (c) Residual significance of the 'probanda'?

Whilst the five requirements stipulated in *Willmott v Barber*[42] do not provide an exhaustive statement of the circumstances in which an estoppel equity will be established, they may retain an important residual significance in cases of acquiescence. This was recognised by Cumming-Bruce LJ in *Swallow Securities Ltd v Isenberg*:

'. . . it has been recognised that the court should regard the formulation by Fry J of the requirement of five probanda as being guidelines, which will probably prove to be the necessary and essential guidelines, to assist the court to decide the question whether it is unconscionable for the plaintiffs to assert their legal rights by taking an advantage of the defendant.'[43]

They were also applied in the more recent case *Matharu v Matharu*,[44] where Roch LJ held that they had been satisfied.

## (3) Application of the modern requirements

Although the approach taken in *Taylor Fashions*[45] explains the doctrine of proprietary estoppel on the general principle of 'unconscionability', to establish an equity the courts have held that the three key elements of 'assurance', 'reliance', and 'detriment or change of position' must be present.[46] Although these elements can be separated for analytical purposes, in *Gillett v Holt*[47] Robert Walker LJ suggested that in practice they are often interrelated because 'the quality of the relevant assurances may influence the issue of reliance' and that 'reliance and detriment are often intertwined'.[48]

### (a) 'Assurance'

No estoppel 'equity' will arise unless the claimant can establish that the legal owner of land made a representation, or created an expectation, that he was presently entitled, or

---

[40] Ibid at 117.     [41] [2000] 2 All ER 289 at 301.     [42] (1880) 15 Ch D 96.
[43] [1985] 1 EGLR 132 at 134.
[44] (1994) 68 P & CR 93, [1994] 2 FLR 597; [1995] Conv 61 (Welstead); (1995) 58 MLR 411 (Milne).
[45] [1982] QB 133n.
[46] See *A-G of Hong Kong v Humphreys Estate (Queen's Gardens) Ltd* [1987] AC 114, PC; *Gillies v Keogh* [1989] 2 NZLR 327 at 346, per Richardson J.
[47] [2000] 2 All ER 289, 301.     [48] See also *Jennings v Rice* (2003) 1 P & CR 8.

would become entitled,[49] to an interest in the land. In some cases the assurance may take the form of an actual agreement between the parties, as in *Yaxley v Gotts*[50] where a builder had entered into an oral agreement to refurbish and convert a house into flats in return for his acquiring the ground floor flats. The Court of Appeal held that, although this agreement was unenforceable as a contract for lack of formalities,[51] it could give rise to a claim by way of proprietary estoppel. However in the majority of cases the assurance will fall far short of any formal agreement between the parties.

An assurance may be given 'actively' through the acts of the legal owner, or 'passively' through his silence and failure to disabuse the claimant of his belief that he is entitled to an interest in the land.[52]

*(i) Active assurance.* In *Pascoe v Turner*[53] the plaintiff made an active assurance to the defendant, a woman with whom he was living. The defendant had moved in with the plaintiff in 1964. In 1973 he left the house when he started an affair with another woman, but the evidence showed that he had visited the defendant and had declared to her that she had nothing to worry about, as the house was hers and everything in it. The Court of Appeal held that the evidence established an assurance sufficient to found an estoppel equity, and since she had acted to her detriment in reliance upon it she was entitled to a remedy by way of proprietary estoppel. In *Inwards v Baker*[54] Mr Baker's son, Jack, was intending to build a bungalow. He was persuaded by his father to build the bungalow on his land, which he subsequently did. The Court of Appeal held that this amounted to a sufficient inducement or encouragement to give rise to an estoppel. In *Griffiths v Williams*[55] the Court of Appeal held that an estoppel equity was established where a mother had assured her daughter that she would be entitled to live in her house for the whole of her life. An active assurance will certainly have been given if the legal owner of property promised that the claimant was, or would become, entitled to some interest in it.[56]

*(ii) Passive assurance.* It seems that if a legal owner merely stands by while the claimant acts to his detriment, in the belief that he is entitled to an interest in the land, this will constitute a sufficient assurance to give rise to an estoppel equity. In *Ramsden v Dyson* Lord Wensleydale said:

'. . . [if a stranger] builds on my land, supposing it to be his own, and I, knowing it to be mine, do not interfere, but leave him to go on, equity considers it to be dishonest in me to remain passive and afterwards to interfere and take the profit.'[57]

Although it is not strictly essential[58] that the owner knew of the plaintiff's action and mistaken belief, and of his own rights to intervene,[59] these are relevant issues and it will be easier to establish an equity where they are present.

---

[49] *Re Basham (Decd)* [1987] 1 All ER 405.    [50] [2000] 1 All ER 711.
[51] Law of Property (Miscellaneous Provisions) Act 1989, s 2.
[52] *Warnes v Headley* (31 January 1984, unreported), CA.
[53] [1979] 1 WLR 431.    [54] [1965] 2 QB 29.    [55] (1977) 248 Estates Gazette 947.
[56] *Wayling v Jones* (1993) 69 P & CR 170.    [57] (1866) LR 1 HL 129 at 168.
[58] *Shaw v Applegate* [1978] 1 All ER 123, CA; *Taylor Fashions Ltd v Liverpool Victoria Trustees Co Ltd* [1982] QB 133n.
[59] Compare *Armstrong v Sheppard & Short Ltd* [1959] 2 QB 384, CA.

*(iii) Assurance relating to specific assets.* Whether the assurance is active or passive it will only generate an equity if given with respect to particular assets. In a sense, this limitation operates as an equivalent of the rule that a trust can only be validly created if there was 'certainty of subject matter'. In *Layton v Martin*[60] a man had given a woman who had moved in with him a general assurance that he would provide her with 'financial security'. It was held that this assurance was too amorphous and insufficiently connected with specific property to give rise to an estoppel equity. Scott J concluded that proprietary estoppel can only arise:

'. . . in connection with some asset in respect of which it has been represented, or is alleged to have been represented that the claimant is to have some interest . . . The present case does not raise that question. A representation that "financial security" would be provided by the deceased to the plaintiff, and on which I will assume she acted, is not a representation that she is to have some equitable or legal interest in any particular asset or assets.'[61]

In *Re Basham (Decd)*[62] it was held that a plaintiff was able to claim a right by way of proprietary estoppel to the residuary estate of the defendant who had made an assurance to that effect. Although the nature of a residuary estate is such that it does not consist of a clearly identified piece of property, Edward Nugee QC held that there was 'no reason in principle or in authority why the doctrine of proprietary estoppel should not apply so as to raise an equity against B in favour of A extending to the whole of A's estate'.[63]

*(iv) Assurance relating to a grant of future rights.* An estoppel equity will arise wherever an assurance is made concerning the future grant of rights in specific property. This will most commonly occur where an owner had made assurances that he will leave property to the claimant in his will. For example, in *Re Basham (Decd)*[64] Edward Nugee QC held that the plaintiff was entitled to a claim by way of proprietary estoppel where the defendant, her step-father, had assured her that a house he owned would be hers on his death. An estoppel equity was also established in *Wayling v Jones*,[65] where the owner of a hotel had promised his partner that he would leave it to him by will on his death.

However in *Taylor v Dickens*[66] it was held that there was no claim by way of proprietary estoppel where an elderly lady had said that she would leave her estate to her gardener, but changed her mind without telling him after he had stopped charging her for his help. Judge Weeks QC held that, in light of the inherent revocability of testamentary dispositions, such an assurance would only give rise to an estoppel equity if it created or encouraged the claimant to believe that the owner would not exercise her right to change her will. This decision was subjected to sever academic criticism[67] which

---

[60] [1986] 2 FLR 227.     [61] [1986] 2 FLR 227 at 238–239.     [62] [1986] 1 WLR 1498.
[63] [1986] 1 WLR 1498 at 1510.     [64] [1986] 1 WLR 1498.
[65] (1993) 69 P & CR 170. See also *Gillett v Holt* [1998] 3 All ER 917 where it was held that an assurance that the defendant would leave his estate to the plaintiff was capable of founding an entitlement by way of proprietary estoppel. However, in the event Carnwath J held that a claim failed because the defendant had only expressed a mere intention to leave his estate by will to the plaintiff and not an irrevocable promise that he would inherit regardless of any changes in circumstances.
[66] [1998] 3 FCR 455.     [67] [1998] Conv 220 (Thomson); [1998] RLR (Swadling).

was accepted by the Court of Appeal in *Gillett v Holt*.[68] In this case Gillett had worked for Holt, who was a gentleman farmer, for nearly forty years. On seven separate occasions Holt had assured him that he would leave his entire estate to him, and that he and his family could therefore be sure of a secure future. Robert Walker LJ explained that these assurances were sufficient to give rise to an estoppel equity even though they did not include an explicit assurance that the owner would not alter his will:

'But the inherent revocability of testamentary dispositions (even if well understood by the parties, as Mr Gillett candidly accepted that it was by him) is irrelevant to a promise or assurance that "all this will be yours" . . . Even when the promise of assurance is in terms linked to the making of a will . . . the circumstances may make clear that the assurance is more than as mere statement of present (revocable) intention, and is tantamount to a promise.'[69]

### (b) 'Reliance'

*(i) 'Reliance' as a causal connection.* Reliance connects the assurance with the detriment. It substantiates that the assurance caused the claimant to act to his detriment. As Balcombe LJ stated in *Wayling v Jones*:

'There must be a sufficient link between the promises relied upon and the conduct which constitutes the detriment.'[70]

*(ii) Burden of proving reliance.* In order to establish an estoppel equity a claimant must demonstrate[71] not merely that an assurance was made by the legal owner of land, but also that he relied upon the assurance made. In *A-G of Hong Kong v Humphreys Estate (Queen's Gardens) Ltd*[72] the Privy Council stated that it was necessary for the claimants to 'show' that they had relied on an expectation which had been encouraged. In *Lim Teng Huan v Ang Swee Chuan*[73] the Privy Council held that the requisite reliance could be established by an 'inevitable'[74] inference drawn from the facts. In *Wayling v Jones* Balcombe LJ held:

'Once it has been established that promises were made, and that there has been conduct by the plaintiff of such a nature that inducement may be inferred then the burden of proof shifts to the defendant to establish that he did not rely on the promises.'[75]

*(iii) Establishing reliance.* A claimant will thus fail to establish an estoppel equity if it can be shown that he acted as he did for reasons other than the assurance. In *Coombes v Smith*[76] Mrs Coombes had an unhappy marriage and fell in love with Mr Smith. He bought a house where it was intended they should live together. She became pregnant

---

[68] [2000] 2 All ER 289.

[69] [2000] 2 All ER 289 at 304. Pawlowski and Brown argue that an estoppel equity would also arise where a testator promises to create a secret trust and then subsequently changes his will so that the property is not left to the secret trustee: 'Constituting a Secret Trust by Estoppel' [2004] Conv 388.

[70] (1993) 69 P & CR 170 at 173. See also *Eves v Eves* [1975] 1 WLR 1338 at 1345, per Brightman J; *Grant v Edwards* [1986] Ch 638 at 648–649, 655–657, 656, per Nourse LJ and per Browne-Wilkinson V-C; *Gillett v Holt* [2000] 2 All ER 289, 306.

[71] See *Greasley v Cooke* [1980] 1 WLR 1306, where Lord Denning MR considered that there is a presumption of reliance once a representation has been established.

[72] [1987] AC 114.      [73] [1992] 1 WLR 113.      [74] [1992] 1 WLR 113 at 118.

[75] (1993) 69 P & CR 170 at 173.      [76] [1986] 1 WLR 808.

by him, and moved into the house. Mr Smith never moved in with her, but visited regularly. The house was sold and another purchased, which Mrs Coombes decorated. After their relationship had broken down, Mrs Coombes claimed an interest in the house by way of proprietary estoppel. Jonathon Parker QC held that even if an assurance had been made Mrs Coombes had not acted in reliance on it. As to her becoming pregnant, he considered:

'. . . it would be wholly unreal, to put it mildly, to find on the evidence adduced before me that the plaintiff allowed herself to become pregnant by the defendant in reliance on some mistaken belief as to her legal rights. She allowed herself to become pregnant because she wished to live with the defendant and bear his child.'[77]

Likewise, leaving her husband was not because of any assurance that Mr Smith had made but because 'she preferred to have a relationship with . . . the defendant rather than continuing to live with her husband . . . There is no evidence that she left her husband in reliance on the defendant's assurance that he would provide for her if and when their relationship came to an end'. Even the decoration failed to demonstrate reliance, since it was done 'by the plaintiff as occupier of the property, as the defendant's mistress, and as [the child's] mother, in the context of a continuing relationship with the defendant . . .'[78]

Similarly, in *Stilwell v Simpson*[79] Douglas Frank QC held that the claimant had not acted to his detriment by carrying out repairs on a house of which he was the tenant in reliance on the defendant's assurance that he would have the property, or first option to purchase, after her death, but for his own benefit because he knew that the defendant could not afford to pay for the work to be done.[80]

However, it should be questioned whether the decision in *Coombes v Smith* is correct. It adopts an unduly restrictive approach to the concept of reliance and an over-optimistic confidence in the ability of the court to determine the true rationale for the claimant's actions. Motives are invariably mixed rather than pure, and it would not be unreasonable to suggest that Mrs Coombes' actions were at least partially influenced by the assurances she had received from her lover. Only with the promise of security was she prepared to continue her relationship and have a child. Subsequent cases have tended to take a more generous attitude towards questions of reliance. In *Matharu v Matharu*[81] a wife returned to live with her husband on the mistaken basis that the matrimonial home was as much hers as his. She later discovered that it was in fact owned by his father. She subsequently acted to her detriment by installing a new kitchen. The Court of Appeal held that this indicated that she had acted in reliance upon an assurance by her father-in-law, through his conduct, that he would abstain from asserting his legal rights to the house, even though the expenditure had been incurred after she was aware of her mistaken assumption as to the ownership of the property. Roch LJ stated:

---

[77] [1986] 1 WLR 808 at 820.

[78] Compare the House of Lords' views of the wife's activities in *Lloyds Bank plc v Rosset* [1991] 1 AC 107.

[79] (1983) 133 NLJ 894.

[80] See also *Philip Lowe (Chinese Restaurant) Ltd v Sau Man Lee* (9 July 1985, unreported), CA; *Layton v Martin* [1986] 2 FLR 227.

[81] (1994) 68 P & CR 93.

'The expenditure on the new kitchen ... being made after the [claimant] knew that the [father-in-law] owned the house cannot be money expended on the faith of the [claimant's] mistaken belief. Nevertheless, it is, in my opinion, conduct by the [claimant] which confirms that the [claimant] had gone to live at 233 Coventry Road under a mistaken belief as to her rights and that the [father-in-law] had by his conduct between 1981 and 1990 led the [claimant] to believe, once she had learned that he was the owner, that he would abstain from asserting his legal rights.'[82]

In *Wayling v Jones*[83] the plaintiff and deceased defendant had cohabited in a homosexual relationship. The defendant ran a hotel business in which he was helped by the plaintiff, who acted as his companion and chauffeur in return for pocket money and the promise that the defendant would leave the business to him on his death. When the defendant died he had left the plaintiff only a motor car valued at £375. At first instance Mr Edward Nugee QC held that although the plaintiff had acted to his detriment by not demanding higher wages, he was not entitled to a claim by way of proprietary estoppel because he had not proved that he had suffered a detriment *in reliance upon* his belief. The Court of Appeal held that sufficient reliance was demonstrated and could be established by inference from the plaintiff's conduct. Balcombe LJ stated the principle:

'The promises relied upon do not have to be the sole inducement for the conduct: it is sufficient if they are an inducement.'[84]

It seems highly likely that if this approach had been adopted in *Coombes v Smith*[85] then the claim by way of proprietary estoppel would have succeeded.

## (c) 'Detriment or change of position'

An estoppel equity calling for a remedy will only be established if a claimant can show that he acted to his detriment in reliance upon the assurance that was made. This final element of detriment renders it 'unconscionable' for the legal owner to assert his strict rights.[86] If the owner had created an expectation on the part of the claimant, but the claimant had done nothing in response, there would be no reason why he should not be entitled to assert his rights. Rights over land are not created by mere representations, which do not amount to either a contract or a declaration of trust.[87] The general principle underlying the doctrine of estoppel was stated by Lord Denning MR in *Amalgamated Investment and Property Co Ltd v Texas Commerce International Bank Ltd (in liquidation)*:[88]

'When the parties to a transaction proceed on the basis of an underlying assumption ... on which they have conducted the dealings between them—neither of them will be allowed to go back on that assumption when it would be unfair or unjust to allow him to do so. If one

---

[82] (1994) 68 P & CR 93 at 103.

[83] (1993) 69 P & CR 170; (1995) 111 LQR 389 (Cooke); [1995] Conv 409 (Davis).

[84] (1995) 69 P & CR 170 at 173.     [85] [1986] 1 WLR 808.

[86] See *Grundt v Great Boulder Pty Gold Mine Ltd* (1937) 59 CLR 641.

[87] It will be remembered that in the case of a declaration of a trust of land there is a need for evidence in writing under s 53(1)(b) of the Law of Property Act 1925. A contract for the creation of an interest in land must be made in writing in accordance with s 1 of the Law of Property (Miscellaneous Provisions) Act 1989.

[88] [1982] QB 84 at 122.

of them does seek to go back on it, the courts will give the other such remedy as the equity of the case demands.'

In more recent cases, the courts have tended to express the requirement of detriment in terms of 'change of position'.[89] In *Lloyds Bank plc v Rosset*[90] Lord Bridge stated that in order to establish a constructive trust or a claim by way of proprietary estoppel, a claimant must:

'. . . show that he or she has acted to his or her detriment or significantly altered his or her position in reliance on the agreement . . .'[91]

In *Watts v Storey*[92] the Court of Appeal held that 'the categories of detriment were not closed'. In *Gillett v Holt* Robert Walker LJ summarised what detriment requires:

'The overwhelming weight of authority shows that detriment is required. But the authorities also show that it is not a narrow or technical concept. The detriment need not consist of the expenditure of money or other quantifiable financial detriment as long as it is something substantial. The requirement must be approached as part of a broad inquiry as to whether repudiation of an assurance is or is not unconscionable in all the circumstances.'[93]

The cases make clear that a wide range of conduct is sufficient 'detriment' to give rise to an equity.

*(i) Improvement of the legal owner's land.* Sufficient detriment will be demonstrated if the claimant had expended money improving the land in respect of which an assurance was given.[94] For example, in *Inwards v Baker*[95] it was a held that a son had acted to his detriment by building a bungalow on his father's land in reliance on an assurance he had received. In *Pascoe v Turner*[96] an equity was raised where the claimant had spent money on redecoration, improvements and repairs to a house that was owned by her former lover, while he passively assured by his acquiescence that she had an interest in the house. Cumming-Bruce J summarised the facts and the conclusion:

'. . . the defendant, having been told that the house was hers, set about improving it within and without. Outside she did not do much . . . Inside she did a good deal more. She installed gas in the kitchen with a cooker, improved the plumbing in the kitchen and put in a new sink. She got new gas fires, putting a gas fire in the lounge. She redecorated four rooms . . . We would describe the work done in and about the house as substantial in the sense that that adjective is used in the context of estoppel.'[97]

In *Matharu v Matharu*[98] it was held that a wife had acted to her detriment when she installed a new kitchen in a house owned by her father-in-law in reliance upon an assurance that it belonged to her husband and that she would have an interest in it. In *Gillett v Holt*[99] one of the ways in which the claimant had acted to his detriment was by incurring substantial expenditure improving the farmhouse he occupied.

---

[89] See *ER Ives Investment Ltd v High* [1967] 2 QB 379, CA; *Bhimji v Salih* (4 February 1981, unreported), CA; In *Re Basham (Decd)* [1986] 1 WLR 1498 at 1504.
[90] [1991] 1 AC 107.   [91] [1991] 1 AC 107 at 132.   [92] (1983) 134 NLJ 631.
[93] [2000] 2 All ER 289 at 308.   [94] See *Voyce v Voyce* (1991) 62 P & CR 290, CA.
[95] [1965] 2 QB 29.   [96] [1979] 1 WLR 431.   [97] [1979] 1 WLR 431 at 435–436.
[98] (1994) 68 P & CR 93.   [99] [2000] 2 All ER 289 at 309–310.

*(ii) Improvement of the claimant's own land.* A claimant will also be held to have acted to his detriment if he improved his own land in reliance upon an assurance that he is to enjoy a right over the land of the legal owner. In *Rochdale Canal Co v King*[100] a mill owner built a mill on his own land after having applied to the canal company to take water from the canal to operate his steam engines. The company did not refuse the application and pipes were laid in the presence of their engineers. The court held that, due to their acquiescence, they were not entitled to an injunction restraining the mill owner from drawing water from the canal.[101]

*(iii) Acquisition of new land by the claimant.* In *Salvation Army Trustees Co Ltd v West Yorkshire Metropolitan County Council*[102] the council informed the Salvation Army that the site of their hall would be required for a proposed road-widening scheme. Although there was no contract for the sale of the hall to the council, the Salvation Army acquired a new site and built a new hall. The council subsequently informed them that the proposed scheme would not be adopted for some years and that they would not therefore be acquiring the old site. Woolf J held that the Salvation Army were entitled to a claim on the basis of proprietary estoppel. He held that the principle of proprietary estoppel was:

'. . . capable of extending to the disposal of an interest in land where that disposal is closely linked by an arrangement that also involves the acquiring of an interest in land.'[103]

*(iv) Working without adequate remuneration.* In *Wayling v Jones*[104] it was held that an estoppel equity was established where the claimant had helped his homosexual partner to run a cafe and hotel in reliance upon the assurance that it would be left to him by will. The fact that he received 'little more than pocket money' as remuneration for his work was sufficient to constitute the necessary element of detriment. Similarly in *Gillett v Holt*[105] the Court of Appeal held that the claimant had acted to his detriment by working for the defendant for forty years at a significantly lower than average remuneration.

*(v) Personal disadvantage.* A claim may arise by way of proprietary estoppel even if the claimant did not act to his detriment financially by incurring the expenditure of money. As Edward Nugee QC stated in *Re Basham (Decd)*:

'. . . it is in my judgment established that the expenditure of A's money on B's property is not the only kind of detriment that gives rise to proprietary estoppel.'[106]

In a number of cases purely personal disadvantage, not connected with the land as such, has been held sufficient to give rise to an equity. In *Jones (AE) v Jones (FW)*[107] a father

---

[100]  (1853) 16 Beav 630.      [101]  See also *Cotching v Bassett* (1862) 32 Beav 101.

[102]  (1980) 41 P & CR 179.        [103]  (1980) 41 P & CR 179 at 192.

[104]  (1993) 69 P & CR 170. See also *Gillett v Holt* [1998] 3 All ER 917 where Carnwath J accepted that a 'lower salary than would otherwise have been appropriate would have been sufficient detriment to establish a claim by way of proprietary estoppel'. However, there was no evidence to prove that the plaintiff had received a lower salary and the claim therefore failed.

[105]  [2000] 2 All ER 289, 309–310.        [106]  [1986] 1 WLR 1498 at 1509.

[107]  [1977] 1 WLR 438.

moved to a house in Suffolk, leaving his son in London. He wanted his son to come and live near him, and bought a house for £4,000 in his own name. The son gave up his job and came to live there with his family. The son paid his father £1,000, but believed, on the basis of assurances that his father gave, that the house was his. On his father's death the property passed to his step-mother, who sought an order for possession. The Court of Appeal held that the son had established an entitlement by way of proprietary estoppel to remain in the house. Moving to be near constituted sufficient detriment.[108] Lord Denning MR stated the principles:

'Old Mr Jones' conduct was such as to lead his son Frederick reasonably to believe that he could stay there and regard Philmona as his home for the rest of his life. On the basis of that reasonable expectation, the son gave up his work at Kingston-upon-Thames and moved to Blundeston . . . it is clear that old Mr Jones would be estopped from turning the son out.'[109]

In *Greasley v Cooke*[110] Doris Cooke moved into the house of Arthur Greasley as a maid-servant in 1938. She lived with one of his sons, Kenneth from 1946. Throughout that time she looked after the son and his mentally disabled sister, Clarice. When Kenneth died in 1975 the members of the family who had inherited the house asked her to leave. The trial judge found that she 'reasonably believed and was encouraged by members of the family to believe that she could regard the property as her home for the rest of her life', but held that she had not acted to her detriment. The Court of Appeal allowed her appeal. Lord Denning MR stated that it was not necessary that the change of position take the form of expenditure of money. He held that:

'It is sufficient if the party, to whom the assurance is given, acts on the faith of it in such circumstances that it would be unjust and inequitable for the party making the assurance to go back on it.'[111]

In *Re Basham (decd)*[112] Jean Bird was the step-daughter of Henry Basham. In 1947 a cottage had been purchased in Henry's name with money provided by Jean's mother. After her death in 1976 he lived in the house. Jean and her husband, who lived nearby, looked after him. He gave her assurances that the house would be hers on his death. Reviewing the facts, Edward Nugee QC held that Jean and her husband had acted to their detriment so as to entitle them to a claim by way of proprietary estoppel:

'. . . the plaintiff did a very great deal for the deceased, and it is clear that she did not receive any commensurate reward for this during his lifetime. There is some evidence, though not very much, of occasions when the plaintiff or husband acted or refrained from acting in a way in which they might not have done but for their expectation of inheriting the deceased's property: I refer to the occasions when the husband refrained from selling his building land, and refrained from taking a job in Lincolnshire which would have made it impossible for the plaintiff to continue caring for her mother and the deceased, and the occasions when the plaintiff instructed solicitors at her own expense in connection with the boundary dispute between the deceased and Mr Kenworthy, and the expenditure of time and money on the house and garden and on carpeting the house, when the deceased had ample means of his

---

[108] See *Watts v Storey* [1983] CA Transcript 319.     [109] [1977] 1 WLR 438 at 442.
[110] [1980] 1 WLR 1306.     [111] [1980] 1 WLR 1306 at 1311.     [112] [1986] 1 WLR 1498.

own to pay for such matters. It may be that none of these incidents, taken by itself, would be very significant, but the cumulative effect of them supports the view that the plaintiff and her husband subordinated their own interests to the wishes of the deceased.'

Such acts 'went well beyond what was called for by natural love and affection', particularly since there was no great love between Jean's husband and the deceased. He was only willing to pay for meals for the deceased and work in the garden because of the expectation that his wife would inherit the estate.

In the more recent case of *Gillett v Holt*[113] the Court of Appeal held that alongside financial detriment the claimant had also suffered personal detriment. On the basis of the assurances that he had received from Holt that his future would be secure he had continued in his employment, not seeking or accepting offers of employment elsewhere or going into business on his own, and he had performed tasks and spent time beyond the normal scope of an employee's duties. He had also failed to take any other steps to secure his future wealth, such as making larger pension contributions. Holt had also exercised significance influence over his family life, so that he and his wife had subordinated their wishes to his, including sending their son to the school of his choice. Robert Walker LJ concluded:

'Mr Gillett and his wife devoted the best years of their lives to working for Mr Holt and his company, showing loyalty and devotion to his business interests, his social life and his personal wishes, on the strength of clear and repeated assurances of testamentary benefits.'[114]

The most important comments regarding the relevance of non-monetary detriment were made by Browne-Wilkinson V-C in *Grant v Edwards*.[115] The case concerned a common intention constructive trust[116] but he considered that 'useful guidance may . . . be obtained from the principles underlying the law of proprietary estoppel'. On the question of detriment he stated:[117]

'In many cases of the present sort, it is impossible to say whether or not the claimant would have done the acts relied on as a detriment even if she thought she had no interest in the house. Setting up house together, having a baby, making payments to general housekeeping expenses (not strictly necessary to enable the mortgage to be paid) may all be referable to the mutual love and affection of the parties and not specifically referable to the claimant's belief that she has an interest in the house. As at present advised, once it has been shown that there was a common intention that the claimant should have an interest in the house, any act done by her to her detriment relating to the joint lives of the parties is, in my judgment, sufficient detriment to qualify.'

Applying the test of 'any act done by her relating to the joint lives of the parties' to proprietary estoppel claims,[118] a whole range of non-monetary detriment would be sufficient to raise an equity.

---

[113] [2000] 2 All ER 289 at 309–310.      [114] [2000] 2 All ER 289 at 310.

[115] [1986] Ch 638; [1986] CLJ 394 (Hayton); [1986] Conv 291 (Warburton).      [116] See Chapter 9.

[117] [1986] Ch 638 at 657.

[118] Although Browne-Wilkinson J did not rest his judgment on the analogy between common intention constructive trusts and proprietary estoppel because the point had not been fully argued.

However, as has been noted above, some cases have taken a much narrower attitude towards non-monetary detriment. In particular, in *Coombes v Smith*[119] Jonathon Parker QC held that a woman who had left her husband to live with her lover, became pregnant by him, gave birth to their child, and looked after the shared property and their daughter had not 'acted to her detriment' in reliance on an assurance that she was entitled to an interest in the house. As has been discussed above, this may be because these acts could not be seen as performed 'in reliance' on an assurance rather than because they were not detrimental per se. Whilst the judgment suggests that acts which are purely integral to the relationship between the parties are not to be regarded as sufficient detriment to establish an equity, it is submitted that this is unduly restrictive and that the case was wrongly decided.[120]

*(vi) Weighing detriment against any benefits derived.* It appears that sometimes the court will weigh any detriment that the claimant has suffered against any benefit that he has received. In *Watts v Storey*[121] the claimant was persuaded by his grandmother to give up a tenancy of a house in Leeds and move into her home, Apple House, in Nottinghamshire, following her move to the Isle of White. He gave up his prospects of finding employment in Leeds. Although the Court of Appeal found that there was an assurance that Apple House would be left to him by will, it held that there was insufficient detriment to found a claim by way of proprietary estoppel:

'. . . when the benefits derived by him from his rent-free occupation . . . are set against any detriments suffered by him as a result of making the move from his Rent Act protected flat in Leeds, he has not on balance suffered any detriment in financial or material terms.'

# 3 Satisfying the equity

## (1) A range of remedial responses

Once a claimant has established an estoppel equity by demonstrating the elements of assurance, reliance and detriment, the question arises as to his remedial entitlement. The mere fact that he has established an equity does not entitle him to any particular remedy, or even to a remedy at all. It is for the court to determine, in its discretion, whether the estoppel equity requires the award of a remedy, and if so the type of remedy that would be appropriate to achieve justice between the parties. This process of determining the appropriate remedial response is described as 'satisfying the equity'. This terminology is long established, as in *Plimmer v Wellington Corpn* the Privy Council stated that:

---

[119]  [1986] 1 WLR 808.

[120]  In the Australian case *W v G* [1996] 20 Fam LR 49 the NSW Supreme Court held that a lesbian partner had acted to her detriment where she had agree to have a child by way of artificial insemination on the basis of an assurance that her partner would assist in the upbringing of the child. The court did not, however, find that having a child per se was a detriment: see (1997) 113 LQR 227 (Bailey-Harris).

[121]  (1983) 134 NLJ 631.

'. . . the court must look at the circumstances in each case to decide in what way the equity can be satisfied.'[122]

Where an estoppel equity has been established, the courts have awarded a wide range of remedies in satisfaction. The process and criteria by which the court determines the appropriate remedy will be examined below.

### (a) Transfer of the legal ownership of land

The most powerful remedy by which the court may satisfy an estoppel equity is to order the legal owner to transfer his land to the claimant. In *Dillwyn v Llewelyn*[123] and *Pascoe v Turner*[124] the legal owner was ordered to convey the fee simple in his house to the claimant.[125] In *Gillett v Holt*[126] the court ordered Holt to transfer the freehold of the farm they occupied to the claimant in part satisfaction of his estoppel interest. The court may also be able to award a conditional or determinable fee simple, specifying the conditions on which the right will come to an end. In *Williams v Staite*[127] Goff LJ stated that:

'. . . the court . . . might hold in any proper case, that the equity is in its nature for a limited period only or determinable upon a condition certain. In such a case the courts must then see whether, in the events which have happened, it has determined or it has expired or been determined by the happening of that condition.'[128]

### (b) Transfer of an undivided share in the land

Where land is held on trust the court may order one joint tenant to transfer his undivided share in the land to another in satisfaction of an estoppel equity. In *Lim Teng Huan v Ang Swee Chuan*[129] the plaintiff and the defendant were the equitable joint tenants of land in Brunei. The defendant built a house on the land believing (wrongly) that a contract had been entered between himself and the plaintiff. The Privy Council held that the plaintiff was therefore estopped from claiming his title to the land, and that the land should belong outright to the defendant, subject to him paying compensation for the value of the land.

### (c) Grant of a lease

In some cases the court has awarded a leasehold estate in satisfaction of proprietary estoppel, as for example in *Siew Soon Wah v Yong Tong Hong*.[130] In *Grant v Williams*[131] a daughter who had lived for most of her life in her mother's house and had cared for her and incurred expenditure improving the property on the basis of a representation that she would be entitled to live in it for the rest of her life was granted a long lease at a nominal rent, determinable on death, in satisfaction of her estoppel equity. In *Yaxley v Gotts*[132] the Court of Appeal upheld the grant of a long lease in satisfaction of an

---

[122] (1883–84) LR 9 App Cas 699 at 714.    [123] (1862) 4 De GF & J 517.    [124] [1979] 1 WLR 431.

[125] See also *Thomas v Thomas* [1956] NZLR 785; *Cameron v Murdoch* [1983] WAR 321; *Riches v Hogben* [1986] 1 Qd R 315; *Re Basham (Decd)* [1987] 1 All ER 405; *Voyce v Voyce* (1991) 62 P & CR 290, CA; *Durant v Heritage and Hamilton* [1994] NPC 117; *Walton v Walton* (20 July 1994, unreported), Ch Div.

[126] [2001] Ch 210.    [127] [1979] Ch 291.    [128] [1979] Ch 291 at 300.

[129] [1992] 1 WLR 113.    [130] [1973] AC 836.    [131] (1977) 248 Estates Gazette 947.

[132] [2000] 1 All ER 711.

estoppel equity where a builder had refurbished and converted a house into flats in reliance upon an assurance from the owner that he would thereby acquire the ground floor flats.

## (d) Right of occupancy

In the majority of cases the courts have stopped short of awarding a claimant full ownership of the property and have granted some form of a right of occupancy. For example, in *Greasley v Cooke*,[133] the Court of Appeal held that the claimant should be entitled to remain in the house rent free for as long as she wished. Similarly, in *Inwards v Baker*[134] the son, who had built his bungalow on his father's land, was held entitled to remain there as long as he wanted. In *Matharu v Matharu*[135] the Court of Appeal held that a claimant was entitled to 'a licence . . . to remain in this house for her life or such shorter period as she may decide'.[136] Such rights of occupation virtually amount to the grant of a 'life interest'. Prior to the introduction of trusts of land under the Trusts of Land and Appointment of Trustees Act 1996, such a right would have tended to create a strict settlement under the provisions of the Settled Land Act 1925.[137] The grant of a lease in *Griffiths v Williams*[138] was a means of avoiding the unsatisfactory consequences of a strict settlement.[139] With the introduction of the trust of land, the courts may become more willing to utilise the equitable life interest as a means of satisfaction of an estoppel equity. Unlike the Irish courts, the English courts have not recognised rights of residence not conferring exclusive possession as proprietary interests in land.

## (e) Financial compensation

In other cases, the courts have awarded a claimant only financial reimbursement in satisfaction of his estoppel equity. In *Dodsworth v Dodsworth*[140] the legal owner of a bungalow allowed the claimants, her brother and his wife, to live in it on their return from Australia. They spent £700 on improvements in the expectation that they would be able to remain in the bungalow as long as they wished. After a breakdown in the relationship between the parties, the Court of Appeal held that the claimants were not entitled to occupy rent-free for life, but were entitled to be repaid their outlay on improvements. The court may award the claimant a lien or a charge over the property to the value of the improvements made.[141] In *Wayling v Jones*[142] the Court of Appeal held that the claimant should be entitled to recover the proceeds of sale of the hotel which his partner had promised to leave him by will. In *Jennings v Rice*[143] the Court of Appeal held that a gardener who had acted to his detriment by looking after an elderly

---

[133] [1980] 1 WLR 1306.     [134] [1965] 2 QB 29.     [135] (1994) 68 P & CR 93.
[136] (1994) 68 P & CR 93 at 103.
[137] See *Dodsworth v Dodsworth* (1973) 228 Estates Gazette 1115; *Ungurian v Lesnoff* [1990] Ch 206; *Costello v Costello* (1994) 70 P & CR 297.
[138] (1977) 248 Estates Gazette 947.
[139] See Stevens and Pearce, *Land Law* (3rd edn, 2005), pp 572–573
[140] (1973) 228 Estates Gazette 1115.
[141] *Unity Joint Stock Mutual Banking Association v King* (1858) 25 Beav 72; *Taylor v Taylor* [1956] NZLR 99.
[142] (1995) 69 P & CR 170.     [143] 2002 WL 45443, [2002] NPC 28.

lady in reliance upon her assurance that she would 'see to it' that he would be alright in her will should received £200,000 from her estate.

### (f)  Grant of an easement

Where appropriate, the courts have held that a claimant is entitled to the grant of an easement over the land of the person estopped, as, for example, in *ER Ives Investment Ltd v High*[144] and *Crabb v Arun District Council.*[145]

### (g)  Composite remedy

On occasion the court has awarded a composite remedy combining. For example, in *Re Sharpe (a bankrupt)*[146] Dorothy Johnson moved into a house, with her nephew Thomas Sharpe, which had been purchased in his name. She provided £12,000 of the purchase price of £17,000 by way of a loan to him. Browne-Wilkinson J held that since the payment was made by way of loan, there was no possibility of a resulting trust, but that she was entitled to an interest under the principles of proprietary estoppel. He held that she should have the right to live in the house until her loan was repaid.[147] As has been seen, in *Gillett v Holt*[148] the Court of Appeal awarded the claimant the freehold of the farm he occupied. In addition he was also awarded a sum of £100,000 to compensate him from his exclusion from the rest of the farming business carried on by Holt.

### (h)  Imposition of a constructive trust

Although the courts have not yet awarded an interest by way of a constructive trust in satisfaction of an estoppel equity, there appears to be no reason in principle why this would not be possible. The effect would be similar to an order to transfer the legal ownership of land, in that the claimant would receive an ownership interest in the property, only in the form of a share of the beneficial ownership behind a trust of land. There are indications in dicta that a constructive trust may be awarded as a remedy. In *Hussey v Palmer*[149] the Court of Appeal considered the case of a woman who had moved into the house of her son-in-law and paid for an extension to be built. In holding that she was entitled to an equitable interest, Lord Denning MR discussed the relevant principle:[150]

'To this I would add *Inwards v Baker*,[151] when a son built a bungalow on his father's land in the expectation that he would be allowed to stay there as his home, although there was no promise to that effect. After the father's death, his trustees sought to turn the son out. It was held that he had an equitable interest which was good against the trustees. In those cases it was emphasised that the court must look at the circumstances of each case to decide in what way the equity can be satisfied. In some by an equitable lien. In others by a constructive trust.'

Although *Hussey v Palmer*[152] is one of a number of cases where Lord Denning enunciated

---

[144] [1967] 2 QB 379, CA.    [145] [1976] Ch 179, CA.    [146] [1980] 1 WLR 219.
[147] See also *Dodsworth v Dodsworth* (1973) 228 Estates Gazette 1115, CA; *Stratulatos v Stratulatos* [1988] 2 NZLR 424.
[148] [2001] Ch 210.    [149] [1972] 3 All ER 744.    [150] [1972] 3 All ER 744 at 747–748.
[151] [1965] 2 QB 29, CA.    [152] [1972] 3 All ER 744.

his now discredited new model constructive trust,[153] his citation of *Inwards v Baker* suggests that he was advocating that the imposition of a constructive trust may be an appropriate remedy where the plaintiff has established the necessary elements of proprietary estoppel. This dictum was approved by the Supreme Court of New South Wales in *Pearce v Pearce*.[154] In the more recent case of *Re Basham (Decd)*[155] Edward Nugee QC also took the view that a constructive trust was an appropriate remedy for cases of proprietary estoppel:

'The plaintiff relies on proprietary estoppel, the principle of which, in its broadest form, may be stated as follows: where one person, A, has acted to his detriment on the faith of a belief, which was known to and encouraged by another person, B, that he either has or is going to be given a right in or over B's property, B cannot insist on his strict legal rights if to do so would be inconsistent with A's belief . . . But in my judgment at all events where the belief is that A is going to be given a right in the future, it is properly to be regarded as giving rise to a species of constructive trust . . .'[156]

In *Matharu v Matharu*[157] the first instance judge held that the claimant was entitled to a share of the beneficial ownership of her matrimonial home by way of proprietary estoppel. Whilst the Court of Appeal held that she should be entitled only to an occupational licence, it was not suggested that a trust interest was a priori inappropriate as a means of satisfaction of an estoppel equity. If the court does possess the jurisdiction to award an equitable interest by way of a constructive trust in satisfaction of an estoppel equity, such a constructive trust would be radically different to the 'institutional' common intention constructive trust generated under the principles set out in *Lloyds Bank plc v Rosset*.[158] A constructive trust imposed by the court by way of proprietary estoppel would be akin to the remedial constructive trust adopted in other jurisdictions, since the claimant's equitable interest would only arise at the date of judgment, and not at the date of the assurance, reliance and detriment.[159]

If a constructive trust was adopted as an appropriate remedy for proprietary estoppel, this would have the effect of significantly widening the circumstances in which it would be possible for the court to grant an equitable interest in shared property. As has been seen, *Lloyds Bank plc v Rosset*[160] demands that the plaintiff demonstrate that there was either an express or an implied common intention regarding the ownership of the property, and that such common intention will only be implied from direct financial contributions. However, if the court can award a constructive trust as a remedy for proprietary estoppel, the plaintiff will only have to demonstrate the lesser requirements of 'assurance', 'reliance' and 'detriment', and the courts have taken account of a much wider range of detriment than pure financial contribution. A clear distinction between the doctrine of the common intention constructive trust and proprietary estoppel was drawn in *Preston and Henderson v St Helens Metropolitan Borough Council*.[161] In 1971 a

---

[153] See Chapter 9.    [154] [1977] 1 NSWLR 170, per Helsham CJ.    [155] [1986] 1 WLR 1498.
[156] [1986] 1 WLR 1498 at 1503–1504.    [157] (1994) 68 P & CR 93.    [158] [1991] 1 AC 107.
[159] If an equitable proprietary interest was created as an automatic consequence of the assurance, reliance and detriment, the constructive trust would similarly arise automatically and would be recognised, rather than created, by the court.
[160] [1991] 1 AC 107.    [161] (1989) 58 P & CR 500.

house was purchased in the name of Mr Preston. Mrs Henderson moved in with him and she paid all the mortgage installments and other expenses associated with the property. At that stage she had gained a half-share in the house by way of a common intention constructive trust. He left in 1976 and apparently said that, as far as he was concerned, the house was hers. After that date she continued to pay all the expenses. The Land Tribunal held that because Mrs Henderson had acted to her detriment on the basis of the assurance that she was to have the house, she was entitled to the whole equitable ownership of the house, which was therefore held on trust for her by Mr Preston.[162]

Any melding of the principles of constructive trusts and proprietary estoppel would perhaps produce something equivalent to the remedial constructive trust adopted in other jurisdictions. As was noted in the previous chapter,[163] recent cases have indeed adopted proprietary estoppel principles so as to determine the share arising by way of a constructive trust where the parties have not reached any agreement as to the way in which the ownership of the land should be shared.[164] However this falls well short of any true melding of the principles, and does not approximate to the remedial construct-ive trust. The court does not possesses any discretion as to whether or not trust interests should be awarded, but merely has a circumscribed discretion to quantify the shares of the parties where a common intention to share has been established in the traditional institutional manner. Although in *Westdeutsche Landesbank Girozentrale v Islington London Borough Council*,[165] Lord Browne-Wilkinson suggested that English law might in future adopt the remedial constructive trust as was noted in the last chapter the most recent cases have rejected the possibility of any such development.[166]

*(i) No remedy because the claimant has already received 'full satisfaction'.* In some cases it appears that the courts may find that a claimant does not require the award of any remedy at all in order to satisfy an estoppel equity because he has already received advantages which have fully satisfied his claim. In *Sledmore v Dalby*[167] Mr Dalby had lived in a house owned by his parents-in-law since 1965. Initially, he and his wife paid rent, but in 1976 they ceased to do so because his wife became seriously ill. He subsequently substantially improved the property, having been encouraged to do so by Mr and Mrs Sledmore. Following the death of his wife, he continued to live in the house, which was then owned by Mrs Sledmore alone, rent free. In 1990 she gave him notice to quit. At first instance Mr Dalby was held entitled to a non-assignable licence to occupy the house for life on the grounds of proprietary estoppel, but the Court of Appeal held that, although he was entitled to an estoppel equity, it had been fully met. Although he had spent money on the property, he had enjoyed the benefits of that expenditure through more than 15 years' rent-free occupation. Roch LJ also took

---

[162] In consequence she was entitled to receive an owner-occupier's supplement on compulsory purchase of the property.

[163] See above p 299 *et seq.*    [164] See *Oxley v Hiscock* [2004] 3 All ER 703.

[165] [1996] AC 669; (1996) 112 LQR 521 (Cape); [1996] CLJ 432 (Jones); [1996] LMCLQ 441 (Stevens). See [1996] RLR 3 (Birks).

[166] *Re Polly Peck (No 2)* [1998] 3 All ER 812. See above p 324.

[167] (1996) 72 P & CR 196; (1997) 113 LQR 232 (Pawlowski).

account of the parties respective situations, weighing the fact that Mrs Sledmore was a widow dependent upon benefit, who urgently wanted to sell the house, against the fact that Mr Dalby was employed and currently making minimal use of the house because he enjoyed accommodation elsewhere.

## (2) Determining the appropriate remedy[168]

As is clear from the preceding section, the courts have awarded a wide range of remedies in satisfaction of estoppel equities. The central question is therefore whether there is any coherent principle underlying the process by which the remedy is selected in each case. Two main opposing views have been advocated to explain the function of the court in the determination of the appropriate remedy. The narrow approach considers that the court is simply required to carry into effect the parties' own 'reasonable expectations'. Under this view, the court is left with a highly circumscribed discretion as to the remedy which is appropriate. The flexible approach argues that the court has a wide discretion to decide the appropriate remedy in the circumstances. In the recent case of *Jennings v Rice*[169] the Court of Appeal considered the merits of these alternatives and concluded that a composite approach should be adopted which would ensure that there was proportionality between the remedy awarded and the detriment experienced.

### (a) Fulfillment of the claimant's 'reasonable expectation'

A number of academics have argued that when the court satisfies an estoppel equity it invariably selects the remedy which as far as possible fulfills the reasonable expectations of the claimant.[170] It is alleged that this analysis is capable of rationally explaining the apparent conflict in outcome between *Dillwyn v Llewelyn*[171] and *Pascoe v Turner*,[172] where the court ordered the transfer of the fee simple to the claimant, and *Inwards v Baker*[173] and *Williams v Staite*,[174] where only a lesser right of occupancy was awarded. The crucial distinguishing feature is said to be the nature of the claimant's expectation raised by the assurance of the legal owner. In *Pascoe v Turner*[175] the assurance given to Mrs Turner was that 'the house is yours and everything in it'. Therefore, her reasonable expectation was that she owned the house and, having acted to her detriment in reliance on that assurance, the court acted to fulfill her expectation. In contrast, in *Inwards v Baker*[176] the father's representation to his son was simply 'Why not put the bungalow on my land and make the bungalow a little bigger?' Although this amounted to a clear indication that the son would be entitled to remain on the land, it cannot be taken as an

---

[168] See especially Gardener, 'The Remedial Discretion in Proprietary Estoppel' (1999) 115 LQR 438; Bright and McFarlane, 'Proprietary Estoppel and Property Rights' [2005] 64 CLJ 449.

[169] 2002 WL 45443, [2002] NPC 28.

[170] See (1984) 100 LQR 376 (Moriarty); (1997) 17 LS 258 (Cooke). However, in *Sledmore v Dalby* (1996) 72 P & CR 196 Hoffmann LJ adopted the view that there must be 'proportionality' between the detriment experienced and the remedy awarded, so that the claimant's expectations will not be fulfilled if to do so would be disproportionate to the amount of detriment he had experienced: see (1997) 113 LQR 232 (Pawlowski). See also [1998] Conv 213, where Mark Thompson suggests that there is no need for an expectation to be satisfied in full where an estoppel equity is raised.

[171] (1862) 4 De GF & J 517.       [172] [1979] 1 WLR 431, CA.       [173] [1965] 2 QB 29, CA.

[174] [1979] Ch 291, CA.       [175] [1979] 1 WLR 431, CA.       [176] [1965] 2 QB 29, CA.

assurance that the son would own the land. The award of a right to occupy for as long as he wished therefore fulfilled the reasonable expectation raised by the assurance he received. Similarly, in *Williams v Staite*[177] the representation was merely that 'you can live here as long as you like', and on the basis of such a representation there could be no reasonable expectation of ownership.

Slightly more difficult to analyse on this 'expectation model' are cases where the claimant was awarded merely monetary compensation for detriment suffered, as for example in *Dodsworth v Dodsworth*.[178] However, in these cases financial compensation seems to operate as a default remedy when the circumstances prevent the fulfillment of the claimant's legitimate expectation. In *Dodsworth*[179] the plaintiff's brother and sister-in-law moved into her bungalow with her on their return from Australia, and spent £700 on improvements in reliance on the assurance by the plaintiff that they would be able to remain in the bungalow as their home for as long as they wished. Obviously, this representation is comparable to that made in *Williams v Staite*[180] and a similar remedy of a right of occupancy would be expected. However, the court awarded the defendants only monetary compensation for their improvements. The explanation must be that it was impossible to fulfill the claimants' reasonable expectation, namely the right to reside in the bungalow with the plaintiff, because the relationship between them had broken down.[181] As Russell LJ observed, the consequence of awarding the defendants a right of occupancy would be that the plaintiff:

'. . . would . . . have to continue sharing her home for the rest of her life with the defendants with whom she was, or thought she was, at loggerheads.'

The award of monetary compensation is therefore a default remedy given where a reasonable expectation of shared occupation is no longer a realistic possibility. This analysis is also capable of explaining the award of monetary compensation in *Hussey v Palmer*,[182] *Re Sharpe*[183] and *Burrows and Burrows v Sharp*.[184] Moriarty summarises the argument as follows:

'The remedies granted [for proprietary estoppel] . . . are not the product of an unpredictable discretion; but are selected in accordance with well-established principles of English property law. Normally, therefore, a remedy will be chosen which gives the party precisely what he has been led to expect, but occasionally, where joint rights to land have been represented, he may get money instead.'[185]

Although the 'fulfillment of the reasonable expectation' analysis has the attractive merit of certainty, a number of criticisms may be made. First, it ignores a large number of judicial statements which emphasise the court's flexibility in determining the

---

[177] [1979] Ch 291, CA.
[178] (1973) 228 Estates Gazette 1115: see also *Taylor v Taylor* [1956] NZLR 99; *Re Sharpe* [1980] 1 WLR 219.
[179] (1973) 228 Estates Gazette 1115.      [180] [1979] Ch 291, CA.
[181] See *Thompson v Park* [1944] KB 408.
[182] [1972] 1 WLR 1286, CA. Although the plaintiff was only claiming monetary compensation, there had been a breakdown of the sharing relationship between the mother-in-law and son-in-law.
[183] [1980] 1 WLR 219. Although the sharing relationship between aunt and nephew had not broken down, it was the nephew's trustee in bankruptcy who was seeking to evict the aunt.
[184] [1991] Fam Law 67; [1992] Conv 54.      [185] (1984) 100 LQR 376 at 412.

appropriate remedy.[186] Secondly, it assumes that it is possible to correctly identify the reasonable expectations of the claimant, whereas the reality is often that the assurance, and therefore the derived expectation, are ambiguous. The informal circumstances and terms in which the assurance is given cannot always be taken as sufficiently certain to determine the remedy. To some extent, the court is engaged in the business of rationalising the claimant's expectation and an element of discretion is simply built into that process. For example, is it strictly accurate to conclude from the language used by the father in *Inwards v Baker*[187] that the son's expectation was only of a right to remain on the land rather than to own it? The extent of his detriment, building a house, could surely indicate that something more substantial than a right of occupancy was expected. As Lord Westbury LC said in *Dillwyn v Llewelyn*:

'No one builds a house for his own life only, and it is absurd to suppose that it was intended by either party that the house at the death of the son, should become the property of the father.'[188]

The heart of the problem is that, in the informal and often family context, the parties rarely formulate precisely the extent of the entitlement being represented, and it is only after the events that the court is called to analyse what has taken place. Determining the claimant's expectation is not therefore an exact science. Moriarty's claim that 'we can get quite some way . . . towards explaining the court's intuitive choice of remedy by merely paying closer attention to the precise content of the representation'[189] is an overstatement.

In the light of such criticisms the Court of Appeal held in *Jennings v Rice*[190] that a pure 'fulfillment of expectations' approach was not the appropriate means of determining the remedy to satisfy an estoppel equity. The case concerned a gardener who had taken care of an elderly lady without remuneration, relying upon her assurance that she would 'see to it' that he was alright, and her statements to him that her house would 'all be yours one day'. At first instance Judge Weeks held that he was entitled to a claim by way of proprietary estoppel, but that he should receive a sum of £200,000 rather than the freehold of the house and its furniture, which was worth considerably more. On appeal it was argued that he should have been entitled to the house and furniture on the grounds that an estoppel equity should be satisfied by making good the expectation of the claimant. The Court of Appeal held that whilst the nature of the expectation was a relevant consideration, it did not alone determine the appropriate remedy. The court was rather required to do justice by ensuring that there was proportionality between the remedy and the detriment.

---

[186] See *Plimmer v Wellington Corpn* (1883–84) LR 9 App Cas 699; *Crabb v Arun District Council* [1976] Ch 179, CA; *Griffiths v Williams* (1977) 248 Estates Gazette 947; *Denny v Jensen* [1977] 1 NZLR 635; *Greasley v Cooke* [1980] 1 WLR 1306, CA; *Morris v Morris* [1982] 1 NSWLR 61.

[187] [1965] 2 QB 29.      [188] (1862) 4 De GF & J 517 at 522.      [189] (1984) 100 LQR 376 at 383.

[190] 2002 WL 45443, [2002] NPC 28.

## (b) Discretionary satisfaction of the estoppel 'equity'

In contrast to the 'expectation' analysis, other academics have argued[191] that the court possesses a broad discretion to select whichever remedy it feels is appropriate in the circumstances of each case. The 'equity' of the claimant arises as a result of the assurance, reliance and detriment, and that equity remains 'inchoate' until the court determines a remedy to satisfy it. In this sense, the court is acting in a similar way to the courts of other jurisdictions where the remedial constructive trust is recognised.[192] The cause of action is proprietary estoppel, and if established the court selects the appropriate remedy

Dicta in a significant number of cases support the suggestion that the court possesses a wide discretion to determine the appropriate remedy. In *Plimmer v Wellington Corpn*[193] Sir Arthur Hobhouse stated that 'the court must look at the circumstances in each case to decide in what way the equity can be satisfied'. In *Crabb v Arun District Council*[194] Lord Denning MR emphasised that in answering the question how an established equity should be satisfied, 'equity is displayed at its most flexible'. He also restated the principle in *Greasley v Cooke*:

'The equity having thus been raised . . . it is for the courts of equity to decide in what way that equity should be satisfied.'[195]

Such flexibility was also emphasised in *Griffiths v Williams*,[196] where Goff LJ answered the question 'what is the relief appropriate to satisfy the equity?' in this way:

'. . . the . . . question is one upon which the court has to exercise a discretion. If it finds that there is an equity, then it must determine the nature of it, and then, guided by that nature and exercising discretion in all the circumstances, it has to determine what is the fair order to make between the parties for the protection of the claimant.'[197]

The wide discretion of the court was also stressed in New Zealand in *Stratulatos v Stratulatos*,[198] where McGehan J said that 'the range of available remedies should not be cluttered by arbitrary rules'.

As with any area in which the court possesses a wide remedial discretion, the key criticism has been that of uncertainty.[199] If the remedy is entirely within the choice of the courts, without any defined criteria as to how that choice will be made, it will not be possible to advise accurately on the likely remedy, which could range from a transfer of the fee simple to mere monetary compensation.[200] The courts seem to be aware of the

---

[191] See [1986] Conv 406 (Thompson); (1986) 49 MLR 741 (Dewar).    [192] See Chapter 9.

[193] (1883–84) LR 9 App Cas 699 at 714.    [194] [1976] Ch 179 at 189.

[195] [1980] 1 WLR 1306 at 1312.    [196] (1977) 248 Estates Gazette 947.

[197] See also *Williams v Staite* [1979] Ch 291 at 298, where Goff LJ said: 'In the normal type of case . . . whether there is an equity and its extent will depend . . . simply upon the initial conduct said to give rise to the equity, although the court may have to decide how, having regard to supervening circumstances, the equity can best be satisfied.'

[198] [1988] 2 NZLR 424.

[199] See *Cowcher v Cowcher* [1972] 1 WLR 425 at 430, where Bagnall J said: '[justice] flows from the application of sure and settled principle for proved or admitted facts'; *Taylor v Dickens* [1998] 1 FLR 806; [1998] Conv 210 (Thompson).

[200] See above, pp 343–349.

danger of uncertainty, as was indicated by Browne-Wilkinson J in *Re Sharpe*.[201] Having held that the claimant entitled to occupy the property until the loan was repaid, he noted:

'I reach this conclusion with some hesitation since I find the present state of the law very confused and difficult to fit in with established equitable principles. I express the hope that in the near future the whole question can receive full consideration in the Court of Appeal, so that, in order to do justice to the many thousands of people who never come into court at all but who wish to know with certainty what their proprietary rights are, the extent to which these irrevocable licences may be defined with certainty. Doing justice to the litigant who actually appears in the court by the invention of new principles of law ought not to involve justice to the other persons who are not litigants before the court but whose rights are fundamentally affected by new principle.'

Such fears of uncertainty also lead the Court of Appeal to reject a purely discretionary approach in *Jennings v Rice*.[202] Whilst it was accepted that equity acts flexibly to do justice by preventing unconscionability, Robert Walker LJ rejected any notion of an unfettered discretion:

'It cannot be doubted that in this as in every other area of the law, the court must take a principled approach, and cannot exercise a completely unfettered discretion according to the individual judge's notion of what is fair in any particular case.'

## (c) Proportionality between the remedy and the detriment[203]

It has now been recognised that it is a false dichotomy to set the two views explained above against each other as if only one were correct. In *Jennings v Rice*[204] the Court of Appeal has confirmed that elements of both are discernible in the decided cases, so that although the courts articulate a flexibility to determine the appropriate remedy to satisfy an estoppel equity, they do so in a circumspect way that takes account of the claimant's expectations. Robert Walker LJ stated the underlying principle as follows:

'. . . once the elements of proprietary estoppel are established an equity arises. The value of that equity will depend upon all the circumstances including the expectation and the detriment. The task of the court is to do justice. The most essential requirement is that there must be proportionality between the expectation and the detriment.'[205]

In applying this underlying principle he drew a distinction between a situation where the assurance and reliance related to specific property and had a consensual character falling not far short of an enforceable contract,[206] and a situation where the claimant's expectation was more uncertain and did not focus on any specific property. In cases falling within the first category, he considered that the court should act to fulfill the expectation of the claimant, on the grounds that the 'consensual element of what has happened suggests that the claimant and the benefactor probably regarded the expected benefit and the accepted detriment as being (in a general, imprecise way) equivalent, or

---

[201] [1980] 1 WLR 219 at 226.    [202] [2003] 1 P & CR 8.
[203] See Bright and McFarlane, 'Proprietary Estoppel and Property Rights' [2005] 64 CLJ 449.
[204] [2003] 1 P & CR 8.    [205] Ibid at [36].    [206] As, for example, in *Yaxley v Gotts* [2000] Ch 162.

at any rate not obviously disproportionate'.[207] He suggested that the situation where an elderly benefactor reaches a clear understanding with the claimant that, if the claimant resides with and cares for the benefactor, the claimant will inherit the benefactor's house, was a typical case where the expectations should be fulfilled. However in cases falling within the second category, where the expectations are uncertain and do not relate to specific property, he considered that the claimant's expectations should be regarded as 'no more than a starting point' for the determination of the remedy:

'But if the claimant's expectations are uncertain, or extravagant, or out of all proportion to the detriment which the claimant has suffered, the court can and should recognise that the claimant's equity should be satisfied in another (and generally more limited) way.'[208]

In such cases the court must exercise 'a wide judicial discretion'[209] to determine the appropriate remedy. Whilst the claimant's expectations remain relevant, the court must also consider the detriment suffered and exercise its discretion so as to ensure that a disproportionate remedy is not awarded. Whilst unwilling to provide a comprehensive enumeration of the factors relevant to the exercise of the court's discretion. Robert Walker LJ did indicate a number of factors which should be taken into account: the misconduct of the claimant; particularly oppressive conduct on the part of the defendant; the court's recognition that it cannot compel people who have fallen out to live peaceably together; alterations in the benefactor's assets and circumstances; the likely effects of taxation; and (to a limited degree) the other claims (legal or moral) on the benefactor or his or her estate.[210]

Having established the appropriate principles, the Court of Appeal concluded that the first instance judge had exercised his discretion correctly in awarding the claimant £200,000 rather than ownership of the benefactor's house and its furniture. He had been unaware as to the extent of her wealth, the actual value of her estate was out of all proportion to what he might reasonably have charged for the services he had provided free, and the nature of the house was such that it was unsuitable for him to reside in on his own.

Other cases also illustrate that the court neither possesses an unbridled discretion, nor determines remedies on a purely mechanistic formula. In *Burrows and Burrows v Sharp*[211] an equity was established when the plaintiff and her family moved in with her grandmother. The relationship broke down and it fell to the court to determine how the equity should be satisfied. The judge at first instance had held that the plaintiff was entitled to continue to reside in the house. The Court of Appeal held that this was unworkable, and instead ordered that the grandmother make financial compensation for the expenditure the plaintiff had incurred. In discussing the appropriate remedy, Dillon LJ emphasised that the court 'had a discretion as to how the equity should be satisfied',[212] and that the appropriate remedy 'had to be decided in the light of the circumstances at the date of the hearing, taking into account, if appropriate, the conduct of the parties up to that date'. As a prime principle he held that:

---

[207] [2003] 1 P & CR 8. at [45].    [208] Ibid at [50].    [209] Ibid at [51].
[210] Ibid.    [211] [1991] Fam Law 67; [1992] Conv 54.
[212] Citing *Griffiths v Williams* (1977) 248 Estates Gazette 947, CA.

'It was often appropriate to satisfy the equity by granting the claimant the interest he was intended to have.'

This emphasises that the claimant's 'reasonable expectation' is the key factor which circumscribes the court's discretion. However, he admitted that in some cases it was not practicable for the court to order that the intention be fulfillled and that in such cases the court must do the best it could. This might mean that 'the way in which an equity should be satisfied might take a wholly different form from what had been intended when the parties were on good terms'. Along with the nature of the claimant's expectations, other factors which should be taken into account in determining the remedy include: the extent of reliance; the relative wealth of the parties; the existence of children; and inequitable conduct by either party.[213]

A similar approach was taken by the Court of Appeal in *Gillett v Holt*.[214] Having concluded that an estoppel equity was established Robert Walker LJ stated that the 'court must decide what is the most appropriate form for the relief to take'.[215] Whilst this might suggest a broad discretion, he proceeded to undertake a two stage process to determine appropriate relief. First he identified the extent of the owners property in respect of which the equity was established. This, it appears, was determined by the expectations that had been generated by the assurances given, namely Holt's farming business. However having established the maximum extent of the equity he held that the court should determine the 'minimum required to satisfy it and do justice between the parties'.[216] Thus the court did not possess an unbridled discretion, but is required to exercise its discretion to determine an appropriate remedy within the limits of the expectations that have been created by the assurances. In exercising its discretion to determine the minimum required he held that the court should look at all the circumstances, including the need to achieve a 'clean break' between the parties and to avoid or minimise future friction.

As was noted above, the principles adopted in *Gillett v Holt* and *Jennings v Rice* were adopted by the Court of Appeal in *Oxley v Hiscock*[217] as the way in which the court should quantify the beneficial interests arising under a common intention constructive trust where the parties had not agreed how the ownership of the property should be shared. This means that cases where the courts exercise their discretion to determine the appropriate share of the beneficial interest arising under such a constructive trust will be useful illustrations as to how the court might exercise its discretion in satisfying an estoppel equity. These cases were discussed in the previous chapter.[218]

---

[213] [1986] Conv 406 (Thompson); Pettit, *Equity and the Law of Trusts* (7th edn, 1993), p 189.
[214] [2000] 2 All ER 289.   [215] [2000] 2 All ER 289 at 311.   [216] [2000] 2 All ER 289 at 312.
[217] [2004] 3 All ER 703.   [218] See above pp 298 *et seq.*

# 11
# Mutual wills

## 1 The nature of mutual wills[1]

### (1) The practical problem

When an owner of property dies, English law permits him to dictate how it should be distributed by means of a will. The cardinal feature of a will is that it remains revocable until the death of the testator, who thus remains free to alter its terms at any time before his demise. As was said in *Vynior's Case*:

'If a man makes his testament and last will irrevocably, yet he may revoke it; for his acts or his words cannot alter the judgement of the law, to make that irrevocable which, of its own nature, is revocable.'[2]

The potential revocability of a will presents a significant obstacle if an owner wishes to leave property to one person absolutely, subject to a requirement that the recipient bequeaths it to an agreed third person. For example, if a husband and wife have one child the husband may want his wife to enjoy all his property if he predeceases her, but also to ensure that it is ultimately left to their daughter. If he simply executes a will leaving his property to his wife, it will become her absolute property on his death and she will be free to execute her own will leaving the property to whoever she chooses, perhaps to the children of a second marriage or to some charitable object. To try to avoid such difficulties they may decide to execute wills with identical terms, leaving their property to each other in the event that they predecease, but to their daughter if they survive. However, even where identical wills have been executed, the survivor will remain free to revoke the former will and leave the property to others.

These practical difficulties are well illustrated by the facts of *Re Cleaver*.[3] Arthur and Flora Cleaver had married in 1967, when he was 78 and she was 74. He had three children by a previous marriage and she had none. They executed identical wills leaving the bulk of their estates[4] to the survivor absolutely, and in default of their survival to the

---

[1] See Oakley, *Constructive Trusts* (3rd edn, 1997), pp 264–274; (1970) 34 Conv (NS) 230 (Burgess); (1979) 24 UTorLJ 390 (Youdan); McFarlane, 'Constructive Trusts Arising on a Receipt of Property *Sub Conditione*' (2004) 120 LQR 667.

[2] (1610) 8 Co Rep 80a.     [3] [1981] 2 All ER 1018.

[4] The remainder after certain specific legacies.

three children.[5] Arthur died in 1975. The will was proved and Florence became entitled to his estate absolutely. She subsequently executed a new will leaving her entire estate, which included the property she had inherited from Arthur, to only one of the children. Whilst Arthur had clearly intended that the property bequeathed to his wife should ultimately be left by her to the children equally,[6] it was impossible to prevent his widow revoking her will and executing a replacement with differing terms. If the terms of the new will were allowed to operate, Arthur's intentions would have been defeated by his wife's subsequent change of mind.

Whilst these difficulties can be avoided by bequeathing property directly to the intended ultimate beneficiaries, or through the use of a life interest which will ensure that the survivor is only entitled to utilise the income derived from the property but not the capital, in reality these are often impracticable solutions. Where the testators do not possess great wealth the survivor may need to make use of the property bequeathed to them, for example to provide retirement income or to pay for nursing care if needed, and solutions which do not enable them to do so are inadequate to fulfill their intentions.[7] What is required is a mechanism which enables the survivor to enjoy the property inherited from the first to die if necessary but which prevents the survivor from making an effective bequest of any of that property remaining at the date of their death to anyone other than the agreed beneficiary. Equity provides such a mechanism through the doctrine of 'mutual wills'.

## (2) The doctrine of mutual wills

The doctrine of 'mutual wills' evolved in equity to overcome the problems presented by the revocability of wills. The essence of this doctrine was stated by Morritt J in *Re Dale (Decd)*:

'The doctrine of mutual wills is to the effect that where two individuals have agreed as to the disposal of their property and have executed mutual wills in pursuance of the agreement, on the death of the first (T1) the property of the survivor (T2), the subject matter of the agreement, is held on an implied trust for the beneficiary named in the wills. The survivor may thereafter alter his will, because a will is inherently revocable, but if he does his personal representatives will take the property subject to the trust.'[8]

Where mutual wills have been executed equity does not prevent the survivor from changing his will.[9] Instead, the executors of the new will hold any property which was intended to be left to the beneficiary of the mutual wills on constructive trust. By means of this trust the property will be held for the beneficiary named in the original mutual wills, and not pass to those named in the new will. As the Privy Council stated in *Gray v Perpetual Trustee Co Ltd*:

---

[5] Two of the children were to receive one-third shares absolutely, with the daughter receiving only a life interest in the remaining third.

[6] [1981] 2 All ER 1018 at 1029. Nourse J described him as 'a very determined man' and that 'everything suggests that he would, so far as he could, have wanted to ensure that anything which was left at [his wife's] death should go back to his side of the family'.

[7] See (1996) NLJ 961 (J Stevens).   [8] [1993] 4 All ER 129 at 132.

[9] See *Re Hey's Estate* [1914] P 192.

'If two persons simultaneously make wills to the same effect, and in that sense mutually, a second will made by one of them after succeeding to the other's estate under the originally made will is precluded from being treated as effective to interfere in equity with the existing disposition.'[10]

Returning to the example of *Re Cleaver*,[11] it was held that the wills executed by Arthur and his wife had been 'mutual wills', so that the equitable doctrine applied and a constructive trust had come into existence. The widow's executors therefore held the property she had received under her husband's will on constructive trust for the three children in equal shares.

## (3) Rationale for the imposition of a constructive trust

A constructive trust will be imposed if the testators executed mutual wills on the basis of an agreement not to revoke. The rationale for imposing a constructive trust in such circumstances is that equity will not permit the survivor to commit a fraud by going back on his agreement. Since the property he received on the death of the first testator had only been bequeathed to him on the basis of the agreement not to revoke his own will, it would be a fraud for him to take the benefit whilst failing to observe the agreement and equity intervenes to prevent this fraud.[12] This rationale is evident from the judgment of Lord Cottenham LC in the early case of *Dufour v Pereira*:

'The parties by the mutual will do each of them devise, upon the engagement of the other, that he will likewise devise in manner therein mentioned. The instrument itself is the evidence of the agreement; and he, that dies first, does by his death carry the agreement on his part into execution. If the other then refuses, he is guilty of a fraud, can never unbind himself, and becomes a trustee of course. For no man shall deceive another to his prejudice. By engaging to do something that is in his power, he is made a trustee for the performance, and transmit that trust to those that claim under him . . .'[13]

The principle was stated in a more modern way by Dixon J in the Australian case *Birmingham v Renfrew*,[14] which was cited with approval in *Re Cleaver*:[15]

'It has long been established that a contract between persons to make corresponding wills gives rise to equitable obligations when one acts on the faith of such an agreement and dies leaving his will unrevoked so that the other takes property under its dispositions. It operates to impose upon the survivor an obligation regarded as specifically enforceable. It is true that he cannot be compelled to make and leave unrevoked a testamentary document and if he dies leaving a last will containing provisions inconsistent with his agreement it is nevertheless a valid testamentary act. But the doctrines of equity attach the obligation to the property. The effect is, I think, that the survivor becomes a constructive trustee and the terms of the trust are those of the will which he undertook would be his last will and testament.'

---

[10] [1928] AC 391 at 399.    [11] [1981] 2 All ER 1018.

[12] See *Re Dale (Decd)* [1993] 4 All ER 129 at 142, per Morrit J.

[13] (1769) 2 Hargreave's Juridical Arguments 304, cited by Morritt J in *Re Dale (Decd)* [1993] 4 All ER 129 at 135–136.

[14] (1937) CLR 666.    [15] [1981] 2 All ER 1018.

The principle was also stated more generally by Nourse J in *Re Cleaver*:

'. . . the principle of all these cases is that a court of equity will not permit a person to whom property is transferred by way of gift, but on the faith of an agreement or clear understanding that it is to be dealt with in a particular way for the benefit of a third person, to deal with that property inconsistently with that agreement or understanding. If he attempts to do so after having received the benefit of the gift equity will intervene by imposing a constructive trust on the property which is the subject matter of the agreement or understanding.'[16]

More recently, in *Re Dale (Decd)* Morrit J reiterated the fraud justification for the imposition of a constructive trust:

'There is a contract between the testators which on the death of T1 is carried into effect by him, that T1 dies with the promise of T2 that the agreement will stand and that it would be a fraud on T1 to allow T2 to disregard the contract which became irrevocable on the death of T1.'[17]

Given that the mutual wills operate to prevent the survivor acting fraudulently, the question has arisen whether the doctrine of mutual wills operates if the surviving testator gains no personal benefit under the will of the first testator who predeceases him. In the majority of cases this problem will not arise because the mutual wills provide that the survivor is to inherit the estate of the predeceasing party absolutely, or receive a life interest in it. However, the problem did arise in *Re Dale (Decd)*.[18] Norman and Monica Dale executed mutual wills in September 1988. They had two children, a son Alan and a daughter Joan. Under the terms of the mutual wills all their property, real and personal, was to be divided equally between their children. They left nothing to each other. Norman died in November 1988 and his estate was worth about £18,500. Monica died in 1990, having made a new will earlier that year leaving £300 to Joan and everything else to Alan. Her estate was valued at £19,000. Joan claimed that the doctrine of mutual wills applied so that Alan, as executor, held Monica's estate on constructive trust in accordance with the terms of the mutual wills. Alan argued that the doctrine could not operate because Monica had derived no personal benefit under Norman's will. After reviewing the authorities, Morritt J concluded that the doctrine of mutual wills could operate even where the surviving testator received no benefit under the first testator's will:

'As all the cases show the doctrine applies when T2 benefits under the will of T1. But I am unable to see why it should be any the less a fraud on T1 if the agreement was that each testator should leave his or her property to particular beneficiaries, for example their children, rather than to each other. It should be assumed that they had good reason for doing so and in any event that is what the parties bargained for. In each case there is the binding contract. In each case it has been performed by T1 on the faith of the promise of T2 and in each case T2 would have deceived T1 to the detriment of T1 if he, T2, were permitted to go back on his agreement. I see no reason why the doctrine should be confined

---

[16] [1981] 2 All ER 1018 at 1024.
[17] [1993] 4 All ER 129 at 136; (1995) 58 MLR 95 (Brierley).
[18] [1993] 4 All ER 129; [1994] NLJ 1272 (O'Hagan).

to cases where T2 benefits when the aim of the principle is to prevent T1 from being defrauded . . .'[19]

# 2  Establishing that wills were mutual

## (1)  A contract not to revoke

### (a)  Necessity of a contract

The doctrine of mutual wills will only operate if the testators had agreed that their wills would not be revoked. In the absence of such an agreement there will be no fraud if the surviving testator revokes his will. As Lord Loughborough LC indicated in *Walpole v Lord Orford*,[20] the principal difficulty in establishing that wills were intended to be mutual is determining whether the testators had entered a legally binding obligation not to revoke their wills rather than a mere 'honourable engagement'. In *Re Cleaver* Nourse J stated:

'I would emphasise that the agreement or understanding must be such as to impose on the donee a legally binding obligation to deal with the property in the particular way.'[21]

More recent cases have held that this agreement between the parties must take the form of a valid contract. In *Re Dale (Decd)*[22] Morrit J held that 'there is no doubt that for the doctrine to apply there must be a contract at law'. The requirement of a contract was reiterated in *Goodchild v Goodchild*,[23] where it had been argued that a contract should not be required because it was not an essential element of the establishment of a constructive trust. The Court of Appeal rejected the purported analogy between the operation of mutual wills and secret trusts and concluded that a contract was required. Morritt LJ stated:

'As Leggatt LJ has pointed out, a consistent line of authority requires that for the doctrine of mutual wills to apply there must be a contract between the two testators. In delivering the advice of the Privy Council in *Gray v Perpetual Trustee Co Ltd*[24] such requirement was made abundantly clear by Viscount Haldane. Counsel . . . suggests that this test is too high. He does so by reference to the requirements for a secret trust or for the imposition of a constructive trust. I do not accept that there is any justification to be found in those areas of equity such as would justify departing from the clear statement of Viscount Haldane.'[25]

Whilst critics have suggested that Morritt LJ misrepresented the earlier cases cited in

---

[19] [1993] 4 All ER 129 at 142. In the Canadian case *Lynch Estate v Lynch Estate* (1993) 8 Alta LR (3d) 291 it was held that a 'disposition agreement' was generally only enforceable against someone who had taken a benefit under it.

[20] (1797) 3 Ves JR 402 at 419. Cited by Nourse J in *Re Cleaver* [1981] 2 All ER 1018 at 1024.

[21] [1981] 2 All ER 1018 at 1024.     [22] [1993] 4 All ER 129 at 133.

[23] [1997] 3 All ER 63; [1997] Conv 153 (Grattan).     [24] [1928] AC 391 at 400.

[25] [1997] 3 All ER 63 at 75

support of his conclusion that a contract is required,[26] and argued that the doctrine of mutual wills should operate whenever testators have reached an agreement or understanding not to revoke their wills,[27] the most recent decisions make clear that a contract will be required.[28] The courts have enjoyed ample opportunity to adopt a lower threshold but have pointedly, and repeatedly, chosen not to do so. Their decision must in principle be correct. The effect of a finding that there are mutual wills is to impose a binding legal obligation in respect of the property affected. To give rise to this, even if a contract is not required, there must be an agreement intended to have legal effect. The difference between such an agreement and a contract is no more than semantic.

## (b) Necessity of consideration

In order to establish that the testators had entered into a binding contract not to revoke their wills, it is necessary to show that consideration was provided. In *Re Dale (Decd)*[29] the defendants argued that consideration was only given for the promise not to revoke if the first testator to die had provided a benefit to the survivor other than his promise not to revoke his own will, because otherwise he would simply bequeath his property in the way that he wished whilst remaining able to change his mind and revoke his will at any time before his death. Morrit J rejected this submission and held that a testator has acted sufficiently to his detriment to constitute consideration where he has performed his promise by executing the mutual will, and not subsequently taken advantage of his legal right to revoke it.

## (c) Absence of any contract

In the absence of a contract the testators' wills will not be mutual, and a constructive trust cannot arise. In *Re Oldham*[30] Mr and Mrs Weldon executed similar wills in 1907. In 1914 the husband died. As a result his estate passed to his wife absolutely. In 1921 she married Mr Oldham, who was some 35 years her junior, and altered her will to grant him a life interest in a large portion of her estate. She died in 1922, leaving some £108,000, all but £10,000 of which had come from her first husband's estate. Astbury J held that there was no evidence of an agreement that the 'mutual' wills should be irrevocable, and therefore there was no trust raised in favour of the beneficiaries named in them.

## (d) Breach of contract by revocation

As mutual wills are executed on the basis of a contract not to revoke, a testator who unilaterally revokes his will before either has died will have acted in breach of his contractual obligations. As such, he will be prima facie liable to pay damages to his fellow testator, and if he has died his estate will be liable to the survivor.[31] There will be

---

[26] *Dufour v Pereira* (1769) 1 Dick 419; *Walpole v Lord Orford* (1797) 3 Ves JR 402; *Gray v Perpetual Trustee Co Ltd* [1928] AC 391; *Birmingham v Renfrew* (1937) CLR 666; *Re Cleaver* [1981] 2 All ER 1018.

[27] [1997] Conv 182 (Harper); [1997] Conv 153 (Grattan).

[28] *Birch v Curtis* [2002] FLR 1158. In New Zealand it was held that the doctrine of mutual wills may be founded either on the basis of contract or restitution: *Re Newey* [1994] 2 NZLR 590.

[29] [1994] Ch 31.    [30] [1925] Ch 75.    [31] *Robinson v Ommanney* (1883) 23 Ch D 285.

no liability for breach if the revocation occurred by operation of law, for example where the testator married or divorced.

## (2) Establishing a contract not to revoke

### (a) The standard of proof

In *Re Cleaver*[32] Nourse J held that the agreement not to revoke the mutual wills can only be established by 'clear and satisfactory evidence' and that the burden of proof is the ordinary civil standard of the balance of probabilities.

### (b) Mere fact of identical wills

In *Dufour v Pereira*[33] Lord Cottenham LC had suggested that, where identical wills had been executed, it was possible to infer that the parties had agreed that they should not be revoked because 'the instrument itself is the evidence of the agreement'. However, it seems clear from more recent cases that the necessary contract not to revoke will not be construed from the mere fact that the testators simultaneously executed identical wills. In *Gray v Perpetual Trustee Co Ltd*[34] the Privy Council concluded that:

'. . . the mere simultaneity of the wills and the similarity of their terms do not appear, taken by themselves, to have been looked on as more than some evidence of an agreement not to revoke. The agreement . . . was a fact which had in itself to be established by evidence, and in such cases the whole of the evidence must be looked at.[35]

This statement of principle was approved by Nourse J in *Re Cleaver*.[36] For this reason, no constructive trust was established in *Re Oldham*,[37] the facts of which were noted above. The only evidence of an agreement came from the fact that the wills had been executed and Astbury J held that this was insufficient. He explained that it was impossible to construe the true intentions of the testators from the mere fact of their identical wills:

'The plaintiff contends that no such agreement need be proved outside the facts of the form of the mutual wills. I regret that I am unable in the circumstances of this case to give effect to that contention, and all the more so because I have no doubt at all that if the husband in 1907 had foreseen that his wife after seven years' survivorship would marry a young man and leave the whole of her first husband's property to that young man and her own relatives he would have made a very different testamentary disposition.'[38]

His rationale for insisting upon a high degree of proof of an agreement is instructive as to the unwillingness of the courts to impose trusts on property in the absence of any clear intention:

'The plaintiff says that each was satisfied to trust the other and made the arrangement only in respect of the property taken by the survivor and not disposed of in the survivor's

---

[32] [1981] 2 All ER 1018 at 1024.
[33] (1769) 1 Dick 419; see also *Walpole v Lord Orford* (1797) 3 Ves JR 402.
[34] [1928] AC 391 at 400.      [35] [1928] AC 391 at 400.      [36] [1981] 2 All ER 1018 at 1022.
[37] [1925] Ch 25.      [38] [1925] Ch 25 at 87.

lifetime. Now this question must be answered. Could these parties have acted as they did with any other object or intent than that the plaintiff asserts? It is impossible to deny that they could. I cannot build up a trust on conjecture, and there are many reasons which may have operated on the minds of these mutual will makers. Each may have thought it quite safe to trust the other, and to believe that, having regard to their ages, nothing was likely to occur in the future substantially to diminish the property taken by the survivor, who could be trusted to give effect to the other's obvious wishes. But that is a very different thing from saying that they bound themselves by a trust that should be operative in all circumstances and in all cases. Suppose that the wife had died first, and the husband not yet sixty had remarried.

It is very difficult to suppose that he had agreed to a course preventing him making a testamentary provision for his second wife except as to one-twentieth of his residue. Again his own relatives to whom he wished his residue to go might, many of them, have pre-deceased the testator and his wife. If the plaintiff's alleged trust is operative there is no means of providing by will for such circumstances, and further I cannot help thinking that any reasonable professional man would have advised against the creation of such a trust if brought to his attention. It is difficult to imagine that when the mutual wills were made, it is intended that under no circumstances should the survivor have any power of altering the trusts except by disposition inter vivos . . . Putting it shortly I have no sufficient means for deciding with certainty what, among many possible inferences, is the sole inference that ought to be drawn from the circumstances of this case.'[39]

Although the mere fact of the execution of mutual wills is not alone sufficient to prove the necessary contract, it may provide a strong indication that a contract had been concluded between the testators.[40] This was recognised even in *Re Oldham*.[41]

## (c) Extrinsic evidence of agreement

Since a contract will not be inferred form the mere execution of identical wills, extrinsic evidence will have to be provided to demonstrate that the testators had concluded a contract not to revoke. A constructive trust will be established if the mutual wills themselves contain a statement that they have been executed on the basis of an agreement, as was the case in *Re Hagger*.[42] Written evidence outside of the wills, for example a memorandum stating the testators' intentions, will also suffice to establish a constructive trust.

However, the majority of recent cases have concerned the difficulties of establishing that there was a constructive trust in the absence of any written evidence concerning the testator's intentions. Whilst oral evidence of the testators' intentions may suffice, it is difficult to establish the existence of the essential contract not to revoke. In *Re Cleaver*[43] Nourse J held that evidence of family conversations entitled him to conclude that that there was 'clear and satisfactory evidence that the testator and the testatrix did make an agreement which they intended should impose mutual legal obligations as to the

---

[39] [1925] Ch 25 at 88–89.

[40] [1925] Ch 25 at 87, where Astbury J said: 'Of course it is a strong thing that these two parties came together, agreed to make their wills in identical terms and in fact so made them. But that does not go nearly far enough.' The approach of Astbury J was approved by the Privy Council in *Gray v Perpetual Trustee Co Ltd* [1928] AC 391 at 400.

[41] [1925] Ch 75.      [42] [1930] 2 Ch 190.      [43] [1981] 2 All ER 1018.

disposal of their property'.[44] This evidence included conversations of Mr Cleaver with his children when Mrs Cleaver was present, and the attitude of Mrs Cleaver after his death, which seemed to suggest that she was aware that she was under an obligation to dispose of her estate in accordance with the terms of their mutual wills, and not merely an honourable engagement.[45] It was only later that she adopted the attitude that she did not have to worry about promises made to her husband because he was dead and could do nothing about it.[46]

In contrast, in *Goodchild v Goodchild*[47] it was held that the evidence had failed to establish that the testators had contractually agreed not to revoke their wills. Dennis Goodchild and his wife Joan executed similar wills in 1988, leaving the majority of their estates to their son Gary. Joan died in 1991 and in 1992 Dennis married Enid, his second wife. He subsequently executed a new will leaving his entire estate to Enid. He died in 1993. Gary claimed that his parents had executed mutual wills in 1988, and that a constructive trust should be imposed over the property left to Enid deriving from his mother. Carnwath J[48] held that there 'was no clear agreement that they were to be mutually binding', a conclusion which was upheld by the Court of Appeal on the grounds that there was inadequate evidence to justify holding that a binding contract had been made.

A variety of evidence had been given in the case. Gary gave evidence from a meeting with his parents which led Carnwath J to conclude that he had no doubt 'he was led to believe by both his parents that he would inherit everything'.[49] Other family friends gave evidence that the wills were intended to be mutually binding.[50] Their housekeeper gave evidence that Joan had wanted to ensure that Gary would 'be all right'. However, this body of anecdotal evidence was weighed against the evidence of the family solicitor who had drawn up the wills in question. He claimed that it was not his normal practice to draw up mutually binding wills but rather to grant a life interest to the survivor. He claimed to have discussed the matter with them and that they clearly intended the survivor to be free to deal with the property during his or her lifetime. Carnwath J summarised the solicitor's evidence:

'He claimed to have discussed this specifically with them. His normal approach was to make something of a joke of the point, for example to ask the wife whether she accepted that, if her husband went off with a blonde nurse he would be able to give her everything (or conversely to ask her husband if he would mind if his wife went off with the milkman). He remembers the visit to the Goodchilds on 13 January, because he had known the house under previous occupants and was interested to see it. He also remembers Mr Goodchild being busy looking after both his wife and her mother, who was also ill and staying with them. His attendance note is in summary form, because as far as he was concerned it was a perfectly straightforward transaction. Had there been instructions to make some form of unusual provision, then he would have noticed that.'[51]

Faced with this conflict of evidence, Carnwath J placed greater weight on the evidence of the solicitor. He concluded that in the circumstances no agreement had been proved:

[44] [1981] 2 All ER 1018 at 1028.    [45] [1981] 2 All ER 1018 at 1027.
[46] [1981] 2 All ER 1018 at 1027–1028.    [47] [1997] 3 All ER 63.    [48] [1996] 1 All ER 670.
[49] [1996] 1 All ER 670 at 678.    [50] [1996] 1 All ER 670 at 679.    [51] [1996] 1 All ER 670 at 681.

'Faced with this conflict of evidence, I have to bear in mind that the onus of proof lies on the plaintiffs, and that, as the cases show, there must be established evidence of a specific agreement outside the wills, not just some loose understanding or sense of moral obligation ... The evidence in this case also shows how difficult it is to rely on the evidence of lay witnesses, when one is dealing with the somewhat technical issue as to whether there has been an agreement for mutually binding wills . . .'[52]

He distinguished *Re Cleaver* on the grounds that the evidence for an agreement in that case had been stronger:

'. . . the facts of each case must be seen in their own context. It would be wrong for me to attempt a detailed analysis of the two cases. I note, however, that in *Re Cleaver* the father and mother had kept their finances separate, and used to deal with their joint financial interests "on a more commercial basis than is sometimes the case". Furthermore, there was specific evidence of their mutual intentions at the time the wills were made. There a meeting with the daughter, immediately following the making of the wills, at which the father—in the presence of his wife—explained to his daughter "what we have put in our wills". It may be that *Re Cleaver* is an extreme example of the circumstances in which an agreement may be found on the basis of oral evidence.'[53]

The Court of Appeal upheld his conclusion that there was insufficient evidence to establish anything beyond a mere moral obligation that the testators' estates would be left to Gary. Leggatt LJ stated:

'Two wills may be in the same form as each other. Each testator may leave his or her estate to the other with a view to the survivor leaving both estates to their heir. But there is no presumption that a present plan will be immutable in the future . . . Dennis and Joy executed wills in the same terms save that each left his or her estate to the other. Thus the survivor was to have both estates. They wanted Gary to inherit the combined estates. But there was no express agreement not to revoke the wills. Nor could any such agreement be implied from the fact that the survivor was in a position to leave both estates to Gary. The fact that each expected that the other would leave them to him is not sufficient to impress the arrangement with a floating trust, binding in equity. A mutual desire that Gary should inherit could not of itself prevent the survivor from resiling from the arrangement. What is required is a mutual intention that both wills should remain unaltered and that the survivor should be bound to leave the combined estate to the son. That is what is missing here.'

It should be noted that the overriding difference between the evidence presented in the cases of *Re Cleaver* and *Goodchild v Goodchild* was as to the evidence of the respective solicitors. In *Re Cleaver* the solicitor's evidence was relatively weak. In contrast, in *Goodchild* the solicitor was adamant that no agreement had been intended, and that he had expressly outlined to the testators the various options as to how they could ensure that the estate passed to the son, and that they had decided to opt for the identical, but not mutual, wills, which he had explained would mean that the survivor was still free to dispose of the property freely as they chose. Thus, in the earlier case the solicitor's evidence was inadequate to rebut the indication from the other oral evidence that an

---

[52] [1996] 1 All ER 670 at 681–682.    [53] [1996] 1 All ER 670 at 683.

agreement had been intended, but of which he had not been made aware, whereas in the latter the solicitor's evidence fully rebutted any inference of an agreement which could be drawn from the other oral evidence presented.

### (3) Certainty of subject and objects

In *Re Cleaver*[54] Nourse J also emphasised that there must be certainty of subject matter and of objects for a constructive trust to arise on the basis of mutual wills. He considered that these requirements 'are as essential to this species of trust as they are to any other'.

## 3 The operation of mutual wills

Whilst English law clearly accepts the doctrine of mutual wills, there are many theoretical and practical difficulties concerning the nature of the trust interest established thereby. In *Goodchild v Goodchild*[55] Morritt LJ emphasised that 'the doctrine of mutual wills is anomalous',[56] and for this reason uncertainties and inconsistencies are tolerated which would render a more conventional trust void.

### (1) Date of creation of the constructive trust[57]

When it is established that wills were intended to be mutual, it has been seen that a constructive trust will arise to prevent the survivor disposing of his property in contravention of his contractual agreement not to vary his will. Whilst it is clear that equity imposes a constructive trust, it is less clear when the trust arises. A number of alternatives present themselves.

### (a) Date the mutual wills are executed

As a matter of logic, this cannot be the date at which the constructive trust arises. The parties remain free to revoke their wills by agreement at any time before the death of the first testator.[58] It may even be that a revocation without agreement will prevent a constructive trust arising. As Sir Gorell Barnes P held in *Stone v Hoskins*,[59] the survivor has no claim to a constructive trust where the testator who has died revoked his mutual will and executed another in a different form.

### (b) Date of the death of the survivor

The date of death of the surviving testator cannot be the relevant date for the establishment of the constructive trust, as it has been held that the interest of a beneficiary of

---

[54] [1981] 2 All ER 1018.     [55] [1997] 3 All ER 63.     [56] [1997] 3 All ER 63 at 76.

[57] See (1951) 14 MLR 137 (Mitchell).

[58] However, if the testator revokes his will before death he will have committed a breach of contract and his estate will be liable to the survivor in damages: see *Robinson v Ommanney* (1883) LR 23 Ch D 285.

[59] [1905] P 194.

a mutual will who survives the first testator but predeceases the second does not lapse. In *Re Hagger*[60] John and Emma Hagger executed mutual wills leaving one-sixth interests in their estates to Edward Adams, Eleanor Palmer and Alice Young. All three survived Emma's death in 1904, but predeceased John, who died in 1928. Clauson J held that their respective interests had not lapsed because the trust took effect from the date of the wife's death.

### (c) Date of the first testator's death

It therefore seems that a constructive trust imposed on the basis of the doctrine of mutual wills arises on the date of the death of the first of the testators who executed them.

## (2) The beneficial interest under the constructive trust

### (a) The property subject to the constructive trust

Although it seems clear that a constructive trust arises on the death of the first testator, it is more difficult to identify the precise nature and extent of the beneficial interest subsisting behind the trust. The property subject to the trust must be determined by the agreement of the testators.[61] One possibility is that the trust only affixes to the property inherited by the survivor under the will of the first testator. In that case it would be possible to hold that, from that moment, the survivor holds it as trustee for the ultimate beneficiary and has no power to dispose of it himself. This view seems to have been accepted in *Re Hagger*,[62] where Clauson J held that from the moment the property came into the hands of the survivor it was held on trust for the beneficiary with the survivor enjoying only a life interest. However, the testators may agree that all of their property, including that owned by the survivor, is covered by the agreement. In *Goodchild v Goodchild*[63] the Court of Appeal indicated that this was a crucial distinguishing feature of the doctrine of mutual wills. The constructive trust arising on the death of the first testator not only affected the property inherited by the survivor, but also the property owned absolutely by the survivor. Morritt LJ explained that for this reason the doctrine of mutual wills was to be distinguished from that of secret trusts, thus explaining the need for a contractual agreement:

'The principles applicable to cases of a fully secret trust do, in substance, require the proof of a contract . . . But if those principles do not require exactly the same degree of agreement as does a contract at law there is no reason to import that lesser requirement into the doctrine of mutual wills. Secret trusts affect the property of the donor not that of the primary donee. Where there are mutual wills the doctrine affects the property of both testators, in particular that of he second to die. If he is to be subjected to an obligation with regard to the property of his own not derived from the other then an agreement should be required.'[64]

It therefore seems that, whenever the essential requirement of a contractual agreement not to revoke is present, a constructive trust will arise at the date of death of the first

---

[60] [1930] 2 Ch 190.    [61] *Re Cleaver* [1981] 2 All ER 1018.    [62] [1930] 2 Ch 190.
[63] [1997] 3 All ER 63.    [64] [1997] 3 All ER 63 at 75.

testator over all the property in the hands of the survivor which it was agreed would be bequeathed to the ultimate beneficiaries of the mutual wills, irrespective of whether it was derived from the first testator's estate or was the survivor's own property. It is unclear whether the trust should extend to encompass property acquired by the survivor after the death of the first testator, for example through receipt of a windfall profit such as gambling winnings. Presumably, this is also a matter which is governed by the terms of the agreement giving rise to the mutual wills and therefore to the trust.

### (b) The beneficiaries' entitlement to the property subject to the constructive trust

Given that a constructive trust arises at the date of death of the first testator over all the property in the hands of the survivor which it was agreed would be bequeathed to the beneficiaries of the mutual wills, the question arises as to the precise nature of that trust interest. It does not seem that the beneficiaries should enjoy the immediate equitable ownership of the trust property in the conventional sense, which would entitle them to compel the survivor to transfer it to them in accordance with the principle of *Saunders v Vautier*.[65] The practical reality is that, in most cases, the underlying intention of the mutual wills is to allow the survivor to use the property inherited for his own support and maintenance during his lifetime. This could be achieved simply by giving the survivor the right to income under a life interest. However, in most cases it will be intended that the survivor can utilise the capital if necessary, but that the residue remaining at his death will be bequeathed to the agreed beneficiaries, rather than to others. As Nourse J observed in *Re Cleaver*,[66] Mr Cleaver wanted Mrs Cleaver to enjoy 'the security after his death which a free power of disposal over his estate would give her' and at the same time 'to ensure that anything which was left at her death should go back to his side of the family'. This means that the property rights of the beneficiaries of the mutual wills cannot crystallise until the date of the death of the survivor. If the trust were to arise on the death of the first testator, ludicrous and unintended results could follow. Whilst the issue was not considered in *Re Dale (Decd)*[67] it is obvious that a trust cannot have been intended to arise on the death of the first testator. If the beneficiaries' interests had crystallised at the date of their father's death, their mother would have held all her property, which was the subject matter of the trust, on trust for the children in equal shares, and she would in effect have no longer owned anything absolutely. At most, she would have enjoyed a right to a life interest thereof.

An alternative model is therefore required to explain the nature of the entitlement of the beneficiaries of a constructive trust arising under mutual wills. The cases have therefore suggested that the property in the hands of the survivor affected by the mutual wills is rendered subject to a floating trust which arises as the date of death of the first testator, but which does not crystallise in favour of the beneficiaries until the death of the survivor. The possibility of such a 'floating trust' was raised by Dixon J in the Australian case *Birmingham v Renfrew*:

'The purpose of an arrangement for corresponding wills must often be, as in this case, to

---

[65] (1841) Cr & Ph 240.    [66] [1981] 2 All ER 1018 at 1029.    [67] [1994] Ch 31.

enable the survivor during his life to deal as absolute owner with the property passing under the will of the party first dying. That is to say, the object of the transaction is to put the survivor in a position to enjoy for his own benefit the full ownership so that, for instance, he may convert it and expend the proceeds if he chooses. But when he dies he is to bequeath what is left in the manner agreed upon. It is only by the special doctrines of equity that such a floating obligation, suspended, so to speak, during the lifetime of the survivor can descend upon the assets at his death and crystallise into a trust.'[68]

The concept of such a 'floating', uncrystallised, trust was raised in England in *Ottaway v Norman*[69] in the context of a fully secret trust.[70] Harry Ottaway left his bungalow by will to Eva Hodges, a woman he had been living with, having communicated his intention that on death she should leave it to his son, William. Although argued and decided on the basis that a fully-secret trust had been created, this does not easily accord with the facts. It was not the intention of Harry that Eva should hold the bungalow on trust for William from the moment of his death. Nor were there mutual wills. Despite an expectation that Eva would leave the bungalow by will to William, she made no simultaneous will alongside Harry. Having held that a secret trust had arisen, Brightman J considered the nature of the beneficiary's rights during the lifetime of Eva, the trustee:

'I am content to assume for present purposes but without so deciding that if property is given to the primary donee on the understanding that the primary donee will dispose by his will of such assets, if any, as he may have at his command at his death in favour of the secondary donee, a valid trust is created in favour of the secondary donee which is in suspense during the lifetime of the primary donee, but attaches to the estate of the primary donee at the moment of the latter's death.'[71]

It therefore seems best to regard mutual wills as creating some type of floating trust, which allows the survivor to dispose of the property subject to it if necessary but crystallising over whatever remains at his death[72] This approach was also assumed by Astbury J in *Re Oldham*.[73] Most significantly, in *Goodchild v Goodchild*[74] Leggatt LJ assumed that mutual wills operated to create a floating trust. In the course of his comments concerning the need for a contractual agreement between the testators, he stated:

'The fact that each expected that the other would leave them to him is not sufficient to impress the arrangement with a floating trust.'[75]

## (c) Use of the property subject to the 'floating' trust by the survivor

Where the doctrine of mutual wills operates so that property in the hands of the surviving testator is subject to a floating constructive trust, the question arises as to duties of the survivor as trustee. The doctrine of mutual wills clearly operates to prevent the survivor disposing of the trust property by will in a manner inconsistent with the mutual wills, but the more significant issue is whether he is prevented from disposing of

---

[68] (1937) CLR 666.    [69] [1972] Ch 698.    [70] See Chapter 7.    [71] [1972] Ch 698 at 713.

[72] As has been seen in Chapter 6, a number of cases hold that such a trust, if created expressly, would fail for lack of certainty.

[73] [1925] Ch 25 at 88.    [74] [1997] 3 All ER 63.    [75] [1997] 3 All ER 63 at 71.

it during his lifetime. In *Re Oldham*[76] Astbury J was of the opinion that the survivor could dispose of the property inter vivos. However, it is clear that there must be limits to the power of the survivor to dispose of the property subject to the trust, otherwise the entire purpose of the arrangement could easily be defeated. This difficulty was recognised by Dixon J in *Birmingham v Renfrew*:

'No doubt gifts and settlements, inter vivos, if calculated to defeat the intention of the compact, could not be made by the survivor and his right of disposition, inter vivos, is, therefore, not unqualified. But, substantially, the purpose of the arrangement will often be to allow full enjoyment for the survivor's own benefit and advantage upon condition that at his death the residue shall pass as arranged.'[77]

Adopting this analysis, the position would be very similar to a floating charge over the assets of a company.[78] So long as the survivor continued to behave in an ordinary way which was in accordance with his means and circumstances, he would continue to have freedom of disposition over the assets subject to the inchoate trust. The trust would, however, crystallise and settle on the assets upon his death, and even during his lifetime he could be called upon to account for any extraordinary transaction inappropriate to his circumstances. In such cases the transaction could be set aside or be held to have no effect. If a purported extraordinary transaction was identified in time, a beneficiary affected by it could presumably take steps to restrain it.

[76] [1925] Ch 25 at 88.      [77] (1937) CLR 666.
[78] *Re Panama, New Zealand and Australian Royal Mail Co* (1870) 5 Ch App 318.

# PART III

# ALLOCATION OF BENEFIT

# 12

# Introduction to allocation

## 1 General

In the preceding chapters it has been seen how equitable mechanisms, which separate the management of property from its ownership, enable owners to deal with their property with great flexibility. Part II has examined the circumstances in which property will be subjected to a trust relationship. In this section, the focus of attention shifts to a consideration of the allocation of the trust fund, in other words how it is decided who has the rights of enjoyment over it.

The nature of the allocation of the fund will be dependent upon the type of equitable obligation which has been created, whether a power of appointment, fixed trust or discretionary trust. The original owner may have specified how the fund should be allocated himself or, alternatively, he may have given to someone else the task of deciding how the allocation should be made by granting a discretion. Each of these mechanisms will be examined in detail in the following chapters. This chapter will sketch some of the recurrent themes that run through the area.

## 2 Certainty of objects

### (1) Nature of the problem

Whenever an equitable mechanism is used to allocate the ownership of a fund, it must be possible for the allocation to be carried out in practice. If it cannot, then the mechanism will fail and the property returns from the fund to the original owner, or his successor in title, by means of a resulting trust.[1] It must also be possible for the court to be able to supervise allocations from the fund to ensure that the owner's wishes are followed and that the fund is not allocated to persons who were never intended to benefit from it. The problem arises particularly where the original owner has defined the potential objects as a class, using a generic description rather than naming them as individuals. For example, if George was to leave £10,000 to his wife, Mildred, to be divided equally amongst his 'good friends', it would be impossible for his directions to

[1] See Chapter 19.

be carried out. How would Mildred know what was meant by a 'good friend'? The concept is not capable of objective definition. To allocate the fund according to his instructions she would have to ascertain the identify of all George's 'good friends' before she could know how much to allocate to each 'good friend'. No doubt there would be many obvious candidates, but that would not be sufficient to make the gift workable. There is bound to be a grey area where it is unclear whether someone is a 'good friend' or not. The rights of any specific 'good friend' cannot be determined until the entire class is known.

If George had given her a discretion to allocate the fund amongst 'which ever of my good friends she chooses', the problem remains, although in a less extreme form. Clearly, the terms of the gift only permit allocation to 'good friends', and to prevent fraud the court must ensure that it is so allocated. If Mildred were to make an allocation of £1,000 to Brian, who was a childhood friend of George but has not seen him for twenty years, how could the court decide whether she had acted within the terms of the discretion? Is Brian a 'good friend' or not?

The very fact that this question is unanswerable is the problem addressed by the requirement that the objects of an equitable obligation to allocate the fund must be certain.[2] This means that the class of people who are potential recipients from the fund are capable of being identified sufficiently clearly for the allocator to carry out his duty and the court to effectively scrutinise any allocations made. Such a term as 'good friends' would not be regarded as sufficiently certain, because it has no clear objective meaning.[3] The precise requirement of certainty of objects differs with the variety of equitable obligation in issue.[4] The test for powers of appointment and discretionary trusts is different from that for fixed trusts. Although the details differ, the principle is the same, namely that the objects (or potential objects) of allocation must be certain.

## (2) Types of certainty

In *Re Baden's Deed Trusts (No 2)*[5] the Court of Appeal drew a distinction between 'conceptual' uncertainty and 'evidential' uncertainty. Understanding this distinction is an essential prerequisite to understanding the requirements of certainty applicable to different equitable obligations.

### (a) Conceptual uncertainty

Conceptual uncertainty refers to any inherent semantic ambiguity in the words used to define a class of objects. If the definition is not objective, so that the court or the allocator can determine without a doubt whether a person is within the class or not, it will be conceptually uncertain. For example, 'tall men' is conceptually uncertain because there is no way of telling what is 'tall'. 'Men over 6 ft' would be conceptually

---

[2] See below for what is meant by certainty in this context.
[3] See *Re Baden's Deed Trusts (No 2)* [1973] Ch 9.
[4] See *McPhail v Doulton* [1971] AC 424, HL
[5] [1973] Ch 9.

certain, because it is possible to say clearly of every man whether he is over 6 ft and within the class, or 6 ft or under and outside it. Similarly, a class of 'old ladies', 'good friends' or 'regulars' at a local pub would be conceptually uncertain. In *Re Baden's Deed Trusts (No 2)*[6] Sachs LJ gave as examples of conceptually certain classes 'first cousins', 'members of the X trade Union', and 'those who have served in the Royal Navy'. Browne-Wilkinson J expressed the problem clearly with regard to the word 'friends' in *Re Barlow's Will Trusts*:

'["Friends"] has a great range of meanings; indeed its exact meaning probably varies from person to person. Some would include only those with whom they had been on intimate terms over a long period; others would include acquaintances who they liked. Some would include people with whom their relationship was primarily one of business; others would not. Indeed, many people, if asked to draw up a complete list of their friends, would probably have some difficulty in deciding whether certain of the people they knew were really "friends" as opposed to "acquaintances" . . .'[7]

No equitable mechanism, whether a power, trust or discretionary trust, is valid if the class of objects is not conceptually certain.[8]

### (b) Evidential uncertainty

Evidential uncertainty refers to the difficulty of actually proving whether a person falls within the specified class of objects of an equitable obligation. The class may be conceptually certain, as for example 'relatives', but unless some scientific process such as genetic fingerprinting can be used, it may be difficult or impossible for some persons to prove whether they are relatives or not. Thus, it may be conceptually certain that any given individual 'is or is not' a relative, but it is impossible to prove to which category a specific person belongs. Fixed trusts require every beneficiary to be identified in fact, and are invalid if evidential certainty is lacking.[9] Powers and discretionary trusts do not require evidential certainty.[10]

## (3) Summary

As has been noted above, different requirements of certainty are applied to different types of equitable obligation. The table below summarises the appropriate test for the main varieties of obligation. These will be examined in more detail in the following chapters.

---

[6] [1973] Ch 9 at 20.

[7] [1979] 1 WLR 278 at 298.

[8] *Re Baden's Deed Trusts (No 2)* [1973] Ch 9. See also (1982) 98 LQR 551 (Emery).

[9] *IRC v Broadway Cottages Trust* [1954] 3 WLR 438; affd [1955] Ch 20, sub nom *Broadway Cottages Trust v IRC* [1954] TR 295, CA. See below, pp 398–402.

[10] *Re Gulbenkian's Settlement Trusts* [1970] AC 508; *McPhail v Doulton* [1971] AC 424; *Re Baden's Deed Trusts (No 2)* [1973] Ch 9. See below, pp 421–425 and 450–455.

| Obligation | Test of certainty | Authority | Requirements |
|---|---|---|---|
| Power | It must be possible to say whether any given individual is or is not a member of the class | *Re Gulbenkian* [1968] Ch 126 | Conceptual certainty |
| Discretionary trusts | It must be possible to say whether any given individual is or is not a member of the class | *McPhail v Doulton* [1971] AC 424 *Re Baden (No 2)* [1972] Ch 607 | Conceptual certainty |
| Fixed trusts | Complete list of all beneficiaries | *IRC v Broadway Cottages Trust* [1955] Ch 20 | Conceptual and evidential certainty |
| Conditional gifts | Condition valid for those who can prove they satisfy the condition | *Re Barlow's Will Trust* [1979] 1 WLR 278 | Individual proof |

# 3 Beneficial entitlement and ownership

A second recurrent theme is the question of the nature of the rights enjoyed by the potential objects of allocation in the fund. This will again depend on the exact nature of the equitable mechanism that has been created, and will range from a subsisting property interest in a share of the fund, to no property right at all in the fund. For example, Oliver has four children, Peter, Quentin, Robert and Stuart. He leaves £100,000 to their godparents, Tristan and Una, to be allocated between them. The exact rights that the children have in the fund will depend on the type of equitable obligation which has been created.

## (1) Fixed trust

At one end of the scale is the fixed trust, where Oliver stipulates that Tristan and Una are to hold the fund on trust for the children in equal shares. From the very moment that the trust is created, when the property comes into the hands of the trustees, the children have an immediate proprietary interest in the fund. They are each the owners in equity of a quarter of the trust property. They are liable for tax on their interest,[11] and it will be protected as against third parties who are not bona fide purchasers for value of a legal estate without notice.[12] The important decision of *Saunders v Vautier*[13] states that, as a consequence of having an immediate proprietary interest in the fund, the beneficiaries of a fixed trust can together demand that the legal title is transferred to them by the

---

[11] See Chapter 5.    [12] See Chapter 3.    [13] (1841) 4 Beav 115.

trustee. This means that if the four children were all of age and mentally competent they could demand that Tristan and Una convey the legal title to them.

## (2) Power of appointment

At the other end of the scale is the power of appointment. If Oliver provides that Tristan and Una are to hold the property and that they have the power to appoint it in favour of such of his children as they may choose, then the children have no immediate proprietary interest in the fund at all.[14] None of them has any interest in the fund unless and until Tristan and Una exercise their power and make an appointment in favour of all or some of them.[15] If they make an appointment of £50,000 in favour of Robert, then Robert will have a proprietary right in the proportion of the fund which has been allocated to him, but he and the others continue to have no interest in the £50,000 comprising the other half of the fund. If there are no appointments the fund will pass by resulting trust[16] to the residuary legatees under Oliver's will.[17]

## (3) Discretionary trust

Between these two extremes lies the discretionary trust, where the exact nature of the potential beneficiaries' right is unclear. The beneficiaries do not have immediate proprietary rights to specific shares of the fund, but they are not without any proprietary right in the fund as a whole. Oliver may have left the fund to Tristan and Una on trust to 'distribute amongst my children as they in their discretion think fit'. As a class, the children have proprietary rights to the fund, but as individuals they could not identify any particular share of the fund as their own, unless and until it was allocated to them by the trustee.

They can, if they all come together, call for the transfer of the legal title under the rule in *Saunders v Vautier*,[18] as was done in *Re Smith*.[19] In practice, this would be almost impossible if the class were a large group, for example in the case of a discretionary trust for the benefit of 'all the employees and ex-employees' of a company. The position taken in *Gartside v IRC*[20] and *Sainsbury v IRC*[21] was that the potential beneficiary of a discretionary trust has no actual proprietary interest in the fund but merely a right to be considered as a beneficiary by the trustees. Once a selection has been made, the beneficiary has entitlement to the share allocated to him. This means that under a discretionary trust the beneficial interest in the property is held 'in the air' without a specific group who have proprietary rights in the fund, until allocations are made by the trustee.

---

[14] *Vestey v IRC* [1980] AC 1148, HL.
[15] *Re Brooke's Settlement Trusts* [1939] Ch 993 at 997.
[16] See Chapter 8.
[17] Unless the rule in *Burroughs v Philcox* (1840) 5 My & Cr 72 applies. See Chapter 15.
[18] (1841) 4 Beav 115.    [19] [1928] Ch 915.    [20] [1968] AC 553.    [21] [1970] Ch 712.

# 4  Purpose trusts[22]

Since a trust creates a proprietary interest in favour of the beneficiaries, it is a cardinal principle that it must have beneficiaries who are capable of owning property and enforcing the trust. For this reason, the law insists that trusts must be for the benefit of legal persons[23] and not merely for the object of carrying out purposes. This limitation is not, however, absolute. By far the most significant exception to this rule is the area of charity, where purpose trusts are upheld as valid and a mechanism to supervise and enforce them is provided by the state for reasons of public policy.[24] There are also several minor exceptions which are considered below.

## (1)  The beneficiary principle

The rule against purpose trusts is long established. In *Morice v Bishop of Durham*[25] Sir William Grant MR stated that:

'Every trust must have a definite object. There must be somebody in whose favour the court can decree specific performance.'

Similarly, in *Bowman v Secular Society*[26] Lord Parker of Waddington said that 'for a trust to be valid it must be for the benefit of individuals'.[27]

### (a)  Rationale for the beneficiary principle

There are three main problems with the validity of purpose trusts which have led to the adoption of the beneficiary principle.

*(i) Without beneficiaries there is no owner.* In its simplest form, a trust makes the beneficiaries into equitable owners. However, as has been seen, the principle that a trust fund 'belongs' to the beneficiaries is not absolute. There are many cases where property may—at least for a time—have no owner in equity. For instance, a trust in favour of Sandra's grandchildren will have no ascertained beneficiaries before at least one grandchild has been born. Similarly, a trust to invest and accumulate a fund for the first woman to land on the moon has no owner in equity until the condition has been satisfied.[28] A discretionary trust in favour of a large class defined in a conceptually certain way, but too large to list, has no identifiable owner. Yet again, it has been held that there is no beneficial owner of the estate of a deceased person until the completion of the administration of the estate. In *Stamp Duties Comr (Queensland) v Livingston*[29] a husband had died, leaving all his property by will to his wife, who had died shortly

---

[22] See Matthews, 'The New Trust: Obligations without Rights?' in Oakley, *Trends in Contemporary Trust Law* (1996).

[23] See Naffine, 'Who are Law's Persons? From Cheshire Cats to responsible Subjects' (2003) 66 MLR 346.

[24] See Chapter 18.        [25] (1805) 10 Ves Jr 522.        [26] [1917] AC 406 at 441.

[27] See also *Leahy v A-G for New South Wales* [1959] AC 457, per Viscount Simmonds: 'a trust may be created for the benefit of persons as cestui que trust but not as a purpose or object unless the purpose or object be charitable'.

[28] The rule against perpetuities requires a perpetuity period to be specified.        [29] [1965] AC 694.

thereafter, and before the administration of her husband's estate had been completed. The Privy Council held that the wife's estate was not liable to pay death duties on the property she was expected to receive on the completion of the administration of her husband's estate because, until the administration was complete, she had no equitable title to the property. The personal representatives were the legal owners and there was no separate equitable owner; the personal representatives merely owed enforceable duties to the 'beneficiaries' of the will or intestacy to see that the administration of the estate was conducted properly. Since the personal representatives had no beneficial interest in the property—they could not keep it for their own use—it follows that, during administration of a deceased's estate, there is no equitable beneficial owner. The concept of property being subject to enforceable obligations but having no immediate beneficial owner is thus well established. This should not be an objection to purpose trusts.

*(ii) The trust cannot be enforced by the court.* Where a trust is created to carry out a purpose there is no person with locus standi to apply to the court to ensure that the terms of the trust are being carried out and that the trustees do not act in breach of trust, for example by misappropriating the trust property for themselves. The supervision of trusts relies first and foremost on the beneficiaries, as the persons most interested in the proper administration of the trust, bringing abuses to the attention of the court.[30]

*(iii) The trust will violate the rule against perpetuity.* The law has always been reluctant to allow property to become subject to restrictions which would unduly prevent its free marketability. Where property is subject to a trust, it is not freely available and the terms of the trust may prevent its most efficient use. For this reason the law provides that property may not be subject to a trust for an excessive period of time. A private trust (as opposed to a charitable trust) must not exceed the perpetuity period, which has been defined to consist of the duration of a human life in being at the date that the trust was established plus an additional period of twenty-one years. If a trust were created for the carrying out of a purpose, there is no guarantee that the purpose would ever be completed so as to bring the trust to an end. The property would therefore be perpetually held on trust. If property is subject to a trust for persons, the perpetuity period is less likely to be violated, as the beneficiary will be a life in being and the trust will not endure beyond his death, although problems may occur if successive interests are created behind a trust. If a trust offends against the perpetuity period it is void ab initio.[31]

## (b) Application of the beneficiary principle

The beneficiary principle was applied so as to invalidate the trust in *Re Astor's Settlement Trusts*.[32] A settlement was made by Viscount Astor of all the issued shares of the *Observer* newspaper. The terms of the trust were that the income was to be applied for

---

[30] See Chapter 27. See also *Re Astor's Settlement Trusts* [1952] Ch 534 at 549; *Re Shaw* [1957] 1 WLR 729 at 744–746.

[31] The more relaxed rules in the Perpetuities and Accumulations Act 1964 only apply to the rule against remoteness of vesting, not to the rule against perpetual trusts.

[32] [1952] Ch 534.

the 'maintenance . . . of good understanding between nations' and 'the preservation of the independence and integrity of the newspapers', purposes which were considered not to be charitable. Roxburgh J held that the trust was invalid on two grounds, first that it offended against the beneficiary principle, and second that the purposes were uncertain. He examined the principle laid down by Lord Parker in *Bowman v Secular Society*[33] and concluded that it was not susceptible to attack from a base of principle,[34] and that it was well established in authority.[35] He referred to *Re Wood*,[36] where Harman J had asserted the orthodox position that 'a gift on trust must have a cestui que trust'.[37] Since the purposes did not fall within any of the exceptions to the beneficiary principle, the trust was void.

In *Re Shaw*[38] George Bernard Shaw left his residuary estate to trustees to apply the income to purposes including research into a proposed 40-letter alphabet, and the transliteration of one of his plays into such an alphabet. These were held not to be charitable purposes, and they failed as purpose trusts. Harman J indicated some dis-satisfaction with the 'beneficiary principle',[39] but felt himself bound by the higher authority of the House of Lords and Court of Appeal.[40] In *Re Endacott*[41] Harman LJ in the Court of Appeal applied the beneficiary principle to a gift by Albert Endacott to the North Tawton Devon Parish Council 'for the purposes of providing some useful memorial to myself'. He did not indicate any of the doubts he had mentioned in *Re Shaw*[42] but instead applauded the 'orthodox sentiments expressed by Roxburgh J in the *Astor* case'.[43] The Court of Appeal held that the gift was a non-charitable purpose trust which did not fall within any of the exceptions to the beneficiary principle.

## (2) Exceptions to the beneficiary principle

Whilst the cases cited above confirm the existence of the 'beneficiary principle' render-ing non-charitable purpose trusts void, English law recognises a number of exceptions where pure non-charitable purpose trusts will be upheld despite the lack of beneficiar-ies. There is no logical rationale for these exceptions, and in this sense they are said to be anomalous. In *Re Astor's Settlement Trusts* Roxburgh J reviewed the exceptions and commented that they were 'anomalous and exceptional . . . concessions to human weakness or sentiment'.[44] In *Re Endacott*[45] Harman LJ confirmed their anomalous nature, and indicated that the number of exceptions should not be increased. They are decisions:

'. . . which are not really to be satisfactorily classified, but are perhaps merely occasions where Homer has nodded, at any rate these cases stand by themselves and ought not to

---

[33] [1917] AC 406.    [34] [1917] AC 406 at 541.    [35] [1917] AC 406 at 546.
[36] [1949] Ch 498.    [37] [1949] Ch 498 at 501.    [38] [1957] 1 WLR 729.
[39] [1957] 1 WLR 729 at 745.
[40] *Bowman v Secular Society* [1917] AC 406; *Re Diplock* [1941] Ch 253 at 259; *IRC v Broadway Cottages Trust* [1955] Ch 20, CA.
[41] [1960] Ch 232.    [42] [1957] 1 WLR 729.    [43] *Re Endacott* [1960] Ch 232 at 250.
[44] [1952] Ch 534 at 547.    [45] [1960] Ch 232, CA.

be increased in number, nor indeed followed, except where the one is exactly like the other.'[46]

Even where a trust falls within the ambit of one of the anomalous exceptions, it will be void if it offends the rule against perpetual trusts because it might exceed the perpetuity period. Opinion differs as to the exact juridical status of the exceptions but they are best regarded as valid unenforceable trusts ('trusts of imperfect obligation').[47] As such, they are not void but the trustees cannot be required to carry out the trust, though the court will prevent them from misapplying the trust property.

## (a) Care of particular animals

A trust for the welfare of animals in general, or of a particular class of animals, will be charitable. A trust for the maintenance of a specific animal is not charitable but may be upheld as an anomalous exception to the beneficiary principle, provided that it does not offend against the perpetuity period. In *Pettingall v Pettingall*[48] a gift by a testator of £50 per annum for the upkeep of his favourite black mare was upheld. In *Mitford v Reynolds*[49] a gift for the upkeep of the testator's horses was upheld. In *Re Dean*[50] William Dean left his eight horses and his hounds to his trustees, and charged his freehold estates with an annuity of £750 per year for fifty years, if they should live that long, to be paid to the trustees for their upkeep. North J held that this was a valid non-charitable trust. However, he seemed to reject the 'beneficiary principle' entirely, stating that he did not assent to the view that a trust is not valid if there is no cestui que trust to enforce it.[51] Although *Re Dean* has been taken as authority for the upholding of trusts for the maintenance of particular animals, the reasoning is incompatible with the beneficiary principle.

Another difficulty with *Re Dean*[52] is that it seems to offend against the perpetuity period. A non-charitable trust must not last beyond the period of lives in being plus twenty-one years. In *Re Dean* the gift to the horses and hounds was for a maximum of fifty years, which exceeds the perpetuity period. One possible solution would be to measure the perpetuity period by reference to an animal life, but this was rejected by Meredith J in *Re Kelly*,[53] who said '. . . there can be no doubt that "lives" means lives of human beings, not of animals or trees in California'. In some cases the courts have taken judicial notice that an animal's life-span is less than twenty-one years,[54] or that the particular animal has less than twenty-one years to live. Again, this approach was questioned in *Re Kelly*.[55] It would still leave problems with animals that clearly have a life-expectancy beyond twenty-one years.

---

[46] [1960] Ch 232 at 250–251.

[47] See (1953) 17 Conv (NS) 46 (Sheridan); (1953) 6 CLP 151 (Marshall); Morris and Leach, *The Rule Against Perpetuities* (2nd edn, 1962) Ch 12; Maudsley, *The Modern Law of Perpetuities* (1979), pp 166–178; (1970) 34 Conv(NS) 77 (Lovell); (1973) 37 Conv(NS) 420 (McKay); (1971) 87 LQR 31 (Harris); (1970) 40 MLR 397 (Gravells); (1977) 41 Conv(NS) 179 (Widdows).

[48] (1842) 11 LJ Ch 176 at 177.     [49] (1848) 16 Sim 105.     [50] (1889) 41 Ch D 552.

[51] (1889) 41 Ch D 552 at 556–557.     [52] (1889) 41 Ch D 552.     [53] [1932] IR 255 at 260–261.

[54] See *Re Haines* (1952) Times, 7 November, Danckwerts J took judicial notice that a cat would not live for more than 21 years and upheld the gift.

[55] Meredith J: 'It was suggested that the last of the dogs could in fact not outlive the testator by more than twenty-one years. I know nothing of that. The court does not enter into the question of a dog's expectation of life. In point of fact neighbours' dogs and cats are unpleasantly long lived . . .'

The most common circumstance in which a trust will be established for a particular animal is where a testator leaves property for the benefit of his favourite pet. It should not be forgotten in such circumstances that the animal also constitutes property and ownership of it will also devolve on the testator's death. The new owner will have the prime responsibility to care for the animal and failure of the trust does not necessarily mean that there is no one to care for the animal.

It must not be forgotten, either, that a gift to an individual with a statement that it is to be used for a particular purpose will often be treated as an absolute gift. The expression of the purpose is considered to be no more than the motive for the gift, imposing a moral obligation rather than a legally binding trust obligation.[56]

### (b)  Maintenance of specific graves and monuments

Trusts to provide for the maintenance of specific graves and monuments have been upheld as valid and unenforceable despite the lack of a beneficiary who can enforce them.[57] In *Mitford v Reynolds*[58] a gift for the erection of a monument was upheld as valid. In *Pirbright v Salwey*[59] a gift of £800 for the upkeep of the burial enclosure of a child in a churchyard for 'as long as the law permitted' was upheld for at least twenty-one years from the testator's death. In *Re Hooper*[60] a testator left £1,000 to his executors to use the income for the upkeep of various family graves and monuments for 'so long as they legally can do so'. Following *Pirbright v Salwey*[61] Maugham J held that the trust was valid for twenty-one years from the testator's death. If the purpose exceeds the perpetuity period, the trust will be void. In *Mussett v Bingle*[62] a testator gave £300 for the erection of a monument and £200 to provide income for its upkeep. This second gift was held void for perpetuity.[63]

This exception did not apply in *Re Endacott* because no specific memorial was identified: 'some useful memorial' was too vague. Even though suitable projects like a bus shelter, a park bench, or public conveniences might come to mind, there was insufficient guidance to enable the trustees to direct the property to a specific project.

### (c)  Saying masses for the dead

According to Catholic theology, on death the soul does not go direct to heaven but to purgatory, a place of punishment where unforgiven sins must be paid for before the soul can go to heaven. The length of time that must be spent in purgatory may be reduced by the saying of masses for the dead soul. Thus, testators may seek to leave money to provide for the saying of masses for the benefit of their own souls, or those of their relatives. The saying of masses for the dead was held to be a charitable activity for

---

[56]  See below, p 384.

[57]  See *Trimmer v Danby* (1856) 25 LJ Ch 424 (testator gave £1,000 to his executors to erect a monument to himself in St Paul's Cathedral).

[58]  (1848) 16 Sim 105.        [59]  [1896] WN 86.        [60]  [1932] 1 Ch 38.        [61]  [1896] WN 86.

[62]  [1876] WN 170.

[63]  By s 1 of the Parish Councils and Burial Authorities (Miscellaneous Provisions) Act 1970 a burial authority may agree, for the payment of a sum, to maintain a grave or monument for a period not exceeding 99 years.

the advancement of religion in *Re Hetherington (Decd)*,[64] provided they are celebrated in public. Thus, a trust for the saying of masses may be valid as a charity. However, it is possible that a gift for the saying of masses in private will be a valid unenforceable purpose trust even though it is not charitable. Such an approach is suggested by the decision of the House of Lords in *Bourne v Keane*.[65] Again, the duration of the gift must not exceed the perpetuity period.

The exception may also extend to the provision of other non-charitable rites. In *Re Khoo Cheng Teow*[66] a gift for the performance of ceremonies called Sin Chew to perpetuate the testator's memory during the perpetuity period was upheld by the Supreme Court of the Straits settlement.

## (3) Policy limitations on purpose trusts

Even if a purpose trust falls within the anomalous exceptions, it appears that it will be invalid if it is for capricious or useless purposes. In *Brown v Burdett*[67] a trust to block up all the rooms of a house for twenty years was held void. The Scottish courts have been astute to hold that trusts for useless purposes are invalid on grounds of public policy. In *M'Caig v University of Glasgow*[68] a trust to erect statues of the testator and 'artistic towers' on his estates was set aside. In *M'Caig's Trustees v Kirk-Session of United Free Church of Lismore*[69] a trust to erect bronze statues of the testatrix's parents and their children was void on grounds of public policy, since it involved 'a sheer waste of money'.[70]

## (4) Trusts for purposes which will benefit an identifiable class of persons

Whilst a non-charitable purpose trust will generally be void unless it falls within the limited categories of the anomalous exceptions, a trust will not be void merely because it is expressed to be for the carrying out of a purpose if it will in fact benefit identifiable individuals who possess sufficient locus standi to enforce it. The central question is whether the carrying out of the specified purpose directly or indirectly benefits an ascertainable and certain group of individuals.

### (a) The rule in *Re Denley's Trust Deed*[71]

In *Re Denley's Trust Deed*[72] the court upheld a gift which appeared to establish a purpose trust. Charles Denley had transferred land to trustees to be maintained and

---

[64] [1990] Ch 1.
[65] [1919] AC 815; see also *Re Hetherington (Decd)* [1989] 2 All ER 129 at 132 (below, p 541).
[66] [1932] Straits Settlements LR 226.      [67] (1882) 21 Ch D 667.      [68] 1907 SC 231.
[69] 1915 SC 426.
[70] Per Lord Salvesen. Other cases include *Aitken's Trustees v Aitken* 1927 SC 374 (erection of a massive bronze equestrian statue); *Lindsay's Executor v Forsyth* 1940 SC 568 (£1,000 on trust to provide weekly supply of flowers to own and mother's graves).
[71] For recent comment on *Re Denley's Trust Deed see* [1996] Conv 24 (Jaconelli); Matthews, 'The New Trust: Obligations without Rights' in Oakley, *Trends in Contemporary Trust Law* (1996), pp 13–15.
[72] [1969] 1 Ch 373.

used as a sports field for the employees of a company. Goff J took the view that, although the trust was expressed to be for a purpose, it was in fact for the benefit of individuals (the employees of the company) because they would benefit, directly or indirectly, from the carrying out of the purpose. As such, it was outside the mischief of the beneficiary principle.[73] Since the employees were an ascertainable and certain class, they had locus standi to apply to the court to enforce the trust. He emphasised that the employees gained a direct benefit from the carrying out of the purposes, and warned that if the benefit was not so direct or intangible the beneficiary principle would invalidate the trust.[74] The trust was therefore upheld because the court could act to enforce it at the suit of the beneficiaries, either negatively by restraining any improper disposition or use of the land, or positively by ordering the trustees to allow the employees to use the land for recreation.[75]

Although the decision prevents the trust falling foul of the beneficiary principle by finding that the employees can enforce the trust, it does not answer the problem of the beneficial ownership of the land. Do the trustees hold the land on trust for the employees? If so, the employees could together demand the transfer of the land to them under the principle of *Saunders v Vautier*,[76] for example if they wanted to sell it to a supermarket for a lucrative development. If that were the case, it would defeat the settlor's intention in establishing the trust. The only other logical conclusion from the decision is that the beneficial interest is suspended for the duration of the trust, which must be limited to the perpetuity period.

### (b) Application of the principle to an unincorporated association

*Re Denley's Trust Deed* was applied in slightly different circumstances by Oliver J in *Re Lipinski's Will Trusts*.[77] Harry Lipinski left his residuary estate to the Hull Judeans (Maccabi) Association in memory of his wife, to be used solely in constructing new buildings for the association. As the gift was made to an unincorporated association the only way it could be upheld was if it was a gift to the individual members of the association.[78] However, it would be difficult to construe a gift for a purpose as a gift to the individual members. Oliver J adopted *Re Denley's Trust Deed* with approval, and concluded that although this gift was expressed as a gift for a purpose (the new buildings) it was directly for the benefit of the members of the Association and could be construed as a gift to them as individuals. He summarised the principle of the case:

'A trust which, though expressed as a purpose, was directly or indirectly for the benefit of an individual or individuals was valid provided those individuals were ascertainable at any one time and the trust was not otherwise void for uncertainty.'[79]

In conclusion, this means that although a gift may be expressed as a gift to a purpose, the court can find that it is really a gift for the benefit of individuals if there is a certain and ascertainable class who will benefit sufficiently directly from its performance. Provided it is not void for perpetuity, it will be upheld.

---

[73] [1969] 1 Ch 373 at 383–384.　　[74] [1969] 1 Ch 373 at 383.　　[75] [1969] 1 Ch 373 at 388.
[76] (1841) 4 Beav 115.　　[77] [1976] Ch 235.　　[78] See Chapter 23.
[79] [1976] Ch 235 at 248.

## (c) Inapplicability of the *Denley* principle to an administratively unworkable class

The principle in *Re Denley's Trust Deed* will not apply if the class of beneficiaries is administratively unworkable through being too wide to form anything like a class.[80] In *R v District Auditor, exp West Yorkshire Metropolitan County Council*[81] a trust was established to assist economic development, youth and community projects and encourage ethnic and minority groups for 'the benefit of all or any or some of the inhabitants of West Yorkshire'. It was held invalid as a private purpose trust, and it could not be upheld on the basis of the *Denley* principle. This is because there were no 'ascertained or ascertainable beneficiaries', as the court had also held that with some 2.5m potential beneficiaries, the trust was administratively unworkable.[82]

## (5) Criticism of the beneficiary principle[83]

The central reason for the beneficiary principle is that if a trust does not have beneficiaries then the court will not be able to enforce and supervise it. As Roxburgh J said in *Re Astor's Settlement Trusts*:

'. . . a court of equity does not recognise as valid a trust which it cannot both enforce and control.'[84]

Where there is no beneficiary, there is no one in whose favour the court can order performance. There is also no one who is interested in the performance of the trust who will apply to the court if the obligation is not being appropriately performed. The court relies on the self-interest of beneficiaries to police trusts and bring any wrongdoing on the part of the trustees to their attention.

However, the force of these objections may have been overstated. Where a trust is made for a purpose, there is always someone who will be entitled to the property in default if the purpose is not carried out,[85] whether the residuary legatee under a will or the owner of the property himself under a resulting trust. Such a person would have sufficient interest to apply to the court if the property were being misapplied by the trustee. This would provide a potential mechanism for control and enforcement. Roxburgh J noted in *Re Astor's Settlement Trusts* that in many of the cases of exceptions to the beneficiary principle there was a residuary legatee who would be able to ensure that the purpose was carried out.[86] Such a mechanism for enforcement seems to have been applied in *Re Thompson*.[87] The testator bequeathed £1,000 to his friend, George

---

[80] See below, p 440.    [81] [1986] RVR 24.    [82] See (1986) 45 CLJ 391 (Harpum).

[83] See Hayton, 'Developing the Obligation Characteristic of the Trust' (2001) 117 LQR 96.

[84] [1952] Ch 534 at 549.

[85] Although that person will not always be immediately ascertainable, as where the residuary beneficiary is whoever happens to be the Vice-Chancellor of the University of Buckingham 21 years from the death of the testator.

[86] *Pettingall v Pettingall* (1842) 11 LJ Ch 176; *Mitford v Reynolds* (1848) 16 Sim 105; *Re Dean* (1889) 41 Ch D 552; *Re Hooper* [1932] 1 Ch 38; *Pirbright v Salwey* [1896] WN 86. See also *Re Astor's Settlement Trusts* [1952] Ch 534 at 542–545.

[87] [1934] Ch 342.

Lloyd, to be applied for the promotion of fox hunting. The residuary legatee under the will was Trinity Hall, University of Cambridge. Clauson J ordered that the executors pay the money to Lloyd, on his giving an undertaking that he would so apply the money. Trinity Hall would be at liberty to apply to the court if the property was misapplied. Although this seems to offer a way of avoiding the beneficiary principle, the case is of limited value. The case was uncontested, and both parties wanted to see the gift upheld. The court only granted the order that they together requested. The result would have been different if the residuary legatee had not wanted to see the purpose performed, but had wanted to see the gift fail so that they would receive the £1,000 as part of the residue.

The problem with this mechanism for enforcement is that in most cases the residuary legatees, who would be able to apply to the court to prevent misapplication of the funds, are the very people who will benefit if the purpose is not carried out and therefore have no incentive to ensure that the testator's wishes are followed. In fact, in most cases they are actively challenging the validity of the purpose trust because they will be entitled to the property in default. Under a trust, the beneficiaries stand to gain if the trust is properly administered, but the residuary legatee under a purpose trust will not gain from the performance of the purpose. The motivation of self-interest is the key to the proper supervision of trusts, and in the case of purpose trusts that self-interest is not present. This mechanism for enforcement would only be able to ensure that the property was not misapplied, but would not be able to ensure that the trustee carried out his duty to perform the trust.

In the light of these difficulties, other jurisdictions have introduced statutory schemes which facilitate the enforcement of non-charitable purposes trusts.[88] The essence of many such schemes is the introduction of a third party 'enforcer' who is empowered to act to ensure that the trustees carry out their duties. For example, under the Cayman Islands Special Trusts (Alternative Regime) Law 1997[89] the 'enforcer' of a trust, who may not himself enjoy any interest in the trust property, is granted 'the same personal and proprietary remedies against the trustee and against third parties as a beneficiary of an ordinary trust'.[90] The enforcer therefore performs a similar function to that of the Crown in relation to the oversight and enforcement of charitable trusts. Whilst such regimes have been adopted in many offshore jurisdictions, no equivalent has yet been adopted in England.[91]

## (6)  The beneficiary principle and certainty of objects

There is a very close relationship between the beneficiary principle and the requirement that the objects of a trust must be certain. In both cases, the requirement follows from the fact that the court must be able to supervise and enforce the operation of the trust. It is possible to re-analyse the cases which have offended against the beneficiary prin-

---

[88]  For example Jersey, Bermuda, Isle of Man, Cayman Islands, British Virgin Islands.
[89]  See Duckworth, *STAR Trusts* (1998, Gostick Hall Publications).          [90]  S 7(1).
[91]  Note also that the Ontario Perpetuities Act 1966 enacts that trusts for non-charitable purposes should be construed as powers, thus overcoming the beneficiary principle, and that the US Uniform Trust Code permits purpose trusts for 21 years.

ciple as cases of uncertainty. Where the purpose is so uncertain that the court could not properly supervise or enforce its execution, then it will not be valid. If the purpose is sufficiently certain and its performance is capable of judicial scrutiny, then it should be valid and upheld.

In *Re Thompson*[92] Clauson J emphasised that the purpose was 'defined with sufficient clearness and is of a nature to which effect can be given'.[93] Similarly, the anomalous exceptions which have been recognised are all sufficiently certain to enable a court to determine whether the property is being applied to the purpose specified. The court can objectively assess whether specified graves are being maintained, animals cared for or masses said. In contrast, *Re Astor's Settlement Trusts*,[94] *Re Shaw*[95] and *Re Endacott*[96] are all explicable on the basis of uncertainty. It would have been impossible for the court to scrutinise whether the trust property was being applied to the 'maintenance . . . of good understanding . . . between nations', or 'the preservation of the independence and the integrity of newspapers', because these concepts are themselves uncertain.[97] Similarly, a trust to provide 'some useful memorial to myself' is unenforceable because it is uncertain.[98] How would the court be able to decide whether the terms of the trust had been carried out?

Although this analysis on the basis of certainty is attractive, and would eliminate the beneficiary principle as an independent requirement, it is not supported by present authority. Uncertainty was a secondary ground for the decision in *Re Astor's Settlement Trusts*[99] and the objection that there were no beneficiaries was treated separately. In *Re Endacott* Lord Evershed MR made absolutely clear that there was a separate 'beneficiary principle':

'No principle perhaps has greater sanction or authority behind it than the general proposition that a trust by English law, not being a charitable trust, in order to be effective must have ascertained or ascertainable beneficiaries.'[100]

# 5  Charitable and benevolent giving

Although purpose trusts are not as a general rule valid, it is often the case that owners wish to allocate their property to purposes rather than to specific individuals. This is particularly so when owners want to support causes that they consider to be worthy. The law provides that certain purposes are charitable and gifts and trusts for these purposes are valid, even though there are no beneficiaries as such. The purposes considered charitable are those which have come to be recognised as for the 'public good',

---

[92] [1934] Ch 342.    [93] [1934] Ch 342 at 344.    [94] [1952] Ch 534.
[95] [1957] 1 WLR 729.    [96] [1960] Ch 232.    [97] See [1952] Ch 534 at 548.
[98] [1960] Ch 232 at 247, per Lord Evershed MR: 'though this trust is specific, in the sense that it indicates a purpose capable of expression, yet it is of far too wide and uncertain a nature . . .'
[99] [1952] Ch 534.    [100] [1960] Ch 232 at 246.

and include the relief of poverty, advancement of education, advancement of religion and other purposes beneficial to the community.[101]

Charitable trusts are not only valid but also enjoy massive financial support through government grants and tax exemptions.[102] The state provides a mechanism by which they can be enforced and supervised, thus preventing their invalidity under the beneficiary principle. They are enforced by the Attorney General[103] in the name of the Crown. The general administration of charities is supervised by the Charity Commissioners.[104] All this state support of purpose trusts is provided in the interests of encouraging giving to worthy causes. The definition of 'charity' is fully considered in Chapter 18 and the control of charities in Chapter 27.

# 6 The duty to act even-handedly

## (1) A general duty

Where a trust has been created for the benefit of multiple beneficiaries, the trustees who have the task of allocating the property have a duty to act even-handedly between them, so that they are all treated impartially and no favouritism is shown to one beneficiary or category of beneficiaries. In *Lloyds Bank plc v Duker*[105] John Mowbray QC stated that there was a general principle that:

'... trustees are bound to hold an even hand among their beneficiaries and not to favour one as against another.'[106]

This clearly means that a trustee must not be partisan to the interests of one beneficiary at the expense of others.[107] The Law Reform Committee in its 23rd Report[108] recommended that trustees be under a statutory duty to hold a fair balance between beneficiaries.[109]

The need to maintain even-handedness between beneficiaries is particularly acute in two contexts: first, in the context of discretionary trusts where the trustee is entitled to decide how the trust property should be allocated amongst the class of beneficiaries; and, secondly, where a trust creates successive interests so that a life tenant is to enjoy the income generated by the trust property for his lifetime, but the person entitled to the remainder interest will receive the capital of the fund on his death.

---

101  *Income Tax Special Purposes Comrs v Pemsel* [1891] AC 531. See below, p 489.
102  See Chapter 18.        103  See Chapter 27.        104  See Chapter 27.
105  [1987] 1 WLR 1324.
106  [1987] 1 WLR 1324 at 1330–1331, citing *Snell's Principles of Equity* (28th edn, 1982), p 225.
107  See *Simpson v Bathurst* (1869) 5 Ch App 193 at 202.        108  Cmnd 8733.
109  Cmnd 8733 at para 3.36.

## (2) The duty to act even-handedly in the context of a discretionary trust

The trustees' duty to act even handedly in the context of a discretionary trust was examined by Scott V-C in the recent case of *Edge v Pensions Ombudsman.*[110] The case concerned a decision by the trustees of a pension scheme to increase the benefits payable to members in service on a particular date. Pensioners who had been in service prior to this date complained to the ombudsman that the changes in the rules introduced were unjust. He concluded that the trustees were under a duty to act impartially between the different beneficiaries, and that they had acted with 'undue partiality' towards those preferred by the rule change. Scott V-C rejected any notion of a general duty to act impartially in the context of a discretionary trust as the very essence of the trust is that the trustees select some to benefit from the wider class of potential beneficiaries. Instead, he held that the trustees were under a duty not to 'take into account irrelevant, irrational or improper factors'.[111] In the circumstances, he held that the trustees properly exercised their discretion and had in fact considered the position of those pensioners who would not benefit. He concluded:

'It was within their discretion to provide benefits to members in service to the exclusion of members no longer in service. They certainly had a duty to exercise their discretionary power honestly and for the purpose for which the power was given and not so as to accomplish any ulterior purposes. But they were the judges of whether or not their exercise of the power was fair as between the benefited beneficiaries and other beneficiaries. Their exercise of the discretionary power cannot be set aside simply because a judge, whether the Pensions Ombudsman or any other species of judge, thinks it was not fair.'[112]

## (3) The duty to act even-handedly in the context of successive interests

Where property is subject to a life interest behind a trust it is important to ensure that both the life tenant and those entitled to the remainder receive a fair share of the fruits of the trust fund, and that the fund is not invested and allocated in such a way that income is generated at the expense of the preservation of the capital, or that the capital is preserved but no income is generated. Equity has tackled this problem by means of rules designed to ensure that the trust fund is invested in such investments as by their very nature will operate fairly in producing income whilst preserving capital.

### (a) The duty to convert investments

*(i) The rule in Howe v Earl of Dartmouth.* As will be seen in Chapter 22, the trustees may be under a duty to convert unauthorised investments. This duty may be expressly imposed in the trust instrument or, in the case of a residuary bequest in a will, implied[113]

---

[110] [1998] 2 All ER 547.

[111] [1998] 2 All ER 547 at 567.     [112] [1998] 2 All ER 547 at 569.

[113] Unless it is excluded by contrary intention of the testator: *Hinves v Hinves* (1844) 3 Hare 609; *Re Pitcairn* [1896] 2 Ch 199.

under the rule in *Howe v Earl of Dartmouth*.[114] This has the effect that the trustee must sell unauthorised investments which by their very nature work an unfairness between the life tenant and the remainderman and reinvest the realised funds in authorised investments. For example, if the trust fund consists of wasting assets, for example copyrights,[115] the consequence of retaining them would be that they would generate a large income for the life tenant, but would be of rapidly depreciating capital value, leaving perhaps little or nothing for the remainderman. The introduction of a general power of trustees to invest as if absolutely entitled to the assets of the trust in the Trustee Act 2000 has vastly extended the range of authorised investments, so that the circumstances in which the rule in *Howe v Earl of Dartmouth* will apply have been significantly restricted.[116]

*(ii) Reform of the rule in Howe v Earl of Dartmouth.* The Law Commission has recently issued a consultation paper recommending that the rule in *Howe v Earl of Dartmouth* requiring the trustees to convert unauthorised investments be abolished in favour of the adoption of a new statutory power for trustees to allocate investment returns and trust expenses as income or capital in so far as in necessary to maintain a balance between income and capital.[117] As a consequence, the implied trust for sale which exists where a trustee is under an obligation to convert unauthorised or hazardous wasting assets would be abolished.[118] This proposal is discussed more fully below.

## (b) Apportionment between income and capital

*(i) The general rules.* Where the trustees are subject to a duty to convert the trust property, it is inevitable that there will be some delay between the time that the trustee receives the property as comprising part of the fund and when he is able to convert it. When the property has been converted and its value realised, the question arises as to how it should then be allocated between the life tenant and the remainderman. It would not be fair for the whole of the proceeds of the converted assets to be applied entirely to capital, since if it was a non-income generating asset the life tenant would have been entitled to receive some income from it during the period of time that it had not yet been converted. The rules of apportionment determine how an allocation is to be made of the realised value of the converted asset between income and capital. Obviously, any express intentions of the testator or settlor will take priority over the implied rules of apportionment. The exact application of the rules will depend upon the type of property which was converted.

The basic position is that when unauthorised investments are converted, the life tenant is entitled to receive the income which he would have received if they had been authorised investments all along. This has been held to an income of 4% per annum on the value of the converted asset from the date of the death of the testator to the date of the conversion.[119] The remainder of the value realised by the conversion is to be

---

[114] (1802) 7 Ves JR 137.     [115] *Re Sullivan* [1930] 1 Ch 84.

[116] *Capital and Income in Trusts: Classification and Apportionment*, Law Comm CP No 175 (2004), para 3.8.

[117] *Capital and Income in Trusts: Classification and Apportionment*, Law Comm CP No 175 (2004), para 1.21.

[118] Ibid.     [119] *Re Fawcett* [1940] Ch 402.

reinvested as capital of the fund. For example, if the asset was of a wasting nature which created a large income, it is possible that the actual income generated between the death of the testator and the conversion would be greater than 4% of the value of the asset. In such a case the life tenant would only be entitled to receive the equivalent of 4% and the remainder would be applied to capital. However, if the asset did not generate income equivalent to 4% the life tenant would be entitled to receive such an amount from the realised value, and the remainder would then be applied to capital.

One crucial question is the date at which the value of the converted asset is to be calculated, so as to enable apportionment to take place. This will depend on whether the trust instrument grants the trustees an express power to postpone conversion. Where there is no power to postpone conversion, the trustees are expected to convert the assets within the 'executor's year'. If the assets are converted within the year, the relevant value is the actual amount realised on conversion.[120] However, if they are not sold within the year, the relevant value is the value one year from the date of death.[121] The life tenant is then entitled to the equivalent of 4% per annum interest on that value and the remainder will be applied to capital. Where the trustees have the power to postpone the conversion, the relevant date for valuing the asset is the date of the testator's death.[122]

The operation of these rules is neatly illustrated by the facts of *Brown v Gellatly*.[123] An estate consisted of several unauthorised assets to which a duty to convert applied, including some ships. With respect to the ships, there was a power to postpone the conversion. Therefore, the relevant date for valuation of the ships was the date of death, but the relevant date for the other unauthorised investments was a year from the testator's death.

*(ii) Rules applicable to a reversionary interest.* Where the assets of the trust include a reversionary interest and there is a duty to convert by selling and reinvesting in authorised investments, a different rule of apportionment applies. In *Re Earl of Chesterfield's Trusts*[124] it was held that the sum to be allocated to capital was the sum which, if it had been invested at 4% per annum compound interest, taking account of income tax, would have produced the sum which was actually realised by the sale of the interest. The remainder of the realised value is then to be paid to the life tenant as income. This rule may be displaced, and if the will demonstrates the testator's intention that the life tenant was to receive the actual income generated he will receive nothing by way of income.[125]

*(iii) Rules applicable to leaseholds.* The rule in *Howe v Earl of Dartmouth*[126] originally applied to leaseholds. However, these are now authorised investments under the Trusts of Land and Appointment of Trustees Act 1996, s 6(3).

*(iv) Reform of apportionment.* The current equitable rules governing apportionment

---

[120] [1940] Ch 402.     [121] *Dimes v Scott* (1828) 4 Russ 195.
[122] *Brown v Gellatly* (1867) 2 Ch App 751; *Re Owen* [1912] 1 Ch 519; *Re Parry* [1947] Ch 23; *Re Berry* [1962] Ch 97.
[123] (1867) 2 Ch App 75l.     [124] (1883) LR 24 Ch D 643.
[125] *Mackie v Mackie* (1845) 5 Hare 70; *Rowlls v Bebb* [1900] 2 Ch 107, CA.     [126] (1802) 7 Ves Jr 137.

can be criticised on the grounds that they are rigid, technical and outdated.[127] They require very complex calculations affecting small amounts of money. The rate of interest used to calculate the respective allocations to income or capital may also be criticised. A figure of 4% may be appropriate in times of low inflation and low interest rates, but is wholly inappropriate when there is high inflation. In other areas a more flexible approach has been developed, for example the interest payable by a trustee for breach of trust is the same as that paid on the court's short-term investment account. In the light of these criticisms a number of proposals for reform have been made. The Law Reform Committee in its 23rd Report recommended that the rules in *Howe v Earl of Dartmouth*[128] and *Re Earl of Chesterfield's Trusts*[129] be 'subsumed in a new statutory duty to hold a fair balance between the beneficiaries, in particular those entitled to income and those entitled to capital'.[130] The Law Commission has recently issued a consultation paper proposing the abolition of all existing equitable rules of apportionment in favour of a statutory power for trustees to allocate investment returns and expenses as income or capital in so far as is necessary to maintain a balance between income and capital.[131] Such a development would be in line with the philosophy of the Trustee Act 2000 which embraced modern portfolio investment theory, in which the main concern of the investor is to balance overall growth and overall risk, by abolishing rigid rules for authorised and unauthorised investments in favour of a general power of investment coupled with a statutory duty of care.[132] The Law Commission provisionally proposed that the personal circumstances of the beneficiaries should not be a relevant factor in the exercise of the statutory power of allocation.[133] The Law Commission recognised that the meaning of 'balance' between income and capital was uncertain due to the scarcity of reported cases, and therefore provisionally propose that there should be a non-exhaustive statutory list of relevant factors to help trustees determine whether or not a balance has been struck between the competing interests of income and capital beneficiaries.[134] It remains to be seen whether these proposals will be implemented.

### (c) Corporate receipts received as a 'windfall' by the trust

Similar problems of allocation between the life tenant and remainderman may arise if the trust receives a 'windfall' because of the assets held. This is particularly the case when the trust holds shares in a company which either makes cash payments to shareholders as a 'capital profits dividend,' capitalises its profits and issues bonus or scrip dividend shares to the existing shareholders, or demerges and gives shares in the new company to the original shareholders.[135] The question arises whether these payments or shares should be allocated to capital or income. In the event of liquidation, all payments to the trustees who hold shares are regarded as capital.[136]

---

[127]  *Capital and Income in Trusts: Classification and Apportionment,* Law Comm CP No 175 (2004), para 1.15.
[128]  (1802) 7 Ves Jr 137.        [129]  (1883) LR 24 Ch D 643.        [130]  (1883) LR 24 Ch D 643 at para 3.36.
[131]  *Capital and Income in Trusts: Classification and Apportionment,* Law Comm CP No 175 (2004), para 1.21.
[132]  Ibid at paras 1.1–1.4.        [133]  Ibid at para 5.66.        [134]  Ibid at para 5.26.
[135]  See *Sinclair v Lee* [1993] Ch 497.
[136]  *Re Armitage* [1893] 3 Ch 337; *IRC v Burrell* [1924] 2 KB 52.

*(i)  Cash payments.* If a company decided to distribute some form of cash bonuses to shareholders, any payments received by trustees who hold shares as part of trust assets are to be regarded as income and therefore allocated to the life tenant. In *Re Bates*[137] a company distributed cash bonuses to shareholders after selling some vessels at prices exceeding their value in the company balance sheets. Eve J held that the life tenant of a trust holding shares in the company was entitled to receive the entire payment as income.[138]

*(ii)  Bonus shares.* If the company decides to capitalise its profits and issue bonus shares to the present shareholders and they are received by trustees, then they are to hold them as part of the capital of the trust. This was so held by the House of Lords in *Bouch v Sproule*,[139] where it was emphasised that the decision whether to distribute cash or to capitalise was for the company alone. The result would no doubt be different if the trustees were entitled to elect to take a dividend either in cash or in the form of additional shares.

*(iii)  Demergers.* The allocation between capital and income where a company demerges is complex, and a distinction may be drawn between a direct and an indirect merger. A direct merger occurs where the original company allocates the shares in the new company to its shareholders. In such cases the Inland Revenue views the shares distributed as income. An indirect merger occurs where the new company allocates its own shares to the shareholders of the original company. In *Sinclair v Lee*[140] it was held that new shares were to be treated as capital assets.

*(iv)  Reform of the allocation of corporate receipts.* The Law Commission considers that the current law regarding the classification of corporate receipts as capital or income does not rest on principle, and fails to deliver either certainty or fairness. It has therefore proposed that the existing rules be abolished and be replaced by a new rule, under which cash distributions to trustee–shareholders by corporate entities, or distributions which the trustees could have taken in cash, should be classified as income, and all other distributions from corporate entities should be classified as capital.[141] If the trustees have a power to allocate the receipt in question to income of capital then the classification will only be a provisional 'default classification', which the trustees will be able to adjust by exercising their power. However if the trustees do not have a power of allocation then this classification will be conclusive. The Law Commission recognised that this new rule would not remove all complexity or every anomaly but considered that it would make the trustee's task easier, and that a simple clear rule would not be a catalyst for disputes.[142] The new rule would eliminate the artificial distinction between direct and indirect demergers, as in both cases the shares would be regarded as capital.[143]

---

[137] [1928] Ch 682.

[138] See also *Re Whitehead's Will Trusts* [1959] Ch 579.

[139] (1887) 12 App Cas 385.     [140] [1993] Ch 497.

[141] *Capital and Income in Trusts: Classification and Apportionment*, Law Comm CP No 175 (2004), para 5.12.

[142] Ibid para 5.11.     [143] Ibid para 5.10.

# 13

# Defined interests

## 1 Introduction

### (1) Meaning of defined interests

This chapter considers those mechanisms for the distribution of a trust fund where the trustees have no discretion as to how the fund is to be allocated. The interests of the objects of the fund, who is to benefit and in what proportions, have already been fixed, or defined, by the creator of the trust. The role of the trustees is merely to carry out those instructions, and carry into effect the owner's intentions. The type of equitable obligation where the interests in the fund are already defined is the fixed trust. The settlor of the trust himself defines the beneficial interests which the beneficiaries under the trust are to enjoy in the trust instrument. The trustee must carry out those terms and distribute the fund as has been specified.

### (a) Example of fixed trusts

If David leaves 10,000 shares in a public company to Elizabeth on trust for his three children, Freida, Graham and Henrietta, in equal shares, Elizabeth has no discretion as to how the fund is to be allocated as the beneficial interests of the three children have already been defined by David. They will each have an immediate beneficial entitlement to a third of the fund. It is Elizabeth's duty to allocate them their respective shares. If David provides that the children should take in unequal proportions, for example that Freida should be entitled to 5,000 shares and the others 2,500 each, Elizabeth would have to allocate in those defined shares.

### (b) Fixed trusts in favour of a class of beneficiaries

The interests granted under a fixed trust may also be specified by means of a class definition rather than by listing each individual who is intended to benefit. Instead of naming Freida, Graham and Henrietta as beneficiaries, David could have left the shares to Elizabeth 'on trust for such of my children who survive me', or alternatively 'to all the present employees at the date of my death' of a particular company. The presumption would be that the members of the class would take the property in equal shares. If such a class definition is used, the trust will only be valid if the objects of the trust are sufficiently certain to enable the trustee, or if necessary the court, to carry out the trust.

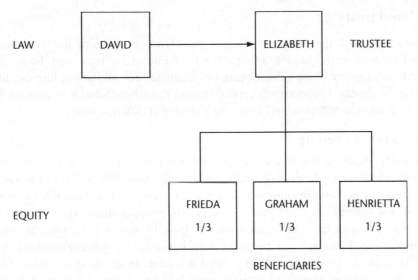

An example of fixed trusts

## 2 Defined interests under trusts

### (1) Bare trusts[1]

A bare trust arises where there is a trustee who holds the trust property on trust for the benefit of a single beneficiary. In a bare trust the trustee has no active duties to perform but merely holds the property on trust for the benefit of the person entitled. The trustee acts exclusively at the direction of the beneficiary, who is able to demand the legal title to be conveyed to him at any time under the principle of *Saunders v Vautier*.[2] The trustee is, in effect, the nominee of the beneficiary and acts at his discretion. For example, in *Vandervell v IRC*[3] the National Provincial Bank held stock in Vandervell Products Ltd for Mr Vandervell. This was a bare trust, and the bank was acting as his nominee. It was obliged to follow his directions, and thus when he asked them to complete a share transfer form to enable him to transfer the shares to the Royal College of Surgeons they acted at his request. The allocation of the fund is not necessarily the prime purpose of a bare trust. It is a very simple mechanism for hiding the true owner of property from the world. The trustee appears to be the legal owner and the beneficiary can remain hidden from the management of the property. In practice, the trustee acts at the beneficiary's direction, who therefore himself keeps control of the management of the property.

---

[1] See Chapter 13.     [2] (1841) 4 Beav 115.     [3] [1967] 2 AC 291, HL.

## (2) Fixed trusts

Unlike a bare trust, the prime purpose of a fixed trust is to allocate the trust fund, or limited interests in the fund, to others. The flexibility of the trust, and the equitable interests in property which subsist behind it, facilitate such allocation. Interests in the fund can be allocated concurrently between two or more beneficiaries, or consecutively, so that different beneficiaries will enjoy the property at different times.

### (a) Concurrent interests

The fixed trust can be used to allocate concurrent interests in the same assets. Often the property which forms the asset of a fund is physically indivisible, and the only way that more than one person can enjoy shares in it is through the allocation of the beneficial interest. For example, it is not possible for people to enjoy shared ownership of land other than behind a trust. If Robert wanted to leave his house to his sons, Steven and Timothy, in equal shares, it is impossible for the house to be physically divided between them. Instead, he can leave it to them on trust as tenants-in-common in equity of equal shares. From the moment that the trust comes into being, they enjoy equal shares of the equitable interest in the house under a trust of land. The fixed trust can also be used to delay allocation of concurrent interests in the trust fund until the future. Rashib, who is dying, has two small children, Khalid and Fatima, and wants to make provision for them. He leaves his property to his brother, Karim, on trust for them until they reach the age of 21. Here Karim would hold the legal title and enjoy the powers of management over the property described in the previous section, but he would be under a duty to allocate the fund to the children equally when they reach the stated age. Whatever the terms of the trust for the timing of the allocation, the trustee must follow them. Karim cannot allocate the fund to his own children when they reach 21, and to do so would be a breach of trust which the court would intervene to prevent or remedy.

### (b) Consecutive interests

Fixed trusts also enable interests in the property to be divided by time, so that one person may enjoy the use of the property for the present, but another has an interest for the future. Alexander dies and leaves his property to trustees on trust for his wife, Becky, for life, and then to his children, Charles and Delia, in equal shares. His wife enjoys an immediate life interest in the property, which will entitle her to the income from it. His children do not have any immediate entitlement to the capital of the fund so they cannot demand that the trustees transfer the legal title to them now, but they enjoy a remainder interest in the fund and will be entitled to the capital in equal shares on the death of their mother. This is a proprietary right which they can sell or assign to others, and if they die it will pass to their own heirs. The task of the trustees is to obey the terms of the trust by investing the fund and by paying the income to Becky, and when she dies by allocating it equally between the children. If they fail to do so they have committed a breach of trust.

## 3 Beneficial entitlement to defined interests

The beneficiaries under a fixed trust may be either immediately ascertainable, or ascertainable only in the future. In the example just given, Alexander identified all of the beneficiaries of his trust by name. They are immediately ascertainable. However, if Sandra creates a trust for her grandchildren equally, the beneficiaries are not yet ascertainable since, even if Sandra already has some grandchildren, she might have more who have not yet been born.

Beneficiaries under a fixed trust may also have vested or contingent interests. They have vested interests where they are immediately ascertainable, and do not have to satisfy any conditions in order to benefit. An interest can be vested even if enjoyment is postponed to a future date. For instance, in Alexander's trust, Charles and Delia have vested interests even though they will only get the capital of the fund when Becky dies. If they die before Becky, they may not be able to enjoy their capital share personally, but it will form part of their estate to be dealt with by will or intestacy. A contingent interest, by contrast, is one where, even though a beneficiary is immediately ascertainable, some further condition has to be satisfied. For instance, if Alexander specified that Charles and Delia had to be living when Becky died in order to take a share of capital, their rights to the capital would be contingent during Becky's life, and would vest only on her death (if they survived her). This is because surviving Becky has been made a condition of taking the gift.

Immediately ascertainable beneficiaries with a vested interest under a fixed trust have an immediate proprietary interest in the assets of the fund. If they are of age, mentally competent and entitled to an immediate interest in the property, they can require the trustee to transfer the legal title to them under the principle of *Saunders v Vautier*.[4] If the beneficiaries are not immediately entitled but have a vested or contingent future interest, they will have to wait until they become immediately entitled to exercise this right. Thus, a remainder interest behind a life interest in the trust fund does not entitle the beneficiary to call for the legal title. However, when the life tenant dies he becomes the sole beneficiary and can demand the conveyance of the legal title.

As the holder of a proprietary interest in the fund, a beneficiary with an immediate vested interest is liable to taxation on his interest.[5] If he dies it will form part of his estate and be subject to inheritance tax. If the property comprising the fund is wrongfully transferred to others by the trustee, not only will all the beneficiaries have personal remedies against the trustee for breach of trust, but their proprietary rights over the fund will be preserved into the hands of all except a bona fide purchaser for value of the fund.[6]

---

[4] (1841) 4 Beav 115.　　[5] See Chapter 4.　　[6] See Chapter 3.

## 4 Certainty of objects

It has already been seen that a valid trust requires certainty of intention,[7] certainty of subject matter and certainty of objects.[8] It is also a cardinal principle that the court must be able to carry out the trust if the trustee is unable and unwilling to do so. This reflects the mandatory nature of the trust obligation. If the objects of the trust are not sufficiently certain, it is impossible for the trustee to carry out his duty of allocation, nor can the court carry out the trust in the event of his default if necessary.

Under a fixed trust the beneficial interests of each and every beneficiary are predefined by the settlor. If these are named then there is no difficulty of uncertainty. The problem arises where the beneficiaries are defined as a class by means of a 'class definition'. Imagine that Wendy leaves £20,000 to Lucy on trust for 'my children in equal shares'. To be able to carry out the trust it must be possible to identify each and every person who falls within the class of 'Wendy's children', because the share of each child in the fund cannot be determined until the full extent to the class is identified. If Lucy were to distribute the fund in equal shares to the first three people who showed themselves to be children of Wendy, she would be in breach of trust if it subsequently came to light that there was a fourth child who should also have received a share. If it fell to the court to carry out the trust and allocate the fund they would also have to be able to identify each and every child.

The problem of uncertainty is generally slight in the context of fixed trusts because they are usually only appropriate for small, well-defined, classes. For larger classes, for example 'all the employees and ex-employees' of a company, a discretionary trust would tend to be used. However, if a fixed trust was intended in such circumstances it would not be possible to carry out the trust and allocate the fund unless each and every employee and ex-employee were identified.

### (1) The 'complete list' test

In order to carry out the terms of the trust and allocate the fund in accordance with the settlor's intentions, the trustee must be able to ascertain each and every person who is entitled to a defined interest in the fund. If he cannot do so then he cannot carry out the terms of the trust. Wynn-Parry J stated in *IRC v Broadway Cottages Trust*[9] that the class must be 'capable of ascertainment'.[10] He took this to mean that the trustee must be able to draw up a 'complete list'[11] of all the beneficiaries of the trust, and that the trust will fail if such a list cannot be drawn up.[12]

The 'complete list' test is almost universally accepted as the requisite test of certainty of objects for fixed trusts, but with little direct authority.[13] *IRC v Broadway Cottage Trust*[14]

---

[7] See Chapter 6.    [8] *Knight v Knight* (1840) 3 Beav 148.    [9] [1954] 1 All ER 878.
[10] [1954] 1 WLR 659 at 664.    [11] [1954] 1 All ER 878 at 881.
[12] See (1971) 29 CLJ 68 (Hopkins) at 81.    [13] See [1984] Conv 22 (Matthews) 22 at 27.
[14] [1954] 1 All ER 878.

is often cited[15] and the judgment at first instance, where the trust was held invalid for lack of certainty, was affirmed by the Court of Appeal.[16] However, the case in fact concerned a discretionary trust,[17] and the test of certainty of objects in discretionary trusts was radically changed by the decision of the House of Lords in *McPhail v Doulton*[18] and it is unlikely that the same result would be arrived at today.

The reasoning of *IRC v Broadway Cottage Trust* was approved by the House of Lords in *Re Gulbenkian's Settlements.*[19] Lord Upjohn stated that:

'. . . the Court of Chancery, which acts in default of trustees, must know with sufficient certainty the objects of the beneficence of the donor so as to execute the trust.'[20]

If the beneficiaries are defined by a class then the class must be certain and capable of ascertainment. He explained:

'Suppose the donor directs that a fund or the income of the fund should be divided equally between members of a class. That class must be as defined as the individual; the court cannot guess at it.'[21]

*Re Gulbenkian's Settlement Trusts (No 1)*[22] concerned a power and not a trust, and pre-dates the decision of the House of Lords in *McPhail v Doulton.*[23]

It has been argued that the 'complete list' test is a 'heresy' which has grown from a misunderstanding of judicial statements,[24] and that the test for fixed trusts should be the same as that for discretionary trusts.[25] However, this runs against principle, logic and authority, and fails to take sufficient account of the differences between the duty to allocate the fund of trustee under a fixed trust and that of trustees under a discretionary trust.[26]

Despite the lack of direct authority, the 'complete list' test is supported both in principle and in logic. The very nature of the fixed trust where the beneficiaries are defined as a class requires that a 'complete list' be drawn up before the trustee can allocate the fund. If such a list cannot be drawn up, it is absolutely impossible for the trustee to carry out his duty to allocate the fund, or for the court of act on his default. Lord Upjohn expressed the problem clearly in *Re Gulbenkian's Settlement*:

'Suppose the donor directs that a fund be divided equally between "my old friends", then unless there is some admissible evidence that the donor has given some special "dictionary" meaning to that phrase which enables the trustees to identify the class with sufficient certainty, it is plainly bad as being too uncertain. Suppose that there appeared before the trustees (or the court) two or three individuals who plainly satisfied the test of being among

---

[15] *IRC v Broadway Cottages Trust* was cited with approval and followed by Upjohn J in *Re Sayer* [1957] Ch 423 at 430.

[16] [1955] Ch 20.

[17] The trustees were to apply the income from the trust fund of £80,000 for the benefit of the beneficiaries specified in the schedule of the trust deed 'in such share proportions and manner as the trustees in their discretion from time to time think fit'.

[18] [1971] AC 424. See Chapter 16.     [19] [1970] AC 508.     [20] [1970] AC 508 at 524.

[21] [1970] AC 508 at 524.     [22] [1970] AC 508.     [23] [1971] AC 424.

[24] [1984] Conv 22 (Matthews).

[25] Requiring only 'conceptual certainty' and not a 'complete list' to be in fact drawn up.

[26] [1984] Conv 304 (Martin); (1984) Conv 307 (Hayton).

"my old friends", the trustees could not consistently with the donor's intentions accept them as claiming the whole or any defined part of the fund. They cannot claim the whole fund for they can show no title to it unless they prove they are the only members of the class, which they cannot do, and so, too, by parity of reasoning they cannot claim any defined part of the fund and there is no authority in the trustees or the court to make any distribution among a smaller class than that pointed to by the donor.'[27]

## (2) Application of the 'complete list' test[28]

Application of the 'complete list' test means that a fixed trust will be void unless the objects are defined with conceptual certainty and can be identified with evidential certainty. Provided that these two elements of certainty are present, it is not necessary that the beneficiaries be immediately ascertainable.

### (a) 'Conceptual certainty'

If a 'complete list' of beneficiaries must be drawn up, it is essential that any class is defined in conceptually certain terms. As was mentioned in the previous chapter,[29] this means that there must be a clear objective definition which will enable the trustee or court to determine whether any given individual falls within the class or is outside it. Without such 'conceptual certainty' it is impossible for a 'complete list' to be drawn up. This was emphasised in the example provided by Lord Upjohn in *Re Gulbenkian's Settlements* above. A trust to divide a fund equally between 'my old friends' is void for uncertainty, because the class is 'conceptually uncertain'. It is impossible to define what is mean by an 'old friend', and it is impossible for the trustee or the court to say of any individual whether he is, or is not, an 'old friend' because they have no criteria on which to make such a judgement.

### (b) 'Evidential certainty'

A 'complete list' of beneficiaries will only be able to be drawn up if it is possible to identify each and every member of the class in fact. This means that there must be absolute 'evidential certainty'. If the trust is created in favour of all the 'employees and ex-employees' of a company, it must be possible to identify each and every employee and ex-employee. In *Re Sayer*[30] a trust in favour of the employees and ex-employees of Sayers (Confectioners) Ltd was held void for uncertainty[31] because it was impossible to draw up a complete list of the persons employed by the company since its incorporation. The company had found it impossible to keep accurate records of its ex-employees.[32] Lord Upjohn also gave an example of a fixed trust void for evidential uncertainty in *Re Gulbenkian's Settlements*:

---

[27] [1970] AC 508 at 524.     [28] [1982] 98 LQR 551 (Emery).     [29] See above, p 374.

[30] [1957] Ch 423.

[31] *Re Sayer* involved what today would be regarded as a discretionary trust and the test adopted in the House of Lords in *McPhail v Doulton* [1971] AC 424, HL would now be applied. As interpreted in *Re Baden (No 2)* [1973] Ch 9 the trust would be upheld, as for a discretionary trust the class of beneficiaries must be 'conceptually' certain but need not be 'evidentially' certain.

[32] [1957] Ch 423 at 430: because of its large number of shops (70), and the nature of its workforce, which consisted of a large number of female shop assistants who tend to change employment frequently.

'If a donor . . . directs trustees to make some specified provision for "John Smith", then to give legal effect to that provision it must be possible to identify "John Smith". If the donor knows three John Smiths then by the most elementary principles of law neither the trustees nor the court in their place can give effect to that provision; neither the trustees nor the court can guess at it. It must fail for uncertainty unless of course admissible evidence is available to point to a particular John Smith as the object of the donor's bounty.'[33]

The relevant date for the drawing up of the complete list is the date of execution of the trust, not the date of its creation.[34]

## (c) 'Ascertainability'

A class may enjoy 'evidential certainty', so that it is possible to draw up a 'complete list' of the beneficiaries, even though it may be impossible to ascertain where some of those who appear on the list are, or whether they are still alive. If Francis leaves all her property to Eric on trust to be divided equally amongst her cousins, this will create a valid fixed trust. The class is conceptually certain, and it is known that Francis had seven cousins. One of the seven, Graham, left for South America in 1987 and has not been seen or heard from since. Would the fact that it is not known whether he is alive or cannot be found, invalidate the trust? Although this looks similar to the problem of 'evidential uncertainty', it is a quite different problem, one of 'ascertainability'.[35] The distinction was drawn by Lord Upjohn in *Re Gulbenkian's Settlements*, where he said:

'If the class is sufficiently defined by the donor the fact that it may be difficult to ascertain the whereabouts or continued existence of some of its members at the relevant time matters not.'[36]

Lord Wilberforce echoed this distinction in *McPhail v Doulton*:

'. . . as to the question of certainty, I desire to emphasise the distinction clearly made and explained by Lord Upjohn, between linguistic or semantic uncertainty . . . and the difficulty of ascertaining the existence or whereabouts of members of the class . . .'[37]

Problems of the 'ascertainability' of beneficiaries will not render the trust void for uncertainty. This is consistent with principle. If a complete list can be drawn up, then the minimum share to which each beneficiary is entitled is known and the fund can be allocated on that basis. In our example, because it is known that Francis had seven cousins, each cousin is certainly entitled to a seventh share in the fund, and Eric can allocate it on that basis. As to the seventh share to which Graham may be entitled, Eric can 'apply to the court for directions or pay a share into court'.[38] In the case of unascertainable beneficiaries who are thought to be dead, the court can make a 'Benjamin order'. This entitles the trustees to allocate the fund on the presumption that

---

[33] [1970] AC 508 at 523.

[34] See eg *Swain v Law Society* [1981] 3 All ER 797. Thus a trust may be created now for the benefit of persons as yet unborn or unascertained, but it must be possible to draw up a complete closed list on the due date of execution.

[35] See [1982] 98 LQR 551 at 556 (Emery).    [36] [1970] AC 508 at 524.

[37] [1971] AC 424 at 457.

[38] *Re Gulbenkian's Settlement Trusts* [1970] AC 508 at 524, per Lord Upjohn.

the beneficiary had predeceased the testator. In *Re Benjamin*[39] David Benjamin left his residuary estate to his children in equal shares. He had twelve children surviving him, but one had disappeared while on holiday in France a year before the testator's death. Joyce J held that, in the absence of any evidence to the contrary, he must be presumed to be dead and his share was to be allocated accordingly. If it subsequently turns out that the unascertained beneficiary is alive, he may trace his share of the fund into the hands of those who received it,[40] and the trustees are not liable for breach of trust.

## (3) Resolving uncertainty

There are some ways in which a gift which would otherwise fail on grounds of uncertainty might be found to be valid. What might appear to be a gift to an ill-defined group such as 'my old friends' might perhaps be treated as a series of separate gifts which can be considered as if they stood alone. For instance, in *Re Barlow's Will Trusts*,[41] Helen Alice Dorothy Barlow died leaving a valuable collection of paintings. She gave instructions in her will that 'any members of my family and any friends of mine' could buy any of the paintings at the prices contained in a catalogue of valuations made some five years before her death. These prices were significantly below the value of the paintings after her death. Browne-Wilkinson J held that the instruction was not invalid for uncertainty. This was not a gift to a class. It was properly to be regarded as a series of individual gifts to persons answering the description of friend or family member. The test which applies to class gifts 'has no application to a case where there is a condition or description attached to one or more individual gifts; in such cases, uncertainty as to some other persons who may have been intended to take does not in any way affect the quantum of the gift to persons who undoubtedly possess the qualification'.[42] Accordingly, 'anyone who can prove that by any reasonable test he or she must have been a friend' of Helen Barlow would be entitled to purchase a picture. Anyone who did not satisfy this stringent test would not be entitled to take advantage of the option created by the will. Similarly, anyone who could prove a blood relationship to Helen Barlow would qualify as a family member. The fact that there might be considerable areas of uncertainty did not defeat the provision for those who clearly satisfied it.

Another way in which problems of uncertainty can be resolved is where the gift itself provides a mechanism for resolving that uncertainty. Thus, a gift to 'intelligent people' would normally fail for lack of certainty because there is no clear definition of intelligence. However, a gift to people who, in the opinion of the President of Mensa, are intelligent, would probably be held to be valid. For instance, in *Re Tuck's Settlement Trusts*,[43] Sir Adolf Tuck, a Jew, was made a baronet in 1910. He wanted to make sure that future descendants inheriting the title of baronet remained in the Jewish faith. To this end, he specified that future baronets would inherit the funds he left by will only if they married a wife of Jewish blood who at the time of her marriage 'continues to worship according to the Jewish faith'. He added that in case of dispute 'the decision of the Chief Rabbi in London shall be conclusive'. Eveleigh LJ in the Court of Appeal had some

---

[39] [1902] 1 Ch 723.      [40] Subject to the Limitation Act 1980, ss 18, 21(3), 22.
[41] [1979] 1 WLR 278.      [42] [1979] 1 All ER 296 at 299.      [43] [1978] Ch 49, [1978] 1 All ER 1047.

doubt as to whether the condition as to the Jewish faith would in itself have been sufficiently clear. However, the reference to the Chief Rabbi made it clear: 'Different people may have different views or be doubtful as to what is "Jewish faith" but the Chief Rabbi knows and can say what meaning he attaches to the words.'[44]

There has been some debate about the reasoning lying behind this decision. Eveleigh J suggested that the Chief Rabbi would have a clear understanding of what was meant by the Jewish faith and could provide it if asked. But it is more than likely that, even for the Chief Rabbi, there could be areas of conceptual doubt. In that case, does reference to him for a decision resolve any uncertainty? It may be that providing for a decision to be made by a third party means that an inherently uncertain concept (for instance, who is intelligent?) is replaced by the certain test (eg those persons stated by the President of Mensa to be intelligent). In that case, what can be done if a decision is taken by the third party arbitrarily—for instance, if the President of Mensa states that someone is intelligent when they are clearly not? The courts are reluctant to see their jurisdiction ousted. If they retain a supervisory jurisdiction, then they need to be able to control the arbitrary exercise of the decision making authority conferred on the third party. Yet they can only decide if the decisions he or she makes have been properly made if the test itself is sufficiently certain to be applied by the court. That takes us back to where we began.

The answer to this problem is contained in the common-sense judgment of Lord Denning. Even if there is conceptual uncertainty, it can be cured by a provision stating that any uncertainty may be resolved by the decision of a competent third party.

'So long as he does not misconduct himself or come to a decision which is wholly unreasonable, I think his decision should stand . . . As this very case shows, the courts may get bogged down in distinctions between conceptual uncertainty and evidential uncertainty . . . The testator may want to cut out all that cackle, and let someone decide it who will really understand what the testator is talking about, and thus save an expensive journey to the lawyers and the courts. For my part, I would not blame him. I would give effect to his intentions.'[45]

# 5 Policy limits

Although a prime purpose of the law of equity is to enable owners to deal with their property as they wish, there are certain policy motivated limits which constrain their freedom. The Rule Against Perpetuities prevents owners tying their property up outside of the market for too long a period of time. Conditional and determinable interests, where the conditions are designed to influence the beneficiaries' behaviour in a way which is contrary to public policy, are also restricted. These limitations are equally applicable to varieties of equitable obligations other than the fixed trust. Legislation also provides that trusts may be set aside if they are established with the object of defrauding the creditors of the settlor.

---

[44] [1978] 1 All ER 1047 at 1057.   [45] [1978] 1 All ER 1047 at 1053–1054.

## (1) The rule against perpetuities

### (a) Remoteness of vesting[46]

The law requires that gifts of property vest within a certain period of time, the perpetuity period. This prevents property being tied up, and hence kept outside the economy, for long periods. At common law, if the property might vest outside of the perpetuity period, the gift would be void. The relevant perpetuity period is a life in being plus twenty-one years. This means that the gift must not vest outside of a period of twenty-one years after the lifetime of a human person living at the date of the creation of the interest.[47]

The rule preventing remoteness of vesting was reformed by the Perpetuities and Accumulations Act 1964. Under s 1, a settlor may specify the relevant perpetuity period in the trust instrument instead of a perpetuity period of a life in being plus twenty-one years, up to a period of eighty years. This is obviously simpler than the requirement of a life in being and is a more attractive option than the royal lives clauses previously regularly used in trust instruments. Where no perpetuity period is specified under s 1, and the trust would have been invalid under the common law rule because it might have vested outside of the perpetuity period,[48] s 3 provides a 'wait and see' procedure. The trust will only be void if it does not in fact vest within the perpetuity period.[49] Section 3 provides its own list of statutory lives by which the perpetuity period is to be measured. It is a great pity that the common law principle with all its complexity was not abolished altogether and replaced by the principle of 'wait and see'.[50] It has been proposed that the rule against perpetuities should be simplified and reformed.[51]

### (b) Rule against inalienability

As well as the rule against remoteness of vesting for reasons of public policy, the law does not allow property to be tied up, and hence become inalienable,[52] forever. A trust must not have a duration longer than the perpetuity period of a life in being plus twenty-one years. This has already been examined in the previous chapter in the context of non-charitable purpose trusts.[53] Charitable trusts are exempt from this

---

[46] See Gray, *The Rule Against Perpetuities* (4th edn, 1942); Morris and Leach, *The Rule Against Perpetuities* (2nd edn, 1962); Maudsley, *The Modern Law of Perpetuities* (1979); Cheshire and Burn, *Modern Law of Real Property* (16th edn, 2000), Ch 13; Megarry and Wade, *The Law of Real Property* (6th edn, 2000), pp 300–356; Hanbury and Martin, *Modern Equity* (17th edn, 2005), pp 355–357.

[47] Gray on Perpetuities, s 201.

[48] It will be invalid even though it may be highly likely in fact to vest within the perpetuity period.

[49] In other words, it is not sufficient to invalidate the gift that it might not vest within the perpetuity period, it must actually fail to vest.

[50] Virtually all trusts which are void under the common law principle are covered by the 'wait and see' provisions of s 3. However, because the statutory lives of s 3 are not identical to common law lives, it is theoretically possible to have a trust which would be valid under the common law principle, but to which the 'wait and see' provisions of s 3 would not apply. For this reason the common law principle is not entirely irrelevant.

[51] Law Commission report No 251 (1998).

[52] This means that the property cannot be transferred or sold (alienated) and enter the general property market.

[53] See above, p 379.

requirement and may be perpetual,[54] as are most pension funds.[55] The Perpetuities and Accumulations Act 1964 has not affected the rule against inalienability (or 'the rule against perpetual trusts', as it is sometimes known).

## (c) Reform of the rule against perpetuities

The rule against perpetuities has been examined by the Law Commission, which has recommended significant legislative reform.[56] The Law Commission recommends that the rule be retained so as to ensure that there is 'some restriction on the freedom of one generation to control the devolution of property at the expense of the generations that follow'. The rule would continue to apply to property held on trust, although it is recommended that it should not apply to pension schemes.[57] However it recommends that the current complex perpetuity period be replaced by a fixed period of 125 years.[58] In respect of the rule against remoteness of vesting the 'wait and see' principle would continue to operate. Any such change would only operate prospectively, so that trusts created prior to the introduction of such a scheme would continue to be governed by the current law. However, the trustees of such a trust would be able to elect by deed that the trust be subject to the new statutory perpetuity period if the trust contains an express perpetuity period of lives in being plus 21 years and they believe that it is difficult or impracticable to ascertain the existence or whereabouts of the measuring lives.[59]

## (2) Conditional and determinable interests[60]

Owners may choose not to make absolute gifts to others, but instead to make gifts which are subject to conditions subsequent or determinable on the happening of a particular event. For example, Terrance may leave his cottage to trustees on trust for his mistress, Joyce, on the condition that she does not marry. This is a very powerful method of controlling a donee's behaviour, since he has a strong financial incentive not to breach the condition and forfeit the interest. However, if the condition is illegal, or one which would constrain the donee's behaviour in a way contrary to public policy, it will be void.

## (a) Conditions void for uncertainty

If the condition or determining event is uncertain, then it will be void. Lord Cranworth stated the principle in *Clavering v Ellison*[61] that the court must be able to 'see from the beginning, precisely and distinctly, upon the happening of what event it was that [the gift] was to determine'.[62] Conditions which have been held void for uncertainty include: a requirement that the donee 'conform to' the Church of England;[63] not marry a person 'not of Jewish parentage';[64] not have a 'social or other relationship with a named

---

[54] See below, p 482.     [55] Pensions Schemes Act 1993, s 163.
[56] Law Com No 251, *The Rules Against Perpetuities and Excessive Accumulations* (1998). See T P Gallanis, 'The Rule Against Perpetuities and the Law Commission's Flawed Philosophy' [2000] 59 CLJ 284.
[57] Para 7.36.     [58] Para 8.13.     [59] Para 8.20.
[60] See Cheshire and Burn, *Modern Law of Real Property* (16th edn, 2000), Ch 15.
[61] (1859) 7 HL Cas 707.     [62] (1859) 7 HL Cas 707 at 725.     [63] *Re Tegg* [1936] 2 All ER 878.
[64] *Clayton v Ramsden* [1943] AC 320, HL.

person';[65] 'continue to reside in Canada'[66] or 'take up permanent residence in England'.[67]

### (b) Conditions void as contrary to public policy

Certain types of condition have also been held to be void because they offend against public policy.

*(i) Conditions restricting alienation.* If a condition attached to a gift is tantamount to a complete restriction on alienation or transfer of the property, it will be void as contrary to public policy.[68] In *Re Brown*[69] a father bequeathed his freehold properties to his four sons in equal shares, with a condition that they were not to alienate their shares other than to each other. Harman J held that this amounted to a general prohibition on alienation because they were a small and diminishing class, and the condition was void.[70]

*(ii) Conditions restraining marriage.* Marriage has always been the fundamental building block of society, and conditions which seek to undermine marriage are void as contrary to public policy.[71] Conditions which completely restrain the donee's freedom to marry are void.[72] However, conditions which restrain the donee's freedom to *remarry* are not void.[73]

Conditions which restrain marriage to particular individuals[74] or classes are also valid. In *Jenner v Turner*[75] a testatrix left property to her brother on condition that he did not marry a 'domestic servant'. This was held to be a valid condition by Bacon V-C. In *Duggan v Kelly*[76] a condition not to marry a 'Papist' was upheld, as was a condition not to marry a 'Scotchman' in *Perrin v Lyon*.[77] Conditions which encourage separation or divorce of husband and wife are void.[78] Thus, in *Re Johnson's Will Trusts*[79] a creator established a trust in favour of his daughter which would pay her £50 per year as long as she continued to be married to her husband, but would pay her the full income from the fund if she were divorced or separated. Buckley J held that the condition was void as it amounted to an incentive to the break-up of the marriage.[80]

---

[65] *Re Jones* [1953] Ch 125.    [66] *Sifton v Sifton* [1938] AC 656.    [67] *Re Gape* [1952] Ch 743.

[68] *Muschamp v Bluet* (1617) J Bridge 132; *Hood v Oglander* (1865) 34 Beav 513; *Re Rosher* (1884) 26 Ch D 801; *Corbett v Corbett* (1888) 14 PD 7; *Re Dugdale* (1888) LR 38 Ch D 176; *Re Cockerill* [1929] 2 Ch 131.

[69] [1954] Ch 39.

[70] Contrast *Re Macleay* (1875) LR 20 Eq 186, where a restriction to alienation within 'the family' was upheld. Harman J considered that this was a large and indeterminable group of people which may increase.

[71] See *Long v Dennis* (1767) 4 Burr 2052 at 2059, per Lord Mansfield: 'conditions in restraint of marriage are odious . . .'

[72] *Low v Peers* (1770) Wilm 364 at 372: an absolute restraint on marriage 'tends to evil and the promoting of licentiousness; it tends to depopulation, the greatest of all political sins . . .'

[73] *Jordan v Holkham* (1753) Amb 209: provision of testator's will that his wife would forfeit her interest if she remarried was upheld. Contrast the Irish case of *Duddy v Gresham* (1878) 2 LR Ir 442 where a condition in the testator's will that his wife not remarry but enter a convent of her choice was held void.

[74] *Re Bathe* [1925] Ch 377; *Re Hanlon* [1933] Ch 254: a gift by testator to her daughter subject to the condition that she does not 'intermarry with AB' upheld by Eve J.

[75] (1880) 16 Ch D 188.    [76] (1848) 10 I Eq R 473.    [77] (1807) 9 East 170.

[78] *Wren v Bradley* (1848) 2 De G & Sm 49; *Re Moore* (1888) 39 Ch D 116; *Re Caborne* [1943] Ch 224; *Re Johnson's Will Trusts* [1967] Ch 387; *Re Hepplewhite Will Trust* [1977] CLY 2710.

[79] [1967] Ch 387.    [80] [1967] Ch 387 at 396.

*(iii) Conditions restraining religion.* Conditions which restrict the choice of religion of a beneficiary have never been regarded as void because they offend against public policy.[81] In *Blathwayt v Baron Cawley*[82] a condition that a beneficiary forfeit his interest if he 'be or become a Roman Catholic' was upheld by the House of Lords. It was neither uncertain nor contrary to public policy. Lord Wilberforce explained that:

'. . . to introduce for the first time a rule of law which would go far beyond the mere avoidance of discrimination on religious grounds . . . would bring about a substantial reduction of another freedom, firmly rooted in our law, namely that of testamentary disposition. Discrimination is not the same thing as choice: it operates over a larger and less personal area, and neither by express provision nor by implication has private selection yet become a matter of public policy.'[83]

However, if the condition restrictive of religion is uncertain it will not be binding. In *Clayton v Ramsden*[84] a provision forfeiting the beneficiary's interest on marriage to a person 'not of Jewish parentage' was held void for uncertainty.[85]

*(iv) Conditions affecting parental duties.* Conditions which seek to separate parent from child are void as contrary to public policy.[86] In *Re Sandbrook*[87] the condition that a gift of the income of a fund was to be forfeited if children lived with their father was held void. Such a condition is void even if the parents are divorced.[88] Some cases have suggested that conditions which interfere with the exercise of parental duties are void. In *Re Borwick*[89] a condition that a minor forfeit an interest if she 'become a Roman Catholic or not be openly or avowedly Protestant' was held void as it operated to interfere with the exercise of a parent's duty in the religious instruction of his children.[90] In *Blathwayt v Baron Cawley*[91] the House of Lords limited the range of this principle, holding that:

'To say that any condition which in any way might affect or influence the way in which a child is to be brought up, or in which parental duties are exercised, is void seems to me to state far too wide a rule.'[92]

*(v) Conditions discriminatory on grounds of race.* The Race Relations Act 1976, s 1 renders discrimination on grounds of colour, race, nationality or ethnic or national origins unlawful. This applies especially in the fields of employment,[93] provision of goods and services and the disposal of property. It does not have any application to

---

[81] The boundary between race and religion is uncertain. In *Mandla v Dowell Lee* [1983] 2 AC 548 Sikhs were held to be a racial group, and in *King-Ansell v Police* [1979] 2 NZLR 531 Jews were also held to be a racial group. However the distinction is of no practical importance for the law of trusts since conditions on grounds of neither religion nor of race are invalid.

[82] [1976] AC 397, HL.    [83] [1976] AC 397 at 426.    [84] [1943] AC 320, HL.

[85] See also *Re Tegg* [1936] 2 All ER 878, where a condition 'to conform' to the Church of England was held void for uncertainty.

[86] See *Re Morgan* (1910) 26 TLR 398; *Re Boulter* [1922] 1 Ch 75.    [87] [1912] 2 Ch 471.

[88] *Re Piper* [1946] 2 All ER 503, which concerned a gift by will to children provided they do not live with their father before attaining the age of 30. Mother had divorced father before the date of the will.

[89] [1933] Ch 657.    [90] The condition was also held void on the grounds of uncertainty.

[91] [1976] AC 397.    [92] [1976] AC 397 at 426, per Lord Wilberforce.    [93] Ss 4–9.

private trusts.[94] The reasoning of Lord Wilberforce in *Blathwayt v Baron Cawley*[95] that legislation against general discrimination had not impinged upon individual selection and choice[96] would be equally applicable to this area. This is reflected in the Race Relations Act, where it is not lawful to discriminate on grounds of race when employment for the purposes of a private household is concerned.[97]

*(vi)  Conditions discriminatory on grounds of sex.* The Sex Discrimination Act 1975 has no application to private trusts.[98]

### (c)  Effect of an invalid condition

The exact consequences of a condition being found to be void will depend on whether the gift was made subject to a condition subsequent or was a determinable interest.

*(i)  Determinable interests.* If the gift is characterised as 'determinable' and the determining event is unlawful for reasons of public policy, the gift will fail and the property reverts to the original owner. Thus, in *Re Moore*[99] a trust to pay a weekly sum to a woman 'whilst . . . living apart from her husband' was held to be a determinable interest and the gift was void.

*(ii)  Conditional interests.* If the gift is subject to a condition subsequent and the condition is unlawful, the gift is not void and the condition is merely struck out. The gift will thus become absolute.[100] In *Re Beard*[101] a testator made a gift of his estates to his nephew, Herbert, 'provided that he does not enter into the naval or military services of the country'. As the condition was held contrary to public policy,[102] it was struck out and the nephew took an absolute interest in the estates.

### (d)  Distinguishing conditional and determinable gifts

Given the different consequences for determinable and conditional gifts if the condition or determining event is unlawful, it is necessary to distinguish between them. The distinction is notoriously difficult to pin-point and was described as 'little short of disgraceful to our jurisprudence'.[103] The essence of the distinction seems to be that in a determinable gift the gift is never contemplated as being absolute, but only as lasting until the determining event occurs.[104] Thus, a gift to George 'until he becomes a brain surgeon' will be a determinable gift. If the determining event occurs, the gift will automatically revert to the original donor.

In a conditional gift, the gift is contemplated as being absolute from the very

---

[94]  Charitable trusts are covered by s 34 of the Act. It is permissible to provide for benefits for a class defined by race, nationality, or ethnic or national origin, but not to provide for a class defined by colour.

[95]  [1976] AC 397.      [96]  See above, p 407.      [97]  S 4(3).

[98]  S 43 provides that charities may provide benefits for one sex only.      [99]  (1888) 39 Ch D 116.

[100]  See *Re Croxon* [1904] 1 Ch 252; *Re Turton* [1926] Ch 96.      [101]  [1908] 1 Ch 383.

[102]  [1908] 1 Ch 383 at 387, per Swinfen Eady J: 'there can be few, if any, provisions more against public good and the welfare of the State than one tending to deter persons from entering the naval or military service of the country'.

[103]  Porter MR in *Re King's Trusts* (1892) 29 LR Ir 401 at 410.

[104]  If the determining event becomes impossible in fact, the gift automatically becomes absolute: *Re Leach* [1912] 2 Ch 422.

beginning, but the occurrence of the condition will cut it short. A gift to George 'unless he becomes a brain surgeon' would be a conditional gift. In cases concerning conditional gifts of land, it has been held that a gift does not end automatically when the condition occurs, but that the donor or his successor in title must 're-enter' by taking steps to terminate the interest.[105] This dogma has no application to a conditional gift by way of trust, where the condition represents a direction to trustees which they will carry out without any further intervention by the original donor.

[105] See Challis's *Real Property* (3rd edn, 1911), pp 219, 261.

# 14

# Powers of advancement and maintenance

## 1 Introduction

In Chapter 13 it was seen that a settlor can create interests under a fixed trust which are contingent upon the happening of some future event. For example, a testator with young children may leave his estate to them subject to a stipulation that they will only become entitled to the property on attaining the age of 21. Although the trustees will hold the fund on trust for them from the time of his death, they will not be entitled to the capital until they attain the specified age and the trustees will be under no duty to transfer it to them. However, whilst the settlor may have created such a contingent interest with the object of preventing his children receiving their inheritance before they are sufficiently mature to manage it for themselves, such an arrangement may cause practical difficulties. In our example, the children may have no actual income on which to live in the interim period before they are entitled to their share of the fund. To overcome such difficulties, the law grants trustees powers which enable them to apply the fund on behalf of beneficiaries even where they have not yet complied with the contingency specified. The power of maintenance allows the trustees to apply the income generated by the fund on behalf of the beneficiary, and the power of advancement allows the trustees to apply part of the capital from the fund to be applied. Although both such powers can be granted expressly in a trust deed, the Trustee Act 1925 grants trustees powers of maintenance[1] and advancement[2] which are usually sufficient. The court also possesses an inherent jurisdiction to provide advancement and maintenance.

## 2 The trustees' power of maintenance

### (1) Express powers of maintenance

A settlor may include express powers of advancement in the trust instrument. However, given the width of the statutory powers it is not usually necessary to do so.

---

[1] Trustee Act 1925, s 31.    [2] Trustee Act 1925, s 32.

## (2) Trustee Act 1925, s 31[3]

Section 31 of the Trustee Act 1925 draws a distinction between the position of a minor who is contingently interested under a trust, and the position of an adult who is similarly contingently interested.[4]

### (a) The position of a contingently interested minor—s 31(1)(i)

Section 31(1)(i) grants the trustees of every trust where property is held for any person, whether their interest is vested or contingent, the power to apply the whole or the part of the income generated by the fund to his parent or guardian for his 'maintenance education or benefit'.[5] This power is to be exercised solely at their discretion.

### (b) The position of a contingently interested adult—s 31(1)(ii)

Section 31(1)(ii) directs that if the beneficiary has reached the age of majority,[6] the trustees are to pay the income generated by the fund to him, until his interest either vests or fails. Payment of such income is not a matter for the trustees' discretion, although it may be excluded if there is a counter-intention indicated by the testator in the trust document.[7]

It has been held that the power to pay over the income to an adult beneficiary who is contingently interested in the fund is excluded if there is a direction in the trust instrument to accumulate the income.[8] Thus, in *Re Turner's Will Trusts*[9] the Court of Appeal held that a beneficiary who was 24 was not entitled to the income from a fund in which he would obtain a vested interest on attaining the age of 28 because the settlor had directed that the income be accumulated.[10] Similarly, in *Re Erskine's Settlement Trusts*[11] a direction to accumulate the income from a fund was held to exclude the power under s 31, even though the direction was itself void under s 164 of the Law of Property Act 1925. Even in the absence of a direction to accumulate, the obligation to pay over the income under s 31(1)(ii) may be excluded. In *Re McGeorge*[12] a gift of agricultural land by a testator to his daughter, which was not to take effect until the death of his wife, was held to express a contract intention because 'by deferring the enjoyment of the devise

---

[3] Trustee Act 1925, s 31 replaces the Conveyancing Act 1881, s 43 (which still applies to instruments coming into force before 1926), which itself replaced a provision in Lord Cranworth's Act of 1860.

[4] By s 31(4) the same principles are applied to income generated by an annuity vested in a minor, with the exception that s 31(2)(ii) has no application and the accumulated income is the absolute property of the infant.

[5] S 31(1)(i). See *Fuller v Evans* [2000] 1 All ER 636.     [6] i.e. 18 years of age.

[7] As the Trustee Act 1925 makes clear by s 69(2): 'All the powers conferred by this Act on trustees are in addition to the powers conferred by the instrument, if any, creating the trust, but those powers unless otherwise stated, apply, if and so far only as a contrary intention is not expressed in the instrument, if any, creating the trust, and have effect subject to the terms of that instrument.'

[8] See *Re Watt's Will Trusts* [1936] 2 All ER 1555; *Re Turner's Will Trusts* [1937] Ch 15; *Re Ransome* [1957] Ch 348; *Re Erskine's Settlement Trusts* [1971] 1 WLR 162.

[9] [1937] Ch 15.

[10] Although he had granted the trustees an express power to apply the income for the 'maintenance, benefit and education' of the beneficiaries, and it was the surplus income which was to be accumulated.

[11] [1971] 1 WLR 162.     [12] [1963] Ch 544.

until after the widow's death the testator has expressed the intention that the daughter shall not have the immediate income'.[13]

## (c) Gifts carrying intermediate income[14]

By s 31(3) the powers of maintenance granted to trustees under s 31(1) are only available if the contingent interest 'carries the intermediate income'. This means that the beneficiary must be entitled to the income earned by the share of the fund to which he is contingently entitled between the date of the gift and the date when his share is paid over to him. Whether a gift carries the intermediate income depends on a series of technical rules, derived from both statute and cases.

*(i) Vested gifts.* A gift which is vested carries the intermediate income unless there is a contrary intention, for example if the income is directed to be applied to someone else.[15]

*(ii) Contingent gifts of residuary personalty.* A contingent gift of residuary personal property[16] made by will always carries the intermediate income from the date of the testator's death.[17] This was explained in *Re Adams*,[18] where North J stated that since the income was 'undisposed of' it would itself become part of the residue. However, if the gift is deferred to 'a future date which must come sooner or later'[19] it does not carry the intermediate income.[20]

*(iii) Specific devises or bequests.* Section 175 of the Law of Property Act 1925 provides that contingent or future specific devices or bequests of property, whether personal or real, carry the intermediate income from the date of the death of the testator unless that income has been otherwise expressly disposed of.[21] The section has been held not to apply to pecuniary legacies.[22]

*(iv) Contingent pecuniary legacies.* Since pecuniary legacies are not included within the scope of s 175, as a general principle a contingent pecuniary legacy will not carry the intermediate income.[23] There are three exceptions to this principle. First, gifts by fathers to their children. If a pecuniary legacy is left by a father to his child, the gift carries the intermediate income if there is no other fund provided for the child's maintenance,[24] and the contingency is the child attaining the age of majority.[25] The rationale behind this exception is clearly similar to that which reveals itself in the presumption of

---

[13] [1963] Ch 544 at 552–553, per Cross J. He also held that s 31 did not apply because the daughter's interest was not contingent, but rather subject to being divested.

[14] (1953) 17 Conv 273 (Ker); (1963) 79 LQR 184 (PVB).

[15] A direction to accumulate merely indicates an exclusion of the power of maintenance, and not that the gift does not carry the intermediate income.

[16] This includes leasehold property, which ranks as personal property: *Guthrie v Walrond* (1883) 22 Ch D 573; *Re Woodin* [1895] 2 Ch 349.

[17] *Countess of Bective v Hodgson* (1864) 10 HL Cas 656; *Re Taylor* [1901] 2 Ch 134.

[18] [1893] 1 Ch 329.        [19] *Re McGeorge* [1963] Ch 544 at 551, per Cross J.

[20] *Re Gillett's Will Trust* [1950] Ch 102; *Re Geering* [1964] Ch 136; *Re McGeorge* [1963] Ch 544; *Re Nash* [1965] 1 All ER 51. Compare also *Re Lindo* (1888) 59 LT 462.

[21] *Re Reade-Revell* [1930] 1 Ch 52; *Re Stapleton* [1946] 1 All ER 323.        [22] *Re Raine* [1929] 1 Ch 716.

[23] *Re George* (1877) 5 Ch D 837, CA.

[24] *Re Moody* [1895] 1 Ch 101; *Re George* (1877) 5 Ch D 837; *Re West* [1913] 2 Ch 345.

[25] *Re Abrahams* [1911] 1 Ch 108.

advancement which rebuts an inference of a resulting trust when a gift is made by a father to his child,[26] namely the obligation of the father to provide. The exception will also apply when a gift of contingent pecuniary legacy is made by a person standing in loco parentis to the minor.[27] Secondly, gifts made with the intention of providing maintenance. If the will expressly or impliedly indicates that the income be used for the maintenance of the minor, the gift will carry the intermediate income. In *Re Churchill*[28] a gift of a pecuniary legacy to a grandnephew was held to carry the intermediate income where the will directed the trustees at their discretion to pay any part of it 'towards the advancement in life or otherwise for the benefit' of the legatee.[29] It is not necessary that the legacy be contingent upon the attainment of majority.[30] Thirdly, gifts set aside. Where a pecuniary legacy is set aside by the testator[31] as a segregated fund for his benefit, to be available on the happening of the contingency, the gift will carry the intermediate income.[32]

## (d) Undistributed income

Since s 31(1)(i) grants the trustee a discretion to pay maintenance out of the intermediate income to the parent or guardian of a minor who has a contingent interest, the question arises as to what should happen to any surplus income the trustees decide not to apply for the beneficiary's maintenance. Such eventuality is covered by the provisions of s 31(2).

*(i) Accumulation of surplus income.* Under s 31(2) the trustees are directed to accumulate and invest any income from the fund which has not been applied to a beneficiary's maintenance. Such accumulated income is then available to be distributed for the beneficiary's maintenance, and may be applied as if it were income arising in the current year.

*(ii) Beneficiary's entitlement to accumulated surplus income.* Section 31(2)(i)(b) provides that if the beneficiary is entitled to a vested interest in the capital of the fund on attaining his majority (or on marriage under that age), he will be entitled to the accumulated surplus income. If, however, his interest is not vested, or liable to be determined, he will not be entitled to the accumulated income.[33] One anomalous result of the wording of s 31(2)(i)(b) is that a distinction is drawn between determinable gifts of realty and personalty. The section states that the beneficiary must be entitled to the property from which the income arose 'in fee simple, absolute or determinable, or absolutely . . .' In *Re Sharp's Settlement Trusts*[34] it was held that the words 'in fee simple, absolute or determinable' apply only to realty, and the word 'absolute' applies exclusively to 'personalty'. This means that a beneficiary has no entitlement on reaching majority to the accumulated income on a fund of personal property in which he has only a determinable interest. On the facts a beneficiary who had attained the age of 21

---

[26] See Chapter 8.     [27] *Re Eyre* [1917] 1 Ch 351.     [28] [1909] 2 Ch 431.
[29] See also *Re Selby-Walker* [1949] 2 All ER 178.     [30] *Re Jones* [1932] 1 Ch 642.
[31] *Re Judkin's Trusts* (1884) 25 Ch D 743.
[32] *Re Medlock* (1886) 54 LT 828; *Re Clements* [1894] 1 Ch 665, *Re Woodin* [1895] 2 Ch 349, CA. Compare also *Re Judkin's Trusts* (1884) 25 Ch D 743.
[33] *Re Sharp's Settlement Trusts* [1973] Ch 331.     [34] [1973] Ch 331; (1972) 36 Conv 436 (Hayton).

was not entitled to the accumulated income from the fund because his contingent interest was liable to be defeated by the exercise of a power of appointment.[35]

*(iii) Death of a minor before attaining a vested interest.* Where a beneficiary dies before attaining majority (or earlier marriage) and income has been accumulated on his behalf, s 31(2)(ii) provides that the accumulated income should be added to the capital of the fund, and not pass as part of the minor's estate.[36] This provision will not apply if a contrary intention is shown from the trust instrument.[37] Thus in *Re Delamere's Settlement Trusts*[38] the trustees of a settlement appointed the income from a trust fund to six infant beneficiaries 'in equal shares absolutely'. The Court of Appeal held that this excluded the operation of s 31(2)(ii) and that the infant beneficiaries had indefeasible interests in the accumulated income.

## (3) The court's inherent jurisdiction

The court has an inherent jurisdiction to allow trust income to be used for a minor's maintenance,[39] and in exceptional circumstances the court may even allow capital to be so used.[40] The courts have generally refused to allow trust income to be used for a child's maintenance where the father has sufficient means to provide for the child.[41] The width of the general statutory power of maintenance has rendered the court's inherent jurisdiction insignificant.

# 3 The trustees' power of advancement

## (1) Meaning of advancement

As has been seen, the power of maintenance enables the trustees to apply the income generated by a trust fund for the maintenance of the beneficiaries, even where they are not as yet entitled to the capital of the fund. A power of advancement enables the trustees to advance part of the capital to beneficiaries who are contingently interested in the trust fund. As Lord Radcliffe observed in *Pilkington v IRC*, the purpose of a power of advancement is that the trustees can in a proper case:

'. . . anticipate the vesting in possession of an intended beneficiary's contingent or reversionary interest by raising money on account of his interest and paying or applying it immediately for his benefit. By so doing they released it from the trusts of the settlement and accelerate the enjoyment of his interest . . .'[42]

---

[35] See also *Phipps v Ackers* (1842) 9 Cl & Fin 583; *Re Heath* [1936] Ch 259; *Re Kilpatrick's Policies* [1966] Ch 730; *Brotherton v IRC* [1978] 1 WLR 610.

[36] *Re Joel's Will Trusts* [1967] Ch 14.    [37] Trustee Act 1925, s 69(2).

[38] [1984] 1 WLR 813; [1985] Conv 153 (Griffith).

[39] *Wellesley v Wellesley* (1828) 2 Bli 124 at 133–134, per Lord Redesdale.

[40] *Ex p Green* (1820) 1 Jac & W 253; *Ex p Chambers* (1829) 1 Russ & M 577; *Robinson v Killey* (1862) 30 Beav 520.

[41] *Douglas v Andrews* (1849) 12 Beav 310 at 311.    [42] [1964] AC 612 at 633.

## (2) Express powers of advancement

A settlor may grant the trustees express powers of advancement in the trust instrument. However, since the enactment of a statutory power,[43] which grants the trustees of a power of advancement modelled on the standard form of such express powers, express powers are only necessary if a settlor wishes the trustees to have wider powers than those granted by the statute.[44]

## (3) Trustee Act 1925, s 32

### (a) Scope of the statutory power of advancement

Section 32(1) grants trustees the power, in their absolute discretion, to apply the capital of a trust fund on behalf of any beneficiary who has an absolute or contingent interest in the fund. It makes no difference that the beneficiary's contingent interest may at some later date be defeated, for example by the exercise of a power of appointment, or that his precise share of the fund may diminish because of an increase in the number of a class to which he belongs.[45] The section introduces some practical limitations on the trustee's power of advancement:

*(i) Proportion of share which may be advanced.* Section 32(1)(a) provides that the trustees must not advance to a beneficiary more than a half of his presumptive or vested interest under the fund.[46]

*(ii) Accounting for advancements in the final distribution of the trust fund.* Where a beneficiary is contingently entitled to a share of the trust fund, s 32(1)(b) provides that any property advanced be taken into account in calculating the size of any share to which he becomes absolutely entitled.[47] This obviously prevents unfairness between the beneficiaries.

*(iii) Protection of those with a prior interest in the trust fund.* Where an advancement would be to the prejudice of those who have a prior life or other interest in the fund, s 32(1)(c) requires that they give consent in writing to any advancement.[48] This protects, for example, a life tenant, who is entitled to the income of the fund during his lifetime. Clearly, if an advancement of capital is made to a contingently entitled remainderman, the life tenant will suffer as the income generated by the fund will decrease with the reduction in the capital.

---

[43] Trustee Act 1925, s 32.

[44] Eg the power to advance more than half a beneficiary's presumptive share. See also Trustee Act 1925, s 32(1)(a).

[45] Eg a trust may grant contingent interests to the children of the settlor, and the class may subsequently increase with the birth of further children.

[46] See *Re Marquess of Abergavenny's Estate Act Trusts* [1981] 1 WLR 843; [1982] Conv 158 (Price). The court may be willing to approve a variation of trusts which will allow the advancement of more than a half of the trust fund if this would be of 'benefit' to the beneficiary: *CD (A Child) v O* [2004] 3 All ER 780. See below p 472.

[47] See *Re Fox* [1904] 1 Ch 480.

[48] The court cannot dispense with the need for consent: *Re Forster's Settlement* [1942] Ch 199. A member of a discretionary class does not need to give consent: *Re Harris's Settlement* (1940) 162 LT 358; *Re Beckett's Settlement* [1940] Ch 279.

### (b) Type of fund where capital may be advanced

Section 32(2) provides that the power of advancement does not apply to funds consisting of capital money under the Settled Land Act 1925.

### (c) The requirement of benefit

The most important restriction of the trustees' power of advancement is the requirement that the application of capital must be for the 'advancement or benefit' of the beneficiary. The meaning of 'benefit' was considered by Lord Radcliffe in *Pilkington v IRC*, where he held that the phrase 'advancement and benefit':

'... means any use of the money which will improve the material situation of the beneficiary.'[49]

The case concerned a proposed advancement of part of the contingent share of an infant beneficiary, Penelope Pilkington. She was entitled to a share of a fund established by her great uncle, provided she reached the age of 21, but the trustees wanted to advance £7,600, to be settled on different trusts in her favour, to avoid death duties. The House of Lords held that this was a proper exercise of the statutory power of advancement, and that there was a benefit to the infant in the avoidance of taxation. Lord Radcliffe observed: 'if the advantage of preserving the funds of a beneficiary from the incidence of death duty is not an advantage personal to that beneficiary, I do not see what is'.[50] It did not matter that the advanced money was to be resettled on different trusts for the infant.[51]

   A wide range of purposes have been held to be sufficiently beneficial to permit an advancement. In the nineteenth century typical examples included the provision of an apprenticeship, the purchase of a commission in the army or an interest in a business.[52] Benefits have included the discharge of the beneficiary's debts,[53] an advancement to a wife who has helped her husband set up in business,[54] an advancement to a girl on her marriage[55] and an advancement to provide for the beneficiary's maintenance and education.[56] In *Re Halstead's Will Trusts*[57] the court approved an advancement to a man so that he could make provision for his wife and child in the future by settling a sum upon himself for life; and after his death for his wife for life, remainder to his children. Farwell J held that this was within the 'very wide terms in which the word "benefit" has been construed in the past'. In *Re Clore's Settlement Trusts*[58] an advancement to enable a contingently entitled beneficiary to make a donation to charity which they felt morally obliged to make was held to be a benefit. The purchases of house and furniture have also been held to be for the benefit of a beneficiary.[59]

---

[49] [1964] AC 612 at 635.   [50] [1964] AC 612 at 640.
[51] *Roper-Curzon v Roper-Curzon* (1871) LR 11 Eq 452; *Re Halstead's Will Trusts* [1937] 2 All ER 57; *Re Ropner's Settlement Trusts* [1956] 1 WLR 902.
[52] *Pilkington v IRC* [1964] AC 612 at 634.   [53] *Lowther v Bentinck* (1874) LR 19 Eq 166.
[54] *Re Kershaw's Trusts* (1868) LR 6 Eq 322.   [55] *Lloyd v Cocker* (1860) 27 Beav 645.
[56] *Re Breed's Will* (1875) 1 Ch D 226; *Re Garrett* [1934] Ch 477.   [57] [1937] 2 All ER 57.
[58] [1966] 1 WLR 955.   [59] *Re Pauling's Settlement Trust* [1964] Ch 303, CA.

## (d) Fiduciary nature of the power of advancement

A power of advancement is a fiduciary power, and must therefore be exercised by the trustee in a fiduciary manner. In *Re Pauling's Settlement Trusts*,[60] in the context of an express power, the Court of Appeal held that this means that before exercising the power the trustees must 'weigh on the one side the benefit of the proposed advancee, and on the other hand the rights of those who are or may hereafter become interested under the trusts of the settlement'.[61] The trustees are also subject to a duty to ensure that money advanced is applied by the beneficiaries for the purposes for which it was advanced.[62]

## (4) The court's inherent jurisdiction

The court possesses an inherent jurisdiction to apply capital[63] for the maintenance or advancement of an infant. For example, in *Clay v Pennington*[64] the court advanced a sum of £125 to cover the cost of an infant's passage to India.[65]

---

[60] [1964] Ch 303.      [61] [1964] Ch 303 at 333, per Willmer LJ.      [62] [1964] Ch 303 at 334.

[63] *Barlow v Grant* (1684) 1 Vern 255.      [64] (1837) 8 Sim 359.

[65] See also *Re Mary England's Estate* (1830) 1 Russ & M 499.

# 15

# Powers of appointment and redistribution

## 1 The nature of powers of appointment

Powers of appointment are one of the equitable mechanisms which facilitate the management and allocation of property.[1] The key feature of a power of appointment is that it is discretionary in character. Unlike a fixed trust[2] or a discretionary trust,[3] the donee of a power is under no enforceable obligation to make any appointments of the fund at all. Even if the donee were never to make any appointments at all, he would not be in breach of a duty owed either to the donor or to the potential objects of the power. The court will not step in to compel the exercise of the power, but it will exercise a supervisory jurisdiction to ensure that, if the donee does decide to exercise the power, he does so properly. Powers of appointment are commonly used as a mechanism to determine the allocation of the surplus remaining of a trust fund after the beneficiaries have received their defined interests. Many older cases concern family trusts where the property of a testator was left on trust for a spouse for life, with a power of appointment granted over the remainder interest.[4] This allows the donee of the power to decide how the capital of the fund should be allocated on the death of the life tenant. The discretionary nature of the power means that the testator does not have to pre-determine how the remainder interest should be distributed, and allows the donee to take account of changing circumstances between the death of the testator and the death of the life tenant. The more recent cases have tended to concern pension funds, where the donee is given a power of appointment over any surplus that remains after the contributors have received their contractual entitlements.[5] The successful investment of many pension funds has meant that their assets exceed their liabilities, so that there is a resulting surplus. The power to allocate the surplus by exercise of a power of appointment, whether to the pensioners or the company, is therefore an extremely valuable right.

---

[1] See Chapters 4 and 5.   [2] See Chapter 13.   [3] See Chapter 16.
[4] *Re Weekes' Settlement* [1897] 1 Ch 289.
[5] *Mettoy Pension Trustees Ltd v Evans* [1990] 1 WLR 1587; *Hillsdown Holdings plc v Pensions Ombudsman* [1997] 1 All ER 862; *Edge v Pensions Ombudsman* [1998] 2 All ER 547.

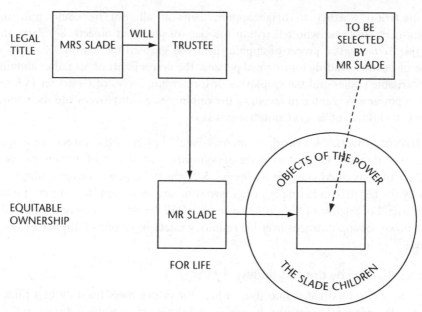

An example of powers of appointment: *Re Weekes' Settlement*

## (1) Classification of powers of appointment

Though all powers of appointment share their discretionary character, several sub-categories of power can be identified, which are differentiated by the nature of the class of potential objects and by the exact duties of the donee.

### (a) Classification by the nature of the class of objects

There are three types of power of appointment: general, special and hybrid powers. They are differentiated by the range of potential objects in whose favour the power may be exercised:

*(i) General powers.* Under a general power of appointment the donee enjoys the right to allocate the property by appointment to anyone he wishes. The donee may even appoint the property to himself. This extremely wide power is tantamount to absolute ownership by the donee.

*(ii) Special powers.* Where the donor of a power has specified that it should only be exercised in favour of a class of people, it is said to be a special power. The donee has absolute discretion whether to make any appointments of the property but any appointments made must be to persons within the specified class. In *Re Weekes' Settlement*[6] Mrs Slade granted a life interest of her estate to her husband and gave him a power of appointment over the reversionary interest in favour of their children. This created a special power in favour of the class of their eight surviving children. Mr Slade

---

[6] [1897] 1 Ch 289.

had discretion whether to make appointments at all, but he could only make appointments to those who fell within the class of potential objects. Similarly, in *Re Gestetner Settlement*[7] a power of appointment was granted by Sigmund Gestetner in favour of a class including four named persons, the descendants of his father and uncle, five charitable bodies and the employees or former employees of Gestetner Ltd. In *Re Sayer*[8] a power was granted in favour of the employees, ex-employees and their widows and infant children of Sayers Confectioners Ltd.

*(iii) Hybrid powers.*[9] A hybrid, or intermediate[10] power is the inverse of a special power. The donee is entitled to make appointments in favour of anyone except the members of a specified class. In *Re Byron's Settlement*[11] a power of appointment was given by the testatrix to her daughter in favour of anyone except 'her present husband or any friend or relative of his'. In *Re Lawrence's Will Trusts*[12] Mr Lawrence granted his wife a power of appointment over his residuary estate in favour of anyone except her relatives.[13]

## (b)  Classification by donee's duties

Powers may also be divided into those where the donee owes no duty of a fiduciary nature to the potential objects of the power, and those where some fiduciary duties are owed. Although in both cases the power remains essentially discretionary, there is a slight difference in the duties owed.

*(i)  Bare or mere powers.*[14] If the donee of the power does not hold the power in a fiduciary capacity, then he owes no duties to the objects concerning its exercise. He is under no duty to exercise it, and need not even consider whether he should exercise the power. He can completely forget that he has it, and never apply his mind to the question whether he should exercise it. This type of power is known as a bare or mere power.

*(ii)  Fiduciary powers.*[15] If the donee holds the power of appointment in a fiduciary capacity, most commonly because it is a power which arises under a trust of which he is the trustee, then he owes limited fiduciary duties to the potential objects of the powers.[16] He must periodically consider whether to exercise the power, although it remains entirely discretionary and he is under no enforceable obligation to make appointments.[17] If he does decide to exercise the power, he must first survey the range of potential objects before making particular appointments.

---

[7] [1953] Ch 672.     [8] [1957] Ch 423.     [9] See *Re Lawrence's Will Trusts* [1972] Ch 418 at 423.

[10] See *Re Manisty's Settlement* [1974] Ch 17, where Templeman J described a power to appoint anyone in the world except the settlor, his wife and other excepted persons as an 'intermediate power'.

[11] [1891] 3 Ch 474.     [12] [1972] Ch 418.

[13] See also *Re Park* [1932] Ch 580; *Re Abrahams' Will Trusts* [1969] 1 Ch 463; *Re Manisty's Settlement* [1974] Ch 17.

[14] See below, p 428.     [15] See below, p 435.

[16] See *Re Hay's Settlement Trusts* [1982] 1 WLR 202.

[17] See *Re Allen-Meyrick's Will Trusts* [1966] 1 WLR 499, where the court refused to intervene to compel trustees to exercise a power that they held over a fund in favour of the settlor's husband.

## (2) Duties of the donees of a power

The donee of a bare power is under no duty to exercise the power because it is entirely discretionary. If he makes no appointments at all he is not in breach of any duty. In *Re Weekes' Settlement*[18] Mr Slade failed to make any appointments in favour of his children and had not committed any breach thereby. The donee does not even have to consider whether or not to exercise the power. By way of exception, if the power is held by someone who is also a trustee then he holds the power in a fiduciary capacity,[19] and although it remains entirely discretionary, he must from time to time consider whether or not to exercise the power in favour of the objects.[20] If the donee does choose to exercise the power, he must not act outside of the terms of the power and appoint in favour of non-objects. Such an appointment to non-objects is known as 'excessive exercise' because it exceeds the scope of the power. He must exercise the power honestly and not fraudulently.[21]

## (3) Rights of the objects of powers

In Chapter 12 it was seen that the beneficiaries of a fixed trust have an immediate proprietary interest in the share of the fund which is earmarked for them and, if of age and legally competent, they can demand that the trustees transfer the property to them.[22] The potential objects of a power of appointment have no immediate proprietary interest in the property over which the donee has power.[23] An object only gains a proprietary interest in any property which is allocated to him by the donee. In *Re Brooks' Settlement Trusts* Farwell J said of the position of a son who was a potential object of a special power under his mother's marriage settlement:

'it is . . . impossible to say that until an appointment has been made in favour of this son that the son had any interest under his mother's settlement other than an interest as one of the people entitled in default of appointment.'[24]

# 2 The validity of powers of appointment

## (1) Certainty of objects

### (a) Comparison with fixed trusts[25]

In the case of a fixed trust it must be possible to draw up a 'complete list' of each and every beneficiary.[26] If this is not possible, the trust is void for uncertainty because neither the trustee nor the court could carry out the trust. If the beneficiaries are

---

[18] [1897] 1 Ch 289.   [19] See below, p 435.

[20] See *Re Abrahams' Will Trusts* [1969] 1 Ch 463 at 474 per Cross J; *Re Hay's Settlement Trusts* [1982] 1 WLR 202.

[21] See below, p 429.   [22] *Saunders v Vautier* (1841) 4 Beav 115.

[23] *Vestey v IRC* [1980] AC 1148, HL.   [24] [1939] Ch 993 at 997.   [25] See Chapter 13.

[26] See above, p 398.

defined as a class, then a complete list can only be drawn up if the class is both conceptually and evidentially certain. In the case of powers, the test of certainty is less stringent. There is no need for the donee to be able to draw up a complete list of every potential object to exercise the power properly. In the case of a general power, such a requirement would entail the production of a list of the entire population of the world! Equally, the court will not step in to exercise the power if the donee defaults because it is purely discretionary. However, the court must be able to supervise any exercise of the power, and in the case of a special power this means that the court must be able to determine whether any person in whose favour the power was exercised was within the class, and therefore entitled to enjoy the benefit of the exercise. As Lord Upjohn observed in *Re Gulbenkian's Settlement*:

'... those entitled to the fund in default [of appointment] must clearly be entitled to restrain the trustees from exercising it save amongst those within the power. So the trustees, or the court, must be able to say with certainty who is within and who without the power.'[27]

If an appointment is made to a person who is outside the class of objects, then the exercise is excessive and void. The test for certainty of objects for powers of appointment has developed to meet this necessity.

## (b)  The 'is or is not' test

The test of certainty for powers of appointment was laid down by the House of Lords in *Re Gulbenkian's Settlement (No 1)*.[28] A special power of appointment was granted in favour of a class consisting of Nubar Gulbenkian, his wife and children, and 'any person or persons in whose house or apartments or in whose company or under whose care or control or by whom or with whom he may from time to time be employed or residing'. This was upheld as sufficiently certain. Lord Upjohn stated the relevant test of certainty:[29]

'... a mere or bare power of appointment among a class is valid if you can with certainty say whether any given individual is or is not a member of the class: you do not have to be able to ascertain every member of the class.'[30]

This test had been propounded by Harman J in *Re Gestetner Settlement*[31] and approved by the Court of Appeal in *IRC v Broadway Cottages Trust*.[32] Lord Upjohn rejected[33] a broader test of certainty put forward by Lord Denning MR in the Court of Appeal that a power of appointment would be valid if it could be said with certainty of any one person that he was clearly within the class, even if it may be difficult to say in other cases

---

[27] [1970] AC 508 at 525.      [28] [1970] AC 508.

[29] Lord Hodson and Lord Guest agreed with Lord Upjohn; Lord Reid delivered a similar opinion; Lord Donovan agreed with Lord Upjohn but reserved his opinion on whether the test proposed by the Court of Appeal that the power should be valid if it could be said of any one person that he was within the class, although he was 'inclined to share' Lord Upjohn's view.

[30] [1970] AC 508 at 521.

[31] [1953] Ch 672; followed by Roxburgh J in *Re Coates (Decd)* [1955] Ch 495 and Upjohn J in *Re Sayer* [1957] Ch 423.

[32] [1955] Ch 20. See also *Re Hain's Settlement* [1961] 1 WLR 440 at 445, per Lord Evershed MR.

[33] [1970] AC 508 at 134.

whether a person is within the class or not.[34] In *Re Gresham*[35] Harman J had held that a power with similar terms to that in *Re Gulbenkian* was void for uncertainty, but the Court of Appeal and House of Lords overruled the decision. Mere difficulty in determining whether an individual is within or without the class is not sufficient to invalidate the power, and the Court can rule on borderline cases.[36] It is only insuperable difficulty that will render the power void for uncertainty.

The *Gulbenkian* test is consistent with established principle and logic. It requires that the court must be able to determine with absolute certainty whether any given individual is or is not a member of the class of potential objects. This is essential if the court is to determine whether the power has been exercised properly. If Toby grants Stephanie a power of appointment over his residuary estate in favour of 'old men', it would be impossible for the court to determine if an appointment in favour of Robert, who is 64, was excessive. It is not possible to say of every individual whether they are 'old' or not, because 'old' has no clear objective meaning. A power in favour of 'men aged over 65' is clearly valid because it is possible to say of every man whether he is over 65 or not. As Lord Reid observed:

'If the class of beneficiaries is not defined with sufficient particularity to enable the court to determine whether a particular person is or is not, on the facts at a particular time, within one of the classes of beneficiaries, then the power must be bad for uncertainty.'[37]

### (c) Application of the 'is or is not' test[38]

The test for certainty of objects for powers laid down in *Re Gulbenkian*[39] was adopted for discretionary trusts by the House of Lords in *McPhail v Doulton*.[40] It was subsequently examined and applied by the Court of Appeal in *Re Baden's Deed Trusts (No 2)*.[41] It follows that, although these cases concerned discretionary trusts, they are the main authorities considering the implications of the *Re Gulbenkian* test for powers of appointment. They indicate that whilst the 'is or is not' test requires conceptual certainty, a special power will not be invalid for reasons of evidential uncertainty.

*(i) 'Conceptual certainty'.* The class of a special power must be defined with conceptual certainty.[42] This means that the class must be defined by objective criteria by which the court can judge whether any given individual is within the class. Thus, a power of appointment in favour of 'my good friends' or 'my business associates' would be void for uncertainty.

*(ii) 'Evidential certainty'.* In *Re Baden's Deed Trusts (No 2)*[43] the majority of the Court of Appeal held that a discretionary trust which was conceptually certain was not defeated by mere evidential uncertainty. In other words, provided the class criteria are clear-cut it does not matter that it is not possible to prove of every individual whether they meet the criteria or not.[44] Since the test is the same for powers of appointment, it is

---

[34] [1968] Ch 126 at 134.      [35] [1956] 1 WLR 573.      [36] [1970] AC 508 at 523.
[37] *Re Gulbenkian's Settlement Trusts (No 1)* [1970] AC 508 at 518.
[38] See [1971] CLJ 68 (Hopkins); (1982) 98 LQR 551 (Emery).      [39] [1970] AC 508.
[40] [1971] AC 424.      [41] [1973] Ch 9.      [42] See Chapter 12.      [43] [1973] Ch 9.
[44] See Chapters 12 and 16.

not necessary that the class of a special power be evidentially certain. The lack of a requirement of strict evidential certainty follows from the fact that the donee of the power does not have to consider every single potential object in exercising his discretion to appoint the property. His complete discretion means that his only duty is to ensure that any appointments are made to persons within the class of objects and not to exercise the power excessively.[45]

### (d) Criticism of the 'is or is not' test

Following *Re Gulbenkian*;[46] *McPhail v Doulton*[47] and *Re Baden (No 2)*,[48] the same requirement of conceptual certainty applies to fixed trusts, discretionary trusts and powers of appointment. Equitable obligations of any of these types will be void if there is no conceptual certainty. This could lead to some unsatisfactory results, and it remains questionable whether the same strict test should apply to powers of appointment, which are discretionary, and trusts, which are in essence mandatory equitable obligations. There is much to commend a modified version of the broader proposition of Lord Denning MR in the Court of Appeal, who proposed that:

'. . . if the [donees] can say of a particular person: "He is clearly within the category", the gift is good, even though it may be difficult in other cases to say whether a person is or is not within the category.'[49]

In *Re Gibbards Will Trusts*[50] a testator gave his trustees a power of appointment over his residuary estate in favour of 'any of my old friends'. Plowman J concluded that 'there is not a sufficient degree of uncertainty about the expression'[51] to hold the power void for uncertainty. Similarly, in *Re Coates (Decd)*[52] a power to appoint a specified sum to 'friends' was upheld as valid. Roxburgh J held that the word 'friend' was not too vague, although he recognised that 'friendship' was a phrase 'particular blurred in outline'.[53] It is unclear whether these cases could be decided similarly today. Definitions such as 'old friends' would probably not be sufficiently conceptually certain[54] under the test propounded in *Re Baden (No 2)*.[55] A fixed trust for 'my old friends' would certainly not be valid as it would not be possible to identify the full extent of the class. *Re Gibbard*[56] was decided on the basis of the test rejected by the House of Lords in *Re Gulbenkian* that it must be possible to say of at least some persons that they are certainly within the class, even if it were not possible to say of others whether they are or not.

Ultimately, it is a question of policy whether a purely discretionary power should fail for lack of complete conceptual certainty. If a donor grants a power to appoint his property in favour of his 'old friends', there are clearly some people who are without

---

[45] With the exception of a fiduciary power where the trustee who holds the power of appointment is under a duty to have an appreciation of the width of the field of potential objects when he exercises it. See *Re Hay's Settlement Trusts* [1982] 1 WLR 202.

[46] [1970] AC 508.      [47] [1971] AC 424.      [48] [1973] Ch 9.

[49] *Re Gulbenkian's Settlement* [1968] Ch 126 at 134.      [50] [1966] 1 All ER 273.

[51] [1966] 1 All ER 273 at 281.      [52] [1955] Ch 495.      [53] [1955] Ch 495 at 499.

[54] See *Re Barlow's Will Trusts* [1979] 1 WLR 278 at 298, per Brown-Wilkinson J: '["Friends"] has a great range of meanings; indeed, its exact meaning probably varies slightly from person to person . . .'

[55] [1973] Ch 9.      [56] [1966] 1 All ER 273.

question within the class. Should the power fail and the donor's intention be defeated merely because there are others about whom it cannot be definitely stated whether they are 'old friends' or not? It would be more in keeping with the donor's intentions that appointments can be made in the donee's discretion to those who are definitely objects. An analogy can be drawn from the requirement of certainty applicable to a gift subject to a condition precedent. In *Re Barlow's Will Trusts*[57] Browne-Wilkinson J held that, if such gifts are made to a class, then they are valid if 'it is possible to say of one or more persons that he or they undoubtedly qualify even though it may be difficult to say of others whether or not they qualify'.[58] The case concerned a testatrix who directed her executor to sell valuable paintings at a considerable undervalue to her family and 'friends'. These gifts were valid because it was possible to say of some people that 'on any reasonable basis' they were friends, and would therefore be entitled to purchase. Provided a potential purchaser satisfied the condition of proving that he was definitely a friend, it did not matter that it was impossible to say whether others were friends or not.

If this approach was applied to powers of appointment it might provide a better balance between upholding the donor's intentions and ensuring that the court can supervise the execution of the power. The court will not intervene if the power is not exercised, so there is no possibility of the court exercising the power itself.[59] The court could prevent excessive exercise by upholding only appointments to those shown definitely to be within the class on any reasonable basis. In cases of doubt, the donee of the power could apply to the court for determination whether a person falls indisputably within the class. Such an approach would be entirely inappropriate for fixed or discretionary trusts where the court may have to carry out the terms of the trust. For powers of appointment it would provide a less stringent test than that declared by the House of Lords in *Re Gulbenkian*,[60] and would be similar to the rejected test applied by the Court of Appeal in that case. One disadvantage is that it would again create a distinction between the test of certainty applying to discretionary trusts and powers which would make the question of whether a particular instrument creates a trust or a power far more significant since that may determine its validity. That danger could be prevented by the court taking a strict view and not succumbing to the temptation of construing an invalid trust as a valid power.[61]

## (2) Capriciousness

Even if a special power of appointment is sufficiently certain, it will be invalid if it is capricious in nature. The principle of capriciousness was considered applicable to special powers in *Re Manisty's Settlement*,[62] where Templeman J suggested that a special power in favour of the 'residents of Greater London' would be capricious 'because the terms of the power negated any sensible intention on the part of the settlor'.[63] Capriciousness does not invalidate a power merely because of its width of the power, as

---

[57] [1979] 1 WLR 278.     [58] [1979] 1 WLR 278 at 281, following *Re Allen* [1953] Ch 810.
[59] Unlike a discretionary trust. See *McPhail v Doulton* [1971] AC 424.     [60] [1970] AC 508.
[61] As was taken in *McPhail v Doulton* [1971] AC 424.     [62] [1974] Ch 17.
[63] [1974] Ch 17 at 27.

a general power is valid even though the donee has the discretion to make appointments to anyone in the whole world. Instead, it invalidates a special power because there is no rational reason why the donor selected the specified class, and consequently the donee has no rational basis on which he can exercise his discretion.[64] 'Residents of Greater London' would be capricious because the class was 'an accidental agglomeration of persons who have no discernible link with the settlor or with any institution'.[65] If there were a link between the donor of the power and the class of potential objects, the power would not be open to the charge of capriciousness. In *Re Hay's Settlement Trusts*[66] Megarry V-C suggested that a power in favour of 'the residents of Greater London' would not be capricious if the donor were a former chairman of the Greater London Council. In *R v District Auditor ex p West Yorkshire Metropolitan County Council*[67] it was held that a discretionary trust created by the council for the benefit of the residents of West Yorkshire was not capricious.[68]

Where a power is found to be capricious it will be rendered void. Capriciousness will only invalidate a special power, and the principle has no application to a general power, or a hybrid power.[69] As both *Re Manisty's Settlement* and *Re Hay's Settlement Trusts* concerned fiduciary powers,[70] where the donee of the power has additional fiduciary duties, the principle may not apply to bare powers where the donee has no obligations of a fiduciary nature.

## 3  Exercise of powers of appointment

### (1)  Formalities

As a general rule, no special formalities are required for the valid exercise of a power of appointment. However, the donee of the power must intend to allocate the fund or part of the fund to an object of the power. Where the power is granted in relation to land an appointment must be evidenced in writing signed by the donee, in accordance with s 51(1)(b) of the Law of Property Act 1925. In some circumstances additional formalities may be required.

### (a)  Formalities required by the terms of the power

The terms of the power may require it to be exercised in a particular form, for example by deed. If so, the power can only be exercised in that form. Where it is stipulated that a

---

[64] [1974] Ch 17 at 27: 'A capricious power negatives a sensible consideration by the trustees of the exercise of the power.'

[65] [1974] Ch 17 at 27.     [66] [1982] 1 WLR 202.     [67] [1986] RVR 24.

[68] It was, however, found to be 'administratively unworkable', demonstrating that 'capriciousness' and 'administrative unworkability' are distinct concepts. See below, p 440.

[69] See *Re Manisty's Settlement* [1974] Ch 17 at 27; *Re Hay's Settlement Trusts* [1982] 1 WLR 202 at 212.

[70] See below, p 435.

power must be exercised by deed, a purported exercise by will, will be ineffective.[71] Similarly, a power which can only be exercised by will cannot be exercised inter vivos.[72]

## (b) Limitations on additional formalities

Although the terms of the power may specify additional formalities, legislation has limited the range of stipulations which must be observed to effect a valid exercise. Under s 159(1) of the Law of Property Act 1925, where a power is exercised inter vivos the exercise will be valid if the donee executed by a valid deed,[73] even though the terms of the power required some 'additional or other form of execution or attestation or solemnity'. This does not exclude the necessity for the donee to comply with any terms of the power requiring him to gain the consent of another individual, or performing an act not relating to the mode of executing the deed.[74] In the case of a will, s 10 of the Wills Act 1837 provides that the exercise of a power by a valid will is effective notwithstanding the absence of any additional formalities required by the terms of the power.[75]

## (2) Defective exercise

In general, a defective exercise of a power is void, and the purported appointment of the fund does not take place. However, equity may validate a defective exercise if the donee 'in discharge of moral or natural obligations shows an intention to execute [a] power'.[76] This will only apply in favour of purchasers for value, creditors, charities, and persons to whom the donee is under a natural or moral obligation to provide. Some key elements must be proved if the defective exercise is to be upheld: 'the intention to pass the property . . . the persons to be benefited . . . the amount of the benefit . . . good consideration'.[77]

## (3) Contracts to exercise

A contract to exercise a power of appointment will operate in equity as a valid exercise of the power, provided that the contract is specifically enforceable. This is an application of the maxim that 'equity treats as done that which ought to be done'. Since a contract to exercise a testamentary power is not specifically enforceable,[78] it does not operate as an effective exercise of the power, and the only remedy available to the disappointed object is an action for damages for breach of contract against the estate.

---

[71] *Re Phillips* (1889) LR 41 Ch D 417.

[72] *Re Evered* [1910] 2 Ch 147 at 156, per Cozens-Hardy MR.

[73] Executed in the presence of and attested by two or more witnesses (Law of Property (Miscellaneous Provisions) Act 1989, s 1).

[74] Law of Property Act 1925, s 159(2).    [75] See also Wills Act 1963, s 2.

[76] *Farwell on Powers* (3rd edn, 1916), p 378; *Chapman v Gibson* (1791) 3 Bro CC 229.

[77] *Farwell on Powers* (3rd edn, 1916), p 379.

[78] *Re Bradshaw* [1902] 1 Ch 436; *Re Cooke* [1922] 1 Ch 292.

## (4) Excessive exercise

The exercise of the power will be excessive if the donee makes an appointment to a person outside of the potential objects of the power. In the case of a special power, appointments can only be made to members of the specified class, whilst in the case of a hybrid power, appointments must not be made to members of the excluded class. Any such excessive appointments are void and of no effect.

If an appointment is made which is partly good and partly bad, the court will sever the good from the bad if possible. In *Re Kerr's Will Trusts*[79] Maria Young had a special power of appointment over a fund in favour of the children of her marriage. By will, she appointed the fund to two of her children, Charlotte and Catherine. Catherine was a child of the marriage and within the power, but Charlotte was an illegitimate child of Maria before she married. The exercise was thus excessive, but the court applied severance and Catherine took the share of the fund appointed to her. The remainder of the fund was divided equally amongst those entitled in default of appointment. In *Re Holland*[80] an appointment was made with attached conditions which rendered the exercise excessive. The conditions were severed from the appointment and it was upheld as a valid exercise.[81] If it is impossible to sever the condition from the appointment the exercise will be excessive and void.[82]

## (5) Effect of valid exercise

The effect of a valid exercise of the power is to allocate the share of the fund appointed to the person in whose favour the donee has exercised the power. The appointee will then be entitled to an immediate proprietary interest in the share of the fund which has been allocated.[83] In *Churchill v Churchill*[84] Lord Romilly MR held that the effect of an appointment by Sir Orford Gordon under a special power of a fund to his three daughters in equal shares was to vest in them absolute interests in the appointed fund.

# 4 Duties of the donee of a bare power of appointment

## (1) No duty to exercise the power

The donee of a bare power of appointment is under no duty to exercise the power and make appointments in favour of the potential objects. He has complete discretion and the court will not compel him to exercise the power, nor even to consider periodically whether he should exercise the power. If he fails to make any appointments at all he is not in breach of any duty owed either to the donor of the power or to the potential objects, and they have no cause for complaint against him.

---

[79] (1878) 4 Ch D 600.    [80] [1914] 2 Ch 595.
[81] See also *Churchill v Churchill* (1866–67) LR 5 Eq 44.    [82] *Re Cohen* [1911] 1 Ch 37.
[83] See *Vestey v IRC* [1980] AC 1148, HL.    [84] (1866–67) LR 5 Eq 44.

## (2) No duty to consider the width of the field

If the donee of the power does decide to exercise it, he has no duty to survey and consider the range of potential objects of the power before exercising his discretion in favour of any one object. He may appoint to whomsoever he wishes, provided they are within the class, without having to take account of others who could benefit if he were to exercise his discretion in their favour. If he is within the scope of the power, the donee may appoint the fund entirely to himself without even considering the other potential objects. In *Re Penrose*[85] an exercise of a special power of appointment by the donee in favour of himself, where he has an object, was upheld. In the case of fiduciary powers, considered below, the donee of the power does have a duty to survey the range of potential objects before exercising his discretion.

## (3) Duty not to delegate the exercise of the power

The donee must not delegate the power of appointment to others except in so far as this is authorised by the terms of the grant: *delegatus non potest delegare*.

## (4) Duty not to exercise the power excessively

The donee of the power is under a duty to make appointments only to those who are objects of the power. As has been seen, any appointments which are excessive will be void.

## (5) Duty not to exercise the power fraudulently

Even if the donee exercises the power and makes appointments which appear to be within the scope of the power, they will be void if the exercise amounts to a 'fraud on the power'. The power must be exercised honestly, and the court will look to the motives and intentions of the donor of the power to ensure that they are not improper. As Lord Parker of Waddington observed in *Vatcher v Paull*:

'. . . The term fraud in connection with frauds on a power does not necessarily denote any conduct on the part of the appointor amounting to fraud in the common law meaning of the term or any conduct which could be properly termed dishonest or immoral. It merely means that the power has been exercised for a purpose or with an intention, beyond the scope of or not justified by the instrument creating the fraud . . .'[86]

Thus, in *Hillsdown Holdings plc v Pensions Ombudsman*[87] an exercise of a power was held to constitute a 'fraud' despite the fact that the donee and all parties had acted honestly and with good intentions. In *Edge v Pensions Ombudsman*[88] Scott V-C held that pension trustees were required to 'exercise their discretionary power honestly and for the purpose for which the power was given and not so as to accomplish any ulterior purpose'.

---

[85] [1933] Ch 793.     [86] [1915] AC 372 at 378.     [87] [1997] 1 All ER 862.
[88] [1998] 2 All ER 547 at 569.

Where the exercise of a power is held invalid on the grounds of fraud, the court acts to protect the interests of those who would be entitled to the fund if no appointments are made. They are the victims of the fraud if appointments are made with improper motives, since they are thereby divested of an interest in the fund to which they would otherwise have become entitled.[89] The effect of fraud is to render the exercise of the power void, not merely voidable.[90]

In *Vatcher v Paull*[91] Lord Parker indicated three circumstances in which the exercise of a power would amount to a fraud. The essence of each is that the benefit is not exclusively conferred upon objects of the power.[92] Clearly, these limitations apply only to special powers and not to general powers, since in the case of a general power there are no persons outside of the scope of the power and the donee may even appoint in his own favour.

### (a)  Where the exercise is due to some bargain between the appointor and the appointee

If an appointment is made on the basis of a prior agreement between the donee/appointor and the appointee as to how the appointed share of the fund should be used, the appointment is void. The purpose of the bargain may be for the donee to gain some benefit for himself, or for a non-object of the power. The objection to such a bargain is 'that the power is used not with the single purpose of benefiting its proper objects'.[93] There is no objection to an appointment made on the basis of a bargain with those who are entitled in default.[94] Where an appointment is a fraud because it was made on the basis of such a bargain, the court may sever the good from the bad provided that it 'can clearly distinguish between the quantum of the benefit bona fide intended to be conferred on the appointee and the quantum of benefit intended to be derived by the appointor or to be conferred on a stranger'.[95] In the recent case *Hillsdown Holdings plc v Pensions Ombudsman*[96] the exercise of a power by a pension fund trustee was held to be a fraud on the power. Hillsdown plc participated in a pension scheme (the FMC scheme) which had accumulated an actuarial surplus of some £20m. The scheme contained no power allowing the trustees to repay any surplus to employers participating in the scheme, and the scheme could not be amended to confer such a power. After an agreement had been negotiated between Hillsdown and the FMC trustees to augment the benefits of FMC pensioners and to transfer to the company £11m of the surplus, the trustees exercised a power under the scheme to transfer the entire fund to another scheme (the HF scheme), the rules of which were changed to allow the surplus to

---

[89]  *Re Brooks' Settlement Trusts* [1939] Ch 993.      [90]  *Cloutte v Storey* [1911] 1 Ch 18, CA.

[91]  [1915] AC 372 at 378.

[92]  *Re Merton* [1953] 1 WLR 1096 at 1100, per Wynn-Parry J: '. . . if, and only if, it appears from the evidence that the object was to secure a benefit for [the appointor] or for some other person not an object of the power, is the transaction to be held invalid', and at 1101: 'The court has to ask itself, what was the appointor's purpose and intention? Was it to secure a benefit for himself or some person not an object of the trust? If the answer is "Yes", there is vice; and if the answer is "No", there is no vice.'

[93]  *Vatcher v Paull* [1915] AC 372 at 379.      [94]  [1915] AC 372 at 379.      [95]  [1915] AC 372 at 378.

[96]  [1997] 1 All ER 862.

be paid to Hillsdown. Knox J held that the FMC trustees' exercise of the power, transferring the assets to HF was a fraud on the power:

'FMC's trustee's exercise of the power . . . constituted a fraud on the power, or in more modern parlance an improper use of the power for a collateral purpose. The purpose for which it was exercised was the composite one of giving effect to the bargain struck with Hillsdown of which a major element was that of a payment of surplus to Hillsdown. That was outside the proper ambit of r 21 which was to enable transfers of obligations and assets to other approved funds securing pension rights for members. In my view the Pensions Ombudsman was right in calling the transfer a fraud on the power.'[97]

### (b) The appointor's purpose and intention is to secure a benefit for himself

Even where there was no explicit bargain between the donee/appointor and appointee, the exercise will constitute a fraud if the purpose of the appointment was to enable the appointor to receive a benefit. Thus, if an appointor makes an appointment in favour of a child they know to be dying, with the intention that they will gain the benefit of that sum on the death of the child, the appointment is a fraud on the power. In *Lord Hinchinbroke v Seymour*[98] a father appointed £10,000 in favour of his daughter who was fourteen and dying of consumption. The intention of the appointment was that the father would take the money as administrator of the child. It was 'as plain a case of gross fraud on a power as can well be imagined', and 'it was quite obvious what the motive was. It could not have been for the benefit of the child, because she was already provided for'.[99] An appointment made to a child who is healthy is not a fraud, even though the appointor stands to gain if the child subsequently dies.[100]

### (c) The appointor's purpose and intention is to secure a benefit for some other person not an object of the power

An appointment in favour of an object of the power will be fraudulent if the real intention of the donee/appointor was to benefit a non-object. In *Re Dick*[101] Mrs Sherman was the donee of a special power of appointment over property left on trust by her father in favour of her brothers or sisters and their issue. She exercised the power by will in favour of her sister, Miss Dick, but contemporaneously with the will executed a formal memorandum desiring her sister provide an annuity of £800 per annum for her gardener Mr Claydon, who was not an object. The memorandum expressly stated that it did not impose a 'trust or legal obligation' on Miss Dick, so that there was no bargain between the appointor and appointee. Nevertheless, the Court of Appeal held that this amounted to an excessive exercise of the power. Evershed MR stated that the central question was:

'. . . whether the right inference is that what Mrs Sherman intended to do, her real deliberate purpose which she wanted and set out by all means that were possible to achieve, was to benefit the Claydons via her relations . . . or whether her purpose was really to benefit her

---

[97] [1997] 1 All ER 862 at 883.      [98] (1784) 1 Bro CC 395.
[99] *Henty v Wrey* (1882) LR 21 Ch D 332 at 342, per Jessel MR.      [100] (1882) LR 21 Ch D 332.
[101] [1953] Ch 343.

relations subject only to this, that she had indicated to them that she hoped . . . they would so something for the Claydons on the lines she had suggested.'[102]

The court held that in all the circumstances the real intention was to benefit the non-object. This case suggests that the court will weigh the appointor's motives and intentions from all the available evidence, a principle that was established by Cohen LJ in *Re Crawshay (Decd) (No 2)*.[103] This is notoriously difficult, as evidenced by the large number of indications and counter-indications considered by the Court of Appeal in *Re Dick*.

# 5 Failure to exercise the power

Since a power of appointment is purely discretionary in nature, a donee is under no obligation to exercise it, and the objects have no rights to the fund unless it is appointed to them. If the power is not exercised, the fund passes to those entitled in default. Usually this will occur where a donee has been granted a power but has died without making any valid appointments, either inter vivos or by will. The persons entitled in default may be specified by the donor in the terms of the power. If no such persons are identified, the general principles of succession or resulting trusts will determine who is entitled.[104] In some circumstances the courts have been willing to imply that the objects themselves are entitled to the fund in default of appointment because there was a 'general intention' on the part of the donor that the objects should benefit.[105]

## (1) Express gift over in default of appointment

The power of appointment may itself contain an express stipulation of who is to receive the fund if no appointments are made. Such an express provision will determine how the fund should be distributed.

## (2) No express gift over in default

If the power does not contain an express gift over in default, the fund will fall to be distributed according to the general principles governing the distribution of surplus funds.[106] If the fund was created by will, the property passes to those entitled to the residuary estate under the will. If the fund was created by an inter vivos settlement, it will result back to the settlor, or his heirs, by a resulting trust.

## (3) An implied trust in default

In some circumstances, even though no appointment has been made the court may hold that the fund should be divided amongst the objects rather than passing to the

---

[102] [1953] Ch 343 at 363.    [103] [1948] Ch 123.    [104] See Chapter 19.
[105] See *Burrough v Philcox* (1840) 5 My & Cr 72.    [106] See Chapter 19.

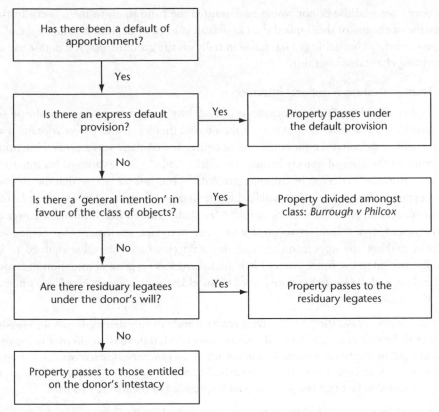

**Effect of default of appointment**

residuary legatees or by resulting trust. This will only be possible if the court can find that there was a 'general intention' by the donee of the power to benefit a class. The leading case is *Burrough v Philcox*.[107] John Walton granted his surviving daughter, Ann, a power of appointment over his property in favour of his nephews and nieces. The power contained no express gift over in default and Ann died without making any appointments. Under the rules of succession, the testator's next of kin would be entitled to the fund. However, Lord Cottenham LC held that the effect of the arrangement was to create a trust in favour of the nephews and nieces subject to Ann's power of selection, so that when Ann died without having made any appointments, they each took an equal share in the fund. The principle was stated by Lord Cottenham:

'... where there appears a general intention in favour of a class, and a particular intention in favour of individuals of a class to be selected by another person, and the particular intention fails, from that selection not being made, the court will carry into effect the general intention in favour of the class.'[108]

The key element is the finding of a general intention in favour of the class. In effect, the court is concluding from the circumstances of the creation of the power that if it has

---

[107]  (1840) 5 My & Cr 72.        [108]  (1840) 5 My & Cr 72 at 92.

not been exercised the donor would have wanted the fund to go to the objects. In this sense the operation of the implied trust in default is somewhat similar to an application cy-pres, where a charitable gift has failed initially on the grounds that the donor had an overriding charitable intention.

### (a) Demonstrating a general intention

An implied trust in default will only arise if it can be shown that the donor of the power possessed a general intention to benefit the objects thereof. If the power contained an express gift in default, then the court cannot conclude that there was a general intention in favour of the class of objects because the donee had already expressed his intention vis-à-vis the fund in default of any appointments.[109] It is not inevitable that the absence of an express gift over in default will lead to the finding of a general intention in favour of the objects. In *Re Weekes' Settlement*[110] Mrs Slade granted her husband a power of appointment over a fund established under her marriage settlement. Mr Slade died without making any appointments, and the children of the marriage claimed to be equally entitled to the fund. Romer J held that there was no general intention in favour of the class, and the fund therefore passed to the eldest son, who was Mrs Slade's heir at law. He stated:

'The authorities do not show . . . that there is a hard and fast rule that a gift to A for life with a power to appoint among a class and nothing more must, if there is no gift over in the will, be held a gift by implication to the class in default of the power being exercised . . . you must find in the will an indication that the testatrix did intend the class or some of the class to take—intended in fact that the power should be regarded in the nature of a trust.'[111]

No general intention in favour of the class was found in *Re Combe*[112] or *Re Perowne (Decd)*.[113] Such a general intention is only likely to be found where the power is in favour of a small and well-defined class, especially a close family group.

### (b) Juridical nature of the implied trust in default

There remains confusion as to the basis under which the fund subject to a power is distributed to the objects under the rule in *Burrough v Philcox*. One analysis is that the power is in fact a discretionary trust under which the donee is under an obligation to make an appointment. Thus in *Burrough v Philcox* Lord Cottenham LC cited the dictum of Lord Eldon in *Brown v Higgs*[114] that the power is given so as to:

'. . . make it the duty of the donee to exercise it; and, in such case, the court will not permit the objects of the power to suffer by the negligence or conduct of the donee, but fastens upon the property a trust for their benefit.'[115]

Similarly, in *Re Weekes' Settlement*[116] Romer J considered that if there had been a general intention in favour of the class this would have rendered the power in the nature of a trust.

A second analysis is that the general intention in favour of the class creates a fixed

---

[109] *Re Mills* [1930] 1 Ch 654.　　[110] [1897] 1 Ch 289.　　[111] [1897] 1 Ch 289 at 292.
[112] [1925] Ch 210.　　[113] [1951] Ch 785.
[114] (1803) 8 Ves 561.　　[115] (1840) 5 My & Cr 72 at 92.　　[116] [1897] 1 Ch 289.

trust in favour of the whole class, so that from the very beginning the objects/ beneficiaries enjoy equal shares in the fund, but that the donor of the power is entitled to divest them of their interests by the exercise of the power.

A third analysis is that the trust in favour of the whole class applies only in default of appointment, just as would be the case if the trust had contained an express gift over in default of appointment. In this situation the beneficiaries of the trust in default of appointment do not have vested, but only contingent, interests which depend for their vesting and fulfillment on the power not being exercised.

The confusion has arisen because the rule only comes into play after there has been a failure on the part of the donee to exercise the power. If appointments had been made, no difficulties would arise. It is better to regard the court as acting *ex post facto*, and implying a trust in favour of the objects of power in the event of no appointment being made, rather than to construe a trust in their favour from the beginning. This was the approach taken by Buckley J in *Re Wills' Trust Deeds*.[117] He considered that a trust in favour of the objects only arose in the event of default:

'A perusal of these cases . . . leads to the conclusion that they really turn on the question whether on the particular facts of each case it was proper to infer that there was a trust in default of appointment for the objects of the power. The court did not, and I think, could not compel the donee personally to exercise the power but carried what it conceived to be the settlor's intention into effect by executing an implied trust in default of appointment.'[118]

It therefore seems that the best analysis is that a power is given to the donee, which he is under no duty to exercise, but that in the event of there being no exercise the court implies a trust in favour of the class on the basis of a general intention in their favour on the part of the donor. The objects thus have no beneficial entitlement to the fund until the trust is implied and the donee of the power has no enforceable duties and is not in breach by failing to make appointments.

# 6 Fiduciary powers

## (1) Definition

If a power of appointment is held by the donee in a fiduciary capacity, the power is a 'fiduciary power'. This will normally occur because the donee is also a trustee of the property subject to the power. In *Re Hay's Settlement Trusts*[119] David Greig and Colin Oliver were the trustees of a settlement made by Lady Hay. As part of the settlement they enjoyed a general power of appointment over the property subject to the trust. As they were trustees, they held their power in a fiduciary capacity.[120] In *Mettoy Pension*

---

[117] [1964] Ch 219.      [118] [1964] Ch 219 at 230.

[119] [1982] 1 WLR 202. Other cases considering fiduciary powers include *Re Gestetner Settlement* [1953] Ch 672; *Re Abraham's Will Trusts* [1969] 1 Ch 463; *Re Gulbenkian's Settlement Trusts (No 1)* [1970] AC 508; *McPhail v Doulton* [1971] AC 424; *Re Manisty's Settlement* [1974] Ch 17; *Mettoy Pension Trustees Ltd v Evans* [1990] 1 WLR 1587.

[120] See also *Breadner v Granville-Grossman* [2001] Ch 523.

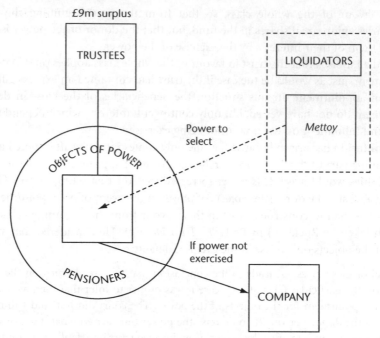

£9m surplus

TRUSTEES

LIQUIDATORS

*Mettoy*

Power to
select

OBJECTS OF POWER

PENSIONERS

If power not
exercised

COMPANY

Fiduciary powers: *Mettoy Pensions v Evans*

*Trustees Ltd v Evans*[121] Warner J described such an obligation as a 'fiduciary power in the full sense',[122] which he defined as:

'. . . comprising any power conferred on the trustees of the property or any other person as a trustee of the power itself.'[123]

The case concerned the pension fund of a company, Mettoy plc, which had gone into liquidation. After the fund had met the fixed entitlements of pensioners, there was a surplus of some £9m remaining in the fund. Rule 13(5) of the fund's rules granted a power of appointment over any surplus, which could be exercised to increase the entitlements of the pensioners. This power was held by the company and not by the separate trustee of the fund. If the power was not exercised, an undistributed surplus would pass to the company itself. In these circumstances Warner J concluded that the power was a fiduciary power even though the trustee was not the donee. He relied on two main factors to reach this conclusion. First, he considered that if the power were a mere power and not a fiduciary power, any supposed discretion by the company to appoint increased entitlements to the pensioners would be 'illusory', since the company would in effect only be making ex gratia gifts from property which they owned abso-lutely.[124] Secondly, the objects of the power were not volunteers, as the fund surplus had

---

[121] [1991] 2 All ER 513. See (1991) Conv 364 (Martin), (1991) 107 LQR 214 (Gardner).
[122] Using the language of Chitty J in *Re Somes* [1896] 1 Ch 250.
[123] [1991] 2 All ER 513 at 545.    [124] [1991] 2 All ER 513 at 547.

arisen partially from their own pension contributions, and not from successful invest-ment or over-contribution by the company alone.[125]

## (2) Duties of the donee of fiduciary powers

The key difference between a 'fiduciary power' and a 'mere power' which is not held in a fiduciary capacity is that the donee of a fiduciary power owes duties to the objects. The scope of these additional duties were considered in *Re Hay's Settlement Trusts*[126] and *Mettoy Pension Trustees Ltd v Evans*.[127] In *Re Hay's Settlement Trusts*[128] Sir Robert Megarry V-C held that there were three additional duties owed by the donee to the objects of a fiduciary power. These duties point to the fact that the donee of a fidu-ciary power must have a greater sensitivity to the nature of the discretion that he holds.

### (a) Duty to consider periodically whether or not he should exercise the power

Unlike a mere power, which the donee need never consider whether or not to exercise, Megarry V-C held that the donee of a fiduciary power cannot 'simply fold his hands and ignore it, for normally he must from time to time consider whether or not to exercise the power'.[129] This duty is enforceable by the court, which may direct the donee to consider whether he should exercise the power.[130]

### (b) Duty to consider the range of objects of the power

The fiduciary nature of the position of the donee also affects the manner in which a donee makes appointments. Following the decision of the House of Lords in *McPhail v Doulton*,[131] which concerned the duties of trustees of a discretionary trust, Megarry V-C held that the donee of a fiduciary power must 'make such a survey of the range of objects' as will enable him to carry out his fiduciary duty.[132] This does not mean that he has to identify every single member of the class of objects before making any allocations of the fund, but that he must find out 'the permissible area of selection'. He cannot make an appointment to the first object who comes to mind.

### (c) Duty to consider the appropriateness of individual appointments

Having considered the range of potential objects, the donee of a fiduciary power must 'then consider responsibly, in individual cases, whether a contemplated beneficiary was within the power and whether, in relation to other possible claimants, a particular grant was appropriate'.[133]

---

[125] [1991] 2 All ER 513 at 550–551. See also *Thrells Ltd v Lomas* [1993] 1 WLR 456; *Re William Makin & Sons Ltd* [1993] OPLR 171.

[126] [1982] 1 WLR 202.     [127] [1991] 2 All ER 513.     [128] [1982] 1 WLR 202.

[129] [1982] 1 WLR 202 at 209.     [130] [1982] 1 WLR 202 at 209.

[131] [1971] AC 424.

[132] Per Lord Wilberforce, quoted by Sir Robert Megarry V-C in *Re Hay's Settlement Trusts* [1982] 1 WLR 202 at 209.

[133] *McPhail v Doulton* [1971] AC 424 at 457, quoted by Sir Robert Megarry in *Re Hay's Settlement Trusts* [1982] 1 WLR 202 at 209.

### (d) Duty to make trust documents available to the objects

In the recent case of *Schmidt v Rosewood Trust Ltd*[134] the Privy Council held that the objects of a fiduciary power of appointment may be entitled to seek disclosure of trust documents of the trust to which the power relates, so as to ensure the proper administration of the trust. However this right is not absolute as disclosure is ordered under the inherent jurisdiction of the court, and the entitlement to disclosure may be limited or safeguarded so as to protect personal or commercial confidentiality, or to balance the competing interests of different beneficiaries, trustees or third parties. At all events the object of a power of appointment will not be granted access to trust documents which would reveal the trustees' reasons for exercising, or not exercising, the power.[135]

## (3) Supervision by the court of fiduciary powers

Since the donee of a fiduciary power owes duties to the objects, the court will ensure that these duties are properly performed.

### (a) Appointments made without due consideration

If appointments are made by the donee without proper consideration of the range of objects and the appropriateness of the particular appointments being made, then such appointments will be void as an invalid exercise of the power. In *Turner v Turner*[136] the trustees of a settlement made appointments by deed under a power of appointment they held in their capacity as trustees. They had executed the deeds at the request of the solicitors acting for the settlor without reading or understanding what they were signing, and without making a decision to appoint. Mervyn Davies J held that these appointments should be set aside because they had been made 'in breach of their duty, in that it was their duty to "consider" before appointing, and this they did not do'.[137]

### (b) Failure to exercise the power

Where the donee of a fiduciary power has failed to make any appointments, the question arises whether the court can intervene to compel them to carry out their duties. In *Re Hay's Settlement Trusts*[138] Sir Robert Megarry V-C indicated that the courts would compel the donee of a fiduciary power to consider exercising it.[139] However, the courts have been reluctant to suggest that they would compel the donee to exercise the power, as this is inconsistent with its discretionary character. In *McPhail v Doulton*[140] Lord Wilberforce cited the judgment of Lord Upjohn in *Re Gulbenkian's Settlement*[141] and stated:

---

[134] [2003] 3 All ER 76.

[135] See also *Foreman v Kingstone* [2004] 1 NZLR 841. See below p 707 for a fuller discussion of the right to disclosure of trust documents.

[136] [1983] 2 All ER 745.      [137] [1983] 2 All ER 745 at 752.      [138] [1982] 1 WLR 202.

[139] [1982] 1 WLR 202 at 209.      [140] [1971] AC 424.      [141] [1970] AC 508.

'. . . although the trustees may . . . be under a fiduciary duty to consider whether or in what way they should exercise their power the court will not normally compel its exercise.'[142]

However, in the *Mettoy*[143] case Warner J considered that in some circumstances the court might be willing to step in and compel the exercise of a fiduciary power. As has been seen, the power was held by Mettoy plc, a company in liquidation. Therefore, the donee was incapable of exercising the power itself, and it was held by the liquidators. They would be unable to exercise it because of a conflict between their duty to give proper consideration to exercising it in favour of the pensioners and their duty to the company's creditors, which would require them to exercise the power to enable the company to take the surplus in default. Warner J held that, since there was no one remaining who could exercise the power, the court should step in. He held that in such circumstances the court could exercise the fiduciary power in the same way that it was entitled to intervene if the trustees of a discretionary trust were failing to carry out their duties. He cited *McPhail v Doulton*,[144] where Lord Wilberforce had suggested a number of means by which the court could intervene to compel the performance of a discretionary trust:

'. . . appointing new trustees, or by authorising or directing representative persons of the classes of beneficiaries to prepare a scheme of distribution, or even, should the proper basis for distribution appear, by itself directing the trustees to so distribute.'[145]

He then suggested that 'the methods [Lord Wilberforce] indicated could be equally appropriate in a case where the court was called upon to intervene in the exercise of a [fiduciary power]'.[146] He therefore held that the court would execute the power of appointment itself, but that, before doing so, further evidence was required to enable it to determine the basis on which an allocation of the surplus fund should be made between the pensioners and the company.[147]

*Mettoy Pension Trustees Ltd v Evans* marks a trend toward the assimilation of discretionary trusts and powers of appointment. The traditional distinction between trusts, which the court will enforce, and powers, which it will not, is all but abolished if the courts are willing to enforce fiduciary powers in exactly the same way that they will enforce discretionary trusts. The limitation seems to be the recognition that this procedure is only available in the limited exceptional circumstances where the power cannot be exercised because there is no donee able to make any appointments.

A different problem arises where the donee of a fiduciary power has failed to make any appointments because he has not fulfilled his duty to consider whether or not to exercise the power. In *Breadner v Granville-Grossman*[148] the two trustees of a discretionary trust were granted a power of appointment in 1976. Under the terms of the trust this power had to be exercised before a specified date, namely 2 August 1989. At a late stage one of the trustees prepared a deed appointing the entire beneficial interest to one beneficiary, which he only explained to his co-trustee on the day that the deed was executed, which was 2 August 1989, in other words after the last day for exercising the

1976 power. The beneficiary claimed that the appointment was still effective in equity, on the grounds that the trustees had failed to comply with their duty to consider exercising it. Park J held that, whilst the trustees had failed to perform their duty to consider exercising the power, the court could not intervene because the power had ceased to be exercisable, even though they would have made the appointment if they had performed their duty. He explained that the willingness of the court to intervene in *Mettoy Pension Trustees Ltd v Evans* did not extend to such a situation:

'In my judgement, however, there is a very big difference between, on the one hand, the courts declaring something which the trustees have done to be void, and on the other hand, the courts holding that a trust takes effect as if the trustees had done something which they had never done at all . . . In the *Mettoy Pension Trustees Ltd* case Warner J observed that, if a case arose where the trustees had done something but, if they had taken all relevant factors into account, would have done something quite different, the court should declare void what they have done. There is no suggestion that the court would or might substitute the different thing which it thinks that the trustees would have done themselves . . . I do not think that Warner J would have done it, and I will not do it either.'[149]

## (4) Validity of fiduciary powers

### (a) Certainty

The test for certainty of objects of a fiduciary power is the same as that for a mere power, namely the 'is or is not' test.[150]

### (b) Capriciousness

It is clear from *Re Manisty's Settlement*[151] and *Re Hay's Settlement Trusts*[152] that a fiduciary power will be void if it is capricious in nature.[153]

### (c) Administrative unworkability[154]

In *McPhail v Doulton*[155] Lord Wilberforce suggested that a discretionary trust which is not void for uncertainty may yet be void for 'administrative unworkability'[156] if the class is 'too wide to form anything like a class'.[157] In *Re Hay's Settlement Trusts*[158] Sir Robert Megarry V-C considered that the principle of 'administrative unworkability' was directed only towards discretionary trusts and had no application to fiduciary powers. However, following the greater assimilation of fiduciary powers and discretionary trusts in *Mettoy Pension Trustees Ltd v Evans*[159] and the willingness of the court to compel their exercise in exceptional circumstances, it may be that the principle will also apply to fiduciary powers. The fiduciary power in the *Mettoy* case would not, however, have been invalidated for 'administrative unworkability' because the class of objects was small and well defined, i.e. the pension fund members.

---

149 [2000] 4 All ER 705 at 723.     150 See above p 421.     151 [1974] Ch 17.
152 [1982] 1 WLR 202.     153 See above, p 425.     154 See (1991) 107 LQR 215.
155 [1971] AC 424.     156 [1971] AC 424 at 444.     157 [1971] AC 424 at 457.
158 [1982] 1 WLR 202.     159 [1991] 2 All ER 513.

# 7 Release of powers

The donor of a power of appointment, whether a bare power or a fiduciary power, may wish to release it. As a consequence of release he will cease to be able to make any appointments of the fund. This has the same effect on the ownership of the property subject to the power as if the power had not been exercised. Therefore, on release those entitled in default will automatically become entitled to the property previously held subject to the power. Sometimes a power may be released to remove persons from the class of potential recipients of the property if the possibility of their receiving a benefit would result in tax disadvantages. For example, it may be advantageous to exclude the settlor from the class of objects of a power to avoid inheritance tax under the 'reservation of benefit' rules.[160] Similarly, a settlement may be liable to income tax if the settlor or his wife may benefit from the exercise of a power of appointment in their favour. In *Muir v IRC*[161] the Court of Appeal held that the trustees had released their power to pay income from the trust towards the payment of premiums of insurance policies held by persons including the settlor, and that therefore the settlor had no interest in the income from the settlement and was not liable to surtax. In *Re Wills' Trust Deeds*[162] property was held on trust for such of the issue of the testator or charitable institutions as the trustees should appoint. The trustees sought to release the power in favour of the testator's issue so that the trust would be for exclusively charitable objects.

## (1) The consequences of release

If property is gifted to persons subject to a power of appointment which may divest them of their interest, on the release of the power their interests will become indefeasible. This was seen in *Re Mills*,[163] which concerned the will of Algernon Mills. His residuary estate was to be held for the benefit of such of his father's children and remoter issue that his brother should appoint or, in default of any such appointment, for his brother absolutely. The brother made a number of appointments and then released the power by deed. The Court of Appeal held that this was a valid release, and the consequence was that the brother became absolutely entitled to the property under the default provision.

## (2) Authority to release

Not every power is capable of being released by the donee. The leading authority concerning the circumstances in which a power may be released is the judgment of Buckley J in *Re Wills' Trust Deeds*.[164] Generally, a donee will only be able to release a power which he is under no obligation to exercise or to consider exercising.

---

[160] See Chapter 5.     [161] [1966] 1 WLR 1269.     [162] [1964] Ch 219.
[163] [1930] 1 Ch 654, CA.     [164] [1964] Ch 219.

## (a) Bare/mere powers

In the case of a mere power, which is not held in any fiduciary capacity and where there is no express or implied trust in favour of the objects in default of appointment, the donee may release the power. As Buckley J said:

'Where a power is conferred on someone who is not a trustee of the property to which the power relates or, if he is such a trustee, is not conferred on him in that capacity, then in the absence of a trust in favour of the objects of the power in default of appointment, the donee is, at any rate prima facie, not under any duty recognisable by the court to exercise a power such as to disenable him from releasing the power.'[165]

Mere powers fall within the ambit of s 155 of the Law of Property Act 1925, which provides:

'A person to whom any power, whether coupled with an interest or not, is given, may by deed release, or contract not to exercise, the power.'[166]

## (b) Mere powers with a trust in favour of the objects in default of appointment

Where a power gives rise to a trust in default of appointment arises, the donee is not entitled to release it so as to defeat the trust. This will be so whether the trust in default is express or implied under the rule in *Burrough v Philcox*.[167] Again, this was explained by Buckley J:

'. . . if a power is granted to appoint among a class of objects and in default of appointment there is a trust, express or implied, in favour of the members of that class, the donee of the power cannot by failure to appoint or by purporting to bind himself not to appoint or, which comes to the same thing, by purporting to release his power, defeat the interests of the members of the class of objects. This proposition really needs only to be stated to be accepted. The problem in such cases, where there is no express trust in default of appointment, is whether such a trust should be inferred . . . [A] power of the kind just mentioned cannot be released, for the donee is under a duty to exercise it, notwithstanding that the court may not be able to compel him personally to perform that duty, and can remedy his default only be executing the trust in default of appointment.'[168]

Buckley J's view that a power cannot be released in this situation is based on the assumption that the trust in favour of the members of the class arises from an obligation to exercise the power. As has already been explained, this may not be the best interpretation of *Burrough v Philcox*. The logic of his statement that the power cannot be released cannot apply to an express trust by way of gift over in default in favour of the class of objects. Such release will accelerate the gift in favour of the class. In *Re Radcliffe*[169] a father held a power of appointment in favour of the class of objects of his children, with an express trust in favour of them equally in default of appointment. One of the three children had died in infancy, and the father was entitled as his

---

[165]   [1964] Ch 219 at 237.
[166]   Law of Property Act 1925, s 160 provides that s 155 applies to 'powers created or arising either before or after the commencement' of the Act.
[167]   (1840) 5 My & Cr 72.          [168]   [1964] Ch 219 at 236.          [169]   [1892] 1 Ch 27.

administrator. The father released the power of appointment by deed and demanded that the trustees pay a third of the trust property to him. The Court of Appeal, following the earlier case of *Smith v Houblon*,[170] held that there had been a valid release and that, subject to the father surrendering his life-interest over the trust, he was entitled to the third to be transferred to him.

## (c) Fiduciary powers

*(i) Fiduciary powers with no authorisation to release.* Where a power is held in a fiduciary capacity, whether by a trustee or other fiduciary, the donee may not release it unless release is authorised by the instrument creating the power. When the predecessor to s 155 of the Law of Property Act 1925 was enacted in 1881,[171] the courts held that it did not apply to trusts held in a fiduciary capacity.[172] This was followed by the Court of Appeal in *Re Mills*[173] and in *Re Wills' Trust Deeds*, where Buckley J said:

'. . . [W]here a power is conferred on trustees virtute officii in relation to their trust property, they cannot release it or bind themselves not to exercise it . . . [T]he same is true if the power is conferred on persons who are in fact trustees of the settlement but is conferred on them by name and not by reference to their office, if on the true view of the facts they were selected as donees of the power because they were the trustees.'[174]

This principle was applied by Millett J in *Re Courage Group's Pension Schemes*,[175] where he held that a committee of management of a pension scheme could not release their powers or discretion so as to deprive their successors of the right to exercise them as they were vested in the committee in a fiduciary capacity. This restriction will also apply where the power is held in a fiduciary capacity, even though the donees are not trustees. As has been seen in *Mettoy Pension Trustees v Evans*,[176] the company, although not a trustee of the fund, held a power of appointment in a fiduciary capacity. Warner J therefore held that it could not be released.

*(ii) Fiduciary powers with authorisation to release.* The donee of a fiduciary power will be entitled to release it if the instrument creating the power gives him the authority to do so. The principle stated by Harman LJ in *Muir v IRC*[177] where he commented on the judgment of Buckley J in *Re Wills' Trusts Deeds*:[178]

'I would agree that, if a power is conferred on trustees virtute officii, that is to say, if it be a [fiduciary] power which the trustees have the duty to exercise, they cannot release it in the absence of words in the trust deed authorising them to do so . . .'[179]

On the facts he found that the trust instrument did authorise a release.[180]

---

[170] (1859) 26 Beav 482.    [171] Conveyancing Act 1881, s 52.
[172] See *Weller v Kerr* (1866) LR 1 Sc & Div 11; *Re Eyre* (1883) 49 LT 259; *Saul v Pattinson* (1886) 55 LJ Ch 831.
[173] [1930] 1 Ch 654.    [174] [1964] Ch 219.    [175] [1987] 1 WLR 495.
[176] [1991] 2 All ER 513.    [177] [1966] 1 WLR 1269.    [178] [1964] Ch 219.
[179] [1966] 1 WLR 1269 at 1283.    [180] See also *Blausten v IRC* [1972] Ch 256, CA.

## (d) Discretionary trusts

Due to the evolutionary development of concepts and terminology, some early cases referring to 'trust powers'[181] would today be recognised as 'discretionary trusts'. Clearly, these cannot be released because the obligation is in the nature of a trust, and the court will compel its exercise.

## (3) Means of release

It seems clear that a purely oral release will be ineffective to release a power.[182] However, it a donee ot a power ot appointment possesses the jurisdiction to release the power, he may do so by deed, as provided in s 155 of the Law of Property Act 1925. Alternatively, a power may be released by the donee entering into a contract not to exercise the power, as also provided in s 155. It seems that a power will also be released where there has been any dealing with the property subject to it which is inconsistent with the exercise of the power. In *Foakes v Jackson*[183] a power was held jointly by a husband and wife, and the survivor had a separate power. A deed was executed in 1886 by the husband, wife and those beneficially entitled to the property assigning it to one of the objects. In 1899, after the wife's death, the husband purported to appoint the property to a different object. Farwell J held that the deed which, with the intention of the donees and the parties entitled in default, had the effect of passing the property absolutely to the object operated as a release of the power. Similarly, in *Re Courtauld's Settlement*[184] Plowman J held that where there had been an application to vary a settlement so that a power was extinguished, there was no need to execute a separate deed of release. Trustees may surrender their trusts and powers by paying the trust property into court, as provided in s 63 of the Trustee Act 1925.

## (4) Release and fraud on a power

The equitable doctrine that will invalidate the fraudulent exercise of a power examined above[185] has no application to the release of a power of appointment, and therefore a donee may release a power even though he thereby derives a personal benefit. In *Re Somes*[186] a father held a power of appointment over property held on his marriage settlement. In default, his daughter was absolutely entitled. He was suffering financial difficulties and therefore released the power and he and his daughter then mortgaged their interests in the fund for £10,000, which was paid to the father. Chitty J held that this was a perfectly valid release:

'. . . it appears to me that there is a fallacy in applying to a release of a power of this kind the doctrines applicable to the fraudulent exercise of such a power. There is no duty imposed on the donee of a limited power to make an appointment; there is no fiduciary relationship

---

[181] See Chapter 16.

[182] See *Re Christie-Miller's Settlement Trusts* [1961] 1 All ER 855n; *Re Courtauld's Settlement* [1965] 2 All ER 544n.

[183] [1900] 1 Ch 807.    [184] [1965] 2 All ER 544n.    [185] See p 000.    [186] [1896] 1 Ch 250.

between him and the objects of the power beyond this, that if he does exercise the power of appointment, he must exercise it honestly for the benefit of an object or the objects of the power, and not corruptly for his own personal benefit; but I cannot see any ground for applying that doctrine to the case of a release of a power; the donee of the power may, or he may not, be acting in his own interest, but he is at liberty, in my opinion, to say that he will never make any appointment under the power, and to execute a release of it.'

Obviously, this will only apply if the power is of a type which may be released.

# 16

# Discretionary trusts

## 1 Introduction

### (1) The nature of discretionary trusts

#### (a) The definition of discretionary trusts

Discretionary trusts were defined by Warner J in *Mettoy Pension Trustees Ltd v Evans* as:

'. . . cases where someone, usually but not necessarily the trustee,[1] is under a duty to select from among a class of beneficiaries those who are to receive, and the proportions in which they are to receive, income or capital of the trust property.'[2]

They are mechanisms by which an owner of property can grant to others the power to allocate a fund amongst a defined group of individuals. As in a power of appointment, the allocator has complete discretion how the fund should be allocated, either or both in terms of the persons who should receive shares of the fund, and the size of the shares they should receive. However, unlike powers of appointment, the allocator is under a mandatory duty to make allocations in accordance with the terms of the trust. The court will intervene to ensure that this duty is discharged.

#### (b) The flexibility of discretionary trusts

The discretionary trust is therefore an extremely flexible mechanism for the distribution of property. It combines all the advantages of the power of appointment in permitting the owner of property not merely to delegate the task of transferring his property to others, but also of delegating the responsibility for deciding how that property should be distributed. Yet it avoids the potential pitfalls of the mere power because the trustees are under a duty to distribute according to the terms of the trust, which is enforceable by the court. This inherent flexibility, coupled with the security of enforcement by the court, has made the discretionary trust ideal as a means of allocating large funds amongst large potential classes of beneficiaries. For example, in the leading case of *McPhail v Doulton*,[3] Bertram Baden established a trust in 1941 to provide benefits for the staff of Matthew Hall & Co Ltd and their relatives and dependants. Clause 9(a) of the deed stated that:

'The trustees shall apply the net income of the fund in making at their absolute dis-

---

[1] This exception is probably intended to recognise the possibility of there being separate management and custodian trustees.     [2] [1991] 2 All ER 513.     [3] [1971] AC 424.

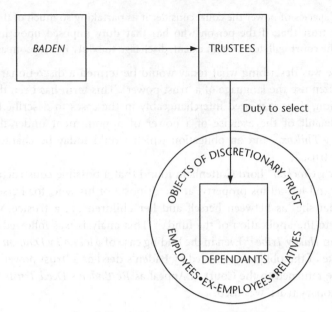

**An example of discretionary trusts:** *McPhail v Doulton*

cretion grants to or for the benefit of any of the officers and employees or ex-officers and ex-employees of the company or to any relative or dependants of any such person in such amounts . . . as they think fit.'

In 1941 the company employed some 1,300 people. By 1962 the fund contained assets valued at £163,000, which had risen to £463,000 in 1972. Clearly, it was never the intention of Mr Baden that each and every member of the specified class should receive payments from the fund, but that those appointed trustees should have the discretion to select some to benefit. Equally, it was not his intention that the trustees be able to sit idly by and fail to make any allocations at all. The language of the deed clearly indicated an obligation, or duty, to distribute the income of the fund. The House of Lords held that a discretionary trust had been created. Although the trustees had complete discretion which particular members of the class specified were to receive shares of the income produced by the fund, they had no freedom to refuse to carry out the trust.

## (2) The development of the discretionary trust[4]

Although the terminology of the 'discretionary trust' is a more recent development, the underlying concept of an equitable obligation which is discretionary in part whilst remaining predominantly mandatory is well established and has a strong historical pedigree. In *Brown v Higgs*[5] Lord Eldon, the Lord Chancellor, held that equitable obligations could not simply be categorised as trusts or powers:

'But there are not only a mere trust and a mere power, but there is also known to this court a power which the party to whom it is given is entrusted and required to execute; and with

---

[4] See also Chapter 4.      [5] (1800) 5 Ves 495.

regard to that species of power the court consider it as partaking so much of the nature and qualities of a trust that, if the person who has that duty imposed upon him does not discharge it, the court will, to a certain extent, discharge the duty in his room and place.'[6]

In essence, he was describing what today would be termed a discretionary trust. The older cases often use the language of a 'trust power'. This term has been the source of some confusion, since it is used interchangeably in the cases to describe both a trust implied in default of the exercise of a power of appointment under the principle of *Burrough v Philcox*,[7] and an obligation which would today be characterised as a discretionary trust.[8]

In *Crockett v Crockett*[9] Lord Cottenham found that a possible construction of a will where a husband left all his property 'at the disposal of his wife, for herself and children', was that she 'as between herself and her children ... a trustee, with a large discretion as to the application of the fund'.[10] This analysis was followed by Sir John Romilly MR in *Hart v Tribe*.[11] Even in the leading case of *McPhail v Doulton*[12] the House of Lords spoke of the obligation created by Baden's deed as a 'trust power',[13] although when the case returned to the Court of Appeal as *Re Baden's Deed Trusts (No 2)*[14] the term 'discretionary trust' was used.

## (3) Types of discretionary trusts

There are two types of discretionary trust, 'exhaustive' and 'non-exhaustive'.

### (a) Exhaustive discretionary trusts

In an exhaustive discretionary trust the trustees are subject to a duty to distribute the whole of the trust fund, or its income, to the potential beneficiaries. They have no power to decide not to distribute part of the fund. An example of an exhaustive discretionary trust is found in *Re Lockers Settlement Trusts*,[15] where a discretionary trust was established in favour of a class of individuals, charities and other institutions. The trustees were regarded as being in breach of trust when they failed to distribute the trust income within a reasonable period of time.[16]

An exhaustive discretionary trust will arise whenever the trustees are not given an express power to retain all or part of the income from the fund, as in *Re Gourju's Will Trusts*.[17]

### (b) Non-exhaustive discretionary trusts

In a non-exhaustive discretionary trust the trustees are not obliged to distribute the whole of the trust fund income amongst the class of beneficiaries but may, in their discretion, decide to accumulate it. This is only possible if the trustees are expressly given the power to retain and accumulate the income, or part of the income, from the

---

[6] (1800) 5 Ves 495 at 570.    [7] (1840) 5 My & Cr 72.
[8] See Pettitt, *Equity and the Law of Trusts* (9th edn, 2001), pp 31–33.    [9] (1848) 2 Ph 553.
[10] (1848) 2 Ph 553 at 561.    [11] (1854) 18 Beav 215.    [12] [1971] AC 424.
[13] Lord Wilberforce did on one occasion refer to 'discretionary trusts': see [1971] AC 424 at 452.
[14] [1973] Ch 9.    [15] [1977] 1 WLR 1323.    [16] [1977] 1 WLR 1323 at 1325.
[17] [1943] Ch 24.

trust fund by the terms of the trust. *McPhail v Doulton*[18] is an example of a non-exhaustive discretionary trust. The trust deed did not require the trustees to distribute all the income generated by the fund to the employees, ex-employees, relatives and dependants, but granted them the power to retain and accumulate it.[19] In many ways a non-exhaustive discretionary trust is extremely similar in practice to a fiduciary power. In neither case is the allocator of the fund obliged to distribute the fund or its income to the class of potential objects or beneficiaries. This leads to the question whether there is any real distinction between them.[20] Analytically, a distinction can be drawn on the basis of the nature of the duties owed by the allocator in each case. Under a non-exhaustive discretionary trust the prime duty of the trustee is to distribute the fund income amongst the class of beneficiaries, although there is a power to retain and accumulate.[21] Whether the trustee has exercised that power properly is open to the supervision of the court under an objective test, that he must have acted in the best interests of the class of beneficiaries. In the case of a power of appointment, the donee of the power has no prime duty, as it is purely within his discretion whether he allocates the property subject to the power. He owes no objective duties that the court can supervise, but purely a subjective duty to act as he thinks best. Provided he acts genuinely, the court cannot question his decision.[22] Although this is a fine distinction, it demonstrates that the non-exhaustive discretionary trust remains in essence a trust, although it is extremely close on the scale of equitable obligations to the fiduciary power.[23] A further distinction is that, under a discretionary trust, the legal title to the trust fund will normally be vested in the trustees, who will thus also be required to invest and manage the trust property. In contrast, a fiduciary power may be held by a person with no rights of ownership to the fund. Thus, in *Mettoy Pension Trustees Ltd v Evans*[24] a power of appointment over a pension fund surplus was held in a fiduciary capacity by a company which was not simultaneously the trustee thereof. However, in the majority of cases a fiduciary power will be held by a trustee since the donee's status as a trustee invests the power with fiduciary characteristics.

## 2 Essential validity of discretionary trusts

A discretionary trust will only be validly created if it satisfies the requirements for the validity of trusts in general. It must have certainty of subject matter and objects, and it must comply with the beneficiary principle. The trust must not exist for a period exceeding the duration of the perpetuity period.[25] Some aspects of these general

---

[18] [1971] AC 424.

[19] Clause 9(b) of deed creating the Matthew Hall Staff trust fund stated: 'The trustees shall not be bound to exhaust the income of any year or other period in making grants . . .' and granted them a power to invest the undistributed surplus under clause 6(a).

[20] See [1970] ASCL 187 (Davies); (1974) 37 MLR 643 (Grbich); (1976) 54 CBR 229 (Cullity).

[21] Compare eg a trust for sale of land, where the trustees are under a duty to sell but have a power to postpone sale. See Chapter 3.

[22] See Chapter 15.     [23] See Chapter 4.

[24] [1991] 2 All ER 513: see (1991) Conv 364 (Martin), (1991) 107 LQR 214 (Gardner).

[25] *Re Coleman* [1936] Ch 528.

requirements warrant detailed attention in the context of discretionary trusts, and there are also some additional requirements which are specific to such trusts, especially that they must not be 'administratively unworkable'.

## (1) Certainty of objects

### (a) The test for certainty prior to *McPhail v Doulton*[26]

When the trust fund is subject to a fixed trust, the trustees hold the fund on trust for the beneficiaries in the shares and proportions determined by the settlor who created the fund. They have no discretion as to how the fund should be allocated. Where the beneficiaries are defined as a class, a fixed trust will be void for uncertainty unless it is possible to draw up a 'complete list' of each and every person who is a member of the specified class. This is because the trustee (or the court in the event of his default) must know the full extent of the class before he is able to determine the individual shares of each beneficiary and carry out the trust. Prior to the leading case of *McPhail v Doulton*,[27] this test was also applied to discretionary trusts. Thus, in *IRC v Broadway Cottages Trust*[28] the Court of Appeal held that a discretionary trust in favour of a class of beneficiaries which could not be completely ascertained at any one moment was void for uncertainty. There were two essential rationales for the application of the 'complete list' test to discretionary trusts:

*(i) The court must be able to exercise the trust.* In *Morice v Bishop of Durham*.[29] Lord Eldon stated that a trust is only valid if the court is able to execute it in the event of a failure by the trustee to carry out their obligation so to do, whether through death, neglect or refusal. The 'complete list test' was applied to discretionary trusts because it was thought that the only method the court could employ to carry out the trust in the event of the trustee's default was to order equal division of the fund between all the potential beneficiaries. Obviously, such equal division would require a complete list of the beneficiaries. However, some early cases had adopted a more flexible approach, holding that the court could exercise its discretion in the event of the trustee's failure. In *Mosely v Mosely*[30] an estate was held on trust by two trustees for such of the testator's relatives as they should think fit. When the trustees failed to exercise their discretion to allocate the property, the court ordered that it be conveyed into court, rather than divided equally amongst the class of potential beneficiaries.[31] In *Warburton v Warburton*[32] trustees held a fund on discretionary trust for the testator's children. The House of Lords ordered that the eldest child be given a double share. In *Hart v Tribe*[33] a testator's wife held £4,000 on discretionary trust for herself and his children. She refused to award any of the income from the fund for the education and maintenance of his son by another marriage. Sir John Romilly MR directed that the boy receive £30 a year from the fund. Although explicable as a case where the trustees' discretion had not

---

[26] [1971] AC 424.    [27] [1971] AC 424.
[28] [1955] Ch 20.    [29] (1805) 10 Ves 522 at 539–540.    [30] (1673) Cas temp Finch 53.
[31] See also *Clarke v Turner* (1694) Freem Ch 198.
[32] (1702) 4 Bro Parl Cas 1.    [33] (1854) 19 Beav 149.

been exercised bona fides, this decision does seem to amount to an exercise of the discretion by the court. In earlier proceedings[34] the Master of the Rolls had indicated that, although the normal means by which the court can execute the trust is equal division between the beneficiaries, this is only one method, and that the court can compel the trustees to exercise their discretion.[35] However, the orthodox position was reiterated in *Gray v Gray*,[36] where Thomas Smith MR held that the only way the court could exercise a discretionary trust where the trustee had failed to do so was by ordering equal division between all the members of the class, and a similar view was taken by Sir Richard Arden in *Kemp v Kemp*.[37] The cases which adopted a more flexible approach were condemned as anomalous by the Court of Appeal in *IRC v Broadway Cottages Trust*.[38] Jenkins LJ asserted the principle that 'a trust for such members of a given class of objects as the trustees shall select is void for uncertainty, unless the whole range of objects eligible for selection is ascertained or capable of ascertainment'.[39] The court rejected the view that it could execute the trust in any way other than by the equal division of the fund amongst all the potential beneficiaries:

'. . . it might be assumed that the trustees for some reason or other might fail or refuse to make any distribution, and see whether the court could execute the trust in that event. Consideration of the case on that assumption shows that the most the court could do would be to remove the inert or recalcitrant trustees and appoint others in their place. That, however, would not be execution of the trust by the court, but a mere substitution for one set of trustees invested with an uncontrollable discretion of another set of trustees similarly invested, who might be equally inert or recalcitrant.'[40]

*(ii) The trustee must be able to exercise his discretion.* In the case of a discretionary trust the trustee is subject to an obligation to exercise his discretion to distribute the fund amongst the class of potential beneficiaries.[41] An underlying assumption of the cases prior to *McPhail v Doulton*[42] was that the trustee would not be able properly to exercise his discretion without drawing up a complete list of the class before making decisions as to how he should allocate the fund. Unlike the donee of a mere power of appointment, who owes no fiduciary duty to the objects, the trustee of a discretionary trust owes the class of beneficiaries fiduciary duties and for this reason would be expected to consider them individually before exercising his discretion. This would require a complete list.

## (b) Criticism of the 'complete list' test

The 'complete list' test applied to discretionary trusts in *IRC v Broadway Cottages Trust*[43] was open to two major criticisms. First, it failed to take account of the developing social function of discretionary trusts. Whilst it might have been appropriate for 'family'-style

---

[34] *Hart v Tribe* (1854) 18 Beav 215.     [35] See also *Richardson v Chapman* (1760) 7 Bro Parl Cas 318.
[36] (1862) 13 I Ch R 404.     [37] (1801) 5 Ves Jr 849.     [38] [1955] Ch 20.
[39] [1955] Ch 20 at 36.     [40] [1955] Ch 20 at 31.
[41] Although in the case of a non-exhaustive discretionary trust he has the power to accumulate rather than distribute.
[42] [1971] AC 424.     [43] [1955] Ch 20, CA.

discretionary trusts where there was a small class of potential beneficiaries, so that in the event of default by the trustee equal division would be a sensible and fair solution, it was entirely inappropriate for discretionary trusts designed to allocate benefits from a fund amongst a large class of potential beneficiaries. The 'complete list' test was simply unworkable for trusts such as that established in *McPhail v Doulton*,[44] since it would never be possible to draw up a list of every single individual who fell within the class of employees, ex-employees and relatives and dependants. The continued application of the 'complete list test' would stagnate the developing social function of the discretionary trust as a means of allocating property. Secondly, it placed too much emphasis on the distinction between trusts and powers of appointment. An inevitable consequence of the adoption of the complete list test for discretionary trusts was that it became essential to tell if a particular obligation was a trust or a power. If it were characterised as a power, then it would probably be valid, as the test of certainty in *Re Gulbenkian's Settlement Trusts*[45] would apply. If it were characterised as a trust, then the much more demanding complete list test would render it void. This placed an undue significance to the question of characterisation especially since the obligations are in essence very similar to each other. This problem is well illustrated by the history of the litigation in *McPhail v Doulton*.[46] Goff J, at first instance, and the majority of the Court of Appeal, held that a valid power had been created. This was despite the fact that the language creating the obligation was clearly of a mandatory character, and therefore the House of Lords unanimously held that it was a discretionary trust. The factor which had influenced the decisions of the lower courts was the problem that, as a result of the *Broadway Cottages*[47] test, to characterise the obligation as a trust would be to render it completely void for uncertainty, as indeed the minority of Lord Hodson and Lord Guest held. It was clearly unsatisfactory that the question of the validity of an obligation should depend upon the fine distinction the between powers and discretionary trusts. As Lord Wilberforce observed:

'It is striking how narrow and in a sense artificial is the distinction, in cases such as the present, between trusts or as the particular type of trust is called, trust powers, and powers . . . It is only necessary to read the learned judgment in the Court of Appeal to see that what to one mind may appear as a power of distribution coupled with a trust to dispose of the undistributed surplus, by accumulation or otherwise, may to another appear as a trust for distribution coupled with a power to withhold a portion and accumulate or otherwise dispose of it. A layman and, I suspect, also a logician would find it hard to understand what the difference is.'[48]

Given this artificiality, the majority of the House of Lords radically altered the test of certainty applicable to discretionary trusts.

### (c) *McPhail v Doulton*[49]

The effect of the decision of the majority of the House of Lords in *McPhail v Doulton*[50] was briefly summarised by Lord Wilberforce:

---

[44] [1971] AC 424.  [45] [1970] AC 508.  [46] [1971] AC 424.  [47] [1955] Ch 20.
[48] *McPhail v Doulton* [1971] AC 424 at 448.  [49] [1971] AC 424.  [50] [1971] AC 424.

'. . . the rule recently fastened upon the courts by *IRC v Broadway Cottages Trust* ought to be discarded and the test for the validity of [discretionary trusts][51] ought to be similar to that accepted by this House in *Re Gulbenkian's Settlement* for powers, namely, that the trust is valid if it can be said with certainty that any given individual is or is not a member of the class.'[52]

Thus, it is no longer necessary that it be possible to draw up a 'complete list' of potential beneficiaries. To reach this conclusion Lord Wilberforce, with whom Lord Reid and Viscount Dilhorne concurred, had to overcome the perceived obstacles which had led to the adoption of the 'complete list test'.

*(i) Equal division was inappropriate if the trustee defaulted in his duty*. The rationale for the adoption of the 'complete list' test was that the court could only intervene to enforce the trust by 'equal division' of the fund between the class of potential beneficiaries. While conceding the applicability of equal division to 'family trusts', Lord Wilberforce demonstrated how it was wholly inappropriate to large scale discretionary trusts of the type in issue:

'As a matter of reason to hold that a principle of equal division applies to trusts such as the present is certainly paradoxical. Equal division is surely the last thing the settlor ever intended: equal division among all may, probably would, produce a result beneficial to none . . .'[53]

This represents a recognition that the social function of discretionary trusts had evolved to enable property owners to 'confer benefits on deserving cases amongst large constituencies—in the same sort of way as charitable trusts'.[54] Clearly, there was never any intention by Bertram Baden that every single employee, ex-employee, relative and dependant should benefit from the fund he had established in their favour, but that the nominated trustees should choose some from that class to receive substantial benefits. The settlor's purpose in creating the fund would be completely defeated if, in the event of the trustees' default, each and every member of the class were to receive an insignificant payment which was far outweighed by the administrative costs of determining the full extent of the class.

*(ii) The Court could enforce the trust other than by ordering equal division*. Although 'equal division' might be inappropriate, cases such as *Gray v Gray*[55] and *Kemp v Kemp*[56] suggested that the courts had no alternative. In *McPhail v Doulton*[57] Lord Wilberforce noted the early cases where the courts had taken a more flexible approach,[58] and concluded that:

'. . . the court, if called upon to execute the [discretionary trust],[59] will do so in the manner best calculated to give effect to the settlor's or testator's intentions . . .'

---

[51] Lord Wilberforce actually used the term 'trust powers'.     [52] [1971] AC 424 at 456.

[53] [1971] AC 424 at 451.

[54] Gardner, *An Introduction to the Law of Trusts* (2nd edn 2003), pp 199–200.

[55] (1862) 13 I Ch R 404.     [56] (1795) 5 Ves 849.     [57] [1971] AC 424 at 457.

[58] [1971] AC 424 at 451. See also *Moseley v Moseley* (1673) Cas temp Finch 53; *Clarke v Turner* (1694) Freem Ch 198; *Warburton v Warburton* (1702) 4 Bro Parl Cas 1; *Richardson v Chapman* (1760) 7 Bro Parl Cas 318, HL.

[59] Lord Wilberforce used the term 'trust powers'.

He suggested three alternative means by which the court is able to ensure that the trust is enforced:

'It may do so by appointing new trustees, or by authorising or directing representative persons to the classes of beneficiaries to prepare a scheme of distribution, or even, should the proper basis for distribution appear by itself directing the trustees so to distribute.'

*(iii) The trustee does not need a 'complete list' of the potential beneficiaries to exercise his discretion.* The suggestion that the trustee must have a complete list of all the potential beneficiaries of the discretionary trust before he can exercise his discretion in favour of any particular beneficiary was also rejected by Lord Wilberforce.

'. . . a trustee with a duty to distribute, particularly among a potentially very large class, would surely never require the preparation of a complete list of names, which anyhow would tell him little that he needs to know.'[60]

Instead, the trustee has a duty of 'inquiry or ascertainment' so 'in each case the trustees ought to make such a survey of the range of objects or possible beneficiaries as will enable them to carry out their fiduciary duty'.[61]

### (d) Application of *McPhail v Doulton*

The House of Lords in *McPhail v Doulton*[62] settled the theoretical question: namely, which test for certainty of objects should govern discretionary trusts? The case was remitted to the Chancery Division for consideration as to whether the terms of the Baden trust met the new requirements, and the case reached the Court of Appeal under the name *Re Baden's Deed Trust (No 2)*.[63] The central question was whether the application of the 'is or is not' test adopted by the House of Lords from *Re Gulbenkian's Settlement Trusts*[64] requires positive proof of the negative limb, so that it can be categorically stated that any individual in the world 'is not' a member of the given class. Counsel[65] for Baden's personal representatives, who claimed the trust was void for uncertainty, argued that as 'relative' in its widest sense means 'descended from a common ancestor' it is impossible to prove that any given individual is not a 'relative'. Therefore, the trust should fail, since it is impossible to say with certainty of any given individual that 'he is not' a member of the class.

The majority of the Court of Appeal took the view that this was not the intended effect of the *Gulbenkian* test, and that it is not necessary to be able to prove that any given individual is not within the class. Sachs and Megaw LLJ distinguished 'conceptual' and 'evidential' certainty,[66] and said that the test is satisfied provided the class is conceptually certain. As Sachs LJ observed:

'. . . "the court is never defeated by evidential uncertainty", and it is in my judgment clear that it is conceptual certainty to which reference was made when the "is or is not a member of the class" test was enunciated . . . The suggestion that such trusts could be invalid because it might be impossible to prove of a given individual that he was not in the relevant class is wholly fallacious . . .'[67]

---

[60] [1971] AC 424 at 449.    [61] [1971] AC 424 at 457.    [62] [1971] AC 424.
[63] [1973] Ch 9.    [64] [1970] AC 508.    [65] John Vinelott QC and Rupert Evans.
[66] See above, p 374.    [67] [1973] Ch 9 at 20.

Both Sachs and Megaw LLJ took the view that since the words 'relatives' and 'dependants' were conceptually certain in their widest possible meanings, the trust was valid and not void for uncertainty. However, they took slightly differing approaches to the problem of 'evidential certainty'.[68] Sachs LJ took the view that if a class was 'conceptually certain' then there was in essence no evidential difficulty because of the operation of a presumption that anyone not positively proved to be within the class is outside of it. The burden falls on potential claimants to prove they fall within the class. Megaw LJ did not employ such a simple evidential presumption, but considered that there were three groups of persons: ie those positively proved within the class; those positively proved to be outside the class; and those about whom, if they were to be considered, it would have to be said they are not proven to be inside or outside the class. He concluded that the trust would be valid provided 'as regards a substantial number of objects, it can be said with certainty that they fall within the test'.[69] Stamp LJ took a differing view to that of the other members of the Court of Appeal. He accepted the argument that it must be possible to say of any individual that 'he is not a member of the class' and on that basis alone would have found the trust void for uncertainty.[70] However, he followed *Harding v Glyn*,[71] a previous authority where 'relations' had been treated by the court as meaning next of kin. He applied this to the Baden trust and concluded that 'relations' meant 'next of kin', which was sufficiently certain.[72]

To summarise, the effect of the decision of the Court of Appeal in *Re Baden's Deed Trusts (No 2)*[73] is that the application of the 'is or is not' test merely requires that the class of potential beneficiaries is conceptually certain. If the class is not conceptually certain then the trust will be void, but it will not be rendered void merely by evidential uncertainty.[74]

## (2) Administrative unworkability

### (a) Definition

Even though a discretionary trust has sufficiently certain objects, it may still be void if it is 'administratively unworkable'. This concept was first proposed by Lord Wilberforce in *McPhail v Doulton*, where he suggested there may be classes where:

'. . . the meaning of the words used is clear but the definition of the beneficiaries is so wide as to not form "anything like a class" so that the trust is administratively unworkable . . .'[75]

He hesitated to give any example, but suggested that a discretionary trust in favour of 'all the residents of Greater London' would fall within the category of administratively unworkable trusts. The principle has been criticised because it is not clear precisely what evil it is seeking to prevent.[76] However, the cases suggest that the sheer size of the class is the most relevant factor. If a class is too vast in number, it is impossible for the trustees to carry out their duty to survey the range of the beneficiaries of the trust

---

[68] Criticised [1973] CLJ 36 (Hopkins); (1972) 36 Conv (NS) 351, 352.
[69] [1973] Ch 9 at 24.    [70] [1973] Ch 9 at 28.    [71] (1739) 1 Atk 469.
[72] [1973] Ch 9 at 28–29.    [73] [1973] Ch 9.    [74] See (1981) 98 LQR 551 (Emery).
[75] [1971] AC 424 at 457.    [76] See (1971) 87 LQR 31 (Harris); (1974) 38 Conv 269 (McKay).

(i)  Sachs LJ

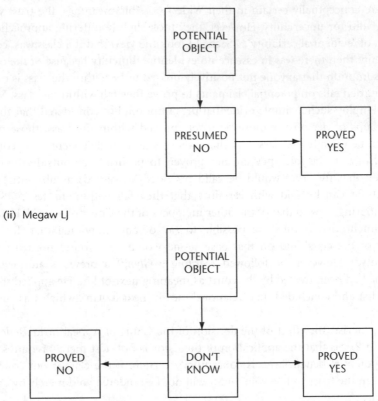

(ii)  Megaw LJ

**Dealing with evidential certainty:** *Re Baden's Deed Trusts (No 2)*

in any real sense, and in the event of their default the court would likewise be unable to carry out the distribution of the fund.

## (b) Application

In *Re Hay's Settlement Trusts*[77] Sir Robert Megarry V-C considered obiter that a discretionary trust with a class similar to that of an intermediate power, namely for all the people in the world except for an excluded class, would be administratively unworkable. In *R v District Auditor ex p West Yorkshire Metropolitan County Council*[78] the Council attempted to create a discretionary trust over a fund of £400,000 in favour of the 'inhabitants of the County of West Yorkshire'. The Council's purpose was to defeat government legislation which prevented them incurring expenditure prior to their being abolished. The Divisional Court held that, although the class was conceptually certain the range of objects, comprising some 2.5m potential beneficiaries, was so wide as to be 'incapable of forming anything like a class'. It was thus administratively unworkable and void. Drawing from Lord Wilberforce's example of 'all the residents of Greater London', and the facts of this case, it can be surmised that 'administrative

---

[77]  [1982] 1 WLR 202.      [78]  [1986] RVR 24; [1986] CLJ 391 (Harpum).

unworkability' will only render discretionary trusts void which have a class ranging in the magnitude of millions. Where the line is to be drawn between trusts falling foul of the principle and those which are valid is impossible to predict. It is easier to understand the concept of administrative unworkability in the context of a fixed trust. There, in the case of a small gift to a large class, the costs of ascertainment and distribution could easily take up the whole, or a disproportionately large part, of the fund. With a discretionary trust it must be rare that a fund would be so small that no rational scheme could be devised. However, it is possible that with a small gift to a large class it might prove impossible to devise any scheme that could have sufficient regard to the interests of the class as a whole, to which the trustees owe fiduciary duties. That would surely then be a case of administrative unworkability. Unworkability could be avoided if, despite the smallness of the gift, the settlor gave some instruction as to the principles upon which the trustees should exercise their discretion.

## (3) Capriciousness[79]

A discretionary trust will also be void if it is capricious. This principle was suggested in *Re Manisty's Settlement*[80] in the context of fiduciary powers, when Templeman J indicated that a power in favour of the 'residents of Greater London' might be capricious. The concept was developed in *Re Hay's Settlement Trusts*,[81] where Sir Robert Megarry V-C suggested that a power in favour of the 'residents of Greater London' would not be void for capriciousness if the donor of the power were, for example, a former mayor of the Greater London Council. It seems that a gift to members of a class will be capricious if there is absolutely no rational reason for making the gift to that class, and that the person charged with allocating the fund has no rational basis on which to make allocations. It is clear that capriciousness is a principle which applies to discretionary trusts and that it is a concept distinct from administrative unworkability. The discretionary trust in *R v District Auditor ex p West Yorkshire Metropolitan County Council*[82] was not regarded as capricious because the Council had every reason to create a fund in favour of its residents.

# 3 Rights of beneficiaries of discretionary trusts

## (1) A proprietary interest in the fund

In the case of a power of appointment it is clear that the objects of the power have no proprietary interest in the fund unless an appointment is made in their favour.[83] In the case of a fixed trust the beneficiaries have equitable title to the property held on trust for them, and may compel the trustees to transfer the legal title to them under the rule

---

[79] See above, p 425.    [80] [1974] Ch 17.    [81] [1982] 1 WLR 202.
[82] [1986] RVR 24.    [83] See above, p 421.

in *Saunders v Vautier*.[84] The position of the beneficiaries of a discretionary trust is not so clear cut, and has led some commentators to suggest that they have a 'quasi-proprietary' right.[85] The rights of the class as a whole are essentially different from the rights of any individual members of the class.

### (a) A proprietary right for the class as a whole

By analogy with fixed trusts, since a discretionary trust is a mandatory equitable obligation and the trustees must distribute the fund amongst the beneficiaries, it would seem logical that the equitable title to the property is vested in the class of potential beneficiaries as a whole. This approach was taken in *Re Smith*,[86] where property was held by trustees on discretionary trust for Mrs Aspinall and her three children. Romer J, following the Court of Appeal decision in *Re Nelson*,[87] held that the class as a whole could have come to the trustees and demanded the transfer of the legal title. He suggested that the principle for the class of such a discretionary trust was to 'treat all the people put together just as though they formed one person, for whose benefit the trustees were directed to apply the whole of a particular fund'.[88] However, despite its credentials in logic, this proprietary interest approach was rejected by the House of Lords in *Gartside v IRC*.[89] The case concerned a non-exhaustive discretionary trust in favour of John Gartside and his wife and children. The central question was whether estate duty was payable on the trust fund, which had not yet been distributed at the date of John's death. The relevant legislation[90] would render the fund liable to estate duty if he was regarded as having an 'interest' in the fund. In these circumstances the House of Lords held that the deceased beneficiary had no 'interest' in the fund and that estate duty was not payable. To reach this conclusion it rejected any possibility of a 'group interest' in the fund. Lord Reid said that 'two or more persons cannot have a single right unless they hold it jointly or in common. But clearly objects of a discretionary trust do not have that: they each have individual rights: they are in competition with each other and what the trustees give to one is his alone'.[91] Lord Wilberforce echoed this thinking, stating that:

'No doubt in a certain sense a beneficiary under a discretionary trust has an "interest": the nature of it may, sufficiently for this purpose be spelt out by saying that he has a right to be considered as a potential recipient of benefit by the trustees and a right to have his interest protected by a court of equity. Certainly that is so, and when it is said that he has a right to have the trustees exercise their discretion "fairly" or "reasonably" or "properly" that indicates clearly enough that some objective consideration . . . must be applied by the trustees and that the right is more than a mere spes.[92] But that does not mean that he has an interest which is capable of being taxed by reference to its extent in the trust's income: it may be a right, with some degree of concreteness or solidity, one which attracts the protection of a court of equity, yet it may still lack the necessary quality of definable extent which must exist before it can be taxed.'[93]

---

[84] (1841) Cr & Ph 240.     [85] [1982] Conv 118.     [86] [1928] Ch 915.
[87] [1928] Ch 920n.     [88] [1928] Ch 920.     [89] [1968] AC 553.
[90] Finance Act 1940, s 43(1).     [91] [1968] AC 553 at 605–606.
[92] A spes is a hope.     [93] [1968] AC 553 at 618.

The case is best understood as a reaction against the prospect of the taxation of the entire balance of the fund which has not yet been allocated every time that a member of the class who is a potential beneficiary dies. This would have been the consequence of holding that the members of the class had a group 'interest' in the trust property.

Whilst the analysis adopted in *Gartside v IRC*[94] was applied to exhaustive discretionary trusts in *Re Weir's Settlement*[95] and *Sainsbury v IRC*,[96] it is arguable that the root problem lay with the drafting of the relevant taxing provisions, which would lead to a ludicrous result, rather than with the suggestion that the class of beneficiaries of a discretionary trust hold the equitable title to the property. As Lord Reid observed in *Gartside*, 'it may be that in 1894 discretionary trusts were not so common that the draughtsman of the legislation must have had them in mind'.[97] The tax has now been abolished. It is submitted that, despite the authority of the House of Lords, the equitable interest of property subject to a discretionary trust does not remain inchoate, or 'in the air', but vests in the class of potential beneficiaries as a whole.[98] There is support for this view in the approach which is taken in relation to the variation of trusts with the consent of the beneficiaries.[99] In the case of an exhaustive discretionary trust, the class would theoretically be able to demand the transfer of the legal title by the trustees. In reality, this will often be impossible, as the class may be incapable of complete ascertainment.

### (b) A proprietary right for individual beneficiaries

Although the class of beneficiaries of a discretionary trust may be regarded as having a collective proprietary entitlement to the fund, it is clear that members of the class cannot claim an individual proprietary entitlement to the fund or any part of the fund unless the trustees exercise their discretion to appoint property in their favour. As Lord Reid observed in *Gartside v IRC*:

'. . . you cannot tell what any one of the beneficiaries will receive until the trustees have exercised their discretion.'[100]

## (2) The right to be considered as a potential beneficiary

The most concrete right that the members of a class of beneficiaries of a discretionary trust possess is the right to be considered as a potential recipient from the fund by the trustees.[101] They also have the right to have the trustees exercise their discretion 'bona fides',[102] 'fairly', 'reasonably', or 'properly'.[103]

---

[94] [1968] AC 553.

[95] [1969] 1 Ch 657 at 682. Cross J stated: 'I do not think that Lord Reid was intending to suggest that the distinction [between exhaustive and non-exhaustive discretionary trusts] was relevant to his discussion of the "group theory". Even if the trust is exhaustive and there is no power to withhold income, the objects have individual competing interests, not concurrent interests in the income.'

[96] [1970] Ch 712.     [97] [1968] AC 553 at 606.

[98] In contrast, Pettit argues that the beneficial interest under a discretionary trust remains 'in suspense' until the trustees exercise their discretion: *Equity and the Law of Trusts* (9th edn, 2001), pp 73–76.

[99] See Chapter 17.

[100] *Gartside v IRC* [1968] AC 553.     [101] *Gartside v IRC* [1968] AC 553 at 606, per Lord Wilberforce.

[102] [1968] AC 533 at 606, per Lord Reid.     [103] [1968] AC 533 at 618, per Lord Wilberforce.

# 4 The duties of trustees of discretionary trusts

As was noted above, the prime obligation of the trustee of a discretionary trust is to carry out the terms of the trust and allocate the fund amongst the class of potential beneficiaries. In the case of an exhaustive discretionary trust, the trustees must allocate the whole of the fund or its income, whereas in the case of a non-exhaustive discretionary trust they have the power to retain and accumulate all or part of the fund or income.[104] The central issues concern the question how the trustees should go about their obligation to allocate in practice.

## (1) The duty to conduct a survey of the range of the objects

The trustees of a discretionary trust are subject to a duty to consider the members of the class as potential recipients of benefit from the trust fund. In the case of a trust with a fairly small class of beneficiaries it may be practicable for the trustees to consider the circumstance of each and every member of the class before deciding on any allocations of benefit. However, in the case of discretionary trusts with a large class it is impossible for the trustees to consider the circumstances of each and every member of the class of potential beneficiaries. For example, the trustees of the Baden trust could not have considered the position of each employee, ex-employee or their relatives and dependants, particularly since many within the class would remain unknown to the trustees at the moment they exercised their discretion.

The requirement that the trustees 'consider' allocations in favour of members of the class of beneficiaries has thus been developed in a way which reflects what can reasonably be expected of them in practice. The exact degree of consideration required of the trustees will depend on the type of the discretionary trust concerned, and in particular the size of the class of potential beneficiaries. The larger the class, the less onerous the duty to consider becomes. In *McPhail v Doulton*[105] Lord Wilberforce stated that trustees must 'make such a survey of the range of objects or possible beneficiaries as will enable them to carry out their fiduciary duty'. In the course of his judgment he sought to elucidate what that duty required:

'Any trustee would surely make it his duty to know what is the permissible area of selection and then consider responsibly, in individual cases, whether a contemplated beneficiary was within the power, and whether, in relation to other possible claimants, a particular grant was appropriate.'[106]

In the case of a discretionary trust with a large class of beneficiaries, the factors that will be taken into account in determining the extent of the trustees' duty to survey the range of objects include the size of the class and the size of the fund available for distribution. As Lord Wilberforce observed:

'. . . a trustee with a duty to distribute, particularly among a potentially very large class, would surely never require the preparation of a complete list of names, which anyhow would

---

[104]  See above, p 448.      [105]  [1971] AC 424 at 457.      [106]  [1971] AC 424 at 449.

tell him little that he needs to know. He would examine the field by class and category; might indeed make diligent and careful enquiries, depending on how much money he had to give away and the means at his disposal, as to the composition and needs of particular categories and of individuals within them; decide upon certain priorities or proportions, and then select individuals according to their needs or qualifications.'[107]

The test is therefore extremely flexible, and appropriate to the modern usage of discretionary trusts as a mechanism to distribute relatively small funds amongst selected members of a potentially vast class. As Sachs LJ observed in *Re Baden's Deed Trusts (No 2)*:

'The word "range" . . . has an inbuilt and obvious element of elasticity, and thus provides for an almost infinitely variable range of vision suitable to the particular trust to be considered. In modern [discretionary] trusts . . . it may be sufficient to know whether the range of potential postulants runs into respectively dozens, hundreds, thousands, tens of thousands or even hundreds of thousands . . . Assessing in a businesslike way "the size of the problem" is what the trustees are called on to do.'[108]

In practical terms, what this means is that the trustee must not make an allocation from the fund to an individual beneficiary without first assessing the appropriateness of that allocation in the light of the claims of other possible beneficiaries. It would be inappropriate for the trustees of a fund of £1m held on an exhaustive discretionary trust for a class of ten beneficiaries to allocate only to three or four individuals without first considering the claims of all the members of the class. In the case of a fund of £1m to be divided amongst a class of a hundred thousand, the trustees would not need to consider the case for each member of the class, provided they bear in mind the number of potential claimants from the class and the purposes of the fund when deciding whether to make any individual allocations.

## (2) The duty not to make allocations outside of the class of potential objects

The trustees must not allocate the trust fund to persons who do not fall within the class of beneficiaries. Any such allocations will be held void by the court because they fall outside of the terms of the trust, and the trustees will be in breach of trust. If such an allocation is made the beneficiaries may enforce remedies against the trustees[109] and the wrongful recipient of the trust property.[110]

---

[107] [1971] AC 424 at 449.
[108] [1973] Ch 9 at 20. See also *Re Hay's Settlement Trusts* [1982] 1 WLR 202 at 210, where Sir Robert Megarry V-C considered that the analogous duties of the trustee of a fiduciary power are to: '. . . consider the range of the objects of the power; and . . . consider the appropriateness of individual appointments.'
[109] See Chapter 28.      [110] See Chapters 30 and 31.

# 17

# Variation of beneficial interests[1]

## 1 Introduction

### (1) Allocation of beneficial interests under trusts

In the case of discretionary trusts the allocation of benefit in the trust fund is within the discretion of the trustee. The original owner of the property who created the trust has not specified precisely how the fund is to be allocated amongst the class of beneficiaries. In the case of a fixed trust the interests of the beneficiaries have been specified by the settlor, and the trustee's obligation is merely to carry out the trust according to its terms. However, it may well be that it is in the interests of the beneficiaries that the trust be carried out in a way which is different to that specified by the settlor. For example, circumstances may have changed since the trust was created so that what was once a tax-advantageous settlement now has disastrous tax consequences.[2] This chapter examines how the allocation of benefit under a trust can be altered from what was originally specified by the settlor.

### (2) The primacy of the settlor's intention?

It is a basic principle that a trust must be carried out according to its terms, and that any deviation from them constitutes a breach of trust. In *Re New* Romer LJ stated that:

'As a rule, the court has no jurisdiction to give, and will not give, its sanction to the performance by the trustees of acts with reference to the trust estate which are not, on the face of the instrument creating the trust, authorised by its terms.'[3]

This 'primacy to the settlor's intention' was also expressed by Farwell J in *Re Walker*,[4] where he declined 'to accept any suggestion that the court has an inherent jurisdiction to alter a man's will because it thinks it beneficial'. However, this commitment to the primacy of the settlor's intention has to be balanced against giving effect to the present wishes and interests of the beneficiaries, and it has never been a principle which has been rigidly applied. Instead, the wishes of the beneficiaries are given primacy over the

---

[1] See Harris, *Variation of Trusts* (1975).
[2] As Lord Denning MR observed in *Re Weston's Settlements* [1969] 1 Ch 223 at 245: 'Nearly every variation that has come before the court has tax avoidance as its principal object.'
[3] [1901] 2 Ch 534 at 544.     [4] [1901] 1 Ch 879 at 885.

intentions of the settlor. In the more recent case of *Goulding v James*[5] the Court of Appeal held that the beneficiaries were entitled to vary a trust in a way which entirely undermined the intentions of the settlor.

## (3) The primacy of the beneficiaries' wishes

It has long been recognised that the beneficiaries of a trust can consent to the execution of the trust in a manner other than that specified by the settlor. A trustee will not be liable for breach of trust if he acts at the request, or with the consent, of the beneficiaries.[6] If the trustees so act and in effect vary the trust by performing it inconsistently with the settlor's intentions, the court will not intervene. At its most dramatic, this enables the beneficiaries to bring the trust to an end. Under the principle of *Saunders v Vautier*[7] the beneficiaries, provided they are absolutely entitled, sui juris and of age, may call for the legal title to the trust property.[8] In *Re Smith*[9] the beneficiaries of a discretionary trust were held able to compel the trustees to transfer the legal title to them. In *Saunders v Vautier*[10] Daniel Vautier was the sole beneficiary of a trust of East India stock established by Richard Wright. The settlor directed in the terms of the trust that dividends from the stock be accumulated by the trustees until Daniel attained the age of 25. The court held that as he was solely entitled to the fund, and the accumulation was for his benefit alone, he was entitled to the fund at the age of twenty-one. In effect, primacy was given to the beneficiary's wishes rather than the settlor's expressed intentions. In *Goulding v James* Mummery LJ identified the principle embodied in the rule in *Saunders v Vautier*.

'The principle recognises the rights of beneficiaries, who are sui juris and together entitled to the trust property, to exercise their proprietary rights to overbear and defeat the intention of a testator or settlor to subject property to the continuing trusts, powers and limitations of a will or trust instrument.'[11]

## (4) Limits to consensual variation

The primacy of the beneficiaries' wishes established by *Saunders v Vautier*[12] enables them to vary the beneficial entitlements under a trusts. However, their right to do so is subject to severe practical restrictions and is often inadequate to authorise a variation of the beneficial interest. A consensual variation of trust can only take place where there is the unanimous consent of all the actual and potential beneficiaries of the trust, since if any beneficiary fails to give consent the trustees will remain open to liability for breach of trust to any who have not consented. Therefore, consensual variation will not be

---

[5] [1997] 2 All ER 239 at 247; (1997) 60 MLR 719 (Luxton). See below p 475.
[6] *Re Pauling's Settlement Trusts* [1964] Ch 303, CA. See below, Chapter 28.
[7] (1841) Cr & Ph 240.
[8] See *Re Chardon* [1928] Ch 464; *Re Smith* [1928] Ch 915; *Re Nelson* [1928] Ch 920n; *Re Beckett's Settlement* [1940] Ch 279; *Re AEG Unit Trusts (Managers) Ltd's Deed* [1957] Ch 415.
[9] [1928] Ch 915.    [10] (1841) Cr & Ph 240.    [11] [1997] 2 All ER 239 at 247.
[12] (1841) Cr & Ph 240.

possible if some of the beneficiaries are minors and unable to give consent, or alternatively unidentifiable or not yet in existence, for example if the class of beneficiaries includes children as yet unborn or the future spouses of present beneficiaries. This will often be the case if the trust creates successive interests, as in *Goulding v James*,[13] itself where the potential beneficiaries of the remainder interest behind a life-interest were the as yet unborn great-grandchildren of the testator. To overcome these limitations the law has developed various means by which the court can approve a variation of trust when the beneficiaries are not able to do so themselves.

# 2 Variation under the inherent jurisdiction of the court

In *Chapman v Chapman*[14] the House of Lords recognised that in four situations the court possesses an inherent jurisdiction to authorise a variation of the terms of a trust.[15] However, even in these situations the court has no real jurisdiction to alter the beneficial interests under the trust.

## (1) Conversion jurisdiction

The court has the power to authorise the conversion of property in which an infant has an equitable interest from personalty or realty.[16] Lord Morton emphasised that even this limited jurisdiction was exceptional in nature,[17] and its exercise would in no way affect the infant's beneficial entitlement.[18]

## (2) Emergency jurisdiction

The court has jurisdiction to authorise transactions involving the trust property which are not authorised by the trust if a 'peculiar set of circumstances arises'[19] for which no provision was made in the trust instrument. In *Re New*[20] the trust fund consisted of ordinary shares in a private limited company. A company reorganisation was proposed in which ordinary shares would be transferred for preference shares and debentures. As the trust instrument did not give the power to invest in such securities, the Court of Appeal authorised the investment acting under their inherent jurisdiction. Romer LJ emphasised that the variation must be for the 'benefit' of the beneficiaries. As in the case of the 'conversion jurisdiction', this 'emergency jurisdiction' does not give the court power to vary the interests of the beneficiaries.

---

[13] [1997] 2 All ER 239 at 247.    [14] [1954] AC 429.
[15] [1954] AC 429 at 445, per Lord Simmonds LC.
[16] See *Earl of Winchelsea v Norcloffe* (1686) 1 Vern 435; *Pierson v Shore* (1739) 1 Atk 480; *Bridges v Bridges* (1752) 12 App Cas 693n; *Inwood v Twyne* (1762) Amb 417; *Lord Ashburton v Lady Ashburton* (1801) 6 Ves 6.
[17] *Re Jackson* (1882) 21 Ch D 786; *Glover v Barlow* (1831) 21 Ch D 788n.
[18] [1954] AC 429 at 451.    [19] *Re New* [1901] 2 Ch 534 at 534, per Romer LJ.
[20] [1901] 2 Ch 534. See also *Re Tollemache* [1903] 1 Ch 955, CA.

## (3) Maintenance jurisdiction

Where the settlor directed that income from the trust fund should be accumulated for the beneficiaries, the court has the jurisdiction to authorise the advancement of the income to provide for their maintenance. Usually, although not necessarily, this will be in the case of infant beneficiaries.[21] The maintenance jurisdiction does not give the court the power to alter the beneficial interests of the beneficiaries.[22]

## (4) Compromise jurisdiction

The court also has inherent jurisdiction to approve on behalf of those who cannot consent for themselves[23] a compromise agreement between the beneficiaries where there has been a 'genuine dispute' about the extent of the rights of the beneficiaries. Prior to the decision of the House of Lords in *Chapman v Chapman*,[24] this 'compromise jurisdiction' had been given a wide meaning so that it could be used to authorise variations in the beneficial interest of the beneficiaries. For example, in *Re Downshire Settled Estates*[25] the Court of Appeal authorised a scheme restructuring the beneficial interests of a settlement for tax reasons. Evershed MR took the view that 'the word "compromise" should not be narrowly construed so as to be confined to "compromises" of disputed rights'.[26] In his dissenting opinion Denning LJ advocated a very general jurisdiction to vary:

'The jurisdiction is not confined to cases where there is a dispute about the extent of the beneficial interests, nor to cases of emergency or necessity, but extends wherever there is a bargain about the beneficial interests which is for the benefit of the infants or unborn persons.'[27]

However, in *Chapman v Chapman*[28] the House of Lords asserted that the court only has the inherent jurisdiction to approve a compromise altering beneficial interests if there is a 'genuine dispute' as to the beneficial entitlements of the beneficiaries. In essence, this means that the court does not possess any jurisdiction to 'vary' the beneficial entitlement of beneficiaries, but merely a jurisdiction to clarify them when there is a dispute about their extent. In the words of Lord Morton:

'. . . the court's jurisdiction to sanction a compromise in the true sense, when the beneficial interests are in dispute, is not a jurisdiction to alter these interests, for they are still unascertained. If, however, there is no doubt as to the beneficial interests, the court is, to my mind, exceeding its jurisdiction if it sanctions a scheme for their alteration . . .'[29]

The decision in *Chapman v Chapman*[30] thus deprived the courts of any real

---

[21] See *Revel v Watkinson* (1748) 1 Ves Sen 93; *Cavendish v Mercer* (1776) 5 Ves 195n; *Greenwell v Greenwell* (1800) 5 Ves 194; *Errat v Barlow* (1807) 14 Ves 202; *Haley v Bannister* (1820) 4 Madd 275; *Havelock v Havelock* (1881) 17 Ch D 807; *Re Collins* (1886) 32 Ch D 229.

[22] *Chapman v Chapman* [1954] AC 429 at 456, per Lord Morton.

[23] [1954] AC 429 at 457, per Lord Morton, the jurisdiction had been exercised on behalf of 'infants interested under a will or settlement and on behalf of possible after-born beneficiaries'.

[24] [1954] AC 429.     [25] [1953] Ch 218.     [26] [1953] Ch 218 at 239.

[27] [1953] Ch 218 at 274.     [28] [1954] AC 429.     [29] [1954] AC 429 at 461.

[30] [1954] AC 429.

jurisdiction to authorise variations in the beneficial interests under trusts. For example, in *Re Powell-Cotton's Resettlement*[31] an alleged dispute over an investment clause in the trust instrument was held not to be a 'genuine dispute' and the Court of Appeal refused to authorise a compromise agreement.[32] The restriction of the court's inherent jurisdiction led to the enactment of the Variation of Trusts Act 1958, which gives the court a 'very wide and, indeed, revolutionary discretion'[33] to approve variations of trusts, including the variation of beneficial interests.

# 3 Statutory powers of variation other than the Variation of Trusts Act 1958

## (1) Trustee Act 1925, s 57[34]

By this section the inherent 'emergency jurisdiction' is extended to cases where a transaction is merely 'expedient' in the opinion of the court. The section is expressly limited to matters of 'the management and administration' of the trust property, and does not enable the variation of beneficial interests under the trust.[35]

## (2) Settled Land Act 1925, s 64(1)

This section enables the court to authorise 'any transaction affecting or concerning the settled land' by the tenant for life, provided that the transaction is, in the opinion of the court, for 'the benefit of the settled land'. Although limited to settled land, this provision allows the court to authorise alterations in beneficial interests, as for example in *Re Downshire Settled Estates.*[36]

## (3) Trustee Act 1925, s 53[37]

This section extends the court's inherent 'maintenance jurisdiction' in favour of infants and gives the court power to order the application of the capital or income from the trust for the 'maintenance, education or benefit of the infant'.

---

[31] [1956] 1 WLR 23.

[32] See also *Allen v Distillers Co (Biochemicals) Ltd* [1974] QB 384; *Mason v Farbrother* [1983] 2 All ER 1078.

[33] *Re Steed's Will Trusts* [1960] Ch 407 at 420–421, per Evershed MR.

[34] See *Re Beale's Settlement Trusts* [1932] 2 Ch 15; *Re Thomas* [1930] 1 Ch 194; *Re Harvey* [1941] 3 All ER 284; *Re Power* [1947] Ch 572; *Re Cockerell's Settlement Trusts* [1956] Ch 372; *Re Shipwrecked Fishermen and Mariners' Royal Benevolent Society* [1959] Ch 220.

[35] *Re Downshire Settled Estate* [1953] Ch 218.

[36] [1953] Ch 218. See also *Hambro v Duke of Marlborough* [1994] Ch 158.

[37] See *Re Meux* [1958] Ch 154; *Re Gower's Settlement* [1934] Ch 365; *Re Bristol's Settled Estates* [1964] 3 All ER 939; *Re Lansdowne's Will Trusts* [1967] Ch 603; *Re Heyworth's Contingent Reversionary Interest* [1956] Ch 364.

## (4) Matrimonial Causes Act 1973

This Act grants the court wide powers to make orders concerning the parties to matrimonial proceedings. By s 24 this includes the powers to order the making of a settlement for the benefit of the 'other part to the marriage and of the children of the family',[38] and to vary the beneficial interests under 'any ante-nuptial or post-nuptial settlement'.[39] This power was exercised by the court in *E v E (Financial Provision)*,[40] where the court ordered that £200,000 should be paid to a wife from a post-nuptial settlement of the matrimonial home on discretionary trusts in favour of the husband, wife and children, on her divorce, thus varying the beneficial interests. It was also exercised in *Brooks v Brooks*,[41] where the House of Lords held that a husband's pension scheme constituted a 'post-nuptial' settlement, thus bringing it within the scope of s 24(1)(c) and allowing the court to vary it so that his ex-wife was entitled to receive a pension from its surplus. However, Lord Nicholls was at pains to stress that this approach did not provide a solution to the problem of splitting pension rights on divorce:

'This decision should not be seen as a solution to the overall pensions problem. Not every pensions scheme constitutes a marriage settlement. And even when a scheme does fall within the court's jurisdiction to vary a marriage settlement, it would not be right for the court to vary one scheme member's rights to the prejudice of other scheme members . . . A feature of the instant case is that there is only one scheme member and, moreover, the wife has earnings of her own from the same employer which will sustain provision of an immediate pension for her. If the court is to be able to split pension rights on divorce in the more usual case of a multi-member scheme where the wife has no earnings of her own from the same employer, or to direct the taking out of life insurance, legislation will still be needed.'[42]

## (5) Mental Health Act 1983, s 96(1)(d)

This section gives the court power to make a settlement of the patient, and to vary it if any material fact was not disclosed when the settlement was made, or if there has been any substantial change in circumstances.

# 4 The Variation of Trusts Act 1958

## (1) Introduction

The Variation of Trusts Act was passed in the aftermath of the decision of the House of Lords in *Chapman v Chapman*,[43] which severely restricted the 'compromise jurisdiction' which the courts had construed to give themselves a wide jurisdiction

---

[38] S 24(1)(a)-(b).    [39] S 24(1)(c)-(d). *C v C (Ancillary relief: Nuptial Settlement* [2005] 2 WLR 241.
[40] [1990] 2 FLR 233.    [41] [1996] AC 375; [1997] Conv 52 (Thomas).
[42] [1996] AC 375 at 396. See Pensions Act 1995; Family Law Act 1996.    [43] [1954] AC 429.

to vary trusts. The matter was referred to the Law Reform Commission, which concluded that:

'. . . the only satisfactory solution to the problem is to give the court the unlimited jurisdiction to sanction such changes which it in fact exercised in the years preceding the decision in *Chapman v Chapman*.'

The subsequently enacted Variation of Trusts Act gives the court a 'very wide . . . discretion'[44] to authorise the variation of trusts, including the adjustment of the beneficial interests thereunder.[45]

## (2) Scheme of the Variation of Trusts Act

The Variation of Trusts Act operates alongside the principle of consensual variation, by which the beneficiaries can consent to the trust being performed in a manner different to that stipulated by the settlor in the trust instrument. The court is given the power to approve 'any arrangement[46] . . . varying or revoking all or any of the trusts, or enlarging the powers of the trustees of managing or administering any of the property subject to the trusts',[47] on behalf of the categories of persons specified in s 1 who are not able to consent on their own behalf.[48] In this sense, the court acts as a 'statutory attorney'[49] for those who cannot consent for themselves, and it enjoys no power to consent on behalf of persons who are able to consent for themselves.[50] As a safeguard to ensure that the interests of those on whose behalf the court can approve a variation are not prejudiced, the arrangement approved must be for their 'benefit'. Thus the Act achieves flexibility, by allowing trusts to be varied to take account of changing circumstances, whilst preserving the right of parties who can consent on their own behalf to make their own decisions, and protecting the interests of those who cannot. The operation of the jurisdiction was most recently considered by the Court of Appeal in *Goulding v James*,[51] where Mummery LJ explained the role of the court and the relationship between the statutory jurisdiction and the rule in *Saunders v Vautier*:

'First, what varies the trust is not the court, but the agreement or consensus of the beneficiaries. Secondly, there is no real difference in principle in the rearrangement of the trusts between the case where the court is exercising its jurisdiction on behalf of the specified class under the 1958 Act and the case where the resettlement is made by virtue of the doctrine in *Saunders v Vautier* and by all the adult beneficiaries joining together. Thirdly, the court is merely contributing on behalf of infants and unborn and unascertained persons the binding

---

[44] *Re Steed's Will Trusts* [1960] Ch 407 at 420–421, per Evershed MR.

[45] The problem of whether an English court might vary a trust governed by a foreign law is examined by Harris in ther light of *Charalambous v Charalambous* [2004] EWCA Civ 1030: (2005) 121 LQR 16.

[46] In *Re Steed's Will Trusts* [1960] Ch 407 Evershed MR held that the word 'arrangement' should be given the 'widest possible sense . . . to cover any proposal . . . put forward'.

[47] S 1(1).      [48] See *Re Holt's Settlement Trusts* [1969] 1 Ch 100.

[49] *Goulding v James* [1997] 2 All ER 239 at 249, per Mummery LJ.

[50] S 1(1) specifically states that the court's power to approve is given irrespective of 'whether or not there is any other person beneficially interested who is capable of assenting thereto'. See also *IRC v Holmden* [1968] AC 685 at 701, per Lord Reid.

[51] [1997] 2 All ER 239 at 247.

assents to the arrangement which they, unlike an adult beneficiary, cannot give. The 1958 Act has thus been viewed by the courts as a statutory extension of the consent principle embodied in the rule in *Saunders v Vautier*.'[52]

Whilst the Variation of Trusts Act enables the courts to approve a proposed variation of the allocation of benefit behind a trust, it has been held that the courts do not possess the jurisdiction to approve a 'resettlement' of the trusts, so that the trust is completely reshaped. There is a line to be drawn somewhere between what amounts to a genuine variation and what is a resettlement.

## (a) A 'resettlement' rather than a 'variation'

On one side of the line falls *Re T's Settlement Trusts*.[53] A trust provided that an infant would become entitled to a quarter of the trust income on attaining her majority. The child was irresponsible and immature, and the court's consent was sought to a variation which would transfer her share of the trust fund to new trustees to be held on protective trust for life, with remainder to her issue. Wilberforce J held that he did not have jurisdiction to approve this arrangement:

'It is obviously not possible to define exactly the point at which the jurisdiction of the court under the Variation of Trusts Act stops or should not be exercised. Moreover, I have no desire to cut down the very useful jurisdiction which this act has conferred upon the court. But I am satisfied that the proposal as originally made to me falls outside it. Though presented as a "variation" it is in truth a complete new resettlement. The former trust funds were to be got in from the former trustees and held upon wholly new trusts such as might be made by an absolute owner of the funds. I do not think that the court can approve this.'[54]

## (b) A genuine variation

*Re Holts Settlement*[55] falls on the other side of the line. A trust had been created for Mrs Wilson for life, with remainder to her children who attained the age of twenty-one. A variation was proposed under which Mrs Wilson would surrender her life-interest in a half of the income in favour of the children, but also to postpone the children's entitlement to capital until each child attained the age of thirty.[56] Megarry J felt that this amounted to a genuine variation and not a resettlement:

'It is not, of course, for the court to draw the line in any particular place between what is a variation and what, on the other hand, is a completely new settlement. A line may, perhaps, one day emerge from a sufficiently ample series of reported decisions; but for the present all that is necessary for me to say is whether the particular case before me is on the right side or the wrong side of any reasonable line that could be drawn. In this case I am satisfied that the arrangement proposed falls on the side of the line which bears the device "Variation".'[57]

---

[52] [1997] 2 All ER 239 at 247.    [53] [1964] Ch 158.
[54] [1964] Ch 158 at 162.    [55] [1969] 1 Ch 100.
[56] See also *Goulding v James* [1997] 2 All ER 239, where the Court of Appeal approved a variation in which the life tenant and remainderman agreed that 90% of the trust capital should be divided between themselves, thus defeating the life interest under the trust.
[57] [1969] 1 Ch 100 at 118.

In the later case of *Re Ball's Settlement Trusts* Megarry J laid down a general test to distinguish between 'variations' and 'resettlements', namely the 'substratum test':

'If an arrangement changes the whole substratum of the trust, then it may well be that it cannot be regarded merely as varying the trust. But if an arrangement, while leaving the substratum, effectuates the purpose of the trust by other means, it may still be possible to regard that arrangement as merely varying the original trusts, even though the means employed are wholly different and even though the form is completely changed.'[58]

The restriction that the court cannot approve a resettlement is a remaining vestige of the 'primacy of the settlor's intention'.

## (3) Persons on whose behalf the court may approve an arrangement

The court may approve a variation of trust on behalf of four groups of persons identified in s 1 of the Variation of Trusts Act 1958.

### (a) Persons incapable of consenting for reasons of infancy or incapacity

By s 1(1)(a) the court can consent on behalf of:

'. . . any person having, directly or indirectly, an interest, whether vested or contingent under the trusts who by reason of infancy or other incapacity is incapable of assenting.'

### (b) Unascertained persons

By s 1(1)(b) the court may consent on behalf of:

'. . . any person (whether ascertained or not) who may become entitled, directly or indirectly, to an interest under the trusts as being at a future date or on the happening of a future event a person of any specified description or a member of any specified class of persons, so however that this paragraph shall not include any person who would be of that description, or a member of that class, as the case may be, if the said date had fallen, or the said event had happened at the date of the application to the court.'

This complicated section is designed to cover the case of beneficiaries who are unascertainable, in the sense that it is not known who they are because the circumstances that would bring them within the class have not yet occurred. Since they are unascertainable, they cannot give consent to variations which affect their position, and the court can consent on their behalf, as for example in *Re Clitheroe's Settlement Trust*,[59] where a variation of a discretionary trust was approved by the court. The trust was established by Lord Clitheroe in favour of 'the descendants of Sir Ralph Cockayne Assheton [his father] or the spouse of any of them'. Consent was given to a tax advantageous variation by the court under s 1(1)(b) on behalf of any future wife that Lord Clitheroe might have, who would thereby become a beneficiary of the trust. Two features of this section are worthy of special attention:

*(i) The court has no jurisdiction on behalf of persons who have an existing contingent interest in the trust.* The court only has jurisdiction under s 1(1)(b) to grant

---

[58] [1968] 1 WLR 899 at 905.      [59] [1959] 1 WLR 1159.

approval on behalf of persons who 'might become entitled . . . to an interest' under the trust in the future. In *Knocker v Youle*[60] it was held that this means that the court cannot consent for persons who have a current interest in the trust, no matter how remote, even though it is impracticable to seek their consent. The case concerned a trust created in 1937 in favour of the settlor's daughter, with default clauses that could cause the property to be held on trust for her cousins. As Warner J noted, these were very numerous[61] and some lived in Australia, so that it was not practical to get their approval to a proposed variation. However, he held that he did not have the jurisdiction to grant approval on their behalf because 'a person who has an actual interest directly conferred upon him or her by a settlement, albeit a remote interest, cannot properly be described as one who "may become" entitled to an interest',[62] and is therefore not within the scope of s 1(1)(b).

*(ii) Section 1(1)(b) implies a 'double contingency' test.* The second part of the definition in s 1(1)(b) adds a 'proviso'[63] that the court cannot consent on behalf of persons who would have interests in the trust if the event that would render them a beneficiary had in fact occurred at the date of the application. This means that the court only has jurisdiction to approve variation on behalf of persons who become entitled in the event of a 'double contingency'. This perceived 'proviso' was applied in *Re Suffert*.[64] A trust was established for Elaine Suffert for life, with the remainder to such of her issue as she should appoint, and in the event of default to those who would be entitled if she died intestate. She was a spinster, without issue, and had three adult cousins. She sought to vary the trust, one cousin consented and the approval of the court was sought on behalf of all unascertained persons who might become entitled under the trusts. Buckley J held that he could not grant approval on behalf of the two adult cousins because they fell within the proviso to s 1(1)(b), since if the event under which they would become entitled, namely the death of Elaine Suffert, had occurred at the date of the application, they would have been beneficiaries of the trust. Similarly, in *Re Moncrieff's Settlement Trusts*[65] a trust was established in favour of Anne Moncrieff, then for such of her issue as she appointed, and in default of appointment, to those entitled on intestacy. The court's approval to a variation was sought on behalf of her adopted son and her next of kin. Buckley J held that there was no jurisdiction to grant approval on behalf of the adopted son, as he fell within the limitation to s 1(1)(b), and would have been entitled at the date of the application if his mother had died. However, the court could consent on behalf of the other next of kin since they would only be entitled on the occurrence of a 'double-contingency', meaning both the death of the mother and the predecease of the adopted son. If the mother alone had died at the date of the application, they would still not have been entitled. *Re Suffert*[66] and *Re Moncrieff's Settlement Trusts*[67] were cited and followed by Warner J in *Knocker v Youle*.[68]

---

[60] [1986] 1 WLR 934; [1987] Conv 144 (Riddall).     [61] There were 17.
[62] [1986] 1 WLR 934 at 937.       [63] [1986] 1 WLR 934 at 937, per Warner J.
[64] [1961] Ch 1.     [65] [1962] 1 WLR 1344.      [66] [1961] Ch 1.
[67] [1962] 1 WLR 1344.      [68] [1986] 1 WLR 934.

## (c) Persons unborn

By s 1(1)(c) the court can consent on behalf of 'any person unborn'. If it is clearly the case that a person is past the age of childbearing and the chance of further beneficiaries arising is an impossible contingency, it is inappropriate to apply to the court to approve a variation under the Variation of Trusts Act. Thus, in *Re Pettifor's Will Trusts*[69] Pennycuick J refused to approve a variation on behalf of the unborn children of a woman of seventy-eight.

## (d) Persons contingently interested under protective trusts[70]

By s 1(1)(d) the court can consent on behalf of:

'. . . any person in respect of any discretionary interest of his under protective trusts where the interest of the principal beneficiary has not failed or determined.'

The important feature of this paragraph is that the court's jurisdiction is not limited to variations which are 'for the benefit' of the person on whose behalf approval is given. If a person falls within the scope of either paras (a)–(c), where the requirement of benefit applies, or para (d), where there is no need to prove benefit, the court may act under paragraph (d).[71]

## (4) The requirement of benefit

Under s 1 the court may only grant approval to a scheme of variation on behalf of a person within the categories set out in s 1(1)(a)–(c) if: 'the carrying out thereof would be for the benefit of that person.'

## (a) Recognised benefits

The courts have recognised that a variety of different types of benefit will be sufficient to allow them to authorise variations:

*(i) Financial benefit.* There is no doubt that the court will grant approval on behalf of persons who would benefit financially from a proposed variation. In *CD (A Child) v O*,[72] for example, Lloyd J approved a variation which would insert a power of advancement into a trust allowing the advancement of the whole capital of the fund to an infant beneficiary to be applied to pay school fees. However the financial benefit sought in most cases has been a reduction in tax liability. As Lord Denning MR observed in *Re Weston's Settlement*, 'nearly every variation that has come before the court has tax-avoidance for its principal object.'[73] In *Re Weston's Settlement*[74] Stamp J did seem to suggest that the court would not sanction 'illegitimate tax avoidance'. He described the proposed variation in a family trust as 'a cheap exercise in tax avoidance which I ought

---

[69] [1966] Ch 257.    [70] See p 138 for an explanation of protective trusts.

[71] *Re Turner's Will Trusts* [1968] 1 All ER 321.

[72] [2004] 3 All ER 780. This would introduce a power of advancement into the trust wider than that conferred by s 32 of the Trustee Act 1925, which gives the trustees discretion to advance up to one half of the presumptive interest of the beneficiary. See above p 415.

[73] [1969] 1 Ch 223 at 245.    [74] [1969] 1 Ch 223.

not to sanction, as distinct from a legitimate avoidance of liability to taxation'.[75] However, the Court of Appeal in *Chapman v Chapman*[76] had not objected to a variation which had as its prime object the reduction of tax liability. In principle all attempts to avoid tax, provided they are lawful, should be legitimate and a 'benefit'.

*(ii) Non-financial benefits.* The courts have also approved variations where the benefit derived is of a social or moral nature. In *Re T's Settlement Trusts*[77] Wilberforce J held that the advantage of postponing the age at which a minor who was irresponsible and immature would become entitled to an interest under the trust was 'the kind of benefit . . . which seems to be within the spirit of the Act'.[78] In *Re Holt's Settlement*[79] Megarry J granted approval to a variation which deferred the interests of the infant beneficiaries until they attained the age of thirty. He considered that 'the word "benefit" . . . is . . . plainly not confined to financial benefit, but may extend to moral or social benefit',[80] and that it would therefore be a benefit to the children not to receive an income from the trust which would make them independent of the need to work before they had become reasonably advanced in their careers and settled in life. In *Re Remnant's Settlement Trusts*[81] a family trust contained a forfeiture clause which would forfeit the interests of members of the family who became, or married, Roman Catholics. A variation removing this clause was approved by the court, which found a benefit to the children in that they would no longer be deterred from marrying a Roman Catholic if they so chose, and that the clause could be a source of future family dissension.[82] Facilitating the administration of the trust will also amount to a benefit, so in *Re Seale's Marriage Settlement*[83] Buckley J approved on behalf of an infant the transfer of a trust to a Canadian trustee where the family had moved permanently to Canada.

### (b) Conflicting benefits

The court may be faced with a situation where the proposed variation is beneficial in some ways but disadvantageous in others. For example, there may be great social or moral benefits, but financial disadvantages. In such circumstances the court will weigh the benefits to determine whether the variation is 'for the benefit' of the persons on whose behalf the court is asked to consent. In *Re Weston's Settlement*[84] the court's approval was sought on behalf of the infant beneficiaries of a marriage settlement to a variation which would transfer the trust to Jersey. Although this would produce a financial benefit of some £800,000, the Court of Appeal held that this was outweighed by the social benefits of the children remaining in England. Lord Denning MR explained how he had weighed the different benefits:

'The court should not consider merely the financial benefit to the infants or unborn children, but also their educational and social benefit. There are many things in life more worthwhile than money. One of these things is to be brought up in this our England, which

---

[75] [1969] 1 Ch 223 at 234.      [76] [1953] Ch 218.      [77] [1964] Ch 158.

[78] [1964] Ch 158 at 162. Wilberforce J held on the facts he did not have the jurisdiction to approve the proposed variation.

[79] [1969] 1 Ch 100.      [80] [1969] 1 Ch 100 at 121.      [81] [1970] Ch 560.

[82] There was also a financial benefit to the children in having their interests under the trust advanced.

[83] [1961] Ch 574.      [84] [1969] 1 Ch 223.

is still "the envy of less happier lands". I do not believe it is for the benefit of children to be uprooted from England and transported to another country simply to avoid tax.'[85]

This weighing of 'benefit' obviously involves a value judgment on the part of the court of the relative merits of the benefits and disadvantages associated with a proposed variation.

## (5) A discretion to vary

The Variation of Trusts Act provides that the court 'may if it thinks fit' approve a proposed variation. This clearly gives the court a discretion, and the court is not obliged to approve a variation even if the requisite element of benefit can be shown. In some recognised circumstances the court will not exercise its discretion to approve a variation.

### (a) Fraud on a power[86]

The court will not approve a variation which amounts to a fraud on a power. Megarry J stated the principle in *Re Wallace's Settlements*:

'If it is clear that a fraud on the power is involved, then plainly the court ought to withhold its approval. The power of the court under the Act is a discretionary power exercisable if the court "thinks fit"; and I cannot conceive that it would be fitting for an arrangement to be approved if that arrangement had been made possible by a manifest fraud on a power, or was in some way connected with such a fraud.'[87]

Difficulty arises where a life tenant holds a life interest over a fund and special power of appointment over the remainder interest. To avoid inheritance tax the life tenant has exercised the power in favour of the objects, and then sought the court's approval to bring the life interest to an end, and divide the fund between himself and the objects of the power. The danger is that the life tenant himself benefits by receiving a share of the capital of the fund, and this may be the prime motivation for exercising the power. In determining whether there has been a fraud on the power an important factor has been the extent to which the life tenant benefits by a division of the fund. If the life tenant receives a share of the fund which is greater than the actuarial value of his life interest[88] then this suggests a fraud on a power. In *Re Brook's Settlement*[89] Stamp J took a very strict approach and held that if the purpose of the exercise of a power of appointment was that the life tenant should gain a share of the fund then there was a fraud on the power even though the life tenant may gain a share of the fund lower than the market value of his life interest.[90] However, a more flexible approach was adopted by Megarry J in *Re Wallace's Settlements*,[91] where he approved a variation when there had been an exercise of a power of appointment, even though the life tenant received a share of the fund slightly greater than the actuarial value of her life interest. On the facts he held that

---

85    [1969] 1 Ch 223 at 245.      86   See Chapter 15.      87    [1968] 1 WLR 711 at 717–718.
88   The actuarial value of the life interest is the sum that would be necessary to purchase an annuity producing the same annual income.
89    [1968] 1 WLR 1661.      90   [1968] 1 WLR 1661 at 1669.      91   [1968] 1 WLR 711.

the exercise of the power had been long intended and was for the benefit of the beneficiaries, and therefore there was no fraud.

## (b) Undermining protective trusts[92]

It seems that the courts will not approve a proposed variation which would have the effect of reducing the protection enjoyed by the beneficiary of a protective trust. In *Re Steed's Will Trusts*[93] the Court of Appeal refused to approve a variation which would effectively remove the protective element from a protective trust of property left by a testator to his housekeeper. The court took the view that the protective element was part of the 'testator's scheme' and it had been his desire and intention that she enjoy that protection.[94]

## (c) Manifest benefit

It is not enough that those on whose behalf the court is asked to grant approval to a proposed variation gain a benefit from the variation. The extent of their benefit must reflect that they are bargaining from a position of strength. This requirement prevents their position being exploited. In *Re Van Gruisen's Will Trusts*[95] Ungoed Thomas J held that it would not be sufficient for the infants and unborn children on whose behalf he was asked to consent merely to receive the actuarial value of their remainder interest in the trust fund. Instead, the court must make 'a practical and business-like consideration of the arrangement including the total amounts of the advantages which the various parties obtain and their bargaining strength'. On the facts he held that the share of the infants and unborn did adequately exceed their actuarial value.

## (d) Relevance of the settlor's intentions

Where the court is requested to grant approval of a variation for persons unable to consent on their own behalf, it is not entitled to refuse a variation which would be for their benefit merely because the variation would contravene the intentions of the original settlor. In such circumstances the intentions and wishes of he original settlor are of 'little, if any, relevance or weight'[96] to the question whether approval should be given. In *Goulding v James* the testatrix left her residuary estate on trust for her daughter for life, with remainder to her grandson on his attaining the age of forty. It was further provided that if he failed to attain the age of forty the residuary estate should pass to such of his children (ie her great-grandchildren) as were living at the date of his death. She had established this trust with the express object of preventing her daughter touching the capital of her estate, because she did not trust her son-in-law. She had postponed her grandson's interest until he was forty because he was presently living with an artistic community in Nantucket and she considered him a 'free spirit' who had not yet settled down. The daughter and grandson sought to vary the trusts under the will so that they would receive a 45% share each of the residuary estate absolutely, with

---

[92] See above, p 138.    [93] [1960] Ch 407.

[94] [1960] Ch 407 at 421–422: the purpose of the protection was to prevent the housekeeper being 'sponged upon' by her brothers.

[95] [1964] 1 All ER 843n.    [96] *Goulding v James* [1997] 2 All ER 239 at 251–252, per Mummery LJ.

the remaining 10% on trusts for any great-grandchildren. As they were adults, the daughter and grandson were perfectly entitled to agree to such variation, but they sought the approval of the court on behalf of the as yet unborn great-grandchildren. Although the variation was for their benefit, because actuarial valuation showed that the current value of the contingent interest of the great-grandchildren was only 1.85% of the residuary estate, Laddie J held that the court should refuse to exercise its discretion to grant approval because the object of the arrangement was the complete opposite of what the testatrix had intended.[97] However, the Court of Appeal held that approval should have been forthcoming. Mummery LJ held that the testatrix's intentions were all but irrelevant in deciding whether the discretion should be exercised:

'In my judgment the legal position is as follows. (1) The court has a discretion whether or not to approve a proposed arrangement. (2) That discretion is fettered by only one express restriction. The proviso to s 1 prohibits the court from approving an arrangement which is not for the benefit of the classes referred to in (a), (b) or (c). The approval of this arrangement is not prevented by that proviso, since it is plainly the case that it is greatly for the benefit of the class specified in s 1(1)(c).'[98]

Ralph Gibson LJ similarly explained that the settlor's original intention was irrelevant:

'Where there is an application under the Variation of Trusts Act 1958 for approval of an arrangement agreed by the beneficiaries, capable of giving assent, it is not clear to me why evidence of the intention of the testator can be of any relevance whatever if it does no more than explain why the testator gave the interests set out in the will and the nature and degree of feeling with which such provisions were selected . . . The fact that a testator would not have approved or would have disapproved very strongly does not alter the fact that the beneficiaries are entitled in law to do it and, if it be proved, that the arrangement is for the benefit of the unborn. If, of course, it can be shown that the arrangement put forward constitutes, for example, a dishonest or inequitable or otherwise improper act on the part of one or more of the beneficiaries, then such evidence would clearly be relevant to the question whether the court would "think fit" to approve it on behalf of a minor or unborn persons. In this case, the evidence of intention of this testatrix seems to me to have been of no relevance.'[99]

The decision in *Goulding v James*[100] is at odds with the decision in *Re Steed's Will Trusts*,[101] where the court refused to vary a protective trust because, amongst other reasons, this was part of the testator's scheme. Whilst the decision in *Goulding v James* may be better founded in logic, the power of the court to approve a variation is discretionary, and it is hard to see why the testator's motives should be wholly disregarded. On the other hand, treating the court as the 'statutory attorney' for those on whose behalf it consents, its task is not to adjudicate on the merits of the scheme as a whole, but only on its impact on those for whom the court acts as a surrogate. From this point of view, why should those beneficiaries lose the benefits in kind they would receive from a variation unless those benefits are more than compensated by the non-pecuniary benefits of knowing that the testator's wishes have been respected?

---

[97] [1996] 4 All ER 854.    [98] [1997] 2 All ER 239 at 249.    [99] [1997] 2 All ER 239 at 252.
[100] [1997] 2 All ER 239 at 251–252, per Mummery LJ.    [101] [1960] Ch 407.

## (e) Widening powers of investment

The Variation of Trusts Act is not limited to the variation of beneficial interest, but may also be used to vary the powers of the trustees under the trust deed. In the past the courts held that they would not grant approval to a variation of the trustee's powers of investment which were wider than those contained in the Trustee Investment Act 1961.[102] However the courts came to recognise that the Act was outdated and approved variations granting wider investment powers.[103] The Trustee Investment Act 1961 has now been replaced by the Trustee Act 2000, which grants trustees the power to make any kind of investment. This new legislative framework is likely to free the courts from any residual unwillingness to grant variations in the trustees' power of investment. The trustees' power of investment is discussed in Chapter 22.

## (6) Effect of an order to vary

The question has arisen as to how precisely a variation of the beneficial interests under a trust take place. Does it occur by the order of the court, or as a result of the arrangement which is consented to by those who are able, and by the court on those who cannot consent for themselves. The difficulty is not merely theoretical because of the implications of s 53(1)(c) of the Law of Property Act, which requires that a disposition of a subsisting equitable interest 'must be in writing signed by the person disposing of the same'.[104] If the variation is considered a 'disposition',[105] and takes effect as a consequence of the arrangement and not the court order, is it necessary that all those who can consent for themselves do so in writing? Although there is some authority to the contrary,[106] the House of Lords has held that the variation takes effect through the arrangement and not by the order of the court. The principle was stated by Lord Reid in *IRC v Holmden*:

'Under the Variation of Trusts Act the court does not itself amend or vary the trusts of the original settlement. The beneficiaries are not bound by variations because the court has made the variation. Each beneficiary is bound because he has consented to the variation. If he was not of full age when the arrangement was made he is bound because the court was authorised to act on his behalf and did so by making an order. If he was of full age and did not in fact consent he is not affected by the order of the court and he is not bound. So the arrangement must be regarded as an arrangement made by the beneficiaries themselves. The court merely acted on behalf of or as representing those beneficiaries who were not in a position to give their own consent and approval.'[107]

Whether the consenting beneficiaries must comply with s 53(1)(c) was considered by Megarry J in *Re Holt's Settlement*,[108] where he adopted two possible solutions to avoid

---

[102] See *Re Kolb's Will Trusts* [1962] Ch 531.

[103] See *Mason v Farbrother* [1983] 2 All ER 1078; *Trustees of the British Museum v A-G* [1984] 1 WLR 418; *Steel v Wellcome Custodian Trustees Ltd* [1988] 1 WLR 167.

[104] See Chapter 6.      [105] *Grey v IRC* [1960] AC 1, HL.

[106] *Re Viscount Hambleden's Will Trusts* [1960] 1 All ER 353n, per Wynn-Parry J.

[107] [1968] AC 685 at 701; *Re Joseph's Will Trusts* [1959] 1 WLR 1019.

[108] [1969] 1 Ch 100. It is worth noting that *Re Holt's Settlement Trusts* was decided prior to the House of Lords' decision in *Re Holmden's Settlement Trusts* and that Megarry J proceeded on the basis that it was the court order which varied the trusts.

the difficulty. First, he accepted that the express granting of the power to vary trusts to the courts by Parliament in the Variation of Trusts Act has 'provided by necessary implication an exception from s 53(1)(c)'.[109] Secondly, if the arrangement is an agreement made for valuable consideration then because it is specifically enforceable the 'beneficial interests pass to the respective purchasers on the making of the agreement', by means of a constructive trust.[110] By virtue of s 53(2), writing is therefore not required.

[109] [1969] 1 Ch 100 at 115: Megarry J accepted that this was not the most natural construction and that he was 'straining a little at the wording in the interests of legislative efficiency'.
[110] [1969] 1 Ch 100 at 116, following *Oughtred v IRC* [1960] AC 206, HL.

# 18

# Charities

## 1 Introduction

### (1) The social context of charitable giving

The majority of trusts and equitable mechanisms examined so far are used by owners to allocate their property to individuals, whether by mechanisms which allocate fixed shares, or those which grant others the discretion how the property should be allocated. Owners do not always wish to dispose of their property to individuals but may also wish to give to purposes that they consider worthy, whether to their school parent-teachers' association, the local animal refuge, an appeal following a major disaster or to a political party which they support. In Chapter 12 it has already been seen that, except for some anomalous exceptions, gifts for purposes will fail by virtue of the 'beneficiary principle'.[1] The most significant exception to this is the area of charitable trusts, where the law upholds and encourages giving to purposes which are regarded in law as charitable.

The significance of charity to society is self-evident. It is a point at which many people have real, if unknowing, contact with the law of trusts, whether they are putting a small donation into collection boxes or envelopes, putting something into a collection at church, contributing regularly through payroll giving schemes or responding to major 'Band Aid'-type disaster appeals. Charity and charitable giving is a growth area. Both the number of charities and the income they receive is increasing, indicating a continued expansion of the charitable sector. The number of charities has been expanding rapidly. When the Nathan Committee reported in 1952 there were some 111,000 charitable trusts,[2] but by 1986 this had grown to 157,902 registered charities, with a suspected further 110,000 unregistered.[3] By 2005 there were 189,531 registered charities[4] (an increase of just under 1,000 since the previous year[5]), with an annual income of over £36bn, almost 600,000 paid staff and around 900,000 trustees.[6] 6279

---

[1] See above, p 378.

[2] *Report of the Committee on the Law and Practice relating to Charitable Trusts* (1952) Cmd 8710), para 103.

[3] *Home Office and HM Treasury, Efficiency Scrutiny of the Supervision of Charities* (1987), Annex E.

[4] *Report of the Charity Commission for England and Wales 2004–2005.*

[5] *Report of the Charity Commission for England and Wales 2003–2004.* The rate of net growth has been similar for two decades.

[6] *Report of the Charity Commission for England and Wales 2004–2005.*

new charities were registered during the year.[7] The sector is dominated by a small number of large charities and by a large number of small charities. The largest 500 charities account for over 46% of total charitable income[8] and approximately 7% of charities receive nearly 90% of recorded income.[9] Conversely, two-thirds of registered charities have an annual income of £10,000 or less, and account for less than 1% of recorded income.[10]

## (2) Mechanisms for charitable giving

Owners of property may decide to apply it for the furtherance of charitable purposes in a variety of ways.

### (a) Outright gifts to charitable organisations

An owner may make a gift to an organisation which enjoys charitable status, whether an unincorporated association, or a charitable corporation. Charitable corporations may be established by Royal Charter (as is the case with many of the older universities); as a company limited by guarantee; by virtue of specific legislation (as is the case with Further Education Corporations); or, following the Charities Bill 2005, as a charitable incorporated organisation registered as such by the Charity Commission.[11] The organisation will receive the property, and apply it to its charitable purposes. A gift to Cancer Research, Oxfam or to a particular educational establishment would be such a gift.

### (b) Fixed trusts in favour of charitable objects

Alternatively, an owner may transfer property to trustees to be used for specified charitable purposes. In such a case the trustees will be subject to a duty to apply the funds to those purposes only. A gift by will to trustees to be applied for the education of the testator's poor relations would be an example.

### (c) Discretionary trusts in favour of charitable objects

An owner may alternatively transfer the property to trustees granting them the discretion as to the charitable purposes to which the fund may be applied. This may be a wide discretion, for example a gift of '£100,000 to trustees to be applied to such charities as they see fit', or the owner may place limits on the width of the discretion, for example 'for such educational charities as they see fit'.

### (d) All charitable institutions are treated similarly

Whether a charity exists as an incorporated or unincorporated body, or as a trust, it is governed by essentially similar rules.

---

[7]  *Report of the Charity Commission for England and Wales 2004–2005.*
[8]  *Report of the Charity Commission for England and Wales 2004–2005.*
[9]  *Report of the Charity Commission for England and Wales 2003–2004.*
[10]  *Report of the Charity Commission for England and Wales 2003–2004.*
[11]  Charities Bill 2005, cl 34 and Sch 7.

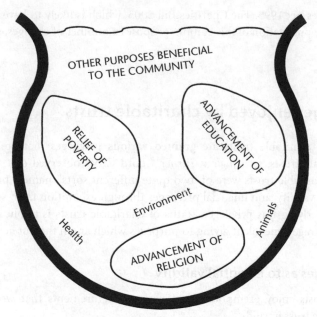

The 'common pot' of charity

## (3) The unity of charity

Although there are numerous charitable organisations, and distinct charitable purposes covering wide ranges of human activity, in some senses the law regards all property dedicated to charity as comprising a single fund, a 'common pot'. This is evident in the way that a gift 'to charity' will be upheld, despite the absence of any indication of the giver's intention as to how it should be used. In such circumstances the Crown disposes of the property to charitable purposes by sign manual. Similarly, if a charity fails, or a charitable purpose comes to an end, any property dedicated to that charity or purpose will be applied to other similar charitable purposes under the principle of cy-près. The property, once dedicated to charity, is seen as placed into the 'common pot', and cannot be removed from it, but will be applied to other purposes.

## (4) Regulation and control of charities

Given both the quantity of money concerned and the dangers of abuse and misuse,[12] the area of charities is regulated by the government. The Attorney General enforces charitable trusts in the name of the Crown, but they are regulated and overseen by the Charity Commission,[13] which plays the predominant role in the supervision and regulation of charities. This regulation and supervision will be examined in Chapter 27. The law concerning the regulation of charities has been consolidated and amended

[12] See eg the case of the Hospital Fund, where some £2.7m of the charity's funds were stolen by the chief fundraiser, reported by the Charity Commissioners in their Report for 1992, paras 91–96.

[13] Prior to the Charities Bill 2005 which constituted the Charity Commission as an incorporated body, the functions of the Commission were vested in the Charity Commissioners.

by the Charities Act 1993. The Charities Bill 2005, which is likely to have been enacted into law by the publication of this edition, proposes a number of changes, some of them significant.

## 2 Privileges enjoyed by charitable trusts

Charities and charitable trusts are granted various privileges that are not enjoyed by other private trusts. In *Dingle v Turner*[14] Lord Cross observed that the privileges enjoyed by charitable trusts were of 'two quite different sorts', namely privileges as to their essential validity, and financial privileges through exemption from some forms of taxation. Underlying this privileged status of charitable trusts is public policy, which seeks to encourage benevolent giving to purposes which are in the public interest.

### (1) Privileges as to essential validity

Charitable trusts enjoy exemption from various requirements that would render a non-charitable trust invalid.

### (a) Purpose trusts

But for a small number of anomalous exceptions, private non-charitable trusts must be for the benefit of persons and not purposes.[15] Charitable trusts are the major exception to this 'beneficiary principle', since by their very nature they are purpose trusts. However, since a mechanism for the enforcement of charitable trusts is provided by the state, the chief objection to purpose trusts (ie that there is nobody in whose favour the court can decree performance of the trust[16]) does not apply. Charitable trusts are enforced by the Charity Commission or by the Attorney General in the name of the Crown.

### (b) Certainty of objects

Whilst non-charitable trusts must have objects which are certain,[17] gifts made exclusively for charitable purposes are valid even though the exact purposes have not been identified with certainty. Thus, a gift to trustees 'for charity' will be valid. This follows from the fact that the law regards 'charity' as if it were a single common pot, and since the gift was certainly intended for that common pot, it will be upheld. If the exact charitable purposes to which the owner of the property intends to give are uncertain, the Charity Commission[18] and the court have jurisdiction to draw up a scheme to apply the funds.

### (c) Perpetuity

Charitable trusts are valid even though they may last for an indefinite period of time. They are exempt from the rule against inalienability, by which trusts requiring capital to

---

[14] [1972] AC 601.      [15] See above, p 378.

[16] *Morice v Bishop of Durham* (1804) 9 Ves 399.      [17] See above, p 373.

[18] Charities Act 1960, s 18(1). Prior to the Charities Bill 2005 which constituted the Charity Commission as an incorporated body, the functions of the Commission were vested in the Charity Commissioners.

be retained for a period longer than the perpetuity period of a life in being plus 21 years are invalid. However, with one exception, the rule against remoteness of vesting applies to gifts to charities as to other gifts. This rule requires that all property given to the trust must vest during the perpetuity period, again a life in being plus 21 years. The exception applies where there is a gift over from one charity to another charity. The gift to the second charity will be valid even though it takes place outside of the perpetuity period. The reason for this exception is that the property has been dedicated forever to charity by the gift to the first charity which vests within the perpetuity period, and it makes no difference that it is subsequently applied for a different charitable purpose. The exception was used in *Re Tyler*[19] to give effect indirectly to a non-charitable purpose. Sir James Tyler left £42,000 of stock to the London Missionary Society, with the condition that they were to maintain his family vault. If the condition was broken there was a gift over in favour of the Blue Coat School. The gift over did not render the gift void for perpetuity, even though it could conceivably have vested outside of the perpetuity period. Although the London Missionary Society could not be compelled to maintain the vault, they would have had a strong financial incentive to do so.

## (2) Financial privileges

Charities and charitable trusts enjoy tremendous financial advantages over private trusts. In 1989 the government white paper *Charities: A Framework for the Future* estimated that charities enjoyed tax exemptions in excess of £2.5bn[20] (with a similar figure being quoted in *The Times* in 2004[21]), though in 1997 the Inland Revenue suggested a figure of £1.75bn.[22] Charities are exempt from income tax on investments and corporation tax.[23] Many charities today participate in profitable trading activities, for example charity shops. These profits may be exempt from income tax.[24] Gifts to charities are exempt from inheritance tax.[25] Charities may recover the income tax paid by donors who give by covenant.[26] Charities are exempt from capital gains tax,[27] stamp duty[28] and National Insurance Surcharge.[29] There is an 80% exemption from non-domestic rates on properties they occupy.[30] Charities are not exempt from VAT. These financial privileges amount to a massive state subsidy of charitable trusts. Some charities may even enjoy exceptional financial privileges. For example, in *Scott v National Trust*[31] Robert Walker J observed that the trust, which was established by

---

[19] [1891] 3 Ch 252, CA.     [20] 1989 (Cm 694), para 1.5.

[21] *The Times* 31 May 2004 quoting a figure of £2.3bn.     [22] Treasury Press Statement, 2 July 1997.

[23] Income and Corporation Taxes Act 1988, s 505.

[24] Provided that the profits are applied solely for the purposes of the charity and that the trade is exercised in the course of carrying out a primary purpose of the charity, or is mainly carried out by beneficiaries of the charity.

[25] Inheritance Tax Act 1984, ss 23, 76.

[26] Income and Corporation Tax Act 1988, s 660(3): provided that the covenant is for four years or more.

[27] Taxation of Chargeable Gains Act 1992, s 256.     [28] Finance Act 1982, s 129.

[29] Finance Act 1977, s 57.

[30] Local Government Finance Act 1988, s 43(5); under s 47 the rating authority has discretion to relieve up to the whole amount payable.

[31] [1998] 2 All ER 705.

statute, is a charity 'whose special place in the affairs of the nation has been recognised by tax exemptions and reliefs (especially in connection with capital taxation) going well beyond those accorded to charities generally'.[32]

## (3) Assessment of the privileges enjoyed by charities

It is clear that charitable trusts enjoy tremendous advantages over non-charitable trusts through their enjoyment of these privileges. The justification for such advantageous treatment is that charitable purposes are of sufficient importance to the community at large that they deserve both to be upheld and encouraged. It is for this reason that the definition of charity focuses on the notion of 'public benefit', for only those purposes which can be said to be of benefit to the public as a whole can be considered worthy of such special treatment. However, it is questionable whether all charities and charitable trusts need be treated alike. At the moment, every charitable trust enjoys not only the privileges as to essential validity, but also the financial privileges. There is no necessary reason why every charitable trust should automatically enjoy the financial privileges, a conclusion which Lord Cross described in *Dingle v Turner*[33] as 'unfortunate'. Obviously, all must receive the privileges as to validity, otherwise many would fail under the beneficiary principle. The proposal that only some charities should enjoy financial privileges was made by the Radcliffe Commission in 1956[34] and, as many charities begin to act more like companies, operating in a commercial manner, running what are often multi-million pound trading operations, it is perhaps time that the question of universal financial privilege was re-examined. The financial privileges available to public schools such as Eton and Harrow are a particularly contentious issue, and have been the subject of extensive debate in the progress of the Charities Bill through Parliament.

It is also an open question whether the availability of financial privilege is a factor to be taken into account when the court is considering if a trust is charitable. In *Dingle v Turner*[35] Lord Cross took the view that, in considering whether a trust was for the benefit of the 'public', regard should be had to the availability of fiscal privileges. However, the other four members of the House expressed doubts as to its relevance. The issue is not resolved by the Charities Bill 2005.

# 3  Defining charitable trusts

## (1) When is a trust charitable?

For a trust to be charitable in law, it must be for a purpose which is considered in law to be prima facie charitable. The purposes considered to be charitable are all purposes

---

[32] [1998] 2 All ER 705 at 710.      [33] [1972] AC 601, HL.

[34] *Royal Commission on Taxation of Profits and Income* (1955) Cmd 9474, ch 7.

[35] [1972] AC 601, HL.

which in a general sense can be considered to be beneficial. In addition to this requirement, the particular application contained in the trust must be for the public benefit. The rationale is that even if a purpose can be considered in a general sense to be beneficial, it should only secure the privileges of charitable status if benefits are conferred upon the public rather than being confined to a small group of private individuals. Finally, if it is possible for funds to be applied in ways which are not considered to be charitable, this will prevent the whole trust from being considered to be charitable, even if parts, taken alone, could have been held charitable.

## (2) Statutory definition of 'charity'

Until the Charities Bill 2005, there had been no statutory definition of charity. Given the significance of the distinction between charitable and non-charitable trusts, this might be thought surprising. Until the enactment of the Charities Bill into law, the meaning of 'charity' as a legal concept is therefore determined by reference to judicial precedents and the decisions of the Charity Commission.

The Charities Bill 2005 for the first time contains a statutory definition of charitable purposes. This definition has made almost no change to the law, and preserves the flexibility which was a fundamental feature of the previous categorisation of charitable purposes. The definition essentially consolidates the previous law, and has the advantage of providing a greater degree of transparency about the range of purposes which are currently considered to be charitable in law. The main drawback with the definition is that, because it incorporates a reference to the previous law, it is impossible to draw a line at the date of the enactment of the Charities Bill 2005 into law: it is also necessary to have regard to most of the case law prior to its enactment.

### (a) Relevance of previous law

The Charities Bill 2005, cl 2(2) provides a list of purposes which are prima facie considered to be charitable, but then states that any purposes which do not fall within the specific categories in the list shall be recognised as charitable if they are 'recognised as charitable purposes under existing charity law'.[36] The statutory definition therefore adds to rather than replacing existing law.

### (b) List is not closed

The Charities Bill retains the dynamism of the previous concept of charitable purposes. The previous law recognised the possibility of development by analogy or because of changes in society and public attitudes. For example, in *Scottish Burial Reform and Cremation Society v Glasgow City Corpn*[37] a trust to promote cremation as a method of disposal of the dead was held charitable by the House of Lords as it was analogous to earlier cases in which it had been held that trusts for the maintenance of graveyards were charitable. Development was possible even where previous case law suggested that a purpose would not, in the past, have been considered to be charitable. For

[36] Cl2(2)(m) and cl 2(4).     [37] [1968] AC 138.

instance in *Funnell v Stewart*[38] Hazel Williamson QC held that faith healing had 'become a recognised activity of public benefit' so as to be charitable even though an earlier decision had held that a trust to promote faith healing was non-charitable.[39]

The concept of development by analogy is recognised by cl 2(4)(b) of the Charities Bill which states that charitable purposes include 'any purposes that may reasonably be regarded as analogous to, or within the spirit of, any purposes falling within' the listed categories or the provision retaining existing charitable purposes. Moreover, development by analogy upon analogy is expressly preserved. Clause 2(4)(c) permits development by analogy from development by analogy and so on ad infinitum. The extraordinary effect of the statutory definition is therefore that it retains all the elements of the previous law. The only change effected by the statutory definition is that the list of purposes which it contains can be changed only by legislation: under the previous law it was possible for a purpose which was once considered to be charitable to cease to be charitable because of changing social conditions. As Lord Wilberforce observed in *Scottish Burial Reform and Cremation Society v Glasgow City Corpn*,[40] 'the law of charity is a moving subject' which evolves over time. This was also recognised by Lord Simmonds in *National Anti-Vivisection Society v IRC*,[41] where a society which promoted the suppression of vivisection was held not to be charitable, as the court found that the advantages of reduced cruelty to animals were outweighed by the detriments to medical research that would be caused if the purpose was accomplished. He said that:

'A purpose regarded in one age as charitable may in another be regarded differently . . . I conceive that an anti-vivisection society might at different times be differently regarded.'

This flexibility to take into account changes in society and in public attitudes is unlikely to be possible for purposes which have been entrenched by legislation.

## (3) The categories of charitable purpose

Prior to the Charities Bill 2005, there were three sources from which the categories of charitable trust were drawn: a long-repealed ancient Act of Parliament which contained a descriptive list; the decisions of the courts, which were categorised into four groups by a leading 19th century judgment; and the determinations of the Charity Commissioners. These original sources can still be discerned in the list provided by the new law.

### (a) The Charitable Uses Act 1601

The Charitable Uses Act 1601[42] did not set out to define charity, but rather to correct abuses in the administration of charitable trusts. However, the preamble to the Act contained a list of the objects which the law regarded as charitable in 1601, which became the guide to which the courts referred to determine whether purposes were charitable. Although the preamble was repealed in 1960,[43] it has continued to provide guidance in defining charity until the changes made by the Charities Bill 2005.

---

[38] [1996] 1 WLR 288.    [39] *Re Hummeltenberg* [1923] 1 Ch 237.    [40] [1968] AC 138.
[41] [1948] AC 31, HL.    [42] 43 Eliz, c 4.    [43] Charities Act 1960, s 38(1).

## (b) Income Tax Special Purposes Comrs v Pemsel[44]

In this case Lord Macnaghten provided an organising classification of charitable purposes. He identified four 'heads' of charity:

'Charity in its legal sense comprises four principal divisions; trusts for the relief of poverty; trusts for the advancement of education; trusts for the advancement of religion; and trusts for other purposes beneficial to the community, not falling under any of the preceding heads.'

This classification was not an exhaustive definition of the law of charity, but a convenient grouping of the cases into areas of benefit which the law regards as charitable, with the exception of the fourth division which is obviously a 'catch-all' category. The categories themselves did not provide the answers as to whether a particular purpose was indeed charitable. In *Scottish Burial Reform and Cremation v Glasgow City Corpn* Lord Wilberforce gave three cautions about its use:

'. . . first that, since it is a classification of convenience, there may well be purposes which do not fit neatly into one or other of the headings; secondly, that the words used must not be given the force of a statute to be construed; and thirdly, that the law of charity is a moving subject which may well have evolved even since 1891.'[45]

## (c) The role of the Charity Commission in defining 'charity'

The Charity Commission plays an increasingly important role in shaping the development of the definition of charitable purposes. The Commission has the legal obligation to keep a register of institutions that are charitable. The Commission has the power to recognise a new purpose as charitable in circumstances where it believes that the courts of law would do so, and it therefore has the same powers as the court to take into account changing social and economic circumstances in determining whether an organisation is charitable or not. The Charity Commission has indicated that it will adopt a 'two-step' test to determine whether a new purpose is charitable, examining whether it is 'analogous to a purpose previously accepted as charitable' and whether it 'satisfies the requirement that the purpose benefits the public'.[46] The Commission has recognised a number of new charitable purposes (such as the promotion of urban and rural regeneration in areas of social and economic deprivation and the conservation of the environment) which have now been included in the list contained in the Charities Bill 2005. The Commission has also decided that some previously charitable purposes should lose their charitable status. For example civilian rifle and pistol clubs had historically enjoyed charitable status on the grounds that they promoted the defence of the realm by encouraging skill in shooting. However in 1993 the Commission decided that gun clubs could no longer be regarded as a reserve for the armed forces.

The role of the Commission in determining whether a purpose is charitable effectively gives it the power to make new law. For instance, using reasoning by analogy, the

---

[44] [1891] AC 531.    [45] [1968] AC 138 at 223.
[46] RR1A, *Recognising New Charitable Purposes* (2001), para 22.

Commissioners decided in 2003–2004 that the promotion of restorative justice was charitable. The Commissioners concluded that 'the promotion of restorative justice was analogous to the charitable purposes of the preservation of public order and the prevention of breaches of the peace, the protection of life and property and the promotion of the sound administration of the law, and as such was for the public benefit'.[47] The Commission has been prepared to make decisions in some potentially contentious areas. For instance, it registered religious charities which do not involve belief in a deity, before there was judicial recognition that this was possible, and even though belief in a deity had been stated as a requirement in the previous case law.[48]

## (4) The new list of charitable purposes

The Charities Bill 2005 sets out a list of charitable purposes in cl 2(2).

'(2) A purpose falls within this subsection if it falls within any of the following descriptions of purposes—

(a) the prevention or relief of poverty;

(b) the advancement of education;

(c) the advancement of religion;

(d) the advancement of health or the saving of lives;

(e) the advancement of citizenship or community development;

(f) the advancement of the arts, culture, heritage or science;

(g) the advancement of amateur sport;

(h) the advancement of human rights, conflict resolution or reconciliation or the promotion of religious or racial harmony or equality and diversity;

(i) the advancement of environmental protection or improvement;

(j) the relief of those in need by reason of youth, age, ill-health, disability, financial hardship or other disadvantage;

(k) the advancement of animal welfare;

(l) the promotion of the efficiency of the armed forces of the Crown;

(m) any other purposes within subsection (4).'

The list is essentially an extended formulation of the classification provided by Lord Macnaghten, even to the extent of including the first three substantive categories, and after an additional group of substantive categories, a 'catch-all' category. This catch-all category includes any other purposes currently considered to be charitable, but which are not included in the previous paragraphs as well as any other purposes which could on the basis of analogy (and by analogy from analogy) be considered to be charitable. The new list, like Lord Macnaghten's, is no more than a classification, although being statutory, it is an authoritative classification. Like Lord Macnaghten's list, it does not follow automatically that because a trust is, for example, for the advancement of animal welfare that it will be charitable. As has already been indicated, the trust must also satisfy the requirement of public benefit.

---

[47]  *Annual Report of the Charity Commissioners for England and Wales 2003–2004*, p 11.
[48]  See below p 495.

The list relies heavily upon existing case law. The Bill states that where the list contains a term which 'has a particular meaning under charity law, the term is to be taken as having the same meaning where it appears in that provision'.[49] Even where this is not the case, previous case law is a guide to the scope and effect of some of the categories. In considering the categories, for convenience, each will be taken separately.

# 4 Charitable purposes

## (1) Trusts for the prevention or relief of poverty

The first general head of charitable purposes identified by Lord Macnaghten and repeated in the list in the Charities Bill 2005 was that of the 'relief of poverty', a description extended to include the prevention of poverty by the Charities Bill 2005. In a social era when there was no welfare state and little other state provision for those at the bottom of society, it was obviously 'beneficial' for private individuals to provide for them. Thus, the law has always regarded the relief of poverty as a charitable purpose to be encouraged, and has tended to be particularly lenient in defining when a gift for the relief of poverty is for the benefit of the 'public,'[50] a leniency which is altered by the Charities Bill 2005.

The preamble to the statute of 1601 referred to the relief of poverty in a wider context, including the 'relief of aged, impotent [i.e. infirm or disabled] and poor people'. As a result, trusts dealing with the relief of problems arising from age or infirmity were recognised as charitable. Trusts for these purposes are now covered by separate categories in the 2005 list.

## (a) The meaning of 'poor'

Poverty is not defined or explained in the Charities Bill 2005. Case law prior to 2005 indicated that it is a relative concept, and that what a society regards as 'poor' will vary with changes in social circumstance and what is regarded as a 'normal' level of income and ownership of consumer products. As a society we are used to images of extreme poverty both at home and abroad. However, apart from these extreme examples, wealth increases through the levels of society and it is almost impossible to draw a line defining the boundary of poverty. Absolute criteria, for example a specified weekly income, would be inadequate as they cannot take account of a person's complete circumstances. In the light of these difficulties the law has not attempted to define poverty but has taken a general, impressionistic approach, which is best illustrated by the examples given in the cases themselves.

The starting point must be *Re Coulthurst,*[51] where Sir Raymond Evershed MR made clear that from the perspective of the law of charity, 'poverty' is not synonymous with destitution:

---

[49] Charities Bill 2005, cl 2(5).   [50] *Dingle v Turner* [1972] AC 601. See below p 000.
[51] [1951] Ch 661, CA.

'It is quite clearly established that poverty does not mean destitution; it is a word of wide and somewhat indefinite import; it may not unfairly be paraphrased for present purposes as meaning persons who have to "go short" in the ordinary sense of that term, due regard being had to their status in life.'

This means that poverty is not to be understood as something experienced only by those at the very bottom of society, and the concept of 'going short'[52] will mean different things to people at different social levels. Those who are middle-class yet have fallen on harder times may well fall within this understanding of poverty, since they 'go short' compared to their social peers, although there may be others with similar financial circumstances who are not regarded as poor, because in the light of their social position they do not 'go short'. Thus, gifts in favour of 'distressed gentlefolk'[53] or persons of 'moderate means'[54] have been held to fall within this understanding of 'poor'. In *Re De Carteret*[55] the Bishop of Jamaica left property on trust to pay an annuity of £40 per annum to widows and spinsters in England whose income was between £80 and £120. Although this excluded widows with an income lower than £80, who seem to be poorer in an absolute sense, the gift was upheld as a valid charitable gift for the relief of poverty. Maugham J expressed some hesitation at this conclusion, and emphasised that the gift expressed the Bishop's preference that the annuities be paid to widows who had children dependent upon them. In contrast, in *Re Gwyon*[56] a gift for the provision of clothing for children was held not charitable since the terms of the gift did not exclude children who were from affluent backgrounds. In *Re Segelman (Decd)*[57] Chadwick J held that the beneficiaries of a trust had been selected on the basis of potential 'poverty' where they were presently 'comfortably off—in the sense that they are able to meet their day-to-day expenses out of income—but not affluent' but where they might need financial help in the future:

'Like many others in similar circumstances, they need a helping hand from time to time in order to overcome an unforeseen crisis: the failure of a business venture, urgent repairs to a dwelling house or expenses brought on by reason of failing health.'[58]

He further considered that minors who became students would be likely to experience 'relative poverty' when their income from grants or parental resources fails to cover their expenditure on 'their actual or perceived needs'.[59]

In *Re Sanders' Will Trusts*[60] money was given to provide dwellings for 'the working classes and their families'. Harman J held this was not charitable, since the term 'the working classes' did not indicate poor persons. In *Re Niyazi's Will Trusts*[61] Megarry V-C held charitable a gift of £15,000 for the construction of a 'working men's hostel' in Cyprus. He distinguished *Re Sanders' Will Trusts* on the basis that 'hostel' meant modest, temporary accommodation for those with a relatively low income, whereas 'dwellings' were ordinary houses which may be inhabited by the well-to-do as much

---

[52] This term was approved by Lightman J in *IRC v Oldham Training and Enterprise Council* [1996] STC 1218 at 1233.
[53] *Re Young* [1951] Ch 344.    [54] *Re Clarke* [1923] 2 Ch 407.    [55] [1933] Ch 103.
[56] [1930] 1 Ch 255.    [57] [1995] 3 All ER 676.    [58] [1995] 3 All ER 676 at 690.
[59] [1995] 3 All ER 676 at 690.    [60] [1954] Ch 265.    [61] [1978] 1 WLR 910.

as the relatively poor. In *IRC v Oldham Training and Enterprise Council* Lightman J held that a trust to help the unemployed would be a charitable trust for the relief of poverty:

'So far as the object . . . is to set up in trade or business the unemployed and enable them to stand on their own feet, that is charitable as a trust for the improvement of the conditions in life of those "going short" in respect of employment and providing a fresh start in life for those in need of it.'[62]

A modern analogy can be drawn from how the courts have reinterpreted the meaning of 'poor' in the equitable doctrine of *Fry v Lane*.[63] The court held that there was a general jurisdiction to set aside a sale made by a 'poor and ignorant man' at a considerable undervalue. This concept was translated into the 20th century in *Cresswell v Potter*[64] where, on divorce, a wife transferred her equitable interest in her matrimonial home to her husband for virtually no consideration. Megarry J set the transaction aside, holding that the wife, who was a Post Office telephonist, fell within the category of 'poor and ignorant'. He considered that the words must be reinterpreted to fit the 20th-century context:

'Eighty years ago when *Fry v Lane* was decided, social conditions were very different from those which exist today. I do not, however, think that the principle has changed, even though the euphemisms of the twentieth century may require the word "poor" to be replaced by "a member of the lower income group".'[65]

Two simple propositions can be drawn from these cases. First, that the legal concept of poverty is itself a relative one, and a person's social position and circumstances will be taken into account in determining if they are 'poor'. Secondly, that to be a valid gift for the relief of poverty, the gift must be exclusively for the benefit of the poor. If those who are not considered poor fall within the scope of the gift then it will not be charitable. The Charity Commission has recently issued guidance for trustees of charities whose purpose included the relief of the poor summarising the current law:

'A person does not have to be destitute to qualify as "poor". Anyone who is in need or suffering hardship or distress might be eligible for help . . . Generally speaking, anyone who cannot afford the normal things in life which most people take for granted would probably qualify for help.' [66]

It is worth noting that the majority of cases which examine the concept of poverty pre-date the creation of the welfare state. It has not been suggested that those in receipt of state benefits are outside of the class of poor people, since they receive the level of income society has decided to grant them, and provision which is additional to state support will still be charitable for the relief of poverty. The Charity Commission has recently stated that people who already receive their full entitlement of state benefits may need additional help,[67] but warned that charity resources should not

---

[62] [1996] STC 1218 at 1233.     [63] (1888) 40 Ch D 312.     [64] [1978] 1 WLR 255n.
[65] [1978] 1 WLR 255n at 257.     [66] CC4, *Charities for the Relief of the Poor* (2001) para 3.
[67] CC4, *Charities for the Relief of the Poor* (2001) para 4.

be used simply to replace state benefits, as this would not make the recipients any better off.[68]

## (b) The meaning of 'relief' or 'prevention'

Under the first category, a gift is not charitable merely because it is for the benefit of the poor. It must also relieve a need that they have as a result of their condition of poverty or must operate to prevent poverty. The concept of relief has been well explored in the courts, but the concept of prevention has been added by the Charities Bill and has therefore not yet been tested. The requirement of relief is best explained in a wider context than that of the relief of poverty. In *Joseph Rowntree Memorial Trust Housing Association Ltd v A-G*[69] the housing association wished to build small dwellings for elderly people, who would be able to purchase them on long leases. The elderly would pay 70% of the purchase price of the premises, with the remainder being paid by the housing association. To be charitable Peter Gibson J emphasised that:

'. . . there must be a need which is to be relieved by the . . . gift, such need being attributable to the aged . . . condition of the person to be benefited.'

Therefore, as counsel for the Attorney General had argued, a gift for the 'aged millionaires of Mayfair' would not be charitable as it would not relieve a need that such millionaires experienced as aged people. The fact that the housing association was providing a specialist type of accommodation for the elderly meant that a need was being relieved and the purpose was charitable.[70] The Charity Commission has recently advised charity trustees that they must 'make every effort to ensure that the benefits given individuals are no more than those actually required to relieve their need.'[71]

## (2) Trusts for the advancement of education

### (a) A broad concept of 'education'

Under the second head of the classification of charity, gifts for the advancement of education will be charitable. The preamble to the 1601 Act included the 'maintenance of schools of learning, free schools and scholars in the universities' and 'the education and preferment of orphans'. The law takes a wide view of what may be regarded as for the advancement of education, and education is not confined to teaching in schools and colleges. In *IRC v McMullen* Lord Hailsham spoke of the education of the young as:

'. . . a balanced and systematic process of instruction, training and practice containing . . . both spiritual, moral, mental and physical elements.'[72]

This wide concept of education has been reflected in the cases which have held that not

---

[68] CC4, *Charities for the Relief of the Poor* (2001) para 17.     [69] [1983] Ch 159.

[70] See also the Garfield Poverty Trust, which provided interest free loans to assist poor members of the Exclusive Brethren to purchase housing; Report of the Charity Commissioners for England and Wales 1990, para 13, App A.

[71] CC4, *Charities for the Relief of the Poor* (2001) para 8.     [72] [1981] AC 1, HL.

only gifts to advance academic study but also for research, culture and sport may be charitable. The Charities Bill 2005 contains separate heads which cover some of these areas.

## (b) Teaching

The advancement of academic teaching and of institutions which provide such teaching is clearly charitable. Charitable gifts have included: the founding of a professorial chair (*A-G v Margaret and Regius Professors in Cambridge*[73]); the endowments of schools and colleges (*A-G v Lady Downing;*[74] *Abbey Malvern Wells Ltd v Ministry of Local Government and Planning*);[75] and the payment of teachers and administrative staff of an institution (*Case of Christ's College Cambridge*).[76] In *Customs and Excise Comrs v Bell Concord Educational Trust Ltd*[77] it was held that trusts endowing fee-paying schools are charitable, provided that the school is non-profit making, or uses its profits for school purposes only. Purposes ancillary to teaching institutions may also be charitable, as for example in *A-G v Ross*,[78] where the students' union at a polytechnic was held charitable as it furthered the educational function of the institution.

## (c) Industrial training and professional bodies

The advancement of industrial and technical training has also been held charitable (*Re Koettgen's Will Trusts*[79] and *Construction Industry Training Board v A-G*[80]). In *IRC v White*[81] an association with the purpose of encouraging craftsmanship and maintaining the standards of the modern and ancient crafts was held to be charitable. The Royal College of Surgeons, which exists to promote the study and practice of the art of surgery, has been held charitable,[82] as has the Royal College of Nursing, whose objects are the better education and training of nurses and to promote nursing as a profession.[83] In contrast, the General Nursing Council, which was established by statute to regulate the nursing profession, has not been held charitable[84] since its objects included the enhancement of the status of nurses, which is analogous to the objectives of trade unions to advance the interests of their members.

## (d) Research

The advancement of education extends beyond mere teaching to include research activity. Despite a general unwillingness to make value judgments which may be subjective, the courts have sought to distinguish research which is of truly educational value and worthy of charitable status, from that which is not. Research which is of no educational value, or of purely esoteric value to the researcher, will not be charitable. The key concept the courts have used is that of public benefit, and only research which is of benefit to the public will be charitable. The three criteria laid down by Slade J in *Re*

---

[73] (1682) 1 Vern 55.     [74] (1766) Amb 550.     [75] [1951] Ch 728.     [76] (1757) 1 Wm Bl 90.
[77] [1990] 1 QB 1040, CA.     [78] [1986] 1 WLR 252.     [79] [1954] Ch 252.
[80] [1973] Ch 173, CA.     [81] [1980] TR 155.
[82] *Royal College of Surgeons of England v National Provincial Bank Ltd* [1952] AC 631, HL.
[83] *Royal College of Nursing v St Marylebone Corpn* [1959] 1 WLR 1077, CA.
[84] *General Nursing Council for England and Wales v St Marylebone Borough Council* [1959] AC 540, HL.

*Besterman's Will Trusts*[85] summarise the present state of the law. For a trust for research to be charitable:

(1) the subject matter of the research must be a useful subject of study;

(2) the knowledge acquired by the research must be disseminated to others;

(3) the trust must be for the benefit of the public, or a sufficiently important section of the public.

The case concerned a trust for research into the works of Voltaire and Rousseau, and since the three criteria were met it was held to be charitable. In the earlier case of *Re Shaw*[86] Harman J had held that a gift by George Bernard Shaw in his will for research into a 40-letter alphabet, and translation of one of his plays into it, was not charitable. However, Harman J seems to have taken a very narrow view of education, stating that:

'. . . if the object [of the research] be merely the increase of knowledge, that is not in itself a charitable object unless it be combined with teaching or education.'[87]

It is questionable whether the same result would have been reached under the principle applied in the later case of *Re Hopkins' Will Trusts*,[88] which concerned a gift to the Francis Bacon Society to be used to find manuscripts proving that the plays of Shakespeare were written by Francis Bacon. Holding the purpose charitable, Wilberforce J stated that the research 'must either be of educational value to the researcher or must be so directed as to lead to something which will pass into the store of educational material, so as to improve the sum of communicable knowledge in an area which education may cover'. This test has now evolved into the three criteria set out by Slade J in *Re Besterman's Will Trusts.*[89]

In summary, it is essential that the subject of proposed research must be of some usefulness. The court will have to make value judgments if it appears that a subject is of absolutely no worth to the educational community. The results of the research must also enter the public domain, usually by publication, and if the information is kept purely for the benefit of the researcher alone it will not be charitable. Therefore, research carried out by companies and intended for their exclusive commercial use will not be charitable. Nor will it be charitable for a university to conduct research on behalf of a corporation if the results of the research cannot enter the public domain.

## (3) The advancement of religion

Trusts for the advancement of religion are the third of Lord Macnaghten's categories which have been retained by the Charities Bill 2005. The law has historically been liberal in granting charitable status to religious purposes and groups, and this reflects the fact that religion was central to the fabric of the nation at the time when many of the cases

---

[85] (1980) Times, 21 January.    [86] [1957] 1 WLR 729.    [87] [1957] 1 WLR 729 at 737.
[88] [1965] Ch 669.    [89] (1980) Times, 21 January.

were decided. The law assumes that any religious activity, provided it is carried on in the public domain,[90] is beneficial to the public. There is no need at this first stage of the test as to whether a purpose is charitable for the particular religion in issue to prove its value, or for the court to weigh the validity of its beliefs. This was emphasised by Lord Reid who stated in *Gilmour v Coats*, that:

'A religion can be regarded as beneficial without it being necessary to assume that all its beliefs are true, and a religious service can be regarded as beneficial to all those who attend it without it being necessary to determine the spiritual efficacy of that service or to accept any particular belief about it.'[91]

Thus, in *Funnell v Stewart*[92] a gift to further the work of a small group of faith healers was not denied charitable status merely because there was no evidence that anyone had ever been healed, as was argued by the testatrix's next of kin, who alleged that the bequest was invalid. Hazel Williamson QC upheld the argument of the Attorney General that there was no need to prove public benefit as it was presumed.

## (a) The meaning of 'religion'

Although the position has now been changed, the courts originally defined religion so as to require belief in a divine being. Indeed, in *Bowman v Secular Society*[93] Lord Parker suggested that only monotheistic faiths would count as religions for the purposes of charity. It therefore follows that groups which merely promote a moral lifestyle without a spiritual dimension will not be charitable for the advancement of religion. This seems somewhat ironic given that the assumed benefit to the public of religion is that citizens will adopt a more moral lifestyle as a result of their beliefs and not the essential validity of the spiritual truths they profess. In *Re South Place Ethical Society*[94] Dillon J expressed the view that religion is 'concerned with man's relations with God' and therefore a society which had the purpose of promoting the 'study and dissemination of ethical principles' did not advance religion.[95] Similarly, in 1999 the Charity Commission rejected the application of the Church of Scientology for registration as a charity. It held that a body would only be charitable for the advancement of religion if it engaged in the worship of the divine being.[96] Whilst it was accepted that the Church of Scientology believed in the existence of a divine being, its activities did not exhibit the defining characteristics of worship, namely the 'reverence or veneration for that supreme being'. The activities of Scientology consisted of 'auditing', which was found to be very much akin to counselling, and 'training', which involved the detailed study of the works of L Ron Hubbard.[97]

The view that religion requires belief in a divine being would rule out the possibility

---

[90] See *Gilmour v Coats* [1949] AC 426.

[91] [1949] AC 426 at 862. See also: *Re Watson* [1973] 1 WLR 1472; *Funnell v Stewart* [1996] 1 WLR 288.

[92] [1996] 1 WLR 288.     [93] [1917] AC 406, HL.     [94] [1980] 1 WLR 1565.

[95] Although it could be, and was, in this particular case, held to be charitable under Lord Macnaghten's fourth category of other purposes beneficial to the public.

[96] Decision of the Charity Commissioners for England and Wales made on 17 November 1999. See also *R v Registrar General, ex p Segerdal* [1970] 2 QB 697.

[97] See also 'Rastafarianism as religion' (2001) 252 NLJ 509 (O'Brien)

of recognising Buddhism as a religion.[98] Equally, if religion requires belief in a single god, then neither could Hinduism be recognised as a religion. This would be an odd conclusion in an open and liberal society in which differences are respected and cherished. It is therefore no surprise that the Charities Bill 2005 states that

' "religion" includes—

>    (i)   a religion which involves belief in more than one god, and
>    (ii)  a religion which does not involve belief in a god;'[99]

This confirms the practice which the Charity Commission had already adopted of registering Hindu and Buddhist trusts,[100] although in many but by no means all cases the organisations included additional objects such as the advancement of education or the relief of poverty, and could therefore have been considered charities on that basis. It is worth noting that even in *Re South Place Ethical Society*,[101] even though Dillon J considered that ethics did not constitute a religion, he considered that the South Place Ethical Society was a charity because the promotion of ethical values and philosophies are charitable as for the advancement of education.

The Charity Commission practice, if tested in the courts, would almost certainly have been approved. For instance in *Varsani v Jesani*[102] the Court of Appeal had to adjudicate on how to deal with the property of a Hindu sect established to follow the teachings of Shree Swaminarayan Bhagwan, who was believed by adherents to have been the incarnation or manifestation of the Supreme Being. The sect had become irretrievably divided. The Court of Appeal had so little doubt that the sect, and both of the divisions which had emerged from it, were charitable that the question of whether Hinduism could be recognised as charitable did not even feature in debate.

### (b)  Equal treatment of different religions

Given that the benefit the court assumes to derive from a trust for the advancement of religion is the benefit of an improved life through religious belief, it follows that the precise nature of the religious belief is not important, and the law does not discriminate between different faiths and traditions. This was expressed by Cross J in *Neville Estates Ltd v Madden*:

'. . . as between different religions the law stands neutral, but it assumes that any religion is at least as likely to be better than none.'

The promotion of the Christian religion in all its denominational forms is clearly charitable, and despite little authority it seems that the mainstream non-Christian religions will be treated similarly.[103] In contrast to their willingness to attempt to assess

---

[98]  See the doubts expressed by Dillon J in *Re South Place Ethical Society* [1980] 1 WLR 1565.

[99]  Clause 2(3)(a).

[100]  See for instance *Gaudiya Mission v Brahmachary* [1997] EWCA Civ 2239; *Varsani v Jesani* [1998] EWCA Civ 630; *Muman v Nagasena* [1999] EWCA Civ 1742. A search of the register of charities discloses many more examples.

[101]  [1980] 1 WLR 1565.       [102]  [1999] 1 Ch 219.

[103]  See the discussion above in relation to Buddhism and Hinduism. *Straus v Goldsmid* (1837) 8 Sim 614, *Re Michel's Trust* (1860) 28 Beav 39 and *Neville Estates Ltd v Madden* [1962] Ch 832 for the promotion of Judaism. The Charity Commission has also registered organisations or trust for the promotion of Islam.

the value of research or supposed art, the courts will not weigh the merits of religious belief. Thus, in *Re Watson*[104] a trust to promote the works of H G Hobbs, the leader of a small group of non-denominational Christians comprising only members of his family, was held charitable despite the unanimous conclusion of expert evidence that they were of no value.

It seems that sects and cults will be charitable provided that they are not destructive to the whole concept of religion or contrary to the foundations of society, no matter how obscure or foolish their beliefs. In *Thornton v Howe*[105] a trust to promote the publication of the works of Johanna Southcote, who claimed that she was the mother of the second messiah was held charitable. The Unification Church (commonly known as the 'Moonies') has been registered as a charity. In contrast to the position in England, in Australia Scientology has been held to be a religion and entitled to charitable status and tax exemptions.[106]

## (c) Purposes ancillary to religion

Purposes ancillary to the advancement of religion will also be charitable. The construction or maintenance[107] of religious buildings, and even the provision of bells,[108] have been held charitable. Provision for the benefit of religious ministers, retired missionaries[109] and the church choir[110] have also been held charitable.

## (d) Gifts to religious leaders

Gifts made to religious leaders in their capacity as such will be considered charitable gifts for the advancement of religion, provided that the gifts are exclusively for the spiritual work of the leader. In *Re Flinn*[111] a gift to the Archbishop of Westminster for 'such purposes as he shall in his absolute discretion think fit' was held charitable, as was a gift to the Bishop of the Windward Islands 'to be used by him as he thinks fit in his dioscese'.[112] In *Farley v Westminster Bank*[113] a gift to a vicar for his 'work in the parish' was held charitable, but in *Re Simson*[114] a gift to a vicar for his 'parish work' was held not to be charitable since as a matter of construction it was held that his 'parish work' may include work which was not exclusively charitable. This distinction is tenuous, if not spurious.

## (e) Advancement not merely belief

A purpose will not be charitable simply because it involves belief in a religion. It must be for the *advancement* of religion. In other words, the activities involved must in some way promote or encourage belief in the faith concerned. In *United Grand Lodge of Ancient Free and Accepted Masons of England v Holborn Borough Council*,[115]

---

104 [1973] 1 WLR 1472.     105 (1862) 31 Beav 125.
106 *Church of the New Faith v Comr of Pay-Roll Tax* (1983) 49 ALR 65.
107 *Re Hooper* [1932] 1 Ch 38—trust to upkeep a tablet and a window in a church.
108 *Re Pardoe* [1906] 2 Ch 184.     109 *Re Mylne* [1941] Ch 204.
110 *Re Royce* [1940] Ch 514.     111 [1948] Ch 241.
112 *Re Rumball* [1956] Ch 105.     113 [1939] AC 430, HL.
114 [1946] Ch 299.     115 [1957] 1 WLR 1080.

freemasonry was held not to be charitable because it did not advance religion as such, but merely encouraged its members to lead a good moral life.

## (4) Advancement of health or the saving of lives

### (a) Medical and healthcare charities

This is the first of the new categories of charitable purpose added by the Charities Bill 2005. It does not represent a new category, but simply a subdivision of what in Lord Macnaghten's classification would have been considered 'other purposes beneficial to the community'. The preamble to the Statute of Charitable Uses referred to the relief of the 'aged, impotent and poor'. The word 'impotent' in this context does not have its modern meaning relating to sexual function, but was used in a more general archaic sense to refer to incapacity, infirmity or illness. In *Joseph Rowntree Memorial Trust Housing Association Ltd v A-G*,[116] it was held that the words of the preamble were to be read disjunctively. It has therefore been recognised for four centuries that the provision of medical care is a charitable purpose.[117] In *Re Smith's Will Trusts*[118] the Court of Appeal held that a gift to be applied to the benefit of such hospitals as the trustees in their absolute discretion thought fit was charitable. The court considered that the testator, who had made his will before the creation of the National Health Service, had meant hospitals dependent on voluntary contributions and not nursing homes run for private profit, which would not be charitable.[119] The provision of healthcare is not confined to conventional treatment. In *Funnell v Stewart*[120] the court held that a trust to further the work of a group offering faith healing was charitable. The view of the Charity Commission is that the promotion of alternative and complementary therapies can be charitable, but evidence is required of its efficacy:

'Assessing the efficacy of different therapies will depend upon what benefits are claimed for it (ie whether it is diagnostic, curative, therapeutic and/or palliative) and whether it is offered as a complement to conventional medicine or as an alternative. Each case is considered on its merits, but the 6th Report of the House of Lords Select Committee on Science and Technology (Session 1999–2000) on complementary and alternative medicine provides a useful guide.'[121]

### (b) Imposition of fees or charges for treatment[122]

It is clear that private hospitals are not non-charitable solely because they charge for their treatment, which is therefore only available to those who are capable of paying or

---

[116] [1983] Ch 159.

[117] See more recently the Charity Commission publication CC6—Charities for the Relief of Sickness (2000).

[118] [1962] 2 All ER 563.    [119] [1962] 2 All ER 563 at 564, per Lord Denning MR.

[120] [1996] 1 WLR 288.

[121] Charity Commission, *Commentary on the Descriptions of Charitable Purposes in the Charities Bill* (December 2005), para 12.

[122] See also the discussion below on the impact of fees upon public benefit.

have insurance. In *Re Resch's Will Trusts*[123] a gift of $8m was made to the St Vincent's Private Hospital. The Privy Council held that this was a valid charitable gift, and that there was sufficient benefit to the community resulting from 'the beds and medical staff of the general hospital, the availability of a particular type of nursing and treatment which supplements that provided by the general hospital and the benefit to the standard of medical care in the general hospital which arises from the juxtaposition of the two institutions'.[124] Again, it was emphasised that if the hospital was carried on as a commercial venture, with a view to making profits for individuals, then it would not be charitable.[125] This means that the majority of privately owned and run nursing homes and old people's homes will not be charitable. This is sensible, since profit-making ventures do not warrant the tax privileges granted to charities.

### (c) Saving lives (and property)

Trusts for the protection of human life and property have been held to be charitable as falling within the scope and intendment of the preamble. For example, in *Re Wokingham Fire Brigade Trusts*[126] the provision of a voluntary fire brigade was held charitable. The Royal National Lifeboat Institution is also charitable.[127] Clearly such services must not exist to make profits for individuals, which would rule out commercial organisations offering emergency services. The Charity Commission considers that a trust for the provision of street lighting or security cameras in public places, or the repair of sea and flood defences, could be considered charitable purposes under this head.[128]

### (d) Analogous and ancillary purposes

The Charities Bill 2005 makes it clear that the advancement of health is to be given an expansive meaning. It states that it 'includes the prevention or relief of sickness, disease or human suffering'.[129] As with trusts for the advancement of education and religion, purposes ancillary to the provision of medical care are charitable, so in *Re Bernstein's Will Trusts*[130] a surgeon's gift of part of his residuary estate to provide extra comforts at Christmas for the nurses of a specified hospital was held charitable. In *London Hospital Medical College v IRC*[131] a students' union at a medical school was held charitable as being a practical necessity to the efficient functioning of the school. The Charity Commission has also decided that the General Medical Council should be registered as a charity on the grounds that it was established for the charitable propose of 'the protection, promotion and maintenance of the health and safety if the community' by ensuring proper standards in the practice of medicine.[132]

---

[123] [1969] 1 AC 514.    [124] [1969] 1 AC 514 at 540, per Lord Wilberforce.
[125] [1969] 1 AC 514.    [126] [1951] Ch 373.    [127] *Re David* (1889) 43 Ch D 27.
[128] Charity Commission, *Commentary on the Descriptions of Charitable Purposes in the Charities Bill* (December 2005), para 15.
[129] Cl 2(3)(b).    [130] (1971) 115 Sol Jo 808.    [131] [1976] 1 WLR 613.
[132] Decision of the Charity Commissioners 2 April 2001.

## (5) Advancement of citizenship or community development

The Charity Commission considers that this head of charity covers a broad range or purposes 'directed towards support for social and community infrastructure which is focused on the community rather than the individual'.[133]

### (a) Rural or urban regeneration

Clause 2(3)(c) of the Charities Bill 2005 states that this head of charitable purpose 'includes rural or urban regeneration'. This is a category of charity recently recognised by the Charity Commission[134] and is an area of activity on which the Commission has issued guidance.[135] In order to attain charitable status an organisation must seek to maintain or improve 'the physical, social and economic infrastructure' and assist people 'who are at a disadvantage because of their social and economic circumstances'. Such purposes might include: providing financial assistance to people who are poor; providing or improving housing standards; helping people find employment; providing education, training and re-training; providing assistance to businesses, including land and buildings on favourable terms; providing and maintaining roads and transport; providing, maintaining and improving recreational facilities; preserving historic buildings in the area; providing public amenities.[136]

### (b) Promotion of community capacity building

The Charity Commission has decided that the promotion of community capacity building in relation to communities which are socially or economically disadvantaged should be recognised as charitable.[137] Community capacity building means 'developing the capacity and skills of the members of a community in such as way that they are better able to identify, and help meet, their needs and to participate more fully in society.'[138] This might involve: equipping people with skills and competencies; realising existing skills and developing potential; promoting people's increased self-confidence; promoting people's ability to take responsibility for identifying and meeting their own, and other people's, needs; encouraging people to become involved in their community and wider society in a fuller way.[139]

### (c) Civic responsibility and good citizenship[140]

Organisations such as the Guides and Scouts would be considered charitable under this category. Another example, reported by the Charity Commission in their Annual Report for 2004–2005 is Funky Dragon, the Welsh youth parliament.

---

[133] Charity Commission, *Commentary on the Descriptions of Charitable Purposes in the Draft Charities Bill* (December 2005), para 16.

[134] See *Charity Commission Annual Report 2003–2004*, p 8.

[135] RR2—Promotion of Urban and Rural Regeneration.

[136] RR2—Promotion of Urban and Rural Regeneration, para 7.

[137] RR5—The Promotion of Community Capacity Building (Nov 2000).

[138] RR5—The Promotion of Community Capacity Building (Nov 2000), para 7.

[139] RR5—The Promotion of Community Capacity Building (Nov 2000), para 13.

[140] The promotion of civic responsibility is specifically included within this head by Charities Bill 2005, cl 2(3)(c)(ii).

### (d) Promoting ethical standards in business and corporate responsibility

Despite the extensiveness of the list of charitable purposes set out in the Charities Bill 2005, there are many examples of charitable activity which are hard to classify. For instance, even though there was no direct judicial authority, the Charity Commission has decided to recognise as charitable organisations which promote the incorporation of ethics into business practice, and which advise and protect vulnerable employees faced with ethical dilemmas in the course of their work. In the light of this the Commission considered that the objects of the Centre of Corporate Accountability, which sought to promote safety by encouraging corporate accountability for breaches of health and safety laws, were capable of being charitable, although the organisation itself was held not to be charitable because its objects were also political.[141]

### (e) Volunteering and the voluntary sector

Volunteering consists of engaging in action which is not compulsory, for which financial reward is not the primary motivation, and which benefits others or society.[142] According to the Home Office Citizenship Survey in 2003, more than 50% of the adult population volunteers.[143] Volunteering makes a very substantial contribution to many areas of life, including culture and the arts, sport and recreation, conservation and regeneration, health and care, and politics. Some volunteering is done on an individual basis, but much operates through what is called the voluntary sector. The voluntary sector comprises organisations which are 'formally constituted, independent of government, self-governing, not profit distributing, primarily non-business and that benefit from voluntarism.'[144] These organisations are established for purposes which add value to the community. Some, but not all voluntary sector organisations are charitable. For instance, housing associations providing social housing for disadvantaged groups and community care associations providing care in the community for individuals with disabilities or mental health problems may be either charitable or non-charitable, depending upon their objects. Clause 2(3)(c)(ii) of the Charities Bill 2005 adds the promotion of volunteering and the voluntary sector to this head of charity.

### (f) Promoting the efficiency of charities

Promoting the effectiveness or efficiency of charities is added to the list of charitable purposes under this head by cl 2(3)(c)(ii) of the Charities Bill 2005. Whilst this is a slightly unusual categorisation, there could be little doubt that trusts seeking to enhance

---

[141] Decision of the Charity Commission for England and Wales, Application for Registration of the Centre for Corporate Accountability, 24 August 2001.

[142] See the definition contained in the United Nations Volunteers Report, prepared for the UN General Assembly Special Session on Social Development, Geneva, June 2004 and cited in the Russell Commission Report 2005, p 13. The Russell Commission was established in May 2004 by the then Home Secretary, David Blunkett, and the Chancellor of the Exchequer, Gordon Brown, to develop a new national framework for youth action and engagement.

[143] Russell Commission Report 2005, p 19.

[144] RR13 – The Promotion of the Voluntary Sector for the Benefit of the Public (September 2004), para 3.

the effectiveness of charities would be recognised as beneficial to the public, since they could only be encouraging the better performance of functions which have already been held, themselves, to be charitable.

## (6) Advancement of the arts, culture, heritage or science

### (a) Art, culture, and education

Trusts which promote an appreciation of the arts and other cultural activities have long been held to be charitable. Prior to the recategorisation of charities by the Charities Bill 2005, this was because such purposes were considered to be extensions of Lord Macnaghten's category of trusts for the advancement of education. A trust to promote the works of William Shakespeare has been held charitable,[145] as has a trust to hold exhibitions of Egyptian archaeological finds.[146] In *Royal Choral Society v IRC*[147] the society, whose purposes were 'to form and maintain a choir in order to promote the practice and performance of choral works', was held charitable by the Court of Appeal. Lord Greene MR rejected the narrow view of education as teaching which had been proposed by counsel for the Inland Revenue, and stated that 'the education of artistic taste is one of the most important things in the development of a civilised human being'. This approach was followed in *Re Delius (Decd)*,[148] where Roxburgh J held charitable a trust to promote the music of the composer Frederick Delius. Purposes which are too vague and uncertain will not be held charitable. So in *Associated Artists Ltd v IRC*[149] the promotion of 'artistic dramatic works' was not considered charitable. In *IRC v White*[150] the Clerkenwell Green Association of Craftsmen, which existed to further crafts and craftsmanship, was held charitable. Charitable purposes within this head can include societies supporting the arts, local or national history or archaeology, the establishment or support of museums, the preservation of ancient sites or buildings, or an individual monument.

### (b) Monuments

A trust to erect a public statue of Earl Mountbatten of Burma was considered charitable by the Charity Commissioners.[151] The chief consideration was that the person to be commemorated could be said to be a figure of historical importance. The public benefit of such a statue was that it would foster patriotism and good citizenship, and act as an incentive to heroic and noble deeds. Memorials to private individuals of no such historical importance will not be charitable.[152] The Charity Commission accepted in 2003 that an appeal to provide a new statue in Banbury to celebrate the nursery rhyme 'Ride a cock horse to Banbury Cross, to see a fine lady upon a white horse' was charitable on the grounds of a trust for the enhancement of a locality and raising

---

[145]  *Re Shakespeare Memorial Trust* [1923] 2 Ch 398.
[146]  *Re British School of Egyptian Archaeology* [1954] 1 WLR 546.      [147]  [1943] 2 All ER 101.
[148]  [1957] Ch 299.       [149]  [1956] 1 WLR 752.       [150]  [1980] TR 155.
[151]  Report of the Charity Commissioners for England and Wales 1981, paras 68–70.
[152]  See *Re Endacott* [1960] Ch 232, CA.

artistic taste, even though it was not accepted that the associated activities proposed in the application for registration were of educational value.[153]

## (c) A requirement of merit

Despite the desire to uphold gifts that genuinely advance artistic and cultural appreciation, the Charity Commission and the courts are astute to ensure that gifts which promote purposes of no artistic merit are not held charitable. The very nature of art makes it difficult for the courts to exercise objective judgments as to what is artistically valuable, and what is not. One man's masterpiece is another man's rubbish. In *Re Delius*[154] it was suggested that the subjective nature of such a judgment would mean that the court would have no option but to hold charitable a trust to promote the work of even an inadequate composer. On the facts the issue did not arise because the high standard of Delius's work was not challenged. However, it is now clear that the court will take expert advice as to the value of work of supposed artistic merit, and if the expert advice is unanimous that it is of no value, then the courts will not find that there is a charity for the advancement of education. In *Re Pinion (Decd)*[155] Harry Pinion had been a prolific collector of paintings, furniture, china, glass and other objets d'art. On his death he left his residuary estate to trustees to open his studio as a museum housing the collection. Expert witnesses considered the merits of the collection, and were unanimous in their conclusion that it was of no value. Indeed, one expert expressed his surprise that such a voracious collector had not even managed to pick up a single meritorious piece by accident. In the light of this evidence the Court of Appeal held that the trust was not charitable. Harman LJ concluded 'I can conceive of no useful object to be served in foisting upon the public this mass of junk'.

## (d) Can the vernacular and the popular have merit?

There is an increasing interest in the study of the vernacular, and of the need to preserve historical evidence of the way of life of ordinary people in the past. The National Trust, for instance, has preserved an ordinary terraced house in the North of England, using it to reflect a comparatively recently bygone way of life.[156] Industrial and folk museums have developed in recent years. No doubt all of these could be considered charitable, even though they reflect 'ordinary' rather than 'high' culture. What the courts have yet to address specifically, however, is whether the promotion and assistance of popular culture and music can be charitable. Why should promoting opera, choral music and the works of Delius be considered charitable if promoting the musical compositions of The Beatles or The Spice Girls is not? Are the only values which the law should uphold as charitable those which are held by the elite and not those held by the masses? The courts have not yet made this clear.

---

[153] *Charity Commission Annual Report 2003–2004*, p 9.
[154] [1957] Ch 299.       [155] [1965] Ch 85.
[156] More recently still, 20 Forthlin Road, Liverpool (Paul McCartney's former council house home) has been opened to the public by the National Trust.

## (7) Advancement of amateur sport

### (a) Promotion of sport per se

It was originally considered that trusts encouraging the playing of sport would not in themselves be considered charitable. The leading case was *Re Nottage*,[157] in which it was held that establishing a prize for ocean yacht racing was not charitable. There had to be some factor other than the playing of sport which justified a conclusion that the purpose was charitable. For instance, in an era when archers formed an essential part of the armed forces, a trust to promote archery practice would have been considered charitable since it helped to promote the defence of the realm by providing a cadre of skilled archers.

### (b) Sport and the advancement of education

A line of authority supported the view that the promotion of sport in schools and universities would be regarded as for the advancement of education, since, as Lord Hailsham indicated in *IRC v McMullen*,[158] education includes 'spiritual, moral, mental and physical elements'. In *Re Mariette*[159] a gift to provide fives and squash courts at a specific school was held charitable. In *IRC v McMullen*[160] the Football Association had established a trust for the promotion of football and other games or sports in schools and universities. This was held charitable as for the advancement of education by the House of Lords, even though the gift was not for the benefit of any specific institution. In contrast, the Charity Commissioners refused charitable status to the Birchfield Harriers, a leading athletic club, on the basis that there was an insufficient element of education in their activities.[161] The promotion of intellectually stimulating games was also held to be charitable, and in *Re Dupree's Deed Trusts*[162] the gift of a prize for chess to boys and young men resident in Portsmouth was held charitable.

### (c) Sport, health and community interest

In November 2002 the Charity Commissioners decided that Community Amateur Sports Clubs (CASCs) should be recognised as charitable.

'As part of our *Review of the Register* project, we have looked at the relationship between sport and charity in the light of modern social conditions. We have taken account of the enormous public interest in sport as a means of promoting health and the vital role that sport plays in improving the health of the nation. We have concluded that, within the law as it stands, we can properly recognise as charitable bodies that set out to encourage community participation in healthy sports.'[163]

By the date of the Charity Commission's Annual Report for 2003–2004, 120 CASCs had

---

[157] [1895] 2 Ch 649, CA. It may be wondered whether the nature of the sport was relevant. Ocean yacht racing has sometimes been described as being as pleasurable as standing under a cold shower tearing up £50 notes. However, cases subsequent to *Re Nottage* have held that even sports of the common man, such as athletics and football, are not charitable.

[158] [1981] AC 1, HL.      [159] [1915] 2 Ch 284.      [160] [1981] AC 1.

[161] Report of the Charity Commissioners for England and Wales 1989, para 52.

[162] [1945] Ch 16.      [163] RR11—Charitable Status and Sport (April 2003), para 5.

been registered.[164] It is this development which has formed the basis for the head of promotion of amateur sport contained in the Charities Bill 2005.

## (d) Healthy recreation

The Charity Commission view was that 'it is the close and obvious connection between physical exercise and physical health that makes the provision of facilities for healthy recreation charitable.'[165] The test which the Charity Commission applied was that

'Sports that are capable of providing "healthy recreation" are those sports which, if practised with reasonable frequency, will tend to make the participant healthier, that is, fitter and less susceptible to disease. Fitness includes elements of stamina, strength and suppleness (there may be others), but it will be enough if a sport contributes to just one of these elements.'[166]

## (e) Statutory extension of the promotion of sport

The Charities Bill 2005 extends the category of sporting activity which can be held to be charitable. By cl 2(2)(g) the promotion of amateur sport is a charitable purpose. Only sports which involve 'physical skill and exertion' are charitable under this head.[167] This reflects the similar restriction which the Charity Commission applied to the recognition of Community Amateur Sports Clubs. It is unlikely that promoting the playing of darts or snooker would be considered to be charitable under this head. More difficulty might be experienced with a game such as lawn bowls, where the extent of exertion required is modest.

## (f) Not all amateur sports clubs are charitable

It does not follow that because it is possible for an amateur sports club to be charitable that all clubs will satisfy the requirements to be charitable. This may be because benefits are confined to a small, private, group of members, as may be the case with some golf clubs. It may be because the sport does not satisfy the test of promoting health or involving physical exertion and skill. It may be because the sport is insufficiently inclusive. For instance, ocean yacht racing has been described as a sport for those who enjoy tearing up £10 notes whilst standing under a cold shower. It is an expensive sport which is generally confined to people with significant means. Without evidence that people from all levels of society have the potential to participate, it is likely that a trust to provide an annual prize for ocean yacht racing would still not be considered to be charitable.[168] Polo and motor racing may also be considered to be 'elite' sports which fail to satisfy the test of public benefit, unless a trust to promote these sports includes measures which enable participation by people who, without the support offered by the trust, could not afford to acquire the expensive equipment needed.[169] The Charity Commissioners refused charitable status to the Birchfield Harriers, a leading athletics club, since they existed to promote competitive sport, rather than to provide sporting

---

[164] *Charity Commission Annual Report for 2003–2004*, p 5.
[165] RR11—Charitable Status and Sport (April 2003), para 8.
[166] RR11—Charitable Status and Sport (April 2003), para 9.     [167] Charities Bill 2005, cl 2(3)(d).
[168] See *Re Nottage* above.     [169] RR11—Charitable Status and Sport (April 2003), para 26.

facilities to the public.[170] Certain amateur sports clubs can register with HM Customs and Revenue in order to gain tax exempt status under Finance Act 2002, Sch 18, but it is not possible following the Charities Bill 2005 for a club to be both registered in this way and to be a registered charity.[171]

## (8) Advancement of human rights, conflict resolution and equality

### (a) A broad category

This new head of charity contained in the Charities Bill 2005 has the longest description. It comprises 'the advancement of human rights, conflict resolution or reconciliation or the promotion of religious or racial harmony or equality and diversity'. This is a category of charitable purpose which, perhaps more than any other, reflects changes in society and social attitudes. The category is clearly of considerable scope.

### (b) Advancement of human rights

The advancement of human rights is now seen as being charitable by analogy with other charitable purposes,[172] a position confirmed by the Charities Bill 2005. The Charity Commission has provided detailed guidance on the recognition of human rights charities, and revised this guidance following the recommendation of the Prime Minister's Strategy Unit in *Private Action, Public Benefit*[173] that the Commission should take a more positive approach to campaigning by charities. The problem is that the promotion of human rights may often require advocating a change in the law, and advocating such a change has been held to be a political purpose which cannot therefore be charitable. By adopting a less cautionary view of what is permissible in relation to political campaigning, the Charity Commission has enabled human rights charities to be registered, even if seeking to influence government policy or to change the law may be activities which the charity will undertake. The Commission has provided a model set of objects for a human rights charity:[174]

'To promote human rights (as set out in the Universal Declaration of Human Rights and subsequent United Nations conventions and declarations)[175] throughout the world by all or any of the following means:

- monitoring abuses of human rights;
- obtaining redress for the victims of human rights abuse;

---

[170]    *Report of the Charity Commissioners for England and Wales 1989*, para 54.

[171]    Charities Bill 2005, cl 5(4).

[172]    RR12—The Promotion of Human Rights (January 2005), para 8: 'Given that respect for human rights is widely regarded as a moral imperative, the well-established charitable purpose of promoting the moral or spiritual welfare and improvement of the community provides a sufficient (but not the only) analogy for treating the promotion of human rights generally as charitable.'

[173]    September 2002.

[174]    Charity Commission RR12—The Promotion of Human Rights (January 2005), para 37.

[175]    Since there are different codes of human rights, it is important that the objects of the charity define which code of human rights it is proposed to promote: RR12—The Promotion of Human Rights (January 2005), para 13.

- relieving need among the victims of human rights abuse;
- research into human rights issues;
- educating the public about human rights;
- providing technical advice to government and others on human rights matters;
- contributing to the sound administration of human rights law;
- commenting on proposed human rights legislation;
- raising awareness of human rights issues;
- promoting public support for human rights;
- promoting respect for human rights among individuals and corporations;
- international advocacy of human rights;
- eliminating infringements of human rights.

In furtherance of that object but not otherwise, the trustees shall have power

- to engage in political activity provided that the trustees are satisfied that the proposed activities will further the purposes of the charity to an extent justified by the resources committed and the activity is not the dominant means by which the charity carries out its objects;'

## (c) Advancement of conflict resolution or reconciliation

This description would include a trust seeking to resolve national or international conflicts, and also a trust promoting restorative justice 'where all the parties with a stake in a particular conflict or offence come together to resolve collectively how to deal with its aftermath and its implications for the future.'[176]

## (d) The promotion of religious or racial harmony or equality and diversity

The promotion of equality between men and women was held charitable in *Halpin v Steear*.[177] The promotion of good community relations has more recently come to be recognised as a charitable purpose, demonstrating that the law of charity is able to develop to meet the social needs of the day, and to reflect the current moral agenda.[178] In *Re Strakosch (Decd)*[179] a gift to be used to appease racial feeling between the Dutch- and English-speaking sections of the South African community was held not to be charitable on the basis that it was a political purpose, too vague, and might include very wide objects some of which would not be charitable. It had been thought that this decision rendered the promotion of racial harmony a non-charitable object. However, the Charity Commissioners have taken the view that the promotion of racial harmony is analogous to other purposes that the courts have held charitable, and have accepted that 'promoting good race relations, endeavouring to eliminate discrimination on

---

[176] Charity Commission Commentary on the Descriptions of Charitable Purposes in the Draft Charities Bill (December 2005), para 26. The promotion of restorative justice was recognised as a charitable purpose by the Charity Commission in 2003: *Charity Commission Annual Report 2003–2004*, p 11.

[177] (27 February 1976, unreported).

[178] RR1—The Review of the Register of Charities (2001), para B1.     [179] [1949] Ch 529, CA.

grounds of race and encouraging equality of opportunity between persons of different racial groups' are charitable purposes.[180] The promotion of religious harmony was accepted as charitable by the Charity Commission in 2002 when it registered The Friends of Three Faiths Forum, an organisation intended to promote religious harmony by enabling people of one faith to understand the religious beliefs of others. The three faiths concerned were Christianity, Judaism and Islam. The Commissioners considered that the purposes were charitable by virtue of the analogy 'to the existing purposes of promoting equality of women with men, promoting racial harmony and promoting the moral or spiritual welfare or improvement of the community.'[181]

## (9) Advancement of environmental protection or improvement

The preservation of national heritage and conservation of the environment are charitable purposes. The National Trust is charitable,[182] since its objects of 'promoting the permanent preservation for the benefit of the nation of lands and tenements (including buildings) of beauty or historic interest and as regards lands for the preservation . . . of their natural aspect features and animal and plant life'[183] are for the public benefit. In their 1973 Annual Report the Charity Commissioners reported that they had registered as charitable the Advisory Committee on Oil Pollution of the Sea, which sought to preserve the sea in general, and especially the seas around the United Kingdom from pollution.[184] In 2001 the Charity Commission recognised the conservation of the environment as a charitable purpose in its own right, including organisations which conserve the environment by promoting biodiversity.[185] Where the organisation is set up to maintain a particular building, site or habitat, the element of public benefit will only be satisfied if the public have access. Whilst there is a presumption that public benefit requires physical access, if there are valid reasons for limiting or excluding such access the public benefit element may be satisfied if the organisation puts in place alternative means of informing the public about its activities.[186] In April 2002 the Charity Commission therefore decided that Recycling in Ottery, a company which sought to 'protect and safeguard the environment particularly through the promotion of re-use and recycling and the provision of recycling facilities', and which ran a scrap yard where members of the public could bring items for recycling, was charitable.[187] However environmental campaign groups which have primarily political purposes will not enjoy charitable status.[188]

---

[180] Report of the Charity Commissioners for England and Wales 1983, paras 18–20.

[181] *Charity Commission Annual Report 2002–2003*, p 22.     [182] *Re Verrall* [1916] 1 Ch 100.

[183] National Trust Act 1907, s 4(1).

[184] Report of the Charity Commissioners for England and Wales 1973, para 40.

[185] RR1—The Review of the Register of Charities (2001), para B9.

[186] RR9—Preservation and Conservation (Feb 2001), paras A18–A20.

[187] Decision of the Charity Commissions for England and Wales, *Application for Registration of Recycling in Ottery*, April 2002.

[188] See below p 518.

## (10) Relief of need

It has already been seen that the Statute of Charitable Uses recognised that charitable purposes included the relief of poverty, infirmity and illness. These are merely examples of need, and other (mainly now archaic) examples are contained in the preamble to the 1601 Statute. The Charities Bill 2005 states that it is a charitable purpose to provide relief for those in need 'by reason of youth, age, ill-health, disability, financial hardship or other disadvantage.'[189] This 'includes relief given by the provision of accommodation or care to the persons mentioned in that paragraph.'[190]

### (a) Examples of the relief of need

There is clearly considerable overlap between this head of charity and the head relating to the relief of poverty and the advancement of health, and many trusts which are charitable under those heads would also be charitable within this category. The category would clearly include the provision of social housing, since this is expressly included in the category. In *Joseph Rowntree Memorial Trust Housing Association Ltd v A-G*,[191] the Housing Association, which wished to build small dwellings for sale to the elderly, was considered charitable even though those who would benefit by purchasing the dwellings would not fall within the definition of 'poor'. Other forms of assistance to disadvantaged groups would also be charitable. For example, the relief of unemploy-ment was not historically a charitable object in itself, though charities have helped unemployed people under the categories of advancing education or relieving poverty. However, as part of its review of the Register, the Charity Commission decided in 1999 that an organisation for the relief of unemployment will be charitable if it can be demonstrated that it is tackling unemployment, either generally or for a significant section of the community. Acceptable activities include the provision of: advice and training to unemployed individuals; practical support for unemployed people by way of accommodation, child care facilities or assistance with travel, land and buildings at below marker or subsidised rents to businesses starting up; capital grants or equip-ment to new businesses; and payment to an existing commercial business to take on additional staff.[192]

It is not necessary that the needs relieved relate only to the United Kingdom. The Charity Commission has held the promotion of trading fairly is a charitable purpose. Thus in 1995 it registered as a charity an organisation which would award a 'fair trade mark' on the packaging of goods sold in supermarkets, which would have the effect of relieving the conditions of life of third world workers.[193]

### (b) Provision of recreational facilities

Until the position was changed by the Recreational Charities Act 1958, the provision of recreational facilities was not, in itself, charitable, even if those facilities are provided to the public at large. This position was established by three decisions of the House of Lords in the mid 20th century. In *Williams' Trustees v IRC*[194] a trust was established to

---

[189] Charities Bill 2005 Clause 2(2)(j).    [190] Clause 2(3)(e)    [191] [1983] Ch 159.
[192] RR3—Charities for the Relief of Unemployment (1999).
[193] RR1—The Review of the Register of Charities (2001), para B17.    [194] [1947] AC 447, HL.

promote Welsh interests in London, including the provision of a meeting place to promote the 'moral, social, spiritual and educational welfare of Welsh people'. The House of Lords held that this was not charitable because of the 'social' purposes, although many of the other purposes of the society would be charitable. In *IRC v City of Glasgow Police Athletic Association*[195] an association which existed 'to encourage and promote all forms of athletic sports and general pastimes' amongst members of the force claimed charitable status and tax exemption on the grounds that it promoted the efficiency of the police force, which would be a charitable object. The House of Lords held that the provision of recreation for the members was not purely incidental to the charitable purpose of promoting the efficiency of the force, and therefore the association was not entitled to charitable status. In *IRC v Baddeley*[196] a gift of land was made to a Methodist Mission, including an area laid out as a playing field complete with a pavilion and groundsman's bungalow. The purposes of the gift included 'the provision of facilities for religious services and instruction and for the social and physical training and recreation' of persons resident in West Ham and Leyton. The House of Lords held that this was not a gift made exclusively for charitable purposes, following *Williams' Trustees v IRC.*[197]

A number of cases have held that gifts for the provision of public recreation grounds can be charitable, for example in *Re Hadden,*[198] where a gift was made for the provision of playing fields, parks and gymnasiums in Vancouver, and in *Re Morgan,*[199] where a gift for the provision of a public recreation ground for a particular parish was held charitable. In *Brisbane City Council v A-G for Queensland*[200] a trust to provide an area or 'a park and recreation purposes' was also held charitable. Viscount Simmonds in *IRC v Baddeley* was careful to stress that the provision of recreation grounds would still be charitable.[201]

The decision in *IRC v Baddeley* gave rise to concern that Women's Institutes and similar organisations, previously considered to be charitable, would no longer qualify for that status. To eliminate any uncertainty the Recreational Charities Act 1958 was enacted. This Act was not intended to enlarge the definition of charity,[202] but instead to give statutory recognition to purposes already recognised as charitable. The statute covers the provision of 'facilities for recreation or other leisure-time occupation'[203] and specific mention is made of facilities at 'village halls, community centres and women's institutes'.[204] The key provision of the Act is that the facilities must be provided in the 'interests of social welfare'.[205] This requirement cannot be met unless the facilities provided have the object of 'improving the conditions of life for the persons for whom the facilities are primarily intended'[206] and those persons must fall within either of the two groups specified:

1.   persons needing such facilities because of their youth, age, infirmity or disability, poverty or social and economic circumstances;[207]

---

[195] [1953] AC 380.     [196] [1955] AC 572.     [197] [1947] AC 447.     [198] [1932] 1 Ch 133.
[199] [1955] 1 WLR 738.     [200] [1979] AC 411, PC.
[201] [1955] AC 572 at 559: 'I think it right to say that, in my opinion, a gift of land for the use as a recreation ground by the community at large or by the inhabitants of a particular geographical area may well be supported as a valid charity.'
[202] Halsbury's Statutes, Vol 5, p 801.     [203] S 1.     [204] S 2.     [205] S 1.     [206] S 1(2)(a).
[207] S 1(2)(b)(i).

2.   the public at large or the male[208] or female members of the public.[209]

Thus, private clubs, such as golf clubs, which provide facilities only for their members, will not attract charitable status and the consequent tax privileges. Only facilities provided for the public in general, for female members of the public (an early example of positive discrimination), and now male members of the public, or to groups in some way disadvantaged will attract charitable status. For example, in their 1984 Report the Charity Commissioners considered as charitable a company with the object of providing an ice-rink in Oxford which would be available to members of the public at large.[210] Although the Act does not specifically mention ethnic or minority groups, the Charity Commission has considered that it would be charitable to set up a community association or other recreational organisation primarily for the use of some identifiable racial minority group.[211] The statute does not exactly define 'social welfare',[212] stating instead the essential elements which must be present. At first instance in *IRC v McMullen*[213] Walton J took the view that 'social welfare' indicates that there must be some kind of deprivation and that as a class, pupils at schools and universities cannot be described as 'deprived'.[214] In the Court of Appeal[215] Bridge LJ rejected that view, stating 'the village hall may improve the conditions of life for the squire and his family as well as for the cottagers'. This was the view of the Charity Commissioners,[216] and was approved by the House of Lords in *Guild v IRC*.[217] Lord Keith expressly stated that Walton J's approach had been incorrect, and that 'persons in all walks of life and all sorts of social circumstances may have their conditions of life improved by the provision of recreational facilities of a suitable character'.[218] A gift for use in connection with a sports centre in North Berwick was therefore held charitable. The fact that patrons must pay reasonable charges for the use of the facilities does not deprive the activity of its charitable status.

The Charity Commission has published its view as to the scope of s 1 of the Recreational Charities Act as part of its review of the Register of Charities.[219] The Commission suggests that an organisation will only be charitable under the Act if it is altruistic in character, meaning that it seeks to provide something for the benefit of others rather than for itself. Thus a social club established by a group of people for their own benefit will not gain charitable status because they are not engaged in 'social welfare.' It also suggests that it will be more difficult to accept that the provision of facilities for the playing of a single sport meets the requirement of social welfare, in

---

[208] Male members of the public were included by Charities Bill 2005, cl 5(2). Prior to this benefits could be confined to female members of the public, but not to male members of the public. Whilst the difference in treatment would now be considered indefensible under the Human Rights Act, at the time of the original enactment of the Recreational Charities Act 1958, it was intended to protect the charitable status of Women's Institutes.

[209] S 1(2)(b)(ii).        [210] *Report of the Charity Commissioners for England and Wales for 1984*, para 19.

[211] RR1A—Recognising New Charitable Purposes (October 2001), para. B14.

[212] See *Valuation Comr for Northern Ireland v Lurgan Borough Council* [1968] NI 104 at 126–127, per Lord MacDermott LCJ.

[213] [1978] 1 WLR 664.        [214] [1978] 1 WLR 664 at 675.        [215] [1979] 1 WLR 130.

[216] *Report of the Charity Commissioners for England and Wales 1989*, para 55.

[217] [1992] 2 AC 310, [1992] 2 All ER 10.        [218] [1992] 2 All ER 10 at 17.

[219] RR4—The Recreational Charities Act 1958 (2000).

contrast to multi-purpose sports facilities provided for the public at large which promote healthy recreation.[220]

## (11) Advancement of animal welfare

Gifts to specific animals may be upheld as valid unenforceable purpose trusts since they are recognised as anomalous exceptions to the beneficiary principle.[221] In contrast, trusts which promote the welfare of animals in general are charitable. In *Re Wedgwood*[222] Frances Wedgwood left property to her brother on secret trust for the protection and benefit of animals. She had discussed with him the possible use of the money to forward the movement for humane slaughtering of animals, which the Court of Appeal held to be a valid charitable object. The necessary element of public benefit was not found in any benefits to the animals themselves, but in the beneficial effects which the relief of cruelty to animals was expected to have on public morality. This was emphasised by all the members of the Court of Appeal. For example, Swinfen Eady LJ explained that:

'. . . a gift for the benefit and protection of animals tends to promote and encourage kindness towards them, to discourage cruelty and to ameliorate the condition of the brute creation, and thus to stimulate humane and generous sentiments in man towards the lower animals, and by these means promote feelings of humanity and morality generally, repress brutality, and thus elevate the human race.'

This reasoning was accepted without question by Nourse J in *Re Green's Will Trusts*.[223] Although it is well established that trusts for the relief of cruelty to animals are charitable, it should not be necessary to justify them on such a convoluted basis. They should be charitable simply because they benefit the animals themselves, the approach taken in Ireland.[224] Such a rationale would reflect current public sentiment towards animals, and would be another example of how the law of charity should not stand trapped by precedents from a previous social era.

In *Re Moss*[225] the welfare of cats and kittens was held charitable, as was a home for lost dogs.[226] In *Tatham v Drummond*[227] the RSPCA was held charitable, and more recently in *Re Green's Will Trusts*[228] a trust for the rescue, maintenance and benefit of cruelly treated animals was held charitable. Gifts for animal sanctuaries have been held charitable, as in *Re Murawski's Will Trusts*,[229] where a gift was made to the Bleakholt Animal Sanctuary, whose constitution adopted the objects of 'the provision of care and shelter for stray, neglected and unwanted animals of all kinds and the protection of animals from ill-usage, cruelty and suffering'. However, it seems that the sanctuary must either relieve cruelty or provide access to the public to view the animals if it is to be regarded as for the benefit of the public. Thus, in *Re Grove-Grady*[230] the Court of Appeal considered that a gift to found the 'Beaumont Animal Benevolent Society' was

---

[220] RR4—The Recreational Charities Act 1958 (2000), paras A24–A25.    [221] See Chapter 12.
[222] [1915] 1 Ch 113.        [223] [1985] 3 All ER 455, at 458.
[224] *Armstrong v Reeves* (1890) 25 LR Ir 325.        [225] [1949] 1 All ER 495.
[226] *Re Douglas* (1887) 35 Ch D 472.        [227] (1864) 4 De GJ & Sm 484.        [228] [1985] 3 All ER 455.
[229] [1971] 1 WLR 707.        [230] [1929] 1 Ch 557.

not charitable. Its purposes were to provide a refuge where animal life of all types might be completely undisturbed by man. The court held that the public derived no benefit from such a refuge, since the purpose was not the reduction of pain or cruelty to the animals and the public could be excluded from entering the area or even looking into it. Russell LJ considered that there was no public benefit when:

'. . . all that the public need know about the matter would be that one or more areas existed in which all animals (whether good or bad from man's point of view) were allowed to live free from any risk of being molested or killed by man; though liable to be molested and killed by other denizens of the area.'

Again, it is questionable whether this attitude should prevail today, when there is greater awareness and concern about environmental and conservation issues (a specific category of charity following the Charities Bill 2005) and of the desirability of maintaining genetic diversity. The establishment of animal sanctuaries kept free from any interference by man could well be regarded as beneficial to the public, the benefit arising simply from the knowledge that such sanctuaries are there, and the heightened awareness of environmental and conservation concerns that they would engender.

## (12) Promotion of the efficiency of the armed forces

Gifts which promote the efficiency of the defence services have been held charitable under the fourth head. This was held to follow from the spirit and intendment of the preamble, which mentioned the 'setting out of soldiers'. Thus, a gift of plate for an officers' mess was held charitable in *Re Good*.[231] In *Re Gray*[232] a gift for the promotion of shooting, fishing, cricket, football and polo for a regiment was held charitable, as it promoted the physical efficiency of the army.[233] The provision of RAF playgroups and ex-servicemen's associations are also charitable.[234] By analogy, it has been held that gifts to promote the efficiency of the police force will also be charitable,[235] although such a charity would not fall within this category.

However, many of the cases in this area date from the early part of the last century and the more recent cases suggest that there will only be a charity if the prime object of the purposes is to promote efficiency. In *IRC v City of Glasgow Police Athletic Association*[236] a gift to promote sport and athletic pastimes in the police force was not held charitable. Although similar to the facts of *Re Gray*,[237] this was held to be a non-charitable purpose, as the promotion of efficiency was only incidental to the promotion of sport.

## (13) Other purposes beneficial to the community

Nothwithstanding the length of the list contained in the Charities Bill 2005, there are many instances of charity which do not fall under any of these categories, but which

---

[231] [1905] 2 Ch 60.    [232] [1925] Ch 362.    [233] [1925] Ch 362 at 365, per Romer J.
[234] Charity Commission for England and Wales, Annual Report 1997, para 90.
[235] *IRC v City of Glasgow Police Athletic Association* [1953] AC 380.
[236] *IRC v City of Glasgow Police Athletic Association* [1953] AC 380.    [237] [1925] Ch 362.

will remain charitable because of the preservation of the current law by cl 2(4). For instance, a number of cases hold that the promotion of trade and industry can be charitable. In *Construction Industry Training Board v A-G*[238] the Board, which was to make provision for the training of those employed in the construction industry, was held charitable. In *IRC v Yorkshire Agricultural Society*[239] the society, which existed for the general promotion of agriculture, was held charitable, as was the provision of a 'showground'[240] which would encourage agriculture. In their annual report for 1973[241] the Charity Commissioners considered that the Council of Industrial Design, which seeks to improve the design of industrial products, was charitable since it was clearly of benefit to the public at large. However, the promotion of the interests of individuals rather than industry in general will not be charitable. In *Hadaway v Hadaway*[242] a trust to 'assist planters and agriculturists' by the provision of loans at favourable rates of interest was held non-charitable by the Privy Council because it was directed at conferring private benefits. Similarly, in *IRC v Oldham Training and Enterprise Council*[243] Lightman J held that a trust to promote 'trade commerce and enterprise' in the Oldham area by providing 'support services and advice to and for new businesses' was not exclusively charitable because they would enable the TEC to 'promote the interests of individuals engaged in trade commerce or enterprise and provide benefits and services to them'.[244]

The list provided by the Charity Commission in its Commentary on the Descriptions of Charitable Purposes in the Draft Charities Bill[245] demonstrates both the difficulty of classifying charities and the extent to which purposes may be charitable under more than one head:

- the provision of public works and services and the provision of public amenities (such as the repair of bridges, ports, havens, causeways and highways, the provision of water and lighting, a cemetery or crematorium, as well as the provision of public facilities such as libraries, reading rooms and public conveniences);
- the relief of unemployment;
- the defence of the country (such as trusts for national or local defence; promoting the efficiency of the emergency services);
- the promotion of certain patriotic purposes, such as war memorials;
- the social relief, resettlement and rehabilitation of persons under a disability or deprivation (including disaster funds);
- the promotion of industry and commerce;
- the promotion of agriculture and horticulture;
- gifts for the benefit of a particular locality (such as trusts for the general benefit

---

[238] [1971] 1 WLR 1303. See also *Crystal Palace Trustees v Minister of Town and Country Planning* [1951] Ch 132, where a trust with the purpose of the promotion of industry commerce and art was held charitable.
[239] [1928] 1 KB 611.    [240] *Brisbane City Council v A-G for Queensland* [1979] AC 411.
[241] *Report of the Charity Commissioners for England and Wales 1973*, paras 69–70.
[242] [1955] 1 WLR 16.    [243] [1996] STC 1218.    [244] [1996] STC 1218 at 1235.
[245] December 2005.

of the inhabitants of a particular place; the beautification of a town; civic societies;

- the promotion of mental or moral improvement;
- the promotion of the moral or spiritual welfare or improvement of the community;
- the preservation of public order;
- promoting the sound administration and development of the law;
- the promotion of ethical standards of conduct and compliance with the law in the public and private sectors;
- the rehabilitation of ex-offenders and the prevention of crime.

# 5 Recognising new charitable purposes

Since the list of charitable purposes is not closed, a question arises as to how new charitable purposes will be recognised. The Charities Bill 2005, cl 2(4) preserves as charitable those purposes 'recognised as charitable under existing charity law' and then, as has already been described, allows the recognition as charitable 'any purposes that may reasonably be regarded as analogous to, or within the spirit of' any purposes listed in the Bill or recognised by existing law as charitable, and so on ad infinitum.

## (1) The 'spirit and intendment' of the Statute of 1601

The Charities Bill appears to exclude a method of reasoning which has been extensively used in the past. Traditionally, the 'spirit and intendment' of the preamble to the Statute of 1601 has acted as the benchmark to determine which purposes benefit the public in ways which are charitable. In *Williams' Trustees v IRC*,[246] where the House of Lords held that a trust for promoting Welsh interests in London was not charitable, Lord Simmonds said that:

'. . . it is still the general law that a trust is not charitable and entitled to the privileges which charity confers, unless it is within the spirit and intendment of the preamble to the Statute of Elizabeth.'

The continued significance of the preamble was reiterated by the Privy Council in *A-G of the Cayman Islands v Wahr-Hansen*,[247] where Lord Browne-Wilkinson took it for granted that it was necessary to decide whether a purpose specified by a donor fell within the spirit and intendment of the preamble. However, the preamble cannot possibly anticipate the needs of society in the 21st century, and is an inadequate vehicle for determining charitable status. As Lord Upjohn commented in *Scottish Burial Reform and Cremation Society Ltd v Glasgow City Corpn*,[248] 'the authorities show that the spirit

---

[246] [1947] AC 447.     [247] [2001] 1 AC 75, [2000] 3 All ER 642.     [248] [1968] AC 138.

and intendment of the preamble to the Statute of Elizabeth have been stretched almost to breaking point'.

## (2) Development by analogy

The practice of development by analogy, incorporated in the Charities Bill, has become the predominant means of ascertaining whether a new purpose can be considered charitable. Lord Wilberforce in the *Scottish Burial Reform* case[249] examined how the principle of the spirit and intendment had been applied in practice:

'... the courts appear to have proceeded first by seeking some analogy between an object mentioned in the preamble and the object with regard to which they had to reach a decision. And then they appear to have gone further and to have been satisfied if they could find an analogy between an object already held to be charitable.'

The Goodman Committee in 1976 recommended that the preamble should be replaced by a modern list of purposes deemed charitable to serve as a new benchmark for further development.[250] Their recommendation has now been implemented some 30 years later.

## (3) Purposes without an analogy

A new situation will occasionally arise in which, although there appears to be a public benefit, there is no obvious analogy. The problem may then arise as to whether this can be considered charitable. In *Williams' Trustees v IRC*, Lord Simmonds said, 'it is not enough to say that the trust in question is for public purposes beneficial to the community or for the public welfare; you must show it to be a charitable trust'.[251] How is this to be done in the absence of any analogy? An approach which has been suggested is that trusts which are for purposes manifestly for the public benefit should be prima facie charitable, unless there are any reasons why they should not be. In *Incorporated Council of Law Reporting for England and Wales v A-G*[252] Russell LJ recognised the inadequacies of the 'spirit and intendment' principle and proposed instead that purposes which 'cannot be thought otherwise than beneficial to the community and of general public utility' should be charitable in law 'unless there are any grounds for holding it to be outside of the equity of the Statute [of 1601]'. This proposal was embraced by Sachs and Buckley LJJ. Applying this principle it was held that the Incorporated Council of Law Reporting was registrable as a charity since its object of the production of law reports, was clearly of general public utility and there were no grounds on which it should not be held charitable.

This approach has much to commend it, as the Privy Council indicated in *A-G of the Cayman Islands v Wahr-Hansen*.[253] It is an honest recognition of how the courts and the Charity Commission actually seem to go about identifying charitable purposes, and it

---

[249] [1968] AC 138.
[250] Report of the Goodman Committee: *Charity Law and Voluntary Organisations* (1976), para 32.
[251] [1947] AC 447.       [252] [1972] Ch 73, CA.       [253] [2001] 1 AC 75, [2000] 3 All ER 642.

retains the safeguard of an option for charitable status to be refused even if the object is in the public interest. However, in *Barralet v A-G* Dillon J expressed doubt whether it is consistent with the decision of the House of Lords in *Williams' Trustees v IRC*[254] and concluded:

'. . . it seems to me that the approach to be adopted in considering whether something is within the fourth category is the approach of analogy from what is stated in the preamble to the Statute of Elizabeth or from what has already been held to be charitable within the fourth category.'[255]

The approach may also no longer be open in view of the way in which cl 2(4) of the Charities Bill 2005 is phrased, although the preservation of 'any purposes . . . recognised as charitable purposes under existing charity law' by cl 2(4) may be capable of being interpreted to include 'other purposes beneficial to the community' as described by Lord Macnaghten in *Pemsel's* case, and therefore allow the use of the reasoning in the *Incorporated Council of Law Reporting* case.

# 6 Charitable purposes overseas

A trust is not denied charitable status merely because any benefit from its execution will be experienced abroad rather than within the jurisdiction. In their Annual Report for 1963 the Charity Commissioners had no doubt that the advancement of religion, the advancement of education and the relief of poverty are charitable in any part of the world, although they indicated that in the case of trusts for the relief of poverty the poverty must be observable and the measures designed to relieve it must have reasonably direct results.[256] For charities within Lord Macnaghten's fourth head of 'other purposes beneficial to the community', they said that there must be some benefit to the community of the United Kingdom, and not merely to the foreign country, reflecting a dictum of Lord Evershed MR in *Camille and Henry Dreyfus Foundation Inc v IRC*.[257] The Commissioners suggested that this might be more easily found in benefits to a Commonwealth country.[258]

With the declining significance of the Commonwealth and the growing importance of links with Europe, Eastern Europe and increased international concern, this distinction is artificial. In their report for 1990, the Commissioners noted the trend toward a European and international dimension in new charities illustrated by the registration of the Gdansk Hospice Fund, the Nairobi Hospice Trust and the USSR Support Charity.[259] Examples of charities with an international dimension include: a gift to the German government for the benefit of soldiers disabled in the Great War;[260] a trust

---

[254] [1947] AC 447.    [255] [1980] 3 All ER 918.
[256] *Report of the Charity Commissioners for England and Wales 1963*, para 72.
[257] [1954] Ch 672 at 684.
[258] *Report of the Charity Commissioners for England and Wales 1963*, para 72.
[259] *Report of the Charity Commissioners for England and Wales 1990*, paras 32, 33.
[260] *Re Robinson* [1931] 2 Ch 122.

for aid to churches, hospitals and schools and for the assistance of the poor and aged in Cephalonia;[261] a trust for planting a grove of olive trees in Israel;[262] and a trust for a working men's hostel in Cyprus.[263]

Commonwealth jurisdictions have also upheld charitable purposes which bring a benefit abroad.[264] In *Re Levy Estate*[265] the Ontario Court of Appeal held that a gift to Israel for charitable purposes under the fourth head was valid even though there was no benefit to the Canadian community. Blair JA rejected earlier English authorities and the views of the Charity Commissioners and concluded:

'The principle that gifts, which are valid for charitable purposes in Canada are equally valid for the same charitable purposes abroad, is deeply embedded in our jurisprudence and also reflects the multinational and multicultural origins of Canadians.'[266]

In their Annual Report of 1992 the Charity Commissioners adopted this approach and rejected the complex concepts of tangible and intangible benefit to the community of the United Kingdom. In future, a charity of any type operating abroad will be presumed charitable in the same way as if its operations were confined to the United Kingdom. This presumption will be rebutted if it would be contrary to public policy to recognise the charity.[267] This simplification of the laws is to be welcomed.

## 7  Trusts with political objects

The fundamental principle behind the definition of charity is that purposes which are charitable must be for the public benefit. However, even if a purpose falls within one of the categories above, and is therefore considered as beneficial, it will not be charitable if it is for political purposes. Lord Parker in *Bowman v Secular Society*[268] stated that equity had always refused to recognise as charitable 'purely political objects'. This restriction was applied by Slade J in *McGovern v A-G.*[269] Amnesty International wanted to set up a trust with four main objects:

(1)  the relief of needy relatives and dependants of prisoners of conscience;

(2)  attempting to secure the release of prisoners of conscience;

(3)  procuring the abolition of torture or inhuman or degrading treatment or punishment;

(4)  undertaking, and disseminating the results of research into the observance of human rights.

---

[261]  *Re Vagliano* [1905] WN 179.        [262]  *Re Jacobs* (1970) 114 Sol Jo 515.

[263]  *Re Niyazi's Will Trusts* [1978] 1 WLR 910.

[264]  *Re Lowin* [1967] 2 NSWR 140, CA; *Re Stone* (1970) 91 WNNSW 704 (SC); *Lander v Whitbread* [1982] 2 NSWLR 530.

[265]  (1989) 58 DLR (4th) 375.        [266]  (1989) 58 DLR (4th) 375 at 383.

[267]  *Report of the Charity Commissioners for England and Wales 1992*, para 76.

[268]  [1917] AC 406.        [269]  [1982] Ch 321.

The Charity Commissioners had refused to register the trust as a charity, and their decision was affirmed by Slade J, who held that the main purpose was political.

## (1) Meaning of 'political objects'

In the course of his judgment Slade J identified the circumstances in which a court would regard a trust as political. The tests he proposed were more recently approved (although in a different context) by the Court of Appeal in *R v Radio Authority, ex p Bull*.[270] A trust will be regarded as political if it has as a direct or principal purpose:

### (a) To further the interests of a political party

Thus, in *Re Ogden*[271] a trust to promote 'Liberal principles' in politics was held not to be charitable.[272] The Charity Commissioners refused to register 'Youth Training' as a charity, since its purpose was to assist the Workers' Revolutionary Party.[273]

### (b) To procure changes in the laws of this country[274]

A ground for the decision of the House of Lords in *National Anti-Vivisection Society v IRC*[275] was that the society's object of the abolition of vivisection would necessitate a change in the law of the land. This, it was held, would not be charitable. Summarising the law and the rationale for this principle, Slade J said:

'. . . the court will not regard as charitable a trust of which the main object is to procure an alteration of the law of the United Kingdom for one of two or both of two reasons; first, the court will ordinarily have no sufficient means of judging as a matter of evidence whether the proposed change will or will not be for the public benefit.[276] Secondly, even if the evidence suffices to enable it to form a prima facie opinion that a change in the law is desirable, it must still decide the case on the principle that the law is right as it stands since to do otherwise would usurp the functions of the legislature.'

This leaves in some doubt the position of campaigns for law reform. The promotion of the present status quo by maintaining the existing law or policy is equally a political purpose,[277] unless the effect of the law or policy concerned is to promote a charitable purpose.[278]

---

[270] [1998] QB 294; [1997] PL 615 (Stevens and Feldman).   [271] [1933] Ch 678.

[272] See also *Bonar Law Memorial Trust v IRC* (1933) 49 TLR 220.

[273] Charity Commissioners for England and Wales Annual Report 1982, paras 451–651.

[274] *IRC v Temperance Council of Christian Churches of England and Wales* (1926) 10 TC 748; *National Anti-Vivisection Society v IRC* [1948] AC 31.

[275] [1948] AC 31.

[276] See *Bowman v Secular Society* [1917] AC 406 at 443, per Lord Parker of Waddington: 'a trust for the attainment of political objects has always been held invalid, not because it is illegal . . . but because the court has no means of judging whether a proposed change in the law will or will not be for the public benefit'. See also [1973] Anglo-American Law Review 47 (Sheridan).

[277] *Re Hopkinson* [1949] 1 All ER 346; *Re Koeppler Will Trusts* [1984] Ch 243.

[278] *Re Vallance* (1876) 2 Seton's Judgements (7th edn) 1304; *Re Herrick* (1918) 52 ILT 213.

### (c) To procure changes in the law of a foreign country

Although there is no obligation on the court to assume that foreign law is right as it stands, Slade J considered that it was still impossible to judge whether a change in foreign law would be beneficial to the community, and therefore such purposes are not charitable. In *R v Radio Authority, ex p Bull*[279] it was held that even the attempt to persuade countries to implement human rights in accordance with their obligations through international treaties was political.

### (d) To procure a reversal of government policy or of particular decisions of governmental authorities in this country

The courts are also unwilling to encroach on the functions of the executive. Therefore, and also because it is impossible to determine whether any changes would result in a public benefit, Slade J held that such purposes would not be charitable.

### (e) To procure a reversal of government policy or of particular decisions of governmental authorities in a foreign country

Similarly the court has no satisfactory means of judging whether there is any public benefit from such a reversal.

## (2) Application of the restriction

Whatever the category of charitable purpose, if a trust or organisation has political purposes, it cannot be recognised as charitable. In *Re Hopkinson*[280] a gift was made for the advancement of adult education on the lines of a Labour Party memorandum. Vaisey J held that the purpose was 'political propaganda masquerading as education' and therefore not charitable.[281] In *Re Bushnell*[282] a trust for the promotion of socialised medicine through the publishing and distribution of books was held to be political rather than for the provision of medical care. In contrast, in *Re Koeppler Will Trusts*[283] a gift to 'Wilton Park', an institution which was not party political and sought to promote greater co-operation in Europe, was held charitable. The Court of Appeal emphasised that the discussions it organised were neither party political nor propagandist. More recently the Charity Commission decided that the Centre for Corporate Accountability was not exclusively charitable because, although it was established for the charitable purpose of promoting public safety, it sought to do so by advocating changes to the law of corporate killing and influencing the prosecutions and investigations policy of the Crown Prosecution Service and the Health and Safety Executive.[284] Charities have been held not to be entitled to engage in public campaigning on political issues unrelated to their charitable objects. In *Baldry v Feintuck*[285] a student union was

---

279 [1998] QB 294; [1997] PL 615 (Stevens and Feldman).      280 [1949] 1 All ER 346.

281 However, in *Re Trust of Arthur McDougall Fund* [1956] 3 All ER 867 it was held that a trust for the education of the public in forms of government and in political matters generally was charitable.

282 [1975] 1 WLR 1596.      283 [1986] Ch 423.

284 Decision of the Charity Commissioners for England and Wales, *Application for Registration of the Centre for Corporate Accountability* (24 August 2001).

285 [1972] 2 All ER 81.

held to have applied money to a non-charitable object when it supported a campaign against the Government policy of ending free milk in schools. Similarly, in *Webb v O'Doherty* [286] support by a student union of a campaign against the Gulf War was held non-charitable.

## (3) Ancillary political activities

Slade J's decision in *McGovern v A-G* [287] initially gave many charities cause for concern. Amnesty International had taken professional advice in drawing up their trust deed. The whole intention was 'that there should be hived off into a trust those purposes which they had been advised would be charitable'.[288] The decision of Slade J was therefore something of a surprise. It affected not just Amnesty International, but also other charities, like Oxfam or Shelter, which, in addition to fulfilling their main purpose of providing relief or care services, would also seek to influence government opinion in favour of the causes which they espoused. Slade J had recognised that a limited degree of political activity was permissible, provided that it was not a main purpose of the trust. He said:

'Trust purposes of an otherwise charitable nature do not lose it merely because the trustees, by way of furtherance of such purposes, have incidental powers to carry on activities which are not themselves charitable . . . If all the main objects of the trust are exclusively charitable, the mere fact that the trustees may have incidental powers to employ political means for their furtherance will not deprive them of their charitable status.'[289]

In *R v Radio Authority, ex p Bull*,[290] Lord Woolf pointed out that this proposition worked both ways, and that therefore an activity which was not in itself political could be considered to become political if it had the objective of promoting a political purpose. 'It takes its nature from the principal objective.'[291]

It is on the basis of the limited 'ancillary purposes' exception that the Charity Commissioners have drawn up guidelines on political activities for charities. In *R v Radio Authority, ex p Bull*, Brooke LJ commented on the impact of this exception:

'Many charitable trusts today—national charities concerned with children, or the physically or mentally disabled, or with housing the homeless, for example—are prominent in their espousal of political means to attain their ends.'[292]

In part, this level of political activity may reflect a softening in the attitude to political activity from the view expressed by Slade J in *McGovern v A-G*.

## (4) Legitimate political activity by charities

It is obviously correct that purposes of a truly political nature should not receive the state subsidy in effect granted to charities through tax privileges. However, it is also the

---

[286] (1991) Times, 11 February.    [287] [1982] Ch 321.

[288] [1981] 3 All ER 493 at 500, per Slade J. Amnesty did ultimately come up with a scheme for a trust which satisfied the Charity Commissioners: see [1997] 2 All ER at 581 and 584.

[289] [1981] 3 All ER 493 at 509 and 511.    [290] [1997] 2 All ER 561.

[291] [1997] 2 All ER 561 at 572.    [292] [1997] 2 All ER 561 at 580.

case that many well-established charities engage in political activity of some type, whether campaigning, lobbying Parliament or advocating changes in the law. For example, the housing charity Shelter may challenge government housing policy, and relief agencies may demand a different attitude by government towards the Third World. A fine balance must be drawn between legitimate political activity by charities, and political activism which is incompatible with the retention of charitable status— any political activity must be purely ancillary to their main charitable objects. This was the theme of the advice given to charity trustees by the Charity Commissioner in guidelines published in their 1981 Report.[293]

In 1999 the Charity Commissioners provided updated comprehensive guidance to charity trustees in their publication *Political Activities and Campaigning by Charities*.[294] Their advice was further updated following the Prime Minister's Strategy Unit report, *Private Action, Public Benefit*—a review of charities and the wider not-for-profit sector.[295] This recommended that the Charity Commission's guidance on political campaigning should place a greater emphasis on the campaigning activities that charities can undertake because:

'• their strong links into local communities means that charities are well placed to monitor, evaluate and comment upon policies as they are implemented;

• the high levels of public trust and confidence they command means that charities are well placed to offer alternative ways of engaging with the public policy debate and the processes of democracy; and

• the diversity of causes they represent, [enables] charities to give voice to a far wider range of political perspectives, including those of minority groups or interests, than might otherwise be heard by government.'[296]

The Commission acknowledges that, whilst an organisation can never be a charity if it is established for political purposes, 'campaigning and political activity may be carried out by recognised charities as a means of furthering their charitable purposes'.[297] Charity trustees are expected to be satisfied on reasonable grounds that:

'• the activities will be an effective means of furthering the purposes of the charity; and

• they will do so to an extent justified by the resources applied.'[298]

The trustees must also comply with the general law and any regulatory requirements and verify that the activities are permitted under the governing trust document.[299] A charity may seek to influence government.[300] It may provide and publish comments on possible or proposed changes in the law or government policy,[301] and advocate a change

---

293  *Report of the Charity Commissioners of England and Wales for 1981*, paras 53–56.
294  CC9—Political Activities and Campaigning by Charities (September 1999).
295  September 2002
296  CC9—Political Activities and Campaigning by Charities (September 2004), para 5.
297  CC9—Political Activities and Campaigning by Charities (September 2004), para 12.
298  CC9—Political Activities and Campaigning by Charities (September 2004), para 16.
299  CC9—Political Activities and Campaigning by Charities (September 2004), para 17.
300  CC9—Political Activities and Campaigning by Charities (September 2004), para 51.
301  CC9—Political Activities and Campaigning by Charities (September 2004), para 55.

in the law or public policy provided that these activities do not become the dominant means by which it carries out its purposes.[302] The Charity Commission indicates that it does not consider seeking to influence public opinion as political activity.[303] A charity may promote or participate in a demonstration or direct action,[304] but must be mindful of the potential risks.[305]

The guidance currently given by the Charity Commission is far less cautious than it was in 1995, when the guidance was first issued. The interpretation given by the Charity Commission of what political activities are permitted go significantly beyond the limits set out by Slade J in *McGovern v A-G*,[306] even as subsequently glossed in *Re Koeppler Will Trusts*.[307] A further indication of the extent to which the Charity Commission has stretched the law is provided in their guidance for Human Rights' Charities.[308] In this publication the Charity Commission indicate that, provided that there is a reasonable expectation that the ends are proportionate to the means and that the activities do not dominate the activities of the charity,[309] it is permissible for the charity to campaign using materials which present only one side of the argument,[310] to campaign for changes in the law,[311] and to press the government of a particular country to adopt particular human rights legislation.[312] It may do this even where a country's domestic law is inconsistent with international standards.[313]

## (5) Critique of the political purposes test

A larger question than the limits on political campaigning, however, is whether the judicial aversion to political trusts is well founded. Slade J in *McGovern v A-G*[314] spoke of the difficulty of judges identifying whether a change in the law is for the public benefit and of the danger of usurping the functions of the legislature. The objection which Slade J gives to party political purposes is that:

'Since their nature would be ex hypothesi be very controversial, the court could be faced with even greater difficulties in determining whether the objects of the trust would be for the public benefit; correspondingly, it would be at even greater risk of encroaching on the functions of the legislature and prejudicing its reputation for political impartiality, if it were to promote such objects by enforcing the trust.'[315]

Slade J gave almost identical reasons for objecting to trusts which sought to achieve their objective through influencing opinion. There would again be no way of telling

---

[302] CC9—Political Activities and Campaigning by Charities (September 2004), para 23
[303] CC9—Political Activities and Campaigning by Charities (September 2004), para 22.
[304] CC9—Political Activities and Campaigning by Charities (September 2004), para 38.
[305] CC9—Political Activities and Campaigning by Charities (September 2004), para 39–41.
[306] [1982] Ch 321.      [307] [1986] Ch 423.
[308] RR12—The Promotion of Human Rights (January 2005).
[309] RR12—The Promotion of Human Rights (January 2005) para 34.
[310] Para 25. In 1999 charities were told that they needed to use well-founded reasoned argument to make their case to government (CC9—Political Activities and Campaigning by Charities (September 1999), para 8).
[311] Para 24.      [312] Para 31.      [313] Para 32.      [314] [1982] Ch 321.
[315] [1981] 3 All ER 493 at 507.

whether a reversal of government policy was for the public benefit 'and in any event [the court] could not properly encroach on the functions of the executive, acting intra vires, by holding that it should be acting in some other manner'.[316]

The objections which Slade J sets out are almost certainly overstated. His aversion to comment on whether the changes in the law are for the public benefit does not seem to have prevented the judges shaping the law through the development of new rules and principles,[317] nor has it prevented them, on occasions, making suggestions for law reform in their judgments. Judges have also taken a leading role in law reform through chairmanship of the Law Commission. Lord Woolf in *R v Radio Authority ex p Bull*[318] acknowledged that a campaign to seek a change in the law would be political even though it could also be commendable. Fine distinctions have also been made. Slade J had no difficulty in reconciling *Jackson v Phillips*[319] with his view of political purposes. There the Massachusetts Supreme Court had upheld as charitable a trust to campaign against slavery before slavery was prohibited in the United States. Slade J took the view that 'the pressure was to be directed by the trustees against individual persons, rather than governments with a view to obtaining the "voluntary manumission" of the slaves belonging to such individuals'.[320]

Much of the objection to the court 'taking sides' would be overcome if, as has been suggested above, the court adopted the policy of accepting purposes as being for the public benefit if they are not immoral, illegal or subversive and are adopted by a significant proportion of the public. It would then be possible for opposing views both to be capable of being considered charitable. It may also be that a distinction needs to be made between propagandist trusts and those which seek to influence public and governmental opinion, and perhaps even influence changes in laws, not through any pre-ordained view of what is right and wrong (which is the position taken in many 'political' activities), but only after careful and considered debate. After all, why should a trust to promote the work of the Law Commission not be held charitable, even though the whole purpose of the Commission is to change the law?

Strong support for the view that such a distinction should be made can be found in *Re Koeppler Will Trusts*.[321] The testator had left a substantial gift to support the work of 'Wilton Park', in making 'a British contribution to the formation of an informed international public opinion and to the promotion of greater co-operation in Europe and the West in general'. The organisation worked by bringing together in conferences a broad range of politicians, academics, civil servants, industrialists and journalists to exchange views on political, economic and social views of common interest. Peter Gibson J, at first instance, having considered the *McGovern* case, held that 'trusts aimed at securing better international relations, including co-operation in a particular part of the world, can properly be called political causes . . . Whether there should be better relations and co-operation and, if so, how it should be achieved and with whom are matters for government decision, not for the court'.[322] This view was overruled by the Court of Appeal. The judgment of the court was given by Slade LJ (who had now been

---

[316] [1981] 3 All ER 493 at 508.    [317] See the discussion in Chapter 1.
[318] [1997] 2 All ER 561 at 571.    [319] 96 Mass 539 (1867).    [320] [1981] 3 All ER 493 at 514.
[321] [1986] Ch 423.    [322] [1984] 2 All ER 111 at 124.

promoted to the Court of Appeal). He distinguished the case from his previous decision in *McGovern*:

'In the present case . . . the activities of Wilton Park are not of a party political nature. Nor, as far as the evidence shows, are they designed to procure changes in the laws or governmental policy of this or any other country: even when they touch on political matters, they constitute, so far as I can see, no more than genuine attempts in an objective manner to ascertain and disseminate the truth. In these circumstances I think that no objections to the trust arise on a political score . . . The trust is, in my opinion, entitled to what is sometimes called a "benignant construction", in the sense that the court is entitled to presume that the trustees will only act in a lawful and proper manner appropriate to the trustees of a charity and not, for example, by the propagation of tendentious political opinions.'[323]

For Slade LJ to say in this case that there was no intention to change laws or governmental policy seems rather disingenuous. A large part of the reason for bringing together distinguished conference participants capable of influencing opinion in Europe and the West must surely have been to act as a driver for co-operation between states and governments. If that is not 'political' at an international level, it is hard to see what could be. The major significance of this judgment must therefore be the recognition that a distinction can be drawn between 'the propagation of tendentious political opinions' which the court will not consider to be charitable, and 'genuine attempts objectively to ascertain and disseminate the truth', even in a political context, which can be charitable. Applying this test, a trust to promote the work of the Law Commission could be charitable, even if a trust to reform the rule against perpetuities would not.

# 8 The requirement of public benefit

## (1) General principles

It is not enough for a trust to be charitable that it is for a purpose which is recognised as charitable. It has also always been the case that the way in which that purpose is achieved must also be for the public benefit. That requirement has been given statutory force by the Charities Bill 2005, cll 2(1)(b) and 3. Public benefit is defined as having the same meaning as under the previous law with one major change, which is that there is no presumption that a purpose of a particular description is for the public benefit, as was the case in some instances under the previous law.

The Charity Commission has issued guidance on its understanding of the public benefit requirement. The guidance indicates that public benefit has the two elements of (a) a benefit of a kind which is recognsed by law, and which (b) is 'provided for or

---

[323] [1985] 2 All ER 869 at 878.

available to the public or a sufficient section of the public.'[324] The Charity Commission further break this analysis down into five principles:[325]

| | |
|---|---|
| **The Benefit:** | i. There must be an identifiable benefit, but this can take many different forms. |
| | ii. Benefit is assessed in the light of modern conditions. |
| **The Public:** | iii. The benefit must be to the public at large, or to a sufficient section of the public. |
| | iv. Any private benefit must be incidental. |
| | v. Those who are less well off must not be entirely excluded from benefit. |

## (2) What is 'identifiable benefit'?

It is so obvious that it hardly needs saying that for a benefit to be recognised by law, it must be of a kind which promotes a purpose which has been recognised by law as charitable. The public benefit in a charity for the advancement of education could not consist of something which has no connection whatever to education. This is simply an application of the principle that the activities of a charity must be consistent with the purposes of the charity.

Even where this requirement is satisfied, there can be difficult issues as to whether the alleged benefit should be recognised. Some purposes or activities may be beneficial in the eyes of some but detrimental in the eyes of others. For example, some members of the community may think that public health would be promoted by campaigning to promote vegetarianism, but others may think that advocating the eating of red meat would be in the public interest for similar reasons. How can the Charity Commission or the court determine whether there is a public benefit without simply making a value judgment?

### (a) A subjective assessment of benefit

One possibility would be for the court to adopt a subjective test, and uphold the gift if the donor thought the activity confers public benefit. This approach seems to have been applied by Chitty J in *Re Foveaux*,[326] where a gift to the International Society for the Total Suppression of Vivisection was held charitable. He acknowledged that vivisection was a practice over which opinion was divided, and said that it was not for the court to 'enter into or pronounce any opinion on the merits of the controversy which subsists between the supporters and opponents of the practice of vivisection'. Instead, when 'humane men and women of a high order of intelligence and education are found in the ranks on either side the law stands neutral'. This reluctance to judge the merits of questions of morals where men's minds reasonably differ was also reflected in the Irish case of *Re Cranston*,[327] which concerned a gift to a vegetarian society. Fitzgibbon LJ took

---

[324] Charity Commission: Public Benefit—the Charity Commission's approach (January 2005), para 14.
[325] Charity Commission: Public Benefit—the Charity Commission's approach (January 2005), para 15. See also Charity Commission: Public Benefit—the legal principles (January 2005), para 3.
[326] [1895] 2 Ch 501.     [327] [1898] 1 IR 431.

the view that it would be charitable provided the purpose was one which the founder of the society believed to be to public advantage, and that his belief 'be at least rational and not contrary either to the general law of the land or to the principles of morality'. The key factor is the subjective belief of the donor, within certain objective limits, that the purpose is beneficial. In neither of these two cases was the court willing to weigh the alleged benefits of the purpose against its alleged drawbacks.

## (b) An objective assessment of benefit

In *National Anti-Vivisection Society v IRC*[328] the House of Lords overruled the decision in *Re Foveaux*[329] and held that a gift to the society, whose object was the suppression of vivisection, was not charitable. They adopted an objective approach to the question of public benefit, and a willingness to weigh the merits of the purpose. Lord Simmonds stated:

'Where on the evidence before it the court concludes that, however well-intentioned the donor, the achievement of his object will be greatly to the public disadvantage, there can be no justification for saying that it is a charitable object.'

The House was faced by the decision of fact of the Special Commissioners for Income Tax that any benefit 'was far outweighed by the detriment to medical science and research and consequently to the public health which would result if the society succeeded in achieving its objects'. This objective approach assumes that the court is competent to make judgments of what is in the public interest. This is questionable, especially when fine moral issues over which there is a real divergence of opinion in society are involved, and at best the court can only give its own value judgment on the issue. The subjective approach, with objective limitations, suggested in *Re Cranston*[330] provides a more attractive alternative. There is no need for the court to make such decisions. Is it not possible that both a trust for the prevention of animal experimentation and a trust for the promotion of medical research could be considered charitable, although their objects are to some extent in conflict? Similarly, could not a trust for the promotion of vegetarianism be charitable alongside a trust for the promotion of meat? All that is really needed is a test which will eliminate those purposes which are in no sense in the public interest or are of benefit only to small and obscure groups and sects. A test which would uphold purposes which a substantial body of public opinion regards as beneficial would be adequate for this purpose. In *Funnell v Stewart*[331] it was held that a trust to advance the practice of faith healing was charitable on the grounds that it had become 'a recognised activity of public benefit'. This suggests that the attitude of the public will be a prime factor in determining whether an activity should be characterised as for the public benefit.

## (3) Different forms of benefit

### (a) Benefit may be practical or moral

The public benefit may consist of practical assistance, as in most cases involving the relief of need, for instance through the provision of housing to the homeless, financial

---

[328] [1948] AC 31.    [329] [1895] 2 Ch 501.    [330] [1898] 1 IR 431.    [331] [1996] 1 WLR 288.

assistance to the poor, or advocacy for those who lack the mental capacity to represent themselves. The benefit may also be of a moral nature. For instance, the promotion of fine music or the preservation of the cultural heritage may have no direct practical benefits, but they may help to improve the human condition in a moral or intellectual sense. It used to be considered that the provision of overseas aid was justified on moral, rather than practical grounds, although a different view is now taken. The Charity Commission has indicated that in deciding whether there are intangible benefits, it will take into account the general consensus of fair-minded and unprejudiced opinion, although public opinion cannot by itself determine what is charitable.[332]

### (b) Benefit may be direct or indirect

It is possible for indirect benefits to be taken into account in deciding whether there is public benefit. A trust to train teachers in the use of sign language provides services directly to the individuals who are trained, but the greater benefits are to the pupils who will benefit from having teachers who have the skills which they need for their education. A hospice providing care for the terminally ill confers benefits not only on the patients who may receive care more closely aligned to their needs than would otherwise be the case; it also relieves the burden which the National Health Service would need to carry, and it provides assistance to the family of the patient who might find it difficult to cope in providing the level of intensive support which a patient needs. All of these factors can be weighed in the balance in deciding whether there is a benefit to the public.

### (c) Benefit must not be 'too remote'

Even where a trust exists to promote an objective which might be thought to be beneficial to the community, it will not be charitable if the benefit received is too remote in nature. In *IRC v Oldham Training and Enterprise Council*[333] a TEC existed to promote 'trade, commerce and enterprise' in the Oldham area by providing 'support services and advice to and for new businesses'. It was argued that although this might involve promotion of the interests of individuals engaged in trade and commerce, this would be charitable because such efforts would 'make the recipients more profitable and thereby, or otherwise, to improve employment prospects in Oldham'. However, Lightman J held that these objects were non-charitable because the 'benefits to the community conferred by such activities are too remote'.[334]

## (4) Assessing benefit in the light of modern conditions

There is not the slightest doubt that the concept of what constitutes a public benefit has changed over the years, and that this is reflected in the decisions of the courts and of the Charity Commission. For instance, it is now recognised that charities which operate overseas can be justified on the basis of the benefits which they confer on their overseas beneficiaries, without needing to show a benefit to the public in the

---

[332] Charity Commission: Public Benefit—the legal principles (January 2005), para 9.
[333] [1996] STC 1218.     [334] [1996] STC 1218 at 1235.

United Kingdom.[335] Views relating to the conservation of the built and natural heritage have changed. There is now, for instance, a belief that the protection of biodiversity could in itself be of value without needing to establish immediate practical benefits.[336]

The assessment of benefit is, however, not free from controversy. A particularly contentious issue which has taken up much time in debate over the Charities Bill 2005 in both Lords and Commons concerns the charitable status of public schools, which is discussed below. The Government has essentially passed this thorny issue to the Charity Commission for resolution. The Charity Commission anticipates that its task will be far from straightforward:

'Applying principles drawn from a small number of cases involving particular charities and situations will involve difficult judgements and interpretations of the law to be made by the Commission. Quite rightly, these will be open to challenge.

For this reason we believe that if changes to the Bill are being considered the development of the law would be enhanced if a future Charities Act included non-exclusive, high level criteria, including issues around fee charging charities, which would clarify the general principles established by the existing law to be taken into account in assessing public benefit.'[337]

## (5) Benefit to the public

### (a) General considerations

It might seem fairly obvious as to whether there is a benefit to the public, but in many cases it is hard to determine whether benefits are genuinely public. For instance, the provision of a park in Birmingham is unlikely to be of much value to the residents of Lampeter. Does it therefore confer benefits on the public? If a trust provides advice and guidance to people suffering from a rare disease, can that be considered to be providing benefits on the public? The answer in both cases is likely to be that the activities concerned are for the public benefit, but they are clearly not for the benefit of the whole of the public, if by that we mean the whole population of England and Wales, or of the United Kingdom. If benefits are available only to part of the public, how can we determine whether those benefits are to the public or merely to a group of private individuals? The cases on public benefit have, in the past, distinguished between different heads of charity. They raise complex issues and are not always easy to reconcile. The abolition of the presumption of public benefit for some categories of charity may result in a harmonisation of the principles of public benefit, but the Charity Commission considers that 'the public benefit requirement is likely in practice to look different for different groups of charities.'[338] Nevertheless, there are some recurrent themes and common principles.

---

[335] *Report of the Charity Commissioners for England and Wales 1992*, para 76.

[336] RR1—The Review of the Register of Charities (2001), para B9.

[337] Public Benefit—The Charity Commission's position on how public benefit is treated in the Charities Bill (July 2005)

[338] Public Benefit—the Charity Commission's approach (January 2005), para 17.

## (b) The 'personal nexus' rule

*(i) Meaning of the 'personal nexus' rule.* The most important case in which a strict test was devised to determine the question of public benefit is the decision of the House of Lords in *Oppenheim v Tobacco Securities Trust Co Ltd*[339] John Phillips was a large shareholder in British American Tobacco (BAT), and on his death he left securities to the trust company to be held upon trust and the income applied to provide for the education of the children of the employees or ex-employees of BAT. The House took the view that this group was not a section of the public but a private class, and that the trust was therefore non-charitable. The principle was stated by Lord Simmonds, who identified two characteristics which would render a class of beneficiaries a 'section of the public'. First, such a class would have to be 'not numerically negligible'. Secondly, the identity of the members of the class could not be defined by means of a personal nexus. He explained that:

'. . . the quality which distinguishes [the potential beneficiaries] from other members of the community, so that they form by themselves a section of it, must be a quality which does not depend on their relationship to a particular individual.'[340]

Thus, although the employees and ex-employees formed a class of some 110,000 persons, they were not a section of the public because they were identified by their personal contractual relationship with BAT. As Lord Simmonds said:

'A group of persons may be numerous but, if the nexus between them is their personal relationship to a single propositus or to several propositi, they are neither the community nor a section of the community for charitable purposes.'[341]

This 'personal nexus' rule provides a conclusive test of whether a class should be regarded as a section of the public. If the identifying feature of the class is their nexus to a particular individual or group of individuals, they cannot constitute a section of the public. So the employees of a company would not constitute a section of the public, nor would the relatives of an individual[342] or the members of a trade union.[343] It is questionable whether, for example, the patients of a particular doctor, clients of a firm of solicitors, members of a university and other similar classes would be excluded by this test. The Charity Commission has recently suggested that any connection would be inappropriate if it was unrelated to the organisation's purpose, for example 'by hair colour or support for a particular football team'.[344]

The rationale behind the test is understandable, namely that purely private groups should not receive the tax privileges enjoyed by charities. If BAT had attempted to set up a similar trust in favour of its own employees, charitable status should not have been granted as the company would have been seeking to provide its employees with a

---

[339] [1951] AC 297.    [340] [1951] AC 297 at 306.    [341] [1951] AC 297.

[342] See *Re Compton* [1945] Ch 123, where the Court of Appeal held that a trust for the education of the descendants of three named persons was not charitable.

[343] *Re Mead's Trust Deed* [1961] 1 WLR 1244.

[344] Public Benefit—the legal principles (January 2005) para 23. See also RR8—The Public Character of Charity (February 2001), para 11.

tax-free benefit. However, the facts of *Oppenheim*[345] were essentially different. The trust was established by a man whose only interest in the company was that he owned a substantial shareholding,[346] and in no sense was there an attempt by the company to give their employees a tax-free perk. In such circumstances, where the gift was made by an outside donor to a substantial class, it is questionable whether there is any reason for refusing charitable status.

The philosophy of providing rigid tests for public benefit is also questionable, since it is impossible to devise a rule which will cover all circumstances and not lead to anomalous results. For this reason, Lord MacDermott dissented from the decision of the other members of the House of Lords in *Oppenheim*, and rejected the personal nexus test. He pointed out that historically there had been no single conclusive test as to what constituted a sufficient section of the public, but that instead:

'The usual way of approaching the issue . . . was . . . to regard the facts of each case and to treat the matter very much as one of degree.'[347]

He pointed out that far from proving conclusive, the 'personal nexus' test would produce unacceptable anomalies:

'Are miners in the service of the National Coal Board now in one category and miners at a particular pit or of a particular district in another?'[348]

The force of Lord MacDermott's criticisms was felt by all members of the House of Lords in *Dingle v Turner*,[349] which is discussed below.

However, despite these criticisms the personal nexus test has continued to be applied and is contained in the Charity Commission guidance on public benefit,[350] although the Commission has indicated that 'whilst the Commission must apply the law as set out in the *Oppenheim* decision unless and until it is over-ruled, it should be both cautious and flexible in the application of the test.'[351] Moreover, the courts have not merely looked to the definition of the class of beneficiaries but to the manner in which the purportedly charitable benefit has been allocated, thus following the time-honoured maxim that equity looks to the substance rather than the form. The personal nexus test was applied by the Court of Appeal in *IRC v Educational Grants Association Ltd.*[352] Metal Box Ltd established and funded the EGA, which had the object of advancing education by providing grants for individuals to attend university or private schools. Between 76% and 85% of the grants made by the EGA were made to children of employees of Metal Box, although Metal Box was not mentioned in the memorandum of association of the EGA. The Court of Appeal held that in practice there was a personal nexus, and that the EGA was not exclusively charitable. This decision seems correct, as it is clear that Metal Box were attempting to provide tax-free benefits for their employees under

---

[345] See above, p 530.
[346] See [1951] AC 297 at 299, where it is recorded that 'no evidence was given of any connection of the grantors with the company except that John Phillips was a large stockholder'.
[347] [1951] AC 297 at 314.     [348] [1951] AC 297 at 318.     [349] [1972] AC 601.
[350] Charity Commission: Public Benefit—the legal principles (January 2005), para 23.
[351] Charity Commission: Public Benefit—the legal principles (January 2005), para A11.
[352] [1967] Ch 993.

the cloak of charity. However, the same conclusion would surely have been reached by a more flexible test looking to all the circumstances of the case. In *Re Koettgen's Will Trusts*[353] an educational trust was open to the public at large, subject to a direction that the trustees were to give preference to the families of employees, up to a maximum of 75% of the income. This was held to be valid, although Pennycuick J in *IRC v Educational Grants Association* expressed considerable difficulty with it. In *Caffoor v Income Tax Comr for Columbo*[354] it was held that a preference for the grantor's family made an educational trust non-charitable. This seems to be the better view, although it must be a question of degree in each case whether the extent of a preference is sufficient to deprive an otherwise charitable trust of its charitable status. The Charity Commission has put forward an interpretation of the personal nexus rule which looks to the substance rather than to the form and therefore helps to modify its most extreme application:

'• there may be a sufficient section of the public in a case where (even though all potential beneficiaries might actually be connected by kin or contract):
   ○ on a general survey of the circumstances and considerations regarded as relevant it is clear that a public class is intended; and
   ○ that class can be (and, as a rule, is in fact) described otherwise than by reference to kin or contractual relationship[356]
• if it is difficult to describe a class using objective and impersonal terms, that would indicate that the body concerned is established for private rather than public benefit; and
• in those cases where the conclusion is that private benefits are intended for a group of individuals who are not together fairly describable as a section of the public or a section of the public, the [personal nexus] rule applies to deny the benefits of charitable status.'[355]

The Charity Commission also expresses the view that to treat groups differently on the basis simply of the way in which the group is defined by the terms of a trust or gift 'would be amenable to challenge under the Human Rights Act 1998 if it leads to an outcome which is not justifiable relationally in the public interest in terms of charity law.'[357]

*(ii) The scope of the 'personal nexus' rule.* The personal nexus test has not been applied to all categories of charity. *Oppenheim v Tobacco Securities Trust Co Ltd* and *IRC v Educational Grants Association* both concerned trusts for the advancement of education, and the test clearly applies to that head. It was also applied to charities within Lord Macnaghten's fourth head of 'other purposes beneficial to the community'.[358] It was not applied to trusts for the advancement of religion, provided that the religiously-affected people lived their lives amongst the community at large (an illustration of the

---

[353] [1954] Ch 252.    [354] [1961] AC 584.
[355] Charity Commission: Public Benefit—the legal principles (January 2005), para A13.
[356] See *Springhill Housing Action Committee v Commissioner of Valuation* [1983] NI 184
[357] Charity Commission: Public Benefit—the legal principles (January 2005), para A15.
[358] See *Re Drummond* [1914] 2 Ch 90, where a gift to provide the holiday expenses of the workpeople of a spinning company was held not charitable since it was not for general public purposes.

acceptance of indirect benefits). Most significantly, it did not apply to charities which fell under the head of relief of poverty. Thus, as Chadwick J observed in *Re Segelman (Decd)*:

'. . . a gift for the relief of poverty is no less charitable because those whose poverty is to be relieved are confined to a particular class limited by ties of blood or employment.'[359]

This exception enjoyed an insurmountable historical pedigree. In *Re Compton*,[360] where the personal nexus test was first suggested, Lord Greene MR referred to a series of cases where gifts to the 'poor relations' of an individual had been held charitable.[361] He concluded that although these cases would fail under the personal nexus test, they were to be regarded as 'anomalous'[362] exceptions to the principle. In *Oppenheim* Lord Simmonds was similarly unwilling to 'harmonise' and overturn the 'poor relations' cases.[363] It might be thought that members of a family are just the type of class which is private rather than public, and therefore not deserving of charitable status. The exception can only be justified on public policy grounds that the relief of poverty is such an important object to society that any gift which seeks to relieve it will be encouraged and upheld.[364] Thus, in *Re Scarisbrick's Will Trusts*[365] Bertha Scarisbrick left her residuary estate to trustees upon trust for her relations 'in needy circumstances'. The Court of Appeal held that this was a valid charitable trust. In *Dingle v Turner*[366] this exception was confirmed by the House of Lords. Frank Dingle left his residuary estate to trustees, the income to be used to pay pensions to the 'poor employees' of E Dingle & Co, a company which he jointly owned. The House of Lords held unanimously that the personal nexus rule had no application to trusts for the relief of poverty.[367] The exemption was re-affirmed in *Re Segelman*,[368] where a testator left property in his will to be used for a period of 21 years for the benefit of the poor and needy members of his family. A schedule was drawn up in which he named six members or his extended family and the issue of five of them as comprising the class of beneficiaries. Chadwick J held that this created a valid charitable gift, falling within the scope of the exception, because it was 'a gift to particular poor persons, the relief of poverty among them being the motive for the gift'.[369]

The special treatment of trusts for the relief of poverty did not seem to apply to trusts relieving needs of other types. Thus, in *Re Mead's Trust Deed*[370] a trust to provide a home for aged members of a trade union and to provide a sanatorium for members

---

[359] [1996] Ch 171, [1995] 3 All ER 676 at 687.      [360] [1945] Ch 123.

[361] *Isaac v DeFriez* (1754) Amb 595; *A-G v Price* (1810) 17 Ves 371; *Bernal v Bernal* (1838) 3 My & Cr 559; *Browne v Whalley* [1866] WN 386; *Gillam v Taylor* (1873) LR 16 Eq 581; *A-G v Duke of Northumberland* (1877) 7 Ch D 745.

[362] [1945] Ch 123 at 139.      [363] [1951] AC 297 at 308.

[364] See *Re Scarisbrick* [1951] Ch 622 at 639, per Evershed MR: 'The "poor relations" cases may be justified on the basis that the relief of poverty is of so altruistic a character that the public element may necessarily be inferred thereby, or they may be accepted as a hallowed, if illogical, exception.'

[365] [1951] Ch 622.      [366] [1972] AC 601.

[367] [1972] AC 601 at 623, per Lord Cross: 'it must be accepted that whatever else it may hold sway the *Compton* rule has no application in the field of trusts for the relief of poverty'.

[368] [1996] Ch 171, [1995] 3 All ER 676; [1996] Conv 379 (Bennett Histed).

[369] [1995] 3 All ER 676 at 688.      [370] [1961] 1 WLR 1244.

(i) 'Personal Nexus'

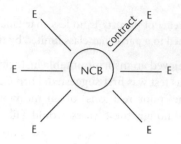

'Employees of the National Coal Board'

(i) 'No Personal Nexus'

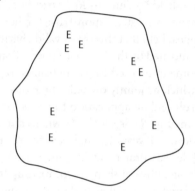

'Miners in a particular geographical area'

### The 'Personal Nexus' rule

suffering from tuberculosis was held not to be charitable because the members of a trade union are not a section of the public.

## (c) Possible harmonization of the personal nexus rule

The future of the anomalous exception of trusts for the relief of poverty from the personal nexus rule is uncertain. The public benefit in having a narrowly defined group of individuals kept in a lifestyle determined by reference to their former conditions of life rather than by reference to any objective assessment of poverty must be tenuous. Nor does a trust for financial provision for the members of one's own family have the characteristic of altruism that is normally the hallmark of charitable activity. It might be thought that such an anomaly could not survive the abolition of the presumption of public benefit in certain cases. Nevertheless, the Charity Commission appears to contemplate the continuation of this strange exception to the personal nexus rule,[371] although the Commission has not yet issued information about how the public benefit test will apply to the different purposes of the different groups of charities.[372]

## (d) The rule against a 'class within a class'

A second rigid and conclusive rule was imposed in *IRC v Baddeley*.[373] As was seen above, in this case a gift to a Methodist Mission in London for the promotion of the 'religious, social and physical training' of persons resident in West Ham and Leyton 'who were or were likely to become members of the Methodist Church' was held non-charitable because of the inclusion of social and recreational purposes. However, the House of Lords also held that the class of potential beneficiaries did not constitute a section of the public, so that there was insufficient 'public benefit'. There is no doubt that the residents of a particular area will be regarded as constituting a section of the public, but Viscount Simmonds drew a distinction between 'a form of relief extended to the whole community yet by its very nature advantageous only to the few and a form of relief accorded to a selected few out of a larger number equally willing and able to take advantage of it'.[374] He said that it would be charitable to provide a bridge, available to the public at large but only used by a very small number. However, it would be different for 'a bridge to be crossed only by impecunious Methodists'. He held that the proposed gift fell within the second category because it was not available to all the residents of West Ham and Leyton but only those who were, or were likely to become, members of the Methodist Church. In effect, he ruled that a class draw within a class will not amount to a section of the public:

'. . . a trust cannot qualify as a charity within the fourth class . . . if the beneficiaries are a class of persons not only confined to a particular area but selected from within it by reference to a particular creed.'[375]

The scope of this particular principle is uncertain. Lord Reid dissented, holding that the members of a particular church were a section of the public and that there should not be a different standard for public benefit between different heads of charity.[376] Lord Tucker[377] and Lord Porter[378] expressed no opinion on the question whether the potential beneficiaries constituted a section of the public. The rule flows from the opinion of Viscount Simmonds, expressed not just in *IRC v Baddeley* but also in *Williams' Trustees v IRC*,[379] that the test for public benefit should be more stringent where it does not fall within a substantively recognised group of charitable purposes.

The description of the limitation as preventing the creation of a 'class within a class' goes too far, since there are many cases where a charitable trust operates despite a double limitation on eligibility. For instance, a trust for poor widows in Rotherhithe was charitable despite there being three limitations on eligibility.[380] The real objection,

---

[371] Charity Commission: Public Benefit—the legal principles (January 2005), paras 23 and A19.
[372] Charity Commission: Public Benefit—the Charity Commission's approach (January 2005), para 18.
[373] [1955] AC 572.      [374] [1955] AC 572 at 592.      [375] [1955] AC 572 at 592.
[376] [1955] AC 572 at 612.      [377] [1955] AC 572 at 614.      [378] [1955] AC 572 at 593.
[379] [1947] AC 447.      [380] *Re Faraker* [1912] 2 Ch 488.

it is submitted, is the introduction of an arbitrary limitation on eligibility. There is no objection to funding a church for the use of Methodists, or a synagogue for the use of Jews. But to limit the use of a bridge to Methodists (even poor Methodists) is an arbitrary and capricious restriction in the use of a facility which should be made available to all.

The continuing relevance of this test for charities under Lord Macnaghten's fourth category has been affirmed by the Charity Commission. In giving guidance about charities for the relief of unemployment the Commission stated:

'It may be that the people living in a particular area of high unemployment belong predominantly to a particular racial, ethnic or religious or other group, and this group will inevitably be the main beneficiary of the organisation's activities. This is unobjectionable in terms of charity law *as long as* the benefits are not additionally *restricted* solely to members of that group. This would constitute a "class within a class", and is too small a beneficial class for charities set up to relieve unemployment.'[381]

The 'class within a class' rule is not, however, reflected in the Charity Commission's statement of the legal principles of public benefit which will apply under the Charities Bill 2005, except to the extent that the Commission indicates that irrational limits on the class of beneficiaries will not be permitted.[382]

### (e)  A flexible approach to public benefit

In contrast to the strict approach to questions of public benefit outlined above, others have advocated a more flexible response, arguing that strict tests are unworkable in practice and lead to anomalous results. They consider that each situation should be considered on its own facts, with a variety of circumstances being taken into account before an impressionistic judgment is made whether a class constitutes a section of the public or not.

As was noted above, in *Oppenheim v Tobacco Securities Trust Co Ltd* Lord Mac-Dermott dissented from the decision of the majority and held that the personal nexus rule should not alone govern the question of public benefit. He considered that to separate the attributes dividing human beings into classes into those purely personal and those purely impersonal was a task 'no less baffling and elusive than the problem to which it is directed, namely, the determination of what is and what is not a section of the public'.[383] He also pointed out the anomalous results that would follow from such a rigid approach, so that a trust framed to provide for the education of children of those employed in the tobacco industry in a named town would be charitable, even though the class of potential beneficiaries may have been appreciably smaller than that under the trust in question. It would also call into question long-standing charities, for example gifts for the education of the daughters of missionaries or children sent to a particular school. He therefore advocated a flexible approach whereby the court would 'regard the facts of each case and . . . treat the matter very much as one of degree', with

---

[381]  RR3—Charities for the Relief of Unemployment (March 1999), para A6. See also RR2—The Promotion of Urban and Rural Regeneration (March 1999), para A20.

[382]  Charity Commission: Public Benefit—the legal principles (January 2005), para 23.

[383]  [1951] AC 297 at 317.

a process of 'reaching a conclusion on a general survey of the circumstances and considerations regarded as relevant rather than of making a single, conclusive test'.[384] On such an approach he would have held the trust charitable, taking into account the numerical size of the class and the fact that it was not limited to present employees but also ex-employees. The intention of the donor was to 'advance the interest of the class described as a class rather than as a collection or succession of particular individuals'.[385]

In *Dingle v Turner*[386] Lord Cross, who delivered the leading judgment, expressed his dissatisfaction with the strict approach taken in *Oppenheim*. He accepted the force of the criticisms of Lord MacDermott, and acknowledged that he himself would 'prefer to approach the problem on much broader lines'.[387] He considered that the distinction between personal and impersonal relationships was unsatisfactory, and concluded that 'at the end of the day one is left where one started with the bare contrast between "public" and "private" '.[388] Like Lord MacDermott, he accepted that the question whether a trust was for the benefit of the public was a question of degree[389] and that a variety of factors would be taken into account. He suggested that a number of factors were significant:

*(i) The size of the class.* Obviously, the larger the class of potential beneficiaries the more likely it is that they will constitute a section of the public. Thus, the employees of a fairly small firm are less likely to be a section of the public than the employees of large companies like ICI and GEC, which employ many thousands of men and women who are largely unknown to each other.[390]

*(ii) The purpose of the trust.* The objects of the trust will exert a major influence on whether it should be regarded as charitable. Lord Cross explained that there was an intrinsic relationship between the size of the class and the objects of the trust:

'It may well be that, on the one hand, a trust to promote some purpose, prima facie charitable, will constitute a charity even though the class of potential beneficiaries might fairly be called a private class and that, on the other hand, a trust to promote another purpose, also prima facie charitable, will not constitute a charity even though the class of potential beneficiaries might seem to some people fairly describable as a section of the public.'[391]

Unfortunately, he did not give any illustration of how this principle might apply in practice.

*(iii) The fiscal privileges enjoyed as a consequence of charitable status.* Lord Cross further indicated that the question of charitable status cannot be determined in isolation from the benefits that such status will bring, so that regard to the fiscal privileges attendant upon charitable status cannot be avoided. He was of the view that the decisions in *Re Compton* and *Oppenheim* were influenced by the 'consideration that if such trusts as were there in question were held valid they would enjoy an

---

[384] [1951] AC 297 at 314.    [385] [1951] AC 297 at 315.    [386] [1972] AC 601.
[387] [1972] AC 601 at 623.    [388] [1972] AC 601 at 623.    [389] [1972] AC 601 at 624.
[390] [1972] AC 601 at 624.    [391] [1972] AC 601 at 624.

undeserved fiscal immunity'.[392] However, Lord MacDermott expressed doubt whether fiscal privilege was a factor to be taken into account in determining whether a class constitutes a section of the public, and Viscount Dilhorne and Lord Hodson concurred with his reservation.

### (f)  The unsatisfactory state of the current law

Whilst the judgment of Lord Cross in *Dingle v Turner*[393] highlights the deficiencies of the *Oppenheim* test, it sadly fails to eliminate the difficulties caused thereby.[394] Its status is in doubt. Although all the members of the House of Lords expressly concurred with his judgment, their comments vis-à-vis the *Oppenheim* test were purely obiter because the trust in question fell within the 'poverty' exception to the personal nexus rule. It is unfortunate that the law is in such a state of uncertainty. It is obvious that the distinction between 'public' and 'private' classes is extremely fine and impossible to capture in any single test or definition. The strict approach advocated by Lord Simmonds should therefore be rejected, and the 'impressionistic' approach advocated by Lord MacDermott and Lord Cross, which takes into account a wide range of factors, should be adopted. There is no reason why fiscal privilege should not be considered as a factor, since the very reason why the law insists that a charity must benefit the public or a section of the public is that private groups should not be entitled to massive state subsidy at the expense of the taxpayer.

## (6)  Private benefit

### (a)  The general principle

By definition, a charity exists for the public benefit. A trust which confers only private benefits cannot be a charitable trust, nor can a trust which provides a mixture of both public and private benefits, unless the private benefits can be seen as being no more than ancillary or subordinate to the public benefits. As the Charity Commission has stated, the purpose of the public benefit requirement is to ensure that 'charities are not used as a means of inappropriately conferring family benefits or fringe benefits on employees'.[395] There can therefore be issues relating to the relative balance of benefits in the case of membership organisations or trusts which confer benefits on a narrow range of beneficiaries. The essential test, as expressed by the Charity Commission, is: 'it is a question of degree; does the organisation exist primarily for the advantage of its members or has the membership structure been adopted solely as an effective way of delivering charitable benefits or for administrative convenience?'[396]

### (b)  Limitations on access to benefits

It is not inconsistent with charitable status for limits to be provided on access to benefits, provided that these limits are not irrational or unreasonable, and they can be

---

[392] [1972] AC 601 at 625.      [393] [1972] AC 601.      [394] (1974) 33 CLJ 63 (Jones).

[395] RR8—The Public Character of Charity (February 2001), para 13.

[396] Charity Commission: Public Benefit—the legal principles (January 2005), para 29

justified by reason of the nature of the charity. It is inevitable that many charitable purposes are not available to every single member of the public. Trusts for the benefit of the blind or the disabled are not available to every member of the community because not every member of the community is blind or disabled. Trusts to provide for sea defences are not of direct benefit to members of the public living inland.[397] There can also legitimately be limits which are not dictated simply by the nature of the benefit conferred. The provision of almshouses or sheltered accommodation could reasonably be confined to residents of a geographical area, since this is a rational way of allocating a limited provision. Participation in an orchestra might be confined to those who reach a satisfactory musical standard, since otherwise the quality of the musical experience might be affected. Membership of a debating society, whilst open to the public as a whole, might be limited at any one time to the number of seats in the debating chamber.[398]

## (c) Incidental private or non-charitable benefits[399]

Although as a general rule a trust will only be charitable if its objects are exclusively charitable, the courts have held that there is an element of leeway such that a trust is not invalidated merely because it contains some non-charitable objects which are subsidiary or ancillary to the main charitable purposes. Thus, in *IRC v City of Glasgow Police Athletic Association*[400] Lord Cohen posed the question whether 'the main purpose of the body . . . is charitable and the only elements in its constitution and operation which are non-charitable are merely incidental to that purpose'.[401] The House of Lords held that, in the circumstances, the promotion of sport was not purely ancillary to the purpose of promoting the efficiency of the police force.

Provided that the extent of such benefits is reasonable in the context of the overall purpose of a charity, it is of no objection that private benefits will also be conferred. It is, for instance, possible for universities as charitable bodies to pay their teaching and support staff, even though this confers private benefits, provided that the payments made represent a fair payment for services rendered. In *Re Coxen*[402] a charitable trust was upheld despite the presence of some non-charitable elements. A previous Lord Mayor of London left some £200,000 to the Court of Aldermen on trust to apply the income to the following purposes:

(a) a sum not exceeding £100 for a dinner for the Court of Aldermen meeting on trust business;

(b) to pay one guinea to each alderman attending a committee in connection with the trust; and

(c) the balance for the benefit of orthopaedic hospitals.

If the first two purposes had not been charitable, Jenkins J would have regarded them as purely ancillary to the main charitable gift. In the event, he held that they were

---

[397] See *IRC v Baddeley* [1955] AC 572.
[398] Charity Commission: Public Benefit—the legal principles (January 2005), para 26.
[399] See [1978] Conv 92 (Gravells).     [400] [1953] AC 380.     [401] [1953] AC 380 at 405.
[402] [1948] Ch 747.

charitable as promoting the better administration of the charity. In *London Hospital Medical College v IRC*[403] a students' union[404] which provided social, cultural and athletic activities for the students of a London teaching hospital was held charitable. Brightman J considered that the prime object of the union was the furtherance of the purposes of the medical college and not the private and personal benefit of the students, which was ancillary.[405] Similarly, in *Re South Place Ethical Society*[406] Dillon J regarded the organisation of social activities by the society as purely ancillary to the society's main object of the promotion of ethical principles.[407] In *Funnell v Stewart*[408] the testatrix had left a substantial sum of money to a faith-healing group which held private religious services but which saw its raison d'être as 'the healing work it did for members of the community'.[409] Hazel Williamson QC held that despite the non-charitable nature of the private services, the trust as a whole was charitable because the private services were 'clearly ancillary or subsidiary to the public faith healing part of the group's work, which was its predominant function'.[410]

In some cases it will be possible to sever the non-charitable or private elements in a trust. Where a gift is made in favour of some charitable and other non-charitable purposes, the court may sever the good from the bad. In *Salusbury v Denton*[411] a gift to the testator's widow was to be applied partly toward charitable objects and the rest to his relatives. The widow died without making any appointments, and the court held that there could be a division of the fund between the charitable and non-charitable objects. Page-Wood V-C applied the maxim 'equality is equity' and divided the fund into two equal shares. However, where severance is possible equal division may not always be the most appropriate solution. In *Re Coxen*[412] Jenkins J held that if he had not been able to find that the object of providing a dinner for the aldermen was charitable, he would have been prepared to divide the fund unequally so as to sever the charitable from the non-charitable objects.

## (7) The exclusion of the less well off

There are many cases which demonstrate that it is not inimical to charitable status for charges to be made by a charity for the services which it provides. It has already been seen above that this has been held to be the case for a housing charity, a healthcare charity, for a sports centre and for educational charities. Nevertheless, there is continuing disquiet in some circles about charities such as public schools or private hospitals which impose charges for their services with the result that benefits are only available to those who can afford to pay for these services. The fact that these organisations make no private profit, or that any profit which they do make is ploughed back into the further enhancement of their provision, does not silence their critics.

---

[403] [1976] 1 WLR 613.
[404] See also *A-G v Ross* [1986] 1 WLR 252, where the students' union of North London Polytechnic was held charitable despite some non-charitable activities which were regarded as ancillary.
[405] [1976] 1 WLR 613 at 623.    [406] [1980] 1 WLR 1565.    [407] [1980] 1 WLR 1565 at 1569.
[408] [1996] 1 WLR 288.    [409] [1996] 1 WLR 288 at 296.    [410] [1996] 1 WLR 288 at 296.
[411] (1857) 3 K & J 529.    [412] [1948] Ch 747.

In *Re Resch's Will Trusts*[413] it was made clear that the assessment of public benefit in the case of a fee-charging organisation need not be confined to an assessment of the benefits to the direct recipients of the services. Indirect benefits to the public can also be taken into account. However, if an organisation excludes the less well-off from both direct and indirect benefits, this is likely to affect its charitable status. In assessing whether the less well off are excluded, the Charity Commission has indicated factors that may be considered:

'• The provision of concessions, subsidised or free places (for example, in the case of schools by offering scholarships, bursaries or assisted places, or in the case of theatres by offering concessionary tickets);

• The existence of accessible insurance or other benefit schemes (for example, medical insurance schemes);

• The provision of wider access to charitable facilities or services. For example some charities may provide additional facilities or services for the less well off people who would otherwise be excluded. Some charities may lend equipment or staff out to other charities or groups which provide the same facilities or services to the less well off. For example, a charitable independent school allowing a state maintained school to use its educational facilities.'[414]

## (8) Public benefit in particular circumstances[415]

### (a) Presumptions of public benefit

*(i) The assumed public benefit of religion.* Until the Charities Bill 2005, it was presumed that, provided religious organisations operated in the public domain, they met the public benefit requirement. The benefit to the public that the court assumed results from religious activity is not the spiritual benefit that a particular religion offers its adherents, but the benefit that comes to the community through the influence and example of its citizens who have adopted and attempted to put into practice the moral and ethical teaching of their religion. This is not a matter on which the courts have ever expected evidence to be presented. In *Neville Estates Ltd v Madden* this attitude was reflected by Cross J, who said:

'. . . the court is . . . entitled to assume that some benefit accrues to the public from the attendance at places of worship of persons who live in this world and mix with their fellow citizens.'[416]

This was echoed by Sir Nicholas Browne-Wilkinson V-C in *Re Hetherington (Decd)*:

'The celebration of a religious rite in public does confer a sufficient public benefit because of the edifying and improving effect of such a celebration on the members of the public who attend.'[417] Similarly, in *Re Hetherington*[418]

---

[413] [1969] 1 AC 514.
[414] Charity Commission: Public Benefit—the legal principles (January 2005), para 36.
[415] See: RR8—The Public Character of Charity (February 2001).      [416] [1962] Ch 832.
[417] [1990] Ch 1.      [418] [1990] Ch 1.

He therefore held that the saying of masses for the dead was prima facie charitable since the invariable practice is that they are said in public, 'which provides a sufficient element of public benefit'. No evidence was presented as to the nature of the benefit either to the dead or to the living.

It us unclear what impact the abolition of the presumption of public benefit will have for religious charities. The fact that the advancement of religion is recognised as a category of charitable purpose means that once a trust or organisation demonstrates that it is established for this purpose, it will satisfy the first part of the two-fold test for charitable status. However, it will still be necessary for the trust or organisation to show that it satisfies the test of public benefit in regard to the way or ways in which it achieves its charitable purpose. Is it legitimate, if the presumption of public benefit has been abolished, for judicial notice still to be taken of the benefits allegedly conferred by the participation in public life of people who attend religious worship? As has already been seen, no presumption is made that a museum collection is of educational value to the public simply because it is available to the public. Why should a presumption be made that religious activity is of public benefit simply because members of the public participate in that activity?

*(ii) The assumed public benefit of animal welfare.* A similar issue arises in relation to the public benefit of animal welfare charities, where judicial notice was taken *Re Wedgwood*[419] of the elevating effect on the human race of providing animal welfare. Will it be sufficient that animal welfare organisations operate in the public domain, or will it be necessary for them to demonstrate through evidence the beneficial impact of their activities? If evidence acceptable to a court of law is required to demonstrate the public benefit of a ban on experimentation on animals, why should there be no need of such proof of the benefits of the provision of animal welfare?

*(iii) Public benefit in the 'poor relations' cases.* The line of authority concerning 'poor relations' has already been considered. Can it really be considered, after the abolition of the presumption of public benefit in certain cases, that the public benefit requirement is satisfied where a person leaves a substantial sum of money for the relief of poverty amongst a class consisting exclusively of his or her immediate family? This situation will surely be altered by the Charities Bill 2005, which is intended to put all charities on the same footing in regard to public benefit.

## (b) 'Cloistered' charities

If a charity has no operation in the public domain, it will be very hard for it to demonstrate public benefit. A trust to promote research will not be charitable unless the results of the research are published or otherwise disseminated. Contemplative religious orders which are cloistered and have no contact with the community at large have been held not to be charitable. In *Gilmour v Coats*[420] a gift of £500 was made to a priory of Carmelite nuns, who were cloistered and devoted their lives to prayer. The House of Lords held that they were not a charity because there was not the necessary element of benefit to the public. There was no interaction between the nuns and the community

---

[419] [1915] 1 Ch 113.     [420] [1949] AC 426.

and Lord Simmonds rejected as 'too vague and intangible' any claimed edification of the public through the example of their spiritual lives and sacrifice. He also rejected the alleged benefit to the community of their intercessory prayer according to Roman Catholic doctrine, as evidenced by an affidavit of the Archbishop of Westminster. This alleged benefit was dismissed as 'manifestly not susceptible of proof', and he stated that the court does not accept as fact whatever a particular religion believes. In *Leahy v A-G of New South Wales*[421] a gift to religious orders which could have included contemplative orders would have been held invalid by the Privy Council as not being exclusively for charitable purposes if it had not been saved by the New South Wales Conveyancing Act 1919–54.

### (c) Absence of public benefit

Any public benefit may be balanced by disbenefits or potential for harm, and it is only if the balance is positive that the public benefit test will be satisfied. This is currently the case even in respect of those types of charity where public benefit is presumed. The Charity Commission recently held that the presumption of public benefit had been rebutted in respect of the activities of the Church of Scientology. The Commission pointed to the fact that Scientology was a new belief system seeking recognition as a religion, whereas the presumption of public benefit has arisen historically in the context of established religions which on the whole conform to a particular pattern involving a theistic belief and a worshipping practice, and to the degree of public and judicial concern which had been expressed about the possible registration of Scientology as a religion.[422]

## 9 Charity Commission guidance on public benefit

Under the Charities Bill 2005, cl 4, the Charity Commission will have a duty to provide guidance as to the operation of the public benefit requirement. The purpose of the guidance is to promote awareness and understanding of the public benefit requirement,[423] but 'the charity trustees of a charity must have regard to any such guidance when exercising any powers or duties to which the guidance is relevant.'[424] The guidance will therefore have authoritative status. The Commission is expected to carry out public and other consultation on any guidance it issues.[425]

## 10 Impact of changes in the law on existing charities

The change in the public benefit requirement made by the Charities Bill 2005 will have an impact upon existing charities. Such trusts or organisations will have essentially one

---

[421] [1959] AC 457.
[422] Decision of the Charity Commissioners for England and Wales made on 17 November 1999.
[423] Charities Bill 2005, cl 4(2).      [424] Charities Bill 2005, cl 4(6).
[425] Charities Bill 2005, cl 4(4).

of two choices. They could amend their purposes and modify their activities in order to comply with the new rules relating to public benefit.[426] They may be required to do this by the Charity Commission. Alternatively, if it is not possible to make such changes, they could cease to be charities and lose their registration. The impact of the latter course of action could be catastrophic for the entity concerned. Under the current law, once assets have irrevocably been devoted to charitable purposes, they cannot be used for any non-charitable purposes, but must, in the event of an organisation ceasing to be charitable, be applied to other charitable purposes.[427] Thus, if a public school lost its charitable status, and wished to operate as a private sector school, it would not be able to transfer its assets to the new non-charitable entity. The new entity would either have to purchase the assets or acquire new premises and facilities. That would inevitably have a dramatic and negative impact upon the level of fees which the new entity would need to charge, or the or upon the quality of the provision which it could offer.

The Charity Commission will be conducting public benefit checks on all existing charities to ensure that they can show positively that they are set up and operate for the public benefit.[428] The Charity Commission has not yet decided how this review will be conducted.[429]

# 11  Interpreting charitable gifts

## (1) 'Exclusively' charitable purposes

For a trust to be upheld as a valid charitable trust it must be for exclusively charitable purposes. None of the trust property must be applicable to non-charitable objects. Similarly, a corporation or unincorporated association will only be a charity if its purposes are exclusively charitable. If there is a combination of purposes, some charitable and others not, then it will not be charitable and will not enjoy the privileges outlined above. Thus, in *IRC v Oldham Training and Enterprise Council*[430] Lightman J held that a TEC was not a charitable body because its objects included some non-charitable elements, including the promotion of the interests of individuals rather than of the community in general. Similarly, in *McGovern v A-G*[431] the trust established by Amnesty International included some charitable objects, but also some non-charitable political purposes and was not held charitable. In *Williams' Trustees v IRC*[432] the objects included many which were charitable, but also the promotion of social activities which are not. In *IRC v Baddeley*[433] the promotion of Methodism was a charitable purpose but the promotion of sport and recreation were not.

---

[426] Charity Commission: Public Benefit—the Charity Commission's approach (January 2005), para 22.
[427] See Charity Commission: Public Benefit—the Charity Commission's approach (January 2005), para 23.
[428] Charity Commission: Public Benefit—the Charity Commission's approach (January 2005), paras 19 and 27.
[429] Charity Commission: Public Benefit—the Charity Commission's approach (January 2005), para 30.
[430] [1996] STC 1218.     [431] [1982] Ch 321.     [432] [1947] AC 447.     [433] [1955] AC 572.

Where the court is required to determine if a gift was for exclusively charitable purposes, it may take a generous approach and give it a 'benignant construction'.[434] This means that, where there is an ambiguity such that a gift is capable of two constructions, one of which would make it void and the other effectual, the court will uphold it. This approach was confirmed by the House of Lords in *Guild v IRC*.[435] The precise scope of the principle permitting a benignant construction was considered by Hazel Williamson QC in *Funnell v Stewart*.[436] She indicated that it would not save a 'dual purpose gift' where one identifiable object was clearly present but plainly not charitable, as the court could not simply ignore the non-charitable element of the trust. However, it would enable the court to save a gift which had a single purpose which was capable of being carried into effect in two different ways, one of which would be charitable and the other of which would not.[437]

## (2) Issues of construction

Common problems arise where a trust is established for a variety of purposes, some of which are charitable and some of which are not. Where such a variety of purposes are listed together, the conjunctions used may determine whether the gift is to be construed as exclusively for charitable purposes. In general, the use of the word 'or' is usually given a disjunctive construction, so that 'charitable or benevolent' purposes are not exclusively charitable. In contrast, the word 'and' is usually given a conjunctive construction so that 'charitable and benevolent' purposes would be exclusively charitable. Although providing a strong prima facie indication, these are not binding rules of construction and each case must be examined in the light of the surrounding circumstances.

### (a) 'And'

In *Re Sutton*[438] a gift to 'charitable and deserving' objects was held exclusively charitable. The word 'and' was given a conjunctive interpretation so that only deserving objects which were also charitable were contemplated. In *Re Best*[439] a gift to 'charitable and benevolent' institutions was similarly held exclusively charitable. The conjunctive construction is only a prima facie guide which may be displaced. In *A-G of the Bahamas v Royal Trust Co,*[440] a gift for purposes connected with the 'education and welfare' of Bahamian children was, in the light of all the circumstances, construed disjunctively and the gift therefore failed since it permitted the application of funds for educational purposes alternatively for welfare purposes which need not necessarily be educational.[441]

---

[434] *IRC v McMullen* [1981] AC 1 at 14, per Lord Hailsham LC; *Weir v Crum-Brown* [1908] AC 162 at 167, per Lord Loreburn LC.

[435] [1992] 2 AC 310 at 322.      [436] [1996] 1 WLR 288 at 296–297.

[437] See also *Re Hetherington* [1990] Ch 1.      [438] (1885) 28 Ch D 464.      [439] [1904] 2 Ch 354.

[440] [1986] 1 WLR 1001.

[441] See also *Re Eades* [1920] 2 Ch 353, 'religious, charitable and philanthropic objects' held not exclusively charitable.

## (b) 'Or'

In *Blair v Duncan*[442] a testatrix gave her trustee discretion to apply part of her residuary estate to 'charitable or public purposes'. The House of Lords held that this was to be read disjunctively, so that the gift included 'public purposes', which may fall outside the scope of charity. The gift therefore failed. A similar result was reached in *Houston v Burns*,[443] where a gift was made for 'public, benevolent or charitable purposes'. In *Chichester Diocesan Fund and Board of Finance v Simpson*[444] a gift in favour of 'charitable or benevolent objects'[445] was reluctantly held not to be exclusively charitable. The House of Lords could not find a more favourable interpretation than that the purposes were to be considered disjunctively.[446] More recently in *A-G of the Cayman Islands v Wahr-Hansen*[447] the Privy Council advised that a trust established for the benefit of 'any one or more religious, charitable or educational institution or instructions or any organisations or institutions operating for the public good' was not exclusively charitable.

In some circumstances, on the construction of a gift as a whole, the word 'or' may not be read in this disjunctive way. In *Re Bennett*[448] a gift to educational purposes and 'other objects of charity, or any other public objects in the parish of Farringdon' was held to be exclusively charitable. Taken as a whole, and especially noting the word 'other', Eve J held that it was not to be construed disjunctively but to mean other public purposes which are also charitable.

## (c) Charitable Trusts (Validation) Act 1954

This Act mitigates the impact of *Chichester Diocesan Fund v Simpson*.[449] It retrospectively validates trusts coming into effect prior to 16 December 1952, where the funds could be used exclusively for charitable purposes, but the terms also permit them to be used for non-charitable purposes. The Act has no application to trusts coming into effect after 15 December 1952. Apart from this, there is no legislation in England allowing a gift which is partly charitable and partly non-charitable to be upheld in so far as it is charitable.[450]

## (d) Trusts for the benefit of a locality

For reasons which have now become obscure, the courts have adopted a benevolent construction towards gifts made in general terms for the benefit of a named locality of its inhabitants. Such gifts are construed to be impliedly limited to charitable purposes in the specified community. Thus a gift to a particular parish,[451] or for the good of a particular country,[452] such as a gift for 'the benefit and advantage of

---

[442] [1902] AC 37.    [443] [1918] AC 337.    [444] [1944] AC 341, HL.

[445] See also *Oxford Group v IRC* [1949] 2 All ER 537, CA.

[446] See also *Re Macduff* [1896] 2 Ch 451, where a gift to charitable or philanthropic purposes was held not exclusively charitable.

[447] [2001] 1 AC 75.    [448] [1920] 1 Ch 305.    [449] [1944] AC 341, HL.

[450] There is legislation to this effect in the Republic of Ireland: Charities Act 1960, s 49. See also *Leahy v A-G for New South Wales* [1959] AC 457, where similar Australian legislation was applied.

[451] *West v Knight* (1669) 1 Cas in Ch 134.

[452] *A-G v Earl of Lonsdale* (1827) 1 Sim 105; *Re Smith* [1932] 1 Ch 153.

Great Britain',[453] will be upheld as a valid charitable trust. However in *A-G of the Cayman Islands v Wahr-Hansen*[454] the Privy Council advised that this generous rule of construction should not be extended to encompass all cases where there are general statements of benevolent or philanthropic objects. It is unlikely that the abolition of the presumption of public benefit will affect this principle of construction.

[453] *Nightingale v Goulburn* (1847) 5 Hare 484.      [454] [2001] 1 AC 75.

# 19
# Winding up of funds

## 1 Surplus funds

When property is held as a fund for the benefit of other persons or purposes, it is inevitable that at some time the fund will come to an end. This may be a result of its exhaustion, as the property is properly applied. Alternatively, the purposes for which the fund was established may have failed or come to an end, leaving a surplus as yet undistributed. This chapter will consider the circumstances in which a fund comes to an end, and especially how the surplus of funds which have failed are applied.

### (1) Exhaustion of the fund

Clearly, the fund will come to an end if all the property within it has been appropriately applied. The most obvious example is a bare trust where the property has been transferred to the beneficiary, thus bringing the trust relationship to an end. Similarly, the trustees of a discretionary trust, either exhaustive or non-exhaustive in character, may have distributed the whole of the fund amongst the class of potential beneficiaries. A charity may have spent all the money it possesses in pursuit of its purposes, and an unincorporated association may have exhausted its funds. In all such cases the fund has come to an end by process of exhaustion, and there is no longer any property left. There is no question of what should happen to an undistributed surplus.

### (2) Failure of the fund

Alternatively, the fund may have to be wound up because of the failure of the purposes of the fund or the organisation holding the fund. For example, a fund may have been established by the transfer of property to trustees on a trust which is subsequently found to be void for uncertainty, or a charitable institution holding funds may have closed.[1] In such circumstances, what happens to the surplus will depend on the nature of the fund and how it was held. In the event that there is no other person who is entitled to the surplus of a fund which has failed, it will pass to the Crown as bona vacantia.

---

[1] *Re Slevin* [1891] 2 Ch 236, CA; *Re Rymer* [1895] 1 Ch 19, CA.

### (a) Failure of trusts

Where a trust fails, any surplus of the fund[2] will generally revert back to the original settlor of the property under a resulting trust.

### (b) Dissolution of unincorporated associations

Where a non-charitable unincorporated association comes to an end, any property held by the association will usually be divided amongst the remaining members of the association in accordance with its rules.

### (c) Failure of charities

When a charitable purpose or particular charitable institution or organisation comes to an end, any surplus held by the charity will be applied cy-près for an alternative charitable purpose.

## 2  Surplus funds on the failure of trusts

### (1) Operation of resulting trusts

When a trust is created, the property subject to it is held by trustees for the beneficiaries, who enjoy the equitable ownership thereof. If the trust fails, the equitable ownership will be returned, or 'result back,' to those who originally owned the property. The trustees will then hold the property on trust for the original owners to whom it has resulted, and it is their duty to transfer it back to them. The essence of a resulting trust was captured by Megarry J in *Re Sick and Funeral Society of St John's Sunday School, Golcar*:

'A resulting trust is essentially a property concept: any property a man does not effectually dispose of remains his own.'[3]

The term 'resulting trust' is used to describe a number of different situations where property will revert back to its original owner, and it is important to distinguish the different senses in which the term is used. Resulting trusts were classified by Megarry J in *Re Vandervell's Trusts (No 2)*[4] into 'presumed' and 'automatic' resulting trusts.[5]

### (a) Presumed resulting trusts'

Presumed' resulting trusts are those which arise as the result of the presumption that a property 'results to the man who advances the purchase money'.[6] For example, in *Tinsley v Milligan*[7] a house was purchased in the sole name of Tinsley, but part of the purchase price was provided by her lesbian lover, Milligan. It was held that there was a resulting trust and that Tinsley held the house on trust for herself and Milligan as joint

---

[2] Or the whole fund in the case of a trust fund void ab initio.     [3] [1973] Ch 51 at 59.
[4] [1974] Ch 269.     [5] [1974] Ch 269 at 289 and 294–296.
[6] *Dyer v Dyer* (1788) 2 Cox Eq Cas 92, per Eyre CB.     [7] [1993] 3 All ER 65.

tenants. The presumptions which give rise to such resulting trusts are not conclusive, and may be rebutted by evidence that the contributor intended to make a gift and not to retain any interest in the property purchased. In some cases, because of the nature of the relationship between the parties, the law presumes that a gift is intended, and a resulting trust does not arise unless the presumption is rebutted by evidence that a gift was not intended.[8]

### (b) Automatic resulting trusts

Megarry J suggested that 'automatic' resulting trusts arise by operation of law, and not on the basis of any presumed intention on the part of the original owner of the property. As he observed:

'What a man fails effectually to dispose of remains automatically vested in him, and no question of a mere presumption can arise.'[9]

Where a trust fails, unless expressly or impliedly excluded,[10] an automatic resulting trust determines how any remaining surplus should be applied.

In *Westdeutsche Landesbank Girozentrale v Islington London Borough Council*,[11] the most significant recent case concerning the law of trusts, this twofold categorisation of resulting trusts was broadly adopted. Both Lord Browne-Wilkinson and Lord Goff explained that resulting trusts arise in two situations corresponding to the presumed and automatic categories previously identified by trusts identified by Megarry J:

'(1) voluntary payments by A to B, or for the purchase of property in the name of B or in his and A's joint names, where there is no presumption of advancement or evidence of intention to make an out and out gift; or (2) property transferred to B on an express trust which does not exhaust the whole beneficial interest.'[12]

However, Lord Browne-Wilkinson doubted that the term 'automatic resulting trust' accurately described the trust arising in favour of the settlor where an express trust fails:

'Under existing law a resulting trust arises in two sets of circumstances ... (B) Where A transfers property to B *on express trusts*, but the trusts declared do not exhaust the whole beneficial interest ... Both types of resulting trust are traditionally regarded as examples of trusts giving effect to the common intentions of the parties. A resulting trust is not imposed by law against the intentions of the trustee (as is a constructive trust) but gives effect to his presumed intention. Megarry J in *Re Vandervell's Trusts (No 2)* suggests that a resulting trust of type (B) does not depend on intention but operates automatically. I am not convinced that this is right. If the settlor has expressly, or by necessary implication, abandoned any beneficial interest in the trust property, there is in my view no resulting trust: the undisposed of equitable interest vests in the Crown as bona vacantia.'[13]

Whilst these comments rightly observe that a resulting trust is not an inevitable result whenever an express trust fails, it is unlikely that Megarry J ever intended the term

---

[8] The presumption of 'advancement'.       [9] [1974] Ch 269 at 289.

[10] See *Davis v Richards and Wallington Industries Ltd* [1991] 2 All ER 563.

[11] [1996] AC 669. See [1996] RLR 3 (Birks); (1996) 112 LQR 521 (Cape); [1996] CLJ 432 (Jones); [1997] LMCLQ 441 (Stevens)

[12] [1996] AC 669 at 689, per Lord Goff.       [13] [1996] AC 669 at 708.

automatic resulting trust to carry this connotation. Such a resulting trust operates in effect as a form of trust implied in default, and whilst it may be rooted in the presumed intention of the settlor, there is a much reduced likelihood that evidence will be adduced that the settlor did not wish to have the equitable interest in the property to revert back to him in the event of such failure. The presumption of his intention is therefore much more resilient than that under a conventional presumed resulting trust, where evidence that a gift was intended will rebut the presumption. Thus, resulting trusts arising in the event of the failure of an express trust do tend to arise automatically in practice, if not in theory, as the trustee will only be able to show that the settlor has expressly, or by necessary implication, abandoned any beneficial interest in the trust property in exceptional circumstances. The law is very slow to recognise abandonment of property by the owner. There are many cases involving chattels on this point[14] and there is no reason to believe that the position should be different for interests behind a trust. However, in the light of Lord Browne-Wilkinson's comments, the terminology of automatic resulting trusts may have to be abandoned. It remains unclear whether a similarly snappy label will emerge. Such trusts could perhaps be termed surplus-funds resulting trusts, which would be more descriptive than Type (B) resulting trusts, which is the best that is offered by Lord Browne-Wilkinson.

This chapter will be concerned with the operation of erstwhile automatic resulting trusts. Presumed resulting trusts have already been considered in Chapter 8.

## (2) Circumstances in which a surplus-fund resulting trust will be implied

### (a) Failure to declare the beneficial interests arising behind an express trust

If property is transferred to trustees upon trust but the settlor makes no effective declaration of the beneficial interests, so that the trustees do not know who they are to hold the property for, they will hold the property transferred on a resulting trust for the settlor, or if he is dead, for his successors in title.[15] The principle was stated by Lord Wilberforce in *Vandervell v IRC*, where an option to repurchase shares was held by a trust company but no indication had been given as to the beneficiaries thereof:

'. . . the option was vested in the trustee company as a trustee on trusts, not defined at the time, possibly to be defined later. But the equitable, or beneficial interest, cannot remain in the air: the consequence in law must be that it remains in the settlor . . .'[16]

The option was therefore held by the trustee company on resulting trust for Mr Vandervell, who had been the original owner of the shares.

The operation of a resulting trust in such circumstances was more recently examined by the Privy Council in *Air Jamaica Ltd v Charlton*. Lord Millett explained that a

---

[14] See *Simpson v Gowers* (1981) 32 OR (2d) 385; *Dennis v North Western Nat Bank* 81 NW 2d 254 (1957).

[15] See *Johnson v Ball* (1851) 5 De G & Sm 85; *Re Keen* [1937] 1 All ER 452 and *Re Boyes* (1884) 26 Ch D 531, where there were ineffective attempts to create secret trusts.

[16] [1967] 2 AC 291 at 329.

resulting trust does not arise because the trustee wanted to retain a beneficial interest in the property:

'Like a constructive trust, a resulting trust arises by operation of law, though unlike a constructive trust it gives effect to intention. But it does arise whether or not the transferor intended to retain a beneficial interest—he almost always does not—since it responds to the absence of any intention on his part to pass a beneficial interest to the recipient. It may arise even where the transferor positively wished to part with the beneficial interest, as in *Vandervell v IRC* . . . The House of Lords affirmed the principle that a resulting trust is not defeated by evidence that the transferor intended to part with the beneficial interest if he has not in fact succeeded in doing so.'[17]

### (b) Failure of an express trust

If a valid trust is created but subsequently fails for some reason, any trust property which remains in the hands of the trustees will be held on resulting trust for the settlor. For example, in *Re Ames' Settlement*[18] Louis Ames created a marriage settlement of £10,000 on the marriage of his son, John, to Miss Hamilton in 1908. The marriage was declared 'absolutely null and void' in 1927 by the Supreme Court of Kenya, on the grounds of the husband's incapacity to consummate the marriage.[19] Vaisey J concluded that, since the marriage had been void ab initio, there was a total failure of the consideration for the marriage settlement and the property should result back to the father's estate. A resulting trust would also arise if a settlement was created in contemplation of a marriage which never took place.[20] In *Re Cochrane*[21] a marriage settlement was created in favour of a wife 'so long as she shall continue to reside with' her husband. They separated and the income was paid to the husband, who then predeceased her. It was held that the income should be held on resulting trust for the settlors in proportion to the contributions they had made to the fund.

Where a trust is void because it fails to comply with all the requirements necessary for the creation of a valid trust, the trust property will again be held on a resulting trust for the settlor or his estate. In *Chichester Diocesan Fund and Board of Finance Inc v Simpson*[22] Caleb Diplock created a discretionary trust in favour of charity. However, because the trust included some non-charitable objects it was invalid and the property resulted back to his estate. In *Re Astor's Settlement Trusts*[23] a trust created in 1945 for the promotion of 'good understanding between the nations' and the 'preservation of the independence and integrity of newspapers' was held void because it contravened the beneficiary principle. The property was therefore held on resulting trust.

Where property has been held on trust for a charity which has failed, it may similarly result back to the settlors or donors. For example, in *Re Ulverston and District New Hospital Building Trusts*[24] a fund had been created for the purpose of building a new hospital. The fund consisted of contributions from named donors, anonymous donors, street collections and the proceeds of entertainments. The purpose became impossible,

---

17 [1999] 1 WLR 1399 at 1412.    18 [1946] Ch 217.
19 See *Re d'Altroy's Will Trusts* [1968] 1 WLR 120; *Re Rodwell* [1970] Ch 726.
20 *Essery v Cowlard* (1884) 26 Ch D 191; *Bond v Walford* (1886) 32 Ch D 238.
21 [1955] Ch 309.    22 [1944] AC 341.    23 [1952] Ch 534.    24 [1956] Ch 622.

and it was held that the fund should be held on resulting trust for its donors. However, often the application of a resulting trust will be excluded by the cy-près doctrine,[25] and the property will be applied to other charitable purposes.

## (c) Trust fund has not been exhausted

Where a trust has been established for a specific purpose, any surplus funds which have not been exhausted on the completion of the purpose should in most cases be returned to the original contributors by way of a resulting trust in proportion to their contributions. The principle was stated by Harman J in *Re Gillingham Bus Disaster Fund*:

'The general principle must be that where money is held upon trust and the trusts declared do not exhaust the fund it will revert to the donor under what is called a resulting trust.'[26]

In *Re Abbott Fund Trusts*[27] a fund of £284 was collected and established in 1890 for the support of two deaf and dumb ladies. On their death in 1899 a surplus of £366 13s 9d remained in the fund. The court held that the surplus should be held for the benefit of those who had subscribed to the fund. Central to the decision was the finding by Stirling J that the fund was never 'intended to become the absolute property of the ladies'.[28] However, in subsequent cases the courts seem to have construed gifts with similar limited purposes as absolute gifts to their beneficiaries, excluding any possibility of a resulting trust to the contributors. In *Re Andrew's Trust*[29] the friends of a deceased clergyman subscribed to a fund for the education of his children. After all the children had completed their education, there was a surplus of some £460 remaining in the fund. Kekewich J held that there should not be a resulting trust to the subscribers, because the gift was to be construed as an absolute gift to the children, with the purpose being merely a motive for the gift. He took the view that the court always[30] construed such gifts in this way.[31] *Re Andrew's Trust*[32] was followed in *Re Osoba (Decd)*,[33] which concerned a trust established by a testator 'for the training of my daughter Abiola up to university grade and for the maintenance of my aged mother'. His mother had died and the daughter had completed her university education, leaving a surplus in the fund. The question arose whether this should pass on a resulting trust to the testator's second wife and daughter, who were the residuary legatees of his estate. The Court of Appeal held that the gift was an absolute gift and the reference to the purpose 'merely a statement of the testator's motive in making the gift'.[34] It is difficult to reconcile[35] *Re*

---

[25] See below, p 568.  [26] [1958] Ch 300 at 310.  [27] [1900] 2 Ch 326.

[28] [1900] 2 Ch 326 at 330.  [29] [1905] 2 Ch 48.

[30] See *Re Sanderson's Will Trust* (1857) 3 K & J 497; *Barlow v Grant* (1684) 1 Vern 255; *Webb v Kelly* (1839) 9 Sim 469; *Lewes v Lewes* (1848) 16 Sim 266; *Presant and Presant v Goodwin* (1860) 1 Sw & Tr 544.

[31] [1905] 2 Ch 48 at 52–53: '. . . If a gross sum be given, or if the whole income of the property be given, and a special purpose be assigned for that gift, this court always regards the gift as absolute, and holds the purpose merely as the motive of the gift, and therefore holds that the gift takes effect as to the whole sum or the whole income, as the case may be.'

[32] [1905] 2 Ch 48.

[33] [1979] 1 WLR 247; [1978] CLJ 219 (Rickett). See also *Re Lipinski's Will Trusts* [1976] Ch 235.

[34] [1979] 1 WLR 247 at 257, per Buckley LJ.

[35] See the judgment of Megarry V-C at first instance in *Re Osoba* [1978] 1 WLR 791.

*Abbott Fund Trusts*[36] with *Re Andrew's Trust.*[37] Ultimately, as was recognised by the Court of Appeal in *Re Osoba*,[38] each turns on its own facts, and it is of perhaps crucial importance that in *Re Abbott Fund Trusts*[39] the beneficiaries of the fund were deceased, and could derive no further benefit from it.[40] The question is whether, on the facts, the intention of the settlor was such as to preclude a resulting trust. It should be noted that the strictness of the beneficiary principle (which invalidates most trusts for non-charitable purposes ab intio) and the cy-près doctrine (which operates in relation to surplus funds of charities) operate to restrict the circumstances in which an express trust is able to be created for a purpose, which may subsequently be accomplished leaving an unexpended surplus.

Special rules apply where an appeal has been made for funds to be applied for a charitable purpose, and there is a failure of the specific purpose for which the appeal was made. These rules are considered below in relation to surplus funds on the failure of a charity.

### (d) Pension fund surplus[41]

Particular problems have arisen concerning the applicability of a resulting trust analysis to a surplus under a pension scheme trust. Although the surplus will often have arisen through the financial contributions of employees, such contributions will have been made on the basis of a contractual relationship between the pension provider and the contributor. The contributions are not simply gifts, and it cannot easily be said that the contributor intended to receive his property back if the fund was wound up whilst in surplus. Rather, the contributor has bargained to receive a contractual benefit in return for his contributions, namely the payment of a contractually agreed pension, thus leaving him with no proprietary claim against the fund if he has received all that he bargained for. Historically it has therefore been suggested that the contractual nature of the relationship between the contributor and the trustees excludes the possibility of a resulting trust.[42] This principle was explained by A L Smith LJ in *Cunnack v Edwards*, which concerned the surplus funds of a society established to provide annuities for the widows of members who died:

'As the member paid his money to the society, so he divested himself of all interest in this money for ever, with this one reservation, that if a member left a widow she was to be provided for during her widowhood. Except as to this he abandoned and gave up the money for ever.'[43]

It was subsequently applied in *Re West Sussex Constabulary's Widows, Children and Benevolent (1930) Fund Trusts*[44] to a fund established to provide payments for the widows and dependants of policemen. When the fund was wound up, leaving a surplus,

---

[36] [1900] 2 Ch 326.  [37] [1905] 2 Ch 48.  [38] [1979] 1 WLR 247 at 251.
[39] [1900] 2 Ch 326.
[40] This was pointed out by Kekewich J in *Re Andrew's Trust* [1905] 2 Ch 48 at 52.
[41] See (2003) TLI 2 (Pollard).
[42] As Megarry J observed in *Re Sick and Funeral Society of St John's Sunday School, Golcar* [1973] Ch 51, many of the difficulties arise because of the confusion of property with contract.
[43] [1896] 2 Ch 679 at 683.  [44] [1971] Ch 1.

Goff J held that the members who had contributed to the fund could not recover back the share of the surplus attributable to their contributions because they had received all the benefit that they had contracted to receive. He similarly held that any fund surplus attributable to the proceeds of entertainments, raffles, sweepstakes and other such fund raising activities, should not be subject to a resulting trust because the participants had acted on the basis of a contractual bargain for services received:

'. . . the relationship is one of contract and not of trust; the purchaser of a ticket may have the motive of aiding the cause or he may not; he may purchase a ticket merely because he wishes to attend the particular entertainment or to try for the prize, but whichever it be, he pays his money as the price of what is offered and what he receives.'[45]

However, in more recent cases it has been held that a resulting trust analysis might be adopted in respect of a pension fund surplus, despite the contractual nature of the contributions made. In *Davis v Richards and Wallington Industries Ltd*[46] Scott J held that it was not inevitable that payments into a fund on the basis of contract would exclude a resulting trust. The case concerned a company pension scheme which, after full provision had been made for pension obligations, contained a surplus of some £3m. This was derived partly from the contributions of employees, who were obliged by their contracts to contribute 5% of their salaries, and partly from the contributions of the employer. On the question whether there should be a resulting trust in favour of those who had contributed, Scott J rejected any blanket principle that contractual payments exclude the possibility of a resulting trust:

'. . . the fact that a payment to a fund has been made under contract and that the payer has obtained all that he or she bargained for under the contract is not necessarily a decisive argument against a resulting trust.'[47]

Instead, he concluded that, whenever a trust fund was involved, any surplus would inevitably pass under a resulting trust unless such a trust was expressly or impliedly excluded.[48] Applying this principle, he held that the employers were entitled to claim the proportion of the surplus attributable to their overpayments by way of a resulting trust. However, in contrast he held that the employees were excluded from claiming a resulting trust. He considered that there were 'unworkable' difficulties of calculating the shares of individual employees,[49] because he considered it necessary to value the benefits that each member had in fact received in order to ascertain his share in the surplus, and also pointed to the legislative rules under which the pension scheme took effect, which placed a maximum on the financial return from the fund to which each employee could become entitled, which would be exceeded if a resulting trust arose in their favour. In the light of these factors a resulting trust was excluded by implication,

---

[45] [1971] Ch 1 at 11.
[46] [1991] 2 All ER 563; [1991] Conv 366 (Martin); [1992] Conv 41 (Gardener).
[47] [1991] 2 All ER 563 at 593.
[48] [1991] 2 All ER 563 at 592–593: following *Jones v Williams* (15 March 1988, unreported), per Knox J.
[49] This was because the value of the benefits of the employees would be different for each employee, depending on how long he had served, how old he was when he joined and how old he was when he left. Two employees may have paid identical sums into the fund, but be entitled to benefits of a different value: see [1991] 2 All ER 563, 595.

and the proportion of the surplus attributable to the employee's overcontributions passed to the Crown as bona vacantia.

*Davis v Richards and Wallington Industries Ltd*[50] thus establishes that where property is held on trust[51] a resulting trust of any surplus will always arise in favour of the contributors unless it is excluded by other considerations.[52] This approach was adopted by the Privy Council in the more recent case of *Air Jamaica Ltd v Charlton*,[53] which also concerned a pension fund surplus attributable to the contributions of the employers and employees of a company. Lord Millett explained that employees should not be excluded from obtaining an interest in a pension fund surplus merely because they had received what they had contracted to receive:

'Their Lordships would observe that, even in the ordinary case of an actuarial surplus, it is not obvious that, when employees are promised certain benefits under a scheme to which they have contributed more than was necessary to fund them, they should not expect to obtain a return of their excess contributions.'[54]

The Privy Council doubted that Scott J had been correct to exclude a resulting trust in favour of the employees. Rather than being required to value the benefits that each member had received in order to ascertain his share, the Privy Council held that the members' share of the surplus should be 'divided pro rata among the members and the estates of deceased members in proportion to the contributions made by each member without regard to the benefits each has received and irrespective of the dates on which the contributions were made'.[55] The company was also held entitled to a resulting trust of the proportion of the surplus attributable to its contributions, despite the presence of a clause in the trust deed stating that 'no moneys which at any time have been contributed by the company under the terms hereof shall in any circumstances be repayable to the company'. The Privy Council considered that this clause only operated to prevent repayments to the company under the terms of the scheme, and did not exclude the possibility of a resulting trust if the scheme came to an end:

'Consequently their Lordships think that clauses of this kind in a pension scheme should generally be construed as forbidding the repayment of contributions under the terms of the scheme, and not as a pre-emptive but misguided attempt to rebut a resulting trust which would arise dehors the scheme. The purpose of such clauses is to preclude any amendment that would allow repayment to the company.'[56]

### (e) Failure of a loan made for a specific purpose where the money was advanced to the borrower subject to a trust[57]

One specialised application of the surplus-funds resulting trust occurs where money has been lent for a specific purpose which has failed. On the failure of the purpose the

---

[50] [1991] 2 All ER 563.

[51] As opposed to the situation where property is held by an unincorporated association.

[52] See also *Palmer ʋ Abney Park Cemetery Co Ltd* (4 July 1985, unreported); *Kerr v British Leyland (Staff) Trustees Ltd* [1986] CA Transcript 286, Fox LJ; *Mihlenstedt v Barclays Bank International Ltd* [1989] IRLR 522.

[53] [1999] 1 WLR 1399.     [54] [1999] 1 WLR 1399 at 1412.     [55] [1999] 1 WLR 1399 at 1413.

[56] [1999] 1 WLR 1399 at 1412.

[57] See Worthington, *Proprietary Interests in Commercial Transactions* (1996), pp 43–70.

borrower will hold the money lent on a resulting trust for the lender. Such a resulting trust is extremely significant if the borrower becomes insolvent, since the lender will be entitled to assert an equitable proprietary claim to the money lent and it will not form part of the assets of the creditor. The lender will not therefore merely rank amongst the general creditors of the borrower, which would have been his position in the absence of a trust because he would only have been entitled to a contractual claim for the repayment of the debt. It is not surprising that the principle originally evolved in cases where lenders were willing to make last-ditch loans to companies in extreme financial peril, since the added security of the resulting trust encourages them to make what would otherwise be extremely risky investments.

The implication of such a resulting trust was first recognised by the House of Lords in *Barclays Bank Ltd v Quistclose Investments Ltd.*[58] A company, Rolls Razor Ltd, was in severe financial difficulties. A financier was willing to lend them £1m if they could meet an ordinary share dividend of some £210,000. They obtained a loan for Quistclose on the agreed condition that it would only be used to pay the dividend, and for that purpose the money was to be kept in a separate bank account. Before the dividends could be paid, Rolls Razor went into voluntary liquidation. The House of Lords held that, because of the exclusive purpose for which the loan was made, the money was received by Rolls Razor in the fiduciary character of a trust to pay the dividend. Since that purpose had failed, there was a resulting trust in favour of the lenders. The principle was explained by Lord Wilberforce:

'There is surely no difficulty in recognising the co-existence in one transaction of legal and equitable rights and remedies: when the money is advanced, the lender acquires an equitable right to see that it is applied for the primary designated purpose: when the purpose has been carried out . . . the lender has his remedy against the borrower in debt: if the primary purpose cannot be carried out, the question arises if a secondary purpose (ie repayment to the lender) has been agreed, expressly or by implication: if it has, the remedies of equity may be invoked to give effect to it . . .'[59]

This principle has been developed and applied in subsequent cases,[60] and the House of Lords recently considered whether such a trust was operative in *Twinsectra Ltd v Yardley.*[61] In this case a finance company agreed to lend £1m to the prospective purchaser of residential land. The money was paid into the client account of the purchaser's solicitor, subject to an express undertaking that the money be utilised 'solely for the acquisition of property on behalf of our client and for no other purpose.'

---

[58] [1970] AC 567. See also [1995] LMCLQ 451 (Mitchell); Matthews, 'The New Trust: Obligations without Rights' in Oakley, *Trends in Contemporary Trust Law* (1996), p 16.

[59] [1970] AC 567 at 581.

[60] *Carreras Rothmans Ltd v Freeman Mathews Treasure Ltd* [1985] Ch 207 at 222, per Peter Gibson J, who explained the trust as arising from the principle 'that equity fastens on the conscience of the person who receives from another property transferred for a specific purpose only and not therefore for the recipient's own purposes, so that such person will not be permitted to treat the property as his own or use it for other than the stated purpose'. See also *Re EVTR* [1987] BCLC 646.

[61] [2002] 2 AC 164; [2002] 2 All ER 377. See [2002] RLR 111 (Ricketts); [2002] Con 387 (Thompson); (2002) 16 TLI 165 (Penner); (2002) 16 TLI 223 (Glister); (2003) 119 LQR 8 (Yeo and Tijo); (2004) 63 CLJ 632 (Glister).

Contrary to the terms of this undertaking £358,000 of the money was used for other purposes. One question was whether the arrangement had given rise to a trust of the money, a crucial prerequisite to the claim of dishonest assistance in a breach of trust which was being maintained by the finance company. The House of Lords held that the money was subject to a trust because it had been paid subject to an undertaking that it would only be used for a specific purpose.

Whilst it is clearly established that a trust will arise where money is lent for a specific purpose which fails, the exact nature of such a trust has been a matter of academic controversy. In particular it has been difficult to determine when the trust comes into existence, the identify of the beneficiary, and how the existence of the trust can be reconciled with the beneficiary principle, since it appears to require the existence of a primary trust under the terms of which money is held for the carrying out of a purpose. These theoretical problems were not explored by the House of Lords in *Quistclose* itself. There are several possibilities, none of which is free from difficulty. Firstly, a loan for a specific purpose may be regarded as creating a primary trust in favour of the persons intended to receive payment, for example specific creditors or shareholders, which gives rise to a resulting trust when the purpose fails. This approach seems to have been adopted by Megarry V-C in *Re Northern Developments (Holdings) Ltd.*[62] However this analysis can be criticised[63] on the grounds that such loans are made to benefit the borrower, and not for the benefit of the creditors or shareholders as such, and that it cannot explain cases where the loan was made for an abstract purpose.[64] Secondly, the loan might create a primary trust to use the money for a purpose, with a resulting trust arising only when the purpose, and hence the primary trust, fails. Under this approach, which was advocated by the Court of Appeal in *Twinsectra Ltd v Yardley*,[65] the equitable interest in the money might be regarded as being 'in suspense' until the stated purpose is carried out, so that neither the lender nor the borrower is, strictly speaking, the beneficiary. However it has the difficulty of appearing to offend the beneficiary principle, and was subjected to criticism in the House of Lords on the grounds that it is unorthodox, fails to have regard to the role which resulting trusts play in equity, and fails to explain why the money is not simply held on resulting trust for the lender from the outset.[66] Thirdly, Chambers has argued that the loan does not create a primary trust at all. Rather, the borrower receives the entire beneficial ownership in the money lent, subject only to a contractual right in the lender to prevent the money being used otherwise than for the stated purpose, and a resulting trust springs into being only if the purpose fails.[67] This view has been criticised because it cannot explain cases of non-contractual payments, and it is inconsistent with the judgments in *Quistclose* which describe the borrower as under a fiduciary duty.[68] Finally, the money lent for a specific purpose may be regarded as being held on resulting trust by the borrower for the lender

---

[62] (6 October 1978, unreported).    [63] *Twinsectra Ltd v Yardley* [2002] 2 All ER 377, [85]–[89].
[64] For example as in *Re EVTR* [1987] BCLC 646.    [65] [1999] Lloyd's Rep Bank 438.
[66] *Twinsectra Ltd v Yardley* [2002] 2 All ER 377, [90], per Lord Millett.
[67] Chambers, *Resulting Trusts* (1997, OUP) pp 68–89.
[68] Ho and Smart, 'Re-interpreting the Quistclose Trust: A Critique of Chambers Analysis' (2001) 21 OJLS 267. See also *Twinsectra Ltd v Yardley* [2002] 2 All ER 377, [95], per Lord Millett.

from the very beginning, the resulting trust arising from the fact that the lender did not intend the borrower to enjoy the beneficial ownership in the money lent. This analysis has been advocated extra judicially by Lord Millett,[69] and was therefore, unsurprisingly, adopted by him in *Twinsectra Ltd v Yardley*.[70] He explained what he considered to be the nature of the *Quistclose* trust:

'As Sherlock Holmes reminded Dr Watson, when you have eliminated the impossible, whatever remains, however improbable, must be the truth. I would reject all the alternative analyses, which I find unconvincing . . . and hold the *Quistclose* trust to be an entirely orthodox example of the kind of default trust known as a resulting trust. The lender pays the money to the borrower by way of loan, but he does not part with the entire beneficial interest in the money, and in so far as he does not it is held on a resulting trust for the lender from the outset. Contrary to the opinion of the Court of Appeal, it is the borrower who has a very limited use of the money, being obliged to apply it for the stated purpose or return it. He has no beneficial interest in the money, which remains throughout in the lender subject only to the borrower's power or duty to apply the money in accordance with the lender's instructions. When the purpose fails, the money is returnable to the lender, not under some new trust in his favour which only comes into being on the failure of the purpose, but because the resulting trust in his favour is no longer subject to any power on the part of the borrower to make use of the money.'[71]

Whilst this analysis has the merit of simplicity, and of avoiding any problem of any conflict with the beneficiary principle, it is submitted that it is somewhat artificial to regard a resulting trust as subsisting from the very moment that the loan is made, prior to the failure of the purpose. It might be better to acknowledge the essentially anomalous and sui generis nature of the *Quistclose* trust, rather than to search for the 'truth' as to its nature by fitting it within 'orthodox' categories. As Potter LJ suggested in the Court of Appeal, the *Quisclose* type trust 'is in truth a "quasi-trust" '.[72]

It remains unclear whether Lord Millett's analysis was authoritatively adopted by majority of the House of Lords. Lord Hoffman held that undertaking had the effect that the money paid into the solicitor's client account was held on trust until such time as it was applied for the acquisition of property in accordance with its terms. He did not specifically refer to the *Quistclose* trust, and he appears to have regarded the arrangement as more akin to an express trust created by the undertaking. Lord Slynn agreed with Lord Hoffman. Lord Hutton agreed with both Lords Hoffman and Lord Millett that the money was subject to a trust, but did not comment further on their reasoning. Lord Steyn agreed with both Lords Hoffman and Lord Hutton. There therefore remains scope for further argument as to whether the trust in *Twinsectra Ltd v Yardley* should properly be regarded as a *Quistclose* trust at all.

The precise criteria that need to be satisfied in order to give rise to a *Qustclose* trust are generally agreed, although their precise import will depend upon which theoretical understating of the nature of the trust is preferred.

---

[69] Sir Peter Millett, 'The Quistclose Trust: Who can enforce it?' (1985) 101 LQR 269.
[70] [2002] 2 All ER 377.      [71] [2002] 2 All ER 377 at 403.
[72] [1999] Lloyd's Rep Bank 438, [76].

*(i)  Loan made for a specific purpose.* A *Quistclose* resulting trust will only arise if the loan was made for an agreed specific purpose which was identified with sufficient certainty. The requirement of certainty will clearly be satisfied where the money was to be used in a precisely identified way, for example for the payment of specific debts or classes of debts. In *Quistclose* the purpose was the payment of a share dividend. In *Carreras Rothmans Ltd v Freeman Mathews Treasure Ltd (in liquidation)*[73] a resulting trust was held to arise where a loan had been made by Rothmans to their advertising agency, who were in financial difficulty, for the purpose of paying third parties with whom Rothmans' adverts had been placed. In *Re EVTR*[74] a resulting trust was found where a loan had been made to a company in financial difficulties for the purchase of new machinery. However in *Twinsectra Ltd v Yardley* the purpose was expressed in vaguer terms, namely that the money was only to be used for the 'acquisition of property',[75] not for the acquisition of specific property. At first instance Carnwarth J held that this purpose was insufficiently certain to generate a trust for the purpose. However the Court of Appeal held that there was a sufficiently clear statement of purpose for the court to decide upon its ambit and whether or not, in any circumstances, it had become frustrated.[76] In the House of Lords Lord Millett held that the undertaking was stated with sufficient certainty, and that there was no difficulty of certainty of objects:

'A trust must have certainty of objects. But the only trust is the resulting trust for the lender. The borrower is authorised (or directed) to apply the money for a stated purpose, but this is a mere power and does not constitute a purpose trust. Provided that the power is stated with sufficient clarity for the court to be able to determine whether it is still capable of being carried out or whether the money has been misapplied, it is sufficiently certain to be enforced. If it is uncertain, however, then the borrower has no authority to make any use of the trust money at all and must return it to the lender under the resulting trust.'[77]

*(ii)  Money kept in a separate bank account?.* In both *Quistclose* and *Carreras Rothmans* the money lent was kept in a separate bank account. However whilst this is obviously extremely clear evidence that the money is intended for the specified purpose only, it is not essential. In *Re EVTR* a resulting trust was found even though the loan had been paid into the company's general account, and in *Twinsectra Ltd v Yardley*[78] a trust was found even though the money lent was held in the solicitor's general client account rather than a separate account.

*(iii)  The purpose has failed.* In cases prior to *Twinsectra Ltd v Yardley* it was held that the resulting trust in favour of the lender only arises where the purpose, and thereby the primary trust, fails. In *Quistclose* and *Carreras Rothmans* this was when the borrower went into liquidation. The meaning of 'failure' was further considered by the Court of Appeal in *Re EVTR*. In that case the money had been advanced to purchase new machinery. The money was paid to the manufacturers, but before the machinery could be delivered EVTR Ltd went into receivership. The machines were never delivered and the manufacturers refunded the purchase price less an amount to compensate for their

---

[73] [1985] Ch 207.    [74] [1987] BCLC 646.    [75] [2002] 2 All ER 377.
[76] [1999] Lloyd's Rep Bank 438, [82].    [77] [2002] 2 All ER 377, [101].    [78] [2002] 2 All ER 377.

loss under the breach of contract. Reversing the decision at first instance, the Court of Appeal held that the purpose had not been completed at the moment the money was paid over to the manufacturers therefore excluding a resulting trust. As Dillon LJ pointed out:

'True it is that the [money] was paid out by the company with a view to the acquisition of new equipment, but that was only at half-time, and I do not see why the final whistle should be blown at half-time.'[79]

A resulting trust will also arise where only a part of the money lent for the specific purpose has been applied to it.[80]

If the explanation of the *Quistclose* trust adopted by Lord Millett in *Twinsectra Ltd v Yardley* is accepted, then it might be better to say that the trust subsists for as long as the purpose has not been carried out, since the resulting trust will simply remain in effect until the money is properly applied.

### (f) Void transactions

In *Westdeutsche Landesbank Girozentrale v Islington London Borough Council*[81] the House of Lords considered whether a resulting trust would arise 'automatically' in situations other than where an express trust had failed. The case concerned an interest rate swap agreement which had been entered between a bank and a local authority, but which was ultra vires the local authority. The bank claimed that as the transaction was void the local authority was not merely subject to a personal common law obligation to make restitution but held the money received under the void contract on resulting trust. In such circumstances, the transfer of money by the bank had never been intended to be subject to an express trust, and therefore the House of Lords held that there were no grounds for finding that it was subject to a resulting trust merely because the contract was void. The argument for a generalised resulting trust to effect restitution was rejected. This has been examined in detail in Chapter 8.

## (3) Counter-intention rebutting the implication of a surplus-funds resulting trust

As Lord Browne-Wilkinson indicated in *Westdeutsche Landesbank Girozentrale v Islington London Borough Council*,[82] the mere fact than an express trust has failed does not inevitably mean that a surplus-funds resulting trust will arise in favour of the settlor/contributor. As has been noted above, where property is contributed to a fund in return for the provision of contractual benefits this may impliedly exclude the possibility of a resulting trust in favour of the contributor. Where no contractual relationship is in issue, the presumption of a resulting trust surplus fund will be rebutted by evidence that the settlor had entirely abandoned his property. Thus, if he no longer intended to retain any interest in it from the moment that it was transferred by him, even by way of

---

[79] [1987] BCLC 646 at 651.     [80] *Latimer v Commissioner of Inland Revenue* [2004] 2 AC 164.
[81] [1996] AC 669.     [82] [1996] AC 669.

reverter in the event of failure of the express trust, any surplus will vest in the Crown as bona vacantia. In the absence of the settlor's express intention against a surplus-funds resulting trust, the most likely circumstance in which such a counter-intention will be implied is where an owner has made a donation which was so small as to indicate that he would not wish it returned in any event. Such cases might include trust surpluses consisting of anonymous small donations from street collections and the like. In *Re Gillingham Bus Disaster Fund*[83] a fund had been established in the aftermath of an accident, in which twenty-four Royal Marine Cadets had been killed, to defray the funeral expenses of the dead and care for the disabled. Some £9,000 was raised, largely by anonymous contributors to street collections. After providing for the funerals and care, there was a large surplus of the fund remaining, and the question before the court was whether that surplus should be returned to the donors on the basis of a resulting trust, be applied cy-près to other charitable purposes, or pass as bona vacantia to the Crown. Harman J held that as the objects of the fund were not exclusively charitable there could be no application cy-près, and the surplus should be held on resulting trust for the contributors. He recognised the tremendous practical difficulty of this solution that many of those who had contributed were unknown, but concluded that this did not make a resulting trust unworkable because the trustees could pay the money into court.[84] However, this appears to be an inappropriate solution. The individual donors surely intended to part with their money when they contributed it to the fund. As such, they should have ceased to enjoy any interest in it, even the possibility of reverter by way of a resulting trust. This more realistic approach was adopted by Goff J in *Re West Sussex Constabulary's Widows, Children and Benevolent (1930) Fund Trusts*[85] in the context of an unincorporated association. He declined to follow the judgment of Harman J in *Re Gillingham Bus Disaster Fund*,[86] but followed the earlier cases of *Re Welsh Hospital (Netley) Fund*[87] and *Re Hillier*,[88] which held that persons contributing to a fund through street collections parted with their money 'out-and-out'[89] and retained no interest in it. As PO Lawrence J had observed in *Re Welsh Hospital*:

'It is inconceivable that any person . . . placing a coin in a collecting-box presented to him in the street should have intended that any part of the money so contributed should be returned to him . . . To draw such an inference would be absurd . . .'[90]

In the light of this analysis it should perhaps be questioned whether a resulting trust should have arisen in favour of the donors in *Re Abbott Fund Trusts*.[91]

Whilst the resulting trust analysis in such cases appears inappropriate, the alternative, whereby the surplus passes as bona vacantia to the Crown, is equally unattractive as an option. The contributors to the *Gillingham Bus Disaster Fund* surely would not have wanted the surplus to pass to the Crown, thus making an involuntary contribution

---

[83] [1958] Ch 300.

[84] [1958] Ch 300 at 314. In 1993 it was announced that the money was to be paid out and used for a memorial to the victims. See Hanbury and Martin, *Modern Equity* (17th edn, 2005), p 245.

[85] [1971] Ch 1.        [86] [1959] Ch 62.        [87] [1921] 1 Ch 655.

[88] [1954] 1 WLR 9; on appeal [1954] 1 WLR 700, CA.

[89] *Re Hillier* [1954] 1 WLR 9 at 21–22, per Upjohn J; [1954] 1 WLR 700 at 714, per Denning LJ.

[90] [1921] 1 Ch 655 at 660.        [91] [1900] 2 Ch 326.

to government income. The central problem with such cases is that they concerned non-charitable purpose trusts, and that there is no equivalent principle to that of cy-près by which any surplus can be applied to similar purposes.[92] If the donors to such purpose trusts are taken to have given their property out-and-out, it is right that a resulting trust should not be implied, but equity should provide a mechanism permitting the application of any such surplus by the trustees in a manner consistent with the original objectives of the trust.

# 3 Surplus funds on the dissolution of unincorporated associations

## (1) Property holding by unincorporated associations

Different problems arise as to what should happen to the assets of an unincorporated association which is dissolved. Because such associations have no legal personality, the basis on which they hold property is complex, and various analyses have been suggested. The modern solution is that the officers of the association hold the assets for the members on the basis of their contract inter se, which is formed by the rules of the association.[93] The members' rights over the assets are therefore governed by contract and not trust. The question of how any assets should be distributed when an association is dissolved has also been subject to a variety of approaches. Early cases decided that any surplus funds would be held on a resulting trust for those who had contributed.[94] However, cases adopting a resulting trust approach pre-date the more recent authorities adopting the contractual analysis of property holding by unincorporated associations, and the modern approach to the distribution of surplus assets is that they should be distributed to the members under that same contract.

## (2) *Re West Sussex Constabulary's Trusts*: partial rejection of the resulting trust approach

In *Re West Sussex Constabulary's Widows, Children and Benevolent (1930) Fund Trusts*[95] a fund to provide benefits to the widows of members of the West Sussex police force was wound up when the force was amalgamated with others, leaving a surplus of £35,000.

---

[92] If *Re Gillingham Bus Disaster Fund* had concerned a charitable trust the surplus remaining after the purposes had been satisfied would have been applied cy-près: *Re Wokingham Fire Brigade Trusts* [1951] Ch 373; *Re Ulverston and District New Hospital Building Trusts* [1956] Ch 622.

[93] *Leahy v A-G for New South Wales* [1959] AC 457, PC; *Neville Estates Ltd v Madden* [1962] Ch 832; *Re Recher's Will Trusts* [1972] Ch 526; *Re Lipinski's Will Trusts* [1976] Ch 235; *Re Grant's Will Trusts* [1980] 1 WLR 360. See p 653.

[94] *Re Printers and Transferrers Amalgamated Trades Protection Society* [1899] 2 Ch 184; *Re Lead Co's Workmen's Fund Society* [1904] 2 Ch 196; *Tierney v Tough* [1914] 1 IR 142; *Re Hobourn Aero Components Air Raid Distress Fund* [1946] Ch 86.

[95] [1971] Ch 1.

The club's revenue was derived from: (a) members' subscriptions; (b) legacies and donations from outsiders; (c) proceeds of entertainments and collecting-boxes. The question arose as to how the surplus should be distributed. Goff J dealt separately with each type of revenue.

## (a) Members' subscriptions[96]

Goff J held that the members were not entitled to take any share of the surplus on the basis of resulting trusts because they had made their contributions on the basis of contract and not trust.[97] They had received all that they had bargained for from their membership of the club. Therefore this property went bona vacantia to the crown.

## (b) Outside legacies and donations[98]

Since these were not given on the basis of contract, Goff J held there should be a resulting trust in favour of those who had contributed, in so far as the surplus was attributable to their contributions. He considered that this aspect of the case was indistinguishable from *Re Abbott Fund Trusts*.[99]

## (c) Proceeds of entertainments and collecting-boxes[100]

As has been considered above,[101] Goff J held that there could be no resulting trust of the surplus attributable to revenue from these sources, and it thus passed bona vacantia to the Crown.

*Re West Sussex Constabulary's Widows, Children and Benevolent (1930) Fund Trusts*[102] rejected a resulting trust solution in relation to members' contributions on the winding up of an unincorporated association. This had the consequence that the majority of the surplus passed bona vacantia to the Crown, with the members seeming to receive nothing for their contributions. The reason for this may be that, although the contractual analysis was argued so as to defeat any claim by the members to a resulting trust, there was no argument that the members had any contractual rights to the surplus. Goff J observed in his judgment:

'The surviving members . . . may well have a right in contract on the ground of frustration or total failure of consideration, and that right may embrace contributions made by past members, though I do not see how it could apply to moneys raised from outside sources. I have not, however, heard any argument based on contract and therefore the declarations I propose to make will be subject to . . . reservation . . .'[103]

---

[96] [1971] Ch 1 at 9–10.

[97] Following *Cunnack v Edwards* [1896] 2 Ch 679; *Re Gillingham Bus Disaster Fund* [1958] Ch 300.

[98] [1971] Ch 1 at 14–16.      [99] [1900] 2 Ch 326.      [100] [1971] Ch 1 at 11–14.

[101] See above, p 564.      [102] [1971] Ch 1.

[103] [1971] Ch 1 at 10: this did not prevent the property being paid over as bona vacantia as the Crown had offered a full indemnity to the trustees.

## (3) *Re Bucks Constabulary Fund (No 2)*: distribution of surplus funds to the members of the association

The reasoning which denied the members any claim in *Re West Sussex Constabulary's Widows, Children and Benevolent (1930) Fund Trusts*[104] was taken a step further in *Re Bucks Constabulary Fund (No 2)*,[105] where it was held that the members of an unincorporated association enjoyed contractual rights to surplus assets. The case concerned a society registered under the Friendly Societies Act 1896, which was wound up because of the amalgamation of the Buckinghamshire Constabulary, leaving a surplus. Given that an unincorporated association derives its existence from an 'implied contract between all the members inter se governed by the rules of the society',[106] Walton J held that this contract should govern the distribution of the surplus:

'... as on dissolution there were members of the society ... in existence, its assets are held on trust for such members to the total exclusion of any claim on behalf of the Crown.'

(i) *Re West Sussex*

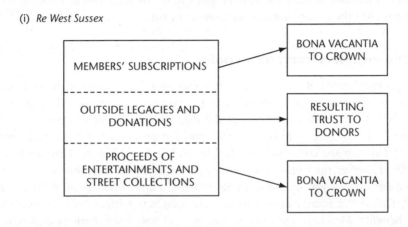

(ii) *Re Bucks Constabulary*

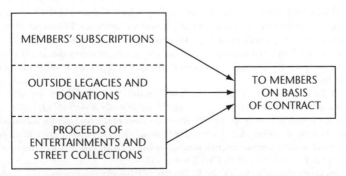

**Distribution of assets on the dissolution of an unincorporated association**

---

[104] [1971] Ch 1.     [105] [1979] 1 WLR 936.     [106] [1979] 1 WLR 936 at 943.

This is entirely consistent with the reasoning that unincorporated associations hold their property on the basis of the contract between the members,[107] and that they must be able to alter the rules of the association so as to put the assets into their own pockets.[108] Since this shows that 'the money was theirs all the time',[109] they should be entitled to what is theirs on the winding-up of the association. This reasoning excludes any possibility of a resulting trust, either of the members' own contributions, or of the donations of outsiders,[110] and provides the members with a basis for entitlement to the surplus which was not found in *Re West Sussex Constabulary's Widows, Children and Benevolent (1930) Fund Trusts.*[111] Therefore, none of the assets of the association, whatever their source, should pass under a resulting trust or as bona vacantia. The only circumstances in which Walton J anticipated the surplus will pass bona vacantia to the Crown is when the society is moribund by being reduced to a single member.[112] The problem with this solution is that, instead of conferring a windfall gain on the Crown (as bona vacantia), it confers a windfall gain on the members, who would never have expected to make a personal profit from a benevolent association. However, this may be no more objectionable than the windfall gains made by members of building societies which have lost their mutual status on takeover or on conversion to a bank.

## (4) The members' contractual rights

The exact entitlement of each surviving member on a distribution of the surplus assets of an association depends on its rules. In the absence of express rules providing for dissolution, the surviving members at the date of dissolution will have prima facie entitlement to the surplus in equal shares, and not proportionately to their contributions.[113] This was the conclusion reached by Walton J in *Re Bucks Constabulary Fund (No 2).*[114] However, the rules of the society may impliedly indicate that something other than equal division was intended. In *Re Sick and Funeral Society of St John's Sunday School, Golcar*[115] a society existed to provide members with sickness allowances and death benefits. Members aged five to twelve paid half contributions and were only

---

[107] *Re Sick and Funeral Society of St John's Sunday School, Golcar* [1973] Ch 51 at 60, per Megarry J: 'membership of a club or association is primarily a matter of contract. The members make their payments, and in return they become entitled to the benefits of membership in accordance with the rules. The sums they pay cease to be their individual property, and so cease to be subject to any concept of resulting trust. Instead, they become the property, through the trustees of the club or association, of all the members for the time being, including themselves.'

[108] See *Re Lipinski* [1976] Ch 235; *Re Grant's Will Trusts* [1980] 1 WLR 360.

[109] *Re Bucks Constabulary Widows' and Orphans' Fund Friendly Society (No 2)* [1979] 1 WLR 936 at 951.

[110] Since these too are held by the association on the basis of the contract for the members absolutely. See *Re Lipinski's Will Trusts* [1976] Ch 235, where Mr Lipinski's gift to the association was held to be a gift to the members subject to their contract inter se, which they could decide to distribute amongst themselves.

[111] [1971] Ch 1.    [112] [1979] 1 WLR 936 at 943.

[113] See *Brown v Dale* (1878) 9 Ch D 78; *Re Printers and Transferrers Amalgamated Trades Protection Society* [1899] 2 Ch 184; *Re Lead Co's Workmen's Fund Society* [1904] 2 Ch 196; *Tierney v Tough* [1914] 1 IR 142; *Feeny and Shannon v MacManus* [1937] IR 23; *Re Blue Albion Cattle Society* [1966] CLY 1274; *Re St Andrew's Allotments Association's Trusts* [1969] 1 WLR 229.

[114] [1979] 1 WLR 936 at 951–955.    [115] [1973] Ch 51.

entitled to half benefits. Megarry J held that since this inequality was written into the rules, dividing the members into different classes, it should be applied to the surplus funds on dissolution. Those paying half contributions were only entitled to half shares in the surplus.[116] The large sums involved in the dissolution of mutual associations can be extremely large: the sale of the RAC rescue service division in 1998 was expected to produce in the order of £30,000 for each of the Club's members.

## (5) Re-emergence of the resulting trust analysis?

*Re Bucks Constabulary Fund (No 2)*[117] marks a clear rejection of the resulting trust analysis in the context of unincorporated associations. However, in the case of *Davis v Richards and Wallington Industries Ltd*,[118] Scott J applied a resulting trust analysis in the context of a company pension fund, which had the effect of denying the employees of the firm any rights to the £3m surplus. This case runs against the grain of the authorities concerned with the surplus assets of unincorporated associations. It seems that Scott J presumed that the only alternatives open to him were a resulting trust or bona vacantia, and he did not consider whether the employees of the firm had any contractual entitlement to the surplus.[119] This may be because occupational pension schemes, to which employees contribute on the basis of their contact and from which they are contractually entitled to benefits, are not analogous to unincorporated associations.[120] The employees do not have sole control of the scheme, and, unlike the members of an unincorporated association, they cannot decide to wind it up and divide the assets amongst themselves. The benefits payable to members are also limited by Inland Revenue rules. The essence of the decision is that the contributors are not deprived of all possible proprietary rights in the fund merely because their contributions and benefits are determined by contract, a principle more recently affirmed by the Privy Council in *Air Jamaica Ltd v Charlton*.[121] It does not undermine the authority of *Re Bucks Constabulary Fund (No 2)*[122] in the context of unincorporated associations, where the general principle remains that the surplus will be divided amongst the surviving members under their contract inter se.

---

[116] See also *Re St Andrew's Allotments Association's Trusts* [1969] 1 WLR 229.

[117] [1979] 1 WLR 936.      [118] [1991] 2 All ER 563; see also above, p 000.

[119] For example, he spoke of 'the principles to be decided between a resulting trust and bona vacantia' (at 519), and *Re West Sussex Constabulary's Widows, Children and Benevolent (1930) Fund Trusts* [1971] Ch 1 was cited in his judgment but *Re Bucks Constabulary Widows' and Orphans' Fund Friendly Society (No 2)* [1979] 1 WLR 936 was not.

[120] Although it was argued by counsel that a pension scheme was merely a species of unincorporated association (at 589).

[121] [1999] 1 WLR 1399.

[122] [1979] 1 WLR 936.

# 4 Surplus funds on the failure of a charity[123]

## (1) The principle of an application cy-près

When a charity comes to an end still holding property on trust, the question arises as to what should happen to that surplus. One possibility is that it should be returned to those who donated it on the basis of a resulting trust, in much the same way as a surplus on the failure of a private trust will return to the original contributors.[124] However, charitable trusts are treated differently from private trusts because they have a public character. Although a whole range of different purposes may fall within the definition of 'charity', it is regarded as a unified area, so that property applied to any particular charitable purpose forms part of the 'common pot' of charity. The law thus regards property given for any specific charitable purpose as given not merely to that particular purpose but dedicated to charity in the general sense. If the particular purpose for which the property was given fails, it will be applied, under a scheme drawn up by the Charity Commissioners,[125] to other similar charitable purposes and will not return to the donor under a resulting trust. This application to alternative charitable purposes is called 'cy-près'. The principle was stated by Roxburgh J in *Re Lucas*:

'. . . once a fund has been devoted to charitable purposes, it cannot be diverted from charity by any supervening impracticality but must be applied cy-près.'[126]

Particular difficulties arise when a testator makes a gift by will to a charity which has ceased to exist. In such circumstances the question arises whether the property bequeathed to the charity should pass to the residuary legatees under a resulting trust, or be applied cy-près to other similar charitable purposes. The principles determining whether the property will be applied cy-près are different, depending upon whether the failure of the charity concerned was 'initial' or 'subsequent'.

## (a) Initial failure

An initial failure occurs if a charity to which property was bequeathed ceased to exist before the testator had died. Since the gift to the charity was never effective, the property concerned will only be applied cy-près to a similar charitable purpose if it can be shown that the testator had a 'general charitable intention'[127] when he made his bequest and not merely the intention to benefit the specific charity which has failed. If no such general charitable intention can be identified, the property will pass to the residuary legatees by way of a resulting trust.

---

[123] See Sheridan and Delaney, *The Cy-près Doctrine* (1959); Sheridan and Keeton, *The Modern Law of Charities* (4th edn, 1992); *Nathan Committee Report* (Cmnd 8710), Ch 9.

[124] See above, p 553.

[125] Formerly, the scheme was drawn up by the court. This 'judicial' cy-près is to be contrasted with 'prerogative' cy-près which is exercised by the Crown where a gift is made to charity but not upon trust.

[126] [1948] Ch 175 at 181.      [127] See *Re Spence* [1979] Ch 483.

## (b) Subsequent failure

A subsequent failure occurs if a charity to which property was bequeathed ceases to exist or if a charitable purpose becomes impossible to implement between the death of the testator and the administration of the estate by the executors. Since the will operates on the death of the testator to transfer an interest in the property to the charity, it is fully dedicated to charity before the failure of the specific charity to which it was given failed. It will therefore be applied cy-près[128] without any need to demonstrate a general charitable intention. Any difficulty is only illusory, and arises because of the time gap between death and the distribution of the estate.

## (c) Failure of charitable appeals

Special statutory rules apply where there is an appeal for funds for a specific charitable purpose but that purpose fails. Where a donor to the appeal cannot be identified or found after advertisement and inquiries, the funds may be applied cy-près as if the funds had been given for charitable purposes generally.[129] The same rule applies where a donor has signed a disclaimer in prescribed form. The Charities Bill 2005 proposes to extend this rule by applying the same principle even to donors who can be identified. Such donors will be treated as having disclaimed their right to have their donation returned if the solicitation by which the appeal was made stated that donors would have no right to the return of their donation in the event of the specific charitable purpose failing unless they make a declaration that they must be consulted before their donation is applied to other purposes.[130] These principles do not apply where an appeal is for non-charitable purposes, as was the case in *Re Gillingham Bus Disaster Fund*,[131] discussed above.

## (2) Circumstances justifying application of surplus funds cy-près

### (a) Impossibility or impracticality

Prior to the Charities Act 1960, property would only be applied cy-près if a charitable purpose had become impossible or impracticable. For example, in *A-G v London Corpn*[132] a trust for 'the propagation of the Christian religion amongst the infidels of Virginia' was found to have become impossible, as Lord Thurlow LC held that there were no infidels left in Virginia. Similarly, in *Ironmongers' Co v A-G*[133] a trust for the redemption of British slaves in Turkey was impossible because there were no such British slaves remaining to be redeemed. In *Re Robinson*[134] a trust had been established to endow an Evangelical church in Bournemouth, subject to a condition that the preacher always wear a black gown. Since this was alienating the congregation, PO

---

[128]   See *Re Slevin* [1891] 2 Ch 236, CA; *Re Wright* [1954] Ch 347, CA.
[129]   Charities Act 1993, s14.
[130]   Charities Bill 2005, cl 17 inserting a new s 14A into the Charities Act 1993.
[131]   [1958] Ch 300.        [132]   (1790) 3 Bro CC 171.        [133]   (1844) 10 Cl & Fin 908.
[134]   [1921] 2 Ch 332. See also *Re Campden Charities* (1881) 18 Ch D 310, CA.

Lawrence J held that this rendered the purpose impracticable[135] and sanctioned a scheme dispensing with the condition.[136]

In order to extend the scope of this narrow jurisdiction, the courts did not insist strictly upon impossibility or impracticality.[137] In *Re Dominion Students Hall Trust*[138] a charity maintained a hostel for male students from the British Empire, but only those of European origin. The charity sought to remove the restriction. Evershed J held that 'the word "impossible" should be given a wide significance'[139] and that in the circumstances the 'colour bar' did render the charity impossible since it would undermine its main objects. He therefore approved a scheme removing the bar. In *Re Lysaght (Decd)*[140] a testatrix left the residue of her estate to the Royal College of Surgeons (RCS) to provide medical studentships. Various limitations were placed on those eligible for the awards, including a provision that they must not be Jewish or Roman Catholic. In view of these restrictions, the RCS refused to accept the trust. Since the trustee would not accept the trust with the condition, Buckley J held that the trust had become impossible, and therefore ordered that the fund be paid to the RCS as trustees without the restriction.[141] In *Re JW Laing Trust*[142] a settlor had created a trust of shares in favour of a variety of evangelical Christian purposes. The trust contained a requirement that the fund was to be distributed during the settlor's lifetime, or within ten years of his death. He died in 1978, by which time the trust was worth some £24m. The types of organisations that the trust had been supporting were unsuited for receiving large sums of capital. It was held that there was no room for application cy-près, but the court removed the restriction under its inherent jurisdiction.

### (b) Charities Act 1993, s 13

Given the restrictive scope of the cy-près jurisdiction, the Nathan Committee recommended that the requirements for impracticality be relaxed.[143] A wider jurisdiction was thus introduced in s 13 of the Charities Act 1960, which has been re-enacted as s 13 of the Charities Act 1993. Section 13 provides for five circumstances in which property given to charitable purposes which have not strictly failed can be applied cy-près:

'(a) where the original purposes, in whole or in part,—
    (i) have been as far as may be fulfilled, or
    (ii) cannot be carried out, or not according to the directions given and to the spirit of the gift; or
(b) where the original purposes provide a use for part only of the property available by virtue of the gift; or
(c) where the property available by virtue of the gift and other property applicable for

---

[135] See also *Re Weir Hospital* [1910] 2 Ch 124.

[136] In essence, he held that the paramount intention was to endow a church, and not to enforce the wearing of a black robe, and that the paramount intention would be rendered impossible by the condition. See *Re Lysaght* [1966] Ch 191 at 208.

[137] See *Re Weir Hospital* [1910] 2 Ch 124.    [138] [1947] Ch 183.

[139] [1947] Ch 183 at 186.    [140] [1966] Ch 191.

[141] See also *Re Woodhams* [1981] 1 WLR 493.    [142] [1984] Ch 143.

[143] *Report of the Committee on the Law and Practice relating to Charitable Trusts* (1952) (Cmd 8710), para 365.

similar purposes can be more effectively used in conjunction, and to that end can suitably, regard being had to *the spirit of the gift*, be made applicable to common purposes; or

(d) where the original purposes were laid down by reference to an area which then was but has since ceased to be a unit for some other purpose, or by reference to a class of persons or to an area which has for any reason since ceased to be suitable, regard being had to *the spirit of the gift*, or to be practical in administering the gift; or

(e) where the original purposes, in whole or in part, have, since they were laid down—

   (i)   been adequately provided for by other means, or

   (ii)   ceased, as being useless or harmful to the community or for other reasons, to be in law charitable, or

   (iii)   ceased in any other way to provide a suitable and effective method of using the property available by virtue of the gift, regard being had to *the spirit of the gift.*'

The Charities Bill 2005 proposes to extend still further the circumstances in which cy-près will be possible by substituting for 'the spirit of the gift' where that phrase is italicised above two factors, namely the spirit of the gift **and** 'the social and economic circumstances prevailing at the time of the proposed alteration of the original purposes'.[144] This amendment would facilitate a cy-près application where, for instance, a trust specified the award of an annual prize which over the years had fallen in value because of the effect of inflation, but which otherwise could still be awarded.

The greater width of the cy-près jurisdiction under s 13 is evident from cases in which it has been considered. In *Re Lepton's Charity*[145] a trust established in 1716 provided for the payment of £3 per annum from the income generated by a piece of land to the minister of a dissenting church, with the remainder distributed amongst the poor. In 1716 the income was £5 but at the date of the case it was some £800. Pennycuick V-C held that, although the purpose of the trust had not failed, the circumstances fell within s 13(1)(a)(ii) and (1)(e)(iii) and directed that £100 per annum be paid to the minister. This decision could more readily have been reached with the amended wording proposed by the Charities Bill 2005. In *Varsani v Jesani*[146] the Court of Appeal applied s 13 in order to deal with the assets of a religious charity that had suffered an irretrievable schism. Chadwick LJ said that under the law as it stood before the Charities Act 1960, the court could not direct a scheme:

'This is because it would still be possible to carry out the original purposes of the charity through the use of its property by the group who . . . had been found to be the adherents to the true faith; and any application of any part of the property for use by the other group would be open to attack as a breach of trust. It is for that reason that, under the old law, the court would have been required to decide the underlying question . . . which (if either) of the views now held by the majority group and the minority group respectively do truly reflect the teachings and tenets of Muktajivandasji.'

He continued by saying that s 13 had changed the position and that it was no longer necessary to examine which group remained true to the original tenets of the faith.

---

[144] Charities Bill 2005 clause 15(3).    [145] [1972] Ch 276.    [146] [1999] Ch 219.

'The original purposes specified in the declaration of trust, that is to say the promotion of the faith of Swaminarayan as practised in accordance with the teachings and tenets of Muktajivandasji, are no longer a suitable and effective method of using the property given in 1967 (or added property held upon the same trusts) because the community is now divided and cannot worship together . . . to appropriate the use of the property to the one group to the exclusion of the other would be contrary to the spirit in which the gift was made.'

The court ordered a scheme for the division of the funds between the two groups.

Section 13 has no application if there would have been no need for a scheme to apply the property prior to the Charities Act 1960. In *Oldham Borough Council v A-G*[147] a council owned a piece of land 'upon trust to preserve and manage the same at all times hereafter as playing fields . . . for the benefit and enjoyment' of local inhabitants. The council wished to sell the land to developers and use the proceeds to purchase a different piece of land with better facilities. The Court of Appeal held that the planned sale and reinvestment for exactly the same purposes did not involve an alternation of the 'original purposes' of the charitable gift. Therefore, since the sale and reinvestment would not have required a scheme before the Charities Act 1960, the trust was not affected by the provisions of s 13 and the court could authorise the sale under its statutory or common law power relating to charities.

### (c) Administrative schemes

The jurisdiction under s 13 does not extend to administrative provisions which cannot be considered as falling within the 'original purposes' specified in s 13(1). Thus, in *Re JW Laing Trust*[148] a stipulation that all the property of the trust be distributed within ten years of the settlor's death was a purely administrative requirement and could not be altered under s 13,[149] and in *Varsani v Jesani*[150] the court held that, even if both groups remained true to the faith as prescribed in the original gift, the court had power to authorise an administrative scheme.

## (3) Subsequent failure of charitable gifts

Where a testator leaves property to a charity in his will which fails after his death but before the administration of the estate is complete, it will be applied cy-près to other charitable purposes rather than resulting back to the residuary legatees, even though it was never in fact received by the charity. This is because the property was fully dedicated to charity from the very moment that the testator died. In such cases the property is applied cy-près, irrespective of whether the testator had a general charitable intention or not, provided that there was an outright and perpetual dedication to charitable purposes, rather than a dedication for a limited period.[151] A number of cases illustrate the operation of cy-près in the context of subsequent failure. In *Re Slevin*[152] a testator

---

[147] [1993] 2 All ER 432.     [148] [1984] Ch 143.

[149] But it was removed by the court under their inherent jurisdiction.

[150] [1998] 3 All ER 273 at 285, per Morritt LJ.

[151] See *Re North Devon and West Somerset Relief Fund Trusts* [1953] 2 All ER 1032; *Re Cooper's Conveyance Trusts* [1956] 1 WLR 1096.

[152] [1891] 2 Ch 236.

left a gift of £200 to St Dominic's Orphanage, Newcastle. The orphanage closed after his death but before the legacy had been paid over. The Court of Appeal held that the property should be applied cy-près, as it had become the property of the charity from the date of the testator's death. The same result was reached in a slightly more complex scenario in *Re Wright*.[153] A testatrix died in 1933, leaving property on trust to found and maintain a convalescent home, subject to a life interest. The life interest came to an end in 1942, but by that date it had become impracticable to carry out the charitable purpose. The question arose whether the property should be applied cy-près or result back to the next-of-kin. The Court of Appeal held that the property should be applied cy-près as the charity gained a right to the property, albeit subject to a life-interest, at the date of the testatrix's death.[154] Property will also be applied cy-près without the need to show a general charitable intention if it was given to accomplish a charitable purpose but the purpose has been completed without the exhaustion of the property given. In *Re King*[155] property worth £1,500 was bequeathed to install a window in a church, the cost of which could not possibly exhaust that sum. Romer J held that the surplus should be applied cy-près.[156] Similarly, in *Re Wokingham Fire Brigade Trusts*[157] a surplus derived from a public appeal was held applicable cy-près without the need to demonstrate any general charitable intention on the part of the donors.[158]

## (4) Initial failure of charitable gifts

A charitable gift will fail initially if the charity has ceased to exist before it receives any interest in the property donated. This will happen when a testator bequeaths property to a charity which ceases to exist before the date of his death. For example, in *Re Spence*[159] a testatrix left part of her estate to 'The Old Folk's Home at Hillworth Lodge Keighley' in a will that was executed in 1968. She died in 1972, but the Old People's Home had closed down in 1971. In cases of initial failure the testator could have changed his will to take account of the failure of the charity but has not done so, perhaps because of his health, or through lack of knowledge that the charity has ceased to exist. The question thus arises whether the property should be applied cy-près to other charitable purposes, or whether it should pass by resulting trust to his residuary legatees. Since the testator cannot be consulted, the law seeks to 'second guess' what he would have wanted to happen to the property. If it can be shown that he had a 'general charitable intention' when he made the gift in his will, the property will be applied cy-près. Such an intention indicates that the testator would have preferred the property to

---

153 [1954] Ch 347.

154 See also *Re Moon's Will Trust* (1948) 64 TLR 123; *Re Tacon* [1958] Ch 447.

155 [1923] 1 Ch 243.

156 See, however, *Re Stanford* [1924] 1 Ch 73 where Eve J held that a similar surplus should pass by way of a resulting trust to the residuary legatees.

157 [1951] Ch 373. See also *Re Ulverston and District New Hospital Building Trusts* [1956] Ch 622.

158 In *Re Welsh Hospital (Netley Fund)* [1921] 1 Ch 655 and *Re North Devon and Somerset Relief Fund Trusts* [1953] 1 WLR 1260 similar surpluses were held applicable cy-près because of the general charitable intention of the donors. However, it is doubtful that such an intention should be necessary, as the donors contributing to a public appeal surely dedicate their donation to charity at he moment it is made.

159 [1979] Ch 483.

be applied to another charity than result back under his will. If there is no general charitable intention, then it is presumed that the testator intended to benefit only the specific charity which has failed, and that in the event of the failure he would have preferred his property to result back to the residuary legatees rather than pass to a replacement charity.

## (a) Has the charity actually failed?

An application cy-près will only be necessary if the charity to which a bequest gift was made has actually failed. In some cases where it appears that a charity has failed the court has found a way of saving the gift by holding that charity has not in fact failed because the charity has in some way continued. If this is the case there is no need to apply the property cy-près and it will be applied to the charitable purposes in their continuing form.

*(i) Amalgamation with other charities.* Where the charity nominated in the testator's will has been amalgamated with other charities it will be held to have continued in that new form, and the property will be applied to the new amalgamated charity without the need for cy-près. In *Re Faraker*[160] a testatrix left £200 to Hannah Bayly's Charity. Hannah Bayly's Charity had been founded in 1756 for the benefit of the poor widows of Rotherhithe, but had ceased to exist as a separate entity in 1905, when it was amalgamated with other charities for the benefit of the poor of Rotherhithe by the Charity Commissioners. The Court of Appeal held that there had been no failure because Hannah Bayly's Charity had not ceased to exist but continued in the form of the amalgamated charity, which encompassed its objects. The principle was applied in *Re Lucas*,[161] where a testatrix, who died in 1942, left £550 to 'the Crippled Children's Home, Lindley Moor, Huddersfield'. The 'Huddersfield Home for Crippled Children' had been founded in 1916, but was closed in 1941. However, its assets were applied to a new charity, 'The Huddersfield Charity for Crippled Children', under a scheme made by the Charity Commissioners. The Court of Appeal applied *Re Faraker*[162] and held that, rather than there being an initial failure, the legacy should pass to the new charity.[163] A more modern example might be the recent merger between the Imperial Cancer Research Fund and the Cancer Research Campaign to form Cancer Research UK.

The principle of *Re Faraker*[164] is limited to cases where there is a genuine amalgamation so that the purposes of the charity have continued in another form. In *Re Roberts*[165] Jane Roberts, who died in 1961, left a share of her residuary estate to the 'Sheffield Boys' Working Home'. The home had closed in 1945, at which point the trustees had transferred the majority of the assets to the 'Sheffield Town Trust', retaining only nominal funds themselves. Wilberforce J held that the property could not be applied to the Sheffield Town Trust on the basis of the principle of *Re Faraker*,[166] as the

---

[160] [1912] 2 Ch 488. Expenditure is not confined to the purposes of the original charity.
[161] [1948] Ch 175; revsd [1948] Ch 24, CA.     [162] [1912] 2 Ch 488.
[163] See also *Re Lucas* [1948] Ch 175; revsd [1948] Ch 242, CA; *Re Bagshaw* [1954] 1 All ER 227; *Re Slatter's Will Trusts* [1964] Ch 512; *Re Stemson's Will Trusts* [1970] Ch 16.
[164] [1912] 2 Ch 488.     [165] [1963] 1 WLR 406.     [166] [1912] 2 Ch 488.

original charity was still in existence, although lacking the machinery to administer the legacy. It was therefore to be applied to the trustees of the home, and then applied cy-près.

Any funds received by the trustees of the amalgamated charity can be used for the general purposes of the charity. They are not limited to the specific purposes contemplated by the testator. It might therefore have surprised the testatrix in *Re Faraker* that not a penny of the funds she left need be spent on widows.

*(ii) Unincorporated associations.* Where a bequest is left to a charitable unincorporated association which ceased to exist before the death of the testator, the courts have held that the gift does not fail because it should be construed as a gift to the continuing purposes of the association and not to the specific association as an entity. The rationale for this principle was considered by Buckley J in *Re Vernon's Will Trusts*:

'Every gift to an unincorporated charity by name without more must take effect as a gift for a charitable purpose. No individual or aggregate of individuals could claim to take such a bequest beneficially.[167] If the gift is to take effect at all, it must be as a bequest for a purpose, viz, that charitable purpose which the named charity exists to serve. A bequest which is in terms made for a charitable purpose will not fail for lack of a trustee . . .'[168]

Since an unincorporated charity has no legal personality,[169] the gift is construed as a gift to the purposes of the association, and those purposes continue even though the particular association has ceased to exist.[170] The gift will only fail if the testator's intention to make the gift was dependent upon the named association to apply the gift.[171]

In contrast, where a bequest is left to a charitable corporation it will be construed as a gift to that particular body, which has legal personality, and therefore if the corporation has ceased to exist the gift fails and the property will only be applied cy-près if a general charitable intention can be shown.[172] These principles were applied in *Re Finger's Will Trusts*.[173] Georgia Finger left a share of her residuary estate to a number of charitable organisations, including The National Radium Commission (NRC), an unincorporated charity, and The National Council for Maternity and Child Welfare (NCMCW), a corporate body. Both had ceased to exist before the death of the testator. Goff J held that since the gift to the NRC was a gift to an unincorporated charity, the gift should be construed as a gift to the purposes of the Commission, which had not failed. The gift to the NCMCW had failed, but the property was applied cy-près because there was a general charitable intention.[174]

It is noteworthy that Australian courts have rejected any difference of construction of

---

[167] Although the usual interpretation of gifts to unincorporated associations is that the members take beneficially (see Chapter 23), this interpretation is excluded in the case of charities since it is inconsistent with charitable status for the members of the charity to take a beneficial interest.

[168] [1972] Ch 300n. See also *Re Morrison* (1967) 111 Sol Jo 758.      [169] See Chapter 23.

[170] This construction was approved by the Court of Appeal in *Re Koeppler Will Trusts* [1986] Ch 423 at 434, per Slade LJ.

[171] Eg *Re Spence* [1979] Ch 483.

[172] *Re Ovey* (1885) 29 Ch D 560; *Liverpool and District Hospital for Diseases of the Heart v A-G* [1981] Ch 193.

[173] [1972] Ch 286; (1972) 36 Conv 198 (Cotterell); (1974) 38 Conv 187 (Martin).

[174] See below, p 576.

gifts made to charitable corporate and unincorporated bodies, and have held that there is a presumption that the gift is made for the purposes of the body in either case.[175] This removes the artificiality of the distinction, which is generated by the unsatisfactory state of English law regarding property holding by unincorporated associations.

*(iii)  Charitable company become insolvent.* There is no cause for an application cy-près where a testator leaves property to a charitable company which has become insolvent and entered into liquidation before the date of his death. In *Re ARMS (Multiple Sclerosis Research) Ltd*[176] testators had left property to a charity which sought to promote research into a cure for multiple sclerosis which had gone into liquidation before their deaths, with debts of just under £1.5m. Neuberger J held that although the testators would not have wanted their gifts to take effect if they had known that the company was in liquidation at the date of their deaths, their gifts took effect because the company was still in existence. Their bequests were therefore available to pay creditors, and were not able to be applied cy-près to other similar charitable purposes.

## (b)  Application cy-près where the charity has failed

Where the charity has in fact failed, the property bequeathed to it will only be applied cy-près if it can be shown that the testator had a 'general charitable intention'. 'General charitable intention' has a technical meaning, which encapsulates the idea that the testator was not so committed to the particular charity nominated in his will that, in the event of its failure, he would have preferred his gift to result back to the residuary legatees under his will rather than to be applied to similar charitable purposes. The principle was outlined by Sir Robert Megarry V-C in *Re Spence*:

'. . . the essence of the distinction is in the difference between particularity and generality. If a particular institution or purpose is specified, then it is that institution or purpose, and no other, that is to be the object of the benefaction. It is difficult to envisage a testator as being suffused with a general glow of broad charity when he is labouring, and labouring successfully, to identify some particular specified institution or purpose as the object of his bounty. The specific displaces the general. It is otherwise where the testator has been unable to specify any particular charitable institution or practicable purpose, and so, although his intention of charity can be seen, he has failed to provide any way of giving effect to it. There, the absence of the specific leaves the general undisturbed . . .'[177]

This makes clear that whether a gift is made with general charitable intention or not is a matter of degree, and there is no single factor which will determine whether a gift falls on the 'particular' or 'general' side of the line. This will be determined in the light of all the circumstances of the gift. In assessing whether a gift was made with 'general charitable intention' the courts have taken account of the following factors.

*(i)  Gifts to specific institutions or bodies.* Where a gift is made to a specific charitable institution or body, this is likely to indicate the absence of any general charitable intention. In *Re Rymer*[178] Horatio Rymer bequeathed a legacy of £5,000 to 'St Thomas'

---

[175]  *Sir Moses Montefiore Jewish Home v Howell & Co (No 7) Pty Ltd* [1984] 2 NSWLR 406.
[176]  [1997] 1 WLR 877.        [177]  [1979] Ch 483 at 493.        [178]  [1895] 1 Ch 19.

Seminary' in Westminster. The seminary had closed before his death, and the students had transferred to a seminary near Birmingham. The Court of Appeal held that there was no general charitable intention because the gift was a gift to a specific seminary.[179] In *Re Spence*[180] Beatrice Spence left half her residuary estate to the 'Old Folk's Home at Hillworth Lodge Keighley'. She died in 1972, and the home had closed in 1971. Megarry V-C held that this was a gift to a specific institution alone, and that there was no general charitable intention.

*(ii) Gifts to a specific institution but with a clear underlying general charitable intention.* Even when a gift is made to a specific institution, if the court can see a 'clear general intention underlying the particular mode' of carrying the charitable purpose out[181] they will find a general charitable intention and apply the property cy-près. Thus, in *Biscoe v Jackson*[182] a gift was made by will for the establishment of a soup kitchen and cottage hospital in Shoreditch. This had become impossible, but Kay J held that the testator had a general charitable intention in that the underlying purpose of the gift was to benefit the poor of Shoreditch through the establishment of the soup kitchen and hospital. In *Re Woodhams (Decd)*[183] the court held that a testator who had left money for the musical education of boys from specific children's homes was held to have a paramount intention to benefit musical education. In *Re Spence*[184] Megarry V-C was unable to find any such underlying general intention because the purpose was to benefit the specific patients of the specific home, and not the aged in general.

*(iii) 'Charity by association'.*[185] Even though a gift is made to a specific institution, the court may find a general charitable intention if the gift is one of a number of charitable bequests, and it is clear that the testator intended all of the property so bequeathed to go to 'charity'. In *Re Knox*[186] Dorothy Knox left her residuary estate to three hospitals and to Dr Barnardo's Homes in equal shares. One hospital, the 'Newcastle-upon-Tyne-Nursing Home', did not exist, and Luxmore J held that the quarter share of the residuary estate should be applied cy-près. He found a general charitable intention in the context of the will, drawing from the fact that the residuary estate was divided amongst four beneficiaries, three of whom were undoubtedly charitable.[187] Similarly, in *Re Satterthwaite's Will Trusts*[188] a testatrix who hated all human beings left her residuary estate to be divided amongst nine specifically named animal charities, including the 'Animal Welfare Service'. There was no such charity. Russell LJ held that a general charitable intention could be discerned from the fact that the other

---

179 See *Fisk v A-G* (1867) LR 4 Eq 521; *Clark v Taylor* (1853) 1 Drew 642.

180 [1979] Ch 483.      181 *Re Spence* [1979] Ch 483 at 495, per Megarry V-C.

182 (1887) 35 Ch D 460. See also *A-G v Boultbee* (1794) 2 Ves 380; *Cherry v Mott* (1836) 1 My & Cr 123.

183 [1981] 1 All ER 202.      184 [1979] Ch 483.

185 The categorisation of these cases by Megarry V-C in *Re Spence* [1979] Ch 483 at 494.

186 [1937] Ch 109.

187 Although the case could equally be explained on the principle of *Re Harwood* [1936] Ch 285, but it was not cited, and the judge reached his conclusion by looking to the other charitable gifts in the context of the will.

188 [1966] 1 WLR 277.

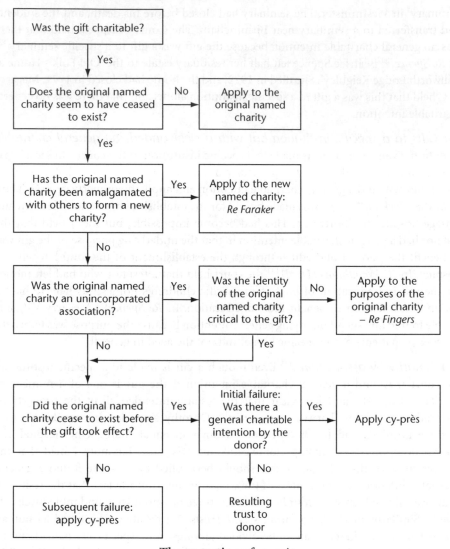

**The operation of cy-près**

eight-ninths of her estate was left to animal charities.[189] The principle of charity by association only applies where a charitable gift fails for lack of certainty or non-existence and has no application where one gift amongst a number of charitable gifts fails because it is non-charitable.

*(iv)  Specific charities which had never existed.* It has been held that it is easier to find a general charitable intention where a gift is made to a specific charity that has never

---

[189]   However, as Megarry V-C noted in *Re Spence*, *Re Satterthwaite's Will Trusts* is not such strong authority as *Re Knox* because Harman LJ had 'the gravest doubts' whether there was general charitable intention, and Diplock LJ agreed with both other judgments.

existed than to a charity which has ceased to exist.[190] In *Re Harwood*[191] a testatrix left bequests to a long list of charitable societies, including those devoted to peace. Amongst these were a gift to the 'Wisbech Peace Society', which had ceased to exist before the testator's death, and the 'Peace Society of Belfast', which the evidence suggested had never existed. Farwell J held that the gift to the Wisbech society failed, and that as it was a gift to a specific institution the testatrix had no general charitable intention. In contrast, he held that because the Belfast society had never existed, she had demonstrated a general charitable intention for the purposes of peace in Belfast, and the gift was applied cy-près. The rationale behind this analysis is probably that, as the testatrix did not check whether a particular charity existed, she must have assumed that it did, and that her intention was therefore to benefit the purposes which the invented name suggested were being pursued.[192]

## (5) Cy-près schemes

Where charity assets are applicable cy-près, the court or the Charity Commission may make or approve a cy-près scheme. The purposes to which those assets are applied should be as close as practicable to the original purposes. The Charities Bill 2005 proposes a wider range of possible applications. It allows the funds to be transferred to a new charity, but subject to 'a duty to secure that the property is applied for purposes which are, so far as is reasonably practicable, similar in character to the original purposes'.[193] It also requires the court or the Charity Commission in making a scheme to have regard to:

'(a) the spirit of the original gift,
(b) the desirability of securing that the property is applied for charitable purposes which are close to the original purposes, and
(c) the need for the relevant charity to have purposes which are suitable and effective in the light of current social and economic circumstances.'[194]

This reduces the importance of the terms and spirit of the original gift by introducing two new criteria which have equal weight. In particular, there is a requirement to consider the relevance of the terms of the scheme to present-day circumstances.

---

[190] *Loscombe v Wintringham* (1850) 13 Beav 87; *Re Clergy Society* (1856) 2 K & J 615; *Re Maguire* (1870) LR 9 Eq 632; *Re Rymer* [1895] 1 Ch 19; *Re Davis* [1902] 1 Ch 876; *Re Harwood* [1936] Ch 285: This construction was rejected by the Court of Appeal of New South Wales in *A-G for New South Wales v Public Trustee* (1987) 8 NSWLR 550, where the court held that there is no rule or principle that it is more difficult to conclude that a testator had a general charitable intention where there is a gift to a named charity which existed at the date of the will but which has ceased to exist before death than in the case where the named charity never existed at all.

[191] [1936] Ch 285.

[192] Two difficulties arise with regard to the decision in *Re Harwood*. First, it was doubted in *Re Koeppler Will Trusts* [1984] 2 All ER 111 whether the purposes of a peace society are charitable because of their political nature. Secondly, in holding that there was no general charitable intention with regard to the gift to the Wisbech society the judge did not consider whether in the context of the will, and the large number of charitable bequests, there was a general charitable intention through the principle of 'charity by association'.

[193] Charities Act 1993, s 14B(4) inserted by Charities Bill 2005, cl 18.

[194] Charities Act 1993, s 14B(3) inserted by Charities Bill 2005, cl 18.

# PART IV

# ASSET MANAGEMENT

# 20

# Holding trusts and nominee holdings

## 1 The nature of nominee holdings

We have seen in Chapter 5 how the trust can be used to enable property to be purchased by a nominee on behalf of a principal. Legal title to the property is held by the nominee or nominees as trustees, but the principal is the beneficial owner. The way in which this arrangement will work in practice is that on any documents relating to legal ownership, it is the nominees' name which will appear. If the property concerned is land, the deed under which the land is acquired will state that it is transferred to the nominees. It is the nominees who will then be registered as owners with the Land Registry, and the Land Certificate will be issued in the name of the nominees. If the property concerned consists of stocks or shares, again the document of transfer will be made out to the nominees, and it is their names which will be recorded in the register of shareholders kept by or on behalf of the company. If the property concerned is money deposited with a bank, the names appearing on the bank account will be that of the nominees.

In consequence of the nominees having legal title, any proceeds from the property, such as rent from land, dividends on shares, or interest on bank deposits, will be payable to the nominees. Only they can give a valid receipt for the income. Similarly, any dealings with the title to the property must be authorised by the nominees. Thus, they must: (a) authorise any withdrawal of funds from a bank account; (b) execute any transfer of land they hold as nominees; and (c) execute any transfer of shares. If the property is disposed of by way of sale, the proceeds of the sale must be paid by the purchaser to the nominees or in accordance with their instructions.

This does not mean, however, that the nominees are free to deal with the proceeds of the assets in any way they choose. The nominees hold the property on behalf of the principal, and must therefore deal with it for the principal's benefit. They must account to the principal both for the original property and for any income or capital derived from it.

Nominees therefore, like Janus, face two ways. As between themselves and the principal, it would not be misleading to describe the principal as the owner. It is he who will benefit from any gain (or lose by any loss) in the value of the property. It is he who is entitled to the capital value of the assets, and to any income or revenue they produce. He may also transfer or otherwise deal with his equitable interest. In *Ingram v IRC*[1] the

---

[1] [1997] 4 All ER 395.

Court of Appeal held that because the nominee is in substance the alter ego of the principal, a nominee holding the freehold of land is unable to grant a lease to the principal. This would amount to the principal granting a lease to herself. This is, however, only one face of the nominees. As between the nominees and the outside world, it is the nominees who are, to most intents and purposes, the owners.

## 2  Rights and obligations of nominees

### (1)  Simple holding trusts

This twin aspect to a nominee holding is typical of the trust, and reflects the distinction which the trust permits to be made between powers of management and beneficial entitlement. The extent of the powers of management of the nominees will depend upon what was agreed at the time the relationship was established. In the usual case, the obligation of the nominees will be to act upon the instructions of the principal: the nominees therefore have no independent right to deal with the property, for instance by sale and reinvestment. An arrangement of this kind, in which the nominees or trustees must simply 'obey orders', may be described as a holding trust. It has two character-istics: the trustees have no discretion as to who will receive the benefit of the trust funds; and they have no authority to deal with the assets except upon instructions from the principal. In many cases the holding trust will be little more than a 'front' for the real beneficial owner. In *Hardoon v Belilios*,[2] for instance, shares were acquired by a firm of stockbrokers in the name of one of their employees. Similarly, in *Arrow Nominees Inc v Blackledge*[3] the 'owner' of shares in a company held his shares via a trust of which Arrow Nominees Inc was the nominee. The same result can arise even if the parties are unaware that their arrangement has created a trust. In *Pennington v Waine (No 1)*[4] the Court of Appeal held that a completed share transfer form, although never submitted to the company for registration, was nevertheless effective as an equitable assignment under which the transferor became a bare trustee for the transferee. Another illustra-tion is provided by *Don King Productions Inc v Warren (No 1)*[5] where the leading boxing promoters in the USA and in the UK entered into a partnership agreement. Lightman J held that the effect of this was to make Frank Warren a trustee of promotion, manage-ment and associated contracts (including a contract with Prince Naseem Hamed) for the benefit of the partnership.[6] Such a trust, where the trustees hold upon trust for a single beneficiary absolutely (ie without conditions or qualifications), is generally described as a bare trust. Where there is more than one beneficiary, but the beneficial entitlements are set out in the trust documents, leaving no discretion as to the division

---

[2] [1901] AC 118.      [3] [2000] 1 BCLC 709.      [4] [2002] EWCA Civ 227, [2002] 1 WLR 2075.
[5] [1998] 2 All ER 608.
[6] The contract of partnership had purported to assign the contracts to the partnership, but the personal nature of the contracts prevented this. The judge held that because the contract of partnership manifested the clear intention that the promotion and management agreements should be held by the partnership absolutely, the agreement should be interpreted as creating a trust: [1998] 2 All ER 608 at 635.

of the property to the trustees, the trust may be described as a fixed trust. It may also be described as an executed trust in that no further act is required to identify the rights of the beneficiaries. That there is more than one beneficiary does not necessarily affect the rights and obligations of the trustees, although it is more likely in such cases that the trustees will be given independent powers of management over the trust assets, and they must, of course, have regard to the interests of all the beneficiaries. Except where otherwise specified in the documents setting up the trusts—for instance, only where all the beneficiaries act unanimously—are they in a position to give binding instructions to the trustees.

The nominee holding trust has become widely used as a means of purchasing shares. Under stock exchange rules, a person selling shares must supply the certificate for the shares sold very promptly after the sale has been made. In order to enable a shareholder to sell rapidly by telephone, many stockbroking firms will now arrange to register shares in the name of a nominee company controlled by the firm. The shares can then be sold by means of a written or oral instruction which simultaneously authorises the nominee to release the share certificate. In some cases the nominee may consolidate the share-holdings of a number of principals under a single share certificate. Although this complicates the issue of identifying the legal title to which the principal's interest relates,[7] it does not affect the legal analysis. The position is not markedly different where ownership of shares is recorded through the new electronic CREST system, rather than in the traditional form of share certificates. Instead of the ownership of the nominee being evidenced by a share certificate, the shareholding is logged on the electronic register kept by the stock exchange. The position of the principal is not affected.

The appointment of nominees by trustees is expressly sanctioned by the Trustee Act 2000.[8] Prior to the enactment of this provision it was not clear whether trustees had the power to appoint a nominee except where there was an express provision in the trust permitting this. With the increasing use of nominees in share dealings, this change was a sensible modernisation. The Trustee Act 2000 also permits the appointment of custodians by trustees.[9] Their function is to undertake safe (physical) custody of trust assets or any documents or records concerning trust assets. This could include, for instance, taking custody of valuable works of art belonging to the trust, bearer securities[10] (which must be deposited with a custodian[11]), or important documents such as share certificates or title documents relating to land. Custodians in this sense should not be confused with custodian trustees, described next. The Act authorises the payment of nominees and custodians by trustees.[12] As with all cases of delegation (of which these are examples), the trustees must keep the arrangement under review.[13]

## (2) Custodian trusts

A special form of holding trust displaying greater complexity than a nominee arrangement is a custodian trust. Whereas with a nominee arrangement the nominee holds a

---

[7] See Chapters 25 and 26 where the rights of a beneficiary to trace into assets acquired with his funds are discussed.     [8] Trustee Act 2000, s 16(1).     [9] Trustee Act 2000, s 17(1).

[10] Ie securities such as investments in a company which are repayable to the person presenting the security document, unlike most investments which are repayable to the person in whose name the investment is made.

[11] Trustee Act 2000, s 18(1).     [12] Trustee Act 2000, s 20.     [13] Trustee Act 2000, ss 21, 22.

single asset or a single class of assets, the function of custodian trustees is to hold all the assets of the trust. The effect is to separate the legal ownership and custody of the trust assets from the function of managing those assets. The *custodian trustees* hold the assets to the order of other *management trustees* who have the powers of management. The custodian trustees hold the legal title to the trust assets, but the management trustees make all the decisions relating to the administration of the trusts. This structure is used for the administration of unit trusts and most pension schemes.[14]

One advantage of a custodian trust is that the management trustees can be changed without the need to transfer all the trust property from the old trustees to the new.[15] Only the Public Trustee, the Official Custodian for Charities and trust corporations[16] are authorised by statute to act as custodian trustees,[17] but there is no reason why a custodian trust should not be established where this is expressly permitted by the terms of the documents establishing a trust.[18] A sports club, for instance, may have taken the lease of a sports field and clubhouse in the names of up to four trustees. The trustees can hold that land upon trust to deal with in accordance with the directions of the club committee. There is no need to change the trustees every time the composition of the committee changes.

Trustees appointed as custodian trustees under the statutory scheme[19] are obliged to follow the instructions of the management trustees, except where to do so would amount to concurring in a breach of trust. Bare trustees may not even have this freedom, for the terms of their appointment might require them to act upon any instruction of the principal.[20] Trustees appointed as custodian trustees without using the statutory scheme will not enjoy the statutory protection afforded to statutory custodian trustees, and they must use their own judgement in deciding whether to follow instructions given to them.[21] Where, however, the terms of the trust are so tightly drawn as to leave no scope for the exercise by them of their own judgement, it will not be a breach

---

[14]  See, for instance, *British Airways Pension Trustees Ltd v British Airways Plc* [2001] EWHC Ch 13 where Lloyd J was asked in litigation between the custodian trustees and the management trustees to resolve doubts and disagreements concerning the construction of the Airways Pension Scheme.

[15]  See S G Maurice. 'The office of custodian trustee' (1960) 24 Conv (ns) 196–204; P Pearce 'Directing the trustee' (1972) 36 Conv (ns) 260–265 at 260–261.

[16]  Trust corporations are companies specially authorised by statute to undertake trust business.

[17]  Public Trustee Rules 1912, r 30. as substituted by the Public Trustee (Custodian Trustee) Rules 1975 (SI 1975/1189) and amended by the Public Trustee (Custodian Trustee) Rules 1976, 1981, 1984 and 1985 (SI 1976/836; SI 1981/358; SI 1984/109; SI 1985/132).

[18]  See *Cadogan v Earl of Essex* (1854) 2 Drew 227 (trustees subject to directions as to investments). Before the enactment of the Companies Acts permitting companies to be incorporated through a registration procedure, a commonly adopted structure for joint stock companies was one in which, under a deed of settlement, the company's assets were held by trustees on trust for the investors in the company, with the firm being managed by a separate committee of directors.

[19]  Established by the Public Trustee Act 1906.

[20]  See *IRC v Silverts Ltd* [1951] Ch 521 where the Court of Appeal distinguished custodian trusts from bare trusts on this ground.

[21]  *Beauclerk v Ashburnham* (1845) 8 Beav 322; *Re Hart's Will Trusts* [1943] 2 All ER 557 (trustees required to be satisfied that a directed investment was purchased at a fair price).

of trust for the trustees to follow binding instructions, even if the transaction would otherwise have been imprudent and so a breach of trust.[22]

## (3) Dealings with the trust assets

Even in trusts where the trustees have no powers over the allocation of beneficial entitlement it is very common for the trustees to be empowered to manage the investment of the trust fund. Such powers of management are not a normal characteristic of a nominee trust. The absence of authorisation to manage the investment of the trust fund will not, however, always prevent the nominees from disposing of the property. Since they have legal title, and appear to the outside world to be the owners, a stranger dealing with them is entitled to treat them as the owners they appear. A transfer from them, by way of cheque on a bank account, or by way of a transfer of land or shares in the proper form, will be effective to give legal title to the transferee. Whether the transferee will acquire that legal title subject to the rights of the principal depends mainly upon whether the transferee was aware of any impropriety at the time of the disposition. If he was not, and the transaction is one in which the stranger gives consideration, then he will normally acquire the property free from any claim of the principal. The extent to which a nominee or other trustee can dispose of the trust property to strangers is considered in Chapters 3 and 31.

Where an unauthorised disposition has been effective to transfer the trust property to a stranger, the principal will not be left without a remedy. An unauthorised transaction on the part of nominees will be a breach of trust and will expose them to personal liability to the principal for any loss which this has occasioned. The principal may also be able to recover, in lieu of the trust property any assets for which it was exchanged. These rights are considered in Part V.

## 3 Execution and performance

The relationship of principal and nominee will continue for so long as the nominees hold the trust assets for the benefit of the principal. By way of agreement between the principal and the nominees (either at the time when the relationship was established, or subsequently) or, in the absence of agreement, under the rule in *Saunders v Vautier*[23] the principal can call for the nominees to transfer the trust property to him. When they do so, the principal will acquire full legal and beneficial ownership, and the trust will be said to be executed (in other words, fully carried out).[24]

Similarly, by virtue of the original arrangement establishing the trust, or by subsequent

---

[22] *Re Hurst* (1890) 63 LT 665. See generally Penelope Pearce, 'Directing the trustees' (1972) 36 Conv (ns) 260–265.

[23] (1841) 4 Beav 115.

[24] Note that a trust can also be described as executed rather than executory because the precise rights of the beneficiaries have already been identified, even though legal ownership has not yet been transferred to the beneficiaries.

agreement, the principal may call upon the nominees to transfer the trust property to a third party, or to deal with it in some other way. Where this is done with the intention of passing full legal and beneficial ownership to the third party, then the trust will equally come to an end. For instance, in *Vandervell v IRC*,[25] the National Provincial Bank Ltd held 100,000 'A' ordinary shares in Vandervell Products Ltd as bare trustees or nominees for the benefit of Guy Vandervell. Mr Vandervell wished to pay for the establishment of a chair in pharmacology at the Royal College of Surgeons. In a scheme devised to minimise his liability to pay tax, Mr Vandervell asked the bank, as his nominees, to transfer the shares to the College. Mr Vandervell then used his controlling interest in the company, through other share-holdings, to pay a dividend on the 'A' ordinary shares large enough to endow the chair in pharmacology. The Inland Revenue argued that Mr Vandervell had retained an equitable interest in the shares after the transfer, so that under the Income Tax Act 1952 he was liable to income tax and surtax (higher-rate income tax) on the dividends. The House of Lords held that the transfer of the shares to the Royal College of Surgeons was effective to give them both the legal title to the shares held by the bank, and Mr Vandervell's equitable beneficial interest. Whether the equitable beneficial interest passed on the transfer depended upon the intention of Mr Vandervell as the person entitled to the beneficial interest. There was no need for some separate transfer of Mr Vandervell's equitable rights. Mr Vandervell had not, therefore, retained an equitable interest in the shares.[26]

## 4 Dealing with the equitable interest

It is possible for the principal or beneficiary under a bare trust to deal with his equitable interest without terminating the trust. The same is true of a beneficiary under a fixed trust. Equity treats the beneficiary under a bare or fixed trust as having a beneficial proprietary interest, and not merely personal rights enforceable against the trustee.[27] That proprietary interest may be sold or given away, used as security for a loan, or itself held upon trust. The alienability of an equitable interest has many times been emphasised. According to Romer RJ in *Timpson's Executors v Yerbury (Inspector of Taxes)*,[28] an equitable interest in property in the hands of a trustee can be disposed of by the person entitled to it in favour of a third party in any one of four different ways:

---

[25] [1967] 1 All ER 1, HL.

[26] This was not enough, however, to enable Mr Vandervell to avoid the taxes. Because the Royal College of Surgeons had given the trustees of a Vandervell family trust an option to repurchase the shares, and there had been no declaration of who was to be the beneficiary of this option, the House of Lords considered that the trustees held the option on Mr Vandervell's behalf until he named some other beneficiary. Because Mr Vandervell therefore retained a power to control who would benefit from the shares once the option was exercised, he had sufficient power of disposition of beneficial entitlement to the shares to subject him to liability to tax. See above p 203.

[27] *Baker v Archer-Shee* [1927] AC 844. For an analysis of the debate as to whether equitable rights are properly characterised as in rem or in personam. See D Waters 'The nature of the trust beneficiary's interest' (1967) 45 Can B R 219–283.

[28] [1936] 1 KB 645 at 664.

'The person entitled to it

(1) can assign it to the third party directly;

(2) can direct the trustees to hold the property in trust for the third party;

(3) can contract for valuable consideration to assign the equitable interest to him; or

(4) can declare himself to be a trustee for him of such interest.'

## (1) Direct assignment

The Law of Property Act 1925, s 136 permits the assignment of choses in action. There is some authority that the section applies to equitable rights, including interests under a trust,[29] although the matter is not entirely free from doubt.[30] For the section to operate, the assignment must be an absolute assignment of the whole interest and not an assignment of part only of the interest or a charge extending only to part of the interest.[31] It must also be made in writing and signed by the assignor, and express notice in writing must be given to the trustee.[32]

Where an assignment fails to comply with the statutory provisions, it may nevertheless be effective as an assignment in equity. An equitable assignment does not need to be in any particular form, or to use any particular set of words or language.[33] It is enough if a clear intention is manifested, by words or conduct, to transfer the benefit of a clearly identified right from the assignor to the assignee.[34] The equitable assignment need not be communicated to the trustee,[35] although if the trustee has notice of the assignment it completes the transaction as to third parties, establishes priority on the part of the assignee, and protects the assignee against any fraudulent receipt by the assignor.[36]

## (2) Directions to the trustees to hold on trust

The alienation may take the form of instructions to the trustee to hold the property upon trust for some other person, as in *Tierney v Wood*.[37] Wood, the principal under a bare trust of property held by his nominee, Tierney, gave directions to his nominee by letter to hold the property upon trust for Wood's wife and daughters.[38] Where the

---

[29] *King v Victoria Insurance Co Ltd* [1896] AC 250 at 254; *Torkington v Magee* [1902] 2 KB 427 at 430–431 per Channell J (reversed on facts [1903] 1 KB 644); *Re Pain, Gustavson v Haviland* [1919] 1 Ch 38 at 44–45 per Younger J.

[30] *Snell's Principles of Equity* (30th edn, Sweet & Maxwell, 2000), pp 84–86.

[31] *Durham Bros v Robertson* [1898] 1 QB 765, CA. A charge operating by way of a mortgage by assignment of the entire interest, with a proviso for reassignment on the discharge of the loan, is, however, within this section: *Tancred v Delagoa Bay and East Africa Rly Co* (1889) 23 QBD 239.

[32] *Campania Colombiana de Seguros v Pacific Steam Navigation Co* [1965] 1 QB 101, [1964] 1 All ER 216 (notice too late if served after commencement of action against debtor).

[33] *William Brandt's Sons & Co v Dunlop Rubber Co* [1905] AC 454 at 462, per Lord MacNaghten.

[34] *Voyle v Hughes* (1854) 2 Sm & G 18. See also *Pennington v Waine* [2002] 1 WLR 2075 where it was held that a share transfer form was capable of operating as an equitable assignment because it demonstrated an immediate and unconditional intention to transfer ownership.

[35] *Kekewich v Manning* (1851) 1 De GM & G 176; *Voyle v Hughes* (1854) 2 Sm & G 18.

[36] *Kekewich v Manning* (1851) 1 De GM & G 176.     [37] (1854) 19 Beav 330.

[38] Similar cases to the same effect are *Rycroft v Christy* (1840) 3 Beav 238; *Bentley v Mackay* (1851) 15 Beav 12; and *Paterson v Murphy* (1853) 11 Hare 88.

directions impose upon the trustee an obligation more onerous than that required by the original terms of the trust, then it may be necessary for the trustee to agree to perform these obligations,[39] but the alienation is valid even if no consideration has been given, provided that the beneficiary has demonstrated an unconditional intention to make an outright transfer.[40] The alienation may also be of part only of the equitable interest in the property,[41] or be in some other way less than an outright transfer.[42]

## (3) Contract to assign

Under the principle that 'equity treats as done that which ought to be done', a contract to transfer property, if specifically enforceable, will normally be effective to pass title in equity to the beneficiary of the contract.[43] Once any conditions which relate to the transfer have been satisfied, such as the identification of the property concerned, equity treats the transfer as if it had already been made.[44] In *Collyer v Isaacs*,[45] for instance, Jessel MR said:

'A man can contract to assign property which is to come into existence in the future, and when it has come into existence, equity, treating as done that which ought to be done, fastens upon that property, and the contract to assign thus becomes a complete assignment.'

Where the contract is for the immediate transfer of existing and identifiable property, equity does not therefore distinguish between an equitable assignment and a contract to assign.[46]

The equitable maxim treating a contract to assign as an actual assignment applies only to contracts for value. It cannot be relied upon by volunteers who have not themselves provided any consideration,[47] possibly even if there may have been someone else who has provided consideration but who does not seek to support the assignment.[48]

---

[39] *Rycroft v Christy* (1840) 3 Beav 238.

[40] *Bentley v Mackay* (1851) 15 Beav 12; *Re Chrimes* [1917] 1 Ch 30.

[41] *Rycroft v Christy* (1840) 3 Beav 238.

[42] *Tierney v Wood* (1854) 19 Beav 330 (life interest followed by entailed interest in land created out of an interest in fee).

[43] *Wright v Wright* (1750) 1 Ves Sen 409 at 412 at (Lord Hardwicke); *Legard v Hodges* (1792) 1 Ves 477 at (Lord Thurlow LC).

[44] *Tailby v Official Receiver* (1888) 13 App Cas 523; *Stephens v Green* [1895] 2 Ch 148, CA.

[45] (1881) 19 Ch D 342 at 351.      [46] *Heap v Tonge* (1851) 9 Hare 90 at 104.

[47] *Re Anstis* (1886) 31 Ch D 596; *Re D'Angibau* (1879) 15 Ch D 228 at 242; *Re Plumptre's Marriage Settlement* [1910] 1 Ch 609 at 616.

[48] *Re Cook's Settlement Trusts* [1965] Ch 902. This case involved a promise to create a trust of the proceeds of sale of certain paintings should they ever be sold, rather than a contract to transfer an existing equitable interest. The judge held that such a promise did not create an existing proprietary interest capable of being held upon trust. The position concerning the assignment of an existing beneficial interest under a trust is therefore distinguishable.

## (4) Declaration of subsidiary trust

Although there may originally have been some doubt as to whether a trust could be created to fasten upon a beneficial interest under an existing trust,[49] it very soon became established that there was no objection to the imposition of such a trust.[50]

As with any trust, however, the trust will come into effect only if there is a clear intention to create an irrevocable trust, and an ineffective attempt to transfer the property will not be construed as a declaration of trust.[51] As Turner LJ observed in *Milroy v Lord*:[52]

'If it [a gift] is intended to take effect by transfer, the Court will not hold the intended transfer to operate as a declaration of trust, for then every imperfect instrument would be made effectual by being converted into a perfect trust.'[53]

[49] See the discussion in Simpson, *An Introduction to the History of the Land Law* (OUP, 1961), pp 189–192.

[50] *Kekewich v Manning* (1851) 1 De GM & G 176. See also *Pulvertoft v Pulvertoft* (1811) 18 Ves 84 at 99, per Lord Eldon LC; *Meek v Kettlewell* (1842) 1 Hare 464 at 470–471, per Wigram VC. See above, p 000.

[51] *Edwards v Jones* (1835) 1 My & Cr 226; *Antrobus v Smith* (1805) 12 Ves 39; *Searle v Law* (1846) 15 Sim 95; *Jones v Lock* (1865) 1 Ch App 25.

[52] (1862) 4 De GF & J 264 at 274.

[53] See further the discussion concerning the constitution of trusts in Chapter 6.

# 21
# Management powers

## 1 Trusts with no management powers

With some kinds of property, such as a valuable painting which it is intended should be kept as a family heirloom, trustees might be directed to hold the property upon trust in its original form without any powers of disposition over the property. The purpose of the trust is to prevent the property—in this case, the painting—from being sold. The beneficial interests have been specified in advance by the settlor, who has left the painting on trust for his eldest child for life, and on her death for her eldest child. Since limited interests cannot be granted directly, the trust is necessary to give effect to the gift, but the trustees have no other real function. The trust can be used in a similar fashion to enable shares to be kept unsold for the benefit of future generations of a family, although in this case the trustees will receive dividend payments from the shareholding which they must pass on to the beneficiaries.

A common form of trust in which the trustee has no powers of disposition or management is a trust of a life insurance policy. When a person takes out a contract of life insurance, under which the insurance company undertakes to pay a sum of money on the death of the person insured, that sum is payable to the personal representatives of the person taking out the insurance contract, and forms part of that person's estate. Since most people taking out this form of life insurance intend their family to benefit from the proceeds of the policy, they may declare that they hold it in trust for their family.[1] The effect of this is that, on their death,[2] the insurance company may make the payment directly to the family members who have been named as beneficiaries,[3] rather than to the personal representatives. This can speed up payment. In addition, the proceeds of the policy do not form part of the estate of the deceased for inheritance tax purposes, and are not available to meet any debts which the insured may have owed.

---

[1] A trust arises wherever a policy of life assurance on the life assured is expressed to be made for the benefit of the spouse or children of the insured: Married Women's Property Act 1882, s 11. In other cases, there must be an express intention to create a trust: compare *Re Webb, Barclays Bank Ltd v Webb* [1941] Ch 225 (trust created) and *Re Engeblach's Estate* [1924] 2 Ch 348 (no trust created).

[2] Or, in the case of an endowment policy, the date of maturity, if earlier: see *Re Ioakimidis' Policy Trusts* [1925] Ch 403.

[3] The spouse or children may be identified by name, in which case the proceeds of the policy are payable to their estate even if they predecease the insured: *Cousins v Sun Life Assurance Society* [1933] Ch 126. If the policy is expressed to be for the insured's spouse or children (or both) without naming them, it is construed as being for the benefit of those in that category who survive the insured: *Re Browne's Policy* [1903] 1 Ch 188.

This is one of the reasons why, in *Foskett v McKeown*,[4] disappointed investors under a land investment scheme sought to trace their misused funds into an insurance policy taken out by the swindler in trust for his family. The proceeds from the policy would not otherwise have been available to meet their claim.

The disadvantages to the insured of creating a trust are that the insured will no longer be able to vary the terms of the policy without obtaining the consent of the beneficiary.[5] The insured must also act in the responsible way required of a trustee, considering the interests of the beneficiaries, for instance in considering whether to surrender the policy.[6]

# 2 The need for management

Unlike paintings and insurance policies, some property cannot be left unmanaged: it requires active management. For instance, if land is held on trust, then, unless it is occupied by the beneficiary, the trustee will need to arrange for it to be let in order to produce an income. The trustee will also need to ensure that the rent is paid promptly and that proper steps have been taken to ensure that the property is properly maintained. Indeed, even a painting may need special measures to be taken to ensure that it is properly conserved, and it would be prudent to insure it. The necessary powers of management might be given to, or retained by, the beneficiaries, as is the case with nominee trusts, which were considered in the last chapter. The powers of management, though, may be conferred upon the trustees holding the title to the property, or in the special case of custodian trusts (also considered in the last chapter) by a separate group of trustees.

A trust might be created expressly for the purpose of conferring responsibility for active management on the trustees, as in the case of property being left on trust for a young child, or an adult who suffers from mental impairment. In other cases, for instance where there is complex beneficial entitlement, the need for powers of management might arise incidentally.

# 3 The extent of the powers

The powers of management conferred upon a trustee are not the same in every case. Quite obviously, the powers of express trustees are likely to differ significantly from those of constructive trustees upon whom a trust has been imposed because of their

---

[4] [1998] Ch 265 (discussed in Chapter 31).

[5] *Re Schebsman* [1944] Ch 83, CA. The contrary view expressed in *Hill v Gomme* (1839) 5 My & Cr 250 is wrong. If the matter remains in simple contract, then the insured will remain at liberty to vary the policy: *Green v Russell* [1959] 2 QB 226.

[6] *Re Equitable Life Assurance Society of US Policy and Mitchell* (1911) 27 TLR 213.

improper conduct. In the latter case, the question of the trustees' powers rarely arises. They are wrongdoers who are, by definition, acting in breach of duty. How far they are authorised to act is therefore unlikely to be in issue.

Even in the case of express trustees, however, the powers of management of the trustees will differ markedly from one situation to another. As is so often the case, the answer to the question about the extent of the management powers of the trustees depends primarily upon the terms of the trust instrument. Failing this, powers may be implied by statute or common law. Finally, the court has statutory and inherent powers to authorise management transactions.

## (1) Express powers

The trust instrument may set out in considerable detail the authority of the trustees. This is particularly likely to be the case with large, professionally drawn trust deeds such as those governing pension funds or unit trusts or even large family trusts, especially where the assets pose distinctive issues of management.[7] For example, if the property which is held upon trust is a controlling interest in a private company which it is intended should be run by the trustees, or if it consists of an author's moral rights in literary works, it would be prudent and usual for the documents establishing the trust to define in detail the powers of the trustees.

Powers of management may or may not include a power to dispose of the property and to reinvest the proceeds. In the case of a trust for sale (described below), the trustees are placed under an express obligation to sell the property and either to distribute or to reinvest the proceeds. Where the trust concerns land, the trustees will, in the absence of any express contrary intention, have both an automatic statutory power to sell the land and to postpone a sale.[8] This does not apply to trusts for sale of other kinds of property, although there can, of course, be an express power to postpone a sale.

## (2) Implied powers

There are some cases where powers or duties can be implied from the context of a trust. Where a trust comprising money or quoted stocks and shares contains an express power of investment, but fails to provide express authority for sale for the purpose of reinvestment, it is reasonable to infer this power. The implication might, in some cases, go beyond the implication of a power and impose a duty on trustees.

The duty to convert under the rule in *Howe v Dartmouth*[9] is the best example of this. This rule requires trustees to sell unauthorised trust assets in order to apply the proceeds into authorised investments. With the greatly increased range of investments which trustees are now permitted to make (see Chapter 22), the circumstances in which this rule might apply are now significantly reduced. There may, however, be some rare

---

[7] Eg in *Re Duke of Norfolk's Settlement Trusts* [1982] Ch 610, CA, the trustees had powers of management which enabled them to carry out a substantial redevelopment of the Strand Estate which formed part of the settlement trusts.

[8] Trusts of Land and Appointment of Trustees Act 1996, ss 4, 6 and 8.        [9] (1802) 7 Ves 137.

situations in which it might still operate. The first issue is whether trustees have acquired unauthorised investments. Where a settlor has transferred specific assets to trustees, as in the case of an inter vivos settlement, it can normally be assumed that he is happy for the assets to be retained in that form. It is different, however, if he has imposed an express duty to sell the assets. The retention of those assets would not then be authorised. The rule in *Howe v Dartmouth* imposes a duty to sell in a second situation. This is where the assets concerned form part of a testator's residuary estate, and, in addition, the terms of the trust provide for successive interests, so that one person is entitled to income and another to capital. In such a case there is the danger that some of the random assets which the trustees have acquired may be in a form which may result in a high income being produced at the expense of capital appreciation or capital security,[10] or conversely, that the assets might have a high or secure capital yield but produce little or no income.[11] For this reason, in order to hold a fair balance between the beneficiaries, the rule in *Howe v Dartmouth* requires the hazardous, wasting or non-income producing assets to be sold and converted into authorised investments.

The rule in *Howe v Dartmouth* does not fit well with modern investment conditions, where a balanced investment portfolio may well include a combination of high-yield and low-yield investments which are intended to keep a balance between income generation and capital growth. The Law Reform Committee recommended[12] that the rule should be replaced with a general duty to hold a fair balance between beneficiaries. Such a rule was, in effect, introduced by s 4 of the Trustee Act 2000 under which trustees are required to keep under review the suitability of the trust investments. This could therefore be interpreted so as to overrule the now outmoded rule in *Howe v Dartmouth*. In any event, the rule can also give way to only the slightest of contrary indications, such as the inclusion of a discretionary power of sale,[13] or an indication that the income or capital beneficiary should be entitled to enjoy or receive the property in specie as the case may be.[14] In the latter instances, the circumstances negate the duty of the trustees to sell which is the basis of the rule. In any event, the introduction of a general power of trustees to invest as if absolutely entitled to the assets of the trust in the Trustee Act 2000 has vastly extended the range of authorised investments so that the circumstances in which the rule in *Howe v Dartmouth* will apply have been significantly restricted.[15]

As was noted in Chapter 12,[16] the Law Commission has recently proposed the abolition of the rule in *Howe v Dartmouth* in favour of a new statutory power for trustees to allocate investment returns and trust expenses as income or capital insofar as is necessary to maintain a balance between income and capital.[17] This reform would be in line

---

[10] Such as copyrights: *Re Sullivan* [1930] 1 Ch 84.

[11] Such as reversionary interests: *Re Pitcairn* [1896] 2 Ch 199.

[12] 23rd Report (1982) Cmnd 8733.     [13] *Re Pitcairn* [1896] 2 Ch 199.

[14] *Boys v Boys* (1860) 28 Beav 436 and *Holgate v Jennings* (1857) 24 Beav 623 respectively.

[15] Capital and Income in Trusts: Classification and Apportionment, Law Comm CP No 175 (2004), para. 3.8.

[16] See above p 388.

[17] Capital and Income in Trusts: Classification and Apportionment. Law Comm CP 175 (2004).

with the philosophy underlying the Trustee Act 2000 in respect of the trustees' powers of investment.

Similarly, other implied powers, such as the power of charity trustees to sell charity land with the consent of the court, will not apply if this is inconsistent with the purpose of the trust. Thus, if a charitable trust is established to retain for the public benefit a particular house once owned by a particular historical figure or a particular building for its architectural merit, then a sale could not take place without altering the terms of the trust 'because after a sale the proceeds or any property acquired with the proceeds could not possibly be applied for the original charitable purpose'.[18]

## (3) Specific statutory powers

Where a trust deed does not set out express powers of management or does not do so comprehensively, and no powers can be implied as a question of fact, the omission may be supplied by statute in one of two ways. First, there are some specific situations in which statutory powers of management are implied. The most notable of these are in trusts of land. Secondly, there are some general powers which are implied into all trusts by the Trustee Act 1925.

### (a) Trusts of land[19]

The policy of the land law reforms of the late nineteenth and early twentieth centuries was to facilitate dealings in land. The Settled Land Act 1925 and the Law of Property Act 1925 chose the mechanism of the trust as the means of achieving this. Since these Acts, a trust has been imposed wherever land is acquired for the benefit of, or transferred to, individuals who are sharing the property either consecutively or concurrently. The Acts established a complex dual system of trusts with one kind of trust (the 'strict settlement') applying in the case of most successive interests in land, and a trust for sale applying in all other cases. Thus, where a testator left the family home which he owned to his wife for life, and on her death to be divided between his children, the house would have been held on a trust, normally governed by the Settled Land Act 1925. And if a husband and wife pooled their resources to acquire jointly the house in which they intended to live, again the property would have been held upon a trust, in this case one regulated by the Law of Property Act 1925.

The rules relating to trusts of land have been considerably simplified by the Trusts of Land and Appointment of Trustees Act 1996 which substitutes a single form of trust, the 'trust of land', for the two types which could previously exist (although preserving strict settlement trusts already in existence). The detailed technical rules governing trusts of land will be found in textbooks on land law, and need not detain us here. A few important features of the trusts are, however, worth pointing out.

---

[18] *Oldham Borough Council v A-G* [1993] 2 All ER 432 at 439, per Dillon LJ.

[19] See Stevens and Pearce, *Land Law* (3rd edn, 2005), Ch 13; Gray & Gray, *Elements of Land Law* (3rd edn, 2001), Ch 8.

## (b) Kinds of trusts of land

Only one kind of trust of land can be created on or after 1 January 1997. This is the trust of land governed by the Trusts of Land and Appointment of Trustees Act 1996. This Act implemented a recommendation of the Law Commission that the law should be simplified in this way.[20] Under this form of trust, the trustees have all the powers of an absolute owner, including the power to sell,[21] and they are given a power to retain the property by postponing the sale for an indefinite period.[22] The power to retain applies even to an express trust to sell land, and is not capable of being excluded.

The only other kind of trust which can still exist but can no longer be created is the strict settlement governed by the Settled Land Act 1925. Under the strict settlement, the person first entitled to a beneficial interest in the land is made a trustee of it for himself or herself and for those who will later succeed to beneficial entitlement. The trustee of the land is called a tenant for life, and in most cases will indeed be entitled to the land for life, although this is not a necessary condition.

All trusts of land other than strict settlements in existence on 1 January 1997 (the date on which the Trusts of Land and Appointment of Trustees Act 1996 came into operation) were subsumed with the new category of trusts of land.

## (c) Powers of trustees of land

Before the creation of the new trust of land under the Trusts of Land and Appointment of Trustees Act 1996, trustees of land had only the limited powers set out by the Settled Land Act 1925. These included the power to sell or exchange the property,[23] to grant leases,[24] to enter into compromises,[25] to raise money by mortgage for a limited number of purposes,[26] to make certain improvements to the property,[27] and a range of other minor and ancillary powers.

As has already been indicated, the powers conferred on trustees by the Trusts of Land and Appointment of Trustees Act 1996 are very much wider since, except where the powers are expressly excluded or curtailed, the trustees have all the powers of an absolute owner.

## (d) Regulating the rights of beneficiaries under trusts of land

The statutory regime established for trusts of land by the Trusts of Land and Appointment of Trustees Act 1996 contains a range of specific and special provisions applicable only to trusts of land. These provisions are discussed fully in textbooks on land law.[28] It is worth just a brief mention one of these special provisions. The 1996 Act makes it clear that a beneficiary with an interest in possession has a prima facie right to occupy the land.[29] Whether beneficiaries under a trust for sale had rights of occupation was not clear under the previous legislation, although the courts took the common sense approach that a beneficiary with an interest in possession was entitled to occupation.[30]

---

[20] Law Commission No 181 *Trusts of Land* (1989); [1990] Conv 12 (Smith).
[21] Trusts of Land and Appointment of Trustees Act 1996, s 6.
[22] Trusts of Land and Appointment of Trustees Act 1996, s 4.     [23] Ss 38–40.     [24] Ss 41–48.
[25] S 58.     [26] S 71.     [27] S 83 and Sch 3.
[28] See eg Stevens and Pearce, *Land Law* (3rd edn, 2005), p361–362.
[29] S 12.     [30] See *Bull v Bull* [1955] 1 QB 234 and *Williams & Glyn's Bank v Boland* [1981] AC 487.

Nor was it clear what rights, if any, the trustees had to regulate occupation by the beneficiaries. The 1996 Act now makes the rights of occupation of the beneficiaries subject to the power of the trustees to exclude or restrict these rights of occupation.[31] Just how useful these powers will prove to be must be open to question. Like all powers exercisable by trustees, except where otherwise provided, the trustees must concur in their exercise. In most trusts of land the same people are both trustees and beneficiaries. This will almost invariably be the case with the purchase of a house by a married or unmarried couple. A need for the trustees to regulate the rights of occupation will only arise where the beneficiaries disagree. In such a case, it follows that if the trustees are the same as the beneficiaries, the disagreement cannot be resolved by the exercise of the powers given to the trustees. Just as before the Act, it may prove necessary for the disagreement to be resolved by the court under its jurisdiction to intervene in cases of dispute.[32]

## (4) General statutory powers

The Trustee Act 1925 contains a small number of powers of management which are incorporated into all trusts. Additional management powers are conferred on trustees by the Trustee Act 2000. The Trustee Act 2000 also replaces the investment provisions of the 1925 Act with a new investment regime. The investment powers are of sufficient importance to merit a separate chapter.[33] The 1925 Act also contains a number of general powers relating to the distribution of trust funds. Since these are allocative rather than management powers, they are considered in Part III.[34]

### (a) Sale

The Trustee Act 1925 contains various provisions governing sale which authorise trustees, for instance, to sell either by auction or by private contract.[35] While these provisions extend and expand upon any trust or power which a trustee may have to sell, they do not confer any authority upon the trustees to sell where it has not arisen in some other way. Similarly, the Trustee Act 2000, which extends the investment powers of trustees, does not include any provision authorising sale except for the purpose of varying an investment.[36] There is therefore no general statutory power of sale except in the case of trusts of land.

### (b) Receipts

By s 14 of the Trustee Act 1925, a trustee may give a receipt in writing 'for any money, securities, or other personal property or effects payable, transferable, or deliverable to him under any trust or power' which is a sufficient discharge to the person making the transfer and which exonerates the transferee from having to enquire into the application of the property by the trustee. This power cannot be excluded by any contrary provision in the trust instrument, if any.[37] If there is more than one trustee, they must

---

[31] S 13.    [32] 9 Trusts of Land and Appointment of Trustees Act 1996, s 14.
[33] See Chapter 22.    [34] Chapter 14.    [35] S 12.
[36] What constitutes investment and reinvestment is discussed in Chapter 22.    [37] S 14(3).

all, it seems, concur in the receipt because of the principle that trustees must act unanimously,[38] except where the trust instrument authorises them to act by a majority[39] or, possibly, authorises them to act individually. Charity and pension trustees are authorised by statute to act by a majority. Where capital money arises on a sale of land held upon trust, a minimum of two trustees are required to give a valid receipt, except where the trustee is a trust corporation.[40]

## (c) Insurance

Trustees had no duty at common law to insure the trust property,[41] nor had they any power to do so. Section 19 of the Trustee Act 1925 conferred a limited power for trustees to take out insurance, and those powers were extended in 1996[42] and again by the Trustee Act 2000, which substituted a new s 19 for the original in the Trustee Act 1925. The new provision authorises trustees to insure any trust property against the risks of loss or damage due to any event, and to pay the premiums out of the income or capital of the trust funds.[43] In the case of trusts where the beneficiaries are all of full age and capacity and together are absolutely entitled to the trust property, this power to insure is subject to any direction given by those beneficiaries.[44] If any payments are made out under the insurance policy, these payments will be treated as capital belonging to the trust, or may be used to reinstate the property lost or damaged.[45] The statutory duty to take reasonable care applies to the exercise of both the statutory and any express power to insure.[46]

## (d) Compromises

A variety of powers relating to the management of property, including some enabling trustees to enter into a compromise or arrangement concerning a dispute, are contained in the Trustee Act 1925, s 15. In *Re Earl of Strafford (Decd)*[47] the sixth Earl of Strafford had left his mansion house, Wrotham Park, and his London home, together with most of his personal property, on a complex trust providing for a series of life interests. The trusts had subsequently been varied by transferring the property to Wrotham Park Settled Estates, an incorporated company.[48] In the light of evidence which emerged after the variation of trusts, there was some confusion as to whether a number of articles, amounting in value to over £170,000, belonged to the Earl of Strafford, and had been settled by him on trust so that they were potentially included in the variation, or whether they belonged to his wife, the Countess. The initial steps in litigation were

---

[38] *Attenborough v Solomon* [1913] AC 76.

[39] *Re Butlin's Settlement Trust* [1976] Ch 251, [1976] 2 All ER 483. Charitable trustees may act by a majority even if there is no express stipulation on the trust instrument: *Re Whiteley* [1910] 1 Ch 600 at 608.

[40] Trustee Act 1925, s 14(2), as amended by the Law of Property (Amendment) Act 1926 and the Trusts of Land and Appointment of Trustees Act 1996, Sch 3. See Settled Land Act 1925, s 94(1) and Law of Property Act 1925, s 27(2), as amended and re-enacted by the Law of Property (Amendment) Act 1926.

[41] *Re McEacharn* (1911) 103 LT 900.

[42] By theTrusts of Land and Appointment of Trustees Act 1996.

[43] Trustee Act 1925, s 19(1) as substituted by Trustee Act 2000, s 34.    [44] Trustee Act 1925, s 19(2).

[45] Trustee Act 1925, s 20.    [46] Trustee Act 2000, s 1 and Sch 1, para 5.    [47] [1979] 1 All ER 513.

[48] Subsequently involved in a leading case concerning the award of damages in lieu of an injunction for breach of a restrictive covenant: *Wrotham Park Estate Co v Parkside Homes Ltd* [1974] 2 All ER 321.

taken in order to resolve the issue before the beneficiaries under the Countess's will proposed a compromise. Under this, they proposed that the trustees would abandon their claim to about half of the assets in return for the other half being held on the trusts declared by the Earl. The beneficiaries of the Countess also offered, in respect of most of those assets, to surrender their life interests under the Earl's trusts. The Court of Appeal held that the trustees were permitted by s 15 to agree to this proposed compromise even if other of their beneficiaries objected, and even though it involved a surrender of beneficial interests by those proposing the compromise. Buckley LJ said:

'The language of s 15 is, it appears to me, very wide. It would, I think, be undesirable to seek to restrict its operation in any way unless legal principles require this, for it seems to me to be advantageous that trustees should enjoy wide and flexible powers of compromising and settling disputes, always bearing in mind that such a power, however wide, must be exercised with due regard for the interests of those whose interests it is the duty of the trustees to protect. I see nothing in the language of the section to restrict the scope of the power.'[49]

The Court of Appeal held that the compromise could be approved provided that, when considered as a whole, it was for the benefit of all the beneficiaries in accordance with their several interests in the trust property. It is not a requirement of approving a compromise that a claim adverse to the trust would otherwise be certain to succeed.[50] There must, nevertheless, be a genuine dispute.[51] The trustees are also required to comply with the statutory duty to take reasonable care imposed by the Trustee Act 2000, s 1.

### (e) Reversionary interests

Trustees are given wide powers under s 22 of the Trustee Act 1925 to enter into arrangements, agreements and other transactions concerning property to which the trust is entitled but which is not yet vested in the trustees. This would include, for instance, property which was payable to the trustees upon the winding-up of a testator's estate. Once again, trustees must comply with the statutory duty to take reasonable care imposed by the Trustee Act 2000, s 1.

## (5) Exceptional authority given by court

The express powers of trustees, as supplemented by the general and special statutory powers, may not cover every transaction which the trustees consider desirable. There is always the possibility of a situation arising which had not been anticipated: a valuable collection of modern art might, for instance, have started to deteriorate owing to the decomposition of some of the materials. Urgent restoration might be required in order to preserve the collection, yet no source of funds may be available to the trustees. In cases such as these, the trustees could enter into some otherwise unauthorised transaction with the consent of all the beneficiaries. If some of the beneficiaries are unascertainable or unable to consent, or perhaps, where they decline consent, the trustees might need to apply to court for approval for an exceptional transaction.

---

[49] [1979] 1 All ER 513 at 520.     [50] *Re Ridsdel* [1947] Ch 597.
[51] *Re Earl of Strafford* [1980] Ch 28; *Chapman v Chapman* [1954] AC 429, CA.

## (a) Statutory jurisdiction

The Trustee Act 1925, s 57 gives the court the jurisdiction to confer additional powers on trustees, either generally or in any particular instance. This jurisdiction may be exercised where the trustees or a beneficiary apply for authority for a transaction which is not otherwise authorised by the trust, and which 'is in the opinion of the court expedient'.[52] This statutory power does not authorise any alteration to the equitable entitlements of the beneficiaries,[53] and it does not require the consent or approval of the beneficiaries. The court would not, however, consider that conferring additional powers upon the trustees was expedient unless it could be considered to be in the interest of the trust estate as a whole.[54] The object of the section is 'to secure that the trust property should be managed as advantageously as possible in the interests of the beneficiaries'.[55] A power conferred on trustees under the section is treated as if it were an overriding power contained in the original trust instrument.[56] The section has been used to extend the investment powers of trustees,[57] to amalgamate two funds held on identical trusts;[58] to authorise a sale of a reversionary interest[59] or other trust property where there was no other power of sale[60] or a necessary consent could not be obtained;[61] to authorise a partition of land.[62] In some cases which come close to trespassing upon the principle that beneficial interests may not be affected, sanction has been given for the release of capital to pay the debts of an income beneficiary, subject to the replacement of the capital on the income beneficiary's death by means of a policy of life assurance.[63]

## (b) Inherent jurisdiction

The jurisdiction conferred upon the court by s 57 of the Trustee Act 1925 complements the inherent jurisdiction which the court has always enjoyed to ensure the good administration of trusts. Lord Morton in the House of Lords in *Chapman v Chapman*[64] suggested that there were four situations in which the court could exercise an inherent jurisdiction. These were: where it authorised the conversion of freehold property to which an infant was beneficially entitled into personal property (which affected the devolution of the property on death until 1926 but is no longer of any significance);

---

[52] A wider jurisdiction for the court to authorise specific transactions for the benefit of settled land or of the persons interested under the settlement is contained in the Settled Land Act 1925, s 64(1). This jurisdiction. which authorises alterations in beneficial interests, applies only to settled land or land held upon trust for sale.

[53] *Re Downshire Settled Estates* [1953] Ch 218, CA.     [54] *Re Craven's Estate* [1937] Ch 423.

[55] *Re Downshire Settled Estates* [1953] Ch 218 at 248 per Evershed MR.

[56] *Re Mair* [1935] Ch 562.

[57] *Re Shipwrecked Fishermen and Mariners Royal Benevolent Society Charity* [1959] Ch 220; *Mason v Farbrother* [1983] 2 All ER 1078; *Anker-Petersen v Anker-Petersen* [1991] 16 LS Gaz R 32.

[58] *Re Harvey* [1941] 3 All ER 284; *Re Shipwrecked Fishermen and Mariners' Royal Benevolent Society Charity* [1959] Ch 220, not following the inconsistent decision in *Re Royal Society's Charitable Trusts* [1956] Ch 87.

[59] *Re Cockerell's Settlement Trusts* [1956] Ch 372.     [60] *Re Hope's Will Trust* [1929] 2 Ch 136.

[61] *Re Beale's Settlement Trusts* [1932] 2 Ch 15.     [62] *Re Thomas* [1930] 1 Ch 194.

[63] *Re Salting* [1932] 2 Ch 57; *Re Mair* [1935] Ch 562.

[64] [1954] AC 429. See also Chapter 17 above.

where it approves a compromise on behalf of an infant or an unborn beneficary;[65] where it authorises the use of accumulated income for the maintenance of an infant (which involves a modification of beneficial entitlement); and where 'the court has allowed the trustees of settled property to enter into some business transaction which was not authorised by the settlement'. Only this last category of the court's inherent jurisdiction is of consequence in this context.

Lord Simonds LC in *Chapman v Chapman* limited the court's inherent jurisdiction to extend the authority of trustees to cases of salvage or emergency. In one series of cases, the court had approved the sale or mortgage of an infant's property to release funds for the preservation of what was retained where such action was absolutely necessary, for instance where buildings were in imminent danger of collapse or ruin.[66] Other cases extended this principle to situations where, although there was no absolute necessity, an emergency had arisen which the creator of the trust had not foreseen or anticipated, and where the best interests of the trust required the granting of exceptional authority. Romer LJ said in *Re New*:

'In the management of a trust estate . . . it not infrequently happens that some peculiar state of circumstances arises for which provision is not expressly made by the trust instrument, and which renders it most desirable, and it may be even essential, for the benefit of the estate and in the interest of all the cestuis que trust, that certain acts should be done by the trustees which in ordinary circumstances they would have no power to do. In a case of this kind, which may reasonably be supposed to be one not foreseen or anticipated by the author of the trust, where the trustees are embarrassed by the emergency that has arisen and the duty cast upon them to do what is best for the estate, and the consent of all the beneficiaries cannot be obtained by reason of some of them not being sui juris or in existence, then it may be right for the court, and the court in a proper case would have jurisdiction, to sanction on behalf of all concerned such acts on behalf of their trustees as we have above referred to.'[67]

In that case the court authorised the trustees to agree to the reconstruction of the capital of a commercial company in which they had an interest. In *Re Tollemache*[68] the Court of Appeal said that *Re New* 'constitutes the high-water mark of the exercise by the court of its extraordinary jurisdiction in relation to trusts', and refused to extend the powers of investment of the trustees to authorise the acquisition of a mortgage which would have enhanced the income of the trust. The fact that a proposed transaction would benefit one or even all of the beneficiaries is insufficient.[69] The jurisdiction which the court exercises in cases falling under the head of salvage or emergency is a jurisdiction to consent on behalf of beneficiaries who are not themselves sui juris by reason of infancy or mental incapacity. Unlike the statutory jurisdiction under s 57 of the Trustee Act 1925, which does not require the consent of adult beneficiaries, the court is probably unable, under its inherent jurisdiction, to override or to supply consent on behalf of those who are themselves legally competent to provide it.

---

[65] Unlike s 15 of the Trustee Act 1925, the inherent jurisdiction permits the approval of a compromise between two beneficiaries which does not directly affect the trustees.

[66] *Re Jackson* (1882) 21 Ch D 786; *Conway v Fenton* (1888) 40 Ch D 512; *Re Montagu* [1897] 2 Ch 8.

[67] [1901] 2 Ch 534 at 544.    [68] [1903] 1 Ch 955.    [69] *Re Montagu* [1897] 2 Ch 8.

## (c) A broader jurisdiction?

There is some authority for suggesting that the inherent powers of the court could extend beyond cases of salvage and emergency. A lengthy series of cases, reviewed in *Re Duke of Norfolk's Settlement Trusts*,[70] establishes beyond doubt that the court has an inherent jurisdiction to authorise the payment of remuneration to trustees, and even, according to the latter case, increase the level of the remuneration. Fox LJ did not consider this to be inconsistent with the principles expressed in *Chapman v Chapman*, which was concerned with the power of the court to authorise variations in beneficial interests as such. He said:

'I appreciate that the ambit of the court's inherent jurisdiction in any sphere may, for historical reasons, be irrational and that logical extensions are not necessarily permissible. But I think that it is the basis of the jurisdiction that one has to consider. The basis, in my view, in relation to a trustee's remuneration is the good administration of trusts . . . [I]t is of great importance to the beneficiaries that the trust should be well administered. If therefore the court concludes, having regard to the nature of the trust, to the experience and skill of a particular trustee and to the amounts which he seeks to charge when compared with what other trustees might require to be paid for their services and to all the other circumstances of the case, that it would be in the interests of the beneficiaries to increase the remuneration, then the court may properly do so.'[71]

The importance of the case in its immediate context is much reduced because the Trustee Act 2000 now allows trustees to be paid reasonable remuneration for services they provide if they are trust corporations or act in a professional capacity.[72] However, the principle of the case remains valid. The influence of the importance of the good administration of a trust is equally capable of application to administrative arrangements other than remuneration. Nor is authorisation of payment for trustees the only instance in which the court enjoys jurisdiction to amend the operating arrangements for trusts. In *Re Ashton's Charity*,[73] followed most recently in *Oldham Borough Council v A-G*,[74] Romilly MR held that, even where there is no applicable statutory authority, the Court of Chancery has a general jurisdiction to authorise the alienation of charity property where the court clearly sees that the transaction is for the charity's benefit and advantage. So, in the *Oldham* case, the Court of Appeal was prepared to authorise the sale for building development of a playing field held upon charitable trusts where the proceeds were to be used to acquire a new site with better facilities. This jurisdiction might relate only to the court's powers regarding the supervision of the administration of charities, and it almost certainly does not extend to authorising a sale which would have the consequence of changing the nature of a trust, as for instance where there is a trust to retain for the public benefit a tract of land of outstanding natural beauty. Nevertheless, when taken in association with the cases on salvage and emergency, the two examples just cited may evidence a wider equitable jurisdiction for the court to

---

[70] [1981] 3 All ER 220.  [71] [1981] 3 All ER 220 at 230.  [72] Ss 28 to 30.
[73] (1856) 22 Beav 288.
[74] [1993] 2 All ER 432. See also *Re Parke's Charity* (1842) 12 Sim 329; *Re North Shields Old Meeting House* (1859) 7 WR 541.

sanction transactions or arrangements which have been approved by all beneficiaries capable of concurring, and which are for the benefit of the trust viewed as a whole, and more particularly for those beneficiaries for whom the court is acting as a surrogate, provided that they do not amount to a rewriting of the beneficial interests.[75]

---

[75] Compare the dissenting judgment of Lord Denning in *Re Chapman's Settlement Trusts* [1953] Ch 218.

# 22

# Investment and reinvestment

## 1 Introduction

Of their non-distributive functions, the powers and duties of trustees in relation to investment are undoubtedly the most important.[1] As has already been explained, except in the very simplest of trusts, it is the duty of the trustee to preserve the trust assets over a period for the benefit of a number of beneficiaries. In many cases, the property which is transferred to the trustee is transferred as a fund, rather than as a set of assets which are to be retained in their original form. The trustee is expected to preserve the value of that fund through proper investment. In some cases, such as with unit trusts, and to some extent with pension funds, investment is the primary purpose of the trust.

It is in the context of investment that the concept of the fund is at its most apparent. The beneficiaries are entitled to share in the wealth which the trust assets represent. The component parts of that wealth are very much less important to the beneficiaries than its aggregate value. Of course, there are exceptions. The member of the landed aristocracy who leaves the family mansion upon trust for future generations of the family will no doubt hope that the home will be preserved intact. The married couple joining together in the purchase of the matrimonial home will no doubt intend to keep it as their dwelling. But even here, the land which constitutes the trust asset will be treated as a fund which can be sold and reinvested: so the new squire can sell some land on the fringe of the estate for building development and invest the proceeds in stocks and shares, or the married couple can 'up sticks' and sell to move to another area where they will buy another house, without in either case dissolving the original trust. The case of land is, perhaps, somewhat special, since the legislature has ensured that trustees of land will always have a power of sale and reinvestment, and as we have already seen in the previous chapter, there is no general power of sale in relation to property other than land which is vested in trustees.

It has already been described how the concept of the fund enables some assets to be disposed of, so that the purchaser acquires the assets free from the trust obligations, the trust obligations instead resting upon the price paid by the purchaser, or with whatever is purchased with the proceeds of the disposal. The issues which have to be addressed in the context of investment are first, when trustees are permitted to dispose of existing trust assets in order to substitute new assets; second, what assets may be substituted for

---

[1] Note that trustees who are conducting investment business must be authorised under s 19 of the Financial Services and Markets Act 2000, or exempted.

the original ones; and third, the principles upon which those investments must be chosen. Overarching these issues is a fundamental question—what is the purpose of investment? It is with that question that we need to begin.

# 2  The purpose of investment

## (1) Even-handedness between beneficiaries

As little as a century ago, one of the more common forms of trust was the family settlement, in which a man of property would settle funds for the benefit of his spouse and children for their lives, with entitlement to the capital then passing to the next generation. The duty of the trustees in such a case was to ensure that the capital was preserved for the benefit of the capital beneficiaries while an income was produced for the settlor's wife and children. The trustees were obliged to keep a fair balance between the two, except where they had been given other instructions by the settlor. This rule of even-handedness between beneficiaries was at the root of the rule in *Howe v Dartmouth*.[2]

## (2) The purpose of the trust

Not all trusts provide for successive interests, therefore requiring both income generation and preservation of capital. It is possible that a trust will provide for the accumulation of income for a limited period, with a view to conferring a lump sum benefit on a beneficiary at a future date. In such a case, it is of greater importance that the trust fund should produce capital appreciation than that it should provide a large income. For instance, in the case of an endowment fund for a major museum and art gallery, 'the desirability of having an increase of capital value which will make possible the purchase of desirable acquisitions for the museum despite soaring prices does something to justify the greater risks whereby capital appreciation may be obtained'.[3] On the other hand, the investment of a pension fund will require a combination of investments which will provide some measure of protection against the ravages of inflation[4] and of investments which will enable the payment of benefits to pensioners as and when they fall due for payment, bearing in mind always the need to make a judgment which takes account of the risks of the investments in question[5] and which has proper regard to the need for security.[6] It may even be that, in considering investment policy, the trustees will need to have regard to the circumstances of individual beneficiaries. Trustees of land, for instance, may invest or apply trust funds in the purchase of property for

---

[2]  See above, p 388.
[3]  *Trustees of the British Museum v A-G* [1984] 1 All ER 337 at 343, per Megarry V-C.
[4]  *Mason v Farbrother* [1983] 2 All ER 1078 at 1086–1087.
[5]  *Cowan v Scargill* [1984] 2 All ER 750 at 760, per Megarry V-C.
[6]  See (1974) 23 ICLQ 748 (Grosh).

occupation by a beneficiary,[7] a decision which can be made only after considering the circumstances of the beneficiaries. And in *Nestlé v National Westminster Bank plc*,[8] Staughton LJ thought that it would be appropriate for trustees to take into account the circumstances of the beneficiaries, as, for example, 'if the life tenant is living in penury and the remainderman already has ample wealth'.

Expressed in general terms, it can be said that the purpose of investment is to enable the fulfillment of the objectives of the trust. In one of the leading cases involving the investment of pension funds, Sir Robert Megarry has said:

'The starting point is the duty of trustees to exercise their powers in the best interests of the present and future beneficiaries of the trust, holding the scales impartially between different classes of beneficiaries. This duty of the trustees towards their beneficiaries is paramount . . . When the purpose of the trust is to provide financial benefits for the beneficiaries, as is usually the case, the best interests of the beneficiaries are normally their best financial interests. In the case of a power of investment, as in the present case, the power must be exercised so as to yield the best return for the beneficiaries, judged in relation to the risks of the investments in question; and the prospects of the yield of income and capital appreciation both have to be considered in judging the return from the investment.'[9]

This statement does not apply only to the exercise by trustees of their powers. The influence of the policy which underlies it can be seen also in the historical approach to trustees' general powers of permitted investment, and in the approach which the courts have in the past adopted in considering extensions to trustees' powers of investment.

# 3  Powers of disposal

## (1)  Assets available for investment

Except where trustees are under an obligation to make an immediate distribution, the trustees will have assets to invest where the funds they receive are in cash or currency. It would rarely be appropriate for the trustees to retain large quantities of banknotes, uncleared cheques, or similar assets. Where the assets which the trustees receive are already in some form of investment, such as shares in a public company, a landholding, or some other enduring form, then it is less clear whether there is a power or even an obligation to realise those assets for the purpose of reinvestment. It has already been noted in the last chapter that there is no general power of sale. The power of sale for the purpose of reinvestment now needs to be examined more closely.

## (2)  Trust for sale

In some trusts, the trustees are placed under an obligation to sell the property in the form in which it is originally received, and either to distribute or to reinvest the

---

[7] Trusts of Land and Appointment of Trustees Act 1996, s 6.    [8] [1994] 1 All ER 118.
[9] *Cowan v Scargill* [1984] 2 All ER 750 at 760, per Megarry V-C.

proceeds of sale. Such a trust is called a trust for sale. A trust for sale may be imposed expressly by the settlor. It used also, in the case of land, to arise by virtue of statutory imposition under the Law of Property Act 1925, although, since the coming into operation of the Trusts of Land and Appointment of Trustees Act 1996, that is no longer the case.

A trust for sale may, finally, arise under the rule in *Howe v Dartmouth*, explained in the previous chapter,[10] where hazardous or wasting assets, or assets generating no income, and which formed part of a testator's residuary estate, are received by a trustee who is to hold the assets for beneficiaries entitled to successive interests. The Law Commission has recently recommended the abolition of the rule in *Howe v Dartmouth* and of the implied trust for sale of unauthorised, hazardous or wasting assets generated thereby.[11] Express and statutory trusts for sale would be unaffected by this reform.

## (3) Other powers of sale and reinvestment

A well-drafted trust will have anticipated the desirability of selling trust assets for the purpose of reinvestment, and will have made express provision. Trusts of land governed by the Settled Land Act 1925 confer upon the tenant for life, as trustee of the land, a power of sale,[12] with the proceeds of sale being treated as capital money which, if not otherwise required, is available for reinvestment.[13] Similarly, there is a power of sale[14] and a power indefinitely to postpone sale[15] in the case of trusts of land governed by the Trusts of Land and Appointment of Trustees Act 1996, in other words in all trusts of land which are created on or after 1 January 1997, and in all trusts of land arising before that date and which are not governed by the Settled Land Act 1925.

Strangely, the Trustee Act 2000, which introduced a new regime for investment of trust funds fails to make clear whether trustees have a power of sale for the purposes of investment. The Act states in s 3 that 'a trustee may make any kind of investment that he could make if he were absolutely entitled to the assets of the trust', but nowhere does it indicate when a trustee may or must make investments. The Trustee Investments Act 1961, which the Trustee Act 2000 largely replaces, did contain the more explicit statement that 'a trustee may invest any property in his hands, whether at the time in a state of investment or not . . . and may from time to time vary such investments'.[16] In the absence of such a general provision, it will be a matter for the proper construction of the trust instrument as to whether the trustees are permitted or expected to invest the trust property. Such a conclusion could readily be reached if the trust assets are to be retained for any length of time, and the conferment of a statutory power of investment could be interpreted as implying a power to sell for the purpose of making an investment.[17]

---

[10] See above, p 594.
[11] Capital and Income in Trusts: Classification and Apportionment, Law Comm CP No 175 (2004)
[12] Settled Land Act 1925, s 38: see Chapter 21.     [13] Settled Land Act 1925, s 73.
[14] Trusts of Land and Appointment of Trustees Act 1996, s 6.
[15] Trusts of Land and Appointment of Trustees Act 1996, s 4.     [16] S 1(1).
[17] See Trustee Act 1925 s 16(1) which could be interpreted as conferring a power of sale in these circumstances. Compare *Hume v Lopes* [1892] AC 112; *Re Pratt's Will Trust* [1943] Ch 326.

However, as has already been explained, there could be circumstances in which the power of sale is excluded because the trust requires the retention of the assets in a particular form.[18] Although there are authorities which suggested that there must be a clear exclusion of the statutory investment powers in express terms,[19] these were cases which sought to limit and not to exclude the trustee's powers of investment. It is submitted that the implied statutory power to sell for the purpose of investment does not apply to property which it is the trustee's duty to retain.[20]

# 4 Authorised investments

## (1) Principles

Except in those rare situations where a person is both trustee and beneficiary (as for instance in the case of co-ownership trusts of land), a trustee is investing property on behalf of others. This requires an approach to risk which may not be the same as that which might be adopted by a person making investments on his or her own behalf. Whilst an individual may consider it appropriate when making decisions in their own behalf to incur a high degree of risk, this is much less appropriate when dealing with the assets of others. To take an extreme example, a person can choose to gamble with their own money by buying lottery tickets, but this would not be a suitable application of trust funds.

There are two different methods which can be used to limit the investment decisions of trustees to investments which are suitable for trust funds. One is to provide a list of investments which are considered to be sufficiently secure and robust to be used for the investment of trust funds, limiting trustees to making a choice from this menu. The other is to impose a general duty on trustees only to select investments which meet the criteria of suitability. The first approach has been the traditional approach in Britain, but the Trustee Act 2000 has implemented a sea change by sweeping away most of the previous restrictions on investment by trustees and adopting the second approach.

## (2) History

The turbulence caused by the bursting of the South Sea Bubble in 1720 was the cause for a serious curtailment by the Court of Chancery of the investments which trustees were permitted to make. From the end of the eighteenth century onwards, it became the rule that a trustee would be liable to bear the deficiency if any loss resulted from

---

[18] See the now repealed s 1(3) of the Trustee Investments Act 1961 which stated that the previous statutory provisions' are exercisable only in so far as a contrary intention is not expressed . . .'

[19] *Re Rider's Will Trusts* [1958] 1 WLR 974; *Re Burke* [1908] 2 Ch 248; *Re Hill* [1914] WN 132.

[20] Compare Settled Land Act 1925, s 67, under which heirlooms (defined as personal chattels settled so as to devolve with settled land) may be sold only pursuant to an order of the court, even where the purpose of sale is to invest the proceeds. In *Re Hope* [1899] 2 Ch 679 the court refused permission under this section to sell the 'Hope' diamond.

making an investment in a way which was not authorised by the settlor or the beneficiaries, and which had gone beyond the range of investments contemplated by the
courts or the legislature. Prior to the Trustee Act 2000, the investments authorised by
the general law were conservative, placing considerable emphasis on the security of
trust funds.

The policy adopted by legislation up to and including the Trustee Investments Act
1961 was to protect beneficiaries by limiting trustees to 'safe' forms of investment. The
Trustee Investments Act 1961 adopted a very much more constrained regulation of
trustee investments than in some other jurisdictions, notably in North America, where
the principal requirement is that in making investments, trustees should act as a prudent man would do when investing on behalf of others.[21] It also lagged substantially
behind the practice of well-advised settlors inserting their own express investment
powers.

In order to avoid the limitations on the powers of investment by trustees, settlors
often included an express power of investment in a settlement. The trustees could also
obtain the consent of the beneficiaries to investments which would not otherwise be
authorised, although this course of action was only available if all the beneficiaries were
capable of giving consent. Finally, the trustees could enlarge their investment powers by
means of an application to court, either under the Variation of Trusts Act 1958 where
the beneficiaries who are capable of consenting concur, or where this is not practicable,
under s 57 of the Trustee Act 1925.

## (3) The new approach

The new approach to investment has been embraced by the Trustee Act 2000. The
approach was described in a Treasury consultation paper.[22] Rather than limit the kinds
of investment which trustees can make, it is seen as more sensible to give the trustees
more extensive powers of investment in relation to the selection of individual investments. The interests of the beneficiaries are then protected by requiring the trustees to
take such expert advice as the nature of the trust requires and by charging them with
responsibility to ensure that the portfolio of investments is properly balanced.

This new approach was first adopted by the Pensions Act 1995. This permits pension
fund trustees to make any kind of investment as if they were absolutely entitled to the
assets.[23] However, the trustees are required to maintain a statement of investment
policy,[24] including information about the policy on risk, expected returns and realisation. The trustees are expected to secure and consider professional advice, to consider
the need to maintain a balanced portfolio and to consider the merits of each individual
investment proposed.[25] The same approach has now been adopted by the Trustee Act

---

[21]  See (1954) 7 Current Legal Problems 139 (Latham); (1974) 23 ICLQ 748 (Grosh).

[22]  Investment Powers of Trustees (May 1996).

[23]  Pensions Act 1995, s 34. Although this appears to confer unlimited scope on the trustees, the use of the
word 'investments' without further definition may in itself impose a restriction. See below.

[24]  Pensions Act 1995, s 35.

[25]  Pensions Act 1995, s 36. There is special provision allowing the trustees to delegate some of these
responsibilities: s 34.

2000 as the general principle for most trusts.[26] Trustees are given the same power to invest trust funds, with some narrow exceptions, as if they owned the assets outright. They are, however, subject to an obligation to act in the best interests of the beneficiaries, to consider the need for diversification of investment, to consider the suitability of individual investments, and to take advice where appropriate.

The power of investment conferred by the Trustee Act 2000, described as the *general power of investment*, extends the powers of investment which may have been conferred upon trustees by other statutory provisions or by the trust instrument, but it can be excluded or restricted by the trust instrument or by legislation.[27] The general power of investment applies to existing trusts, not just those created after the passing of the 2000 Act.[28]

## (4) Express powers of investment

### (a) Interpretation

The need for express powers of investment is significantly reduced by the general power of investment conferred by Trustee Act 2000. Nevertheless, it is still common practice for professionally drafted trusts to contain express investment powers. The approach to the interpretation of such powers is demonstrated *by Re Harari's Settlement Trusts.*[29] Sir Victor Harari had transferred assets to trustees which fell outside the categories authorised by the general rules for trustees. Under an express provision in the trust deed, it was declared that:

'The trustees shall hold the said investments so transferred to them as aforesaid upon trust that they may either allow the same to remain in their present state of investment so long as the trustees may see fit or may at any time or times . . . realise the said investments . . . and . . . invest the money produced thereby . . . in or upon such investments as to them may seem fit with power . . . to vary or transpose any investments for or into others.'

It was argued before the judge that the investments which the trustees could select under this clause were limited to those generally authorised by law (which of course at the time were much narrower than they are now), since the clause did not clearly and unambiguously extend the range of investments beyond those permitted by statute. Jenkins J held, however, that the trustees were given a wider power of investment. In his view, he was free to construe the settlement according to what he considered to be the natural and proper meaning of the words used in their context, and he saw no justification for implying any restriction on the wide construction which the words themselves were sufficient to bear.[30]

---

[26] The general investment powers do not apply to occupational pension schemes, authorised unit trusts or certain schemes under the Charities Act 1993: see Trustee Act 2000, ss 36–38. There are special statutory rules applying to these forms of collective investment.

[27] Trustee Act 2000, s 6.      [28] Trustee Act 2000, s 7.      [29] [1949] 1 All ER 430.

[30] See, to similar effect, *Re Peczenik's Settlement* [1964] 2 All ER 339.

### (b) Limits to investment powers

Although it is clear from *Re Harari's Settlement Trusts* that investment clauses will not be given a restrictive interpretation, there are still pitfalls for the draftsman. If the draftsman seeks to impose a limit on the range of permissible investments, that limit should be clearly and unambiguously expressed. Difficulties have occurred in the past with clauses limiting investments to stocks in 'any British colony or dependency' because of changes in the status of Commonwealth and former Commonwealth countries.[31] A clause authorising investment in 'blue chip' securities has also been held to be ineffective on grounds of uncertainty.[32]

### (c) Meaning of 'investment'

A number of cases, discussed in relation to the Trustee Act 2000, below, have considered what is meant by the word 'investment'. The cases suggest that an application of funds will not be considered to be an investment unless the assets produce an income. It may be that in the light of changing investment practice, a different view would be taken today and that assets expected to produce a capital gain could be considered to be investments even if they were producing no income.[33] Nevertheless, good drafting will make clear that applications in non-income generating assets are permitted. The Universities' Superannuation Scheme Rules (the pension scheme for academic staff within the old universities), for instance, state that the trustee may apply its assets for the purchase of 'investments or other property of whatsoever nature and wheresoever . . . and whether producing income or not'.[34]

### (d) Loans

In *Khoo Tek Keong v Ch'ng Joo Tuan Neoh*[35] the Privy Council held that trustees were not authorised to make an unsecured personal loan under a clause which permitted them 'to invest all moneys liable to be invested in such investments as they in their absolute discretion think fit'. Where security is given for the loan, it may be classed as an investment under such a clause and, again, a suitably drafted clause can authorise the application of trust funds in unsecured personal loans.[36]

## (5) General power of investment under Trustee Act 2000

### (a) Meaning of 'investment'

The general power of investment conferred by the Trustee Act 2000 states that 'a trustee may make any kind of investment that he could make if he were absolutely entitled to

---

[31] *Re Maryon-Wilson's Estate* [1912] 1 Ch 55, CA; *Re Brassey's Settlement* [1955] 1 WLR 192; *Re Rider's Will Trusts* [1958] 1 WLR 974.

[32] *Re Kolb's Will Trusts* [1962] Ch 531.

[33] See *Cook v Medway Housing Society* [1997] STC 90 at 98 for support for this view.

[34] Universities' Superannuation Scheme Rules, r 20.8(a).      [35] [1934] AC 529.

[36] *Re Laing's Settlement* [1899] 1 Ch 593. The Universities' Superannuation Scheme Rules state that the trustee may apply funds 'upon such personal credit with or without security as the trustee company shall in its absolute discretion see fit' (r 20.8(a)).

the assets of the trust'.[37] The Act does not define what is meant by an investment, and this is therefore something to be resolved by reference to general principles of interpretation. The explanatory note to the Act states that an investment is something which is expected to produce an income or capital return. The caselaw on the use of the word in express investment clauses shows a narrower interpretation being adopted. In *Re Wragg*[38] P O Lawrence J held that a clause authorising investment in 'stocks funds shares and securities or other investments' was wide enough to include the purchase of land which was to be rented out to produce an income. He stated that 'to invest' includes as one of its meanings 'to apply money in the purchase of some property from which interest or profit is expected and which property is purchased in order to be held for the sake of the income which it will yield'. However, in *Re Power*,[39] the court considered that the purchase of a house for occupation by a beneficiary was not permitted under a clause providing that 'All moneys requiring to be invested under this my will may be invested by the trustee in any manner in which he may in his absolute discretion think fit in all respects as if he were the sole beneficial owner of such moneys including the purchase of freehold property in England or Wales'. The reason for this was that land being occupied by a beneficiary would not be generating income, and it could not therefore appropriately be described as an investment.[40] Strict application of this interpretation of the meaning of 'investment' would preclude trustees from purchasing, in the absence of the conferral of an express power in trust instrument, assets for investment which only have potential to appreciate in capital value but do not produce any income, for example precious metals, works of art, fine wine or antiques. Premium bonds would also not be considered an investment.

The Trustee Act 2000 failed to resolve this problem, since it utilises the terminology of 'investment' without further definition. The Law Commission in its report on the powers and duties of trustees which preceded the Act expressed the view that avoiding any definition of investment would permit the concept to evolve in ways which might be constrained were a definition to be given.[41] The explanatory notes accompanying the Act state that the power of investment conferred by the Act permits trustees to invest so as to produce an income or capital return, but these do not form part of the Act and cannot be regarded as having overruled the definition of 'investment' in *Re Power*.[42] It would, however, be inconvenient if the word 'investment' in the Trustee Act 2000 were to be interpreted in the same restrictive way. Changing patterns of investment now mean that it is not uncommon for applications of funds to carry no rights to income. For instance, some companies adopt a policy of making no declaration of a dividend in order to reinvest profits with the intention of increasing the value of their shares; it is possible to purchase units in authorised unit trusts where all income is reinvested rather than being paid out to investors, again with the intention of producing capital growth; and it is possible to purchase capital bonds which are redeemable after a fixed period at a value higher than the purchase price, compensating for the lack of interest by this capital growth. All of these applications of funds generate potential capital growth

---

[37] Trustee Act 2000, s 3(1).    [38] [1919] 2 Ch 58.    [39] [1947] Ch 572.
[40] See also *Re Peczenik's Settlement Trusts* [1964] 1 WLR 720.
[41] Law Commission Report No 260 (1999), *Trustees Powers and Duties*, p 22.    [42] [1947] Ch 572.

and can have a place in a properly constructed investment portfolio. It would be unfortunate if trustees were not able to take advantage of them. As has already been indicated, it is possible that were the issue to be addressed today, a court would adopt the view set out in the explanatory memorandum and hold that the expression 'investment' included any application of funds which produced either potential income or potential capital returns.[43]

## (b) Traditional investments

There are certain types of investment which undoubtedly fall within the expression 'investment' as used in the Trustee Act 2000. This would include deposits in a bank or building society, the purchase of government stock, and the purchase of shares in publicly quoted companies. All of these forms of investment were permitted by the Trustee Investments Act 1961, which contained the list of authorised trustee investments prior to the enlargement of investment powers given to trustees by the 2000 Act. The 1961 Act was the first Act to allow trustees to invest in company shares. This was a significant step, as a short analysis of different types of investment will indicate.

Where money is invested by deposit with a bank, the bank pays annual or other periodic interest, but undertakes only to return the sum originally deposited when the account is closed. Government stock is not repayable on demand, but is usually repayable at a fixed future date. Again, interest is payable periodically, but when the date for repayment of the stock falls due, it is repaid only at face value. Pending the date of repayment, the price at which the stock is traded will fluctuate in accordance with prevailing market interest rates and the period before redemption. A stock which offers a high fixed rate of interest on its nominal value, compared with market rates, will tend to trade at a premium (ie at a higher price than its nominal value), reflecting the advantage of the holder receiving the high income. Conversely, a stock which offers a low rate of nominal interest will tend to trade at a discount against its nominal value, reflecting the low yield of interest.

Shares in public companies offer the advantage, compared with fixed interest securities and deposits, of offering the potential for both income and capital growth. The policy of most companies is to pay an annual dividend out of the profits which the company makes, while also retaining assets and profits which will enable the underlying capital value of the company to grow. As the net worth of the company increases, so its stock market value will tend to increase. The shareholder will thus receive an income and hope to participate in capital gains. The stock market can be volatile, particularly in the short term, so that, as investment advisers are required to warn, 'the value of your investment can fall as well as rise'. The share market crash of October 1987 shows how dramatic the falls can be. Nevertheless, over the longer term, investments in shares this century have consistently outperformed bank and building society deposits and purchases of fixed interest securities. Having said this, however, the average value of company shares as measured by one of the standard indices, the Financial Times index of the top 100 companies, did not increase between 1997 and 2002.

---

[43] This view was taken in a different context in *Cook v Medway Housing Society* [1997] STC 90 at 98. See also (2001) 15 TLI (Hicks) for the view that the 'portfolio' theory of investment permits more flexibility.

The ability of trustees, even in the absence of express extended powers of investment, to invest in shares, has been of considerable importance in enabling astute trustees to produce a reasonable income while providing a good measure of protection against inflation through capital appreciation.

## (c) Financial instruments

The relatively recent past has seen an increase in the variety of financial instruments available. Some of these were created expressly for the purpose of providing investment vehicles, whilst others originated as mechanisms to help in managing the risks of exchange rate or share price fluctuations. It is not clear whether all of these financial instruments would be considered to be investments permitted by the Trustee Act 2000. Some should fall within the meaning of the term provided that it is not given too narrow an interpretation. Capital bonds, under which a company undertakes to repay a given sum at a fixed date in the future, but without any payment of interest in the meantime, have already been referred to. Since these bonds are sold at a price below their redemption value, the capital gain makes up for the loss of interest. There should be no reason why these capital bonds should not be considered valid trustee investments.

There are other financial instruments which are less readily considered to be investments within the ordinary meaning of the term. This includes, for instance, the so-called 'derivatives'. One form of derivative is the 'future' under which a person commits to the sale or purchase of shares or currency at a given date in the future at a fixed price. The other principal form is the 'option' under which the holder has the right, but not an obligation, to buy (purchase) or sell (put) at a fixed price on a future date. These instruments allow a jeweller, for instance, to reduce the risks of the price of gold going up or down by entering into an advance purchase contract or option. They would allow an exporter who knows that he will receive payment in a foreign currency in a year's time to reduce the risk of currency fluctuation by entering into a contract which effectively fixes the exchange rate. However, they also allow speculators to gamble on whether prices will go up or down.[44] There may be a place for this kind of speculation in some trusts, and banks are offering dealings in derivatives to private clients with substantial funds to invest. However, since they are extremely risky compared to most other forms of investment, they could well be considered to be outside the scope of authorised investment. Even if they were held to be 'investments' as that term is used in the Trustee Act 2000, a trustee would have to show that a properly informed decision had been made to apply trust funds in this fashion.

## (d) Purchase of land

The general power of investment does not in itself authorise trustees to invest in the purchase of land.[45] Section 8 of the Trustee Act 2000, however, contains authority for

---

[44] Trustee Act 2000, s 3(3).

[45] It is also possible to gamble on prices going up or down through 'spread betting' where a gambler stakes money against the future price of a given share. If the share falls within the agreed band or spread of prices at the set date, the betting company pays out on the bet. It is unlikely that any convincing argument could be made that spread betting constitutes an investment within the meaning of the Trustee Act 2000.

trustees (with some exceptions[46]) to purchase land. This extends to all trustees the power to apply trust funds to the purchase of land which was first conferred by statute on trustees of land by the Trusts of Land and Appointment of Trustees Act 1996.[47] There is now no distinction between trustees of land and trustees of personal property in this regard. Trustees may purchase land as an investment, for occupation by a beneficiary, or for any other reason. The purchase may be of a legal freehold or leasehold estate in the United Kingdom.[48] Trustees have no statutory authority to purchase land overseas, but the power to acquire such land could be conferred expressly by the trust instrument. Trustees who acquire land under the statutory power conferred by the Trustee Act 2000, s 8 have all the powers of an absolute owner in relation to the land for the purpose of exercising their functions as trustees.[49]

### (e) Loans

Trustees have been permitted to invest in loans secured by way of a mortgage over the borrower's land for over one hundred years.[50] The Trustee Act 2000 continues to allow trustees to invest by way of loans secured on land,[51] but there is nothing in the Act which expressly confers any power to make unsecured loans. *Khoo Tek Keong v Ch'ng Joo Tuan Neoh*[52] suggests that unsecured loans would not be considered as investments without some express authority.

### (f) Modification of the general power of investment

The general power of investment conferred on trustees by the Trustee Act 2000 is in addition to any express powers which might be conferred upon trustees,[53] but may also be restricted or excluded by an express provision.[54] It goes almost without saying that the general power of investment can be modified by legislation, although, out of an abundance of caution, the Act makes this clear.[55]

As was indicated earlier, the Act applies to trusts created before the commencement of the Act as well as to those created subsequently.[56] Where a trust instrument contains a phrase such as 'the trustees may invest in any investment authorised by law for the investment of trust property', this will be treated as conferring on trustees the general power of investment, whether the trust was made before or after the 2000

---

[46] The power does not apply to trustees of settled land, who have the power to apply trust funds to the purchase of land under the Settled Land Act 1925, ss 73, 75. Similarly, the power does not apply to occupational pension funds, authorised unit trusts and certain charity investment funds: Trustee Act 2000, ss 36–38.

[47] S 6.

[48] Or the equivalent of a legal estate in the case of land in Scotland; Trustee Act 2000, s 8(2).

[49] This means, for instance, that trustees are able to grant leases, borrow against the security of the land, carry out building works, and so on.

[50] See Trustee Act 1925, s 8; Trustee Investments Act 2000, Sch 1, Pt II, para 13. Similar provisions appeared in the legislation which these Acts replaced.

[51] Although Trustee Act 1925, s 8 has been repealed, Trustee Act 2000, s 3(3) acknowledges that trustees may make loans secured on land.

[52] [1934] AC 529. The case is referred to above in relation to express powers of investment.

[53] Trustee Act 2000, s 6(1)(a).   [54] Trustee Act 2000, s 6(1)(b).   [55] Trustee Act 2000, s 6(1)(b).

[56] Trustee Act 2000, s 7(1).

Act.[57] Express provisions contained in trust instruments made before 3 August 1961 (the day on which the Trustee Investments Act 1961 came into operation) are not to be treated as restricting or excluding the general power of investment.[58]

# 5 Widening of powers of investment

The substantial increase in the investment powers given to trustees by the Trustee Act 2000 should mean that it will be rare that they will consider their powers to be too narrow. However, there may be some instances in which they seek wider investment powers, for instance permitting the purchase of property overseas, or clarifying whether they are permitted to invest in assets which produce no income. There are a number of ways in which this may be possible.

## (1) Power of variation in trust deed

Some trust deeds contain provisions under which alterations or amendments to the deed can be made. For instance, the Universities' Superannuation Scheme Rules provide that the rules can be altered by deed, with certain restrictions concerning maintaining the purpose of the scheme to provide pensions and other benefits for eligible employees, and subject to certain consents.[59]

## (2) Consent of beneficiaries

Where all the beneficiaries of a trust are ascertainable, and, being competent to do so, give their consent, then new powers of investment proposed by the trustees may be adopted.

## (3) Variation of Trusts Act 1958

Where it is not possible to obtain consent from all the beneficiaries of a trust, or some of the beneficiaries of the trust are not competent to give consent, and in certain other cases, the Variation of Trusts Act 1958 will apply. This enables the court to approve a variation of trust, including a variation of investment powers, on behalf of the unascertainable or incompetent beneficiaries.[60] The Act does not permit the court to consent to a variation on behalf of ascertainable and competent beneficiaries who have

---

[57] See Trustee Act 2000, s 7(3). A trust instrument made after the 2000 Act which stated that trustees could invest in the manner authorised by the Trustee Investments Act 1961 would, however, be treated as limiting the investment powers of trustees to those permitted under the old rules set out in that Act.

[58] Trustee Act 2000, s 7(2).

[59] USS Rules, s 21. See also British Coal Corpn v *British Coal Staff Superannuation Scheme Trustees Ltd* [1995] 1 All ER 912.

[60] See Chapter 18.

not been consulted (even where to do so would be inconvenient) or to override a refusal of consent by such a beneficiary.

## (4) Trustee Act 1925, s 57

This section authorises the court to approve a transaction, either exceptionally or generally,[61] and has been held to be wide enough in scope to authorise extended investment powers.[62] It has an advantage over the Variation of Trusts Act 1958 in that it does not require the beneficiaries to be consulted or to agree to the enlargement of the investment powers, although the court will not approve the variation unless it can be seen as being in the general interests of all the beneficiaries. In *Anker-Petersen v Anker-Petersen*[63] it was suggested that applications for extending powers of investment were more appropriately brought under s 57 than under the Variation of Trusts Act 1958. This was because it was more realistic for the court to consider the matter on behalf of the beneficiaries as a group rather than individually, as the 1958 Act required.

## (5) Principles on which court grants approval

In a case decided shortly after the passing of the Trustee Investments Act 1961, *Re Kolb's Will Trusts*,[64] it was said that the investment powers in that Act should 'be taken to be prima facie sufficient and ought only to be extended if, on the particular facts, a special case for extending them can be made out'.[65] Subsequent cases departed from that view, and showed a greater willingness to entertain requests for enlarging powers of investment. Thus, in *Mason v Farbrother*,[66] Blackett Ord V-C approved a considerable widening of the powers of investment of the trustees of the Co-Operative Wholesale Society pension fund, and in *Trustees of the British Museum v A-G*[67] Megarry V-C approved the enlargement of the investment powers of the trustees of a museum of international importance. The first case was dealt with under the provisions of the Trustee Act 1925, s 57, and the latter under the Variation of Trusts Act 1958, but there does not seem to have been a difference in approach. Relevant factors included the quality of the advice available to the trustees, and the measures which were to be taken to balance risk and safety. The division of the trust fund into separate parts with different risk profiles was considered to be an important factor in granting approval. In *Steel v Wellcome Custodian Trustees*,[68] Hoffmann J approved almost unfettered investment powers with no obligation to divide the fund into divisions for the trustees of an extremely large charitable foundation. He had regard to the size of the fund, the eminence and experience of the trustees, and the provisions in the proposed scheme for obtaining advice.

It is only possible to speculate what approach would now be taken by the courts in

---

[61]  The Act applies to private trusts. The court has similar powers in respect of charitable trusts under the Charitable Trusts Acts 1853–1925.
[62]  *Mason v Farbrother* [1983] 2 All ER 1078.      [63]  [1991] 16 LS Gaz R 32.      [64]  [1962] Ch 531.
[65]  [1962] Ch 531 at 540.      [66]  [1983] 2 All ER 1078.      [67]  [1984] 1 All ER 337.
[68]  [1988] 1 WLR 167.

deciding whether to grant extended powers of investment. The width of the powers given by the 2000 Act might mean that there would be the same kind of reluctance to entertain an application as happened in *Re Kolb's Will Trusts*. Since the current legislative regime does not require any division of the trust fund, it is unlikely that a court would insist on it if granting enlarged powers, but the factors identified by Hoffmann J would still surely be relevant in deciding whether an extension of powers was appropriate.

# 6 Portfolio investment theory

## (1) The responsibilities of trustees

The duties of trustees in relation to investment are considered in detail below. Foremost in those duties are a requirement to have regard to the fact that they are dealing with money belonging to others, and therefore have a duty to safeguard it. They must also consider the appropriate balance between capital and income, and the need to protect the trust assets against erosion through inflation. If the trustees are holding only a small fund which they are expected to distribute in the near future, then the principal consideration will be safeguarding the assets in the short term whilst keeping the ability to draw on the fund for the purposes of distribution. Investing the money by way of deposit in a bank might be the simplest and most appropriate way of doing this. However, if the funds are larger and are to be retained for a longer period, then other considerations affecting the choice of investments come into play.

## (2) Risk management

The advantage of depositing money with a bank is that the bank undertakes to return the same amount as was deposited with it, together with interest. The depositor runs only a very small risk that if the bank becomes insolvent, it may not be able to meet its obligations in full. The disadvantage is that the effect of inflation reduces the purchasing power of the cash sum which the bank returns to the depositor. How then is it possible for an investor to safeguard against inflation? A traditional means of doing this is to purchase company shares, which over the long term can be expected to increase in value in money terms, as well as providing an income through the dividends which the company pays. However, the risks associated with company shares are greater. The company may not flourish: it may be badly managed, or it may be operating in a sector which is generally in decline. In consequence, the risks that a single shareholding will fall in value are much greater than is the case with a bank deposit. The greater potential return from company shares is balanced by a greater element of risk. Trustees are permitted to take risks with trust funds. No investment is entirely risk free. However, it is the function of the trustees to manage the risks so that the balance of risk and profit is appropriate for the nature of the trust.

## (3) Investment portfolios

One of the principles of investment policy is that you should not 'put all your eggs in one basket'. By investing in several companies, not just one, there is less chance that all will fail (although equally less chance that all will thrive). The risks are further reduced if the investments are made in different market sectors—for instance buying shares in companies operating in different fields such as banking, oil distribution, business services or supplying utilities. Portfolio investment theory is that where an investment fund is large enough, different parts of the fund should be invested in different ways to provide a balance of growth or income potential, and of security and risk. Instead of evaluating the profile or risk of individual investments, what matters is the balance across the portfolio as a whole—higher risks in some parts of the fund may be balanced by lower risks, or compensating considerations, in other parts of the fund. The exact balance will vary according to individual requirements. A pension fund investing for existing pensioners needs to tilt more towards income and security than, say, a trust fund which is designed to accumulate to pay out a sum to a beneficiary in 20 years' time. The portfolio theory of investment was examined and discussed in *Nestlé v National Westminster Bank plc*.[69]

## (4) Trustee Investments Act 1961

The Trustee Investments Act 1961 espoused the portfolio investment theory, but did so in a rigid way. Investments authorised for trustees were divided into three categories, and trustees who wished to invest in the riskier categories were obliged to take advice, and for certain investments (called wider-range investments) to create a separate part of the trust fund. The enlargement of the categories of permitted investment were welcome, but the way in which the Act required trustees to allocate investments was mechanical, cumbersome, and arbitrarily inflexible.[70] Certain aspects of the operation of the Act were rightly described as 'curious'.[71]

## (5) Trustee Act 2000

The rigidity and capriciousness of the investment rules in the 1961 Act have been swept away by the 2000 Act. This permits trustees to invest in the way most appropriate for the circumstances of their trust with none of the arbitrary limitations of the 1961 Act. In reviewing whether trustees have acted properly, the courts are likely to take account of the current theory of portfolio investment.

---

[69] [1994] 1 All ER 118; (1992) 142 NLJ 1279 (Martin); [1993] Conv 63 (Kenny); [1998] Con 352 (Watt and Stauch).

[70] The Act initially required a division of the trust fund into two equal parts to enable the wider powers of investment to take effect (Trustee Investments Act 1961, s 2(1)), and this was later varied by the Trustee Investments (Division of Trust Fund) Order 1996, SI 1996/845 to permit three-quarters of the fund to be applied in the wider range of investments. Trustees could not choose some other division, such as two-thirds.

[71] *Nestlé v National Westminster Bank Ltd* [1993] 1 WLR 1260 at 1278, per Staughton LJ.

# 7 Duties of trustees in relation to investment

## (1) The general duty of care

There is a substantial body of case law considering the duties of trustees in relation to investment, much of which remains relevant although the Trustee Act 2000 imposes some statutory duties. The first of these statutory duties is the statutory duty of care. Trustees are required to exercise such care and skill in relation to investments as is reasonable in the circumstances.[72] As is explained elsewhere, a higher standard of care is expected from trustees acting in a professional capacity and where the trustee claims to have special knowledge or experience.[73] This is no more than a statutory restatement of the principles which had been established by the cases, with a clarification of the position of professional trustees. In *Speight v Gaunt*[74] Lord Blackburn stated that the general duty of trustees was to act honestly and fairly and to take 'all those precautions which an ordinary prudent man of business would take in managing similar affairs of his own'. In *Re Whiteley*[75] Lindley LJ refined this dictum as it applies to investment. He said:

'The duty of the trustee is not to take such care only as a prudent man would take if he had only himself to consider, the duty is rather to take such care as an ordinary prudent man would take if he were minded to make an investment for the benefit of other people for whom he felt morally bound to provide.'[76]

Lord Watson on appeal to the House of Lords explained:

'Business men of ordinary prudence may, and frequently do, select investments which are more or less of a speculative character; but it is the duty of a trustee to confine himself to the class of investments which are permitted by the trust, and likewise to avoid all investments of that class which are attended by hazard.'[77]

In addition to the specific duties relating to investment, trustees remain subject in making investment decisions, to their general fiduciary duties. This means that they should not act in a way which gives rise to a conflict of interest. Thus, in a Canadian case, it was held that the trustees were in breach of trust where they made a loan to a company owned by one of the trustees. Even though this application of the trust funds did not fall outside the investment powers of the trustees, the conflict of interest made the loan an improper investment.[78]

We have already seen how the rule in *Howe v Dartmouth*,[79] if it has not been superseded by the Trustee Act 2000, may require immediate disinvestment by trustees of hazardous investments received under a residuary testamentary gift which is to be held for beneficiaries with successive interests. However, in accordance with portfolio

---

[72] Trustee Act 2000, s 1(1).      [73] Trustee Act 2000, s 1(1). See the discussion in Chapter 28.

[74] (1883) 9 App Cas 1.

[75] (1886) 33 Ch D 347; affd sub nom *Learoyd v Whiteley* (1887) 12 App Cas 727.

[76] (1886) 33 Ch D 347 at 355.      [77] (1887) 12 App Cas 727 at 733.

[78] *Re David Feldman Charitable Foundation* (1987) 58 OR (2d) 626.      [79] See above, p 388.

investment theory, as has already been explained, trustees may be entitled to retain or to make an investment which involves a measure of risk (as most investments inevitably do), provided that the risk involved in that investment is balanced by other elements in the portfolio. That is the tenor of most recent judgments on the investment powers of trustees. In *Nestlé v National Westminster Bank plc*[80] Hoffmann J said that 'an investment which in isolation is too risky and therefore in breach of trust may be justified when held in conjunction with other investments'.

## (2) The standard investment criteria

The Trustee Act 2000, s 4 requires all trustees exercising a power of investment, including trustees exercising express investment powers, to have regard to what are described as the *standard investment criteria*.[81] There are two such criteria. First, the trustees must have regard to the suitability of the investment concerned, and secondly to the need for diversification. The trustees must have regard to these standard investment criteria both in making investments,[82] and also in periodically reviewing the investments.[83] The responsibilities of trustees in relation to investments are ongoing—they cannot invest funds and then forget them. They must keep the investment portfolio under periodic review.

When looking at the suitability of investments, the Trustee Act 2000 envisages a two-stage process. The trustees must both consider the suitability for the trust of a particular kind of investment. For instance, should the trust invest in purchasing shares in a unit trust? The trustees must then consider the suitability of the particular investment proposed. For instance, having decided that investing in a unit trust would be suitable, which fund manager and which of that manager's investment funds should be selected?

## (3) The need for advice

A further requirement of the Trustee Act 2000 is that trustees must normally take proper advice on investment decisions.[84] The Trustee Investments Act 1961 required trustees always to take advice before making all but a very limited range of investments. This requirement has been changed by the 2000 Act. Trustees can dispense with seeking advice if they reasonably conclude that in all the circumstances it is unnecessary or inappropriate to do so.[85] For instance, the trustees may consider the sums involved to be too small, or they may already have sufficient expertise available to them through fellow trustees or employees of the trust. However, for trustees to dispense with advice requires a conscious decision on the part of the trustees. It would be a breach of trust for trustees to fail to seek advice through oversight, even in a situation where advice was unneces-

---

[80] [1994] 1 All ER 118.
[81] These criteria are not new. They first appeared in the Trustee Investments Act 1961, s 6(1).
[82] Trustee Act 2000, s 4(3).        [83] Trustee Act 2000, s 4(1).
[84] Trustee Act 2000, s 5(1) (new investments) and s 5(2) (review of existing investments).
[85] Trustee Act 2000, s 5(3).

sary, although it is hardly likely in such an instance that any action for breach of trust would be pursued.

'Proper advice' is defined by the Act as 'the advice of a person who is reasonably believed by the trustee to be qualified to give it by his ability in and practical experience of financial and other matters relating to the proposed investment'.[86] The trustees are not obliged to follow the advice which they are given. Their obligation is only to obtain and consider it. They would not be discharging their function if they followed the advice without applying their own minds to it,[87] but equally it would be unwise to disregard the advice without good reason.[88]

## (4) Financial considerations

The object of investment is to produce a financial return from trust assets. The trustees are expected to adopt an investment strategy which has regard to the nature and purpose of the trust. This will affect whether the trustees should be maximising income, maximising capital growth, or balancing the two, and what balance there should be between risk and return. Where there are both income and capital beneficiaries, the trustees must seek a balance between high income and capital growth. It has been said that in all but the smallest fund, this will require a high proportion of the trust assets to be invested in company shares.[89] Where an income beneficiary would not be liable to tax on certain kinds of investment, however, this also should be considered by the trustees and would legitimately influence their investment decisions.[90] Because trustees must consider how to achieve a fair and proper balance between all the different classes of beneficiary, they will not be in breach of trust simply because their investment policy has resulted in greater erosion of the real capital value of the trust fund than would have been the case with a different investment strategy. Trustees are not under an absolute obligation to ensure that the capital value of the fund is maintained.[91] For instance, in *Nestlé v National Westminster Bank plc*[92] the heiress to the chocolate family fortune complained that, had the trustees invested differently, she could have received an inheritance four times greater than was the case. The Court of Appeal held that, although there had been errors of judgement on the part of the trustees, including a misunderstanding of the width of their powers of investment, and a failure to review the investments sufficiently often, there had not been any breach of trust resulting in liability to the heiress. It was also said that even if trustees had acted for the wrong reasons, they would still not be liable if their decision could be justified objectively by other, valid, reasons.[93] The case illustrates the difficulty which

---

[86] Trustee Act 2000, s 5(4). A person acting as an investment adviser must be authorised under s19 Financial Services and Markets Act 2000.

[87] See *Jones v AMP Perpetual Trustee Co NZ Ltd* [1994] 1 NZLR 690.

[88] See *Cowan v Scargill* [1984] 2 All ER 750 at 762 (discussed below).

[89] *Nestlé v National Westminster Bank plc* [1994] 1 All ER 118.

[90] *Nestlé v National Westminster Bank plc* [1994] 1 All ER 118.

[91] See *Jones v AMP Perpetual Trustee Co NZ Ltd* [1994] 1 NZLR 690.     [92] [1993] 1 WLR 1260.

[93] See also *Cowan v Scargill* [1984] 2 All ER 750.

the beneficiary faces in seeking to prove a breach of trust in relation to investment by trustees.[94]

## (5) Ethical considerations[95]

The extent to which trustees may have regard to ethical considerations was explored by Megarry V-C in *Cowan v Scargill*.[96] The National Coal Board pension fund was controlled by both management-appointed and union-appointed trustees. The union-appointed trustees objected to a proposed annual investment plan unless it adopted the policy of withdrawing from overseas investment and from investment in industries in competition with coal. This led to a direct clash between the union-appointed trustees, led by Arthur Scargill—the National Union of Mineworkers General Secretary and a veteran of industrial disputes—and the other trustees, leading to the hearing in court. Eschewing the use of a barrister, Arthur Scargill chose to represent himself in court. Sir Robert Megarry held that the action of the union trustees was unreasonable. The duty of trustees was to optimise the benefits which the beneficiaries would receive. In the vast majority of cases, financial considerations would prevail. There could be rare cases where this was not so.

'Plainly the present case is not one of this rare type of case. Subject to such matters, under a trust for the provision of financial benefits, the paramount duty of the trustees is to provide the greatest financial benefits for the present and future beneficiaries.'[97]

Trustees were not to be deflected from this duty to the beneficiaries merely because the policy of seeking the best financial returns conflicted with their personal opinions.

'Trustees may have strongly held social or political views. They may be firmly opposed to any investment in South Africa[98] or other countries, or they may object to any form of investment in companies concerned with alcohol, tobacco, armaments or other controversial products. In the conduct of their own affairs, of course, they are free to abstain from making any such investments. Yet under a trust, if investments of this type would be more beneficial to the beneficiaries than other investments, the trustees must not refrain from making the investments by reason of the views that they hold.'[99]

It was not enough that they were honest and sincere in their cause. The general standard of conduct required of trustees demanded more.

'Honesty and sincerity are not the same as prudence and reasonableness. Some of the most sincere people are the most unreasonable; and Mr Scargill told me that he had met quite a few of them. Accordingly, although a trustee who takes advice on investments is not bound to accept and act on that advice, he is not entitled to reject it merely because he sincerely

---

[94] See also *Jones v AMP Perpetual Trustee Co NZ Ltd* [1994] 1 NZLR 690, where trustees were held not liable for retaining shares in a falling market.

[95] See Lord Nicholls, 'Trustees and their broader community; where duty, morality and ethics converge' (1995) 9 TLI 71; (1992) 55 MLR 587 (Luxton)

[96] [1984] 2 All ER 750.      [97] [1984] 2 All ER 750 at 762.

[98] This remark was made before the end of apartheid.      [99] [1984] 2 All ER 750 at 761.

disagrees with it, unless in addition to being sincere he is acting as an ordinary prudent man would act.'[100]

One of the cases which Megarry V-C thought might be exceptional and where ethical or moral considerations could legitimately sway the decision of the trustees was where all the beneficiaries were adults who shared the same moral values who 'might well consider that it was far better to receive less than to receive more money from what they consider to be evil and tainted sources'.[101]

Such a situation arose in *Harries v Church Comrs for England*,[102] which concerned the investment policy of the body controlling the investment funds of the Church of England. The revenue from these funds, together with contributions from parishes, was used to maintain churches and to meet the stipends of the clergy. The Church Commissioners operated an ethical investment policy, under which they chose not to invest in businesses which might be offensive to the Church, including armaments, gambling, tobacco, newspapers and South Africa.[103] Sir Donald Nicholls V-C considered that these exclusions were appropriate and justified for a religious charity whose members were likely to support such a policy, but he rejected a call by the Bishop of Oxford for a much wider group of exclusions. Even though ethical considerations were legitimate for the Church Commissioners, provided that they left an adequate width of investment, where charity trustees held assets for investments, their principal duty was to seek the maximum return consistent with commercial prudence. If they did not do this, they would not be discharging their duty of furthering the purposes of the trust. If the Church Commissioners used their funds otherwise than for investment, how in the long term could they ensure that the clergy were paid and the Church's buildings maintained?

The danger of blind adherence to a political policy without considering the interests of the beneficiaries is illustrated by *Martin v Edinburgh District Council*,[104] where Lord Murray held that trustees were in breach of trust for pursuing a policy of disinvestment in South Africa prior to the end of apartheid 'without considering expressly whether it was in the best interests of the beneficiaries and without obtaining professional advice'. Trustees would only be entitled to adopt a blind policy of this nature where it was expressly permitted or required by the instrument establishing the trust.

## (6) Periodic review of investments

The duty of trustees in relation to investment is a continuing one. They do not discharge their duty merely by giving proper consideration to the appropriateness of an investment at the time it is made or the asset acquired. They must also consider periodically whether the balance of investment is correct, and whether individual investments are retained. This responsibility is specifically imposed by the Trustee Act 2000, s 4(2), but would in any event apply on general trust principles. In *Bartlett v Barclays Bank Trust Co Ltd (No 2)*[105] trustees held a controlling shareholding in a property investment

---

[100] [1984] 2 All ER 750 at 762.   [101] [1984] 2 All ER 750 at 761.
[102] [1993] 2 All ER 300. See [1992] Conv 115 (Nobles).
[103] A very similar list of exclusions to those given by Megarry V-C in the passage cited above, p 624.
[104] 1988 SLT 329.   [105] [1980] 1 All ER 139.

company. It was held that they were in breach of trust in failing to review the activities of the company and in permitting the directors to engage in a speculative and inadvisable development scheme.

Provided that the trustees have given proper consideration to whether an investment should be retained, they will not be liable because it can be seen, with the benefit of hindsight, that they made a mistake. In *Re Chapman*[106] the trustees had properly invested in mortgages of agricultural land. The value of the land fell, placing the security of the mortgages at risk. The trustees nevertheless decided to retain them, hoping that the market would improve. Instead, land values fell still further. The Court of Appeal refused to find the trustees liable.

'There is no rule of law which compels the court to hold that an honest trustee is liable to make good loss sustained by retaining an authorised security in a falling market, if he did so honestly and prudently, in the belief that it was the best course to take in the interests of all parties. Trustees acting honesty, with ordinary prudence and within the limits of their trust, are not liable for mere errors of judgment.'[107]

It is believed that this will continue to be the case notwithstanding the omission by the Trustee Act 2000 of s 4 of the Trustee Act 1925, under which trustees were not to be held liable for breach of trust by reason only of continuing to hold an investment which has ceased to be authorised either by the trust instrument or by the general law.

## (7) Special rules for particular investments

### (a) Mortgages of land

In the nineteenth century, before building societies played the major role which they did in the first half of the twentieth century in financing the purchase of residential property, private mortgages were very common and a frequent type of investment for trustees. Modern conditions of inflation, and the ready availability of commercial funds from the building societies and banks make this form of investment much less popular for trustees, although it still occurs to a limited extent, and is envisaged by the Trustee Act 2000, s 3(3). Special rules used to be provided by the Trustee Act 1925, s 8 for trustees lending on mortgage. These rules protected trustees against liability for advancing too high a proportion of the value of the property if they lent no more than two-thirds of a valuation made by an independent surveyor or valuer. These rules have now been removed by the Trustee Act 2000 so that the question of whether a mortgage transaction was prudent and appropriate must be decided without recourse to any such guidelines.[108] It is not considered advisable for trustees to lend on the security of anything other than a first legal mortgage,[109] although it is possible that a loan on a properly registered second mortgage would not, in itself, be a breach of trust. The trust instrument may, of course, permit a loan on a second mortgage, or even an unsecured loan.

---

[106] [1896] 2 Ch 763.
[107] See also *Jones v AMP Perpetual Trustee Co NZ Ltd* [1994] 1 NZLR 690.
[108] See *Re Solomon* [1912] 1 Ch 261; *Re Dive* [1909] 1 Ch 328; *Shaw v Cates* [1909] 1 Ch 389.
[109] See *Chapman v Browne* [1902] 1 Ch 785, CA.

## (b) Controlling interest in a company

Trustees who have a shareholding which gives them a controlling interest in a company are expected to take more than a passive interest in the affairs of the company. They should either ensure that one of the trustees is a member of the board (if not an executive director) or, at the very least, they should keep a watching brief lest the company seeks to act in an improvident way.[110]

## (8) Special considerations for charity investment

The Charities Act 1993, s 24 authorises the court or the Charity Commissioners to approve schemes for the establishment of common investment funds where trustees wish to pool the investments of two or more charitable trusts.[111] There should normally be some connection between the participating charities. Section 25 of the Act contains provisions for the establishment of common deposit schemes for charities.

# 8 Delegation of investment decisions

## (1) Authority to delegate investment management

Investment decisions and their execution are so complex that in many cases it will not be appropriate for trustees to manage the investment of trust funds themselves. This is more likely to be the case where large funds are under investment, or where the trustees do not themselves have investment experience. In such cases, the management of the investments might be delegated by the trustees. For instance, as the case of *Cowan v Scargill*[112] illustrated, the National Coal Board pension fund, one of the largest such funds, was not invested directly by the trustees. Instead, it was managed by professional financial advisers on behalf of the trustees, subject to the approval of an annual investment plan giving direction which was prepared by the advisers for consideration by the board of trustees.

Prior to the Trustee Act 2000 it was not clear whether the delegation of investment management was permitted by general law, so that it was considered wise for a trust instrument expressly to authorise the delegation by trustees of investment management to professional portfolio managers.[113] The Pensions Act 1995 contains provisions enabling trustees to delegate certain of their functions concerning investment subject to a number of safeguards.[114] The Trustee Act 2000 has now extended to all trustees the explicit authority to delegate investment management.[115] This implements a proposal

---

[110] *Re Lucking's Will Trusts* [1967] 3 All ER 726.
[111] For a common investment scheme approved under previous legislation see *Re University of London Charitable Trusts* [1964] Ch 282.
[112] [1985] Ch 270.     [113] See (1990) 106 LQR 88 (Hayton).     [114] Pensions Act 1995, s 34.
[115] The powers granted in the Trustee Act 2000 do not, therefore, apply to pension trusts.

made by the Law Commission.[116] The change has been achieved by authorising trustees to delegate any function relating to the trust, with certain exceptions.[117] Investment management is one of the functions which can be delegated.[118]

## (2) Conditions

Where trustees do choose to delegate investment management, or *asset management,* to use the wider phrase used in the Trustee Act 2000, certain conditions must be satisfied. These conditions probably apply even in cases where this is done under an express power in the trust instrument rather than under the statutory power to delegate. First, the delegation to the agent must be in writing, or must be evidenced in writing.[119] Secondly, the trustees must produce a policy statement in writing, or evidenced in writing, which gives guidance as to how the asset management functions should be exercised.[120] This policy statement should, for instance, indicate what level of risk the trustees consider acceptable, what balance is being sought between income and capital growth, and whether there are any types of investment that should be avoided. Third, the contract with the agent must require the agent to comply with the current policy statement given by the trustees.[121] Finally, the trustees must exercise reasonable care in the selection of the agent, since the selection of agents is one of the functions to which the statutory duty of care applies.[122]

In addition, the Act specifically imposes on the agent the obligation to have regard to the standard investment criteria, described above.[123] However, the agent is dispensed from the need to obtain advice if the agent is the sort of person from whom it would have been proper to seek advice.[124] Thus, where, as will often be the case, the trustees delegate investment management to a professional fund manager (such as an investment bank), the agent does not have to seek advice from other professionals. Professional fund managers will sometimes insist on a limitation of liability, or permission to act where there may be a potential conflict of interest, and the trustees are authorised by the Act to agree to such terms if it is reasonably necessary to do so.[125] The appointment of an agent will be valid notwithstanding any failure by the trustees to comply with the limits relating to the appointment,[126] but the trustees will thereby expose themselves to potential liability for breach of trust.

---

[116] Law Commission Report No 260 (1999), *Trustees Powers and Duties.* This proposal adopts a recommendation of the Trust Law Revision Committee.

[117] Trustee Act 2000, s 11.

[118] Investment functions are included in the list of functions which can be delegated by trustees of a charitable trust, and are not excluded from the general authority given to other trustees.

[119] Trustee Act 2000, s 15(1).     [120] Trustee Act 2000, s 15(2)(a).

[121] Trustee Act 2000, s 15(2)(b).     [122] Trustee Act 2000, s 1 and Sch 1, para 3.

[123] Trustee Act 2000, s 13(1).     [124] Trustee Act 2000, s 13(2).

[125] Trustee Act 2000, s 14(2) and (3).     [126] Trustee Act 2000, s 24.

## (3) Supervision and review

Just as the functions of trustees are not completed once they have made the initial investments of the trust fund, so their functions are not completed where they have appointed an agent. The trustees must keep the arrangement under review,[127] they must intervene if necessary by giving directions or terminating the agency,[128] and they must review and revise the investment policy statement.[129]

## (4) Related functions

In addition to the delegation of investment management, trustees may also appoint nominees to act on their behalf, custodians to hold documents relating to trust assets or the trust assets themselves, and custodian trustees in whom the trust assets are vested. These arrangements are described in Chapter 20.

---

[127] Trustee Act 2000, s 22(1).    [128] Trustee Act 2000, s 22(1) and (4).
[129] Trustee Act 2000, s 22(2).

# 23

# Collective assets and investments

## 1 Introduction

We have already seen how the conceptual creation of equity, the fund, enables a benefi-ciary's wealth to be considered to have an identity which is distinct from the assets in which that wealth may at any particular time have been invested. The fund can also be used to enable a number of individuals to pool their assets, the advantage being that the combined assets of the investors can be used more effectively than the separate assets of the individuals. The group can take advantage of economies of scale, thereby reducing dealing and other management costs. It may also, because of the size of the combined fund, benefit from a wider spread of investments, both in order through diversification to reduce the risk of a narrower range of investment, and also through a balanced portfolio, to take greater risk with parts of the fund which would be unacceptable without the balance of another part which is being employed more conservatively.

The issues which arise from the establishment of groups for collective investment are similar to those which are raised by other forms of association. Not every association, whether for investment or other purposes, requires the assistance of equity. There are some forms of association which can enjoy the benefits of collective investment in other ways. These are considered briefly below. Most rely upon the association acquiring some form of independent legal status. The great advantage of equity's fund and trust concepts is that the members of the group can enjoy the benefits of scale which have been described above and yet retain the security of direct beneficial ownership of the investments.

Most collective investment vehicles are now subject to regulation under the Financial Services and Markets Act 2000. The provisions of this Act are intended to safeguard the public, and a detailed consideration of the rules set out by the Act falls outside the scope of this book.

## 2 Incorporation of a company

One way in which a group of like-minded individuals can form an association is to establish a company which is incorporated under the Companies Acts.[1] The company

---

[1] Companies Act 1985.

then has an independent legal status, but is owned by the subscribing shareholders who can control the company by using the votes which most shareholdings confer. They will participate in the annual profits which the company makes through a distribution of dividends, and can benefit in any capital appreciation of the company's assets either through special distributions, or through a winding-up, dissolution and distribution of the company's assets, or, more commonly, through the sale of their shareholding to a willing purchaser. Equity plays no special role in such arrangements although, before the introduction of the modern company through legislation, lawyers used the trust concept as the basis for the creation of the joint stock company,[2] the predecessor of the modern limited liability company. However, although the directors of the company are no longer to be considered to be trustees for the shareholders,[3] they are treated as being in a fiduciary position, and in this respect are subject to some of the obligations and liabilities which apply to trustees.

Most companies are established for trading purposes. They enable a group of individuals to combine their assets for this purpose by subscribing for shareholdings in the company, and to share in the benefits which derive from the profits made by the trading operations. The shareholdings in most large companies are bought and sold on the stock exchange. It is therefore possible for investors who have little interest in the trading activities of the company to buy its shares in the hope of making profits through capital appreciation and the income derived from dividend payments (the annual or twice yearly distribution of profits to shareholders). The trading operations in which the company is involved may relate to the provision of financial services, so it is also possible for third parties to enter into contracts with the company to obtain these financial services. For instance, most banks and insurance companies are incorporated under the Companies Acts. A person putting money on deposit with a bank is in fact entering into a contract under which ownership of that money is transferred to the bank and the depositor retains no proprietary interest in it. However, in return the bank contractually undertakes to repay a different but equivalent sum with interest. The law of trusts has no part to play in such a transaction, unless there is some special term in the contract which gives the depositor a proprietary interest.

# 3 Investment trusts

Despite the misleading nomenclature, these are not trusts at all, but companies quoted on the stock exchange whose purpose is not to trade directly, but instead to purchase shares in manufacturing or service companies. The word 'investment' is descriptive of the purpose of the corporation; the word 'trust' reflects the way in which joint stock

---

[2] The Joint Stock Companies Act 1856 allowed joint stock companies to be established with limited liability.

[3] See *Saloman v A Saloman & Co Ltd* [1897] AC 22. Compare the earlier case of *Smith v Anderson* (1880) 15 Ch D 247 in which the directors of a joint stock company were considered to be in the position of trustees for the members of the company.

companies were originally established, prior to modern company legislation permitting the statutory incorporation of companies.

The original investments of an investment trust are acquired through the sale of shares for which subscriptions are invited from the public. Further investments may be acquired through subsequent issues of shares, and from profits made from capital growth and the retention of dividends payable out of the company's own shareholdings, and which have not been fully distributed. The company may also be empowered to borrow, being able to use its shareholdings as security or collateral. Provided that the return from the investments made with the borrowings is greater than the cost of the loan, the investment trust company will increase its underlying asset value. The market capitalisation of the company (ie the total value of the shares in the company) will normally tend to follow the underlying asset value of the company, but the market capitalisation will sometimes exceed the value of the company (when its shares are said to trade at a premium), and will sometimes fall below it (when the shares are said to trade at a discount). A rise in the asset value of the company is not necessarily reflected directly in a rise in the value of the company's shares: their value is instead determined by how many investors wish to purchase them on the market, and how much they are prepared to pay.

## 4 **Open-ended investment companies**[4]

Investment trusts are closed-ended in that the company issues a fixed number of shares. If an investor who originally subscribed for those shares decides to realise his investment, he does so by selling his shareholding to a new investor. The company does not normally buy back the shareholding. Unless the company seeks exceptional power to buy back shares, or new shares are issued to raise additional capital, the number of shares issued remains unchanged.

Open-ended investment companies (or OEICs) operate differently. The only purpose of an OEIC is to provide a vehicle for collective investment. The company issues shares to prospective investors, and uses the funds so raised to make investments through the purchase of shares and other securities. These assets are held by a depositary (effectively a custodian trustee) on behalf of the OEIC.[5] If, after the initial launch of the company, new investors wish to join, then this is done by issuing additional shares which are sold at the average asset value of the existing shares. The additional funds so raised are used to make additional investments. When an investor wants to realise his investment, this is done by cancelling the shares in return for payment to the investor of the average asset value per share. Of course, where the number of buyers and sellers is equal, the shares of one are in effect transferred to the other. In this respect the OEIC operates similarly to an investment trust company, but the difference is that where the number of

---

[4] See the Open-Ended Investment Companies Regulations 2001, SI 2001/1228, replacing the Open-Ended Investment Companies (Investment Companies with Variable Capital) Regulations 1996, SI 1996/2827.

[5] The Open-Ended Investment Companies Regulations 2001, SI 2001/1228, reg 5.

buyers and sellers are not in balance, the number of issued shares changes. OEICs are thus quite similar in operation to unit trusts (see below), and are indeed marketed on that basis. Although only introduced in 1996, by 2000 OEICs accounted for approximately 20% of investment through collective investment schemes, and that proportion was expected to rise.[6]

# 5 Mutual societies

English law does not automatically accord to clubs or societies a status of legal personality which is independent of the membership. Clubs, societies or other unincorporated associations operate in a similar way to partnerships. Legal actions must be brought by one member of the association on behalf of the others,[7] and legal actions are defended in a similar way.

This legal dogma produced difficulties for associations which wished to engage in commercial or quasi-commercial activities such as co-operative societies wishing to engage in retail trading, insurance companies which wished to provide insurance benefits for members,[8] credit unions which would take deposits from members and make short-term loans to depositing members at favourable rates of interest, and building societies which take longer-term deposits and loans. To overcome these difficulties, legislation was enacted which enabled these mutual associations, through a simple process of registration, to obtain limited independent legal personality, although they continued to be owned and governed by their members in accordance with their rules.[9] The legislation provided for a variety of different forms of association, for instance friendly societies set up to provide mutual insurance benefits;[10] and co-operative societies established to provide not-for-profit trading activities.[11] An example of the latter is the International Exhibition Co-operative Wine Society which was set up in 1874 to supply good wines at fair prices to its members. Additional legislation covers specialist

---

[6] HM Treasury consultation document preceding enactment of the Financial Services and Markets Act 2000 and associated regulations.

[7] See eg *Verrall v Great Yarmouth Borough Council* [1981] QB 202, CA, where an action seeking specific performance of a contract for the hire of a conference hall for the National Front was brought by the association's secretary.

[8] Often on a very small scale: mutual insurance societies were frequently established to provide funeral benefits for members. Small premiums were collected weekly, often by a representative calling door-to-door, and in return for these, the policy would pay enough on the death of a policy-holder to meet the costs of a modest funeral.

[9] See, for example, Friendly Societies Act 1896, s 49(1), which states: 'All property belonging to a registered society, whether acquired before or after the society is registered, shall vest in the trustees for the time being of the society, for the use and benefit of the society and the members thereof, and of all persons claiming through the members according to the rules of the society.'

[10] Friendly Societies Act 1829; Friendly Societies Act 1896. The current legislation is the Friendly Societies Act 1974 and the Friendly Societies Act 1992.

[11] Industrial and Provident Societies Act 1852; Industrial and Provident Societies Act 1862. See now the Industrial and Provident Societies Acts 1965 and 1978.

types of association, for instance credit unions,[12] building societies,[13] and housing associations.[14] Registration of an association as an industrial and provident society or as a friendly society was a convenient alternative to incorporation under the Companies' Acts for mutual groups, many of which remain in operation today.

Most industrial and provident or friendly societies (collectively called *mutual societies*, a phrase sometimes used in the society's name) were, in origin, local self-help organisations. In the early part of the 20th century and onwards, however, some of them expanded considerably, as is particularly evident with building societies. They expanded their operations outside their local areas, often distanced themselves in practice from their original mutual ethos, with full-time, often self-perpetuating, professional management. By retaining rather than distributing some of each year's trading profit, the society would be able to build up substantial reserves, and through the acquisition of property could control assets of considerable value. In most practical respects, some mutual societies have become indistinguishable from companies incorporated under the Companies Acts. When the society is wound up, merged with another similar society, or taken over by a company incorporated under the Companies Acts, these assets are available for distribution between the members. There is a difference, however, in the way in which members can deal with their share in the society whilst it remains in being. In most companies, the shareholder is able to sell his interest upon leaving membership, and thereby gain a benefit from the surplus and capital appreciation of the asset base which has taken place during his membership. By comparison, the member of a mutual society loses all claim to the society's assets on leaving membership, normally without receiving any payment on ceasing to be a member. This can result in windfall gains accruing to those who happen to be members at the time that a society is wound up, privatised or taken over, even though they may have been members for a very short period.

No doubt because they are endowed by statute with limited legal personality independent of the individual members, the only problems concerning the ownership or management of a mutual society's assets which have received recent judicial attention concern their dissolution, when such societies are treated in the same way as unincorporated associations.[15] Mutual societies receiving deposits or engaging in offering other financial services are subject to regulation under the Financial Services and Markets Act 2000.

The relevance of mutual societies in the present context—that of collective investment—is that many mutual societies have operated as vehicles for collective investment, albeit generally with some other social purpose. This is particularly evident with credit unions and building societies, both of which provided convenient vehicles for saving by small investors. It is also the case with many of the mutual insurance and tontine societies which have increasingly developed a range of financial services which differ little from those offered by banks or incorporated insurance companies.

---

[12] Now governed by the Credit Unions Act 1979.    [13] Building Societies Act 1986.
[14] Housing Acts 1985 and 1988.    [15] See below p 653 and Chapter 19.

# 6 Building societies

Although they now operate in a very similar way to banks,[16] building societies were originally mutual organisations established for the purpose of enabling their members to build or acquire houses for residential use. The members would pool their savings. The fund thereby created would be used to make loans on mortgage to members for house purchase. Some building societies were set up for a limited period and were dissolved once the original membership had all acquired homes. Others were established on a permanent basis, and this was reflected in the name of the society, such as the Leeds Permanent Building Society.

Some early building societies took advantage of friendly society legislation although they now have their own legislation.[17] Thus, they were able to obtain legal personality for the purpose of holding and managing property, for entering into contractual arrangements and for bringing and defending legal actions. Nevertheless, as mutual organisations, they were—and in theory remain—controlled by their members (ie qualifying depositors and borrowers) without separate shareholders. The consequence of the controlling interest of the membership can be seen in what happens when it is proposed that a building society should merge with another, or be taken over by a public limited company. The members have to give their approval through a ballot to the proposed merger or takeover. Any payment made to the society will be distributed between the society's borrowers and depositors. The possibility of making a windfall gain is so attractive that some investors are attracted to a society as 'carpetbaggers'. Some societies have taken measures to inhibit such activity by a variety of means, in some cases by requiring new depositors to agree to donate to charity any windfall gains they receive if the society converts to company status or is sold.

It has been argued that building societies have an unfair advantage over banks: although they are accountable to their members in a similar way to that in which banks are accountable to their shareholders, the building societies do not have to pay a rent on the capital which they employ, although the banks pay a dividend to their shareholders. Despite this advantage, it has been said, most building societies do not offer their members preferential rates on loans or deposits. Some building societies have met this objection by paying a bonus to their members. Many of the remaining building societies are therefore taking a more aggressive approach to protecting their mutual status.

# 7 Endowment policies

The purchase of an endowment policy represents an indirect way of investing in the stock market and other assets. In return for either a single lump sum premium, or periodical premium payments, an insurance company offers a combination of life

---

[16] The Abbey National and the Halifax are former building societies which have been incorporated as banks with public limited company status.

[17] Building Societies Act 1986.

insurance and investment. In return for the life insurance element, the insurance company guarantees a lump sum payment if the policy-holder dies during a specified period. If the policy-holder does not die during that period, then the insurance company instead makes a lump sum payment to the policy-holder. This could either be a predetermined fixed sum (normally the same as that guaranteed on death), or a variable sum ('with profits') depending on the success of the investments made by the insurance company. With this latter form, each year the insurance company distributes a proportion of its profits between qualifying policy-holders. The policy-holders are not entitled to withdraw their allocated share of profits until their policy matures at the end of the specified period or earlier death. The allocated profits are therefore retained by the insurance company for this period and are available for it to lend at interest, to use for the purchase of property, or to invest on the stock market. These investments, in turn, will help to increase the insurance company's profits, which are again available for distribution between eligible policy-holders. Because it is almost certain that if an insurance company is conducting its affairs properly it will make profits each year, it is possible in 'low-cost' endowments to provide insurance benefits which are greater than the guaranteed lump sum payable if the policy matures at its full term. It is anticipated with this kind of arrangement that, by the time the policy matures, the profits allocated to the policy will bring the final capital sum up to at least the level of the insurance benefits payable if the investor dies before the policy matures.

For many years, endowment policies were a popular way of repaying mortgages on residential property. When income tax relief was available on life insurance premiums, holders of endowment policies were also able to benefit from this tax relief. Endowment policies have now lost in popularity to unit trust arrangements.

# 8  Unit trusts

A unit trust is a complex form of equitable co-ownership.[18] An initial fund is established through subscriptions from investors. The fund thus established is used for the purchase of investments by the fund manager, the investments being held by a custodian trustee. The fund is valued, and on the basis of this valuation, notionally divided into units of equal value. Each investor is allocated a number of units proportionate to the amount which that investor originally subscribed. Although it is possible for a unit trust to contain no power of reinvestment,[19] most unit trusts permit the fund manager to alter the portfolio of investments, although often within special limits.

The fund would not normally be closed for further investment. Further subscriptions normally remain possible: for each new unit acquired the investor must pay a sum equivalent to the current unit value. The fund manager will, by means of such subscriptions, acquire further funds for investment. Equally, subscribers will normally be able to

---

[18]  See *Costa & Duppe Properties Ltd v Duppe* [1986] VR 90.
[19]  See *Re Municipal and General Securities Co Ltd's Trust* [1950] Ch 212.

withdraw from the fund without the whole fund being closed.[20] The investor wishing to realise his investment will either sell his units, via the fund manager, to someone else wishing to enter the fund, or the fund manager will realise sufficient of the collective pool of investments to meet the cost of repaying the investor the current unit value of the units which are being cashed in. Provision for such dealings will be made in the trust deed.

The fund manager covers the costs of operating the unit trust by fixing the price of units available for purchase at a higher level than the price which will be given to an investor surrendering units. This difference between the 'offer' price[21] and the 'bid' price[22] is known as the 'turn'. The fund manager and fund trustee also make an annual charge for the administration of the investment fund, usually by taking a percentage of the capital value. All of these matters are regulated by the trust deed governing the unit trust.

The rights of investors in a unit trust are a mix of contract and trust. The investment itself is made pursuant to a contract which defines the basis upon which units are bought and sold. It is common for the contract to state that the investor acquires no proprietary right in the underlying assets in which investments are made. The basis of the scheme, however, as its name suggests, is a trust, and this is confirmed by the Financial Services and Markets Act 2000.[23] The effect of the contractual term is that no individual participant in a unit trust can call for the vesting in him or her of the property held in the scheme. Although the matter is not free from doubt, however, it is likely that the effect of the trust on which the assets are held is that all of the participants, when combined together, command the whole beneficial interest in the fund. In theory they could therefore call for the termination of the fund and the vesting of ownership in themselves as beneficiaries under the principle in *Saunders v Vautier*.[24] More importantly, in the event of the insolvency of the fund manager, the assets of the fund should not be available to meet any general debts of the insolvent manager. Moreover, the fund manager is likely to be subject to all the obligations of a trustee in relation to the discharge of the manager's functions, including the obligation to comply with the duty of care in making investment decisions.[25]

# 9 Investment club

With this form of arrangement, a number of investors group into a syndicate. Each member of the syndicate subscribes an agreed amount each month or other agreed period. The members of the syndicate meet periodically and agree which investment will be acquired from the accumulated subscribed funds. The investment is purchased

---

[20] See Financial Services and Markets Act 2000, s 243.  [21] The price fixed for the purchase of units.
[22] The price for which units may be cashed in.  [23] S 237.
[24] (1841) 4 Beav 115. See also *Re AEG Unit Trust Managers Ltd's Deed* [1957] Ch 415.
[25] It is not possible for this liability to be excluded in the case of authorised unit trusts (ie unit trusts for which subscribers are solicited by means of advertisement): Financial Services and Markets Act 2000 s253.

in the name of one or more of the syndicate who holds it upon trust for the others. The club rules provide what is to happen if the members of the syndicate fail to reach agreement, if they wish to wind the club up, or if one of them wishes to resign. An investment club is one type of unincorporated association, which will be considered later in this chapter. As described in Chapter 5, a syndicate purchasing tickets in the National Lottery works in a similar way. The organiser collects subscriptions from the members, and uses them to purchase tickets on behalf of the members. Any winnings will be held in trust for division between the members.

# 10  Pension funds[26] and provision for retirement

## (1)  Methods of providing for retirement

In addition to the retirement pensions which are offered by the state and funded out of taxation,[27] individuals may make their own arrangements. They may do this either individually or through an occupational pension scheme, or through a combination of both. A very simple way of making individual provision is to save until retirement, and either to draw income and capital from the accumulated fund after retirement, or to use it to purchase an annuity. This is an arrangement with an insurance company under which the insurance company, in return for a lump sum, agrees to make periodic or annual[28] payments at an agreed rate, either fixed or with provision for annual increases to allow for inflation, for the remainder of the annuitant's life. The arrangement is purely contractual. On the basis of actuarial information and advice, and a knowledge of current investment market conditions and returns, the insurance company can make a fairly accurate calculation of the cost of making the payments. In some cases, of course, the annuitant will live longer than expected, which will cost the insurance company more than the sum it received. If the insurance company has made its calculations correctly, however, these costs will be balanced by other cases in which the annuitant dies prematurely. The effect of an annuity is therefore to pass the risks of mortality on the erosion of the capital to the insurance company.

## (2)  Types of pension scheme

### (a)  Personal pensions

Instead of saving independently to raise the capital to purchase an annuity, most people planning to provide an income for retirement will do so through an arrangement

---

[26] See generally *Report of the Pension Law Review Committee*, Chairman Professor Roy Goode (1993 Cm 2342) (The Goode Report); Nobles, *Pensions, Employment and the Law* (1993); Inglis-Jones, *The Law of Occupational Pension Schemes* (1989); Ellison, *Pensions Law and Practice* (1987); Hayton, 'Pension Trusts and Traditional Turst: Drastically Different Species of Trusts' [2005] Conv 229.

[27] Including National Insurance contributions.     [28] Hence the term 'annuity'.

with an insurance company. One reason for doing this is that very substantial tax relief is available for qualifying pension savings plans. The investor gains the benefit of this tax relief, but is obliged to use the savings made through the plan exclusively for the purpose of providing benefits on retirement. Part may be taken in the form of a capital sum, but the remainder must be used for the purchase of an annuity. Recent changes in legislation have made it possible for the person retiring to defer the purchase of an annuity for a short period, since low interest rates at the time an annuity is purchased significantly reduce the periodical payments which insurance companies are prepared to offer. The savings vehicles which are used in pension savings schemes are either endowment policies, or, increasingly frequently, unit trust schemes. Apart from the fact that the proceeds of the savings plan must be used to purchase retirement benefits, there is no material difference between an endowment or unit trust scheme used as a part of a pension plan and an endowment or unit trust used in any other way.

### (b) Occupational pensions

Occupational pensions were first introduced in the late nineteenth century, but became very much more important over the course of the twentieth century. It has been calculated that in 1991, 10.7 million employees in the United Kingdom were active members of occupational pension schemes, representing 57% of working men and 37% of working women.[29] A variety of forms were used for the introduction of such schemes. Some were, and in the public sector remain, unfunded. The pensions are then payable out of the annual revenue of the enterprise. The overwhelming majority of private occupational pension schemes, however, are funded.

### (c) Funded schemes

Under a funded occupational pension scheme the employee and the employer generally both make contributions to an investment fund. That fund is then used to finance the payment of the pensions when they fall due. Although other means of providing for pensions are possible, the overwhelming majority of private sector pension funds are held by trustees under irrevocable trusts. One substantial reason for this is that the tax privileges accorded to approved schemes are available only to pension schemes established in this way.[30] Funded schemes themselves divide into two main groups: money purchase schemes and defined benefit schemes.[31] There can in addition be special arrangements such as an 'executive pension plan' for a single employee.[32]

*(i) Money purchase schemes.* With a money purchase scheme, although the employee's and the employer's contributions are normally invested through a single investment fund, a separate individual account is kept for each member to record

---

[29] The Goode Report, para 2.2.4.

[30] Income and Corporation Taxes Act 1988, s 592, re-enacting a provision first found in Finance Act 1921.

[31] The Goode Report, paras 2.2.11–2.2.23. Some hybrid schemes have features of both defined-benefit and money-purchase.

[32] As in *Brooks v Brooks* [1996] AC 375. In this case the House of Lords considered that special features of this bespoke pension plan meant that it constituted a marriage settlement which could be varied on divorce.

the value of that member's share of the total value of the fund. On an employee's retirement the whole[33] of the capital value of the employee's portion of the fund (ie the sum standing to his credit in the individual account) is used to provide pension benefits on his retirement. Part may be used to provide a lump sum, and the remainder is generally used to purchase an annuity from an insurance company. A money purchase scheme is therefore like an independently arranged pension savings plan used to purchase retirement benefits. The principal differences are, first, that the employer contributes at a rate which is agreed with the employee (or the employees generally) and, secondly, that (depending upon the size of the scheme) the collective investment fund may be maintained as a separate investment fund for the particular occupational scheme, rather than being pooled with funds from other sources and managed as a general fund by an insurance company (as would be the case with most personal pension schemes). Because the rate contributed by the employer is fixed, money purchase schemes are sometimes called defined contribution schemes.

Money purchase schemes are on the whole less attractive to employees than defined benefit schemes and represent a minority of occupational pension schemes,[34] although money purchase schemes may be more advantageous to the early leaver: that is, the employee who leaves the scheme before having worked until retirement age. The original pension plan for university staff—the Federated Superannuation Scheme for Universities (FSSU)—was a money purchase plan in which participating employees were able to make choices themselves about the way in which their contributions would be invested. The scheme failed to make adequate provision for inflation, and was therefore superseded by a defined benefits scheme (USS) introduced in the early 1970s.

Changes to pensions rules made by the Pensions Act 1995 mean that money purchase schemes are increasing in popularity. Unlike defined benefit schemes, there is no statutory obligation on an employer to increase contributions if investment returns prove to be lower than had been anticipated when contribution levels had previously been agreed. The significant decline in the value of shares in the period to 2002 has accelerated the move by employers to close defined benefit schemes and to move into defined contribution or money purchase schemes.

*(ii) Defined benefit schemes.* These represent the majority of managed occupational pension funds.[35] Most such schemes offer a pension which is related to the employee's salary in the last few years preceding leaving the scheme or retirement, and for this reason are called 'final salary' schemes. Pensions are usually paid at the rate of one-eightieth or one-sixtieth of final salary for each year of pensionable service. Such schemes are generally funded by means of each employee contributing a fixed percentage of salary with the employer making up whatever sum an actuary calculates is

---

[33] The sum available might be affected by the need for the pension trustees to make provision for certain guaranteed benefits, for example to a surviving spouse or dependants.

[34] According to figures supplied by the National Association of Pension Funds Annual survey of Pension Schemes 1993 Table 66, only 11% of occupational pension schemes were money-purchase funded schemes.

[35] Some 89% of funded occupational schemes fell into this category, according to the National Association of Pension Funds Annual Survey of Pension Schemes 1993, Table 66. The proportion is likely to have fallen because of trends by employers to close such schemes because of the uncertain costs of funding them.

necessary to ensure that the scheme has sufficient assets to meet its liabilities.[36] The liabilities of the fund will depend, amongst other variables, upon the number of employees, their likelihood of retiring at a salary higher than their current earnings, their life expectancy, the benefits offered to surviving spouses and other dependants, and the provision made by the scheme for increases in pensions to allow for inflation.[37] The assets needed to cover these liabilities will depend, amongst other variables, upon the assumptions which can be made about future returns from investment. Although actuaries can make estimates of these liabilities and necessary assets, the science is not an exact one, and it cannot be predicted accurately what contributions are required simply on the basis of current earnings. The calculations also make assumptions about future investment returns which may turn out to be too conservative or too optimistic. Actuarial reviews will therefore sometimes indicate that a pension fund is in deficit (i.e. that the liabilities exceed the available assets) and sometimes that it is in surplus (i.e. that the assets exceed the liabilities). In the former case, contributions will have to be increased if the fund is to continue to be able to meet its obligations. The Pensions Act 1995 contains detailed rules imposing an obligation on the trustees of defined benefit pension schemes to conduct regular actuarial reviews and on employers to make good any serious deficiencies which these reveal.[38] Where the actuarial review reveals that the fund has more assets than are required to meet its liabilities, an issue may arise as to who should benefit from the superfluity of assets. It is in relation to this last issue that the legal debate concerning occupational pensions has been at its fiercest. We return to this question later.

## (3) Trusts and pension schemes

### (a) The use of trusts in pension schemes

The use of the trust as a means of providing for pensions enables the fund assets to be kept separate from the assets and liabilities of the employer. This offers some security in the event of the insolvency of the employer. The trust also means that where benefits are payable to someone other than the employee who is a member of the scheme, such as the employee's surviving spouse, the beneficiary has an enforceable claim which will not be barred by an absence of privity of contract. As explained above, it also means that the scheme can qualify for tax benefits. Where the scheme is a defined benefit scheme, it might be wondered whether the trust vehicle is necessary at all. The benefits which the members will receive are defined by the rules of the scheme: the contributions which they make, and the benefits they will receive, are fixed. A simple contract could achieve the same. As to the protection against the insolvency of the employer, this could equally be safeguarded by obtaining a guarantee from some third party, such as an insurance company or, indeed, by the contract for the provision of the pension being made directly by a third party such as an insurance company. The rights of beneficiaries

---

[36] Goode Report, para 2.2.13.    [37] The Pensions Act 1995, s 76 requires annual increases.

[38] Pensions Act 1995, ss 56–59; Occupational Pension Schemes (Minimum Funding Requirement and Actuarial Valuations) Regulations 1996, SI 1996/1536.

who are strangers to the contract could be protected by simple legislation, such as that which applies to non-contracting parties who are covered by a certificate of motor insurance, and is now conferred generally by the Contracts (Rights of Third Parties) Act 1999. The value of the trust as a means of securing the independence of pension funds from employers fell into question following the Maxwell affair, where it was discovered that Robert Maxwell had misappropriated large sums of money forming part of the Mirror Newspaper Group pension scheme. Even where there are employee representatives on the board of trustees, they may be influenced in the decisions which they make by the presence of employer trustees who have the power to hire and fire.[39]

There are special features of the trusts employed in occupational pension schemes.[40] The size of pension funds can be very considerable.[41] Pension schemes are not established by way of the generosity of a settlor, but as the result of contractual contributions which both the employer and the employee are contractually obliged to make. The beneficiaries therefore help to finance their own benefits: 'Even in a non-contributory scheme, the employer's payments are not bounty. They are part of the consideration for the services of the employee.'[42] The trustees are frequently interested in a pension fund as employers or employees,[43] rather than being wholly independent as they typically would be in a family trust. Under the Pensions Act 2004 at least one-third of the total number of trustees must be trustees appointed by the members of the scheme (member-nominated trustees).[44] The membership is not fixed, but open-ended. There is generally a wide power to alter the terms of the trust[45] and it is not uncommon for the pension fund to be established by an interim trust deed which is then replaced by a subsequent definitive trust instrument. It has been held that such a definitive trust deed operates retrospectively from the date of the establishment of the scheme,[46] but this has been described as 'controversial', and not applicable to alter vested rights.[47]

The special features of pension schemes could be expected to produce differences in the way in which trust law applies, and this is evident in the special statutory rules[48] and

---

[39] See House of Commons Paper (1991–1992) No 61, *The Operation of Pension Funds*, para 48 (cited by Moffat, *Trusts Law Text and Materials* (3rd edn, 1999), p 507).

[40] See generally [1992] 6 Trust Law International 119 (Lord Browne-Wilkinson).

[41] Although there is very considerable variation. Less than 0.1% of all pension schemes accounted for over 20% of pension scheme members, while 75% of the total number of schemes, with twelve members or fewer accounted for just 3% of all scheme members: see Goode Report, para 2.2.6.

[42] *McDonald v Horn* [1995] 1 All ER 961 at 973, per Hoffmann LJ.

[43] There is no reason why the trustees should not also be beneficiaries of the scheme: *Edge v Pensions Ombudsman* [1998] 2 All ER 547.

[44] Pensions Act 2004, s 241. The Act makes it clear (in s 39) that such trustees are not affected by the ordinary rule that trustees cannot put themselves in a position where their duties and personal interest conflict merely because they may benefit as scheme members from the exercise of a power conferred on the trustees; see also *Edge v Pensions Ombudsman* [1998] 2 All ER 547 and *National Grid Co plc v Laws* [1997] PLR 157 (compare *Re Drexel Burnham Lambert UK Pension Plan* [1995] 1 WLR 32 on the position before the Act).

[45] Pensions Act 1995, s 67 limits the extent to which such powers can be exercised. Ss 68 and 69 provide for pension schemes to be modified to implement the requirements of the Act.

[46] *Re Imperial Foods Ltd Pension Scheme* [1986] 2 All ER 802 Walton J, Pen Schemes 23: Feb 2000.

[47] *Trustee Corpn Ltd v Nadir* [2000] EWHC Ch 41 (Lawrence Collins J).

[48] Including regulation by the statutory Occupational Pensions Regulatory Authority established by the Pensions Act 1995, s 1. The Authority can prohibit a person from acting as a trustee, impose financial penalties and restrain the misuse of assets: ss 3–11. The Act also created the role of Pensions Ombudsman.

in some of the emerging case law,[49] although there are judges who have said that the administration of pension trusts should not be treated differently from the administration of other trusts. Speaking of investment, for instance, Sir Robert Megarry said:

'I can see no reason for holding that different principles apply to pension fund trusts from those which apply to other trusts. Of course, there are many provisions in pension schemes which are not to be found in private trusts, and to these the general law of trusts will be subordinated. But subject to that, I think that the trusts of pension funds are subject to the same rules as other trusts.'[50]

Similarly, in *Re Trusts of Scientific Pension Plan* Ratee J, faced with a question as to the interpretation of a clause in a pension scheme, said:

'I accept that, as was said in *Mettoy Pension Trustees Ltd v Evans*,[51] "the court's approach to the construction of documents relating to a pension scheme should be practical and purposive, rather than detached and literal", though I also accept that the ordinary principles of trust law apply to the terms of such a scheme once so construed.'

The note, sounded in this statement, that a slightly different approach might be required from the ordinary for pension scheme deeds, was echoed in *Stevens v Bell*,[52] where Lady Justice Arden, giving the sole opinion of the Court of Appeal on a complex issue of interpretation of the Airways Pension Scheme, said:

'A pension scheme should be construed so to give a reasonable and practical effect to the scheme. The administration of a pension fund is a complex matter and it seems to me that it would be crying for the moon to expect the draftsman to have legislated exhaustively for every eventuality.'[53]

The Goode Committee, established to review the framework for occupational pension schemes in the wake of the Maxwell affair, favoured the retention of trust law as the basis for providing and regulating such pensions.[54] The committee observed that 'trust law is indeed of considerable antiquity, but it has shown a remarkable ability to adapt itself to modern commercial requirements'.[55] The value of trust law lay in segregating assets for the protection of the beneficiaries; in providing a mechanism for the collective representation and protection of members of a group of people linked by a common interest; and in the embodiment of highly developed concepts of fiduciary responsibility. The committee therefore concluded:

'We therefore endorse the view expressed in the great weight of evidence submitted to us that trust law in itself is broadly satisfactory and should continue to provide the foundation for interests, rights and duties arising in relation to pension schemes. But, some of the principles of trust law require modification in their application to pensions.'[56]

The committee recommended the introduction of a Pensions Act to place curbs on the

---

[49] See eg *Mihlenstedt v Barclays Bank plc* [1989] IRLR 522 and *Mettoy Pension Trustees Ltd v Evans* [1991] 2 All ER 513.
[50] In *Cowan v Scargill* [1985] Ch 270.　　[51] [1991] 2 All ER 513 at 537.　　[52] [2002] EWCA 672.
[53] [2002] EWCA 672 at para 28.　　[54] The Goode Report, para 4.1.14.
[55] The Goode Report, para 4.1.9.　　[56] The Goode Report, para 4.1.14.

permissible content of scheme rules, to secure the solvency of schemes, the monitoring of pension funds, and other matters of regulation. Some of the recommendations of the committee were implemented by the Pensions Act 1995, which has now been amended and supplemented by the provisions of the Pensions Act 2004, which introduces a new Pensions Regulator. The regulation of pensions funds under this new regime is discussed below.

### (b) Special duty of pension fund trustees

Most occupational pension schemes confer a wide measure of discretion upon the trustees. In accordance with ordinary principles of trust law, any powers which are held by a trustee will prima facie be held by them in a fiduciary capacity.[57] The trustees must therefore consider the best interests of the beneficiaries and exercise the power impartially and in accordance with its purpose.[58] The power will not be validly exercised if it has been exercised for an improper purpose, or as a result of illegitimate threats.[59] In *Re Courage Group's Pension Schemes* the Courage brewing group of companies had been taken over by Hanson Trust plc as part of the purchase of the Imperial Group. Hanson sought to be substituted as principal employer under the Courage Group scheme so that it could retain a surplus of approximately £70m on a sale of the Courage Group to Elders IXL Ltd, the brewers of Castlemaine XXXX. This surplus could then be used to fund pensions for other Hanson employees. Hanson sought to do this under a power in the pension trust deed which permitted variations which did not affect the main purpose of the fund. Millet J held that the power in the trust deed could be exercised only with the consent of the trustees,[60] and also that it would be improper for the trustees to give consent since the exercise of the power in the present circumstances would be for a purpose inconsistent for that for which it was conferred.[61] The trustees were under an obligation to protect the interests of the employed members, pensioners and deferred pensioners.[62] They would not be doing so if they permitted a variation in the trusts by the unilateral decision of a takeover raider. The employees, while having no legal right to any pension fund surpluses were entitled to have them dealt with by consultation and negotiation.

The Pensions Act 2004 requires pension trustees to have high level of knowledge and understanding. Under s 247 they must be conversant with the trust deed and the rules of the scheme, any statement of investment principles maintained by the trust, the statement of funding principles prepared for the trust and any other document recording policy for the time being adopted by the trustees relating to the administration of

---

[57] *Re Hay's Settlement Trusts* [1981] 3 All ER 786.

[58] See Chapter 22 for a consideration on the exercise of powers by trustees.

[59] *Hillsdown Holdings plc v Pensions Ombudsman* [1997] 1 All ER 862.

[60] See also *Stannard v Fisons Pension Trust Ltd* [1992] IRLR 27, where the Court of Appeal held that transfer payments made in respect of a group of employees transferring to another scheme could not be determined solely by the scheme actuary, but had to be approved as fair by the trustees. See also *Re Imperial Food Ltd's Pension Scheme* [1986] 1 WLR 717.

[61] See also *Lock v Westpac Banking Corpn* (1991) 25 NSWLR 593.

[62] Deferred pensioners are members of a pension scheme who leave it before retiring age, but are entitled under the rules of the scheme to receive a pension upon reaching normal retirement age. It is a requirement of legislation that retirement schemes should contain such a provision.

the scheme generally.[63] They are also required to have a knowledge and understanding of the law relating to pensions and trusts and the principles relating to the funding of occupational pension schemes and the investment of the assets of such schemes.[64] Corporate trustees of pension schemes are required to secure that each individual who exercises any function which the company has as a trustee of the scheme is conversant with these matters.[65]

### (c) Duty to act in good faith

An attempt by Hanson Trust plc to capture a pension fund surplus again arose in *Imperial Group Pension Trust Ltd v Imperial Tobacco Ltd.*[66] The Imperial Group was taken over by Hanson plc. The Imperial Group pension scheme was very substantially in surplus. Hanson offered members the chance to transfer to a new pension scheme with enhanced guarantees against inflation, but under which the surplus could be transferred to Hanson instead of being used to augment pensions. Hanson did not appear to be prepared to consent to an amendment to the Imperial Group scheme to provide similar guarantees. Browne-Wilkinson V-C considered that it was a reasonable inference, although not a proven one, that Hanson was withholding its consent to the augmentation amendment under the Imperial scheme in order to seek control of the pension fund surplus by persuading members to transfer to the other scheme. In his view, if that were the case, Hanson would be withholding consent for a collateral purpose and would be acting unlawfully. Although in his view the power of the company to consent to variations in the scheme was not a fiduciary power, nor was it subject to an implied test of reasonableness, nevertheless pension schemes fell to be judged against the background of an employment relationship. As a matter of trust law:

'. . . the pension trust deed and rules themselves are to be taken as being impliedly subject to the limitation that the rights and powers of the company can only be exercised in accordance with the implied obligation of good faith . . . the company's right to give or withhold its consent to an amendment . . . is subject to the implied obligation that the right shall not be exercised so as to destroy or seriously damage the relationship of confidence and trust between the company and its employees and former employees.'[67]

There is a similar contractual obligation upon a company to act in good faith in regard to pension matters affecting employees and former employees.[68]

### (d) Certain powers fiduciary

Browne-Wilkinson V-C held in the *Imperial Group* case that the power which the employer held was not fiduciary or subject to a test of reasonableness because such a limitation was not necessary to give business efficacy to the scheme. The question of implied limitations on powers held by employers must, however, be looked at in relation to each power individually. In *Mettoy Pension Trustees Ltd v Evans* a provision in a pension trust provided that any surplus on dissolution 'may at the absolute discretion

---

[63] S 247(3).     [64] S 247 (4).     [65] S 248(3).     [66] [1991] 2 All ER 597.
[67] [1991] 2 All ER 597 at 606.
[68] *Mihlenstedt v Barclays Bank plc* [1989] IRLR 522; *National Grid plc v Mayes* [2001] 2 All ER 417, HL.

of the employer be applied to secure further benefits . . . and any further balance thereafter remaining' shall be paid to the employer. The company went into compulsory winding-up on insolvency. Warner J held that the power just set out was a fiduciary power. If the power was a beneficial one which the company was free to exercise or not as it chose, then it was meaningless. If there had been no power, and the company had been the beneficial owner under the rules of any surplus, then it would still have been able to augment the benefits of members if it chose. The company had therefore to be under some obligation in relation to the power if the rule was to have any consequence. Secondly, the members of the pension scheme were contributories, not volunteers. The power to augment pensions out of any surplus was something which they had contracted for; it was also unrealistic to suggest that their contributions had not played at least some role in the generation of the surplus.

Having concluded that the power was fiduciary, Warner J held that it would not vest in a receiver under a debenture issued by the company since it did not form part of the company's beneficial assets. Neither could it be exercised or released by the liquidator whose duties were to have regard primarily to the interests of the creditors and contributories of the company, which would create a conflict of interest between those persons and the beneficiaries under the pension scheme to whom the person exercising the power was also to have regard. Nor could the power be exercised by the directors of the company, since they lost all their powers on the appointment of the liquidator. Warner J was therefore led to the conclusion that in the absence of any other person to exercise the fiduciary power, it was for the court to do so.[69]

It has been suggested by one commentator that the recent cases concerning the exercise by trustees and employers of powers relating to the application of a pension fund surplus are swayed not just by ordinary principles of trust law, but also by the deeper-lying consideration that such surpluses should not be left at the mercy of company creditors and take-over predators.[70] Where an employer becomes insolvent, the position of scheme members is strengthened by the requirement under the Pensions Act 1995 that an independent trustee be appointed[71] and only this trustee can exercise any fiduciary powers of the employer and any discretionary powers of the trustees under the scheme.[72]

### (e) Investment of pension funds

The principles applicable to the investment of pension funds were considered in the previous chapter. Trustees of pensions funds benefit from two advantages: they have the same power to make investments as if they were beneficially entitled to the funds,[73] and they have no vicarious liability for the default of a qualified fund manager[74] to whom they delegate investment decisions[75] In *Cowan v Scargill* Sir Robert Megarry V-C

---

[69] This was one of the options identified for the exercise of discretionary trusts by Lord Wilberforce in *McPhail v Doulton* [1970] 2 All ER 228 at 247. See Chapter 16.

[70] (1991) 107 LQR 214 Gardner.       [71] Pensions Act 1995, ss 22–24.       [72] Pensions Act 1995, s 25.

[73] Pensions Act 1995, s 34(1).

[74] Ie a fund manager authorised to conduct investment business under the Financial Services Act 1986.

[75] Pensions Act 1995, s 34(2). Similar provisions now apply to the majority of trusts under the Trustee Act 2000. Where the trusts assets include investments a fund manager must be appointed: Pensions Act 1995, s 47.

opined that the investment of pension funds was governed by the ordinary principles of trust law, although bearing in mind that the size of some pension funds he emphasised the need for diversification and expert advice. In his view, despite indications in an earlier case,[76] it would normally be improper for trustees to invest in the employer's own business since it would not be fulfilling the duty of the trustees to have regard to the best financial interests of the beneficiaries. Only where a clause in the trust deed or rules permitted investment in the parent company on favourable terms would it be legitimate to show this kind of preference to the employer.[77]

### (f) Information

Members of pension schemes, like the beneficiaries under any trust, have the right to be given information about the administration of the trust.[78] Statutory regulations give flesh to that obligation so far as accounts and other financial information is concerned.[79] David Hayton has recently argued that the common law should be developed, in recognition of the differences between pension trusts and conventional private trusts, so as to impose a duty on pension trustees to give beneficiaries reasons for their decisions.[80]

### (g) Liability of trustees

It is common for the rules of pension schemes to confer exceptionally broad discretions on the trustees, and also to contain provisions exempting the trustees from liability for breaches of trust except those which have been committed knowingly or in bad faith. The Pensions Act 1995 now clarifies the position in relation to the delegation of investment decisions,[81] and prevents trustees from being exempt from liability for failure to take reasonable care. However, issues can easily arise concerning other functions of the trustees. The Goode Committee recommended that there should be a statutory statement of the responsibilities of pension trustees with an irreducible minimum core.[82] Even where discretions are conferred on trustees in the widest possible terms, the court will retain its jurisdiction to review the exercise of those discretions.[83]

## (4) Pension fund surpluses

### (a) Entitlement to a surplus while the scheme continues[84]

The question of entitlement to pension fund surpluses has arisen as an incidental issue in the cases which have just been described. The notional surplus in a pension fund is, as has already been indicated, the amount by which the assets of the fund exceed the

---

[76] *Evans v London Cooperative Society* reported in Ellison, *Private Occupational Pension Schemes* (1979), p 356.

[77] Regulations under the Pension Schemes Act 1993 currently restrict self-investment by pension funds to 5% of the fund's resources.

[78] *Re Londonderry's Settlement* [1965] Ch 918, CA discussed below, p 705.

[79] Pensions Act 1995, s 41 and Occupational Pension Schemes (Disclosure of Information) Regulations 1996, SI 1996/1655.

[80] [2005] Conv 229. See below p 705 for an explanation of the current absence of any obligation on trustees to provide their beneficiaries with reasons for their decisions.

[81] Ss 33 and 34.     [82] The Goode Report, paras 4.5.55–4.5.56.

[83] *See Boe v Alexander* (1987) 41 DLR (4th) 520.     [84] See (1994) 14 LS 345–363 (Nobles).

liabilities. While the fund continues, there is always the possibility that some of the assumptions made by the actuary were mistaken. The salaries of scheme members might rise faster than the actuary has allowed, or the return on the fund's investments may be poorer than projected. Even a small difference in the assumptions in these matters can turn an apparently large actuarial surplus into a significant actual deficit. This phenomenon was seen when returns from investments fell in the 1990s[85] and again in the early years of the 21st century. In the case of one pension fund,[86] it was estimated that a reduction of 0.5% in the assumed rate of future dividend growth would reduce the actuarial surplus from £460m to £293m, a reduction of more than 35%. There has already been litigation which has involved the appropriate basis for calculating the solvency of a pension fund.[87] It is likely that there will be greater emphasis on this issue in future litigation.

The calculation of surplus is an imprecise matter. But if it is agreed that there is a surplus, who is entitled to it? The Inland Revenue requires that a surplus should be eliminated within a set period[88] but it imposes no requirement as to how the surplus should be reduced. That is a matter for the rules of the trust or for any approved amendment.[89] The rules may permit augmentation of pension benefits, a suspension or reduction of the contributions payable by the employer and sometimes also of the employee, or a cash payment to the employer. In most instances, more than one of these options will be available, although in every case concerning the application of a surplus, the answer will depend upon the proper interpretation of the scheme rules.[90] For instance, in *British Coal Corpn v British Coal Staff Superannuation Scheme Trustees Ltd*[91] a question arose relating to a substantial actuarial surplus which had been built up within the coal industry pension scheme. Under the rules of the scheme, a surplus was to be applied, first, to provide full indexation for any pensions payable;[92] secondly, to reduce the contributions of the employer until the employer was reimbursed for any payments which had been made in respect of actuarial deficiencies in the fund; thirdly, to meet any increase in pensions to reflect the cost of living in the next calendar year; and, finally, after retaining whatever reserve was considered desirable, to apply any remaining balance in equal parts for the benefit of members (by reducing contributions or increasing benefits) and for the benefit of the employer. The scheme contained a provision which permitted alterations to the rules, although a proviso prohibited any alteration 'making any of the moneys of the Scheme payable to any of the Employers'.

---

[85]  See the Goode Report, para 2.4.19.

[86]  The LRT Pension Fund: see *London Regional Transport Pension Fund Trustee Co Ltd v Hatt* [1993] PLR 227.

[87]  See *Stannard v Fisons Pension Trust Ltd* [1992] IRLR 27, CA.

[88]  The period allowed for the elimination of the surplus depends upon the means used to reduce it. For an account of the rules and recommendations for change see the Goode Report, paras 4.3.20–4.3.37.

[89]  In addition to any express power of amendment conferred by the trust rules which may be subject to approval or consultation under the principles explained above, certain modifications may be made by order by the Occupational Pensions Board which has a statutory power in this regard: Social Security Act 1973, s 64(1A) (as amended by Social Security Act 1986, Sch 10, para 3).

[90]  Subject to limits imposed by the Pensions Act 1995, s 37.

[91]  [1995] 1 All ER 912.

[92]  In other words, to increase pensions fully in line with any increase in the cost of living.

As part of its plans to reduce its workforce, the Coal Corporation had entered into an agreement with the pension fund trustees to increase the benefits of employees made redundant by offering enhanced pensions. The Corporation agreed to fund these additional benefits by paying the additional costs to the pension fund trustees in install-ments over a ten-year period. Before all the payments had been made, a revaluation of the fund showed that there was a surplus. The Corporation claimed to be able to set off the outstanding balance of the additional payments it had agreed to make against the part of the actuarial surplus which was to be applied to the employer. Vinelott J held that this was prohibited by the rules of the scheme. The Corporation had agreed to pay the trustees a lump sum. That could not be repaid to the Corporation under the rules. It made no difference that the sum was payable in installments, since relieving the Corporation from liability in respect of an installment would have the same effect as a repayment of an installment already made. An almost identical issue arose in *National Grid Co plc v Mayes*[93] where the House of Lords was asked to rule whether the National Grid and International Power could use part of a pension fund surplus to meet the cost of supporting enhanced early retirement pensions which the companies had already agreed to pay by installments, although they had not completed making those install-ments. The House of Lords held that Vinelott J had come to the wrong conclusion in the *British Coal* case. The purpose of the prohibition on payments to the employers was to meet Inland Revenue restrictions which forbade the repayment of money contri-buted to the pension scheme, since those contributions had benefited from taxation privileges. That fiscal consideration did not apply to payments which, although agreed to be made, had not at that stage been paid. Moreover, it was not in dispute that the employer could take advantage of a surplus to reduce future contributions, if this was permitted by the rules of the scheme. There was no practical difference between reducing the standard rate of future contributions and cancelling installment payments which had previously been agreed. Both actions had the same effect of reducing the total value of the fund.

In the *National Grid* case, the House of Lords considered that, if it was necessary, the rules of the pension scheme could be amended to permit the payment of the surplus to the employers since the rules conferred a power to make amendments, and did not forbid the use of the power to allocate the surplus in these circumstances. We have already seen that the employer and trustees have at least a duty to act in good faith in relation to any such powers. But there is no principle that any surplus automatically belongs either to the employer or to the scheme members. Knott J in *London Regional Transport Pension Fund Trustee Co Ltd v Hatt*[94] has said that it is 'quite impossible, as well as simplistic, to try to identify the owner or owners of a surplus'.

The argument for the employees and pensioners is that an occupational pension represents deferred wages. An employee who was not in receipt of an occupational pension would expect higher pay if he was to be required to make his own provision for retirement. An occupational pension is therefore an earned reward for employment.[95] The European Court of Justice has held that occupational pensions are to be regarded

---

[93] [2001] WLR 864.      [94] [1993] PLR 227.

[95] See *Parry v Cleaver* [1970] AC 1 at 16, per Lord Reid; *McDonald v Horn* [1995] 1 All ER 961 at 973.

as deferred pay within the equal pay provisions of EU law.[96] Against this, it may be argued for the employers that the employees under a defined benefit scheme receive all to which they are entitled in return for their contributions if the defined benefits are paid. In most schemes, once the employee has made a fixed contribution, it is the employer who undertakes to meet the balance of the cost. If the employer bears the risk of having to increase contributions if the fund falls into deficit, then it is just that the employer should, by compensation, reap the benefit of any accrued surplus. An alternative but similar argument in a balance of cost scheme is that a surplus represents a mistaken overpayment by the employer which should be refunded.

In every case but one, which will shortly be considered,[97] the courts have refused to fall sharply on one side of the divide or the other. For instance, in *Mettoy*, Warner J refused to allow the employer to claim beneficial ownership of the fund surplus, since this would be inconsistent with a power to augment pensions. But in the *Courage* case, Millet J emphasised that the members 'have no legal right to participate in the surpluses'. There is, in any event, the difficulty that since most pension schemes make provision for widows, widowers and children or other dependants, some of the potential beneficiaries remain unidentifiable until the pension scheme has run its full course. The true position with pension schemes may therefore be that the search for an 'owner' of the fund, in the sense that is possible with fixed trusts, is illusory. Just as with discretionary trusts,[98] or with the administration of estates,[99] it may be that the real claim of both employers and members of a pension scheme is not to ownership, but to the due administration of the scheme and trust. In that context, it is likely that there will be further importation of principles from employment law and perhaps also of public and company law where the courts have long sought to defend legitimate expectations and minority rights.

## (b) Entitlement to pension fund surplus on liquidation of employer

When an employer ceases business, any associated pension scheme is likely to be closed to new members unless it either formed part of an industry-wide or group-wide scheme, or the whole scheme is transferred to another continuing scheme. When a pension fund closes, it becomes much easier to quantify any surplus, since some of the variables affecting the calculation are eliminated. A number of possibilities arise. The scheme might be merged with another, transferring all assets and liabilities. Alternatively, the scheme could continue in existence until all pension entitlements are discharged in full. Or the trustees could use the assets of the fund to purchase cover from an insurance company for the pensions which have or may become payable. In the latter two cases, if the scheme is solvent, a surplus will arise for distribution. One possibility is that the surplus is property without an owner which should pass as bona vacantia to the Crown. The courts are generally reluctant to choose this as a solution.[100]

---

[96]  *Barber v Guardian Royal Exchange Insurance Group* [1991] 1 QB 344, ECJ.
[97]  *Davis v Richards and Wallington Industries Ltd* [1991] 2 All ER 563.
[98]  See *McPhail v Doulton* [1971] AC 424, HL.
[99]  *Stamp Duties Comr (Queensland) v Livingston* [1965] AC 694, PC.
[100]  *Jones v Williams* (15 March 1988, unreported) (Knox J), cited by Scott J in *Davis v Richard and Wallington Industries Ltd* [1991] 2 All ER 563; *Air Jamaica Ltd v Charlton* [1999] 1 WLR 1399.

The question then remains as to how the balance should be divided between the only two other groups of potential claimant, the employers and the scheme members. In *Davis v Richards and Wallington Industries Ltd*,[101] Scott J chose to adopt a resulting trust analysis in allocating the surplus of a pension scheme being wound up and where, on one of the assumptions which he had to consider, no express rule had provided for that eventuality. The pension fund had been created by contributions from both employers and employees. In the absence of some term in the trust deed or rules excluding a resulting trust,[102] any surplus should revert to them as contributors.[103] The employees had received all the benefits for which they had contracted, although that was not conclusive against retaining an interest under resulting trust. However, it was unlikely that funds deriving from the employees themselves would have been sufficient to finance the payment of the pensions. Their contributions, Scott J said, could therefore be seen as exhausted. The surplus had therefore been generated by contributions from the employer who, with hindsight, had contributed more than was necessary under the balance of cost provisions in the scheme. Moreover, it would probably be unworkable to seek to apportion a surplus fairly and equitably among the various classes of member, and, in any event, further payments to some members might exceed Inland Revenue limits. The whole of the surplus was therefore held upon trust for the employers.

The decision of Scott J in this case does not fit well with the tenor of most other decisions, which seek to draw a balance between the interests of employers and scheme members. It may also be based on a misunderstanding of the current approach to the allocation of funds on the winding up of benevolent funds.[104] The decision has been criticised by Lord Millet in *Air Jamaica Ltd v Charlton* where the Privy Council took the view that a surplus resulted just as much from the contributions of the employees as they did from the contributions of the employer. In the *Air Jamaica* case the employees had not received all the benefits they anticipated because certain provisions of the pension trust were void for perpetuity.[105] This was therefore no bar to a resulting trust in their favour, nor was it a bar to a resulting trust that it might confer benefits on the employees which exceeded the limits allowed by tax law. So far as the employers were concerned, an express term in the pension deed that no moneys contributed by the company 'shall in any circumstances be repayable to the company' equally did not bar a resulting trust in favour of the employer, since the resulting trust arose outside or *dehors* the pension scheme. The Privy Council therefore held that the surplus was held on resulting trust for the employees and the employer in proportion to the ratio of contributions, which happened to be equal proportions.

---

[101] [1991] 2 All ER 563. See also Chapter 19.

[102] As in the decision of Foster J in *Re ABC Television Pension Scheme* [1989] PLR 21 to which he referred.

[103] Compare *Re Gillingham Bus Disaster Fund* [1958] Ch 300 and *Re West Sussex Constabulary's Widows, Children and Benevolent (1930) Fund Trusts* [1971] Ch 1, discussed above.

[104] See the subsequent decision on this matter of Warner J in *Re Bucks Constabulary Widows' and Orphans' Fund Friendly Society (No 2)* [1979] 1 WLR 936, discussed below in relation to unincorporated associations.

[105] The Pensions Schemes Act 1993 s 163 exempts qualifying approved occupational schemes from the rule against perpetutities. There was no such exemption for the pension scheme in the *Air Jamaica* case.

## (5) Enforcement of rights by members

Employees, former employees and pensioners are all beneficiaries under the trust deed in a pension scheme and therefore have the rights of any beneficiary to bring actions for breach of trust or in relation to the administration of the trust. The costs of the litigation can be substantial,[106] with little direct benefit to an individual plaintiff. Plaintiffs might be assisted in bringing an action by a trade union, and there is also the possibility of the court ordering that the costs of a hearing should be borne out of the pension fund assets whatever the outcome at trial.[107] Members of a pension scheme may also take complaints to the Pensions Ombudsman, who has statutory powers to deal with complaints concerning occupational and personal pension schemes.[108] The Pensions Ombudsman has substantial authority to resolve disputes, subject to appeal on points of law to the High Court.[109] Advice is also available through an independent conciliation agency, the Occupational Pensions Advisory Service. It should not be forgotten that in some cases a member of a pension scheme who has been given careless advice or has suffered in some other way by the negligence of a financial adviser might have a claim in negligence or other rights conferred by the Financial Services and Markets Act 2000.

## (6) Regulation of pension funds

### (a) The Pensions Regulator

The Pensions Act 2004 has created a new body to regulate pension funds, the Pensions Regulator.[110] The Pensions Regulator replaces the Occupational Pensions Regulatory Authority set up by the Pensions Act 1995. The key objectives of the Pensions Regulator are set out in s 5 and include the protection of the benefits of the members of personal and occupational pension schemes, reducing the risk that such pension schemes may be under-funded or misappropriated by fraud, and promoting and improving understanding of the good administration of work-based pension schemes. To this end the Pensions Regulator has the statutory power to prohibit a person from serving as a pension trustee if it is 'satisfied that he is not a fit and proper person to be a trustee of the scheme,'[111] and may impose financial penalties on trustees who breach their statutory duties.[112] The Regulator can order a scheme to be wound up so as to protect the interests of the members,[113] and may issue a freezing order pending consideration of winding up if there is 'an immediate risk to the interests of members under the scheme or the assets of the scheme'.[114] The Regulator must also ensure that pension schemes are adequately funded so that they are able to meet their liabilities. Every scheme must meet

---

[106] Moffat, *Trusts Law Text and Materials* (3rd edn, 1999), p 535 provides examples.

[107] See *McDonald v Horn* [1995] 1 All ER 961.

[108] Pension Schemes Act 1993, ss 146–151; Pensions Act 1995, s 157.

[109] For an example of an appeal against a decision of the Pensions Ombudsman see *Newham London Borough Council v Skingle* [2002] 3 All ER 287.

[110] Pensions Act 2004, s 1.

[111] Ibid, s 33(1).      [112] Pensions Act 1995, s 10.      [113] Ibid, s 11.

[114] Pensions Act 2004, s 23.

the 'statutory funding objective', which requires the fund to have 'sufficient and appropriate assets to cover its technical provisions,'[115] meaning 'the amount required on an actuarial calculation, to make provision for the scheme's liabilities.'[116] The trustees and managers of the fund must prepare, and from time to time review, a 'written statement of funding principles' which will state their policy for securing that the funding objective is met.[117] An actuarial valuation of the fund must be obtained at least annually,[118] and the actuary must certify whether the funding objective has been met.[119] If the funding objective has not been met the trustees must prepare and implement a 'recovery plan' which sets out 'the steps to be taken to meet the statutory funding objective.'[120] If the trustees fail to prepare and implement a recovery plan the Regulator may require increased contributions to be made to the fund to ensure that the funding objective is met.[121] A scheme which cannot be rescued may be wound up by the Regulator.[122]

### (b) The Pension Protection Fund

The Pensions Act 2004 also establishes a statutory Pension Protection Fund[123] to compensate the members of occupational pension schemes who suffer as a result of fraud,[124] or because the company to which they relate becomes insolvent and the assets of the pension fund are insufficient to meets its liabilities.[125] The Pension Protection Fund is funded by a risk-based protection levy imposed on defined benefit occupational pension scheme by the Pension Protection Fund Board.[126]

## 11 Clubs and societies

### (1) Types of clubs and societies

English law, as has already been observed,[127] does not accord automatically an independent status to clubs, societies or other unincorporated associations. The question which therefore arises is how a society which has no legal status as such can hold or manage property. As so often in relation to the management of property, equity has sought to supply the answer. It is desirable first, however, to distinguish four different kinds of club or society.

### (a) Proprietary clubs

A proprietary club is privately owned by an individual or company. The owner permits members to use the facilities in return for membership and other fees. A hotel with leisure facilities which permits members of the public to use the swimming pool and exercise rooms in return for an annual fee, describing those subscribing in terms such as

---

115 Ibid, s 222(1).    116 Ibid, s 222(2).    117 Ibid, s 223.    118 Ibid, s 224.
119 Ibid, s 225.    120 Ibid, s 226.    121 Ibid, s 231.    122 Ibid, s 154.
123 Ibid, s 107.    124 Ibid, s 182.    125 Ibid, ss 126, 127 and 131.
126 Ibid, ss 173 and 174.    127 See above, section 5 (p 633).

members of the 'Park Hotel Health Club' would be a club of this kind. Since all the club assets belong to the owner, there are no special considerations for the involvement of equity.

### (b) Incorporated clubs and societies

A variant of the proprietary club is where the proprietor which owns the club assets is a company and its shareholders are also the members of the club. In such a case, each member of the club may be required to acquire a share in the company owning the club assets at the time of being admitted as a member. On leaving membership, the member may then be required to surrender the share. In this way, only members of the club are shareholders and through their shareholdings, they own and control the club assets, although it is the company which will be treated as owner for such legal purposes as bringing and defending legal actions. On the dissolution of the club, any club assets will be distributed in accordance with company law.

### (c) Members' club

Another type of club is a members' club. The club assets are not owned by a company or individual, whether associated with the membership or not. It is in this situation that the problem arises of who owns and controls the club assets. Clubs and societies belonging to this category are generally described as unincorporated associations. They are a group of individuals, bound together in some way by club rules, but without having acquired separate legal personality for the group by incorporation or in some other way such as registration as a friendly society.

### (d) Societies which are not unincorporated associations

After we have considered the theory upon which unincorporated associations legally own and manage property, we shall see that there is, in fact, a further type of association or society which cannot fit within the ordinary principles created by equity, and a further set of extraordinary principles have had to be developed to cover this situation.

## (2) The 'problem' of asset holding and management

The absence of an independent legal personality for an unincorporated association creates only a theoretical problem of asset holding and management. Most clubs and societies get along perfectly well, raising funds by subscriptions from members and by fund-raising events such as cake sales, car boot sales and other activities. They will find little difficulty in opening a bank or building society account. A problem arises only when someone leaves a legacy by will to an unincorporated association, and the next of kin or residuary beneficiary challenges the validity of the legacy; or when the association is being wound up and there is a dispute between the members; or in some similar, comparatively unusual, situation.

The courts have been prevented by precedent and English legal tradition from saying that an unincorporated association, as such, is capable of owning property. Yet were the courts to say that the association is incapable of enjoying or managing property, they would be flying in the face of reality. The courts have therefore had to invent or construct[128] a solution to the 'problem' in order to justify the fact that in practice unincorporated associations can enjoy and manage, and receive by subscription or gift, sometimes substantial funds and assets.

## (3) The purpose trust theory

It has been seen in Chapter 12 that, except in the case of charities, English law does not permit the creation of a trust which has no beneficiaries, with the exception of a few narrowly defined categories. One such exception used to apply to gifts to unincorporated associations[129] which were considered valid as gifts for the purposes of the association provided that the association was free to dispose of its assets at any time.[130] If the terms of the gift, or the rules of the association to which it was made, did not permit the association to be wound up and its assets disposed of within a period of lives in being, plus up to a further 21 years, then the disposition would be invalid for infringing the rule against perpetual trusts, otherwise known as the rule against inalienability.[131]

Judicial doubt has been expressed as to whether, even if the gift to an unincorporated association were limited to the perpetuity period, it could take effect as a gift for the purposes of the society. In *Leahy v A-G of New South Wales* Viscount Simonds expressed the firm opinion that a gift upon trust for the purposes of an unincorporated association would be invalid for want of beneficiaries. Viscount Simonds believed that the cases upholding gifts to unincorporated associations could be upheld on a different principle, namely that they were beneficial gifts to the members of the society. This analysis is considered below.

More recently, it has been suggested by Goff J in *Re Denley's Trust Deed* that a gift for non-charitable purposes would be outside the mischief of the beneficiary principle if the purposes are directly or indirectly for the benefit of an individual or individuals. This may mean that, subject to the gift being confined to the perpetuity period, a gift for the purposes of an unincorporated association which benefits the members of that association can be valid notwithstanding Viscount Simonds' observations.

## (4) Gift to members

The theory which Lord Simonds believed explained the unincorporated association cases was that they all treated a gift to an association as valid if a gift could be treated as to the present members rather than upon trust for the purposes of the society. The case before the Privy Council in *Leahy v A-G of New South Wales* concerned a gift by will of a homestead and land upon trust to whatever order of Roman Catholic nuns or Christian Brothers his executors might select. Because his executors were at liberty to

---

[128] See Hackney, *Understanding Equity and Trusts* (1987), pp 75–82.
[129] See *Re Endacott* [1960] Ch 232.
[130] *Re Drummond* [1914] 2 Ch 90; *Re Clarke* [1901] 2 Ch 110; *Re Taylor* [1940] Ch 481; *Re Price* [1943] Ch 422.
[131] *Carne v Long* (1860) 2 De GF & J 75; *Re Macaulay' Estate* [1943] Ch 435n.

select a purely contemplative order of nuns, the gift could not be treated as wholly charitable.[132] Could the gift be treated as a valid private trust in favour of a contemplative order of nuns if the executors wished to choose such a group? The Privy Council advised that it could not. The gift could not be valid as a gift for the purposes of such a group. It could therefore be upheld only if it were a gift to the members of the chosen order. In the opinion of the Privy Council, a gift to an unincorporated association was to be treated prima facie as a gift to the individual members of that association at the time of the gift so that they can together dispose of it as they think fit. On that footing, a gift to an unincorporated association would be valid.

But that interpretation of the gift was not possible in this case, and the gift was invalid in so far as a contemplative order of nuns could be selected. The testator had not made a gift to the members of a selected order, but upon trust for the order itself; the order could be numerically very large and spread over the whole world, and although the homestead had 20 rooms and there were 730 acres of land, it was unrealistic to expect this to be shared beneficially by the members of a religious order. The Privy Council believed that:

'. . . however little the testator understood the effect in law of a gift to an unincorporated body of persons by their society name, his intention was to create a trust not merely for the benefit of the existing members of the selected order but for its benefit as a continuing society and for the furtherance of its work.'

To give effect to this, the gift would have to include future as well as present members of the order. It would then fail for perpetuity. The statement by Viscount Simonds exposes one of the difficulties with the theory which he adopted. The court was obliged to frustrate the intentions of the testator because of the lack of an adequate theory to explain how a contemplative order of nuns could receive, hold, and manage assets. Yet there are contemplative orders with substantial property interests. The theory is clearly inadequate to explain this.

There are other problems. If a gift to a club or society is treated as a gift to the individual members beneficially, it enables them to deal with it collectively however they wish. But if they are tenants-in-common of the gift, each member could claim payment directly of his share, and if joint tenants, each member could do the same after an act of severance converting his interest into that of a tenant-in-common. Again, the theory does not explain how club or society assets should be dealt with when new members join or existing members resign. An existing member with a share as tenant-in-common or joint tenant of property derived from gifts to which the *Leahy* analysis applies would continue to be entitled to it even after leaving membership of the club, unless there was an assignment of the share to the continuing members, which would require writing.[133]

---

[132] See Chapter 18.
[133] The assignment of any existing equitable interest requires a written disposition: Law of Property Act 1925, s 53(1)(c). See Chapter 6.

## (5) Gift subject to the rules of the association

In *Neville Estates Ltd v Madden* Cross J put forward a refined version of the *Leahy* theory which goes some way to meet the objections. He said that a gift could be construed as:

'. . . a gift to the existing members not as joint tenants, but subject to their respective contractual rights and liabilities towards one another as members of the association. In such a case a member cannot sever his share. It will accrue to the other members on his death or resignation, even though such members include persons who became members after the gift took effect. If this is the effect of the gift, it will not now be open to objection on the ground of perpetuity or uncertainty unless there is something in its terms or circumstances or in the rules of the association which precludes the members at any given time from dividing the subject of the gift between them on the footing that they are solely entitled to it in equity.'[134]

Cross J did not need to apply the analysis to the case before him, since he was concerned with a charitable association in relation to which it is clear that property may validly be held upon trust for the purposes of the association. The analysis was, however, adopted by Brightman J in *Re Recher's Will Trusts*,[135] the case with which this theory is most frequently associated. In that case, Brightman J held that a gift by will to the London and Provincial Anti-Vivisection Society would have been valid on this interpretation if the society had still been in existence at the date of the testatrix's death. Other cases subsequently have adopted the same analysis and it is now generally accepted as the proper way in which to explain how unincorporated associations receive gifts, hold their assets, and distribute them on the winding-up of the association.[136] As Walton J said in *Re Bucks Constabulary Fund (No 2)*:[137]

'I can see no reason for thinking that this analysis is any different whether the purpose for which the members of the association associate are a social club, a sporting club, to establish a widows' and orphans' fund, to obtain a separate Parliament for Cornwall, or to further the advance of alchemy. It matters not. All the assets of the association are held in trust for its members (of course subject to the contractual claims of anybody having a valid contract with the association) save and except to the extent to which valid trusts have otherwise been declared of its property.'

The theory allows the club or society to own assets by deeming them to be vested beneficially in the members, although legal title will normally be held by some trustee, such as the treasurer, who will hold the assets upon trust to deal with them in accordance with the instructions of the committee of management;[138] but it prevents members from withdrawing their share of the assets from the society by giving paramountcy to the rules of the society which members have mutually agreed by contract to observe.[139]

---

[134] [1962] Ch 832 at 849.    [135] [1972] Ch 526.
[136] See above Chapter 19.    [137] [1979] 1 All ER 623.
[138] It is desirable that a gift by will to an unincorporated association should provide that the receipt of the treasurer or other officer is a sufficient discharge, for if this is not provided for by the rules of the society, the administrators of the estate should technically obtain the discharge by way of receipt from every member.
[139] As in *Clarke v Earl of Dunraven and Mount-Earl* [1897] AC 59.

## (6) Limits to the mutual contract theory

The mutual contract theory explained in *Neville Estates Ltd v Madden* and *Re Recher's Will Trusts* can only apply, as Cross J explained, where there is nothing in the terms of the gift or in the rules of the society which will prevent the distribution of the association's assets. If there is, then even under this analysis, any gift will fail under the rule against perpetual trusts. In *Carne v Long* a testator had made a gift of his house to the trustees of the Penzance Public Library, a subscription library. The rules of the library provided that it could not be broken up as long as ten members remained. The House of Lords held that, under the rules, the library was intended to be a perpetual institution, so that the gift could not be upheld. More recently, in *Re Grant's Will Trusts* a testator left property 'to the Labour Party Property Committee for the benefit of the Chertsey Headquarters of the Chertsey and Walton Constituency Labour Party'. Under the rules of the Constituency Labour Party, its constitution could not be altered without the consent of the National Labour Party, to which it was subordinate. Vinelott J held that the element of control by an outside body meant that the gift infringed the rule against perpetual trusts since the Constituency Party was not at liberty to dissolve itself.[140]

The theory can only apply where there is an identifiable membership who are capable (in theory) of being beneficial owners subject to the rules of membership. This presented a problem in *Conservative and Unionist Central Office v Burrell*.[141] The party was considered by the Court of Appeal to be a combination of a number of elements which could not be considered an unincorporated association because of the lack of a body of mutual rights and duties binding those elements together.

## (7) Conditions attached to gifts to unincorporated associations

There may be something in the terms of a gift rather than in the rules of an association that makes the mutual contract theory inapplicable. The theory cannot apply if the terms of the gift exclude the possibility of the members of the association taking beneficially. When this will be so was considered by Oliver J in *Re Lipinski's Will Trusts*.[142] Harry Lipinski had left his residuary estate to an unincorporated association, the Hull Judeans (Maccabi) Association, 'in memory of my late wife to be used solely in the work of constructing new buildings for the association and/or improvements to the said buildings'. The next-of-kin disputed the validity of this gift. Their counsel argued that the terms of the gift meant that the members of the association could not take beneficially, since the money had to be used for a particular purpose and because there was an intention to create a permanent endowment. Oliver J rejected the argument that the words of the gift showed an intention to create a permanent endowment: the whole

---

[140] Compare *News Group Newspapers Ltd v Society of Graphical and Allied Trades 1982* [1986] ICR 716, CA, where, although the local branch of a trade union was subordinate to the national union, it was in theory possible for the local branch to secede from the union and dissolve itself. It may be that even where there is no provision under the rules of an association for amendment and dissolution, this would be permitted by the unanimous agreement of the members: see *Universe Tankships Inc of Monrovia v International Transport Workers Federation* [1983] 1 AC 366, HL.

[141] [1982] 1 WLR 522.    [142] [1976] Ch 235.

of the money could be spent immediately. Nor did he think that the direction of Harry Lipinski as to how the money should be spent was binding on the association. The association was free within its rules to alter its constitution and to divide the whole of its assets between the members.[143] Oliver J therefore believed that there was nothing to prevent the application of the mutual contract theory. As an alternative, he considered that, even if the association was bound to apply the money for a particular purpose, on the authority of *Re Denley's Trust Deed* 'a trust which, though expressed as a purpose, was directly or indirectly for the benefit of an individual or individuals was valid provided that those individuals were ascertainable at any one time and the trust was not otherwise void for uncertainty'.[144]

The latter analysis might ensure that Harry Lipinski's bounty was used as he intended, although even in this case some of Oliver J's remarks suggest that the members of the association would be free as both trustees and beneficiaries of the gift to treat it as an absolute one.[145] In order to sustain the validity of Harry Lipinski's gift, Oliver J is thus permitting the association to disregard his directions. One wonders if Harry Lipinski would have turned in his grave at the suggestion that the members of the association would be free to divide the legacy among themselves rather than building as he requested. If he intended an absolute gift to the members, why did he seek to impose a direction as to how it was to be used?

There might be situations in which the addition of a direction in a gift to an unincorporated association could not be overcome in one of the ways suggested by Oliver J in *Re Lipinski's Will Trusts*. If a gift to an unincorporated association imposes in clear terms a trust to use that gift in a way which is neither directly nor indirectly for the benefit of the members, it would be rather more difficult to treat the gift as an absolute one to the members of the association subject to its rules, since the members would not also be beneficiaries. Even in this case, however, if the purposes of the trust were within the purposes of the society it might be possible to take the view that the direction to hold upon trust was otiose and could therefore be disregarded. There is persuasive authority that in the case of benevolent associations established for altruistic purposes the mutual contract analysis is the one which prima facie applies to the assets of the association.[146]

## (8) Associations without mutual contract status

Mention has already been made of *Conservative and Unionist Central Office v Burrell*,[147] a case which involved the tax status of the Conservative Party. If it was an

---

[143] He drew an analogy with *Re Bowes* [1896] 1 Ch 507, where it was held that a gift by will to be used for planting trees on the Wemmergill Estate could be used in any way which the landowner chose.

[144] This analysis of the gift appears to represent a return to the purpose trust theory which was rejected in *Leahy v A-G for New South Wales*.

[145] By analogy with *Re Turkington* [1937] 4 All ER 501. This appears to be an application of the rule in *Saunders v Vautier* (1841) 10 LJ Ch 354.

[146] *Re Bucks Constabulary Widows' and Orphans' Fund Friendly Society (No 2)* [1979] 1 All ER 623, where Walton J believed that nothing turned upon the status of the benevolent fund as a Friendly Society for the purpose of deciding how its property was held for the purpose of distribution on its dissolution.

[147] [1982] 1 WLR 522, CA.

unincorporated association, then the treasurer would have been liable to pay corporation tax on behalf of the association. The Court of Appeal held that the Conservative Party was not an unincorporated association because, although it was an association of individuals, it lacked a set of rules regulating its affairs and binding its members together by means of mutually enforceable rights and obligations.[148] Since the existence of such a body of rules is essential to the mutual contract analysis of property-holding by clubs and societies, the court felt obliged to offer a solution as to how the Conservative Party was legally entitled to manage its finances. In the High Court,[149] Vinelott J put forward the suggestion that a person making a donation to the party entered into a contract with the treasurer under which the latter would be in breach of contract if he failed to apply the sums received for the purposes of the party, and that the treasurer might also be under some special equitable obligation akin to that of an executor. Without commenting on these possibilities, Brightman LJ in the Court of Appeal put forward another possibility. He suggested that the contributor would confer an irrevocable mandate on the party treasurer[150] to add the donation or subscription to the general funds of the party. The contributor would have the right to prevent a misapplication of the general funds, or to have a misapplication remedied, until on ordinary accounting principles no part of the contributor's donation is represented in the general funds.

Brightman LJ acknowledged that the mandate theory could not easily support donations by will, since mandate and agency relationships can subsist only during the lifetime of the principal.[151] It would, however, be possible for a testator to authorise his personal representatives to enter into a mandate on his behalf.

The potential of the mandate theory to explain and justify gifts where there is no obvious beneficiary has yet to be fully explored or exploited. For instance, there is no reason why mandate or agency theory could not equally apply to gifts to unincorporated associations with clear rules as it does to less formally constituted groups. The mandate theory could also make a gift for purposes effective even without any ascertainable human beneficiaries.[152] The willingness of the court to put the theory forward in the *Conservative Central Office* case, even though any such theory is unlikely to have been in the mind of many Conservative Party members, is an indication of how the courts will stretch legal theory to solve a problem which legal theory has itself created.

---

[148] The Court of Appeal also suggested that an unincorporated association required a defined date upon which it had come into existence, and that members should be free to join or to leave at will. The necessity for these requirements may be doubted.

[149] [1980] 3 All ER 42.

[150] The effect of the mandate would be to make the treasurer the contributor's agent in relation to the funds transferred.

[151] See *Re Wilson* [1908] 1 Ch 839. There might also be difficulty where a new treasurer took office since the relationship between principal and agent is essentially a personal one.

[152] See Chapter 12.

# 24

# Delegation by trustees

## 1 Introduction

As a consequence of his position, a trustee enjoys powers of control and management over the trust fund. In some situations, for example where property is subject to a discretionary trust, the trustee even enjoys the discretion to choose how the trust fund should be allocated amongst the beneficiaries. The precise duties and powers that a trustee will have depend upon the express terms of the trust deed creating the trust, or those which are implied by statute. In some circumstances it will be clear that the trustee is not the appropriate person to perform all the functions required of him as trustee, perhaps because he lacks the necessary expertise. He could obviously take advice and then carry out the function, but the question arises whether he can delegate his power to an agent who can perform it for him. Traditionally, equity has been reluctant to permit delegation by trustees of their powers, but statutory powers of delegation have increasingly been available to trustees. The position for most trusts is now governed by the Trustee Act 2000 which has substantially changed the approach to delegation.

It should be noted that there are two forms of delegation. The trustees, acting together, may decide to delegate collectively a function to an agent. Alternatively, a single trustee may seek, for instance during a temporary period of absence, to assign his individual functions to a person to exercise on his behalf. This chapter looks first at collective delegation before considering individual delegation, although some elements of the discussion apply to both forms of delegation.

## 2 Delegation at common law

### (1) The general principle: no delegation of trustees' duties

Traditionally, equity took the view that a trustee had no power to delegate his powers to an agent, either individually or collectively. As the Latin maxim expresses it: *delegatus non potest delegare*. This was emphasised by Lord Langdale MR in *Turner v Corney*,[1] which involved a trust where there was an express power of delegation. He stated that:

---

[1] (1841) 5 Beav 515. See also *Robson v Flight* (1865) 4 De GJ & SM 608 at 613, per Lord Westbury LC; *Speight v Gaunt* (1883) 22 Ch D 727 at 756, per Lindley LJ.

'trustees who take on themselves the management of property for the benefit of others have no right to shift their duty on other persons; and if they employ an agent, they remain subject to responsibility toward their cestui que trust, for whom they have undertaken the duty.'

The rationale for this restriction was that the settlor had placed his confidence in the trustees he had chosen to perform the trust obligations.[2] As Lord Westbury stated in *Robson v Flight*:

'such trusts and powers are supposed to have been committed by the [settlor] to the trustees he appoints by reason of his personal confidence in their discretion, and it would be wrong to permit them to be exercised by [another].'[3]

However, in consequence of the evolution of the law, this general principle must now be replaced by the more moderate position stated by Lord Radcliffe in *Pilkington v IRC*:[4] 'the law is not that trustees cannot delegate: it is that trustees cannot delegate unless they have authority to do so'. Thus, the central question is as to the circumstances in which trustees enjoy the authority to delegate their responsibilities.

## (2) A limited entitlement to delegate

### (a) Delegation in the ordinary course of business

During the eighteenth century the courts came to accept that, in some circumstances, delegation to an agent was required for reasons of commercial practicality. In *Learoyd v Whiteley Lord Watson* therefore stated a general principle permitting trustees to delegate their functions

'. . . whilst trustees cannot delegate the execution of the trust, they may . . . avail themselves of the services of others wherever such employment is according to the usual course of business.'[5]

### (b) Scope of the right to delegate

The common law power of trustees to delegate within the ordinary course of business did not, however, entitle trustees to delegate all of their functions or duties. The right to delegate extended only in respect of their ministerial acts, in other words those which did not require an exercise of discretion on their part. Trustees were not permitted to delegate their discretions,[6] such as the selection of trust investments,[7] or the decision whether or not to sell[8] or lease[9] trust property. Thus, whilst trustees were able to

---

[2] *Speight v Gaunt* (1883) 9 App Cas 1 at 29, per Lord Fitzgerald.

[3] (1865) 4 De GJ & SM 608 at 613.        [4] [1964] AC 612, HL.

[5] (1887) 12 App Cas 727 at 734.

[6] *Speight v Gaunt* (1883) 9 App Cas 1. This limitation was recently restated in *Scott v National Trust* [1998] 2 All ER 705 at 717, per Robert Walker J.

[7] *Rowland v Witherden* (1851) 3 Mac & G 568.

[8] *Clarke v Royal Panopticon* (1857) 4 Drew 26; *Green v Whitehead* [1930] 1 Ch 38.

[9] *Robson v Flight* (1865) 4 De GJ & SM 608.

delegate the implementation of their decisions and the routine administration of the trust, they were required to continue to take all the basic decisions themselves.

## (3) Trustees' liability for the acts of their agent

The mere fact that trustees were entitled to appoint an agent, whether because such an appointment was within the ordinary course of business or for reasons of necessity, did not mean that they were free from personal liability for any loss caused by the acts of the agent. They would be personally liable for breach of trust if the agent they appointed was not appropriate, or if they failed to exercise adequate supervision, on the grounds that they had acted other than as reasonably prudent men of business.

### (a) Agent employed outside of the scope of his business

A trustee who had legitimately delegated to an agent was liable to the trust if he employed an agent to carry out functions which were outside of the scope of his ordinary business.[10] As Kay J said in *Fry v Tapson*:

'*Speight v Gaunt* did not lay down any new rule, but only illustrated a very old one, viz., that trustees acting according to the ordinary course of business, and employing agents as a prudent man of business would do on his own behalf are not liable for the default of an agent so employed. But an obvious limitation to that rule is that the agent must not be employed out of the ordinary scope of his business. If the trustee employs an agent to do that which is not the ordinary business of such an agent, and he performs that unusual task improperly, and loss is thereby occasioned, the trustee would not be exonerated.'[11]

The trustees, who were considering investing trust funds on a mortgage, had delegated the task of selecting a valuer for the land concerned to their solicitors. The solicitors recommended a London surveyor, who did not have local knowledge of the area where the land was situated,[12] and who also had a pecuniary interest in the grant of the mortgage as he would receive a commission of £75 if the mortgage was granted. He overvalued the property and the trustees lent £5,000, which was lost when the mortgagor became bankrupt. The trustees were held liable to replace this loss to the trust fund because it was out of the ordinary course of business of solicitors to appoint a valuer.

### (b) Trustees' duty to supervise agents

Trustees who appointed an agent were under a duty properly to supervise his activities. The standard of care required was that of the ordinary prudence which a man uses in his own affairs.[13] For example, in *Rowland v Witherden*[14] trustees had committed the

---

[10]  See *Re Earl of Litchfield* (1737) 1 Atk 87; *Ghost v Waller* (1846) 9 Beav 497; *Rowland v Witherden* (1851) 3 Mac & G 568; *Re Gasquoine* [1894] 1 Ch 470.

[11]  (1884) 28 Ch D 268 at 280.       [12]  See also *Budge v Gummow* (1872) 7 Ch App 719.

[13]  *Munch v Cockerell* (1840) 5 My & Cr 178; *Mendes v Guedalla* (1862) 2 John & H 259; *Speight v Gaunt* (1883) 22 Ch D 727.

[14]  (1851) 3 Mac & G 568.

management of a trust fund completely to a solicitor, who had misapplied it. The Lord Chancellor held that the trustees were liable for their failure properly to supervise the solicitor's activities:

'The short result of the case is, that the trustees, instead of themselves seeing to the investment of the trust fund, delegated that duty to their solicitor, who misapplied the money . . . The trustees were bound to satisfy themselves in some way other than by the mere assurances of their solicitor, and by payments made by him as for interests, that the money was really advanced on mortgage. But they did not even require a sight of the mortgage deed, but simply paid the money to their solicitor and implicitly relied on his integrity . . .'

Similarly, in *Fry v Tapson*[15] Kay J held that the trustees would be liable for their acceptance of the valuation 'without attempting to check it'.[16]

## 3  Trustee Act 1925: A statutory right to delegate

Prior to the Trustee Act 1925 it has been seen that trustees were only entitled to appoint an agent when this was reasonably necessary or was within the ordinary course of business. The Trustee Act 1925[17] considerably extended the powers of trustees to delegate functions to agents by dispensing with the requirement that the delegation be reasonably necessary or in the ordinary course of business. However, the powers were still relatively restrictive—for instance only ministerial functions could normally be delegated—and the provisions of the Act relating to the liability of trustees where they had delegated a function were obscure to the point of unintelligibility. The leading case on the liability of trustees who had delegated functions to an agent was *Re Vickery*,[18] but even though this was reported in 1931, questions remained about the interpretation both of the statutory provisions and of this case some 70 years later. Few doubted that the position under the Act was unsatisfactory, not least the students who were required to grapple in examinations with the problems created by the statutory provisions.

In 1982 the Law Reform Committee considered whether the scope for delegation should be widened to encompass the trustees' discretions as well as ministerial functions, but concluded that the distinction between the delegation of administrative and managerial functions and of their discretions should be maintained.[19] However, in its Consultation Paper, *Trustees' Powers and Duties*, the Law Commission suggested that the climate of opinion had changed and that trustees should be entitled to delegate the task of managing the trust property to a fund manager, who would be entitled to make investment decisions within the context of an investment policy determined by the trustees:

'We consider that there is no longer any continued justification for the existing restrictions on trustees' powers of collective delegation. The principal objection to the present law is that trustees' powers of investment and certain of their powers of management (such as the

---

[15]  (1884) 28 Ch D 268.      [16]  (1884) 28 Ch D 268 at 282.      [17]  S 23 (now repealed).

[18]  [1931] 1 Ch 572.      [19]  Law Reform Committee, 23rd report (Cmnd 8733) para 4.3.

power to sell, lease or mortgage trust property) are regarded in all respects as fiduciary. As such they must be exercised by the trustees alone and are non-delegable. This position was the product of a time when the decisions which trustees had to take were both comparatively straightforward and infrequent. However, it is increasingly unrealistic, given that many of these tasks (particularly in relation to investment) now arise regularly and often require speedy professional advice and execution. We consider that the "exigencies of business" now justify the delegation of these discretions because adherence to the present restrictions is likely to frustrate the trustees' paramount duty to act in the best interests of the trust.'[20]

Judicial notice was also taken of the difficulty caused by the inability of the trustees to delegate their discretions. In *Scott v National Trust*[21] Robert Walker J stated:

'. . . trustees may not (except in so far as they are authorised to do so) delegate the exercise of their discretions, even to experts. This sometimes creates real difficulties, especially when lay trustees have to digest and assess expert advice on a highly technical matter (to take merely one instance, the disposal of actuarial surplus in a superannuation fund).'

# 4 The current statutory framework

The Trustee Act 2000 now provides the framework for delegation by trustees. It distinguishes between two principal situations: delegation by charity trustees, and delegation by other trustees. The position the Act takes is much more radical in the latter case than it is in the former. There is also special provision for pension scheme trustees and some other special situations. Although not so described in the Act, the power of delegation conferred on most trustees can conveniently be called the general power of delegation.

## (1) General power of delegation

The approach adopted by the Trustee Act 2000 to most trustees is radically new. Instead of specifying when trustees may appoint agents, the Act confers a general power to delegate any function other than certain non-delegable functions.[22] This is a complete reversal of the previous position.

The functions which *cannot* be delegated by trustees to an agent are:

(a) decisions concerning the distribution of the trust assets;[23]

(b) decisions as to whether costs or fees should be debited to capital or to income;[24]

(c) the appointment of new trustees;[25]

(d) any power to delegate trustee functions or to appoint a nominee or custodian.[26]

---

[20] *Trustees' Powers and Duties* (1997) Law Comm Consultation Paper No 146, para 5.16.
[21] [1998] 2 All ER 705 at 717.   [22] Trustee Act 2000, s 11(1) and (2).
[23] Trustee Act 2000, s 11(2)(a).   [24] Trustee Act 2000, s 11(2)(b).
[25] Trustee Act 2000, s 11(2)(c).   [26] Trustee Act 2000, s 11(2)(d).

In addition, trustees of land who are obliged to consult the beneficiaries before exercising any of their powers may not delegate the obligation to carry out this consultation.[27] Should they delegate any function which involves a duty to consult, it must be on terms which enable the trustees to conduct that consultation and to give effect to the wishes of the beneficiaries.[28]

The connecting link between the matters which the trustees cannot delegate is that they are functions which lie at the heart of trusteeship and have a clear fiduciary content. The functions which can be delegated include all ministerial acts (ie the implementation of decisions already taken), including the implementation of decisions relating to the distribution of trust funds. However, unlike the previous position, it is also possible for the trustees to delegate functions which may require the exercise of discretions or decisions. For instance if Andrew and Brenda are appointed as trustees of a valuable collection of antiquarian books, some of which need rebinding, they could delegate to a librarian acquaintance the task of finding a craftsman with the appropriate skills. Similarly, they can delegate their investment functions, including the choice of which investments to make, although there are special rules applying to the delegation of asset management which were considered in Chapter 22.

## (2) Delegation by charity trustees

The Act maintains for charity trustees the position under the pre-existing law that the trustees can delegate only in prescribed situations.[29] The reason for limiting the powers of charity trustees to delegate is that there are some functions which are so central to the trust that it would not be appropriate for anyone other than the trustees to exercise them. For instance the decision as to how to distribute funds by a charity established to make grants is something which should be under the immediate control of the trustees. The Explanatory Memorandum to the Act suggests that to have conferred a general authority on charity trustees to delegate, but to prohibit the delegation by charity trustees of distributive functions, or even of 'charitable functions', could unduly have narrowed the powers of charity trustees to appoint agents.

The delegable functions of charity trustees are:

(a)  carrying out a decision already made by the charity trustees;[30]

(b)  investing the trust assets, or carrying out any function relating to investment;[31]

(c)  carrying out any function relating to fund raising other than the raising of funds 'by means of profits of a trade which is an integral part of carrying out the trust's charitable purpose', the trade being something which is carried out as a primary purpose of the trust or is mainly carried out by the beneficiaries of the trust.[32]

This short list of delegable functions can be extended by delegated legislation made by the Secretary of State.[33]

---

[27]  Trustee Act 2000, ss 13(3), (4) and (5).
[28]  Trustee Act 2000, s 13(4).      [29]  Trustee Act 2000, s 11(3).      [30]  Trustee Act 2000, s 11(3)(a).
[31]  Trustee Act 2000, s 11(3)(b).      [32]  Trustee Act 2000, s 11(3)(c) and s 11(4).
[33]  Trustee Act 2000, s 11(3)(d) and s 11(5).

The policy adopted by the Act is to allow the delegation of ministerial acts (executing decisions already taken). So far as discretions are concerned, the Act distinguishes between the functions of charity trustees relating to the generation of income to finance the charitable purposes (which can be delegated) and those relating to carrying out of the charitable purposes (which cannot be delegated). The proviso in s 13(3)(c) relating to trades which are conducted mainly by beneficiaries or which are a primary purpose of the trust is designed to prevent, say, the trustees of a school operating under a charitable trust from delegating their discretions relating to the running of the school. The trustees of a charitable housing association operating by way of trust would be in a similar position.

## (3) Delegation by pension fund trustees and other special cases

The general power of delegation described above is restricted in its application to pension scheme trustees. Pension scheme trustees are not permitted to delegate investment functions under the general power,[34] nor to appoint nominees or custodians,[35] although in other respects pension fund trustees may employ the general power of delegation. Another restriction on pension scheme trustees is that, in order to avoid potential conflicts of interest, they may not appoint as an agent an employer or a person who is connected with or an associate of an employer.[36]

The reason for excluding the power to delegate investment functions is that there are special provisions dealing with this in the Pensions Act 1995, which contains special safeguards to protect the rights of occupational pension scheme members. Section 34(2)(a) of the Pensions Act 1995 provides that the trustees of a pension trust scheme may delegate any decision about investments to a fund manager. Such a fund manager must be authorised to conduct investment business under the Financial Services and Markets Act 2000. Where such delegation occurs the trustees are required to prepare, maintain and from time to time revise a written statement of the principles governing decisions about investments for the purpose of the scheme outlining their policy about the following matters: the kinds of investments to be held; the balance between different kinds of investments; risk; the expected return on investments; the realisation of investments.[37] Thus, the trustees are required to set the general policy that investment decisions should follow, but they can delegate the selection of specific investments to meet such a strategy to the fund manager. The trustees may also delegate decisions about investments to two or more of their number,[38] or to a fund manager operating outside the United Kingdom in respect of overseas investment business.[39]

The general power of delegation does not apply to trustees of authorised unit trusts[40] nor to trustees of a common investment scheme or of a common deposit scheme made under the Charities Act 1993.[41]

---

[34] Trustee Act 2000, s 36(5).     [35] Trustee Act 2000, s 36(8).     [36] Trustee Act 2000, s 36(7).
[37] Pensions Act 1995, s 35(1)–(3).     [38] Pensions Act 1995, s 34(5)(a).
[39] Pensions Act 1995, s 34(5)(b).     [40] Trustee Act 2000, s 37.     [41] Trustee Act 2000, s 38.

## (4) Who may be appointed agent

The trustees have a wide discretion as to whom they may to appoint as an agent. They may even appoint one or more of the trustees as agent[42] (for instance four trustees might wish to delegate to one of their number the task of negotiating the terms of a lease for premises to be occupied by the trust), or a person who has already been appointed as a nominee or custodian.[43] The trustees may not authorise two different people to undertake the same function[44] unless they are appointed to exercise the function jointly. That is a matter of common sense. The trustees are also prohibited from appointing a beneficiary as an agent,[45] even if the beneficiary is also a trustee. This particular restriction does not apply to trusts of land, where under the Trusts of Land and Appointment of Trustees Act 1996, s 9 it is possible for trustees of land to delegate to a beneficiary of full age 'any of their functions as trustees which relate to the land'. This provision would enable trustees of land to delegate the functions relating to the management of the land to the beneficiary who is tenant for life for the time being. It would not permit them to delegate to the beneficiary any function relating to the application of the proceeds from any dealings with the land.

## (5) Terms of agency

The appointment of an agent by trustees does not have to be in writing, or evidenced in writing, except in the case of the delegation of asset management functions.[46] The terms of the appointment, including the remuneration of the agent, are at the discretion of the trustees[47] (although the amount of the remuneration must be reasonable),[48] with a number of significant caveats. The special restrictions applicable to the delegation of asset management functions are explained in Chapter 22. Another limitation on the power of trustees to set their own terms is that where a function being delegated is subject to any specific duties or restrictions attached to that function, then those duties or restrictions apply to the agent as they would have done to the trustee,[49] although if that restriction relates to obtaining advice, there is no need for the agent to seek advice if he is the kind of person who could have given it to the trustees.[50] For instance, a trust might authorise the trustees to take out insurance on buildings belonging to the trust only after consulting a qualified surveyor or valuer. If the trustees delegate this function to a chartered surveyor, there is no need for that agent to consult another valuer.

There are certain terms relating to the appointment of agents which can be agreed by trustees only if 'it is reasonably necessary for them to do so'.[51] These are terms:

(a)  allowing the agent to appoint a substitute;[52]

(b)  exemption clauses limiting the liability of the agent;[53]

---

[42] Trustee Act 2000, s 12(1).    [43] Trustee Act 2000, s 12(4).    [44] Trustee Act 2000, s 12(2).
[45] Trustee Act 2000, s 12(3).    [46] Trustee Act 2000, s 15, see above p 627.
[47] Trustee Act 2000, s 14.    [48] Trustee Act 2000, s 32(2).    [49] Trustee Act 2000, s 13.
[50] Trustee Act 2000, s 13(2).    [51] Trustee Act 2000, s 14(2).    [52] Trustee Act 2000, s 14(3)(a).
[53] Trustee Act 2000, s 14(3)(b).

(c)  terms permitting the agent to act in circumstances giving rise to a conflict of interest.[54]

No definition is given in the Act of what is meant by reasonable necessity. Trustees will therefore need to act cautiously and to be prepared to demonstrate the basis on which they considered the inclusion of one of these terms to be reasonably necessary. This might be that it was usual business practice for specialists operating in a particular field to require such a provision. The Explanatory Memorandum to the Act provides an example:

'The appointment of a fund manager will often be essential to the efficient and effective management of the assets of the trust . . . As the standard terms of business of fund managers generally require limits on liability and the ability to act despite a conflict of interest, the ability to appoint a manager would amount to little in practice if trustees were unable to accept such terms.'

## (6) Liability of agent

It has already been noted that powers and functions delegated to agents are subject to the same conditions and restrictions as applied to that power or function in the hands of the trustees. The Act does not apply any special statutory duty upon agents, so their position is governed by the contractual principles of agency. In most situations these will impose a duty upon the agent to exercise due care and diligence in the exercise of the functions assigned to him. Because these duties arise in contract, the agent's principal liability is to the trustees who appointed him. An unresolved issue is whether there might be some circumstances in which the agent might be directly liable to the beneficiaries, whether under the Contracts (Rights of Third Parties) Act 1999 or under common law or equitable principles arising from interference with the rights of third parties.[55] An analogous situation is where a solicitor negligently draws up a will for a testator, with the result that a beneficiary fails to obtain the benefit intended by the testator. It is now well established that the solicitor owes a duty of care in tort to the beneficiary which is directly enforceable, in addition to the contractual duty owed to the testator.[56] However, a difference in this situation is that the testator (or his estate), although having a cause of action, has suffered no loss, and it is only if the beneficiary can sue that the wrongdoing solicitor can be held to account. In the case of a trust, any action brought by the trustees against an agent will enlarge the trust assets and so normally benefit the beneficiaries, reducing or even eliminating one of the justifications for conceding a direct cause of action. In addition, if the beneficiaries have a direct cause of action against an agent, it could give rise to potential double jeopardy, a matter which was of concern to the Court of Appeal in *Carr-Glyn v Frearsons*[57] when dealing with an action by a beneficiary under a will. The court in

---

[54]  Trustee Act 2000, s 14(3)(c).
[55]  For a discussion of the liability of third parties who cause loss to a trust see Chapter 30.
[56]  See *Ross v Caunters* [1980] Ch 297; *White v Jones* [1995] 2 AC 207; *Carr-Glyn v Frearsons* [1999] Ch 326.
[57]  [1999] Ch 326. See also *Worby v Rosser* [2000] PNLR 140.

that case was able to resolve the issue by holding that any action by the testatrix's estate could only be complementary to that by the beneficiary: each could sue for their own loss only.

## (7) Liability of trustees

### (a) Liability in deciding whether or not to delegate

The Trustee Act 2000 adopts the same approach to the liability of trustees as at common law. Essentially trustees are obliged to exercise care in both the appointment and in the supervision of agents. This is achieved by the imposition of the statutory duty of care. The Act says nothing, however, about the duty of trustees in deciding whether or not to delegate. Trustees are therefore under no *statutory* duty to exercise due care in deciding whether or not to delegate any of their functions, except in relation to decisions by trustees of land to delegate to a beneficiary.[58] They do not, for instance, need to demonstrate that it was reasonably necessary to delegate, nor that delegation was in the best interests of the beneficiaries. The fact that trustees can delegate even where there is no need to do so has been criticised, on the basis that it is unfair that the trustee should be able to delegate tasks to agents at the expense of the trust which he could easily and reasonably undertake himself. For this reason the Law Reform Committee recommended in their 23rd Report in 1982 that trustees should only be able to charge the trust for the expenses of delegation which were reasonably incurred.[59] There could also be the converse problem, where trustees unreasonably decide to undertake a specialist activity without appointing an agent. It remains to be seen whether the courts will impose a duty of care in such situations on the basis that the trustees are in breach of their general duty to act in the best interests of the beneficiaries.

### (b) Duty of care in selection and appointment

Having made a decision to appoint an agent, the trustees are subject to the statutory duty to take reasonable care in selecting the agent, in determining the terms on which the agent is to act, and in preparing the investment policy statement where investment functions are delegated.[60] So, for instance, the trustees would be liable for appointing an agent to sell trust property who did not have the relevant expertise, if this is something which the trustees could reasonably have been expected to discover. Suppose that Stephanie is the trustee of a shop, which had been let to Rufus before Stephanie was appointed as a trustee. She needs to negotiate an increase in the rent under a rent review clause in the lease. Having no experience herself, she appoints a local estate agent to act on the trust's behalf. She fails to ask if he has any experience of dealing with commercial property, and his lack of experience causes a loss because the rent obtained on review is far below the level it should be. Stephanie will be liable for breach of trust (and the agent will be liable for breach of his contractual duty of care).

---

[58] Trusts of Land and Appointment of Trustees Act 1996, s 9A (added by Trustee Act 2000, Sch 2).
[59] Law Reform Committee, 23rd report (Cmnd 8733), para 4.6.
[60] Trustee Act 2000, s 1 and Sch 1, para 3.

## (c) Duty of care in supervision

The trustees are also under a statutory duty to keep an eye on the activities of the agent by keeping the arrangements for the delegation under review, monitoring the actions of the agent, considering whether to intervene, and taking appropriate action where necessary.[61] Imagine, for instance, that Veronica has employed an antiquarian book specialist to catalogue and value a collection of rare books which she holds on trust. Veronica allows the specialist free access to the collection for this purpose. When a scholar asks to see a book, it is discovered that this book and several others are missing. Veronica takes no action, and it later transpires that the specialist had yielded to temptation by stealing a number of the books, something which would not have happened if his access had been supervised. Veronica could be liable for breach of trust for failure to review the arrangements if it is considered that in the circumstances she failed to exercise reasonable care. The position in this respect is just as it was at common law. For instance, in *Re Lucking's Will Trusts,*[62] Mr Lucking was the sole trustee of a trust fund which consisted of a majority shareholding in a private company. He appointed a Lieutenant-Colonel Dewar to manage the company, who sent a blank cheque which Lucking signed. Dewar subsequently misappropriated some £16,000. Cross J held that Lucking was liable for his own breach of trust in failing to supervise the activities of Dewar after he became aware of reasons to doubt his honesty.[63] The standard of care applied was that of *Speight v Gaunt,*[64] namely that the trustee is 'bound to conduct the business of the trust in such a way as an ordinary prudent man of business would conduct a business of his own'.[65] The duty so expressed is effectively the same duty as the statutory duty of care.

## (d) Liability for failure to observe restrictions

Where trustees have failed to comply with one of the restrictions on the appointment of agents, for instance where they have agreed to a clause limiting the liability of the agent where it was not reasonably necessary to do so, the trustees will be in breach of trust. There may also be limitations on the appointment of agents contained in the trust instrument which they are required to observe at pain of committing a breach of trust. The fact that the trustees have exceeded their powers in authorising a person to act as their agent does not, however, invalidate the appointment.[66]

## (e) Vicarious liability

Where the trustees have exercised due care in the appointment and supervision of an agent, however, they are not liable merely because the agent does something which causes a loss to the trust. Section 23 of the Trustee Act 2000 exempts trustees who are not personally in breach of the statutory duty of care from what may be called vicarious

---

[61] Trustee Act 2000, ss 21, 22.

[62] [1968] 1 WLR 866. *Bartlett v Barclays Bank Trust Co Ltd (Nos 1 & 2)* [1980] Ch 515 provides another example.

[63] Cross J considered that the statutory protection for trustees then in force gave no indemnity to trustees who were themselves at fault.

[64] (1833) 22 Ch D 727.      [65] (1833) 22 Ch D 727 at 874.      [66] Trustee Act 2000, s 24.

liability.[67] For instance, in the example above of the theft by a specialist of books from a valuable collection of which Veronica was the trustee, Veronica is not automatically liable because her agent was dishonest and stole the books. To hold her liable it has to be shown that she did not exercise reasonable care in selecting the specialist (perhaps she should have taken up references from other clients) or that she did not take appropriate action in supervising him.

Section 23 may not be happily worded. It states that 'a trustee is not liable for any act or default of the agent' unless the trustee has failed to comply with the statutory duty 'when entering into the arrangements under which the person acts as agent' or 'when carrying out his duties' of keeping the appointment under review. On a literal interpretation, a trustee who fails to conduct a review at all, rather than carrying out a review badly, would not be liable. This interpretation, however, would undoubtedly be contrary to the policy of the Act, and it is likely that the courts will give the section a purposive interpretation to make trustees liable for unreasonable omissions as well as careless commissions.

## (8) Liability of pension fund trustees

If the trustees of a pension fund exercise their right to delegate investment decisions to a fund manager their liability for the acts of their agent are specified by Pensions Act 1995, s 34(4):

'The trustees are not responsible for the act or default of any fund manager in the exercise of any discretion delegated to him . . . if they have taken all such steps as are reasonable to satisfy themselves or the person who made the delegation on their behalf has taken all such steps as are reasonable to satisfy himself—

  (a) that the fund manager has the appropriate knowledge and experience for managing the investments in the scheme, and

  (b) that he is carrying out his work competently and complying with section 36.'[68]

Although the language used is not identical, these obligations are very similar to the statutory duty of care imposed on other trustees who have appointed an agent.

## (9) Liability of trustees of land for the acts of their agents

Where trustees of land have delegated their functions to a beneficiary under the special power to do so in the Trusts of Land and Appointment of Trustees Act 1996[69] they are subject to the statutory duty of care in respect of the decision to delegate and in the supervision of the arrangement.[70]

---

[67] The Law Commission in *Trustees' Powers and Duties* (1997) Law Com Consultation Paper No 146, paras 4.29–4.31 suggest that this description is not particularly helpful or accurate since there is no case in which a trustee has been held vicariously liable. However, the expression accurately conveys the concept of liability for the fault of others even where there is no personal fault.

[68] Ie s 36 of the Pensions Act 1995 which requires the trustees to consider the need for diversification and to the suitability of investments.

[69] Trusts of Land and Appointment of Trustees Act 1996, s 9.

[70] Trusts of Land and Appointment of Trustees Act 1996, s 9A (inserted by Trustee Act 2000).

# 5 Individual delegation

In addition to the trustees acting together to appoint an agent, it is also possible for an individual trustee to delegate by appointing a substitute to exercise all or any of his powers. This was not something which was possible at common law, because of the principle *delegatus non potest delegare*. There is now statutory authority contained in Trustee Act 1925, s 25. As originally enacted, this section permitted delegation only during the absence of a trustee overseas. The section was substantially enlarged by the Powers of Attorney Act 1971 to confer a general authority to delegate trustee functions (including discretions), but only for a period not exceeding 12 months. The current provisions date from the Trustee Delegation Act 1999 which made further minor amendments. Section 25(1) of the Trustee Act 1925 (as amended) provides that:

'Notwithstanding any rule of law or equity to the contrary, a trustee may, by power of attorney,[71] delegate the execution or exercise of all or any of the trusts, powers and discretions vested in him as trustee either alone or jointly with any other person or persons.'

The delegation may not exceed 12 months,[72] must be by made by deed,[73] and notice must be given to the other trustees and to the person entitled to appoint new trustees.[74] The purpose of this last requirement is to enable the trustees to consider whether the trustee making the delegation should be replaced. Where a trustee delegates his functions under s 25(1), he remains strictly liable for any losses caused by the agent, as s 25(7) provides that the donor of the power of attorney '. . . shall be liable for the acts or defaults of the donee in the same manner as if they were the acts or defaults of the donor'. Appointment of an agent under this section is thus a far less satisfactory course of action for a trustee than appointment of an agent under the powers of collective delegation provided by the Trustee Act 2000.

A delegation by means of a power of attorney will, like all such appointments of an agent, lapse should the principal cease to have full mental capacity, but the Trustee Delegation Act 1999[75] permits the power to be executed as an enduring power, which remains valid despite the incapacity of the principal.

[71] See Chapter 5.    [72] Trustee Act 1925, s 25(2)(a) (as amended).
[73] This is a requirement of all powers of attorney.
[74] Trustee Act 1925, s 25(4) (as amended).
[75] Trustee Delegation Act 1999, ss 6 and 9. The Act repeals Enduring Powers of Attorney Act 1985, s 3(3) which previously permitted the delegation of trustee functions by enduring power of attorney.

# 25

# Appointment, removal and retirement of trustees

## 1 The appointment of the original trustees of a trust fund

### (1) Appointment by the settlor

### (a) Express trusts[1]

When a trust of property is created, generally the settlor will appoint the initial trustees of the settlement. If he creates the trust inter vivos by declaring that he holds the property on trust for the beneficiaries, he will be the trustee. If he transfers the property to a third party subject to a trust, that person will become the trustee. Usually, the deed creating the trust will appoint the trustees. If the trust is testamentary, so that it is only created after his death, the testator will usually nominate the trustees in his will.

### (b) Implied trusts[2]

A trust may also come into being without the express intention of the original legal owner of the property. In some instances the recipient of the legal title of property will be deemed to hold it on trust for someone else. As has been seen, trusts which arise by implication from the circumstances or conduct of the parties are known as 'resulting' and 'constructive' trusts. The person who is deemed to hold property on either a constructive or resulting trust becomes a trustee, even though he may not be aware of the fact of the trust, provided he was aware of the circumstances affecting his conscience which gave rise to the trust.[3]

---

[1] See Chapter 6.    [2] See Chapters 8 and 9.

[3] *Westdeutsche Landesbank Girozentrale v Islington London Borough Council* [1996] AC 669 at 705, per Lord Browne-Wilkinson. Although this judgment causes problems by suggesting that a person does not become a trustee of property until he is aware that he is intended to hold the property for the benefit of others, or of the factors which affect his conscience, it is probably better to regard Lord Browne-Wilkinson's comments as intimating that the trustee is not subject to the full fiduciary duties of trusteeship until he was aware of the existence of the trust. The trust exists irrespective of his knowledge in the sense that the property belongs in equity to the beneficiaries. However, the mere fact that there is a 'trust' in this sense does not mean that the trustee will be subject to personal liability for breach of trust if he acts in a manner inconsistent with the existence of the trust.

## (c)  Capacity to act as a trustee

Any legal person, whether an individual or corporation,[4] with legal capacity may act as a trustee. However, the Law of Property Act 1925, s 20 provides that: 'The appointment of an infant to be a trustee in relation to any settlement or trust shall be void . . .' This restriction only applies in respect of express trusts, and if a minor receives property in circumstances which would create a resulting or constructive trust he will become a trustee of the property.[5] However, this will only be possible in the case of personal property, as s 1(6) of the Law of Property Act 1925 provides that an infant cannot hold a legal estate in land. If a minor is appointed trustee of an express trust there are mechanisms which will enable the minor to be removed from his position and replaced.[6]

## (d)  A trust will not fail for want of a trustee[7]

If a trust has been validly created by the transfer of the trust property to the trustees, or by the death of the testator who has specified trusts in his will, the trust will not fail if the nominated trustees either disclaim the trust,[8] are incapable of acting as trustees,[9] or have predeceased the testator. Equity will not permit a trust to fail for want of a trustee and will seek to carry the settlor's intentions into effect as far as is possible. This principle operates in different ways depending on whether the trust was created by an inter vivos or testamentary transfer.

*(i) Inter vivos transfer of property to trustees upon trust.* If the settlor effectively transferred the trust property to trustees by means of an inter vivos conveyance and the trustees disclaim, the trust property will revest in the settlor subject to the trusts. For example, in *Mallott v Wilson*[10] the settlor transferred land in 1866 to a trustee on trust. When the trustee executed a deed of disclaimer in 1867, it was held that the trust did not fail but that the property was automatically revested in the settlor by operation of law, and that he held the land subject to the trusts that had been validly created.[11] If the settlor has died since the trust was created, the property will revest in his personal representatives, who will again hold it subject to the trusts.

*(ii) Testamentary transfers of property upon trust.* If the trust was intended to be created by the testamentary transfer of the trust property to trustees and they predecease the testator, the deceased's personal representatives will hold the property on the terms of the trust that he had intended to create. For example, in *Re Willis*[12] a

---

[4]  See *A-G v St John's Hospital Bedford* (1865) 2 De GJ & Sm 621; *Re Thompson's Settlement Trust* [1905] 1 Ch 229; *Bankes v Salisbury Diocesan Council of Education Inc* [1960] Ch 631.

[5]  See *Re Vinogradoff* [1935] WN 68.

[6]  Eg Trustee Act 1925, s 36(1). See below, p 676.

[7]  *Robson v Flight* (1865) 4 De GJ & Sm 608.

[8]  A person appointed trustee can disclaim the trust at any time before he has accepted it. He may disclaim by deed although that is not necessary and a disclaimer can be inferred from his conduct: *Stacey v Elph* (1833) 1 My & K 195; *White v Barton* (1854) 18 Beav 192; *Holder v Holder* [1968] Ch 353. Once the trust has been accepted the trustee cannot disclaim: *Re Sharman's Will Trusts* [1942] Ch 311. A trustee cannot disclaim part of a trust, and therefore acceptance of part will amount to an acceptance of the whole: *Re Lord and Fullerton's Contract* [1896] 1 Ch 228; *Re Lister* [1926] Ch 149, CA.

[9]  See *Re Armitage* [1972] Ch 438.     [10]  [1903] 2 Ch 494.

[11]  See also *Jones v Jones* [1874] WN 190.     [12]  [1921] 1 Ch 44.

testatrix had left property on discretionary trusts for various charities. The trustee, who was to select how the property was to be allocated between the charities, had predeceased her. However, the court held that the trust did not fail but that the fund would vest in her executors and the court would select how the fund should be allocated.[13] Similarly, if the trustee survives the testator but then disclaims the trust the property will also revest in the settlor's personal representatives, again subject to the trusts.

In either case the trust will not fail and the court has the power to appoint new trustees.[14] However, this principle is subject to the qualification that the trust will fail if the identity of the disclaiming trustee was essential to the trust. In *Re Lysaght (Decd)*[15] a testator left the residue of her estate to the Royal College of Surgeons to provide scholarships which were not to be awarded to Jews or Roman Catholics. In these circumstances the RCS, as trustee, refused to accept the trust. Buckley J held that the trust therefore failed, stating that:

'If it is of the essence of a trust that the trustees selected by the settlor and no one else shall act as the trustees of it and those trustees cannot or will not undertake the office, the trust must fail.'

In the circumstances, because the gift was charitable and had failed, it was applied cy-près.[16]

### (e)  Limitation on the number of trustees

Where the trust fund consists of personal property there is no limit on the number of trustees that the settlor may appoint when the trust is created. However, in the case of a trust of land, the property legislation of 1925 restricts the number of persons who may hold the legal title. This restriction was introduced with the objective of increasing conveyancing efficiency. The Trustee Act 1925, s 34(2)[17] provides that for settlements created after 1925:

'(a)  the number of trustees thereof shall not in any case exceed four, and where more than four persons are named as such trustees, the four first named (who are able and willing to act) shall alone be the trustees, and the other persons named shall not be trustees unless appointed on the occurrence of a vacancy.

(b)  the number of trustees shall not be increased beyond four.'[18]

It is to be noted that those who are named after the first four named as trustees do not automatically become trustees if a vacancy arises, and they will only become a trustee if they are properly appointed by whoever has the authority to appoint replacement trustees. In the context of land it is also worth noting that although it is possible

---

[13]  See also *Moggridge v Thackwell* (1803) 7 Ves 36.

[14]  *A-G v Stephens* (1834) 3 My & K 347; *Jones v Jones* (1874) 31 LT 535; *Mallott v Wilson* [1903] 2 Ch 494.

[15]  [1966] Ch 191: see also *Reeve v A-G* (1843) 3 Hare 191; *Re Lawton* [1936] 3 All ER 378.

[16]  See Chapter 19.        [17]  See also Law of Property Act 1925, s 34(2), (3).

[18]  There are a number of very limited exceptions to the principle in s 34(3), primarily being land held on trust for 'charitable, ecclesiastical, or public purposes'.

to have a sole trustee, overreaching of equitable trust interests cannot take place unless there is a payment to two trustees of land.[19] This is the case even where there are two trustees, but one has appointed the other as his attorney so that the attorney is acting in two capacities—on his own behalf and on behalf of the trustee for whom he is attorney.[20]

# 2 Retirement of trustees

## (1) Voluntary retirement of trustees

Once a trustee has been appointed and has taken up his office, he may subsequently wish to retire from the trust. Although it is possible for the trust to contain an express power permitting retirement, s 39 of the Trustee Act 1925 provides a general power which is usually adequate:

'Where a trustee is desirous of being discharged from the trust, and after his discharge there will be either a trust corporation or at least two individuals to act as trustees to perform the trust, then, if such trustee as aforesaid by deed declares that he is desirous of being discharged from the trust, and if his co-trustees and such other person, if any, as is empowered to appoint trustees, by deed consent to the discharge of the trustee, and to the vesting in the co-trustees alone of the trust property, the trustee desirous of being discharged shall be deemed to have retired from the trust, and shall, by the deed, be discharged therefrom under this Act, without any new trustee being appointed in his place.'

This provision permits the retirement of a trustee without a replacement being appointed, but this will only be possible if at least two trustees, or a trust corporation remain. Where these conditions are not satisfied, a trustee may retire and be replaced under the power contained in s 36 of the Trustee Act 1925, which is considered below. Retirement will not protect a trustee from liability for breaches of trust that he committed whilst he was a trustee, and he will be liable for breaches of trust committed after his retirement if he retired to facilitate those breaches.[21]

## (2) Compulsory retirement of trustees at the direction of the beneficiaries

Historically, trustees could not be forced to retire by the beneficiaries of a trust, no matter how much the beneficiaries may have wished to have them replaced, and they could only be forcibly removed on grounds of incapacity or maladministration. However, where the beneficiaries are of age and legally competent it has been seen that they can demand that the trust be brought to an end under the rule in *Saunders v Vautier*.[22]

---

[19] See Law of Property Act 1925, ss 2, 27.

[20] Trustee Delegation Act 1999 s 7. The same applies where the attorney acts for two or more trustees and is not acting with another trustee.

[21] See Chapter 28.     [22] (1841) 4 Beav 115.

If they wish they could therefore effectively remove the trustees and replace them by settling the property on new trusts. However, this process may be both costly (including potential liability to additional tax) and inefficient, as it requires a transfer of the legal title to the trust property from the original trustees to the beneficiaries, and then from the beneficiaries to the new trustees. The Trusts of Land and Appointment of Trustees Act 1996 therefore introduced a new statutory power enabling the beneficiaries of a trust to require a trustee to retire in circumstances where they could have taken advantage of the rule in *Saunders v Vautier* to achieve the same result. By s 19(2)(a) the beneficiaries of a trust may give a written direction to a trustee or trustees to retire from the trust. This right is only exercisable if there is no person nominated for the purpose of appointing new trustees by the trust instrument,[23] and if the beneficiaries of the trust are of full age and capacity and, taken together, are absolutely entitled to the property subject to the trust.[24] This means that the right to direct retirement will not be available where there are infant beneficiaries of the trust, which will often be the case in respect of a discretionary trust. Where a trustee has been directed to retire by the beneficiaries, s 19(3) provides that he will be required to make a deed declaring his retirement and shall be deemed to have retired and be discharged from the trust. However, he will only be required to retire if three conditions are satisfied: (i) reasonable arrangements have been made for the protection of any rights he has in connection with the trust;[25] (ii) after he has retired there will be either a trust corporation or at least two persons to act as trustees to perform the trust;[26] and (iii) either another person is to be appointed a new trustee on his retirement, or the continuing trustees consent by deed to his retirement.[27] The power to compulsorily retire trustees under s 19 thus enables the beneficiaries to defeat the intentions of the settlor, who may have intended that a specific individual act as trustee. This ability to undermine the settlor's express intentions is the inevitable consequence of the rule in *Saunders v Vautier*. However, a settlor can expressly exclude the right to compulsorily retire trustees under s 19,[28] and in reality a standard exclusion may be utilised in express trusts so that the provision will only be applicable in respect of resulting and constructive trusts, especially of the family home.[29] Where trusts have come into existence before the commencement of the Act, the power to direct retirement can be excluded by the execution of a deed to that effect by the settlor, or surviving settlors, who created the trust.[30] If such a deed is executed, it is irrevocable in effect.[31]

---

[23] S 19(1)(a).      [24] S 19(1)(b).

[25] S 19(3)(b). This would include, for example, unpaid fees and expenses.

[26] S 19(3)(c). This is consistent with s 39 of the Trustee Act 1925.

[27] S 19(3)(d). In the event that the co-trustees refuse to consent to the retirement directed by the beneficiaries the only means of removal of the trustee will be by order of the court exercising its jurisdiction under s 41 of the Trustee Act 1925.

[28] S 21(5).

[29] Although, even here, the provision cannot be exercised if one of the beneficiaries (who may also be the trustee) does not agree.

[30] S 21(6).      [31] S 21(7).

# 3 The appointment of replacement or additional trustees

## (1) The need for new appointments

Although the original trustees of a trust are usually appointed by the settlor, it is inevitable that in the lifetime of many trusts circumstances may arise where it is necessary to appoint new trustees.

### (a) Appointment of additional trustees

It may be necessary or beneficial for the number of original trustees appointed by the settlor to be increased by the appointment of additional trustees. This may be because of the workload that the trustees are experiencing or for simple reasons of convenience. In the case of land, if the settlor has created a trust for sale with a single trustee it may be necessary to appoint at least one additional trustee so that, if the land is sold, the purchaser can gain the benefit of overreaching.[32]

### (b) Appointment of replacement trustees

It may be necessary to appoint new trustees as replacements for those who are no longer able to act as such, for example because of death or mental incapacity, or who have retired from the trust.

### (c) Removal of trustees

In some circumstances it may be necessary to remove a trustee from the trust against his will, for example if he proves to be incompetent or is frustrating the efficient exercise of the trust.

## (2) Power to appoint new trustees

Having recognised that there may be a need in some circumstances to appoint new trustees, the central question is how such appointments can be made: i.e. who has the power to select and appoint new trustees, and in what circumstances can such powers be exercised? Although there would be advantages in making a thematic survey of the reasons why new appointments may need to be made and the powers that could be used to make them, because of an overlap between the scope of the various powers it is better to consider the different jurisdictions that enable the appointment of new trustees.

### (a) Express powers

In keeping with the fundamental philosophy that, as far as possible the settlor's intentions will be carried out, the trust deed may contain an express power authorising the

---

[32] The Trustee Delegation Act 1999 section 7 makes it clear that the two trustee rule is not satisfied if all of the trustees are represented by a single person acting under a power of attorney, or where the same single person is both a trustee and acts under a power of attorney for the other trustees.

appointment of new trustees. Such a power will be strictly construed.[33] There is some question whether the donee of such a power can appoint himself as trustee of the settlement. In *Re Skeats' Settlement*[34] a trust contained an express power granting certain persons the power to appoint 'any other person' to be trustee. They exercised the power to appoint themselves. Kay J held that this was invalid since the power was fiduciary in character:

'The universal rule is that a man should not be judge in his own cause; that he should not decide that he is the best possible person, and say that he ought to be the trustee. Naturally no human being can be imagined who would not have some bias one way or the other as to his own personal fitness, and to appoint himself among other people, or excluding them to appoint himself would certainly be an improper exercise of any power of selection of a fiduciary character such as this is. In my opinion it would be extremely improper for a person who has a power to appoint or select new trustees to appoint or select himself . . .'[35]

This principle was followed by Kekewich J in *Re Newen*,[36] but was doubted by Buckley J in *Montefiore v Guedalla*,[37] where he stated that:

'On the cases, I am clearly of opinion that it has not been laid down that the appointors are outside the class who can be appointed, although it has been said, and it is a very salutary rule, than an appointor ought not, save in exceptional circumstances, to appoint himself.'[38]

However, in *Re Sampson*[39] Kekewich J considered that the decision in *Montefiore v Guedalla*[40] might require future reconsideration.[41]

Today, express powers are of little significance because of the statutory powers that are available to provide for the appointment of new trustees. These statutory powers were themselves modelled on the express powers which had previously been included in trust deeds. If there is an express power providing for the removal of trustees from the trust, s 36(2) of the Trustee Act 1925 applies, which provides:

'Where a trustee has been removed under a power contained in the instrument creating the trust, a new trustee or trustees may be appointed in the place of the trustee who is removed, as if he were dead, or, in the case of a corporation, as if the corporation desired to be discharged from the trust, and the provisions of this section shall apply accordingly, but subject to the restriction imposed by this act on the number of trustees.'

### (b) Statutory powers

There are three important statutory provisions granting the power of appointment of new trustees.

### (i) Trustee Act 1925, s 36. This section provides for the appointment of new trustees in a wide range of circumstances by persons either nominated in the trust deed by the settlor, or, in the absence of any such nomination, by the persons provided for by the section. The intervention of the court is not required for appointments made under the power contained in s 36.

---

[33] *Stones v Rowton* (1853) 17 Beav 308; *Re Norris* (1884) 27 Ch D 333.
[34] (1889) 42 Ch D 522.    [35] Ibid at 527.    [36] [1894] 2 Ch 297.    [37] [1903] 2 Ch 723.
[38] [1903] 2 Ch 723 at 725.    [39] [1906] 1 Ch 435.    [40] [1903] 2 Ch 723.
[41] *Re Sampson* concerned a statutory rather than an express power to appoint new trustees.

*(ii) Trustee Act 1925, s 41.* This section grants the court a wide power to appoint new trustees either in addition to or in substitution for present trustees. The power is discretionary and may be exercised whenever the court considers it is expedient.

*(iii) Trusts of Land and Appointment of Trustees Act 1996, ss 19 and 20.* It has already been noted how the Trusts of Land and Appointment of Trustees Act 1996 has introduced a new statutory right enabling the beneficiaries of a trust to direct the compulsory retirement of a trustee. Section 19(2)(b) also grants the beneficiaries the right to direct the appointment of new trustees, and s 20 provides for the appointment of a replacement trustee where a trustee is mentally incapable of acting and there is no person willing and able to appoint a replacement under s 36(1) of the Trustee Act 1925.

# 4 Trustee Act 1925, s 36

## (1) Appointing substitute trustees

### (a) The power to appoint substitute trustees

The Trustee Act 1925, s 36(1) provides:

'Where a trustee, either original or substituted, and whether appointed by a court or other-wise, is dead, or remains out of the United Kingdom for more than twelve months, or desires to be discharged from all or any of the trusts or powers reposed in or conferred on him, or refuses or is unfit to act therein, or is incapable of acting therein, or is an infant, then subject to the restrictions imposed by this Act on the number of trustees—

    (a) the person or persons nominated for the purpose of appointing new trustees by the instrument, if any, creating the trust; or

    (b) if there is no such person, or no such person able and willing to act, then the surviving or continuing trustees or trustee for the time being, or the personal representatives of the last surviving or continuing trustee;

may, by writing, appoint one or more other person (whether or not being the persons exercising the power) to be a trustee or trustees in the place of the trustee so deceased, remaining out of the United Kingdom, desiring to be discharged from the trust, and the provisions of this section shall apply accordingly, but subject to the restrictions imposed by this Act on the number of trustees.'

### (b) Circumstances in which the power may be exercised

Section 36 provides that the power to appoint new trustees may be exercised in seven well-defined circumstances, which cover many of the most likely situations in which new trustees would need to be appointed. It is to be noted that s 36 applies only to trustees and not to personal representatives.[42]

---

[42] See *Re Cockburn's Will Trust* [1957] Ch 438; *Re King's Will Trusts* [1964] Ch 542. However, the court has power to appoint substituted person representative under the Administration of Justice Act 1985, s 50.

*(i) The trustee is dead.* By s 36(8) the power of appointment under s 36(1) is also exercisable where a person who is nominated trustee in a will, predeceases the testator. There is some authority[43] that the sections will also be operative in the unlikely event that the settlor attempts an inter vivos transfer to a trustee who is already dead. However, this will only be the case if the dead trustee was one of a number of others who were alive, since an attempt by the settlor to transfer property inter vivos to trustees who are all dead will not create a trust in the first place.

*(ii) The trustee remains out of the United Kingdom for more than 12 months.* The rationale for this provision was that the limited and slow means of communication and travel would prevent a trustee who was absent from the country being able to properly carry out the trust business. As has already been seen, under s 25 of the Trustee Act 1925 a trustee may delegate his managerial functions and discretions by a power of attorney for up to 12 months, for instance, during absence abroad. Today, with such instant means of communication as e-mail, telephone and fax, and with the availability of rapid air transport, it is questionable whether the absence of a trustee abroad inevitably prevents him from conducting the business of the trust. The absence from the UK must be for a continuous period of 12 months. In *Re Walker*[44] Mr Walker was co-trustee of a settlement with Mrs Walker. He was out of the UK for more than a year from spring 1899, with the exception of one week in London in November 1899. In these circumstances Farwell J held that Mrs Walker could not exercise the power of appointment under what is now s 36(1).[45] The power enables a trustee to be removed against his will, as was held by Danckwerts J in *Re Stoneham's Settlement Trusts*.[46]

*(iii) The trustee desires to be discharged from all or any of the trusts or powers reposed in or conferred on him.* This provision means that a trustee can be discharged from only part of his trust responsibility, which prior to the Act was only possible through the court.[47]

*(iv) The trustee refuses to act.* This clearly covers the case where a trustee disclaims the trust.

*(v) The trustee is unfit or incapable.* This refers to any personal incapacity that would prevent the trustee acting as such. It clearly includes mental incapacity, so in *Re East*[48] the court held that there was a valid exercise of a power to appoint new trustees where one of three co-trustees became of unsound mind.[49] Similarly, in *Re Lemann's Trust*[50] age and infirmity were considered sufficient 'incapacity'. A trustee will also be considered unfit to act if he is bankrupt, as was held in *Re Wheeler and De Rochow*.[51]

---

[43] See *Re Hadley* (1851) 5 De G & Sm 67.      [44] [1901] 1 Ch 259.

[45] Previously, Trustee Act 1893, s 10.      [46] [1953] Ch 59.

[47] See *Savile v Couper* (1887) 36 Ch D 520; *Re Moss's Trusts* (1888) 37 Ch D 513.

[48] (1873) 8 Ch App 735.

[49] It is possible for a trustee to execute an enduring power of attorney before becoming of unsound mind which has the effect of delegating to an agent his functions as a trustee of land and which operates in the event of his incapacity: Trustee Delegation Act 1999 s 1.

[50] (1883) 22 Ch D 633.

[51] [1896] 1 Ch 315. See also *Re Roche* (1842) 1 Con & Law 306; *Re Hopkins* (1881) 19 Ch D 61.

It seems that a trustee is not unfit to act merely through absence abroad.[52] However, in *Mesnard v Welford*[53] a trustee who had been absent in New York for 20 years was held to be incapable of acting for the purposes of an express power of appointment.[54] The cases holding that a trustee resident overseas may be incapable of acting all date from the 19th century, and improvements in communications and in the speed of international travel cast their current reliability into doubt.[55] In the case of the dissolution of a corporate trustee, s 36(3) provides:

'Where a corporation being a trustee is or has been dissolved . . . then, for the purposes of this section . . . the corporation shall be deemed to be and to have been from the date of the dissolution incapable of acting in the trusts or powers reposed in or conferred on the corporation.'

*(vi) The trustee is an infant.* Such an eventuality is only likely to arise in respect of a constructive or resulting trust of personal property, since in other cases the appointment of an infant as trustee is void.[56]

*(vii) The trustee has been removed under an express power.* If the trust instrument includes an express provision for the removal of trustees, any trustee who is so removed may be replaced under the powers of appointment of s 36 as if he were a trustee who had died.[57]

## (c) Persons who may exercise the power to appoint new trustees

As well as defining the circumstances in which new trustees may be appointed, s 36 of the Trustee Act also specifies who is to make any such appointments. The section adopts an order of priority as to who can exercise the power. It emphasises the settlor's intentions by giving priority to any person nominated for the purpose in the trust instrument, but provides alternative mechanisms for appointment if there is no such person nominated.

*(i) The person or persons nominated by the trust instrument.* By s 36(1)(a), if the settlor has nominated a person or persons in the instrument creating the trust to exercise the power of appointment of new trustees then it is they who can exercise the power to appoint under s 36(1). Such persons only fall within s 36(1) if they have a general power to make appointments[58] and not a power which is only granted in specific circumstances. In *Re Sichel's Settlements*[59] the nominated persons were given the power to appoint new trustees in the event of the present trustees becoming 'incapable to act'. Neville J held, following the decision of Kekewick J in *Re Wheeler and De Rochow*,[60] that they were not the appropriate persons to appoint a new trustee where

---

[52] See *Withington v Withington* (1848) 16 Sim 104; *O'Reilly v Alderson* (1849) 8 Hare 101; *Re Harrison's Trusts* (1852) 22 LJ Ch 69; *Re Bignold's Settlement Trusts* (1872) 7 Ch App 223.

[53] (1853) 1 Sm & G 426.

[54] See also *Re Lemann's Trusts* (1883) 22 Ch D 633, where Chitty J gave the residence of a trustee abroad as one instance of incapacity.

[55] See the remarks by Millet J in *Richard v Mackay* (1997) 11 Trust Law International 22.

[56] Law of Property Act 1925, s 20.     [57] S 36(2).

[58] *Re Walker and Hughes' Contract* (1883) 24 Ch D 698.     [59] [1916] 1 Ch 358.

[60] [1896] 1 Ch 315. However, he did express his disagreement with the decision.

one of the existing trustees was 'unfit' to act. Where several persons are jointly nomi-nated, in the absence of a contrary intention[61] the survivor or survivors cannot exercise the power.[62] In that event, the power to appoint will be exercisable by those indicted in s 36(1). The same result will follow if the nominated persons are incapable of acting, for example because of disagreement.[63]

*(ii) The surviving or continuing trustee or trustees.* If there are no persons nominated in the trust instrument, or if such persons are unable or unwilling to act, s 36(1)(b) provides that it is the 'surviving or continuing trustee or trustees for the time being' who may appoint new trustees. It has been held that the last surviving or continuing trustee includes a sole trustee.[64] The central difficulty concerns the questions as to who are the 'continuing trustees' where it is intended to remove a trustee who is alive and capable, since it is a basic principle that trustees must act with unanimity. It would prove impos-sible to remove a trustee against his will if he was to be regarded as a 'continuing trustee' and therefore had to be party to the decision to remove and replace him. The position is complicated by s 36(8), which provides that the continuing trustees include 'a refusing or retiring trustee, if willing to act in the execution of the provisions of this section'. This has the effect that a retiring sole trustee or retiring group of trustees are able to appoint their successors, although s 37(1)(c) means that two retiring trustees cannot be replaced by one, not being a trust corporation.[65] Whether a trustee should be regarded as 'refus-ing or retiring' was considered by Danckwerts J in *Re Stoneham's Settlement Trusts*.[66] He took the general view that a trustee who is being removed from the trust is not retiring and therefore does not fall within the scope of s 36(8):

'It seems to me, in the absence of any authority which binds me to decide otherwise, that a person who is compulsorily removed from a trust is not a person who retires and is not a retiring trustee.'

Similarly, following *Re Coates to Parsons*,[67] he held that a trustee who has been abroad for more than 12 months was not a 'refusing or retiring trustee' within the meaning of s 38, and that therefore he was not a 'continuing trustee' and his concurrence was not needed for the appointment of a new trustee.

*(iii) The personal representatives of the last surviving or continuing trustee.* As a last resort, if there are no nominated persons who can make new appointments and there are no 'surviving or continuing' trustees the statute pragmatically provides in

---

[61] *Re Harding* [1923] 1 Ch 182.

[62] This is subject to the exceptions that the survivors can exercise the power if the property is vested in them (*Re Bacon* [1907] 1 Ch 475), they hold the power as trustees (Trustee Act 1925, s 18(1)) or the power was granted to a class of which two or more members survive (*Jefferys v Marshall* (1870) 19 WR 94).

[63] *Re Sheppard's Settlement Trust* [1888] WN 234. Alternatively, because they cannot be found: *Cradock v Witham* [1895] WN 75.

[64] *Re Shafto's Trusts* (1885) 29 Ch D 247. *Adam and Company International Trustees Ltd v Theodore Goddard (a firm)* [2000] WTLR 349; [2003] Con 15 (Barlow)

[65] *Adam and Company International Trustees Ltd v Theodore Goddard (a firm)* [2000] WTLR 349; [2003] Con 15 (Barlow).

[66] [1953] Ch 59.        [67] (1886) 34 Ch D 370.

s 36(1)(a) that the 'personal representatives of the last surviving or continuing trustee' have the power to appoint new trustees.

### (d) No one is able to appoint a substitute trustee

In some extreme circumstances, even where there is a jurisdiction to appoint a substitute trustee under s 36 there will be no one who is capable of exercising it. Such a problem is especially likely where property is held by sole trustee who has become mentally incapable. Since a sole incapable trustee is a surviving trustee, he alone is entitled to exercise the power to appoint a substitute for himself, and yet is incapable of so doing. In such circumstances where the power to appoint under s 36 is moribund, the court may exercise its jurisdiction to appoint new trustees under s 41. The Trusts of Land and Appointment of Trustees Act 1996 has conferred upon the beneficiaries of the trust the right to direct the appointment of a substitute. This jurisdiction is examined later in this chapter.

## (2) Appointing additional trustees

### (a) The power to appoint additional trustees

The Trustee Act 1925, s 36(6)[68] also provides for the appointment of additional trustees:

'Where, in the case of any trust, there are not more than three trustees—

    (a) the person or persons nominated for the purpose of appointing new trustees by the instrument, if any, creating the trust; or

    (b) if there is no such person, or no such person able and willing to act, then the trustee or trustees for the time being;

may, by writing appoint another person or other persons to be an additional trustee or additional trustees, but it shall not be obligatory to appoint any additional trustees, unless the instrument, if any creating the trust, or any statutory enactment provides to the contrary, nor shall the number of trustees be increased beyond four by virtue of any such appointment.'

### (b) Circumstances in which the power may be exercised

Section 36(6) gives the trustee of a trust the option to increase the number of trustees to a maximum of four through the appointment of additional trustees. This power is subject to any express terms in the trust or by statute requiring the number of trustees to be increased.

### (c) Persons who may appoint additional trustees

The mechanisms by which such appointments may be made are almost identical to those adopted under s 36(1).

*(i) The person or persons nominated by the trust instrument.* Priority is given to the settlor's express intention in the form of persons nominated for the purpose of

---

[68] As amended by Trusts of Land and Appointment of Trustees Act 1996, Sch 3, para 3(11).

appointing trustees in the trust instrument. Providing they are willing and able to act they alone can exercise the power.

*(ii) The trustee or trustees for the time being.* In the absence of any nominated persons the other trustees, whether a sole trustee or co-trustees, may appoint additional trustees. Obviously, if there are no trustees remaining because of death, the provisions of s 36(1) will operate. A limited power is available to the donee of a registered enduring power of attorney to exercise the functions of the trustees to appoint a new trustee if to do so is necessary to ensure that there are two trustees to receive capital money arising from a disposition of land.[69]

## (3)  Making appointments under s 36

### (a)  Persons who may be appointed

In the case of substitute appointments, under s 36(1) the persons who may exercise the power can appoint whoever they desire as trustees and it is specifically provided that they may appoint themselves if they wish. However, due to a slight difference in drafting, persons who are nominated to appoint additional trustees are not specifically permitted to appoint themselves under s 36(6), and in *Re Power's Settlement*[70] it has been held that they cannot appoint themselves. Where there are already two trustees, it is not possible for them to retire and to be replaced by a single trustee, unless that trustee is a trust corporation recognised under English law.[71]

### (b)  Relevance of the beneficiaries' wishes

The person (or persons) entitled to appoint new trustees are under no obligation to consult the beneficiaries of the trust and ascertain their wishes as to who should be appointed. In *Re Brockbank*[72] Vaisey J held that the person entitled to appoint under s 36 could not be compelled to do what the beneficiaries wanted, as the right to appoint belonged solely to those whom it was given by the statute and the court was unwilling to interfere with its exercise.[73] The only means by which the beneficiaries could compel the appointment of the persons they wanted to be trustees would be to put an end to the trust[74] under the rule in *Saunders v Vautier* or to make a direction under the Trusts of Land and Appointment of Trustees Act 1996.[75] The power to make a direction under the 1996 Act does not apply if the person entitled to appoint new trustees was nominated by the trust instrument.

### (c)  Formalities of appointment

The appointment of new trustees, whether substitute trustees under s 36(1) or additional trustees under s 36(6), must be made in writing. However, an appointment made

---

[69]  Trustee Act 1925, s 36(6A)–(6D) as inserted by the Trustee Delegation Act 1999.
[70]  [1951] Ch 1074, CA.
[71]  See *Adam and Co International Trustees Ltd v Theodore Goddard* (2000) ITELR 634.
[72]  [1948] Ch 206.
[73]  See also *Re Gadd* (1883) 23 Ch D 134; *Re Higginbottom* [1892] 3 Ch 132.
[74]  [1948] Ch 206 at 210.        [75]  Section 19. This jurisdiction is discussed later in this Chapter.

by deed will have the effect of vesting the trust property in the new trustees under s 40 of the Trustee Act 1925, subject to registration of the trustees as legal owners in the case of land and shares.

## (d) Effect of appointment

Section 36(7) provides that:

'Every new trustee appointed under this section as well before as after all the trust property becomes by law, or by assurance, or otherwise vested in him, shall have the same powers, authorities and discretions, and may in all respects act as if he had been originally appointed a trustee by the instrument, if any, creating the trust.'

This provision applies equally to the appointment of additional or substitute trustees.

# 5 Trustee Act 1925, s 41

## (1) The power of the court to appoint new trustees

Section 41(1) of the Trustee Act 1925 provides:

'The court may, whenever it is expedient to appoint a new trustee or new trustees, and if it is found inexpedient difficult or impracticable so to do without the assistance of the court, make an order appointing a new trustee or new trustees either in substitution for or in addition to any existing trustee or trustees, or although there is no existing trustee.'

## (2) Scope of the power under s 41

This provision gives the court a very wide discretion to appoint trustees, either in substitution for, or in addition to, existing trustees. However, a number of features should be noted.

### (a) Relation to other powers of appointment of trustees

Appointments will generally only be made under the jurisdiction of s 41 where they cannot be made through the exercise of an express power within the trust instrument, nor under the statutory power granted by s 36 of the Trustee Act 1925.[76]

### (b) 'Whenever it is expedient to appoint . . . and if it is found inexpedient difficult or impractical so to do without the assistance of the court'

This double-limbed test sets down the circumstances in which the court may exercise the power of appointment. It must be both expedient for a substitute or additional trustee to be appointed and in some sense, because of the circumstances, the assistance

---

[76] *Re Soulby's Trusts* (1873) 21 WR 256; *Re Gibbon's Trusts* (1882) 45 LT 756; *Re Sutton* [1885] WN 122.

of the court must be necessary. Section 41(1) itself specifies some such circumstances where the jurisdiction may need to be exercised:

'In particular . . . the court may make an order appointing a new trustee in substitution for a trustee who is incapable by reason of mental disorder within the meaning of the Mental Health Act 1983, of exercising his functions as trustee, or is a bankrupt, or is a corporation which is in liquidation or has been dissolved.'

A number of illustrations can be given of other circumstances in which the power has been exercised. In *Re Smirthwaite's Trust*[77] the court exercised its statutory power[78] to appoint new trustees when all of the trustees named in the settlor's will had pre-deceased him. In *Re May's Will Trust*[79] one of three trustees of a will was in Belgium during the time of the German invasion and had not escaped. It was held that there was no evidence that she was 'incapable of acting' within the meaning of s 36(1) so that she could not be replaced by the continuing trustees, but the court appointed a new trustee under s 41. The court may also act where an express power or the power under s 36 is incapable of being exercised, for example if the donee of an express power is an infant.[80] In *Re Rendell's Trusts*[81] the court exercised its power to appoint a trustee where one of the surviving trustees was opposed to the appointment.

### (c) Removal of trustees against their will

It is clear that s 41 permits the court to remove trustees from the trust against their will. In *Re Henderson* Bennet J stated:

'I do not think that it is open to doubt that on the language of the sub-section the court has jurisdiction to displace a trustee against his will and to appoint a new trustee in substitution for him. Take the case of a trustee who is a convicted felon or a bankrupt whom the beneficiaries desire to have replaced by a new trustee. On the language of the sub-section, in my judgement, the court has a discretion, which it can exercise, if it regards it as expedient so to do, by appointing a new trustee in place of the trustee who has been convicted of felony, or who is a bankrupt . . . I do not doubt that the section gives the court jurisdiction in a proper case to appoint new trustees in place of and against the will of an existing trustee. Before exercising that jurisdiction the court must be satisfied that it is expedient to make such an appointment.'[82]

He held that a trustee who had refused to retire in place of the Public Trustee should be removed against her will because she had previously agreed to retire but had changed her mind for no reason of substance. This was followed by Roxburgh J in *Re Solicitor, A*[83] where a bankrupt solicitor was replaced by the court acting under s 41.

One limitation to the principle that the court can remove a trustee against his will under s 41 is that there must be no dispute as to the facts. This was emphasised by Cotton LJ in *Re Combs*[84] and accepted by Bennet J in *Re Henderson*.[85]

---

[77] (1871) LR 11 Eq 251.    [78] Under the Trustee Act 1850.    [79] [1941] Ch 109.
[80] *Re Parson's* [1940] Ch 973.    [81] (1915) 139 LT Jo 249.
[82] [1940] Ch 764 at 767.    [83] [1952] Ch 328.    [84] (1884) 51 LT 45.
[85] [1940] Ch 764. See also *Popoff v Actus Management Ltd* [1985] 5 WWR 660.

## (3) Exercise of the court's discretion

The court's power to appoint under s 41 is discretionary, and it must be satisfied that any appointments are 'expedient'. The question whether an appointment was 'expedient' was raised in *Re Weston's Settlement*,[86] where there was an attempt to move a trust from England to Jersey for tax reasons, and to replace the English trustees with trustees in Jersey. Applications were made under the Variation of Trusts Act 1958[87] in favour of the infant beneficiaries of the trust and under s 41 for the appointment of new trustees. The court refused to exercise its discretion under either of these provisions. As to s 41, Lord Denning MR said:

'. . . with the appointment of new trustees the Trustee Act 1925 gives no guide. It simply says that the court may appoint new trustees "whenever it is expedient". There being no guidance in the statute, it remains for the court to do the best it can.'[88]

Several reasons for the refusal of the court to appoint appear from the judgment. First, the proposed move of the trust to Jersey was solely for reasons of tax avoidance. Secondly, there was a relatively slight connection between the beneficiaries and Jersey. They had lived there for only a short time, and there was a high probability that they would move after the trust had been transferred. As Harman LJ said, they 'cannot be said to have proved that they truly intend to make Jersey their home'.[89] Finally, the court referred to the inadequacy of the law in Jersey for dealing with trusts. Harman LJ said:

'[Jersey] law has never had any experience of trusts and so far as appears, the courts of Jersey have never made an order executing the trusts of a settlement. There is not, it appears, any Trustee Act in Jersey at all, and the effect of this last transaction must, so far as I can see, have nothing to recommend it from a trust point of view.'

In these circumstances the court refused to appoint trustees, and instead held that 'these are English settlements and they should . . . remain so unless some good reason connected with the trusts themselves can be put forward'.[90]

In contrast, it should be noted that in *Re Windeatt's Will Trusts*[91] the court was willing to approve a scheme for the variation of a trust, including the appointment of new trustees in Jersey, where the family had lived there for some nineteen years. In such circumstances it seem likely that the court would have equally found it 'expedient' to appoint new trustees under s 41 if that had been necessary. Given the significant improvement in communications, and the increased recognition of trusts overseas, it is quite possible that the courts would now be more willing to entertain the appointment of trustees overseas than they have in the past where there is some real overseas connection or other justification.[92] In *Richard v The Hon A.B. Mackay*,[93] Millet J suggested that where trustees were exercising their own discretion to appoint an overseas trustee and

---

[86] [1969] 1 Ch 223.    [87] See Chapter 18.    [88] [1969] 1 Ch 223 at 245.

[89] [1969] 1 Ch 223 at 248.    [90] [1969] 1 Ch 223 at 284.    [91] [1969] 1 WLR 692.

[92] See *Re Beatty's WT (No 2)* (1997) 11 Trust Law International 77; *Richard v Mackay* (1997) 11 Trust Law International 22 (decided 1987).

[93] (1997) 11 Trust Law International 22.

seek merely approval from the court, the court should only need to be satisfied that the decision was 'not so inappropriate that no reasonable trustee could entertain it'. He recognised that social conditions had moved on and that international families with international interests 'are as likely to make their home in one country as in another and as likely to choose one jurisdiction as another for the investment of their capital'. The court should not act in a way that frustrated this.

## (4) Persons the court will appoint trustees

### (a) General principles guiding the court's selection

In *Re Tempest*,[94] which concerned the appointment of new trustees under a predecessor to s 41,[95] the Court of Appeal laid down three criteria that the court will apply in exercising its discretion to appoint new trustees. These were set out by Turner LJ.

*(i) Regard to the wishes of the settlor.* 'First, the court will have regard to the wishes of the persons by whom the trust has been created, if expressed in the instrument creating the trust, or clearly to be collected from it.'[96]

*(ii) Regard to the interests of the beneficiaries.* 'Another rule which may, I think, safely be laid down is this—that the court will not appoint a person to be a trustee with a view to the interest of some of the persons interested under the trust, in opposition either to the wishes of the testator or to the interests of the other cestuis que trust. I think so for this reason that it is of the essence of the duty of every trustee to hold an even hand between the parties interested under a trust.'[97]

*(iii) Regard to the effective execution of the trust.* 'A third rule which, I think, may safely be laid down is this—that the court in appointing a trustee will have regard to the question, whether his appointment will promote or impede the execution of the trust, for the very purpose of the appointment is that the trust may be better carried into execution.'[98]

The Court of Appeal held that the proposed trustee, Mr Petre, should not be appointed. Although there could be no objection to him 'in point of character, position or ability', he fell foul of the rules proposed. First, he was the nominee of the beneficiary of the trust, Charles Tempest, and the testator's intentions had been to exclude him 'from all connection with his estate'. Secondly, the court considered that he had been 'proposed as a trustee . . . with a view to his acting in the trust in the interests of some only of the objects of it . . . and not with a view to his acting as an independent trustee for the benefit of all the objects of the trusts'.

### (b) Persons the court will not normally appoint trustees

There are some persons who, irrespective of their abilities, the court will not normally appoint as trustees because of their relationship to the trust and the likelihood of a

---

[94] (1866) 1 Ch App 485.    [95] Trustee Act 1850.    [96] (1866) 1 Ch App 485 at 487.
[97] (1866) 1 Ch App 485 at 487.    [98] (1866) 1 Ch App 485 at 488.

conflict of interest. The court will not appoint, except in exceptional circumstances,[99] a beneficiary or a beneficiary's spouse as trustee,[100] nor the solicitor to the life tenant or the solicitor to an existing trustee.[101] Nor, according to a number of cases, will the court appoint a person living abroad unless the trust's property or the beneficiaries are also abroad,[102] although it may be that this attitude is changing.[103]

# 6 Trusts of Land and Appointment of Trustees Act 1996

## (1) Appointment of trustees at the direction of the beneficiaries

It has been seen that ss 36 and 41 of the Trustee Act 1925 provide mechanisms for the appointment of new trustees, whether additional or replacement, in specified circumstances. However, in neither case do the beneficiaries of the trust have the right to require the appointment of a specific person as a trustee, as the right to appoint is vested in either other persons (the surviving or continuing trustees, or the personal representatives of the last surviving trustee) or the court. However, the Trusts of Land and Appointment of Trustees Act 1996, s 19 has granted the beneficiaries of a trust the right to direct the appointment of new trustees. Section 19(2)(b) provides that the beneficiaries can give:

'a written direction to the trustees or trustee for the time being (or, if there are none, to the personal representative of the last person who was a trustee) to appoint by writing to be a trustee or trustees the person or persons specified in the direction.'

As in the case of the power to direct the retirement of trustees, this right to direct appointment can only be exercised if the beneficiaries would otherwise be entitled to take advantage of the rule in *Saunders v Vautier*[104] because they are of age, legally competent and collectively entitled to the trust property.[105] The right to direct appointments is also excluded if the trust instrument expressly nominates a person for the purpose of appointing new trustees,[106] or if the right has been expressly excluded.[107] The beneficiaries' right to direct the appointment of new trustees cannot be exercised

---

[99] Eg where no independent person can be found to take up the office: *Ex p Clutton* (1853) 17 Jur 988; *Re Clissold's Settlement* (1864) 10 LT 642; *Re Burgess' Trusts* [1877] WN 87; *Re Parrott* (1881) 30 WR 97; *Re Lightbody's Trusts* (1884) 33 WR 452.

[100] *Ex p Clutton* (1853) 17 Jur 988; *Ex p Conybeare's Settlement* (1853) 1 WR 458; *Re Orde* (1883) 24 Ch D 271; *Re Kemp's Settled Estate* (1883) 24 Ch D 485, CA; *Re Coode* (1913) 108 LT 94.

[101] *Re Kemp's Settled Estates* (1883) 24 Ch D 485 27; *Re Norris* (1884) 27 Ch D 333; *Re Earl of Stamford* [1896] 1 Ch 288; *Re Spencer's Settled Estates* [1903] 1 Ch 75.

[102] *Re Guibert's Trust Estate* (1852) 16 Jur 852; *Re Hill's Trusts* [1874] WN 228; *Re Drewe's Settlement Trusts* [1876] WN 168; *Re Freeman's Settlement Trusts* (1887) 37 Ch D 148; *Re Liddiard* (1880) 14 Ch D 310; *Re Whitehead's Will Trusts* [1971] 1 WLR 833.

[103] See *Re Beatty's WT (No 2)* (1997) 11 Trust Law International 77; *Richard v Mackay* (1997) 11 Trust Law International 22.

[104] (1841) 4 Beav 115.     [105] S 19(1)(b).     [106] S 19(1)(a).     [107] S 21(5)–(8).

so as to appoint more than the maximum number of trustees permitted under the Trustee Act 1925.[108]

Problems remain concerning the practical implementation of the beneficiaries' right to direct the appointment of new trustees. Whereas s 19(3) makes clear that a trustee who is directed to retire must do so, there is no equivalent provision requiring the trustees (or the personal representative of the last surviving trustee) to carry into effect a direction to appoint. If the trustees are required to make the directed appointment, it is unclear whether they would be liable if the person nominated by the beneficiaries was unsuitable and the trust suffered a loss in consequence of the appointment. Presumably, the appointing trustees would be exempt from any liability for breach of trust in such circumstances because the appointment would have been made at the unanimous instigation of the beneficiaries.

## (2) Appointment of a substitute for a mentally incapable trustee

It has already been noted that, where a trustee has become mentally incapable, the right to appoint a substitute trustee may have become moribund. This may be because the persons enjoying the right to appoint, whether under an express power or under s 36 of the Trustee Act 1925, are unwilling to do so, or because there is no one entitled to appoint a substitute: for example, where there is a sole trustee who has become incapable and the trust instrument does not include an express power of appointment. In order to facilitate the appointment of a substitute without the need for the court to intervene, s 20(2) of the Trusts of Land and Appointment of Trustees Act 1996 provides that the beneficiaries of the trust may give 'a written direction to appoint by writing the person or persons specified in the direction to be a trustee or trustees in place of the incapable trustee'. The right to give such a direction only arises where a trustee is incapable by reason of mental disorder of exercising his functions as trustee,[109] and there is no person who is both entitled and willing and able to appoint a trustee in place of him under s 36(1) of the Trustee Act 1925.[110] The right to direct an appointment in such circumstances is only conferred upon the beneficiaries if they would otherwise be entitled to take advantage of the rule in *Saunders v Vautier:* ie they are of age, legally competent and collectively entitled to the trust property.[111] The direction to appoint must be made to either a receiver of the incapable trustee,[112] or a person acting for him under an enduring power of attorney,[113] or a person with authority to act under the Mental Health Act 1983.[114] The beneficiaries' right to direct an appointment under s 20 may be expressly excluded in the trust instrument,[115] or, in the case of a trust created

---

[108]  Trusts of Land and Appointment of Trustees Act 1996, s 19(5).

[109]  S 20(1)(a). Mental disorder is defined by Mental Health Act 1983, s 1: see Trusts of Land and Appointment of Trustees Act 1996, s 23(2).

[110]  S 20(1)(b).        [111]  S 20(1)(c).        [112]  S 20(2)(a).

[113]  S 20(2)(b). See above, Chapter 5 for an explanation of the nature of an enduring power of attorney. It is possible for a trustee to delegate all his functions to another person to exercise on his behalf by means of an enduring power of attorney: see Trustee Delegation Act 1999.

[114]  S 20(2)(c).        [115]  S 21(5).

before the commencement of the Act, may be excluded by the execution of a deed to that effect by all the surviving settlors.[116]

# 7 Appointment of special trustees

A number of statutory provisions provide for the appointment of special trustees.

## (1) Judicial Trustees Act 1896

### (a) Nature of a judicial trustee

A judicial trustee is a trustee appointed by the court under s 1 of the Judicial Trustees Act 1896. The person appointed a judicial trustee is an officer of the court, and is therefore subject to its control and supervision. The purpose of appointing a judicial trustee is to ensure the proper execution of the trust, but without incurring the full expense of having the trust administered by the court. This was explained by Jenkins J in *Re Ridsdel*:

'The object of the Judicial Trustees Act 1896 . . . was to provide a middle course in cases where the administration of the estate by the ordinary trustees had broken down, and it was not desired to put the estate to the expense of a full administration of the estate . . . a solution was found in the appointment of a judicial trustee, who acts in close concert with the court and under conditions enabling the court to supervise his transactions.'[117]

Although the judicial trustee may be given special directions by the court, and he may apply for the court's directions in his decisions, the purpose is not to 'reduce the administration of an estate by a judicial trustee to very much the same position as where an estate is being administered by the court and every step has to be taken in pursuance of the court's directions'.[118]

The appointment of a judicial trustee was particularly important prior to the enactment of s 50 of the Administration of Justice Act 1985, since it was the only way that a personal representative could be replaced. Although a judicial trustee is largely in the same position as any other trustee, for example he has the power to compromise claims,[119] he cannot appoint his successor under the provisions of s 36 of the Trustee Act 1925.

### (b) Appointment of a judicial trustee

*(i) The power to appoint.* The Judicial Trustees Act 1896, s 1(1) provides that:

'Where application is made to the court by or on behalf of the person creating or intending to create a trust, or by or on behalf of a trustee or beneficiary, the court may, in its discretion, appoint a person (in this Act called a judicial trustee) to be a trustee, either jointly with any

---

[116] S 21(6).      [117] [1947] Ch 597 at 605.      [118] *Re Ridsdel* [1947] Ch 597.
[119] *Re Ridsdel* [1947] Ch 597.

other person or as sole trustee, and if sufficient cause is shown, in place of any existing trustees.'

The power to appoint a judicial trustee is therefore purely discretionary. It is also clear that a trustee may be removed against his will and replaced by a judicial trustee.

*(ii) Persons who may be appointed.* Section 1(3) provides that:

'Any fit and proper person nominated for the purpose in the application may be appointed a judicial trustee, and, in the absence of such nomination, an official of the court may be appointed, and in any case a judicial trustee shall be subject to the control and supervision of the court as an officer thereof.'

*(iii) Remuneration of judicial trustees.* Section 1(5) provides that the court may direct that the judicial trustee be remunerated for his services from the trust property.

## (2) Public Trustee Act 1906

### (a) Nature of the public trustee

The Public Trustee is a corporation sole which may act as an ordinary trustee, custodian trustee[120] or judicial trustee.[121] He was established by the Public Trustee Act 1906, and one main function is to administer small estates. Once appointed, he has the same powers and duties, rights and liabilities as an ordinary trustee.

### (b) Appointment of the public trustee

*(i) Appointment as an ordinary trustee.* Section 5(1) provides that the Public Trustee may be appointed trustee of any will or settlement:

'either as an original or as a new trustee, or as an additional trustee, in the same cases, and in the same manner, and by the same persons or court, as if he were a private trustee, with this addition, that, though the trustees originally appointed were two or more, the public trustee may be appointed sole trustee.'

This is subject to the limitations that he may decline to accept any trust, although not on the grounds of the small value of the trust fund,[122] that he may not act as the trustee of any trust under a deed of arrangement for the benefit of creditors or as administrator of an insolvent estate,[123] and that he shall not accept any trust exclusively for religious or charitable purposes.[124] The court may order the appointment of the Public Trustee even if the trust instrument prohibits his appointment.[125]

*(ii) Appointment as a custodian trustee.* Section 4(1) provides that:

'Subject to rules under this Act the public trustee may, if he consents to act as such, and

---

[120] A custodian trustee holds the property of the trust fund and the documents relating to such property, but leaves the administration of the trust to the managing trustee. See Public Trustee Act 1906, s 4(2). See also Chapter 20.

[121] Public Trustee Act 1906, s 2(1).     [122] S 2(3).     [123] S 2(4).     [124] S 2(5).

[125] S 5(3).

whether or not the number of trustees has been reduced below the original number, be appointed to be custodian trustee of any trust—

(a) by order of the court made on the application of any person on whose application the court may order the appointment of a new trustee; or

(b) by the testator, settlor or other creator of any trust; or

(c) by the person having power to appoint new trustees.'

*(iii) Intestate estates.* The Public Trustee holds the estate of a person who dies intestate, pending the appointment of an administrator.[126]

## 8 The court's inherent jurisdiction to remove trustees

As well as the statutory power to remove trustees under s 41 of the Trustee Act 1925, the court possesses an inherent jurisdiction to remove trustees in an action begun by writ for the administration or execution of a trust.[127] Although there is little authority as to the exercise of this jurisdiction, the overriding consideration seems to be the welfare of the beneficiaries and the trust estate. Some guidance was provided by the Privy Council in *Letterstedt v Broers*, where Lord Blackburn said:

'The reason why there is so little to be found in the books on this subject is probably that suggested by Mr Davey in his argument. As soon as all questions of character are as far settled as the nature of the case admits, if it appears clear that the continuance of the trustee would be detrimental to the execution of the trusts, even if for no other reason than that human infirmity would prevent those beneficially interested, or those who act for them, from working in harmony with the trustee, and if there is no reason to the contrary from the intentions of the framer of the trust to give this trustee a benefit or otherwise, the trustee is always advised by his own counsel to resign, and does so. If, without any reasonable ground, he refused to do so, it seems to their Lordships that the court might think it proper to remove him . . .'[128]

The court may act under its inherent jurisdiction even where the facts are in dispute.[129] The inherent jurisdiction was used to remove three trustees against their will in *Clarke v Heathfield (No 2)*.[130] The case concerned a trust fund of money belonging to the National Union of Mineworkers. The three trustees transferred the funds abroad to prevent them being sequestrated as a result of the illegal industrial action by the union. Members of the NUM sought to have the trustees removed by the court. Mervyn Davies J held that the court should exercise its power to remove the trustees under its inherent jurisdiction. A number of factors influenced his decision to remove, including the trustees' refusal to obey orders of the court and that the transfer of the funds abroad

---

[126] Law of Property (Miscellaneous Provisions) Act 1994, s 14.
[127] *Re Wrightson* [1908] 1 Ch 789; *Re Henderson* [1940] Ch 764.
[128] (1884) 9 App Cas 371 at 386.
[129] *Re Chetwynd's Settlement* [1902] 1 Ch 692; *Re Wrightson* [1908] 1 Ch 789; *Re Henderson* [1940] Ch 764.
[130] [1985] ICR 606.

rendered them unavailable for the purposes for which they were contributed by the membership of the union.

## 9 Summary

Having considered the range of powers by which trustees may be appointed, it is possible to summarise how they may operate in practice. This is illustrated by means of the following table.

| Circumstances | Relevant power | Exercised by? |
|---|---|---|
| Initial appointment | Own choice | Settlor/testator Court (if original trustee disclaims the trust, or if the trust would otherwise fail for want of a trustee) |
| Appointment of additional trustee | Express power<br>Trustee Act 1925, s 36(6)<br>TOLATA* 1996, s 19 | Person nominated<br>Trustees for the time being<br>Beneficiaries |
| Replacement of existing trustee | Express power<br>Trustee Act 1925, s 36 (in specified circumstances)<br><br>TOLATA 1996, s 19<br>TOLATA 1996, s 20 (Mentally incapable trustee)<br>Trustee Act 1925, s 41 | Person nominated<br>'Surviving or continuing trustees' or personal representatives of last such<br>Beneficiaries<br>Beneficiaries<br><br>Court |
| Retirement without replacement | Trustee Act 1925, s 39<br><br>TOLATA 1996, s 19 | Retiring trustee with consent of others<br>Beneficiaries with consent of remaining trustees |
| Removal of trustee | Trustee Act 1925, s 36<br><br><br>TOLATA 1996, s 19<br><br><br>Trustee Act 1925, s 41<br>Inherent jurisdiction | 'Surviving or continuing trustees' or personal representatives of last such<br>Beneficiaries (with consent of remaining trustees if not being replaced)<br>Court<br>Court |

* Trusts of Land and Appointment of Trustees Act 1996

# 26

# Accountability of trustees

## 1 Introduction

Throughout Part IV it has been seen that trustees, by virtue of their legal ownership, enjoy powers of management and control over the trust property. They are under a duty to act in the best interests of the beneficiaries of the trust, but inevitably their position opens to them tremendous possibilities for abuse. Part V of this book considers the question of how the trustees of a trust are controlled and supervised, and in particular Chapter 27 details the general mechanisms by which such control is effected. It will be seen that the prime responsibility for supervising the activities of the trustees falls to the beneficiaries, who are able to complain to the court if they believe the trustees have committed, or are about to commit, a breach of trust. If the beneficiaries are able to apply to the court before the alleged breach has taken place they may obtain an injunction against the trustees to restrain them from committing the contemplated breach.[1] If the breach has already occurred there are a number of other remedies which may be available to the beneficiaries.[2]

Trustees are also subject to a number of duties which enable the beneficiaries to keep a better check on their activities by entitling them to obtain information which will inform them of the trustees' actions and may enable the beneficiaries to detect breaches of trust. This chapter will consider those duties.

## 2 The duty to act unanimously

One safeguard to the proper conduct of a trust is the appointment of joint trustees. Where the trust property is held by a sole trustee the opportunities for abuse will be greater, since a co-trustee cannot act alone without the collusion of his fellow trustees. For this reason, in the context of land, overreaching, which defeats the interests of the beneficiaries of a trust of land, is only permitted by statute where the legal title to the land is held by more than two trustees.[3] The two trustee rule has been clarified and strengthened by the Trustee Delegation Act 1999 under which, if one of two trustees has delegated his powers relating to the sale of land to the other trustee, the sole

---

[1] See Chapter 2.      [2] See Chapters 28–31.
[3] Law of Property Act 1925, ss 2, 27. See also *State Bank of India v Sood* [1997] 1 All ER 169.

trustee-cum-attorney cannot give a valid receipt without a second person being added as trustee.[4]

Except in the case of pension fund trusts[5] and charity trusts, co-trustees must generally act unanimously.[6] They cannot act on the basis of a majority decision.[7] The principle was stated by Jessel MR in *Luke v South Kensington Hotel Ltd*:[8]

'There is no law that I am acquainted with which enables the majority of trustees to bind the minority. The only power to bind is the act of [them all].'

Illustrations of the application of the requirement of unanimity can be drawn from a number of areas. If one of several co-trustees enters into a contract to sell trust property to a third party, the duty to act unanimously means that the contract cannot be enforced against the trust.[9] Similarly, the trustees must act unanimously in the exercise of their discretions. In *Tempest v Lord Camoys*[10] one of two trustees wished to exercise their discretion to purchase land with the trust property, but the other trustee refused to concur in the purchase. The Court of Appeal held that, as the refusing trustee had properly exercised his discretion, the court could not interfere and the purchase could not take place as the trustees were not unanimous. However, in *Messeena v Carr*[11] Lord Romilly MR held that there was no breach of trust where a discretion was exercised by one of two trustees and the other 'approved and sanctioned what was done'. A receipt which is given for money by only one of two trustees will be ineffective to discharge the payor unless this is done by way of an express term in the trust instrument. Therefore, in *Lee v Sankey*[12] a firm of solicitors was held not to have been discharged when it paid over proceeds of a testator's real estate and was given a receipt by one of the two trustees of the will, who misappropriated the money and died insolvent.

In some exceptional circumstances it seems that the duty to act unanimously will not apply. For example, in *Nicholson v Smith*[13] it was held that notice of the intention to renew a lease by one of two trustees was sufficient. Where the trust assets include shares, it is generally the case that the company's articles provide that the trust should not be recognised, and that the first named of joint holders can give an effectual receipt for dividends paid on the shares.

---

[4] Trustee Delegation Act 1999, s 7. The same is true where there are two or more trustees all of whom have delegated their powers to the same agent.

[5] S 32 Pensions Act 1995 provides that trustees of an occupational pension scheme may make decisions by a majority.

[6] The trust instrument may specify circumstances in which the trustees do not need to be unanimous.

[7] See *Leyton v Sneyd* (1818) 8 Taunt 532; *Tempest v Lord Camoys* (1882) 21 Ch D 571, CA; *Astbury v Astbury* [1898] 2 Ch 111; *Boardman v Phipps* [1967] 2 AC 46. HL.

[8] (1879) 11 Ch D 121 at 125.

[9] *Naylor v Goodall* (1877) 47 LJ Ch 53.

[10] (1882) 21 Ch D 571.

[11] (1870) LR 9 Eq 260.

[12] (1873) LR 15 Eq 204.

[13] (1882) 22 Ch D 640.

# 3 The duty to exercise discretions properly

## (1) The duties of trustees relating to the exercise of discretion

Where trustees have discretion as to how the trust property should be managed or allocated, they must exercise their discretion properly. Although the courts will not force the trustees to reach a particular conclusion in the exercise of their discretion, it will intervene if they exercise their discretion improperly or improperly fail to exercise it. In *Tempest v Lord Camoys*[14] Jessel MR said:

'It is settled law that when a [settlor] has given a pure discretion to trustees as to the exercise of a power, the court does not enforce the exercise of the power against the wish of the trustees, but it does prevent them from exercising it improperly.'[15]

## (2) The trustees' duty to consider exercising a discretion

Trustees are under a duty to consider whether they should exercise any discretion that they hold with regard to the trust property, even though the court cannot compel how the discretion should be exercised. These principles were applied in *Tempest v Lord Camoys*.[16] Mr Fleming, one of the trustees, had properly considered the exercise of his discretion and had refused to invest the trust property in land or to raise money by way of a mortgage. As Brett LJ said:

'. . . there was undoubtedly an absolute discretion in the trustees as to what land they should purchase. Mr Fleming has not refused to exercise the power at all, but has objected to purchase this particular property. It needs no authority to induce us to hold that if a discretion is given to trustees as to what property they should purchase the Court will not take it out of their hands.'

In *Turner v Turner*[17] the court set aside deeds of appointment which had been exercised by the trustees on the grounds that, although they appeared to be valid, the trustees had not even read them. In effect, there had been no real consideration whether or not the power should be exercised. In *Klug v Klug*,[18] a trustee had refused to concur in an advancement because the beneficiary (her daughter) had married without her consent. Neville J held that the court would intervene to direct the payment because the trustee 'has not exercised her discretion at all'.

## (3) Relevance of the beneficiaries' wishes in the exercise of the trustees' discretion

Where the trustees of a trust hold discretionary powers it is they alone who must decide whether or not to exercise the discretion. Except in respect of a trust of

---

[14] (1882) 21 Ch D 571.    [15] Ibid, at 578.    [16] Ibid.    [17] [1984] Ch 100.
[18] [1918] 2 Ch 67.

land,[19] trustees are not subject to an obligation to consult their beneficiaries before they exercise their discretions, nor are they obliged to follow beneficiaries' wishes. In *Re Brockbank*[20] Vaisey J refused to compel a trustee to exercise his power to appoint new trustees under s 36 of the Trustee Act 1925[21] in the manner demanded by the beneficiaries and other trustees. He emphasised the discretionary nature of the power:

'The power of nominating a new trustee is a discretionary power, and, in my opinion is no longer exercisable and, indeed, can no longer exist if it has become one of which the exercise can be dictated by others.'

This statement no longer holds completely true following the Trusts of Land and Appointment of Trustees Act 1996, which gives beneficiaries a limited authority to direct the appointment of new trustees.[22] However, the proposition set out remains accurate in respect of other trustee discretions, even in situations where the beneficiaries can call for the appointment of new trustees or bring the trust to an end under the rule in *Saunders v Vautier*.[23] The beneficiaries cannot dictate how the trustees should exercise their discretion.

## (4) Improper exercise of discretion

### (a) General principles

Given that the courts will intervene if trustees exercise, or threaten to exercise, their discretion improperly, the question naturally arises as to the circumstances in which an exercise will be regarded as improper. The difficulty, similar to that faced in the judicial review of administrative decisions, is that the court does not act as the judge of whether trustees make the 'right' decision. The court will only interfere in limited circumstances. This was explained by Lord Truro LC in *Re Beloved Wilkes' Charity*:

'. . . it is to the discretion of the trustees that the execution of the trust is confided, that discretion being exercised with an entire absence of indirect motive, with honesty of intention, and with a fair consideration of the subject. The duty of supervision on the part of the court will thus be confined to the question of the honesty, integrity, and fairness with which the deliberation has been conducted, and will not be extended to the accuracy of the conclusion arrived at . . .'[24]

However, it is clear that trustees do not enjoy an absolute discretion. The ability of the court to intervene and impugn an exercise of the trustees' discretion was recognised by the House of Lords in *Dundee General Hospital Board of Management v Walker*,[25] where Lord Reid stated:

'If it can be shown that the trustees considered the wrong question, or that, although they

---

[19] Trusts of Land and Appointment of Trustees Act 1996, s 11. See Stevens and Pearce, *Land Law* (2nd edn, 2000), p 249.

[20] [1948] Ch 206.    [21] See Chapter 25.

[22] See Chapter 25. Trusts of Land and Appointment of Trustees Act 1996, ss 19–21 enables the beneficiaries of a trust to direct the trustees to make appointments, or compel retirements, if they would otherwise be able to bring the trust to an end under the rule in *Saunders v Vautier*.

[23] (1841) 4 Beav 115.    [24] (1851) 3 Mac & G 440.    [25] [1952] 1 All ER 896.

purported to consider the right question they did not really apply their minds to it or perversely shut their eyes to the facts or that they did not act honestly or in good faith, then there was no true decision and the court will intervene.'[26]

The principles under which the court will be willing to intervene to set aside an improper exercise of a discretion by a trustee have been undergoing continual development and are still not finally settled.[27]

Because, as is described later, trustees are not normally under an obligation to provide reasons for a decision, it will not often be possible to demonstrate that they have ignored relevant considerations or taken into account irrelevant considerations. However, recent formulations of the circumstances in which the courts will intervene suggest that there will be occasions when the facts may speak for themselves. Thus, a court would be prepared to intervene if the trustees' decision 'can be said to be one that no reasonable body of trustees properly directing themselves could have reached'.[28] If the decision of the trustees is not so much at odds with any sensible expectation of the person creating the trust, the court will not intervene merely because it would have reached a different decision.[29]

## (b) Fraudulent exercise

The court will clearly intervene if it can be shown that the discretion was exercised fraudulently.

## (c) Improper motives

The court will intervene if the trustee exercises or refuses to exercise the power for irrelevant and extraneous motives. For example, in *Klug v Klug*[30] the court intervened where one of two trustees refused to exercise her discretionary power of advancement[31] in favour of her daughter because she had married without her consent. In the Irish case of *Tomkin v Tomkin*[32] a valuable house and land near Dublin had been left under a family trust. The trustee, who was also a beneficiary, had a power to postpone sale. TC Smyth J held that the trustee 'by deliberate inaction, was content to let matters lie so that at a future date he could more conveniently acquire the trust property without having explored or realized its development potential.' He also allowed members of his family to occupy the property without payment of rent. It was held that the trustee was in breach of trust for acting as if he were the sole owner and for disregarding

---

[26] [1952] 1 All ER 896 at 905. This formulation was cited with approval by Robert Walker J in *Scott v National Trust* [1998] 2 All ER 705 at 717–718.

[27] See *Re Hastings-Bass* [1975] Ch 25; *Mettoy Pension Trustees Ltd v Evans* [1990] 1 WLR 1587; *Stannard v Fisons Pension Trust* [1992] IRLR 27; *Breadner v Granville-Grossman* [2000] 4 All 705; *Re Barr's Settlement Trusts* [2003] 1 All ER 763; *Sieff v Fox* [2005] 3 All ER 693.

[28] *Edge v Pensions Ombudsman* [1998] Ch 512 at 534 per Scott VC; an approach confirmed by the Court of Appeal [2000] Ch 602. The language used reflects the standard laid down for the review of decisions made by administrative bodies in *Associated Provincial Picture House v Wednesbury Corpn* [1948] 1 KB 223.

[29] See *Edge v Pensions Ombudsman* [1998] Ch 512 and *Breadner v Granville-Grossman* [2000] 4 All ER 705 at 732–733 where Park J refused to overturn the exercise of a power because, even if they were fully informed, 'it is at least possible that the trustees . . . would still have gone ahead'.

[30] [1918] 2 Ch 67.   [31] See Chapter 16.   [32] 1998/6924P (8 July 2003).

the interests of the other beneficiaries. The judge indicated that the property should be sold.

## (d) Failure to take account of relevant matters

Since the decision in *Re Hastings-Bass (decd)*,[33] it has been clear that the court can set aside an exercise of discretion by a trustee which was made improperly, either because the trustee took into account irrelevant considerations, or failed to take account of relevant considerations. As Robert Walker J stated in *Scott v National Trust*,[34] trustees are under a duty to take account of all relevant matters when they decide whether or not to exercise their discretion:

'Trustees must act in good faith, responsibly and reasonably. They must inform themselves, before making a decision, of matters which are relevant to the decision. These matters may not be limited to simple matters of fact but will, on occasion (indeed quite often) include taking advice from appropriate experts, whether the experts are lawyers, accountants, actuaries, surveyors, scientists or whomsoever.'[35]

However, the precise scope of what has become known as the *Hastings-Bass* principle has been continually evolving, and has yet to be definitively clarified. The principle has been restated a number of times in different cases,[36] most recently by Lloyd LJ, sitting as a judge of the Chancery Division, in *Sieff v Fox*.[37] He stated the principle as follows:

'Where trustees act under a discretion given to them by the terms of the trust, in circumstances in which they are free to decide whether or not to exercise that discretion, but the effect of the exercise is different from that which they intended, the court will interfere with their action if it is clear that they would not have acted as they did had they not failed to take into account considerations which they ought to have taken into account, or taken into account considerations which they ought not to have taken into account.'[38]

The most significant aspect of this formulation is the assertion that an exercise of discretion will only be set aside if it is clear that the trustees would have decided differently if they had considered appropriately.[39] Only in cases where the trustees were under obliged to act would the lesser requirement that they 'might' have acted differently apply.[40] Lloyd LJ therefore held that the exercise of a discretionary power of appointment could be set aside because the trustees had failed to take into account the true consequences of the appointment as regards capital gains tax, because they had been wrongly advised, and they would not have acted as they did if they had known the correct position.

In *Re Barr's Settlement Trusts*[41] Lightman J held that the principle will only apply where

---

[33] [1974] 2 All ER 193.    [34] [1998] 2 All ER 705.    [35] [1998] 2 All ER 705 at 717.
[36] *Mettoy Pension Trustees Ltd v Evans* [1990] 1 WLR 1587 at 1621; *Re Barr's Settlement Trusts* [2003] 1 All ER 763.
[37] [2005] 3 All ER 693; (20060 122 LQR 35 (Mitchell).    [38] Ibid, at [119].
[39] Contra to the formulation adopted by Lightman J in *Re Barr's Settlement Trusts* [2003] 1 All ER 763.
[40] [2005] 3 All ER 693 at [119].
[41] [2003] 1 All ER 763. See [2004] 63 CLJ 283 (Conaglen); [2005] Conv 208 (Hilliard).

the trustee failed to consider what he was under a duty to consider, and not merely because he made a mistake or by reason of ignorance or mistake did not take into account a relevant consideration.[42]

It has not yet been finally determined whether a discretion exercised without proper consideration of relevant matters is voidable or void. In *Re Barr's Settlement Trusts* Lightman J held that the effect was to render the exercise voidable.[43] Whilst attracted to this conclusion, Lloyd LJ did not have to decide whether an improper exercise was void or voidable in *Seiff v Fox*.[44] However he opined that the proposition would require further consideration in the light of earlier authority. He stated what he considered to be the main ways at present open to the court to control the application of the principle:

'(a) to insist on a stringent application of the tests as they have been laid down; (b) to take a reasonable and not over-exigent view of what it is that the trustees ought to have taken into account, and (c) to adopt a critical approach to contentions that the trustees would have acted differently if they had realised the true position, perhaps especially so in cases (unlike the present) where it is in the interests of all who are before the court that the appointment should be set aside.'[45]

### (e) Capriciousness

*Re Manisty's Settlement*[46] suggests that the court will intervene if trustees exercise a discretion capriciously. Templeman J stated that:

'The court may also be persuaded to intervene if the trustees act "capriciously", that is to say, act for reasons which I apprehend could be said to be irrational, perverse or irrelevant to any sensible expectation of the settlor; for example, if they chose a beneficiary by height or complexion or by the irrelevant fact that he was a resident of Greater London.'

### (f) Unreasonableness

The extent to which the courts will interfere with the exercise of a discretion by trustees merely on the grounds that it can be considered as unreasonable remains relatively uncertain, but there appears to be a growing willingness on the part of the courts to intervene. Some of the older authorities suggested that a distinction could be drawn between discretions which were stated in the trust instrument to be 'uncontrollable' and those which contained no such provision. Where the discretion given to the trustees is expressly stated to be 'uncontrollable' by the trust instrument, there are authorities which suggest that the court cannot interfere unless the trustees have exercised their discretion mala fides.[47] In the absence of such an express declaration, some nineteenth-century cases suggested a wide jurisdiction to intervene, so for example in *Re Roper's Trust*[48] Fry J considered that the court could intervene if the trustees had 'not exercised a sound discretion'.[49] However, cases in the mid 20th century favoured the view that the

---

[42] Ibid, at 770.   [43] Ibid, at 774.   [44] [2005] 23 All ER 693 at [82], [119]
[45] Ibid, at [82].   [46] [1974] Ch 17.
[47] See *Gisborne v Gisborne* (1877) 2 App Cas 300; *Tabor v Brooks* (1878) 10 Ch D 273.
[48] (1879) 11 Ch D 272.
[49] See also *Re Hodges* (1878) 7 Ch D 754; *Re Lofthouse* (1885) 29 Ch D 921, CA.

court would not intervene merely on the grounds that the exercise was unreasonable if it was made in good faith.[50] In the Scottish case *Dundee General Hospitals v Walker*[51] the trustees had accepted that the test for the exercise of their discretion was whether it was reasonable, but the House of Lords doubted that this was appropriate. Lord Normand concluded:

'I desire to reserve the question whether the trustee's decision . . . was . . . open to question on any other grounds save that it was dishonest, or that it involved a trespass beyond the limits of what was committed to them by the [settlor] . . . [I]t is one thing to say that the trustees must honestly discharge their trust and keep within the bounds of the powers and duties entrusted to them, and quite another to say that they must not fall into errors which other persons, including a court of law, might consider unreasonable.'[52]

The House of Lords reiterated its unwillingness to question the trustees' exercise of their discretion on the grounds of unreasonableness in *Re Gulbenkian's Settlement Trusts*.[53] The trustees had a discretion whether or not to pay income from the trust fund to certain beneficiaries. Lord Reid said of their position:

'They are given an absolute discretion. So if they decide in good faith at appropriate times to give none of the income to any of the beneficiaries the court cannot pronounce their reasons to be bad. And similarly if they decide to give some or all of the income to a particular beneficiary the court will not review their decision. That was decided by this House in *Gisborne v Gisborne*[54] . . .'

At the turn of the 21st century there are indications that the courts might be willing to go a little further. This is reflected in the *Hastings-Bass* principle adopted by Park J in *Breadner v Granville-Grossman*[55] and which he described as having 'obvious affinities to the much more developed area of the principles which the courts will apply when judicially reviewing the exercises of statutory powers by public authorities'.[56] Similarly, in *Scott v National Trust*,[57] Robert Walker J described the public law concept of legitimate expectation as being potentially relevant in reviewing the decisions of trustees, and in *Edge v Pensions Ombudsman* Scott V-C, in speaking of the basis on which a court would review trustees' decisions, said:

'The judge may disagree with the manner in which the trustees have exercised their discretion, but unless they can be seen to have taken into account irrelevant, improper or irrational factors, or unless their decision can be said to be one that no reasonable body of trustees properly directing themselves could have reached, the judge cannot intervene.'[58]

The language used is the language of the *Wednesbury*[59] test of reasonableness used in reviewing the decisions of public bodies. This importation of public law principles has

---

[50]  See *Re Steed's Will Trusts* [1960] Ch 407 at 418.     [51]  [1952] 1 All ER 896.
[52]  [1952] 1 All ER 896 at 901.       [53]  [1970] AC 508.       [54]  (1877) 2 App Cas 300.
[55]  [2000]4 All ER 705.       [56]  Ibid at 721 and 732.       [57]  [1998] 2 All ER 705.
[58]  [1998] Ch 512 at 534.
[59]  *Associated Provincial Picture Houses v Wednesbury Corpn* [1948] 1 KB 223, CA, per Lord Greene MR: 'It must be proved to be unreasonable in the sense that the court considers it to be a decision that no reasonable body could have come to. It is not what the court considers unreasonable, a different thing altogether.'

been criticised as unnecessary and potentially misleading,[60] since it could result in the importation of principles such as the need to hear both sides before reaching a decision, a concept which has not so far formed part of the law of trusts. It remains to be seen how far the analogy will be pursued. Even in cases which have made the analogy with judicial review, limits are recognised. For instance, in *Edge v Pensions Ombudsman*,[61] Scott V-C reaffirmed that the court would not subject to an objective test of fairness an exercise by the trustees of a discretionary power to provide additional benefits to members of a pension scheme:

'It was within their discretion to provide benefits to members in service to the exclusion of members no longer in service. They certainly had a duty to exercise their discretionary power honestly and for the purpose for which the power was given and not so as to accomplish any ulterior purposes. But they were the judges of whether or not their exercise of the power was fair as between the benefited beneficiaries and other beneficiaries. Their exercise of the discretionary power cannot be set aside simply because a judge . . . thinks it was not fair.'[62]

### (g) Compelling action

According to Park J in *Breadner v Granville-Grossman*,[63] there is a substantial distinction 'between on the one hand, the courts declaring something which the trustees have done to be void, and, on the other hand, the courts holding that a trust takes effect as if the trustees had done something which they never did at all'. He considered that he had no jurisdiction to treat as effective the purported exercise of a power outside the time limits for its exercise where the trustees had made a mistake about the last date for its exercise. The power in that instance was a mere power, which in his view lapsed when the time limit expired. Fiduciary powers may be treated differently by the courts. It was recognised in *McPhail v Doulton*[64] that there were various ways in which the courts could secure the performance of discretionary trusts, and those methods may be equally applicable to fiduciary powers. They include directing the trustees to act in a particular way. For instance in *Klug v Klug*[65] the court ordered a payment to be made to a beneficiary despite the improper refusal of one trustee to concur in the decision; and in *Mettoy Pension Trustees Ltd v Evans*[66] Warner J was prepared to exercise a fiduciary power himself where there was no other person able to do so by reason of a conflict of interest.

## (5) Are trustees' required to give reasons for their decisions?

### (a) No duty to give reasons

The basic rule was stated by Harman LJ in *Re Londonderry's Settlement*:[67] 'trustees exercising a discretionary power are not bound to disclose to their beneficiaries the

---

[60] By Professor Hayton in *Hayton and Marshall: Cases and Commentary on the Law of Trusts and Equitable Remedies* (12th edn, 2005), pp 656–657.
[61] [1998] 2 All ER 547.    [62] [1998] 2 All ER 547 at 569.    [63] [2000] 4 All ER 705 at 723.
[64] [1971] AC 424    [65] [1918] 2 Ch 67.    [66] [1991] 2 All ER 513.
[67] [1965] Ch 918 at 928.

reasons actuating them in coming to a decision'. This statement accords with a long line of authorities establishing that trustees, who have decided either to exercise or not to exercise their discretion, are under no duty to provide the beneficiaries with reasons for their decision, and was more recently reaffirmed by Scott V-C in *Edge v Pensions Ombudsman*.[68] The absence of a requirement to give reasons for a decision was applied by Lord Truro LC in *Re Beloved Wilkes' Charity*,[69] which concerned a trust to provide for the education of a boy from one of three named parishes, or, if there was no suitable candidate from those parishes, a boy from any parish. The trustees decided to use the funds to support a boy, Charles Joyce, who was outside of the parish, and their exercise of discretion was challenged on the grounds that there was a suitable boy, William Gale, from within the parishes. Lord Truro held that the trustees were under no duty to disclose the 'particulars' of why they had exercised the discretion in that way, and that there was no ground for imputing bad motives to the trustees from the affidavits. This principle was confirmed by the Court of Appeal in *Re Gresham Life Assurance Society, ex p Penney*[70] in the context of the directors of a company who, under the deed of settlement, had the discretion whether to accept a proposed transferee of the company shares. The court held that they were not obliged to provide reasons for their decision to refuse to accept a transferee and that in the absence of contrary evidence the court would take it for granted that they had acted bona fide.

## (b) Justification for the rule

In *Re Londonderry's Settlement*[71] Salmon LJ provided a number of justifications for the rule that trustees were not obliged to provide the beneficiaries with reasons for their decisions:

'So long as the trustees exercise [the power] . . . bona fide with no improper motive, their exercise of the power cannot be challenged in the courts – and their reasons for acting as they did are, accordingly, immaterial. This is one of the grounds for the rule that trustees are not obliged to disclose to beneficiaries their reasons for exercising a discretionary power. Another ground for this rule is that it would not be for the good of the beneficiaries as a whole, and yet another that it might make the lives of trustees intolerable should an obligation rest upon them . . . Nothing would be more likely to embitter family feelings and the relationship between the trustees and members of the family, were the trustees obliged to state their reasons for the exercise of the powers entrusted to them. It might indeed well be difficult to persuade any persons to act as trustees were a duty to disclose their reasons, with all the embarrassment, arguments and quarrels that might ensue, added to their present not inconsiderable burdens.'

## (c) Trustees voluntarily provide reasons

Although there is no obligation on the trustees to give reasons for decisions regarding the exercise of their discretion, if they do choose to give reasons this may reveal grounds for the court to intervene. As Lord Truro LC said in *Re Beloved Wilkes' Charity*:

---

[68] [1998] 2 All ER 547 at 568. See also *Wilson v Law Debenture Trust Corpn* [1995] 2 All ER 337.
[69] (1851) 3 Mac & G 440.    [70] (1872) 8 Ch App 446.    [71] [1965] Ch 918, CA.

'If, however, as stated by Lord Ellenborough in *R v Archbishop of Canterbury*,[72] trustees think fit to state a reason and the reason is one which does not justify their conclusion, then the Court may say that they have acted by mistake and in error, and that it will correct their decision; but if, without entering into details, they simply state, as in many cases it would be most prudent and judicious for them to do, that they have met and considered and come to a conclusion, the Court has then no means of saying that they have failed in their duty, or to consider the accuracy of their conclusion.'[73]

## (d) Reasons required where trustees decide to deprive a beneficiary of a legitimate expectation?

Whilst there has been no general relaxation of the rule that beneficiaries are not entitled to be informed by trustees of their reason for a decision, in the recent case of *Scott v National Trust*[74] Robert Walker J suggested that where the beneficiaries of a trust enjoy a legitimate expectation that a discretion will be exercised in their favour, they may be entitled to be given the reasons for a change of policy. He stated:

'. . . if (for instance) trustees (whether of a charity, or a pension fund, or a private family trust) have for the last ten years paid £1,000 per quarter to an elderly, impoverished beneficiary of the trust it seems at least arguable that no reasonable body of trustees would discontinue the payment, without any warning, and without giving the beneficiary the opportunity of trying to persuade the trustees to continue the payment, at least temporarily. The beneficiary has no legal or equitable right to continued payment, but he or she has an expectation. So I am inclined to think that legitimate expectation may have some part to play in trust law as well as in judicial review cases.'[75]

It has yet to be seen how far such a principle may be taken in the context of private trusts. However, it might perhaps have led to a different result in *Wilson v Law Debenture Trust Corpn plc*,[76] where it was held that pension trustees were not required to disclose their reasons for reversing a policy that they had pursued in the preceding years concerning the transfer of a fund surplus.

## (e) Access to trust documents

The beneficiaries of a trust are prima facie entitled to have access to inspect trust documents. However the raises a potential conflict of principles where the exercise of a right of access to trust documents would disclose the trustees' reasons for the exercise of their discretions to the beneficiaries.

*(i) The right of beneficiaries to disclosure of trust documents.* The beneficiaries of a trust were historically regarded as enjoying the entitlement to access to trust documents on the basis of their proprietary right in the trust property. In *O'Rourke v Darbishire*[77] Lord Parmoor stated that a beneficiary 'is generally entitled to the production for inspection of all documents relating to the affairs of the trust.'[78] The rationale for this entitlement was explained by Lord Wrenbury:

---

[72] (1812) 15 East 117.   [73] (1851) 3 Mac & G 440.   [74] [1998] 2 All ER 705.
[75] [1998] 2 All ER 705 at 718.   [76] [1995] 2 All ER 337.   [77] [1920] AC 581.
[78] [1920] AC 581 at 619.

'The beneficiary is entitled to see all trust documents because they are trust documents and because he is a beneficiary. They are in this sense his own . . . The proprietary right is a right to access to documents which are your own.'[79]

However the rationale for permitting access to trust documents was recently reconsidered by the Privy Council in *Schmidt v Rosewood Trust Ltd*,[80] which concerned an appeal from the Isle of Man by the object of a power of appointment under a trust who sought access to the trust documents. The Privy Council rejected the contention that an object of a power of appointment could not obtain disclosure of trusts documents because he did not have a proprietary interest under the trust, and preferred to regard the right to seek disclosure of trust documents as an aspect of the inherent jurisdiction of the court to supervise the administration of trusts. This relocation of the entitlement to disclosure of trust documents to the inherent jurisdiction of the court, rather than in the proprietary right of the beneficiaries, means that a beneficiary will not enjoy an absolute right to disclosure of trust documents, as the court may exercise its inherent jurisdiction so as to limit disclosure. Lord Walker stated:

'. . . no beneficiary (and least of all a discretionary object) has any entitlement as of right to disclosure of anything which can plausibly be described as a trust document. Especially when there are issues as to personal or commercial confidentiality, the court may have to balance the competing interests of different beneficiaries, the trustees' themselves and third parties. Disclosure may have to be limited and safeguards may have to be put in place. Evaluation of the claims of a beneficiary (and especially of a discretionary object) may be an important part of the balancing exercise which the court has to perform on the materials placed before it'[81]

The case did not require the Privy Council to decide whether the object of the power of appointment in question should be entitled to the disclosure sought, as this was remitted to the High Court of the Isle of Man for further consideration. The Privy Council did not provide comprehensive guidance as to the circumstances in which a request for disclosure might be denied. However it did suggest that limits and safeguards may have to be put in place where there are issues of personal confidentiality and a need to balance the competing interests of different beneficiaries, the trustees and third parties.[82]

*(ii)  The meaning of trust documents.* It has proved difficult to provide any definition of trust documents.

On one reckoning, they would be any documents which relate to the administration of the trust. This was not, however, the view taken in *Re Londonderry's Settlement*, where Salmon LJ observed that 'the category of trust documents has never been comprehensively defined'.[83] He went on to suggest some common characteristics of 'trust documents':

---

[79]  [1920] AC 581 at 626–627.

[80]  [2003] 3 All ER 76; (2004) 120 LQR 1 (Davies). Hayton argues that the courts should take a lead from this decision and regard it as appropriate to insist on pension trustees providing reasons for their decisions: [2005] Conv 229.

[81]  Ibid, at [67].

[82]  See also *Foreman v Kingstone* [2004] 1 NZLR 841 for further examination of the circumstances in which the court may refuse to limit disclosure of trust documents to beneficiaries.

[83]  [1965] Ch 918 at 938.

'(1) they are documents in the possession of the trustees as trustees; (2) they contain information about the trust which the beneficiaries are entitled to know; (3) the beneficiaries have a proprietary interest in the documents and, accordingly, are entitled to see them.'

The assignment of these characteristics to trust documents is circular. Salmon LJ appears to suggest that a document is trust document because the trustee is entitled to see it, but that he is entitled to see it because it is a trust document in which he has a proprietary right. In any event, in the light of *Schmidt v Rosewood Trust Ltd*[84] it is no longer the case that the entitlement to disclosure of trust documents is founded upon the proprietary right of the beneficiary. In *Hartigan Nominees Pty Ltd v Rydge*[85] it was held that the beneficiaries of a discretionary trust were not entitled to see the settlor's confidential memorandum of wishes stating how he wanted the trustees to exercise their discretion, as this was of no legal force.

It would be better to treat the obligation of disclosure by trustees as being based upon the nature of trusteeship and their fiduciary obligations than upon any artificial characterisation of the documents held by trustees.[86] This would permit the policy issues relating to disclosure of information by trustees to be more openly addressed, and it is policy considerations that lie at the heart of the question of disclosure.

*(iii) No disclosure of trust documents which would reveal the trustees' reasons for exercising their discretion.* Despite the remaining uncertainties as to the definition of trust documents and the manner in which the court will exercise its inherent jurisdiction to order disclosure of trust documents, it seems clear that beneficiaries will not be entitled to disclosure of trust documents which would reveal the trustees' reasons for the exercise of their discretions. In *Re Londonderry's Settlement*[87] the Court of Appeal held that the beneficiaries would not be entitled to have access to trust documents which would reveal the reasons for the trustees decisions. Concerning the minutes of trustees meetings, Harman LJ concluded:

'I would hold that even if documents of this type ought properly to be described as trust documents, they are protected for the special reason which protects the trustees' deliberations on a discretionary matter from disclosure. If necessary, I hold that this principle overrides the ordinary rule . . .'[88]

The change in the understanding of the basis for the beneficiaries' entitlement to the disclosure of trust documents in *Schmidt v Rosewood Trust Ltd*[89] has not affected this principle, since the revelation of the reasons for the exercise of a discretion would be an issue of personal confidentially which would cause the court to limit the right to disclosure. In the New Zealand case of *Foreman v Kingstone* Potter J expressly stated that the decision in *Schmidt v Rosewood Trust Ltd* would not affect the subordination of the right to disclosure of trust documents to the right of the trustees to confidentiality for their reasons:

[84] [2003] 3 All ER 76.      [85] (1992) 29 NSWLR 405
[86] See the discussion in *Hartigan Nominees Ltd v Rydge* (1992) 29 NSWLR 405. See also *Re Murphy's Settlements* [1998] 3 All ER 1.
[87] [1965] Ch 918.      [88] [1965] Ch 918 at 933.      [89] [2003] 3 All ER 76.

'Approached as a matter of principle, the entitlement of the beneficiaries to disclosure of trust documents pursuant to the trustees' fundamental obligation to be accountable to beneficiaries, must be measured against another fundamental principle that the autonomy of trustees in the exercise of their discretions under the trust must be ensured. Hence trustees are not obliged to disclose to beneficiaries their reasons for exercising their discretionary power.'[90]

The decisions relating to disclosure by trustees of reasons for their decisions have therefore shown a higher regard for the principle that the trustees should be able to keep these reasons confidential than for the interest of the beneficiaries in seeing that the discretions are properly exercised. In *Wilson v Law Debenture Trust Corpn plc*,[91] two members of a pension scheme asked the trustees to disclose all the trust documents in their possession, including the minutes of their meetings, which might indicate the reasons for their decision not to transfer the whole of a fund surplus, as had been done in preceding years. The trustees refused to disclose these documents on the basis that they were not required to disclose documents which would divulge their reasons for exercising their discretion. Rattee J held that he was required to give effect to settled principles of trust law, so that in the absence of any evidence of impropriety the court would not compel the trustees of a pension scheme to disclose their reasons for the exercise of a discretion.[92] There is no reported English case dealing with the issue of whether beneficiaries are entitled to see a 'letter of wishes' expressing a settlor's wishes which has been given to the trustees but is not intended to be legally binding.[93] Despite the importance of such a document to beneficiaries in understanding the intentions of the settlor and the purpose of the trust of which they are beneficiaries, both Australian[94] and Jersey[95] decisions have held that if the settlor intended this expression of wishes to remain confidential from the beneficiaries, in the interests of family harmony this confidentiality should be respected.

## (f) Reform required?

The rule that trustees are not obliged to provide reasons for their decisions may mean that it is almost impossible for the beneficiaries to challenge a decision because they do not have sufficient evidence to sustain a claim that the trustees acted dishonestly, took irrelevant matters into consideration, or failed to take account of all relevant factors. For example, in *Re Beloved Wilkes' Charity*[96] one suggestion was that the trustees had chosen Charles Joyce rather than William Gale because Joyce was the brother of a clergyman who had been in contact with one of the trustees, who was also a clergyman. However, without a comprehensive statement of the trustees deliberations and reasons

---

[90] [2004] 1 NZLR 841 at [89].     [91] [1995] 2 All ER 337.

[92] [1995] 2 All ER 337 at 347. But see the comments of Robert Walker J in *Scott v National Trust* [1998] 2 All ER 705 at 718 that trustees can be compelled to disclose their reasons if challenged in legal proceedings, and his implicit criticism of the National Trust's failure to record any details of the long debate on the controversial decision to ban stag hunting.

[93] If a letter by a settlor is intended to be legally binding, then logically it should be subject to the same requirement of disclosure as the trust instrument.

[94] *Hartigan Nominees Ltd v Rydge* (1992) 29 NSWLR 405.

[95] *Re Rabaiotti's 1989 Settlement* [2001] WTLR 953.     [96] (1851) 3 Mac & G 440.

it was impossible to demonstrate that the discretion had been improperly exercised. In the contrasting case of *Klug v Klug*[97] a daughter was able to show that her mother had acted improperly because she had letters where she had made clear that she would not exercise the discretion because of the daughter's marriage.

Thus, the present law creates an inherent inconsistency. Whilst equity seeks to prevent trustees acting improperly, it also fails to provide the beneficiaries with the right to know how decisions were reached so as to enable them to be subjected to proper scrutiny. This inconsistency runs deeper than this. Where a beneficiary takes legal action to challenge the exercise of a discretion, it is likely that he will be able to force the trustees to disclose their reasons. As Robert Walker J observed in *Scott v National Trust*:

'If a decision taken by trustees is directly attacked in legal proceedings, the trustees may be compelled either legally (through discovery or subpoena) or practically (in order to avoid adverse inferences being drawn) to disclose the substance of the reasons for their decision.'[98]

However, it is submitted that the real need for reasons arises before any question relating to an exercise of discretion is brought to court. At present, the beneficiary is required to decide whether there are sufficient grounds to mount a legal challenge to an exercise of discretion – and to provide evidence to support this claim – whilst remaining in the dark as to the formal reasons for it. In some circumstances the facts themselves may prima facie indicate that the discretion was wrongly exercised, but in many cases there may be no such external indications. In such circumstances the presumption that, in the absence of evidence to the contrary, a trustee has exercised his discretion properly, operates so as to present an insurmountable obstacle to effective scrutiny of the trustees' decision making. The problems facing beneficiaries were well captured in a submission of counsel for the plaintiffs in *Wilson v Law Debenture Trust Corpn plc*[99] where he argued that the trustee of a pension scheme was:

'. . . in fact bound to give reasons for the exercise of discretions conferred upon the trustee by the relevant trust instrument because . . . it would be unreasonable that members of the scheme who had bought their interests should not be able to see that the trustee has exercised its discretion properly – which they cannot see in the absence of reasons given for the trustee's actual exercise of its discretion.'[100]

In contrast to the reluctance of equity to oblige trustees to provide reasons for their decisions the law relating to the scrutiny of decision making by public bodies has developed rapidly over the past fifty years, including the emergence of a duty to give reasons for decisions.[101] There is clear evidence in the recent trusts cases that the principles under which administrative decisions may be judicially reviewed have cross-fertilised the equity principles determining the duty of trustees in the exercise of their duties. It remains to be seen how far these developments will be carried. One possibility is that the general principle that trustees are not required to give reasons for their

---

[97] [1918] 2 Ch 67.   [98] [1998] 2 All ER 705 at 719.   [99] [1995] 2 All ER 337.
[100] [1995] 2 All ER 337 at 348, summarised by Rattee J.
[101] See *Padfield v Minister of Agriculture, Fisheries and Food* [1968] AC 997; *R v Secretary of State for the Home Department, ex p Doody* [1994] 1 AC 531; *R v Secretary of State for the Home Department, ex p Fayed* [1997] 1 All ER 228.

decisions may be abandoned, irrespective of the type of trust concerned. Alternatively, the principle could be abandoned for certain types of trusts, including pension funds and other quasi-public trusts where the argument that trustees required the safety of secrecy to enable them to perform their duties is less compelling than in respect of small family trusts. At all events, it is submitted that today equity should not be bound by nineteenth century cases which place the interests of the trustees above those of the beneficiaries, and that no discretion should be able to be exercised without proper scrutiny.

# 4  The duty to keep accounts and records

## (1)  Accounts and their availability to beneficiaries

Trustees are under a duty to keep accounts of the trusts and to allow the beneficiaries to inspect them as requested. This was so held in *Pearse v Green*,[102] where Plumer MR said that: 'It is the first duty of an accounting party, whether an agent, trustee, a receiver or executor . . . to be constantly ready with his accounts.'[103] The beneficiaries, who include for this purpose the potential beneficiaries of a discretionary trust[104] are entitled to a copy of the accounts at their own expense.[105] If the trustee fails to deliver accounts he will be liable to pay the costs of any application to the court to enforce the performance of his duty.[106] The beneficiaries of a trust are entitled to be told who the trustees are and given their addresses since otherwise the right to be informed of the state of the trust funds and how they have been distributed would be meaningless.[107]

## (2)  Audit

There is no general duty on trustees to have the trust accounts audited. However, a number of statutory provisions permit either the trustees or the beneficiaries to obtain an audit of the accounts. Audits may also be required by the trust instrument.

### (a)  The Trustee Act 1925, s 22(4)

This section enables the trustees in their absolute discretion to have the trust account audited once every three years:

'Trustees may, in their absolute discretion, from time to time, but not more than once in every three years unless the nature of the trust or any special dealings with the trust

---

[102] (1819) 1 Jac & W 135.
[103] See also *Clarke v Lord Ormonde* (1821) Jac 108; *Springett v Dashwood* (1860) 2 Giff 521.
[104] *Chaine-Nickson v Bank of Ireland* [1976] IR 393.
[105] See *Ottley v Gilby* (1845) 8 Beav 602; *Kemp v Burn* (1863) 4 Giff 348; *Re Watson* (1904) 49 Sol Jo 54.
[106] *Re Skinner* [1904] 1 Ch 289.
[107] *Re Murphy's Settlements* [1998] 3 All ER 1, a case where the settlor was required to provide this information to the objects of a discretionary trust.

property make a more frequent exercise of the right reasonable, cause the accounts of the trust property to be examined or audited by an independent accountant, and shall, for that purpose, produce such vouchers and give such information to him as he may require.'

The costs of such an audit may be met from the capital and income of the trust property.

### (b) The Public Trustee Act 1906, s 13(1)

This section enables the trustees or the beneficiaries to apply for an audit of the trust accounts:

'Subject to rules under this Act and unless the court otherwise orders, the condition and accounts of any trust shall, on an application being made and notice thereof given in the prescribed manner by any trustee or beneficiary, be investigated and audited by such a solicitor or public accountant as may be agreed on by the applicant and the trustees or, in default of agreement, by the public trustee or some person appointed by him:

Provided that (except with the leave of the court) such an investigation or audit shall not be required within 12 months after any such previous investigation or audit, and that a trustee or beneficiary shall not be appointed under this section to make an investigation of audit.'

This section has been described as an 'exceedingly drastic enactment'[108] as it establishes the right to an audit. However, if an improper application is made the applicant may be ordered to bear the costs of the audit.[109]

### (c) Pensions

The Pensions Act 2004 imposes special requirements for periodic actuarial valuations.[110]

## (3) Information regarding the trust property

Trustees are subject to a general duty to provide their beneficiaries with information concerning the trust property. As Lindley LJ said in *Low v Bouverie*,[111] the trustees must: 'give all his cestui que trust, on demand, information with respect to the mode in which the trust fund has been dealt with, and where it is'. Lindley LJ went on to indicate that there was some information that the trustee was not obliged to provide to the beneficiary:

'But it is no part of the duty of a trustee to tell his cestui que trust what incumbrances the latter has created, nor which of his incumbrancers have given notice of their respective charges.'

However, s 137(8) of the Law of Property Act 1925 now provides that the beneficiaries can require the production of any notice concerning the dealing with the equitable

---

[108] *Re Oddy* [1911] 1 Ch 532, per Parker J.
[109] *Re Oddy* [1911] 1 Ch 532; *Re Utley* (1912) 106 LT 858.     [110] S 224.
[111] [1891] 3 Ch 82 at 99.

interest which has been served upon them. Special provisions are applicable to pension funds under the Pensions Act 1995, s 41 and regulations made thereunder.

## (4) Advice

The duty of the trustees is simply to provide the beneficiaries with information, not to provide them with advice. As Megarry V-C said in *Tito v Waddell (No 2):*[112]

'... trustees ... are under a duty to answer inquiries by the beneficiaries about the trust property ... But that is a far remove from saying that trustees have a duty to proffer information and advice to their beneficiaries; and I think the courts should be very slow to advance along the road of imposing such a duty. I say nothing about what may be kindly or helpful; I deal only with a duty for the breach of which the trustees may be held liable in equity. Short of the alter ego type of case I do not think that trustees can be said to be under any duty to proffer information to their beneficiary, or to see that he has proper advice, merely because they are trustees for him and know that he is entering into a transaction with his beneficial interest with some person or body connected in some way with the trustees, such as a company in which the trustees own some shares beneficially.'

[112] [1977] Ch 106 at 242–243.

# PART V

# CHECKS AND CONTROLS

# 27

# Control of trusts and trustees

## 1 The need for control

### (1) The potential for abuse

In Parts III and IV it has been seen how the mechanisms developed by equity, primarily the trust and the power, enable the separation of the management and the ownership of property. It is obvious that whenever one person has the effective control of property but is required to act for the benefit of another there is a possibility that he will misuse the powers that he holds. For example, a trustee may be tempted to apply the trust property for his own benefit rather than for the benefit of the beneficiaries, or the donee of a special power of appointment may attempt to appoint to someone outside of the class. The exact limits that circumscribe the actions of a person enjoying the responsibility to manage and allocate property are determined by the nature of the relationship that has been created. He will have a range of rights and duties, some of which are imposed by the general principles of equity, and others of which may have been imposed expressly when the mechanism was created. The question arises as to how to ensure that the holder of the management responsibility carries out his duties properly.

### (2) The reality of abuse

Human nature being what it is, the reports are littered with cases where trustees enjoying the responsibility to manage trust property have abused their position and failed to carry out their duties. For example, in *Lipkin Gorman v Karpnale Ltd*[1] a solicitor misappropriated money from his firm's client account to finance his gambling habit. *Bishopsgate Investment Management Ltd v Maxwell (No 2)*[2] concerned the infamous Maxwell pension fraud. Ian and Kevin Maxwell were directors of a company which held assets on trust for the pension schemes of companies owned by Robert Maxwell. To support other private companies which Robert Maxwell owned, property was misappropriated from the trust fund. Kevin and Ian, as directors, were responsible for signing transfer forms authorising the misappropriations. This was a classic case where those who held the management power over the property by virtue of their position as directors and trustees abused their position and were able to apply the property for improper purposes rather than for the benefit of the pensioners.

---

[1] [1987] 1 WLR 987.    [2] [1994] 1 All ER 261.

## (3) Preventing abuse

It is often impossible to prevent those who are dishonest from taking advantage of the opportunities for abuse that their position brings, and the crucial question is generally whether an adequate remedy is available when an abuse has taken place. However, the legal system possesses some mechanisms by which to attempt to prevent abuses occurring.

### (a) Supervision and regulation

The law could introduce methods requiring the ongoing supervision of trustees, by the court or by independent regulators, so that their dealings are closely scrutinised and the potential for abuse is greatly reduced. It might be possible to establish regulatory bodies with the responsibility of ensuring that trustees do their duty, although in practice this would prove impossible because of the number and range of trusts that exist. However, in the case of charitable trusts a sophisticated scheme of regulation is in place through the Charity Commissioners. Regulatory regimes have been introduced in specific contexts where trust relationships may play an important part, for example to oversee the financial services industry and especially pension fund managers. The Pensions Act 1995 introduced the Occupational Pensions Regulatory Authority with the object of reducing the opportunities for fraud.

Generally, abuse occurs because of the dishonesty of an individual trustee or trustees. The choice of trustee is therefore of the utmost importance. At present, there is no general provision disqualifying certain individuals from holding office as trustees, although the Charities Act 1993 does disqualify certain persons from serving as charity trustees. Following the recommendations of the Pension Law Review Committee, which sat under the chairmanship of Professor Roy Goode after the Maxwell scandal, s 29(1) of the Pensions Act 1995 provides that a person is disqualified for being a trustee of any pension trust scheme if he has been convicted of any offence involving dishonesty or deception, is an undischarged bankrupt, or is disqualified to act as a company director.[3] A company cannot serve as trustee of a pension fund if any of its directors is disqualified from acting as trustee under the section.

Obviously, the greatest dangers of abuse arise where the trust property is held and managed by a sole trustee. Where there are multiple trustees the general rule that all decisions must be unanimous provides a measure of protection for the beneficiaries.

### (b) Deterrence and remedies

Rather than supervising trustees so as to prevent abuse occurring, equity has put in place powerful remedies which are available when an abuse occurs, which therefore act to deter those who might consider abusing their position. If the remedies available to the beneficiaries of a trust operate to deprive a trustee of any gain made through abuse of his position, this will act as a disincentive to abuse in the first place. Some abuses, particularly the misappropriation of trust property, also constitute criminal offences, in which case the possibility of criminal conviction will also act as a deterrent.

---

[3] Under the Company Directors' Disqualification Act 1986.

# 2 The means of control

## (1) Criminal sanctions

Some measure of control over the conduct of trustees is provided by the general criminal law. In particular, if a trustee misappropriates trust property he will be guilty of theft. The Theft Act 1968 defines theft in s 1(1):

'A person is guilty of theft if he dishonestly appropriates property belonging to another with the intention of permanently depriving the other of it . . .'

'Property belonging to another' is defined in s 5(2) to include property held on trust so that 'where property is subject to a trust, the persons to whom it belongs shall be regarded as including any person having a right to enforce the trust, and an intention to defeat the trust shall be regarded accordingly as an intention to deprive of the property any person having that right'. Thus, the trustee, or anyone else who misappropriates the trust property, will be guilty of theft.[4] However, although the prospect of a conviction for theft may serve as a deterrent to abuse, it does not restore the trust property to the beneficiaries, which is often their prime concern.

## (2) Supervision by the court

Every trust is technically under the jurisdiction and the supervision of the court. However, in practice the court does not exercise a day-to-day function of supervising the activities of trustees, ensuring that they do not abuse their powers and that they carry out their duties properly. The court is dependent on the beneficiaries of the trust to bring complaints regarding the trustees' conduct to their attention. If the beneficiaries approach the court before a trustee acts improperly, it will be able to issue an injunction to restrain the proposed breach of trust. Where a breach has already occurred, the beneficiaries will be awarded an appropriate remedy.

Even though it does not act as a day-to-day watchdog over trustees, the court serves the very important function of setting the standard of probity that trustees are required to observe in their dealings, by which their conduct will be tested if a claim is made against them by the beneficiaries. The higher the standard of care that is required, the greater the probability that the trustee will not be able to gain by abusing his position, and the greater the deterrent effect. Traditionally, the courts have set extremely high standards for the conduct of trustees, and the remedies available border on the draconian.

### (a) The fiduciary position of the trustee

Trustees stands in a fiduciary position to the beneficiaries of the trust. This means that they are always expected to act in the interests of the beneficiaries, with the implication that they are not permitted to take advantage of their position for their own benefit. As

---

[4] See *Re A-G's Reference (No 1 of 1985)* [1986] QB 491; (1986) 102 LQR 486; (1986) 45 CLJ 367 (Gearty); (1986) 136 NLJ 913 (Smart); [1987] Conv 209 (Martin).

such, they owe a duty of exclusive loyalty to the beneficiaries. Trustees are not the only persons deemed fiduciaries in equity. Those occupying positions of trust and responsibility for the affairs of others, such as company directors, agents and partners, are also regarded as fiduciaries. Equity imposes a rigid rule that a fiduciary must not benefit by virtue of his position, which thus acts as a safeguard to ensure that there is no possibility that he is abusing it. A fiduciary will be forced to disgorge any profits that he may have made in breach of his fiduciary duty by making restitution of them to the persons to whom the duty was owed. The standard of probity expected of a fiduciary is extremely high, as was confirmed in *Boardman v Phipps*,[5] where the majority of the House of Lords held that a fiduciary was liable to make restitution of profits he had made if there had been a mere possibility of a conflict between his duty and his personal interests.

### (b) The standard of care expected of trustees

Equity imposes an objective standard of care on the way that trustees carry out their duties. They are expected to act with the standard of care of an ordinary prudent man of business who is dealing on behalf of someone else.[6] If the trustee fails to exercise the requisite standard of care, or fails to carry out his duties, or acts outside of his powers or the terms of the trust, he will have committed a breach of trust and will be liable to compensate the beneficiaries for any loss caused by his breach.

## (3) Supervision by the beneficiaries

As the court cannot supervise the activities of every trustee, the prime responsibility for such supervision falls to the beneficiaries of the trust. They are expected to monitor the trustee's activities, and to complain to the court if there is any breach of fiduciary duty or breach of trust. It is entirely appropriate that this burden should fall to them, as they are the very people who are most interested in the proper performance of the trust. It is they who will be most anxious to ensure that the trustee carries out his duties properly, that trust property is not misapplied, and that the trustee does not use his position to his own advantage at their expense. A number of principles, which have been examined earlier in this book, confirm that the beneficiaries are the persons primarily responsible for the supervision of the trustees.

### (a) Beneficiary principle

The beneficiary principle examined in Chapter 12 is predicated on the understanding that the beneficiaries are primarily responsible for supervising the trustees. The very reason equity requires a trust to have identifiable legal persons as beneficiaries is that in the absence of such a beneficiary no one possesses the necessary locus standi to apply to the court in the event of a breach by the trustees, and there is no one in whose favour the court can decree specific performance of the trust.[7] If the trust is created in

---

[5] [1967] 2 AC 46.
[6] *Speight v Gaunt* (1883) 9 App Cas 1, HL; *Bartlett v Barclay's Bank Trust Co Ltd* [1980] Ch 515.
[7] *Morice v Bishop of Durham* (1804) 9 Ves 399; *Bowman v Secular Society Ltd* [1917] AC 406; *Re Astor's Settlement* [1952] Ch 534; *Re Shaw* [1957] 1 WLR 729.

favour of a pure purpose, who can enforce the trust? In the case of charitable trusts this problem has been overcome, as they are enforced by the Attorney General, acting on behalf of the Crown. It is notable that the limited anomalous exceptions to the beneficiary principle give rise to valid but unenforceable trusts.

## (b) Beneficiaries' entitlement to information

As was seen in Chapter 26, although the beneficiaries of a trust cannot require the trustees to provide reasons for the exercise, or non-exercise, of their discretions,[8] they are entitled to receive information detailing how the trust assets are held.[9] The fact that the beneficiaries are entitled to obtain such information enables them to supervise to some measure the activities of the trustees. The court will intervene if a trustee can be shown to have exercised his discretion wrongly.[10] The general effectiveness of the beneficiaries' supervision of the trustees' exercise of their discretion is limited by the fact that they are not entitled to reasons from the trustees for their decisions. This means that, although a beneficiary may suspect that a discretion has been exercised wrongly, he is unable to gain the evidence necessary to make out his case.

## (c) Beneficiaries may approve breaches of trust

Whilst it might be expected that trustees are subject to an absolute obligation to carry out the terms of a trust as specified by the original settlor, this is not in fact the case. If the beneficiaries consent to the trustees acting otherwise than in accordance with the terms of the trust, then they will not attract liability for their breach. Trustees may vary the terms of the trust with the consent of the beneficiaries, or even bring the trust to an end.[11] The courts have no jurisdiction to step in and prevent a breach of trust which is made with the full consent of all the beneficiaries, even if this defeats the intentions of the settlor.

## (d) Beneficiaries entitled to seek remedies

Where a trustee has abused his powers or position the trustees may come to the court to seek a remedy. There are a variety of remedies that may be available to them, each of which will be examined in detail in the following chapters.

*(i) Compensation for breach of trust.* Where trustees have committed a breach of trust, the beneficiaries are prima facie entitled to recover compensation from them for any loss the trust has sustained as a result of the breach. The remedy of damages for breach of trust is purely personal against the trustee, and will therefore be ineffective if the trustee is insolvent. The nature and scope of the remedy for breach of trust is considered in Chapter 28.

*(ii) Account of profits for breach of fiduciary duty.* If the trustee has made an unauthorised profit for himself by allowing his duty and his personal interest to conflict,

---

[8] *Re Beloved Wilkes' Charity* (1851) 3 Mac & G 440; *Re Londonderry's Settlement* [1965] Ch 918, CA; *Wilson v Law Debenture Trust Corpn* [1995] 2 All ER 337.
[9] *Low v Bouverie* [1891] 3 Ch 82 at 99. [10] *Klug v Klug* [1918] 2 Ch 67.
[11] *Saunders v Vautier* (1841) Cr & Ph 240; see also Chapter 18 and Chapter 22.

he will be in breach of his fiduciary duty and the beneficiaries will be able to recover from him any profit that he has made. The duty to account for profits made is a purely personal duty, although the beneficiaries may have a proprietary claim to any profits remaining in the hands of the trustee, or property which can be regarded as the proceeds of such profits.[12] The nature and scope of the equitable duty to account for profits received in breach of fiduciary duty is considered in Chapter 29.

*(iii) Proprietary remedies.* If the trustee who has committed a breach of trust or made an unauthorised profit is insolvent, any personal remedies of the beneficiaries will be rendered largely ineffective. They will merely rank amongst the trustee's general creditors. However, if they can show that the trustee has property amongst his assets which was trust property, or if he has assets which can be shown to be the product of trust property by application of the rules of tracing, the beneficiaries will be able to claim those assets as belonging to the trust. They will not fall to be considered as comprising part of his general assets, and in effect the trust will gain priority over the interests of the general creditors. The availability of proprietary remedies, and the rules used to identify trust property, are considered in Chapter 31.

*(iv) Remedies against strangers to the trust.* Where a breach of trust involves third parties who are strangers to the trust, the beneficiaries may have both personal and proprietary remedies against them. If such a stranger has received and retained property which was misappropriated from the trust, the beneficiaries will be able to assert their equitable entitlement to it unless he had acquired it as a bona fide purchaser for value without notice of the existence of the trust. This is also the case if he can be shown to have property amongst his assets which is the product of trust property he received by the rules of tracing. If, however, he received property from the trust but has subsequently dissipated it, or its proceeds, he may yet be liable to account to the trust for the value of the property he received. The obligation to account for the value of such property is a restitutionary remedy and at present only a recipient who acted dishonestly will be obliged to make restitution, although there are increasing calls by academics for the adoption of a strict liability to make restitution against the recipients of trust property. A stranger who has not himself received trust property, but who had assisted the trustees in a misappropriation of trust property, may also be liable to compensate the trust for the value of the misappropriated property. This liability is analogous to the tort of conversion. Such an assistor will only attract liability if he acted dishonestly. The remedies available to the beneficiaries against strangers to a trust are considered in Chapter 30.

## (4) Evaluating the effectiveness of supervision by the beneficiaries

It is obvious that the beneficiaries of a trust have a strong vested interest in ensuring that it is properly carried out according to its terms, and that the trustees do not abuse their position. However, the effectiveness of their supervision depends upon the nature

---

[12] *A-G for Hong Kong v Reid* [1994] 1 All ER 1.

of the trust. In the case of a small family trust, where the trustees and the terms of the trust are well known to the beneficiaries, such scrutiny is likely to be close and effective. In the case of large modern trust funds, with many thousands of beneficiaries and millions of pounds of assets, the beneficiaries are not in a position to scrutinise the day-to-day conduct of the trustees, both because of the enormity of the task, and the complexity of the situations involved. In such circumstances it is not realistic to expect the beneficiaries effectively to supervise the trustees' performance of their duties. To take the Maxwell pension fraud as an example: could the employees entitled to pensions realistically be expected to scrutinise the dealings of the directors of the companies holding the assets on trust so as to prevent the wrongful transfer of trust asses to the Maxwell private companies? Another limitation is that the trustees' misconduct often only comes to light after the event, when it is too late to prevent it, and when the beneficiaries' remedies may be all but ineffective because of the trustees' insolvency and because the trust property has been dissipated. Both these problems demonstrate the limitation of the effectiveness of supervision by the beneficiaries, and emphasise the importance of appointing appropriate persons to act in that capacity.

## 3 Controlling and supervising charitable trusts

Just as the trustees of a private trust have the potential to breach their duty and act in their own interests rather than in the interests of their beneficiaries, the trustees of charitable trusts have the opportunity to defraud both the charity for which they act as trustee and the public at large who make donations. It is essential to protect against spurious charities, and to ensure that the funds of genuine charities are properly applied. In 1992 the Charity Commissioners reported two examples of fraud by charity trustees which illustrate the kind of abuse that the law seeks to prevent. In the case of the Hospital Fund, a registered charity, two trustees were investigated after the Commissioners learnt of their lifestyle. It was found that the charity was raising some £0.5m per annum by the sale of tickets for a prize draw, door to door in Kent, but that only some 20% of the money raised was being applied to the hospitals. The trustees were arrested and convicted of false accounting. In the case of the National Hospital for Neurology and Neurosurgery Development Foundation, an employee, Miss Rosemary Aberdour, was in charge of fund raising and stole some £2.7m. Abuse may also take a less dramatic form. In 2001 the Charity Commission reported how it had undertaken an investigation of the Devon Sheltered Homes Trust, a charity which was responsible for running a residential care home for people with learning disabilities, after complaints from residents had not been dealt with satisfactorily by the management. New management was appointed and the quality of service provided was greatly improved. The following year, responding to concerns raised by a local authority's trading standards department, the Charity Commission investigated the relationship between the Happy Society, a charity for disabled people in Wolverhampton, and three publishing companies. The contracts between the society and the companies were terminated in view of the Commission's conclusion that the trustees had exercised no meaningful control over the commercial participators' activities, the funds they raised, and how much the Happy Society received.[13]

In the case of private trusts the primary task of supervising the trustees and ensuring that they do not abuse their position falls to the beneficiaries. Charitable trusts do not have beneficiaries as such since, by their very nature, they are purpose trusts[14] and an exception to the beneficiary principle,[15] although there may obviously be persons who are interested in seeing that assets held on trust for charity are properly applied, for example donors.[16] Historically, charities were supervised and controlled by the Attorney General acting on behalf of the Crown. However, his function has largely been replaced by a regulatory system which has a statutory footing. The law was revised by the Charities Act 1993 and is further revised by the Charities Bill 2005.

## (1) Features of the regulatory system

The main feature of the regulatory mechanism for charities is the role of the Charity Commission, which will be made a body corporate on the enactment of the Charities Bill 2005[17]. The Charity Commission has the task of overseeing charities in general and investigating abuses. It is obliged to maintain a register of charities. One of the Charity Commissioners is also required to act as the Official Custodian for Charities. The legislation provides that some persons are disqualified from holding office as trustees and requires charity trustees to maintain accounts and to submit an annual report of the charity's activities and an annual statement of accounts to the Commissioners. The report and accounting requirements enable the Commissioners to supervise the conduct of charities, and they are also open to public inspection. Some charities are under the jurisdiction of visitors, although the authority of visitors to universities has been significantly reduced by legislation and no longer applies to employment matters or to complaints by students. Disputes relating to the former fall within the jurisdiction of employment tribunals, and student complaints are now within the jurisdiction of the Independent Adjudicator for Higher Education, an office established by the Higher Education Act 2004.

The Charities Bill 2005 further extends the role of the Charity Commission in the regulation of charities, conferring on it extended powers to suspend or remove trustees,[18] to give specific directions for the protection of charity,[19] and to direct the application of charity property.[20] The Commission is given the power, on issue of a search warrant, to enter premises.[21] There is, however, an obligation on the Charity Commission to have regard to the principles of best regulatory practice, 'including the principles under

---

[13]  Charity Commission Annual Report 2002–2003.       [14]  See Chapter 19.       [15]  See Chapter 13.
[16]  See also [1997] Conv 106 (Warburton).
[17]  Charities Bill 2005, cl 6. Whilst the functions of the Commission are to be exercised on behalf of the Crown, cl 6(4) states that it shall not be subject to control by a government department or any Minister of the Crown.
[18]  Charities Act 1993, s18A inserted by Charities Bill 2005, cl 19.
[19]  Charities Act 1993, s19A inserted by Charities Bill 2005, cl 20.
[20]  Charities Act 1993, s19B inserted by Charities Bill 2005, cl 21.
[21]  Charities Act 1993, s31A inserted by Charities Bill 2005, cl 26.

which regulatory activities should be proportionate, accountable, consistent, transparent and targeted only at cases in which action is needed'.[22]

## (2) The Crown

The Crown is parens patriae of charity,[23] and therefore protector of charity in general.[24] However, this function is exercised on behalf of the Crown by the Attorney General.

## (3) The Attorney General

Historically, the main mechanism for the supervision and control of charitable trusts was the Attorney General, acting on behalf of the Crown. As Hoffmann J stated in *Bradshaw v University College of Wales, Aberystwyth*: 'So far as the enforcement of the trust is a matter of public interest, the guardian of that interest is the Attorney General.'[25]

Prior to the Charities Act 1993 the Attorney General was generally a necessary party to charity proceedings[26] because he represented the beneficial interest,[27] in other words the charitable purposes of the trust. As Lord Simmonds observed in *National Anti-Vivisection Society v IRC*,[28] it is the right and duty of the Attorney General to inform the courts if the trustees of a charity fall short of their duty,[29] and to help the court formulate schemes for the execution of charitable trusts.[30]

Prior to the 1993 Act, only the Attorney General was entitled to bring an action to determine whether a trust was charitable. However, s 32 of the Charities Act 1993 grants the Charity Commission the same powers as the Attorney General to take legal proceedings with reference to charities, or the property affairs of charities, and to compromise claims to avoid or end proceedings. This emphasises that the primary responsibility for controlling and enforcing charitable trusts falls today to the Commission.

## (4) The court

### (a) The jurisdiction of the court

The court possesses a general inherent jurisdiction[31] over charitable trusts. It has the power to draw up schemes for the administration of a charity,[32] particularly where there

---

[22] Charities Act 1993, s1D inserted by Charities Bill 2005, cl 7.

[23] *Wallis v Solicitor-General for New Zealand* [1903] AC 173 at 181–182.

[24] *A-G v Glegg* (1738) 1 Atk 356; *Moggridge v Thackwell* (1803) 7 Ves 36; *Incorporated Society v Richards* (1841) 1 Dr & War 258; *A-G v Compton* (1842) 1 Y & C Ch Cas 417; *National Anti-Vivisection Society v IRC* [1948] AC 31, HL; *Re Belling* [1967] Ch 425; *Hauxwell v Barton-upon-Humber UDC* [1974] Ch 432.

[25] [1987] 3 All ER 200 at 203.

[26] See *Wellbeloved v Jones* (1822) 1 Sim & St 40; *National Anti-Vivisection Society v IRC* [1948] AC 31, HL; *Hauxwell v Barton-upon-Humber UDC* [1974] Ch 432.

[27] *Ware v Cumberlege* (1855) 20 Beav 503; *Re King* [1917] 2 Ch 420.     [28] [1948] AC 31 at 62.

[29] *A-G v Brown* (1818) 1 Swan 265; *National Anti-Vivisection Society v IRC* [1948] AC 31.

[30] *National Anti-Vivisection Society v IRC* [1948] AC 31; *Re Harpur's Will Trusts* [1962] Ch 78, CA.

[31] *Mills v Farmer* (1815) 1 Mer 55; *A-G v Sherborne Grammar Schools Governors* (1854) 18 Beav 256.

[32] See *A-G v Coopers' Co* (1812) 19 Ves 187; *A-G v St Olave's Grammar School* (1837) Coop Pr Cas 267; *A-G v Dedham School* (1857) 23 Beav 350.

is a need to administer a fund cy-près,[33] and it remedies breaches of trust by charity trustees. This jurisdiction derives from the court's general jurisdiction over trusts. If a gift has been made to charity in general, or simply to one of the heads of charity, for example 'the poor', the court has the jurisdiction to draw up a scheme for the application of the property if a trust was intended, but if no trust was intended the Crown applies the property under the sign manual.[34] The court has no jurisdiction in the case of a charity founded by Royal Charter[35] or over a charity completely regulated by statute.[36] However, the court does have jurisdiction to ensure that the terms of the charter or statute are properly kept. The court retains an inherent jurisdiction over corporate charities, even though, in the strict sense, a company required to apply its assets for charitable purposes does not hold those assets on trust.[37] The Court of Appeal has held that the court has no jurisdiction under the Charities Act 1993 in respect of charities established outside England and Wales under a foreign legal system.[38]

An example of the exercise of the court's supervisory jurisdiction over charitable trusts is provided by *Royal Society for the Prevention of Cruelty to Animals v A-G.*[39] The Society sought to exclude members and applicants for membership who had joined for the ulterior purpose of changing its anti-hunting policy. Members and applicants who fell within defined categories would be treated as conclusively proved deserving of exclusion, without the need to consider the merits of their individual cases. Lightman J held that whilst the policy of exclusion did not contravene the Human Rights Act, the Society should not operate its chosen method of implementing its membership policy. He considered that it was 'arbitrary and unattractive' and that it was not necessary to exclude from membership persons to whom no conceivable objection could be taken if the full facts were allowed to be taken into account. Given that emergency action was not required, the 'plight of the innocent' needed to be given greater weight. He also considered that the 'public image and reputation' of the Society had not been sufficiently taken into account in adopting such a draconian policy.

### (b) Concurrent jurisdiction of the Charity Commission

The primacy of the role of the Charity Commission in the supervision and control of charitable trusts is also evident, in that the Commission enjoys concurrent jurisdiction alongside that of the court. It is thus able to exercise many of the functions formerly the exclusive preserve of the court. By s 16(1) of the Charities Act 1993 the Charity Commission enjoys the same jurisdiction and powers that are exercisable by the High Court in charity proceedings for the purposes of: (a) establishing a scheme for the

---

[33] See Chapter 19.

[34] *Moggridge v Thackwell* (1803) 7 Ves 36; *Paice v Archbishop of Canterbury* (1807) 14 Ves 364; *Spiller v Maude* (1881) 32 Ch D 158n; *Re Slevin* [1891] 2 Ch 236, CA; *Re White* [1893] 2 Ch 41, CA; *Re Bennett* [1960] Ch 18.

[35] *A-G v Smart* (1748) 1 Ves Sen 72; *A-G v Middleton* (1751) 2 Ves Sen 327; *A-G v Governors of the Foundling Hospital* (1793) 2 Ves 42. If the charity was granted a Royal Charter subsequent to its foundation to provide an incorporated trustee, the court retains its inherent jurisdiction: *A-G v Dedham School* (1857) 23 Beav 350.

[36] *Re Shrewsbury Grammar School* (1849) 1 Mac & G 324.

[37] *Liverpool and District Hospital for Diseases of the Heart v A-G* [1981] 1 All ER 994.

[38] *Gaudiya Mission v Brahmachary* [1998] Ch 341.　　[39] [2001] 3 All ER 530.

administration of a charity; (b) appointing, discharging or removing a charity trustee or trustee for a charity, or removing an officer or employee; (c) vesting or transferring property, or requiring or entitling any person to call for or make any transfer of property or any payment.

## (c) Charity proceedings

The effectiveness of the supervision of charitable trusts by the court depends on those who might have some interest being able to start an action. Other than the Attorney General and the Charity Commission, s 33(1) of the Charities Act 1993 provides that:

'Charity proceedings may be taken with reference to a charity either by the charity, or by any of the charity trustees, or by any person interested in the charity, or by any two or more inhabitants of the area of the charity if it is a local charity, but not by any other person.'

*(i) Any person interested in the charity.* The definition of this phrase has been considered in a number of cases. *Re Hampton Fuel Allotment Charity*[40] concerned a charity relieving hardship and distress amongst residents of Hampton. The charity sought to sell land which it owned to a supermarket for £8m. A minority of the trustees felt that the sale was at a gross undervalue, and that the real value was some £14m. They started an action seeking orders concerning the administration of the charity along with Richmond Council, which had the power to appoint three of the trustees and in whose borough the charity operated. At first instance the council was struck out as not being a person 'interested in the charity'. However, the Court of Appeal held that it did enjoy sufficient interest to maintain an action. It was unwilling to attempt a comprehensive definition of 'any person interested in the charity' but stated that:

'If a person has an interest in securing the due administration of a trust materially greater than, or different from, that possessed by ordinary members of the public . . . that interest may, depending on the circumstances, qualify him as a "person interested . . ." '[41]

The council had an interest greater than that of the ordinary public because it had a functional role with regard to the charity, in that it appointed three of the eleven trustees, and it was the local authority of the area benefited by the carrying out of the purposes. The Court of Appeal referred to *Haslemere Estates Ltd v Baker*,[42] where Megarry V-C had held that enjoyment of an adverse interest against a charity did not necessarily equate with having a good reason for seeking to enforce the trust. Thus, he suggested that not even tenants of charity land, or those with easements, profits, mortgages or restrictive covenants, or those who had contracted to repair or decorate charity houses or had agreed to buy or sell goods to the charity, would have sufficient interest. It seems that a donor to a charity may have sufficient interest,[43] but not the executors of a donor.[44]

*Haslemere Estates Ltd v Baker*, which concerned a claim by a property developer against the trustees of Dulwich College, was distinguished by Robert Walker J in *Scott v*

---

[40] [1989] Ch 484.      [41] [1989] Ch 484 at 494.      [42] [1982] 1 WLR 1109.
[43] *Brooks v Richardson* [1986] 1 WLR 385.
[44] *Bradshaw v University College of Wales, Aberystwyth* [1988] 1 WLR 190.

*National Trust*[45] on the grounds that it concerned a wholly commercial dispute which had no real connection with the internal or functional administration of charitable trusts.[46] In contrast, he held that held the hunts and tenant farmers which were affected by a decision of the National Trust not to allow the hunting of deer with hounds on its land in Devon and Somerset were sufficiently interested in the charity to bring proceedings. He pointed out that they had been hunting there since long before the land had belonged to the Trust, and that they had been partners with the National Trust in the management of its land.[47]

The ambit of s 33(1) was most recently considered in *Royal Society for the Prevention of Cruelty to Animals v A-G.*[48] The RSPCA sought to change its membership rules so as to exclude members who had been campaigning to persuade the Society to change its anti-hunting stance and prevent applicants becoming members who shared this objective. Lightman J held that an existing member of the Society did have sufficient interest in the charity to commence charity proceedings challenging the propriety of the Society's actions, but that a mere applicant for membership did not:

'But I do not think that a disappointed applicant for membership has any such sufficient interest. Any member of the public is free to apply for membership; the exercise of that liberty cannot elevate the status of a non-member into that of a person interested. To extend the right of suit to any such applicant would be to cast the net too wide.'[49]

*(ii) Consent of the Charity Commission.* Section 33(2) provides that no proceedings shall be taken in any court without the authorisation of the Charity Commission. The Commission is not to authorise proceedings if the case could be dealt with under their own powers.[50] The reason for these limitations is to prevent pointless actions which would simply waste the charity's money.

## (5) The Charity Commission

The Charity Commissioners were first appointed under the Charitable Trusts Act 1853. Their position was modernised by the Charities Act 1960, which implemented the recommendations of the Nathan Committee Report.[51] It is now enshrined in the Charities Act 1993, which followed the Woodfield Report[52] and which is further amended by the Charities Bill 2005. The Charity Commission will become a body corporate with a membership and structure specified in a new schedule to the Charities Act 1993, and with newly specified objectives:[53]

1. to increase public trust and confidence in charities;

2. to promote awareness and understanding of the operation of the public benefit requirement;

---

45  [1998] 2 All ER 705.      46  [1998] 2 All ER 705 at 715.      47  [1998] 2 All ER 705.
48  [2001] 3 All ER 530.      49  [2001] 3 All ER 530 at [21].      50  S 33(3).
51  The Committee on the Law and Practice relating to Charitable Trusts, Cmnd 8710 of 1952.
52  Efficiency Scrutiny of the Supervision of Charities, 1987; National Audit Office Report, House of Commons Paper 380, 1986–87; Annual Report 1987.
53  Charities Act 1993, Sch 1B inserted by Charities Bill 2005, cl 7.

3. to promote compliance by charity trustees with their legal obligations in exercising control and management of the administration of their charities;

4. to promote the effective use of charitable resources; and

5. to enhance the accountability of charities to donors, beneficiaries and the general public.

The functions of the Charity Commission, which are set out in a further new schedule, underline the importance of the role of the Charity Commission in applying and developing charity law, regulating charities, disseminating information, and providing information and advice.

## (a) Annual report

The Commission has the duty to make an annual report to the Secretary of State, which must be laid before Parliament. These reports provide a review of the administration of charities and bring attention to any particular problems. The Commissioners also provide precedents for purposes that they have registered as charitable, and any changes in their requirements.

## (b) Power to institute inquiries

By s 8(1) the Commission has the power to 'institute inquiries with regard to charities, or a particular charity or class of charities'. In connection with this power they have wide-ranging ancillary powers to obtain relevant information. They may order any person to furnish accounts and statements and to return answers in writing to any questions or inquiries,[54] to furnish copies of documents under his control[55] and to give evidence,[56] which may be taken under oath.[57] By s 11 of the Act it is a criminal offence knowingly or recklessly to provide the Commission with false or misleading information, or to wilfully alter, suppress, conceal or destroy any document required to be produced to the Commission. As has been noted above, under the Charities Bill 2005 the Commission may obtain a warrant to search premises.

In 2001 the Charity Commissioners published 123 inquiry reports.[58] The Commission also monitored 96.5% of all charities with an income over £250k, 94.5% of charities with an income of £100k–£250k and 87.6% of charities with an income of £10k–£100k.[59] In the year ending March 2005, the Charity Commission undertook 325 investigations into charities, and as a result, reported that it safeguarded or recovered over £34 million of charitable funds.[60] The Charity Commission is increasingly adopting a risk-based approach in order to concentrate its engagement with charities where it is most needed and which takes account of the risk involved to the charity and its beneficiaries, and the capacity of the charity to comply.[61]

## (c) Power to act for the protection of charities

Section 18 grants the commissioners wide-ranging powers to take action where they have instituted an inquiry and are satisfied:

---

[54] S 8(3)(a).    [55] S 8(3)(b).    [56] S 8(3)(c).    [57] S 8(4).
[58] Annual Report 2001, p 12.    [59] Annual Report 2001, p 13.
[60] Annual Report 2004–2005, p 5.    [61] Annual Report 2004–2005, p 5.

'(a) that there is or has been any misconduct or mismanagement in the administration of the charity; or

(b) that it is necessary or desirable to act for the purpose of protecting the property of the charity or securing a proper application for the purposes of the charity of that property or of property coming to the charity.'[62]

The action they may take includes: the suspension of any trustee pending consideration of his removal;[63] appointing additional trustees;[64] vesting the property of the charity in the Official Custodian;[65] restraining persons who hold property on behalf of the charity from parting with it without their approval;[66] restricting the transactions and payments that may be entered or made without approval;[67] and appointing a receiver and manager.[68] In addition, where the trustees are satisfied that both criteria (a) and (b) above are met, they have the power to: (i) remove any trustee, charity trustee, officer, agent or employee of the charity who has been responsible for or privy to the misconduct or mismanagement or has by his conduct contributed to it or facilitated it; (ii) by order establish a scheme for the administration of the charity.[69] Additional powers will be conferred on the Charity Commission by the Charities Bill 2005, including the power to give specific directions for the protection of charity and to direct the application of charity property.[70]

### (d)  Duty to maintain a register of charities

Section 3 requires the Commissioners to maintain a register of all charities. The scope and purpose of this register is considered below.

### (e)  Duty to inform the Attorney General of the desirability of bringing legal proceedings

Section 33(7) places the trustees under a duty to inform the Attorney General if it is desirable for him to take legal proceedings with reference to any charity.

### (f)  Power to give advice to charity trustees

Section 29 empowers the Commissioners to give their opinion or advice to a charity trustee 'on any matter affecting the performance of his duties as such'. A charity trustee who acts in accordance with such advice is deemed 'to have acted in accordance with his trust', unless he knew or had reasonable cause to suspect that the advice had been given in ignorance of material facts.

### (g)  The official custodian

By s 2 of the Charities Act 1993 (as amended by the Charities Bill 2005) the Charity Commission is required to designate a person to act as the Official Custodian for charitable trusts, so that charity trustees could vest charity property in him as custodian trustee, thereby obviating the need for property (and, in particular, land) to be transferred to the new trustees every time the trustees of a charity change.

---

[62] S 18(1).        [63] S 8(1)(i).        [64] S 8(1)(ii).        [65] S 8(1)(iii).        [66] S 8(1)(iv).
[67] S 8(1)(vi).        [68] S 8(1)(vii).        [69] S 18(2)(i)–(ii).
[70] Charities Bill 2005, inserting ss 19A and 19B into the Charities Act 1993.

## (h) Cost

In 1999–2000 the Commission was allocated £21.8m.[71] In its Annual Report for 2004–05 the Commission reports that it spent a total £29.8m on operating activity and capital investment in the year ending in March 2005.

## (6) The Charities Register

A scheme of general registration of charities was first introduced by the Charities Act 1960. It is now the duty of the Commissioners to maintain such a register, which by s 3(3) of the Charities Act 1993 Act shall contain the name of the charity and any other information the Commissioners think fit. Some charities are not required to register, namely: the 'exempt' charities listed in Sch 2;[72] charities which are exempted by order or regulations and which, following the Charities Bill 2005, have an income of less than £100,000 per annum;[73] charities with a low income, currently less than £1,000 per annum,[74] but to increase under the Charities Bill 2005 to £5,000 per annum.[75] Registered charities are required to provide a copy of their trusts when they apply for registration[76] and the register, including the copies of the charities' trust instruments, is open to public inspection at all reasonable times.[77] The register can be inspected online.

It was formerly the case that exempt charities were exempt not only from the requirement to register, but they were also exempt from many of the regulatory provisions contained in the Charities Acts. This was because they were drawn from sectors which had alternative forms of regulation. The Charities Bill 2005 significantly changes the position. It makes some changes (by clause 11) to the categories of institution with exempt charity status. It also requires a 'principal regulator' to be appointed for all exempt charities.[78] The principal regulator is charged with 'promoting compliance by the charity trustees with their legal obligations in exercising control and management of the administration of the charity.' By clause 12, the Bill increases the degree of regulation of exempt charities, giving the Charity Commission, *inter alia* the power to institute inquiries. This power to institute an inquiry can only be exercised at the request of the principal regulator.

Universities are exempt charities, and as such are not required to register with the Charity Commission. Universities are already subject to detailed scrutiny by the Higher Education Funding Councils in England and Wales, and it is likely that the funding councils will be appointed as the principal regulator for this group of exempt charities.

## (7) The Charity Tribunal

The Charities Bill 2005 establishes a new body, the Charity Tribunal.[79] Under the previous law, a person who was unhappy with a decision of the Charity Commission, for

---

[71] Annual Report 1999, para 6.3.9.    [72] S 3(5)(a).

[73] S 3(5)(b). to be replaced by s 3(2) by the Charities Bill 2005.

[74] S 3(5)(c).

[75] The requirement that small charities must register if they hold land or have a permanent endowment is not being re-enacted by the Charities Bill 2005.

[76] S 3(6).    [77] S 3(8).    [78] Cl 13.    [79] Charities Bill 2005, cl 8.

instance because of a refusal to register a body or a trust as a charity, could ask the Commission to review the decision using its own internal review processes and, if still unhappy, could appeal to the High Court. Under the Charities Bill there is now in many cases a right of appeal to the Charity Tribunal following a final decision, direction, or order of the Charity Commission.[80] There is then a further right of appeal to the High Court, but only on points of law.[81] The Bill gives the Attorney General the right to refer certain matters to the Tribunal.[82] The Attorney General is also given the power to intervene in proceedings before the Tribunal, to which he is not a party.[83]

The membership of the tribunal will include both legally-qualified members and other members who have knowledge or experience relating to charities.[84] The tribunal may sit in panels, but in each such case at least one member of the panel must be a legally-qualified member (or the President, who must be legally qualified).[85] The sorts of matter over which the Tribunal will have jurisdiction are appeals against decisions to register or to refuse to register an institution as a charity, to institute an inquiry with regard to a particular institution or group of institutions, a decision to appoint or remove a charity trustee, and many other decisions listed in Sch 1C.

The Tribunal will clearly have a very important role to play in the future. Many disputed decisions made by the Charity Commission go no further than the internal review process. Since the Tribunal will offer a relatively cheap and speedy alternative to an appeal to the High Court, it is likely that more decisions will be appealed, but since a further appeal to the High Court is possible only where a point of law is involved, fewer cases will be dealt with by the courts. The role of the Charity Tribunal in the development and interpretation of charity law, and in particular the recognition of charitable purposes, is likely to be considerable.

## (8)  Control of charity trustees

The legislative framework recognises the importance of the role of the trustees of charities, and that they enjoy the major opportunities for abuse. Some persons are disqualified from serving as charity trustees, whilst those who can occupy such positions are subject to onerous duties.

### (a)  Disqualification

The Charities Act 1993, s 72 disqualifies certain individuals from serving as charity trustees. The main circumstances in which a person will be so disqualified are:[86] (i) previous conviction of any offence involving dishonesty or deception; (ii) undischarged bankruptcy; (iii) previous removal from the office of a charity trustee by an order of the Commissioners; (iv) previous disqualification from serving as a company director under the Company Directors' Disqualification Act 1986. Any person who serves as a charity trustee while disqualified commits a criminal offence.[87]

---

[80]  S 2A(4)(a) and Sch 1C inserted by the Charities Bill 2005, cl 8.
[81]  S 2C inserted by the Charities Bill 2005, cl 8.
[82]  S 2A(4)(b) and Sch 1D inserted by the Charities Bill 2005, cl 8.
[83]  S 2D inserted by the Charities Bill 2005, cl 8.        [84]  Sch 1B inserted by the Charities Bill 2005.
[85]  Ibid.        [86]  See s 72(1)(a)–(f).        [87]  Charities Act 1993, s 73.

## (b) Duties of charity trustees

The trustees of most charities are under a duty to keep proper financial records and to provide an annual report to the Charity Commissioners. However, the trustees of exempt charities are merely under a duty to keep proper books of account which must be preserved for six years.[88] Where the charity is a company the trustees are exempt from the accounting requirements of the Charities Act 1993[89] but must comply with the company law provisions relating to accounts. Under the Charities (Accounts and Reports) Regulations 1995[90] a new framework was introduced for charity accounting requiring charities to produce annual accounts and a trustee report. The presentation of this information will be required to be uniform, thus allowing people to see more clearly how charities are spending their money. A system of thresholds ensures that the heaviest burden falls to the larger charities, where a stricter regime of external scrutiny will apply. Smaller charities will be subject to less demanding requirements. Charities are required to make their accounts available to the public on request.[91]

*(i) Duty to apply for registration.* Under s 3(7) the trustees of a charity which is not registered and is not exempted or excepted from the requirement to be registered are under a duty to apply for it to be registered.

*(ii) Duty to keep accounts.* Charity trustees are under a duty to keep accounting records which are sufficient to show and explain all the charity's transactions.[92]

*(iii) Duty to prepare annual accounts.* They are also under a duty to prepare an annual statement of accounts in accordance with the regulations made by the Secretary of State.[93]

*(iv) Duty to have an annual audit.* If the annual income of the charity exceeds a specified limit the accounts must be audited, but if it does not exceed that amount they can be examined by an independent examiner. If an audit is not carried out the Commissioners may order an audit at the expense of the charity or the charity trustees.[94]

*(v) Duty to prepare an annual report.* The trustees of a charity are under a duty to prepare an annual report for each financial year containing a report on the activities of the charity during the past year and other information as may be prescribed by regulation. The annual report must be transmitted to the charity commissioners and have attached the statement of accounts[95] and where appropriate the auditor or independent examiner's report.[96] The annual report is to be kept open to public inspection by the commission.[97]

## (9) Local authorities and local charities

Although the Charity Commission operates a national scheme for the registration and supervision of charities, the Charities Act 1993 also makes provision for localised

---

[88] S 46.      [89] Ss 41(5); s 42(7); s 43(9); s 45(5); Companies Act 1985, Pt VII.      [90] SI 1995 2724.
[91] Annual Report 1996, paras 43–47.      [92] S 41.      [93] S 42.      [94] S 43.
[95] With the exception of charities which are companies: s 46(5).      [96] S 46.      [97] S 47.

schemes. Under s 76 county and district councils, London borough councils and the Common Council of the City of London may maintain an index of local charities, from which they may publish information, summaries or extracts, and which is to be open to public inspection. They are entitled to receive from the Commission copies of entries on the register which are relevant for the index.

## (10) Visitors

### (a) Charities under the jurisdiction of visitors

Ecclesiastical and eleemosynary corporations are under the jurisdiction of visitors. Ecclesiastical corporations are those which exist for the furtherance of religion and the perpetuation of the rites of the Church.[98] The visitor is generally the ordinary,[99] although in the case of Royal Foundations or free chapels, the visitor is the patron. Eleemosynary corporations are corporations constituted for the perpetual distribution of free alms or bounty of the founder to such persons as he has directed. They are generally hospitals[100] or colleges. They include the majority of the older universities which were created by Royal Charter. The visitor for such corporations may be appointed by the founder, or if no such appointment was made, the founder and his heirs are the visitor.[101] Where the visitor is the Crown the powers are exercised by the Lord Chancellor.

### (b) Extent of the jurisdiction of the visitor

The visitor only enjoys jurisdiction over the internal affairs of the charity, and has no application to relations between the members of corporations and those outside.[102] In the case of universities created by Royal Charter, the visitor formerly had jurisdiction over matters between the university and students who are members of the university[103] although the visitor's jurisdiction to consider complaints from students has now been transferred by the Higher Education Act 2004 to the Independent Adjudicator for Higher Education. The visitor's jurisdiction, in those instances where it remains, is sole and exclusive,[104] although he must act within his jurisdiction and the rules of natural justice.[105] The visitor is subject to control by the courts through judicial review.

---

[98]   1 Bl Com (16th edn), p 470; *A-G v St Cross Hospital* (1853) 17 Beav 435.

[99]   1 Bl Comm (16th edn), p 479; *Re Dean of York* (1841) 2 QB 1; *R v Dean of Rochester* (1851) 17 QB 1; *Revised Canons Ecclesiastical*, Canon C18, para 4.

[100]   See *Dilworth v Stamps Comrs* [1899] AC 99; *Moses v Marsland* [1901] 1 KB 668.

[101]   *Phillips v Bury* (1694) Skin 447.

[102]   This includes the undergraduates at the majority of Colleges of Oxford and Cambridge, where only the master, fellows and exhibitioners are members of the college. See also *R v Industrial Disputes Tribunal, ex p Queen Mary College, University of London* [1957] 2 QB 483; *Herring v Templeman* [1973] 3 All ER 569, CA; *Casson v University of Aston in Birmingham* [1983] 1 All ER 88; *Thomas v University of Bradford* [1987] 1 All ER 834, HL.

[103]   *Patel v Bradford University Senate* [1978] 1 WLR 1488; *Oakes v Sidney Sussex College, Cambridge* [1988] 1 WLR 431; *R v HM the Queen in Council, ex p Vijayatunga* [1990] 2 QB 444.

[104]   *A-G v Harrow School Governors* (1754) 2 Ves Sen 551; *A-G v Magdalen College, Oxford* (1847) 10 Beav 402; *Thomson v University of London* (1864) 33 LJ Ch 625; *Thorne v University of London* [1966] 2 QB 237, CA; *Patel v Bradford University Senate* [1978] 1 WLR 1488.

[105]   *R v Lord President of the Privy Council, ex p Page* [1993] AC 682.

## (c) Statutory limitation of the visitor's jurisdiction

In the case of universities the jurisdiction of the visitor has been greatly curtailed by the Education Reform Act 1988. Section 206 provides that the visitor has no jurisdiction in respect of any dispute relating to a member of the academic staff which concerns his appointment or employment or the termination of his appointment or employment.[106] The visitor's former jurisdiction over student complaints has also been removed by statute.

## (11) Judicial review of decisions taken by charities

In *Scott v National Trust*[107] Robert Walker J considered the question whether a decision of the National Trust to ban deer hunting with hounds on its land was amenable to judicial review. He noted that charitable trusts involved a public element and that the charity enjoyed powers and discretions which might affect different sections of the public directly or indirectly. Whilst he was unwilling to consider whether any charity, or even any charity specially established by statute is subject to judicial review, he stated his opinion that the National Trust would be susceptible:

'. . . the National Trust is a charity of exceptional importance to the nation, regulated by its own special Acts of Parliament. Its purposes and functions are of high public importance, as is reflected by the special statutory provisions (in the fields of taxation and compulsory acquisition) to which I have already referred. It seems to me to have all the characteristics of a public body which is, prima facie, amenable to judicial review, and to have been exercising its statutory public functions in making the decision which is challenged.'[108]

However, he held that the availability of judicial monitoring through charity proceedings in the Chancery Division meant that judicial review would not be appropriate in all but the most exceptional cases, which he suggested might include where a local authority held land on charitable trusts and questions about its dealings with that land were caught up with other questions about its dealings with land which it owned beneficially.[109] The case suggests that the process of judicial review may have some minor role to play in the control of charities and the activities of charity trustees.

In contrast in *Royal Society for the Prevention of Cruelty to Animals v A-G*[110] Lightman J held that disappointed applicants for membership of the Society were not entitled to seek judicial review. He held that, whilst the Society was a very important charity and its activities were of great value to society, it could be distinguished from the National Trust on the grounds that it had no statutory or public law role. Thus, although it is the largest non-governmental law enforcement agency in England and Wales, in carrying out these activities it is in no different position from that of any citizen or other organisation.

---

[106] See (1991) 54 MLR 137 (Pettit); *Thomas v University of Bradford* [1987] 1 All ER 834; *Pearce v University of Aston in Birmingham* [1991] 2 All ER 461 and *(No 2)* [1991] 2 All ER 469; *Hines v Birkbeck College (No 2)* [1992] Ch 33, CA.

[107] [1998] 2 All ER 705.    [108] [1998] 2 All ER 705 at 716.

[109] [1998] 2 All ER 705 at 717–718.    [110] [2001] 3 All ER 530.

# 28

# Remedies against the trustee for breach of trust

## 1 Meaning of breach of trust

### (1) General definition

It is difficult to provide a simple definition of a breach of trust. Although Sir Robert Megarry V-C was unwilling to attempt any 'comprehensive definition of a breach of trust' in *Tito v Waddell (No 2)*,[1] he referred to two American definitions which had found approval in the courts. First, *Pomeroy's Equity Jurisprudence*[2] states that 'every omission or violation by a trustee of a duty which equity lays on him . . . is a breach of trust'. Secondly, Professor Scott states that a trustee 'commits a breach of trust if he violates any duty which he owes as trustee to the beneficiaries'.[3] These two definitions demonstrate that the essence of a breach of trust is the failure of the trustees properly to carry out the duties expected of them. Their duties may either be expressly required of them by the trust deed creating the trust, or imposed by the general principles of equity. It is also clear that trustees are liable for breach of trust both for their acts and omissions.

### (a) Acts of trustees in breach of trust

If trustees act in a manner inconsistent with the terms of the trust they will have committed a breach of trust.[4] For example, if the trustees of a discretionary trust allocate the trust property to a person outside the class of potential beneficiaries they will be acting in breach of trust.[5] Similarly, if a trustee exceeds the powers that he has been granted by the trust he will be liable.[6] For example, if a trust deed contains an express power of investment which excludes the general power of investment granted in s 3 of the Trustee Act 2000[7] the trustee will commit a breach of trust if he invests the trust fund in investments other than those which are authorised by the trust deed.

---

[1] [1977] 3 All ER 129. He regarded such an attempt as a 'perilous task' (at 247).
[2] As adopted by Corpus Juris Secundum (1955) vol 90, pp 225, 228, para 247.
[3] *Scott on Trusts* (3rd edn 1967), vol 3, p 1605, para 201.
[4] *Pye v Gorges* (1710) Prec Ch 308; *Mansell v Mansell* (1732) 2 P Wms 678; *Charitable Corpn v Sutton* (1742) 9 Mod Rep 349; *Clough v Bond* (1838) 3 My & Cr 490; *Harrison v Randall* (1851) 9 Hare 397; *Reid v Thompson and M'Namara* (1851) 2 I Ch R 26; *Dance v Goldingham* (1873) 8 Ch App 902.
[5] See Chapter 16.
[6] *Adair v Shaw* (1803) 1 Sch & Lef 243; *Collier v M'Bean* (1865) 34 Beav 426.
[7] Trustee Act 2000, s 6(1).

## (b) Omissions of trustees in breach of trust

If trustees fail to fulfill their duties to the trust through neglect or omission, they will also commit a breach of trust.[8] Historically the standard of care required of trustees was the objective standard of the 'ordinary prudent man of business'. As Brightman J said in *Bartlett v Barclays Bank Trust Co Ltd*:[9]

'The cases establish that it is the duty of a trustee to conduct the business of the trust with the same care as an ordinary prudent man of business would extend towards his own affairs.'[10]

A higher standard of care was demanded of professional trustees, such as trust corporations. This is entirely appropriate since such corporations, which carry on a specialised business of trust management, hold themselves out as having a level of expertise beyond that of the 'ordinary prudent man of business'. They will be held liable 'if loss is caused to the trust fund because it neglects to exercise the special care and skill which it professes to have'.[11]

More recently the duty of care demanded of trustee in respect of the performance of some of their duties has been placed on a statutory footing. Section 1(1) of the Trustee Act 2000 provides that:

'Whenever the duty under this subsection applies to a trustee, he must exercise such care and skill as is reasonable in the circumstances, having regard in particular—

    (a) to any special knowledge or experience that he has or holds himself out as having, and

    (b) if he acts as trustee in the course of a business or profession, to any special knowledge or experience that it is reasonable to expect of a person acting in the course of that kind of business or profession.'

This statutory duty of care applies to certain specific situations which are outlined in Schedule 1 to the Trustee Act 2000 and include the exercise of the power of investment, review of the trust investments, obtaining advice about trust investments, the exercise of powers in relation to land (including the power to acquire land) and the appointment of agents custodians or nominees.

If a trustee has failed to exercise the required standard of care, and loss is caused to the trust, he will be liable for breach of trust. For example, in *Re Lucking's Will Trusts*[12] a trustee was held liable for his failure adequately to supervise the management of a

---

[8] *Charitable Corpn v Sutton* (1742) 9 Mod Rep 349; *Lord Montfort v Lord Cadogan* (1810) 17 Ves 485; *Moyle v Moyle* (1831) 2 Russ & M 710; *Taylor v Tabrum* (1833) 6 Sim 281; *Clough v Bond* (1838) 3 My & Cr 490; *Fenwick v Greenwell* (1847) 10 Beav 412; *Dix v Burford* (1854) 19 Beav 409; *Stone v Stone* (1869) 5 Ch App 74; *Jefferys v Marshall* (1870) 19 WR 94; *Re Brogden* (1888) 38 Ch D 546, CA; *Evans v London Co-operative Society* (1976) Times, 6 July; *Bartlett v Barclays Bank Trust Co Ltd* [1980] Ch 515.

[9] [1980] Ch 515 at 531.

[10] *Re Speight* (1883) 22 Ch D 727; affd sum nom *Speight v Gaunt* (1883) 9 App Cas 1; *Learoyd v Whiteley* (1887) 12 App Cas 727, HL; *Re Godfrey* (1883) 23 Ch D 483; *Re Chapman* [1896] 2 Ch 763, CA; *Re Lucking's Will Trusts* [1967] 3 All ER 726, [1968] 1 WLR 866.

[11] [1980] Ch 515 at 531, per Brightman J. See also *Re Waterman's Will Trusts* [1952] 2 All ER 1054; *Nestlé v National Westminster Bank plc* (29 June 1988, unreported).

[12] [1967] 3 All ER 726, [1968] 1 WLR 866.

company in which the trust held a controlling interest. Similarly, in *Bartlett v Barclays Bank Trust Co Ltd (No 2)*[13] a bank was held liable for its failure to supervise two land development projects undertaken by a company of which the bank held 99.8% of the shares as trustee for the Bartlett Trust.[14] The investment subsequently proved to have been imprudent and hazardous and wholly unsuitable for a trust. It may not always be easy to determine whether a trustee's breach was one of commission or omission, as was seen in *Bishopsgate Investment Management Ltd v Maxwell (No 2)*,[15] but the distinction may be important, especially as to the issue of causation.[16]

## (c) Exemption clauses

Whilst trustees are subject to the general duty to act with the prudence of an ordinary man of business, the trust instrument may specifically exclude their liability for conduct which was not dishonest. Even the new statutory duty of care introduced by s 1 of the Trustee Act 2000 many be expressly excluded by the trust instrument.[17] Where such a clause is included in the trust deed it has the effect of lowering the standard of care required of the trustees in the conduct of their business. In *Armitage v Nurse*[18] the Court of Appeal considered the efficacy of a term of a trust instrument which provided that:

'No trustee shall be liable for any loss or damage which may happen to Paula's fund or any part thereof or the income thereof at any time or from any cause whatsoever unless such loss or damage shall be caused by his own actual fraud . . .'

Millett LJ rejected the submission that a trustee exemption clause which purports to exclude all liability except for actual fraud is void, either because it is repugnant or contrary to public policy. Whilst he accepted that there was an irreducible core of obligations owed by trustees to the beneficiaries of a trust, he held that these did not include the obligation to act without negligence:

'But I do not accept the further submission that these core obligations include the duties of skill and care, prudence and diligence. The duty of the trustee to perform the trusts honestly and in good faith for the benefit of the beneficiaries is the minimum necessary to give substance to the trusts, but in my opinion it is sufficient.'[19]

He therefore held that the clause was effective to exclude the trustees from liability for loss or damage to the trust property no matter how indolent, imprudent, lacking in diligence, negligent or wilful he may have been, so long as he has not acted dishonestly.[20] However, he did express his opinion that such exemption clauses had gone too far,[21] with the result that professional trustees charging for their services were able to exclude liability for gross negligence when they would not dream of excluding liability for ordinary professional negligence, but thought that it was for Parliament to deny them effect.[22]

---

[13] [1980] Ch 515.    [14] See also *Armitage v Nurse* [1997] 2 All ER 705 at 716.
[15] [1994] 1 All ER 261.    [16] See below, p 744.    [17] Sch 1, para 7.
[18] [1997] 2 All ER 705; (1997) 11 TLI 52 (Pollard and Walsh); [1998] CLJ 33 (Nicholas J McBride).
[19] [1997] 2 All ER 705 at 713.    [20] [1997] 2 All ER 705 at 711.    [21] [1997] 2 All ER 705 at 715.
[22] See Hayton, 'The Irreducible Core Content of Trusteeship' in Oakley, *Trends in Contemporary Trust Law* (1996); [1998] Conv 100 (McCormack).

The operation of such exemption clauses was further elucidated by the Court of Appeal in the recent case of *Walker v Stones*.[23] The central issue concerned the application of an exclusion clause which purported to protect trustees from liability arising other than through 'wilful fraud or dishonesty'. At first instance Rattee J, relying on *Armitage v Nurse*, had held that this clause would protect a trustee who had knowingly acted in breach of trust, providing that he had acted in a genuine (even if misguided) belief that what he was doing was for the benefit of the beneficiaries, on the grounds that this would not amount to dishonesty. The Court of Appeal rejected this approach, holding that the test for dishonesty could not be limited to an inquiry into the subjective state of mind of the trustee, but included an irreducible objective standard.[24] Giving the judgment of the court Sir Christopher Slade held that the exclusion clause must be interpreted so as to 'take account of the case where the trustee's so-called "honest belief", though actually held, is so unreasonable that, by any objective standard, no reasonable solicitor trustee could have thought that what he did or agreed to was for the benefit of the beneficiaries.'[25] He considered that that such clauses should be construed 'no more widely than their language on a fair reading suggests' and concluded:

'That clause in my judgement would not exempt the trustees from liability for breaches of trust, even if committed in the genuine belief that the course taken was in the best interests of the beneficiaries, if such belief was so unreasonable that no reasonable solicitor-trustee could have held that belief.'[26]

Sir Christopher Slade expressly confined his construal of the exclusion clause to the case of a solicitor-trustee, noting that the test of honesty may vary from case to case, depending upon the role and calling of the trustee.[27]

Subsequent to these decisions the Law Commission has conducted a review of the operation of trustee exemption clauses and issued a consultation paper.[28] The Law Commission found that it was relatively common to find express provision for exclusion of liability in modern trust instruments and that professional trustees have come to rely on them as a means of affording protection from liability for breach of trusts. However, whilst many professional trustees considered such clauses to be a necessary component of modern trust practice, and the inclusion of an exclusion clause is likely to lead to lower liability insurance premiums, the Law Commission concluded that there was a very strong case for some regulation of trustee exemption clauses. It rejected an absolute prohibition on all trustee exemption clauses on the grounds that denying settlers all power to modify or restrict the extent of the obligations and liabilities of trustees would undermine the flexibility and adaptability of the trust relationship. However it proposed that a distinction should be drawn between professional trustees and 'lay' trustees, and that the power of professional trustees to exclude liability be circumscribed. It proposed that professional trustees should not be able to rely on clauses which exclude their liability for breach of trust arising from negligence, and that

---

[23] [2001] QB 902.

[24] Applying the test of dishonesty adopted by the House of Lords in *Royal Brunei Airlines Sdn Bhd v Tan* [1995] 3 All ER 97 and by the Court of Appeal in *Twinsectra Ltd v Yardley* [1999] Lloyd's Rep Bank 438.

[25] [2000] 4 All ER 412 at 443.     [26] [2000] 4 All ER 412 at 446.     [27] [2000] 4 All ER 412 at 443.

[28] *Trustee Exemption Clauses*, Law Commisison Consultation Paper No 171 (2003).

in so far as professional trustees may not exclude liability for breach of trust, that they should not be permitted to claim indemnity from the trust fund. Further the Law Commission proposed that in determining whether professional trustees have been negligent the court should have power to disapply duty exclusion clauses or extended powers clauses where reliance on such clauses would be unreasonable in the circumstances for the trustee to be exempted from liability. The Law Commission sought views on other possible options for reform, including the possible restriction of reliance on a trustee exemption clause to circumstances where the clause satisfies the test of reasonableness. It remains to be seen whether any of these proposals will be implemented, all would require legislation.

### (d) Breach of trust in the context of constructive and resulting trusts

Whereas the trustees of an express trust are liable for breach of trust, the position of a trustee of a resulting or constructive trust is more complex. The essential difference relates to the nature of the duties of such trustees, since in many cases they will not be expected to perform the ordinary functions of express trustee such as the investment of the trust fund. As Millet LJ observed in *Lonrho plc v Al-Fayed (No 2)*:

'It is a mistake to suppose that in every situation in which a constructive trust arises the legal owner is necessarily subject to all the fiduciary obligations and disabilities of an express trustee.'[29]

The primary duty of a constructive trustee is often simply to preserve the trust property for the benefit of the beneficiaries, and to ensure that it is not dissipated. If the trust property is dissipated by the trustee he may be liable to compensate the beneficiaries for their loss: i.e. the value of the trust property. However, it appears that a constructive trustee will only be personally liable in this way if, at the time that the property was dissipated, he was consciously aware of his obligations as a trustee, so that he had acted contrary to them. In *Westdeutsche Landesbank Girozentrale v Islington London Borough Council*, Lord Browne-Wilkinson stated:

'Since the equitable jurisdiction to enforce trusts depends upon the conscience of the holder of the legal interest being affected, he cannot be a trustee of the property if and so long as he is ignorant of the facts alleged to affect his conscience, i.e. until he is aware that he is intended to hold the property for the benefit of others in the case of an express trust, or, in the case of a constructive trust, of the factors which are alleged to affect his conscience.'[30]

Whilst the precise import of this analysis is somewhat obscure, the best interpretation is probably that a person who receives property as a trustee cannot be held liable for any breach of trust, or breach of fiduciary duty, if he was unaware of the fact that he was such a trustee, or of the circumstances making him a trustee. Thus, a third party recipient of trust property who is not a bona fide purchaser thereby becomes a constructive trustee of it, and the beneficial interest of the beneficiaries is preserved. However, the fact that he is a trustee does not mean that he will attract personal liability for breach of trust if he dissipates the property in circumstances where he was unaware

---

[29] [1992] 1 WLR 1 at 12.    [30] [1996] AC 669.

of the constructive trust. In *Bristol and West Building Society v Mothew* Millett LJ adopted this analysis as a summary of the practical outworking of Lord Browne-Wilkinson's comments:

'In *Westdeutsche Landesbank Girozentrale v Islington London Borough Council* Lord Browne-Wilkinson expressly rejected the possibility that a recipient of trust money could be personally liable, regardless of fault, for any subsequent payment away of the moneys to third parties even though, at the date of such payment, he was ignorant of the existence of any trust.'[31]

## (2) Nature of liability for breach of trust

### (a) A compensatory remedy

The remedy for breach of trust is essentially compensatory. When a breach has been committed the trustee responsible is liable to compensate the trust for all the loss flowing directly or indirectly from the breach.[32]

### (b) A personal remedy

The liability of a trustee who has committed a breach to compensate the trust is entirely personal. It is only available against him as an individual and it is not a proprietary remedy against specific assets in his hands. If the trustee retains trust property in his hands due to his breach of trust, or has made a profit because of such a breach and still holds the profit in his hands, the beneficiaries may seek proprietary remedies. These are considered in Chapters 29 and 31, and will be particularly important if the trustee in breach is bankrupt, since the beneficiaries' claim to compensation for breach of trust will only rank alongside the claims of his other general creditors. If the trustee in breach has died the liability continues against his estate.[33]

### (c) Election between compensatory and restitutionary remedies

Whereas a trustee who commits a breach of trust will be liable to compensate the trust for any loss sustained, a trustee who receives an unauthorised profit in breach of his fiduciary duty will be liable to make restitution of the profit received, which constitutes an unjust enrichment. Difficulties arise where a trustee's conduct constitutes both a breach of trust and a breach of fiduciary duty. In such circumstances it is essential to determine whether the potential remedies for breach of trust and breach of fiduciary duty are cumulative—in which case the beneficiaries will be entitled to recover both compensation (for the loss they have suffered) and restitution (of the profit received by the trustee)—or alternative—in which case the beneficiaries must elect between them. In *Tang Man Sit (Decd) v Capacious Investments Ltd*[34] the Privy Council held that the

---

[31] [1996] 4 All ER 698 at 716.

[32] *Bateman v Davis* (1818) 3 Madd 98; *Lander v Weston* (1855) 3 Drew 389; *Knott v Cottee* (1852) 16 Beav 77; *Re Miller's Deed Trusts* [1978] LS Gaz R 454; *Bartlett v Barclays Trust Co Ltd* [1980] Ch 515.

[33] See *Fry v Fry* (1859) 27 Beav 144.

[34] [1996] AC 514, [1996] 1 All ER 193. See [1995] RLR 117 (Stevens); (1996) 112 LQR 375 (Birks).

remedies of compensation for breach of trust and restitution where a trustee has breached his fiduciary duty are alternative, and that the beneficiaries must elect between them to prevent double recovery. The case concerned a planned joint venture for the development of land. The defendant provided land for the development, which was funded by the plaintiff company. It was agreed that the defendant would assign legal title to sixteen of the houses built to the plaintiffs. From the time of this agreement the defendant held the house on trust for the plaintiffs, and in breach of trust the title was never assigned. Over a period of years he let the houses to tenants and received a profit of some HK$2m in the form of rent. The plaintiffs claimed that they were entitled to an equitable account of these profits on the grounds that they were unauthorised remuneration received by the defendant trustee in breach of its fiduciary duty, and also damages for breach of trust for the rent that they could have obtained from the houses if they had been assigned at the appropriate time, a sum which was assessed at HK£17m. The defendant had paid HK$1.8m to the plaintiffs by way of account of the profit received, and the plaintiffs subsequently sought the damages due. The defendant argued that by accepting the account of profits the plaintiffs had made an irrevocable election between the restitutionary and compensatory remedies. The Privy Council held that in the circumstances no election had been made, so that the plaintiffs were entitled to recover full damages, less the KH$1.8m they had already received. The Privy Council clearly stated that where a defendant's conduct can be characterised both as a breach of trust and a breach of fiduciary duty the respective remedies are alternative and the plaintiff must choose between them:

'Faced with alternative and inconsistent remedies a plaintiff must choose, or elect, between them. He cannot have both . . . to some extent at least the remedies claimed by the plaintiff included two alternative and inconsistent remedies. An account of the profits Mr Tang had made from the lettings is an alternative remedy to damages for the loss of use of the houses.'[35]

## (3) Scope of a trustee's liability for breach of trust

### (a) Trustees are liable only for their own breaches of trust

Trustees are only liable for their own breaches of trust and not for the breaches of their co-trustees.[36] However, where several trustees are liable for a breach of trust they are jointly and severally liable. Thus, in *Bishopsgate Investment Management Ltd v Maxwell (No 2)*[37] Kevin and Ian Maxwell, who had both signed transfers misappropriating assets held on trust for the pensions of the employees of Maxwell-owned companies, were jointly and severally liable for their breaches. Joint and several liability means that the beneficiary can recover the entire loss to the trust from any one of the trustees alone.[38] Even where the beneficiary has obtained a judgment against all the trustees he may

---

[35] [1996] 1 All ER 193 at 197 and 201, per Lord Nicholls.    [36] *Townley v Sherborn* (1634) J Bridg 35.
[37] [1994] 1 All ER 261, CA.
[38] *Walker v Symonds* (1818) 3 Swan 1; *Re Harrison* [1891] 2 Ch 349; *McCheane v Gyles (No 2)* [1902] 1 Ch 911.

choose to execute it against any one.[39] As Leach MR stated in *Wilson v Moore*:[40] 'all parties to a breach of trust are equally liable; there is between them no primary liability'.

Although the beneficiaries may be able to recover the entire loss suffered by the trust from just one of the trustees in breach, that trustee may be able to recover a contribution to the damages he has had to pay from his fellow trustees who are in breach under the Civil Liability (Contribution) Act 1978.[41]

### (b) Trustees are generally not liable for breaches committed before they were appointed

A trustee is not liable for breaches of trust which were committed before his appointment.[42] On appointment he is obliged to make reasonable inquiries to ensure that the trust affairs are in order,[43] but, except in so far as a discrepancy appears, he 'is entitled to assume that everything has been duly attended to up to the time of his becoming trustee'.[44] However, if he does discover such a breach he should take proceedings against the former trustees responsible.

### (c) Trustees continuing liability after they have retired from the trust

Retirement does not save a trustee from liability for breaches of trust committed whilst he was a trustee. He will also be liable if he retired to enable a breach of trust to take place. The principle was stated by Kekewich J in *Head v Gould*:

'. . . in order to make a retiring trustee liable for a breach of trust committed by his successor you must show, and show clearly, that the breach of trust which was in fact committed was not merely the outcome of the retirement and new appointment, but was contemplated by the further trustee when such retirement and appointment took place.'[45]

The key factor which renders a retired trustee liable is the fact that he was fully aware of, and connived in, the subsequent breach of trust.

### (d) Trustees generally not vicariously liable for the acts of others

Until recently the liability of trustees for the actions of his fellow trustees or properly appointed agents was limited by s 30(1) of the Trustee Act 1925, which provided that:

'A trustee . . . shall be answerable and accountable only for his own acts, receipts, neglects, or defaults, and not for those of any other trustee, nor for any banker, broker, or other person with whom any trust money or securities may be deposited, nor for the insufficiency or deficiency of any securities, nor for any other loss, unless the same happens through his own wilful default.'

However this provision was repealed by Trustee Act 2000, with the effect that trustees will be liable when they have failed to act in accordance with their duty of care.

---

[39] *A-G v Wilson* (1840) Cr & Ph 1; *Fletcher v Green* (1864) 33 Beav 426.
[40] (1833) 1 My & K 126 at 146.      [41] See below.
[42] *Re Strahan* (1856) 8 De GM & G 291.
[43] *Harvey v Oliver* (1887) 57 LT 239; *Re Lucking's Will Trusts* [1968] 1 WLR 866.
[44] *Re Strahan* (1856) 8 De GM & G 291 at 309, per Turner LJ.      [45] [1898] 2 Ch 250 at 273–274.

## 2 The remedy for breach of trust

### (1) General principle

#### (a) Compensation for loss[46]

A trustee who acts in breach of trust will be liable to compensate the trust for any loss suffered as a result of his breach.[47] As Street J said in *Re Dawson*:

'. . . the trustee is liable to place the trust estate in the same position it would have been in if no breach had been committed.'[48]

In some recent cases, for example *Target Holdings Ltd v Redferns*[49] this compensation has been described as 'restitution' of the trust estate.[50] However, this usage is not strictly accurate, and is liable to be confused with the recently recognised law of restitution. As a legal term of art, restitution is the response which consists in a defendant giving up to the plaintiff any unjust gain, known as an enrichment, which he has received at his expense.[51] A trustee may not have received any personal gain from his breach, in which case it is impossible to regard him as 'enriched'. Whilst the compensatory remedy does in effect restore the trust fund, it is not a restitutionary remedy. The trustee is required to compensate the trust for the loss it has sustained in consequence of his conduct, not to return an enrichment he has received. As Lord Browne-Wilkinson observed in *Target Holdings Ltd v Redferns*:

'. . . in the case of a breach of such a trust involving the wrongful paying away of trust assets, the liability of the trustee is to restore to the trust fund, often called the trust estate, what ought to have been there.'[52]

#### (b) Causation

A trustee who has acted in breach is only liable to compensate the trust for loss which was caused by his breach. If there is no causal link between the breach and the loss, the trustee will not be liable. This is clear from the decision of the Court of Appeal in *Bishopsgate Investment Management Ltd v Maxwell (No 2)*.[53] This case arose out of the Maxwell pension fraud. Ian Maxwell was the director of the plaintiff company, which acted as trustee of a number of pension schemes for the employees of companies owned by Robert Maxwell. Assets held by the company had been misappropriated and applied to the benefit of Robert Maxwell's private companies. Ian Maxwell, as a director, had

---

[46]   See Oakley, 'The Liberalising Nature of Remedies for Breach of Trust' in Oakley, *Trends in Contemporary Trust Law* (1996), pp 219–230; [1997] Conv 14 (Capper); (2000) 59 CLJ 31 (L Sealey); P Birks and F Rose (eds), *Restitution and Equity, Vol 1: Resulting Trusts and Equitable Compensation*.

[47]   See also [1996] Conv 186 (Baxter).        [48]   [1966] 2 NSWLR 211 at 215.

[49]   [1995] 3 All ER 785.

[50]   [1995] 3 All ER 785 at 793, per Lord Browne-Wilkinson. See also Hanbury & Martin, *Modern Equity* (16th edn, 2001) which describes the liability as 'restitutionary' (at p 652).

[51]   Birks, *Introduction to the Law of Restitution* (1985), pp 9–27.

[52]   [1995] 3 All ER 785 at 793.        [53]   [1994] 1 All ER 261.

signed transfers beneath the signature of his brother, Kevin, and had also signed blank transfers. He had made no inquiry about the transactions and had signed the transfers because his brother had done so. The plaintiff obtained summary judgment against him, and an order for an interim payment of £500,000 while damages were assessed. He appealed on the basis that the plaintiff had not shown that his inactivity had caused the loss. The Court of Appeal made it clear that where a fiduciary has committed a breach of duty by omission, the plaintiff claiming damages must prove that the omission caused the loss, in the sense that compliance would have prevented the damage.[54] However, the court held that this was not a case where the breach was in the nature of an omission, but that the breach was simply the improper transfer of the shares to Robert Maxwell Group plc. Causation was thus clearly established and the summary judgment was upheld.

The requirement of causation was considered at length by the House of Lords in *Target Holdings Ltd v Redferns.*[55] The case concerned the purchase of properties in Birmingham by a company, Crowngate Developments Ltd, which was owned by Mr Kohli and Mr Musafir. The vendor was Mirage Properties Ltd, and the purchase was made through two companies registered in Jersey, Panther Ltd and Kholi & Co, also owned by Kohli and Musafir. Redferns was a firm of solicitors acting for the purchasers. Crowngate applied for a loan of £1.7m to purchase the properties from Target, which was granted on the basis of a £2m valuation of the properties made by a firm of estate agents. In fact, Mirage had agreed to sell the properties to Crowngate for £775,000 but Target were not aware of this. The loan was paid into Redferns' client account on 28 June 1989, without any express instructions as to the release of the funds. On 29 June £1.25m was transferred to the account of Panther in Jersey, although at this stage the contract for the purchase of the properties had not yet been entered, and it was not until July that the contracts and mortgages in favour of Target were executed. Subsequently, the value of the properties dropped sharply and Target sought to recover their loss.

Any action against the estate agents, who had carried out the valuation, was of little value because they were in liquidation. Target therefore sought to recover their loss (less anything they would realise from the sale of the property) from Redferns, on the grounds that the transfer of funds before the contracts for sale and the mortgages had been entered had constituted a breach of trust. There was no doubt that this payment was made in breach of trust, and the central question was whether the solicitors should be liable for all the loss suffered by Target on the loans when the most immediate cause was the drop in property prices. At first instance Warner J gave Redferns leave to defend the claim upon condition that they make an interim payment of £1m to Target. Target appealed to the Court of Appeal, claiming that they should have been given final judgment. The majority of the Court of Appeal held that Warner J should have granted final judgment in their favour. They held that Target were entitled to recover the whole

---

[54] Ibid at 264, per Hoffmann LJ.

[55] [1995] 3 All ER 785: (1996) 112 LQR 27 (Rickett); [1996] LMCLQ 161 (Nolan); [1997] Conv 14 (Capper); (1995) 9 TLI 86 (Ulph). See also (1998) 114 LQR 214 (Sir Peter Millett).

of their loss from Redferns, since the payment of the trust money to a stranger in breach of trust had caused their loss. Peter Gibson LJ[56] concluded:

'The cause of action is constituted simply by the payment away of Target's moneys in breach of trust and the loss is quantified in the amount of those moneys, subject to Target giving credit for the realisation of the security it received. It was for Redferns to justify their action or otherwise show why Target was not entitled to compensation in the sum claimed.'[57]

He approved a number of authorities which upheld the view that the principles of remoteness of damage as applied in the context of damages for breach of contract or tort have no application to breach of trust.[58] In particular he referred to the judgment of Street J in *Re Dawson*, who explained the operation of the rule:

'... The principles ... do not appear to involve any inquiry as to whether the loss was caused by or flowed from the breach. Rather the inquiry in each instance would appear to be whether the loss would have happened if there had been no breach ... The cases ... demonstrate that the obligation to make restitution, which the courts of equity have from very early times imposed on defaulting trustees and other fiduciaries is of a more absolute nature than the common law obligation to pay damages for tort or breach of contract.'[59]

However, Ralph Gibson LJ delivered a powerful dissenting judgment, in which he held that Warner J had been correct to refuse to give Target final judgment. He did not dissent on the issue of remoteness, but took the view that there was an arguable defence that the breach had not caused the loss. Although he felt that Target was likely to succeed, he held that it was arguable that they would have gone ahead with the transaction in any event, relying on the valuation of the properties by the estate agents, and that in such circumstances the breach of trust by Redferns would not have been the cause of the loss:

'If it appears just to the court, having regard to [the fiduciary relationship between the parties] and its purpose, and the obligations of the parties within it, and to the way in which the parties would have behaved, for the court to regard the breach as having caused no loss to the plaintiff, because the loss would have happened if there had been no breach, then the court can and must so hold.'[60]

As Redferns had made out an arguable defence, he felt that Warner J had correctly granted them conditional leave to defend.

Redferns appealed to the House of Lords, which held that Target was not entitled to final judgment. Lord Browne-Wilkinson stated the underlying principle as follows:

'... there does have to be some causal connection between the breach of trust and the loss to the trust estate for which compensation is recoverable, viz the fact that the loss would not have occurred but for the breach.'[61]

---

[56] With whom Hirst LJ agreed.        [57] [1994] 2 All ER 337 at 353.

[58] *Clough v Bond* (1838) 3 My & Cr 490; *Re Dawson* [1966] 2 NSWLR 211; *Alliance and Leicester Building Society v Edgestop Ltd* [1994] 2 All ER 38; *Bishopsgate Investment Management Ltd v Maxwell (No 2)* [1994] 1 All ER 261, CA.

[59] [1966] 2 NSWLR 211 at 215–216.        [60] [1994] 2 All ER 337 at 347.

[61] [1995] 3 All ER 785 at 794. See also *Re Miller's Deed Trusts* [1978] LS Gaz 454; *Nestlé v National Westminster Bank plc* [1994] 1 All ER 118.

He went on to conclude that, on the assumption that the transaction would have gone ahead irrespective of the breach of trust, the breach had not been the cause of the loss suffered:

'Target has not demonstrated that it is entitled to any compensation for breach of trust. Assuming that moneys would have been forthcoming from some other source to complete the purchase from Mirage if the moneys had not been wrongly provided by Redferns in breach of trust, Target obtained exactly what it would have obtained had no breach occurred, i.e. a valid security for the sum advanced.'[62]

In the course of his judgment he rejected Target's argument that Redferns were under an immediate duty to restore the trust fund, holding that in a commercial conveyancing context a client has no right to have the solicitor's client account reconstituted after the transaction is completed.[63] He also rejected the argument that the quantum of compensation was to be fixed at the date that the alleged breach occurred. Instead he held:

'The quantum is fixed at the date of judgment, at which date, according to the circumstances then pertaining, the compensation is assessed as the figure then necessary to put the trust estate or the beneficiary back into the position it would have been in had there been no breach.'[64]

Despite concluding that Target had not proved causation, the House of Lords was doubtful whether Redferns would ultimately be able to show that their breach had not caused the loss. Lord Browne-Wilkinson summarised:

'There must be a high probability that, at trial, it will emerge that the use of Target's money to pay for the purchase from Mirage and the other intermediate transactions was a vital feature of this transaction . . . If the moneys made available by Redfern's breach of trust were essential to enable the transaction to go through, but for Redfern's breach of trust Target would not have advanced any money. In that case the loss suffered by Target by reason of the breach of trust will be the total sum advanced to Crowngate less the proceeds of the security.'[65]

For this reason, although Redferns were granted leave to defend the action, the order requiring them to pay £1m into court was not set aside.

In conclusion, the decision of the House of Lords in *Target Holdings Ltd v Redferns* requires a plaintiff seeking compensation when trust property has been transferred contrary to the terms of the trust (or in the case of a bare trust contrary to the instructions of the beneficiary) to demonstrate that, but for the alleged breach of trust, he would not have suffered the loss sustained. Conversely, the defendant can escape liability by demonstrating that the loss would have been sustained even if the breach had not occurred, and the transaction would have been entered irrespectively.

By way of qualification to this general proposition, in *Bristol and West Building Society v May May & Merrimans (No 1)*[66] it was held that a mortgagee claiming

---

[62] [1995] 3 All ER 785 at 799.    [63] [1995] 3 All ER 785 at 795–796.

[64] [1995] 3 All ER 785 at 796.    [65] [1995] 3 All ER 785 at 799–800.

[66] [1996] 2 All ER 801; [1997] LMCLQ 26 (Alcock).

compensation from a solicitor who paid over money advanced on completion—where the money had been received in response to a request based upon a warranty or misrepresentation which the solicitor knew[67] to be misleading—need not demonstrate that the transaction would not have gone ahead but for the misrepresentation. Chadwick J held that there was no need for the plaintiff to answer the 'what if' question:

'It would, as it seems to me, be a strange principle of equity which allowed a solicitor who, in breach of the duty of good faith owed to his client, had given a warranty which he knew to be false with the intention that the client should act upon it, to say, in answer to a claim for compensation in respect of loss which had resulted from the client relying on the warranty and acting as he intended, that the client must establish that he would not have so acted if he had been told the true facts. After all, a common reason for giving a warranty which the warrantor knows to be false is the fear that, without the false warranty, the lender will refuse to proceed. If it were not for that fear the warrantor would have no reason to withhold the truth . . . [W]here a fiduciary has failed to disclose material facts, he cannot be heard to say, in answer to a claim for equitable compensation, that disclosure would not have altered the decision to proceed with the transaction.'[68]

He held that this approach was supported by the earlier decision of the Privy Council in *Brickenden v London Loan & Savings Co,*[69] which he considered had not been overruled by the House of Lords in *Target Holdings Ltd v Redferns.* In *Swindle v Harrison*[70] the Court of Appeal held that the mere fact that a fiduciary had failed to disclose material facts did not establish liability if the transaction would have proceeded irrespective, unless the fiduciary had acted fraudulently.

### (c) Remoteness and foreseeability of loss

Although *Target Holdings Ltd v Redferns (a firm)*[71] demonstrates a need to establish causation in order to render a trustee liable to compensate for breach of trust, the further question arises whether, where such causation is established, a trustee is liable for all the loss which flows from his breach, directly or indirectly, or whether some principle of remoteness operates to limit his liability to such losses as were reasonably foreseeable as a result of the breach. Traditionally it has been held that the trustee's liability is not mitigated by such principles as remoteness of damage.[72] However, in *Canson Enterprises Ltd v Boughton & Co*[73] the majority of the Supreme Court of Canada held that a claim for compensation for breach of fiduciary duty could be subject to the same principle of remoteness and foreseeability applied to claims in contract and tort.[74] This conclusion was justified on the grounds that, although equity had not developed its own principles of remoteness and foreseeability, it was entitled to draw from the relevant common law principles. Equity and law had been fused and, in relation to compensation, they shared the same policy objectives. However, the majority clearly felt that there was a distinction to be drawn between situations where a fiduciary in

---

[67] Or must be taken to have known.      [68] [1996] 2 All ER 801 at 825–826.
[69] [1934] 3 DLR 465.      [70] [1997] 4 All ER 705, [1998] RLR 135 (Elliott).      [71] [1996] AC 421.
[72] Underhill and Hayton, *Law Relating to Trusts and Trustees* (16th edn, 2003), p 855.
[73] (1991) 85 DLR (4th) 129.
[74] See the judgment of La Forest J, with whom Sopinka, Gonthier and Cory JJ concurred.

breach had received trust property, and where he had merely failed to fulfill a fiduciary obligation which he owed. La Forest J said:

'There is a sharp divide between a situation where a person has control of property which in the view of the court belongs to another, and one where a person is under a fiduciary duty to perform an obligation where equity's concern is simply that the duty be performed honestly and in accordance with the undertaking the fiduciary has taken on . . . In the case of a trustee relationship, the trustee's obligation is to hold the res or object of the trust for his cestui que trust, and on breach the concern of equity is that it be restored to the cestui que trust, or if that cannot be done, to afford compensation for what the object would be worth. In the case of a mere breach of duty, the concern of equity is to ascertain the loss resulting from the breach of the particular duty.'[75]

The case concerned a solicitor who had acted for the purchaser of property and received a secret profit on the sale. The land was subsequently developed by the purchasers, who built a warehouse, but the warehouse suffered extensive damage because of the negligence of the soil engineer overseeing its construction. The purchasers claimed that they would not have gone ahead with the purchase if they had known of the secret profit, and sought to recover the loss they had suffered from the solicitor. Borrowing the tort concept of intervening cause, the Supreme Court limited the solicitor's liability to the loss that was caused before the intervention of the negligent third party engineers. Thus, the Canadian Supreme Court has accepted the principle of limitation of damages to those which were reasonably foreseeable in the case of loss caused by a breach of a mere fiduciary duty.

In *Target Holdings Ltd v Redferns*[76] the House of Lords held that the common law principle of remoteness of damage has no application to liability where trust property was wrongly transferred by the trustee in breach of the terms of the trust. Lord Browne-Wilkinson stated:

'If specific restitution of the trust property is not possible, then the liability of the trustee is to pay sufficient compensation to the trust estate to put it back to what it would have been had the breach not been committed. Even if the immediate cause of the loss is the dishonesty or failure of a third party the trustee is liable to make good that loss to the trust estate if, but for the breach, such loss would not have occurred. Thus the common law rules of remoteness of damage and causation do not apply.'[77]

However, where a trustee has acted without due care, thus causing a loss to the trust, it is possible that the principles of remoteness may apply. In *Bristol and West Building Society v Mothew*[78] the Court of Appeal considered the nature of the equitable liability of a fiduciary in breach of his duty to act with due skill and care. Millett LJ stated:

'Although the remedy which equity makes available for breach of the equitable duty of skill and care is equitable compensation rather than damages, this is merely the product of

---

[75]  (1991) 85 DLR (4th) 129 at 146.      [76]  [1995] 3 All ER 785.

[77]  [1995] 3 All ER 785 at 794. For criticism of this position see: *Bank of New Zealand v New Zealand Guardian Trust Co Ltd* [1999] 1 NZLR 213; aff'd [1999] 1 NZLR 664; *Collins v Brebner* [2000] Lloyd's Rep PN 587; Elliott, 'Remoteness Criteria in Equity' (2002) 65 MLR 588.

[78]  [1996] 4 All ER 698.

history and in this context is in my opinion a distinction without a difference. Equitable compensation for breach of the duty of skill and care resembles common law damages in that it is awarded by way of compensation to the plaintiff of his loss. There is no reason in principle why the common law rules of causation, remoteness of damage and measure of damages should not be applied by analogy in such a case.'[79]

### (d) Accounting for tax liability

The rule that tax liability is to be taken into account when calculating damages for personal injury in tort[80] is not applied, and in *Re Bell's Indenture*[81] it was held that a trustee should restore the value of misappropriated property to the trust without allowance for the tax that would have had to be paid on it by the trust if it had not been misappropriated.

## (2) Specific situations—investment[82]

In a number of common examples of breach of trust, the loss to the trust is calculated on the basis of settled principles.

### (a) Trustee purchases unauthorised investments

Where the trustee has purchased unauthorised investments he will be liable for any loss resulting from the purchase. In *Knott v Cottee*[83] an executor who had an express power to invest in British Government Stocks or land invested in foreign stock and Exchequer bills which were subsequently sold by order of the court at a loss. It was held that the trustee was liable to compensate for the loss caused by the unauthorised investment, even though had they been retained they would have produced a profit for the trust because of a subsequent rise in value following the order of the court to sell.

### (b) Trustee retains unauthorised investments

If the trustee retains unauthorised investments he will be liable to the beneficiaries for any loss that the trust suffers as a result. The measure of loss will be the amount that the investments could have realised if they had been sold at the proper time, less the value that they actually realised. In *Fry v Fry*[84] trustees received the Longford Inn on trust in 1834. The testator's will stated that they were to sell it 'as soon as convenient after his decease . . .' In 1836 they refused an offer of £900. By 1859 the inn remained unsold, and had dramatically fallen in value because of the opening of a railway, depriving it of much of its business. Romilly MR held that the estates of the now dead trustees were liable for any loss to the trust, which would be the difference between the £900 offer they had refused and the price eventually obtained.[85]

### (c) Trustee retains authorised investments

Under s 5 of the Trustee Act 2000 a trustee is under duty to review the investments of the trust and to obtain and consider proper advice about whether they should be varied.

---

[79] [1996] 4 All ER 698 at 711.     [80] *British Transport Commission v Gourley* [1956] AC 185, HL.
[81] [1980] 1 WLR 1217.     [82] See Chapter 22.     [83] (1852) 16 Beav 77.
[84] (1859) 27 Beav 144.     [85] See *Jaffray v Marshall* [1994] 1 All ER 143.

If he fails to fulfill this duty, or fails to exercise the requisite duty of care, he will be liable to compensate the trust for the resulting loss.

## (d) Trustee sells authorised investments

If the trustee improperly sells an authorised investment he will be liable to the trust for any loss. In *Re Massingberd's Settlement*[86] the trustees had power to invest in government stock. In 1875 they sold Consols, which were authorised investments, and reinvested in unauthorised mortgages. In proceedings, begun in 1887, the Court of Appeal held that although the whole of the money invested on the mortgages was recovered, the trustees must replace the Consols which had been sold even though they now stood at a higher price.

## (e) Mortgages

Where a trustee has invested in mortgages he will be liable to the trust if the security subsequently proves insufficient. However, the trustee may enjoy some protection under ss 8 and 9 of the Trustee Act 1925. Section 9 provides that if the trustee makes an investment on a mortgage which is unauthorised merely because of the amount that has been advanced, the security shall be deemed an authorised investment for the sum that could properly have been advanced, and the trustee 'shall only be liable to make good the sum advanced in excess thereof with interest'. If the trustee has chosen to follow the procedure of s 8,[87] and obtained a valuation and advanced a loan of not more than two-thirds of the amount of the valuation on the advice of the valuer, he 'shall not be chargeable with breach of trust by reason only of the proportion borne by the amount of the loan to the value of the property at the time when the loan was made'.

## (3) Assessing compensation

As has been noted, in *Target Holdings Ltd v Redferns*[88] it was held that the quantum of equitable compensation payable in respect of a breach of trust is to be assessed not at the date that the breach occurred, but at the date of judgment. The House of Lords overruled the decision in *Jaffray v Marshall*,[89] where it had been held that a trustee who committed an ongoing breach of trust by failing to restore trust property to the trust fund was required to compensate the beneficiaries to the level of the best possible price that he could have obtained for the property during the period when it was not restored. A settlement had been created in favour of Lady Jaffray for life, remainder to her children. In 1979 Lady Jaffray wished to purchase a new house for £75,000 but did not have sufficient funds. The trustees provided some £35,000 toward the purchase from the trust and it was agreed that the house should be shared between Lady Jaffray and the trust as tenants-in-common in shares of eight-fifteenths and seven-fifteenths. At the same time as the purchase was completed, the purchasers executed a mortgage in favour of Coutts & Co. This was admitted to be in breach of trust. The question at issue

---

[86] (1890) 63 LT 296.    [87] Which is not obligatory.    [88] [1995] 3 All ER 785.
[89] [1994] 1 All ER 143.

concerned the appropriate measure of compensation for the breach. If the compensation was to be assessed at the date the writ was issued in 1989 the value of the house would have been £160,000. However due to a fall in property prices by the date of the judgment it was only worth £117,000. Nicholas Stewart QC, sitting as a deputy judge of the High Court, held that the compensation was to be assessed on the basis that the trustees could have sold the property at the date of the writ, and that the trust had only failed to realise the increased value of the property because of their continuing breach of trust in not selling.[90] However, Lord Browne-Wilkinson held that the case had been decided by an application of the wrong principle:

'... the principles applicable in an action for an account of profits were, to my mind, wrongly applied to a claim for compensation for breach of trust. In my judgment [*Jaffray v Marshall*] was wrongly decided not only because the wrong principle was applied but also because the judge awarded compensation by assessing the quantum on an assumption (viz that the house in question would have been sold at a particular date) when he found as a fact that such sale would not have taken place even if there had been no breach of trust.'[91]

## (4) Offsetting losses and gains

### (a) The general rule

It is a basic principle that each breach of trust is to be treated independently of the trustee's other activities. A loss suffered by the trust as a result of a breach in one transaction cannot be off set against a gain achieved for the trust in another. The trustee remains liable for the loss caused by his breach irrespective of the gain. This principle was accepted in *Bartlett v Barclays Bank Trust Co Ltd (No 2)*,[92] where Brightman J stated:

'The general rule ... is that where a trustee is liable in respect of distinct breaches of trust, one of which resulted in a loss and the other in a gain, he is not entitled to set the gain against the loss, unless they arise in the same transaction.'[93]

This rule was applied in *Dimes v Scott*,[94] where the trustees of a settlement created on the death of Captain Piercey in 1802 failed to sell an investment in the East India Company which they had been directed to convert into money by the Captain's will. When the investment was realised in 1813 the proceeds were used to purchase Consuls. As the price of the Consuls had fallen since the date of the testator's death they were able to purchase more than they would have been able to at that time. It was held that the gain to the beneficiaries of the extra Consuls could not be offset against their liability for excessive payments made to the life tenant while the unauthorised investment was retained. Under the rule in *Howe v Dartmouth*[95] the life tenant was only entitled to a 4% return on the value of the investment as income, whereas it had in fact produced a 10% return which was paid to the life tenant by the trustees.[96]

---

[90] [1994] 1 All ER 143 at 154.    [91] [1995] 3 All ER 785 at 799.

[92] [1980] Ch 515; [1980] Conv 155 (Shindler); [1983] Conv 127 (Pearce and Samuels).

[93] [1980] Ch 515 at 538. See also *Adye v Feuilleteau* (1783) 3 Swan 84n; *Robinson v Robinson* (1848) 11 Beav 371; *Wiles v Gresham* (1854) 2 Drew 258.

[94] (1828) 4 Russ 195.    [95] (1802) 7 Ves 137.    [96] See Chapter 21.

## (b) Distinct breaches of trust

The rule preventing any set-off between losses and gains only applies if there are distinct, independent breaches of trust. If the breaches occur in the course of one indivisible transaction then any gain will be taken into account. This provides an adequate explanation for *Fletcher v Green.*[97] Here the trustee of a settlement committed a breach of trust by lending money on a mortgage which proved insufficient security. When the security was realised the money was invested in Consuls, which rose in value producing a gain of £251. The court held that this gain must be set off against the trustee's liability for the failure of the security.

## (c) Set-off in exceptional circumstances

In *Bartlett v Barclays Bank Trust Co Ltd (No 2)*[98] the general principle that there should be no set-off between gains and losses flowing from a breach of trust was reaffirmed. However on the specific facts Brightman J did permit the defendant bank to set off the gain that had been made in one investment in breach of trust against a loss made in another. A company owned by the trust made two investments in property development schemes which were wholly inappropriate, and the bank was liable for having failed adequately to supervise the operations of the company. On one project, the 'Old Bailey Project', the company lost £580,000 capital and a great deal of income. On another project, the 'Guildford Development', which was entered under exactly the same policy of investment, the company made a profit of some £271,000. Brightman J held that this profit could be offset against the liability of the bank for the loss incurred by the 'Old Bailey Project'. However he failed to provide an adequate explanation of why the set-off was permitted. Having stated the general principle, he continued:

'. . . the relevant cases are . . . not altogether easy to reconcile. All are centenarians and none is quite like the present. The Guildford development stemmed from exactly the same policy and (to a lesser degree because it proceeded less far) exemplified the same folly as the Old Bailey project. Part of the profit was in fact used to finance the Old Bailey disaster. By sheer luck the gamble paid off handsomely, on capital account. I think it would be unjust to deprive the bank of this element of salvage in the course of assessing the cost of the shipwreck. My order will therefore reflect the bank's right to an appropriate set-off.'[99]

Despite the fact that the developments took place under the same policy, it cannot be said that they were effectively part of the same transaction so as not to be 'distinct' breaches of trust. It seems that the judge recognised a residuary power to grant a set-off on the basis of the balance of justice between the parties in the particular circumstances.

---

[97] (1864) 33 Beav 426.    [98] [1980] Ch 515.    [99] [1980] Ch 515 at 538.

## (5) Interest

### (a) General principle

Where a trustee is liable to compensate the trust for loss caused by his misapplication of trust property, the trust is also entitled to recover interest on the sum misapplied. The rationale for this was explained by Buckley LJ in *Wallersteiner v Moir (No 2)*:

'It is well established in equity that a trustee who in breach of trust misapplies trust funds will be liable not only to replace the misapplied principal fund but to do so with interest from the date of the misapplication. This is on the notional ground that the money so applied was in fact the trustee's own money and that he has retained the misapplied trust money in his own hands and used it for his own purposes.'[100]

The court assumes that the trustee has retained the misapplied property and has therefore had the opportunity to earn interest on it.

### (b) Rate of interest

Historically the rate of interest awarded was 4% per annum,[101] with an increase to 5% if the trustee was guilty of fraud[102] or had used the money to pursue his own trade.[103] If the trustee had in fact received a higher rate of interest than that he had to pay the beneficiary whatever he had received.[104] However, in times of high inflation such a low rate fails to reflect the conditions of the lending market. As Brightman LJ observed in *Bartlett v Barclays Bank Trust Co Ltd (No 2)*:

'In these days of huge and constantly changing interest rates[105] (the movement being usually upwards so far) I think it would be unrealistic for a court of equity to abide by the modest rate of interest which was current in the stable times of our forefathers.'[106]

He therefore concluded that the proper rate of interest ought to be that allowed from time to time on the court's short-term investment account, established under s 6(1) of the Administration of Justice Act 1965. Other cases have held that the rate should be 1% above bank base rate.[107] In *Guardian Ocean Cargoes Ltd v Banco do Brasil (No 3)*[108] Hirst J awarded interest at 1% above the New York prime rate. Ultimately the determination of the appropriate rate of interests is a matter for the discretion of the court. In the recent case of *Jaffray v Marshall*[109] Nicholas Stewart QC, sitting as a deputy High

---

[100]   [1975] QB 373 at 397.

[101]   *Hall v Hallet* (1784) 1 Cox Eq Cas 134; *Jones v Foxall* (1852) 15 Beav 388; *A-G v Alford* (1855) 4 De GM & G 843; *Fletcher v Green* (1864) 33 Beav 426; *Imperial Mercantile Credit Association (liquidators) v Coleman* (1873) LR 6 HL 189; *Re Beech* [1920] 1 Ch 40.

[102]   *A-G v Alford* (1855) 4 De GM & G 843.

[103]   If the trustee has made a profit the beneficiaries have the option of claiming the profit instead. See *Vyse v Foster* (1872) 8 Ch App 309; *Re Davis* [1902] 2 Ch 314; *Gordon v Gonda* [1955] 2 All ER 762.

[104]   *Jones v Foxall* (1852) 15 Beav 388. See also *Mathew v TM Sutton Ltd* [1994] 4 All ER 793.

[105]   He noted how in the years 1963–80 the bank rate of minimum lending had changed 80 times, varying between 4% and 17%, and the bank deposit rate had changed 70 times, varying between 2% and 15%.

[106]   [1980] Ch 515 at 547.

[107]   *Wallersteiner v Moir (No 2)* [1975] QB 373, 508n; *Belmont Finance Corpn Ltd v Williams Furniture Ltd (No 2)* [1980] 1 All ER 393, CA; *O'Sullivan v Management Agency and Music Ltd* [1985] QB 428, CA.

[108]   [1992] 2 Lloyd's Rep 193.        [109]   [1994] 1 All ER 143.

Court judge, took judicial notice that 'the period since 1989 has not been a period of the very high level of inflation that has been seen at times in fairly recent years. Accordingly, the rate of return needed to preserve capital is not as high'.[110] He held that compensation should be paid with interest at the special account rate. In *Re Evans (decd)*[111] Richard McCombe QC awarded interest of 8% to satisfy equity in a case involving the non-professional administrator of a small estate in time of gentle inflation, where interest rates had varied between 8% and 14.5% during the relevant period.

### (c) Simple or compound interest?

Whereas the common law only enjoys the jurisdiction to award simple interest on damages awarded, in equity the court may award compound interest.[112] Whether compound or simple interest should be paid on the equitable compensation due to the trust is also a matter for the court's discretion. Historically, compound interest was usually awarded because of the trustee's fraud, or his having used misapplied property in his trade.[113] In *Wallersteiner v Moir (No 2)*,[114] where a company director misused company funds for his own purposes, Lord Denning MR rejected the view that interest was awarded 'by way of a punishment'.[115] Instead, he held that compound interest should be awarded where this represents what the trustee should reasonably have obtained with the trust property if it has been misapplied:

'Should it be simple interest or compound interest? On general principles I think it should be presumed that the company (had it not been deprived of the money) would have made the most beneficial use open to it: cf *Armory v Delamirie*[116] . . . It may be that the company would have used it in its own trading operation; or that it would have used it to help its subsidiaries. Alternatively it should be presumed that the wrongdoer made the most beneficial use of it. But, whichever it is, in order to give adequate compensation, the money should be replaced at interest with yearly rests, ie, compound interest.'

Since it will almost always be the case that either the trust or the wrongdoer would have made 'most beneficial use' of the property by obtaining compound interest, there is a virtual presumption in favour of awarding compound interest. Although the Law Commission has made proposals for the reforms of the statutory jurisdiction to award compound interest on debts and damages, it has not proposed any change to the inherent equitable jurisdiction, which will continue to operate alongside the statutory jurisdiction.[117]

---

[110] [1994] 1 All ER 143 at 154.   [111] [1999] 2 All ER 777.

[112] See *Westdeutsche Landesbank Girozentrale v Islington London Borough Council* [1996] AC 669, where the House of Lords held that the court did not possess the jurisdiction to award compound interest on a common law claim to restitution.

[113] *Piety v Stace* (1799) 4 Ves 620; *Heathcote v Hulme* (1819) 1 Jac & W 122; *Brown v Sansome* (1825) M'Cle & Yo 427; *Jones v Foxall* (1852) 15 Beav 388; *Penny v Avison* (1856) 3 Jur NS 62; *Re Davis* [1902] 2 Ch 314.

[114] [1975] QB 373, 508n.

[115] See *Jones v Foxall* (1852) 15 Beav 388; *Gordon v Gonda* [1955] 2 All ER 762, CA.

[116] (1722) 1 Stra 505.

[117] Law Com No 287 (2004), Pre-Judgment Interest on Debts and Damages, para 5.50.

## 3 Defences to liability for breach of trust

Even if a trustee has committed a breach of trust which has caused loss to the trust, it is not inevitable that he will be required to pay equitable compensation to the trust. A number of defences are available to trustees which may wholly or partially protect them from liability.

### (1) Beneficiaries' consent or concurrence

#### (a) General principle

A beneficiary cannot complain of a breach of trust by a trustee to which he consented, or in which he actively concurred or passively acquiesced.[118] As Wilmer LJ stated in the context of an advance of trust property made by a trustee bank to the beneficiaries in breach of trust in *Re Pauling's Settlement Trusts*:[119]

'... if the bank can establish a valid request or consent by the advanced beneficiary to the advance in question, that is a good defence on the part of the bank to the beneficiary's claim, even though it can be plain that the advance was made in breach of trust.'

The case concerned a marriage settlement created in 1919 on the marriage of Violet Pauling and Commander Younghusband. The trustees were the bank Coutts & Co. By an express provision of the trust deed the trustees had the power to advance up to one-half of the beneficiaries' presumptive share under the trust for their advancement or absolute use. The family consistently lived beyond its means, and Violet's current account with the trustees was often overdrawn. Between 1948 and 1954 a number of advancements were made to the children of the marriage, Francis, George, Anne and Anthony, who were all of age by 1951, ostensibly for such purposes as improvements to their homes and the purchase of furniture. However, the money advanced was generally paid into Violet's overdrawn current account. The children subsequently complained that the bank had acted in breach of trust in making these advancements.

In respect of an advance of £2,000 to George and Francis in 1949, stated to be for improvements to a house in the Isle of Man, and of advances of some £5,350 to Francis, George and Ann between September 1953 and June 1954, the Court of Appeal held that the bank was not liable because the beneficiaries had validly consented to the advances being made, with full knowledge that the money would be applied to reduce their mother's overdraft.

If a trustee wishes to avoid liability completely he must have gained the consent of all the beneficiaries of the trust. If only some had consented the remainder will retain the right to maintain an action against him for his breach.

---

[118] *Walker v Symonds* (1818) 3 Swan 1; *Stafford v Stafford* (1857) 1 De G & J 193; *Ghillingworth v Chambers* [1896] 1 Ch 685, CA.
[119] [1964] Ch 303 at 335.

## (b) Requirements for relief from liability

*(i) The beneficiary must be of age.* A beneficiary's consent to a breach of trust will only be effective to protect the trustee from liability if he had reached the age of majority. The consent of a minor is ineffective.[120] However, a minor who fraudulently misrepresents his age to persuade trustees to pay trust money over to him will not be permitted to deny that his consent was effective because of his age.[121]

*(ii) The beneficiary must not have consented whilst under any other incapacity.* If the beneficiary is under any incapacity which would invalidate his consent a trustee remains liable.[122] Therefore, a beneficiary who is of age but under a mental incapacity cannot give an effective consent to a breach of trust. In *Re Pauling's Settlement Trusts*[123] one son, Francis, was a schizophrenic, but it was held that his mental condition was not sufficiently serious to render his consent invalid.

*(iii) The beneficiary must have freely given consent.* Only the freely given consent of a beneficiary will be sufficient to protect a trustee from liability. In *Re Pauling's Settlement Trusts*[124] it was held that the trustees could not rely on the beneficiaries' consent where it was given while the children were acting under the undue influence of their parents. It was only when they were 'emancipated' from parental control that their consent was effective. However, in such circumstances a trustee will only be liable 'if he knew, or ought to have known that the beneficiary was acting under the undue influence of another'.[125]

*(iv) The beneficiary must have given an informed consent.* A trustee will only be protected if the beneficiary's consent to the breach of trust was an informed consent.[126] The principle was stated by Wilberforce J, at first instance, in *Re Pauling's Settlement Trusts*:

'. . . the court has to consider all the circumstances in which the concurrence of the cestui que trust was given with a view to seeing whether it is fair and equitable that, having given his concurrence, he should afterwards turn round and sue the trustees: that subject to this, it is not necessary that he should know that what he is concurring in is a breach of trust, provided that he fully understands what he is concurring in . . .'[127]

This principle was also adopted by Harman J in *Holder v Holder*[128] and Goff LJ in *Re Freeston's Charity*.[129]

*(v) The beneficiary need not have benefited from the breach of trust.* In *Fletcher v Collis*[130] it was held that a trustee will be protected from liability where a beneficiary has

---

[120] *Adye v Feuilleteau* (1783) 3 Swan 84n; *Lord Montfort v Lord Cadogan* (1816) 19 Ves 635; *Wilkinson v Parry* (1828) 4 Russ 272; *March v Russell* (1837) 3 My & Cr 31.

[121] *Overton v Banister* (1844) 3 Hare 503; *Wright v Snowe* (1848) 2 De G & Sm 321.

[122] *Crosby v Church* (1841) 3 Beav 485; *Mara v Manning* (1845) 2 Jo & Lat 311; *Fletcher v Green* (1864) 33 Beav 426.

[123] [1961] 3 All ER 713 at 731–732; on appeal [1964] Ch 303 at 347–348.

[124] [1964] Ch 303.     [125] [1964] Ch 303 at 338, per Willmer LJ.

[126] There must be a full and frank disclosure by the trustee. See *Phipps v Boardman* [1964] 2 All ER 187.

[127] [1961] 3 All ER 713 at 730.     [128] [1968] Ch 353.     [129] [1979] 1 All ER 51.

[130] [1905] 2 Ch 24.

consented to the breach even if he did not obtain any personal benefit from that breach.[131]

## (2) Subsequent condonation of the breach by the beneficiaries

A trustee is similarly protected from liability if, after a breach has been committed, the beneficiaries condone it, release him from liability, or indemnify him. This principle is subject to the same qualifications as apply to the rule that a trustee is not liable to a beneficiary who has consented to a breach of trust: ie the condoning or releasing beneficiary must be of age;[132] the condoning or releasing beneficiary must not be under any other incapacity; the beneficiary must freely condone the breach or release the trustee from liability;[133] the beneficiary must have known what he was condoning or from what he was releasing the trustee. Condonation obtained through undue influence will be of no effect. As Westbury LC stated in *Farrant v Blanchford*:[134]

'Where a breach of trust has been committed from which a trustee alleges that he has been released, it is incumbent on him to show that such release was given by the cestui que trust deliberately and advisedly, with full knowledge of all the circumstances, and of his own rights and claims against the trustee . . .'[135]

## (3) The discretion of the court to grant relief from liability

### (a) Trustee Act 1925, s 61[136]

Section 61 confers upon the court a general discretion to grant a trustee relief from liability for breach of trust. The section provides:

'If it appears to the court that a trustee, whether appointed by the court or otherwise, is or may be personally liable for any breach of trust . . . but has acted honestly and reasonably, and ought fairly to be excused for the breach of trust and for omitting to obtain the direction of the court in the matter in which he committed such breach, then the court may relieve him either wholly or in part from personal liability for the same.'

This section clearly grants a wide discretion to the court, both as to whether a trustee should be relieved at all and, if so, the extent to which he should be relieved. This enables the court to take account of the circumstances in which the breach occurred and to assess the culpability of the trustee in the light of them. However, the starting

---

[131] See also *Re Pauling's Settlement Trusts* [1961] 3 All ER 713 at 730; *Allen v Rea Brothers Trustees Ltd* [2002] WTLR 625.

[132] *Wade v Cox* (1835) 4 LJ Ch 105; *Parker v Bloxam* (1855) 20 Beav 295.

[133] Westbury LC stated in *Farrant v Blanchford* that a trustee must be able to show that the beneficiary 'gave the release freely and without pressure or undue influence or any description'. See also *Lloyd v Attwood* (1859) 3 De G & J 614; *Reade v Reade* (1881) 9 LR Ir 409.

[134] (1863) 1 De GJ & Sm 107 at 119.

[135] See also *Ramdsen v Hylton* (1751) 2 Ves Sen 304; *Hore v Becher* (1842) 12 Sim 465; *Pritt v Clay* (1843) 6 Beav 503; *Thomson v Eastwood* (1877) 2 App Cas 215, HL; *Re Garnett* (1885) 31 Ch D 1, CA.

[136] Trustee Act 1925, s 61 re-enacts s 3 of the Judicial Trustees Act 1896, and many of the cases below consider the effect of s 3.

point of the law is that a trustee is prima facie liable even for honest technical breaches of trust, and the burden falls to the trustee to demonstrate that he should be granted relief.[137]

## (b) Pre-conditions for the grant of relief under s 61

The courts have emphasised that the discretion conferred by s 61 is not to be exercised on the basis of strict and narrow interpretations. As Bryne J observed in *Re Turner*:[138]

'It would be impossible to lay down any general rules or principles to be acted on in carrying out the provisions of the section, and I think that each case must depend on its own circumstances.'[139]

However, for the court even to consider relief the trustee must show that he had acted 'honestly and reasonably', and that he 'ought fairly to be excused'. Although there is little authority, some consideration has been given to the meaning of these requirements.

*(i) 'Honesty'.* It is clear that a trustee cannot be granted relief from liability if he has acted dishonestly. However, as Kekewich J observed in *Perrins v Bellamy*,[140] in a large majority of cases where a breach of trust has been committed the trustee will not have acted dishonestly and the real question will concern whether the trustee had acted 'reasonably':

'The legislature has made the absence of all dishonesty a condition precedent to the relief of the trustee from all liability. But that is not the grit of the section. The grit is in the words "reasonably, and ought fairly to be excused for the breach of trust" . . .'[141]

*(ii) 'Reasonably'.* A trustee will only be granted relief from liability if he had acted reasonably. As Kekewich J pointed out in *Perrins v Bellamy*[142] this means that the trustees must have 'acted reasonably in their breach of trust'. It will therefore be very hard for a trustee to gain relief if the very basis of his breach of trust was that he had failed to observe the appropriate standard of care expected of a trustee.[143] For example, in *Bartlett v Barclays Bank Trust Co Ltd (No 2)*[144] the bank was liable because they had failed adequately to supervise the management of the company owned by the trust. Since the very grounds of their liability was their negligence they could not be said to be entitled to relief under s 61 as they had not acted 'reasonably'.

Even where trustees have committed a breach of trust by exceeding their powers, for example by misappropriation of trust property or unauthorised investment, relief can only be granted if they acted reasonably.[145] In *Re Turner*[146] Byrne J was not prepared to

---

[137] *Re Stuart* [1897] 2 Ch 583.    [138] [1897] 1 Ch 536 at 542.

[139] See also *Re Pauling's Settlement Trusts* [1964] Ch 303 at 359, per Upjohn LJ: 's 61 is purely discretionary, and its application necessarily depends on the particular facts of each case'.

[140] [1898] 2 Ch 521.    [141] [1898] 2 Ch 521 at 527–528.    [142] [1898] 2 Ch 521 at 529.

[143] The appropriate standard of care will either be the new statutory duty of care under s 1 of the Trustee Act 2000 or, if this does not apply, the common law standard of the 'ordinary prudent man of business'.

[144] [1980] Ch 515.

[145] See *Re Turner* [1897] 1 Ch 536; *Re Stuart* [1897] 2 Ch 583; *Re Dive* [1909] 1 Ch 328; *Shaw v Cates* [1909] 1 Ch 389; *Re Mackay* [1911] 1 Ch 300.

[146] [1897] 1 Ch 536.

find that a trustee who had invested trust money upon an equitable mortgage, which was not an authorised investment, had acted 'reasonably'. He had not acted as he would have done if it had been a transaction of his own. He had relied on his co-trustee, who was a solicitor. In *Re Stuart*[147] a trustee who had invested money on a mortgage where the security had proved insufficient was held not to have acted reasonably because the mortgage had been granted outside the terms of (what is now) s 8 of the Trustee Act 1925.[148] No proper valuation had been obtained and the amount lent was greater than two-thirds of the amount stated in the valuation. Although Stirling J held that this 'was not necessarily fatal' to the application of s 61, the legislature had laid down a standard by which the trustee was to be judged. He concluded that, if the trustee had been dealing with his own money, he would not have advanced the mortgage without further inquiry.[149] In *Ward-Smith v Jebb*[150] a trustee had paid trust money to a person he assumed was a beneficiary because of the effect of the Adoption of Children Act 1949, when in fact the Act had no application to the person. Buckley J applied the test of reasonableness of an ordinary man of business acting on his own behalf and said that 'a prudent man, whose affairs were affected by a statute would either satisfy himself that he fully understood its effect or would seek legal advice'. There were therefore no grounds for the court to grant relief under s 61. In contrast relief was granted in the recent case of *Re Evans*.[151] The defendant had administered her mother's small estate by distributing it to herself on the assumption that her brother, from whom she had not heard for thirty years, was no longer alive. Prior to the distribution she had sought legal advice and purchased a missing-beneficiary policy to cover the value of approximately half of the capital value of the assets. Richard McCombe QC held whilst the mere fact that a trustee has acted on legal advice does not automatically entitle relief under s 61[152] the defendant had acted reasonably. The estate was relatively small, she was a lay person who was at all times willing to abide by the advice of her solicitors, and some provision had been made for her brother's potential claims.

It is clear that s 61 applies to professional as well as non-professional trustees.[153] However, in the case of a 'professional trustee', the courts have held that a higher standard of care is expected,[154] and they are more reluctant to grant relief under s 61. As the Court of Appeal said in *Re Pauling's Settlement Trusts*:

'Where a banker undertakes to act as a paid trustee of a settlement created by a customer, and so deliberately places itself in a position where its duty as trustee conflicts with its interest as a banker, we think that the court should be very slow to relieve such a trustee under [s 61].'[155]

---

[147] [1897] 2 Ch 583.    [148] Then s 4 of the Trustee Act 1888 and s 8 of the Trustee Act 1893.
[149] [1897] 2 Ch 583 at 591–592.    [150] (1964) 108 Sol Jo 919.    [151] [1999] 2 All ER 777.
[152] *Marsden v Regan* [1954] 1 All ER 475, at 482, per Evershed MR.
[153] In *Re Pauling's Settlement Trusts* [1964] Ch 303 at 338 the Court of Appeal said that 'it would be a misconstruction of the section to say that it does not apply to professional trustees'; and (at 356) Wilmer LJ said that 'all of us are agreed that in the very special circumstances of this case the bank should be accorded some relief notwithstanding the fact that they were professional trustees paid for their services'.
[154] *National Trustees Co of Australia Ltd v General Finance Co of Australasia Ltd* [1905] AC 373; *Bartlett v Barclays Bank Trust Co Ltd* [1980] Ch 515.
[155] [1964] Ch 303 at 339.

*(iii) 'Ought fairly to be excused'.* The difficulty with this requirement is to identify precisely what it adds over and above the requirement that the trustee must have acted 'reasonably'. As Kekewich J observed in *Perrins v Bellamy*:

'I venture . . . to think that, in general and in the absence of special circumstances, a trustee who has acted "reasonably" ought to be relieved, and that it is not incumbent on the Court to consider whether he ought "fairly" to be excused, unless there is evidence of a special character showing that the provisions of the section ought not to be applied in his favour.'[156]

However, he seemed to contradict himself in *Davis v Hutchings*,[157] where he held that a trustee who had acted both honesty and reasonably ought not to be relieved from liability. The trustees had distributed a share of the trust fund to their solicitor, who claimed that he was the assignee of the share. They failed to investigate his title, which would have revealed that the assignment was subject to the plaintiff's charge over the share. He held that it would be impossible for them to be excused 'without departing from well-established rules'[158] and there was no justification for the trustees being 'let off'.[159] However, the case can perhaps be better explained on the grounds that the trustees' conduct was unreasonable. Surely a prudent man of business acting on his own behalf would not fail to investigate the assignee's alleged title in such circumstances, particularly when that would be the well-established rule. Ultimately the inclusion of the expression 'ought fairly to be excused' emphasises the wide discretion given to the court as to whether, in all the circumstances, the trustee should be granted relief. The preconditions are that he acted honestly and reasonably, but it is then a matter for the court. As Evershed MR said in *Marsden v Regan*, having found that the trustee had acted honestly and reasonably:

'There still remains the question: Ought she fairly to be excused? That is the most difficult point of all. But it is essentially a matter within the discretion of the judge . . .'[160]

In *Re Wightwick's Will Trusts*[161] trustees had paid over money to the National Anti-Vivisection Society on the basis of the generally held view that the gift was a valid charitable gift, even though the gift was in fact invalid. Wynn-Parry J held that because the trustees had acted bona fides throughout it was 'proper to declare under s 61 Trustee Act 1925, that they acted honestly and reasonably and ought fairly to be excused for any breach of trust which they might have committed'.[162]

## (c) The extent of relief

If the court finds that the conditions for granting relief are met, the extent to which the trustee may be relieved is a matter for the discretion of the court. Section 61 provides that the trustee may be relieved 'wholly or in part'. In *Re Pauling's Settlement Trusts*[163] one breach of trust by the bank involved the advance of £2,600 to Francis and George to pay off a debt owed by their mother secured on her life interest, known as the 'Hodson

---

[156] [1898] 2 Ch 521 at 529.
[157] [1907] 1 Ch 356. But see *Re Allsop* [1914] 1 Ch 1 where the Court of Appeal, whilst accepting that *Davis v Hutchings* may have been right on its facts, rejected the wider dicta of Kekewich J.
[158] [1907] 1 Ch 356 at 364.    [159] [1907] 1 Ch 356 at 365.    [160] [1954] 1 WLR 423 at 435.
[161] [1950] Ch 260.    [162] [1950] Ch 260 at 266.    [163] [1964] Ch 303.

Loan'. In return, the mother assigned to them life policies with a surrender value of £650, on which she promised to continue to pay the premiums, and which would pay £3,000 on her death. There was a division between the members of the Court of Appeal as to the extent to which the bank should be relieved of liability in respect of this transaction. The majority found that, in the circumstances, the bank had acted honestly and reasonably, but that it should only be relieved to the extent of the surrender value of the policies which had been assigned to them. Willmer J, dissenting, held that they should be relieved from all liability.

'. . . whereas my brethren think that the bank should be relieved only in part, I take the view that if relief is to be accorded to all, it should be accorded in full. I can see no logical reason for stopping short of relief in full.'[164]

In *Re Evans (decd)*[165] Richard McCombe QC held that the defendant was entitled to relief from liability to pay interest to her brother on the sum that had not been distributed to him on the administration of their mother's estate, but only to the extent that his claim would not be able to be satisfied out of the proceeds of the sale of a house which had derived from the estate and was still at her disposal.

## (4) Limitation[166]

### (a) General principle

Section 21(3) of the Limitation Act 1980 provides:

'Subject to the preceding provisions of this section, an action by a beneficiary to recover trust property or in respect of any breach of trust, not being an action for which a period of limitation is prescribed by any other provision of this Act shall not be brought after the expiration of six years from the date on which the right of action accrued.'

This has the effect that a beneficiary cannot bring an action for a breach of trust which occurred more than six years ago. Some details of the provision require further examination.

*(i) 'Trustees'.* Section 21 concerns remedies available against 'trustees' who commit breaches of trust. By s 38(1), 'trustee' is given the same definition as in the Trustee Act 1925, and therefore includes express trustees, personal representatives and trustees holding property on implied or constructive trusts.[167]

*(ii) 'Breach of trust'.* The period of limitation applies only to breaches of trust. In *Tito v Waddell (No 2)*[168] Megarry V-C held that it did not apply to claims made against

---

[164] [1964] Ch 303 at 356.     [165] [1999] 2 All ER 777.
[166] See Birks and Pretto (eds), *Breach of Trust*, Chs 11 and 12.
[167] Trustee Act 1925, s 68(17). It has also been held to include fiduciary agents: *Burdick v Garrick* (1870) 5 Ch App 233; company directors: *Re Lands Allotment Co* [1894] 1 Ch 616, CA; a mortgagee in respect of the proceeds of sale: *Thorne v Heard* [1895] AC 495; but not a trustee in bankruptcy: *Re Cornish* [1896] 1 QB 99; nor the liquidator of a company in voluntary liquidation: *Re Windsor Steam Coal Co (1901) Ltd* [1928] Ch 609.
[168] [1977] Ch 106 at 249.

trustees who had acted in breach of fiduciary duty by purchasing property from the trust in contravention of the self-dealing rule, or by purchasing the beneficiaries' beneficial interest in contravention of the fair-dealing rule.[169] In such cases the doctrine of laches may operate to protect a trustee from unduly tardy proceedings.[170]

*(iii) 'The date on which the right of action accrued'*. Section 21(3) provides that 'for the purposes of this subsection, the right of action shall not be treated as having accrued to any beneficiary entitled to a future interest in the trust property until the interest fell into possession'. This means that time does not begin to run against a remainderman, or beneficiary with a reversionary interest, until his interest has fallen into possession.

## (b) Exceptions

In some circumstances the Limitation Act 1980 provides for a period of limitation other than the standard six years applicable to claims for breach of trust.

*(i) Trustee was party to fraud*. Section 21(1)(a) provides that there is no limitation period to an action by the beneficiary 'in respect of any fraud or fraudulent breach of trust to which the trustee was a party or privy'.[171] The meaning of fraud was considered in *Re Sale Hotel and Botanical Gardens Co*,[172] where it was held that a promoter of a company who himself received £250 from the sale was not entitled to protection under the section.[173] Wright J stated:

'It would be impossible to hold that moral fraud ... is required for the purposes of that section. That section seems to me directed to the relief of trustees from what may be called innocent or negligent breaches of trust, and not breaches of trust in which, for their own personal gain, the trustees have committed knowingly acts from the nature of which the law imputes to them knowledge that they are doing wrong.'[174]

However in *Armitage v Nurse*[175] Millett LJ stated that the section was only applicable in cases involving dishonesty. The exception will only apply if the fraud was committed by the trustee himself. In *Thorne v Heard*[176] the trustees allowed a solicitor who was acting for them to retain the proceeds of sale of trust property, which he then fraudulently applied to his own use. The Court of Appeal held that the plaintiff's action was barred by the Statute of Limitations and that the case did not fall within the exception because the fraud was the fraud of the solicitor and not of the trustees, who were therefore neither party nor privy to the fraud.

*(ii) Trustee who retains trust property in his hands*. Section 21(1)(b) provides that there is no limitation period to an action by the beneficiary 'to recover from the trustee

---

[169] See Chapter 29.     [170] See below, p 765.
[171] This subsection enacts the rule of permanent liability which was applied by equity to express trustees. See *North American Land and Timber Co Ltd v Watkins* [1904] 1 Ch 242; affd [1904] 2 Ch 233, CA.
[172] (1897) 77 LT 681. See also *Vane v Vane* (1873) 8 Ch App 383; *North American Land and Timber Co Ltd v Watkins* [1904] 2 Ch 233, CA.
[173] Then the Trustee Act 1888, s 8.
[174] See *Collings v Wade* [1896] 1 IR 340, where it was held that fraud must amount to dishonesty.
[175] [1998] Ch 241.     [176] [1894] 1 Ch 599.

trust property or the proceeds of trust property in the possession of the trustee, or previously received by the trustee and converted to his use'. There is no requirement here that the trustee be guilty of fraud. The action lies due to the mere fact that the trustee still holds trust property, or its proceeds, in his hands. The exception was applied in *Re Howlett*,[177] where a trustee occupied trust property without paying any occupational rents to the beneficiary. Dankwerts J held that the beneficiary could recover such rent from the trustee even after the limitation period had expired because the situation fell within the exception. The trustee should have obtained a rent from the property, and since he had not done so he 'must be considered as having it in his own pocket at the material date'.[178] If the trust property has been dissipated by the trustee, for example if it has been lost,[179] spent on the maintenance of an infant beneficiary[180] or applied in the discharge of a debt,[181] the exception will not apply.

*(iii) Claims to the personal estate of a deceased person.* Section 22(1)(a) provides that:

'No action in respect of any claim to the personal estate of a deceased person or to any share or interest in any such estate (whether under a will or on intestacy) shall be brought after the expiration of twelve years from the date on which the right to receive the share or interest accrued.'

Since a personal representative may also be a trustee the question has arisen whether in such circumstances the six-year limitation period in s 21(3), or the twelve-year period in s 22(1)(a), should apply. Under the preceding legislation,[182] it was essential to determine whether the personal representative had become a trustee. If he had, then the six-year period would displace the twelve-year period.[183] The better view seems to be that under the Limitation Act 1980 the period of twelve years will apply to all actions concerning the personal estate of a deceased person, whether or not the personal representative became a trustee.[184]

*(iv) Actions to account.* Section 23 prescribes the time limit for actions for an account:

'An action for an account shall not be brought after the expiration of any time limit under this Act which is applicable to the claim which is the basis of the duty to account.'

Until recently it was thought that this provision had the effect that no statutory limitation period operated in respect of an action for an account of unauthorised profits from

---

[177] [1949] Ch 767.    [178] [1949] Ch 767 at 778.

[179] *Re Tufnell* (1902) 18 TLR 705; *Re Fountaine* [1909] 2 Ch 382.

[180] *Re Page* [1893] 1 Ch 304; *Re Timmis* [1902] 1 Ch 176.

[181] Even when the trustee was a partner in the bank to which the debt was owed. See *Re Gurney* [1893] 1 Ch 590.

[182] Real Property Limitation Act 1874, s 8; Trustee Act 1888, s 8.

[183] See *Re Swain* [1891] 3 Ch 233; *Re Timmis* [1902] 1 Ch 176; *Re Richardson* [1920] 1 Ch 423, CA; *Re Oliver* [1927] 2 Ch 323; *Re Diplock* [1948] Ch 465, CA; affd sub nom *Ministry of Health v Simpson* [1951] AC 251, HL.

[184] See Pettit, *Equity and the Law of Trusts* (9th edn, 2001), pp 518–519; Preston and Newsom, *Limitation of Actions* (4th edn, 1989), p 51.

a fiduciary.[185] However, in *Coulthard v Disco Mix Club Ltd*[186] it was held that an action for an account against a fiduciary was subject to the same limitation period as a common law action for damages. Thus an action for account for breach of fiduciary duty will be subject to a six year limitation period unless it involved a genuine misappropriation of trust property by the fiduciary, in which circumstances s 21(1)(a) will apply and there will be no limitation period.[187] Where there is no limitation period the equitable doctrine of laches may apply to protect fiduciaries from unduly delayed proceedings.[188] This is discussed more fully in the following chapter.

*(v) Postponement of limitation period.* Section 32(1) provides that the date from which the Limitation Act shall run may be postponed to a date later than the date of the cause of action:

'. . . where in the case of any action for which a period of limitation is prescribed by this Act, either—

(a) the action is based upon the fraud of the defendant; or
(b) any fact relevant to the plaintiff's right of action has been deliberately concealed from him by the defendant; or
(c) the action is for relief from the consequences of a mistake;

the period of limitation shall not begin to run until the plaintiff has discovered the fraud, concealment or mistake (as the case may be) or could with reasonable diligence have discovered it.'

It has been held that this section applies to actions against trustees.[189]

## (c) Reform of limitation

The Law Commission has recently recommended sweeping reform of the limitation period applicable to claims for a remedy for a wrong in its Report *Limitation of Actions*,[190] which, if implemented, would simplify and radically alter the limitation period applicable to actions for breach of trust. The Law Commission proposes the introduction of a single core limitation regime applicable to all claims. This would consist of a primarily limitation period of three years starting from the date on which the claimant knows, or ought reasonably to know (a) the facts which give rise to the cause of action; (b) the identity of the defendant; and (c) if the claimant has suffered injury, loss or damage or the defendant has received a benefit, that the injury, loss, damage or benefit was significant. This primary limitation period would be supplemented by a long-stop limitation period of ten years, starting from the date of the accrual of the cause of action, or from the date of the act or omission which gives rise to the cause of action. It is proposed that this core regime should apply to all claims for breach of trust and claims to recover trust property,[191] and to claims for breach of

---

[185] *A-G v Cocke* [1988] Ch 414; *Nelson v Rye* [1996] 2 All ER 186; [1997] Conv 225 (Stevens).
[186] [2000] 1 WLR 707.      [187] *Paragon Finance v DB Thakerar & Co* [1999] 1 All ER 400.
[188] See below p 766.
[189] *Beaman v ARTS Ltd* [1949] 1 KB 550, CA; *Kitchen v Royal Air Forces Association* [1958] 1 WLR 563; *Phillips-Higgins v Harper* [1954] 1 QB 411; *Bartlett v Barclays Bank Trust Co Ltd* [1980] Ch 515.
[190] Law Com No 270 (2001).      [191] Law Com No 270 (2001) para 4.94.

fiduciary duty.[192] No distinction would be made between fraudulent and non-fraudulent breaches of trust,[193] nor would a special limitation period operate where the claimant was bringing a claim to recover property against his or her trustee.[194] A special rule would operate in the case of a claim for the recovery of property held on a bare trust so that the cause of action shall not accrue unless and until the trustee acts in breach of trust.[195]

## (5) Laches

If a plaintiff delays bringing his action, the court may consider it inequitable for him to succeed, and the defendant will be protected from any liability. The doctrine was explained by the Privy Council in *Lindsay Petroleum Co v Hurd*:

'. . . the doctrine of laches in courts of equity is not an arbitrary or a technical doctrine. Where it would be practically unjust to give a remedy, either because the party has, by his conduct, done that which might fairly be regarded as equivalent to waiver of it, or where by his conduct and neglect he has, though perhaps not waiving that remedy, yet put the other party in a situation in which it would not be reasonable to place him if the remedy were afterwards to be asserted, in either of these cases, lapse of time and delay are most material.'[196]

In *Nelson v Rye*[197] Laddie J rejected a submission that delay per se is insufficient to raise the defence unless the defendant shows that he had suffered substantial prejudice or detriment. He stated that there were no defined hurdles over each of which a litigant must struggle before the defence is made out,[198] and instead identified a number of main factors which should be taken in to account by the court:

'The courts have indicated over the years some of the factors which must be taken into consideration in deciding whether the defence runs. Those factors include the period of the delay, the extent to which the defendant's position has been prejudiced by the delay, and the extent to which the prejudice was caused by the actions of the plaintiff.'[199]

In some circumstances the defence of laches may even operate so as to prevent a beneficiary from asserting their equitable interest in the trust property because it would be unconscionable for them to do so.[200] In *Patel v Shah*[201] commercial properties had been purchased in the late 1980s in circumstances which gave rise to a resulting trust in favor of the claimants. However, following the property slump in the early 1990s, when the properties were in negative equity and the rental income was insufficient to meet the mortgage installments, the claimants left the defendants to deal with everything relating to the properties, and the defendants took on the whole burden of keeping the properties afloat. The claimants only sought to assert their beneficial interest in the properties in 2002 when market prices had recovered and the properties were

---

[192] Law Com No 270 (2001) para 4.95.    [193] Law Com No 270 (2001) paras 4.97–4.101.
[194] Law Com No 270 (2001) paras 4.102–4.106.    [195] Law Com No 270 (2001) para 4.105.
[196] (1874) LR 5 PC 221 at 239–240.    [197] [1996] 2 All ER 186; [1997] Conv 225 (Stevens).
[198] [1996] 2 All ER 186 at 200.    [199] [1996] 2 All ER 186 at 201.
[200] See *Frawley v Neill* [2000] CP Reports 20.    [201] [2005] EWCA Civ 157.

producing income and capital gains. The Court of Appeal held that in these circumstances the claimants were barred from asserting their equitable interest by the defense of laches. They had acted unconscionably by leaving the defendants to deal with the properties, and had departed from their commercial arrangements by ceasing to bear any risk or expense. In effect the venture between the defendants and the claimants had ceased to be joint.

### (a) Relation to statutory limitation periods

The doctrine of laches has no application where a statutory period of limitation applies.[202] Thus, in *Re Pauling's Settlement Trusts*[203] Wilberforce J held that there was no room for the operation of the equitable doctrine of laches because there was an express statutory provision.[204] The doctrine will therefore have limited application because of the general limitation period for breach of trust in s 21(3) of the Limitation Act 1980. However, it will continue to apply to those situations where there is no statutory limitation period, particularly those falling within the scope of s 21(3).

### (b) Knowledge of the right of action

It seems that the doctrine of laches will only apply if the plaintiff had knowledge of the rights he failed to pursue. In *Lindsay Petroleum Co v Hurd*[205] the Privy Council stated that 'in order that the remedy should be lost by laches or delay, it is . . . necessary that there should be sufficient knowledge of the facts constituting the title to relief'.

### (c) Length of delay

There is no set length of time that will cause the court to apply the doctrine of laches. Instead the court must determine whether, given the circumstances, it would be inequitable to allow the claim to succeed. Very short periods, if not accompanied by acts of acquiescence by the plaintiff, will not be sufficient. In *Lindsay Petroleum Co v Hurd*[206] the Privy Council held that a delay of fifteen months was insufficient, as was a delay of two and a quarter years in *Re Sharpe*.[207] In *Weld v Petre*,[208] in the context of the redemption of a mortgage, the Court of Appeal suggested a period of 20 years, therefore holding that a delay of 18 years and four months was 'not of itself sufficient to disentitle the plaintiffs to relief'.[209]

### (d) Prejudice to the defendant

The doctrine of laches operates very closely with the principle of acquiescence. As the Privy Council noted in *Lindsay Petroleum Co v Hurd*,[210] equity will grant relief where to allow the plaintiff his remedy would be practically unjust because he has 'by his conduct, done that which might fairly be regarded as equivalent to a waiver'.

---

[202]  *Gwembe Valley Devlopment Co Ltd v Koshy* [2004] WTLR 97 at [140].          [203]  [1961] 3 All ER 713.
[204]  [1961] 3 All ER 713 at 735. Affirmed by the Court of Appeal [1964] Ch 303.
[205]  (1874) LR 5 PC 221 at 241.          [206]  (1874) LR 5 PC 221.
[207]  [1892] 1 Ch 154. In *Bunn v BBC* [1998] 3 All ER 552 Lightman J refused to grant an injunction preventing a television broadcast because it had been delayed until the last minute. This would not, however, have affected any remedy in damages for the alleged breach of confidence.
[208]  [1929] 1 Ch 33 at 54–55.          [209]  [1929] 1 Ch 33 at 55, per Lawrence LJ.
[210]  (1874) LR 5 PC 221 at 239–240.

Whilst the authorities recognise that the defence may apply where in the absence of an conduct by the plaintiff other than delay,[211] the mere fact of a delay in commencing proceedings is not usually sufficient to give rise to the defence of laches. As Laddie J observed in *Nelson v Rye*:

'I accept that mere delay alone will almost never suffice, but the court has to look at all the circumstances . . . and then decide whether the balance of justice or injustice is in favour of granting the remedy or withholding it. If substantial prejudice will be suffered by the defendant, it is not necessary to prove that it was caused by the delay. On the other hand, the plaintiff's knowledge that the delay will cause such prejudice is a factor to be taken into account.'[212]

He held that, in the circumstances, Nelson had caused an unreasonable delay by ignoring Rye's advice that they should get around the table to see how the figures worked out, but that he had done this because he did not want to hear Rye's warnings that he was living beyond his means. He further held that Rye would be prejudiced by the proceedings because he had not retained documents relating to the receipt of earnings for the entire period of the claim, having cleared them out to make space after a six-year period. He would be incapable of remembering the details of the accounts, especially relating to any expenses incurred that he would be entitled to set off against the gross earnings received.

# 4 Contribution and indemnity where a trustee is liable

Although a trustee may be liable to the beneficiaries for breach of trust without any defence, in some circumstances he may be entitled to a contribution or indemnity from his co-trustees, or from the beneficiaries of the trust, which will have the practical effect of partially or completely alleviating his obligation to provide equitable compensation.

## (1) Indemnity from co-trustees

As was noted above, trustees who together commit a breach of trust are jointly and severally liable for that breach. However, in some circumstances a trustee may be entitled to receive a full indemnity from liability for his breach from his fellow trustees.

## (a) Co-trustee acted fraudulently

Where one of several trustee acts fraudulently the others are entitled to a complete indemnity from liability. In *Re Smith*[213] two trustees invested in debentures. One, who was also the tenant for life of the settlement, invested because he believed that this would increase his income from the trust, whilst the other invested because he had

---

[211] *Lindsay Petroleum Co v Hurd* (1874) LR 5 PC 221; *Erlanger v New Sombrero Phosphate Co* (1878) 3 App Cas 1218; *Brooks v Muckleston* [1909] 2 Ch 519.
[212] [1996] 2 All ER 186 at 201.     [213] [1896] 1 Ch 71.

received a bribe to do so. Kekewich J held that, because of his dishonesty, the bribed trustee alone was liable.

### (b) Co-trustee is a professional

A trustee may be entitled to an indemnity if his co-trustee was a professional whose advice he could reasonably be expected to rely on. This has most often been the case where a co-trustee was a solicitor.[214] In *Re Partington*[215] the two trustees of a settlement invested in a mortgage which was an improper investment for the trust. Stirling J held that Mr Allen, who was a solicitor, was liable to indemnify his co-trustee, Mrs Partington, because she had 'been misled by her co-trustee by reason of his not giving her full information as to the nature of the investments which he was asking her to advance the money upon'. For an indemnity the trustee must have acted purely on the basis of the solicitor trustee. In *Head v Gould*[216] Kekewich J said that there was no right to an indemnity merely because a co-trustee is a solicitor when the trustee 'was an active participator in the breach of trust complained of, and is not proved to have participated merely in consequence of the advice and control of the solicitor'.[217]

### (c) Co-trustee has personally benefited from the breach of trust

The general principle was considered by the Court of Appeal in *Bahin v Hughes*.[218] Cotton LJ said that a trustee is entitled to an indemnity from his co-trustee either when they are both liable to the beneficiary because the co-trustee got trust money into his own hands and made use of it,[219] or 'against a trustee who has himself got the benefit of the breach of trust'.[220] Where the trustee is also a beneficiary, and has benefited by the breach of trust, he is liable to indemnify his co-trustees to the extent of his beneficial interest. The principle was stated by Kay J in *Chillingworth v Chambers*:

'. . . the weight of authority is in favour of the holding that a trustee who, being also a [beneficiary], has received, as between himself and his co-trustee, an exclusive benefit by the breach of trust, must indemnify his co-trustee to the extent of his interest in the trust fund, and not merely to the extent of the benefit which he has received.'[221]

The trustees of a will invested in mortgages which proved to provide insufficient security. Chillingworth had also become a beneficiary, and the purposes of the investment had been to produce a higher rate of interest from the trust property, which was for his benefit. The court held that the deficit of £1,580 was to be made good from Chillingworth's beneficial interest, and that Chambers was indemnified from liability. If the trustee-beneficiary's interest is insufficient to cover the total loss, the trustees will be equally liable for the remaining loss.

---

[214] See *Lockhart v Reilly* (1856) 25 LJ Ch 697; *Bahin v Hughes* (1886) 31 Ch D 390, CA.
[215] (1887) 57 LT 654.      [216] [1898] 2 Ch 250.      [217] [1898] 2 Ch 250 at 265.
[218] (1886) 31 Ch D 390.      [219] See *Thompson v Finch* (1856) 25 LJ Ch 681.
[220] (1886) 31 Ch D 390 at 396.      [221] [1896] 1 Ch 685 at 707.

## (2) Contribution from co-trustees

### (a) Position pre-1979

Prior to the enactment of the Civil Liability (Contribution) Act 1978 trustees who were jointly and severally liable for a breach of trust were equally liable, irrespective of the degree of blame warranted by their conduct. A trustee who had been held liable to the beneficiaries could recover equal contributions from his co-trustees. The effect of this rule was seen in *Bahin v Hughes*,[222] where an unauthorised investment was made by two of the three trustees of a settlement, with the third trustee, Mr Edwards, taking no active part. He claimed that he was not liable to contribute, but the Court of Appeal held that the trustees were equally liable and there was no ground for an indemnity. As Cotton LJ concluded:

'. . . in my opinion it would be laying down a wrong rule to hold that where one trustee acts honestly, though erroneously, the other trustee is to be held entitled to an indemnity who by doing nothing neglects his duty more than the acting trustee.'[223]

### (b) Civil Liability (Contribution) Act 1978[224]

The Civil Liability (Contribution) Act 1978 gives the court a wide discretion to apportion liability between trustees who are jointly and severally liable for breach of trust.[225] Section 1(1) states the general principle of contribution:

'. . . any person liable in respect of any damage suffered by another person may recover contribution from any other person liable in respect of the same damage (whether jointly with him or otherwise).'

The general discretion of the court is found in s 2(1):

'. . . in any proceedings for contribution under s 1 . . . the amount of the contribution recoverable from any person shall be such as may be found by the court to be just and equitable having regard to the extent of that person's responsibility for the damage in question.'

The court can therefore reflect the respective blameworthiness of co-trustees in the extent to which they permit contribution. Under s 2(2) the court has the power to find that a trustee is exempt from making contributions to his co-trustee, or that a trustee is entitled to a complete indemnity from his co-trustee.

## (3) Indemnity from a beneficiary

As has already been noted, a trustee will not incur any liability for a breach of trust to a beneficiary who consented to it, or subsequently concurred in it.[226] The trustee remains

---

[222] (1886) 31 Ch D 390.    [223] (1886) 31 Ch D 390 at 396.

[224] For the comparable position in Australia see: *Alexander v Perpetual Trustees WA Ltd* [2003] 216 CLR 109;. [2006] 122 LQR 563 (Vann).

[225] S 6(1) makes clear that the statute applies to damage caused by breach of trust. *Friends' Provident Life Office v Hillier Parker May & Rowden (a firm)* [1997] QB 85; *Dubai Aluminium Co Ltd v Salaam* [2003] 2 AC 366.

[226] See above, p 756.

liable to any beneficiaries who did not so consent or concur. However, the trustee may be entitled to be indemnified from the beneficial interest of any trustee who requested, or consented to the breach.

## (a) The court's inherent jurisdiction

If a trustee commits a breach of trust at the instigation or the request of a beneficiary the court has the power, under its inherent jurisdiction, to impound the beneficiary's beneficial interest to indemnify the trustee for any liability he might incur.[227] There is no need for the request or instigation to be made in writing.[228] However, the trustee will not be entitled to an indemnity unless the beneficiary knew the facts of what was happening. Where the beneficiary has not requested or instigated the breach of trust but merely consented to it, the trustee may still be entitled to an indemnity from his beneficial interest. This will only be the case if the consent was given in writing and the beneficiary gained a personal benefit from the breach.[229] The indemnity will only extend to the amount of that benefit.[230]

## (b) Trustee Act 1925, s 62

This section grants the court a wide discretion to impound the beneficial interest of a beneficiary who has instigated, requested or consented to a breach of trust, to indemnify the trustee. Section 62(1) provides:

'Where a trustee commits a breach of trust at the instigation or request or with the consent in writing of a beneficiary, the court may, if it thinks fit, make such orders as the court thinks just, for impounding all or any part of the interest of the beneficiary in the trust estate by way of indemnity to the trustee or persons claiming through him.'

In *Re Pauling's Settlement Trusts (No 2)*[231] Wilberforce J stated that the purpose of the section was to extend the courts' inherent jurisdiction, and in *Bolton v Curre*[232] Romer J said that the forerunner to s 62[233] 'was intended to enlarge the power of the court as to indemnifying trustees, and to give greater relief to trustees, and was not intended and did not operate to curtail the previously existing rights and remedies of trustees, or to alter the law except by giving greater power to the court'. It has been held that the requirement of writing applies only to a beneficiary's consent,[234] and the court may impound the beneficiary's interest under s 62 where there has been instigation or a request irrespective of the absence of writing. The court will only impound the beneficiary's interest if he had sufficient knowledge. In *Re Somerset* Smith LJ stated:

---

[227]   *Booth v Booth* (1838) 1 Beav 125; *Lincoln v Wright* (1841) 4 Beav 427; *Raby v Ridehalgh* (1855) 7 De GM & G 104; *Bentley v Robinson* (1859) 9 I Ch R 479; *Sawyer v Sawyer* (1885) 28 Ch D 595, CA; *Ricketts v Ricketts* (1891) 64 LT 263; *Chillingworth v Chambers* [1896] 1 Ch 685.

[228]   *Griffiths v Hughes* [1892] 3 Ch 105; *Mara v Browne* [1895] 2 Ch 69.

[229]   *Booth v Booth* (1838) 1 Beav 125; *Chillingworth v Chambers* [1896] 1 Ch 685.

[230]   *Raby v Ridehaigh* (1855) 7 De GM & G 104.       [231]   [1963] Ch 576.

[232]   [1895] 1 Ch 544 at 549.

[233]   Trustee Act 1888, s 6; repeated by the Trustee Act 1893, s 45.

[234]   *Griffiths v Hughes* [1892] 3 Ch 105; *Re Somerset* [1894] 1 Ch 231.

'. . . upon the true reading of this section, a trustee in order to obtain the benefit conferred thereby, must establish that the beneficiary knew the facts which rendered what he was instigating, requesting or consenting to in writing a breach of trust.'[235]

It is not necessary that he actually know that those facts amount to a breach of trust. In *Re Pauling's Settlement Trusts (No 2)*[236] Wilberforce J held that the protection of the section was not only available to existing trustees of the trust, but also to former trustees who had since retired from the trust or been replaced. The only requirement is that the person seeking the indemnity was a trustee at the time of the breach.

[235] [1894] 1 Ch 231.    [236] [1963] Ch 576.

# 29

# Fiduciary position of trustees

## 1 Fiduciary relationships[1]

### (1) The trustee as a fiduciary

In the previous chapter it was seen that a trustee will be liable to pay equitable compensation for any loss suffered in consequence of a breach of trust. Such a breach will occur if he acts in a manner inconsistent with the express terms of the trust, or if he fails to act as required with insufficient care. However, the duties of a trustee are not confined solely to his obligation not to act in breach of trust. A further essential aspect of the multifaceted nature of trusteeship is that a trustee stands in a fiduciary relationship to the beneficiaries of the trust.[2] The fiduciary position of a trustee subjects him to onerous negative obligations in equity, which are designed to prevent him from abusing his position by acting in his own interests at the expense of the interests of his beneficiaries. It has already been seen how the division between legal and equitable ownership effected by a trust separates the control and management of property from the entitlement to its ultimate enjoyment. Although this separation provides great flexibility, it also obviously provides opportunity for abuse. The trustee who controls the property can thereby use it for his own advantage, for example by selling himself the trust property at an undervalue. To prevent the trustee gaining personal advantages at the expense of the beneficiaries' equity characterises the relationship as a 'fiduciary,' which entitles the beneficiaries to a remedy if the trustee makes unauthorised personal gains by virtue of his position. A trustee in breach of his fiduciary duty will be required to make restitution to the beneficiaries of any unauthorised profits he has received through the abuse of his position.

### (2) Fiduciary relationships

#### (a) Types of fiduciary relationship

The fiduciary relationship has been described as 'one of the most ill-defined, if not altogether misleading terms in our law'.[3] And it has been said that 'there are few

---

[1] See Glover, *Commercial Equity: Fiduciary Relationships* (1995); Goff and Jones, *The Law of Restitution* (6th edn, 2002), Ch 33; Oakley, *Constructive Trusts* (3rd edn, 1997), Ch 3; Finn, *Fiduciary Obligations* (1977); (1968) 84 LQR 472 (Jones); (1981) 97 LQR 51 (Shepherd).

[2] *Keech v Sandford* (1726) Sel Cas Ch 61; *Price v Blakemore* (1843) 6 Beav 507.

[3] Finn, *Fiduciary Obligations* (1977), p 1.

legal concepts more frequently invoked but less conceptually certain than that of the fiduciary relationship'.[4] As Frankfurter J said in the American case *SEC v Chenery Corpn*:[5]

'To say that a man is a fiduciary only begins analysis; it gives direction to further inquiry. To whom is he a fiduciary? What obligations does he owe as a fiduciary? In what respect has he failed to discharge these obligations? And what are the consequences of his deviation from duty?'[6]

It is important to recognise that a fiduciary relationship may arise in a number of ways. In *LAC Minerals Ltd v International Corona Resources Ltd*,[7] a decision of the Canadian Supreme Court, Wilson J distinguished between relationships which in their very nature are fiduciary, and those which take on a fiduciary character because of the particular relationship between the parties:

'It is ... my view of the law that there are certain relationships which are almost per se fiduciary, such as trustee and beneficiary, guardian and ward, principal and agent, and that where such relationships subsist they give rise to fiduciary duties. On the other hand, there are relationships which are not in their essence fiduciary, such as the relationship brought into being by the parties in the present case by virtue of their arm's length negotiations towards a joint venture agreement, but this does not preclude a fiduciary duty from arising out of specific conduct engaged in them or either of them within the confines of the relationship.'[8]

## (b) Relationships fiduciary per se

English law has never provided a comprehensive definition of fiduciary relationships. Instead, certain relationships, because of their very nature, have come to be regarded as fiduciary. This obviously allows for flexibility as circumstances and commercial practice change. As Finn stated, a fiduciary 'is, simply, someone who undertakes to act for or on behalf of another in some particular matter or matters'.[9] In the unusual case of *Reading v A-G*[10] the House of Lords held that an army sergeant who had used his uniform to enable lorries smuggling spirits and drugs to pass through army checkpoints was a fiduciary, and therefore he was obliged to account to the Crown for the money he had received from the smugglers for his services. In the Court of Appeal Asquith LJ attempted a summary of the characteristics of a fiduciary relationship:

'... a fiduciary relationship exists (a) whenever the plaintiff entrusts to the defendant property ... and relies on the defendant to deal with such property for the benefit of the plaintiff or purposes authorised by him, and not otherwise, and (b) whenever the plaintiff entrusts to the defendant a job to be performed ... and relies on the defendant to procure for the plaintiff the best terms available ...'[11]

---

[4]  *LAC Minerals Ltd v International Corona Resources Ltd* (1989) 61 DLR (4th) 14 at 26, per La Forest J.
[5]  518 US 80 (1943) at 85–86.
[6]  Cited by Goff and Jones, *The Law of Restitution* (6th edn, 2002), p 709, and by the Privy Council in *Re Goldcorp Exchanges Ltd* [1994] 2 All ER 806.
[7]  (1989) 61 DLR (4th) 14.      [8]  (1989) 61 DLR (4th) 14 at 16.
[9]  Finn, *Fiduciary Obligations* (1977), p 201.      [10]  [1951] AC 507.      [11]  [1949] 2 KB 232 at 236.

The relationship of trustee and beneficiary is not the only one that is characterised as fiduciary by equity. Other recognised fiduciary relationships include: mortgagee and mortgagor;[12] principal and agent;[13] solicitor and client;[14] partners and co-partners;[15] company directors and the company;[16] senior management and their employer company;[17] confidential employees and their employers;[18] government employees and the Crown;[19] and pawnbroker and pawnor.[20] The essence of all these relationships is that one person occupies a position in which he has a duty to act on behalf of another, thereby enjoying the potential to abuse his position by acting for his own interests. They are relationships in which there is an inherent element of 'trust and confidence'[21] between the parties. In Canada it has been held that the relationship between doctor and patient[22] and between child-abuser and victim[23] are also fiduciary, and it has been suggested that the relationship between priest and parishioner should likewise be fiduciary.[24] English law has not yet adopted these relationships as fiduciary per se, although individual relationships of this type could be found to be fiduciary if the circumstances suggested that there was a sufficient degree of reliance between the parties.

---

[12] *Farrars v Farrars Ltd* (1888) 40 Ch D 395, CA.

[13] *De Bussche v Alt* (1878) 8 Ch D 286; *Kirkham v Peel* (1880) 43 LT 171; *Lamb v Evans* [1893] 1 Ch 218, CA; *New Zealand Netherlands Society Oranje Inc v Kuys* [1973] 1 WLR 1126, PC; *English v Dedham Vale Properties Ltd* [1978] 1 WLR 93; *Korkontzilas v Soulos* (1997) 146 DLR (4th) 214.

[14] *Re Hallet's Estate* (1880) 13 Ch D 696, CA; *McMaster v Bryne* [1952] 1 All ER 1362; *Brown v IRC* [1965] AC 244, HL; *Oswald Hickson Collier & Co v Carter-Ruck* [1984] AC 720n; *Swindle v Harrison* [1997] 4 All ER 705; *Logstaff v Birtles* [2002] 1 WLR 470. In *Conway v Ratiu* [2006] 1 All ER 571 the Court of Appeal said, contra Lord Millett in *Prince Jefri Bolkiah v KPMG (a firm)* [1999] 2 AC 222, that the fiduciary relationship of a solicitor to his client is distinct from the contractual obligations arising under his retainer. As such the fiduciary duty is not necessarily to be found or confined to the terms of the contractual retainer, so that the fiduciary relationship may outlive the contractual solicitor/client relationship. See also *Hilton v Barker Booth and Eastwood (a firm)* [2005] 1 All ER 651 at [28]–[29] per Lord Walker; (2006) 122 LQR 1 (Getzler).

[15] *Bentley v Craven* (1853) 18 Beav 75; *Aas v Benham* [1891] 2 Ch 244; *Thompson's Trustee in Bankruptcy v Heaton* [1974] 1 WLR 605. See also *Holiday Inns Inc v Yorkstone Properties (Harlington)* (1974) 232 Estates Gazette 951.

[16] *Sinclair v Brougham* [1914] AC 398; *Regal (Hastings) v Gulliver* [1967] 2 AC 134n; *Selangor United Rubber Estates Ltd v Craddock* (No 3) [1968] 1 WLR 1555; *Industrial Development Consultants Ltd v Cooley* [1972] 1 WLR 443; *Cowan de Groot Properties Ltd v Eagle Trust plc* [1992] 4 All ER 700; *Item Software (UK) Ltd v Fassihi* [2004] EWCA 1244. See (2005) 121 LQR 213 (Berg); (2003) MLR 852 (Scott) and 894 (Koh). See also Koh, 'Once a Director, Always a Fiduciary?' [2003] 62 CLJ 403 for a consideration whether a director continue to be a fiduciary even after he ceases to be a director of the company.

[17] *Sybron Corpn v Rochem Ltd* [1984] Ch 112; *Canadian Aero-Services v O'Malley* (1973) 40 DLR (3d) 371; *Agip (Africa) Ltd v Jackson* [1990] Ch 265.

[18] *Triplex Safety Glass Co Ltd v Scorah* [1938] Ch 211; *British Celanese Ltd v Montcrieff* [1948] Ch 564; *British Syphon Co v Homewood* [1956] 1 WLR 1190; *A-G v Guardian Newspapers Ltd (No 2)* [1990] 1 AC 109, HL; *A-G v Blake* [1998] 1 All ER 833.

[19] *Reading v A-G* [1951] AC 507; *A-G v Guardian Newspapers Ltd (No 2)* [1990] 1 AC 109; *A-G for Hong Kong v Reid* [1994] 1 All ER 1, PC; *A-G v Blake* [1998] 1 All ER 833.

[20] *Mathew v TM Sutton Ltd* [1994] 4 All ER 793.   [21] [2006] 1 All ER 571 at [71] per Auld LJ.

[22] *Norberg v Wynrib* (1992) 92 DLR (4th) 449.   [23] *M (K) v M (H)* (1992) 96 DLR (4th) 289.

[24] Frankel, *Equity, Fiduciaries and Trusts*, ed Waters (1993).

### (c) Fiduciary duties arising within the context of a relationship which is not fiduciary per se[25]

The majority of commercial relationships cannot be characterised as fiduciary per se, as the parties simply bargain with each other at arm's length. However, the specific nature of a particular relationship may bring about a fiduciary relationship between the parties. This was the case in *LAC Minerals Ltd v International Corona Resources Ltd*,[26] where two companies were negotiating at arm's length about the possibility of a joint venture of exploit minerals from land over which the plaintiff company (LAC) owned mining rights. In the course of these negotiations it was clear to the defendants from results of the plaintiffs' drilling that adjacent land was also likely to include mineral deposits. The defendants then purchased the adjacent land, defeating a competing bid from the plaintiffs, and developed a mine alone. Although the relationship between the defendants and the plaintiffs was not fiduciary per se, the Supreme Court held that fiduciary duties were owed because the defendants had received confidential information from the plaintiffs in the course of the negotiations. In *A-G v Blake*[27] Lord Woolf MR similarly suggested that a fiduciary relationship arises whenever information is imparted by one person to another in confidence,[28] although he noted that in the majority of cases such information will be imparted in the context of a relationship which is already fiduciary, for example where the recipient of the information was an employee.

In contrast in *Re Goldcorp Exchange Ltd (in receivership)*[29] the Privy Council held that a relationship had remained exclusively commercial so that it had not become fiduciary. The case concerned a company in New Zealand which dealt in gold bullion and other precious metals. Customers purchased what was described as 'non-allocated metal' which would be held for them by the company free of charge. They were entitled to take physical delivery of the metal by giving seven days' notice, at which point it would be appropriated from the metal which the company held in bulk. It was argued that the company stood in a fiduciary relationship to the customers, but the Privy Council held that their relationship was purely contractual. As Lord Mustill explained:

'No doubt the fact that one person is placed in a particular position vis-à-vis another through the medium of a contract does not necessarily mean that he does not also owe fiduciary duties to that other by virtue of being in that position. But the essence of a fiduciary relationship is that it creates obligations of a different character from those deriving from the contract itself. Their Lordships have not heard in argument any submission which went beyond suggesting that by virtue of being a fiduciary the company was obliged honestly and conscientiously to do what it had by contract promised to do . . . It is possible, without misuse of language to say that the customers put faith in the company, and that their trust has not been repaid. But the vocabulary is misleading; high expectations do not necessarily lead to equitable remedies.'[30]

---

[25]  See Oakley, 'The Liberalising Nature of Remedies for Breach of Trust' in Oakley, *Trends in Contemporary Trust Law* (1996), pp 230–233.

[26]  (1989) 61 DLR (4th) 14.      [27]  [1998] 1 All ER 833.      [28]  [1998] 1 All ER 833 at 842.

[29]  [1994] 2 All ER 806.      [30]  [1994] 2 All ER 806 at 821–822.

## (3) The function of fiduciary relationships in English law[31]

It has been seen that it is difficult to define fiduciary relationships with comprehensive accuracy. This difficulty is compounded by the varied functions that they perform in English law at present. They operate so as to impose duties which restrict the fiduciary's ability to act in his own interests, and also as a trigger which may lead to the creation of an equitable trust interest in property by way of a constructive trust.

### (a) Fiduciary duties[32]

A person who stands in a fiduciary relationship may owe a range of duties to his principal. Not all of these duties can properly be characterised as fiduciary in nature. For example a trustee, who is by definition also a fiduciary, will owe duties of care regarding his conduct of the trust business to the beneficiaries alongside his fiduciaries duties. In *Bristol and West Building Society v Mothew*[33] Millett LJ commented:

'The expression fiduciary duty is properly confined to those duties which are peculiar to fiduciaries and the breach of which attracts legal consequences differing from those consequent upon the breach of other duties. Unless the expression is so limited it is lacking in practical utility. In this sense it is obvious that not every breach of duty by a fiduciary is a breach of fiduciary duty.'[34]

He therefore held that it was inappropriate to apply the expression fiduciary to the obligation of a trustee to use proper skill and care in the discharge of his duties. In *A-G v Blake*[35] the Court of Appeal similarly held that an employee who had published an unauthorised biography had acted in breach of contract but not in breach of fiduciary duty. In *Swindle v Harrison*[36] the Court of Appeal considered that the duties imposed by equity upon a fiduciary go beyond the common law duties of skill and care.[37]

Given that not every duty owed by a fiduciary to his principal can be characterised as fiduciary in nature, the question arises as to the content of his specifically fiduciary duties. In *Bristol and West Building Society v Mothew*[38] Millett LJ identified the core content of the fiduciary duty:

'A fiduciary is someone who has undertaken to act for or on behalf of another in a particular matter in circumstances which give rise to a relationship of trust and confidence. The distinguishing obligation of a fiduciary is the obligation of loyalty. The principal is entitled to the single-minded loyalty of his fiduciary. This core liability has several facets: a fiduciary must act in good faith; he must not make a profit out of his trust; he must not place himself in a position where his duty and his interest may conflict; he may not act for his own benefit or the benefit of a third person without the informed consent of his principal. This is not intended to be an exhaustive list, but it is sufficient to indicate the nature of fiduciary obligations.'[39]

---

[31] See Conaglen, 'The Nature and Function of Fiduciary Loyalty' (2005) 121 LQR 452.

[32] See Austin, 'Moulding the Content of Fiduciary Duties' in Oakley, *Trends in Contemporary Trust Law* (1996).

[33] [1996] 4 All ER 698; [1997] CLJ 39 (Nolan). [34] [1996] 4 All ER 698 at 710.

[35] [1998] 1 All ER 833. [36] [1997] 4 All ER 705. [37] [1997] 4 All ER 705 at 716, per Evans LJ.

[38] [1996] 4 All ER 698.

[39] [1996] 4 All ER 698 at 711–712. See also *A-G v Blake* [1998] 1 All ER 833 at 842, per Lord Woolf MR.

Whilst the core content of a fiduciary duty can be identified as an obligation of exclusive loyalty, the precise content of specific fiduciary relationships will vary. As Lord Browne-Wilkinson observed in *Henderson v Merrett Syndicates Ltd*,[40] the phrase 'fiduciary duties' is a dangerous one, giving rise to a mistaken assumption that all fiduciaries owe the same duties in all circumstances. In *A-G v Blake* Lord Woolf MR stated:

'There is more than one category of fiduciary relationship, and the different categories possess different characteristics and attract different kinds of fiduciary obligations.'[41]

The duration of the core fiduciary duty of loyalty is also determined by the context of the relationship in which the fiduciary duty arose. The mere fact that a person once occupied a fiduciary position does not necessarily mean that they will be subject to a lifelong duty of loyalty. *A-G v Blake* concerned the nature of the fiduciary duties of a former secret service agent. George Blake had served as a member of the security forces from 1944 until 1960. In 1951 he had become an agent for the Soviet Union. He was arrested and imprisoned, but escaped to live in Moscow. He subsequently wrote an autobiography entitled *No Other Choice* which was published in England. The Crown sought to recover the profits derived from the book on the grounds that the publication was in breach of fiduciary duty. The Court of Appeal held that, although Blake's employment had rendered him subject to a fiduciary duty, his fiduciary duties did not endure beyond the termination of his employment. Lord Woolf MR explained:

'We do not recognise the concept of a fiduciary obligation which continues notwithstanding the determination of the particular relationship which gives rise to it. Equity does not demand a duty of undivided loyalty from a former employee to his former employer . . . A former employee owes no duty of loyalty to his former employer. It is trite law that an employer who wishes to prevent his employee from damaging his legitimate commercial interests after he has left his employment must obtain contractual undertakings from his employee to this effect. He cannot achieve his object by invoking the fiduciary relationship which formerly subsisted between them.'[42]

Whether Blake was a fiduciary or not was not an issue which arose in the subsequent appeal to the House of Lords.[43] However Lord Nicholls[44] and Lord Steyn[45] were both at pains to stress that the position he occupied was at least very closely akin to a fiduciary relationship, suggesting that this might have been a fruitful avenue for appeal.

### (b) Remedies for breach of fiduciary duties

Where a fiduciary acts in breach of his duty he will have committed an equitable wrong against his principal. As such, his principal will be able to recover either equitable compensation or restitution from his fiduciary.

*(i) Equitable compensation for loss sustained.*[46] If a fiduciary commits a breach of

---

[40] [1995] 2 AC 145 at 206.     [41] [1998] 1 All ER 833 at 842.
[42] [1998] 1 All ER 833 at 841–842.     [43] [2000] 4 All ER 385.
[44] [2000] 4 All ER 385 at 400.     [45] [2000] 4 All ER 385 at 404.
[46] See Conaglen, 'Equitable Compensation for Breach of Fiduciary Dealing Rules' (2003) 119 LQR 246.

duty his principal will be entitled to recover equitable damages to compensate him for any loss he has suffered. Where the fiduciary was a trustee his breach will probably have constituted a breach of trust, entitling the beneficiaries to receive compensation. A right to receive equitable compensation for breach of fiduciary duty will arise where the fiduciary was not also a trustee. The principal will be entitled to recover such compensation as would put him in the position he would have been in if the wrong had not been committed. To establish the right to compensation, the principal must demonstrate that the alleged breach of fiduciary duty caused the loss sustained. In *Swindle v Harrison*[47] Mrs Harrison mortgaged her house in order to enable her son to purchase and restore a hotel. Further finance was required to complete the transaction which it was expected would be provided by way of a loan from a brewery. At the date of completion the loan had not been forthcoming and the plaintiff solicitors therefore offered her a bridging loan to complete the hotel purchase. She wished to go ahead with the transaction because she felt the purchase would be advantageous to her and her son. However the solicitors failed to disclose to her that they would be making a profit for themselves from the bridging loan, and that her son's bank was unlikely to provide him with the references needed to obtain the brewery loan. The hotel business was unsuccessful and the solicitors sought possession. Mrs Harrison counterclaimed that she was entitled to receive equitable compensation for the equity she had lost in her home on the grounds that the solicitors has committed a breach of their fiduciary duty. The Court of Appeal held that the solicitors had breached their duty by failing to make full disclosure of the circumstances and that they were therefore liable to compensate her for any loss suffered. However the essential issue was whether her loss had been caused by the breach. Mrs Harrison submitted that she was not required to prove that she would not have completed the purchase in any event,[48] and that she should be compensated merely because the bridging loan had enabled her to complete the purchase. The Court of Appeal rejected this submission and held that, unless the breach could properly be regarded as the equivalent of fraud,[49] she was required to demonstrate causation. In the circumstances it concluded that she would have completed the transaction anyway. Evans LJ explained that she had failed to establish causation:

'The failure to disclose cannot be said to have led to the making of the loan, even on a but for basis, precisely because disclosure of the true facts would not have affected her decision to accept it. Since she would have accepted the loan and completed the purchase, even if full disclosure had been made to her, she would have lost the value of the equity in her home in any event. She cannot recover damages or compensation for that loss, in my judgement, except on proof *either* that the plaintiffs acted fraudulently or in a manner equivalent to fraud *or* that she would not have completed the purchase if full disclosure had been made, i.e. if the breach of duty had not occurred.'[50]

---

[47] [1997] 4 All ER 705; (1998) 114 LQR 181 (Tjio and Yeo); [1998] RLR 135 (Elliott). See also (1998) 114 LQR 214 (Sir Peter Millett).

[48] Cf *Target Holdings v Redferns* [1996] AC 421. See above pp 709–713.

[49] [1997] 4 All ER 705 at 717, per Evans LJ.     [50] [1997] 4 All ER 705 at 718.

The obligation to pay equitable compensation for breach of fiduciary duty is a purely personal remedy.

*(ii) Restitution of the unauthorised profit.* Where a fiduciary breaches his duty of exclusive loyalty and receives an unauthorised profit he will be liable to make restitution[51] to his principal by way of an equitable duty to account for the profit received. He is obliged to pay over to his principal a sum of money equivalent to the amount of profit received, though not necessarily the actual money (or its proceeds) which comprised the profit. It is sometimes said that the fiduciary is required to disgorge his unauthorised profit. The obligation to account operates as a personal remedy.

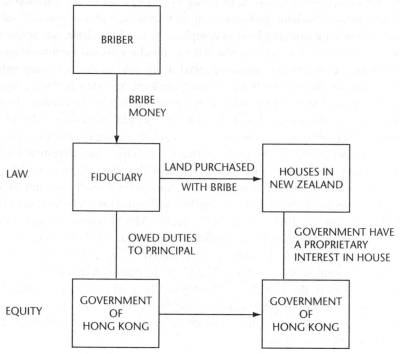

**Proprietary claims to profits made in breach of fiduciary duty:**
*A-G of Hong Kong v Reid*

*(iii) Constructive trust of the unauthorised profit.* The fact that a fiduciary is under a personal obligation in equity to account for the profit received may also give rise to a constructive trust of the specific property comprising the profit. The ability to establish such a constructive trust will prove especially significant if the fiduciary is insolvent, since otherwise the principal will merely rank as a general creditor of the fiduciary, in which case the personal duty to account is unlikely to provide an adequate remedy. If

---

[51] See Goff and Jones, *The Law of Restitution* (6th edn, 2002), pp 707–739; Birks, *Introduction to the Law of Restitution* (1985), pp 313–357; Burrows, *The Law of Restitution* (2nd edn, 2002), pp 493–508; (1989) CLJ 302 (Jackman). See also: R C Nolan, 'Conflicts of Interest, Unjust Enrichment and Wrongdoing', Chap 7 in Cornish, Nolan, O'Sullivan & Virgo (eds) *Restitution Past, Present and Future* (1998).

the actual profit, or its proceeds,[52] can be identified in the fiduciary's hands, his principal will be entitled to it in equity, and will be able to claim priority ahead of any other general creditors. A constructive trust of an unauthorised profit obtained in breach of fiduciary duty was held to have arisen in *A-G of Hong Kong v Reid*.[53] Reid, the acting Director of Public Prosecutions for Hong Kong, had accepted bribes in the course of his duties. The Privy Council held that three houses which Reid had purchased in New Zealand with the bribe money were held on trust for the Crown. However in *Paragon Finance v DB Thakerar & Co*[54] Millett LJ held that no constructive trust would arise if the fiduciary was an agent who received payments on behalf of his principal which he was entitled to pay into his own account and mix with his own money. Such an agent would not have been subject to a duty to keep the receipts separate from his own and to apply them exclusively to the benefit of his principal. Thus a manager of a musician who had received royalty payments on behalf of his client, which had been paid into his own account, mixed with his own money, and from which his commission had been deducted, would be liable to account to his client for any underpayments, but no constructive trust would arise.[55]

## (c) Fiduciary relationships and equitable property rights

It is thus clear that a fiduciary relationship is capable of generating equitable interests in property by way of a constructive trust. If a fiduciary receives property (whether money or not) as an unauthorised profit, he will hold it on constructive trust for his principal, even though it was not previously subject to any trust. Thus, the money received by the DPP in *A-G of Hong Kong v Reid* was not previously subject to any trust relationship, but was the absolute property of the briber. The Crown enjoyed no prior interest in it and only derived an entitlement because the DPP stood in a fiduciary relationship. Alongside this principle that any unauthorised profit received by a fiduciary is subjected to a constructive trust, it seems that property which is misappropriated by a fiduciary from his principal will also be subject to a constructive trust, irrespective of whether the property was received by the fiduciary or a third party. For example, in *Agip (Africa) Ltd v Jackson*[56] a company was defrauded by its chief accountant, Zdiri, who altered the name of the payees of genuine payment orders so that they were payable to dummy companies he had created. Millett J held that as the accountant was a fiduciary of the company by virtue of his senior position and responsibility, the misappropriated money was held on constructive trust by the recipient dummy companies and Agip was enabled to trace it. The money paid to such companies was not previously subject to a trust but had been the absolute property of the company. Similarly, in *Brinks Ltd v Abu-Saleh (No 3)*[57] Rimmer J held that gold bullion which had been stolen was

---

[52] Whether the fiduciary retain in his hands any property that is or represents the profit received will depend on the laws of tracing. See Chapter 31.

[53] [1994] 1 All ER 1.       [54] [1999] 1 All ER 400.

[55] Thus rejecting the earlier decision of Laddie J in *Nelson v Rye* [[1996] 2 All ER 186.

[56] [1990] Ch 265, [1992] 4 All ER 385; (1989) 105 LQR 528 (Birks); (1991) 107 LQR 71 (Sir Peter Millett); [1991] Ch 547, [1992] 4 All ER 451; (1991) 50 CLJ 409 (Harpum); [1992] Conv 367 (Goulding); All ER Rev 1992, 258–265 (Swadling).

[57] (1995) Times, 23 October; [1996] Conv 447 (Stevens).

subject to a constructive trust in favour of its corporate owners because the robbery had been carried out with the assistance of a security guard who stood in a fiduciary relationship.

Whilst it is clear that an unauthorised profit received by a fiduciary, and property misappropriated from a principal by (or with the assistance) of a fiduciary, will be held subject to a constructive trust in favour of the principal, some cases have held that the mere fact that a transaction was subject to a vitiating factor entitling the transferor to restitution from the transferee will establish a fiduciary relationship between them, so that the transferee holds the property received subject to a constructive trust in favour of the transferor. In *Chase Manhattan Bank NA v Israel-British Bank (London) Ltd*[58] the plaintiff bank paid $1m to the defendant bank by mistake, having forgotten that they had previously made an identical payment. Goulding J held that as a consequence of the mistaken payment the defendant bank had become a fiduciary of the plaintiff bank, so that the $1m was held on constructive trust for them. By means of this reasoning, the plaintiff could maintain a proprietary claim to $1m in the assets of the defendant, which was insolvent, thus negating the value of any personal right to restitution at common law on the grounds of mistake. However, it is far from clear that this approach is correct. In *Westdeutsche Landesbank Girozentrale v Islington London Borough Council*[59] Lord Browne-Wilkinson considered that, whilst the decision in *Chase-Manhattan* could be regarded as rightly decided, the reasoning of Goulding J was erroneous. He considered that a constructive trust was constituted not by the mere receipt of the mistaken payment, but by the fact that the bank to whom the payment had been made knew of the mistake within two days of their receipt of the money:

'Although the mere receipt of the moneys, in ignorance of the mistake, gives rise to no trust, the retention of the moneys after the recipient bank learned of the mistake may well have given rise to a constructive trust.'[60]

However, it is submitted that even this reasoning does not adequately explain the creation of an equitable proprietary interest in the money mistakenly paid. The central question should focus rather on the proprietary effects of the mistaken payment. If the mistake was sufficient to prevent property in the money passing to the payee, then the payee will hold it subject to an immediate constructive trust from the moment that it was received. He may not become a fiduciary for the payor until he becomes aware that the mistake had been made and he was conscious of the circumstances giving rise to the constructive trust. But the mere fact that he becomes aware of a mistake rendering him subject to a personal obligation to make restitution should neither make him a fiduciary of the payor nor subject the money in his hands to a constructive trust.

### (d)  The artificial use of fiduciary relationships

The power of a fiduciary relationship to generate proprietary rights and remedies has provided a major incentive for the encroachment of such relationships into the

---

[58] [1981] Ch 105.      [59] [1996] AC 669.      [60] [1996] AC 669 at 715.

commercial arena. For example, increasingly, the employment relationship has come to be characterised as fiduciary and not merely contractual. The lack of a clear definition has enabled the courts to manipulate fiduciary relationships as a means of achieving remedial justice, so that the use of the term 'fiduciary' has often seemed artificial. It has already been argued that the finding of a fiduciary relationship in *Chase Manhattan Bank NA v Israel-British Bank (London) Ltd*[61] was artificial, and the reason for it was to ensure that the mistaken payor bank was entitled to a proprietary remedy so as to gain priority over the payee's general creditors. This artificiality was recognised by the Supreme Court of Canada in *LAC Minerals Ltd v International Corona Resources Ltd*,[62] where La Forest J said that there was a third category of the usage of 'fiduciary':

'. . . [the] third usage of "fiduciary" stems, it seems, from a perception of remedial inflexibility in equity. Courts have resorted to fiduciary language because of the view that certain remedies, deemed appropriate in the circumstances, would not be available unless a fiduciary relationship was present. In this sense, the label fiduciary imposes no obligations, but is rather merely instrumental or facilitative in achieving what appears to be the appropriate result.'

He regarded the use of 'fiduciary' in *Chase-Manhattan* as an example of this 'third usage'. It was not that the relationship between the banks was genuinely 'fiduciary', as they were simply businesses operating at arm's length. Rather the characterisation of the relationship as fiduciary was an essential prerequisite to the availability of tracing in equity, and the relationship was so characterised merely to facilitate the availability of such tracing as the foundation of a proprietary claim. The requirement of a fiduciary relationship with regard to tracing will be fully discussed in Chapter 31.

## (4) Abuse of position

### (a) Fiduciaries owe a duty of exclusive loyalty to their principals

As Millett LJ indicated in *Bristol and West Building Society v Mothew*,[63] a fiduciary owes a duty of exclusive loyalty to his principal. This duty of loyalty applies to prevent the fiduciary abusing his position. It operates to deter fiduciaries from acting in breach and to provide restitution for the principal if a breach is committed. Where the fiduciary is a trustee the potential for abuse of position arises because the trustee may use his powers of management over the trust property for his own benefit rather than in the best interest of the beneficiaries. This danger was recognised in early cases. In *Keech v Sandford*[64] a trustee held the lease of a market on trust for an infant. When the lease came to an end the lessor refused to renew it to the trust and the trustee took it personally. King LC held that the trustee could not take the lease for himself and noted the danger of the trustee abusing his position at the expense of the interests of the beneficiary:

[61] [1981] Ch 105.   [62] (1989) 61 DLR (4th) 14.   [63] [1998] Ch 1.
[64] (1726) Sel Cas Ch 61.

'. . . I very well see, if a trustee, on the refusal to renew, might have a lease for himself, few trust estates would be renewed to the [beneficiary].'

Similarly, if the trustee wishes to sell part of the trust property he may be tempted to sell it to himself at an undervalue. In his capacity as trustee his duty would be to gain the best possible price for the beneficiaries, but as an individual he would obviously wish to obtain the lowest price to enjoy the best bargain for himself. As trustee he would be both the purchaser, who offers a price, and the seller, who agrees to the price. It would be easy for him to abuse his position so that he benefits at the expense of the beneficiaries by selling to himself at an undervalue.[65]

In the recent case of *Item Softwear (UK) Ltd v Fassihi*[66] the Court of Appeal held that a fiduciary was under a duty to disclose his own misconduct to his principal, even though he had not obtained any unauthorised profit. However this decision has been criticised,[67] and it remains unclear whether such an extension of the fiduciary duty is consistent with earlier authorities.[68]

## (b) The difficulty of weighing motives

If a trustee does act in circumstances where it could be suggested that he had abused his position to gain a personal benefit, it may be impossible to weigh his true motives: ie whether he was in fact allowing his own interests to prevail over those of the beneficiaries. As Lord Eldon LC observed in *Ex p James*,[69] 'no court is equal to the examination and ascertainment' of these facts. Because of the practical impossibility of discovering a fiduciary's true motives, equity has taken the very strict view that a fiduciary is liable to account for any profits he makes whenever there was an objective possibility of a conflict between his interests and his duty.[70] There is no need to demonstrate that the fiduciary acted with the subjective intention of benefiting himself at the expense of the beneficiaries. This is a blunt instrument applied in the beneficiaries' favour. As Lord Herschell stated in *Bray v Ford*:

'It is an inflexible rule of a Court of Equity that a person in a fiduciary position . . . is not, unless otherwise expressly provided, entitled to make a profit; he is not allowed to put himself in a position where his interest and duty conflict.'[71]

The duty of exclusive loyalty imposed by a fiduciary duty is not absolute. The fiduciary is not prevented from ever acting in his own interests and receiving a benefit by virtue of his position. He is only prevented from retaining unauthorised profits for himself. A fiduciary will not be liable to make restitution if he breaches his duty with the full informed consent of his principal.

---

[65]  See *Holder v Holder* [1968] Ch 353; *Re Thompson's Settlement* [1986] Ch 99.

[66]  [2004] EWCA 1244; [2005] 64 CLJ 48 (Conaglen).       [67]  (2005) 121 LQR 213 (Berg).

[68]  See *Horcal Ltd v Gartland* [1984] BCLC 549 at 554, per Robert Goff LJ.

[69]  (1803) 8 Ves 337 at 345.

[70]  See *Regal (Hastings) Ltd v Gulliver* [1967] 2 AC 134n, [1942] 1 All ER 378, HL; *Boardman v Phipps* [1967] 2 AC 46, HL.

[71]  [1896] AC 44.

# 2 Unauthorised remuneration

## (1) General principle[72]

As a general rule a trustee is not entitled to receive remuneration for his work unless authorised by the trust deed appointing him, or by statute.[73] The rationale for this principle was stated by Lord Normand in *Dale v IRC*:

'. . . it is not that reward for services is repugnant to the fiduciary duty, but that he who has the duty shall not take any secret remuneration or any financial benefit not authorised by the law . . . or by the trust deed under which he acts . . .'[74]

This statement makes clear that the bar on remuneration is not absolute, so that properly authorised remuneration may be retained by the trustee. In the modern commercial world, where the majority of trusts are administered by professional trustees, the general principle still stands, but it has been recognised that there are other competing objectives. As Fox LJ observed in *Re Duke of Norfolk's Settlement Trusts*:

'. . . the court has to balance two influences which are to some extent in conflict. The first is that the office of trustee is, as such, gratuitous; the court will accordingly be careful to protect the interests of the beneficiaries against claims by the trustees. The second is that it is of great importance to the trust that the trust should be well administered.'[75]

To balance these objectives the courts have a wide inherent jurisdiction to permit trustees to receive remuneration.

## (2) Reimbursement of trustee's expenses

Although a trustee is not prima facie entitled to receive remuneration, he is entitled to the reimbursement of any expenses incurred by him in the work of the trust.[76] Section 31(1)(a) of the Trustee Act 2000 provides that a trustee is entitled to be reimbursed from the trust funds for 'expenses properly incurred by him when acting on behalf of the trust'.

## (3) Authorised remuneration

A trustee is perfectly entitled to retain remuneration which he was authorised to receive, and he is therefore not liable to make restitution of it to the trust.

---

[72] (1983) 46 MLR 289 (Bishop and Prentice).

[73] *How v Godfrey and White* (1678) Cas temp Finch 361; *Bonithon v Hockmore* (1685) 1 Vern 316; *Robinson v Pett* (1734) 3 P Wms 249; *Re Ormsby* (1809) 1 Ball & B 189; *Taylor v Taylor* (1843) 4 Dr & War 124; *Re Barber* (1886) 34 Ch D 77; *Re Bedingfield* (1887) 57 LT 332; *Barrett v Hartley* (1866) LR 2 Eq 789; *Re Accles Ltd* [1902] WN 164.

[74] [1954] AC 11 at 27.     [75] [1982] Ch 61 at 79.

[76] *Stott v Milne* (1884) 25 Ch D 710; *Re Chapman* (1894) 72 LT 66, CA; *Hardoon v Belilios* [1901] AC 118; *Holding and Management Ltd v Property Holding and Investment Trust plc* [1990] 1 All ER 938, CA; see also *Boardman v Phipps* [1967] 2 AC 46, HL, where the fiduciary received payment 'on a liberal scale' for his work and skill in obtaining a profit for himself and the trust.

## (a) Trust instrument

A trustee is not accountable for remuneration he is entitled to receive under the trust instrument.[77] Such provisions are extremely common, and professional trustees will only act if the trust deed contains such a provision. Section 28 of the Trustee Act 2000 provides that a trustee who is acting in a professional capacity is entitled to receive payment for his services on behalf of the trust even if those services are capable of being provided by a lay trustee.

## (b) Statute

Section 29 of the Trustee Act 2000 provides that, in the absence of an express entitlement in the trust instrument, a trust corporation, or a professional trustee who is not a sole trustee,[78] is entitled to receive reasonable remuneration for any services provided on behalf of the trust. Such a professional trustee will only be entitled to reasonable remuneration if 'each other trustee has agreed in writing that he may be remunerated for the services'. It should be noted that different rules apply to the remuneration of the trustees of a charitable trust.[79]

Other statutory provisions govern the remuneration of certain specialised trustees. The Public Trustee may charge fees fixed by the Treasury,[80] as may anybody appointed a custodian trustee.[81] The court may grant remuneration to a person appointed a judicial trustee.[82] If the court appoints a corporation to be a trustee, then it may authorise the corporation to receive remuneration for its services.[83]

## (c) Court's inherent jurisdiction

The court enjoys an inherent jurisdiction to authorise a trustee to receive remuneration, both in respect of work already done and for future work.[84] However, as Lord Goff recognised in *Guinness plc v Saunders*,[85] this jurisdiction is irreconcilable with the rule that a trustee is not entitled to remuneration for services rendered by him to the trust except as expressly provided in the trust deed. He therefore held that the exercise of the jurisdiction should be 'restricted to those case where it cannot have the effect of encouraging the trustees in any way to put themselves in a position where their interests conflict with their duties as trustees'.

The scope of the inherent jurisdiction was examined in *Re Duke of Norfolk's Settlement Trusts*.[86] The Court of Appeal accepted 'without doubt' that the court pos-

---

[77] *Webb v Earl of Shaftesbury* (1802) 7 Ves 480; *Willis v Kibble* (1839) 1 Beav 559; *Public Trustee v IRC* [1960] AC 398, HL; *Space Investments Ltd v Canadian Imperial Bank of Commerce Trust Co (Bahamas) Ltd* [1986] 1 WLR 1072, PC.

[78] S 29(1),(2).        [79] Ss 28(3), 29(1), 29(2) and 30 of the Trustee Act 2000.

[80] *Re Masters* [1953] 1 WLR 81.

[81] Public Trustee Act 1906, s 9, as amended by the Public Trustee (Fees) Act 1957 and subsequent orders.

[82] Public Trustee Act 1906, s 4(3).        [83] Judicial Trustees Act 1896, s 1(5).

[84] *Brown v Litton* (1711) 1 P Wms 140; *Re Masters* [1953] 1 All ER 19; *Re Worthington* [1954] 1 WLR 526; *Re Jarvis* [1958] 2 All ER 336; *Boardman v Phipps* [1967] 2 AC 46, HL; *Re Duke of Norfolk's Settlement Trusts* [1982] Ch 61, CA; *O'Sullivan v Management Agency and Music Ltd* [1985] QB 428, CA.

[85] [1990] 1 All ER 652 at 667.

[86] [1982] Ch 61; (1981) 40 CLJ 243 (Ockleton); (1982) 45 MLR 211 (Green); (1982) 98 LQR 181 (PVB); [1982] Conv 231 (Hodkinson); (1982) 126 Sol Jo 195 (Fox).

sesses an inherent jurisdiction to authorise the payment of remuneration to trustees, both in the case of prospective trustees for future services and in the case of an unpaid trustee who has already accepted office and has embarked on his fiduciary duties on a voluntary basis. It also held that the court had the jurisdiction to increase the level of remuneration to which a trustee was entitled under the trust instrument. Fox LJ indicated the factors that the court should take into account in exercising this jurisdiction:

'If therefore the court concludes, having regard to the nature of the trust, the experience and skill of a particular trustee and to the amounts which he seeks to charge when compared with what other trustees might require to be paid for their services and to all the other circumstances of the case, that it would be in the interests of the beneficiaries to increase the remuneration, then the court may properly do so.'[87]

### (d) Solicitor-trustees

A solicitor-trustee who acts in legal proceedings on behalf of the trust, himself and his co-trustees, or himself and his beneficiaries, is entitled to receive the usual costs under the rule in *Cradock v Piper*.[88] In *Re Worthington*[89] Upjohn J said that this rule was 'exceptional, anomalous and not to be extended'.[90]

## 3 Purchase of trust property by trustees

As was explained above, the court is keen to ensure that fiduciaries do not gain any advantage by exploiting their position at the expense of those for whose benefit they are supposed to be acting. One of the most obvious dangers is that the trustee, who has control over the trust property, will sell it to himself at an undervalue. A similar difficulty is that the trustee may use the advantages of his position to purchase the beneficial interest from the beneficiaries at an undervalue. Equity has applied two rules, or presumptions, which are designed to prevent the trustee abusing his position. They were summarised by Megarry V-C in *Tito v Waddell (No 2)*:

'. . . there are two separate rules. The self-dealing rule is that if a trustee sells the trust property to himself the sale is voidable by any beneficiary ex debito justitiae, however fair the transaction. The fair-dealing rule is that if a trustee purchases the beneficial interest of any of his beneficiaries, the transaction is not voidable ex debito justitiae, but can be set aside by the beneficiary unless the trustee can show that he has taken no advantage of his position and has made full disclosure to the beneficiary, and that the transaction is fair and honest.'[91]

These two rules therefore differ in their sphere of operation and standard of liability.

---

[87] [1982] Ch 61 at 79.

[88] (1850) 1 Mac & G 664; *Lincoln v Windsor* (1851) 9 Hare 158; *Broughton v Broughton* (1855) 5 De GM & G 160; *Whitney v Smith* (1869) 4 Ch App 513; *Pince v Beattie* (1863) 9 Jur NS 1119; *Re Corsellis* (1887) 34 Ch D 675; *Re Worthington* [1954] 1 All ER 677.

[89] [1954] 1 WLR 526.       [90] [1954] 1 All ER 677 at 678.       [91] [1977] Ch 106.

## (1) The self-dealing rule[92]

### (a) Application of the self-dealing rule

The self-dealing rule applies when a trustee purchases property from the trust. As Arden MR stated in *Campbell v Walker*:

'Any trustee purchasing the trust property is liable to have the purchase set aside, if in any reasonable time the [beneficiary] trust chooses to say, he is not satisfied with it.'[93]

The self-dealing rule also applies against a trustee who has retired from the trust with the object of buying trust property[94] and a trustee who has recently retired.[95] However, in *Re Boles and British Land Co's Contract*[96] it was held that it did not apply where a trustee had retired for twelve years. It will have no application against trustees with no active duties to perform[97] or who have disclaimed the trust.[98] The rule will not catch a transaction completed by a trustee if the contract was entered before he became a fiduciary.[99]

The leading authority concerning the application of the self-dealing rule is *Holder v Holder*.[100] Frank Holder died, leaving an estate which included two farms. He appointed as his executors his wife, one of his daughters, and one of his sons, Victor. Victor was the tenant of one of the two farms, 'Lower Farm'. He renounced his executorship to enable him to buy the farm, although beforehand he had performed some minor acts in the administration of the estate including signing a few cheques for trivial sums and endorsing a few insurance policies. He subsequently purchased the farm at public auction. His brother sought to have the sale set aside on the basis that he had, as executor, purchased trust property. The Court of Appeal held that although the purported renunciation of his executorship was technically ineffective he had never assumed the duties of an executor and had not interfered in any way with the administration of the estate. He had not therefore been in the position of both vendor and purchaser of the farm and the sale was not set aside.[101]

The self-dealing rule was also recently applied in *Kane v Radley-Kane*.[102] The defendant was the administrator of her husband's estate and stepmother to his three sons. He had died intestate leaving amongst his assets shares in a software company which were valued at £50,000 at the date of his death. Since the entire estate was worth only £93,000, and the defendant was entitled by statute to a legacy of £125,000, she trans-

---

[92] See McPherson J, 'Self-dealing Trustees' in Oakley, *Trends in Contemporary Trust Law* (1996).

[93] (1800) 5 Ves 678 at 680.

[94] *Spring v Pride* (1864) 4 De GJ & Sm 395; *Re Mulholland's Will Trusts* [1949] 1 All ER 460.

[95] *Wright v Morgan* [1926] AC 788.      [96] [1902] 1 Ch 244.

[97] *Parkes v White* (1805) 11 Ves 209.      [98] *Stacey v Elph* (1833) 1 My & K 195.

[99] *Vyse v Foster* [1874] LR 7 HL 318; *Re Mulholland's Will Trusts* [1949] 1 All ER 460.

[100] [1968] Ch 353.

[101] This explanation of the case was preferred by Vinelott J in *Re Thompson's Settlement* [1986] Ch 99; see below, p 790. See also *In Plus Group Ltd v Pyke* [2002] 2 BCLC 201; [2003] 62 CLJ 42 (Koh) where the Court of Appeal held that a company director was not in breach of his fiduciary duties by competing with the company in circumstances where he had been wholly excluded from the management of the company such that his position was entirely nominal.

[102] [1999] Ch 274, [1998] 3 All ER 753.

ferred the shares into her own name. Some three years later she sold them for £1,131,438. The plaintiff, one of her stepsons, sought a declaration that the transaction by which the defendant had appropriated the shares to herself was rendered void by the self-dealing rule. Sir Richard Scott V-C held that the self-dealing rule applied to the transaction. He explained that it had involved a conflict of interest:

'There is no doubt that, in appropriating or purporting to appropriate the Shiredean shares to herself in or towards satisfaction of the £125,000 statutory legacy due to herself, Mrs Radley-Kane was effecting a transaction in which her duty and interest were in conflict. It was her duty as a personal representative owed to the other beneficiaries in the intestate estate, that is to say, to the three sons, to realise the assets of the estate as advantageously as she properly could, and not to apply a greater part of those assets towards payment or discharge of any liability or charge payable out of the estate than was necessary for that purpose. If she had been a creditor of the estate and, as I understand it, she may well be, and had purported to take some asset of the estate in satisfaction of her debt, that would have been a transaction in which her duty and interest would have conflicted. Similarly, in taking the Shiredean shares in satisfaction of her £125,000 statutory legacy she was entering into a transaction in which her duty and interest conflicted.'[103]

As the transaction was not expressly or impliedly authorised by statute, and the beneficiaries had not consented to it, it was held to be void. The proceeds of sale were therefore to be treated as part of the assets of the state and the defendant entitled merely to the legacy of £125,000.

## (b) Standard required by the self-dealing rule

From the earliest cases the self-dealing rule has been applied strictly, and the courts have been unwilling to enter into any consideration of whether the trustee in fact abused his position. An affected transaction is liable to be set aside whenever a trustee has purchased trust property, no matter whether the purchase was to all intents and purposes fair. As Lord Eldon LC stated in *Ex p James*:

'This doctrine as to purchase by trustees, assignees, and persons having a confidential character, stands more upon general principle than upon the circumstances of any individual case. It rests upon this: that the purchase is not permitted in any case, however honest the circumstances; the general interests of justice requiring it to be destroyed in every instance.'[104]

In *Ex p Lacey* he explained how the court would not enter into consideration of whether such a transaction was fair in fact:

'. . . whether [the trustee] makes advantage, or not, if the connection does not satisfactorily appear to have been dissolved, it is the choice of the [beneficiaries] whether they will take back the property, or not . . . It is founded upon this; that though you may see in a particular case, that he has not made advantage, it is utterly impossible to examine upon satisfactory evidence in the power of the court, by which I mean, in the power of the parties, in ninety-nine cases out of a hundred, whether he has made advantage or not.'[105]

---

[103] [1998] 3 All ER 753 at 757.    [104] (1803) 8 Ves 337 at 344.    [105] (1802) 6 Ves 625 at 626a.

The law has therefore adopted a strict objective approach that whenever a trustee is both vendor and purchaser the transaction may be set aside. Thus even a purchases by a trustee at public auction can be set aside by the beneficiaries.[106] In *Wright v Morgan*[107] the Privy Council held that a sale of land to the trustee at a price fixed by independent valuers must be set aside.

Some doubt was cast upon this strict application of the self-dealing rule by the Court of Appeal in *Holder v Holder*.[108] Sachs LJ took the view that there was no longer any need for the court to be shackled by a rigid rule of an irrebuttable presumption 'which stems from the alleged inability of a court to ascertain the state of mind of a trustee',[109] and that it should be treated merely as a rule of practice. Danckwerts LJ seemed, similarly, to take the view that the rule was a matter for the discretion of the judge. However in *Re Thompson's Settlement*[110] Vinelott J seemed to prefer to view the decision in *Holder v Holder* as turning on the fact that the brother had never acted as executor in a way which could be taken to amount to acceptance of a duty to act in the interests of the beneficiaries under the will. He affirmed the more traditional approach:

'... The principle is applied stringently in cases where a trustee concurs in a transaction which cannot be carried into effect without his concurrence and who also has an interest or owes a fiduciary duty to another in relation to the same transaction. The transaction cannot stand if challenged by a beneficiary because in the absence of an express provision in the trust instrument the beneficiaries are entitled to require that the trustees act unanimously and that each brings to bear a mind unclouded by any contrary interest or duty in deciding whether it is in the interests of the beneficiaries that the trustees concur in it.'

The application of a strict approach was also supported by Sir Richard Scott V-C in *Kane v Radley-Kane* where he stated that it was 'a general and highly salutary principle of law that a trustee cannot validly contract with himself and cannot exercise his trust powers to his own advantage'.[111]

### (c) Exceptions to the self-dealing rule

The self-dealing rule will not apply if the trust instrument authorises the trustee to purchase trust property.[112] Similarly, if the beneficiaries consent[113] to the purchase, they cannot subsequently have it set aside. The court also possesses the discretion to permit a purchase.[114] Where land is subject to a strict settlement,[115] s 68 of the Settled Land Act 1925 provides that the tenant for life of settled land may purchase the property.

---

[106] *Whichcote v Lawrence* (1798) 3 Ves 740; *Campbell v Walker* (1800) 5 Ves 678; *Dyson v Lum* (1866) 14 LT 588.

[107] [1926] AC 788.    [108] [1968] Ch 353.    [109] [1968] Ch 353 at 402.

[110] [1986] Ch 99.    [111] [1998] 3 All ER 753 at 757.

[112] *Sargeant v National Westminster Bank plc* (1990) 61 P & CR 518.    [113] See below, p 817.

[114] *Farmer v Dean* (1863) 32 Beav 327.

[115] Following the introduction of the trust of land in the Trusts of Land and Appointment of Trustees Act 1996, no new strict settlements can be created, but existing settlements will continue.

## (d) Remedies of the beneficiary

Where trust property has been acquired by a trustee in contravention of the self-dealing rule, the transaction is voidable at the option of the beneficiaries. If the trustee has resold the property he will be required to make restitution to the trust of any profits he made.[116] If he has retained the property the beneficiary may insist that it is reconveyed to the trust, or a new sale may be ordered.

## (2) The fair-dealing rule

The fair-dealing rule applies where a trustee purchases the beneficial interest from one or more of the beneficiaries. Since such a transaction is the result of negotiation between the trustee and the beneficiary, there is less risk that the trustee will exploit his position. Equity therefore adopts a less strict approach than under the self-dealing rule. Transactions entered in violation of the fair-dealing rule are voidable by the beneficiary unless the trustee can show that he has not taken any advantage by virtue of his position.[117] The rule was stated by Lord Eldon in *Coles v Trecothick*:

'. . . a trustee may buy from the [beneficiary], provided that there is a distinct and clear contract, ascertained to be such after a jealous and scrupulous examination of all the circumstances, proving that the [beneficiary of the] trust intended the trustee should buy; there is no fraud, no concealment, no advantage taken, by the trustee of information acquired by him in the character of trustee.'[118]

In *Thomson v Eastwood*[119] Lord Cairns stated that a court of equity would examine such a transaction and 'ascertain that value paid by the trustee, and will throw upon the trustee the onus of proving that he gave full value, and that all information was laid before the [beneficiary] when it was sold'.

# 4 Incidental profits

As a trustee stands in a fiduciary relationship to the beneficiaries of the trust, he will not be permitted to retain unauthorised profits which he receives as a result of holding his position.[120] He must not permit his interests and his duties to conflict. The rationale for this rule was clearly expressed by Lord Herschell in *Bray v Ford*:

---

[116] *Hall v Hallet* (1784) 1 Cox Eq Cas 134; *ex p James* (1803) 8 Ves 337.

[117] *Clarke v Swaile* (1762) 2 Eden 134; *Coles v Trecothick* (1804) 9 Ves 234; *Randall v Errington* (1805) 10 Ves 423; *Morse v Royal* (1806) 12 Ves 355; *Sanderson v Walker* (1807) 13 Ves 601; *Dover v Buck* (1865) 5 Giff 57.

[118] (1804) 9 Ves 234.

[119] (1877) 2 App Cas 215.

[120] A vendor of land who holds the property on constructive trust for the purchaser as a result of the specifically enforceable contract for sale is not required to account for benefits received from the trust property in the absence of agreement to the contrary: *Engelwood Properties v Patel* [2005] 3 All ER 307.

'It is an inflexible rule of a court of equity that a person in a fiduciary position, such as the respondent, is not, unless otherwise expressly provided, entitled to make a profit; he is not allowed to put himself in a position where his interest and his duty conflict. It does not appear to me that this rule is as has been said, founded upon principles of morality. I regard it rather as based on the consideration that, human nature being what it is, there is danger, in such circumstances, of the person holding a fiduciary position being swayed by interest rather than by duty, and thus prejudicing those whom he was bound to protect. It has, therefore, been deemed expedient to lay down this positive rule.'[121]

The concept of conflict of interest, which the rule aims to prevent, was explained by Lord Cranworth LC in *Aberdeen Rly Bros v Blaikie*:[122]

'And it is a rule of universal application, that no one, having such duties to discharge, shall be allowed to enter into engagements in which he has, or can have, a personal interest conflicting, or which possibly may conflict, with the interests of those whom he is bound to protect.'[123]

It is necessary to consider first the circumstances in which the courts have held trustees liable to account for incidental profits which they have made as a result of their conflict of interest, and, secondly the standard of liability required by the rule.

## (1) Renewal of a lease

A trustee who renews for himself a lease which was previously held on trust for the beneficiaries will hold the lease on trust for them. This rule was applied in *Keech v Sandford*.[124] The trustee held the profits of Romford market on trust for a minor. When the lease expired, the landlord refused to renew the lease to the trust. Instead, he renewed the lease to the trustee personally. King LC held that the lease should be assigned by the trustee to the infant and that he should account for the profits he had made. He recognised that it 'may seem hard that the trustee is the only person of all mankind who might not have the lease', but justified the result in the light of general policy considerations:

'. . . it is very proper that the rule should be strictly pursued, and not in the least relaxed; for it is very obvious what would be the consequences of letting trustees have the lease, on refusal to renew to the [beneficiary].'

The principle of *Keech v Sandford* applies only where a lease owned by a trust is renewed to a fiduciary. In *Re Biss*[125] a man rented premises for his business. When he died his widow, who was the administratrix of his estate, continued the business with the help of their adult son. The landlord refused to renew the lease to the widow but

---

[121] [1896] AC 44 at 51.    [122] (1854) 2 Eq Rep 1281.
[123] See also *Richardson v Chapman* (1760) 7 Bro Parl Cas 318, HL; *Phayre v Peree* (1815) 3 Dow 116, HL; *Shallcross v Oldham* (1862) 2 John & H 609; *Bennett v Gas Light and Coke Co* (1882) 52 LJ Ch 98; *Lagunas Nitrate Co v Lagunas Syndicate* [1899] 2 Ch 392; *Costa Rica Rly Co v Forwood* [1901] 1 Ch 746; *Re Thomson* [1930] 1 Ch 203.
[124] (1726) Sel Cas Ch 61.    [125] [1903] 2 Ch 40.

granted it to the adult son. It was held that the son did not hold the lease on trust for the estate because he did not stand in a fiduciary relationship with the estate. He was therefore under no personal incapacity to take the benefit, the renewal was not an accretion to the original term and it had not been renewed to him until there had been an absolute refusal by the landlord to renew to the administratrix for the estate.

In *Don King Productions Inc v Warren*[126] the principle of *Keech v Sandford* was applied by analogy to the renewal of a contract held on trust for a partnership to one of the partners in a personal capacity. The case concerned a partnership established between boxing promoters Don King and Frank Warren in 1994. The partnership was subsequently dissolved in 1997. As partners stand in a fiduciary relationship the Court of Appeal held that the entire benefit of any management or promotion agreements concluded by a partner after the date of the dissolution but before the conclusion of the winding up of the partnership affairs with a boxer with whom he already has such an agreement would be held on trust for the partnership.

## (2) Purchase of a freehold reversion

The principle of *Keech v Sandford* has been extended to include the purchase by a trustee of the freehold reversion of land leased to the trust. Until recently there were doubts whether the rule operated in the same absolute manner. In *Protheroe v Protheroe*[127] the rule was applied strictly to a husband who purchased the freehold reversion of a house he held on trust jointly with his wife, but earlier cases suggested that the rule will only apply if the lease was renewable to the trust by law or custom.[128] However it was applied without any such qualification in *Thompson's Trustee in Bankruptcy v Heaton*,[129] where a partner had purchased the freehold reversion of a farm which was a partnership asset. Following *Protheroe v Protheroe*,[130] Pennycuick V-C held that:

'. . . it is also well established that where someone holding a leasehold interest in a fiduciary capacity acquires the freehold reversion, he must hold that reversion as part of the trust estate.'[131]

*Thompson's Trustee in Bankruptcy v Heaton* was cited with approval by the Court of Appeal in *Don King Productions Inc v Warren*[132] suggesting that the rule will be applied equally strictly where a trustee acquires the freehold reversion.

---

[126] [2000] Ch 291.

[127] [1968] 1 WLR 519; (1968) 32 Conv 220 (Crane); (1968) 31 MLR 707 (Jackson); (1968) 84 LQR 309 (Megarry).

[128] *Re Lord Ranelagh's Will* (1884) 26 Ch D 590; *Phillips v Phillips* (1885) 29 Ch D 673, CA; *Longton v Wilsby* (1897) 76 LT 770; *Bevan v Webb* [1905] 1 Ch 620; *Phipps v Boardman* [1964] 1 WLR 993 at 1009; (1969) Conv (NS) 161 (Cretney).

[129] [1974] 1 WLR 605.    [130] [1968] 1 WLR 519.    [131] [1968] 1 WLR 519 at 521.

[132] [2000] Ch 291, at 340.

## (3) Remuneration received as a director

Where the trust assets include company shares the trustees control the associated voting rights at company meetings. If the trustees exploit this power to appoint themselves as directors of the company they will be liable to account for any remuneration they thereby receive. The position was considered in *Re Macadam*,[133] where the trustees of a will were granted the power to appoint two directors of a company. They duly appointed themselves and received remuneration for their services. Cohen J held that they were accountable to the trust for the remuneration they had received, and stated the general principles which apply:

'I think the root of the matter really is: did [the trustee] acquire the position in respect of which he drew the remuneration by virtue of his position as trustee? In the present case there can be no doubt that the only way in which the plaintiffs became directors was by the exercise of the powers vested in the trustees of the will . . . although the remuneration was remuneration for services as director of the company, the opportunity to receive that remuneration was gained as a result of the exercise of a discretion vested in the trustees, and they had put themselves in a position where their interest and duty conflicted.'

It follows from this that a trustee will not be accountable for any remuneration he received from a directorship if he did not in fact use his position to obtain it.[134] Thus in *Re Dover Coalfield Extension Ltd*[135] it was held that a trustee would be able to retain remuneration received from a directorship to which he had been appointed before becoming a trustee, as it would not have been obtained by use of his position. In *Re Gee*[136] it was held that a trustee who is elected to a directorship would be entitled to retain any remuneration he received if he would still have been elected a director even if the trust shares he controlled had been voted against him, since he would not then have obtained his position through the use of the trust share. However, he would not be protected from liability merely because he abstained from using the trust shares.

Trustees will not be liable to make restitution if the trust instrument permits them to appoint themselves directors and receive remuneration.[137] The court also possesses an inherent jurisdiction to permit trustees to retain remuneration they receive as directors on a similar basis to the inherent jurisdiction accepted in *Re Duke of Norfolk's Settlement Trusts*.[138] Goulding J considered that the court would permit a trustee 'to retain reasonable remuneration for effort and skill applied by him in performing the duties of the directorship over and above the effort and skill ordinarily required of a director appointed to represent the interests of a substantial shareholder'.[139]

## (4) Commission earned

A trustee who receives a commission for introducing trust business will be liable to account for the commission he has received as unauthorised profit. In *Williams v*

---

[133] [1946] Ch 73. See also *Re Francis* (1905) 74 LJ Ch 198; *Re Orwell's Will Trusts* [1982] 1 WLR 1337.
[134] *Re Lewis* (1910) 103 LT 495.    [135] [1907] 2 Ch 76.    [136] [1948] Ch 284.
[137] *Re Llewellin's Will Trusts* [1949] Ch 225.    [138] [1979] Ch 37.
[139] [1979] Ch 37 at 162–163.

*Barton*[140] a trustee was employed as a clerk at a firm of stock brokers. The firm was employed to value the trust securities and the trustee received a commission for introducing the business. Russell J held that the commission received was to be treated as part of the trust estate.

## (5) Competition

If the trust assets include a business the trustee must not set up in competition. In *Re Thomson*[141] Clauson J held that it would be a breach of fiduciary duty for a trustee of a yacht broking business to set up independently as a yacht broker because he would have been 'entering into an engagement in which he would have a personal interest conflicting or which possibly might conflict with the interests of those he was bound to protect'.[142] The rationale for this decision may be the relatively specialised nature of the yacht broking business, where it was inevitable that brokers would be in competition with each other. In *Aas v Benham*[143] it was held that there was no breach of fiduciary duty where a member of a partnership of shipbrokers formed a company to build ships. The two operations would not be in competition. In *In Plus Group Ltd v Pyke*[144] Sedley LJ considered that a director of a company could not simply become involved with a competing third party without the consent of the company because of his fiduciary duty,[145] although on the facts of the case he held that the fiduciary duty had not been breached.

## (6) Bribes

A trustee or other fiduciary who receives a bribe by virtue of his position will not be entitled to retain it. He will be required to make restitution to the trust, or his principal, by way of an equitable liability to account. His liability to make personal restitution in this way is uncontroversial. However, in *A-G of Hong Kong v Reid*[146] the Privy Council held that a fiduciary also holds such a bribe on constructive trust for principal. This important decision will be discussed more fully below.

## (7) Opportunities

A fiduciary is liable to make restitution to his principal if he obtains a profit by exploiting an opportunity which rightfully belonged to his principal. A fiduciary who exploits such an opportunity for his own benefit without the authorisation of his principal will be liable to account even where principal could not have taken advantage of the opportunity himself.[147]

---

[140] [1927] 2 Ch 9.    [141] [1930] 1 Ch 203.    [142] [1930] 1 Ch 203 at 216.
[143] [1891] 2 Ch 244; *Moore v M'Glynn* [1894] 1 IR 74.
[144] [2002] 2 BCLC 201; (2003) 66 MLR 109 (Grantham).
[145] Rejecting dicta to the opposite effect in *London and Marshonaland Exploration Co Ltd v New Marshonaland Exploration Co Ltd* [1891] WN 165.
[146] [1994] 1 All ER 1. See [1994] LMCLQ 189 (Pearce).
[147] See *Regal (Hastings) Ltd v Gullier* [1967] 2 AC 134n, [1942] 1 All ER 378; *Industrial Development Consultants Ltd v Cooley* [1972] 1 WLR 443; *Boardman v Phipps* [1967] 2 AC 46, HL.

## (a) Company directors

One of the most common situations in which fiduciaries exploit opportunities belonging to their principals is that of company directors who take up opportunities properly belonging to their company, to which they stand in a fiduciary relationship. In *Cook v Deeks*[148] three of the four directors of a company who were negotiating for a contract to construct a railway took the contract for themselves in their private capacity so as to exclude the fourth director. The Privy Council held that this amounted to a breach of their fiduciary duty, and that they were liable to account to the company for the profits they made from the transaction. In the leading case, *Regal (Hastings) Ltd v Gulliver*,[149] a company which owned cinemas wanted to acquire two other cinemas in Hastings. To enable the company to achieve this objective it formed a subsidiary with 5,000 shares. The company was financially only able to take up 2,000 of the shares in the subsidiary. Since the owner of the cinemas refused to sell them unless the share capital was completely taken up, the directors of the company purchased the remaining 3,000 shares and the deal went ahead. The company was subsequently sold and the directors made a profit of £2 16s 1d on each of the shares they had taken up. The House of Lords held that the directors were accountable to the purchasers of the company for the profit they had made on the shares because they had obtained it by reason of their fiduciary position. As Lord Russell of Killowen concluded:

'The directors standing in a fiduciary relationship to Regal . . . and having obtained these shares by reason and only by reason of the fact that they were directors of Regal and in the course of the execution of that office, are accountable for the profits which they have made out of them.'[150]

It made no difference that the company could not have taken up the opportunity itself for lack of finance, nor that the directors had acted bona fides without fraud.[151]

In *Industrial Development Consultants Ltd v Cooley*[152] Neville Cooley was the managing director of Industrial Development Consultants Ltd, a company which provided construction consultancy services. He entered into negotiations on behalf of the company with the Eastern Gas Board for a contract to build new depots. The Board refused to enter into a contract with the company because of their policy of not employing development companies, but they offered a contract to Cooley in his personal capacity, which he accepted. He then gained release from his position as managing director by representing that he was suffering from a serious illness. Roskill J held that Cooley was liable to account for the profit he had gained from the contract because in entering it he had allowed his duty and his interests to conflict.

Although directors are prima facie liable to make restitution of any profit they receive by appropriating an opportunity belonging to their company, they will be protected from liability if they were authorised to take up the opportunity. This seems to be the correct analysis of the decision of the Privy Council in *Queensland Mines Ltd v*

---

[148] [1916] 1 AC 554.     [149] [1967] 2 AC 134n, [1942] 1 All ER 378.
[150] [1942] 1 All ER 378 at 389.     [151] See below, p 797.     [152] [1972] 1 WLR 443.
[153] (1978) 18 ALR 1; (1979) 42 MLR 711 (Sullivan). See also *Island Export Finance Ltd v Umunna* [1986] BCLC 460; *In Plus Group Lyd v Pyke* [2002] 2 BCLC 201.

*Hudson.*[153] Hudson was the managing director of Queensland Mines, a company which was investigating the possibility of mining iron ore in Tasmania. Two licences were obtained from the Tasmanian government, but the company was not able to start mining operations because of lack of finance. Instead Hudson resigned as managing director and exploited the licences himself, eventually selling them to an American company from which he received royalties on the ore mined. The company argued that he should account for the profits he had made, but the Privy Council held that he was not liable. As Lord Scarman observed, the difficulty of the case lay 'not in the formulation of the law but in the analysis of the facts'.[154] On the facts the Privy Council concluded that by 1962 the board of directors, 'fully informed as to all the relevant facts, had reached a firm decision to renounce all interest in the exploitation of the licence and had assented to Mr Hudson taking over the venture for his own account'. The basis of the decision thus seems to be that the directors had decided that the company would not take up the opportunity, and that Hudson was therefore free to take it up himself. Although this reasoning is attractive it is open to the objection that the board of directors is not the appropriate organ of the company to reject such an opportunity and permit a director to take it up for himself. The only organ of the company competent to grant such authorisation is the shareholders' meeting.[155]

## (b) Trustees

Since a trustee is a fiduciary vis-à-vis the beneficiaries of the trust he will similarly act in breach of duty if he takes personal advantage of opportunities which properly belong to the trust. For example if a trust includes shares amongst its assets, and a rights issue is proposed, the trustees cannot purchase the shares offered under the rights issue for themselves unless authorised to do so by the beneficiaries. If they do purchase the shares without authorisation they will be held on constructive trust for the beneficiaries.

## (c) Other fiduciaries

Fiduciaries other than company directors and trustees will also be held liable to account for any unauthorised profits their receive through exploiting an opportunity belonging to their principal. This can be seen from the leading case of *Boardman v Phipps*.[156] A trust had been established by Charles Phipps on behalf of his wife for life, and after her death for his four children. The trustees were his widow, daughter and a professional trustee. One asset of the trust was a 27% holding in a private company, Lester & Harris Ltd. Thomas Boardman was the solicitor to the trust and the Phipps family. Boardman and one of the beneficiaries, Thomas Phipps, were unhappy with the way that the company was being run and decided that the only way to protect the trust asset was to acquire a controlling interest in the company. Boardman suggested this to the managing trustee, who made it clear that he was against the trustees buying such a controlling

---

[154] (1978) 18 ALR 1 at 3.
[155] (1979) MLR 711 (Sullivan). See also *Prudential Assurance Co v Newman Industries (No 2)* [1980] 2 All ER 841 at 862; *Shaker v Al-Bedrawi* [2002] 4 All ER 835.
[156] [1967] 2 AC 46, HL.

interest and that, without applying to the court, they had no power to do so. Boardman and Phipps, having informed two of the trustees but not the third, who was the testator's elderly widow, subsequently purchased a controlling interest in the company. They then capitalised some of the company's assets, making a profit of some £47,000 for the trust and £75,000 for themselves. One of the other beneficiaries, John Phipps, claimed that they should account for this profit to the trust. By a bare majority the House of Lords held that Boardman was liable to account. He had stood in a fiduciary relationship to the trust and, although he had acted honestly throughout, in exploiting the opportunity there had been a possibility of a conflict between his duty and his interest.

## (8)  Use of confidential information[157]

A fiduciary who makes use of confidential information belonging to his principal will be liable for any profit that he makes.[158] In *A-G v Guardian Newspapers Ltd (No 2)*[159] the House of Lords held that the Sunday Times was liable to account for the profits made by its publication of extracts of 'Spycatcher', a book written by a former member of the British security services, who stood in a fiduciary relationship to the Crown, and which contained confidential information.[160] In *Peter Pan Manufacturing Corpn v Corsets Silhouette Ltd*[161] the defendant company's designer was shown a sample copy of the design of a new brassiere in confidence by the plaintiff company. When the defendants subsequently manufactured it Pennycuick J ordered that they account for their profits. Liability on the basis of the exploitation of confidential information was also established in the Canadian case of *LAC Minerals Ltd v International Corona Resources Ltd*.[162] LAC received confidential information from Corona during the course of negotiations with a view to establishing a joint venture to exploit minerals from land owned by Corona, which indicated that adjacent land was also likely to contain mineral deposits. LAC subsequently purchased the adjacent land in their own right, and exploited the minerals themselves. The Supreme Court held that there was a fiduciary relationship between the parties, and that LAC should hold the land on constructive trust for Corona because of their breach of confidence.[163]

The exploitation of confidential information provides a further possible explanation for the decision in *Boardman v Phipps*.[164] In the course of negotiations for the purchase of the majority shareholding in the company Boardman, while purporting to act as the trust solicitor on the business of the trust, received essential information about the value of the company's assets and the prices at which shares had recently changed hands. This information enabled him to put forward his offer for the majority share-holding. Lord Hodson and Lord Guest held that Boardman was accountable for the

---

[157]  See Glover, 'Is breach of confidence a fiduciary wrong?' (2001) 21 LS 595.
[158]  *York and North Midland Rly Co v Hudson* (1853) 16 Beav 485; *Kirkham v Peel* (1881) 44 LT 195.
[159]  [1990] 1 AC 109.        [160]  See [1989] CLP 49 (Jones).        [161]  [1964] 1 WLR 96.
[162]  (1989) 61 DLR (4th) 14.
[163]  See also Chapter 9. Tang argues that there was no justification for a constructive trust in *LAC Minerals v International Corona Resources*: 'Confidence and the constructive trust' (2003) 23 LS 135.
[164]  [1967] 2 AC 46, HL.

profit he made because he had acquired the shares using this confidential information, which they considered to be trust property. However Lord Cohen took the view that the information that had been obtained was not 'property in the strict sense'[165] and decided the case on the basis of the rule in *Regal (Hastings) Ltd v Gulliver*,[166] and Lord Upjohn rejected the argument that the information was to be regarded as part of the trust assets.[167]

However, it is clear that the duty not to profit from confidential information only subsists for so long as the information received retains its confidential status. Once it has entered the public sphere, the obligation of confidentiality no longer subsists. Thus, in *A-G v Blake*[168] the Court of Appeal held that a former spy was not in breach of any fiduciary duty when he had published an autobiography which contained information concerning his work which had entered the public sphere prior to publication. Lord Woolf MR commented:

'The duty to respect confidence is also a fiduciary duty, but it subsists only as long as the information remains confidential.'[169]

This was subsequently confirmed by the House of Lords.[170] It has also been held that a third party who receives confidential information disclosed by a fiduciary in breach of his duty is not automatically liable to account for any profits resulting from his exploitation of that information. In *Satnam Ltd v Dunlop Heywood & Co Ltd*[171] a development company owned an option to purchase a site which was determinable by the site owners if it went into receivership. The company of surveyors acting for the development company subsequently told a rival developer that their client had been placed into receivership and that the local authority was favourable towards development. On the basis of this information the rival developers purchased the site. Whilst the surveyors had clearly breached their fiduciary duty in revealing this confidential information the Court of Appeal held that the rival developers did not hold the land acquired on constructive trust for the original developers, nor were they liable to account for their profits. Nourse LJ, giving the judgment of the Court, explained that mere knowledge of a breach of fiduciary duty was insufficient to render a person who was not himself a fiduciary a constructive trustee. He held that the third party would only have been liable to make an account of profits if it had acted dishonestly.

## 5  Liability for breach of fiduciary duty

Having examined the circumstances in which a fiduciary will be held to have acted in breach of his duty it is possible to extrapolate from the cases the standard of liability

---

[165] [1967] 2 AC 46 at 103. Note that in *Crown Dilmun plc v Sutton* [2004] 1 BCLC 468 it was accepted that confidential information was not property. See also *Douglas v Hello!* [2005] EWCA Civ 595.

[166] [1967] 2 AC 134n, [1942] 1 All ER 378.        [167] [1967] 2 AC 46 at 127–128.

[168] [1998] 1 All ER 833 at 842.        [169] [1998] 1 All ER 833 at 842.

[170] [2000] 4 All ER 385.        [171] [1999] 3 All ER 652.

required to trigger a remedy. It appears that the courts have adopted a strict test of liability which does not require the principal to demonstrate that the fiduciary in fact permitted his duty and his interest to conflict. Instead a fiduciary will be liable to account if there was a mere possibility that his duty and his interests would conflict. The adoption of such a strict approach has attracted criticism. Whilst in the majority of cases a fiduciary who has profited from his position will have acted dishonestly and without regard for the interest of his principle, in some cases a fiduciary who received a profit may have been entirely innocent of any wrongdoing or fraudulent conduct, especially if he exploited an opportunity which his principal could not have exploited, or where the danger of a conflict of interest had been so remote that there was no realistic possibility that such a conflict had occurred. In such cases it may seem questionable whether the fiduciary should be liable to make restitution of his profits. Such difficulties were evident in *Boardman v Phipps*,[172] the facts of which were discussed above. The House of Lords consistently emphasised that Boardman and his colleague had been entirely innocent of any misconduct. Lord Cohen for example said that their integrity was 'not in doubt' and that they had acted 'with complete honesty throughout'.[173] However it nevertheless held that Boardman was required to make restitution of the profits he had received by way of an equitable account. Given the success of the defendants' venture, which it must be remembered also resulted in a considerable profit for the trust, the plaintiff was, as Lord Cohen observed, a 'fortunate man in that the rigour of equity enables him to participate in the profits'.[174]

## (1) Strict liability

Despite the potential for unfairness in some cases, English law has adopted a strict principle that a fiduciary is liable to account for any unauthorised profits obtained in circumstances where there was a mere possibility that his duty and his interest had conflicted. In *Bray v Ford*[175] Lord Herschell described this as 'an inflexible rule of equity'. In *Regal (Hastings) Ltd v Gulliver*[176] Lord Russell of Killowen stressed that the fiduciary was required to give up the profit he had made irrespective of his honesty:

'The rule of equity, which insists on those, who by use of a fiduciary position make a profit, being liable to account for that profit, in no way depends on fraud, or absence of bona fides; or upon such questions or considerations as whether the profit would or should otherwise have gone to the plaintiff, or whether the profiteer was under a duty to obtain the source of the profit for the plaintiff, or whether he took a risk or acted as he did for the benefit of the plaintiff, or whether the plaintiff has in fact been damaged or benefited by his action. The liability arises from the mere fact of a profit having, in the stated circumstances, been made. The profiteer, however honest and well intentioned, cannot escape the risk of being called upon to account.'

---

[172] [1967] 2 AC 46.    [173] [1967] 2 AC 46 at 104.    [174] [1967] 2 AC 46 at 104.
[175] [1896] AC 44 at 51.    [176] [1942] 1 All ER 378.

In reaching this conclusion he drew upon the language of Lord King LC in *Keech v Sandford*,[177] and of Lord Eldon LC in *Ex p James*,[178] who had said that the self-dealing rule 'rests upon this: that the purchase is not permitted in any case however honest the circumstances'. More recently in *Guinness plc v Saunders*[179] the House of Lords held that a company director who had received an unauthorised payment of £5.2m was liable to account to his company because he had allowed his duty and his interest to conflict, even though he had acted in complete good faith throughout.[180]

A divergence of views was apparent in the House of Lord in *Boardman v Phipps*[181] as to the degree of likelihood of a real conflict of interest required to render a fiduciary liability to account. It was alleged that Boardman had allowed his duty and his interest to conflict by purchasing a controlling interest in a company partially owned by the trust whilst there was a possibility that, as the trust solicitor, he could be called upon by the trustees to advise whether it would be wise for them to seek to acquire the power to pursue a similar investment. Lord Upjohn, dissenting, took the view that a fiduciary should only be required to disgorge his profits where there had been a 'real sensible possibility' of a conflict of interest. In the circumstances he considered that the possibility of a conflict was simply too remote to render Boardman liable:

'The relevant rule for the decision of this case is the fundamental rule of equity that a person in a fiduciary capacity must not make a profit out of his trust which is a part of the wider rule that a trustee must not place himself in a position where his duty and his interest may conflict. It is perhaps most highly against trustees or directors in the celebrated speech of Lord Cranworth LC in *Aberdeen Rly Bros v Blaikie Bros*, where he said: "And it is a rule of universal application, that no one, having such duties to discharge, shall be allowed to enter into engagements in which he has, or can have, a personal interest conflicting, or which possibly may conflict, with the interests of those whom he is bound to protect." The phase "possibly may conflict" requires consideration. In my view it means that the reasonable man looking at the relevant facts and circumstances of the particular case would think that there was a real sensible possibility of conflict; not that you could imagine some situation arising which might, in some conceivable possibility in events not contemplated as real sensible possibilities by any reasonable person, result in a conflict.'[182]

He therefore concluded that Boardman had not acted in breach of his duty because there had been no 'real sensible possibility' of a conflict of interest, and that he should not be required to disgorge his profits.

In contrast the majority of the House of Lords held that the remoteness of the possibility of a genuine conflict of interest was irrelevant to the liability of a fiduciary. Lord Cohen,[183] Lord Hodson and Lord Guest cited with approval the statement of principle of Lord Russell in *Regal (Hastings) Ltd v Gulliver*.[184] As Lord Hodson observed:

'No doubt it was but a remote possibility that Mr Boardman would ever be asked by the

---

[177] (1726) Sel Cas Ch 61.  [178] (1803) 8 Ves 337.  [179] [1990] 2 AC 663.
[180] [1990] 2 AC 663 at 710, per Lord Goff.  [181] [1967] 2 AC 46.  [182] [1967] 2 AC 46 at 124.
[183] Who had read the speeches to be delivered by Lord Hodson and Lord Guest and agreed in substance with them.
[184] [1967] 2 AC 134n, [1942] 1 All ER 378.

trustees to advise on the desirability of an application to the court in order that the trustees might avail themselves of the information obtained. Nevertheless, even if the possibility of conflict is present between personal interest and the fiduciary position the rule of equity must be applied.'[185]

In consequence of the decision of the majority in *Boardman v Phipps* English law imposes a very strict liability for breach of fiduciary duty so that a fiduciary is liable to account for profits he has received whenever there was a mere possibility, no matter how remote, that his duty and his interest might conflict.

A number of arguments can be put forward in defence of the strict liability of fiduciaries. First, it should be remembered that a fiduciary is only required to make restitution of unauthorised profits. He is able to protect himself from liability by full disclosure of his proposed activities to his principal, which in the case of a trust will mean the beneficiaries. If the principal consents or acquiesces in the conduct disclosed the fiduciary will not be held accountable for any profits he receives thereby. However, where a fiduciary fails to fully disclose his intended course of action to his principal it is not unfair to presume that he was acting in a manner that he did not expect would be condoned. Secondly, it has already been noted that it is impossible to conduct an inquiry into the subjective motives which influenced a fiduciary's conduct to determine whether a genuine conflict of interest occurred.[186] The court can only look to the objective reality of external appearances, and the mere possibility of such a conflict triggers a remedial response in favour of the principal. This ensures that a situation can never arise where the fiduciary does in fact profit from a breach of his duty. Thirdly, it has to be remembered that the rule has implications beyond any immediate case in point. It operates to deter fiduciaries who may consider abusing their position. This has been described as the prophylactic function of the rule: equity does not wait to see whether the principal has suffered any detriment as a result of the fiduciaries conduct but imposes a duty which will hold the fiduciary accountable if he might have been tempted to sacrifice the interests of the beneficiary.[187] This prophylactic approach appeared to be to the fore in the reasoning of the House of Lords in *Guinness plc v Saunders*,[188] where Lord Goff emphasised that the court must not act in a manner which would provide any encouragement to trustees to put themselves in a position where their duty would conflict with their personal interests.

## (2) Amelioration of the consequences of strict liability

Whilst the adoption of a strict liability to make restitution of unauthorised profits may sometimes be perceived to operate unfairly against an honest fiduciary, such unfairness may partially be alleviated at the remedial stage. Whereas, prima facie, a fiduciary in breach will be required to disgorge the entirety of the profit he received, in some circumstances the courts have held that a fiduciary may be permitted to retain a

---

[185] [1967] 2 AC 46 at 111.    [186] *Ex p James* (1803) 8 Ves 337.
[187] P Birks, *Introduction to the Law of Restitution* (1985), pp 332–333, 339–343.
[188] [1990] 2 AC 663.

proportion thereof for himself.[189] The exercise of such relief is akin to the inherent jurisdiction to authorise a trustee to retain past remuneration, and to recoup his expenses from the trust. For example, in *Boardman v Phipps*[190] the majority of the House of Lords held that although Boardman was liable to account for the profits he had received, he should enjoy an allowance to represent his work and skill, which had contributed substantially to the making of the profit. This allowance was to be calculated 'on a liberal scale'.

It remains unclear, however, whether the allowance granted in *Boardman v Phipps* included any share of the profits made, or whether it was intended solely to reflect the expenses he had incurred. In *O'Sullivan v Management Agency and Music Ltd*[191] the court expressly permitted a fiduciary to retain a share of the profit it had received. An exclusive management contract between a musician and a management company was set aside on the grounds of undue influence. The Court of Appeal held that whilst the company was required to account for the profits that it had received under contract, it should be permitted it to retain an allowance of reasonable remuneration for their skill and labour. This allowance explicitly included a small share of the profits made. The principle was stated by Fox LJ:

'Once it is accepted that the court can make an appropriate allowance to a fiduciary for his skill and labour I do not see why, in principle, it should not be able to give him some part of the profit of the venture if it was thought that justice as between the parties demanded that.'[192]

The allowance is therefore entirely within the court's discretion, and on the facts it was held that a profit element should be included to recognise the contribution that the company had made to the singer's success, but that this would be less than the profit they might have made if the contract had been properly negotiated in the first place to reflect disapprobation of their conduct in obtaining the contract through undue influence.[193]

The stated objective was to 'achieve substantial justice between the parties'.[194] It might be thought that this would provide a way of adjusting the harsh consequences of the strict approach taken in *Boardman v Phipps*.[195] However *Guinness plc v Saunders*[196] suggests that the courts will be unlikely to award a share of the profits to directors or trustees who allow their duty and their interests to conflict. The case concerned a director, Mr Ward, who received £5.2m under a contract he had entered to provide his services to help with a take-over bid. He was held liable to account for this money because he had acted in breach of fiduciary duty and had not disclosed his interest to

---

[189] In *Warman International v Dwyer* (1995) 128 ALR 201 the High Court suggested that where a fiduciary had acted in breach of his duty in the context of a business rather than through the receipt of a specific asset it may well be inappropriate and inequitable to compel the errant fiduciary to account for the whole of the profit of his conduct of the business or exploitation of the principal's goodwill over an indefinite period of time. In such a case it might therefore be appropriate to allow the fiduciary a proportion of the profits, depending upon the particular circumstances.

[190] [1967] 2 AC 46.      [191] [1985] QB 428.      [192] [1985] QB 428 at 468.

[193] [1985] QB 428 at 469, per Fox LJ: 'the defendants must suffer . . . because of the circumstances in which the contracts were procured.'

[194] [1985] QB 428 at 469, per Fox LJ.      [195] [1967] 2 AC 46.      [196] [1990] 2 AC 663, HL.

the company board. The question arose whether he should receive any allowance for the services he had performed. The House of Lords held that he should not. Lord Goff analysed the rationale for the award of an allowance on a liberal scale in *Boardman v Phipps*[197] and concluded:

'The decision has to be reconciled with the fundamental principle that a trustee is not entitled to remuneration for services rendered by him to the trust except as expressly provided in the trust deed. Strictly speaking, it is irreconcilable with the rule so stated. It seems to me therefore that it can only be reconciled with it to the extent that the exercise of the equitable jurisdiction does not conflict with the policy underlying the rule. As I see it, such a conflict will only be avoided if the exercise of the jurisdiction is restricted to those cases where it cannot have the effect of encouraging trustees in any way to put themselves in a position where their interests conflict with their duties as trustees.'[198]

The allowance in *Boardman v Phipps* was therefore justified because of the 'equity underlying Mr Boardman's claim', and as such it would not provide any encouragement to trustees to put themselves in a position where their duties as trustees conflicted with their interests. In the case of Mr Ward, remuneration would be inappropriate because he had agreed to provide his services in return for a substantial fee and 'was most plainly putting himself in a position in which his interests were in stark contrast with his duty as a director'.[199]

## (3)  A higher threshold before a fiduciary is liable for breach of duty?

Some Commonwealth jurisdictions have not adopted the strict penal approach exemplified in England by *Regal (Hastings) Ltd v Gulliver*[200] and *Boardman v Phipps*.[201] They have been more willing to examine whether a conflict of interest had arisen so as to prejudice the principal. In the Canadian case *Peso Silver Mines v Cropper*[202] a less strict approach was taken towards the fiduciary duty of company directors. Cropper was a member of the Board of Peso, a mining company which was offered 126 prospecting claims near their own mines. The company board decided bona fides not to purchase the claims and Cropper then joined a syndicate which formed a company and purchased them. Peso claimed that Cropper was liable to account for the profit he had made. The British Columbia Court of Appeal[203] held that he was not accountable, and rejected the approach adopted in *Regal (Hastings) v Gulliver*. It considered that the strict rules of equity had been carried far enough and were not appropriate for a modern country in a modern era. The Supreme Court of Canada[204] subsequently also held that Cropper was not accountable, but on the narrower ground that the facts fell outside the rule in *Regal (Hastings) v Gulliver* because the board had bona fides come to the conclusion that the investment was not one the company should make,

---

[197] [1967] 2 AC 46.     [198] [1990] 2 AC 663 at 701.     [199] [1990] 2 AC 663 at 702.
[200] [1967] 2 AC 134n, [1942] 1 All ER 378.     [201] [1967] 2 AC 46.
[202] (1966) 58 DLR (2d) 1; (1967) 30 MLR 450 (Prentice); (1971) 49 Can B Rev 80 (Beck); (1975) 53 Can B Rev 771 (Beck).
[203] (1966) 56 DLR (2d) 117.     [204] (1966) 58 DLR (2d) 1.

and that the director could not therefore be treated as having made the investment on behalf of the company.[205]

In Australia the High Court has adopted the approach taken by Lord Upjohn in *Boardman v Phipps*. Thus, in *Consul Development Pty Ltd v DPC Estates Pty Ltd*[206] Gibbs J specifically cited Lord Upjohn's suggestion that the words 'possibly may conflict' require consideration.[207] In *Chan (Kak Loui) v Zacharia*[208] Deane J suggested that it might still be arguable in the High Court that 'the liability to account for a personal benefit or gain obtained or received by use or by reason of fiduciary position, opportunity or knowledge will not arise in circumstances where it would be unconscientious to assert it or in which, for example, there is no possible conflict between personal interest and fiduciary duty . . .'[209]

However, as yet there is no indication that the English courts will move away from the strict liability advocated in *Boardman v Phipps*,[210] which was applied by the House of Lords in *Guinness plc v Saunders*.[211]

## (4) Conclusion

It might be thought that in practice there is very little difference between the two standards of liability propounded by the House of Lords in *Boardman v Phipps*.[212] Lord Upjohn's 'real sensible possibility' of a conflict of interest test will exclude only those cases where it seems there is absolutely no danger of the beneficiaries in fact being prejudiced by the fiduciary's conduct. It is an objective test and therefore there is still no need to inquire into actual motives, and it is sufficiently harsh to serve as an adequate deterrent to trustees who might contemplate abusing their position. However although Lord Upjohn's test has much to commend it, and it has found favour with academic commentators,[213] the strict approach that a fiduciary will be liable to account whenever there was a mere possibility of a conflict of interest, no matter how remote or unlikely the circumstances, represents the present position of English Law. The only way that the fiduciary can avoid liability, no matter how honest he may have been, is by ensuring that his profit-making activities are authorised by his principal following full disclosure.

---

[205] Citing Lord Greene MR in the Court of Appeal, which was referred to by Lord Russell in the House of Lords.

[206] (1975) 5 ALR 231.   [207] (1975) 5 ALR 231 at 249.   [208] (1983) 154 CLR 178.

[209] (1983) 154 CLR 178 at 204–205. See also *Warman International v Dwyer* (1995) 128 ALR 201, discussed by Oakley, 'The Liberalising Nature of Remedies for Breach of Trust' in Oakley, *Trends in Contemporary Trust Law* (1996), pp 236–239.

[210] [1967] 2 AC 46.

[211] [1990] 2 AC 663. Note however the dicta of Sedley LJ in *In Plus Group Ltd v Pyke* [2002] 2 BCLC 201 that a company director would not commit a breach of fiduciary duty by serving a competing company without consent if he had been treated unfairly. Grantham argues that this is inconsistent with the strict duty imposed on fiduciaries: (2003) 66 MLR 109.

[212] [1967] 2 AC 46.

[213] (1968) 84 LQR 472 (Jones); Goff and Jones, *The Law of Restitution* (6th edn, 2002), p 730–731; Finn, *Fiduciary Obligations* (1997), pp 130–168.

## 6 Remedies against a fiduciary who has received an unauthorised profit

As has been noted above, a fiduciary who has made an unauthorised profit will be required to make restitution thereof to his principal. Such restitution or disgorgement can be effected either by a personal or a proprietary remedy. It has often proved difficult to determine whether a personal or proprietary remedy is available, and in many cases the courts have not clearly identified the remedy awarded. The problem was stated clearly in the Australian High Court by Gibbs J in *Consul Development Pty Ltd v DPC Estates Pty Ltd*:

'The question whether the remedy which the person to whom the duty is owed may obtain against the person who has violated the duty is proprietary or personal may sometimes be one of some difficulty. In some cases the fiduciary has been declared a trustee of the property which he has gained by his breach; in others he has been called upon to account for his profits and sometimes the distinction between the two remedies has not . . . been kept clearly in mind.'[214]

In many cases it will not be necessary to determine whether the principal is entitled to a proprietary remedy as a personal remedy will suffice. However the availability of a proprietary remedy will be of crucial importance if the fiduciary is insolvent,[215] or if he has invested the profit received in assets which have appreciated in value. In the case of insolvency a principal will gain priority over the general creditors of the fiduciary if he can demonstrate a proprietary entitlement to any assets which represent the profit received. In the case of asset appreciation the principal will only be able to claim entitlement to the increased value by means of a proprietary right.

It should be noted that if a trustee has received a profit in breach of fiduciary duty his conduct may also constitute a breach of trust. If so, his obligations to make restitution of his profit gained in breach of fiduciary duty and to compensate the trust for any loss suffered in consequence of his breach are alternative remedies. The beneficiaries are required to elect between them and cannot recover both, otherwise they would gain double recovery. The need to elect was identified by the Privy Council in *Tang Man Sit (Decd) v Capacious Investments*,[216] which was discussed in detail in Chapter 28.[217]

### (1) Personal remedies

Whenever a fiduciary receives an unauthorised profit in breach of his fiduciary duty he is subject to a personal obligation to make restitution of the amount of the profit received to his principal. This personal restitutionary obligation is effected through the equitable duty to account. The personal remedy of account will be adequate to effect

---

[214] (1975) 5 ALR 231 at 249.    [215] See [1995] CLJ 377 (Oakley).
[216] [1996] AC 514, [1996] 1 All ER 193. See [1995] RLR 117 (Stevens); (1996) 112 LQR 375 (Birks).
[217] See p 736, above.

restitution where the fiduciary remains solvent and able to pay his principal an amount of money equivalent to the profit he received. Such a personal remedy appears to have been awarded in *Boardman v Phipps*.[218] In many cases where an equitable account of profits was ordered there was no need to determine whether a proprietary remedy by way of a constructive trust was also available because the personal remedy provided adequate satisfaction of the principal's right to receive restitution. As Professor Birks notes,[219] 'the vital fact is that [Boardman] was not insolvent. It was not necessary, therefore, for the plaintiff to claim any right in rem'.[220] A personal remedy will also be preferred to a proprietary claim if the fiduciary is solvent but the assets remaining in his hands representing the profit he received have fallen in value. As Lord Tempelman stated in *A-G of Hong Kong v Reid*:

'If the property representing the [profit[221]] decreases in value the fiduciary must pay the difference between that value and the initial amount of the [profit] . . .'[222]

The relevant date for the assessment of the quantum of the personal remedy is the date that the profit was received. The principal will only be entitled to recover the actual or net profit which was received by the fiduciary.[223]

## (2) Proprietary remedies

### (a) A constructive trust of unauthorised profits

It has always been clear that in some circumstances a constructive trust is imposed when a fiduciary receives an unauthorised profit in breach of his duty. This is evident in *Keech v Sandford*,[224] where the court held that a lease which had been renewed to a trustee in his personal capacity, rather than on behalf of the trust, should be assigned to the infant beneficiary. This suggests that the infant enjoyed an equitable entitlement to the lease from the moment that the trustee had acquired it. The trustee was also obliged to account for the profits he had received in the meantime. This account of profits is also explicable on the basis that the lease was always the property of the trust. In *Cook v Deeks*[225] the Privy Council similarly held that a contract entered by directors personally, in breach of their fiduciary duty, was held 'on behalf of the company',[226] such that 'it belonged in equity to the company and ought to have been dealt with as an asset of the company'.[227] In *Williams v Barton*[228] the court held that a commission received by a trustee in breach of fiduciary duty was to be treated as part of the estate of which he was executor, as he held it on constructive trust. In *Boardman v Phipps*[229] the House of Lords seems to have come to the conclusion that the majority shareholding which had been acquired in breach of fiduciary duty was

---

[218] [1967] 2 AC 46.      [219] Birks, An Introduction to the Law of Restitution (Oxford, 1985).
[220] Birks, An Introduction to the Law of Restitution, p 388.
[221] In fact, Lord Tempelman used the term 'bribe', since this was what the fiduciary had in fact received, but the principle remains the same irrespective of the source of the profit received.
[222] [1994] 1 All ER 1.      [223] *Patel v London Borough of Brent* [2003] EWHC 3081.
[224] (1726) Sel Cas Ch 61.      [225] [1916] 1 AC 554.      [226] [1916] 1 AC 554 at 563.
[227] [1916] 1 AC 554 at 564.      [228] [1927] 2 Ch 9.      [229] [1967] 2 AC 46.

held on constructive trust for the beneficiaries of the trust.[230] More recently in *Guinness plc v Saunders*[231] the House of Lords held that a £5.2m fee received by a director in breach of fiduciary duty was held on constructive trust for the company. He was therefore required to 'restore that money'[232] to the company.[233]

Although these cases established that a fiduciary may sometimes hold any unauthorised profits he has received on constructive trust, it remained unclear whether such a trust would arise in all such circumstances. In particular there was long established authority that a fiduciary who had received a bribe would not hold it on constructive trust for his principal. The resulting inconsistency was only recently resolved by the decision of the Privy Council in *A-G of Hong Kong v Reid*.[234]

### (b) Constructive trust of a bribe received by a fiduciary

Whereas a proprietary remedy by way of a constructive trust has always been available in some instances where a fiduciary has received an unauthorised profit, in the case of bribes it was historically held that no such proprietary remedy was available to a principal. A bribed fiduciary did not hold the bribe received on constructive trust, and the principal was confined to a personal remedy of account.[235] In *Lister & Co v Stubbs*[236] Stubbs, the foreman dyer of Lister & Co, received £5,500 in bribes from another company with whom he placed business while acting as agent for Lister. The Court of Appeal held that the money he received was not held on constructive trust, and that Lister & Co therefore had had no proprietary claim to it. Stubbs was under a personal duty to account for the money he had received, and the relationship between Stubbs and the company was simply one of debtor and creditor.

*Lister & Co v Stubbs* was followed in *A-G's Reference (No 1 of 1985)*.[237] A pub landlord was contractually obliged to sell only goods supplied by a brewery. He moved barrels of his own beer into the pub at night. He was charged under s 25(1) of the Theft Act 1968 with going equipped for theft. The trial judge ruled that there was no case to answer, and it was referred to the Court of Appeal by the Attorney General. The central issue was whether the landlord would have been a constructive trustee of any money paid to him by customers for beer sold in breach of his contract. The Court of Appeal held that this did not fall within the ambit of s 5 of the Theft Act because 'a person in a fiduciary

---

[230] [1967] 2 AC 46 at 117, per Lord Guest: 'I have no hesitation in coming to the conclusion that the appellants hold the Lester & Harris shares as constructive trustees . . .' This understanding of the claim in *Boardman v Phipps* was also expressed by the Privy Council in *A-G for Hong Kong v Reid* [1994] 1 All ER 1 at 11.

[231] [1990] 2 AC 663.    [232] [1990] 2 AC 663 at 702, per Lord Goff.

[233] See also *Neptune (Vehicle Washing Equipment) Ltd v Fitzgerald* [1996] Ch 274; *CMS Dolphin Ltd v Simonet* [2001] BCLC 704.

[234] [1994] 1 All ER 1.    [235] *Metropolitan Bank v Heiron* (1880) 5 Ex D 319, CA.

[236] (1890) 45 Ch D 1.

[237] [1986] QB 491; (1986) 102 LQR 486; (1986) 45 CLJ (Gearty); (1986) 136 NLJ 913 (Smart); [1987] Cov 209 (Martin). See also *Powell and Thomas v Evans Jones & Co* [1905] 1 KB 11, CA; *A-G's Reference (No 1 of 1985)* [1986] QB 491; *Logicrose Ltd v Southend United Football Club Ltd* [1988] 1 WLR 1256; *A-G for Hong Kong v Reid* [1992] 2 NZLR 385. For those who supported the decision in *Lister v Stubbs*, see Birks, *An Introduction to the Law of Restitution* (1985), p 388; (1987) 103 LQR 433 (Goode).

position who uses that position to make a secret profit . . . is not a trustee'.[238] Lord Lane CJ concluded that:

'A trustee is not permitted to make a profit from his trust. Therefore if he uses trust property to make a profit from the trust, he is accountable for that profit. If and when such a profit is identified as a separate piece of property, he may be a constructive trustee of it. However, until the profit is identifiable as a separate piece of property, it is not trust property and his obligation is to account only.'[239]

However, it is contended that little weight should be placed upon this decision. It is clearly correct that a proprietary remedy cannot subsist when specific property cannot be identified as representing the profit received, but it does not follow that no such proprietary entitlement exists at the moment that such a profit is received. The property is specifically identifiable when the customer pays over the price of the beer, although if mixed with other money it may then prove impossible to identify it subsequently in the assets of the recipient.

Although the rule in *Lister & Co v Stubbs*[240] was supported by some academics,[241] it was subjected to heavy criticism by others.[242] In *A-G of Hong Kong v Reid*[243] the Privy Council considered that it should no longer be followed. Reid received bribes exceeding NZ$2.5m in the course of his work as a public prosecutor in Hong Kong. Part of this money was used to purchase three freehold properties in New Zealand. The Privy Council considered that, since Reid had acted in breach of his fiduciary duty, he held the money he received on constructive trust for the Crown. Since the houses were the traceable proceeds of the bribes received, they were also held on trust for the Crown. Lord Templeman, delivering the advice of the Board, explained the rationale for the decision:

'The decision in *Lister & Co v Stubbs* is not consistent with the principles that a fiduciary must not be allowed to benefit from his own breach of duty, that the fiduciary should account for the bribe as soon as he receives it and that equity regards as done that which ought to be done. From these principles it would appear to follow that the bribe and the property from time to time representing the bribe are held on a constructive trust for the person injured.'[244]

The rejection of *Lister & Co v Stubbs* eliminated an anomaly in the law. As can be seen from *Boardman v Phipps*,[245] an 'honest' fiduciary will be held to be a constructive

---

[238] [1986] QB 491 at 503, citing *Reading v A-G* [1951] AC 507, HL; In *Re Sharpe* [1980] 1 WLR 219; *R v Governor of Pentonville Prison, ex p Tarling* (1978) 70 Cr App Rep 77; *Lister & Co v Stubbs* (1890) 45 Ch D 1.

[239] [1986] QB 491 at 506.     [240] (1890) 45 Ch D 1.     [241] (1987) 103 LQR 433 (Goode).

[242] Underhill and Hayton, *Law Relating to Trust and Trustees* (15th edn, 1995), p 877; Oakley, *Constructive Trusts* (2nd edn, 1997), p 56; Goff and Jones, *The Law of Restitution* (6th edn, 2002), pp 740–742; Pettit, *Equity and the Law of Trusts* (9th edn, 2001), p 143; Meagher, Gummow and Lehane, *Equity Doctrines and Remedies* (3rd edn,1992), para 1323; Sir Anthony Mason, *Essays in Equity* (1985), 246; Finn, *Fiduciary Obligations* (1977), para 513; Jacobs, *Law of Trusts in Australia* (5th edn), p 297; (1979) 95 LQR 536 (Needham); [1980] Conv 200 (Braithwaite); [1993] RLR 7 (Sir Peter Millett).

[243] [1994] 1 All ER 1; (1995) 58 MLR 87 (Allen);

[244] [1994] 1 All ER 1 at 9. See also *Sumitomo Bank Ltd v Kartika Rathna Thahir* (1993) 1 SLR 735.

[245] [1967] 2 AC 46, HL.

trustee of any unauthorised profit received if there was the mere possibility of a conflict between his interest and his duty. It was unacceptable that a proprietary remedy was available against an honest fiduciary but not against a 'dishonest' fiduciary who had accepted a bribe.[246]

The exact status of the decision in *A-G of Hong Kong v Reid* has continued to be debated, since it is a Privy Council decision, and some cases have suggested that *Lister & Co v Stubbs* continue to be binding on English courts.[247] However in *Daraydan Holdings Ltd v Solland International Ltd*,[248] which concerned a defendant who had received a secret commission of £1.8m from the claimants on contracts for the luxurious refurbishment of properties sin London and Qatar, Lawrence Coliins J held that *A-G of Hong Kong v Reid* ought to be applied:

'The system of precedent would be shown in a most unfavourable light if a litigant in such a case were forced by the doctrine of binding precedent to go to the House of Lords in order to have the decision of the Privy Council affirmed. That would be particularly so where the decision of the Privy Council is recent, where it was a decision on the English common law, where the Board consisted mainly of serving Law Lords, and where the decision had been made after full argument on the correctness of the earlier decision.'[249]

Strictly speaking these comments were themselves obiter, since the case was distinguishable from *A-G of Hong Kong v Reid* because the bribe involved had been derived directly from the claimant's property because the price paid by the claimant had been increased by the amount of the bribe, but they reflect a strong judicial sentiment that *Lister v Stubbs* has been overruled in practice.

## (c) Constructive trust of unauthorised profits in all circumstances

It is hard to overestimate the significance of *A-G for Hong Kong v Reid*.[250] The rejection of *Lister & Co v Stubbs* and the reasoning of Lord Templeman suggest that in all situations in which a fiduciary receives an unauthorised profit a constructive trust will be imposed in favour of his principal. The constructive trust arises as an inexorable consequence of the equitable duty to account. As Lord Templeman explained:

'As soon as the bribe was received it should have been paid or transferred instanter to the person who suffered from the breach of duty. Equity considers as done that which ought to be have been done. As soon as the bribe was received, whether in cash or in kind, the false fiduciary held the bribe on a constructive trust for the person injured.'[251]

The imposition of the constructive trust is therefore analogous to the trust that arises when a specifically enforceable contract for the creation or transfer of an equitable interest is entered. For example, a contract for the sale of land creates an immediate

---

[246] See below.
[247] *A-G v Blake* [1997] Ch 84; *Halifax Building Society v Thomas* [1996] Ch 217. See, however, *Ocular Sciences Ltd v Aspect Vision Care Ltd* [1997] RPC 289 and *Fyffes Group Ltd v Tempelman* [2000] Lloyd's Rep 643 where *A-G for Hong Kong v Reid* was applied.
[248] [2005] 4 All ER 73.       [249] Ibid at [85]–[86].       [250] [1994] 1 All ER 1.
[251] [1994] 1 All ER 1 at 5. See also *MacIntosh v Fortex Group Ltd* [1997] 1 NZLR 711. See Worthington, *Proprietary Interests in Commercial Transactions* (1996), pp 192–194; (1998) 18 OJLS 361 (Chambers).

constructive trust in favour of the purchaser, and a contract for the grant of a legal lease will create an equitable lease.[252] If this analysis is correct, a constructive trust would certainly have been available as a remedy in *Boardman v Phipps*.[253] Boardman had received an unauthorised profit in breach of his fiduciary duty, and he was therefore subject to an equitable duty to account to his principal. Since equity would treat as done that which ought to be done, namely payment over of the profit received, he would hold the profit on constructive trust. It is also difficult to see how the decision of the Court of Appeal in *A-G's Reference (No 1 of 1985)*[254] can survive as good authority in the light of *A-G of Hong Kong v Reid*.[255] The publican would have held any profit derived from the sale of his own beer in breach of the exclusive supply contract on constructive trust, as he was admittedly subject to a personal duty to account.

## (d) No constructive trust where an agent was not required to apply money received on behalf of his principal exclusively for the benefit of his principal

Although *A-G for Hong Kong v Reid* seems to suggest that a fiduciary will always hold any unauthorised profits he has received on constructive trust for his principal, it has been recently questioned whether such a constructive trust will arise where an agent has failed to account to his principal for money received on his behalf if he was not subject to a duty to keep the money received separate from his own, and to apply it exclusively for the benefit of his principal. In *Nelson v Rye*[256] the manager of a musician had agreed to receive all the income arising from his client's activities, and to account annually to him for the income received, less his agreed commission and expenses. Laddie J held that in these circumstances the manager was a constructive trustee of any income he had failed to pay to his client in accordance with their agreement, citing with approval an academic article authored by Sir Peter Millett.[257] Somewhat ironically, in *Paragon Finance plc v Thakerar & Co*[258] Millett LJ suggested that *Nelson v Rye* had been wrongly decided, and that the income wrongly retained could not have been held on constructive trust for the client. Millett LJ explained that, in his opinion, the nature of the agency agreement had rendered it impossible to establish a constructive trust:

'Unless I have misunderstood the facts or they were very unusual it would appear that the defendant was entitled to pay receipts into his own account, mix them with his own money, use them for his own cash flow, deduct his own commission, and account for the balance to the plaintiff only at the end of the year. It is fundamental to the existence of a trust that the trustee is bound to keep the trust property separate from his own and apply it exclusively for the benefit of the beneficiary. Any right on the part of the defendant to mix the money which he received with his own and use it for his own cash flow would be inconsistent with the existence of a trust.'[259]

---

[252] *Walsh v Lonsdale* (1882) 21 Ch D 9; see also *Job v Job* (1877) 6 Ch D 562; *Lowe v Dixon* (1885) 16 QBD 455.

[253] [1967] 2 AC 46.    [254] [1986] QB 491.    [255] See (1994) 110 LQR 180 (Smith).

[256] [1996] 2 All ER 186.    [257] 'Bribes and Secret Commissions' [1993] RLR 7.

[258] [1999] 1 All ER 400.    [259] [1999] 1 All ER 400 at 416.

The limitation suggested in *Paragon Finance plc v Thakerar & Co,* which was followed by Jules Sher QC in *Coulthard v Disco Mix Club Ltd,*[260] will only apply in a very narrow range of circumstances. In the vast majority of cases where a fiduciary has received an unauthorised profit he will be subject to an immediate duty to account to his principal, thus generating a constructive trust.

### (e) Identifying assets subject to a constructive trust

A proprietary right can only subsist in respect of specific property. A principal will therefore only be able to assert his equitable ownership against assets in the hands of his fiduciary (or a third party) which he can identify as representing the profit received, or the proceeds of the profit received. Whether such identification is possible will be determined by the equitable rules of tracing. In some cases it will be relatively straight-forward to identify assets representing the profit received, as for example in *A-G of Hong Kong v Reid,* where the houses claimed could be shown to have been purchased with the bribe received. If it is not possible to identify any traceable proceeds of the profit received, the principal will be confined to seeking a personal remedy by way of an equitable account. The rules of tracing will be examined in Chapter 31.

## (3) Criticism of the present remedial structure

As has been argued above, it seems clear that at present in English law, in consequence of the decision in *A-G of Hong Kong v Reid,* a constructive trust will arise whenever a fiduciary receives an unauthorised profit. However, this general availability of a propri-etary remedy has been subjected to criticism, on both theoretical and practical grounds, and alternative approaches have been advocated.

### (a) Criticism of *A-G of Hong Kong v Reid*[261]

It is somewhat ironic that, whereas *Lister & Co v Stubbs*[262] had been subjected to strong criticism before it was set aside by the Privy Council, *A-G of Hong Kong v Reid* has since become the subject of equally vociferous criticism. The imposition of a constructive trust in that case was clearly motivated by policy considerations. As Lord Templeman observed:

'Bribery is an evil practice which threatens the foundation of any civilised society. In particu-lar, bribery of policemen and prosecutors brings the administration of justice into disrepute. Where bribes are accepted by a trustee, servant, agent or other fiduciary, loss and damage are caused to the beneficiaries, master or principal whose interests have been betrayed. The amount of loss or damage resulting from the acceptance of a bribe may or may not be quantifiable.'[263]

It therefore seemed morally unacceptable that an honest fiduciary might hold an

---

[260] [2000] 1 WLR 707.
[261] See (1994) 53 CLJ 31 (Oakley); [1994] RLR 57 (Crilley); (1995) 54 CLJ 60 (Gardner). See also R Goode, 'Proprietary Restitutionary Claims' Chap 5 in Cornish, Nolan, O'Sullivan & Virgo (eds) *Restitution Past, Present & Future* (1998).
[262] (1890) 45 ChD 1.    [263] [1994] 1 All ER 1 at 4.

unauthorised profit on constructive trust but a blatantly dishonest fiduciary who had accepted a bribe would not. Surely the morally more repugnant conduct demands the more powerful remedy. Whilst *Lister & Co v Stubbs* was largely criticised by property lawyers on grounds of inconsistency, *A-G of Hong Kong v Reid* has largely been criticised by restitution lawyers on the grounds of proprietary overkill.[264] The main criticism concerns the perceived danger of unfairness to other creditors of the fiduciary if he is insolvent and assets representing the bribe received are subject to a constructive trust, thus gaining the principal priority. This danger did not in fact arise in *Reid* because he was not insolvent. Lord Templeman considered that the right of the principal should prevail over the entitlements of other general creditors:

'. . . it is said that if the false fiduciary holds property representing the bribe in trust for the person injured, and if the false fiduciary is or becomes insolvent, the unsecured creditors of the false fiduciary will be deprived of their right to share in the proceeds of that property. But the unsecured creditors cannot be in a better position than their debtor. The authorities show that property acquired by a trustee innocently but in breach of trust and the property from time to time representing the same belong in equity to the cestui que trust and not to the trustee personally, whether he is solvent or insolvent. Property acquired by a trustee as a result of a criminal breach of trust and the property from time to time representing the same must also belong in equity to the cestui que trust and not to the trustee whether he is solvent or insolvent.'[265]

Central to the criticism of the constructive trust analysis adopted in *Reid* is the perception that there was insufficient nexus between the principal and the bribe received by the fiduciary to justify the imposition of a proprietary right, irrespective of the fact that the relationship between the fiduciary and his principal justifies a personal obligation to make restitution. If the automatic constructive trust founded upon the equitable duty to account is to be rejected, an alternative analysis is needed by which to differentiate the circumstances in which a constructive trust will be imposed over profits received in breach of fiduciary duty, and situations where the principal will be confined to a personal remedy.

## (b)  Constructive trust only justified if there was a proprietary nexus between the principal and the unauthorised profit

Some academics have suggested that an unauthorised profit received by a fiduciary should only be subject to a constructive trust if the profit was obtained through a misuse of the principal's property. Professor Birks has argued that a proprietary remedy should only be available where there was a sufficient 'proprietary base' connecting the profit and the principal.[266] Hanbury and Martin[267] argued that a constructive trust should only arise where a profit has been made by the fiduciary's use of trust property, and that in all other circumstances there should only be a personal duty to account. If a proprietary nexus were to be required between the profit and the principal the proceeds

---

[264]  See [1994] RLR 57 (Crilley); [1997] CFILR 43 (Rotherham); Burrows, *The Law of Restitution* (2nd edn, 2002), pp 72 and 499–500.

[265]  [1994] 1 All ER 1 at 5.     [266]  An Introduction to the Law of Restitution (1985), pp 378–393.

[267]  *Modern Equity* (14th edn, 1993), p 598. See now (17th edn, 2005) pp 630–633..

of a bribe could not be subject to a constructive trust as the principal had no prior connection with the property constituting the bribe, nor was it received by the fiduciary as a product of property belonging to the principal.[268] If this analysis were to be applied to the earlier case of *Boardman v Phipps*[269] a constructive trust would only have been justified if the confidential information exploited to generate the profit was characterised as trust property.

Whilst this approach would certainly restrict the scope of proprietary claims, it is predicated upon a distinction between abuse of property and abuse of position. Where a fiduciary had received a profit through abuse of his principal's property the principal would be entitled either to a proprietary claim by way of constructive trust or a personal restitutionary remedy. If the fiduciary had merely exploited his position, but not the principal's property, the principal would be confined to a personal right to receive restitution. In *A-G of Hong Kong v Reid*[270] the Privy Council was unwilling to draw such a distinction, so that any abuse by a fiduciary, whether of property or position, will give rise to a constructive trust. The constructive trust arises from the mandatory nature of the equitable duty to account.

### (c) A remedial constructive trust

Under the approach adopted in *Reid,* the court possesses no discretion to determine whether a principal should be entitled to a proprietary claim if his fiduciary received an unauthorised profit. The constructive trust arises automatically, without the intervention of the court, at the moment that the profit was received. The constructive trust operates in what has been described as an institutional manner. However, other jurisdictions, and especially Canada, have adopted a more flexible form of constructive trust, termed the remedial constructive trust. The remedial constructive trust has two significant characteristics. First, it is a trust imposed to reverse unjust enrichment. Secondly, where unjust enrichment is identified it is for the court to determine whether a constructive trust would be an appropriate remedy to effect restitution. Thus, if a fiduciary has received an unauthorised profit in breach of duty he will have been unjustly enriched thereby, and the court will enjoy the discretion to decide whether the principle should be entitled to a proprietary remedy. No trusts arises at the moment that the profit was received, but only when the court determines that a constructive trust should be imposed. In this way the interests of third parties, for example other general creditors of an insolvent fiduciary, can be taken into account. In *LAC Minerals Ltd v International Corona Resources Ltd*[271] the defendant had acted in breach of fiduciary duty by misusing confidential information to purchase land which contained substantial mineral deposits. A majority of the Supreme Court of Canada held a constructive trust should be imposed. A remedial constructive trust was also utilised in *Korkontzilas v Soulos,*[272] where a gratuitous agent acting for the potential purchaser of land had failed to deliver her offer to the vendor and arranged to sell the property to his own wife instead. The majority of the Supreme Court held that a constructive trust

---

[268] See also Tang, 'Confidence and the constructive trust' (2003) 23 LS 135.
[269] [1967] 2 AC 46.    [270] [1994] 1 All ER 1.    [271] (1989) 61 DLR (4th) 14.
[272] (1997) 146 DLR (4th) 214.

should be imposed. The discretionary nature of the remedy was stressed, so that a constructive trust would not be imposed if it would be unjust, for example if the interests of intervening creditors would be affected. The operation of such a remedial constructive trust is so different from the present English approach that *A-G of Hong v Reid* was not even cited.

Whilst the remedial constructive trust offers the attraction of flexibility, this is gained at the expense of certainty. For this reason English law has so far refused to adopt the remedial constructive trust. In *Westdeutsche Landesbank Girozentrale v Islington London Borough Council*[273] Lord Browne-Wilkinson tentatively suggested that it may conceivably be introduced when an appropriate case arises for decision. However in *Re Polly Peck (No 2)*[274] the Court of Appeal strongly indicated that the remedial constructive trust should not be introduced into English law without the intervention of Parliament. If in the future the remedial constructive trust is adopted, the present orthodoxy found in *A-G of Hong Kong v Reid* will have to be revised. The nature and operation of the remedial constructive trust has been discussed in detail in Chapter 9 above.

## (d)  Redefining the fiduciary relationship

Whilst much debate has concerned the nature of the remedies available to a principal whose fiduciary has received an unauthorised profit, many of the difficulties in this area have been caused by the extension of the concept of the 'fiduciary relationship' into commercial relationships. The proprietary remedies triggered by a fiduciary relationship may be justified in the context of a trust but are less clearly applicable where the fiduciary is an employee who has committed a breach of contract which has generated a profit. In such circumstances it may be difficult to determine whether the employee's breach caused any loss to his employer, or to assess the quantum of such loss. It is much simpler to identify the extent of the gain received by the employee. If an employee were liable to make restitution to his employer of any profit earned by his breach of contract, this would provide the employer with adequate remedial satisfaction whilst eliminating the need to demonstrate a fiduciary relationship. Historically, such an alternative analysis was impossible because it had been held that a defendant in breach of contract was not subject to an obligation to make restitution of his profit.[275] If the breach enabled the defendant to enter a more profitable contract with someone else,[276] the availability of restitution would have the effect of undermining the incentive to commit efficient breach. However, in *A-G v Blake*[277] the House of Lords held that in exceptional circumstances a contract breaker could be required to account for the profits he had derived from his breach. Lord Nicholls examined the relevant authorities and concluded:

'My conclusion is that there seems to be no reason, *in principle*, why the court must in all

---

[273] [1996] AC 669.        [274] [1998] 3 All ER 812.

[275] *Surrey County Council v Beredo Homes Ltd* [1993] 1 WLR 1361.

[276] *Teacher v Calder* [1899] AC 451.

[277] [2000] 4 All ER 385. See also *Experience Hendrix LLC v PXX Enterprises Inc* [2003] 1 All ER (Comm) 830; [2003] RLR 101 (Edleman); [2003] LMCLQ 301 (Lee). Note the criticisms of *A-G v Blake* in Campbell, 'The treatment of *Teacher v Calder* in *AG v Blake*' (2002) 65 MLR 256, and Campbell and Harris, 'In. defence of breach: a critique of restitution and the performance interest' (2002) 22 LS 208.

circumstances rule out an account of profits as a remedy for breach of contract. . . . When, exceptionally, a just response to a breach of contract so requires, the court should be able to grant the discretionary remedy of requiring a defendant to account to the plaintiff for the benefits he has received from his breach of contract.'[278]

The case concerned a traitorous former member of the security services who had published an autobiography without the consent of his former employers, in contravention of an express term of his contract. In the Court of Appeal Lord Woolf MR had suggested that restitution of profits obtained by a breach of contract should only be required where a defendant had done the very thing he contracted not to do, or had saved himself expenditure by skimping on the performance required under his contract.[279] However the House of Lords was unwilling to adopt any specific guidelines as to when the remedy of account should be awarded, other than that the usual remedies of damages, specific performance and injunction must be 'inadequate.' Lord Nicholls stated:

'It will only be in exceptional cases, where those remedies are inadequate, that any question of accounting for profits will arise. No fixed rules can be prescribed. The court will have regard to all the circumstances, including the subject matter of the contract, the purpose of the contractual provision which has been breached, the circumstances in which the breach occurred, the consequences of the breach and the circumstances in which relief is being sought. A useful guide, although not exhaustive, is whether the plaintiff had a legitimate interest in preventing the defendant's profit-making activity and, hence, in depriving him of his profit. It would be difficult, and unwise, to attempt to be more specific.'[280]

The adoption of a restitution remedy to recover profits obtained by a breach of contract may allow for a contraction of the scope of relationships which need to characterised as fiduciary in nature, especially in the context of employment relationships. In such cases the duty of exclusive loyalty will be replaced by specific contractual obligations of loyalty. An employee such as Reid could thus be required to make restitution of unauthorised profits received in breach of contract, which would certainly include a bribe, without inevitably requiring the imposition of a constructive trust. The remedy would be personal and the principal would stand alongside other general creditors in the event of an insolvency.

## (4) Conclusion

Despite criticism and alternatives, the overwhelming weight of English principle and authority favours the view that a fiduciary who receives an unauthorised profit will hold it on constructive trust for his principal. His principal will therefore enjoy an immediate equitable interest in the profit received, which may be maintained against any assets which can be identified as its product by the rules of tracing. In the event that the fiduciary is insolvent, he will be able to obtain priority over other general creditors. Similarly, his proprietary rights enable him to claim any appreciation in the value of

---

[278] [2000] 4 All ER 385 at 396.    [279] [1998] 1 All ER 833 at 846. See [1998] RLR 118 (Virgo).
[280] [2000] 4 All ER 385 at 398.

property representing the profit. However, in the majority of cases the fiduciary will be solvent, so that will be little advantage in asserting a proprietary claim. The fiduciary will be subject to a personal obligation to account for the profit received. The appropriateness of the imposition of a constructive trust where a fiduciary has received an unauthorised profit was recently defended by Lawrence Collins J in *Daraydan Holdings Ltd v Solland International Ltd:*

'There are powerful policy reasons for ensuring that a fiduciary does not retain gains acquired in violation of fiduciary duty, and I do not consider that it should make any difference whether the fiduciary is insolvent. There is no injustice to the creditors in their not sharing in an asset for which the fiduciary has not given value, and which the fiduciary should not have had.'[281]

# 7 Defences to an action for breach of fiduciary duty

## (1) Conduct authorised by principal

As has been noted, a fiduciary is not subject to an absolute duty of self-denial preventing him from retaining any benefits for himself. He will only be required to make restitution of unauthorised profits which were obtained without the consent or acquiescence of his principal. He will only be entitled to rely on such consent or acquiescence if he made full disclosure of the course he intended to pursue. In *Boardman v Phipps*[282] the House of Lords accepted that if Boardman had acted with the consent of the trustees and beneficiaries he would not have been in breach of fiduciary duty and would not therefore have been liable to account for the profits he had received.[283] However he had failed to obtain the consent of one of the trustees,[284] and had not sought the approval of the plaintiff beneficiary. By contrast, in *Queensland Mines Ltd v Hudson*[285] a company director who had taken up an opportunity initially offered to the company was not held liable to account for his profits because he had acted after full disclosure to the other directors.

## (2) Limitation

The defence of limitation in regard to an action for compensation for breach of trust was examined in the previous chapter.[286] It has proved more difficult to apply the provisions of the Limitation Act 1980 to actions against fiduciaries who have received an unauthorised profit, because the legislation does not make any express provision for such claims. Instead provisions designed primarily with express trusts in mind have had

---

[281] [2004] EWHC 622 at [86]. See also Goff & Jones, *The Law of Restitution* (6<sup>th</sup> edn, 2002) who argue at p739 that *A-G for Hong King v Reid* should be followed.

[282] [1967] 2 AC 46.    [283] [1967] 2 AC 46 at 93, per Viscount Dilhorne.

[284] Who was, incidentally, suffering from senile dementia.

[285] (1978) 18 ALR 1; (197) 42 MLR 711 (Sullivan).    [286] See above p 762.

to be interpreted so as to provide a limitation period for actions for breach of fiduciary duty and the concomitant constructive trusts of unauthorised profits which arise from them. The relevant principles have been considered and clarified by a number of recent decisions,[287] culminating in the decision of the Court of Appeal in *Gwembe Valley Development Company Ltd (in receiveship) v Koshy*.[288]

Until recently it was thought that no limitation period was applicable to an action for an account, as s 23 of the Limitation Act 1980 was thought not to apply to such a claim.[289] However in *Coulthard v Disco Mix Club Ltd*[290] it was held that an action for an account against a dishonest fiduciary should be subject to the same limitation period as a common law action for damages, namely six years. The case concerned an agency agreement between a disc-jockey and a manager for the commercial exploitation of his beat-mixed recordings. It was alleged that the defendant manager had dishonestly failed to pay the plaintiff everything he was entitled to receive under the agreement. The central question was whether the claim was time-barred by the limitation period. Jules Sher QC held that, applying s 36 of the Limitation Act 1980,[291] the claim founded on breach of fiduciary duty was subject to the six-year limitation period because it was an equitable jurisdiction equivalent to a common law claim of fraud. He explained as follows:

'Now, in my judgement, the true breaches of fiduciary duty, i.e. the allegations of deliberate and dishonest under accounting, are based on the same factual allegations as the common law claims of fraud. The breaches of fiduciary duty are thus no more than the equitable counterparts of the claims at common law. The court of equity, in granting relief for such breaches would be exercising a concurrent jurisdiction with that of the common law. I have little doubt but that to such a claim the statute would have applied. . . . I am happy to come to what seems to be the sensible conclusion that no distinction in point of limitation can be made between an action for damages for fraud at common law and its counterpart in equity based on the same facts.'[292]

*Coulthard v Disco Mix Club Ltd* concerned an action for an account but did not involve trust property because the defendant had not been obliged to keep the money in question separate from his own. Different principles apply where a fiduciary has held an unauthorised profit on constructive trust for his principal. In such cases the claim against the fiduciary may be regarded as analogous to an action by a beneficiary for breach of trust and so fall within the scope of s 21 of the Limitation Act 1980. In *Bristol*

---

[287] *Bristol and West Building Society v Mothew* [1998] Ch 1; *Paragon Finance plc v DB Thackerar* [1999] 1 All ER 400; *Cia De Seguros Imperio v Heath (REBX) Ltd* [2001] 1 WLR 112; *JJ Harrison v Harrison* [2002] BCLC 162.

[288] [2004] WTLR 97.

[289] *A-G v Cocke* [1988] Ch 414; *Nelson v Rye* [1996] 2 All ER 186; [1997] Conv 225 (Stevens). See above, p 000.

[290] [2000] 1 WLR 707.

[291] Whilst in *Nelson v Rye* [1996] 2 All ER 186 Laddie J, relying on the authority of *A-G v Cocke* [1988] Ch 414, had held that and action for breach of fiduciary duty was not subject to a period of limitation, Jules Sher QC considered that the case was 'unsafe' because the possible application of s 36 of the Limitation Act 1980 had not been argued.

[292] [2000] 1 WLR 707 at 730.

*and West Building Society v Mothew*[293] and *Paragon Finance plc v Thackerar & Co*[294] Millett LJ held that for the purposes of limitation it was necessary to distinguish between a fiduciary who had enjoyed a pre-exiting relationship with the principal under which he had assumed the duties of a trustee, even though he had not been expressly appointed as such, and a situation in which a constructive trust of an unauthorised profit was only the response of equity in supplying a remedial formula for dealing with the consequences of a fraud. Where a constructive trust of an unauthorised profit arose in the context of such a pre-existing duty the limitation provisions of s 21 would apply, so that the action would be subject to a six-year limitation period, unless the fiduciary had acted fraudulent or dishonestly,[295] or retained the profit or its traceable proceeds in his possession,[296] in which case there would be no applicable limitation period. Where there was no such pre-existing duty the action would be subject to a six-year limitation period since s 21 would not apply. These principles were adopted and affirmed by the Court of Appeal in the more recent case of *Gwembe Valley Development Company Ltd v Koshy* where Mummery LJ stated:

'In the light of those cases, in our view, it is possible to simplify the court's task when considering the application of the 1980 Act to claims against fiduciaries. The starting assumption should be that a six-year limitation period will apply—under one or other provision of the Act, applied directly or by analogy—unless it is specifically excluded by the Act or established case-law. Personal claims against fiduciaries will normally be subject to limits by analogy with claims in tort or contract . . . By contrast, claims for breach of fiduciary duty, in the special sense explained in Mothew, will normally be covered by section 21. The six-year time limit under section 21(3) will apply, directly or by analogy, unless excluded by subsection 21(1)(a) (fraud) or (b)'[297]

The case concerned a company director who had received undisclosed profits from a contract with the company. The court held that his position meant that he had had 'trustee-like responsibilities' in the exercise of his powers of management of the property of the company and in dealing with the application of its property, and that therefore the claim for an account was within the scope of s 21, Since he had acted dishonestly in breaching his fiduciary duty s 21(1)(a) applied to exclude the six-year limitation period and he was not entitled to any defence of limitation.

The equitable doctrine of laches will only be available where a claim to an account is not subject to a statutory limitation period, in which case it may protect a fiduciary from unduly delayed proceedings if it would be inequitable to allow them to proceed, for example because he would suffered substantial prejudice or detriment. The defence of laches will not therefore be available where s 21(1) of the Limitation Act 1980 applies. Thus in *Gwembe Valley Development Co Ltd v Koshy* the Court of Appeal held that the defence of laches was not available as a defence to the action for dishonest breach of fiduciary duty.[298] The operation of the doctrine of laches was examined in detail in Chapter 28[299] in the context of actions for breach of trust.

[293]  [1998] Ch 1.        [294]  [1999] 1 All ER 400.        [295]  S 21(1)(a).        [296]  S 21(1)(b).
[297]  [2004] WTLR 97, at [111].        [298]  [2004] WTLR 97 at [140].        [299]  See above, p 766.

# 30

# Remedies against strangers to the trust

## 1 Introduction

### (1) Relationship to remedies against trustees

The previous two chapters have examined the remedies which beneficiaries may pursue against a trustee who acts in breach of trust, or in breach of his fiduciary duty. However, if a trustee commits a breach of trust which involves a third party who was a stranger to the trust,[1] either as a participant in the breach or as the recipient of trust property transferred to him in breach of trust, the beneficiaries of the trust may be entitled to pursue remedies against the stranger. Such remedies may prove more attractive to the beneficiaries than their remedies against the trustee in breach. The availability of remedies against a stranger to the trust will be especially important if the trustee is insolvent, thus rendering direct remedies against him ineffective. Whilst a stranger to a trust may be liable at common law in tort, for example if he provides the trustee with negligent advice,[2] beneficiaries may enjoy equitable remedies against a stranger who has wrongfully received trust property or wrongfully involved himself in the administration of the trust.

### (2) Personal and proprietary remedies against strangers to the trust

Where a stranger is liable in equity to the beneficiaries of a trust, the beneficiaries may enjoy either personal or proprietary remedies.

### (a) Proprietary remedies

It is a basic axiom of the law of property that a third party who receives property subject to a subsisting equitable interest cannot take free from that interest unless he is a bona fide purchaser for value without prior notice of the interest.[3] Since the beneficiaries of a trust enjoy the equitable ownership of the trust property[4] it follows that, if the trustee transfers trust property to a stranger in breach of trust, the stranger will acquire the

---

[1] The third party is termed a 'stranger to the trust' because he was not a trustee and therefore was not subject to any obligations prior to his involvement in the breach.

[2] See *Royal Brunei Airlines v Tan* [1995] 3 All ER 97 at 108.     [3] See Chapter 3.

[4] See above, Chapter 4.

legal title subject to the beneficiaries' equitable pre-existing interests, unless he was a bona fide purchaser for value without notice thereof.[5] The beneficiaries' equitable interests in the trust property will be preserved and they will be able to claim the property in the stranger's hands as their own in equity. If the stranger has subsequently dealt with the trust property he received, for example by exchanging it for different property or mixing it with other property (whether his own or also belonging to a third party), the beneficiaries will be entitled to assert their equitable interest against any assets in his hands which can be shown to represent the trust property originally received. Equity has developed a complex set of rules to enable it to determine whether any such property can be identified in the hands of the stranger, known as the rules of tracing. These rules and their application are examined in detail in Chapter 31.[6]

*Re Diplock*[7] provides an example of the circumstances in which a proprietary claim may be available against the strangers to a trust who have received trust property. The executors of Caleb Diplock had wrongfully distributed his residuary estate amongst various charities.[8] Since the charities were innocent volunteers, who had not provided valuable consideration, they received the money subject to the pre-existing equitable interests of the beneficiaries to whom it should have been allocated. His next of kin were therefore able to claim from the charities any assets that could be shown to represent the trust property by the rules of tracing.

If the stranger who receives trust property in breach of trust has disposed of it, so that no assets remain in his hands which can be said to represent the trust property, the property is said to have been dissipated. Once the trust property has been dissipated it is no longer possible for the beneficiaries to maintain any proprietary claim against the stranger who had received it. However, the stranger may still be subject to a personal liability to make restitution of the value of the property he had received in breach of trust.

## (b) Personal remedies

Where a stranger has participated in the commission of a breach of trust, but has not received any trust property into his hands, it will not be possible for the beneficiaries to seek a proprietary remedy against him. Similarly, if a stranger did received trust property, but it has been dissipated so that no traceable proceeds remain in his hands, the beneficiaries cannot enjoy any proprietary remedy. They will be confined to a personal action for restitution. If the stranger has only partially dissipated the trust property he received, or it is traceable into assets which have fallen in value, a personal action may also be preferred. The personal liability of the stranger who has assisted in the commission of a breach of trust or who has received trust property is by way of an equitable action of account. He is often said to be 'liable to account as a constructive

---

[5] In the context of the equitable doctrine of notice, 'valuable consideration' means money or money's worth, and includes marriage consideration. The consideration need not be adequate and may be nominal. See *Bassett v Nosworthy* (1673) Cas temp Finch 102; *Midland Bank Trust Co Ltd v Green* [1981] AC 513, HL.

[6] Together, in some circumstances, with the common law.     [7] [1948] Ch 465, CA.

[8] The executors acted under the mistaken belief that their power under the will to distribute the residuary estate amongst 'such charitable institutions or other charitable or benevolent object or objects in England' was valid. The court held that it was void as it was not exclusively charitable.

trustee'. In effect the stranger is held liable to account to the trust just as if he had been a properly appointed trustee, even though in fact he was not. In *Polly Peck International plc v Nadir (Asil) (No 2)*[9] Scott LJ described this remedy as 'the in personam constructive trust claim'. The personal nature of the claim can also be seen from cases such as *Re Montagu*[10] and *Lipkin Gorman v Karpnale Ltd*,[11] which are considered below. The equitable liability to account as a constructive trustee is essentially fault-based, so that a stranger will only be required to account if he acted with the requisite degree of fault.

(i)  The personal duty to account

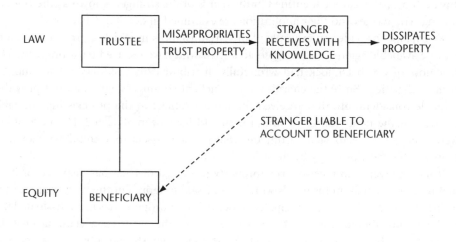

(ii)  Holding the property on constructive trust

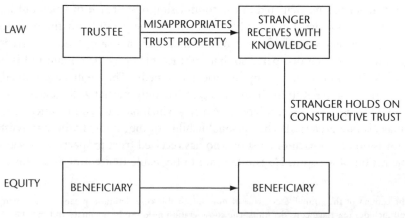

**The contrast between personal and proprietary claims**

9  [1992] 4 All ER 769 at 781.    10  [1987] Ch 264, [1992] 4 All ER 308.
11  [1992] 4 All ER 331, [1987] 1 WLR 987.

## (3) Circumstances in which a stranger will be liable as a constructive trustee

The circumstances in which a stranger may be held liable as a 'constructive trustee' were identified by Lord Selbourne LC in *Barnes v Addy*.[12]

'. . . those who create a trust clothe the trustee with a legal power and control over the trust property, imposing on him a corresponding responsibility. That responsibility may no doubt be extended in equity to others who are not properly trustees, if they are found either making themselves trustees de son tort, or actually participating in any fraudulent conduct of the trustee to the injury of the [beneficiary]. But, on the other hand, strangers are not to be made constructive trustees merely because they act as agents of trustees in transactions within their legal powers, transactions, perhaps of which the Court of Equity may disapprove, unless those agents receive and become chargeable with some part of the trust property, or unless they assist with knowledge in a dishonest and fraudulent design on the part of the trustees . . .'

More modern terminology is now used to describe the three circumstances in which a stranger will be held liable.

### (a) Trustee de son tort

Where a stranger who had not been appointed as a trustee takes it upon himself to act as a trustee, and deals with the trust property accordingly, he will be held liable for any breach of trust that was committed just as if he were in fact a properly appointed trustee.

### (b) Dishonest assistance in a breach of trust

Where a stranger dishonestly participates in a breach of trust committed by the trustees he will be liable to account personally as a constructive trustee for any loss suffered by the trust.

### (c) Knowing/dishonest receipt of trust property

Where a stranger receives trust property, knowing that it is trust property, he will be liable to account as a constructive trustee to the trust for the value of the property received.

## (4) The nomenclature of personal remedies

Whilst the liability of a stranger to a trust has historically been termed 'liability to account as a constructive trustee' the language of constructive trusteeship has recently been subjected to criticism on the grounds of artificiality. In *Paragon Finance plc v Thakerar & Co* Millett LJ considered that it had been unfortunate that such liability was described in this way:

---

[12]  (1874) 9 Ch App 244 at 251–252.

'In such a case the expressions "constructive trust" and "constructive trustee" are mis-leading, for there is no trust and usually no possibility of a proprietary remedy; they are "nothing more than a formula for equitable relief": *Selangor United Rubber Estates Ltd v Craddock (No 3)* [1968] 2 All ER 1073 at 1097 per Ungoed Thomas J.'[13]

Whilst this is certainly true in respect of the liability of a stranger who has dishonestly assisted in a breach of trust, it is questionable whether the criticism applies equally forcefully to the liability of strangers who have dealt with the trust property as a trustee de son tort, or who have knowingly received and misapplied trust property. In such cases the stranger is liable to account because of his conscious misdealing with the trust property. It is not artificial to regard him as a 'constructive trustee', and the language of constructive trusteeship is not operating as a mere formula for equitable relief.[14] In *Dubai Aluminium Co Ltd v Salaam* Lord Millett further suggested that the terminology 'accountable in equity' should replace the terminology 'accountable as a constructive trustee.'[15]

# 2 Stranger who takes it upon himself to act as a trustee

## (1) Definition

A person who has not been appointed a trustee but intermeddles in the administration of a trust by taking it upon himself to act as if he were a trustee, will be held liable as if he were in fact a properly appointed trustee. He is known as a trustee de son tort. The principle was explained by Smith LJ in *Mara v Browne*:

'. . . if one, not being a trustee and not having authority from a trustee, takes upon himself to intermeddle with trust matters or to do acts characteristic of the office of trustee, he may thereby make himself what is called in law a trustee of his own wrong—i.e. a trustee de son tort, or, as it is also termed a constructive trustee.'[16]

More recently, the same essential characteristics were identified by Ungoed-Thomas J in *Selangor United Rubber Estates Ltd v Cradock (No 3)*:

'Those who, though not appointed trustees, take on themselves to act as such and to possess and administer trust property for the beneficiaries, become trustees de son tort. Distinguish-ing features . . . are (a) they do not claim to act in their own right but for the beneficiaries, and (b) their assumption to act is not itself a ground of liability . . . and so their status as trustees precedes the occurrence which may be the subject of a claim against them.'[17]

The principle that an intermeddling stranger may become a trustee de son tort is an application to the law of trusts of the principle that anyone who takes it upon himself to act in a fiduciary capacity will be treated and held accountable as if he in fact held the fiduciary position he assumed. Thus, a person who takes it upon himself to act as an

---

[13] [1999] 1 All ER 400 at 409.
[14] See 'Recipient Liability After Westdeutsche' [1998] Conv. 13 (Jill Martin).
[15] [2003] 2 AC 366.    [16] [1896] 1 Ch 199 at 209.    [17] [1968] 2 All ER 1073 at 1095.

agent for another will be held liable to account to his principal just as if he had been properly appointed.[18] The principle was applied in *Blyth v Fladgate*,[19] where a firm of solicitors, Fladgates, held Exchequer bills which were assets of a marriage settlement. After all three trustees of the settlement had died, the moneys were advanced by the firm on a mortgage at the instigation of the husband. The securities proved to be insufficient and it was held that the partners of the firm were liable to make good the shortfall. The rationale for this was that when the Exchequer bills were sold, the firm (meaning each and every partner) became a constructive trustee of the money. They could not possibly be seen as acting as the agents of the trustees[20] because at that stage there were no trustees. By their actions they had assumed upon themselves the position of trustees and it was their duty to see that the moneys were properly applied. They were therefore liable.[21]

One limitation to the principle seems to be that a person will only be held liable as a trustee de son tort if he had the trust property vested in him or had the right to call for its transfer. This was made clear in *Re Barney*,[22] where Kekewich J held that it was essential to the character of a trustee that 'he should have trust property actually vested in him, or so far under his control that he has nothing to do but require that . . . it should be vested in him', and that 'if that is true of a trustee properly appointed, why is it not also true of a trustee de son tort'.[23] However, it should be noted that he may be using the concept of a trustee de son tort in the wider sense of a constructive trustee rather than the more limited modern usage of an intermeddling stranger.

## (2) Remedies

In *Soar v Ashwell* Lord Esher MR took the view that an intermeddling stranger must be treated, and therefore held liable, as if he were a properly appointed trustee:

'Where a person has assumed, either with or without consent, to act as a trustee of money or other property . . . a Court of Equity will impose upon him all the liabilities of an express trustee . . .'[24]

The prime liability of the express trustee is not to act in breach of trust, and the trustee de son tort will likewise be held personally liable to account for any such breach. In particular, if he has wrongfully transferred or dissipated trust property he will have to account for it to the trust. As already illustrated in *Blyth v Fladgate*,[25] the partners of a firm of solicitors who had become trustees de son tort were held liable to the trust for

---

[18] See *Lyell v Kennedy* (1889) 14 App Cas 437, HL; *English v Dedham Vale Properties Ltd* [1978] 1 WLR 93.
[19] [1891] 1 Ch 337.
[20] A person who receives and deals with trust property as an agent of the trustees will not be held liable as a trustee de son tort when he deals with the property. In *Williams-Ashman v Price and Williams* [1942] Ch 219 Bennett J held that *Mara v Browne* [1896] 1 Ch 199, CA, was authority that 'an agent in possession of money which he knows to be trust money, so long as he acts honestly, is not accountable to the beneficiaries interested in the trust money unless he intermeddles in the trust by doing acts characteristic of a trustee and outside the duties of an agent'. Any liability will be governed by the principle concerned delegation: see Chapter 24.
[21] Following the explanation of the case by Vinelott J in *Re Bell's Indenture* [1980] 3 All ER 425 at 433–435.
[22] [1892] 2 Ch 265.   [23] [1892] 2 Ch 265 at 272–273.   [24] [1893] 2 QB 390 at 394.
[25] [1891] 1 Ch 337.

the loss caused by an investment in a mortgage. If the trustee de son tort has trust property, or property which can be shown to represent the original trust property,[26] in his hands the trust will be able to claim that property as its own. This will be particularly important if the trustee de son tort is insolvent.

# 3 Strangers who assist a breach of trust[27]

## (1) Definition

Where a trustee commits a breach of trust he will be personally liable to compensate the trust for any loss suffered in consequence of his breach. His liability is a primary liability, as he was subject to the trust obligations. However, equity will also hold liable a stranger who participates in a breach of trust by assisting a trustee in action which constitutes a breach. The liability of such an assisting stranger is a secondary liability. The stranger is liable as an accessory to the breach of trust. Such accessory liability may provide the only effective remedy for the beneficiaries if the trustee is insolvent. Equity will hold a stranger who assisted a breach of trust liable to account as a constructive trustee. This was recognised in *Barnes v Addy*[28] where Lord Selbourne stated that the responsibilities and liabilities of a trustee may be 'extended to those who are not properly trustees, if they are found . . . actually participating in any fraudulent conduct of the trustees to the injury of the [beneficiary] trust'. The rationale for the imposition of accessory liability against strangers to a trust was more recently examined by the Privy Council in *Royal Brunei Airlines Sdn Bhd v Tan*,[29] where Lord Nicholls stated:

'Beneficiaries are entitled to expect that those who become trustees will fulfill their obligations. They are also entitled to expect, and this is only a short step further, that those who become trustees will be permitted to fulfill their obligations without deliberate intervention from third parties. They are entitled to expect that third parties will refrain from intentionally intruding in the trustee-beneficiary relationship and thereby hindering a beneficiary from receiving his entitlement in accordance with the terms of the trust instrument. There is here a close analogy with breach of contract. A person who knowingly procures a breach of contract, or knowingly interferes with the due performance of a contract, is liable to the innocent party. The underlying rationale [of accessory liability] is the same.'[30]

The accessory liability may prove particularly important if a misappropriation of trust property was perpetrated by a trustee in breach of trust and a financial institution, such

---

[26] See Chapter 31, where the equitable rules of tracing are examined.

[27] See (1996) 112 LQR 56 (Gardner); A J Oakley, 'The Liberalising Nature of Remedies for Breach of Trust' in Oakley, *Trends in Contemporary Trust Law* (1996), pp 239–247; Elliott and Mitchell, 'Remedies for Dishonest Assistance' (2004) 67 MLR 16.

[28] (1874) 9 Ch App 244 at 251–252.

[29] [1995] 2 AC 378, [1995] 3 All ER 97; (1995) 111 LQR 545 (Harpum); [1995] Conv 339 (Halliwell); (1995) 54 CLJ 505 (Nolan); [1995] RLR 105 (Stevens); [1996] LMCLQ 1 (Birks); (1996) 112 LQR 56 (Gardner); (1997) 60 MLR 443 (Berg).

[30] [1995] 3 All ER 97 at 103–104.

as a bank, was involved in the transaction. For example in *Lipkin Gorman v Karpnale Ltd*[31] Cass, a partner in a firm of solicitors, had used money from the firm's client account to finance his gambling habit. As well as seeking a remedy against the club in which the money had been spent[32] the firm claimed that the bank at which the client account was held was liable as an accessory to the partner's breach of trust. The manager of the bank, which also held Cass's personal account, had been aware that Cass had been cashing cheques at the casino and had warned him that his gambling was not controlled. At first instance it was held that the bank had sufficient knowledge of Cass's misuse of funds to render them liable to account for the money that had been misappropriated. The claim against the bank was, however, subsequently dismissed by the Court of Appeal[33] on the grounds that the bank had not been sufficiently aware that a breach of trust was being committed.

## (2) A personal remedy

A stranger who acts as an accessory to a breach of trust will generally only be subject to a personal liability to account to the trust for the loss suffered in consequence of the breach. Ordinarily he will not have received any trust property, and consequently the beneficiaries will be unable to identify any assets in his hands which could be the subject of a proprietary claim.[34] As has been noted above, it is highly artificial to describe the liability of a stranger who has assisted a breach of trust as 'liability to account as a constructive trustee'. Nor can his liability be characterised as genuinely restitutionary. Since he did not receive any trust property he was not enriched at the expense of the beneficiaries by his assistance. By definition restitution is only available to reverse an unjust enrichment. This was recognised by the Privy Council in *Royal Brunei Airlines Sdn Bhd v Tan*:

'Liability as an accessory is not dependent upon receipt of trust property, It arises even though no trust property has reached the hands of the accessory. It is a form of secondary liability in the sense that it only arises where there has been a breach of trust.'[35]

## (3) Requirements of accessory liability

A stranger will only be held liable as an accessory to a breach of trust if four requirements are satisfied. These requirements were identified by Peter Gibson J in *Baden*

---

[31]  [1992] 4 All ER 331, [1987] 1 WLR 987.      [32]  See below, p 842.

[33]  [1992] 4 All ER 409: on the grounds that the bank could not be liable to account as a constructive trustee unless it was also liable for breach of contract to its customer and that there had been wholly inadequate material on which to base a finding of fraud or dishonesty on the part of the bank manager.

[34]  However, many of the cases concern banks or other financial organisations where the trust property has passed through their hands. See *Baden Delvaux and Lecuit v Société Générale pour Favoriser le Développement du Commerce et de l'Industrie en France SA* [1983] BCLC 325; *Lipkin Gorman v Karpnale Ltd* [1987] 1 WLR 987; *Agip (Africa) Ltd v Jackson* [1990] Ch 265.

[35]  [1995] 3 All ER 97 at 99–100.

*Delvaux v Société Générale*[36] and subjected to significant revision by the Privy Council in *Royal Brunei Airlines Sdn Bhd v Tan*.

## (a) The existence of a trust

A stranger can only be held liable as an accessory to a breach of trust if there was in fact a trust in existence. This requirement is generally uncontroversial. For example, in *Royal Brunei Airlines v Tan* the plaintiffs were an airline which employed a firm to act as their agents for the sale of tickets. Under the contract between the parties, the firm agreed to hold any money received from the sale of tickets on trust for the airline until it was paid over. The defendant was the founder and principal shareholder of the firm. In breach of the terms of the contract the firm, authorised by the defendant, used money received from ticket sales for its own purposes. On the insolvency of the firm the airline claimed that the defendant was liable to account as an accessory to the breach of trust that had been committed by the firm. In these circumstances there was clearly an express trust, thus opening the possibility of accessory liability. There is no need for the defendant to have known of the existence of the trust.[37]

## (b) A breach of trust

A stranger will almost certainly[38] only be liable as an accessory if a breach of trust was committed by a trustee. In *Baden Delvaux v Société Générale*[39] Peter Gibson J had held that a stranger would only be liable if the trustee had assisted in a dishonest and fraudulent design of the trustees.[40] In *Royal Brunei Airlines v Tan*[41] the defendant therefore claimed that he should not be liable as an accessory because the firm, which had misused money held on trust, had not acted fraudulently or dishonestly.[42] As was seen in Chapter 28, a trustee may commit a breach of trust innocently or negligently. The Privy Council rejected this argument and held that there was no need to demonstrate that the trustee had acted dishonestly or fraudulently.[43] All that was required was a breach of trust, irrespective of whether it had been committed honestly or dishonestly. A stranger will therefore be liable as an accessory if he acted with a sufficient degree of personal fault, irrespective of the degree of fault of the trustee in breach:

---

[36] *Baden, Delvaux and Lecuit v Société Générale pour Favoriser le Développement du Commerce et de l'Industrie en France SA* [1983] BCLC 325.

[37] *Barlow Clowes v Eurotrust* [2006] 1 All ER 333.

[38] The cases so far indicate that there must be a breach of trust but, by analogy with the tort of interference with contract, there is no reason why a dishonest assistor could not be liable even if a trustee is protected by a valid trust provision excluding liability.

[39] *Baden, Delvaux and Lecuit v Société Générale pour Favoriser le Développement du Commerce et de l'Industrie en France SA* [1983] BCLC 325.

[40] This position was also supported in *Barnes v Addy* (1874) 9 Ch App 244 and *Belmont Finance Corpn Ltd v Williams Furniture Ltd* [1979] Ch 250.

[41] [1995] 3 All ER 97.

[42] The Privy Council held that, in fact, the company had acted dishonestly since the state of mind of the defendant could be imputed to it: [1995] 3 All ER 97 at 109.

[43] The Privy Council relied on earlier authorities to reach this conclusion: *Fyler v Fyler* (1841) 3 Beav 550; *A-G v Leicester Corpn* (1844) 7 Beav 176; *Eaves v Hickson* (1861) 30 Beav 136. In Canada it has been held that a fraudulent and dishonest breach must have been committed by the trustee: *Air Canada v M & C Travel Ltd* (1993) 108 DLR (4th) 592; *Gold v Rosenberg* (1995) 25 OR (3d) 601.

'... what matters is the state of mind of the third party sought to be made liable, not the state of mind of the trustee. The trustee will be liable in any event for the breach of trust, even if he acted innocently, unless excused by an exemption clause in the trust instrument or relieved by the court. But *his* state of mind is essentially irrelevant to the question whether the *third party* should be made liable to the beneficiaries for the breach of trust. If the liability of the third party is fault-based, what matters is the nature of his fault, not that of the trustee. In this regard dishonesty on the part of the third party would seem to be a sufficient basis for his liability, irrespective of the state of mind of the trustee who is in breach. It is difficult to see why, if the third party dishonestly assisted in a breach, there should be a further prerequisite to his liability, namely that the trustee also must have been acting dishonestly. The alternative view would mean that a dishonest third party is liable if the trustee is dishonest, but if the trustee did not act dishonestly that of itself would excuse a dishonest third party from liability. That would make no sense.'[44]

## (c) Assistance in the breach of trust

A stranger will only be liable as an accessory if he in fact assisted the commission of a breach of trust. In *Royal Brunei Airlines Sdn Bhd v Tan*[45] the defendant had authorised the use of trust money by the firm for its ordinary business purposes, including the paying of salaries and expenses and keeping its bank overdraft down. He had clearly assisted in the commission of the breach. However, where it cannot be shown that the stranger has assisted the breach of trust there will be no grounds for any accessory liability. In *Brinks Ltd v Abu-Saleh (No 3)*[46] the defendant's husband had couriered some of the proceeds of the Brinks-Matt gold robbery to Switzerland. It was claimed that the defendant had knowingly assisted in a breach of trust by accompanying her husband on his trips so as to give the impression that they were enjoying a family holiday, thus cloaking the illegal nature of his activities and making it easier for him to cross borders. Rimer J held that she had not in fact assisted the breach of trust, and that she was not therefore liable to account for the £3m her husband had couriered. He held that she had not participated in the breach because she was not party to the couriering agreements entered by her husband, and he had carried out all elements of the couriering exercise. Her only role had been to provide him with company on the long and tiring drives. In essence, Rimmer J seems to have held that a stranger will only be liable as an accessory if he participates in the breach by performing positive acts of assistance. Mere passive acquiescence in the activity alleged to constitute a breach of trust will thus be insufficient to establish liability. It is submitted that this reasoning is unduly narrow, and that a person should be liable as an accessory whenever his or her conduct passively encourages the commission of a breach of trust, provided that it was dishonest.

## (d) Dishonesty

The equitable liability of a stranger as an accessory to a breach of trust is fault-based.[47] It operates as a species of equitable wrong, similar to a common law tort. Much of the debate over the years has concerned the degree of fault which must be demonstrated

---

[44] [1995] 3 All ER 97 at 102.      [45] [1995] 3 All ER 97.
[46] (1995) Times, 23 October; [1996] Conv 447 (Stevens); (1996) 10 TLI 53 (Oakley).
[47] *Twinsectra v Yardley* [2002] 2 All ER 377 at [107], per Lord Millett.

before an assistor will be held liable as an accessory. Prior to *Royal Brunei Airlines Sdn Bhd v Tan*,[48] this debate was couched in the language of 'knowledge'. In some cases it had been held that a stranger would be liable as a knowing assistor if he had participated in a breach of trust without any actual knowledge but in circumstances where he had been negligent in not realising, or discovering, that he was assisting a breach of trust.[49] However, increasingly it came to be held that a higher standard of fault than mere negligence was required to establish accessory liability. In *Agip (Africa) Ltd v Jackson*[50] Millett J held a firm of accountants liable to account to the plaintiff company because they had knowingly participated in the laundering of money defrauded by its chief accountant.[51] He warned against over-refinement of the shades of knowledge required to establish accessory liability and suggested instead that the assistor must have acted with 'dishonesty'.[52] This higher threshold for liability was adopted by the Court of Appeal in *Lipkin Gorman v Karpnale Ltd*[53] and *Polly Peck International plc v Nadir (Asil) (No 2)*.[54] In *Royal Brunei Airlines Sdn Bhd v Tan*[55] the Privy Council held that accessory liability was founded upon the dishonesty of the assistor.[56] Lord Nicholls explained why the requirement of dishonesty was to be preferred to that of knowledge:

'To inquire . . . whether a person dishonestly assisted in what is later held to be a breach of trust is to ask a meaningful question, which is capable of being given a meaningful answer. That is not always so if the question is posed in terms of knowingly assisted. Framing the question in the latter form all too often leads one into tortious convolutions about the sort of knowledge required, when the truth is that knowingly is inapt as a criterion when applied to the gradually darkening spectrum where the differences are of degree and not kind.'[57]

In *Twinsectra Ltd v Yardley*[58] the House of Lords confirmed that dishonesty was the necessary condition for the imposition of accessory liability, thus affirming the decision in *Royal Brunei Airlines Sdn Bhd v Tan*.

---

[48] [1995] 3 All ER 97.

[49] *Selangor United Rubber Estates Ltd v Cradock (No 3)* [1968] 1 WLR 1555; *Karak Rubber Co Ltd v Burden (No 2)* [1972] 1 WLR 602; *Rowlandson v National Westminster Bank Ltd* [1978] 1 WLR 798; *Baden, Delvaux and Lecuit v Société Générale pour Favoriser le Développement du Commerce et de l'Industrie en France SA* [1983] BCLC 325.

[50] [1990] Ch 265, [1992] 4 All ER 385; (1991) 107 LQR (Sir Peter Millett); affd [1991] Ch 547, [1992] 4 All ER 451; (1991) 50 CLJ 409 (Harpum); [1992] Conv 367 (Goulding); (1992) 12 LS 332 (Norman).

[51] Whilst the Court of Appeal held that the lower negligence threshold was applicable, subsequent cases demonstrate that the approach of Millett J has prevailed. See also *Eagle Trust plc v SBC Securities Ltd* [1992] 4 All ER 488; *Cowan de Groot Properties Ltd v Eagle Trust plc* [1992] 4 All ER 700 at 754.

[52] (1989) 105 LQR 528 (Birks).    [53] [1992] 4 All ER 409, [1989] 1 WLR 1340.

[54] [1992] 4 All ER 769 at 777, per Scott LJ.    [55] [1995] 3 All ER 97.

[56] *Royal Brunei Airlines v Tan* was followed by the Court of Appeal in *Satnam Ltd v Dunlop Hetwood Ltd* [1999] 3 All ER 652 and applied in *Cigna Life Insurance New Zealand Ltd v Westpac Securities Ltd* [1996] 1 NZLR 80.

[57] [1995] 3 All ER 97 at 107.

[58] [2002] 2 All ER 377; [2002] 10 RLR 112 (Rickett); [2002] Con 303 (Kenny) and 387 (Thompson); (2002) 16 TLI 165 (Penner); [2003] Con 398 (Andrews); (2004) 120 LQR 208 (Yeo). See also *Barlow Clowes v Eurotrust* [2006] 1 All ER 333.

## (4) The meaning of 'dishonesty'

Whilst it is easy to specify that the dishonesty of the assistor is the requisite degree of fault to establish accessory liability, it is more difficult to identify precisely what conduct will be characterised as dishonest, and whether the test is objective or subjective. In *Royal Brunei Airlines Sdn Bhd v Tan* the Privy Council gave some indications as to how the concept should be applied. The nature of dishonesty was then thoroughly examined by the House of Lords in *Twinsectra Ltd v Yardley* and most recently re-examined by the Privy Council in *Barlow Clowes International Ltd (in liquidation) v Eurotrust.*[59]

### (a) Dishonesty an objective criterion for liability

There has been much debate in the years since the decision in *Royal Brunei Airlines Sdn Bhd v Tan* as to the precise meaning of dishonesty, and especially whether it is objective or subjective in nature, and therefore whether the defendant must have been consciously aware that he was acting wrongly. In *Royal Brunei Airlines v Tan* Lord Nicholls was at pains to explain that dishonesty provided an objective criterion for assessment of the defendant's conduct:

'Whatever may be the position in some criminal or other contexts . . . in the context of the accessory liability principle acting dishonestly, or with a lack of probity, which is synonymous, means simply not acting as an honest person would in the circumstances. This is an objective standard. At first sight this might seem surprising. Honesty has a connotation of subjectivity, as distinct from the objectivity of negligence. Honesty, indeed, does have a strong subjective element in that it is a description of a type of conduct assessed in the light of what a person actually knew at the time, as distinct from what a reasonable person would have known or appreciated. Further, honesty and its counterpart dishonesty are mostly concerned with adverting conduct, not inadvertent conduct. Carelessness is not dishonesty. Thus for the most part dishonesty is to be equated with conscious impropriety.'[60]

He held that these inherently subjective characteristics of dishonesty did not mean that individuals were free to set their own standards. Honesty is not an optional scale, with higher and lower values according to the moral standards of each individual. Therefore, a person who knowingly appropriates a person's property will not escape a finding of dishonesty simply because he sees nothing wrong in such behaviour.[61] He considered that in the majority of circumstances there would be little difficulty identifying how an honest person would behave. For example, he stated:

'Unless there is a very good and compelling reason, an honest person does not participate in a transaction if he knows it involves a misapplication of trust assets to the detriment of the beneficiaries. Nor does an honest person in such a case deliberately close his eyes and ears, or deliberately not ask questions, lest he learn something he would rather not know, and then proceed regardless.'[62]

He also indicated that any assessment of dishonesty would have to be contextual, taking

---

[59] [2006] 1 All ER 333.      [60] [1995] 3 All ER 97 at 106.
[61] Ibid, at 106. See also *Walker v Stones* [2000] All ER 412 at 443 per Sir Christopher Slade.
[62] Ibid, at 106.

account of the circumstances of the transaction which constituted a breach of trust and the personal attributes of the assistor, including his experience and intelligence,[63] and that strangers should not generally be liable as assistors if they had acted negligently.[64] Strangers who owe a duty of care to the trust (for example advisers, consultants, bankers and agents) are liable in tort if they fail to exercise reasonable skill and care, and there is no compelling reason to impose any additional liability in equity.

### (b) Dishonesty a subjective criterion for liability?

In *Twinsectra Ltd v Yardley* the House of Lords subjected the comments of Lord Nicholls to careful scrutiny in order to identify the essential elements of dishonesty, and made comments which appeared to require a subjective awareness of wrongdoing on the part of the defendant. Lord Hutton identified three ways in which the standard of dishonesty may be applied, varying by whether the concept is viewed subjectively or objectively. First, dishonesty may operate as a purely subjective standard, 'whereby a person is only dishonest if he transgresses his own standard of honesty, even if that standard is contrary to that of reasonable and honest people'.[65] This purely subjective standard has been rejected by the courts, for example in *Walker v Stones* Sir Christopher Slade LJ considered that a solicitor-trustee would have acted dishonestly even though he held an 'honest belief' that his actions were in the best interests of his beneficiaries if his belief was 'so unreasonable that, by any objective standard, no reasonable solicitor-trustee could have thought that what he did or agreed to do was for the benefit of the beneficiaries'.[66] Secondly, dishonesty may operate as a purely objective standard, 'whereby a person acts dishonestly if his conduct is dishonest by the ordinary standards of reasonable and honest people'.[67] Finally dishonesty may operate in a manner which combines elements of objectivity and subjectivity. Lord Hutton explained:

'Thirdly, there is a standard which combines an objective and a subjective test, and which requires that before there can be a finding of dishonesty it must be established that the defendant's conduct was dishonest by the standards of reasonable and honest people and that he himself realised that by those standards his conduct was dishonest. I will term this "the combined test".'[68]

The majority of the House of Lords held that this combined test should be adopted as the standard of dishonesty necessary for the imposition of accessory liability. Lord Millett dissented in favour of the adoption of a purely objective test which does not require the defendant to have realised that he was acting dishonestly.

### (c) The meaning of dishonesty clarified as a primarily objective criterion for liability

The test adopted by the majority in *Twinsectra Ltd v Yardley* was thus ambiguous, and open to a possible interpretation whereby a defendant would not be regarded as dishonest if he had acted dishonestly according to the objective standards of honest men, but had personally set himself a different standard of honesty such that he was not

---

[63] Ibid, at 107.    [64] Ibid, at 108.    [65] [2002] 2 All ER 377 at [27].
[66] [2000] 4 All ER 412 at 443.    [67] [2002] 2 All ER 377 at [27].    [68] Ibid, at [27].

consciously aware that his conduct would be regarded as dishonest by ordinary standards.[69] In the light of this ambiguity and uncertainty the exact meaning and application of the test of dishonesty propounded by the House of Lords in in *Twinsectra Ltd v Yardley* was clarified by the Privy Council in *Barlow Clowes International Ltd v Eurotrust International Ltd.*[70] The central issue in this case was whether liability on the basis of dishonesty required the court to conduct an inquiry into the defendant's views as to what the ordinary standards of honesty would be, so as to then determine whether he had consciously reflected that he was transgressing them. Lord Hoffman stated that, although some of the comments made in *Twinsectra Ltd v Yardley* might have contained an 'element of ambiguity', they had not intended to be different from the principles stated in *Royal Brunei Airlines Sdn Bhd v Tan.*[71] Lord Hoffman therefore explained that Lord Hutton, who had stated in *Twinsectra v Yardley* that a defendant should not escape liability 'because he sets his own standards of honesty and does not regard as dishonest what he knows would offend the normally accepted standards of honest conduct',[72] had not intended to impose a requirement that the defendant must have had reflections about what the normally accepted standards were. He further indicated that his own comments in *Twinsectra Ltd v Yardley* that a dishonest state of mind meant 'consciousness that one is transgressing ordinary standards of honest behavior'[73] were only intended 'to require consciousness of those elements of the transaction which make participation transgress ordinary standards of honest behaviour.'[74] They did not, therefore, 'also require him to have thought about what those standards were.'[75] The Privy Council therefore accepted the following statement of the trial judge as a correct statement of the law:

'. . . liability for dishonest assistance requires a dishonest state of mind on the part of the person who assists in a breach of trust. Such a state of mind may consist in knowledge that the transaction is one in which he cannot honestly participate (for example, a misappropriation of other people's money), or it may consist in suspicion combined with a conscious decision not to make inquiries which might result in knowledge[76] . . . Although a dishonest state of mind is a subjective mental state, the standard by which the law determines whether it is dishonest is objective. If by ordinary standards a defendant's mental state would be characterised as dishonest, it is irrelevant that the defendant judges by different standards.'[77]

## (d) The application of the criterion of dishonesty

In the light of the most recent cases, it therefore appears that a defendant will be held liable if he had clear reasons to be suspicious about a transaction, and consciously ignored these suspicions, even though he was not consciously aware that by so doing he was transgressing ordinary standards. In *Barlow Clowes v Eurotrust*[78] the defendant, Mr Henwood, had been one of the principal directors of an Isle of Man company

---

[69] The Court of Appeal of New Zealand expressed obiter reservations about the subjective element of the combined test in *US International Marketing Ltd v National Bank of New Zealand Ltd,* 28 October 2003; (2004) 120 LQR 208 (Yeo).

[70] [2006] 1 All ER 333.     [71] [1995] 2 AC 378.     [72] [1995] 2 AC 378.     [73] Ibid, at [20].

[74] [2006] 1 All ER 339 at [16].     [75] Ibid.

[76] Citing *Manifest Shipping Co Ltd v Uni-Polaris Insurance Co Ltd* [2001] 1 All ER 743; [2003] 1 AC 469.

[77] [2006] 1 All ER 333 at [10].     [78] [2006] 1 All ER 33 [2006] Conv 188 (Ryan).

providing offshore financial services, which paid away money that had been misappropriated from investors by Peter Clowes and one of his associates, a Mr Cramer. The Privy Council held that there was sufficient evidence to conclude that Mr Henwood had acted dishonestly. The evidence indicated that he had been made fully aware of the Barlow Clowes business, such that it must have come home to him that there was a real possibility that the large amount of money being put through the company could well be the investors' money. He also knew of previous dishonesty by Mr Cramer, and told lies in evidence, denying that he had any knowledge of the Barlow Clowes business and the money laundering transactions which passed through the company. In contrast in *Twinsectra Ltd v Yardley* the defendant solicitor was held not to have acted dishonestly. The claimant lenders, had advanced £1m to a firm of solicitors subject to an undertaking that the money would be retained until it was applied in the acquisition of property by the borrower, Yardley. In breach of this undertaking the firm of solicitors subsequently paid the money to Leach, another solicitor who was acting for Yardley in respect of the transaction. Leach then failed to ensure that the money was utilised solely for the acquisition of property in accordance with the undertaking, and Yardley used £358,000 for other purposes. At first instance Carnwath J held that the money had not been held on trust, and that Leach had not acted dishonestly, although he had been 'misguided'. Whilst he had been aware of all the facts he had 'simply shut his eyes to the problems' and had considered it a matter for the other solicitors whether he could release the money to his client. The Court of Appeal reversed these findings, holding that Leach had acted dishonestly because he had shut his eyes to the rights of Twinsectra. The House of Lords held by a majority that Leach had not acted dishonestly. Lords Hutton and Hoffman considered it unfortunate that Carnwath J had referred to Leach as having shut his eyes to the obvious, but considered that this alone did not render him dishonest. Instead the crucial question was whether 'Leach realised that his action was dishonest by the standards of responsible and honest solicitors'.[79] The majority held that Carnwath J had not applied an incorrect test, and there was no justification for taking the exceptional step of reversing a finding by the trial judge on a question of fact, as he had had the advantage of seeing the party give evidence in the witness box. In *Barlow Clowes v Eurotrust*[80] the Privy Council affirmed the decision in *Twinsectra Ltd v Yardley*, but seemed to do so for very different reasons than those that had been given in the judgments. Lord Hoffman explained:

'On the facts of the *Twinsectra* case, neither the judge who acquitted Mr Leach of dishonesty nor the House undertook any inquiry into the views of the defendant solicitor Mr Leach about ordinary standards of honest behaviour. He had received on behalf of his client a payment from another solicitor who he knew had given an undertaking to pay it to Mr Leach's client only for a particular use. But the other solicitor had paid the money to Mr Leach without requiring any undertaking. The judge found that he was not dishonest because he honestly believed that the undertaking did not, so to speak, run with the money and that, as between him and his client, he held it for his client unconditionally. He was therefore bound to pay it upon his client's instructions without restriction on its use. The

---

[79] [2002] 2 All ER 377 at [49], per Lord Hutton. See also at [20], per Lord Hoffman.
[80] [2006] 1 All ER 333.

majority of the House of Lords considered that a solicitor who held this view of the law, even though he knew all the facts, was not by normal standards dishonest.'[81]

It is hard to avoid the conclusion that this is a re-rationalisation of the decision. The Privy Council appears to claim that the House of Lords held that Leach was honest because his conduct would not have been regarded as dishonest by the objective criteria of 'normal standards' for solicitors. In fact the House of Lords repeatedly stressed that he was not dishonest because he had not subjectively realised that his conduct was dishonest by normal standards. Since the rationale given for the decision in *Twinsectra* is dubious, it appears that the Privy Council in *Barlow Clowes v Eurotrust* has changed the test for dishonesty without admitting that the House of Lords had been mistaken in the earlier case. Nevertheless the clarification of the requirements of dishonesty, and the reassertion of a primarily objective understanding, is to be welcomed.

## (5) Alternatives to dishonesty as the criteria for accessory liability[82]

Whilst *Royal Brunei Airlines Sdn Bhd v Tan* and *Twinsectra Ltd v Yardley* have firmly established dishonesty as the touch-stone for accessory liability in English law, alternative approaches have been adopted in other jurisdictions, and Lord Millett has advocated a return to the concept of 'knowing assistance' in his dissenting judgment in the latter case.

### (a) Unconscionability

Whilst English law had moved from a requirement of knowledge to one of dishonesty, the courts in New Zealand[83] have held that the accessory liability should be seen as rooted in the concept of 'unconscionability'. In *Powell v Thompson* Thomas J stated:[84]

'In turning to the knowing assistance class of cases, the focus of the court's scrutiny shifts squarely to the conduct of the third party. Was it unconscionable? The key question is whether his or her behaviour was such that the obligations of the trust should be imposed upon them. The language of imposition is now apt. These trust obligations are imposed, not because the third party has received and benefited from the receipt of property which is subject to a trust, but because they deserve to be treated as if they were a trustee in respect of the trust in issue. They too, along with the trustee, can be called to account for the abuse of the trust.'

He rejected the English authorities which had held that mere negligence was insufficient to ground accessory liability,[85] stating that there was no sound reason why the negligent conduct of a third party who assisted the trustee to commit a breach of trust should be put beyond the purview of unconscionable conduct which should attract the burden of trusteeship.[86] Subsequent cases considered that a higher threshold of fault

---

[81] Ibid, at [17].    [82] See also [2003] Con 398 (Andrews).    [83] See [1991] NZLJ 90.
[84] [1991] 1 NZLR 597 at 610.
[85] *Carl-Zeiss-Stiftung v Herbert Smith & Co (No 2)* [1969] 2 Ch 276, CA; *Re Montagu's Settlement Trusts* [1987] Ch 264.
[86] [1991] 1 NZLR 597 at 612.

should be required to establish liability.[87] In *Equiticorp v Hawkins*[88] Wylie J agreed that liability was founded on the principle of 'unconscionability' but felt unable to accept that mere negligence, or constructive knowledge, would be sufficient:

'In principle I accept the test of unconscionability . . . But it is on the standards by which unconscionability is to be measured that my view differs from his. I adhere to the concept of want of probity. In my opinion mere carelessness, neglect or oversight, which is not wilful or reckless, is not unconscionable . . . I prefer the more conservative approach indicated by so many judges in England since *Baden Delvaux* . . .'[89]

In *Royal Brunei Airlines Sdn Bhd v Tan*[90] the Privy Council considered the viability of unconscionability as a touchstone for liability but felt that it was either synonymous with dishonesty, or if not, that it was too vague:

'. . . unconscionable is not a word in everyday use by non-lawyers. If it is to be used in this context, and if it is to be the touchstone for liability as an accessory, it is essential to be clear on what, *in this context*, unconscionable *means*. If unconscionable means no more than dishonesty, then dishonesty is the preferable label. If unconscionable means something different, it must be said that it is not clear what that something different is. Either way, therefore, the term is better avoided in this context.'[91]

## (b) Knowing assistance

As has been noted already, Lord Millett delivered a dissenting opinion in *Twinsectra Ltd v Yardley*[92] rejecting the 'combined test' for dishonesty adopted by the majority in favour of a purely objective test. He gave three reasons for preferring such an objective approach:

'(1) consciousness of wrongdoing is an aspect of mens rea and an appropriate condition of criminal liability: it is not an appropriate condition of civil liability. This generally results from negligent or intentional conduct. For the purpose of civil liability, it should not be necessary that the defendant realised that his conduct was dishonest; it should be sufficient that it constituted intentional wrongdoing. (2) The objective test is in accordance with Lord Selbourne LC's statement in *Barnes v Addy* and traditional doctrine. This taught that a person who knowingly participates in the misdirection of money is liable to compensate the injured party. While negligence is not sufficient condition of liability, intentional wrongdoing is. Such conduct is culpable and falls below the standards of honesty adopted by ordinary people. (3) The claim for 'knowing assistance' is the equitable counterpart of the economic torts. They are intentional torts; negligence is not sufficient and dishonesty is not necessary. Liability depends on knowledge. A requirement of subjective dishonesty introduces an unnecessary and unjustified distinction between the elements of the equitable claim and those of the tort of wrongful interference with the performance of a contract.'[93]

In his opinion the adoption of such an objective standard for liability should lead to a

---

87  *Equiticorp Industries Group Ltd v Hawkins* [1991] 3 NZLR 700; *Marshall Futures Ltd v Marshall* [1992] 1 NZLR 316.
88  [1991] 3 NZLR 700.    89  Ibid, at 728.    90  [1995] 3 All ER 97.    91  Ibid, at 108.
92  [2002] 2 All ER 377.    93  Ibid, at [127].

return to the traditional nomenclature of the equitable claim as liability for 'knowing assistance':

'For my own part, I have no difficulty in equating the knowing mishandling of money with dishonest conduct. But the introduction of dishonesty is an unnecessary distraction, and conducive to error. Many judges would be reluctant to brand a professional man as dishonest where he was unaware that honest people would consider his conduct to be so. If the condition of liability is intentional wrongdoing and not conscious dishonesty as understood in the criminal courts, I think we should return to the traditional description of this head of equitable liability as arising from "knowing assistance".'[94]

It seems somewhat ironic that Lord Millet, who had begun the task of cutting the Gordian knot of 'knowledge' and replacing it with 'dishonesty' in *Agip (Africa) Ltd v Jackson* should now seek a return to the earlier terminology. It also appears to be self contradictory to advocate abandonment of the language of dishonesty to avoiding slurring the reputations of professionals who have committed intentional wrongdoing, whilst at the same time stating that such intentional wrongdoing is 'culpable and falls below the objective standards of honesty adopted by ordinary people'.

# 4 Strangers who receive trust property in breach of trust

The prime obligation of trustees is to allocate the trust property to those entitled to it under the terms of the trust. If they misappropriate the trust property and transfer it to third party strangers to the trust they will clearly have acted in breach. However, if the trustees are insolvent, any remedy which the beneficiaries might be able to maintain against them for breach of trust will be useless as a means of restoring the trust fund. In such circumstances the beneficiaries may instead seek a remedy against the stranger who received the trust property. A stranger who has received trust property may be liable as a constructive trustee, and the beneficiaries may be able to pursue either proprietary or personal remedies against him.

## (1) Remedies against a stranger who has received trust property

### (a) Proprietary remedies

Where property is subject to a pre-existing trust, the beneficiaries are already entitled to the equitable ownership of the trust property. They enjoy a proprietary interest in the trust fund which is capable of enduring through changes in the legal ownership thereof. Whilst the trustees are able to transfer the legal title to the trust property, mere transfer of the legal title does not defeat the interests of the beneficiaries. Their equitable interest in the trust property will be preserved against a transferee of the legal title unless the transferee was a bona fide purchaser for value without notice. Thus, if trust property is

---

[94] Ibid, at [134].

transferred by trustees to a stranger in breach of trust, the beneficiaries may be able to assert a proprietary interest in such of the property (or its traceable proceeds[95]) as remains in the hands of the stranger. If the stranger is insolvent, any assets identifiable in his hands as representing the trust property will continue to belong to the trust in equity, and they will not therefore be available to satisfy the claims of his creditors.

## (b) Personal remedies

Where a stranger to a trust has received trust property but no longer retains it (or any traceable proceeds) in his hands, the beneficiaries will not longer be able to assert any proprietary claim against him. The trust property has been dissipated. However, in such circumstances the stranger may be required to account as a constructive trustee for the value of the trust property he had received. The obligation to account in equity operates as a personal restitutionary remedy.[96] The stranger who received the trust property in breach of trust was thereby unjustly enriched, and is required to make restitution to the trust of the value of his enrichment, i.e. the value of the trust property he received. The personal equitable liability of a stranger to account for the value of trust property he received is, like the liability of an accessory to a breach of trust examined above, a fault-based liability. There has been a great deal of controversy as to the requisite threshold of fault necessary before a stranger will be required to account for the value of the property he received. Some cases have indicated that a high degree of fault should be required, whereas others have argued that the recipients of trust property should be subject to a strict liability to make restitution. Beneficiaries may also prefer to seek restitution by way of a personal equitable account if a stranger has only partially dissipated the trust property he received.

## (2) Proprietary remedies where a stranger to a trust retains trust property or its traceable proceeds

A stranger who receives trust property transferred in breach of trust will not gain priority over the equitable interests of the beneficiaries unless he was a bona fide purchaser for value without notice. The interests of the beneficiaries will therefore be preserved if the stranger was a volunteer who had provided no consideration in return for receipt of the trust property, irrespective of whether he was aware of the existence of the trust or not. If the stranger had provided valuable consideration, the interests of the beneficiaries will only be preserved if he purchased the property with notice that it was subject to a trust. In essence, the burden falls to the recipient of trust property to demonstrate that his conscience was not affected so as to require him to observe the trust. He will only be able to do this if he can satisfy all the elements of the equitable doctrine of notice.

---

[95] See Chapter 31.

[96] This was made clear by Megarry V-C in *Re Montagu's Settlement Trusts* where he described the imposition of liability to account as a constructive trustee as imposing 'a personal obligation on a man' in contrast to the equitable doctrine of notice which determines 'the burdens on property': [1987] Ch 264 at 272–273.

## (a) Stranger was a volunteer

A stranger who receives trust property as an innocent volunteer will hold it subject to the beneficiaries' pre-existing equitable interest, irrespective of whether he had knowledge that it was trust property. The beneficiaries will be able to demand that he returns it or its traceable proceeds. As Lord Browne-Wilkinson observed in *Westdeutsche Landesbank Girozentrale Bank v Islington London Borough Council*:

'Even if the [third party recipient] is not aware that what he has received is trust property [the beneficiary] is entitled to assert his title in that property.'[97]

The preservation of the beneficiaries' proprietary rights to the trust property is not therefore determined by the fault of the recipient, and it provides extremely important protection of their interests. In *Re Diplock*[98] the executors of a will transferred a testator's residuary estate to charities in the belief that valid charitable bequests had been made. As the recipient charities were innocent volunteers, who had provided no consideration in return for the gifts received, the Court of Appeal held that beneficiaries under the will were entitled to recover any trust property, or its traceable proceeds, remaining in their hands. Where the recipient of trust property was an innocent volunteer, the beneficiaries' proprietary interests therein will be preserved in any asset identifiable in his hands by the rules of tracing, but he will not be subject to a personal liability to account as a constructive trustee. As Megarry V-C explained in *Re Montagu's Settlement Trusts*:

'Suppose . . . a trustee transfers trust property to a person who takes it in all innocence, believing that he is entitled to it as a beneficiary . . . He cannot claim to be a purchaser for value without notice, for he is a mere volunteer. If when the truth emerges he still has the property he must restore it, whereas if he no longer has either the property or its traceable proceeds, he is under no liability, unless he has become a constructive trustee.'[99]

As will be seen below, liability as a constructive trustee is imposed only if the stranger had received the trust property with the requisite degree of fault. The position of an innocent volunteer who has received trust property without fault therefore clearly highlights the dichotomy between the proprietary and personal remedies which may be available against a stranger who receives trust property.[100]

## (b) Stranger provided valuable consideration

A stranger who acquires trust property for valuable consideration will still hold it subject to the pre-existing equitable interest of the beneficiaries if, at the time he acquired it, he had sufficient knowledge that it was trust property to affect his conscience. He is not protected by the equitable doctrine of notice and must yield priority to the beneficiaries. If he still possesses the property received (or its traceable proceeds[101]) he will hold it on constructive trust for the beneficiaries. The beneficiaries' equitable interests will be preserved if the purchaser acquired the trust property with actual, implied or constructive notice of the existence of the trust. Such constructive notice

---

[97] [1996] AC 669 at 707.    [98] [1948] Ch 465, CA.    [99] [1987] Ch 264 at 271.
[100] See Birks, *Introduction to the law of Restitution* (1985), pp 411–412 and 439–447.
[101] See Chapter 31.

includes notice of everything that he would have known about the property if he had made all the inspections and investigations expected of a reasonably prudent man of business.[102] As Millett J stated in *Macmillan Inc v Bishopsgate Investment Trust plc*:

'In English law notice ... includes not only actual notice (including wilful blindness or contrived ignorance, where the purchaser deliberately abstains from an inquiry in order to avoid learning the truth) but also constructive notice, that is to say notice of such facts as he would have discovered if he had taken proper measures to investigate them.'[103]

This amounts to a negligence standard, so that a purchaser will be affixed with constructive notice if he negligently failed to realise that the property was trust property. It is important to note that, whilst this negligence standard of constructive notice is sufficient to prevent a purchaser acquiring trust property free from the equitable interest of the beneficiaries, it is insufficient to fix the purchaser with a liability to account as a constructive trustee for the property he received. As Megarry V-C observed in *Re Montagu's Settlement Trusts*:

'... one has to be very careful to distinguish the notice that is relevant in the doctrine of purchase without notice from the knowledge that suffices for the imposition of a constructive trust.'[104]

Although the doctrine of constructive notice might seem to place a very heavy burden upon a purchaser of property to satisfy himself that it was not subject to a trust, in reality the extent of inquiries necessary to discharge that burden will vary with the nature of the property concerned and the circumstances of the transaction. Whilst a purchaser of land is required to make comprehensive investigations into the title of the vendor there has been a reluctance to carry a similarly onerous requirement into commercial transactions, where the speed of transfer does not permit such extensive pre-acquisition inquiries.[105] In *Macmillan Inc v Bishopsgate Investment Trust plc*[106] Millett J was reluctant to impose an onerous duty to investigate title to shares offered for sale when commercial custom and practice did not require close investigation of the transferor's title. He therefore held that banks which had acquired shares which were held on trust for the plaintiff, having been wrongly transferred as part of the attempt to support the ailing Maxwell business empire, were not affixed with constructive notice because they had not acted with actual knowledge or suspicion that the transferee was not the beneficial owner.[107] In *El Ajou v Dollar Land Holdings plc (No 1)*[108] he had cautioned that a commercial party was not expected to be unduly suspicious.[109]

---

[102] See types (iv) and (v) of knowledge categorised by Peter Gibson J in *Baden Delvaux and Lecuit v Société Générale pour Favoriser le Développement du Commerce et de l'Industrie en France SA* [1983] BCLC 325. See also *Northern Bank Ltd v Henry* [1981] IR 1.

[103] [1995] 3 All ER 747 at 769.

[104] [1987] Ch 264, [1992] 4 All ER 308 at 324–325, citing the Court of Appeal in *Re Diplock* [1948] Ch 465 at 478–479.

[105] See *Manchester Trust v Furness* [1895] 2 QB 539; *Greer v Downs Supply Co* [1927] 2 KB 28.

[106] [1995] 3 All ER 747

[107] [1995] 3 All ER 747 at 780–781. See: N Gegal 'Cross-Border Security Enforcement, Restitution and Priorities' Chapter 7 in Rose (ed), *Restitution and Banking Law* (1998), pp 112–119.

[108] [1993] 3 All ER 717.      [109] Ibid, at 739.

## (c)  Stranger was a bona fide purchaser

Where trust property is received by a stranger to the trust who was a bona fide purchaser for value without knowledge of the existence of the trust (whether actual or constructive), the stranger will acquire the property free from any interests of the beneficiaries. They will no longer be able to maintain any proprietary claim to the erstwhile trust property (or its proceeds) in the stranger's hands.

# (3)  Personal remedies against a stranger who received trust property

## (a)  A stranger who received trust property may be required to account for its value as a constructive trustee

As was noted above, if a stranger receives trust property in breach of trust and subsequently dissipates it so that there are no traceable proceeds in his hands, the beneficiaries of the trust will not be able to pursue a proprietary claim against him. They may, however, be entitled to seek a personal remedy requiring him to return to the trust the value of the property he received. This remedy is restitutionary, in that it requires him to restore the enrichment he received at the expense of the beneficiaries, who were entitled to the property under the trust. If the trust property has been partially dissipated the beneficiaries may likewise seek a personal remedy in respect of the value of the property which has been dissipated. The remedy by which such restitution is effected is the imposition of an equitable duty to account as a constructive trustee. Equity requires a stranger who has received trust property to restore equivalent value to the trust fund if he has wrongfully dissipated it. His liability is fault-based and rooted in equitable notions of conscience. Unless the stranger was aware that the property he received was subject to a trust he was entitled to treat it as his own, for example by disposing of it, consuming it on services which leave no traceable end product, or transferring it to others. His conscience will only be affected if he knew that the property was subject to a trust, in which case he will have become subject to an obligation to preserve it for the beneficiaries. As Lord Browne-Wilkinson stated in *Westdeutsche Landesbank Girozentrale v Islington London Borough Council*:

'Since the equitable jurisdiction to enforce trusts depends upon the conscience of the holder of the legal interest being affected, he cannot be a trustee of the property if and so long as he is ignorant of the facts alleged to affect his conscience, i.e. until he is aware that he is intended to hold the property for the benefit of others in the case of an express or implied trust, or, in the case of a constructive trust, of the factors which are alleged to affect his conscience.'[110]

This seems to mean that a recipient of trust property will not be subject to a duty to preserve the trust fund unless and until he knew that it was subject to a trust. If he dissipates the property after becoming aware that it was trust property he acts in breach of his duty to preserve the trust fund, which is imposed by equity because he is a constructive trustee. He will therefore be liable to account to the beneficiaries. As was noted above the language of liability to account as a constructive trustee has been

---

[110]  [1996] AC 669 at 705.

criticised on the grounds of artificiality. Whilst this criticism is admittedly accurate in the case of the liability of strangers who have assisted in a breach of trust, it is less justified in the case of the liability of strangers who receive trust property. Their liability derives from the fact that they held the property on trust for the beneficiaries and failed to carry out their duties as trustee.

## (b) Examples where a personal remedy was claimed against a stranger who had received trust property

The operation of the personal liability to account can be illustrated by four leading cases. In *Re Montagu's Settlement Trusts*[111] the beneficiaries of a trust sought to render a stranger liable to account for the value of trust property he had received and subsequently dissipated. In 1923 the tenth Duke of Manchester promised to create a trust of the chattels to which he would become entitled on the death of the ninth Duke. The trustees were supposed to draw up an inventory of such chattels, but failed to do so. After the death of the ninth Duke in 1947 they released all the chattels to the tenth Duke, who disposed of a number of them during his lifetime. On the death of the tenth Duke in 1977 the eleventh Duke claimed that his estate was liable to account for the value of the items which had been sold. As the tenth Duke had received the chattels as a volunteer he had received them subject to the trust because he was not a bona fide purchaser. His estate was therefore required to return any remaining chattels or their traceable proceeds. However, his estate was only liable to account for the value of the chattels which had been sold if the tenth Duke had sold them with knowledge that they were subject to the 1923 settlement. Megarry V-C held that, in the circumstances, the Duke had not known that the chattels were subject to the trust when he had disposed of them. In *Lipkin Gorman v Karpnale Ltd*[112] Norman Cass was a partner in a firm of solicitors who used some £223,000 from the firm's client account to finance his gambling at the Playboy Club. The firm subsequently sought to recover the money that had been paid to the club. It alleged that the club was liable to account as a constructive trustee for the money received, which was no longer identifiable by the rules of tracing because it had become mixed with its other receipts. It was held that the club had not received the money with sufficient knowledge that it was subject to a trust to render it liable to account as a constructive trustee. In *Eagle Trust plc v SBC Securities Ltd*[113] the defendants had received some £13.5m from the plaintiff company through the fraud of its chief executive as part of the underwriting of a rights issue or cash alternative in the course of a takeover. It claimed that the defendants were liable to account for what they had received in equity because they had received it knowing that it had been misappropriated. It was held that the defendants had not received the property with sufficient knowledge to render them liable as constructive trustees. In the most recent case of *BCCI (Overseas) Ltd v Akindele*[114] the liquidators of BCCI claimed that an investor was liable to account as a constructive trustee for over $16 million which he had received in performance of an investment agreement he had entered with a company controlled by the BCCI group, purportedly to buy and sell shares in BCCI, which was alleged to have

---

[111]  [1987] Ch 264.       [112]  [1992] 4 All ER 331, [1987] 1 WLR 987.       [113]  [1992] 4 All ER 488.
[114]  [2001] Ch 437.

been a sham. Although the agreement was not found to have been a sham, the payments were held to have been procured in consequence of a fraudulent breach of fiduciary duty by directors of BCCI, and they were therefore impressed with a constructive trust. As such the investor had received trust property. The Court of Appeal held, however, that he was not personally liable to account for the trust money he had received because he had not acted 'unconscionably'. He had not been aware of the internal arrangements within BCCI which had rendered the payment a breach of fiduciary duty. These four cases clearly illustrate that the duty to account as a constructive trustee is a personal remedy, available against a person who has received property that he knew was trust property, with which he has subsequently dealt in a manner inconsistent with his duty to observe the trust. They also show how difficult it can be to establish liability in practice.

## (c) Fault required to render a recipient of trust property liable to account

There is currently a great deal of debate, which foments inevitable uncertainty, regarding the requirements which must be satisfied before a recipient of trust property will be held personally liable to account for the value of what he received. In his dissenting opinion in *Twinsectra Ltd v Yardley*, Lord Millett recently asserted that the personal liability of a recipient was not founded upon fault:

'Liability for "knowing receipt" is receipt-based. It does not depend on fault. The cause of action is restitutionary and is available only where the defendant received or applied the money in breach of trust for his own use and benefit. There is no basis for requiring actual knowledge of the breach of trust, let alone dishonesty, as a condition of liability. Constructive notice is sufficient, and may not even be necessary. There is powerful academic support for the proposition that the liability of the recipient is the same as in other cases of restitution, that is to say strict but subject to a change of position defence.'[115]

However these obiter comments are inconsistent with the tenor of the leading judgments of the House of Lords and Court of Appeal which have consistently held that the equitable obligation to account as a constructive trustee for the value of property received in breach of trust is founded upon the fault of the recipient, and in only one exceptional situation have the courts found that liability should be strict. As Lord Browne-Wilkinson stated in *Westdeutsche Landesbank Girozentrale v Islington London Borough Council*:

'. . . unless [the recipient of trust property] has the requisite degree of knowledge he is not personally liable to account as trustee.'[116]

In the four cases discussed above, this crucial element was found to be lacking, demonstrating how difficult it can be to establish entitlement to a personal remedy.

The most controversial issue in relation to the personal liability to account has concerned the degree of fault required to establish liability. It is clear that the level of fault sufficient to found a personal liability to account as a constructive trustee is not synonymous with the element of notice which will determine whether a recipient of

[115] [2002] 2 All ER 377, at [105].
[116] [1996] AC 669 at 707. In support of this proposition he cited *Re Diplock* [1948] Ch 465 and *Re Montagu's Settlement Trusts* [1987] Ch 264.

property acquired it free from pre-existing equitable rights. As Megarry V-C observed in *Re Montagu's Settlement Trusts*:

'It should be remembered that the doctrine of purchaser without notice and constructive trust are concerned with matters which differ in important respects. The former is concerned with the question whether a person takes property subject to or free from some equity. The latter is concerned with whether or not a person is to have imposed upon him the personal burdens and obligations of trusteeship.'[117]

A stranger may therefore receive property subject to a trust because he is affixed with notice thereof, yet not attract any personal liability if he dissipates the trust property.

Whilst some cases have indicated that liability can be founded upon the mere negligence of the recipient, or in very narrow circumstances that liability may even be strict, the majority of more recent cases have required a higher threshold of fault, which is consistent with the developments in the context of accessory liability examined above, where the Privy Council has stated that an assisting stranger will only be liable if he acted dishonestly. Many cases have addressed the requirement of fault in terms of the knowledge of the stranger who received trust property, and this terminology was utilised by Lord Browne-Wilkinson in *Westdeutsche Landesbank Girozentrale v Islington London Borough Council*.[118] A scale of the knowledge which a recipient might have possessed was provided by Peter Gibson J in *Baden Delvaux v Société Général*.[119] Having considered all the previous decisions, and drawing heavily from the doctrine of notice operating in the context of land conveyancing, including the definition of constructive notice provided in s 199 of the Law of Property Act 1925, he identified five classes of knowledge:[120] (i) actual knowledge; (ii) wilfully shutting one's eyes to the obvious; (iii) wilfully and recklessly failing to make such inquiries as an honest and reasonable man would make; (iv) knowledge of circumstances which would indicate the facts to an honest and reasonable man; (v) knowledge of circumstances which would put an honest and reasonable man on inquiry.

It is clear from this analysis that the concept of knowledge for these purposes includes not only facts that the recipient of trust property actually knew, but also facts that he could and should have known. Subsequent cases have sought to distinguish between knowledge of types (i)–(iii) and knowledge of types (iv) and (v). Whereas knowledge of types (i)–(iii) are rooted in some degree of conscious moral culpability on the part of the recipient, knowledge of types (iv) and (v) derive from his negligence. The majority of recent cases suggest that mere negligence on the part of the recipient should not be sufficient to give rise to liability to account as a constructive trustee. However, each of the degrees of fault which have been proposed as the touchstone for liability will be examined.

*(i) Strict liability.* In general the courts have held that imposition of a liability to account as a constructive trustee against a recipient of trust property requires some

---

[117] [1987] Ch 264 at 272–273, [1994] 4 All ER 308 at 320.    [118] [1996] AC 669 at 707.

[119] *Baden, Delvaux and Lecuit v Société Général pour Favoriser le Développement du Commerce et de l'Industrie en France SA* [1983] BCLC 325.

[120] [1983] BCLC 325 at 407, considered at 408–421.

degree of fault. However in *Re Diplock*[121] the Court of Appeal held that charities which had mistakenly received money from an estate, because the executors had erroneously believed that a valid charitable bequest had been made, were personally liability to account to the estate for the property they had received, irrespective of the fact that they had acted entirely innocently. Their liability was affirmed by the House of Lords.[122] The decision amounts to the imposition of a strict liability to account as a constructive trustee, and it has not found favour in subsequent decisions. Such strict liability has been confined to claims involving the administration of estates, or analogous circumstances. In *Ministry of Health v Simpson*[123] Lord Simmonds was careful to limit the principle to the administration of an estate. He started his judgment with a warning that it was 'important in the discussion of this question to remember that the particular branch of the jurisdiction of the Court of Chancery with which we are concerned relates to the administration of assets of a deceased person.'[124] He based his judgment on the principle stated by Lord Davey in *Harrison v Kirk*:

'The Court of Chancery in order to do justice and to avoid the evil of allowing one man to retain what is really and legally applicable to the payment of another man devised a remedy by which where the estate had been distributed without regard to the rights of a creditor, it has allowed the creditor to recover back what has been paid to the beneficiaries or the next of kin who derive title from the deceased testator or intestate.'[125]

He then extended this principle to the facts of *Re Diplock*:

'It would be strange if a court of equity, whose self-sought duty it was to see that the assets of a deceased person were duly administered and came into the right hands and not into the wrong hands, devised a remedy for the protection of the unpaid creditor but left the unpaid legatee or next of kin unprotected.'[126]

Subsequent cases have extended the personal liability imposed in *Re Diplock*[127] to circumstances analogous to the administration of estates.[128] In *Butler v Broadhead*[129] and *Re J Leslie Engineers Co Ltd (in liquidation)*[130] it was held that there was sufficient analogy between the position of the executor of an estate and the liquidator of a company to entitle a creditor to recover from overpaid contributories in a winding-up. However the claim did not succeed in either case,[131] and there has been no general extension of the principle to all trust situations.

The strict liability of the recipients in *Re Diplock* was also ameliorated by a requirement that the claimants first exhaust their personal remedies against the executors who had wrongly paid the charities. The Court of Appeal stated:

'Since the original wrong payment was attributable to the blunder of the personal representatives, the right of the unpaid beneficiary is in the first instance against the wrongdoing

---

[121] [1948] Ch 465.    [122] *Ministry of Health v Simpson* [1951] AC 251.
[123] [1951] AC 251.    [124] [1951] AC 251 at 265.    [125] [1904] AC 1.
[126] [1951] AC 251 at 266.    [127] [1948] Ch 465.
[128] See also Smith, 'Unjust Enrichment, Property and the Structure of Trusts' (2000) 116 LQR 412.
[129] [1975] Ch 97.    [130] [1976] 1 WLR 292.
[131] In *Butler v Broadhead* the claim was barred by the Companies Act, and in *Re J Leslie Engineers Co Ltd* the creditors exhausted their claim against the liquidators.

executor or administrator; and the beneficiary's direct claim in equity against those overpaid or wrongly paid should be limited to the amount which he cannot recover from the party responsible.'[132]

As the court observed, this may mean that in some circumstances the whole amount will have to be recovered from the innocent volunteers, for example if the executors are insolvent, have acted under a court order, or are protected by s 27 of the Trustee Act 1925.[133] The strict liability imposed in *Re Diplock* has left the law in a state of confusion. The scope of the liability appears extremely limited if other remedies against the blundering executor must be exhausted first. It is submitted that the imposition of a strict liability to account as a constructive trustee is inconsistent with the equitable nature of the remedy. In *Westdeutsche Landesbank Girozentrale v Islington London Borough Council* Lord Browne-Wilkinson stressed that equity operates on the conscience of the owner of the legal interest,[134] but in *Re Diplock* the entirely innocent recipients of property, who had committed no wrong by disposing of it because they honestly believed that they were entitled to it, were required to account.

In reality the award of an equitable account in *Re Diplock* was a consequence of an inadequacy in the availability of common law restitution at the time that the case was decided. Until the recent decision of the House of Lords in *Kleinwort Benson Ltd v Lincoln City Council*[135] a plaintiff was only entitled to recover restitution from the payee of money paid under a mistake of fact,[136] but not of money paid under a mistake of law.[137] The executors in *Re Diplock* had paid money to persons they believed were legally entitled to receive because of their misconstruction of the relevant law, and would not therefore have been entitled to recover restitution on the grounds of mistake. However now that the barrier preventing recovery of money paid under a mistake of law has been removed,[138] such beneficiaries would be entitled to receive restitution from the wrongly paid charities, but the charities would also be entitled to claim the defence of change of position.[139] Provided that the charities had acted in good faith, it is unlikely that they would have to make restitution of the money they had dissipated, since such dissipation would constitute a change of position.

---

[132] [1948] Ch 465 at 503.

[133] Trustee Act 1925, s 23 provides that the personal representatives may gain protection where they advertise their intention to distribute in the Gazette and a newspaper.

[134] [1996] AC 669 at 705.      [135] [1999] 2 AC 349, [1998] 4 All ER 513.

[136] See *Barclays Bank v W J Simms* [1980] QB 677; *Rover International Ltd v Cannon Film Sales Ltd (No 3)* [1989] 1 WLR 912, CA; *Lipkin Gorman v Karpnale Ltd* [1991] 2 AC 548, HL.

[137] See *Bilbie v Lumley* (1802) 2 East 469; *Brisbane v Dacres* (1813) 5 Taunt 143; *William Whiteley v R* (1909) 101 LT 741; *Sawyer and Vincent v Window Brace Ltd* [1943] 1 KB 32; *Avon County Council v Howlett* [1983] 1 All ER 1073, CA; *R v Tower Hamlets London Borough Council, ex p Chetnik Developments Ltd* [1988] AC 858; *Woolwich Building Society v IRC* [1993] AC 70, CA.

[138] The decision of the House of Lords to abrogate the distinction between mistakes of fact and law in *Kleinwort Benson v Lincoln City Council* [1999] 2 AC 349, [1998] 4 All ER 513 had been presaged in other jurisdictions. See: Judicature Amendment Act 1958, s 2 (New Zealand); *Air Canada v British Columbia* (1989) 59 DLR (4th) 161 (Canada); *David Securities Pty Ltd v Commonwealth Bank of Australia* (1992) 109 ALR 57 (Australia); *Morgan Guaranty Trust Co of New York v Lothian Regional Council* 1995 SLT 299 (Scotland).

[139] *Lipkin Gorman v Karpnale Ltd* [1991] 2 AC 548.

They would therefore only be liable to make restitution in full if they had not acted in good faith, which is tantamount to the introduction of a species of fault-based liability.

Whilst the general attitudes of the courts towards *Re Diplock* has been hostile,[140] so that it has been characterised as exceptional and its scope has not been extended, more recently some academics have suggested that it should provide the paradigm for the availability of personal restitutionary remedies against a stranger who received trust property. Although this proposal has not yet been adopted, it is discussed at the end of this chapter.

*(ii) Negligence of the recipient.* Some English cases[141] have held that a stranger should be liable to account as a constructive trustee if he received trust property with knowledge of any of the five types identified in *Baden Delvaux*,[142] including mere negligence. In *El Ajou v Dollar Land Holdings plc*[143] Millett J suggested, albeit obiter, that liability could be founded upon the mere negligence of the recipient of property:

'. . . I am content to assume, without deciding, that dishonesty or want of probity involving actual knowledge (whether proved or inferred) is not a precondition of liability; but that a recipient is not expected to be unduly suspicious and is not to be held liable unless he went ahead without further inquiry in circumstances in which an honest and reasonable man would have realised that the money was probably trust money and was being misapplied.'[144]

In New Zealand the courts have also held that knowledge of all five types identified in *Baden Delvaux*, therefore including negligence, are sufficient to give rise to liability.[145] Until the recent judgment of the Court of Appeal in *BCCI (Overseas) Ltd v Akindele*[146] it was generally thought that the criteria of negligence had been rejected in favour of a requirement of conscious wrongdoing. However Nourse LJ, whilst rejecting the formulation of a test of liability in terms of 'knowledge' in favour of a generalised requirement of 'unconscionability', held that dishonesty was not a 'necessary ingredient of liability in knowing receipt'.[147] He approved those English and New Zealand authorities favouring liability on the basis of the lower threshold of 'constructive knowledge', which thus favours the adoption of a negligence standard. However it will be argued below that the test propounded by Nourse LJ, and the purported reintroduction of a negligence test, is inconsistent with other authorities, so that a requirement of dishonesty is to be preferred.

*(iii) Conscious wrongdoing.* The requisite degree of fault for the imposition of liability to account as a constructive trustee was examined by Megarry V-C in *Re Montagu's*

---

[140]  See the recent comments of Nourse LJ in *BCCI Ltd v Akindele* [2000] 4 All ER 221 at 236.

[141]  *Selangor United Rubber Estates v Cradock (No 3)* [1968] 1 WLR 1555; *Karak Rubber Co Ltd v Burden (No 2)* [1972] 1 All ER 1210; *Rowlandson v National Westminster Bank Ltd* [1978] 3 All ER 370; *Belmont Finance Corpn v Williams Furniture Ltd* [1979] 1 All ER 118, CA.

[142]  [1983] BCLC 325.        [143]  [1993] 3 All ER 717.        [144]  [1993] 3 All ER 717 at 739.

[145]  *Westpac Banking Corpn v Savin* [1985] 2 NZLR 41; *Powell v Thompson* [1991] 1 NZLR 597; *Equiticorp Industries Group v Hawkins* [1991] 3 NZLR 700; *Lankshear v ANZ Banking Group* [1993] 1 NZLR 481; *Nimmo v Westpac Banking Corpn* [1993] 3 NZLR 218; *Springfield Acres (in liquidation) v Abacus (Hong Kong)* [1994] 3 NZLR 502.

[146]  [2000] 4 All ER 221.        [147]  [2000] 4 All ER 221 at 231.

*Settlement Trusts*,[148] the facts of which were considered above.[149] He held that the tenth Duke of Manchester should only be held liable to account for the value of the chattels sold in breach of trust if he had acted with 'want of probity'.[150] He considered that knowledge stemming from negligence would not establish sufficient fault to justify liability:

'. . . knowledge is not confined to actual knowledge, but includes at least knowledge of types (ii) and (iii) in the *Baden* case . . . for in such cases there is a want of probity which justifies imposing a constructive trust . . . Whether knowledge of the *Baden* types (iv) and (v) suffices for this purpose is at best doubtful; in my view it does not, for I cannot see that the carelessness involved will normally amount to a want of probity.'[151]

He referred to authorities decided prior to *Baden Delvaux* where it had been held that negligence was insufficient to give rise to a constructive trust,[152] and emphasised that the requirement of 'knowledge' was essentially different from the concept of 'notice' used to determine whether equitable property rights had been defeated. Subsequent cases followed the approach of Megarry V-C. In *Lipkin Gorman v Karpnale Ltd*[153] Alliott J held that 'want of probity is the key aspect in the approach the court should take'.[154] This was affirmed by the Court of Appeal.[155] In *Eagle Trust plc v SBC Securities Ltd*[156] Vinelott J reiterated that in the context of a commercial transaction:

'. . . to make a defendant liable as a constructive trustee, it must be shown that he knew, in one of the senses set out in categories (i), (ii) and (iii) of Peter Gibson J's analysis in *Baden*, that the moneys were misapplied.'[157]

In *Cowan de Groot Properties v Eagle Trust*[158] Knox J similarly held that it was essential for a plaintiff to demonstrate that the recipient of trust property had knowledge within categories (i), (ii) and (iii).[159] *Re Montagu* was also endorsed by Lord Browne-Wilkinson in *Westdeutsche Landesbank Girozentrale v Islington London Borough Council*[160] and by Knox J in *Hillsdown Holdings plc v Pensions Ombudsman*.[161]

**(iv) Dishonesty.** Whilst *Re Montagu* held that liability to account as a constructive

---

[148]  [1987] Ch 264, [1992] 4 All ER 308; (1986) 102 LQR 267 and (1987) 50 MLR 217 (C Harpum); [1987] CLJ 385 (Hayton).

[149]  See above, p 844.

[150]  This picks up the language of Sachs LJ in *Carl-Zeiss-Stifung v Herbert Smith & Co (No 2)* [1969] 2 All ER 367 at 379 that there must be an 'element . . . of dishonesty or of consciously acting improperly', as opposed to an innocent failure to make what a court may later decide to have been proper enquiry', and Edmund Davies LJ who spoke of 'want of probity'.

[151]  [1987] Ch 264 at 285. For a description of the types of knowledge identified in *Baden* see above.

[152]  *Carl-Zeiss-Stifung v Herbert Smith & Co (No 2)* [1969] 2 Ch 276; *Competitive Insurance Co Ltd v Davies Investments Ltd* [1975] 1 WLR 1240.

[153]  [1992] 4 All ER 331, [1987] 1 WLR 987.         [154]  [1992] 4 All ER 331 at 349.

[155]  [1992] 4 All ER 409 at 420, per May LJ; [1990] CLJ 17 (Jones).

[156]  [1992] 4 All ER 488, [1991] BCLC 438.         [157]  [1991] BCLC 438 at 509.

[158]  [1992] 4 All ER 700.

[159]  [1992] 4 All ER 700 at 760. He also held that if it was necessary to have regard to knowledge of types (iv) and (v) that there still was no knowledge on the facts.

[160]  [1996] AC 669 at 707. See also *Hillsdown Holdings plc v Pensions Ombudsman* [1997] 1 All ER 862.

[161]  [1997] 1 All ER 862 at 902–903.

trustee would only be imposed against a conscious wrongdoer, the standard of liability would perhaps better be expressed as a requirement of dishonesty. In *Agip (Africa) Ltd v Jackson*[162] Millett J warned against an 'over refinement or a too ready assumption that categories (iv) and (v) are necessarily cases of constructive notice only' and suggested that the 'true distinction is between honesty and dishonesty', which is essentially a jury question.[163] As was discussed above, in the context of liability of a stranger as an accessory to a breach of trust the Privy Council has adopted dishonesty as the touch-stone of liability in preference to knowledge.[164] In the context of the liability of a recipient of trust property it is likely that dishonesty is synonymous with the want of probity identified in *Re Montagu*. Both terms were used by the Court of Appeal in *Carl-Zeiss-Stifung v Herbert Smith & Co (No 2)*.[165] More recently the requirement of dishonesty was applied by the Court of Appeal in *Twinsectra Ltd v Yardley*.[166] As was noted above, the requirement of dishonesty was rejected by the Court of Appeal in *BCCI (Overseas) v Akindele* in favour of a requirement of 'unconscionability' which might encompass elements of constructive notice. However *Twinsectra Ltd v Yardley* was not considered by the Court, and it is submitted that the stronger line of authorities favours the continued requirement of conscious wrongdoing. Furthermore, although Nourse LJ rejected the language of dishonesty he did accept that at least some degree of fault would be required to render it unconscionable for the defendant to retain the benefit he had received, and it is very difficult to determine where this line is to be drawn. At all events it is clear that no personal liability to account can be maintained against an innocent volunteer who has received trust property except in the anomalous situations where *Re Diplock* may still apply.

*(v) Unconscionability.* The determination of an appropriate standard of personal liability applicable to a stranger who has received trust property has been bedevilled by terminological debates. The recent decision of the Court of Appeal in *BCCI (Overseas) v Akindele*[167] has sought to cut through this Gordian knot by means of the introduction of a new test of 'unconscionability'.[168] Nourse LJ rejected previous attempts to provide a categorisation of different types of notice and proposed a new generalised test of liability:

'I have come to the view that, just as there is now a single test of dishonesty for knowing assistance, so ought there to be a single test of knowledge for knowing receipt. The recipient's state of knowledge must be such as to make it unconscionable for him to retain the benefit of the receipt.'[169]

However it must be questioned whether this new approach provides a more comprehensible means of determining liability. Nourse LJ himself noted that it would not

---

[162] [1990] Ch 265, [1992] 4 All ER 385 at 405.

[163] See also *Metall und Rohstoff AG v Donaldson Lufkin & Jenrette Inc* [1990] 1 QB 391 at 474; *Polly Peck International plc v Nadir (No 2)* [1992] 4 All ER 769 at 781–782.

[164] *Royal Brunei Airlines v Tan* [1995] 3 All ER 97; *Barlow Clowes v Eurotrust* [2006] 1 All ER 333.

[165] [1969] 2 All ER 367.    [166] [1999] Lloyd's Rep Bank 438.; (2000) 59 CLJ 444 (D. Fox).

[167] [2000] 4 All ER 221; [2001] RLR 99 (Stevens).

[168] See, Barkehall, ' "Goodbye" knowing receipt. "Hello" unconscientious receipt' (2001) 21(2) OJLS 239.

[169] [2000] 4 All ER 221 at 235.

avoid 'difficulties of application', although he felt that it would 'avoid those difficulties of definition and allocation to which the previous categorisations have led'.[170] Whilst Nourse LJ appears to acknowledge the difficulties associated with the adoption of 'knowledge' as a criterion for liability he reintroduces them by requiring the court to determine if the recipient's 'state of knowledge' would render it unconscionable to retain the benefit. As was noted above, in *Royal Brunei Airlines Sdn Bhd v Tan* Lord Nicholls strongly doubted the usefulness of unconscionability as a criterion of liability. His comments are of such significance that it is worth repeating them in full:

'. . . unconscionable is not a word in everyday use by non-lawyers. If it is to be used in this context, and if it is to be the touchstone for liability as an accessory, it is essential to be clear on what, *in this context*, unconscionable *means*. If unconscionable means no more than dishonesty, then dishonesty is the preferable label. If unconscionable means something different, it must be said that it is not clear what that something different is. Either way, therefore, the term is better avoided in this context.'[171]

These criticisms are borne out by the application of the unconscionability test in *BCCI (Overseas) Ltd v Akindele* itself. In concluding that the investor in that case had not acted 'unconscionably' Nourse LJ stated that the first instance judge had held that he had not acted dishonestly, and that he would have held that he 'did not have actual or constructive knowledge' that his receipt was traceable to a breach of fiduciary duty.[172] Thus the language of unconscionability could only operate parasitically upon the language of dishonesty of traditional notice. It is therefore submitted that the proposed criteria of 'unconscionability' should be rejected in favour of the less opaque requirement of 'dishonesty', as applied by the Court of Appeal in *Twinsectra Ltd v Yardley*.[173] The already weak authority of the dicta in *BCCI (Overseas) Ltd v Akindele* have been further undermined by the decision of the House of Lords in *Criterion Properties plc v Stratford UK Properties LLC*,[174] where it was held that the Court of Appeal had fallen into error by considering the issue to have been one of equitable 'knowing receipt' at all. A claim to recover benefits conferred under a contract which is set aside does not involve any trust property, and hence is a matter for the common law of restitution, where the personal liability is strict, subject to the defence of change of position.

### (d) Establishing dishonesty

As has been explained above, the best interpretation of current case law is that a stranger who has received trust property will only be liable to account as a constructive trustee if he acted dishonestly. The conceptual characteristics of dishonesty identified in *Royal Brunei Airlines Sdn Bhd v Tan*,[175] *Twinsectra Ltd v Yardley*[176] and *Barlow Clowes v Eurotrust*[177] were discussed above in relation to dishonest assistance,[178] and they are equally relevant in this context. Several additional observations can be made regarding the application of the criteria of dishonesty to those who have received trust property.

---

[170] [2000] 4 All ER 221 at 236.    [171] [1995] 3 All ER 97, at 108.
[172] [2000] 4 All ER 221 at 238.    [173] [1999] Lloyd's Rep Bank 438.
[174] [2004] 1 WLR 1846; [2004] LMCLQ 421.    [175] [1995] 2 AC 378.
[176] [2002] 2 All ER 377.    [177] [2006] 1 All ER 333.    [178] See above, p 833.

*(i) Distinguishing commercial and non-commercial settings.* The determination whether a person acted dishonestly must take account of the particular circumstances in which the events occurred. In *Cowan de Groot Properties v Eagle Trust*[179] Knox J pointed out that the duty of the directors of a purchasing company is to buy as cheaply as they can.[180] This, after all, fits the philosophy of profit: buy cheap and sell dear. In the view of Knox J, it would be unduly onerous to impose upon directors of a company a positive duty to inquire into the reasons for a sale to them at a bargain price. His view is supported by *Eagle Trust plc v SBC Securities Ltd*,[181] where Vinelott J emphasised that the doctrines of constructive notice had developed 'in the field of property transactions' and that the courts had been particularly reluctant to extend the doctrine of constructive notice to cases where moneys are paid in the ordinary course of business to the defendant in discharge of a liability.[182] The question which therefore arises is when dishonesty will be found in the context of a commercial transaction. In *Cowan de Groot Properties v Eagle Trust* Knox J considered that liability would be imposed against a person guilty of commercially unacceptable conduct in the particular context involved.[183] This approach was cited with approval by Lord Nicholls in *Royal Brunei Airlines Sdn Bhd v Tan*.[184] In *BCCI (Overseas) Ltd v Akindele* it was held that the decision of an investor to enter into an agreement with a commercial bank was to be treated as an 'arm's length business transaction'. The investor was not therefore put on notice that some fraud or breach of trust was being perpetrated merely because the agreement was artificial in nature and offered a high rate of interest.[185]

*(ii) Relevance of the recipient's personal attributes in determining whether he was dishonest.* In *Re Clasper Group Services Ltd*[186] it was held that in determining whether a defendant had the requisite knowledge to justify the imposition of liability to account as a constructive trustee the court must take his personal 'attributes'[187] into account. Whereas a mature and experienced person might be held to have had sufficient knowledge, an innocent and inexperienced person might not. The case concerned a boy employed by his father's company who was given a cheque for £2,000 by his father a month before the company went into voluntary liquidation. He paid it into his bank account and then lent £3,000 from the account to another company which his father had acquired. Warner J held that, bearing in mind the youth of the boy,[188] the fact that his only experience was his work in a lowly position for a group of companies owned by his father, and the fact that he was not particularly bright, he did not have sufficient knowledge affecting his conscience to justify the imposition of a constructive trust. In *Royal Brunei Airlines Sdn Bhd v Tan*[189] the Privy Council likewise held that in determining whether a person had acted dishonestly the court should have regard to the personal attributes of the person concerned, including his experience and intelligence.

*(iii) Timing of dishonesty.* A recipient of trust property will only be held liable to account as a constructive trustee if he acted dishonestly when he received it or disposed

---

[179] [1992] 4 All ER 700 at 761.    [180] [1992] 4 All ER 700 at 761.    [181] [1992] 4 All ER 488.
[182] [1992] 4 All ER 488 at 507.    [183] [1992] 4 All ER 700 at 761.
[184] [1995] 3 All ER 97 at 107.    [185] [2000] 4 All ER 221 at 237.    [186] [1989] BCLC 143.
[187] Following Lawson J in *International Sales and Agencies Ltd v Marcus* [1982] 3 All ER 551 at 558.
[188] Who was 17.    [189] [1995] 3 All ER 97 at 107.

of it. A recipient of trust property will not therefore be liable to account if he had been aware of the existence of the trust before he received the property, but had honestly forgotten that it was subject to a trust at the time that it was received. Thus in *Re Montagu's Settlement Trusts*[190] Megarry V-C held that the tenth Duke of Manchester was not liable to account for the value of the trust chattels he had received because he had not been aware of the existence of the trust at the date that he had received them. He explained:

'If a person once has clear and distinct knowledge of some fact, is he treated as knowing that fact for the rest of his life, even after he has genuinely forgotten all about it? . . . it seems to me that a person should not be said to have knowledge of a fact that he once knew if at the time in question he has genuinely forgotten all about it, so that it could not be said to operate on his mind any longer.'[191]

He suggested a cautious approach, stating that the court should be slow to conclude that what was once known had been forgotten. Conversely, a stranger who received property without any awareness that it was subject to the trust, but without having given value for it, will still be held liable to account as a constructive trustee if he subsequently disposed of it after having become aware that it was trust property.[192] This follows from the comment of Lord Browne-Wilkinson in *Westdeutsche Landesbank Girozentrale v Islington London Borough Council*[193] that a person is liable as a trustee from such time as he becomes aware that it was intended to be held on trust.[194] He will not be liable to account for any part of such property dissipated before he became aware of the trust, as his conduct would not, to that extent, have been dishonest. Nor will he be liable, despite subsequent knowledge if, at the time of acquiring the property, he was a bona fide purchaser for value without notice.[195]

## (4) Restitution:[196] an alternative approach to the liability of a stranger who received trust property

### (a) Restitution and the receipt of trust property

Restitution is a technical term describing the remedy by which a defendant is required to return to a plaintiff the amount of an enrichment he received at the plaintiff's

---

[190] [1987] Ch 264.    [191] [1987] Ch 264 at 284.

[192] See *Karak Rubber Co Ltd v Burden (No 2)* [1972] 1 WLR 602 at 632, per Brightman J.

[193] [1996] AC 669 at 705.

[194] See *Sheridan v Joyce* (1844) 1 Jo & Lat 401, where a trustee loaned trust money in breach of trust. The recipient, Fair, did not initially know that the money was trust money, but later discovered. The Court of Chancery of Ireland held that he had become a constructive trustee of the money as soon as he had become aware of the facts.

[195] See above.

[196] Birks, *An Introduction to the Law of Restitution* (1985), pp 140–146, 445–446; Burrows, *The Law of Restitution* (2nd edn, 2002), pp 182–210; Goff & Jones, *The Law of Restitution* (6th edn, 2002) 739–746; Virgo, *The Principles of the Law of Restitution* (1999) 666–672, Gerard McMeel, *The Modern Law of Restitution* (2000), pp 384–396. See also Payne, 'Unjust Enrichment Trusts and Recipient Liability for Unlawful Dividends' (2003) 119 LQR 583, who argues for a restitutionary rather than a trusts approach to unlawfully paid dividends. Her views are criticised by Tham, 'Unjust Enrichment and Unlawful Dividends: A Step too Far?' [2005] 64 CLJ 177.

expense. Unlike a compensatory remedy, the quantum of recovery is not assessed by reference to any loss suffered by the plaintiff, but is determined by the gain received by the defendant. Where a defendant receives value at the expense of the plaintiff he may be required to make restitution of equivalent value to him. Restitution is only available where the enrichment of the defendant was unjust, in the sense that the law regards it as inappropriate that he should be entitled to retain it. Thus, the unjust enrichment of a defendant is the cause of action which leads to the award of restitution. Until recently, English law did not recognise an autonomous cause of action in unjust enrichment. However, in *Lipkin Gorman v Karpnale Ltd*[197] the House of Lords affirmed that unjust enrichment is an independent cause of action alongside breach of contract, tort, or breach of trust.

Although the precise scope of unjust enrichment has yet to be determined, there are many areas where it is clear that restitution is available, for example where a plaintiff has paid money to a defendant by mistake. Prior to the recognition of unjust enrichment, English law did award restitutionary remedies, both at common law (by means of the action for money had and received) and in equity. In consequence of the legitimisation of unjust enrichment as an autonomous cause of action it has been argued that all such restitutionary remedies should be re-analysed under the single rubric of unjust enrichment, irrespective of their historical pedigree. Inevitably integration into such a unitary principle would require harmonisation of the ingredients necessary for a claim to succeed, which may involve the abandonment of traditional precedents and doctrines. This process has ramifications in respect of strangers who have received trust property because the personal liability to account as a constructive trustee is a species of restitutionary remedy. The stranger who is liable to account is required to make restitution of the value he received from the trust (i.e. the value of the trust property he received) at the expense of the beneficiaries. As has been seen above, this equitable obligation to make restitution is currently only imposed if the recipient was at fault. In contrast, at common law an unjustly enriched defendant is required to make restitution irrespective of whether he was at fault. Liability is strict. Some academic writers have therefore suggested that a stranger who receives trust property in breach of trust, and is thereby unjustly enriched, should be strictly liable to make restitution subject to defences intended to prevent injustice.

In New Zealand[198] the equitable liability of a stranger receiving trust property to account as a constructive trustee has been analysed as a right to restitution on the grounds of unjust enrichment. The courts have held that knowledge of all five categories identified in *Baden* will be sufficient to give rise to a constructive trust. In *Powell v Thompson*[199] Thomas J considered that the observations of Sir Robert Megarry V-C in *Re Montagu's Settlement Trusts*[200] did not accurately reflect the present law. In *Equiticorp*

---

[197] [1991] 2 AC 548.

[198] See *Westpac Banking Corpn v Savin* [1985] 2 NZLR 41; *Elders Pastoral Ltd v Bank of New Zealand* [1989] 2 NZLR 180; *Powell v Thompson* [1991] 1 NZLR 597; *Equiticorp Industries Group Ltd v Hawkins* [1991] 3 NZLR 700.

[199] [1991] 1 NZLR 597.

*Industries Group Ltd v Hawkins*[201] Wylie J held that all five types of knowledge apply to cases of knowing receipt. The courts have held that the underlying basis of the liability to account as a constructive trustee for knowing receipt of trust property is 'the unjust enrichment of the defendant at the expense of the plaintiff'.[202] Since the basis of the remedy is unjust enrichment, the court must conduct a general inquiry whether in the circumstances it would be inequitable not to require the defendant to account to the plaintiff. This analysis clearly affects the issue of the knowledge required, as Thomas J explained in *Powell v Thompson*:

'. . . in certain circumstances a Court of Equity could be persuaded to examine the equities of the competing claims where the defendant was not aware that he or she was receiving or dealing with the property in a way which was inconsistent with a trust. Because liability in this class of case stems from equity's unwillingness to accept the enrichment of the third party at the expense of the beneficiary, and not any particular conduct or misconduct on the part of either the trustee or the third party, such knowledge may not be necessary in order to activate equity's jurisdiction with the objective of ensuring a result which is consonant with good conscience.'[203]

In consequence, the New Zealand position differs greatly from that currently taken by the English courts. However, the New Zealand courts have also taken a completely different approach to the development of constructive trusts. As Thomas J had observed in *Elders Pastoral Ltd v Bank of New Zealand*:[204]

'Unquestionably, in New Zealand the constructive trust has become a broad equitable remedy for reversing that which is inequitable or unconscionable. With this approach it is unlikely that the courts of New Zealand will be encouraged to adopt the more restricted approach evident in Great Britain.'[205]

## (b) Restitution at common law: strict liability subject to defences

As has been noted, at common law the obligation to make restitution is imposed against a defendant irrespective of whether he was at fault. If a defendant receives money from a payor who was acting under a mistake, it is irrelevant whether he was aware that the payor was mistaken. He is obliged to make restitution merely because he has been enriched in circumstances where the enrichment was unjust because the payor's consent to the payment was vitiated by the mistake. Similarly, where a contract is set aside a defendant who has received benefits under the contract will be strictly liable to make restitution subject to the defence of change of position.[206] The factor requiring restitution (termed the unjust factor) is intrinsically one-sided, in the sense that it is the payor's lack of true consent to the transaction which rendered the enrichment unjust.

---

[200] [1987] Ch 264.
[201] [1991] 3 NZLR 700.
[202] *Powell v Thompson* [1991] 1 NZLR 597 at 607, per Thomas J.
[203] [1991] 1 NZLR 597 at 608.
[204] [1989] 2 NZLR 180.
[205] [1991] 1 NZLR 597 at 615.
[206] *Criterion Properties plc v Stratford UK Properties LCC* [2004] 1 WLR 1846.

Provided that the defendant can be demonstrated to have been enriched, his liability to make restitution is strict. Whilst such liability might appear unduly harsh, the enriched defendant is protected from an unjust outcome by the availability of the defence of change of position.[207] This defence is available only in response to restitutionary claims and it allows the court to hold that a defendant should not be required to make full restitution of the entire enrichment he received. This defence was also recognised by the House of Lords in *Lipkin Gorman v Karpnale Ltd.*[208] The rationale for the defence was outlined by Lord Goff: 'where an innocent defendant's position is so changed that he will suffer an injustice if called upon to repay or to repay in full, the injustice of requiring him so to repay outweighs the injustice of denying the plaintiff restitution'.[209] Although he did not provide a comprehensive analysis of how the defence would apply in all situations, he went on to formulate a broad general principle:

'At present I do not wish to state the principle any less broadly than this: that the defence is available to a person whose position has so changed that it would be inequitable in all the circumstances to require him to make restitution or alternatively to make restitution in full. I wish to stress however that the mere fact that the defendant has spent the money, in whole or in part, does not of itself render it inequitable that he should be called upon to repay, because the expenditure might in any event have been incurred by him in the ordinary course of things. I fear that the mistaken assumption that mere expenditure of money may be regarded as amounting to a change of position for present purposes has led in the past to opposition by some to recognition of a defence which in fact is likely to be available only on comparatively rare occasions.'[210]

He provided examples of circumstances in which he thought that the defence of change of position would apply, including a defendant who makes a donation to charity in good faith having received a payment of money from a plaintiff acting under a mistake of fact, and a third party who similarly gives money to a charity which he had received from a thief.

## (c)  Distinguishing restitution at common law from restitution in equity

The history of the litigation in *Lipkin Gorman Ltd v Karpnale* provides a useful illustration of the differences between the strict liability of the common law restitutionary claim and the fault-based liability in equity. It will be remembered that the case concerned a solicitor who had stolen money from his firm's client account to finance his gambling at the Playboy Club. The firm initially claimed that the club was liable to account in equity as a constructive trustee for the money it had received. This claim was rejected at first instance because the club had not lacked probity in its receipt of the money. In essence, the club was not at fault in receiving the money. In contrast, the House of Lords held that the club was liable at common law to make restitution

---

[207]  See Goff and Jones, *The Law of Restitution* (6th edn, 2002) pp 821–837; Burrows, *The Law of Restitution* (2nd edn, 2002), pp 510–529; Mitchell, 'Change of position: the developing law' [2005] 1 LMCLQ 168.

[208]  [1991] 2 AC 548.

[209]  [1991] 2 AC 548 at 579.

[210]  [1991] 2 AC 548 at 580.

of the stolen money it had received. The money received had belonged at common law to the firm and the club had not provided good consideration when it was received in return for gambling chips.[211] Although no traceable proceeds of the money were identifiable amongst the club's assets, it had been unjustly enriched by the receipt thereof and was therefore strictly liable to make restitution. However, the House of Lords went on to hold that the club's liability to make restitution should be ameliorated by application of the defence of change of position. Lord Goff held that it would be inequitable to require the club to repay the money it had received in full without making allowance for the winnings that it had paid on some of the bets placed by Cass. Thus, although the club had received £222,909, they were required to make restitution of only £150,960.

### (d) Identifying an unjust factor requiring the recipient of trust property to make restitution

Whilst it is clear that the liability of a defendant to make restitution at common law is strict, it is less easy to identify the unjust factor which requires a third party receiving trust property to make restitution. When a trustee transfers the trust property to a stranger in breach of trust, the stranger receives good legal title irrespective of the breach. The trustee is able to transfer the trust property by virtue of his legal ownership and the powers of management attendant thereon. As Lord Browne-Wilkinson explained in *Hammersmith and Fulham London Borough Council v Monk*, 'the fact that a trustee acts in breach of trust does not mean that he has no capacity to do the act he wrongly did'.[212] Restitution theorists have therefore sought to identify an unjust factor which would justify the award of restitution where a stranger has received trust property. Whilst there is general agreement that the mere receipt of trust property should give rise to a right to restitution there is disagreement as to the identification of an appropriate unjust factor. Some academics have favoured the adoption of 'ignorance' as an unjust factor, by which it is meant that the property was misdirected to the defendant without the consent or knowledge of the owner.[213] Such misdirection may be perpetrated with dishonesty, for example where a thief steals the plaintiff's money and passes it to the defendant, or it may occur through an honest mistake, for example where a trustee misunderstands his duty and pays money to the defendant which ought to go to the plaintiff. Others have rejected ignorance in favour of restitution to vindicate a property right.[214] In either case the right to receive restitution arises irrespective of any fault on the part of the recipient. Although liability is strict, the recipient will be protected from injustice by the defence of change of position.

---

[211]  [1991] 2 AC 548 at 575. Lord Goff explained: '. . . when Cass placed a bet, he received nothing in return which constituted valuable consideration. The contract of gaming was void; in other words, it was binding in honour only . . . Even when a winning bet is has been paid, the gambler does not receive valuable consideration for his money. All he receives is, in law, a gift from the club.'

[212]  [1992] 1 AC 478, 493

[213]  [1989] LMCLQ 296 (Birks).

[214]  See, for example, Virgo, *The Principles of the Law of Restitution* (1999), pp 128–129, 666–672.

## (e) Ignorance as an unjust factor at common law

No case has yet adopted the language of ignorance to justify the imposition of an obligation to make restitution.[215] Whilst the recipient club in *Lipkin Gorman v Karpnale Ltd*[216] was required to make restitution, the precise factor making its enrichment unjust was left unclear. Lord Goff seemed to indicate that the right to restitution arose simply because the club had received legal title to the firm's money without having provided valuable consideration:

'. . . here the money had been paid to the respondents by a third party, Cass; and in such a case the [plaintiff] has to establish a basis on which he is entitled to the money. This (at least as a general rule) he does by showing that the money is his legal property . . . If he can do so, he may be entitled to succeed in a claim against a third party for money had and received to his use, though not if the third party has received the money in good faith and for a valuable consideration.'[217]

In the earlier case of *Banque Belge pour l'Etranger v Hambrouck*,[218] a mistress was held liable to make restitution at common law of money she had received from her lover, who had stolen it from his employer. The plaintiffs claimed restitution of £315 remaining in her bank account, which was traceable as their money. Although they sought a personal action for money had and received, they only claimed the amount that remained and not the amount that she had received. In principle, they would have been entitled to receive restitution of all the money that she had received, subject to a defence of change of position. It should be noted that the availability of restitution at common law is severely limited, not merely by the defence of change of position, but also by the restrictive common law rules of tracing by which it can be demonstrated that the defendant received the plaintiff's money. As Lord Goff indicated in *Lipkin Gorman v Karpnale Ltd*,[219] the fact that at common law property in money is lost as such when it is mixed with other money has made the number of successful claims to restitution founded on mere receipt of the plaintiff's property very rare.[220]

## (f) Criticisms of the proposed adoption of strict liability restitution in equity

The central question is thus whether the current fault-based personal liability of a recipient of trust property should be re-explained as a strict liability to make restitution of the value of the property received, subject to the availability of a defence of change of position. This would entirely eliminate the need to demonstrate fault, whether characterised as knowledge, dishonesty or unconscionability, as a prerequisite of liability. Although such a radical departure from the traditional analysis of equity was initially

---

[215]  See (1992) 55 MLR 377 (McKendrick); [1996] LMCLQ 63 (Swadling); [1996] LMCLQ 463 (Grantham and Rickett); [1998] LMCLQ 18 (Bant).

[216]  [1991] 2 AC 548.

[217]  [1991] 2 AC 548 at 572.

[218]  [1921] 1 KB 321.

[219]  [1991] 2 AC 548.

[220]  [1991] 2 AC 548 at 572.

greeted with hostility by equity lawyers,[221] some have come to advocate it.[222] In effect, it would amount to the adoption of the strict personal liability of the charities in *Re Diplock* in every situation in which a stranger receives trust property, subject to the modification that they would be entitled to the defence of change of position.[223] Such a development has been advocated by Lord Nicholls, speaking extra judicially.[224] Despite the recent bare unsubstantiated assertion of Lord Millett in *Twinsectra Ltd v Yardley* that liability for 'knowing receipt' is receipt based and does not depend upon fault,[225] at present English law has not adopted such a strict liability right to restitution against a stranger who has received trust property in place of the equitable liability to account as a constructive trustee, and the leading authorities strongly support the current approach. In *Westdeutsche Landesbank Girozentrale v Islington London Borough Council*[226] Lord Browne-Wilkinson reiterated the fault-based approach of *Re Montagu*. In *BCCI (Overseas) Ltd v Akindele* Nourse LJ openly doubted the prevailing academic orthodoxy that the adoption of strict liability coupled with a change of position defence would be preferable to the current fault-based liability.[227]

The advantages of a strict liability claim in restitution, whether based on ignorance or the vindication of property rights, are said to be the harmonisation of the equitable and common law rules, the elimination of unhelpful terminology (such as liability to account as a constructive trustee) and the prevention of injustice. In particular, the debate has focused on the position of an innocent donee who has dissipated the property he received. Following the common law approach, such a person would be strictly liable to make restitution, subject to the defence of change of position. In equity he would attract no personal liability at all. However, it is not obvious that in reality the position in equity is less adequate than that at common law. Where trust property has been received by an innocent donee, but not dissipated by him, the beneficiaries will be able to recover it from him. As a volunteer, he will not enjoy the protection of the doctrine of notice and the beneficiaries' equitable interest will have been preserved. Where the property has been dissipated, leaving no traceable proceeds, the innocent donee will not be liable to make restitution under the current law.[228] At common law

---

[221] (1986) 102 LQR 114 (Harpum).

[222] Harpum, 'The Basis of Equitable Liability', in Birks (ed), *The Frontiers of Liability* (1994); Oakley, 'The Liberalising Nature of Remedies for Breach of Trust' in Oakley, *Trends in Contemporary Trust Law* (1996), pp 247–251; [1998] Conv 13 (Martin).

[223] See also Smith, 'Unjust Enrichment, Property and the Structure of Trusts' (2000) 116 LQR 412, who argues that the strict liability principle adopted in *Re Diplock* might properly be confined to situations involving the administration of an estate.

[224] Lord Nicholls, 'Knowing Receipt: The Need for a New Landmark' Chapter 17 in Cornish, Nolan, O'Sullivan and Virgo, *Restitution Past, Present and Future* (1998).

[225] [2002] 2 All ER 377, at [105].

[226] [1996] AC 669 at 705.

[227] [2000] 4 All ER 221.

[228] It should also be remembered that, where property subject to a trust has been received by a stranger the trustees, or a person owing a fiduciary relationship, will have acted in breach of trust, whether innocently or dishonestly, and will therefore be liable to restore the misdirected trust fund. However, it does not seem that the beneficiaries are required to exhaust their remedies against the mis-directing trustee first: *Omar v Omar* (29 November 1996, unreported), Blackburne J; [1997] RLR 139.

the act of dissipation may itself give rise to a defence of change of position. The only circumstances in which the common law and equitable approaches would produce different results are therefore where an innocent donee had dissipated the property he received in circumstances in which he would not be entitled to the benefit of the defence of change of position, for example where it had been utilised to cover his ordinary living expenses. The scope of the defence of change of position is thus the crucial element which will determine the availability of restitution in practice. In equity, an innocent donee is not required to account as a constructive trustee even if the specific money received has been dissipated by ordinary expenditure. In *Lipkin Gorman v Karpnale Ltd*[229] Lord Goff seemed to suggest that the dissipation of property received through ordinary expenditure would not operate as a defence. Only exceptional expenditure which could be related to the receipt of the enrichment would suffice. In *Scottish Equitable plc v Derby*[230] the Court of Appeal held that the defence was not limited to specific items of expenditure, and that it may be right for the court not to apply too demanding a standard of proof when an honest defendant says that he has spent an overpayment by improving his lifestyle but cannot produce any detailed accounting. However it held that the defence did not apply to an overpayment made to reduce a mortgage, as it was not a detriment to pay off a debt which would have to be paid sooner of later.

At the heart of the debate is a desire to harmonise the rules of equity and the common law. Although this might seem superficially attractive, it is questionable whether the philosophy underlying equity and the common law are truly compatible.[231] It is easy to assume that a restitutionary right founded on the receipt of property should operate identically, irrespective of whether the property received was legal or equitable. In reality, the very nature of legal and equitable ownership differ. Equitable ownership is a product of the historic bifurcation of English law which led to the evolution of a concept of double-ownership through the trust. Unlike legal ownership, equitable ownership only arises because the conscience of the legal owner is affected in such a way as to require him to observe the interests of the beneficiaries. The idea of fault is inherent in the creation, or imposition, of trusts, and is clearly operative through the equitable doctrine of notice which determines when equitable ownership rights are defeated. The remedy requiring a stranger to account as a constructive trustee is similarly rooted in the concept of conscience, and the overriding presumption is that a recipient of the legal title of property is entitled to enjoy security of receipt until such time as he becomes aware that it was subject to a trust, and that he should therefore be entitled to treat it as if it was his own. From the perspective of equity he is not unjustly enriched by the mere receipt of trust property. His enrichment only becomes unjust from such time as he was aware that he had received trust property and was therefore subject to an obligation to preserve it for the beneficiaries. The philosophies of equity and the common law in this respect are different. The common law right to restitution has

---

[229] [1991] 2 AC 548.
[230] [2001] 3 All ER 818.
[231] See, for example, Jaffey, *The Nature and Scope of Restitution* (2000), pp 327–346, who argues that the nature of equitable property rights does not demand the imposition of strict liability.

developed so that liability is strict but defences are broad. It should be noted that this does not eliminate entirely the need to assess fault. It merely changes the stage of the process at which fault must be considered. The defence of change of position only operates if the defendant acted bona fides. A dishonest defendant would not be able to take advantage of the defence, for example if he gave money to charity knowing that it had been paid to him by mistake. In contrast, equity regards the element of fault as crucial to liability itself. The charge that such notions as dishonesty are uncertain and difficult to apply can be met with the equally valid criticism that the defence of change of position is vague, underdeveloped and arbitrary. The adoption of strict liability in place of the current fault based liability would also effect a change in the allocation of the burden of proof where a claim is made against a recipient of trust property. Currently the burden of proof falls to the claimant, who must establish that the recipient dishonestly received trust property. If strict liability were to be adopted instead, the claimant would merely have to demonstrate that the property had been received, passing the burden to the recipient to establish a defence by way of change of position.

In the light of such criticisms Nourse LJ recently expressed his opinion that the current fault-based liability should not be superseded by strict liability restitution in *BCCI (Overseas) Ltd v Akindele.* Although his remarks were strictly obiter they are a significant counter-voice advocating the maintenance of the current position:

'While in general it may be possible to sympathise with a tendency to subsume a further part of our law under the principle of unjust enrichment, I beg leave to doubt whether strict liability coupled with a change of position defence would be preferable to fault-based liability in many commercial transactions, for example where, as here, the receipt is of a company's funds which have been misapplied by its directors. Without having heard argument it is unwise to be dogmatic, but in such a case it would appear to be commercially unworkable and contrary to the spirit of the rule in *Royal British Bank v Turquand*,[232] that, simply on proof of an internal misapplication of the company's funds, the burden should shift to the recipient to defend the receipt either by a change of position or perhaps in some other way.'[233]

In the light of these arguments, the contention of Professor Birks that 'there is no rational argument for depriving the equitable owner of the claim in unjust enrichment based on strict liability'[234] is clearly overstated and cannot be accepted as anything other than a polemical assertion.

### (g) Wider implications of the adoption of strict liability restitution in equity

If equity is forced to abandon its present commitment to fault as the basis of liability to make personal restitution, the implications may be yet further reaching. It is presently alleged to be inconsistent that an innocent donee of trust property is under no obligation to make restitution. Might it not equally be argued that it would be inconsistent if

---

[232]  (1856) 6 E & B 327.
[233]  [2000] 4 All ER 221 at 236. Goff and Jones do not share his doubt: *The Law of Restituton* (6th edn, 2002), p 744.
[234]  Birks and Pretto (eds), *Breach of Trust*, p 239.

an innocent donee were entitled to enjoy a defence of change of position to a strict liability to make restitution if he had dissipated trust property, but that if he had retained it the beneficiaries could recover it as their property, even though he might have changed his position in good faith on the basis that he thought he had received a valid gift? For example, imagine that a person owned 1,000 shares in a public company and then received a further 1,000 shares in the same company which were subject to a trust. He was entirely innocent and, in the light of his windfall, he gave his original block of shares to charity. Since he was not a bona fide purchaser the beneficiaries would be able to claim the 1,000 shares remaining in his hands as subject to the trust, and it would be no defence to their proprietary claim that he had changed his position.[235] It would then, no doubt, be argued that the defence of change of position should be utilised to entitle the court to re-apportion equitable proprietary interests, and the entire concept of the equitable ownership of property would be reduced to a subset of a rampant law of unjust enrichment. The law of unjust enrichment should rather be seen as subordinate to the law of property and parasitic upon it. A recipient is only unjustly enriched because he receives property belonging to another. Where that property is equitable in character, it should be for the principles of equity to determine the circumstances in which the recipient was enriched. Given that the very nature of equitable property is founded upon notions of conscience, it is perfectly logical to find that a recipient is not unjustly enriched until he dishonestly dissipates such property. The mere fact that this result is inconsistent with a common law approach does not render it unacceptable. Inconsistency is only illogical where there is a real similarity between the things which are allegedly inconsistent. Legal title and equitable title are different, and therefore there is no reason to expect them to adopt identical rules regarding the circumstances in which a recipient of property will be unjustly enriched so as to oblige him to make restitution. It is quite clear that equity and the common law have different rules concerning the circumstances in which a third party will acquire property free from pre-existing property rights. In equity a bona fide purchaser of trust property is not unjustly enriched because the pre-existing equitable property right of the beneficiaries is brought to an end by the process of the acquisition. In contrast, legal ownership is generally not destroyed by bona fide purchase and the *nemo dat* rule operates, subject to limited exceptions. As the decision of the majority of the House of Lords in *Westdeutsche Landesbank Girozentrale v Islington London Borough Council*[236] demonstrates, differences between common law rights and remedies and equitable rights and remedies cannot be ignored merely by the invocation of the language of restitution and unjust enrichment.

In *El Ajou v Dollar Land Holdings plc (No 1)*[237] Millett J, stated that a personal remedy based on knowing receipt was the counterpart in equity of the common law claim for money had and received. He noted that the common law action was a receipt-based

---

[235] Unless the defence of change of position extends to proprietary interests. See *Re Diplock* [1948] Ch 465; (1991) 107 LQR 71 (Millett LJ); Birks, 'Change of Position and Surviving Enrichment', in Swadling (ed), *The Limits of Restitutionary Claims* (1997).

[236] [1996] AC 669 at 705.

[237] [1993] 3 All ER 717.

claim to restitution and concluded: 'So, in my judgment, is the [personal remedy based on knowing receipt], unless arbitrary and anomalous distinctions between the common law and equitable claims are to be insisted upon.'[238] However, it is submitted that the present distinctions are not arbitrary and anomalous but reflect the intrinsic difference in the character of legal and equitable proprietary rights. It is entirely appropriate for equity, which reflects conscience, to retain a fault-based liability to make restitution, and this is the present position in English law.

---

[238]  [1993] 3 All ER 717 at 738.

# 31

# Tracing

## 1 What is tracing?[1]

### (1) Tracing is a process by which property is identified

Tracing describes the process by which the law allows the original owner of property to identify assets in the hands of a third party which represent it because they are its exchange product or proceeds. For example, if a car is stolen and the thief sells it for cash which he uses to purchase shares in a company, the car owner will be entitled to identify the shares as the product of his original property. In *Foskett v McKeown*, the most significant recent case concerning the nature of tracing, Lord Millett distinguished between 'following' and 'tracing' as follows:

'Following is the process of following the same asset as it moves from hand to hand. Tracing is the process of identifying a new asset as the substitute for the old.'[2]

If tracing is the process by which such proceeds of property can be identified, the rules of tracing provide the framework of principles which determine whether such identification is possible. In some cases, for example where there was a clean substitution of one type of property for another, the identification of assets representing the original property is relatively easy. In the example given above, the car was swapped for money, which was in turn swapped for the shares. Thus the shares can be identified as representing the car. However, in most cases the transactions which have occurred will have been far more complex, especially where the property sought to be traced was money. There may have been numerous exchanges, and at various stages in the chain of exchange the property may have become mixed with other property. Where such mixing occurs the process of identification becomes much more difficult. For example, if the car was stolen and then sold for cash, which was paid into a bank account of the thief which already contained a substantial balance, and shares were then purchased using money from the bank account, it is much less easy to demonstrate that the shares are the proceeds of the car. The shares could equally have been purchased using the money that was already in the account which was not the product of the car. The rules

---

[1] For extensive recent considerations of tracing see: Birks (ed), *Laundering and Tracing* (1995); Smith, *The Law of Tracing* (1997).

[2] [2001] 1 AC 102, [2000] 3 All ER 97, 119; [2001] Conv 94 (Stevens); [2000] 63 MLR 905 (Grantham and Rickett); (2001) 117 LQR (Berg); [2000] RLR 573 (Sir Robert Walker); (2000) 14 Tru LI 194 (Jaffey).

of tracing have evolved to try to determine the circumstances in which property can be traced through more complicated exchanges and mixed funds.

## (2)  Tracing at common law and in equity

A variety of rules and presumptions have been developed to enable the identification of specific property, and to determine whether it has continued to be identifiable as such through transfers, substitutions and mixing. The distinction between legal and equitable ownership is fundamental to English property law. This historic bifurcation has led to the development of two separate bodies of rules for tracing property, one operative for tracing ownership at common law, and the other for tracing the equitable beneficial ownership which arises under a trust. Whilst the common law rules have little application beyond the most simple of dealings with property, the equitable rules are considerably more generous and facilitate tracing through more complex transactions. The rules in equity have developed particularly to trace property through mixed funds. The equitable rules also have a moral dimension, operating more harshly against a wrongdoer who misappropriates property than an innocent party. Whilst many have argued that the common law rules of tracing are unduly restrictive, and that the rules should be harmonised for both legal and equitable ownership, at present it is not possible to utilise the equitable rules to trace property unless it is held on trust.

## (3)  Tracing and claiming

Tracing is merely a process which enables an owner of property to identify assets as representing his original property. As such, the process of tracing does not itself determine the rights that the original owner may assert in any assets identified by the rules of tracing. Tracing is not therefore a remedy but a mechanism. However, tracing as a process is pursued with the object of providing a foundation for the assertion of a right or a remedy. The original owner may seek to assert a proprietary right to any assets identified by the rules of tracing, with the consequence that they are his property and they do not belong to the holder. Alternatively, he may seek a purely personal remedy requiring that the holder of the identified assets make restitution of the value of the property he had received. The assertion of an appropriate remedy in respect of assets identified by the rules of tracing has been termed 'claiming'.[3] This purpose and nature of tracing was explained by Lord Millett in *Foskett v McKeown*:

'Tracing is thus neither a claim nor a remedy. It is merely the process by which a claimant demonstrates what has happened to his property, identifies its proceeds and the persons who have handled or received them, and justifies his claim that the proceeds can properly be regarded as representing his property.'[4]

Whether an original owner will be able to assert a proprietary claim to any assets identified by the tracing process as representing his property will depend upon a number of factors, including the nature of his interest in the original asset, and whether

---

[3]  See Smith, *The Law of Tracing* (1997), pp 284–369.    [4]  [2000] 3 All ER 97 at 120.

any intervening defences negate his ability to claim. Where he can assert such a proprietary claim his right of ownership is, in effect, preserved into the exchange product of his original property. The claiming of specific assets will be especially significant in two circumstances. First, the person presently holding the identified assets may be insolvent.[5] If the identified assets are subject to a proprietary claim they will not fall to be distributed amongst his general creditors, and as such a claiming owner will enjoy a priority which could not be achieved through a personal claim. Secondly, the identified assets may be more valuable than the original property which has been traced into them. If so, a proprietary claim will enable the original owner to take the benefit of the appreciation which has occurred.[6]

Given the distinction between tracing and claiming, this chapter will examine in turn the rules of tracing at common law and in equity, and then the ensuing claiming rights of an original owner who has been able to identify assets which represent his original property.

## (4) The nature of the tracing process[7]

### (a) Tracing and restitution

There has been a great deal of debate in recent years as to the conceptual nature of the tracing process. Traditionally tracing was understood to form part of the law of property, and to operate by preserving title to property through substitutions and mixtures. However some academics have argued that the tracing process should be understood rather as part of the law of restitution.

Restitution is the response which consists in a defendant giving up to a plaintiff an unjust enrichment which he has received at his expense. Generally, restitution will be effected by means of a personal remedy, so that the defendant will be ordered to pay to the plaintiff a sum of money equivalent to the enrichment he has received. In his seminal work *Introduction to the Law of Restitution*, Professor Birks classified this remedy as 'restitution in the first measure', and the measure of the restitution is the 'value received', i.e. the extent to which he was unjustly enriched. However, he has argued that restitution will sometimes be effected by means of a proprietary remedy, so that the defendant is forced to give up to the plaintiff any property in his hands which represents the enrichment he received. This is termed 'restitution in the second measure', and the measure of restitution is the 'value surviving' in the defendant's hands.[8] Tracing is regarded merely as a process by which 'value surviving' is identified. This is not a matter of mere semantics as this analysis has important consequences for the understanding of the nature of the tracing process.

---

[5] See [1995] CLJ 377 (Oakley).

[6] Re *Tilley's Will Trust* [1967] Ch 1179; *Jones (FC) & Sons v Jones* [1996] 4 All ER 721; *Foskett v McKeown* [2000] 3 All ER 97.

[7] See (1992) 45 CLP 69 (Birks); Moriarty, 'Tracing, Mixing and Laundering' in Birks (ed), *Laundering and Tracing* (1995), pp 73–94; Smith, *The Law of Tracing* (1997); (1997) 11 TLI 2 (Birks); Smith, *Unjust Enrichment, Property and the Structure of Trusts* (2000) 116 LQR 412; Burrows, *Proprietary Restitution: Umasking Unjust Enrichment* (2001) 117 LQR 412.

[8] Birks, *Introduction to the Law of Restitution* (1985), pp 75–98 and 358–401.

This restitutionary analysis cuts to the very heart of the nature of tracing. Traditionally, tracing has been understood to operate by descent of title, or 'vested interest'. A plaintiff is entitled to trace because he initially had title to property, which title he is able to follow into mixtures and exchange products because it was never lost. This analysis is rejected because of the perceived danger of a 'geometric multiplication'[9] in the plaintiff's wealth as he gains interests in all the exchange products for his property as well. For example, if a trustee takes £5,000 from the trust and purchases a diamond ring, which he sells for £10,000 and then purchases a car with the money, the beneficiary could have equitable title to the ring, the car and the £10,000 in the hands of the seller of the car, all at the same time. As an alternative to this 'vested interest' approach, Professor Birks has argued that the original owner of property has only a 'power in rem which he can bring down on assets that by the rules of tracing are identified as the surviving enrichment'.[10] The original owner has no proprietary rights to any mixed fund or to assets purchased out of a mixed fund, but only a 'power to crystallise such a right'.[11]

More recently Professor Burrows has also argued that tracing operates not as a proprietary process but to prevent unjust enrichment. He asserts that the tracing of rights into substitute assets cannot be explained on a proprietary basis:

'Ownership of a pig can explain ownership of the piglets but does not explain why P can be said to own the horse that D has obtained in substitution for the pig stolen from P. To reason from one to the other is to apply a very tempting but, in truth, fictional notion of property.'[12]

In his view, where a substitution occurs the owner of the original property is given a new title to reverse the unjust enrichment of the third party who has substituted it. Unmasking the underlying principle of unjust enrichment thus opens the door to consideration whether the act of substitution should automatically entitle an original owner to obtain title to the new asset. However it can be countered that it is well established in English law that an original owner has an automatic right to claim entitlement to assets which are substituted for his property. Given that both 'unjust enrichment' and 'property' are both essentially rhetorical constructs it is perfectly legitimate for a legal system to characterise such an automatic entitlement as an aspect of property. The ownership of piglets produced by a pig is equally determined by long established conventions which are characterised as property, and is no more or less fictitious that the conventions which dictate entitlements to substitute property.

In his final work before his untimely death, Professor Birks reiterated his long-held view that tracing is merely a power to vest a currently traceable substitute in himself, not a right, although he acknowledged that this view is not uncontroversial.[13]

---

[9] Birks, *Introduction to the Law of Restitution*, p 394. See also Burrows, *The Law of Restitution* (2nd edn, 2002), p 92.

[10] See (1992) 45(2) CLP 69 at 89–95 (Birks).

[11] Birks, *Introduction to the Law of Restitution* (1985), p 393. See also *Re J Leslie Engineers Co Ltd* [1976] 1 WLR 292.

[12] 'Proprietary Restitution: Unmasking Unjust Enrichment' (2002) 117 LQR 412 at 418. See also Craig Rotherham, 'The Metaphysics of Tracing: Substituted Title and Property Rhetoric' (1996) 34 Osgoode Hall LJ 321.

[13] Birks, *Unjust Enrichment* (2nd edn, 2005), p198. See also Hedley & Halliwell (eds), *The Law of Restitution* (2002) p 58.

## (b) Tracing as a proprietary process

Whist the use of tracing as a means of identifying the receipt of enrichment is unquestioned, it is submitted that the relegation of tracing to a mere process without proprietary implications is unduly reductionist and at odds with both authority and principle. Whilst tracing may functionally operate to demonstrate receipt, and thus as the foundation for a personal claim to restitution at common law or in equity, the process of tracing is intrinsically proprietary in nature. Value cannot exist in the abstract but only in the form of specific assets or property. The leading cases concerning the right to trace at common law and in equity support the view that tracing operates by 'descent of title' so that a plaintiff can trace his property through mixtures and substitutions.[14] At every stage of the chain of events he continues to be the owner, whether at law or in equity, of the assets identified by the rules of tracing. If at any point he ceases to be the owner, his right to trace comes to an automatic end, as when trust property is acquired by a bona fide purchaser.

In *Lipkin Gorman v Karpnale Ltd*, the leading case concerning common law tracing, Lord Goff held that the implication of tracing money from a solicitor's client account was that it remained 'their property at common law'.[15] He therefore understood the tracing claim to operate on a proprietary basis. In *Jones (FC) & Sons (a firm) v Jones*[16] the Court of Appeal similarly held that money was traceable at common law because the recipient had not obtained title to it. In the recent case of *Foskett v McKeown*, which concerned the tracing of trust property in equity, the House of Lords clearly stated that the tracing process was to be viewed as part of the law of property rather than restitution. Lord Millett explained:

'The transmission of a claimant's property rights from one asset to its traceable proceeds is part of our law of property, not of the law of unjust enrichment. There is no "unjust factor" to justify restitution (unless "want of title" be one, which makes the point). The claimant succeeds if at all by virtue of his own title, not to reverse unjust enrichment. Property rights are to be determined by fixed rules and settled principles, they are not discretionary. They do not depend upon ideas of what is "fair, just or reasonable". Such concepts, which in reality mask decisions of legal policy, have no place in the law of property. A beneficiary of a trust is entitled to a continuing beneficial interest not merely in the trust property but in its traceable proceeds also, and his interest binds every one who takes the property or its traceable proceeds except a bona fide purchaser for value without notice.'[17]

Professor Burrows[18] considers this affirmation of proprietary nature of tracing to have

---

[14] Except for the judgment of Robert Walker J in *El Ajou v Dollar Land Holdings plc (No 2)* [1995] 2 All ER 213, who suggested (at 223) that: 'tracing claims depend not on equitable ownership as such but on the concept of an equitable charge.'

[15] [1992] 4 All ER 512 at 529.     [16] [1997] Ch 159.

[17] [2000] 3 All ER 97 at 119–120. Similar sentiments were also expressed by Lord Browne-Wilkinson at p. 101–102. Earlier cases supporting the proprietary nature of tracing in equity include: *Sinclair v Brougham* [1914] AC 398; *Re Diplock* [1948] Ch 465; *Chase Manhattan Bank NA v Israeli-British Bank (London) Ltd* [1981] Ch 105; *Agip v Jackson* [1992] 4 All ER 451. For criticism of such a proprietary understanding of the tracing process see Burrows, 'Proprietary Restitution: Unmasking Unjust Enrichment' (2001) 117 LQR 412.

[18] Burrows, *The Law of Restitution* (2nd edn, 2002), p 81. See also (2001) 117 LQR 412 and (2001) 54 CLP 231.

been unfortunate. He argues that it is a fiction to say that a claimant is given ownership of traced property because his or her ownership of the original property continues through the substitute property, and he argues that the truth it that the claimant may be given a new title to the traced property to reverse the defendant's unjust enrichment at the claimant's expense.[19] However the rules of tracing, which will be examined below, have evolved specifically to identify property. Their one object is to identify specific assets in which the plaintiff has a continuing proprietary interest. This is evident from rules such as the 'lowest intermediate balance', which prevents tracing into money added later to an account which has been depleted, because that additional money is not in equity the property of the plaintiff. Similarly, the limitation that property will not be traced into the hands of a bona fide purchaser for value without notice demonstrates that the basis is descent of title. Tracing is impossible in such circumstances because the proprietary chain is broken at the point where the equitable interest is defeated. The right of a plaintiff to take advantage of any increase in value of assets identified by the rules of tracing also points to the proprietary nature of the tracing process.[20]

It is questionable whether the supposed fear of 'geometric multiplication' of the plaintiff's property is justified in practice. The danger is only apparent at common law in consequence of the principle *nemo dat quod non habet*. The well-established limitation that the common law cannot trace into a mixed fund itself prevents such 'geometric progression'. In equity, 'geometric multiplication' is curtailed by the principle that the right to trace is lost as against a bona fide purchaser for value. Geometric multiplication is also inhibited by the principle that a plaintiff cannot recover twice for the same loss. Geometric multiplication provides a plaintiff with a choice of trails of ownership, from amongst which he can choose. It is therefore no more of a problem than other situations in which a plaintiff has a choice of remedies, as for example where the purchaser of a defective product can choose to sue either the manufacturer or the retailer.

Whilst restitution theorists have helpfully clarified the distinction between 'tracing' and 'claiming', so that tracing is seen as a process and not a remedy in itself, it is submitted that the tracing process is inherently proprietary in nature. What is traced is not abstract value but property in specific assets.[21] When specific assets are identified as representing the plaintiff's original property, the plaintiff is able to assert a proprietary entitlement to them and claim them as belonging to himself. If assets are identified by the equitable rules of tracing, the present legal owner will be treated as holding them on a constructive trust for the plaintiff, or, alternatively, the plaintiff may be entitled to

[19]  See also Rotherham, 'Tracing Misconceptions in *Foskett v McKeown*' [2003] RLR 57.

[20]  See also the arguments of Grantham and Rickett, 'Property Rights as a Legally Significant Event' (2003) 62 CLJ 717.

[21]  See also *Westdeutsche Landesbank Girozentrale v Islington London Borough Council* [1996] AC 669 at 709, where Lord Browne-Wilkinson stated in respect of Professor Birk's argument that unjust enrichment would give rise to an automatic resulting trust: 'First, the argument elides rights in property (which is the only proper subject matter of a trust) into rights in "the value transferred". A trust can only arise where there is defined property: it is therefore not consistent with trust principles to say that a person is a trustee of property which cannot be defined. The same argument applies to the right to trace in equity. It can only subsist in respect of identified property which is held on trust for the person tracing and not in respect of some abstract concept of value.'

vindicate his proprietary right by means of an equitable charge.[22] Similarly, where specific assets are identified by the common law rules of tracing the plaintiff will be entitled to claim them as his property.[23] In many cases the plaintiff will be forced to resort to a personal claim to restitution because the specific assets have been dissipated in whole or in part. In such circumstances the restitutionary claim is parasitic upon the proprietary tracing process, which operates to demonstrate that the defendant was enriched at the expense of the plaintiff.

## 2 Tracing and claiming at common law[24]

### (1) Common law tracing through clean substitutions

The common law rules of tracing are clearly capable of following the ownership of property through a clean substitution, in other words through an exchange which did not involve any mixing of the original property being traced with other property. This was established in the leading early case, *Taylor v Plumer*.[25] Sir Thomas Plumer had entrusted a stockbroker, Walsh, with money for investment in Exchequer bills. Walsh instead misappropriated the money and used it to purchase bullion and American bonds. He was apprehended and surrendered the property. The central issue was whether the bullion and bonds were rightly the property of Sir Thomas or Walsh's trustee in bankruptcy. Lord Ellenborough held that the money which Sir Thomas had given to Walsh could be traced into the bullion and securities, and that they were properly the property of Sir Thomas. He stated the principle:

'It makes no difference in reason or law into what other form, different from the original, the change may have been made . . . for the product or the substitute for the original thing still follows the nature of the thing itself . . .'

### (2) Common law tracing of tangible property into a mixed bulk

Alongside tracing property through clean substitutions, the common law is also able to trace tangible property which is mixed with identical property so as to create a bulk. Where such mixing occurs the owners of the goods which have been mixed become tenants in common of the whole in the proportions which they have contributed to it.[26]

---

[22] *Boscawen v Bajwa* [1995] 4 All ER 769: *Foskett v McKeown* [2001] 1 AC 102.

[23] *Jones (FC) & Sons v Jones* [1997] Ch 159.

[24] See Worthington, *Proprietary Interests in Commercial Transactions* (1996), pp 133–144; Smith, *The Law of Tracing* (1997), pp 162–174; Matthews, 'The Legal and Moral Limits of Common Law Tracing', in Birks (ed), *Laundering and Tracing* (1995), pp 23–72; Burrows. *The Law of Restitution* (2nd ed, 2002), pp 83–93; (1966) 7 WALR 463 (Scott); (1976) 92 LQR 360 (Goode); (1976) 40 Conv (NS) 277 (Pearce); (1979) 95 LQR 78 (Khurshid and Matthews); [1997] LMCLQ 65 (Band).

[25] (1815) 3 M & S 562. It has recently been argued that this case has been fundamentally misinterpreted: see below, p 874.

[26] *Spence v Union Marine Insurance Co* (1868) LR 3 CP 427.

In *Indian Oil Corpn Ltd v Greenstone Shipping Co SA (Panama) (The Ypatianna)*[27] an owner's crude oil was mixed with other crude oil belonging to a shipowner which was already on board a vessel. Staughton J held that the owner was entitled to trace his oil into the bulk. In *Glencore International AG v Metro Trading International Inc (No 2)*[28] Moore-Bick J extended this principle to a situation where oil was blended with oil of a different grade or specification with the result that a new product was produced. The original owner was held able to trace his oil into the mixture, identifying a proportion in the new blend which takes account of both the quantity and the value of the oil contributed to the new bulk. However the right to trace will be lost where tangible property is not merely mixed to form a bulk but is consumed in the manufacture of an entirely new product so as to lose its identity altogether. Thus in *Borden (UK) Ltd v Scottish Timber Products Ltd*[29] it was not possible to trace resin which was mixed with other materials so as to manufacture chipboard. Where tangible property is mixed so as to form a bulk the rights of the original owner will vary depending upon whether the mixing was wrongful or innocent, and whether the property can be divided between the parties.

### (3) Common law tracing of money through mixed funds

Whilst *Taylor v Plumer* demonstrates that the common law can trace property through clean substitutions, it also established the limitation that the common law is incapable of tracing money through a mixed fund. Lord Ellenborough stated that it was only possible to follow assets where they are able to be 'ascertained' to represent the original property, and that such ascertainment becomes impossible 'when the subject is turned into money, and mixed and confounded in a general mass of the same description'.

Subsequent cases have thus held that the common law cannot trace money through a mixed fund.[30] Say, for example, that an agent holds shares on behalf of his principal. If the agent sells the shares and uses the proceeds to purchase a diamond ring, the common law can trace his property into the ring. However, if the agent sells the shares and then mixes the proceeds with money of his own to create a mixed fund, and then uses money from the fund to purchase the ring, the common law can no longer trace because of the mixing which had taken place. The rationale for this limitation was said by Lord Ellenborough to be a difficulty of fact, not law. Money has no ear-mark and therefore cannot be distinguished within a mixed fund, whereas 'money in a bag, or otherwise kept apart from other money' is ear-marked and so outside of the limitation.

The limitation was accepted by the Court of Appeal in *Banque Belge Pour l'Etranger v Hambrouck*.[31] The case concerned a man who obtained cheques by fraud from his employers, which were paid into his bank account. He then passed the money to his mistress, Mlle Spanoghe, who paid it into her bank account. The Court of Appeal held that it was possible to trace the money at common law into Mlle Spanoghe's account.

---

[27] [1988] QB 345.     [28] [2001] 1 Lloyd's Rep 284.     [29] [1981] Ch 25.

[30] See *Re Diplock* [1948] Ch 465 at 519–520; *Agip (Africa) Ltd v Jackson* [1990] Ch 265; *El Ajou v Dollar Land Holdings plc* [1993] BCLC 735; *Bank Tejarat v Hong Kong and Shanghai Banking Corpn* [1995] 1 Lloyd's Rep 239; *Jones (FC) & Sons v Jones* [1996] 4 All ER 721.

[31] [1921] 1 KB 321.

Previously it had been thought that the common law would not trace money into a bank account at all, but the court held that, following the equity case *Re Hallet's Estate,*[32] there was nothing to prevent the court examining the details of a bank account.[33] The mere fact that the money had been paid into a bank account did not itself cause a failure of the means of ascertainment.[34] However in granting the claim, the court stressed that there had been no mixing of the money in the bank accounts concerned. If there had been mixing, then it seems that common law tracing, unlike equitable tracing, would not have been available.[35] Similarly, in *Lipkin Gorman v Karpnale Ltd*[36] common law tracing was only possible because the defendants had conceded that there had been no mixing of the misappropriated money.

It is important to note that whilst the common law is incapable of tracing money through a mixed fund, it is capable of tracing money into a mixed fund so as to establish that the recipient was enriched by the receipt of that property.

## (4) Common law tracing of money through the banking system[37]

Whilst the common law is prima facie capable of tracing money through a bank account, provided that it remains unmixed, more recent cases have found that tracing is not possible at common law where money has been transferred between bank accounts and the means of exchange has inevitably involved some element of mixing. In *Agip (Africa) Ltd v Jackson*[38] the plaintiff firm was defrauded by its chief accountant, Zdiri. He altered the names of the payee on genuine payment orders in favour of dummy companies he had created. One payment of $518,000 was made to a dummy company, Baker Oil Services Ltd, who held an account at a branch of Lloyds Bank in London. On receiving the payment order Agip's bankers telegraphed instructions to Lloyds Bank Overseas Division to credit the account of Baker Oil at their London Branch with a corresponding amount. At the same time, their correspondent bank in New York debited their account and credited Lloyds Bank's correspondent bank in New York. The next day the money was transferred from the Baker Oil account to the account of the defendants, who were a firm of accountants in the Isle of Man. All but $45,000 was then paid out. There had been no mixing of the money in the Baker Oil account. At first instance Millett J held that Agip could not trace the money at common law. One reason for this denial focused on the nature of the transfer. He held that:

'The money was transmitted by telegraphic transfer. There was no cheque or any equivalent. The payment order was not a cheque or its equivalent . . . Nothing passed between Tunisia

---

[32]  (1880) 13 Ch D 696.

[33]  See *Jones (FC) & Sons v Jones* [1997] Ch 159 where money was traced at common law into a bank account.

[34]  As Atkin LJ graphically said: 'But if in 1815 the common law halted outside the banker's door, by 1879 equity had the courage to lift the latch, walk in and examine the books . . . I see no reason why the means of ascertainment so provided should not now be available both for common law and equity proceedings.'

[35]  [1921] 1 KB 321 at 336, per Atkin LJ; at 330, per Scrutton LJ.     [36]  [1991] 2 AC 548.

[37]  See Smith, *The Law of Tracing* (1997), pp 249–262.

[38]  [1990] Ch 265, [1992] 4 All ER 385; (1989) 105 LQR 528 (Birks); (1991) 107 LQR 71 (Sir Peter Millett); [1991] Ch 547, [1992] 4 All ER 451; (1991) 50 CLJ 409 (Harpum); [1992] Conv 367 (Goulding); All ER Rev 1992, pp 258–265 (Swadling).

and London but a stream of electrons. It is not possible to treat the money as received by Lloyds Bank of London, or its correspondent bank in New York, as representing the proceeds of the payment order or of any other physical asset previously in its hands . . .'[39]

This argument was rejected by the Court of Appeal, where Fox LJ took the view that it did not matter that the transfer had been by order rather than cheque.[40] More significantly, however, Millet J had held that the plaintiffs were not entitled to trace at common law because the money must have been mixed with other money when the transfer took place through the New York clearing system between Agip and Lloyds' correspondent banks. This reasoning was supported by the Court of Appeal,[41] and tracing at common law was thus prevented.

Similar reasoning was employed in *Bank Tejarat v Hong Kong and Shanghai Banking Corpn (CI) Ltd*,[42] where the plaintiff had paid the defendants DM3.4m via the Frankfurt clearing system. Tuckey J applied the principle identified in *Agip (Africa) Ltd v Jackson* and held that, as the plaintiff's money would inevitably have become mixed with other money through the Frankfurt deutschmark clearing system, it was impossible to trace the money at common law into the hands of the defendants.[43] The plaintiff's claim to personal restitution at common law by way of an action for money had and received therefore failed.

In both case the inadequacy of the common law rules of tracing required the plaintiffs to turn instead to equity, asserting that the misappropriated money was subject to a trust and that the respective defendants were liable on the grounds of knowing assistance.[44] It is submitted that the refusal to allow common law tracing on the grounds of inevitable mixing during the process of transfer of funds involves an unduly literalistic analysis of the tracing process. Whenever transfers occur between banks, whether by virtue of an electronic transfer or a cheque which is presented through the clearing system, it is not as if the specific money held in the account from which the funds are drawn is transferred to the bank holding the account into which it is to be paid. Where money is held in a bank account, the nature of the relationship between the bank and its customer is one of debtor and creditor, so that there is no real connection between the balance in account and any specific money as such. Where money is debited from one account and credited to another there should simply be an evidential presumption that the money represented thereby has passed from one account to the other. The means of transfer operative between the banks holding the accounts should not prevent that inference.

Unless such an inference is operative there is no reason why the common law should ever be able to trace into or through a bank account. The mere transfer of money between accounts held at different domestic banks is effected through the clearing system and yet this does not seem to have prevented common law tracing. It has been seen that in *Jones (FC) & Sons (a firm) v Jones*[45] the partner of the plaintiff firm drew

---

[39] [1990] Ch 265 at 399.     [40] [1992] 4 All ER 451 at 465.
[41] [1992] 4 All ER 451 at 465, per Fox LJ.
[42] [1995] 1 Lloyd's Rep 239; (1995) 9 TLI 91 (Birks); [1996] LMCLQ 1 (Birks).
[43] [1995] 1 Lloyd's Rep 239 at 245.
[44] Now dishonest assistance: *Royal Brunei Airlines v Tan* [1995] 2 AC 378, [1995] 3 All ER 97.
[45] [1996] 4 All ER 721.

cheques totalling £11,700 on a joint account at the Midland Bank which were paid into an account opened in the name of his wife with a firm of commodity brokers. She then received cheques for £50,760 from the commodity brokers which she paid into a deposit account. The Court of Appeal held that the firm's trustee in bankruptcy should be entitled to trace at common law and that it was not necessary to take account of the reality of the clearing system which lay behind the transaction. Millett LJ stated that:

'The trustee can follow the money in the joint account at Midland Bank, which had been vested by statute in him, into the proceeds of the three cheques which Mrs Jones received from her husband. The trustee does not need to follow money from one recipient to another or follow it through the clearing system; he can follow the cheques as they pass from hand to hand. It is sufficient for him to be able to trace the money into the cheques and the cheques into their proceeds.'[46]

However, if this reasoning is correct, there is equally no reason why the court should have been concerned with the means of transfer through the clearing system in *Agip (Africa) Ltd v Jackson* and *Bank Tejarat v Hong Kong and Shanghai Banking Corpn (CI) Ltd*. Surely it is enough to identify a debit from one account echoed by a corresponding receipt by another. This is as much a swap of one chose in action for another as if a cheque had physically changed hands. Millett LJ seems to lay great stress upon the presence of a physical cheque, which would suggest a return to his argument in *Agip (Africa) Ltd v Jackson*[47] that the common law cannot trace through an electronic transfer, which was rejected by the Court of Appeal.

The nature of a bank account is also a cause for difficulty in relation to common law tracing. As has been noted, the relationship between banker and customer is one of debtor and creditor. In *R v Preddy*,[48] a criminal case concerning mortgage fraud, the House of Lords held that where money was debited from one account and paid into another account, the second account holder had not obtained the property of the first account holder so as to render him liable to conviction for theft under s 15(1) of the Theft Act 1968.[49] Lord Goff explained:

'The question remains . . . whether the debiting of the lending institution's bank account, and the corresponding crediting of the bank account of the defendant or his solicitor, constitutes obtaining of that property. The difficulty in the way of that conclusion is simply that, when the bank account of the defendant (or his solicitor) is credited, he does not obtain the lending institution's chose in action. On the contrary that chose in action is extinguished or reduced pro tanto, and a chose in action is brought into existence representing a debt in an equivalent sum owed by a different bank to the defendant or his solicitor. In these circumstances it is difficult to see how the defendant or thereby obtained *property belonging to another*, i.e. to the lending institution.

Professor Sir John Smith has suggested that "Effectively, the victim's property has been changed into another form and now belongs to the defendant. There is the gain and equivalent loss which is characteristic of, and perhaps the substance of, obtaining".[50] But even if

---

[46] [1996] 4 All ER 721 at 728.     [47] [1990] Ch 265, [1992] 4 All ER 385.
[48] [1996] AC 815; [1996] LMCLQ 456 (Fox).     [49] Obtaining property by deception.
[50] [1995] Crim LR 564, 565–566.

this were right, I do not for myself see how this can properly be described as obtaining property belonging to another. In truth the property which the defendant has obtained is the new chose in action constituted by the debt now owed to him by his bank, and represented by the credit entry in his own bank account. This did not come into existence until the debt so created was owed to him by his bank, and so never belonged to anyone else. True, it corresponded to the debit entered in the lending institution's bank account; but it does not follow that the property which the defendant acquired can be identified with the property which the lending institution lost when its account was debited.'[51]

If this analysis is correct, it appears to remove any ability of the common law to trace money through bank accounts. If the increased balance in the credited account cannot be identified with the corresponding reduction in the balance of the debited account, then it is untraceable into that account. This is fundamentally inconsistent with the decision of the Court of Appeal in *Jones (FC) & Sons (a firm) v Jones*,[52] where it was held that the money credited to Mrs Jones's account belonged at law to the firm from whose account it had been debited. It is equally inconsistent with *Banque Belge Pour l'Etranger v Hambrouck*.[53] Even though the plaintiffs were seeking a personal remedy, their right to restitution was dependent upon establishing that the defendant had received their money into her bank account. It is also submitted that it is inconsistent with the judgment of the House of Lords in *Lipkin Gorman v Karpnale Ltd*,[54] where Lord Goff held that the plaintiff firm of solicitors was entitled to trace money misappropriated from their client account:

'There is in my opinion no reason why the solicitors should not be able to trace their property at common law in that chose in action, or in any part of it, into its products, ie cash drawn by Cass from their client account at the bank. Such a claim is consistent with their assertion that the money so obtained by Cass was their property at common law.'[55]

It would be utterly illogical if the firm were permitted to trace if Cass withdrew cash from their client account, and presumably also if he subsequently paid the cash into his own bank account, but not if he arranged for a direct transfer of money from their client account to his own bank account. Yet this would seem to be the implication of the decision in *R v Preddy*.[56] The ramifications of this case for the ability to trace through bank accounts at common law have yet to be fully considered by the courts.[57] However, the decision prompted statutory reform of the law of theft to ensure that defendants who received mortgage funds by fraud would be guilty of an offence.[58]

## (5) Criticism of the common law rules of tracing

Whilst the authorities have consistently held that the common law is incapable of tracing property through a mixed fund, this limitation has been subject to much criticism. The very origins of this limitation have been challenged by Lionel Smith, who has

---

[51] [1996] AC 815 at 834.    [52] [1996] 4 All ER 721.    [53] [1921] 1 KB 321.
[54] [1991] 2 AC 548.    [55] [1991] 2 AC 548 at 574.    [56] [1996] AC 815.
[57] For comment on the implications of *R v Preddy* in the context of tracing, see [1996] LMCLQ 456 (Fox).
[58] Theft (Amendment) Act 1996.

argued that in *Taylor v Plumer*[59] the common law court was in fact considering the equitable rules of tracing, with the implication that there was therefore no reason for the common law to consider itself limited in subsequent cases.[60] Whilst this misunderstanding was acknowledged by Millett LJ in *Jones (FC) & Sons (a firm) v Jones*,[61] he made clear that this alone did not permit the overthrow of the settled common law principle which had emerged despite the misunderstanding.[62]

Given that the limitation cannot be eliminated merely because of historical misunderstanding of *Taylor v Plumer*, it is open to objections on its own terms. It appears to be rooted in the perception that the common law cannot identify property in a mixed fund but, as commentators have pointed out,[63] there is no reason why the common law cannot recognise joint title to a mixed fund through a tenancy-in-common. This possibility was recognised in *Spence v Union Marine Insurance Co Ltd*,[64] where bales of wool were mixed and it was not possible to identify their owners because the identifying marks had been lost in a shipwreck. The court held that there was a tenancy-in-common.

Although in principle the recognition of a tenancy in common at law should enable the common law to trace into mixtures, the cases have not adopted this analysis. The inability of the common law to trace into mixed funds has had the effect of turning plaintiffs to seek relief in equity, since the equitable rules permit tracing through a mixed fund. Whilst this might achieve practical justice, equitable tracing is dependent upon the existing of a trust relationship. The desire to trace in equity has therefore tended to lead to an expansion of the circumstances in which misappropriated property will be treated as subject to a constructive trust, usually through the medium of a fiduciary relationship. It is questionable whether the expansion of equitable rights and interests in the commercial field is appropriate, and this view seems to have been reflected in more recent cases.[65] The common law rules of tracing have also restricted the availability of common law restitution through the action for money had and received, since it cannot be demonstrated that a defendant was enriched by the receipt of the plaintiff's property where it has passed through a mixed fund. Thus, in *Bank Tejarat v Hong Kong and Shanghai Banking Corpn (CI) Ltd*[66] the plaintiff's claim for common law restitution on the grounds of mistake failed because it was not able to trace its money into the hands of the defendants because it had become mixed in the Frankfurt clearing system. At present it is impossible to utilise the equitable rules of tracing to found a common law claim to restitution.[67]

It is therefore submitted that there is no reason in principle, or in practice, for the emasculated common law rules that do not permit tracing through a mixed fund. If the common law rules were to develop so as to enable such tracing, there would be less need for an expansion of equity, trusts and fiduciary relationships into the commercial sphere as adequate restitutionary remedies would be available to a plaintiff whose

---

[59] (1815) 3 M & S 562.    [60] (1995) LMCLQ 240 (Smith).    [61] [1996] 4 All ER 721.

[62] [1996] 4 All ER 721 at 729.    [63] (1976) Conv (NS) 277 (Pearce).    [64] (1868) LR 3 CP 427.

[65] Eg: *Re Goldcorp Exchange* [1995] 1 AC 74; *Westdeutsche Landesbank Girozentrale v Islington London Borough Council* [1996] AC 669.

[66] [1995] 1 Lloyd's Rep 239; (1995) 9 TLI 91 (Birks).

[67] See *Jones (FC) & Sons v Jones* [1996] 4 All ER 721 at 729, per Millett LJ.

property had been misappropriated or misdirected. In *Jones (FC) & Sons (a firm) v Jones*[68] Millett LJ expressed dissatisfaction with the present position:

'There is no merit in having distinct and different tracing rules at law and in equity, given that tracing is neither a right nor a remedy but merely the process by which the plaintiff establishes what has happened to his property and makes good his claim that the assets which he claims can properly be regarded as representing his property. The fact that there are different tracing rules at law and in equity is unfortunate through probably inevitable, but unnecessary differences should not be created where they are not required by the different nature of legal and equitable doctrines and remedies. There is, in my view, even less merit in the present rule which precludes the invocation of the equitable tracing rules to support a common law claim; until that rule is swept away unnecessary obstacles to the development of a rational and coherent law of restitution will remain.'

In *Foskett v McKeown* he re-iterated his dissatisfaction with the current position in the House of Lords, and stated:

'Given its nature, there is nothing inherently legal or equitable about the tracing exercise. There is thus no sense in maintaining different rules for tracing at law and in equity. One set of tracing rules is enough ... There is certainly no logical justification for allowing any distinctions between them to produce capricious results in cases of mixed substitutions by insisting on the existence of a fiduciary relationship as a precondition for applying equity's tracing rules. The existence of such a relationship may be relevant to the nature of the claim which the plaintiff can maintain, whether personal or proprietary, but that is a different matter.'[69]

However, given that the case involved a straightforward situation where a trustee had misappropriated trust property, and that the equitable tracing rules were therefore undoubtedly available, he concluded that it was not the occasion to explore the relationship between equitable and common law tracing rules further. His comments are therefore strictly obiter, and the traditional dichotomy between the rules of tracing in equity and at common law remains intact, albeit on notice of impending demise.

## (6) Claiming at common law

It has been seen that the common law enables legal owners to trace their property though clean substitutions, and to trace tangible property into a mixed bulk. Once the tracing process has identified assets which represent the original property the original owner may be able to assert a claim thereto. The original owner may be entitled to assert a proprietary right, or he may be entitled to claim restitution, which is a personal remedy.

### (a) Claiming assets which are the product of a clean substitution

Common law tracing through clean substitutions operates on the basis of the preservation of the plaintiff's title to the property being traced. The plaintiff had legal title

---

[68] [1996] 4 All ER 721.    [69] [2000] 3 All ER 97 at 121.

before any clean substitutions took place, and such substitutions are not able to deprive him of his title. Except in the case of currency (banknotes and coins) to which special rules apply,[70] even a bona fide purchaser will not take free from the plaintiff's original title because his legal title is good against the world and cannot be defeated. This seems to have been the rationale of *Taylor v Plumer*,[71] where Lord Ellenborough said that Sir Thomas had simply 'repossessed himself of that, of which . . . he had never ceased to be the lawful proprietor'. More recently, in *Lipkin Gorman v Karpnale Ltd*, where a solicitor had taken money for gambling from the client account of his firm, Lord Goff held that the firm could trace at common law:

'There is in my opinion no reason why the solicitors should not be able to trace their property at common law in that chose in action [the client account], in any part of it, into its product, i.e. cash drawn by Cass from their client account at the bank. Such a claim is consistent with their assertion that the money so obtained by Cass was their property at common law.'[72]

Historically the common law did not possess adequate remedies to enable the plaintiff to vindicate his proprietary entitlement to assets identified as representing his original property. Whilst the common law developed real actions to enable a plaintiff to recover land, there were no equivalent actions to enable an owner to recover a specific chattel. As Professor Goode[73] has pointed out, the common law was only ever able to offer a personal remedy in damages for detinue or conversion. By statute the court enjoyed the discretion to award specific recovery in an action in detinue.[74] Section 3 of the Torts (Interference with Goods) Act 1977 entitles the court to order the delivery of goods. However in some older cases the owner was able to recover his property[75] and more recent cases have now established beyond doubt that an original owner may claim legal title to any assets identified by the rules of tracing.[76]

It is thus now clear that where a legal owner can identify assets in the hands of a third party as representing his original property he will be entitled to claim them as his own. In *Lipkin Gorman v Karpnale Ltd*[77] Lord Goff stated that the legal owner of property was entitled to trace or follow his property into its product. This principle was applied by the Court of Appeal in *Jones (FC) & Sons (a firm) v Jones*,[78] where the defendant had received money drawn from the bank account of a firm which had committed an act of bankruptcy before it had been adjudicated bankrupt. The money was invested in an account held by a firm of commodity brokers which dealt in potato futures. The investment was highly successful and the account contained almost five times as much

---

[70] See [1996] CLJ 547 (Fox); [1996] RLR 60 (Fox).     [71] (1815) 3 M & S 562.

[72] [1991] 2 AC 548 at 529, [1992] 4 All ER 512; (1991) Lloyd's MCLQ 473 (P Birks); (1991) 107 LQR 521 (P Watts); [1992] Conv 124 (M Halliwell); (1992) 55 MLR 377 (E McKendrick); (1992) 45(2) CLP 69 (P Birks).

[73] (1976) LQR 360 (Goode).

[74] Common Law Procedure Act 1854, s 78. Detinue was abolished by s 2 of the Torts (Interference with Goods) Act 1977.

[75] As in *Taylor v Plumer* (1815) 3 M & S 562.

[76] See *Jones (FC) & Sons v Jones* [1996] 4 All ER 721.     [77] [1991] 2 AC 548 at 573.

[78] [1996] 4 All ER 721, (1997) 113 LQR 21 (Andrews and Beatson); [1997] CLJ 30 (M Fox). See also [1997] RLR 92–96 (Davern).

money as had been initially invested. The Court of Appeal held that, as the firm could trace the money at common law into the account with the brokers, its trustee in bankruptcy was entitled to the money in the account (which had been paid into court). Beldam LJ stated:

'There is now ample authority for the proposition that a person who can trace his property into its product, provided the product is identifiable as the product of his property, he may lay legal claim to that property.'[79]

Where an owner is entitled to claim specific assets at common law he will be entitled to take advantage of any appreciation in value which they have experienced.

### (b) Claiming assets where tangible property has been mixed to form a bulk

As was noted above, the common law permits the tracing of tangible property into a mixed bulk. Where a mixed bulk has been created the rights of an original owner will vary depending upon whether the bulk is able to be separated into proportionate shares representing the assets of the contributors.

*(i) Claiming where the bulk can be divided into proportionate shares.* Where the bulk is capable of division a contributor will be entitled to claim the proportionate share which represents his original property, and of which he is a tenant in common. Such division will usually be possible if the property is fungible in nature, such as when it consists of grain, oil or wine.[80] The principle was stated by Staughton J in *Indian Oil Corpn Ltd v Greenstone Shipping Co SA (Panama)(The Ypatianna)*:

'. . . where B wrongfully mixes the goods of A with goods of his own, which are substantially of the same nature and quality, and they cannot in practice be separated, the mixture is held in common and A is entitled to receive out of it a quantity equal to that of his goods which went into the mixture, any doubt as to that quantity being resolved in favour of A.'[81]

*(ii) Claiming where the bulk cannot be divided into proportionate shares.* In contrast, where property was wrongfully mixed to form a bulk which cannot be divided into the proportionate shares of the contributors, the original owner will be entitled to claim the entire bulk. The right to claim the entire bulk in such circumstances was recognised by the House of Lords in *Foskett v McKeown*,[82] on the grounds that a pro rata division of the property is the best that the wrongdoer can hope for. Such circumstances are admittedly likely to be rare, but Lord Millet referred to the Canadian case of *Jones v De Marchant*[83] by way of example. In that case a husband had wrongfully used eighteen beaver skins belonging to his wife, together with fours skins of his own, to have a fur coat made up, which he gave to his mistress. Since the skins were no longer able to be separated it was held that the wife was entitled to ownership of the entire coat.

### (c) Claiming personal restitution at common law

The process of tracing may also provide a foundation for a personal claim to restitution. Where property is misappropriated or misdirected a recipient will be treated as having been unjustly enriched. The extent of his enrichment is the value of the property that he

---

[79] [1996] 4 All ER 721 at 731.    [80] *Foskett v McKeown* [2000] 3 All ER 97 at 125, per Lord Millett.
[81] [1988] QB 345, 371.    [82] [2000] 3 All ER 97.    [83] (1916) 28 DLR 561.

had received. If nothing remains in his hands which can be said to represent the property he received then a proprietary claim will not be available because the property has been dissipated. A proprietary claim can only subsist in relation to some specific identifiable asset. As Lord Lane CJ observed in *A-G's Reference (No 1 of 1985)*,[84] there can be no proprietary remedy unless there is an asset which can be 'identified as a separate piece of property'. The original owners may, however, be entitled to claim personal restitution from the recipient. In the context of such a claim, tracing is operating as a process by which it can be demonstrated that a defendant was in fact enriched at the expense of the original owner by receipt of his property. A personal restitutionary claim may also be more advantageous to an original owner than a proprietary claim even where the property has not been dissipated if the assets which represent his property have subsequently fallen in value, since the measure of restitution will be determined by the value of the property at the point of receipt. However such a personal remedy will only be more advantageous in practice if the recipient is solvent and able to discharge the obligation to make restitution.

As was noted in the previous chapter, the liability of a person who has received property belonging to another to make restitution at common law is strict, subject to the availability of the defence of change of position. The role of common law tracing as a foundation for a personal liability to make restitution is evident in *Lipkin Gorman v Karpnale Ltd*,[85] where a solicitor had misappropriated money from his firm's client account in order to finance his gambling at the Playboy Club. His firm sought to recover restitution from the club of the misappropriated money it had received. The firm could not make a proprietary claim to any assets in the club's hands as none could be identified which were the product of the money received. The common law rules would not permit tracing once the money had become mixed with other money of the club. However, the rules of common law tracing did establish that the club had received money which belonged to the firm, and thus entitled them to maintain the common law action for money had and received. As Lord Goff explained:

'It is well established that a legal owner is entitled to trace his property into its product, provided that the latter is indeed identifiable as the product of his property . . . Before Cass drew upon the solicitor's client account at the bank, there was of course no question of the solicitor's having any legal property in any cash lying at the bank. The relationship of the bank with the solicitors was essentially that of debtor and creditor; and since the client account was at all material times in credit, the bank was the debtor and the solicitors were its creditors. Such a debt constitutes a chose in action, which is a species of property; and since the debt was enforceable at common law, the chose in action was legal property belonging to the solicitors at common law. There is in my opinion no reason why the solicitors should not be able to trace their property at common law in that chose in action, or in any part of it, into its product, i.e. cash drawn by Cass from their client account at the bank. Such a claim is consistent with their assertion that the money obtained by Cass was their property at

---

[84] [1986] QB 491 at 506.      [85] [1991] 2 AC 548.

common law . . . it further follows, from the concession made by the respondents,[86] that the solicitors can follow their property into the hands of the respondents when it was paid to them at the club.'[87]

Thus, the firm's ability to trace the money drawn from the client account into the hands of the club, via the activities of the misappropriating solicitor, was vital to the establishment of their entitlement to restitution by way of an action for money had and received. Lord Goff stressed that the firm's claim was not proprietary, although it was founded upon the receipt of property:

'. . . the solicitors seek to show that the money in question was their property at common law. But their claim in the present case for money had and received is nevertheless a personal claim; it is not a proprietary claim, advanced on the basis that money remaining in the hands of the respondents is their property.'[88]

# 3 Tracing and claiming in equity[89]

## (1) The scope of equitable tracing

Whereas the common law rules of tracing have remained restrictive, equity developed rules which are much more flexible. There is no barrier preventing the tracing of equitable proprietary interests through a mixed fund. The rules, which originated in the context of the misappropriation of property subject to an express trust, are derived from evidential presumptions which enable the court to determine whether property has survived through mixing, and whether any assets purchased with money from a mixed fund can be said to represent property contributed to the mixture. The equitable rules are particularly designed to deal with mixing of funds in a bank account. By necessity they are rough and ready and not overly sophisticated. The presumptions on which they are founded also take account of the moral blameworthiness of the parties whose funds have been mixed. If a mixed fund consists of misappropriated trust property and the property of the wrongdoing trustee, the rules operate harshly against the wrongdoer. In contrast, if the mixture is comprised of misappropriated trust property and that of an innocent volunteer they seek to do justice between the two innocent parties.

---

[86] The respondents had conceded that if it could be shown that the firm enjoyed legal title to the money from the client account in the hands of the solicitor then that tile was not defeated by mixing of that money with other money in his hands.

[87] [1991] 2 AC 548 at 572–573.　　[88] [1991] 2 AC 548 at 572.

[89] Hayton, 'Equity's Identification Rules', in Birks (ed), *Laundering and Tracing* (1995), pp 1–22; Worthington, *Proprietary Interests in Commercial Transactions* (1996), pp 173–186; Burrows, *The Law of Restituion* (2nd edn, 2002), pp 93–104.

## (2) The right to trace in equity

Equitable tracing is not available in every situation in which property has been misappropriated or misapplied. Historically equity has taken the view that tracing is only possible where there was an initial fiduciary relationship. Whilst the language of a fiduciary relationship is somewhat imprecise and opaque what is really required is that the property sought to be traced was subject to a trust and thus belonged to the plaintiff in equity. This follows from the fact that the equitable rules of tracing seek to identify trust property. The question whether tracing in equity is possible is therefore closely connected to the question whether the original property was subject to a trust. Many of the early cases concerning equitable tracing concerned the misappropriation of property held under an express trust, as for example in *Re Hallet's Estate*[90] and *Re Oatway*.[91] Problems have occurred where plaintiffs have sought to trace property in equity which was not subject to a pre-existing trust and where the very circumstances of misappropriation or transfer are alleged to have given rise to a constructive trust, thus entitling the plaintiff to trace. In many commercial contexts the inadequacy of the common law rules of tracing has forced plaintiffs to turn to equity, which has tended to exert pressure on the court to find a trust relationship through the artificial use of fiduciary relationships.

### (a) The requirement of a fiduciary relationship

The present position of the English cases is that an initial fiduciary relationship is a prerequisite of the right to trace in equity. This was reaffirmed in *Westdeutsche Landesbank Girozentrale v Islington London Borough Council*.[92] Whilst the House of Lords overruled the earlier decision of *Sinclair v Brougham*,[93] Lord Browne-Wilkinson was at pains to stress that this did not amount to a rejection of the requirement of a fiduciary relationship since the House of Lords was not wishing to cast any doubt on the principles of tracing established in the later case of *Re Diplock*.

In *Re Diplock*[94] charities had wrongly received payments of £203,000 under a will. The next of kin were held entitled to trace the money in equity into the charities' hands, because the executors clearly stood in a fiduciary relationship to the estate. The Court of Appeal had examined the judgments of the House of Lords in *Sinclair v Brougham*[95] and concluded that a fiduciary relationship was a pre-requisite to tracing inequity. Lord Greene MR stated:

'Lord Parker and Lord Haldane both predicate the existence of a right of property recognised by equity which depends upon there having existed at some stage a fiduciary relationship of some kind (though not necessarily a positive duty of trusteeship) sufficient to give rise to the equitable right to trace property. Exactly what relationships are sufficient to bring such an equitable right into existence for the purposes of the rule which we are considering is a matter which has not been precisely laid down. Certain relationships are clearly

---

[90] (1880) 13 Ch D 696.    [91] [1903] 2 Ch 356.

[92] [1996] AC 669. In *Dublin Corpn v Building and Allied Trade Union* [1996] 1 IR 468 the Irish Supreme Court doubted that *Sinclair v Brougham* was authority for the proposition that a fiduciary relationship was a prerequisite of equitable tracing.

[93] [1914] AC 398.    [94] [1948] Ch 465.    [95] [1914] AC 398.

included; eg trustee (actual or constructive) and cestui que trust; and "fiduciary" relationships such as that of principal and agent . . .'

In *Sinclair v Brougham* a building society had operated an ultra vires banking business.
The case concerned the rights of the depositors who had invested their money with the
bank when the building society had become insolvent. The House of Lords held that
they were not entitled to claim restitution at common law through the action for money
had and received, which would have meant that they would have stood as creditors in
the insolvency and they would have ranked pari passu with the other general creditors
of the society. At that time the right to restitution was said to be founded upon an
implied contract to repay money had and received. The House of Lords held that, since
the building society had acted ultra vires in conducting the banking business, any
contract to repay the depositors would also have been ultra vires and was therefore void
and unenforceable. Since this would have the consequence that the depositors would
have no entitlement to claim as creditors in the insolvency, the House of Lords held that
the building society had received their deposits as a fiduciary and that they were entitled
to trace their money in equity into its remaining assets. In subsequent cases the implied
contract theory was rejected as artificial, and the right to restitution is now available
through the autonomous cause of action in unjust enrichment. In *Westdeutsche Landesbank Girozentrale v Islington London Borough Council*[96] the House of Lords therefore
held that, if the same facts had arisen for decision today, the depositors would have been
entitled to personal restitution on the grounds that the building society had been
unjustly enriched by the receipt of their deposits when there had been a total failure of
consideration because their promise to repay was ultra vires and void. There would
therefore be no need to trace in equity and, in as far as the House of Lords had found
that the deposits were held on trust for the depositors by the building society so as to be
traceable in equity, it was overruled.

Other cases also support the view that a fiduciary relationship is an essential prerequisite for equitable tracing. In *Agip (Africa) Ltd v Jackson*,[97] Fox LJ observed:

'Equity . . . will follow money into a mixed fund and charge the fund. There is, in the present
case, no difficulty about the mechanics of tracing in equity. The money can be traced
through the various bank accounts to Baker Oil and onwards. It is, however, a prerequisite to
the operation of the remedy in equity that there must be a fiduciary relationship which calls
the equitable jurisdiction into being . . .'[98]

On the facts this presented no difficulty, because it was held that the plaintiff's fraudulent accountant stood in a fiduciary relationship to them. A fiduciary relationship was
also held to be a prerequisite of the right to trace in equity by the Court of Appeal in
*Boscawen v Bajwa*,[99] and in *Jones (FC) & Sons (a firm) v Jones*[100] the misappropriated
money was traced at common law rather than in equity because Mrs Jones had not
received it in a fiduciary capacity so that it was not subject to a constructive trust.
Whilst in *Foskett v McKeown*[101] Lord Millett considered that there was no logical

---

[96] [1996] AC 669.     [97] [1992] 4 All ER 451.     [98] [1992] 4 All ER 451 at 466.
[99] [1995] 4 All ER 769 at 777, per Millett LJ.     [100] [1997] Ch 159.
[101] [2000] 3 All ER 97 at 121.

justification for insisting upon the existence of a fiduciary relationship as a precondition for applying equity's tracing rules, the requirement was not overruled because the case concerned a straightforward case of the misappropriation of trust money.

Where trust property has been misappropriated or misdirected the essential requirement of a fiduciary relationship will be satisfied. The trustee stood in a fiduciary relationship vis-à-vis the beneficiary who is seeking to trace in equity. However, it is also clear that the fiduciary relationship need not have existed prior to the misappropriation or misdirection of the property concerned, since the circumstances of the misappropriation or misdirection may themselves give rise to a fiduciary relationship entitling the original owner to trace in equity. In *Chase Manhattan Bank NA v Israeli-British Bank (London) Ltd*[102] Chase Manhattan paid the Israeli-British Bank $1m. Due to a clerical error the same amount was paid again later the same day. The Israeli-British bank became insolvent and Chase Manhattan sought to trace the second mistaken payment money into its assets. Although they would clearly have had a personal action for restitution of the sum paid by mistake, it was essential that they could maintain a proprietary claim, because they would otherwise merely rank amongst the general creditors. However, the banks were two commercial organisations, dealing with each other at arm's length, and as such they did not stand in a fiduciary relationship, nor was the money paid subject to a pre-existing trust. Despite this, Goulding J held that the very fact that the payment had been made by mistake brought about a fiduciary relationship which entitled Chase Manhattan to trace. He stated his rationale:

'. . . a person who pays money to another under a factual mistake retains an equitable property in it and the conscience of that other is subjected to a fiduciary duty to respect his proprietary right.'[103]

However, this decision was subjected to criticism by the House of Lords in *Westdeutsche Landesbank Girozentrale v Islington London Borough Council*,[104] where Lord Browne-Wilkinson stated that he could not agree that the mere fact that the payment had been made by mistake meant that the payor retained the equitable interest in the money paid when it had not previously been subject to a trust.[105] Although the judge's reasoning was doubted, Lord Browne-Wilkinson felt that the case may have been rightly decided:

'The defendant bank knew of the mistake made by the paying bank within two days of the receipt of the moneys. The judge treated this fact as irrelevant but in my judgement it may well provide a proper foundation for the decision. Although the mere receipt of the moneys, in ignorance of the mistake, gives rise to no trust, the retention of the moneys after the recipient bank learned of the mistake may well have given rise to a constructive trust.'[106]

It is submitted, however, that this reasoning is spurious. If the mistaken payment effected a transfer of the ownership of the money to the payee when it was received, there is no reason why a trust should have been imposed when the bank discovered that a mistake had occurred. The bank was clearly subject to an obligation to make restitution at common law, but the mere fact that it should have to make restitution does not

---

[102] [1981] Ch 105.     [103] [1981] Ch 105 at 119.     [104] [1996] AC 669.
[105] [1996] AC 669 at 714.     [106] [1996] AC 669 at 715.

generate a constructive trust. Whilst the equitable obligation to account has been held to give rise to a constructive trust because of the operation of the maxim that equity treats as done that which ought to be done, there is no equivalent principle at common law. It is submitted that the crucial question should focus on the proprietary consequences of the mistaken payment at the moment it was made, in other words, whether the mistake prevented title in the money passing to the payee. Lord Goff indicated that a fundamental mistake might prevent the beneficial interest in property passing to a payee.[107]

The requirement of an initial fiduciary relationship has been subject to heavy criticism, both on the grounds that it is not supported in authority and that it is not justified in principle.[108] The major criticism is that the requirement is artificial, the courts being willing to find, or 'discover',[109] a fiduciary relationship whenever they feel that tracing is justified, as in *Chase Manhattan Bank NA v Israeli-British Bank (London) Ltd.*[110] For this reason, Goff and Jones suggested in an earlier edition of their seminal text that whether tracing (which they call a 'restitutionary proprietary claim') should be available should 'depend on whether it is just, in the particular circumstances of the case, to impose a constructive trust on, or an equitable lien over, particular assets . . .'[111] However, this proposal is equally unsuitable because of its arbitrary nature and it has not been maintained in subsequent editions, where it is regretted that the courts have not taken opportunities which have been presented to overrule the requirement.[112]

In practice it seems that the requirement of a 'fiduciary relationship' is less of a limitation than some critics have suggested. In any case involving property that was held upon trust there will be no difficulty and equitable tracing will always be available. It is the commercial situations which have generated difficulty. However, even in the commercial context the requirement is easily circumvented. As Millet J observed in *Agip (Africa) Ltd v Jackson*[113] it is 'readily satisfied in most cases of commercial fraud, since the embezzlement of a company's funds almost invariably involves a breach of fiduciary duty on the part of one of the company's employees or agents'.[114] Although he noted the criticism, he felt that it was not for a court of first instance to reconsider the requirement, and as has been seen the Court of Appeal merely reasserted it.[115]

## (b) Equitable ownership of the property traced

Although the requirement of a fiduciary relationship has not prevented tracing in practice, the language is confusing because it conceals the true basis of equitable tra-

---

[107] [1996] AC 669 at 690.

[108] See Goff and Jones, *The Law of Restitution* (6th edn, 2002), pp 104–106; Birks, *Introduction to the Law of Restitution* (1985), pp 377–385; (1976) 40 Conv 277 (Pearce). It is argued that *Sinclair v Brougham* [1914] AC 398 did not require an initial fiduciary relationship and that the case was misunderstood by the Court of Appeal in *Re Diplock* [1948] Ch 465.

[109] Goff and Jones, *The Law of Restitution* (6th edn, 2002), p 105.    [110] [1981] Ch 105.

[111] Goff and Jones, *The Law of Restitution* (3rd edn, 1987), p 79.

[112] Goff and Jones, *The Law of Restitution* (6th edn, 2002), pp 104–106. In this most recent edition, Goff and Jones argue that the comments of the House of Lords in *Foskett v McKeown* [2000] 3 All ER 97 that 'there is no sense in maintaining different rules for tracing at law and in equity' lead to the conclusion that the courts should no longer insist on a fiduciary relationship before a claimant can trace in equity.

[113] [1992] 4 All ER 385.    [114] [1992] 4 All ER 385 at 402.    [115] [1992] 4 All ER 451.

cing. Equity is not concerned with the presence of a fiduciary relationship per se, but rather with the identification of a trust. A person will only be entitled to trace property in equity of which he was the equitable owner. Where trust property was misappropriated or misdirected, the beneficiaries are entitled to trace the trust property which belongs to them in equity. Where the property of an absolute owner is misappropriated or misdirected, he will only be entitled to trace if the circumstances of the misappropriation or misdirection gave rise to a trust in his favour.[116] This analysis of tracing was propounded by Pearce, who argued that equitable tracing should be available whenever there is a 'continuing right of property recognised in equity'.[117] More recently, Professor Birks has argued that equitable tracing should be available whenever there is a sufficient 'proprietary base'. By this he means that:

'. . . the circumstances of the original receipt by the defendant must be such that, either at law or in equity, the plaintiff retained or obtained the property in the matter received by the defendant, and then continued to retain it until the moment at which the substitution or intermixture took place.'[118]

The trust analysis of the right to trace in equity was supported by the Privy Council in *Re Goldcorp Exchange Ltd (in receivership)*.[119] The customers who had purchased 'non-allocated metal' were not entitled to trace their purchase money into the bulk of metal held by the company because they could not be shown to have any equitable proprietary interest in it arising through the contract of sale.[120]

It is submitted that the 'trust' analysis should be adopted in place of the current requirement of a 'fiduciary relationship'. However, such a development would not lead to any significant practical change in the operation of equitable tracing since there is such a close connection between equitable ownership and a fiduciary relationship that two terms could almost be seen to be synonymous. As much is admitted by Birks:

'. . . the requirement of a fiduciary relationship is, in this context one and the same as the requirement of an undestroyed proprietary base . . . a plaintiff who wants to assert an equitable proprietary interest in the surviving enrichment must show facts such that the property in the original receipt did not pass at law and in equity to the recipient. If he can show such facts, so that, at least in equity, he retained the property in the res, he will, after identifying the surviving enrichment, be able to raise an equitable proprietary interest in those different assets. Where such facts are shown, the relationship between him and the recipient can, rightly, be described as "fiduciary" in that it will resemble the relationship between cestui que trust and trustee.'[121]

---

[116] See *Westdeutsche Landesbank Girozentrale v Islington London Borough Council* [1996] AC 669 at 706, per Lord Browne-Wilkinson.

[117] (1976) 40 Conv 275.      [118] Birks, *Introduction to the Law of Restitution* (1985), p 378.

[119] [1994] 2 All ER 806.

[120] See [1995] RLR 83–93 (Birks). Compare *El Ajou v Dollar Land Holdings plc (No 2)* [1995] 2 All ER 213, where Robert Walker J suggested that tracing depends on the concept of an equitable charge and not equitable ownership.

[121] Birks, *Introduction to the Law of Restitution* (1985), p 381. The latest edition of Goff & Jones, *The Law of Restitution* (1998) asserts at p 103 that the requirement of a fiduciary relationship is a recognition that the plaintiff must have an equitable title to the asset he is claiming.

Whilst the trust analysis may be little more than an alternative label for the present search for a 'fiduciary relationship', it has the merit of de-mythologising the process because it is a more accurate and precise description of what the court is looking for. However, the mere fact that a different label is used does not answer the difficult questions as to the circumstances in which a trust will arise so as to justify tracing in equity.

### (c) Circumstances in which it will be possible to trace in equity

*(i) Misappropriation of trust property by a trustee.* Equitable tracing will always be available against a trustee who has wrongfully misappropriated trust property, because the beneficiary retains his equitable title to the trust property. Thus equitable tracing was permitted in *Foskett v McKeown*[122] where a trustee had wrongfully used trust money to pay the premiums due under his insurance policy.

*(ii) Receipt of trust property by a stranger to a trust.* Where property subject to a trust is transferred to a stranger in breach of trust, the beneficiary will be entitled to trace the trust property into the hands of the stranger unless he was a bona fide purchaser for value without notice, in which case the beneficiary's equitable title will be defeated.

*(iii) Profits received by a fiduciary in breach of duty.* As unauthorised profits received by a fiduciary are held on constructive trust for his principal, the principal will be entitled to trace them in equity. Thus, in *A-G of Hong Kong v Reid*[123] the Crown was able to trace the bribes that had been received by a fiduciary into the houses he had purchased with them.

*(iv) Stolen or misappropriated property.* In *Lipkin Gorman v Karpnale Ltd*[124] Lord Templeman approved Australian authorities which hold that a thief does not gain title to his property, but holds it on trust. He cited with approval O'Connor J in *Black v S Freedman & Co*:

'Where money has been stolen, it is trust money in the hands of the thief and he cannot divest it of that character. If he pays it over to another person, then it may be followed into that person's hands. If, of course, that other person shows that it has come to him bona fides for valuable consideration, and without notice, it then may lose its character as trust money and cannot be recovered . . .'[125]

In *Westdeutsche Landesbank Girozentrale v Islington London Borough Council*[126] Lord Browne-Wilkinson also held that theft would generate a constructive trust sufficient to give rise to the right to trace in equity. He considered whether a resulting trust would arise when a thief stole a bag of coins:

'I agree that the stolen moneys are traceable in equity. But the proprietary interest which equity is enforcing in such circumstances arises under a constructive, not a resulting, trust. Although it is difficult to find clear authority for the proposition, when property is obtained by fraud equity imposes a constructive trust on the fraudulent recipient; the property is

---

[122] [2001] 1 AC 102.    [123] [1994] 1 All ER 1.    [124] [1991] 2 AC 548, [1992] 4 All ER 512.
[125] (1910) 12 CLR 105.    [126] [1996] AC 669.

recoverable and traceable in equity . . . Money stolen from a bank account can be traced in equity.'[127]

This principle is sufficient to justify tracing in equity in *Agip (Africa) Ltd v Jackson*[128] without having to find that the accountant, Zdiri, was a fiduciary. He was simply a thief who never gained title to the money he misappropriated, so it was possible to follow it into Baker Oil's account and beyond. The principle that a constructive trust arises from the fraudulent receipt of property was applied to establish a right to trace by Lawrence Collins J in *Commerzbank Aktiengesellschaft v IMB Morgan plc*,[129] where a stockbroker in Nigeria had received money into its accounts which had been obtained as a result of fraud.

It may be noted that, although the authorities now support the view that the thief holds on trust, it is an unusual kind of trust since, so far as the property originally stolen is concerned, the thief does not normally have legal title. This is always the case where tangible property is stolen, and may even be the case in relation to certain intangible property, such as money.[130] Because of this unusual characteristic, there is much to be said for the view that the right to trace exists because of the continuing equitable proprietary rights of the true owner rather than because of the existence of a trust in the conventional sense.[131]

*(v) Payments made under a void contract.*[132] A recent area of controversy has concerned the question whether a payment made under a contract void ab initio is traceable in equity. It had been argued that such a payment would give rise to a resulting trust in favour of the payor, thus entitling him to trace the payment into the assets of the payee. However, this analysis was comprehensively rejected by the House of Lords in *Westdeutsche Landesbank Girozentrale v Islington London Borough Council*,[133] where it was held that money paid under a void interest rate swap agreement was not subject to a resulting trust. Lord Goff stated:

'. . . there is no general rule that the property in money paid under a void contract does not pass to the payee; and it is difficult to escape the conclusion that, as a general rule, the beneficial interest in the money likewise passes to the payee.'[134]

---

[127] [1996] AC 669 at 716. The following cases were cited in favour of this proposition: *Stocks v Wilson* [1913] 2 KB 235; *R Leslie Ltd v Sheill* [1914] 3 KB 607; *Bankers Trust Co v Shapira* [1980] 1 WLR 1274; *McCormick v Grogan* (1869) LR 4 HL 82. The proposition has been doubted in a number of a number of subsequent authorities including *Halifax Building Society v Thomas* [1996] Ch 217; *Paragon Finance v DB Thakerar* [1999] 1 All ER 400 and *Shalson v Russo* [2003] WTLR 1165. In *Sinclair Investment Holding SA v Versailles Trade Finance Ltd* [2005] EWCA Civ 722 the Court of Appeal expressed reservations about the principle but refused to strike out a claim founded upon it on the grounds that there was at least an arguable cause of action based on a constructive trust of property obtained by fraud or theft.

[128] [1990] Ch 265; affd [1992] 4 All ER 451.     [129] [2004] EWHC 2771.

[130] Where intangible property is obtained by fraud, legal title may pass to the thief, as for instance if shares or registered land are registered in his name.

[131] See above, p 884.

[132] See Worthington, Proprietary Interests in Commercial Transactions (1996), pp 148–161.

[133] [1996] AC 669.     [134] [1996] AC 669 at 690.

The House of Lords reversed the decision of the Court of Appeal[135] that a resulting trust had arisen, and overruled *Sinclair v Brougham*.[136] It therefore seems that it will generally be impossible to trace money paid under a void contract in equity and that the payor will be confined to seeking restitution at common law. However, Lord Browne-Wilkinson did seem to suggest that a trust would be imposed if the recipient of the payment was aware of the invalidity of the contract so as to affect his conscience and justify the imposition of a constructive trust, and that such a trust could arise even after receipt if the payee became aware of the invalidity whilst the payment was still identifiable in his hands.

*(vi)  Payments made under a voidable contract.*[137] In *El Ajou v Dollar Land Holdings plc (No 1)*[138] Millett J held that a resulting trust arose when a payment had been made under a voidable contract. The case concerned a fraudulent share selling scheme operated by three Canadians. The plaintiffs' money was invested in the scheme after their agent was bribed to invest in it. The proceeds were eventually invested in a property development project carried on with the defendants, Dollar Land Holdings. The plaintiffs sought to recover their money from the defendants. Millett J held that although they could not trace at common law, because the money had been mixed, they could trace in equity because there was a fiduciary relationship between them and their agent, who was bribed. However, Millett J went on to consider the position of other victims of the fraud who had not invested through a fiduciary and concluded that they too would be entitled to trace:

'Other victims, however, were less fortunate. They employed no fiduciary. They were simply swindled. No breach of any fiduciary obligation was involved. It would, of course, be an intolerable reproach to our system of jurisprudence if the plaintiff were the only victim who could trace and recover his money. Neither party before me suggested that this is the case; and I agree with them. But if the other victims of the fraud can trace their money in equity it must be because, having been induced to purchase the shares by false and fraudulent mis-representations, they are entitled to rescind the transaction and revest the equitable title to the purchase money in themselves, at least to the extent necessary to support an equitable tracing claim . . .'[139]

Whilst this neatly emphasises that the essence of the right to trace is not a fiduciary relationship per se but the need to demonstrate a trust, the judgment of the Privy Council in *Re Goldcorp Exchange Ltd (in receivership)*[140] casts doubt upon the proposition. The purchasers of 'non-allocated metal' argued that they were entitled to

---

[135] [1994] 1 WLR 938; [1994] RLR 73 (Swadling). Dillon LJ had adopted the following conclusion: 'Since, contrary to the expectation of the parties, the swap transaction and contract are, and were from the outset, ultra vires and void, the purpose for which the £2.5 million was paid by the bank to the council has wholly failed, and the £2.5 million has, from the time the council received it, been held on a resulting trust for the bank.'

[136] [1914] AC 398.

[137] See Worthington, Proprietary Interests in Commercial Transactions (1996), pp 161–168.

[138] [1993] BCLC 735; revsd [1994] BCLC 464, CA. See also: *Daly v Sydney Stock Exchange* (1986) 160 CLR 371; *Lonrho plc v Fayed (No 2)* [1992] 1 WLR 1; *Halifax Building Society v Thomas* [1996] Ch 217.

[139] [1993] BCLC 735 at 753.    [140] [1994] 2 All ER 806.

rescind the contract on the grounds of misrepresentation. Although they had not in fact rescinded their contracts, the Privy Council suggested that even if they had they would not have been entitled to an equitable proprietary right. As Lord Mustill explained:

'. . . even if this fatal objection could be overcome, the argument would, in their Lordships' opinion, be bound to fail. Whilst it is convenient to speak of the customers "getting their money back" this expression is misleading. Upon payment by the customers the purchase moneys became, and recission or no recission remained, the unencumbered property of the company. What the customers would recover on recission would not be "their" money, but an equivalent sum . . .'[141]

In the light of *Westdeutsche Landesbank Girozentrale v Islington London Borough Council*[142] it seems that the mere fact that a contract is avoided will not give rise to a trust entitling a payor to trace in equity.[143]

*(vii) Payments made by mistake.* As has already been seen in *Chase Manhattan Bank NA v Israeli-British Bank (London) Ltd*,[144] it was held that a payor was entitled to trace in equity a payment caused by his mistake of fact. However, it remains unclear why equitable tracing was permitted. In *Westdeutsche Landesbank Girozentrale v Islington London Borough Council*[145] Lord Browne-Wilkinson doubted that the payor could be said to have retained the equitable title to his money when it was not subject to a trust prior to the payment, and the payee had not known at the moment that the payment was made that the payor was acting under a mistake. He seemed to suggest that a trust only arose because the payee became aware of the mistake two days later, thus affecting his conscience and leading to the imposition of a trust. This analysis has been subject to criticism[146] and, as was noted above, the true question should be whether the payee received good title to the money paid at the moment that it was transferred to him. If so, no trust arises and, whilst the recipient may be required to make restitution of the amount of the payment, the payor should not be entitled to trace. Tracing should only be possible if the money was paid under a mistake of fact so fundamental as to prevent property passing. The real difficulty is in identifying mistakes sufficiently fundamental to prevent property passing. As Robert Goff J said in *Barclays Bank Ltd v W J Simms*[147] in the majority of cases property will pass in payments made under a mistake of fact.[148] In *Re Goldcorp Exchange Ltd*[149] the Privy Council emphasised that the mistake in *Chase Manhattan* was a mistake whereby one party mistakenly made the same payment twice.[150] In *Westdeutsche* Lord Goff suggested that only a fundamental mistake of fact might prevent the equitable interest in money passing to a payee.[151]

---

[141] [1994] 2 All ER 806 at 825–826.     [142] [1996] AC 669.
[143] See also *Criterion Properties plc v Stratford UK Properties LLC* [2004] 1 WLR 1846.
[144] [1981] Ch 105.     [145] [1996] AC 669.     [146] [1996] RLR 3 (Birks), pp 21–23.
[147] [1980] QB 677.     [148] See [1994] RLR 73 (Swadling).     [149] [1994] 2 All ER 806.
[150] [1994] 2 All ER 806 at 826.     [151] [1996] AC 669 at 690.

### (3) Equitable tracing through clean substitutions

Where trust property has been exchanged for other property the beneficiaries are entitled to trace into the exchange product. Thus, if a trustee uses trust money to purchase a diamond ring, the beneficiaries will be able to trace their equitable ownership into the ring.

### (4) Equitable tracing of tangible property into a mixed bulk

If the trust property consists of tangible property, for example if it is a quantity of crude oil, it is possible that the trustee may wrongfully allow the trust property to be mixed with other property so as to form a bulk. In such circumstances the beneficiaries would be entitled to trace the trust property into the bulk, and they would be entitled to a share of the equitable ownership proportionate to their contribution.[152]

### (5) Equitable tracing of money through a mixed fund

More difficult problems present themselves if misappropriated trust property is mixed with other property so that it can no longer be identified as such. Assets purchased from the mixed fund cannot then be regarded as solely the product of the trust property. Unlike the rules of tracing at common law, the equitable rules of tracing permit the trust property to be traced through a mixed fund of money and into assets acquired from it. *Foskett v McKeown*[153] involved just such a situation. The case concerned a Mr Murphy, who in 1986 had taken out a unit-linked life insurance policy, which provided for the payment of a death benefit of £1million. The initial annual premiums due under this policy were paid by Mr Murphy using his own money. However the premiums due in 1989 and 1990 were paid using money from a bank account which he held on trust for the customers of a company he controlled which had contracted to buy land on their behalf in Portugal. The proceeds of the life insurance policy were written in trust for the benefit of his children. In 1991 Mr Murphy committed suicide, and the death benefit was paid. The question at issue was whether the beneficiaries were entitled to trace their misappropriated money into the proceeds of the policy. The House of Lords held, by a bare majority, that the beneficiaries were entitled to a share of the proceeds proportionate to the contribution of the trust money to the payment of their premiums. Lord Millett explained that the beneficiaries were able to trace their trust money into the insurance policy itself, and thence into the proceeds of the policy:

'It is, however, of critical importance in the present case to appreciate that the purchasers do not trace the premiums directly into the insurance money. They trace them first into the policy and thence into the proceeds of the policy. It is essential not to elide the two steps. In this context, of course, the word "policy" does not mean the contract of insurance. You do not trace the payment of a premium into the insurance contract any more than you trace a payment into a bank account in to the banking contract. The word "policy" is here used to describe the bundle of rights to which the policyholder is entitled in return for the premiums. These rights, which may be very complex, together constitute a chose in action, viz

---

[152] *Foskett v McKeown* [2000] 3 All ER 97 at 125.    [153] [2001] 1 AC 102.

the right to payment of a debt payable on a future event and contingent upon the continued payment of further premiums until the happening of the event. That chose in action represents the traceable proceeds of the premiums; its current value fluctuates from time to time. When the property matures, the insurance money represents the traceable proceeds of the policy and hence indirectly of the premiums. It follows that, if a claimant can show that premiums were paid with his money, he can claim a proportionate share of the policy.'[154]

*Foskett v McKeown* involved a somewhat unusual mixture of funds in the form of the payment of premiums of an insurance policy. More commonly misappropriated funds will become mixed in a bank account. Equity has developed special rules to determine whether trust property can be traced through a mixture of funds in a bank account.

## (6) Equitable tracing of money through the banking system

Whilst equity is capable of tracing property through a mixed fund, the process of identification can be extremely complex where money has become mixed with funds in a bank account. Where trust property was paid into a bank account it may be essential to determine whether the remaining balance, or assets purchased from it, can be seen as representing the original trust property. Of necessity, this inquiry is often conducted ex post facto, only after the misappropriation of the trust property has been discovered and the transactions have taken place. The rules that have evolved are simply rough and ready presumptions which operate to determine whether any remaining balance, or property purchased, can be identified as the product of the trust money. They operate differently depending upon whether the mixture consisted of trust money and the money of the wrongdoing trustee, or the money of the trust and of another innocent party, for example money misappropriated from another trust. The rules emerged in the last century, and they are only really appropriate for simple bank accounts.

### (a) Mixture in a bank account consisting of the trust property and the trustee's own property

Where a wrongdoing trustee has mixed trust property with his own property in a bank account, the rules operate harshly against him. If the mixed fund has been partially dissipated, any remaining balance, or assets acquired from the account, are presumed to belong to the trust. The burden is on the wrongdoer to show that the asset or balance represents his own money.[155] Where the account balance has been reduced by withdrawals which have been dissipated, the court will presume that the remaining balance represents the trust property and that the wrongdoer's own money has been dissipated. The wrongdoer will not be permitted to assert that it represents his own money and that the money he has spent and dissipated was the trust money. As Millett LJ stated in *Boscawen v Bajwa*:

'A trustee will not be allowed to defeat the claim of his beneficiaries by saying that he has resorted to trust money when he could have made use of his own.'[156]

---

[154] [2000] 3 All ER 97 at 126.  [155] *Lupton v White* (1808) 15 Ves 432.
[156] [1995] 4 All ER 769 at 778.

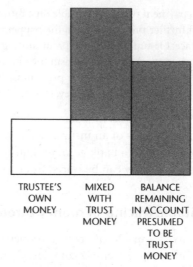

TRUSTEE'S
BANK
ACCOUNT

| TRUSTEE'S OWN MONEY | MIXED WITH TRUST MONEY | BALANCE REMAINING IN ACCOUNT PRESUMED TO BE TRUST MONEY |

Equitable tracing: *Re Hallet's Estate*

This presumption was applied in *Re Hallet's Estate*. A solicitor, who was a trustee of his own marriage settlement, was entrusted with money by a client for investment. He paid money from the trust and his client's money into his bank account, which also contained some of his own money. He made various payments out, which had been dissipated. On his death the account contained enough money to satisfy the claims of the trust and the client, but not his other creditors. The central question was whether the money in the account could be said to be the property of the trust and client, in which case they would gain priority over the general creditors. The Court of Appeal held that the trustee must be presumed to have spent his own money first, and to have preserved the trust moneys. Jessel MR stated the principle applying to a trustee who has blended trust moneys with his own:

'. . . it seems to me perfectly plain that he cannot be heard to say that he took away the trust money when he had a right to take away his own money . . . His money was there, and he had a right to draw it out, and why should the natural act of simply drawing out the money be attributed to anything except to his ownership of money which was at the bankers.'[157]

If the presumption adopted in *Re Hallet's Estate* were absolute, it would produce an anomalous result if the wrongdoing trustee purchased assets from the account and then dissipated the remaining balance. The trustee would be able to claim that the assets had been acquired with his own money since he was deemed to spend this first. However, the presumption that the trustee withdraws and spends his own money first is not absolute but a specific application of the general maxim that 'everything is presumed

---

[157] (1880) 13 Ch D 696 at 727–728.

against a wrongdoer'. Whatever the circumstances and the order of events, the wrong-doer is presumed to have acted so as to preserve the trust money. Thus, assets acquired before the remaining balance of the account was dissipated may be claimed to represent the trust property. As Millett LJ stated in *Boscawen v Bajwa*:

'. . . if the beneficiary asserts that the trustee has made use of the trust money there is no reason why he should not be allowed to prove it.'[158]

Thus in *Re Oatway*,[159] where application of the presumption in *Re Hallet's Estate* would have worked an injustice, exactly the opposite presumption was applied, namely that the trustee had spent the trust money first. Lewis Oatway was a solicitor and the trustee of a will. He misappropriated £3,000 from the trust and paid this into a bank account where it was mixed with his own money. He purchased Oceana shares for £2,137 using money from the account. At the time that he purchased them there would have been enough of his own money in the account to purchase the shares. After the purchase he dissipated the balance of the account and died insolvent, leaving the shares, now valued at £2,474. If the rule in *Re Hallet* were applied the shares would have been purchased with his money, and therefore form part of his general assets. However, Joyce J held that the shares were to be regarded as the product of the trust money. Having examined the rule in *Re Hallet's Estate* he concluded:

'It is, in my opinion, equally clear that when any of the money drawn out has been invested, and that investment remains in the name or under the control of the trustee, the rest of the balance having been afterwards dissipated by him, he cannot maintain that the investment which remains represents his own money alone, and that what has been spent and can no longer be traced and recovered was the money belonging to the trust.'[160]

The contrasting decisions in *Re Hallet's Estate*[161] and *Re Oatway*[162] are not in conflict with each other, but can be seen as applications of a general principle that the trustee is estopped from asserting that he has dissipated trust money before his own. This principle will operate differently depending on the individual facts of each situation. Although this rule works to the advantage of the beneficiaries of the trust, it must be remembered that it acts to the detriment of the general creditors, who will inevitably receive a lower dividend from the insolvency. It is questionable whether this priority is always just.

There seems little authority as to the position if a trustee wrongfully mixes trust property with his own in a bank account, from which assets are purchased, and either those assets or the balance remaining in the account are sufficient to cover the money taken from the trust. This would be of particular significance if the asset purchased has increased in value, because if the beneficiaries can show that the property was purchased with their money they would be entitled to claim the increase in value. There is no direct authority. Possibly, the court could apply the rule in *Re Hallet's Estate* and hold that the trustee spent his own money first, leaving the trust to the balance in the

---

[158] [1995] 4 All ER 769 at 778.   [159] [1903] 2 Ch 356.
[160] [1903] 2 Ch 356 at 360.   [161] (1880) 13 Ch D 696.   [162] [1903] 2 Ch 356.

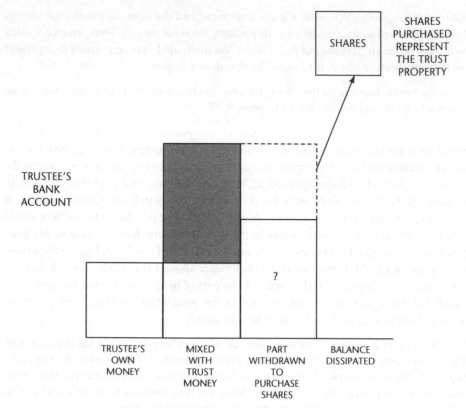

**Equitable tracing: *Re Oatway***

account. In *Re Tilley's Will Trusts*[163] it seems to have been accepted that if the beneficiary could show that the asset had been purchased with trust money, or partially with trust money, they could claim the increase in value proportionately. However, the difficulty is that it is impossible to show whose money was used. In such circumstances Professor Birks suggests that the principles operating in the case of funds consisting of the mixed money of innocent volunteers should apply so that the trust would share any gain with the wrongdoer pari passu[164] unless the account was a current account, in which case the rule in *Clayton's Case* would apply: i.e. 'first in, first out'.

### (b) Mixture in a bank account consisting of the trust property and property of an innocent volunteer

The harsh presumptions which operate against a wrongdoer who has mixed trust property with his own are not applied where trust property has been mixed with that of other innocent volunteers. In such a case the rules reflect the moral blamelessness of the parties whose money has been mixed, and they aim to do substantive justice between them. However, a distinction is made between different types of account. Where the money of innocent parties has been mixed in a current account the rule in

---

[163] [1967] Ch 1179.    [164] Birks, *Introduction to the Law of Restitution* (1985), p 370.

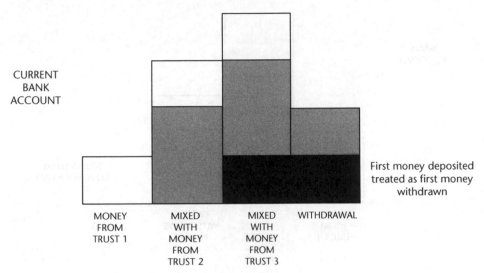

CURRENT
BANK
ACCOUNT

First money deposited
treated as first money
withdrawn

MONEY
FROM
TRUST 1

MIXED
WITH
MONEY
FROM
TRUST 2

MIXED
WITH
MONEY
FROM
TRUST 3

WITHDRAWAL

**The rule in *Clayton's Case*: 'first in, first out'**

*Clayton's Case*[165] will prima facie apply.[166] *Clayton's Case* presumes that money is paid out of a current account in the same order in which it had been paid in. In other words, that the first money to be spent from the account represents the first money that was paid in, hence the rule is known as 'first in, first out'. This is a rough and ready rule which originally developed in the banker and client context. It reflects the fact that current accounts are often extremely active. However, the presumption is not absolute, and it will not be applied if the result would be unjust. Starting with the decision in *Barlow Clowes International Ltd (in liquidation) v Vaughan*,[167] the trend of recent cases has been to consider that application of the rule would be unjust in almost all circumstances where the money of innocent volunteers has been mixed in a bank account, such that the 'rule' will only apply in the most exceptional circumstances. In *Barlow Clowes International Ltd v Vaughan* the Court of Appeal was faced with the consequences of the collapse of the Barlow Clowes investment company in Gibraltar. Depositors had paid into investment plans, but the money had been misapplied and the company was left owing some £115m to investors, with assets far less than that amount. Some investors argued that the rule in *Clayton's Case* should be applied, with the consequence that the late investors would recover virtually all their money, leaving the early investors with nothing. After a wide-ranging examination of the authorities, the court held that the rule was well established and that it was not open to them to overrule it. As Dillon LJ observed:

'. . . the decisions of this court . . . establish and recognise a general rule of practice that *Clayton's Case* is to be applied when several beneficiaries' moneys have been blended in one

---

[165] (1816) 1 Mer 572.

[166] See *Re Hallett's Estate* (1879) 13 Ch D 696 (Fry J); *Hancock v Smith* (1889) 41 Ch D 456; *Re Stenning* [1895] 2 Ch 433; *Mutton v Peat* [1899] 2 Ch 556; *Re Diplock* [1948] Ch 465, CA.

[167] [1992] 4 All ER 22. See Fox, 'Legal title as a Ground of Restitutionary Liability' [2000] RLT 465.

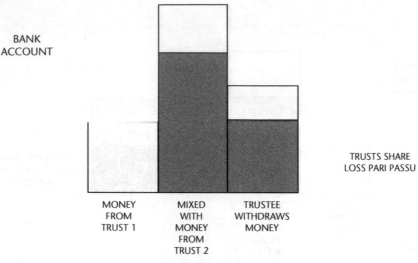

BANK
ACCOUNT

TRUSTS SHARE
LOSS PARI PASSU

MONEY
FROM
TRUST 1

MIXED
WITH
MONEY
FROM
TRUST 2

TRUSTEE
WITHDRAWS
MONEY

**Sharing pari passu**

bank account and there is a deficiency. It is not ... for this court to reject that long established general practice.'

However, the court felt free to depart from the rule in the circumstances of the case, because it would work injustice. The principle governing the application of the rule was stated by Woolf LJ:

'The rule need only be applied when it is convenient to do so and when its application can be said to do broad justice having regard to the nature of the competing claims ... It is not applied if this is the intention or presumed intention of the beneficiaries. The rule is sensibly not applied when the costs of applying it is likely to exhaust the fund available for the beneficiaries.'[168]

On the facts it was held that the rule would not be applied because the investment fund was regarded by the investors as a common pool, and that they should share pari passu in what remained because they had experienced a common misfortune. It would have been wholly inequitable to apply the rule in *Clayton's Case*, which would have meant some investors recovering everything to the exclusion of the rest, who would recover nothing. The court also considered an alternative and more sophisticated version of the rule. The 'North American' approach would treat each withdrawal from the account as a withdrawal in the same proportions as the different interests in the account at the moment of withdrawal. Woolf LJ accepted that this solution could have advantages over a distribution pari passu, but the complications made it impracticable to apply in these circumstances.[169] Subsequent cases have continued to reject the application of the rule.[170] In *Russell-Cooke Trust Co v Prentis* Lindsay J went so far as to suggest that the

---

[168] [1992] 4 All ER 22 at 39.

[169] See also *Re Eastern Capital Futures Ltd* [1989] BCLC 371.

[170] See also the discussion of the rule in *Re French Caledonia Travel* (2004) 22 ACLC 498; [2003] NSWSC 1008; [2005] 64 CLJ 45 (Conaglen).

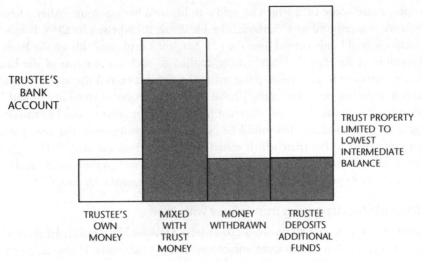

TRUSTEE'S
BANK
ACCOUNT

TRUST PROPERTY
LIMITED TO
LOWEST
INTERMEDIATE
BALANCE

| TRUSTEE'S OWN MONEY | MIXED WITH TRUST MONEY | MONEY WITHDRAWN | TRUSTEE DEPOSITS ADDITIONAL FUNDS |

**The lowest intermediate balance:** *Roscoe v Winder*

fact that the first-in first-out principle will not usually be applied where beneficiaries have shared a common misfortune means that it might be 'more accurate to refer to the exception that is, rather than the rule in *Clayton's case*.'[171] Lawrence Collins J also refused to apply the rule in *Commerbank Aktiengesellschaft v IMB Morgan plc*[172] where money obtained by fraud had been paid into the account of a firm of stockbrokers, where it had become mixed so that it was not possible to identify any part of the funds as belonging to a particular client. He held that the rule would be 'impracticable and unjust' to apply, and held that the balance in the account should be divided in proportion amongst the clients. The rule in *Clayton's Case* has no application to mixtures of tangible property, where any abatement in the mixture must be shared pari passu.[173]

Where the mixing of the trust property and the property of an innocent volunteer takes place in a bank account other than a current account, the rule in *Clayton's Case* will not apply. In *Sinclair v Brougham*[174] and *Re Diplock*[175] it was held that the parties will share pari passu in any assets that have been purchased from the mixed fund and any balance remaining in the account. They will also bear any increase or loss in value in proportion to their contributions.

## (c) The lowest intermediate balance

Whether a fund consists of a mixture of trust money with the wrongdoer's own, or the money of an innocent volunteer, if money has been dissipated from the account and then further money is paid into the account, the trust has no claim to any of that other money. The trust is limited to what is known as the lowest intermediate balance, because it is impossible that anything in the account above that figure represents trust property. The operation of this rule is seen in *Roscoe v Winder*.[176] A wrongdoer

---

[171] [2003] 2 All ER 478, [2005] 64 CLJ 45 (Conaglen)    [172] [2004] EWHC 2771.
[173] *Re Goldcorp Exchange Ltd* [1995] 1 AC 74, HC New Zealand (Thorp J).
[174] [1914] AC 398.    [175] [1948] Ch 465, CA.    [176] [1915] 1 Ch 62.

misappropriated some £455 which he paid into his own bank account. After a few days the balance was reduced to £25, though by his death it had risen to £358. It was held that a charge could only extend over the £25. Sargant J explained this on the basis that the principle of *Re Hallet's Estate*[177] only applied to such an amount of the balance ultimately standing to the credit of the trustee as did not exceed the lowest balance of the account during the intervening period. If the subsequent payments in had been specifically intended to replenish the trust funds, then the trust would be entitled to a charge over them because this would be expressly imposing upon the later payment a trust equivalent to the trust which rested on the previous balance.[178] The rule preventing tracing beyond the lowest intermediate balance was more recently reaffirmed by the Court of Appeal in *Bishopsgate Investment Management v Homan*.[179]

### (d) Bank trustee depositing trust money with itself

The above situations have all involved cases where a trustee has mixed trust money with either his own or that of innocent volunteers in bank accounts. However, given that banks may themselves act as trustees, they may deposit trust money with themselves. If they then become insolvent the question may arise as to whether the beneficiaries can trace the money in the hands of the bank. This issue was considered by the Privy Council in *Space Investments Ltd v Canadian Imperial Bank of Commerce Trust Co (Bahamas) Ltd*.[180] The case concerned a bank, the Mercantile Bank Trust Co Ltd, which was the trustee of various settlements. The trust instruments contained clauses permitting the trustee to open and maintain savings accounts with any bank, including itself. The bank deposited trust money with itself, and then became insolvent. The question was whether the beneficiaries were entitled to trace the trust money into the bank accounts and therefore gain priority over the other unsecured creditors of the bank. The Privy Council held that they were not entitled to do so because the deposit was entirely lawful and not in breach of trust. The beneficiaries were to be treated like all the other depositors of the bank who were restricted to proving in the liquidation as unsecured creditors for the amount which ought to have been credited to their accounts at the date of liquidation. However, the Privy Council considered that the position would have been different if the bank trustee had misappropriated the trust money and had acted in breach of trust by depositing the trust property with itself. In such circumstances the beneficiaries would be entitled to an equitable charge over all the assets of the bank. Lord Templeman explained the Board's reasoning:

'A bank in fact uses all deposit moneys for the general purposes of the bank . . . in these circumstances it is impossible for the beneficiaries interested in trust money misappropriated from their trust to trace their money to any particular asset belonging to the trustee

---

[177] (1880) 13 Ch D 696.

[178] Sargant J took the view that if the account was a separate trust account then, the mere fact of a payment in would be sufficient indication of an intention to substitute the additional moneys (see eg *Re Hughes* [1970] IR 237), but there was no such intention in the case of a payment into a general trading account.

[179] [1995] 1 All ER 347; (1994) 8 TLI 102 (Smith). See also *British Columbia v National Bank of Canada* (1994) 119 DLR (4th) 669.

[180] [1986] 1 WLR 1072.

bank. But equity allows the beneficiaries, or a new trustee appointed in place of an insolvent bank trustee to protect the interests of the beneficiaries, to trace the trust money to all the assets of the bank and to recover the trust money by the exercise of an equitable charge over all the assets of the bank.'[181]

This accorded the beneficiaries priority over all the unsecured creditors of the bank. This was justified by the Board on the grounds that the settlor and beneficiaries of the trust had never accepted the risks involved in the possible insolvency of the bank, whereas the unsecured other creditors had voluntarily accepted that risk. In conclusion the distinction between the beneficiaries' position where the deposit was authorised and where it was not was justified on the basis that:

'Equity . . . protects beneficiaries against breaches of trust. But equity does not protect beneficiaries against the consequences of the exercise in good faith of powers conferred by the trust instrument.'[182]

This decision has been criticised, since in effect it enables the beneficiaries to maintain a security interest over assets that could not possibly be the product of the trust property.[183] In *Re Goldcorp Exchange Ltd*[184] the Privy Council referred to *Space Investments* and the criticisms which had been levelled at the judgment but concluded that:

'In the present case it is not necessary or appropriate to consider the scope and ambit of the observations in *Space Investments* or their application to trustees other than bank trustees . . .'

The exact scope and application of the principle therefore awaits further clarification.

## (7) Equitable tracing into assets acquired prior to receiving misappropriated trust property[185]

The question has arisen whether misappropriated money can be traced in equity into an asset acquired before the trust property was received. Such a process has been described as 'backward tracing'. In *Bishopsgate Investment Management v Homan*[186] Dillon LJ was willing to accept that in some circumstances trust money could be traced into a pre-acquired asset. The first instance judge had suggested that tracing would be possible if property had been acquired with borrowed money, either by way of loan or overdraft, and there was an inference that when the borrowing was incurred it was the intention that it should be repaid[187] with the misappropriated money. He considered that the beneficiary would be entitled to a charge over the asset acquired provided that the connection between the misappropriation and the asset was sufficiently proved. In contrast, Leggatt LJ entirely dismissed the possibility of such backward tracing:

'. . . there can be no equitable remedy against an asset acquired *before* misappropriation of money takes place, since ex hypothesi it cannot be followed into something which

---

[181] [1986] 1 WLR 1072 at 1974.   [182] [1986] 1 WLR 1072.   [183] (1987) 103 LQR 433 (Goode).
[184] [1994] 2 All ER 806.
[185] (1995) 111 LQR 517 (Sir Peter Millett); (1995) 9 TLI 78 (Oliver); (1995) 54 CLJ 377 (Oakley).
[186] [1995] 1 All ER 347.   [187] [1995] 1 All ER 347 at 351.

existed and so had been acquired before the money was received and therefore without its aid.'[188]

In *Foskett v McKeown*[189] Scott V-C expressed the opinion that it should be possible to trace into assets acquired with borrowed money if the trust money was used to repay the borrowing and it had always been the intention that the trust money would be used to acquire the asset.

## (8) The limits of equitable tracing

Whilst the right to trace in equity is not lost merely because the property becomes mixed with other property, there are circumstances in which it will no longer be possible to identify assets as representing the original property.

### (a) Bona fide purchase

It is not possible to trace trust property into the hands of a bona fide purchaser for value without notice. In such circumstances the equitable ownership of the property is entirely defeated and the purchaser receives the absolute ownership thereof. The beneficiaries may, however, be able to trace into the consideration provided by the purchaser, since this will represent the proceeds of the property.

### (b) Dissipation

Once property and its proceeds have been dissipated, or used up, tracing is impossible because there is clearly no asset that represents the original property. The principle was stated by the Court of Appeal in *Re Diplock*:

'The equitable remedies presuppose the continued existence of the money either as a separate fund or as part of a mixed fund or as latent in property acquired by means of such a fund. If, on the facts of any individual case, such continued existence is not established, equity is as helpless as the common law itself.'[190]

Therefore, beneficiaries would be unable to trace if a trustee used trust property to pay for a meal which he consumed, or a foreign holiday which he has taken, as no asset would remain. Similarly, if the property has been used to discharge a debt, nothing would be left that could be said to represent the trust property.[191] A debt is a chose in action and once it has been paid it ceases to exist. There is no longer a relationship of debtor and creditor. In *Re Diplock*[192] the Court of Appeal held that it was not possible to trace trust money wrongfully transferred to two charities who had used it to discharge debts. In *Re Tilley's Will Trusts*[193] it was held that it was not possible to trace money paid into an overdrawn bank account, because such payment only goes to reduce the amount of the overdraft, which is simply a debt owed by the customer to the bank. The inability to trace money paid into an overdrawn account was also accepted by the Court

---

[188] [1995] 1 All ER 347 at 355.     [189] [1997] 3 All ER 392 at 409.     [190] [1948] Ch 465 at 521.
[191] For an alternative view see [1995] 54 CLJ 290 (Smith).     [192] [1948] Ch 465.
[193] [1967] Ch 1179.

of Appeal in *Bishopsgate Investment Management Ltd v Homan*[194] and by the Privy Council in *Re Goldcorp Exchange.*[195]

However, where a beneficiary's money is used in breach of trust to discharge a secured debt the beneficiary will be entitled to be subrogated to the position of the secured creditor and therefore able to recover the amount of the discharged loan from the debtor. This was so held in *Boscawen v Bajwa.*[196] Money was held on trust by a solicitor for the Abbey National, which had advanced it intending that it be used to complete the purchase of a house owned by Mr Bajwa which was subject to a charge in favour of the Halifax. In breach of trust the money was used to discharge the charge but the purchase fell through. The Court of Appeal held that the Abbey National's money could be traced into the discharge of the debt and that they should be subrogated to the position of the Halifax, which had been the creditor of the legal charge. Millett LJ explained that the Abbey National was entitled to subrogation because they had intended to retain the beneficial interest in its money unless and until that interest was replaced by a first legal mortgage on the property[197] and that in the circumstances Mr Bajwa could not claim that the charge had been discharged for his benefit as this would be unconscionable.[198] Whilst subrogation may provide some answer to the problem of dissipation where money has been used to discharge a debt, it will only operate to the plaintiff's advantage if the debt was secured. Despite these authorities supporting the view that it is impossible to trace into an overdrawn bank account, in *Foskett v McKeown*[199] Scott V-C considered that it remained an open question whether it was possible to trace into assets acquired from an overdrawn bank account:

'The availability of equitable remedies ought, in my view, to depend upon the substance of the transaction in question and not upon the strict order in which associated events happen . . . I would wish, for my part, to make it clear that I regard the point as still open and, in particular, that I do not regard the fact that an asset is paid for out of borrowed money with the borrowing subsequently repaid out of trust money as being necessarily fatal to an equitable tracing claim by the trust beneficiaries. If, in such a case, it can be shown that it was always the intention to use the trust money to acquire the asset, I do not see why the order in which the events happen should be regarded as critical to the claim.'[200]

In *Re Diplock*[201] the Court of Appeal suggested that the use of trust property to improve a house where the improvement added no value to the house, or even caused a loss in value, would amount to a dissipation preventing tracing. In such circumstances there is nothing to trace, because 'the money will have disappeared leaving no monetary trace behind'. If the property has been dissipated, the only possible remedy will be a personal remedy against the trustee for breach of trust, or if it was received by a

---

[194] [1995] Ch 211; [1995] LMCLQ 446 (Gullifer).

[195] [1995] 1 AC 74. See also *Boscawen v Bajwa* [1995] 4 All ER 769 at 775; *PMPA v PMPS* (27 June 1994, unreported) [1995] RLR 217, HC of Ireland.

[196] [1995] 4 All ER 769; (1995) 9 TLI 124 (Birks); [1995] LMCLQ 451 (Mitchell); (1996) 55 CLJ 199 (Andrews); [1997] Conv 1 (Oakley).

[197] [1995] 4 All ER 769 at 782    [198] [1995] 4 All ER 769 at 784.    [199] [1997] 3 All ER 392.

[200] [1997] 3 All ER 392 at 409. In support of this proposition he cited *Agricultural Credit Corpn of Saskatchewan v Pettyjohn* (1991) 79 DLR (4th) 22 and (1995) 54 CLJ 290 (Smith).

[201] [1948] Ch 465 at 547.

stranger who is liable to account for its value as a constructive trustee because he acted dishonestly.

### (c) Unascertained goods

It seems that it is not possible to trace in equity into unascertained goods, because the purchaser does not gain title to those goods under the contract of sale until they have been separated from the bulk. This was so held in *Re London Wine Co (Shippers) Ltd*[202] and by the Privy Council in *Re Goldcorp Exchange Ltd*.[203] In the latter case a company dealing in precious metals sold customers 'non-allocated metal' which the company stored as a bulk on their behalf. The customers were entitled to physical delivery of the metal on seven days' notice. The company became insolvent and, after the payment of the secured creditors, there would be nothing left for the customers who had bought 'non-allocated metal'. The customers sought to claim a proprietary right to the gold that was held by the company by way of equitable tracing, but the Privy Council held that they had no proprietary rights. One reason was that the customers had purchased unascertained goods and that title, including equitable title, would not pass until the goods were ascertained by the seller from the bulk. Clearly, there could be a declaration of trust on behalf of the purchaser of unascertained goods by the seller, but on the facts the Privy Council held that was not the intention of the company:

'The company cannot have intended to create an interest in its general stock of gold which would have inhibited any dealings with it otherwise than for the purpose of delivery under the non-allocated sale contracts.'[204]

It follows that if trust property is used to purchase unascertained goods, there will be no possibility of tracing into the bulk unless the relationship is such that it can be shown that there was a trust in favour of the purchaser.[205]

### (d) Inequitable to trace

In *Re Diplock*[206] the Court of Appeal considered that there should be no tracing if an innocent volunteer has used trust property to improve land. To impose a charge over the land for the increase in value in such circumstance would not, in the court's view, produce an equitable result.[207] The reason for this is that a charge is enforceable by sale, and the result is that the innocent volunteer could be compelled to sell his house. This limitation may perhaps be seen as an example of the general defence of change of position, which was recognised by the House of Lords in *Lipkin Gorman Ltd v Karpnale*.[208] Whether it will be inequitable to trace will depend on the circumstances of each case. *Re Diplock*[209] concerned charities who were innocent volunteers. As Goff and

---

[202] (1975) 126 NLJ 977.     [203] [1994] 2 All ER 806.     [204] [1994] 2 All ER 806 at 815.
[205] See *Hunter v Moss* [1994] 3 All ER 215.     [206] [1948] Ch 465.
[207] [1948] Ch 465 at 546–548. The inability to trace where money has been expended on maintaining or improving land was accepted by Lord Browne-Wilkinson in *Foskett v McKeown* [2000] 3 All ER 97 at 102. Where property is used for such purposes he considered that it would 'at most' give rise to a proprietary lien to recover the money expended.
[208] [1991] 2 AC 548.     [209] [1948] Ch 465.

Jones suggest,[210] the result might have been different if the innocent volunteer had been a rich banker who had used trust money wisely to increase the value of his country house, and he has ample liquid assets to discharge any charge over the house without having to sell it. It may now be the case that the Trusts of Land and Appointment of Trustees Act 1996 contains sufficient safeguards to protect the innocent volunteer against the unfair pursuit of a claim to an interest in land through the rules of tracing.

## (9) Claiming in equity

Once the equitable tracing process has identified assets which represent the original trust property the beneficiaries may be able to assert a claim thereto. The potential claims available to beneficiaries in equity are wider than at common law. Depending upon the precise circumstances the beneficiaries may either be able to assert a proprietary claim to the assets identified, an equitable lien to restore the trust fund, or a personal claim to restitution.

### (a) Claiming assets identified as representing the original trust property

Where assets have been identified as representing the original trust property the beneficiaries may wish to claim a proprietary entitlement to them by asserting their equitable ownership. The ability to make such a claim will be especially important if the person who possesses the assets is insolvent, since this will gain the beneficiaries priority over their other creditors. Beneficiaries may also wish to assert a proprietary claim in order to take advantage of any rise in value of the assets identified.[211] A proprietary claim may therefore enable them to gain a windfall benefit. In *Foskett v McKeown*[212] Lord Millet considered that if A misappropriates B's money and uses it to buy a winning ticket in the lottery, B is entitled to claim the winnings. In the same case the House of Lords has recently clarified the entitlement of beneficiaries to claim assets which are identified by the equitable tracing process as representing their original trust property, thus eliminating previous uncertainty as to the rights of beneficiaries.

*(i) Claiming assets which were cleanly substituted for the trust property*. It has long been established that where trust property has been misappropriated the beneficiaries will be entitled to claim any assets which can be identified as the product of a clean substitution.[213] Lord Millett explained as follows:

'The simplest case is where a trustee wrongfully misappropriates trust property and uses it exclusively to acquire other property for his benefit. In such a case the beneficiary is entitled *at his option* either to assert his beneficial ownership of the proceeds or to bring a personal claim against the trustees for breach of trust and enforce an equitable lien or charge on the

---

[210] Goff and Jones, *The Law of Restitution* (6th edn, 2002), p 111.

[211] Some earlier cases, such as the decision of the House of Lords in *Sinclair v Brougham* [1914] AC 398 suggested that a beneficiary was not able to assert a proprietary claim so as to take advantage of an increase in the value of the property. However this was questioned by in *Re Tilley's Will Trusts* [1967] 1 Ch 1179, and in *Foskett v McKeown* [2000] 3 All ER 97 the House of Lords finally held definitively that beneficiaries are entitled to gain the advantage of an increase in value of assets acquired from the trust property.

[212] [2000] 3 All ER 97.  [213] *Re Hallett's Estate* (1880) 13 Ch D 696.

proceeds to secure restoration of the trust fund. He will normally be able to exercise the option in the way most advantageous to himself.'[214]

*(ii) Claiming assets which were acquired from a mixed fund.* Prior to *Foskett v McKeown* a distinction appears to have been drawn between the rights of beneficiaries where assets identified as representing the original trust property were acquired from a mixed fund consisting of the trust property and the property of another innocent party, and where they had been acquired from a mixed fund consisting of the trust property and the property of the wrongdoing trustee. Where the mixed fund had consisted of the trust property and the property of another innocent party, for example another trust or an innocent volunteer, the assets acquired would be shared *pari passu* and the beneficiaries would be entitled to claim a share of the equitable ownership proportionate to their contribution. However where the mixed fund consisted of the misappropriated trust property and the property of the wrongdoing trustee it was thought that the beneficiaries were not able to claim a proportionate share of any assets acquired. Instead they were limited to claiming an equitable lien over the property to secure the restoration of the trust fund. This distinction originated with the judgment of Jessel MR in *Re Hallet's Estate*,[215] and was applied by Scott V-C in the Court of Appeal in *Foskett v McKeown*.[216] However, in the House of Lords Lord Millett held that no such distinction was to be drawn between the right of beneficiaries to claim a proportionate share of assets acquired from a mixed fund:

'In my view the time has come to state unequivocally that English law has no such rule. It conflicts with the rule that a trustee must not benefit from his trust. I agree with Burrows that the beneficiary's right to elect to have a proportionate share of a mixed substitution necessarily follows once one accepts, as English law does, (i) that a claimant can trace in equity into a mixed fund and (ii) that he can trace unmixed money into its proceeds and assert ownership of the proceeds.

Accordingly, I would state the basic rule as follows. Where a trustee wrongfully uses trust money to provide part of the cost of acquiring an asset, the beneficiary is entitled at his option either to claim a proportionate share of the asset or to enforce a lien upon it to secure his personal claim against the trustee for the amount of the misapplied money.'[217]

*(iii) Claiming assets where tangible property has been mixed to form a bulk.* If the trust property consists of tangible property which has been mixed so as to form a physical bulk, the beneficiary will be entitled to claim a share of the equitable ownership of the bulk proportionate to his contribution. In the event that pro rata division is impossible the beneficiary will be entitled to take the whole bulk.[218] However, given the greater ability of equity to facilitate the co-ownership of property through the medium of a trust, it is much less likely that such a situation will arise than at common law.

## (b) Enforcing an equitable lien to secure a personal claim restore the trust fund

Beneficiaries are able to claim a proportionate share of assets acquired from a mixed

[214] [2000] 3 All ER 97 at 122.     [215] (1880) 13 Ch D 696.
[216] [1998] Ch 265.     [217] [2000] 3 All ER 97 at 123–124.
[218] *Foskett v McKeown* [2000] 3 All ER 97 at 125, per Lord Millett.

fund which included the trust property. In many cases this proprietary claim will prove most advantageous to the beneficiaries, since it will enable them to gain priority over other general creditors in the event of an insolvency, or to take advantage of any increase in value of the assets. Such a proprietary claim will not, however, be advantageous if the assets acquired from the mixed fund have fallen in value, since a proprietary claim will force the beneficiaries to bear a rateable share of the loss. In order to protect the beneficiaries in such circumstances, they are entitled to choose to claim to enforce an equitable lien against the mixed fund to secure their personal claim against the trustee to have the trust fund restored. The availability of such a lien was recognised in *Re Hallet's Estate.*[219] As was noted above, in *Foskett v McKeown* the House of Lords asserted a general rule that a beneficiary has the right to elect between claiming a proportionate share of an asset acquired from a mixed fund and enforcing an equitable lien. However Lord Millett explained that a lien will only be available where the mixed fund consisted of the trust property and the wrongdoing trustee's own property, and not where the mixed fund consisted of the property of equally innocent parties:

'Innocent contributors, however, must be treated equally inter se. Where the beneficiary's claim is in competition with the claims of other innocent contributors, there is no basis upon which any of the claims can be subordinated to any of the others. Where the fund is deficient, the beneficiary is not entitled to enforce a lien for his contribution; all must share rateably in the fund. The primary rule in regard to a mixed fund, therefore, is that gains and losses are borne by the contributors rateably. The beneficiary's right to elect instead to enforce a lien to obtain repayment is an exception to the primary rule, exercisable where the fund is deficient and the claim is made against the wrongdoer and those claiming through him.'[220]

Thus if a trustee misappropriates £5,000 from a trust fund and mixes it with £5,000 of his own money and purchases shares for £10,000, the beneficiaries will either be able to claim off the equitable interest in the shares or enforce a lien for £5,000 against the shares. If the shares have risen in value to £12,000 the assertion of a proportionate proprietary interest will be more advantageous. If they have fallen in value to £8,000 the enforcement of a lien will ensure that the trust fund is fully restored, and that the beneficiaries do not have to bear the consequences of the wrongdoer's poor investment.

## (c) Claiming personal restitution in equity

Where trust property has been misapplied and dissipated so that there are no longer any assets remaining which can be identified as its traceable proceeds, the beneficiaries will not be able to assert a proprietary claim. However they may be able to claim personal restitution from a stranger who received the trust property. In this context the rules of tracing operate as a process by which it can be established that a stranger had in fact received trust property. This was recognised by Millett LJ in *Boscawen v Bajwa*:

'Tracing properly so-called . . . is neither a claim nor a remedy but a process. Moreover, it is not confined to the case where the plaintiff seeks a proprietary remedy; it is equally necessary where he seeks a personal remedy against the knowing recipient or knowing assistant.'[221] The personal liability of a stranger who has received trust property to make

---

[219] (1880) 13 Ch D 696.     [220] [2000] 3 All ER 97 at 124.     [221] [1995] 4 All ER 769 at 776.

restitution was considered in the previous chapter. As was seen, unlike at common law the mere fact of receipt alone is presently insufficient to generate a personal liability to make restitution in equity. The equitable liability to account as a constructive trustee is fault-based, so that a recipient will only be liable to make restitution if he acted 'dishonestly' in receiving and dissipating trust property. If the present position is abandoned in favour of a strict liability to make restitution subject to the defence of change of position, the rules of equitable tracing will still serve the same purpose of demonstrating receipt.

# Index